MORAL PHILOSOPHY

Selected Readings
SECOND EDITION

MORAL PHILOSOPHY

Selected Readings

SECOND EDITION

GEORGE SHER
Rice University

HARCOURT BRACE COLLEGE PUBLISHERS

Fort Worth Philadelphia San Diego New York Orlando Austin San Antonio
Toronto Montreal London Sydney Tokyo

Publisher	TED BUCHHOLZ
Editor in Chief	CHRISTOPHER P. KLEIN
Senior Acquisitions Editor	DAVID C. TATOM
Developmental Editor	J. CLAIRE BRANTLEY
Project Editor	TAMARA NEFF VARDY
Production Manager	DIANE GRAY
Art Director	BURL DEAN SLOAN

Address editorial correspondence to:
Harcourt Brace College Publishers
301 Commerce Street, Suite 3700
Fort Worth, TX 76102

Address orders to:
Harcourt Brace & Company
Permissions Department
6277 Sea Harbor Drive
Orlando, FL 32887-6777
1-800-782-4479 or 1-800-433-0001 (in Florida)

Printed in the United States of America

ISBN: 0-15-501755-1

Library of Congress Catalog Card Number: 95-78578

5 6 7 8 9 0 1 2 3 4 016 9 8 7 6 5 4 3 2 1

Preface

This second edition of *Moral Philosophy: Selected Readings* is substantially revised in both content and structure. Of its 56 selections, 20 are new. Some new selections provide additional clarification of difficult material such as Kant's moral theory, others offer improved statements of important views, and still others take positions not adequately represented in the first edition. Moreover, the book has been reorganized to clarify the relationships among the readings: I have divided the section on normative ethics into two, one on consequentialism and one on deontology; the section on moral psychology and moral education has been replaced by a more focused section on virtue; the section that was entitled "Moral Epistemology" now bears the more accurate title "Objectivity and Knowledge"; and I have added a separate section on the meaning of moral language.

Despite these changes, the book's basic aims remain the same. *Moral Philosophy* is intended to introduce the reader to the full range of problems of moral philosophy, from metaethics to applied ethics. It combines substantial chunks of the classics, which everyone should read, with some of the best of the extremely interesting work of the recent past and the present. In general, my principle of selection has been simply to include as much of what seems best and most important. However, in what is now Part VIII, Applications, I have purposely not included any of the fine recent work on social policy and the justice of institutions. Essays on these topics would not mesh well with the preceding sections, which focus mostly on individual behavior.

Some very important positions in moral philosophy are inherently complex, while others presuppose sophisticated views from other areas of philosophy. As a result, any collection of this type must strike some balance between comprehensiveness and comprehensibility. In establishing my own balance, I have included a few essays that seem too difficult to assign to beginning students. But I think the great majority of the book's essays—far more than can be taught in any single semester—fall well within the grasp of the beginning student. Thus, the anthology is compatible with a variety of styles of introductory ethics courses. At the same time, it should be suitable for an intermediate or even an advanced course in moral theory.

Although I shall not mention them all again, I remain grateful to all those who helped me in putting together the first edition. I also want to add a word of thanks to my former colleague Robert Hall, who helped me to compile the selections that make up the Nietzsche reading, and whose assistance I neglected to acknowledge in the first edition. In addition, I want to thank my current colleague Baruch Brody, who read most of the new introductory material and made a number of very helpful suggestions. I also owe a debt of gratitude to the reviewers who commented on sections of the manuscript in draft form. They include the following: Don Loeb, University of Vermont; Bridget Newell, University of Utah; Paul A. Roth, University of Missouri; Stephen Scales, University of San Diego; Earl Spurgin, University of North Carolina; and William Wilcox, California Polytechnic State University. Any errors, of course, remain mine alone. I would, finally, like to acknowledge the contributions of David Tatom, Claire Brantley, and the others at Harcourt Brace College Publishers with whom I have worked. Their able assistance transformed what can be a difficult and taxing process into a smooth and enjoyable one.

Contents

III   OBJECTIVITY AND KNOWLEDGE   191

IV   NORMATIVE ETHICS: CONSEQUENTIALISM   295

V   NORMATIVE ETHICS: DEONTOLOGY   371

VIII   APPLICATIONS   691

I

THE JUSTIFICATION
FOR BEING MORAL

To act morally, a person must consider the interests of others. He must keep his promises, act fairly, and not cause harm. But acting in these ways is often not the best way of achieving our own goals. Whether we want to win an election, succeed in business, or just move quickly through a grocery line, we sometimes seem to fare better by doing what is wrong. Why, then, should we do what is right?

Before we can answer this question, we must ask another. It does no good to offer someone a reason for being moral that he will not accept. Moreover, according to some, the only reasons that anyone accepts are reasons of self-interest. If so, then the only way to convince anyone to act morally is to show that being moral *is* in a person's overall interest. Thus, our first question must be whether people *do* act only to further their own interests.

The view that they do is known as *psychological egoism,* and versions of it can be found in the thought of Thomas Hobbes (reading 3), Jeremy Bentham (reading 43), and, although less consistently, John Stuart Mill (reading 23). Because there are many different views about what is in one's interest, there are also many versions of the view that people always *pursue* our own interests. However, Joel Feinberg (reading 1) and others have mounted powerful arguments against all versions of that view. Given these arguments, the case for psychological egoism seems weaker than many believe.

Even if we are not entirely self-interested, self-interest remains one powerful motive among others. Thus, showing that being moral is in each person's interest remains one good way of convincing someone to do the right thing. And, as Plato notes in reading 2, virtue often does bring honor and rewards.

More importantly, Thomas Hobbes argues forcefully in reading 3 that conformity to moral rules is necessary for self-preservation. Although Hobbes believes that in the absence of government, "every man has a right to every thing," he insists that where there is civil order, we best protect our interests by keeping agreements, displaying gratitude, and, generally, treating others as we wish to be treated. By not mistreating others, we avoid mistreatment by them. At first glance, this seems to invite the reply that we sometimes *can* benefit by acting wrongly. But Hobbes' position may be that it is difficult to know in advance which immoral acts will benefit us and that the costs of finding out are often prohibitive. For these reasons, the cautiously self-interested person may do best by consistently following morality.

Quite clearly, these suggestions contain much truth. Yet because they appeal to such facts as our inability to know when our wrongdoing will be discovered, they do not rule out wrongdoing under all conceivable circumstances. In reading 2, Plato tells the story of the ancestor of Gyges, who found a ring that made him invisible. If someone had such a ring, he *would* know that he could get away with doing what is wrong. Thus, if self-interest is to prevent him from acting wrongly, it must do so on some further grounds. As David Gauthier notes in reading 4, it may well be that each person is better off when everyone follows the rules of morality than when everyone does not follow them. However, as Gauthier also notes, this does not mean that each person is always better off when he follows the rules of morality himself. When following the rules does not make one better off, the question of why one ought to follow them remains open.

One extremely influential answer was proposed by Immanuel Kant. As Kant argues in reading 30, even when acting morally is in one's interest, self-interest appears to be the wrong reason for doing the right thing. For example, when a shopkeeper's only reason for dealing honestly with a child is to preserve his reputation, his actions seem to lack moral worth. Though not immoral, they are not motivated by respect for the moral law. But if respect for moral law is different from mere desire, then the justification for following the moral law must also be independent of any agent's desires. The justification must appeal to considerations accessible to all rational beings. It must, in Kant's view, be supplied by reason itself.

The Kantian idea that it is somehow inconsistent or irrational to ignore the interests of others has been developed in various ways. For example, in reading 5, Alan Gewirth attempts to ground morality in reason by appealing to the requirements of purposive action. In his view, anyone who acts is committed to believing that he has a right to act, and thus also that he has a right to the freedom and well-being that make action possible. These rights are violated when others act immorally toward him. Because each person's reason for believing that he has rights is simply that he acts, and because each person knows that all others are agents as well, each person must be committed to believing that all others have similar rights. And because our status as agents is unavoidable, the resulting commitment to morality must be unavoidable too.

So far, we have considered two kinds of efforts to justify morality. One appeals to the desire to further one's self-interest, while a second appeals to reason rather than any kind of desire. But it is also possible to envision an intermediate approach—one which, like the first, attempts to show that being moral will satisfy one's desires, but which, like the second, does not appeal to self-interest. Along these lines, Philippa Foot argues in reading 6 that the moral life can be defended only to those who already want to be kind, fair, and just. Many people do have such desires and find such lives inspiring. But one who lacks a commitment to charity, justice, and honesty does not frustrate his own purposes by acting immorally. For that person, being immoral is not irrational.

When we ask for a reason to be moral, we are in effect seeking guidance for our actions. But, according to Jean-Paul Sartre (reading 7), there is no guidance to be had. Whatever reasons we are given, we ourselves will have to interpret them, and only we can decide how much weight to assign them. As Sartre puts it, "in the bright realm of values, we have no excuse behind us, nor justification before us." Thus, according to Sartre, the question "Why should I be moral?" is beside the point. If we follow some particular version of morality, it is not because we have compelling reason to do so, but simply because that is our choice.

1

Psychological Egoism

JOEL FEINBERG

Joel Feinberg (b. 1926), Professor of Philosophy at the University of Arizona, has done influential work in social and legal philosophy. His books include Doing and Deserving, Social Philosophy, *and a recent quadrilogy with the overall title* The Moral Limits of the Criminal Law. *This essay is reprinted from Feinberg's anthology* Reason and Responsibility.

In the essay, Feinberg examines psychological egoism—the view that we never want or pursue anything except our own happiness or self-interest. Although this view claims to explain why we act as we do, Feinberg points out that it is rarely supported by empirical evidence. Instead, it trades on certain arguments that are seldom carefully examined. Psychological egoism is, for example, often thought to hold because each person is motivated by his own desires and no one else's. However, as Feinberg notes, the fact that my desires are my own implies nothing about what I desire. Thus, it does not imply that I desire only my own happiness or satisfaction. Again, defenders of the view sometimes note that we get pleasure from helping others (or feel pangs of conscience about not helping). Yet far from supporting psychological egoism, this fact actually tells against it. For why should we feel such pleasure, if not that helping others satisfies a desire to help them—a desire that is emphatically not aimed only at our own happiness?

These examples do not exhaust the arguments considered by Feinberg. Throughout his discussion, however, the main point is clear. When we consider the matter carefully, we find no good reason to accept psychological egoism. We are free, therefore, to accept the commonsense view that people often act not to increase their own happiness, but simply to help others or to do the right thing.

THE THEORY

1. "Psychological egoism" is the name given to a theory widely held by ordinary men, and at one time almost universally accepted by political economists, philosophers, and psychologists, according to which all human actions when properly understood can be seen to be motivated by selfish desires. More precisely, psychological egoism is the doctrine that the only thing anyone

is capable of desiring or pursuing ultimately (as an end in itself) is his *own* self-interest. No psychological egoist denies that men sometimes do desire things other than their own welfare—the happiness of other people, for example; but all psychological egoists insist that men are capable of desiring the happiness of others only when they take it to be a *means* to their own happiness. In short, purely altruistic and benevolent actions and desires do not exist; but people sometimes appear to be acting unselfishly and disinterestedly when they take the interests of others to be means to the promotion of their own self-interest.

2. This theory is called *psychological* egoism to indicate that it is not a theory about what *ought* to be the case, but rather about what, as a matter of fact, *is* the case. That is, the theory claims to be a description of psychological facts, not a prescription of ethical ideals. It asserts, however, not merely that all men do as a contingent matter of fact "put their own interests first," but also that they are capable of nothing else, human nature being what it is. Universal selfishness is not just an accident or a coincidence on this view; rather, it is an unavoidable consequence of psychological laws.

The theory is to be distinguished from another doctrine, so-called "ethical egoism," according to which all men *ought* to pursue their own well-being. This doctrine, being a prescription of what *ought* to be the case, makes no claim to be a psychological theory of human motives; hence the word "ethical" appears in its name to distinguish it from *psychological* egoism.

3. There are a number of types of motives and desires which might reasonably be called "egoistic" or "selfish," and corresponding to each of them is a possible version of psychological egoism. Perhaps the most common version of the theory is that apparently held by Jeremy Bentham.[1] According to this version, all persons have only one ultimate motive in all their voluntary behavior and that motive is a selfish one; more specifically, it is one particular kind of selfish motive—namely, a desire for one's own *pleasure*. According to this version of the theory, "the only kind of ultimate desire is the desire to get or to prolong pleasant experiences, and to avoid or to cut short unpleasant experiences for oneself."[2] This form of psychological egoism is often given the cumbersome name—*psychological egoistic hedonism*.

PRIMA FACIE REASONS IN SUPPORT OF THE THEORY

4. Psychological egoism has seemed plausible to many people for a variety of reasons, of which the following are typical:

---

1 See his *Introduction to the Principles of Morals and Legislation* (1789), Chap. 1, first paragraph: "Nature has placed mankind under the governance of two sovereign masters, *pain* and *pleasure*. It is for them alone to point out what we ought to do, as well as to determine what we shall do. . . . They govern us in all we do, in all we say, in all we think: every effort we can make to throw off our subjection will serve but to demonstrate and confirm it."

2 C. D. Broad, *Ethics and the History of Philosophy* (New York: The Humanities Press, 1952), Essay 10—"Egoism As a Theory of Human Motives," p. 218. This essay is highly recommended.

a. "Every action of mine is prompted by motives or desires or impulses which are *my* motives and not somebody else's. This fact might be expressed by saying that whenever I act I am always pursuing my own ends or trying to satisfy my own desires. And from this we might pass on to—'I am always pursuing something for myself or seeking my own satisfaction.' Here is what seems like a proper description of a man acting selfishly, and if the description applies to all actions of all men, then it follows that all men in all their actions are selfish."[3]

b. It is a truism that when a person gets what he wants he characteristically feels pleasure. This has suggested to many people that what we really want in every case is our own pleasure, and that we pursue other things only as a means.

c. *Self-Deception.* Often we deceive ourselves into thinking that we desire something fine or noble when what we really want is to be thought well of by others or to be able to congratulate ourselves, or to be able to enjoy the pleasures of a good conscience. It is a well-known fact that people tend to conceal their true motives from themselves by camouflaging them with words like "virtue," "duty," etc. Since we are so often misled concerning both our own real motives and the real motives of others, is it not reasonable to suspect that we might *always* be deceived when we think motives disinterested and altruistic? . . .

d. *Moral Education.* Morality, good manners, decency, and other virtues must be teachable. Psychological egoists often notice that moral education and the inculcation of manners usually utilize what Bentham calls the "sanctions of pleasure and pain." Children are made to acquire the civilizing virtues only by the method of enticing rewards and painful punishments. Much the same is true of the history of the race. People in general have been inclined to behave well only when it is made plain to them that there is "something in it for them." Is it not then highly probable that just such a mechanism of human motivation as Bentham describes must be presupposed by our methods of moral education?

CRITIQUE OF PSYCHOLOGICAL EGOISM: CONFUSIONS IN THE ARGUMENTS

5. *Non-Empirical Character of the Arguments.* If the arguments of the psychological egoist consisted for the most part of carefully acquired empirical evidence (well-documented reports of controlled experiments, surveys, interviews, laboratory data, and so on), then the critical philosopher would have no business carping at them. After all, since psychological egoism purports to be a scientific theory of human motives, it is the concern of the experimental psychologist, not the philosopher, to accept or reject it. But as a matter of

---

[3] Austin Duncan-Jones, *Butler's Moral Philosophy* (London: Penguin Books, 1952), p. 96. Duncan-Jones goes on to reject this argument. See pp. 512f.

fact, empirical evidence of the required sort is seldom presented in support of psychological egoism. Psychologists, on the whole, shy away from generalizations about human motives which are so sweeping and so vaguely formulated that they are virtually incapable of scientific testing. It is usually the "armchair scientist" who holds the theory of universal selfishness, and his usual arguments are either based simply on his "impressions" or else are largely of a nonempirical sort. The latter are often shot full of a very subtle kind of logical confusion, and this makes their criticism a matter of special interest to the analytic philosopher.

6. The psychological egoist's first argument (see 4a) is a good example of logical confusion. It begins with a truism—namely, that all of my motives and desires are *my* motives and desires and not someone else's. (Who would deny this?) But from this simple tautology nothing whatever concerning the nature of my motives or the objective of my desires can possibly follow. The fallacy of this argument consists in its violation of the general logical rule that analytic statements (tautologies),* cannot entail synthetic (factual) ones.† That every voluntary act is prompted by the agent's own motives is a tautology; hence, it cannot be equivalent to "A person is always seeking something for himself" or "All of a person's motives are selfish," which are synthetic. What the egoist must prove is not merely:

(i) Every voluntary action is prompted by a motive of the agent's own.

but rather:

(ii) Every voluntary action is prompted by a motive of a quite particular kind, viz. a selfish one.

Statement (i) is obviously true, but it cannot all by itself give any logical support to statement (ii).

The source of the confusion in this argument is readily apparent. It is not the genesis of an action or the *origin* or its motives which makes it a "selfish" one, but rather the "purpose" of the act or the *objective* of its motives; *not where the motive comes from* (in voluntary actions it always comes from the agent) but *what it aims at* determines whether or not it is selfish. There is surely a valid distinction between voluntary behavior, in which the agent's action is motivated by purposes of his own, and *selfish* behavior in which the agent's motives are of one exclusive sort. The egoist's argument assimilates all voluntary action into the class of selfish action, by requiring, in effect, that an unselfish action be one which is not really motivated at all.

• • •

7. But if argument 4a fails to prove its point, argument 4b does no better. From the fact that all our successful actions (those in which we get what we were after) are accompanied or followed by pleasure it does not follow, as the

---

* Traditionally, analytic statements have been taken to be statements that are true by virtue of the meanings of words, and hence convey no information about the world.

† Traditionally, statements that do convey information about the world.

egoist claims, that the *objective* of every action is to get pleasure for oneself. To begin with, the premise of the argument is not, strictly speaking, even true. Fulfillment of desire (simply getting what one was after) is no guarantee of satisfaction (pleasant feelings of gratification in the mind of the agent). Sometimes when we get what we want we *also* get, as a kind of extra dividend, a warm, glowing feeling of contentment; but often, far too often, we get no dividend at all, or, even worse, the bitter taste of ashes. Indeed, it has been said that the characteristic psychological problem of our time is the *dissatisfaction* that attends the fulfillment of our very most powerful desires.

Even if we grant, however, for the sake of argument, that getting what one wants *usually* yields satisfaction, the egoist's conclusion does not follow. We can concede that we normally get pleasure (in the sense of satisfaction) when our desires are satisfied, *no matter what our desires are for;* but it does not follow from this roughly accurate generalization that the only thing we ever desire is our own satisfaction. Pleasure may well be the usual accompaniment of all actions in which the agent gets what he wants; but to infer from this that what the agent always wants is his own pleasure is like arguing, in William James's example,[4] that because an ocean liner constantly consumes coal on its trans-Atlantic passage that therefore the *purpose* of its voyage is to consume coal. The immediate inference from even constant accompaniment to purpose (or motive) is always a *non sequitur.*

Perhaps there is a sense of "satisfaction" (desire fulfillment) such that it is certainly and universally true that we get satisfaction whenever we get what we want. But satisfaction in this sense is simply the "coming into existence of that which is desired." Hence, to say that desire fulfillment always yields "satisfaction" in this sense is to say no more than that we always get what we want when we get what we want, which is to utter a tautology like "a rose is a rose." It can no more entail a synthetic truth in psychology (like the egoistic thesis) than "a rose is a rose" can entail significant information in botany.

8. *Disinterested Benevolence.* The fallacy in argument 4b then consists, as Garvin puts it, "in the supposition that the apparently unselfish desire to benefit others is transformed into a selfish one by the fact that we derive pleasure from carrying it out."[5] Not only is this argument fallacious; it also provides us with a suggestion of a counter-argument to show that its conclusion (psychological egoistic hedonism) is false. Not only is the presence of pleasure (satisfaction) as a by-product of an action no proof that the action was selfish; in some special cases it provides rather conclusive proof that the action was *unselfish.* For in those special cases the fact that we get pleasure from a particular action *presupposes that we desired something else*—something other than our own pleasure—as an end in itself and not merely as a means to our own pleasant state of mind.

This way of turning the egoistic hedonist's argument back on him can be illustrated by taking a typical egoist argument, one attributed (perhaps apocryphally) to Abraham Lincoln, and then examining it closely:

---

[4] *The Principles of Psychology* (New York: Henry Holt, 1890), Vol. II, p. 558.

[5] Lucius Garvin, *A Modern Introduction to Ethics* (Boston: Houghton Mifflin, 1953), p. 39.

Mr. Lincoln once remarked to a fellow-passenger on an old-time mud-coach that all men were prompted by selfishness in doing good. His fellow-passenger was antagonizing this position when they were passing over a corduroy bridge that spanned a slough. As they crossed this bridge they espied an old razor-backed sow on the bank making a terrible noise because her pigs had got into the slough and were in danger of drowning. As the old coach began to climb the hill, Mr. Lincoln called out, "Driver, can't you stop just a moment?" Then Mr. Lincoln jumped out, ran back and lifted the little pigs out of the mud and water and placed them on the bank. When he returned, his companion remarked: "Now Abe, where does selfishness come in on this little episode?" "Why, bless your soul Ed, that was the very essence of selfishness. I should have had no peace of mind all day had I gone on and left that suffering old sow worrying over those pigs. I did it to get peace of mind, don't you see?"[6]

If Lincoln had cared not a whit for the welfare of the little pigs and their "suffering" mother, but only for his own "peace of mind," it would be difficult to explain how he could have derived pleasure from helping them. The very fact that he did feel satisfaction as a result of helping the pigs presupposes that he had a preexisting desire for something other than his own happiness. Then when *that* desire was satisfied, Lincoln of course derived pleasure. The *object* of Lincoln's desire was not pleasure; rather pleasure was the *consequence* of his preexisting desire for something else. If Lincoln had been wholly indifferent to the plight of the little pigs as he claimed, how could he possibly have derived any pleasure from helping them? He could not have achieved peace of mind from rescuing the pigs, had he not a prior concern—on which his peace of mind depended—for the welfare of the pigs for its own sake.

In general, the psychological hedonist analyzes apparent benevolence into a desire for "benevolent pleasure." No doubt the benevolent man does get pleasure from his benevolence, but in most cases, this is only because he has previously desired the good of some person, or animal, or mankind at large. Where there is no such desire, benevolent conduct is not generally found to give pleasure to the agent.

9. *Malevolence.* Difficult cases for the psychological egoist include not only instances of disinterested benevolence, but also cases of "disinterested malevolence." Indeed, malice and hatred are generally no more "selfish" than benevolence. Both are motives likely to cause an agent to sacrifice his own interests— in the case of benevolence, in order to help someone else, in the case of malevolence in order to harm someone else. The selfish man is concerned ultimately only with his own pleasure, happiness, or power; the benevolent man is often equally concerned with the happiness of others; to the malevolent man, the *injury* of another is often an end in itself—an end to be pursued sometimes with no thought for his own interests. There is reason to think that men have as often sacrificed themselves to injure or kill others as to help or to save others, and with as much "heroism" in the one case as in the other. The unselfish nature of malevolence was first noticed by the Anglican Bishop

---

6 Quoted from the *Springfield* (Illinois) *Monitor*, by F. C. Sharp in his *Ethics* (New York: Appleton-Century, 1928), p. 75.

and moral philosopher Joseph Butler (1692–1752), who regretted that men are no more selfish than they are.[7]

10. *Lack of Evidence for Universal Self-Deception.* The more cynical sort of psychological egoist who is impressed by the widespread phenomenon of self-deception (see 4c) cannot be so quickly disposed of, for he has committed no *logical* mistakes. We can only argue that the acknowledged frequency of self-deception is insufficient evidence for his universal generalization. His argument is not fallacious, but inconclusive.

No one but the agent himself can ever be certain what conscious motives really prompted his action, and where motives are disreputable, even the agent may not admit to himself the true nature of his desires. Thus, for every apparent case of altruistic behavior, the psychological egoist can argue, with some plausibility, that the true motivation *might* be selfish, appearance to the contrary. Philanthropic acts are really motivated by the desire to receive gratitude; acts of self-sacrifice, when truly understood, are seen to be motivated by the desire to feel self-esteem; and so on. We must concede to the egoist that all apparent altruism might be deceptive in this way; but such a sweeping generalization requires considerable empirical evidence, and such evidence is not presently available.

11. *The "Paradox of Hedonism" and Its Consequences for Education.* The psychological egoistic Hedonist (e.g., Jeremy Bentham) has the simplest possible theory of human motivation. According to this variety of egoistic theory, all human motives without exception can be reduced to one—namely, the desire for one's own pleasure. But this theory, despite its attractive simplicity, or perhaps because of it, involves one immediately in a paradox. Astute observers of human affairs from the time of the ancient Greeks have often noticed that pleasure, happiness, and satisfaction are states of mind which stand in a very peculiar relation to desire. An exclusive desire for happiness is the surest way to prevent happiness from coming into being. Happiness has a way of "sneaking up" on persons when they are preoccupied with other things; but when persons deliberately and single-mindedly set off in pursuit of happiness, it vanishes utterly from sight and cannot be captured. This is the famous "paradox of hedonism": the single-minded pursuit of happiness is necessarily self-defeating, for *the way to get happiness is to forget it;* then perhaps it will come to you. If you aim exclusively at pleasure itself, with no concern for the things that bring pleasure, then pleasure will never come. To derive satisfaction, one must ordinarily first desire something other than satisfaction, and then find the means to get what one desires.

To feel the full force of the paradox of hedonism the reader should conduct an experiment in his imagination. Imagine a person (let's call him "Jones") who is, first of all, devoid of intellectual curiosity. He has no desire to acquire any kind of knowledge for its own sake, and thus is utterly indifferent to questions of science, mathematics, and philosophy. Imagine further that the

---

7 See his *Fifteen Sermons on Human Nature Preached at the Rolls Chapel* (1726), especially the first and eleventh.

beauties of nature leave Jones cold: he is unimpressed by the autumn foliage, the snow-capped mountains, and the rolling oceans. Long walks in the country on spring mornings and skiing forays in the winter are to him equally a bore. Moreover, let us suppose that Jones can find no appeal in art. Novels are dull, poetry a pain, paintings nonsense and music just noise. Suppose further that Jones has neither the participant's nor the spectator's passion for baseball, football, tennis, or any other sport. Swimming to him is a cruel aquatic form of calisthenics, the sun only a cause of sunburn. Dancing is coeducational idiocy, conversation a waste of time, the other sex an unappealing mystery. Politics is a fraud, religion mere superstition; and the misery of millions of underprivileged human beings is nothing to be concerned with or excited about. Suppose finally that Jones has no talent for any kind of handicraft, industry, or commerce, and that he does not regret that fact.

What then is Jones interested in? He must desire something. To be sure, he does. Jones has an overwhelming passion for, a complete preoccupation with, his own happiness. The one exclusive desire of his life is *to be happy*. It takes little imagination at this point to see that Jones's one desire is bound to be frustrated. People who—like Jones—most hotly pursue their own happiness are the least likely to find it. Happy people are those who successfully pursue such things as aesthetic or religious experience, self-expression, service to others, victory in competitions, knowledge, power, and so on. If none of these things in themselves and for their own sakes mean anything to a person, if they are valued at all then only as a means to one's own pleasant states of mind—then that pleasure can never come. The way to achieve happiness is to pursue something else.

Almost all people at one time or another in their lives feel pleasure. Some people (though perhaps not many) really do live lives which are on the whole happy. But if pleasure and happiness presuppose desires for something other than pleasure and happiness, then the existence of pleasure and happiness in the experience of some people proves that those people have strong desires for something other than their own happiness—egoistic hedonism to the contrary.

The implications of the "paradox of hedonism" for educational theory should be obvious. The parents least likely to raise a happy child are those who, even with the best intentions, train their child to seek happiness directly. How often have we heard parents say:

> I don't care if my child does not become an intellectual, or a football star, or a great artist. I just want him to be a plain average sort of person. Happiness does not require great ambitions and great frustrations; it's not worth it to suffer and become neurotic for the sake of science, art, or do-goodism. I just want my child to be happy.

This can be a dangerous mistake, for it is the child (and the adult for that matter) without "outer-directed" interests who is the most likely to be unhappy. The pure egoist would be the most wretched of persons.

The educator might well beware of "life adjustment" as the conscious goal of the educational process for similar reasons. "Life adjustment" can be achieved only as a by-product of other pursuits. A whole curriculum of "life adjustment courses" unsupplemented by courses designed to incite an interest in things other than life adjustment would be tragically self-defeating.

As for moral education, it is probably true that punishment and reward are indispensable means of inculcation. But if the child comes to believe that the *sole* reasons for being moral are that he will escape the pain of punishment thereby and/or that he will gain the pleasure of a good reputation, then what is to prevent him from doing the immoral thing whenever he is sure that he will not be found out? While punishment and reward then are important tools for the moral educator, they obviously have their limitations. Beware of the man who does the moral thing only out of fear of pain or love of pleasure. He is not likely to be wholly trustworthy. Moral education is truly successful when it produces persons who are willing to do the right thing *simply because it is right,* and not merely because it is popular or safe.

12. *Pleasure as Sensation.* One final argument against psychological hedonism should suffice to put that form of the egoistic psychology to rest once and for all. The egoistic hedonist claims that all desires can be reduced to the single desire for one's own *pleasure.* Now the word "pleasure" is ambiguous. On the one hand, it can stand for a certain indefinable, but very familiar and specific kind of sensation, or more accurately, a property of sensations; and it is generally, if not exclusively, associated with the senses. For example, certain taste sensations such as sweetness, thermal sensations of the sort derived from a hot bath or the feel of the August sun while one lies on a sandy beach, erotic sensations, olfactory sensations (say) of the fragrance of flowers or perfume, and tactual and kinesthetic sensations from a good massage, are all pleasant in this sense. Let us call this sense of "pleasure," which is the converse of "physical pain," pleasure$_1$.

On the other hand, the word "pleasure" is often used simply as a synonym for "satisfaction" (in the sense of gratification, not mere desire fulfillment). In this sense, the existence of pleasure presupposes the prior existence of desire. Knowledge, religious experience, aesthetic expression, and other so-called "spiritual activities" often give pleasure in this sense. In fact, as we have seen, we tend to get pleasure in this sense whenever we get what we desire, no matter what we desire. The masochist even derives pleasure (in the sense of "satisfaction") from his own physically painful sensations. Let us call the sense of "pleasure" which means "satisfaction"—pleasure$_2$.

Now we can evaluate the psychological hedonist's claim that the sole human motive is a desire for one's own pleasure, bearing in mind (as he often does not) the ambiguity of the word "pleasure." First, let us take the hedonist to be saying that it is the desire for pleasure$_1$ (pleasant sensation) which is the sole ultimate desire of all people and the sole desire capable of providing a motive for action. Now I have little doubt that all (or most) people desire their own pleasure, *sometimes.* But even this familiar kind of desire occurs, I think, rather rarely. When I am hungry, I often desire to eat, or, more specifically, to eat this piece of steak and these potatoes. Much less often do I desire to eat certain morsels simply for the sake of the pleasant gustatory sensations they might cause. I have, on the other hand, been motivated in the latter way when I have gone to especially exotic (and expensive) French or Chinese restaurants; but normally, pleasant gastronomic sensations are simply a happy consequence or by-product of my eating, not the antecedently desired objective of my eating. There are, of course, others who take gustatory sensations far more seriously: the *gourmet* who eats only to savor the textures and flavors of fine foods, and the wine fancier who "collects" the exquisitely subtle and very pleasant tastes of rare old wines. Such men are truly absorbed in their taste sensations when they eat and drink, and there may even be some (rich) persons whose desire for such sensations is the sole motive for eating and drinking. It should take little argument, however, to convince the reader that such persons are extremely rare.

Similarly, I usually derive pleasure from taking a hot bath, and on occasion (though not very often) I even decide to bathe simply for the sake of such sensations. Even if this is equally true of everyone, however, it hardly provides grounds for inferring that *no one ever* bathes for *any* other motive. It should be empirically obvious that we sometimes bathe simply in order to get clean, or to please others, or simply from habit.

The view then that we are never after anything in our actions but our own pleasure—that all men are complete "gourmets" of one sort or another—is not only morally cynical; it is also contrary to common sense and everyday experience. In fact, the view that pleasant sensations play such an enormous role in human affairs is so patently false, on the available evidence, that we must conclude that the psychological hedonist has the other sense of "pleasure"—satisfaction—in mind when he states his thesis. If, on the other hand, he really does try to reduce the apparent multitude of human motives to the one desire for pleasant sensations, then the abundance of historical counterexamples justifies our rejection out of hand of his thesis. It surely seems incredible that the Christian martyrs were ardently pursuing their own pleasure when they marched off to face the lions, or that what the Russian soldiers at Stalingrad "really" wanted when they doused themselves with gasoline, ignited themselves, and then threw the flaming torches of their own bodies on German tanks, was simply the experience of pleasant physical sensations.

13. *Pleasure as Satisfaction.* Let us consider now the other interpretation of the hedonist's thesis, that according to which it is one's own pleasure₂ (satisfaction) and not merely pleasure₁ (pleasant sensation) which is the sole ultimate objective of all voluntary behavior. In one respect, the "satisfaction thesis" is even less plausible than the "physical sensation thesis"; for the latter at least is a genuine empirical hypothesis, testable in experience, though contrary to the facts which experience discloses. The former, however, is so confused that it cannot even be completely stated without paradox. It is, so to speak, defeated in its own formulation. Any attempted explication of the theory that all men at all times desire only their own satisfaction leads to an *infinite regress* in the following way:

"All men desire only satisfaction."
"Satisfaction of what?"

"Satisfaction of their desires."
"Their desires for what?"
"Their desires for satisfaction."
"Satisfaction of what?"
"Their desires."
"For what?"
"For satisfaction."—etc., *ad infinitum.*

In short, psychological hedonism interpreted in this way attributes to all people as their sole motive a wholly vacuous and infinitely self-defeating desire. The source of this absurdity is in the notion that satisfaction can, so to speak, feed on itself, and perform the miracle of perpetual self-regeneration in the absence of desires for anything other than itself.

To summarize the argument of sections 11 and 12: The word "pleasure" is ambiguous. Pleasure$_1$ means a certain indefinable characteristic of physical sensation. Pleasure$_2$ refers to the feeling of satisfaction that often comes when one gets what one desires whatever be the nature of that which one desires. Now, if the hedonist means pleasure$_1$ when he says that one's own pleasure is the ultimate objective of all of one's behavior, then his view is not supported by the facts. On the other hand, if he means pleasure$_2$, then his theory cannot even be clearly formulated, since it leads to the following infinite regress: "I desire only satisfaction of my desire for satisfaction of my desire for satisfaction ... etc., *ad infinitum.*" I conclude then that psychological hedonism (the most common form of psychological egoism), however interpreted, is untenable.

• • •

2

The Ring of Gyges

PLATO

Plato (427–347 B.C.) wrote a series of dialogues that immortalized his teacher Socrates. In these dialogues, Plato poses in striking form many of the issues and competing answers that have been at the center of philosophical study for more than two thousand years.

In this selection from his dialogue The Republic, Book 2, *Plato articulates a central challenge to morality: Why should anyone do what is just (or, more generally, what is right)? If, like Gyges, we had a ring that could render us invisible, why should we not do whatever foul deeds we pleased? If what matters is worldly reward and honor, then it is not important to act justly, but only to appear just. In that case, we should feign justice, but secretly practice injustice whenever possible. If we are to avoid this conclusion, our justification of morality must go deeper. We must ask, "In what way does its very possession benefit a man?"*

When I had said this I thought I had done with the discussion, but evidently this was only a prelude. Glaucon on this occasion too showed that boldness which is characteristic of him, and refused to accept Thrasymachus' abandoning the argument. He said: Do you, Socrates, want to appear to have persuaded us, or do you want truly to convince us that it is better in every way to be just than unjust?

I would certainly wish to convince you truly, I said, if I could.

Well, he said, you are certainly not attaining your wish. Tell me, do you think there is a kind of good which we welcome not because we desire its consequences but for its own sake: joy, for example, and all the harmless pleasures which have no further consequences beyond the joy which one finds in them?

Certainly, said I, I think there is such a good.

Further, there is the good which we welcome for its own sake and also for its consequences, knowledge for example and sight and health. Such things we somehow welcome on both counts.

Yes, said I.

Are you also aware of a third kind, he asked, such as physical training, being treated when ill, the practice of medicine, and other ways of making money? We should say that these are wearisome but beneficial to us; we should not want them for their own sake, but because of the rewards and other benefits which result from them.

There is certainly such a third kind, I said, but why do you ask?

Under which of these headings do you put justice? he asked.

I would myself put it in the finest class, I said, that which is to be welcomed both for itself and for its consequences by any man who is to be blessed with happiness.

That is not the opinion of the many, he said; they would put it in the wearisome class, to be pursued for the rewards and popularity which come from a good reputation, but to be avoided in itself as being difficult.

I know that is the general opinion, I said. Justice has now for some time been objected to by Thrasymachus on this score while injustice was extolled, but it seems I am a slow learner.

Come then, he said, listen to me also to see whether you are still of the same opinion, for I think that Thrasymachus gave up before he had to, charmed by you as by a snake charmer. I am not yet satisfied by the demonstration on either side. I am eager to hear the nature of each, of justice and injustice, and what effect its presence has upon the soul. I want to leave out of account the rewards and consequences of each. So, if you agree, I will do the following: I will renew the argument of Thrasymachus; I will first state what people consider the nature and origin of justice; secondly, that all who practise it do so unwillingly as being something necessary but not good; thirdly, that they have good reason to do so, for, according to what people say, the life of the unjust man is much better than that of the just.

It is not that I think so, Socrates, but I am perplexed and my ears are deafened listening to Thrasymachus and innumerable other speakers; I have never heard from anyone the sort of defence of justice that I want to hear, proving that it is better than injustice. I want to hear it praised for itself, and I think I am most likely to hear this from you. Therefore I am going to speak at length in praise of the unjust life and in doing so I will show you the way I want to hear you denouncing injustice and praising justice. See whether you want to hear what I suggest.

I want it more than anything else, I said. Indeed, what subject would a man of sense talk and hear about more often with enjoyment?

Splendid, he said, then listen while I deal with the first subject I mentioned: the nature and origin of justice.

They say that to do wrong is naturally good, to be wronged is bad, but the suffering of injury so far exceeds in badness the good of inflicting it that when men have done wrong to each other and suffered it, and have had a taste of both, those who are unable to avoid the latter and practice the former decide that it is profitable to come to an agreement with each other neither to inflict injury nor to suffer it. As a result they begin to make laws and covenants, and the law's command they call lawful and just. This, they say, is the origin and essence of justice; it stands between the best and the worst, the best being to do wrong without paying the penalty and the worst to be wronged without the power of revenge. The just then is a mean between two extremes; it is welcomed and honoured because of men's lack of the power to do wrong. The man who has that power, the real man, would not make a compact with anyone not to inflict injury or suffer it. For him that would be madness. This then, Socrates, is, according to their argument, the nature and origin of justice.

Even those who practice justice do so against their will because they lack the power to do wrong. This we could realize very clearly if we imagined ourselves granting to both the just and the unjust the freedom to do whatever they liked. We could then follow both of them and observe where their desires led them, and we would catch the just man redhanded travelling the same road as the unjust. The reason is the desire for undue gain which every organism by nature pursues as a good, but the law forcibly sidetracks him to honour equality. The freedom I just mentioned would most easily occur if these men had the power which they say the ancestor of the Lydian Gyges possessed. The story is that he was a shepherd in the service of the ruler of Lydia. There was a violent rainstorm and an earthquake which broke open the ground and created a chasm at the place where he was tending sheep. Seeing this and marvelling he went down into it. He saw, besides many other wonders of which we are told, a hollow bronze horse. There were window-like openings in it; he climbed through them and caught sight of a corpse which seemed of more than human stature, wearing nothing but a ring of gold on its finger. This ring the shepherd put on and came out. He arrived at the usual monthly meeting which reported to the king on the state of the flocks, wearing the ring. As he was sitting among the others he happened to twist the hoop of the ring towards himself, to the inside of his hand, and as he did this he became invisible to those sitting near him and they went on talking as if he had gone. He marvelled at this and, fingering the ring, he turned the hoop outward again and became visible. Perceiving this he tested whether the ring had this power and so it happened: if he turned the hoop inwards he became invisible, but was visible when he turned it outwards. When he realized this, he at once arranged to become one of the messengers to the king. He went, committed adultery with the king's wife, attacked the king with her help, killed him, and took over the kingdom.

Now if there were two such rings, one worn by the just man, the other by the unjust, no one, as these people think, would be so incorruptible that he would stay on the path of justice or bring himself to keep away from other people's property and not touch it, when he could with impunity take whatever he wanted from the market, go into houses and have sexual relations with anyone he wanted, kill anyone, free all those he wished from prison, and do the other things which would make him like a god among men. His actions would be in no way different from those of the other and they would both follow the same path. This, some would say, is a great proof that no one is just willingly[1] but under compulsion, so that justice is not one's private good, since wherever either thought he could do wrong with impunity he would do

---

[1] This of course directly contradicts the famous Socratic paradox that no one is willingly bad and that people do wrong because they have not the knowledge to do right, which is virtue.—TRANS.

so. Every man believes that injustice is much more profitable to himself than justice, and any exponent of this argument will say that he is right. The man who did not wish to do wrong with that opportunity, and did not touch other people's property, would be thought by those who knew it to be very foolish and miserable. They would praise him in public, thus deceiving one another, for fear of being wronged. So much for my second topic.

As for the choice between the lives we are discussing, we shall be able to make a correct judgment about it only if we put the most just man and the most unjust man face to face; otherwise we cannot do so. By face to face I mean this: let us grant to the unjust the fullest degree of injustice and to the just the fullest justice, each being perfect in his own pursuit. First, the unjust man will act as clever craftsmen do—a top navigator for example or physician distinguishes what his craft can do and what it cannot; the former he will undertake, the latter he will pass by, and when he slips he can put things right. So the unjust man's correct attempts at wrongdoing must remain secret; the one who is caught must be considered a poor performer, for the extreme of injustice is to have a reputation for justice, and our perfectly unjust man must be granted perfection in injustice. We must not take this from him, but we must allow that, while committing the greatest crimes, he has provided himself with the greatest reputation for justice; if he makes a slip he must be able to put it right; he must be a sufficiently persuasive speaker if some wrongdoing of his is made public; he must be able to use force, where force is needed, with the help of his courage, his strength, and the friends and wealth with which he has provided himself.

Having described such a man, let us now in our argument put beside him the just man, simple as he is and noble, who, as Aeschylus put it,[2] does not wish to appear just but to be so. We must take away his reputation, for a reputation for justice would bring him honour and rewards, and it would then not be clear whether he is what he is for justice's sake or for the sake of rewards and honour. We must strip him of everything except justice and make him the complete opposite of the other. Though he does no wrong, he must have the greatest reputation for wrongdoing so that he may be tested for justice by not weakening under ill repute and its consequences. Let him go his incorruptible way until death with a reputation for injustice throughout his life, just though he is, so that our two men may reach the extremes, one of justice, the other of injustice, and let them be judged as to which of the two is the happier.

Whew! My dear Glaucon, I said, what a mighty scouring you have given those two characters, as if they were statues in a competition.

I do the best I can, he replied. The two being such as I have described, there should be no difficulty in following the argument through as to what kind of life awaits each of them, but it must be said. And if what I say sounds rather boorish, Socrates, realize that it is not I who speak, but those who praise

2 In *Seven Against Thebes*, 592–594, it is said of Amphiaraus that "he did not wish to appear but to be the best," and it continues with the words quoted below: "He harbours in his heart a deep furrow, from which good counsels grow."—TRANS.

injustice as preferable to justice. They will say that the just man in these circumstances will be whipped, stretched on the rack, imprisoned, have his eyes burnt out, and, after suffering every kind of evil, he will be impaled and realize that one should not want to be just but to appear so. Indeed, Aeschylus' words are far more correctly applied to the unjust than to the just, for we shall be told that the unjust man pursues a course which is based on truth and not on appearances; he does not want to appear but to be unjust:

> He harvests in his heart a deep furrow
> from which good counsels grow.

He rules his city because of his reputation for justice, he marries into any family he wants to, he gives his children in marriage to anyone he wishes, he has contractual and other associations with anyone he may desire, and, beside all these advantages, he benefits in the pursuit of gain because he does not scruple to practise injustice. In any contest, public or private, he is the winner, getting the better of his enemies and accumulating wealth; he benefits his friends and does harm to his enemies. To the gods he offers grand sacrifices and gifts which will satisfy them, he can serve the gods much better than the just man, and also such men as he wants to, with the result that he is likely to be dearer to the gods. This is what they say, Socrates, that both from gods and men the unjust man secures a better life than the just.

After Glaucon had thus spoken I again had it in mind to say something in reply, but his brother Adeimantus intervened: You surely do not think that enough has been said from this point of view, Socrates?

Why not? said I.

The most important thing, that should have been said, has not been said, he replied.

Well then, I said, let brother stand by brother. If Glaucon has omitted something, you come to his help. Yet what he has said is sufficient to throw me and to make me incapable of coming to the help of justice.

Nonsense, he said. Hear what more I have to say, for we should also go fully into the arguments opposite to those he mentioned, those which praise justice and censure injustice, so that what I take to be Glaucon's intention may be clearer. When fathers speak to their sons, they say one must be just—and so do all who care for them, but they do not praise justice itself, only the high reputations it leads to, in order that the son, thought to be just, shall enjoy those public offices, marriages, and the rest which Glaucon mentioned, as they belong to the just man because of his high repute; they lay even greater emphasis on the results of reputation. They add popularity granted by the gods, and mention abundant blessings which, they say, the gods grant to the pious. So too the noble Hesiod and Homer declare,[3] the one that for the just the gods make "the oak trees bear acorns at the top and bees in the middle and their

---

3 The two quotations which immediately follow are from Hesiod's *Works and Days*, 232–233, and Homer, *Odyssey*, 19, 109.—TRANS.

fleecy sheep are heavy with their burden of wool" and many other blessings of like nature. The other says similar things:

> (like the fame) of a goodly king who, in his piety,
> upholds justice; for him the black earth bears wheat
> and barley and the trees are heavy with fruit; his
> sheep bear lambs continually and the sea provides its fish.

Musaeus[4] and his son grant from the gods more robust pleasures to the just. Their words lead the just to the underworld, and, seating them at table, provide them with a banquet of the saints, crown them with wreaths, and make them spend all their time drinking, as if they thought that the finest reward of virtue was perpetual drunkenness. Others stretch the rewards of virtue from the gods even further, for they say that the children and the children's children and the posterity of the pious man who keeps his oaths will survive into the future. Thus, and in other such ways, do they praise justice. The impious and unjust they bury in mud in the underworld, they force them to carry water in a sieve, they bring them into disrepute while still living, and they attribute to them all the punishments which Glaucon enumerated in the case of the just with a reputation for injustice, but they have nothing else to say. This then is the way people praise and blame justice and injustice.

Besides this, Socrates, look at another kind of argument which is spoken in private, and also by the poets, concerning justice and injustice. All go on repeating with one voice that justice and moderation are beautiful, but certainly difficult and burdensome, while incontinence and injustice are sweet and easy, and shameful only by repute and by law. They add that unjust deeds are for the most part more profitable than just ones. They freely declare, both in private and in public, that the wicked who have wealth and other forms of power are happy. They honour them but pay neither honour nor attention to the weak and the poor, though they agree that these are better men than the others.

What men say about the gods and virtue is the most amazing of all, namely that the gods too inflict misfortunes and a miserable life upon many good men, and the opposite fate upon their opposites. Begging priests and prophets frequent the doors of the rich and persuade them that they possess a god-given power to remedy by sacrifices and incantations at pleasant festivals any crime that the rich man or one of his ancestors may have committed. Moreover, if one wishes to harass some enemy, then at little expense he will be able to harm the just and the unjust alike, for by means of spells and enchantments they can persuade the gods to serve them. They bring the poets as witnesses to all this, some harping on the easiness of vice, that

> Vice is easy to choose in abundance, the path is
> smooth and it dwells very near, but sweat is placed by
> the gods on the way to virtue,

---

4 Musaeus was a legendary poet closely connected with the mystery religion of Orphism.—TRANS.

and a path which is long, rough, and steep;[5] others quote Homer as a witness that the gods can be influenced by men, for he too said:[6]

the gods themselves can be swayed by prayer, for
suppliant men can turn them from their purpose by
sacrifices and gentle prayers, by libations and burnt offerings
whenever anyone has transgressed and sinned.

They offer in proof a mass of writings by Musaeus and Orpheus, offspring, as they say, of Selene and the Muses. In accordance with these they perform their ritual and persuade not only individuals but whole cities that, both for the living and for the dead, there are absolutions and purifications for sin by means of sacrifices and pleasurable, playful rituals. These they call initiations which free from punishment yonder, where a dreadful fate awaits the uninitiated.

When all such sayings about the attitudes of men and gods toward virtue and vice are so often repeated, what effect, my dear Socrates, do we think they have upon the minds of our youth? One who is naturally talented and able, like a bee flitting from flower to flower gathering honey, to fit over these sayings and to gather from them an impression of what kind of man he should be and of how best to travel along the road of life, would surely repeat to himself the saying of Pindar: should I by justice or by crooked deceit scale this high wall and thus live my life fenced off from other men? The advantages said to be mine if I am just are of no use, I am told, unless I also appear so; while the troubles and penalties are obvious. The unjust man, on the other hand, who has secured for himself a reputation for justice, lives, they tell me, the life of a god. Therefore, since appearance, as the wise men tell me, forcibly overwhelms truth and controls happiness, this is altogether the way I should live. I should build around me a façade that gives the illusion of justice to those who approach me and keep behind this the greedy and crafty fox of the wise Archilochus.[7]

"But surely" someone objects, "it is not easy for vice to remain hidden always." We shall reply that nothing is easy which is of great import. Nevertheless, this is the way we must go if we are to be happy, and follow along the lines of all we have been told. To protect our secret we shall form sworn conspiratorial societies and political clubs. Besides, there are teachers of persuasion who make one clever in dealing with assemblies and with the courts. This will enable us to use persuasion here and force there, so that we can secure our own advantage without penalty.

"But one cannot force the gods nor have secrets from them." Well, if either they do not exist or do not concern themselves with human affairs, why should we worry about secrecy? If they do exist and do concern themselves, we have heard about them and know them from no other source than our laws and

---

5 Hesiod, *Work and Days*, 287–289.—TRANS.

6 Homer, *Iliad*, 9, 497–501.—TRANS.

7 I.e., the fox mentioned by Archilochus. The fable in question is not extant.—TRANS.

our genealogising poets, and these are the very men who tell us that the gods can be persuaded and influenced by gentle prayers and by offerings. We should believe both or neither. If we believe them, we should do wrong and then offer sacrifices from the proceeds. If we are just, we shall not be punished by the gods but we shall lose the profits of injustice. If we are unjust we shall get the benefit of sins and transgressions, and afterwards persuade the gods by prayer and escape without punishment. "But in Hades we will pay the penalty for the crimes committed here, either ourselves or our children's children." "My friend," the young man will reply as he does his reckoning, "mystery rites have great potency, and so have the gods of absolution, as the greatest cities tell us, and the children of the gods who have become poets and prophets tell us that this is so."

For what reason then should we still choose justice rather than the greatest injustice? If we practice the latter with specious decorum we shall do well at the hands of gods and of men; we shall live and die as we intend, for so both the many and the eminent tell us. From all that has been said, Socrates, what possibility is there that any man of power, be it the power of mind or of wealth, of body or of birth, will be willing to honour justice and not laugh aloud when he hears it praised? And surely any man who can show that what we have said is untrue and has full knowledge that justice is best, will be full of forgiveness, and not of anger, for the unjust. He knows that only a man of godlike character whom injustice disgusts, or one who has superior knowledge, avoids injustice, and that no other man is willingly just, but through cowardice or old age or some other weakness objects to injustice, because he cannot practice it. That this is so is obvious, for the first of these men to acquire power is the first to do wrong as much as he is able.

The only reason for all this talk, Socrates, which led to Glaucon's speech and mine, is to say to you: Socrates, you strange man, not one of all of you who profess to praise justice, beginning with the heroes of old, whose words are left to us, to the present day—not one has ever blamed injustice or praised justice in any other way than by mentioning the reputations, honours, and rewards which follow justice. No one has ever adequately described, either in poetry or in private conversation, what the very presence of justice or injustice in his soul does to a man even if it remains hidden from gods and men; one is the greatest evil the soul can contain, while the other, justice, is the greatest good. If you had treated the subject in this way and had persuaded us from youth, we should then not be watching one another to see we do no wrong, but every man would be his own best guardian and he would be afraid lest, by doing wrong, he live with the greatest evil.

Thrasymachus or anyone else might say what we have said, and perhaps more in discussing justice and injustice. I believe they would be vulgarly distorting the effect of each. To be quite frank with you, it is because I am eager to hear the opposite from you that I speak with all the emphasis I can muster. So do not merely give us a theoretical proof that justice is better than injustice, but tell us how each, in and by itself, affects a man, the one for good, the other for evil. Follow Glaucon's advice and do not take reputations into account, for if you do not deprive them of true reputation and attach false reputations to them, we shall say that you are not praising justice but the reputation for it, or blaming injustice but the appearance of it, that you are encouraging one to be unjust in secret, and that you agree with Thrasymachus that the just is another's good, the advantage of the stronger, while the unjust is one's own advantage and profit, though not the advantage of the weaker.

Since you have agreed that justice is one of the greatest goods, those which are worthy of attainment for their consequences, but much more for their own sake—sight, hearing, knowledge, health, and all other goods which are creative by what they are and not by what they seem—do praise justice in this regard: in what way does its very possession benefit a man and injustice harm him? Leave rewards and reputations for others to praise.

For others would satisfy me if they praised justice and blamed injustice in this way, extolling the rewards of the one and denigrating those of the other, but from you, unless you tell me to, I will not accept it, because you have spent your whole life investigating this and nothing else. Do not, therefore, give us a merely theoretical proof that justice is better than injustice, but tell us what effect each has in and by itself, the one for good, the other for evil, whether or not it be hidden from gods and men.

I had always admired the character of Glaucon and Adeimantus, and on this occasion I was quite delighted with them as I listened and I said: You are the sons of a great man, and Glaucon's lover began his elegy well when he wrote, celebrating the repute you gained at the battle of Megara:

Sons of Ariston, godlike offspring of a famous man.

That seems well deserved, my friends; you must be divinely inspired if you are not convinced that injustice is better than justice, and yet can speak on its behalf as you have done. And I do believe that you are really unconvinced by your own words. I base this belief on my knowledge of the way you live, for, if I had only your words to go by, I would not trust you. The more I trust you, however, the more I am at a loss what to do. I do not see how I can be of help; I feel myself incapable. I see a proof of this in the fact that I thought what I said to Thrasymachus showed that justice is better than injustice, but you refuse to accept this as adequate. On the other hand I do not see how I can refuse my help, for I fear it is even impious to be present when justice is being charged and to fail to come to her help as long as there is breath in one's body and one is still able to speak. So the best course is to give her any assistance I can.

•   •   •

3

Morality and Self-Interest

THOMAS HOBBES

Thomas Hobbes (1588–1679) made important contributions in metaphysics and psychology as well as political theory and ethics. The following selection is from his masterpiece Leviathan, *chapters 13, 14, 15, 17, 18, and 21.*

According to Hobbes, morality is ultimately grounded in self-interest. In his view, people act solely to achieve gratification and to avoid being harmed. If this view is correct (it is criticized by Joel Feinberg in reading 1), the only effective reason for being moral is that morality serves each person's interest. And this is, in fact, Hobbes's position. He argues that justice, gratitude, and other elements of morality serve to ward off strife and disorder. For this reason, conformity to them is dictated by various "laws of nature."

Do such laws always apply? According to Hobbes, they do not. When we keep an agreement without assurance that others will do likewise, we needlessly jeopardize ourselves. Since this is not reasonable, moral requirements apply only when backed by force. As Hobbes himself puts it, "covenants without the sword are but words." To provide the required force, we need a government, or "sovereign," that is stronger than any citizen or group of citizens. By imposing severe penalties for disobedience, the government removes incentives to attack or betray others for gain or through fear. It thus makes possible both morality and peace.

OF THE NATURAL CONDITION OF
MANKIND AS CONCERNING THEIR FELICITY AND MISERY

Nature hath made men so equal, in the faculties of the body, and mind; as that though there be found one man sometimes manifestly stronger in body, or of quicker mind than another; yet when all is reckoned together, the difference between man, and man, is not so considerable, as that one man can thereupon claim to himself any benefit, to which another may not pretend, as well as he. For as to the strength of body, the weakest has strength enough to kill the strongest, either by secret machination, or by confederacy with others, that are in the same danger with himself.

And as to the faculties of the mind, setting aside the arts grounded upon words, and especially that skill of proceeding upon general, and infallible rules, called science; which very few have, and but in few things; as being not a native faculty, born with us; nor attained, as prudence, while we look after somewhat else, I find yet a greater equality amongst men, than that of strength. For prudence, is but experience; which equal time, equally bestows on all men, in those things they equally apply themselves unto. That which may perhaps make such equality incredible, is but a vain conceit of one's own wisdom, which almost all men think they have in a greater degree, than the vulgar; that is, than all men but themselves, and a few others, whom by fame, or for concurring with themselves, they approve. For such is the nature of men, that howsoever they may acknowledge many others to be more witty, or more eloquent, or more learned; yet they will hardly believe there be many so wise as themselves; for they see their own wit at hand, and other men's at a distance. But this proveth rather that men are in that point equal, than unequal. For there is not ordinarily a greater sign of the equal distribution of any thing, than that every man is contented with his share.

From this equality of ability, ariseth equality of hope in the attaining of our ends. And therefore if any two men desire the same thing, which nevertheless they cannot both enjoy, they become enemies; and in the way to their end, which is principally their own conservation, and sometimes their delectation only, endeavour to destroy, or subdue one another. And from hence it comes to pass, that where an invader hath no more to fear, than another man's single power; if one plant, sow, build, or possess a convenient seat, others may probably be expected to come prepared with forces united, to dispossess, and deprive him, not only of the fruit of his labour, but also of his life, or liberty. And the invader again is in the like danger of another.

And from this diffidence of one another, there is no way for any man to secure himself, so reasonable, as anticipation; that is, by force, or wiles, to master the persons of all men he can, so long, till he see no other power great enough to endanger him: and this is no more than his own conservation requireth, and is generally allowed. Also because there be some, that taking pleasure in contemplating their own power in the acts of conquest, which they pursue farther than their security requires; if others, that otherwise would be glad to be at ease within modest bounds, should not by invasion increase their power, they would not be able, long time, by standing only on their defence, to subsist. And by consequence, such augmentation of dominion over men being necessary to a man's conservation, it ought to be allowed him.

Again, men have no pleasure, but on the contrary a great deal of grief, in keeping company, where there is no power able to over-awe them all. For every man looketh that his companion should value him, at the same rate he sets upon himself: and upon all signs of contempt, or undervaluing, naturally endeavours, as far as he dares, (which amongst them that have no common power to keep them in quiet, is far enough to make them destroy each other), to extort a greater value from his contemners, by damage; and from others, by the example.

So that in the nature of man, we find three principal causes of quarrel. First, competition; secondly, diffidence; thirdly, glory.

The first, maketh men invade for gain; the second, for safety; and the third, for reputation. The first use violence, to make themselves masters of other men's persons, wives, children, and cattle; the second, to defend them; the third, for trifles, as a word, a smile, a different opinion, and any other sign of undervalue, either direct in their persons, or by reflection in their kindred, their friends, their nation, their profession, or their name.

Hereby it is manifest, that during the time men live without a common power to keep them all in awe, they are in that condition which is called war; and such a war, as is of every man, against every man. For WAR, consisteth not in battle only, or the act of fighting; but in a tract of time, wherein the will to contend by battle is sufficiently known: and therefore the notion of *time,* is to be considered in the nature of war; as it is in the nature of weather. For as the nature of foul weather, lieth not in a shower or two of rain; but in an inclination thereto of many days together; so the nature of war, consisteth not in actual fighting; but in the known disposition thereto, during all the time there is no assurance to the contrary. All other time is PEACE.

Whatsoever therefore is consequent to a time of war, where every man is enemy to every man; the same is consequent to the time, wherein men live without other security, than what their own strength, and their own invention shall furnish them withal. In such condition, there is no place for industry; because the fruit thereof is uncertain: and consequently no culture of the earth; no navigation, nor use of the commodities that may be imported by sea; no commodious building; no instruments of moving, and removing, such things as require much force; no knowledge of the face of the earth; no account of time; no arts; no letters; no society; and which is worst of all; continual fear, and danger of violent death; and the life of man, solitary, poor, nasty, brutish, and short.

It may seem strange to some man, that has not well weighed these things; that nature should thus dissociate, and render men apt to invade, and destroy one another: and he may therefore, not trusting to this inference, made from the passions, desire perhaps to have the same confirmed by experience. Let him therefore consider with himself, when taking a journey, he arms himself, and seeks to go well accompanied; when going to sleep, he locks his doors; when even in his house he locks his chests; and this when he knows there be laws, and public officers, armed, to revenge all injuries shall be done him; what opinion he has of his fellow-subjects, when he rides armed; of his fellow citizens, when he locks his doors; and of his children, and servants, when he locks his chests. Does he not there as much accuse mankind by his actions, as I do by my words? But neither of us accuse man's nature in it. The desires, and other passions of man, are in themselves no sin. No more are the actions, that proceed from those passions, till they know a law that forbids them: which till laws be made they cannot know: nor can any law be made, till they have agreed upon the person that shall make it.

It may peradventure be thought, there was never such a time, nor condition of war as this; and I believe it was never generally so, over all the world: but there are many places, where they live so now. For the savage people in many places of America, except the government of small families, the concord whereof dependeth on natural lust, have no government at all; and live at this day in that brutish manner, as I said before. Howsoever, it may be perceived what manner of life there would be, where there were no common power to fear, by the manner of life, which men that have formerly lived under a peaceful government, use to degenerate into, in a civil war.

But though there had never been any time, wherein particular men were in a condition of war one against another; yet in all times, kings, and persons of sovereign authority, because of their independency, are in continual jealousies, and in the state and posture of gladiators; having their weapons pointing, and their eyes fixed on one another; that is, their forts, garrisons, and guns upon the frontiers of their kingdoms; and continual spies upon their neighbors; which is a posture of war. But because they uphold thereby, the industry of their subjects; there does not follow from it, that misery, which accompanies the liberty of particular men.

To this war of every man, against every man, this also is consequent; that nothing can be unjust. The notions of right and wrong, justice and injustice have there no place. Where there is no common power, there is no law: where no law, no injustice. Force, and fraud, are in war the two cardinal virtues. Justice, and injustice are none of the faculties neither of the body, nor mind. If they were, they might be in a man that were alone in the world, as well as his senses, and passions. They are qualities, that relate to men in society, not in solitude. It is consequent also to the same condition, that there be no propriety, no dominion, no *mine* and *thine* distinct; but only that to be every man's, that he can get: and for so long, as he can keep it. And thus much for the ill condition, which man by mere nature is actually placed in; though with a possibility to come out of it, consisting partly in the passions, partly in his reason.

The passions that incline men to peace, are fear of death; desire of such things as are necessary to commodious living; and a hope by their industry to obtain them. And reason suggesteth convenient articles of peace, upon which men may be drawn to agreement. These articles, are they, which otherwise are called the Laws of Nature: whereof I shall speak more particularly, in the two following chapters.

OF THE FIRST AND SECOND
NATURAL LAWS, AND OF CONTRACTS

The RIGHT OF NATURE, which writers commonly call *jus naturale,* is the liberty each man hath, to use his own power, as he will himself, for the preservation of his own nature; that is to say, of his own life; and consequently, of doing any thing, which in his own judgment, and reason, he shall conceive to be the aptest means thereunto.

By LIBERTY, is understood, according to the proper signification of the word, the absence of external impediments: which impediments, may oft take away part of a man's power to do what he would; but cannot hinder him from using the power left him, according as his judgment, and reason shall dictate to him.

A LAW OF NATURE, *lex naturalis,* is a precept or general rule, found out by reason, by which a man is forbidden to do that, which is destructive of his life, or taketh away the means of preserving the same; and to omit that, by which he thinketh it may be best preserved. For though they that speak of this subject, use to confound *jus,* and *lex, right* and *law:* yet they ought to be distinguished; because RIGHT, consisteth in liberty to do, or to forbear: whereas LAW, determineth, and bindeth to one of them: so that law, and right, differ as much, as obligation, and liberty; which in one and the same matter are inconsistent.

And because the condition of man, as hath been declared in the precedent chapter, is a condition of war of every one against every one; in which case every one is governed by his own reason; and there is nothing he can make use of, that may not be a help unto him, in preserving his life against his enemies; it followeth, that in such a condition, every man has a right to every thing; even to one another's body. And therefore, as long as this natural right of every man to every thing endureth, there can be no security to any man, how strong or wise soever he be, of living out the time, which nature ordinarily alloweth men to live. And consequently it is a precept, or general rule of reason, *that every man, ought to endeavour peace, as far as he has hope of obtaining it; and when he cannot obtain it, that he may seek, and use, all helps, and advantages of war.* The first branch of which rule, containeth the first, and fundamental law of nature; which is, *to seek peace, and follow it.* The second, the sum of the right of nature; which is, *by all means we can, to defend ourselves.*

From this fundamental law of nature, by which men are commanded to endeavour peace, is derived this second law; *that a man be willing, when others are so too, as far-forth, as for peace, and defence of himself he shall think it necessary, to lay down this right to all things; and be contented with so much liberty against other men, as he would allow other men against himself.* For as long as every man holdeth this right, of doing any thing he liketh; so long are all men in the condition of war. But if other men will not lay down their right, as well as he; then there is no reason for any one, to divest himself of his: for that were to expose himself to prey, which no man is bound to, rather than to dispose himself to peace. This is that law of the Gospel; *whatsoever you require that others should do to you, that do ye to them.* And that law of all men, *quod tibi fieri non vis, alteri ne feceris.*

To *lay down* a man's *right* to any thing, is to *divest* himself of the *liberty,* of hindering another of the benefit of his own right to the same. For he that renounceth, or passeth away his right, giveth not to any other man a right which he had not before; because there is nothing to which every man had not right by nature: but only standeth out of his way, that he may enjoy his own original right, without hindrance from him; not without hindrance from another. So that the effect which redoundeth to one man, by another man's defect of right, is but so much diminution of impediments to the use of his own right original.

Right is laid aside, either by simply renouncing it; or by transferring it to another. By *simply* RENOUNCING; when he cares not to whom the benefit thereof redoundeth. By TRANSFERRING; when he intendeth the benefit thereof to some certain person, or persons. And when a man hath in either manner abandoned, or granted away his right; then he is said to be OBLIGED, or BOUND, not to hinder those, to whom such right is granted, or abandoned, from the benefit of it: and that he *ought,* and it is his DUTY, not to make void that voluntary act of his own: and that such hindrance is INJUSTICE, and INJURY, as being *sine jure;* the right being before renounced, or transferred. So that *injury,* or *injustice,* in the controversies of the world, is somewhat like to that, which in the disputations of scholars is called *absurdity.* For as it is there called an absurdity, to contradict what one maintained in the beginning: so in the world, it is called injustice, and injury, voluntarily to undo that, which from the beginning he had voluntarily done. The way by which a man either simply renounceth, or transferreth his right, is a declaration, or signification, by some voluntary and sufficient sign, or signs, that he doth so renounce, or transfer; or hath so renounced, or transferred the same, to him that accepteth it. And these signs are either words only, or actions only; or, as it happeneth most often, both words, and actions. And the same are the BONDS, by which men are bound, and obliged: bonds, that have their strength, not from their own nature, for nothing is more easily broken than a man's word, but from fear of some evil consequence upon the rupture.

Whensoever a man transferreth his right, or renounceth it; it is either in consideration of some right reciprocally transferred to himself; or for some other good he hopeth for thereby. For it is a voluntary act: and of the voluntary acts of every man, the object is some *good to himself.* And therefore there be some rights, which no man can be understood by any words, or other signs, to have abandoned, or transferred. As first a man cannot lay down the right of resisting them, that assault him by force, to take away his life; because he cannot be understood to aim thereby, at any good to himself. The same may be said of wounds, and chains, and imprisonment; both because there is no benefit consequent to such patience; as there is to the patience of suffering another to be wounded, or imprisoned: as also because a man cannot tell, when he seeth men proceed against him by violence, whether they intend his death or not. And lastly the motive, and end for which this renouncing, and transferring of right is introduced, is nothing else but the security of a man's person, in his life, and in the means of so preserving life, as not to be weary of it. And therefore if a man by words, or other signs, seem to despoil himself of the end, for which those signs were intended; he is not to be understood as if he meant it, or that it was his will; but that he was ignorant of how such words and actions were to be interpreted.

The mutual transferring of right, is that which men call CONTRACT.

There is difference between transferring of right to the thing; and transferring, or tradition, that is delivery of the thing itself. For the thing may be delivered together with the translation of the right; as in buying and selling with ready-money; or exchange of goods, or lands: and it may be delivered some time after.

Again, one of the contractors, may deliver the thing contracted for on his part, and leave the other to perform his part at some determinate time after, and in the mean time be trusted; and then the contract on his part, is called PACT, or COVENANT: or both parts may contract now, to perform hereafter: in which cases, he that is to perform in time to come, being trusted, his performance is called *keeping of promise,* or faith; and the failing of performance, if it be voluntary, *violation of faith.*

• • •

If a covenant be made, wherein neither of the parties perform presently, but trust one another; in the condition of mere nature, which is a condition of war of every man against every man, upon any reasonable suspicion, it is void: but if there be a common power set over them both, with right and force sufficient to compel performance, it is not void. For he that performeth first, has no assurance the other will perform after; because the bonds of words are too weak to bridle men's ambition, avarice, anger, and other passions, without the fear of some coercive power; which is the condition of mere nature, where all men are equal, and judges of the justness of their own fears, cannot possibly be supposed. And therefore he which performeth first, does but betray himself to his enemy; contrary to the right, he can never abandon, of defending his life, and means of living.

But in a civil estate, where there is a power set up to constrain those that would otherwise violate their faith, that fear is no more reasonable; and for that cause, he which by the covenant is to perform first, is obliged so to do.

The cause of fear, which maketh such a covenant invalid, must be always something arising after the covenant made; as some new fact, or other sign of the will not to perform: else it cannot make the covenant void. For that which could not hinder a man from promising, ought not to be admitted as a hindrance of performing.

• • •

A covenant not to defend myself from force, by force, is always void. For, as I have showed before, no man can transfer, or lay down his right to save himself from death, wounds, and imprisonment, the avoiding whereof is the only end of laying down any right; and therefore the promise of not resisting force, in no covenant transferreth any right; nor is obliging. For though a man may covenant thus, *unless I do so, or so, kill me;* he cannot covenant thus, *unless I do so, or so, I will not resist you, when you come to kill me.* For man by nature chooseth the lesser evil, which is danger of death in resisting; rather than the greater, which is certain and present death is not resisting. And this is granted to be true by all men, in that they lead criminals to execution, and prison, with armed men, notwithstanding that such criminals have consented to the law, by which they are condemned.

• • •

OF OTHER LAWS OF NATURE

From that law of nature, by which we are obliged to transfer to another, such rights, as being retained, hinder the peace of mankind, there followeth a third; which is this, *that men perform their covenants made:* without which, covenants are in vain, and but empty words; and the right of all men to all things remaining, we are still in the condition of war.

And in this law of nature, consisteth the fountain and original of JUSTICE. For where no covenant hath preceded, there hath no right been transferred, and every man has right to every thing; and consequently, no action can be unjust. But when a covenant is made, then to break it is *unjust:* and the definition of INJUSTICE, is no other than *the not performance of covenant.* And whatsoever is not unjust, is *just.*

But because covenants of mutual trust, where there is a fear of not performance on either part, as hath been said in the former chapter, are invalid; though the original of justice be the making of covenants; yet injustice actually there can be none, till the cause of such fear be taken away; which while men are in the natural condition of war, cannot be done. Therefore before the names of just, and unjust can have place, there must be some coercive power, to compel men equally to the performance of their covenants, by the terror of some punishment, greater than the benefit they expect by the breach of their covenant; and to make good that propriety, which by mutual contract men acquire, in recompense of the universal right they abandon: and such power there is none before the erection of a commonwealth. And this is also to be gathered out of the ordinary definition of justice in the Schools: for they say, that *justice is the constant will of giving to every man his own.* And therefore where there is no *own,* that is no propriety, there is no injustice; and where there is no coercive power erected, that is, where there is no commonwealth, there is no propriety; all men having right to all things: therefore where there is no commonwealth, there nothing is unjust. So that the nature of justice, consisteth in keeping of valid covenants: but the validity of covenants begins not but with the constitution of a civil power, sufficient to compel men to keep them: and then it is also that propriety begins.

The fool hath said in his heart, there is no such thing as justice; and sometimes also with his tongue; seriously alleging, that every man's conservation, and contentment, being committed to his own care, there could be no reason, why every man might not do what he thought conduced thereunto: and therefore also to make, or not make; keep, or not keep covenants, was not against reason, when it conduced to one's benefit. He does not therein deny, that there be covenants; and that they are sometimes broken, sometimes kept; and that such breach of them may be called injustice, and the observance of them justice: but he questioneth, whether injustice, taking away the fear of God, for the same fool hath said in his heart there is no God, may not sometimes stand with that reason, which dictateth to every man his own good; and particularly then, when it conduceth to such a benefit, as shall put a man in a condition, to neglect not only the dispraise, and revilings, but also the power of other men. The kingdom of God is gotten by violence: but what if it could be gotten by unjust violence? were it against reason so to get it, when it is impossible to receive hurt by it? and if it be not against reason, it is not against justice; or else justice is not to be approved for good. From such reasoning as this, successful wickedness hath obtained the name of virtue: and some that in all other things have disallowed the violation of faith; yet have allowed it, when it is for the getting of a kingdom. And the heathen that believed, that Saturn was deposed by his son Jupiter, believed nevertheless the same Jupiter to be the avenger of injustice: somewhat like to a piece of law in Coke's *Commentaries on Littleton;* where he says, if the right heir of the crown be attainted of treason; yet the crown shall descend to him, and *eo instante* the attainder be void: from which instances a man will be very prone to infer; that when the heir apparent of a kingdom, shall kill him that is in possession, though his father; you may call it injustice, or by what other name you will; yet it can never be against reason, seeing all the voluntary actions of men tend to the benefit of themselves; and those actions are most reasonable, that conduce most to their ends. This specious reasoning is nevertheless false.

For the question is not of promises mutual, where there is no security of performance on either side; as when there is no civil power erected over the parties promising; for such promises are no covenants: but either where one of the parties has performed already; or where there is a power to make him perform; there is the question whether it be against reason, that is, against the benefit of the other to perform, or not. And I say it is not against reason. For the manifestation whereof, we are to consider; first, that when a man doth a thing, which notwithstanding any thing can be foreseen, and reckoned on, tendeth to his own destruction, howsoever some accident which he could not expect, arriving may turn it to his benefit; yet such events do not make it reasonably or wisely done. Secondly, that in a condition of war, wherein every man to every man, for want of a common power to keep them all in awe, is an enemy, there is no man who can hope by his own strength, or wit, to defend himself from destruction, without the help of confederates; where every one expects the same defence by the confederation, that any one else does: and therefore he which declares he thinks it reason to deceive those that help him, can in reason expect no other means of safety, than what can be had from his own single power. He therefore that breaketh his covenant, and consequently declareth that he thinks he may with reason do so, cannot be received into any society, that unite themselves for peace and defence, but by the error of them that receive him; nor when he is received, he retained in it, without seeing the danger of their error; which errors a man cannot reasonably reckon upon as the means of his security: and therefore if he be left, or cast out of society, he perisheth; and if he live in society, it is by the errors of other men, which he could not foresee, nor reckon upon; and consequently against the reason of his preservation; and so, as all men that contribute not to his destruction, forbear him only out of ignorance of what is good for themselves.

• • •

Whatsoever is done to a man, conformable to his own will signified to the doer, is no injury to him. For if he that doeth it, hath not passed away his original right to do what he please, by some antecedent covenant, there is no breach of covenant; and therefore no injury done him. And if he have; then his will to have it done being signified, is a release of that covenant: and so again there is no injury done him.

Justice of actions, is by writers divided into *commutative,* and *distributive:* and the former they say consisteth in proportion arithmetical; the latter in proportion geometrical. Commutative therefore, they place in the equality of value of the things contracted for; and distributive in the distribution of equal benefit, to men of equal merit. As if it were injustice to sell dearer than we buy; or to give more to a man than he merits. The value of all things contracted for, is measured by the appetite of the contractors: and therefore the just value, is that which they be contented to give. And merit (besides that which is by covenant, where the performance on one part, meriteth the performance on the other part, and falls under justice commutative, not distributive) is not due to justice; but is rewarded of grace only. And therefore this distinction, in the sense wherein it useth to be expounded, is not right. To speak properly, commutative justice, is the justice, of a contractor; that is, a performance of covenant, in buying, and selling; hiring, and letting to hire; lending, and borrowing; exchanging, bartering, and other acts of contract.

And distributive justice, the justice of an arbitrator; that is to say, the act of defining what is just. Wherein, being trusted by them that make him arbitrator, if he perform his trust, he is said to distribute to every man his own: and this is indeed just distribution, and may be called, though improperly, distributive justice; but more properly equity; which also is a law of nature, as shall be shown in due place.

As justice dependeth on antecedent covenant; so does GRATITUDE depend on antecedent grace; that is to say, antecedent free gift: and is the fourth law of nature; which may be conceived in this form, *that a man which receiveth benefit from another of mere grace, endeavour that he which giveth it, have no reasonable cause to repent him of his good will.* For no man giveth, but with intention of good to himself; because gift is voluntary; and of all voluntary acts, the object is to every man his own good, of which if men see they shall be frustrated, there will be no beginning of benevolence, or trust; nor consequently of mutual help; nor of reconciliation of one man to another; of *war;* which is contrary to the first and fundamental law of nature, which commandeth men to *seek peace.* The breath of this law, is called *ingratitude;* and hath the same relation to grace, that injustice hath to obligation by covenant.

A fifth law of nature, is COMPLAISANCE; that is to say, *that every man strive to accommodate himself to the rest*. For the understanding whereof, we may consider, that there is in men's aptness to society, a diversity of nature, rising from their diversity of affections; not unlike to that we see in stones brought together for building of an edifice. For as that stone which by the asperity, and irregularity of figure, takes more room from others, than itself fills; and for the hardness, cannot be easily made plain, and thereby hindereth the building, is by the builders cast away as unprofitable, and troublesome: so also, a man that by asperity of nature, will strive to retain those things which to himself are superfluous, and to others necessary; and for the stubbornness of his passions, cannot be corrected, is to be left, or cast out of society, as cumbersome thereunto. For seeing every man, not only by right, but also by necessity of nature, is supposed to endeavour all he can, to obtain that which is necessary for his conservation; he that shall oppose himself against it, for things superfluous, is guilty of the war that thereupon is to follow; and therefore doth that, which is contrary to the fundamental law of nature, which commandeth *to seek peace*. The observers of this law, may be called SOCIABLE, the Latins call them *commodi*; the contrary, *stubborn, insociable, forward, intractable*.

A sixth law of nature, is this, *that upon caution of the future time, a man ought to pardon the offences past of them that repenting, desire it*. For PARDON, is nothing but granting of peace; which though granted to them that persevere in their hostility, be not peace, but fear; yet not granted to them that give caution of the future time, is sign of an aversion to peace; and therefore contrary to the law of nature.

A seventh is, *that in revenges*, that is, retribution of evil for evil, *men look not at the greatness of the evil past, but the greatness of the good to follow*. Whereby we are forbidden to inflict punishment with any other design, than for correction of the offender, or direction of others. For this law is consequent to the next before it, that commandeth pardon, upon security of the future time. Besides, revenge without respect to the example, and profit to come, is a triumph, or glorying in the hurt of another, tending to no end; for the end is always somewhat to come; and glorying to no end, is vain-glory, and contrary to reason, and to hurt without reason, tendeth to the introduction of war; which is against the law of nature; and is commonly styled by the name of *cruelty*.

• • •

And because, though men be never so willing to observe these laws, there may nevertheless arise questions concerning a man's action; first, whether it were done, or not done; secondly, if done, whether against the law, or not against the law; the former whereof, is called a question *of fact*; the latter a question *of right*, therefore unless the parties to the question, covenant mutually to stand to the sentence of another, they are as far from peace as ever. This other to whose sentence they submit is called an ARBITRATOR. And therefore it is of the law of nature, *that they that are at controversy, submit their right to the judgment of an arbitrator.*

And seeing every man is presumed to do all things in order to his own benefit, no man is a fit arbitrator in his own cause; and if he were never so fit; yet equity allowing to each party equal benefit, if one be admitted to be judge, the other is to be admitted also; and so the controversy, that is, the cause of war, remains, against the law of nature.

For the same reason no man in any cause ought to be received for arbitrator, to whom greater profit, or honour, or pleasure apparently ariseth out of the victory of one party, than of the other: for he hath taken, though an unavoidable bribe, yet a bribe; and no man can be obliged to trust him. And thus also the controversy, and the condition of war remaineth, contrary to the law of nature.

And in a controversy *of fact,* the judge being to give no more credit to one, than to the other, if there be no other arguments, must give credit to a third; or to a third and fourth; or more: for else the question is undecided, and left to force, contrary to the law of nature.

These are the laws of nature, dictating peace, for a means of the conservation of men in multitudes; and which only concern the doctrine of civil society. There be other things tending to the destruction of particular men; as drunkenness, and all other parts of intemperance; which may therefore also be reckoned amongst those things which the law of nature hath forbidden; but are not necessary to be mentioned, nor are pertinent enough to this place.

And though this may seem too subtle a deduction of the laws of nature, to be taken notice of by all men; whereof the most part are too busy in getting food, and the rest too negligent to understand; yet to leave all men inexcusable, they have been contracted into one easy sum, intelligible even to the meanest capacity; and that is, *Do not that to another, which thou wouldest not have done to thyself;* which sheweth him, that he had no more to do in learning the laws of nature, but, when weighing the actions of other men with his own, they seem too heavy, to put them into the other part of the balance, and his own into their place, that his own passions, and self-love, may add nothing to the weight; and then there is none of these laws of nature that will not appear unto him very reasonable.

The laws of nature oblige *in foro interno;* that is to say, they bind to a desire they should take place: but *in foro externo;* this is, to the putting them in act, not always. For he that should be modest, and tractable, and perform all he promises, in such time, and place, where no man else should do so, should but make himself a prey to others, and procure his own certain ruin, contrary to the ground of all laws of nature, which tend to nature's preservation. And again, he that having sufficient security, that others shall observe the same laws towards him, observes them not himself, seeketh not peace, but war; and consequently the destruction of his nature by violence.

And whatsoever laws bind *in foro interno,* may be broken, not only by a fact contrary to the law, but also by a fact according to it, in case a man think it contrary. For though his action in this case, be according to the law; yet his purpose was against the law; which, where the obligation is *in foro interno,* is a breach.

The laws of nature are immutable and eternal; for injustice, ingratitude, arrogance, pride, iniquity, acception of persons, and the rest, can never be made lawful. For it can never be that war shall preserve life, and peace destroy it.

The same laws, because they oblige only to a desire, and endeavour, I mean an unfeigned and constant endeavour, are easy to be observed. For in that they require nothing but endeavour, he that endeavoureth their performance, fulfilleth them; and he that fulfilleth the law, is just.

And the science of them, is the true and only moral philosophy. For moral philosophy is nothing else but the science of what is *good,* and *evil,* in the conversation, and society of mankind. *Good,* and *evil,* are names that signify our appetites, and aversions; which in different tempers, customs, and doctrines of men, are different: and divers men, differ not only in their judgment, on the senses of what is pleasant, and unpleasant to the taste, smell, hearing, touch, and sight; but also of what is conformable, or disagreeable to reason, in the actions of common life. Nay, the same man, in divers times, differs from himself; and one time praiseth, that is, calleth good, what another time he dispraiseth, and calleth evil: from whence arise disputes, controversies, and at last war. And therefore so long a man is in the condition of mere nature, which is a condition of war, as private appetite is the measure of good, and evil: and consequently all men agree on this, that peace is good, and therefore also the way, or means of peace, which, as I have shewed before, are *justice, gratitude, modesty, equity, mercy,* and the rest of the laws of nature, are good; that is to say; *moral virtues;* and their contrary *vices,* evil. Now the science of virtue and vice, is moral philosophy; and therefore the true doctrine of the laws of nature, is the true moral philosophy. But the writers of moral philosophy, though they acknowledge the same virtues and vices; yet not seeing wherein consisted their goodness; nor that they come to be praised, as the means of peaceable, sociable, and comfortable living, place them in a mediocrity of passions: as if not the cause, but the degree of daring, made fortitude; or not the cause, but the quantity of a gift, made liberality.

These dictates of reason, men used to call by the names of laws, but improperly: for they are but conclusions, or theorems concerning what conduceth to the conservation and defence of themselves; whereas law, properly, is the word of him, that by right hath command over others. But yet if we consider the same theorems, as delivered in the word of God, that by right commandeth all things; then are they properly called laws.

OF THE CAUSES, GENERATION, AND DEFINITION OF A COMMONWEALTH

The final cause, end, or design of men, who naturally love liberty, and dominion over others, in the introduction of that restraint upon themselves, in which we see them live in commonwealths, is the foresight of their own preservation, and of a more contented life thereby; that is to say, of getting themselves out from that miserable condition of war, which is necessarily consequent, as hath been shown (chapter 13), to the natural passions of men, when there is no visible power to keep them in awe, and tie them by fear of punishment to the performance of their covenants, and observation of those laws of nature set down in the fourteenth and fifteenth chapters.

For the laws of nature, as *justice, equity, modesty, mercy,* and, in sum, *doing to others, as we would be done to,* of themselves, without the terror of some power, to cause them to be observed, are contrary to our natural passions, that carry us to partiality, pride, revenge, and the like. And covenants, without the sword, are but words, and of no strength to secure a man at all. Therefore notwithstanding the laws of nature (which every one hath then kept, when he has the will to keep them, when he can do it safely) if there be no power erected, or not great enough for our security; every man will, and may lawfully rely on his own strength and art, for caution against all other men. And in all places, where men have lived by small families, to rob and spoil one another, has been a trade, and so far from being reputed against the law of nature, that the greater spoils they gained, the greater was their honour; and men observed no other laws therein, but the laws of honour; that is, to abstain from cruelty, leaving to men their lives, and instruments of husbandry. And as small families did then; so now do cities and kingdoms which are but greater families, for their own security, enlarge their dominions, upon all pretences of danger, and fear of invasion, or assistance that may be given to invaders, and endeavour as much as they can, to subdue, or weaken their neighbours, by open force, and secret arts, for want of other caution, justly; and are remembered for it in after ages with honour.

· · ·

It is true, that certain living creatures, as bees, and ants, live sociably one with another, which are therefore by Aristotle numbered amongst political creatures; and yet have no other direction, than their particular judgments and appetites; not speech, whereby one of them can signify to another, what he thinks expedient for the common benefit: and therefore some man may perhaps desire to know, why mankind cannot do the same. To which I answer,

First, that men are continually in competition for honour and dignity, which these creatures are not; and consequently amongst men there ariseth on that ground, envy and hatred, and finally war; but amongst these not so.

Secondly, that amongst these creatures, the common good differeth not from the private; and being by nature inclined to their private, they procure thereby the common benefit. But man, whose joy consisteth in comparing himself with other men, can relish nothing but what is eminent.

Thirdly, that these creatures, having not, as man, the use of reason, do not see, nor think they see any fault, in the administration of their common business;

whereas amongst men, there are very many, that think themselves wiser, and abler to govern the public, better than the rest; and these strive to reform and innovate, one this way, another that way; and thereby bring it into distraction and civil war.

Fourthly, that these creatures, though they have some use of voice, in making known to one another their desires, and other affections; yet they want that art of words, by which some men can represent to others, that which is good, in the likeness of evil; and evil, in the likeness of good; and augment, or diminish the apparent greatness of good and evil; discontenting men, and troubling their peace at their pleasure.

Fifthly, irrational creatures cannot distinguish between *injury,* and *damage;* and therefore as long as they be at ease, they are not offended with their fellows: whereas man is then most troublesome, when he is most at ease: for then it is that he loves to shew his wisdom, and control the actions of them that govern the commonwealth.

Lastly, the agreement of these creatures is natural; that of men, is by covenant only, which is artificial: and therefore it is no wonder if there be somewhat else required, besides covenant, to make their agreement constant and lasting; which is a common power, to keep them in awe, and to direct their actions to the common benefit.

The only way to erect such a common power, as may be able to defend them from the invasion of foreigners, and the injuries of one another, and thereby to secure them in such sort, as that by their own industry, and by the fruits of the earth, they may nourish themselves and live contentedly; is, to confer all their power and strength upon one man, or upon one assembly of men, that may reduce all their wills, by plurality of voices, unto one will: which is as much as to say, to appoint one man, or assembly of men, to bear their person; and every one to own, and acknowledge himself to be author of whatsoever he that so beareth their person, shall act, or cause to be acted, in those things which concern the common peace and safety; and therein to submit their wills, every one to his will, and their judgments, to his judgment. This is more than consent, or concord; it is a real unity of them all, in one and the same person, made by covenant of every man with every man, in such manner, as if every man should say to every man, *I authorize and give up my right of governing myself, to this man, or to this assembly of men, on this condition, that thou give up thy right to him, and authorize all his actions in like manner.* This done, the multitude so united in one person, is called a COMMONWEALTH, in Latin CIVITAS. This is the generation of that great LEVIATHAN, or rather, to speak more reverently, of that *mortal god,* to which we owe under the *immortal God,* our peace and defence. For by this authority, given him by every particular man in the commonwealth, he hath the use of so much power and strength conferred on him, that by terror thereof, he is enabled to form the wills of them all, to peace at home, and mutual aid against their enemies abroad. And in him consisteth the essence of the commonwealth; which, to define it, is *one person, of whose acts a great multitude, by mutual covenants one with another, have made themselves every one the author, to the end he may use the strength and means of them all, as he shall think expedient, for their peace and common defence.*

And he that carrieth this person is called SOVEREIGN, and said to have *sovereign power;* and every one besides, his SUBJECT.

•   •   •

4

Morality and Advantage

DAVID GAUTHIER

David Gauthier (b. 1932) is Distinguished Service Professor of Philosophy at the University of Pittsburgh. His book Morals by Agreement *is an important contemporary contribution to ethics. This essay appeared in* The Philosophical Review *(October 1967).*

Adapting an example from the mathematical theory of games, Gauthier shows that what is individually rational may be collectively irrational. If each person does what is best for him, the overall result may not be best for anyone. Gauthier suggests further that immorality may exhibit just this structure. Even if each person can sometimes benefit by acting immorally, it may be that each would do better if everyone were moral than if everyone were not. In that case, it will be true in one sense, but false in another, that morality is in each person's interest.

I

Hume asks, rhetorically, "What theory of morals can ever serve any useful purpose, unless it can show, by a particular detail, that all the duties which it recommends, are also the true interest of each individual?"[1] But there are many to whom this question does not seem rhetorical. Why, they ask, do we speak the language of morality, impressing upon our fellows their duties and obligations, urging them with appeals to what is right and good, if we could speak to the same effect in the language of prudence, appealing to considerations of interest and advantage? When the poet, Ogden Nash, is moved by the muse to cry out:

O Duty,
Why hast thou not the visage of a sweetie or a cutie?[2]

---

[1] David Hume, *An Enquiry Concerning the Principles of Morals*, sec. ix, pt. ii.

[2] Ogden Nash, "Kind of an Ode to Duty."

we do not anticipate the reply:

> O Poet,
> I really am a cutie and I think you ought to know it.

The belief that duty cannot be reduced to interest, or that morality may require the agent to subordinate all considerations of advantage, is one which has withstood the assaults of contrary-minded philosophers from Plato to the present. Indeed, were it not for the conviction that only interest and advantage can motivate human actions, it would be difficult to understand philosophers contending so vigorously for the identity, or at least compatibility, of morality with prudence.

Yet if morality is not true prudence it would be wrong to suppose that those philosophers who have sought some connection between morality and advantage have been merely misguided. For it is a truism that we should all expect to be worse off if men were to substitute prudence, even of the most enlightened kind, for morality in all of their deliberations. And this truism demands not only some connection between morality and advantage, but a seemingly paradoxical connection. For if we should all expect to suffer, were men to be prudent instead of moral, then morality must contribute to advantage in a unique way, a way in which prudence—following reasons of advantage—cannot.

Thomas Hobbes is perhaps the first philosopher who tried to develop this seemingly paradoxical connection between morality and advantage. But since he could not admit that a man might ever reasonably subordinate considerations of advantage to the dictates of obligation, he was led to deny the possibility of real conflict between morality and prudence. So his argument fails to clarify the distinction between the view that claims of obligation reduce to considerations of interest and the view that claims of obligation promote advantage in a way in which considerations of interest cannot.

More recently, Kurt Baier has argued that "being moral is following rules designed to overrule self-interest whenever it is in the interest of everyone alike that everyone should set aside his interest."[3] Since prudence is following rules of (enlightened) self-interest, Baier is arguing that morality is designed to overrule prudence when it is to everyone's advantage that it do so—or, in other words, that morality contributes to advantage in a way in which prudence cannot.[4]

Baier does not actually demonstrate that morality contributes to advantage in this unique and seemingly paradoxical way. Indeed, he does not ask how it is possible that morality should do this. It is this possibility which I propose to demonstrate.

---

3 Kurt Baier, *The Moral Point of View: A Rational Basis of Ethics* (Ithaca, 1958), p. 314.

4 That this, and only this, is what he is entitled to claim may not be clear to Baier, for he supposes his account of morality to answer the question "Why should we be moral?" interpreting "we" distributively. This, as I shall argue in Sec. IV, is quite mistaken.

II

Let us examine the following proposition, which will be referred to as "the thesis": *Morality is a system of principles such that it is advantageous for everyone if everyone accepts and acts on it, yet acting on the system of principles requires that some persons perform disadvantageous acts.*[5]

What I wish to show is that this thesis *could be true,* that morality could possess those characteristics attributed to it by the thesis. I shall not try to show that the thesis is true—indeed, I shall argue in Section V that it presents at best an inadequate conception of morality. But it is plausible to suppose that a modified form of the thesis states a necessary, although not a sufficient, condition for a moral system.

Two phrases in the thesis require elucidation. The first is "advantageous for everyone." I use this phrase to mean that *each* person will do better if the system is accepted and acted on than if *either* no system is accepted and acted on *or* a system is accepted and acted on which is similar, save that it never requires any person to perform disadvantageous acts.

Clearly, then, the claim that it is advantageous for everyone to accept and act on the system is a very strong one; it may be so strong that no system of principles which might be generally adopted could meet it. But I shall consider in Section V one among the possible ways of weakening the claim.

The second phrase requiring elucidation is "disadvantageous acts." I use this phrase to refer to acts which, in the context of their performance, would be less advantageous to the performer than some other act open to him in the same context. The phrase does not refer to acts which merely impose on the performer some short-term disadvantage that is recouped or outweighed in the long run. Rather it refers to acts which impose a disadvantage that is never recouped. It follows that the performer may say to himself, when confronted with the requirement to perform such an act, that it would be better *for him* not to perform it.

It is essential to note that the thesis, as elucidated, does not maintain that morality is advantageous for everyone in the sense that each person will do *best* if the system of principles is accepted and acted on. Each person will do better than if no system is adopted, or than if the one particular alternative mentioned above is adopted, but not than if any alternative is adopted.

Indeed, for each person required by the system to perform some disadvantageous act, it is easy to specify a better alternative—namely, the system modified so that it does not require *him* to perform any act disadvantageous to himself. Of course, there is no reason to expect such an alternative to be better than the moral system for everyone, or in fact for anyone other than the person granted the special exemption.

---

5 The thesis is not intended to state Baier's view of morality. I shall suggest in Sec. V that Baier's view would require substituting "everyone can expect to benefit" for "it is advantageous to everyone." The thesis is stronger and easier to discuss.

A second point to note is that each person must gain more from the disadvantageous acts performed by others than he loses from the disadvantageous acts performed by himself. If this were not the case, then some person would do better if a system were adopted exactly like the moral system save that it never requires *any* person to perform disadvantageous acts. This is ruled out by the force of "advantageous for everyone."

This point may be clarified by an example. Suppose that the system contains exactly one principle. Everyone is always to tell the truth. It follows from the thesis that each person gains more from those occasions on which others tell the truth, even though it is disadvantageous to them to do so, than he loses from those occasions on which he tells the truth even though it is disadvantageous to him to do so.

Now this is not to say that each person gains by telling others the truth in order to ensure that in return they tell him the truth. Such gains would merely be the result of accepting certain short-term disadvantages (those associated with truth-telling) in order to reap long-term benefits (those associated with being told the truth). Rather, what is required by the thesis is that those disadvantages which a person incurs in telling the truth, when he can expect neither short-term nor long-term benefits to accrue to him from truth-telling, are outweighed by those advantages he receives when others tell him the truth when they can expect no benefits to accrue to them from truth-telling.

The principle enjoins truth-telling in those cases in which whether one tells the truth or not will have no effect on whether others tell the truth. Such cases include those in which others have no way of knowing whether or not they are being told the truth. The thesis requires that the disadvantages one incurs in telling the truth in these cases are less than the advantages one receives in being told the truth by others in parallel cases; and the thesis requires that this holds for everyone.

Thus we see that although the disadvantages imposed by the system on any person are less than the advantages secured him through the imposition of disadvantages on others, yet the disadvantages are real in that incurring them is *unrelated* to receiving the advantages. The argument of long-term prudence, that I ought to incur some immediate disadvantage *so that* I shall receive compensating advantages later on, is entirely inapplicable here.

III

It will be useful to examine in some detail an example of a system which possesses those characteristics ascribed by the thesis to morality. This example, abstracted from the field of international relations, will enable us more clearly to distinguish, first, conduct based on immediate interest; second, conduct which is truly prudent; and third, conduct which promotes mutual advantage but is not prudent.

A and *B* are two nations with substantially opposed interests, who find themselves engaged in an arms race against each other. Both possess the latest in weaponry, so that each recognizes that the actual outbreak of full scale war between them would be mutually disastrous. This recognition leads A and B to agree that each would be better off if they were mutually disarming instead of mutually arming. For mutual disarmament would preserve the balance of power between them while reducing the risk of war.

Hence A and B enter into a disarmament pact. The pact is advantageous for both if both accept and act on it, although clearly it is not advantageous for either to act on it if the other does not.

Let A be considering whether or not to adhere to the pact in some particular situation, whether or not actually to perform some act of disarmament. A will quite likely consider the act to have disadvantageous consequences. A expects to benefit, not by its own acts of disarmament, but by B's acts. Hence if A were to reason simply in terms of immediate interest, A might well decide to violate the pact.

But A's decision need be neither prudent nor reasonable. For suppose first that B is able to determine whether or not A adheres to the pact. If A violates, then B will detect the violation and will then consider what to do in the light of A's behavior. It is not to B's advantage to disarm alone; B expects to gain, not by its own acts of disarmament, but by A's acts. Hence A's violation, if known to B, leads naturally to B's counterviolation. If this continues, the effect of the pact is entirely undone, and A and B return to their mutually disadvantageous arms race. A, foreseeing this when considering whether or not to adhere to the pact in the given situation, must therefore conclude that the truly prudent course of action is to adhere.

Now suppose that B is unable to determine whether or not A adheres to the pact in the particular situation under consideration. If A judges adherence to be in itself disadvantageous, then it will decide, both on the basis of immediate interest and on the basis of prudence, to violate the pact. Since A's decision is unknown to B, it cannot affect whether or not B adheres to the pact, and so the advantage gained by A's violation is not outweighed by any consequent loss.

Therefore, if A and B are prudent they will adhere to their disarmament pact whenever violation would be detectable by the other, and violate the pact whenever violation would not be detectable by the other. In other words, they will adhere openly and violate secretly. The disarmament pact between A and B thus possesses two of the characteristics ascribed by the thesis to morality. First, accepting the pact and acting on it is more advantageous for each than making no pact at all. Second, in so far as the pact stipulates that each must disarm even when disarming is undetectable by the other, it requires each to perform disadvantageous acts—acts which run counter to considerations of prudence.

One further condition must be met if the disarmament pact is to possess those characteristics ascribed by the thesis to a system of morality. It must be the case that the requirement that each party perform disadvantageous acts be essential to the advantage conferred by the pact; or, to put the matter in the way in which we expressed it earlier, both A and B must do better to adhere to this pact than to a pact which is similar save that it requires no disadvantageous acts. In terms of the example, A and B must do better to adhere to the pact than to a pact which stipulates that each must disarm only when disarming is detectable by the other.

We may plausibly suppose this condition to be met. Although A will gain by secretly retaining arms itself, it will lose by B's similar acts, and its losses may well outweigh its gains. B may equally lose more by A's secret violations than it gains by its own. So, despite the fact that prudence requires each to violate secretly, each may well do better if both adhere secretly than if both violate secretly. Supposing this to be the case, the disarmament pact is formally analogous to a moral system, as characterized by the thesis. That is, acceptance of and adherence to the pact by A and B is more advantageous for each, either than making no pact at all or than acceptance of and adherence to a pact requiring only open disarmament, and the pact requires each to perform acts of secret disarmament which are disadvantageous.

Some elementary notation, adapted for our purposes from the mathematical theory of games, may make the example even more perspicuous. Given a disarmament pact between A and B, each may pursue two pure strategies—adherence and violation. There are, then, four possible combinations of strategies, each determining a particular outcome. These outcomes can be ranked preferentially for each nation; we shall let the numerals 1 to 4 represent the ranking from first to fourth preference. Thus we construct a simple matrix,[6] in which A's preferences are stated first:

		B	
		adheres	violates
	adheres	2,2	4,1
A			
	violates	1,4	3,3

The matrix does not itself show that agreement is advantageous to both, for it gives only the rankings of outcomes given the agreement. But it is plausible to assume that A and B would rank mutual violation on a par with no agreement. If we assume this, we can then indicate the value to each of making and adhering to the pact by reference to the matrix.

The matrix shows immediately that adherence to the pact is not the most advantageous possibility for either, since each prefers the outcome, if it alone violates, to the outcome of mutual adherence. It shows also that each gains less from its own violations than it loses from the other's, since each ranks mutual adherence above mutual violation.

Let us now use the matrix to show that, as we argued previously, public adherence to the pact is prudent and mutually advantageous, whereas private adherence is not prudent although mutually advantageous. Consider first the case when adherence—and so violation—are open and public.

6 Those familiar with the theory of games will recognize the matrix as a variant of the Prisoner's Dilemma. In a more formal treatment, it would be appropriate to develop the relation between morality and advantage by reference to the Prisoner's Dilemma. This would require reconstructing the disarmament pact and the moral system as proper games. Here I wish only to suggest the bearing of game theory on our enterprise.

If adherence and violation are open, then each knows the strategy chosen by the other, and can adjust its own strategy in the light of this knowledge—or, in other words, the strategies are interdependent. Suppose that each initially chooses the strategy of adherence. A notices that if it switches to violation it gains—moving from 2 to 1 in terms of preference ranking. Hence immediate interest dictates such a switch. But it notices further that if it switches, then B can also be expected to switch—moving from 4 to 3 on its preference scale. The eventual outcome would be stable, in that neither could benefit from switching from violation back to adherence. But the eventual outcome would represent not a gain for A but a loss—moving from 2 to 3 on its preference scale. Hence prudence dictates no change from the strategy of adherence. This adherence is mutually advantageous; A and B are in precisely similar positions in terms of their pact.

Consider now the case when adherence and violation are secret and private. Neither nation knows the strategy chosen by the other, so the two strategies are independent. Suppose A is trying to decide which strategy to follow. It does not know B's choice. But it notices that if B adheres, then it pays A to violate, attaining 1 rather than 2 in terms of preference ranking. If B violates, then again it pays A to violate, attaining 3 rather than 4 on its preference scale. Hence, no matter which strategy B chooses, A will do better to violate, and so prudence dictates violation.

B of course reasons in just the same way. Hence each is moved by considerations of prudence to violate the pact, and the outcome assigns each rank 3 on its preference scale. This outcome is mutually disadvantageous to A and B, since mutual adherence would assign each rank 2 on its preference scale.

If A and B are both capable only of rational prudence, they find themselves at an impasse. The advantage of mutual adherence to the agreement when violations would be secret is not available to them, since neither can find it in his own overall interest not to violate secretly. Hence, strictly prudent nations cannot reap the maximum advantage possible from a pact of the type under examination.

Of course, what A and B will no doubt endeavor to do is eliminate the possibility of secret violations of their pact. Indeed, barring additional complications, each must find it to his advantage to make it possible for the other to detect his own violations. In other words, each must find it advantageous to ensure that their choice of strategies is interdependent, so that the pact will always be prudent for each to keep. But it may not be possible for them to ensure this, and to the extent that they cannot, prudence will prevent them from maximizing mutual advantage.

IV

We may now return to the connection of morality with advantage. Morality, if it is a system of principles of the type characterized in the thesis, requires that some persons perform acts genuinely disadvantageous to themselves, as a means to greater mutual advantage. Our example shows sufficiently that such a system is possible, and indicates more precisely its character. In particular, by an argument strictly parallel to that which we have pursued, we may show that men who are merely prudent will not perform the required disadvantageous acts. But in so violating the principles of morality, they will disadvantage themselves. Each will lose more by the violations of others than he will gain by his own violations.

Now this conclusion would be unsurprising if it were only that no man can gain if he alone is moral rather than prudent. Obviously such a man loses, for he adheres to moral principles to his own disadvantage, while others violate them also to his disadvantage. The benefit of the moral system is not one which any individual can secure for himself, since each man gains from the sacrifices of others.

What is surprising in our conclusion is that no man can ever gain if he is moral. Not only does he not gain by being moral if others are prudent, but he also does not gain by being moral if others are moral. For although he now receives the advantage of others' adherence to moral principles, he reaps the disadvantage of his own adherence. As long as his own adherence to morality is independent of what others do (and this is required to distinguish morality from prudence), he must do better to be prudent.

If all men are moral, all will do better than if all are prudent. But any one man will always do better if he is prudent than if he is moral. There is no real paradox in supposing that morality is advantageous, even though it requires the performance of disadvantageous acts.

On the supposition that morality has the characteristics ascribed to it by the thesis, is it possible to answer the question "Why should we be moral?" where "we" is taken distributively, so that the question is a compendious way of asking, for each person, "Why should I be moral?" More simply, is it possible to answer the question "Why should I be moral?"

I take it that this question, if asked seriously, demands a reason for being moral other than moral reasons themselves. It demands that moral reasons be shown to be reasons for acting by a noncircular argument. Those who would answer it, like Baier, endeavor to do so by the introduction of considerations of advantage.

Two such considerations have emerged from our discussion. The first is that if all are moral, all will do better than if all are prudent. This will serve to answer the question "Why should we be moral?" if this question is interpreted rather as "Why should we all be moral—rather than all being something else?" If we must all be the same, then each person has a reason—a prudential reason—to prefer that we all be moral.

But, so interpreted, "Why should we be moral?" is not a compendious way of asking, for each person, "Why should I be moral?" Of course, if everyone is to be whatever I am, then I should be moral. But a general answer to the question "Why should I be moral?" cannot presuppose this.

The second consideration is that any individual always does better to be prudent rather than moral, provided his choice does not determine other choices. But in so far as this answers the question "Why should I be moral?" it leads to the conclusion "I should not be moral." One feels that this is not the answer which is wanted.

We may put the matter otherwise. The individual who needs a reason for being moral which is not itself a moral reason cannot have it. There is nothing surprising about this; it would be much more surprising if such reasons could be found. For it is more than apparently paradoxical to suppose that considerations of advantage could ever of themselves justify accepting a real disadvantage.

V

I suggested in Section II that the thesis, in modified form, might provide a necessary, although not a sufficient, condition for a moral system. I want now to consider how one might characterize the man who would qualify as moral according to the thesis—I shall call him the "moral" man—and then ask what would be lacking from this characterization, in terms of some of our commonplace moral views.

The rationally prudent man is incapable of moral behavior, in even the limited sense defined by the thesis. What difference must there be between the prudent man and the "moral" man? Most simply, the "moral" man is the prudent but trustworthy man. I treat trustworthiness as the capacity which enables its possessor to adhere, and to judge that he ought to adhere, to a commitment which he has made, without regard to considerations of advantage.

The prudent but trustworthy man does not possess this capacity completely. He is capable of trustworthy behavior only in so far as he regards his *commitment* as advantageous. Thus he differs from the prudent man just in the relevant respect; he accepts arguments of the form "If it is advantageous for me to agree[7] to do x, and I do agree to do x, then I ought to do x, whether or not it then proves advantageous for me to do x."

Suppose that A and B, the parties to the disarmament pact, are prudent but trustworthy. A, considering whether or not secretly to violate the agreement, reasons that its advantage in making and keeping the agreement, provided B does so as well, is greater than its advantage in not making it. If it can assume that B reasons in the same way, then it is in a position to conclude that it ought not to violate the pact. Although violation would be advantageous,

---

7 The word "agree" requires elucidation. It is essential not to confuse an advantage in agreeing to do x with an advantage in saying that one will do x. If it is advantageous for me to agree to do x, then there is some set of actions open to me which includes both saying that I will do x and doing x, and which is more advantageous to me than any set of actions open to me which does not include saying that I will do x. On the other hand, if it is advantageous for me to say that I will do x, then there is some set of actions open to me which includes saying that I will do x, and which is more advantageous to me than any set which does not include saying that I will do x. But this set need not include doing x.

consideration of this advantage is ruled out by *A*'s trustworthiness, given the advantage in agreeing to the pact.

The prudent but trustworthy man meets the requirements implicitly imposed by the thesis for the "moral" man. But how far does this "moral" man display two characteristics commonly associated with morality—first, a willingness to make sacrifices, and second, a concern with fairness?

Whenever a man ignores his own advantage for reasons other than those of greater advantage, he may be said to make some sacrifice. The "moral" man, in being trustworthy, is thus required to make certain sacrifices. But these are extremely limited. And—not surprisingly, given the general direction of our argument—it is quite possible that they limit the advantages which the "moral" man can secure.

Once more let us turn to our example. *A* and *B* have entered into a disarmament agreement and, being prudent but trustworthy, are faithfully carrying it out. The government of *A* is now informed by its scientists, however, that they have developed an effective missile defense, which will render *A* invulnerable to attack by any of the weapons actually or potentially at *B*'s disposal, barring unforeseen technological developments. Furthermore, this defense can be installed secretly. The government is now called upon to decide whether to violate its agreement with *B*, install the new defense, and, with the arms it has retained through its violation, establish its dominance over *B*.

A is in a type of situation quite different from that previously considered. For it is not just that *A* will do better by secretly violating its agreement. *A* reasons not only that it will do better to violate no matter what *B* does, but that it will do better if both violate than if both continue to adhere to the pact. *A* is now in a position to gain from abandoning the agreement; it no longer finds mutual adherence advantageous.

We may represent this new situation in another matrix:

		B	
		adheres	*violates*
	adheres	3,2	4,1
A			
	violates	1,4	2,3

We assume again that the ranking of mutual violation is the same as that of no agreement. Now had this situation obtained at the outset, no agreement would have been made, for *A* would have had no reason to enter into a disarmament pact. And of course had *A* expected this situation to come about, no agreement—or only a temporary agreement—would have been made; *A* would no doubt have risked the short-term dangers of the continuing arms race in the hope of securing the long-run benefit of predominance over *B* once its missile defense was completed. On the contrary, *A* expected to benefit from the agreement, but now finds that, because of its unexpected development of a missile defense, the agreement is not in fact advantageous to it.

The prudent but trustworthy man is willing to carry out his agreements, and judges that he ought to carry them out, in so far as he considers them advantageous. *A* is prudent but trustworthy. But is *A* willing to carry out its agreement to disarm, now that it no longer considers the agreement advantageous?

If *A* adheres to its agreement in this situation, it makes a sacrifice greater than any advantage it receives from the similar sacrifices of others. It makes a sacrifice greater in kind than any which can be required by a mutually advantageous agreement. It must, then, possess a capacity for trustworthy behavior greater than that ascribed to the merely prudent but trustworthy man (or nation). This capacity need not be unlimited; it need not extend to a willingness to adhere to any commitment no matter what sacrifice is involved. But it must involve a willingness to adhere to a commitment made in the expectation of advantage, should that expectation be disappointed.

I shall call the man (or nation) who is willing to adhere, and judges that he ought to adhere, to his prudentially undertaken agreements even if they prove disadvantageous to him, the trustworthy man. It is likely that there are advantages available to trustworthy men which are not available to merely prudent but trustworthy men. For there may be situations in which men can make agreements which each expects to be advantageous to him, provided he can count on the others' adhering to it whether or not their expectation of advantage is realized. But each can count on this only if all have the capacity to adhere to commitments regardless of whether the commitment actually proves advantageous. Hence, only trustworthy men who know each other to be such will be able rationally to enter into, and so to benefit from, such agreements.

Baier's view of morality departs from that stated in the thesis in that it requires trustworthy, and not merely prudent but trustworthy, men. Baier admits that "a person might do better for himself by following enlightened self-interest rather than morality."[8] This admission seems to require that morality be a system of principles which each person may expect, initially, to be advantageous to him, if adopted and adhered to by everyone, but not a system which actually is advantageous to everyone.

Our commonplace moral views do, I think, support the view that the moral man must be trustworthy. Hence, we have established one modification required in the thesis, if it is to provide a more adequate set of conditions for a moral system.

But there is a much more basic respect in which the "moral" man falls short of our expectations. He is willing to temper his singleminded pursuit of advantage only by accepting the obligation to adhere to prudentially undertaken commitments. He has no real concern for the advantage of others, which would lead him to modify his pursuit of advantage when it conflicted with the similar pursuits of others. Unless he expects to gain, he is unwilling to accept restrictions on the pursuit of advantage which are intended to equalize the opportunities open to all. In other words, he has no concern with fairness.

---

[8] Baier, op. cit., p. 314.

We tend to think of the moral man as one who does not seek his own well-being by means which would deny equal well-being to his fellows. This marks him off clearly from the "moral" man, who differs from the prudent man only in that he can overcome the apparent paradox of prudence and obtain those advantages which are available only to those who can display real restraint in their pursuit of advantage.

Thus a system of principles might meet the conditions laid down in the thesis without taking any account of considerations of fairness. Such a system would contain principles for ensuring increased advantage (or expectation of advantage) to everyone, but no further principle need be present to determine the distribution of this increase.

It is possible that there are systems of principles which, if adopted and adhered to, provide advantages which strictly prudent men, however rational, cannot attain. These advantages are a function of the sacrifices which the principles impose on their adherents.

Morality may be such a system. If it is, this would explain our expectation that we should all be worse off were we to substitute prudence for morality in our deliberations. But to characterize morality as a system of principles advantageous to all is not to answer the question "Why should I be moral?" nor is it to provide for those considerations of fairness which are equally essential to our moral understanding.

5

The 'Is-Ought' Problem Resolved

ALAN GEWIRTH

Alan Gewirth (b. 1912) taught philosophy for many years at the University of Chicago. He is the author of Reason and Morality *and many essays on ethical theory and is a past president of the American Philosophical Association's Western Division. This selection was originally his presidential address to that body. Its middle section is omitted here.*

The "is-ought problem" to which Gewirth's title refers was first posed by David Hume (see reading 8). Hume asked how it can ever be legitimate to draw conclusions about what we ought to do, or what ought to happen, from premises about what is the case. In other words, how can we derive normative conclusions from factual premises?

In this essay, Gewirth first refines this problem and then proposes a solution to it. To reach that solution, Gewirth employs what he calls the "dialectically necessary method." His method is dialectical because, like Plato in the Socratic dialogues, he starts from the claims of others. But unlike Plato, Gewirth does not begin with claims that people just happen to make. Instead, he proceeds from assumptions to which we commit ourselves merely by acting. Since we cannot avoid acting, these assumptions are, for practical purposes, necessary.

What, then, are the assumptions? Since all action is purposive, all agents must regard their purposes as valuable. And since freedom and well-being are needed to achieve any purposes, all agents must also regard their freedom and well-being as valuable. Because of this, all agents must see themselves as having rights to freedom and well-being. And because these rights are seen to follow from agency alone, each agent must ascribe them to all other agents. But if all other agents have these rights, then we ought not to harm or interfere with them. Thus, the transition from "is" to "ought" is made.

When I told one of my philosophical friends the title of this paper, he suggested that I make a slight addition, so that the title would read: "The 'Is-Ought' Problem Resolved—Again?!" Indeed, I agree with his implied conviction that on certain interpretations of it the 'Is-Ought' Problem has already been resolved several times; and I wish to emphasize that these resolutions and the polemical exchanges generated by them have done much to sharpen the issues. Nevertheless, I also maintain that the real 'Is-Ought' Problem has not yet been resolved. I therefore want to do three main things in this paper. First, I shall present what I take to be the real 'Is-Ought' Problem and shall indicate why it is the real one. Second, I shall review the main recent attempts to resolve the Problem and shall show that none of these has succeeded so far as the real 'Is-Ought' Problem is concerned. Third, I shall give my resolution of this real Problem.

I

First, then, what is the real 'Is-Ought' Problem? It will come as no surprise that the Problem is concerned with moral 'oughts'. After all, it was in the context of a discussion of the basis of "moral distinctions" that Hume wrote his famous passage about the need for explaining and justifying the transition from 'is' to 'ought' as copulas of propositions.[1] And in the introduction to a recent anthology devoted to the subject, the editor writes that the 'Is-Ought' Problem is "the central problem in moral philosophy."[2]

Now the word 'moral' is used in several different senses. While taking account of these differences, I shall focus on certain paradigm cases of what are undeniably moral 'ought'-judgments which persons have sought to derive from 'is'-statements. These judgments are of two main kinds. One kind sets forth negative moral duties to refrain from inflicting serious harm on other persons. Their paradigm uses have been of this form: "A tends to do X to B in order to gratify A's inclinations although he knows this will bring only great suffering to B; therefore, A ought not to do X to B." The other kind sets forth positive duties to perform certain actions for the benefit of other persons, especially where the latter would otherwise suffer serious harm. Their paradigm uses have been of this sort: "B is drowning and A by throwing him a rope can rescue him; therefore A ought to throw the rope to B;" or "B is starving while A has plenty of food; therefore A ought to give some food to B;" and so forth. In addition to such individual moral duties, persons have also sought to derive more specifically sociopolitical moral 'oughts' from 'is'-statements; for example, "That society is characterized by great inequalities of wealth and power; therefore it ought to be changed;" or "This state respects civil liberties; therefore we ought to that extent to support it;" and so forth.

The 'oughts' presented in these judgments have five important formal and material characteristics, which will constitute five interrelated conditions or tests that must be satisfied by any solution of the real 'Is-Ought' Problem. First, the 'oughts' are moral ones in the sense that they take positive account of the interests of other persons as well as the agent or speaker, especially as

---

1 *Treatise of Human Nature,* III.i.1 (ed. Selby-Bigge, pp. 469–470).

2 W.D. Hudson, ed., *The Is-Ought Question* (London: Macmillan and Co., 1969), p. 11.

regards the distribution of what is considered to be basic well-being. It is this well-being, indicated in the antecedent 'is'-statements, that provides the reasons for the actions urged in the 'ought'-judgments.

Second, these 'oughts' are prescriptive in that their users advocate or seek to guide or influence actions, which they set forth as required by the facts presented in the antecedents. Although not all uses of 'ought' are prescriptive, such advocacy marks the unconditional use of 'ought' as in the above cases, where the antecedent empirical statements serve not to qualify or restrict the 'oughts' but rather to indicate the facts or reasons which make them mandatory.

Third, the 'oughts' are egalitarian in that they require that at least basic well-being be distributed equally as between the agent addressed and his potential recipients, or as among the members of a society. Although such egalitarianism is sometimes made part of the definition of 'moral', and I shall myself sometimes use 'moral' to include both this and the prescriptiveness just mentioned, it seems best to distinguish these considerations, since there may, after all, be non-egalitarian moralities.

A fourth important characteristic of these 'oughts' is that they are determinate. By this I mean that the actions they prescribe have definite contents such that the opposite contents cannot be obtained by the same mode of derivation. Thus, in my above example, the 'oughts' require, respectively, rescuing, feeding, not harming; at the same time they are opposite-excluding in that one cannot, by the mode of derivation in question, obtain as conclusions 'oughts' which permit or require not rescuing, not feeding, or harming.

A fifth characteristic of these 'oughts', which to some extent encompasses some of the other characteristics, is that they are categorical, not merely hypothetical. By this characteristic, which applies more directly to the individual 'ought'-judgments, I mean that the requirements set forth therein are normatively overriding and ineluctable or necessary, in that their bindingness cannot be removed by, and hence is not contingent on or determined by, variable, escapable features either of the persons addressed or of their social relations. These escapable, non-determining features include the self-interested desires of the persons addressed, their variable choices, opinions, and attitudes, and institutional rules whose obligatoriness may itself be doubtful or variable.

Now it is with 'ought'-judgments having these five characteristics of being moral, prescriptive, egalitarian, determinate, and categorical that the real 'Is-Ought' Problem is concerned. The Problem is this: how can 'ought'-judgments having these five characteristics be logically derived from, or be justified on the basis of, premises which state empirical facts? As this question suggests, a sixth condition which must be satisfied by any solution of the real 'Is-Ought' Problem is that of non-circularity, especially in the respect that the premises from which the 'ought'-conclusions are derived must not themselves be moral or prescriptive. The resolution of the Problem calls not only for presenting a derivation which satisfies these six conditions but also for a theory which adequately explains why this derivation is successful and why previous attempts at derivation have been unsuccessful. There may indeed be problems about deriving from empirical statements 'ought'-judgments which lack one or more of these five characteristics; but they are not the real 'Is-Ought' Problem, not only because, having fewer conditions to satisfy, they are easier to resolve, but also because they necessarily fail to cope with the issue of justifying categorical moral 'ought'-judgments, judgments which bear on the most basic requirements of how persons ought to live in relation to one another.

It is the decisive importance of this issue of justification that makes the real 'Is-Ought' Problem at once so central and so difficult for moral philosophy. There is a familiar sequence of considerations at this point. The moral 'ought'-judgments of the sort I mentioned above are not self-evident; hence if they are to be justified at all they must be derived in some way from other statements. These other, justifying statements must themselves be either moral or nonmoral (where 'moral' here includes also the characteristics of prescriptiveness and categoricalness). If the justifying statements are moral ones, then there recurs the question of how *they* are to be justified, since they too are not self-evident, and the question continues to recur as we mount through more general moral rules and principles. If, on the other hand, the statements from which the moral 'ought'-judgments are to be derived are non-moral ones, such as the empirical statements that figured in my paradigm cases, then there is the difficulty that the 'ought'-judgments are not derivable from those statements either inductively or deductively, unless we define 'ought' in empirical terms; and such a definition raises many questions of adequacy, including how the 'ought'-judgments can pass the tests of prescriptiveneses and categoricalness. But it seems clear that if the moral 'ought'-judgments cannot in any way be justified on the basis of empirical and logical considerations, i.e. by logical derivation from 'is'-statements, then they cannot be definitively justified at all. Hence the crucial importance of the real 'Is-Ought' Problem.

I shall use the expression *external model* and *internal model* to distinguish the two chief positions on this issue. The external model holds that 'ought' is external to 'is' in that there is a basic logical gap between them: 'ought' cannot be correctly defined in terms of empirical and logical considerations alone, nor can these considerations constitute determinate criteria of 'ought' because any facts adduced as such criteria must ultimately reflect personal and hence variable decisions; consequently, 'ought' cannot be logically derived from 'is.' The internal model upholds the opposite position. The external model asserts also that 'ought'-judgments are not self-evident, so it concludes that they are not capable of any definitive justification at all; they reflect decisions or attitudes to which, at least at an ultimate level, questions of justification are inapplicable. Although logical gaps of some sort have also been held to underlie various other philosophical Problems—for example, in the Problem of Induction there is the logical gap between particular observation-statements and general laws, and in the Mind-Body Problem there is the logical gap between statements about bodily movements and statements about intentional human actions— the 'is-ought' gap is declared by the external model to be much wider than any of these others, for while both sides of the other gaps fall within the 'is', the 'is-ought' gap involves a difference between 'is' and something belonging to an entirely separate category.

• • •

III

In this final section I want to show how 'ought'-judgments which are categorical, determinate, prescriptive, egalitarian, and moral can be logically and noncircularly derived from 'is'-statements which describe empirical facts about the world. I shall do this by presenting a certain version of what I have called the internal model. But my version differs in important respects from those considered above. The main bases of these differences comprise two interrelated points, one about the context, the other about method.

The factual context within which my argument will proceed is that of the generic features of action. This context is both logically prior to and more invariable and inescapable than the other contexts appealed to in the attempted material 'is-ought' derivations considered above. In those derivations, as we have seen, there were two sorts of variabilities, each of which made the 'ought'-conclusions hypothetical rather than categorical. The arguments went as follows: Given a certain structured context, certain actions are necessary or required by that context. The necessities here were hence hypothetical in that, while one had first to accept the respective contexts as normatively binding, as justifiably setting forth requirements for action, this acceptance was not itself necessary, but was rather a matter of one's choice. I shall call this the acceptance-variability of the respective contexts. In addition, the specific contents of each context could vary; that is, even if one accepted the context in general, one might adopt different ends, participate in different institutions, have different conceptions of well-being, and these diversities generated quite different and even opposed 'ought'-conclusions. I shall call this the content-variability of the respective contexts. So there was a double hypotheticalness in these arguments, and this accounted for their failure to satisfy the conditions of categoricalness and determinacy.

In the context of the generic features of action, on the other hand, neither of these variabilities is found. There is no acceptance-variability, for it is not open to any person intentionally to evade or reject the context of action. To be sure, one might try to carry out such rejection by intentionally committing suicide, ingesting sleep-inducing drugs, selling oneself into slavery, and so forth. But not only would this intentional removal of oneself from the context of action obviously carry a crushing price, but moreover the very acts of taking these evading steps would themselves be actions, and hence the necessary conditions of actions, their generic features, would be fulfilled in the very process of removing oneself from further involvement in the context of action.

Similarly, if one views actions in terms of their generic features there is no content-variability in the context of actions; for although actions may, of course, be of many different sorts, they all have certain generic features in common, features which are necessarily exhibited by any instance of action, and these necessary features logically generate certain requirements or 'oughts' regardless of the specific differences of kinds of action. Because of this lack of acceptance-variability and content-variability, the 'oughts' derived from the context of the generic features of action have a necessity which enables them to satisfy the conditions of categoricalness and determinacy. I shall, in fact, try to show that the relation of the theory of action to moral philosophy is much closer and more substantive than has hitherto been thought.

It is to be noted that I am here using the word 'action' in a quite strict sense. In this sense, human movements or behaviors are not actions if they occur from one or more of the following kinds of cause: (a) direct compulsion by someone or something external to the person; (b) causes internal to the person, such as reflexes, ignorance, or disease, which decisively contribute, in ways beyond his control, to the occurrence of the behavior; (c) indirect compulsion whereby the person's choice to emit behavior is forced by someone else's coercion. In contrast to such behaviors, actions in the strict sense have the generic features of being voluntary and purposive. By 'voluntary' I mean that the agent occurrently or dispositionally controls his behavior by his unforced choice, knowing the various proximate circumstances of his action. By 'purposive' I mean that the agent intends to do what he does, envisaging some purpose or goal which may consist either in the performance of the action itself or in some outcome of that performance; in either case, insofar as it is the purpose of his action the agent regards it as some sort of good. These generic features also mean that actions are characterized by freedom and relative well-being on the part of the agent: by freedom in virtue of their uncoerced character and the agent's control over them; by well-being in the relative sense that the agent's purpose is to do or obtain something he regards as good, although not necessarily good in terms either of morality or even of his own self-interest.

The direct relevance of action in the strict sense to the 'Is-Ought' Problem can be seen from the fact that 'ought'-judgments are primarily concerned with action in this sense. When it is said, not only in moral or political precepts but also in prudential, technical, institutional, and other practical precepts, that some person ought to do something, the assumption of the speaker, at least prospectively, is that the person addressed is an actual or potential agent who can control his behavior with a view to achieving the objective set forth in the precept, and that the agent will set some sort of preferred priority either on this objective or on the ones for which he would otherwise act. As this last point indicates, actions in the strict sense include behaviors whereby agents may violate as well as fulfill moral, political, and other practical precepts, and they also include behaviors which are indifferent in relation to such precepts.

In addition to this consideration, the direct rational justification for focusing on the generic features of action is that, being invariable, they impose themselves on every agent, as against the particular contents of his actions which vary with his different and possibly arbitrary inclinations, and also that, being necessary to all action, they take priority for the agent over the particular purposes for which he may contingently act.

Before proceeding to the derivation, I must say something about the method I shall follow. Philosophers have, of course, dealt with and disagreed over the nature of their operations and results; in this regard they have used such phrases as 'rational reconstruction', 'conceptual analysis', 'criteriological connection', 'phenomenological description', 'inductive generalization', and so forth. I cannot, of course, deal with this issue here. But in order to facilitate understanding of what I shall try to do, I should point out that I shall use what I call a dialectically necessary method. My method is dialectical in a sense closely related to that referred to in the Socratic dialogues and in Aristotle: that is, it begins from assumptions, statements, or claims made by protagonists—in this case, the agent—and it examines what these logically imply. The method is dialectically necessary, however, in that the assumptions or claims in question are necessarily made by agents; they reflect not some protagonist's variable opinions, interests, or ideals but rather the necessary structure of purposive action as viewed by the agent. One aspect of this necessity has already been suggested in my statements about the invariability of the context of the generic features of action. On the basis of these necessary contents, I shall show that every agent is logically committed to making or at least accepting certain determinate, categorical moral 'ought'-judgments. Although I shall characterize the steps leading to this logical commitment as entailments, my argument will not be materially affected if the connections in question are interpreted in some less stringent way, so long as their necessary connection with the context of the generic features of action is kept in view.

It will constitute no objection to my use of this method that agents do not necessarily perform speech acts or make linguistic utterances. For on the basis of their actions certain thought-contents can be attributed to them in either direct or indirect discourse. If we see someone running very hard in order to catch a bus, we can safely infer, without stopping him and asking him, that he thinks it is worth his effort to try to catch that bus, just as if we see someone reading a book with avid interest we don't have to see whether he is moving his lips in order to attribute to him such a judgment as, "It is worth my attention reading this book," according to whatever criterion of worth is involved in his purpose of reading. Moreover, although there is in general a difference between entailment-relations among propositions and relations of belief of those propositions—if p entails $q,$ this does not entail that someone's believing that p entails his believing that q—nevertheless I shall here attribute to the agent belief in or acceptance of certain propositions on the basis of their being entailed by other propositions he accepts. The justification for this is that the entailments in question are so direct that awareness of them can safely be attributed to any person who is sufficiently rational to be able to control his behavior by his unforced choice with a view to achieving his purposes.

Enough of preliminaries. I shall now undertake to show how 'ought'-judgments having the five required characteristics are logically derivable from 'is'-statements which describe the occurrence of actions in the strict sense defined above. Although the argument will involve various complexities, some of which I have treated in detail elsewhere, I can indicate enough of the main lines in what follows.

To begin with, that purposive actions occur or that some person performs an action is an empirical fact which can be stated in descriptive, empirical propositions regardless of whether the statements are made by the agent himself or by other persons. As made by the agent himself, the statement may be put formally as, "I do X for purpose E." Although there has been an abortive attempt to argue that assertions of the performance or occurrence of actions are ascriptive rather than descriptive in that they make moral or legal judgments about the agent's responsibility, this attempt has, by general agreement, been definitively refuted.[3] And although some utterances of this form are performatory in Austin's sense, most are not. In a somewhat different direction we can also disregard here Cartesian doubts about the possibility of empirically ascertaining that the choices and purposes involved in action are in fact occurrently or dispositionally present. This disregard is especially warranted because, in accordance with my dialectical method, I shall be considering actions as they are viewed and referred to by the agent himself.

From this empirical premiss, the agent's statement that he performs an action, the derivation will now proceed in four main steps. The first step involves the point that the action as viewed by the agent has, in virtue of its purposiveness, a certain evaluative element. To see this, we must note that action is not a mere physical occurrence in which the entities concerned make no choices and guide themselves for the sake of no purposes. Nor is the agent's attitude toward his action merely a passive or contemplative one; the action is not something that happens to him from causes beyond his control. On the contrary, the agent's relation to the action he brings about is conative and evaluative, for he acts for some purpose which seems to him to be good. In acting, the agent envisages more or less clearly some preferred outcome, some objective or goal which he wants to achieve, where such wanting may be either intentional or inclinational. This goal is regarded by the agent as worth aiming at or pursuing; for if he did not so regard it he would not unforcedly choose to move from quiescence or non-action to action with a view to achieving the goal. This conception of worth constitutes a valuing on the part of the agent; he regards the object of his action as having at least sufficient value to merit his acting to attain it, according to whatever criteria are involved in his action. These criteria of value need not be moral nor even hedonic; they run the full range of the purposes for which the agent acts. Now 'value' in this broad sense is synonymous with 'good' in a similarly broad sense encompassing a wide range of nonmoral as well as moral criteria. Hence, since the agent values, at least instrumentally, the purposes or objects for which he acts, it can also be said that he regards these objects as at least instrumentally good according to whatever criteria lead him to try to achieve his purpose. He may, of course,

3 See H. I. A. Hart, "The Ascription of Rights and Responsibilities," *Proceedings of the Aristotelian Society*, vol. 49 (1948–49); P. T. Geach, "Ascriptivism," *Philosphical Review*, vol. 69 (1960), pp. 221 ff.; Hart, *Punishment and Responsibility* (Oxford: Clarendon Press, 1968), Preface.

also regard his purpose as bad on other criteria, and he may regret the narrow range of alternatives open to him among which he chooses. Still, so long as his choice is not forced, by the very fact that he chooses to act he shows that he regards his action as worth performing and hence as good at least relatively to his not acting at all or to his acting for other purposes which are open to him. The presence of choice and purpose in action thus gives it a structure such that, from the standpoint of the agent, "I do X for purpose E" entails "X and E are good." Since the latter statement is a value-judgment, or at least the function of such a judgment, to this extent from the standpoint of the agent the 'fact-value' gap, even if not the 'is-ought' gap, is already bridged in action.

The agent's positive evaluative judgment extends not only to his particular action and purpose but also to the generic features which characterize all his actions. Since his action is a means to attaining something he regards as good, even if this is only the performance of the action itself, he regards as good the voluntariness or freedom which is an essential feature of his action, for without this he would not be able to act for any purpose at all. He also regards as good those basic aspects of his well-being which are the necessary conditions both of the existence and of the success of all his actions, and which hence are not relative to his particular purposes and not subject to the disagreements that we saw earlier attach to different interpretations of well-being as a whole. This basic well-being comprises certain physical and psychological dispositions ranging from life and physical integrity to a feeling of confidence as to the general possibility of attaining one's goals.

In connection with this point, it should be noted that whereas the eudaemonist derivation considered above, like other naturalistic doctrines, left itself open to the objection that what it regards as well-being is not really good or is not considered good by some persons, my present argument does not incur this objection. For, being dialectical, the argument proceeds from within the standpoint of the agent himself and his own purposes and conceptions of well-being, whatever they may be. But as against the means-end derivation considered above, my argument, being dialectically *necessary,* does not depend for its direct content upon the contingent and variable purposes which different persons may have and the means required for these; it depends rather upon the necessary means which are required for any purposive actions, and which any agent must therefore regard as good. Thus, because freedom and basic well-being are at least instrumentally necessary to all the agent's actions for purposes, from the agent's standpoint his statement, "I do X for purpose E" entails not only "X and E are good" but also "My freedom and basic well-being are good as the necessary conditions of all my actions."

From this first main step there follows a second, bearing on justifications and right-claims. In virtue of his positive evaluations the agent regards himself as justified in performing his actions and in having the freedom and basic well-being which generically figure in all his actions, and he implicitly makes a corresponding right-claim. To regard something as justified on some criterion is to hold that its rightness is or can be established according to that criterion, and to have toward it a corresponding attitude of endorsement. Now an important, even if not the only, basis of an action's being right from the standpoint of its agent is that he regards it as having a good purpose. The agent therefore regards his action as justified by this goodness. But, *a fortiori,* he especially regards himself as justified in having freedom and basic well-being, since these are the necessary conditions of all his actions and hence of any purposes or goals he may attain or pursue through action.

This justificatory attitude takes the logical form of a claim on the part of the agent that he has a right to perform his actions and to have freedom and basic well-being. Even if there is not in every case a correct inference from an agent's regarding X as good to his claiming a right to X, the inference does hold from within the agent's standpoint insofar as X consists in freedom and basic well-being, because of the strategic relation of these goods to all his purposive actions. In the case of every claim to have a right to X, a necessary condition is that X seem directly or indirectly good to the claimant, and a sufficient condition is that he regard X as a basic good such as is required for his pursuit of any other goods. For it is central to the concept of a right, at least where it is advanced as a claim by individuals, that its primary, even if not its only, application is to the proximate prerequisites of any purposive actions, since without the direct capacity for such action the claimant, beyond making the claim itself, would not be able to move toward anything he regards as good. It is this elemental aspect of right-claims that seems to me to underlie Jefferson's asserting as self-evident that all men have inalienable rights to life, liberty, and the pursuit of happiness. Put in the dialectically necessary terms I am using here, this says that since every agent regards as basic goods the freedom and basic well-being which are the proximate necessary conditions of his acting for the achievement of any of his purposes, and since the criterion of claiming justifications and rights, so far as the agent is concerned, consists in the first instance in such proximate necessary conditions, it follows that any agent must claim, at least implicitly, that he has a right to freedom and basic well-being. And this right-claim is prescriptive: it carries the agent's advocacy or endorsement.

According to this second main step, then, action as viewed by the agent has a normative as well as an evaluative structure, in that it involves right-claims as well as judgments of good. From the agent's standpoint, his judgment "My freedom and basic well-being are good as the necessary conditions of all my actions" entails "I have a right to freedom and basic well-being."[4] This second step is, of course, crucial for the 'is-ought' derivation, since the normative concept of having a right either already is, or is directly translatable into, a deontic concept. Nevertheless, in order to show how all five conditions of the real 'Is-Ought' Problem are to be satisfied, I must go through two further steps.

---

4 For more detailed arguments for the above two steps, see my "The Normative Structure of Action," *Review of Metaphysics,* vol. 25 (1971), pp. 238 ff.

The third main step involves the consideration that, given the agent's claim that he has a right to freedom and basic well-being, he is logically committed to a generalization of this right-claim to all prospective agents and hence to all persons. To see this, we must note that every right-claim is made on behalf of some persons or group with an at least implicit recognition of the description or sufficient reason which is held to ground the right. This description or sufficient reason may be quite general or quite particular, but in any case the person who claims some right must admit, on pain of contradiction, that this right also belongs to any other persons to whom that description or reason applies. This necessity is an exemplification of the logical principle of universalizability: if some predicate P belongs to some subject S because S has the property Q (where the 'because' is that of sufficient reason or condition), then P must also belong to all other subjects S_1, S_2, . . . S_n which have Q. If one denies this implication in the case of some individual, such as S_1, which has Q, then one contradicts oneself, for in saying that P belongs to S because S has Q one implies that all Q is P, but in denying this in the case of S_1, which has Q, one says that some Q is not P.

The crucial question in the present context concerns the description or sufficient reason which the agent adduces as decisively relevant in claiming that he has a right to freedom and basic well-being. Many philosophers have held that there is no logical limit in this respect, that any agent can choose whatever description or sufficient reason he likes without committing any logical error. He may claim that he has the rights in question because and only because, for example, he is white or male or American or a philosopher or an atheist, or for that matter because he is named Wordsworth Donisthorpe or because he was born on such and such a date at such and such a place, and so forth. And, of course, depending on the property he adduces as a sufficient reason for his right-claim, he will be logically required to grant only that these rights belong to all other persons who have this property, including, at the extreme, the class consisting only of one member, himself.

In opposition to this view, I hold that the agent logically must adduce only a certain description or sufficient reason as the ground of his claim that he has a right to freedom and basic well-being. This description or sufficient reason is that he is a prospective agent who has purposes he wants to fulfill. If the agent adduces anything less general than this as his exclusive justifying description, then, by the preceding argument, he can be shown to contradict himself. Let us designate by the letter R such a more restrictive description. Examples of R would include, "My name is Wordsworth Donisthorpe" and the other descriptions just mentioned. Now let us ask the agent whether, while being an agent, he would still claim to have the rights of freedom and basic well-being even if he were not R. If he answers yes, then he contradicts his assertion that he has these rights only insofar as he is R. He would hence have to admit that he is mistaken in restricting his justificatory description to R. But if he answers no, i.e. if he says that while being an agent he would not claim these rights if he were not R, then he can be shown to contradict himself with regard to the generic features of action. For, as we have seen, it is necessarily true of every agent both that he requires freedom and basic well-being in order to act and that he hence implicitly claims the right to have freedom and basic well-being. For an agent not to claim these rights would mean that he does not act for purposes he regards as good at all and that he does not regard his actions, with their necessary conditions of freedom and basic well-being, as justified by the goodness of his purpose. But this in turn would mean that he is not an agent, which contradicts the initial assumption. Thus, to avoid contradicting himself, the agent must admit that he would claim to have the rights of freedom and basic well-being even if he were not R, and hence that the description or sufficient reason for which he claims these rights is not anything less general than that he is a prospective agent who has purposes he wants to fulfill.[5]

It is also this generality that explains why, in the necessary description or sufficient reason of his having these rights, I have referred to a *'prospective* agent who has purposes he wants to fulfill.' For the agent claims these rights not only in his present action with its particular purpose but in all his actions. To restrict to his present purpose his reason for claiming the rights of freedom and basic well-being would be to overlook the fact that he regards these as goods in respect of all his actions and purposes, not only his present one.

Since, then, the agent, in order to avoid contradicting himself, must claim that he has the rights of freedom and basic well-being for the sufficient reason that he is a prospective agent who has purposes he wants to fulfill, he logically must accept the generalization that all prospective agents who have purposes they want to fulfill, and hence all persons, have the rights of freedom and basic well-being. This generalization is a direct application of the principle of universalizability; and if the agent denies the generalization, then, as we have seen, he contradicts himself. For on the one hand in holding, as he logically must, that he has the rights of freedom and basic well-being because he is a prospective purposive agent, he implies that all prospective purposive agents have these rights; but on the other hand he holds that some prospective purposive agent does not have these rights.

I shall henceforth refer to the agent who avoids such contradictions, and who hence accepts the opposed logically necessary statements, as a 'rational agent.' It will be noted that this is the minimal and most basic sense of 'rational' as applied to persons and that its criterion is a purely logical one, involving consistency or the avoidance of self-contradiction. Thus we have seen that, by virtue of accepting the statement "I have a right to freedom and basic well-being," the rational agent must also accept "I have these rights for the sufficient reason that I am a prospective purposive agent," and hence that "All prospective purposive agents have a right to freedom and basic well-being." The rational

---

5 I have presented this and related arguments more fully in "The Justification of Egalitarian Justice," *American Philosophical Quarterly*, vol. 8 (1971), pp. 331 ff., and in *Moral Rationality*, The Lindley Lecture for 1972 (University of Kansas, 1972).

agent must therefore advocate or endorse these rights for all other persons on the same ground as he advocates them for himself.

The fourth and final main step moves directly from this generalized right-claim to a correlative 'ought'-judgment. For all rights are logically correlative with at least negative duties or 'oughts', in that for any person A to have a right to have or do something X entails that all other persons ought to refrain from interfering either with A's having or doing X or at least with A's trying to have or do X. Hence, since the agent logically had to admit that "All prospective purposive agents have a right to freedom and basic well-being," he must also logically accept the 'ought'-judgment, "I ought to refrain from interfering with the freedom and basic well-being of all prospective purposive agents," and hence of all persons. Interference with their freedom would constitute coercion; interference with their basic well-being would constitute basic harm. Thus we have seen that from the initial empirical premiss, "I do X for purpose E," there logically follows the 'ought'-judgment, "I ought to refrain from coercing other persons or inflicting basic harm on them." The agent is logically compelled to admit these 'oughts', on pain of contradiction.

The general principle of these 'oughts' or duties may be expressed as the following precept addressed to every agent: *Apply to your recipient the same generic features of action that you apply to yourself.* I shall call this the *Principle of Generic Consistency (PGC),* since it combines the formal consideration of consistency, as found in the above universalization argument, with the material consideration of the generic features of action, including the right-claims which the agent necessarily makes. The *PGC* is an egalitarian universalist moral principle since it requires an equal distribution of the most basic rights of action. It says to every agent that just as, in acting, he necessarily applies to himself and claims as rights for himself the generic features of action, voluntariness or freedom and purposiveness at least in the sense of basic well-being, so he ought to apply these same generic features to all the recipients of his actions by allowing them also to have freedom and basic well-being and hence by refraining from coercing them or inflicting basic harm on them. This means that the agent ought to be impartial as between himself and other persons when the latter's freedom and basic well-being are at stake, so that he ought to respect other persons' freedom and basic well-being as well as his own. And as we have seen, if the agent denies or violates this principle, then he contradicts himself.

The *PGC* has as direct or indirect logical consequences egalitarian moral 'ought'-judgments of the paradigmatic sort that I presented at the outset. Given the *PGC*, there directly follows the negative duty not to inflict serious gratuitous harm on other persons. There also directly follows the positive duty to perform such actions as rescuing drowning persons or feeding starving persons, especially when this can be done at relatively little cost to oneself. For the *PGC* prohibits inflicting basic harms on other persons; but to refrain from performing such actions as rescuing and feeding in the circumstances described would be to inflict basic harms on the persons in need and would hence violate the

impartiality required by the *PGC*. It would mean that while the agent partici-
pates in the situation voluntarily and with basic well-being, not to mention
his other purposes, he prevents his recipients from doing so. Although there
is indeed a distinction between causing a basic harm to occur and merely
permitting it to occur by one's inaction, such intentional inaction in the described circumstances is itself an action that interferes with the basic well-
being of the persons in need. For it prevents, by means under the agent's control
and with his knowledge, the occurrence of transactions which would remove
the basic harms in question.

The *PGC* also has as its indirect consequences sociopolitical moral 'ought'-
judgments requiring actions in support of civil liberties and in opposition to
great inequalities of wealth and power. While I do not have the time now to
go into such institutional applications, the general point is that since the *PGC*
requires an equal distribution of the most basic rights of action, freedom and
basic well-being, it also requires legal, political, and economic institutions
which foster such libertarian and egalitarian rights, and it hence requires actions which support such institutions. Unlike the direct institutional derivations
considered earlier, if the obligations grounded in various institutions are to be
justified, then the institutions themselves must first be justifiable through the
PGC.[6] And it is by rules based on such justified institutions that conflicts arising
from agents' use of their freedom are to be resolved.

This, then, concludes my argument. So far as concerns the particular paradigmatic moral 'ought'-judgments which I presented at the outset, I have not
derived them directly from their antecedent 'is'-statements about B's starving
and so forth; rather I have treated these combinations as enthymemes having
such specific 'ought'-premises as: "Whenever some person is starving and
someone else can relieve him at no comparable cost to himself, he ought to
do so." These 'ought'-premises, however, follow from the *PGC*, and the *PGC*
in turn follows, through the steps I have indicated, from the 'is'-statement
made by the agent that he performs actions for purposes. Hence, the particular
moral 'ought'-judgments have been derived, through several intermediate steps,
from an empirical 'is'-statement.

I have here presented, then, a complex version of what I have called the
internal model of the relation between 'ought' and 'is'. I have not directly
defined 'ought' in terms of 'is'; rather, I have held that the application of 'ought'
is entailed by the correlative concept of having a right. The agent's application
of this concept, in turn, has been derived from the concept of goods which are
the necessary conditions of all his actions, since he necessarily claims that he
has a right to at least these goods. And the agent's application of the concept
of good, finally, has been derived from his acting for purposes. Since the agent's
assertion that he acts for purposes is an empirical, descriptive statement, I have

---

6 For fuller discussion of how institutional obligations are derived from the *PGC*, see my "Obligation: Political, Legal, Moral," op. cit., (above, n. 10). See also my "Categorical Consistency in
Ethics," *Philosophical Quarterly,* vol. 17 (1967), pp. 289 ff.

in this indirect way derived 'ought' from 'is'. Whether the derivation is at each point definitional or is rather of some other non-arbitrary sort does not materially affect my argument, so long as its necessary relation to the context of action is recognized.

If this derivation has been successful, if it constitutes a resolution of the real 'Is-Ought' Problem, then the 'ought'-judgments which I have derived have the five characteristics indicated in my first section. Let us examine whether this is so. We have already seen that the PGC and the more specific 'ought'-judgments that follow from it are moral and egalitarian. They are also prescriptive, since they follow logically from the agent's prescriptive claim that he has a right to freedom and basic well-being. And they are determinate, for they rule out the coercion and basic harm which we saw were permitted by other 'is-ought' derivations.

It may be questioned, however, whether the condition of categoricalness has been satisfied. The objection would be that there is a conflict between the categorical and the dialectical. Since my argument has been dialectical in that it proceeds from within the standpoint of the agent, including the evaluations and right-claims he makes, the PGC and the ensuing ought-judgments I have derived are valid, so holds the objection, only relatively to the agent's standpoint, but not absolutely. Even if the agent is logically compelled to uphold certain 'ought'-judgments, given his initial statement that he performs actions for purposes, this does not establish that those judgments are really correct or binding. Hence, their 'oughts' are not categorical.

My reply to this objection is that the dialectically *necessary* aspect of my method gives the 'ought'-conclusions a more than contingent or hypothetical status. Since moral 'oughts' apply only or primarily to the context of action and hence to agents, to have shown that certain 'ought'-judgments logically must be granted by all agents, on pain of contradiction, is to give the judgments an absolute status since their validity is logically ineluctable within the whole context of their possible application. It will be recalled that in my original specification I said that for 'ought'-judgments to be categorical the normative bindingness of the requirements they set forth cannot be removed or evaded by variable, escapable features of the persons addressed, including their self-interested desires or their contingent choices, opinions, and attitudes. This condition of categoricalness is fulfilled by the PGC's 'ought'-judgment.

This necessity also explicates the respect in which moral judgments have truth-value. The PGC and the moral judgments that follow from it are true in that they correspond to the concept of a rational agent, for they indicate what logically must be admitted by such an agent. As I noted above, the criterion of 'rational' here is a purely logical one.

Finally, what of the condition of non-circularity? Although my argument began from the agent's empirical statements that he performs actions, I then pointed out that actions as viewed by him have certain ineluctable evaluative and normative elements. Doesn't this mean that I have reached a normative or at least a prescriptive 'ought'-conclusion only by putting normativeness or prescriptiveness into my premiss about action? It was this question that figured in the 'dilemma of commitment' that I presented above. Now an assumption of this dilemma was that for any person who undertakes to derive 'ought' from 'is' within some context, it is open to him to choose or to refrain from choosing to commit himself to that context with its requirements. As we have seen, however, it is impossible intentionally to refrain from committing oneself to the context of the generic features of action, for any such refraining would itself exhibit those features. Hence, the 'ought' which is derived within that context is prescriptive; but nevertheless the derivation is not circular, because the derived 'ought' reflects not a dispensable choice or commitment but rather a necessity which is not subject to any choice or decision on the part of the agent. The objector hence cannot say, "You've reached a commitment or prescription in the conclusion only because you've already chosen to put the commitment or prescription into your premiss;" for the latter commitment in the premiss is not one that the deriver has *chosen* or has *put into* the premiss. Rather, the commitment is there in the nature of the case, and all he is doing is recognize it; but he cannot evade it. In any event, as already noted, the initial premiss of the derivation is the agent's empirical statement that he performs actions for purposes; and the prescriptiveness of the moral 'ought'-conclusion is accounted for more specifically by the advocacy embodied in his right-claim together with its logical generalization.

What I have tried to show here, then, is that the 'is' of the performance of actions having the generic features logically generates the 'ought' of categorical moral judgments; or, in other words, that the fact of being a purposive agent logically requires, on pain of self-contradiction, an acknowledgment that one ought to act in certain basic moral ways. To summarize: Because actions are conative and value-pursuing, they commit the agent to advocate or endorse for himself the rights of freedom and basic well-being which are the proximate necessary prerequisites of all his acting; hence, he makes judgments which fulfill the condition of prescriptiveness. Because the agent must advocate these rights for general reasons stemming from his simply being a prospective purposive agent, his advocacy must logically be extended to all other persons; hence, his judgments fulfill the conditions of being moral and egalitarian. And because this extension is based on the generic and hence inescapable features of action, it logically cannot be evaded or reversed regardless of any variable desires, choices, or attitudes on the part of the agent; hence, his judgments fulfill the conditions of determinacy and categoricalness. In this way, then, by an analysis of the generic features of action and their normative implications, I have argued that the real 'Is-Ought' Problem is resolved.

6

Morality as a System of Hypothetical Imperatives

PHILIPPA FOOT

Philippa Foot (b. 1920) is Professor of Philosophy Emerita at the University of California at Los Angeles and Senior Research Fellow at Somerville College, Oxford. She has published influential articles on free will, the problem of abortion, and other topics in moral philosophy. Some of her essays are collected under the title Virtues and Vices.

In this essay from that collection, Foot takes issue with the central Kantian claim that morality must be grounded in categorical rather than in hypothetical imperatives. Kant's position (see reading 30) is that any genuinely moral reason for acting must operate independently of any desires or inclinations that an agent merely happens to have. Foot disagrees. She acknowledges that it may make sense to say that a person should do something that will not further his desires, as when we say that even a person who cares nothing about etiquette should, according to the rules, not eat peas with a knife. However, Foot insists that the rules of etiquette provide no reason for acting unless one wants to obey them, and that the rules of morality are precisely similar in this regard. Contrary to what Kantians say, an amoral person can rationally and consistently disregard moral rules.

If moral rules do not compel rational assent, then do they not lose all their force and special status? According to Foot, they do not. Even if moral considerations provide reasons for acting only when someone wants to act morally, it hardly follows that the desire to act morally must be shallow or transient. To the contrary, among those who have it, that desire is often extremely deep and stable. If we reject psychological hedonism and other forms of psychological egoism (see reading 1), we will have to agree that such a desire can lead people to make great sacrifices to achieve moral ends. This, Foot argues, is all that any moralist needs or should ask.

There are many difficulties and obscurities in Kant's moral philosophy, and few contemporary moralists will try to defend it all. Many, for instance, agree in rejecting Kant's derivation of duties from the mere form of the law expressed in terms of a universally legislative will. Nevertheless, it is generally supposed, even by those who would not dream of calling themselves his follow-ers, that Kant established one thing beyond doubt—namely, the necessity of distinguishing moral judgements from hypothetical imperatives. That moral judgements cannot be hypothetical imperatives has come to seem an unques-tionable truth. It will be argued here that it is not.

In discussing so thoroughly Kantian a notion as that of the hypothetical imperative, one naturally begins by asking what Kant himself meant by a hypothetical imperative, and it may be useful to say a little about the idea of an imperative as this appears in Kant's works. In writing about imperatives Kant seems to be thinking at least as much of statements about what ought to be or should be done, as of injunctions expressed in the imperative mood. He even describes as an imperative the assertion that it would be 'good to do or refrain from doing something'[1] and explains that for a will that 'does not always do something simply because it is presented to it as a good thing to do' this has the force of a command of reason. We may therefore think of Kant's imperatives as statements to the effect that something ought to be done or that it would be good to do it.

The distinction between hypothetical imperatives and categorical impera-tives, which plays so important a part in Kant's ethics, appears in characteristic form in the following passages from the *Foundations of the Metaphysics of Morals:*

> All imperatives command either hypothetically or categorically. The former pre-sent the practical necessity of a possible action as a means to achieving something else which one desires (or which one may possibly desire). The categorical impera-tive would be one which presented an action as of itself objectively necessary, without regard to any other end.[2]

> If the action is good only as a means to something else, the imperative is hypotheti-cal; but if it is thought of as good in itself, and hence as necessary in a will which of itself conforms to reason as the principle of this will, the imperative is categorical.[3]

The hypothetical imperative, as Kant defines it, 'says only that the action is good to some purpose' and the purpose, he explains, may be possible or actual. Among imperatives related to actual purposes Kant mentions rules of prudence, since he believes that all men necessarily desire their own happiness. Without committing ourselves to this view it will be useful to follow Kant in classing together as 'hypothetical imperatives' those telling a man what he ought to do because (or if) he wants something and those telling him what he ought to do on grounds of self-interest. Common opinion agrees with Kant in insisting that a moral man must accept a rule of duty whatever his interests or desires.

1 *Foundations of the Metaphysics of Morals*, Sec. II, trans. by L. W. Beck.

2 Ibid.

3 Ibid.

Having given a rough description of the class of Kantian hypothetical imperatives it may be useful to point to the heterogeneity within it. Sometimes what a man should do depends on his passing inclination, as when he wants his coffee hot and should warm the jug. Sometimes it depends on some long-term project, when the feelings and inclinations of the moment are irrelevant. If one wants to be a respectable philosopher one should get up in the mornings and do some work, though just at that moment when one should do it the thought of being a respectable philosopher leaves one cold. It is true nevertheless to say of one, at that moment, that one wants to be a respectable philosopher, and this can be the foundation of a desire-dependent hypothetical imperative. The term 'desire' as used in the original account of the hypothetical imperative was meant as a grammatically convenient substitute for 'want', and was not meant to carry any implication of inclination rather than long-term aim or project. Even the word 'project', taken strictly, introduces undesirable restrictions. If someone is devoted to his family or his country or to any cause, there are certain things he wants, which may then be the basis of hypothetical imperatives, without either inclinations or projects being quite what is in question. Hypothetical imperatives should already be appearing as extremely diverse; a further important distinction is between those that concern an individual and those that concern a group. The desires on which a hypothetical imperative is dependent may be those of one man, or may be taken for granted as belonging to a number of people engaged in some common project or sharing common aims.

Is Kant right to say that moral judgements are categorical, not hypothetical, imperatives? It may seem that he is, for we find in our language two different uses of words such as 'should' and 'ought', apparently corresponding to Kant's hypothetical and categorical imperatives, and we find moral judgements on the 'categorical' side. Suppose, for instance, we have advised a traveller that he should take a certain train, believing him to be journeying to his home. If we find that he has decided to go elsewhere, we will most likely have to take back what we said: the 'should' will now be unsupported and in need of support. Similarly, we must be prepared to withdraw our statement about what he should do if we find that the right relation does not hold between the action and the end—that it is either no way of getting what he wants (or doing what he wants to do) or not the most eligible among possible means. The use of 'should' and 'ought' in moral contexts is, however, quite different. When we say that a man should do something and intend a moral judgement we do not have to back up what we say by considerations about his interests or his desires; if no such connexion can be found the 'should' need not be withdrawn. It follows that the agent cannot rebut an assertion about what, morally speaking, he should do by showing that the action is not ancillary to his interests or desires. Without such a connexion the 'should' does not stand unsupported and in need of support; the support that *it* requires is of another kind.

There is, then, one clear difference between moral judgements and the class of 'hypothetical imperatives' so far discussed. In the latter 'should' is 'used hypothetically', in the sense defined, and if Kant were merely drawing attention to this piece of linguistic usage his point would easily be proved. But obviously Kant meant more than this; in describing moral judgements as non-hypothetical—that is, categorical imperatives—he is ascribing to them a special dignity and necessity which this usage cannot give. Modern philosophers follow Kant in talking, for example, about the 'unconditional requirement' expressed in moral judgements. These, they say, tell us what we have to do whatever our interests or desires, and by their inescapability they are distinguished from hypothetical imperatives.

The problem is to find proof for this further feature of moral judgements. If anyone fails to see the gap that has to be filled it will be useful to point out to him that we find 'should' used non-hypothetically in some non-moral statements to which no one attributes the special dignity and necessity conveyed by the description 'categorical imperative'. For instance, we find this non-hypothetical use of 'should' in sentences enunciating rules of etiquette, as, for example, that an invitation in the third person should be answered in the third person, where the rule does not *fail to apply* to someone who has his own good reasons for ignoring this piece of nonsense, or who simply does not care about what, from the point of view of etiquette, he should do. Similarly, there is a non-hypothetical use of 'should' in contexts where something like a club rule is in question. The club secretary who has told a member that he should not bring ladies into the smoking-room does not say, 'Sorry, I was mistaken' when informed that this member is resigning tomorrow and cares nothing about his reputation in the club. Lacking a connexion with the agent's desires or interests, this 'should' does not stand 'unsupported and in need of support'; it requires only the backing of the rule. This use of 'should' is therefore 'non-hypothetical' in the sense defined.

It follows that if a hypothetical use of 'should' gave a hypothetical imperative, and a non-hypothetical use of 'should' a categorical imperative, then 'should' statements based on rules of etiquette, or rules of a club would be categorical imperatives. Since this would not be accepted by defenders of the categorical imperative in ethics, who would insist that these other 'should' statements give hypothetical imperatives, they must be using this expression in some other sense. We must therefore ask what they mean when they say that 'You should answer . . . in the third person' is a hypothetical imperative. Very roughly the idea seems to be that one may reasonably ask why anyone should bother about what should (from the point of view of etiquette) be done, and that such considerations deserve no notice unless reason is shown. So although people give as their reason for doing something the fact that it is required by etiquette, we do not take this consideration as *in itself giving us reason to act*. Considerations of etiquette do not have any automatic reason-giving force, and a man might be right if he denied that he had reason to do 'what's done'.

This seems to take us to the heart of the matter, for, by contrast, it is supposed that moral considerations necessarily give reasons for acting to any man. The difficulty is, of course, to defend this proposition which is more often repeated than explained. Unless it is said, implausibly, that all 'should' or 'ought' statements give reasons for acting, which leaves the old problem of assigning a special categorical status to moral judgement, we must be told what it is that makes the moral 'should' relevantly different from the 'shoulds' appearing in normative statements of other kinds.[4] Attempts have sometimes been made to show that some kind of irrationality is involved in ignoring the 'should' of morality: in saying "Immoral—so what?" as one says "Not *comme il faut*—so what?' But as far as I can see these have all rested on some illegitimate assumption, as, for instance, of thinking that the amoral man, who agrees that some piece of conduct is immoral but takes no notice of that, is inconsistently disregarding a rule of conduct that he has accepted; or again of thinking it inconsistent to desire that others will not do to one what one proposes to do to them. The fact is that the man who rejects morality because he sees no reason to obey its rules can be convicted of villainy but not of inconsistency. Nor will his action necessarily be irrational. Irrational actions are those in which a man in some way defeats his own purposes, doing what is calculated to be disadvantageous or to frustrate his ends. Immorality does not *necessarily* involve any such thing.

It is obvious that the normative character of moral judgement does not guarantee its reason-giving force. Moral judgements are normative, but so are judgements of manners, statements of club rules, and many others. Why should the first provide reasons for acting as the others do not? In every case it is because there is a background of teaching that the non-hypothetical 'should' can be used. The behaviour is required, not simply recommended, but the question remains as to why we should do what we are required to do. It is true that moral rules are often enforced much more strictly than the rules of etiquette, and our reluctance to press the non-hypothetical 'should' of etiquette may be one reason why we think of the rules of etiquette as hypothetical imperatives. But are we then to say that there is nothing behind the idea that moral judgements are categorical imperatives but the relative stringency of our moral teaching? I believe that this may have more to do with the matter than the defenders of the categorical imperative would like to admit. For if we look at the kind of thing that is said in its defence we may find ourselves puzzled about what the words can even mean unless we connect them with the feelings that this stringent teaching implants. People talk, for instance, about the 'binding force' of morality, but it is not clear what this means if not that we *feel*

---

4 To say that moral considerations are *called* reasons is blatantly to ignore the problem.

   In the case of etiquette or club rules it is obvious that the non-hypothetical use of 'should' has resulted in the loss of the usual connexion between what one should do and what one has reason to do. Someone who objects that in the moral case a man cannot be justified in restricting his practical reasoning in this way, since every moral 'should' gives reasons for acting, must face the following dilemma. Either it is possible to create reasons for acting simply by putting together any silly rules and introducing a non-hypothetical 'should,' or else the non-hypothetical 'should' does not necessarily imply reasons for acting. If it does not necessarily imply reasons for acting we may ask why it is supposed to do so in the case of morality. Why cannot the indifferent amoral man say that for him 'should$_m$' gives no reason for acting, treating 'should$_m$' as most of us treat 'should$_e$'? Those who insist that 'should$_m$' is categorical in this second 'reason-giving' sense do not seem to realise that they never prove this to be so. They sometimes say that moral considerations 'just do' give reasons for acting, without explaining why some devotee of etiquette could not say the same about the rules of etiquette.

ourselves unable to escape. Indeed the 'inescapability' of moral requirements is often cited when they are being contrasted with hypothetical imperatives. No one, it is said, escapes the requirements of ethics by having or not having particular interests or desires. Taken in one way this only reiterates the contrast between the 'should' of morality and the hypothetical 'should', and once more places morality alongside of etiquette. Both are inescapable in that behaviour does not cease to offend against either morality or etiquette because the agent is indifferent to their purposes and to the disapproval he will incur by flouting them. But morality is supposed to be inescapable in some special way and this may turn out to be merely the reflection of the way morality is taught. Of course, we must try other ways of expressing the fugitive thought. It may be said, for instance, that moral judgements have a kind of necessity since they tell us what we 'must do' or 'have to do' whatever our interests and desires. The sense of this is, again, obscure. Sometimes when we use such expressions we are referring to physical or mental compulsion. (A man has to go along if he is pulled by strong men and he has to give in if tortured beyond endurance.) But it is only in the absence of such conditions that moral judgements apply. Another and more common sense of the words is found in sentences such as 'I caught a bad cold and had to stay in bed' where a penalty for acting otherwise is in the offing. The necessity of acting morally is not, however, supposed to depend on such penalties. Another range of examples, not necessarily having to do with penalties, if found where there is an unquestioned acceptance of some project or rôle, as when a nurse tells us that she has to make her rounds at a certain time, or we say that we have to run for a certain train. But these too are irrelevant in the present context, since the acceptance condition can always be revoked.

No doubt it will be suggested that it is in some other sense of the words 'have to' or 'must' that one has to or must do what morality demands. But why should one insist that there must be such a sense when it proves so difficult to say what it is? Suppose that what we take for a puzzling thought were really no thought at all but only the reflection of our *feelings* about morality? Perhaps it makes no sense to say that we 'have to' submit to the moral law, or that morality is 'inescapable' in some special way. For just as one may feel as if one is falling without believing that one is moving downward, so one may feel as if one has to do what is morally required without believing oneself to be under physical or psychological compulsion, or about to incur a penalty if one does not comply. No one thinks that if the word 'falling' is used in a statement reporting one's sensations it must be used in a special sense. But this kind of mistake may be involved in looking for the special sense in which one 'has to' do what morality demands. There is no difficulty about the idea that we feel we *have to* behave morally, and given the psychological conditions of the learning of moral behaviour it is natural that we should have such feelings. What we cannot do is quote them in support of the doctrine of the categorical imperative. It seems, then, that in so far as it is backed up by statements to the effect that the moral law *is* inescapable, or that we *do* have to do what is morally required of us, it is uncertain whether the doctrine of the categorical imperative even makes sense.

The conclusion we should draw is that moral judgements have no better claim to be categorical imperatives than do statements about matters of etiquette. People may indeed follow either morality or etiquette without asking why they should do so, but equally well they may not. They may ask for reasons and may reasonably refuse to follow either if reasons are not to be found.

It will be said that this way of viewing moral considerations must be totally destructive of morality, because no one could ever act morally unless he accepted such considerations as in themselves sufficient reason for action. Actions that are truly moral must be done 'for their own sake', 'because they are right', and not for some ulterior purpose. This argument we must examine with care, for the doctrine of the categorical imperative has owed much to its persuasion.

Is there anything to be said for the thesis that a truly moral man acts 'out of respect for the moral law' or that he does what is morally right because it is morally right? That such propositions are not prima facie absurd depends on the fact that moral judgement concerns itself with a man's reasons for acting as well as with what he does. Law and etiquette require only that certain things are done or left undone, but no one is counted as charitable if he gives alms 'for the praise of men', and one who is honest only because it pays him to be honest does not have the virtue of honesty. This kind of consideration was crucial in shaping Kant's moral philosophy. He many times contrasts acting out of respect for the moral law with acting from an ulterior motive, and what is more from one that is self-interested. In the early *Lectures on Ethics* he gave the principle of truth-telling under a system of hypothetical imperatives as that of not lying *if it harms one to lie*. In the *Metaphysics of Morals* he says that ethics cannot start from the ends which a man may propose to himself, since these are all 'selfish'.[5] In the *Critique of Practical Reason* he argues explicitly that when acting not out of respect for moral law but 'on a material maxim' men do what they do for the sake of pleasure or happiness.

> All material practical principles are, as such, of one and the same kind and belong under the general principle of self love or one's own happiness.[6]

Kant, in fact, was a psychological hedonist[*] in respect of all actions except those done for the sake of the moral law, and this faulty theory of human nature was one of the things preventing him from seeing that moral virtue might be compatible with the rejection of the categorical imperative.

If we put this theory of human action aside, and allow as ends the things that seem to be ends, the picture changes. It will surely be allowed that quite apart from thoughts of duty a man may care about the suffering of others, having a sense of identification with them, and wanting to help if he can. Of course he must want not the reputation of charity, nor even a gratifying rôle

---

5 Pt. II, Introduction, sec. II.

6 Immanuel Kant, *Critique of Practical Reason*, trans. L. W. Beck, p. 133.

* One who believes that actions are performed to gain pleasure or avoid pain. For discussion, see Joel Feinberg, "Psychological Egoism," *reading 1.*

helping others, but, quite simply, their good. If this is what he does care about, then he will be attached to the end proper to the virtue of charity and a comparison with someone acting from an ulterior motive (even a respectable ulterior motive) is out of place. Nor will the conformity of his action to the rule of charity be merely contingent. Honest action may happen to further a man's career; charitable actions do not *happen* to further the good of others.[7]

Can a man accepting only hypothetical imperatives possess other virtues besides that of charity? Could he be just or honest? This problem is more complex because there is no end related to such virtues as the good of others is related to charity. But what reason could there be for refusing to call a man a just man if he acted justly because he loved truth and liberty, and wanted every man to be treated with a certain respect? And why should the truly honest man not follow honesty for the sake of the good that honest dealing brings to men? Of course, the usual difficulties can be raised about the rare case in which no good is foreseen from an individual act of honesty. But it is not evident that a man's desires could not give him reason to act honestly even here. He wants to live openly and in good faith with his neighbours; it is not all the same to him to lie and conceal.

If one wants to know whether there could be a truly moral man who accepted moral principles as hypothetical rules of conduct, as many people accept rules of etiquette as hypothetical rules of conduct, one must consider the right kind of example. A man who demanded that morality should be brought under the heading of self-interest would not be a good candidate, nor would anyone who was ready to be charitable or honest only so long as he felt inclined. A cause such as justice makes strenuous demands, but this is not peculiar to morality, and men are prepared to toil to achieve many ends not endorsed by morality. That they are prepared to fight so hard for moral ends—for example, for liberty and justice—depends on the fact that these are the kinds of ends that arouse devotion. To sacrifice a great deal for the sake of etiquette one would need to be under the spell of the emphatic 'ought'. One could hardly be devoted to behaving *comme il faut*.

In spite of all that has been urged in favour of the hypothetical imperative in ethics, I am sure that many people will be unconvinced and will argue that one element essential to moral virtue is still missing. This missing feature is the recognition of a *duty* to adopt those ends which we have attributed to the moral man. We have said that he *does* care about others, and about causes such as liberty and justice; that it is on this account that he will accept a system of morality. But what if he never cared about such things, or what if he ceased to care? Is it not the case that he *ought* to care? This is exactly what Kant would say, for though at times he sounds as if he thought that morality is not concerned with ends, at others he insists that the adoption of ends such as the happiness of others is itself dictated by morality.[8] How is this proposition to

---

7 It is not, of course, necessary that charitable actions should *succeed* in helping others; but when they do so they do not *happen* to do so, since that is necessarily their aim. (Footnote added, 1977.)

8 See e.g., *The Metaphysics of Morals*, pt. II, sec. 30.

be regarded by one who rejects all talk about the binding force of the moral law? He will agree that a moral man has moral ends and cannot be indifferent to matters such as suffering and injustice. Further, he will recognise in the statement that one *ought* to care about these things a correct application of the non-hypothetical moral 'ought' by which society is apt to voice its demands. He will not, however, take the fact that he ought to have certain ends as in itself reason to adopt them. If he himself is a moral man then he cares about such things, but not 'because he ought'. If he is an amoral man he may deny that he has any reason to trouble his head over this or any other moral demand. Of course he may be mistaken, and his life as well as others' lives may be most sadly spoiled by his selfishness. But this is not what is urged by those who think they can close the matter by an emphatic use of 'ought'. My argument is that they are relying on an illusion, as if trying to give the moral 'ought' a magic force.[9]

This conclusion may, as I said, appear dangerous and subversive of morality. We are apt to panic at the thought that we ourselves, or other people, might stop caring about the things we do care about, and we feel that the categorical imperative gives us some control over the situation. But it is interesting that the people of Leningrad were not struck by the thought that only the *contingent* fact that other citizens shared their loyalty and devotion to the city stood between them and the Germans during the terrible years of the siege. Perhaps we should be less troubled than we are by fear of defection from the moral cause; perhaps we should even have less reason to fear it if people thought of themselves as volunteers banded together to fight for liberty and justice and against inhumanity and oppression. It is often felt, even if obscurely, that there is an element of deception in the official line about morality. And while some have been persuaded by talk about the authority of the moral law, others have turned away with a sense of distrust.

[9] See G. E. M. Anscombe, "Modern Moral Philosophy," *Philosophy* (1958). My view is different from Miss Anscombe's, but I have learned from her.

7

Existentialism Is a Humanism

JEAN-PAUL SARTRE

Jean-Paul Sartre (1905–1980) was an influential French intellectual with interests spanning philosophy, literature, and politics. His most important philosophical work is Being and Nothingness. *He also wrote a number of well-received novels and plays, including* Nausea, The Flies, *and* No Exit.

In this essay from his book Existentialism and Human Emotions, *Sartre argues that we create our own moral values. As an atheist, he denies that God is the source of moral obligations. (For a different sort of argument for this conclusion, see Plato's* Euthyphro, *reading 14.) But, unlike many other moralists, Sartre also denies that moral values exist independently of God. He contends that appealing to such independent values is just a way of evading our own responsibility. In support of this, he argues that no principle can be binding on us unless we choose to adopt it. Furthermore, he contends that traditional moral theories are too vague to provide guidance. For example, before we can apply Kant's principle, "treat persons as ends rather than means" (reading 30), we must decide whether our proposed action will treat anyone as a means. In thus interpreting the principle, we are in effect making the decision. Similarly, when we ask advice, we decide the issue through our choice of adviser. Neither independent values nor "human nature" can predetermine our choices. Thus, in choosing, we create both our values and ourselves.*

What is meant by the term *existentialism?*

Most people who use the word would be rather embarrassed if they had to explain it, since, now that the word is all the rage, even the work of a musician or painter is being called existentialist. A gossip columnist in *Clartés* signs himself *The Existentialist*, so that by this time the word has been so stretched and has taken on so broad a meaning, that it no longer means anything at all. It seems that for want of an advance-guard doctrine analogous to surrealism, the kind of people who are eager for scandal and flurry turn to this philosophy which in other respects does not at all serve their purposes in this sphere.

Actually, it is the least scandalous, the most austere of doctrines. It is intended strictly for specialists and philosophers. Yet it can be defined easily. What complicates matters is that there are two kinds of existentialist; first, those who are Christian, among whom I would include Jaspers and Gabriel Marcel, both Catholic; and on the other hand the atheistic existentialists, among whom I class Heidegger, and then the French existentialists and myself. What they have in common is that they think that existence precedes essence, or, if you prefer, that subjectivity must be the starting point.

Just what does that mean? Let us consider some object that is manufactured, for example, a book or a paper-cutter: here is an object which has been made by an artisan whose inspiration came from a concept. He referred to the concept of what a paper-cutter is and likewise to a known method of production, which is part of the concept, something which is, by and large, a routine. Thus, the paper-cutter is at once an object produced in a certain way and, on the other hand, one having a specific use; and one can not postulate a man who produces a paper-cutter but does not know what it is used for. Therefore, let us say that, for the paper-cutter, essence—that is, the ensemble of both the production routines and the properties which enable it to be both produced and defined—precedes existence. Thus, the presence of the paper-cutter or book in front of me is determined. Therefore, we have here a technical view of the world whereby it can be said that production precedes existence.

When we conceive God as the Creator, He is generally thought of as a superior sort of artisan. Whatever doctrine we may be considering, whether one like that of Descartes or that of Leibnitz, we always grant that will more or less follows understanding or, at the very least, accompanies it, and that when God creates He knows exactly what He is creating. Thus, the concept of man in the mind of God is comparable to the concept of paper-cutter in the mind of the manufacturer, and, following certain techniques and a conception, God produces man, just as the artisan, following a definition and a technique, makes a paper-cutter. Thus, the individual man is the realization of a certain concept in the divine intelligence.

In the eighteenth century, the atheism of the *philosophes* discarded the idea of God, but not no much for the notion that essence precedes existence. To a certain extent, this idea is found everywhere; we find it in Diderot, in Voltaire, and even in Kant. Man has a human nature; this human nature, which is the concept of the human, is found in all men, which means that each man is a particular example of a universal concept, man. In Kant, the result of this universality is that the wild-man, the natural man, as well as the bourgeois, are circumscribed by the same definition and have the same basic qualities. Thus, here too the essence of man precedes the historical existence that we find in nature.

Atheistic existentialism, which I represent, is more coherent. It states that if God does not exist, there is at least one being in whom existence precedes essence, a being who exists before he can be defined by any concept, and that this being is man, or, as Heidegger says, human reality. What is meant here by saying that existence precedes essence? It means that, first of all, man exists, turns up, appears on the scene, and, only afterwards, defines himself. If man, as the existentialist conceives him, is indefinable, it is because at first he is nothing. Only afterward will he be something, and he himself will have made what he will be. Thus, there is no human nature, since there is no God to conceive it. Not only is man what he conceives himself to be, but he is also only what he wills himself to be after this thrust toward existence.

Man is nothing else but what he makes of himself. Such is the first principle of existentialism. It is also what is called subjectivity, the name we are labeled with when charges are brought against us. But what do we mean by this, if not that man has a greater dignity than a stone or table? For we mean that man first exists, that is, that man first of all is the being who hurls himself toward a future and who is conscious of imagining himself as being in the future. Man is at the start a plan which is aware of itself, rather than a patch of moss, a piece of garbage, or a cauliflower; nothing exists prior to this plan; there is nothing in heaven; man will be what he will have planned to be. Not what he will want to be. Because by the word "will" we generally mean a conscious decision, which is subsequent to what we have already made of ourselves. I may want to belong to a political party, write a book, get married; but all that is only a manifestation of an earlier, more spontaneous choice that is called "will." But if existence really does precede essence, man is responsible for what he is. Thus, existentialism's first move is to make every man aware of what he is and to make the full responsibility of his existence rest on him. And when we say that a man is responsible for himself, we do not only mean that he is responsible for his own individuality, but that he is responsible for all men.

The word subjectivism has two meanings, and our opponents play on the two. Subjectivism means, on the one hand, that an individual chooses and makes himself; and, on the other, that it is impossible for man to transcend human subjectivity. The second of these is the essential meaning of existentialism. When we say that man chooses his own self, we mean that every one of us does likewise; but we also mean by that that in making this choice he also chooses all men. In fact, in creating the man that we want to be, there is not a single one of our acts which does not at the same time create an image of man as we think he ought to be. To choose to be this or that is to affirm at the same time the value of what we choose, because we can never choose evil. We always choose the good, and nothing can be good for us without being good for all.

If, on the other hand, existence precedes essence, and if we grant that we exist and fashion our image at one and the same time, the image is valid for everybody and for our whole age. Thus, our responsibility is much greater than we might have supposed, because it involves all mankind. If I am a workingman and choose to join a Christian trade-union rather than be a communist, and if by being a member I want to show that the best thing for man is resignation, that the kingdom of man is not of this world, I am not only involving my own case—I want to be resigned for everyone. As a result, my action has involved all humanity. To take a more individual matter, if I want to marry, to have children; even if this marriage depends solely on my own circumstances or passion or wish, I am involving all humanity in monogamy and not merely myself. Therefore, I am responsible for myself and for everyone else. I am creating a certain image of man of my own choosing. In choosing myself, I choose man.

This helps us understand what the actual content is of such rather grandiloquent words as anguish, forlornness, despair. As you will see, it's all quite simple.

First, what is meant by anguish? The existentialists say at once that man is anguish. What that means is this: the man who involves himself and who realizes that he is not only the person he chooses to be, but also a lawmaker who is, at the same time, choosing all mankind as well as himself, can not help escape the feeling of his total and deep responsibility. Of course, there are many people who are not anxious; but we claim that they are hiding their anxiety, that they are fleeing from it. Certainly, many people believe that when they do something, they themselves are the only ones involved, and when someone says to them, "What if everyone acted that way?" they shrug their shoulders and answer, "Everyone doesn't act that way." But really, one should always ask himself, "What would happen if everybody looked at things that way?" There is no escaping this disturbing thought except by a kind of double-dealing. A man who lies and makes excuses for himself by saying "not everybody does that," is someone with an uneasy conscience, because the act of lying implies that a universal value is conferred upon the lie.

Anguish is evident even when it conceals itself. This is the anguish that Kierkegaard called the anguish of Abraham. You know the story: an angel has ordered Abraham to sacrifice his son; if it really were an angel who has come and said, "You are Abraham, you shall sacrifice your son," everything would be all right. But everyone might first wonder, "Is it really an angel, and am I really Abraham? What proof do I have?"

There was a madwoman who had hallucinations; someone used to speak to her on the telephone and give her orders. Her doctor asked her, "Who is it who talks to you?" She answered, "He says it's God." What proof did she really have that it was God? If an angel comes to me, what proof is there that it's an angel? And if I hear voices, what proof is there that they come from heaven and not from hell, or from the subconscious, or a pathological condition? What proves that they are addressed to me? What proof is there that I have been appointed to impose my choice and my conception of man on humanity? I'll never find any proof or sign to convince me of that. If a voice addresses me, it is always for me to decide that this is the angel's voice; if I consider that such an act is a good one, it is I who will choose to say that it is good rather than bad.

Now, I'm not being singled out as an Abraham, and yet at every moment I'm obliged to perform exemplary acts. For every man, everything happens as if all mankind had its eyes fixed on him and were guiding itself by what he does. And every man ought to say to himself, "Am I really the kind of man who has the right to act in such a way that humanity might guide itself by my actions?" And if he does not say that to himself, he is masking his anguish.

There is no question here of the kind of anguish which would lead to quietism, to inaction. It is a matter of a simple sort of anguish that anybody who has had responsibilities is familiar with. For example, when a military officer takes the responsibility for an attack and sends a certain number of men to death, he chooses to do so, and in the main he alone makes the choice. Doubtless, orders come from above, but they are too broad; he interprets them, and on this interpretation depend the lives of ten or fourteen or twenty men. In making a decision he can not help having a certain anguish. All leaders know this anguish. That doesn't keep them from acting; on the contrary, it is the very condition of their action. For it implies that they envisage a number of possibilities, and when they choose one, they realize that it has value only because it is chosen. We shall see that this kind of anguish, which is the kind that existentialism describes, is explained, in addition, by a direct responsibility to the other men whom it involves. It is not a curtain separating us from action, but is part of action itself.

When we speak of forlornness, a term Heidegger was fond of, we mean only that God does not exist and that we have to face all the consequences of this. The existentialist is strongly opposed to a certain kind of secular ethics which would like to abolish God with the least possible expense. About 1880, some French teachers tried to set up a secular ethics which went something like this: God is a useless and costly hypothesis; we are discarding it; but, meanwhile, in order for there to be an ethics, a society, a civilization, it is essential that certain values be taken seriously and that they be considered as having an *a priori* existence. It must be obligatory, *a priori*, to be honest, not to lie, not to beat your wife, to have children, etc., etc. So we're going to try a little device which will make it possible to show that values exist all the same, inscribed in a heaven of ideas, though otherwise God does not exist. In other words—and this, I believe, is the tendency of everything called reformism in France—nothing will be changed if God does not exist. We shall find ourselves with the same norms of honesty, progress, and humanism, and we shall have made of God an outdated hypothesis which will peacefully die off by itself.

The existentialist, on the contrary, thinks it very distressing that God does not exist, because all possibility of finding values in a heaven of ideas disappears along with Him; there can no longer be an *a priori* Good, since there is no infinite and perfect consciousness to think it. Nowhere it is written that the Good exists, that we must be honest, that we must not lie; because the fact is we are on a plane where there are only men. Dostoevsky said, "If God didn't exist, everything would be possible." That is the very starting point of existentialism. Indeed, everything is permissible if God does not exist, and as a result man is forlorn, because neither within him nor without does he find anything to cling to. He can't start making excuses for himself.

If existence really does precede essence, there is no explaining things away by reference to a fixed and given human nature. In other words, there is no determinism, man is free, man is freedom. On the other hand, if God does not exist, we find no values or commands to turn to which legitimize our conduct.

So, in the bright realm of values, we have no excuse behind us, nor justification before us. We are alone, with no excuses.

That is the idea I shall try to convey when I say that man is condemned to be free. Condemned, because he did not create himself, yet, in other respects is free; because, once thrown into the world, he is responsible for everything he does. The existentialist does not believe in the power of passion. He will never agree that a sweeping passion is a ravaging torrent which fatally leads a man to certain acts and is therefore an excuse. He thinks that man is responsible for his passion.

The existentialist does not think that man is going to help himself by finding in the world some omen by which to orient himself. Because he thinks that man will interpret the omen to suit himself. Therefore, he thinks that man, with no support and no aid, is condemned every moment to invent man. Ponge, in a very fine article, has said, "Man is the future of man." That's exactly it. But if it is taken to mean that this future is recorded in heaven, that God sees it, then it is false, because it would really no longer be a future. If it is taken to mean that, whatever a man may be, there is a future to be forged, a virgin future before him, then this remark is sound. But then we are forlorn.

To give you an example which will enable you to understand forlornness better, I shall cite the case of one of my students who came to see me under the following circumstances: his father was on bad terms with his mother, and, moreover, was inclined to be a collaborationist; his older brother had been killed in the German offensive of 1940, and the young man, with somewhat immature but generous feelings, wanted to avenge him. His mother lived alone with him, very much upset by the half-treason of her husband and the death of her older son; the boy was her only consolation.

The boy was faced with the choice of leaving for England and joining the Free French Forces—that is, leaving his mother behind—or remaining with his mother and helping her to carry on. He was fully aware that the woman lived only for him and that his going-off—and perhaps his death—would plunge her into despair. He was also aware that every act that he did for his mother's sake was a sure thing, in the sense that it was helping her to carry on, whereas every effort he made toward going off and fighting was an uncertain move which might run aground and prove completely useless; for example, on his way to England he might, while passing through Spain, be detained indefinitely in a Spanish camp; he might reach England or Algiers and be stuck in an office at a desk job. As a result, he was faced with two very different kinds of action: one, concrete, immediate, but concerning only one individual; the other concerned an incomparably vaster group, a national collectivity, but for that very reason was dubious, and might be interrupted en route. And, at the same time, he was wavering between two kinds of ethics. On the one hand, an ethics of sympathy, of personal devotion; on the other hand, a broader ethics, but one whose efficacy was more dubious. He had to choose between the two.

Who could help him choose? Christian doctrine? No. Christian doctrine says, "Be charitable, love your neighbor, take the more rugged path, etc., etc." But which is the more rugged path? Whom should he love as a brother? The fighting man or his mother? Which does the greater good, the vague act of fighting in a group, or the concrete one of helping a particular human being to go on living? Who can decide *a priori?* Nobody. No book of ethics can tell him. The Kantian ethics says, "Never treat any person as a means, but as an end." Very well, if I stay with my mother, I'll treat her as an end and not as a means; but by virtue of this very fact, I'm running the risk of treating the people around me who are fighting, as means; and, conversely, if I go to join those who are fighting, I'll be treating them as an end, and, by doing that, I run the risk of treating my mother as a means.

If values are vague, and if they are always too broad for the concrete and specific case that we are considering, the only thing left for us is to trust our instincts. That's what this young man tried to do; and when I saw him, he said, "In the end, feeling is what counts. I ought to choose whichever pushes me in one direction. If I feel that I love my mother enough to sacrifice everything else for her—my desire for vengeance, for action, for adventure—then I'll stay with her. If, on the contrary, I feel that my love for my mother isn't enough, I'll leave."

But how is the value of a feeling determined? What gives his feeling for his mother value? Precisely the fact that he remained with her. I may say that I like so-and-so well enough to sacrifice a certain amount of money for him, but I may say so only if I've done it. I may say "I love my mother well enough to remain with her" if I have remained with her. The only way to determine the value of this affection is, precisely, to perform an act which confirms and defines it. But, since I require this affection to justify my act, I find myself caught in a vicious circle.

On the other hand, Gide has well said that a mock feeling and a true feeling are almost indistinguishable; to decide that I love my mother and will remain with her, or to remain with her by putting on an act, amount somewhat to the same thing. In other words, the feeling is formed by the acts one performs; so, I can not refer to it in order to act upon it. Which means that I can neither seek within myself the true condition which will impel me to act, nor apply to a system of ethics for concepts which will permit me to act. You will say, "At least, he did go to a teacher for advice." But if you seek advice from a priest, for example, you have chosen this priest; you already knew, more or less, just about what advice he was gong to give you. In other words, choosing your adviser is involving yourself. The proof of this is that if you are a Christian, you will say, "Consult a priest." But some priests are collaborating, some are just marking time, some are resisting. Which to choose? If the young man chooses a priest who is resisting or collaborating, he has already decided on the kind of advice he's going to get. Therefore, in coming to see me he knew the answer I was going to give him, and I had only one answer to give: "You're free, choose, that is, invent." No general ethics can show you what is to be done; there are no omens in the world. The Catholics will reply, "But there are." Granted—but, in any case, I myself choose the meaning they have.

When I was a prisoner, I knew a rather remarkable young man who was a Jesuit. He had entered the Jesuit order in the following way: he had had a number of very bad breaks; in childhood, his father died, leaving him in poverty, and he was a scholarship student at a religious institution where he was constantly made to feel that he was being kept out of charity; then, he failed to get any of the honors and distinctions that children like; later on, at about eighteen, he bungled a love affair; finally at twenty-two, he failed in military training, a childish enough matter, but it was the last straw.

This young fellow might well have felt that he had botched everything. It was a sign of something, but of what? He might have taken refuge in bitterness or despair. But he very wisely looked upon all this as a sign that he was not made for secular triumphs, and that only the triumphs of religion, holiness, and faith were open to him. He saw the hand of God in all this, and so he entered the order. Who can help seeing that he alone decided what the sign meant?

Some other interpretation might have been drawn from this series of set-backs; for example, that he might have done better to turn carpenter or revolutionist. Therefore, he is fully responsible for the interpretation. Forlornness implies that we ourselves choose our being. Forlornness and anguish go together.

As for despair, the term has a very simple meaning. It means that we shall confine ourselves to reckoning only with what depends upon our will, or on the ensemble of probabilities which make our action possible. When we want something, we always have to reckon with probabilities. I may be counting on the arrival of a friend. The friend is coming by rail or street-car; this supposes that the train will arrive on schedule, or that the street-car will not jump the track. I am left in the realm of possibility; but possibilities are to be reckoned with only to the point where my action comports with the ensemble of these possibilities, and no further. The moment the possibilities I am considering are not rigorously involved by my action, I ought to disengage myself from them, because no God, no scheme, can adapt the world and its possibilities to my will. When Descartes said, "Conquer yourself rather than the world," he meant essentially the same thing.

The Marxists to whom I have spoken reply, "You can rely on the support of others in your action, which obviously has certain limits because you're not going to live forever. That means: rely on both what others are doing elsewhere to help you, in China, in Russia, and what they will do later on, after your death, to carry on the action and lead it to its fulfillment, which will be the revolution. You even *have* to rely upon that, otherwise you're immoral." I reply at once that I will always rely on fellow-fighters insofar as these comrades are involved with me in a common struggle, in the unity of a party or a group in which I can more or less make my weight felt; that is, one whose ranks I am in as a fighter and whose movements I am aware of at every moment. In such a situation, relying on the unity and will of the party is exactly like counting on the fact that the train will arrive on time or that the car won't jump the track. But, given that man is free and that there is no human nature for me to depend on, I can not count on men whom I do not know by relying on human goodness or man's concern for the good of society. I don't know what will become of the Russian revolution; I may make an example of it to the extent that at the present time it is apparent that the proletariat plays a part in Russia that it plays in no other nation. But I can't swear that this will inevitably lead to a triumph of the proletariat. I've got to limit myself to what I see.

Given that men are free and that tomorrow they will freely decide what man will be, I can not be sure that, after my death, fellow-fighters will carry on my work to bring it to its maximum perfection. Tomorrow, after my death, some men may decide to set up Fascism, and the others may be cowardly and muddled enough to let them do it. Fascism will then be the human reality, so much the worse for us.

Actually, things will be as man will have decided they are to be. Does that mean that I should abandon myself to quietism? No. First, I should involve myself; then, act on the old saw, "Nothing ventured, nothing gained." Nor does it mean that I shouldn't belong to a party, but rather that I shall have no illusions and shall do what I can. For example, suppose I ask myself, "Will socialization, as such, ever come about?" I know nothing about it. All I know is that I'm going to do everything in my power to bring it about. Beyond that, I can't count on anything. Quietism is the attitude of people who say, "Let others do what I can't do." The doctrine I am presenting is the very opposite of quietism, since it declares, "There is no reality except in action." Moreover, it goes further, since it adds, "Man is nothing else than his plan; he exists only to the extent that he fulfills himself; he is therefore nothing else than the ensemble of his acts, nothing else than his life."

According to this, we can understand why our doctrine horrifies certain people. Because often the only way they can bear their wretchedness is to think, "Circumstances have been against me. What I've been and done doesn't show my true worth. To be sure, I've had no great love, no great friendship, but that's because I haven't met a man or woman who was worthy. The books I've written haven't been very good because I haven't had the proper leisure. I haven't had children to devote myself to because I didn't find a man with whom I could have spent my life. So there remains within me, unused and quite viable, a host of propensities, inclinations, possibilities, that one wouldn't guess from the mere series of things I've done."

Now, for the existentialist there is really no love other than one which manifests itself in a person's being in love. There is no genius other than one which is expressed in works of art; the genius of Proust is the sum of Proust's works; the genius of Racine is his series of tragedies. Outside of that, there is nothing. Why say that Racine could have written another tragedy, when he didn't write it? A man is involved in life, leaves his impress on it, and outside of that there is nothing. To be sure, this may seem a harsh thought to someone whose life hasn't been a success. But, on the other hand, it prompts people to understand that reality alone is what counts, that dreams, expectations, and hopes warrant no more than to define a man as a disappointed dream, as miscarried hopes, as vain expectations. In other words, to define him negatively and not positively. However, when we say, "You are nothing else than your life," that does not imply that the artist will be judged solely on the basis of his works of art; a thousand other things will contribute toward summing him up. What we mean is that a man is nothing else than a series of undertakings, that he is the sum, the organization, the ensemble of the relationships which make up these undertakings.

II
THE MEANING OF
MORAL LANGUAGE

When they think about morality, many people assume both that there is a truth of the matter and that they have some chance of discovering what it is. However, many philosophers contest both assumptions. In this and the next section, we will consider some of the challenges they pose.

The most radical challenge denies that any ethical utterance *can* be true. According to this view, someone who says that keeping promises is right, or that pain is bad, is attempting neither to state any fact nor to assert any truth. Instead, he is only expressing a personal attitude *toward* promise-keeping or pain. If we take his utterance to have any other meaning, we are misled by the grammatical similarity between "*X* is right" and "*X* is good" on the one hand, and "*X* is rectangular" and "*X* is red" on the other. Thus, according to the proposed view, the reason we cannot know what is right or good is simply that there is *nothing to know*. Because this view asserts that ethical utterances lack cognitive content, it is often called *non-cognitivism*.

Non-cognitivism is at least foreshadowed in the theory of the great eighteenth-century Scottish philosopher David Hume. In his *Treatise of Human Nature* (excerpted in reading 8), Hume argued that no form of reason can ever supply any motive for acting, but that morality often does move us to act. He concluded that moral characteristics—goodness and rightness—cannot be revealed by reason. Instead, when we say that someone has a good character, or that he has done the right thing, our assertion must originate in our own feelings. As Hume put it, "when you pronounce any action or character to be vicious, you mean nothing, but that from the constitution of your nature you have a feeling or sentiment of blame from the contemplation of it." However, Hume also wrote that if persons are to "converse together on any reasonable terms," each must adjust his ethical utterances, not merely to the feelings that he *does* have toward the relevant actions or characters, but also to the feelings that he *would* have toward them if they affected him more or less immediately. Here Hume implies that ethical utterances can be used to communicate, and so also that there is something *that* they can communicate. Whether this commits him to holding that ethical utterances can be true, and hence whether it makes him a kind of cognitivist, are questions that cannot be settled here.

In the twentieth century, non-cognitivism has been developed in a variety of ways. According to A. J. Ayer (reading 10), when we say that a cruel act is wrong, or that the agent should not have behaved cruelly, we are either expressing our own disapproval of cruelty or exhorting others to refrain from cruel acts. Because Ayer assimilates ethical utterances to expressions of emotion such as moans or cheers, his account is known as *the emotive theory*. More recently, R. M. Hare (reading 11) has maintained that when we say that we ought to do something, we are both committing ourselves to doing it and prescribing similar acts for all others who are similarly situated. Thus, if some-one says that he ought to cheat another, he is prescribing that he himself be cheated when the roles are reversed. Since few are willing to prescribe this, Hare's view implies that most who say that they ought to cheat others, or who act on that conviction, are being inconsistent. More recently yet, Alan Gibbard (reading 12) has sought to locate morality within a broader non-cognitivist framework. For Gibbard, the fundamental notion is not morality but rational-ity. He suggests that "to call something rational is to express one's acceptance of norms that permit it." Moral notions, in turn, are defined in terms of norms that make it appropriate to respond to certain kinds of acts with guilt (if one is the agent) or resentment (if one is not).

Despite their differences, all non-cognitivists agree that instead of attempting to say anything true, ethical utterances merely express, prescribe, or assert. However, as David Brink points out in reading 13, many of the claims we make using ethical terms do not lend themselves to such an analysis; if we adopted this analysis, we would have to stop making such claims. Consider, for example, the assertion "A person should not be held responsible for actions he could not have known were wrong." If someone who says "X is wrong" is merely expressing his feelings toward X, then what could a speaker mean by the embedded phrase "actions he could not have known were wrong"? To preserve consistency, a non-cognitivist must somehow reinterpret this use of "wrong" in expressive terms. However, after examining several possibilities, Brink concludes that no such interpretation is plausible.

If we reject non-cognitivism in favor of the view that ethical utterances can be true or false, we must explain what *makes* ethical claims true. This requires that we understand what "good" and related terms mean. To answer this question, some have sought to define moral expressions in nonmoral terms— for example, by equating "good" with "productive of pleasure." However, according to G. E. Moore (reading 9), whatever combination of "natural" properties we choose, it always makes sense to ask, "But *is* something with those properties good?" Moreover, it is always conceivable that the answer will turn out to be no. Thus, Moore concludes that the property of being good (and, by extension, of being right, wrong, etc.) is distinct from everything in the natural realm. To mark the distinction, Moore calls these *nonnatural* properties. However, even if moral properties *are* distinct from all natural properties, it may still be true that everything with a given set of natural properties will always have all the *same* moral properties. In more technical terms, moral properties may *supervene* on natural ones. For a brief statement of this important view, see Nicholas Sturgeon's discussion in reading 18.

Whatever the relations between moral and nonmoral properties, there are many candidates for the roles of good- and right-making features. A number of important possibilities will be discussed in later sections, but one can be discussed here. This is the *divine command theory*, which holds that what is right depends on the wishes or commands of God. Because God is not a part of the natural world, this theory is, strictly speaking, not a form of naturalism. It is, however, a form of supernaturalism.

One obvious virtue of the divine command theory is that it invests morality with God's authority and majesty. Yet just because of this, the theory cannot convince those who doubt God's existence. Moreover, before accepting it, even believers must respond to a dilemma first noticed by Plato. In reading 14, Plato asks, in effect, whether actions are made right by the fact that God commands them or whether God commands acts because they are independently right. If we accept the first alternative, God's commands will appear arbitrary, while if we accept the second, then what is right will not depend on God's commands. However, in reading 15, Robert M. Adams proposes a version of the divine command theory which may avoid the difficulty. Drawing on recent results from other areas of philosophy, Adams argues that it is "most plausible to identify wrongness with the property of being contrary to the commands of a loving God." Because the relevant commands must stem from God's love, Adams implies that they are not arbitrary in any damaging sense. In this way, he in effect grasps the first horn of Plato's dilemma.

8

Morality and
Natural Sentiment

DAVID HUME

*David Hume (1711–1776) made enduring contributions to ethics, social
philosophy, the theory of knowledge, and the philosophy of religion. His
masterpiece,* A Treatise of Human Nature, *was published when he was
twenty-eight.*

*Hume's theory of ethics is elaborate and subtle. This selection, excerpted
from Books 2 and 3 of the* Treatise, *presents some of its main elements. To
begin, Hume examines the view that morality is grounded in reason. Since
morality sometimes moves us to act, this view implies that reason can
motivate actions. But Hume argues that reason supplies no motives. At
best, it tells us how to achieve what we independently desire. Since reason
"is, and ought only to be, the slave of the passions," it is not the source of
moral judgments.*

*What, then, is? According to Hume, the crucial role is played by the
passions themselves. When we judge a character to be virtuous or vicious,
or an act to be good or bad, we are projecting our own feelings upon it.
These feelings are not merely reactions to the fact that we are benefited or
harmed. Rather, they reflect pleasures and pains we feel through
sympathetic identification with other affected parties. In stressing the
connection between moral judgments and the judge's own feelings, Hume
anticipates Ayer's emotive theory (reading 10). In stressing the role of
sympathetic identification with others, he anticipates theories like Hare's
(reading 11).*

*Although Hume's general theory applies to all moral judgments, he
makes an important distinction between natural and artificial virtues. Such
traits as beneficence and generosity are always beneficial and thus are
natural virtues. But other virtues, such as justice, are different. If goods
were plentiful or not easily transferred, or if people were less covetous than
they are, there would be no need for justice. But given the world as it is,
rules of ownership are in everyone's interest. For this reason, we develop
conventions that each person observes in expectation that others will do
likewise. Since justice is the observation of such conventions, it is an
artificial virtue.*

OF THE INFLUENCING MOTIVES OF THE WILL

Nothing is more usual in philosophy, and even in common life, than to talk of the combat of passion and reason, to give the preference to reason, and assert that men are only so far virtuous as they conform themselves to its dictates. Every rational creature, it is said, is obliged to regulate his actions by reason; and if any other motive or principle challenge the direction of his conduct, he ought to oppose it till it be entirely subdued or at least brought to a conformity with that superior principle. On this method of thinking the greatest part of moral philosophy, ancient and modern, seems to be founded; nor is there an ampler field as well for metaphysical arguments as popular declamations than this supposed pre-eminence of reason above passion. The eternity, invariableness, and divine origin of the former have been displayed to the best advantage; the blindness, inconstancy, and deceitfulness of the latter have been as strongly insisted on. In order to show the fallacy of all this philosophy, I shall endeavor to prove, *first*, that reason alone can never be a motive to any action of the will; and, *secondly*, that it can never oppose passion in the direction of the will.

The understanding exerts itself after two different ways, as it judges from demonstration or probability; as it regards the abstract relations of our ideas, or those relations of objects of which experience only gives us information. I believe it scarce will be asserted that the first species of reasoning alone is ever the cause of any action. As its proper province is the world of ideas, and as the will always places us in that of realities, demonstration and volition seem upon that account to be totally removed from each other. Mathematics, indeed, are useful in all mechanical operations, and arithmetic in almost every art and profession: but it is not of themselves they have any influence. Mechanics are the art of regulating the motions of bodies *to some designed end* or *purpose;* and the reason why we employ arithmetic in fixing the proportions of numbers is only that we may discover the proportions of their influence and operation. A merchant is desirous of knowing the sum total of his accounts with any person: why? but that he may learn what sum will have the same *effects* in paying his debt, and going to market, as all the particular articles taken together. Abstract or demonstrative reasoning, therefore, never influences any of our actions, but only as it directs our judgment concerning causes and effects; which leads us to the second operation of the understanding.

It is obvious that when we have the prospect of pain or pleasure from any object, we feel a consequent emotion of aversion or propensity, and are carried to avoid or embrace what will give us this uneasiness or satisfaction. It is also obvious that this emotion rests not here, but, making us cast our view on every side, comprehends whatever objects are connected with its original one by the relation of cause and effect. Here then reasoning takes place to discover this relation; and according as our reasoning varies, our actions receive a subsequent variation. But it is evident in this case that the impulse arises not from reason, but is only directed by it. It is from the prospect of pain or pleasure that the aversion or propensity arises towards any object: and these emotions extend themselves to the causes and effects of that object, as they are pointed out to us by reason and experience. It can never in the least concern us to know that such objects are causes, and such others effects, if both the causes and effects be indifferent to us. Where the objects themselves do not affect us, their connection can never give them any influence; and it is plain that, as reason is nothing but the discovery of this connection, it cannot be by its means that the objects are able to affect us.

Since reason alone can never produce any action or give rise to volition, I infer that the same faculty is as incapable of preventing volition or of disputing the preference with any passion or emotion. This consequence is necessary. It is impossible reason could have the latter effect of preventing volition, but by giving an impulse in a contrary direction to our passions; and that impulse, had it operated alone, would have been ample to produce volition. Nothing can oppose or retard the impulse of passion but a contrary impulse; and if this contrary impulse ever arises from reason, that latter faculty must have an original influence on the will and must be able to cause as well as hinder any act of volition. But if reason has no original influence, it is impossible it can withstand any principle which has such an efficacy, or ever keep the mind in suspense a moment. Thus it appears that the principle which opposes our passion cannot be the same with reason, and is only called so in an improper sense. We speak not strictly and philosophically when we talk of the combat of passion and of reason. Reason is, and ought only to be, the slave of the passions, and can never pretend to any other office than to serve and obey them. As this opinion may appear somewhat extraordinary, it may not be improper to confirm it by some other considerations.

A passion is an original existence or, if you will, modification of existence, and contains not any representative quality which renders it a copy of any other existence or modification. When I am angry, I am actually possessed with the passion, and in that emotion have no more a reference to any other object than when I am thirsty, or sick, or more than five feet high. It is impossible, therefore, that this passion can be opposed by, or be contradictory to, truth and reason; since this contradiction consists in the disagreement of ideas, considered as copies, with those objects which they represent.

What may at first occur on this head is that as nothing can be contrary to truth or reason, except what has a reference to it, and as the judgments of our understanding only have this reference, it must follow that passions can be contrary to reason only so far as they are *accompanied* with some judgment or opinion. According to this principle, which is so obvious and natural, it is only in two senses that any affection can be called unreasonable. First, when a passion, such as hope or fear, grief or joy, despair or security, is founded on the supposition of the existence of objects which really do not exist. Secondly, when, in exerting any passion in action, we choose means sufficient for the designed end, and deceive ourselves in our judgment of causes and effects. Where a passion is neither founded on false suppositions, nor chooses means insufficient for the end, the understanding can neither justify nor condemn it. It is not contrary to reason to prefer the destruction of the whole world to the scratching of my finger. It is not contrary to reason for me to choose my total ruin to prevent the least uneasiness of an Indian, or person wholly unknown to me. It is as little contrary to reason to prefer even my own acknowledged lesser good to my greater, and have a more ardent affection for the former than the latter. A trivial good may, from certain circumstances, produce a desire superior to what arises from the greatest and most valuable enjoyment; nor is there anything more extraordinary in this than in mechanics to see one pound weight raise up a hundred by the advantage of its situation. In short, a passion must be accompanied with some false judgment in order to its being unreasonable; and even then it is not the passion, properly speaking, which is unreasonable, but the judgment.

• • •

MORAL DISTINCTIONS NOT DERIVED FROM REASON

• • •

Those who affirm that virtue is nothing but a conformity to reason; that there are eternal fitnesses and unfitnesses of things which are the same to every rational being that considers them; that the immutable measure of right and wrong impose an obligation, not only on human creatures, but also on the Deity himself: all these systems concur in the opinion that morality, like truth, is discerned merely by ideas, and by their juxtaposition and comparison. In order, therefore, to judge of these systems, we need only consider whether it be possible from reason alone to distinguish betwixt moral good and evil, or whether there must concur some other principles to enable us to make that distinction.

If morality had naturally no influence on human passions and actions, it were in vain to take such pains to inculcate it; and nothing would be more fruitless than that multitude of rules and precepts with which all moralists abound. Philosophy is commonly divided into *speculative* and *practical*; and as morality is always comprehended under the latter division, it is supposed to influence our passions and actions, and to go beyond the calm and indolent judgments of the understanding. And this is confirmed by common experience, which informs us that men are often governed by their duties, and are deterred from some actions by the opinion of injustice, and impelled to others by that of obligation.

Since morals, therefore, have an influence on the actions and affections, it follows that they cannot be derived from reason, and that because reason alone, as we have already proved, can never have any such influence. Morals excite passions, and produce or prevent actions. Reason of itself is utterly impotent in this particular. The rules of morality, therefore, are not conclusions of our reason.

No one, I believe, will deny the justness of this inference; nor is there any other means of evading it than by denying that principle on which it is founded. As long as it is allowed that reason has no influence on our passions and actions, it is in vain to pretend that morality is discovered only by a deduction of reason. An active principle can never be founded on an inactive; and if reason be inactive in itself, it must remain so in all its shapes and appearances, whether it exerts itself in natural or moral subjects, whether it considers the powers of external bodies or the actions of rational beings.

It would be tedious to repeat all the arguments by which I have proved that reason is perfectly inert and can never either prevent or produce any action or affection. It will be easy to recollect what has been said upon that subject. I shall only recall on this occasion one of these arguments, which I shall endeavour to render still more conclusive and more applicable to the present subject.

Reason is the discovery of truth or falsehood. Truth or falsehood consists in an agreement or disagreement either to the *real* relations of ideas, or to *real* existence and matter of fact. Whatever, therefore, is not susceptible of this agreement or disagreement is incapable of being true or false, and can never be an object of our reason. Now, it is evident our passions, volitions, and actions, are not susceptible of any such agreement or disagreement; being original facts and realities, complete in themselves, and implying no reference to other passions, volitions, and actions. It is impossible, therefore, they can be pronounced either true or false, and be either contrary or conformable to reason.

This argument is of double advantage to our present purpose. For it proves *directly* that actions do not derive their merit from a conformity to reason, nor their blame from a contrariety to it; and it proves the same truth more *indirectly*, by showing us that as reason can never immediately prevent or produce any action by contradicting or approving of it, it cannot be the source of moral good and evil, which are found to have that influence. Actions may be laudable or blamable, but they cannot be reasonable or unreasonable: laudable or blamable, therefore, are not the same with reasonable or unreasonable. The merit and demerit of actions frequently contradict, and sometimes control our natural propensities. But reason has no such influence. Moral distinctions, therefore, are not the offspring of reason. Reason is wholly inactive, and can never be the source of so active a principle as conscience, or a sense of morals.

• • •

But, to be more particular, and to show that those eternal immutable fitnesses and unfitnesses of things cannot be defended by sound philosophy, we may weigh the following considerations.

If the thought and understanding were alone capable of fixing the boundaries of right and wrong, the character of virtuous and vicious either must lie in some relations of objects, or must be a matter of fact which is discovered by our reasoning. This consequence is evident. As the operations of human understanding divide themselves into two kinds—the comparing of ideas and the inferring of matter of fact—were virtue discovered by the understanding, it must be an object of one of these operations; nor is there any third operation of the understanding which can discover it. There has been an opinion very industriously propagated by certain philosophers that morality is susceptible of demonstration; and though no one has ever been able to advance a single step in those demonstrations, yet it is taken for granted that this science may be brought to an equal certainty with geometry or algebra. Upon this supposition vice and virtue must consist in some relations, since it is allowed on all hands that no matter of fact is capable of being demonstrated. Let us therefore begin with examining this hypothesis and endeavour, if possible, to fix those moral qualities which have been so long the objects of our fruitless researches, point out distinctly the relations which constitute morality or obligation, that we may know wherein they consist, and after what manner we must judge of them.

If you assert that vice and virtue consist in relations susceptible of certainty and demonstration, you must confine yourself to those *four* relations which alone admit of that degree of evidence; and in that case you run into absurdities from which you will never be able to extricate yourself. For as you make the very essence of morality to lie in the relations and as there is no one of these relations but what is applicable not only to an irrational but also to an inanimate object, it follows that even such objects must be susceptible of merit or demerit. *Resemblance, contrariety, degrees in quality*, and *proportions in quantity and number*; all these relations belong as properly to matter as to our actions, passions, and volitions. It is unquestionable, therefore, that morality lies not in any of these relations, nor in the sense of it in their discovery.[1]

Should it be asserted that the sense of morality consists in the discovery of some relation distinct from these, and that our enumeration was not complete when we comprehended all demonstrable relations under four general heads; to this I know not what to reply, till some one be so good as to point out to me this new relation. It is impossible to refute a system which has never yet been explained. In such a manner of fighting in the dark, a man loses his blows in the air and often places them where the enemy is not present.

· · ·

Nor does this reasoning only prove that morality consists not in any relations that are the objects of science; but, if examined, will prove with equal certainty

---

1 As a proof how confused our way of thinking on this subject commonly is, we may observe that those who assert that morality is demonstrable do not say that morality lies in the relations, and that the relations are distinguishable by reason. They only say that reason can discover such an action in such relations to be virtuous, and such another vicious. It seems they thought it sufficient if they could bring the word "relation" into the proposition, without troubling themselves whether it was to the purpose or not. But here, I think, is plain argument. Demonstrative reason discovers only relations. But that reason, according to this hypothesis, discovers also vice and virtue. These moral qualities, therefore, must be relations. When we blame any action, in any situation, the whole complicated object of action and situation must form certain relations, wherein the essence of vice consists. This hypothesis is not otherwise intelligible. For what does reason discover, when it pronounces any action vicious? Does it discover a relation or a matter of fact? These questions are decisive, and must not be eluded.

that it consists not in any *matter of fact* which can be discovered by the understanding. This is the *second* part of our argument; and if it can be made evident, we may conclude that morality is not an object of reason. But can there be any difficulty in proving that vice and virtue are not matters of fact whose existence we can infer by reason? Take any action allowed to be vicious— wilful murder, for instance. Examine it in all lights, and see if you can find that matter of fact or real existence which you call *vice*. In whichever way you take it, you find only certain passions, motives, volitions, and thoughts. There is no other matter of fact in the case. The vice entirely escapes you, as long as you consider the object. You never can find it till you turn your reflection into your own breast and find a sentiment of disapprobation which arises in you towards this action. Here is a matter of fact; but it is the object of feeling, not of reason. It lies in yourself, not in the object. So that when you pronounce any action or character to be vicious, you mean nothing, but that from the constitution of your nature you have a feeling or sentiment of blame from the contemplation of it. Vice and virtue, therefore, may be compared to sounds, colours, heat, and cold, which, according to modern philosophy, are not quali- ties in objects but perceptions in the mind: and this discovery in morals, like that other in physics, is to be regarded as a considerable advancement of the speculative sciences; though, like that too, it has little or no influence on practice. Nothing can be more real, or concern us more, than our own senti- ments of pleasure and uneasiness; and if these be favourable to virtue, and unfavourable to vice, no more can be requisite to the regulation of our conduct and behaviour.

I cannot forbear adding to these reasonings an observation which may, perhaps, be found of some importance. In every system of morality which I have hitherto met with, I have always remarked that the author proceeds for some time in the ordinary way of reasoning, and establishes the being of a god, or makes observations concerning human affairs; when of a sudden I am surprised to find that instead of the usual copulations of propositions *is* and *is not*, I meet with no proposition that is not connected with an *ought* or an *ought not*. This change is imperceptible, but is, however, of the last conse- quence. For as this *ought* or *ought not* expresses some new relation or affirma- tion, it is necessary that it should be observed and explained; and at the same time that a reason should be given for what seems altogether inconceivable, how this new relation can be a deduction from others which are entirely different from it. But as authors do not commonly use this precaution, I shall presume to recommend it to the readers; and am persuaded that this small attention would subvert all the vulgar systems of morality and let us see that the distinction of vice and virtue is not founded merely on the relations of objects, nor is perceived by reason.

MORAL DISTINCTIONS DERIVED FROM A MORAL SENSE

Thus the course of the argument leads us to conclude that since vice and virtue are not discoverable merely by reason, or the comparison of ideas, it must be by means of some impression or sentiment they occasion, that we are able to mark the difference betwixt them. Our decisions concerning moral rectitude and depravity are evidently perceptions; and as all perceptions are either impressions or ideas, the exclusion of the one is a convincing argument for the other. Morality, therefore, is more properly felt than judged of; though this feeling or sentiment is commonly so soft and gentle that we are apt to confound it with an idea, according to our common custom of taking all things for the same which have any near resemblance to each other.

The next question is of what nature are these impressions, and after what manner do they operate upon us? Here we cannot remain long in suspense, but must pronounce the impression arising from virtue to be agreeable, and that proceeding from vice to be uneasy. Every moment's experience must convince us of this. There is no spectacle so fair and beautiful as a noble and generous action; nor any which gives us more abhorrence than one that is cruel and treacherous. No enjoyment equals the satisfaction we receive from the company of those we love and esteem; as the greatest of all punishments is to be obliged to pass our lives with those we hate or contemn. A very play or romance may afford us instances of this pleasure which virtue conveys to us; and pain which arises from vice.

Now, since the distinguishing impressions by which moral good or evil is known are nothing but *particular* pains or pleasures, it follows that in all inquiries concerning these moral distinctions it will be sufficient to show the principles which make us feel a satisfaction or uneasiness from the survey of any character, in order to satisfy us why the character is laudable or blamable. An action, or sentiment, or character, is virtuous or vicious; why? because its view causes a pleasure or uneasiness of a particular kind. In giving a reason, therefore, for the pleasure or uneasiness, we sufficiently explain the vice or virtue. To have the sense of virtue is nothing but to *feel* a satisfaction of a particular kind from the contemplation of a character. The very *feeling* constitutes our praise or admiration. We go no further; nor do we inquire into the cause of the satisfaction. We do not infer a character to be virtuous because if pleases; but in feeling that it pleases after such a particular manner we in effect feel that it is virtuous. The case is the same as in our judgments concerning all kinds of beauty, and tastes, and sensations. Our approbation is implied in the immediate pleasure they convey to us.

I have objected to the system which establishes eternal rational measures of right and wrong, that it is impossible to show in the actions of reasonable creatures any relations which are not found in external objects; and therefore, if morality always attended these relations, it were possible for inanimate matter to become virtuous or vicious. Now it may, in like manner, be objected to the present system, that if virtue and vice be determined by pleasure and pain, these qualities must in every case arise from the sensations; and consequently any object, whether animate or inanimate, rational or irrational, might become morally good or evil, provided it can excite a satisfaction or uneasiness. But though this objection seems to be the very same, it has by no means the same force in the one case as in the other. For, *first*, it is evident that under the term *pleasure* we comprehend sensations which are very different from each other, and which have only such a distant resemblance as is requisite to make them be expressed by the same abstract term. A good composition of music and a bottle of good wine equally produce pleasure; and, what is more, their goodness is determined merely by the pleasure. But shall we say, upon that account, that the wine is harmonious, or the music of a good flavour? In like manner, an inanimate object and the character or sentiments of any person may, both of them, give satisfaction; but, as the satisfaction is different, this keeps our sentiments concerning them from being confounded, and makes us ascribe virtue to the one and not to the other. Nor is every sentiment of pleasure or pain, which arises from characters and actions, of that *peculiar* kind which makes us praise or condemn. The good qualities of an enemy are hurtful to us, but may still command our esteem and respect. It is only when a character is considered in general, without reference to our particular interest, that it causes such a feeling or sentiment as denominates it morally good or evil. It is true, those sentiments from interest and morals are apt to be confounded, and naturally run into one another. It seldom happens that we do not think an enemy vicious, and can distinguish betwixt his opposition to our interest and real villainy or baseness. But this hinders not but that the sentiments are in themselves distinct, and a man of temper and judgment may preserve himself from these illusions. In like manner, though it is certain a musical voice is nothing but one that naturally gives a *particular* kind of pleasure, yet it is difficult for a man to be sensible that the voice of an enemy is agreeable, or to allow it to be musical. But a person of a fine ear, who has the command of himself, can separate these feelings and give praise to what deserves it.

Secondly, we may call to remembrance the preceding system of the passions, in order to remark a still more considerable difference among our pains and pleasures. Pride and humility, love and hatred, are excited when there is anything presented to us that both bears a relation to the object of the passion and produces a separate sensation related to the sensation of the passion. Now, virtue and vice are attended with these circumstances. They must necessarily be placed either in ourselves or others, and excite either pleasure or uneasiness; and therefore must give rise to one of these four passions, which clearly distinguishes them from the pleasure and pain arising from inanimate objects that often bear no relation to us; and this is, perhaps, the most considerable effect that virtue and vice have upon the human mind.

It may now be asked *in general* concerning this pain or pleasure that distinguishes moral good and evil, *from what principle is it derived, and whence does it arise in the human mind?* To this I reply, *first*, that it is absurd to imagine that, in every particular instance, these sentiments are produced by an *original* quality and *primary* constitution. For as the number of our duties is in a manner infinite, it is impossible that our original instincts should extend to each of them, and from our very first infancy impress on the human mind all that multitude of precepts which are contained in the completest system of ethics. Such a method of proceeding is not conformable to the usual maxims by which nature is conducted, where a few principles produce all that variety we observe in the universe, and everything is carried on in the easiest and most simple manner. It is necessary, therefore, to abridge these primary impulses and find some more general principles upon which all our notions of morals are founded.

But, in the *second* place, should it be asked, whether we ought to search for these principles in *nature*, or whether we must look for them in some other origin? I would reply that our answer to this question depends upon the definition of the word *nature*, than which there is none more ambiguous and equivocal. If *nature* be opposed to miracles, not only the distinction betwixt vice and virtue is natural, but also every event which has ever happened in the world, *excepting those miracles on which our religion is founded*. In saying, then, that the sentiments of vice and virtue are natural in this sense, we make no very extraordinary discovery.

But *nature* may also be opposed to rare and unusual; and in this sense of the word, which is the common one, there may often arise disputes concerning what is natural or unnatural; and one may in general affirm that we are not possessed of any very precise standard by which these disputes can be decided. Frequent and rare depend upon the number of examples we have observed; and as this number may gradually increase or diminish, it will be impossible to fix any exact boundaries betwixt them. We may only affirm on this head that if ever there was anything which could be called natural in this sense, the sentiments of morality certainly may; since there never was any nation of the world, nor any single person in any nation, who was utterly deprived of them, and who never, in any instance, showed the least approbation or dislike of manners. These sentiments are so rooted in our constitution and temper that, without entirely confounding the human mind by disease or madness, it is impossible to extirpate and destroy them.

But *nature* may also be opposed to artifice as well as to what is rare and unusual; and in this sense it may be disputed whether the notions of virtue be natural or not. We readily forget that the designs, and projects, and views of men are principles as necessary in their operation as heat and cold, moist and dry; but, taking them to be free and entirely our own, it is usual for us to set them in opposition to the other principles of nature. Should it therefore be demanded whether the sense of virtue be natural or artificial, I am of opinion that it is impossible for me at present to give any precise answer to this question. Perhaps it will appear afterwards that our sense of some virtues is artificial, and that of others natural. The discussion of this question will be more proper, when we enter upon an exact detail of each particular vice and virtue.[2]

Meanwhile, it may not be amiss to observe from these definitions of *natural* and *unnatural* that nothing can be more unphilosophical than those systems which assert that virtue is the same with what is natural, and vice with what is unnatural. For in the first sense of the word "nature," as opposed to miracles, both vice and virtue are equally natural; and in the second sense, as opposed to what is unusual, perhaps virtue will be found to be the most unnatural. At

---

2 In the following discourse, *natural* is also opposed sometimes to *civil*, sometimes to *moral*. The opposition will always discover the sense in which it is taken.

least it must be owned that heroic virtue, being as unusual, is as little natural as the most brutal barbarity. As to the third sense of the word, it is certain that both vice and virtue are equally artificial and out of nature. For, however it may be disputed whether the notion of a merit or demerit in certain actions be natural or artificial, it is evident that the actions themselves are artificial, and performed with a certain design and intention; otherwise they could never be ranked under any of these denominations. It is impossible, therefore, that the character of natural and unnatural can ever, in any sense, mark the boundaries of vice and virtue.

Thus we are still brought back to our first position that virtue is distinguished by the pleasure, and vice by the pain, that any action, sentiment, or character, gives us by the mere view and contemplation. This decision is very commodious; because it reduces us to this simple question, *why any action or sentiment, upon the general view or survey, gives a certain satisfaction or uneasiness*, in order to show the origin of its moral rectitude or depravity, without looking for any incomprehensible relations and qualities which never did exist in nature, nor even in our imagination, by any clear and distinct conception? I flatter myself I have executed a great part of my present design by a state of the question which appears to me so free from ambiguity and obscurity.

OF THE ORIGIN OF JUSTICE AND PROPERTY

We now proceed to examine two questions, viz., *concerning the manner in which the rules of justice are established by the artifice of men;* and *concerning the reasons which determine us to attribute to the observance or neglect of these rules a moral beauty and deformity*. These questions will appear afterwards to be distinct. We shall begin with the former.

• • •

There are three different species of goods which we are possessed of: the internal satisfaction of our minds, the external advantages of our body, and the enjoyment of such possessions as we have acquired by our industry and good fortune. We are perfectly secure in the enjoyment of the first. The second may be ravished from us, but can be of no advantage to him who deprives us of them. The last only are both exposed to the violence of others, and may be transferred without suffering any loss or alteration; while at the same time there is not a sufficient quantity of them to supply every one's desires and necessities. As the improvement, therefore, of these goods is the chief advantage of society, so the *instability* of their possession, along with their *scarcity*, is the chief impediment.

In vain should we expect to find in *uncultivated nature* a remedy to this inconvenience; or hope for any inartificial principle of the human mind which might control those partial affections, and make us overcome the temptations arising from our circumstances. The idea of justice can never serve to this purpose, or be taken for a natural principle capable of inspiring men with an equitable conduct towards each other. That virtue, as it is now understood, would never have been dreamed of among rude and savage men. For the notion of injury or injustice implies an immorality or vice committed against some other person. And as every immorality is derived from some defect or unsoundness of the passions, and as this defect must be judged of, in a great measure, from the ordinary course of nature in the constitution of the mind, it will be easy to know whether we be guilty of any immorality with regard to others, by considering the natural and usual force of those several affections which are directed towards them. Now, it appears that in the original frame of our mind our strongest attention is confined to ourselves; our next is extended to our relations and acquaintance; and it is only the weakest which reaches to strangers and indifferent persons. This partiality, then, and unequal affection must not only have an influence on our behaviour and conduct in society, but even on our ideas of vice and virtue; so as to make us regard any remarkable transgression of such a degree of partiality, either by too great an enlargement or contraction of the affections, as vicious and immoral. This we may observe in our common judgments concerning actions, where we blame a person who either centers all his affections in his family, or is so regardless of them as, in any opposition of interest, to give the preference to a stranger or mere chance acquaintance. From all which it follows that our natural uncultivated ideas of morality, instead of providing a remedy for the partiality of our affections, do rather conform themselves to that partiality and give it an additional force and influence.

The remedy, then, is not derived from nature but from *artifice;* or, more properly speaking, nature provides a remedy in the judgment and understanding for what is irregular and incommodious in the affections. For when men, from their early education in society, have become sensible of the infinite advantages that result from it, and have besides acquired a new affection to company and conversation, and when they have observed that the principal disturbance in society arises from those goods which we call external, and from their looseness and easy transition from one person to another, they must seek for a remedy by putting these goods as far as possible on the same footing with the fixed and constant advantages of the mind and body. This can be done after no other manner than by a convention entered into by all the members of the society to bestow stability on the possession of those external goods, and leave every one in the peaceable enjoyment of what he may acquire by his fortune and industry. By this means every one knows what he may safely possess; and the passions are restrained in their partial and contradictory motions. Nor is such a restraint contrary to these passions; for if so, it could never be entered into nor maintained; but it is only contrary to their heedless and impetuous movement. Instead of departing from our own interest, or from that of our nearest friends, by abstaining from the possessions of others, we cannot better consult both these interests than by such a convention; because it is by that means we maintain society, which is so necessary to their well-being and subsistence as well as to our own.

This convention is not of the nature of a *promise;* for even promises themselves, as we shall see afterwards, arise from human conventions. It is only a general sense of common interest; which sense all the members of the society express to one another, and which induces them to regulate their conduct by certain rules. I observe that it will be for my interest to leave another in the possession of his goods, *provided* he will act in the same manner with regard to me. He is sensible of a like interest in the regulation of his conduct. When this common sense of interest is mutually expressed and is known to both, it produces a suitable resolution and behaviour. And this may properly enough be called a convention or agreement betwixt us, though without the interposition of a promise; since the actions of each of us have a reference to those of the other, and are performed upon the supposition that something is to be performed on the other part. Two men who pull the oars of a boat do it by an agreement or convention, though they have never given promises to each other. Nor is the rule concerning the stability of possessions the less derived from human conventions, that it arises gradually, and acquires force by a slow progression and by our repeated experience of the inconveniences of transgressing it. On the contrary, this experience assures us still more that the sense of interest has become common to all our fellows, and gives us a confidence of the future regularity of their conduct; and it is only on the expectation of this that our moderation and abstinence are founded. In like manner are languages gradually established by human conventions, without any promise. In like manner do gold and silver become the common measures of exchange, and are esteemed sufficient payment for what is of a hundred times their value.

After this convention concerning abstinence from the possessions of others is entered into, and every one has acquired a stability in his possessions, there immediately arise the ideas of justice and injustice; as also those of *property, right,* and *obligation.* The latter are altogether unintelligible without first understanding the former. Our property is nothing but those goods whose constant possession is established by the laws of society—that is, by the laws of justice. Those, therefore, who make use of the words *property,* or *right,* or *obligation,* before they have explained the origin of justice, or even make use of them in that explication, are guilty of a very gross fallacy, and can never reason upon any solid foundation. A man's property is some object related to him. This relation is not natural but moral, and founded on justice. It is very preposterous, therefore, to imagine that we can have any idea of property without fully comprehending the nature of justice, and showing its origin in the artifice and contrivance of men. The origin of justice explains that of property. The same artifice gives rise to both. As our first and most natural sentiment of morals is founded on the nature of our passions, and gives the preference to ourselves and friends above strangers, it is impossible there can be naturally any such thing as fixed right or property, while the opposite passions of men impel them in contrary directions, and are not restrained by any convention or agreement.

• • •

. . . I have already observed that justice takes its rise from human conventions, and that these are intended as a remedy to some inconveniences which proceed from the concurrence of certain *qualities* of the human mind with the *situation* of external objects. The qualities of the mind are *selfishness* and *limited generosity*; and the situation of external objects is their *easy change*, joined to their *scarcity* in comparison of the wants and desires of men. But however philosophers may have been bewildered in those speculations, poets have been guided more infallibly by a certain taste or common instinct which, in most kinds of reasoning, goes further than any of that art and philosophy with which we have been yet acquainted. They easily perceived, if every man had a tender regard for another, or if nature supplied abundantly all our wants and desires, that the jealousy of interest, which justice supposes, could no longer have place; nor would there be any occasion for those distinctions and limits of property and possession which at present are in use among mankind. Increase to a sufficient degree the benevolence of men, or the bounty of nature, and you render justice useless by supplying its place with much nobler virtues and more valuable blessings. The selfishness of men is animated by the few possessions we have in proportion to our wants; and it is to restrain this selfishness that men have been obliged to separate themselves from the community, and to distinguish betwixt their own goods and those of others.

Nor need we have recourse to the fictions of poets to learn this, but, beside the reason of the thing, may discover the same truth by common experience and observation. It is easy to remark that a cordial affection renders all things common among friends, and that married people in particular mutually lose their property and are unacquainted with the *mine* and *thine*, which are so necessary and yet cause such disturbance in human society. The same effect arises from any alteration in the circumstances of mankind; as when there is such a plenty of anything as satisfies all the desires of men; in which case the distinction of property is entirely lost, and everything remains in common. This we may observe with regard to air and water, though the most valuable of all external objects; and may easily conclude that if men were supplied with everything in the same abundance, or if *every one* had the same affection and tender regard for *every one* as for himself, justice and injustice would be equally unknown among mankind.

•   •   •

. . . Though the rules of justice are established merely by interest, their connection with interest is somewhat singular, and is different from what may be observed on other occasions. A single act of justice is frequently contrary to *public interest*; and were it to stand alone, without being followed by other acts, may in itself be very prejudicial to society. When a man of merit, of a beneficent disposition, restores a great fortune to a miser or a seditious bigot, he has acted justly and laudably; but the public is a real sufferer. Nor is every single act of justice, considered apart, more conducive to private interest than to public; and it is easily conceived how a man may impoverish himself by a single instance of integrity, and have reason to wish that, with regard to that single act, the laws of justice were for a moment suspended in the universe. But however single acts of justice may be contrary either to public or private interest, it is certain that the whole plan or scheme is highly conducive, or indeed absolutely requisite, both to the support of society and the well-being of every individual. It is impossible to separate the good from the ill. Property must be stable, and must be fixed by general rules. Though in one instance the public be a sufferer, this momentary ill is amply compensated by the steady prosecution of the rule and by the peace and order which it establishes in society. And even every individual person must find himself a gainer on balancing the account; since without justice society must immediately dissolve, and every one must fall into that savage and solitary condition which is infinitely worse than the worst situation that can possibly be supposed in society. When, therefore, men have had experience enough to observe that, whatever may be the consequence of any single act of justice performed by a single person, yet the whole system of actions concurred in by the whole society is infinitely advantageous to the whole and to every part, it is not long before justice and property take place. Every member of society is sensible of this interest; every one expresses this sense to his fellows along with the resolution he has taken of squaring his actions by it, on condition that others will do the same. No more is requisite to induce any one of them to perform an act of justice, who has the first opportunity. This becomes an example to others; and thus justice establishes itself by a kind of convention or agreement, that is, by a sense of interest, supposed to be common to all, and where every single act is performed in expectation that others are to perform the like. Without such a convention no one would ever have dreamed that there was such a virtue as justice, or have been induced to conform his actions to it. Taking any single act, my justice may be pernicious in every respect; and it is only upon the supposition that others are to imitate my example that I can be induced to embrace that virtue; since nothing but this combination can render justice advantageous, or afford me any motives to conform myself to its rules.

We come now to the *second* question we proposed, viz., *Why we annex the idea of virtue to justice, and of vice to injustice.* This question will not detain us long after the principles which we have already established. All we can say of it at present will be dispatched in a few words; and for further satisfaction the reader must wait till we come to the third part of this book. The *natural* obligation to justice, viz., interest, has been fully explained; but as to the *moral* obligation, or the sentiment of right and wrong, it will first be requisite to examine the natural virtues before we can give a full and satisfactory account of it.

After men have found by experience that their selfishness and confined generosity, acting at their liberty, totally incapacitate them for society, and at the same time have observed that society is necessary to the satisfaction of those very passions, they are naturally induced to lay themselves under the restraint of such rules as may render their commerce more safe and commodious. To the imposition, then, and observance of these rules, both in general and in every particular instance, they are at first induced only by a regard to interest; and this motive, on the first formation of society, is sufficiently strong and forcible. But when society has become numerous and has increased to a tribe or nation, this interest is more remote; nor do men so readily perceive that disorder and confusion follow upon every breach of these rules, as in a more narrow and contracted society. But though in our own actions we may frequently lose sight of that interest which we have in maintaining order, and may follow a lesser and more present interest, we never fail to observe the prejudice we receive either mediately or immediately from the injustice of others, as not being in that case either blinded by passion or biassed by any contrary temptation. Nay, when the injustice is so distant from us as no way to affect our interest, it still displeases us, because we consider it as prejudicial to human society and pernicious to every one that approaches the person guilty of it. We partake of their uneasiness by *sympathy;* and as everything which gives uneasiness in human actions, upon the general survey, is called *vice,* and whatever produces satisfaction, in the same manner, is denominated *virtue,* this is the reason why the sense of moral good and evil follows upon justice and injustice. And though this sense in the present case be derived only from contemplating the actions of others, yet we fail not to extend it even to our own actions. The *general rule* reaches beyond those instances from which it arose; while at the same time we naturally *sympathize* with others in the sentiments they entertain of us.

• • •

OF THE ORIGIN OF THE NATURAL VIRTUES AND VICES

We come now to the examination of such virtues and vices as are entirely natural, and have no dependence on the artifice and contrivance of men. The examination of these will conclude this system of morals.

• • •

We have already observed that moral distinctions depend entirely on certain peculiar sentiments of pain and pleasure, and that whatever mental quality in ourselves or others gives us a satisfaction by the survey or reflection is of course virtuous; as everything of this nature that gives uneasiness is vicious. Now, since every quality in ourselves or others which gives pleasure always causes pride or love, as every one that produces uneasiness excites humility or hatred, it follows that these two particulars are to be considered as equivalent with regard to our mental qualities; *virtue* and the power of producing love or pride; *vice* and the power of producing humility or hatred. In every case, therefore, we must judge of the one by the other, and may pronounce any *quality* of the mind virtuous which causes love or pride, and any one vicious which causes hatred or humility.

If any *action* be either virtuous or vicious, it is only as a sign of some quality or character. It must depend upon durable principles of the mind which extend over the whole conduct and enter into the personal character. Actions themselves, not proceeding from any constant principle, have no influence on love or hatred, pride or humility; and consequently are never considered in morality.

This reflection is self-evident and deserves to be attended to as being of the utmost importance in the present subject. We are never to consider any single action in our inquiries concerning the origin of morals, but only the quality or character from which the action proceeded. These alone are *durable* enough to affect our sentiments concerning the person. Actions are indeed better indications of a character than words, or even wishes and sentiments; but it is only so far as they are such indications that they are attended with love or hatred, praise or blame.

To discover the true origin of morals, and of that love or hatred which arises from mental qualities, we must take the matter pretty deep and compare some principles which have been already examined and explained.

We may begin with considering anew the nature and force of *sympathy*. The minds of all men are similar in their feelings and operations; nor can any one be actuated by any affection of which all others are not in some degree susceptible. As in strings equally wound up the motion of one communicates itself to the rest, so all the affections readily pass from one person to another, and beget correspondent movements in every human creature. When I see the *effects* of passion in the voice and gesture of any person, my mind immediately passes from these effects to their causes, and forms such a lively idea of the passion as is presently converted into the passion itself. In like manner, when I perceive the *causes* of any emotion, my mind is conveyed to the effects, and is actuated with a like emotion. Were I present at any of the more terrible operations of surgery, it is certain that, even before it begun, the preparation of the instruments, the laying of the bandages in order, the heating of the irons, with all the signs of anxiety and concern in the patient and assistants, would have a great effect upon my mind, and excite the strongest sentiments of pity and terror. No passion of another discovers itself immediately to the mind. We are only sensible of its causes or effects. From *these* we infer the passion; and consequently, *these* give rise to our sympathy.

• • •

No virtue is more esteemed than justice, and no vice more detested than injustice; nor are there any qualities which go further to the fixing the character, either as amiable or odious. Now, justice is a moral virtue, merely because it has that tendency to the good of mankind, and indeed is nothing but an artificial invention to that purpose. The same may be said of allegiance, of the laws of nations, of modesty, and of good manners. All these are mere human contrivances for the interest of society. And since there is a very strong sentiment of morals, which in all nations and all ages has attended them, we must allow that the reflecting on the tendency of characters and mental qualities is sufficient to give us the sentiments of approbation and blame. Now, as the means to an end can only be agreeable where the end is agreeable, and as the good of society, where our own interest is not concerned or that of our friends, pleases only by sympathy, it follows that sympathy is the source of the esteem which we pay to all the artificial virtues.

Thus it appears that *sympathy* is a very powerful principle in human nature, that it has a great influence on our taste of beauty, and that it produces our sentiment of morals in all the artificial virtues. From thence we may presume that it also gives rise to many of the other virtues, and that qualities acquire our approbation because of their tendency to the good of mankind. This presumption must become a certainty, when we find that most of those qualities which we *naturally* approve of have actually that tendency and render a man a proper member of society; while the qualities which we *naturally* disapprove of have a contrary tendency and render any intercourse with the person dangerous or disagreeable. For having found that such tendencies have force enough to produce the strongest sentiment of morals, we can never reasonably, in these cases, look for any other cause of approbation or blame; it being an inviolable maxim in philosophy that where any particular cause is sufficient for an effect, we ought to rest satisfied with it, and ought not to multiply causes without necessity. We have happily attained experiments in the artificial virtues, where the tendency of qualities to the good of society is the *sole* cause of our approbation, without any suspicion of the concurrence of another principle. From thence we learn the force of that principle. And where that principle may take place, and the quality approved of is really beneficial to society, a true philosopher will never require any other principle to account for the strongest approbation and esteem.

That many of the natural virtues have this tendency to the good of society, no one can doubt of. Meekness, beneficence, charity, generosity, clemency, moderation, equity, bear the greatest figure among the moral qualities, and are commonly denominated the *social* virtues, to mark their tendency to the good of society.

• • •

The only difference betwixt the natural virtues and justice lies in this, that the good which results from the former rises from every single act, and is the object of some natural passion; whereas a single act of justice, considered in itself, may often be contrary to the public good; and it is only the concurrence of mankind in a general scheme or system of action which is advantageous. When I relieve persons in distress, my natural humanity is my motive, and so far as my succour extends, so far have I promoted the happiness of my fellow creatures. But if we examine all the questions that come before any tribunal of justice, we shall find that, considering each case apart, it would as often be an instance of humanity to decide contrary to the laws of justice as conformable to them. Judges take from a poor man to give to a rich; they bestow on the dissolute the labour of the industrious; and put into the hands of the vicious the means of harming both themselves and others. The whole scheme, however, of law and justice is advantageous to the society; and it was with a view to this advantage that men, by their voluntary conventions, established it. After it is once established by these conventions, it is *naturally* attended with a strong sentiment of morals which can proceed from nothing but our sympathy with the interests of society. We need no other explication of that esteem which attends such of the natural virtues as have a tendency to the public good.

• • •

Before I proceed further, I must observe two remarkable circumstances in this affair which may seem objections to the present system. The first may be thus explained. When any quality or character has a tendency to the good of mankind, we are pleased with it and approve of it because it presents the lively idea of pleasure; which idea affects us by sympathy, and is itself a kind of pleasure. But as this sympathy is very variable, it may be thought that our sentiments of morals must admit of all the same variations. We sympathize more with persons contiguous to us than with persons remote from us; with our acquaintance, than with strangers; with our countrymen, than with foreigners. But notwithstanding this variation of our sympathy, we give the same approbation to the same moral qualities in China as in England. They appear equally virtuous and recommend themselves equally to the esteem of a judicious spectator. The sympathy varies without a variation in our esteem. Our esteem, therefore, proceeds not from sympathy.

To this I answer, the approbation of moral qualities most certainly is not derived from reason or any comparison of ideas; but proceeds entirely from a moral taste and from certain sentiments of pleasure or disgust which arise upon the contemplation and view of particular qualities or characters. Now, it is evident that those sentiments, whencever they are derived, must vary according to the distance or contiguity of the objects; nor can I feel the same lively pleasure from the virtues of a person who lived in Greece two thousand years ago that I feel from the virtues of a familiar friend and acquaintance. Yet I do not say that I esteem the one more than the other; and therefore, if the variation of the sentiment without a variation of the esteem be an objection, it must have equal force against every other system, as against that of sympathy. But to consider the matter aright, it has no force at all; and it is the easiest matter in the world to account for it. Our situation with regard both to persons and things is in continual fluctuation; and a man that lies at a distance from us may in a little time become a familiar acquaintance. Besides, every particular man has a peculiar position with regard to others; and it is impossible we could ever converse together on any reasonable terms, were each of us to consider characters and persons only as they appear from his peculiar point of view. In order, therefore, to prevent those continual *contradictions* and arrive at a more *stable* judgment of things, we fix on some *steady* and *general* points of view, and always in our thoughts, place ourselves in them, whatever may be our present situation. In like manner, external beauty is determined merely by pleasure; and it is evident a beautiful countenance cannot give so much pleasure when seen at a distance of twenty paces as when it is brought nearer us. We say not, however, that it appears to us less beautiful; because we know what effect it will have in such a position, and by that reflection we correct its momentary appearance.

In general, all sentiments of blame or praise are variable, according to our situation of nearness or remoteness with regard to the person blamed or praised, and according to the present disposition of our mind. But these variations we regard not in our general decisions, but still apply the terms expressive of our liking or dislike in the same manner as if we remained in one point of view. Experience soon teaches us this method of correcting our sentiments, or at least of correcting our language, where the sentiments are more stubborn and unalterable. Our servant, if diligent and faithful, may excite stronger sentiments of love and kindness than Marcus Brutus, as represented in history; but we say not upon that account that the former character is more laudable than the latter. We know that, were we to approach equally near to that renowned patriarch, he would command a much higher degree of affection and admiration. Such corrections are common with regard to all the senses; and, indeed, it were impossible we could ever make use of language or communicate our sentiments to one another, did we not correct the momentary appearances of things and overlook our present situation.

•   •   •

. . . When we form our judgments of persons merely from the tendency of their characters to our own benefit, or to that of our friends, we find so many contradictions to our sentiments in society and conversation, and such an uncertainty from the incessant changes of our situation, that we seek some other standard of merit and demerit which may not admit of so great variation. Being thus loosened from our first station, we cannot afterwards fix ourselves so commodiously by any means as by a sympathy with those who have any commerce with the person we consider. This is far from being as lively as when our own interest is concerned, or that of our particular friends; nor has it such an influence on our love and hatred; but being equally conformable to our calm and general principles, it is said to have an equal authority over our reason, and to command our judgment and opinion. We blame equally a bad action which we read of in history, with one performed in our neighbourhood the other day; the meaning of which is that we know from reflection that the former action would excite as strong sentiments of disapprobation as the latter, were it placed in the same position.

I now proceed to the *second* remarkable circumstance which I propose to take notice of. Where a person is possessed of a character that in its natural tendency is beneficial to society, we esteem him virtuous, and are delighted with the view of his character, even though particular accidents prevent its operation and incapacitate him from being serviceable to his friends and country. Virtue in rags is still virtue; and the love which it procures attends a man into a dungeon or desert, where the virtue can no longer be exerted in action and is lost to all the world. Now, this may be esteemed an objection to the present system. Sympathy interests us in the good of mankind; and if sympathy were the source of our esteem for virtue, that sentiment of approbation could only take place where the virtue actually attained its end and was beneficial to mankind. Where it fails of its end, it is only an imperfect means and, therefore, can never acquire any merit from that end. The goodness of an end can bestow a merit on such means alone as are complete and actually produce the end.

To this we may reply that, where any object, in all its parts, is fitted to attain any agreeable end, it naturally gives us pleasure and is esteemed beautiful, even though some external circumstances be wanting to render it altogether effectual. It is sufficient if everything be complete in the object itself. A house that is contrived with great judgment for all the commodities of life pleases us upon that account, though perhaps we are sensible that no one will ever dwell in it. A fertile soil and a happy climate delight us by a reflection on the happiness which they would afford the inhabitants, though at present the country be desert and uninhabited. A man whose limbs and shape promise strength and activity is esteemed handsome, though condemned to perpetual imprisonment. The imagination has a set of passions belonging to it upon which our sentiments of beauty much depend. These passions are moved by degrees of liveliness and strength, which are inferior to *belief*, and independent of the real existence of their objects. Where a character is in every respect fitted to be beneficial to society, the imagination passes easily from the cause to the effect, without considering that there are still some circumstances wanting to render the cause a complete one. *General rules* create a species of probability which sometimes influences the judgment, and always the imagination.

It is true, when the cause is complete and a good disposition is attended with good fortune which renders it really beneficial to society, it gives a stronger pleasure to the spectator, and is attended with a more lively sympathy. We are more affected by it; and yet we do not say that it is more virtuous, or that we esteem it more. We know that an alteration of fortune may render the benevolent disposition entirely impotent; and therefore we separate as much as possible the fortune from the disposition. The case is the same as when we correct the different sentiments of virtue which proceed from its different distances from ourselves. The passions do not always follow our corrections; but these corrections serve sufficiently to regulate our abstract notions, and are alone regarded when we pronounce in general concerning the degrees of vice and virtue.

•   •   •

9

Goodness As Simple and Indefinable

G. E. MOORE

G. E. Moore (1873–1958) taught for many years at Cambridge University. An influential figure in twentieth-century philosophy, he made important contributions both in the theory of knowledge and in ethics. His major works include Principia Ethica, Ethics, *and* Philosophical Studies.

In this selection, taken from Principia Ethica, *Chapter 1, Moore asks what sort of thing goodness is. His question has important implications for moral knowledge. If goodness is a property in the natural world—if, for instance, it is the tendency to make people happy—then we can discover its existence by using ordinary empirical methods. But if goodness is not a natural property, then our knowledge of it must take some other form.*

Moore believes that goodness is neither a simple nor a composite natural property. Rather than being definable in any simpler terms, goodness is one of the simple elements in terms of which other things may be defined. But it cannot be identified with any of the simple things that are found in nature. If goodness could be defined as pleasure, then the question "Is pleasure good?" would boil down to the triviality "Is pleasure pleasant?" But the two questions are not the same. In general, Moore is more explicit about what goodness is not than about what it is. However, the core of his view—that goodness differs from anything that is empirically discoverable, yet still has some sort of objective existence—is clear enough. According to many, this view contains an important element of truth.

• • •

That which is meant by 'good' is, in fact, except its converse 'bad,' the *only* simple object of thought which is peculiar to Ethics. Its definition is, therefore, the most essential point in the definition of Ethics; and moreover a mistake with regard to it entails a far larger number of erroneous ethical judgments than any other. Unless this first question be fully understood, and its true answer clearly recognised, the rest of Ethics is as good as useless from the point of view of systematic knowledge. True ethical judgments, of the two kinds last dealt with, may indeed be made by those who do not know the answer to this question as well as by those who do; and it goes without saying that the two classes of people may lead equally good lives. But it is extremely unlikely that the *most general* ethical judgments will be equally valid, in the absence of a true answer to this question: I shall presently try to shew that the gravest errors have been largely due to beliefs in a false answer. And, in any case, it is impossible that, till the answer to this question be known, any one should know *what is the evidence* for any ethical judgment whatsoever. But the main object of Ethics, as a systematic science, is to give correct *reasons* for thinking that this or that is good; and, unless this question be answered, such reasons cannot be given. Even, therefore, apart from the fact that a false answer leads to false conclusions, the present enquiry is a most necessary and important part of the science of Ethics.

6. What, then, is good? How is good to be defined? Now, it may be thought that this is a verbal question. A definition does indeed often mean the expressing of one word's meaning in other words. But this is not the sort of definition I am asking for. Such a definition can never be of ultimate importance in any study except lexicography. If I wanted that kind of definition I should have to consider in the first place how people generally used the word 'good'; but my business is not with its proper usage, as established by custom. I should, indeed, be foolish, if I tried to use it for something which it did not usually denote: if, for instance, I were to announce that, whenever I used the word 'good,' I must be understood to be thinking of that object which is usually denoted by the word 'table.' I shall, therefore, use the word in the sense in which I think it is ordinarily used; but at the same time I am not anxious to discuss whether I am right in thinking that it is so used. My business is solely with that object or idea, which I hold, rightly or wrongly, that the word is generally used to stand for. What I want to discover is the nature of that object or idea, and about this I am extremely anxious to arrive at an agreement.

But, if we understand the question in this sense, my answer to it may seem a very disappointing one. If I am asked 'What is good?' my answer is that good is good, and that is the end of the matter. Or if I am asked 'How is good to be defined?' my answer is that it cannot be defined, and that is all I have to say about it. But disappointing as these answers may appear, they are of the very last importance. To readers who are familiar with philosophic terminology, I can express their importance by saying that they amount to this: That propositions about the good are all of them synthetic and never analytic; and that is plainly no trivial matter. And the same thing may be expressed more popularly, by saying that, if I am right, then nobody can foist upon us such an axiom as that 'Pleasure is the only good' or that 'The good is the desired' on the pretence that this is 'the very meaning of the word.'

7. Let us, then, consider this position. My point is that 'good' is a simple notion, just as 'yellow' is a simple notion; that, just as you cannot, by any manner of means, explain to any one who does not already know it, what yellow is, so you cannot explain what good is. Definitions of the kind that I was asking for, definitions which describe the real nature of the object or notion denoted by a word, and which do not merely tell us what the word is used to mean, are only possible when the object or notion in question is

something complex. You can give a definition of a horse, because a horse has many different properties and qualities, all of which you can enumerate. But when you have enumerated them all, when you have reduced a horse to his simplest terms, then you can no longer define those terms. They are simply something which you think of or perceive, and to any one who cannot think of or perceive them, you can never, by any definition, make their nature known. It may perhaps be objected to this that we are able to describe to others, objects which they have never seen or thought of. We can, for instance, make a man understand what a chimaera is, although he has never heard of one or seen one. You can tell him that it is an animal with a lioness's head and body, with a goat's head growing from the middle of its back, and with a snake in place of a tail. But here the object which you are describing is a complex object; it is entirely composed of parts, with which we are all perfectly familiar—a snake, a goat, a lioness; and we know, too, the manner in which those parts are to be put together, because we know what is meant by the middle of a lioness's back, and where her tail is wont to grow. And so it is with all objects, not previously known, which we are able to define: they are all complex; all composed of parts, which may themselves, in the first instance, be capable of similar definition, but which must in the end be reducible to simplest parts, which can no longer be defined. But yellow and good, we say, are not complex: they are notions of that simple kind, out of which definitions are composed and with which the power of further defining ceases.

8. When we say, as Webster says, 'The definition of horse is "A hoofed quadruped of the genus Equus," ' we may, in fact, mean three different things. (1) We may mean merely: 'When I say "horse," you are to understand that I am talking about a hoofed quadruped of the genus Equus.' This might be called the arbitrary verbal definition: and I do not mean that good is indefinable in that sense. (2) We may mean, as Webster ought to mean: 'When most English people say "horse," they mean a hoofed quadruped of the genus Equus.' This may be called the verbal definition proper, and I do not say that good is indefinable in this sense either; for it is certainly possible to discover how people use a word: otherwise, we could never have known that 'good' may be translated by 'gut' in German and by 'bon' in French. But (3) we may, when we define horse, mean something much more important. We may mean that a certain object, which we all of us know, is composed in a certain manner: that it has four legs, a head, a heart, a liver, etc., etc., all of them arranged in definite relations to one another. It is in this sense that I deny good to be definable. I say that it is not composed of any parts, which we can substitute for it in our minds when we are thinking of it. We might think just as clearly and correctly about a horse, if we thought of all its parts and their arrangement instead of thinking of the whole; we could, I say, think how a horse differed from a donkey just as well, just as truly, in this way, as now we do, not only so easily; but there is nothing whatsoever which we could so substitute for good; and that is what I mean, when I say that good is indefinable.

9. But I am afraid I have still not removed the chief difficulty which may prevent acceptance of the proposition that good is indefinable. I do not mean

to say that *the* good, that which is good, is thus indefinable; if I did think so, I should not be writing on Ethics, for my main object is to help towards discovering that definition. It is just because I think there will be less risk of error in our search for a definition of 'the good,' that I am now insisting that *good* is indefinable. I must try to explain the difference between these two. I suppose it may be granted that 'good' is an adjective. Well 'the good, that which is good,' must therefore be the substantive to which the adjective 'good' will apply: it must be the whole of that to which the adjective will apply, and the adjective must *always* truly apply to it. But if it is that to which the adjective will apply, it must be something different from that adjective itself; and the whole of that something different, whatever it is, will be our definition of *the* good. Now it may be that this something will have other adjectives, beside 'good,' that will apply to it. It may be full of pleasure, for example: it may be intelligent: and if these two adjectives are really part of its definition, then it will certainly be true, that pleasure and intelligence are good. And many people appear to think that, if we say 'Pleasure and intelligence are good,' or if we say 'Only pleasure and intelligence are good,' we are defining 'good.' Well, I cannot deny that propositions of this nature may sometimes be called definitions; I do not know well enough how the word is generally used to decide upon this point. I only wish it to be understood that that is not what I mean when I say there is no possible definition of good, and that I shall not mean this if I use the word again. I do most fully believe that some true proposition of the form 'Intelligence is good and intelligence alone is good' can be found; if none could be found, our definition of *the* good would be impossible. As it is, I believe *the* good to be definable; and yet I still say that good itself is indefinable.

10. 'Good,' then, if we mean by it that quality which we assert to belong to a thing, when we say that the thing is good, is incapable of any definition, in the most important sense of that word. The most important sense of 'definition' is that in which a definition states what are the parts which invariably compose a certain whole; and in this sense 'good' has no definition because it is simple and has no parts. It is one of those innumerable objects of thought which are themselves incapable of definition, because they are the ultimate terms by reference to which whatever *is* capable of definition must be defined. That there must be an indefinite number of such terms is obvious, on reflection; since we cannot define anything except by an analysis, which, when carried as far as it will go, refers us to something, which is simply different from anything else, and which by that ultimate difference explains the peculiarity of the whole which we are defining: for every whole contains some parts which are common to other wholes also. There is, therefore, no intrinsic difficulty in the contention that 'good' denotes a simple and indefinable quality. There are many other instances of such qualities.

Consider yellow, for example. We may try to define it, by describing its physical equivalent; we may state what kind of light-vibrations must stimulate the normal eye, in order that we may perceive it. But a moment's reflection is sufficient to shew that those light-vibrations are not themselves what we mean by yellow. *They* are not what we perceive. Indeed we should never have been able to discover their existence, unless we had first been struck by the patent difference of quality between the different colours. The most we can be entitled to say of those vibrations is that they are what corresponds in space to the yellow which we actually perceive.

Yet a mistake of this simple kind has commonly been made about 'good.' It may be true that all things which are good are *also* something else, just as it is true that all things which are yellow produce a certain kind of vibration in the light. And it is a fact, that Ethics aims at discovering what are those other properties belonging to all things which are good. But far too many philosophers have thought that when they named those other properties they were actually defining good; that these properties, in fact, were simply not 'other,' but absolutely and entirely the same with goodness. This view I propose to call the 'naturalistic fallacy' and of it I shall now endeavour to dispose.

11. Let us consider what it is such philosophers say. And first it is to be noticed that they do not agree among themselves. They not only say that they are right as to what good is, but they endeavour to prove that other people who say that it is something else, are wrong. One, for instance, will affirm that good is pleasure, another, perhaps, that good is that which is desired; and each of these will argue eagerly to prove that the other is wrong. But how is that possible? One of them says that good is nothing but the object of desire, and at the same time tries to prove that it is not pleasure. But from his first assertion, that good just means the object of desire, one of two things must follow as regards his proof:

(1) He may be trying to prove that the object of desire is not pleasure. But, if this be all, where is his Ethics? The position he is maintaining is merely a psychological one. Desire is something which occurs in our minds, and pleasure is something else which so occurs; and our would-be ethical philosopher is merely holding that the latter is not the object of the former. But what has that to do with the question in dispute? His opponent held the ethical proposition that pleasure was the good, and although he should prove a million times over the psychological proposition that pleasure is not the object of desire, he is no nearer proving his opponent to be wrong. The position is like this. One man says a triangle is a circle: another replies 'A triangle is a straight line, and I will prove to you that I am right: *for*' (this is the only argument) 'a straight line is not a circle.' 'That is quite true,' the other may reply; 'but nevertheless a triangle is a circle, and you have said nothing whatever to prove the contrary. What is proved is that one of us is wrong, for we agree that a triangle cannot be both a straight line and a circle: but which is wrong, there can be no earthly means of proving, since you define triangle as straight line and I define it as circle.'—Well, that is one alternative which any naturalistic Ethics has to face; if good is *defined* as something else, it is then impossible either to prove that any other definition is wrong or even to deny such definition.

(2) The other alternative will scarcely be more welcome. It is that the discussion is after all a verbal one. When A says 'Good means pleasant' and B says 'Good means desired,' they may merely wish to assert that most people

have used the word for what is pleasant and for what is desired respectively. And this is quite an interesting subject for discussion: only it is not a whit more an ethical discussion than the last was. Nor do I think that any exponent of naturalistic Ethics would be willing to allow that this was all he meant. They are all so anxious to persuade us that what they call the good is what we really ought to do. 'Do, pray, act so, because the word "good" is generally used to denote actions of this nature': such, on this view, would be the substance of their teaching. And in so far as they tell us how we ought to act, their teaching is truly ethical, as they mean it to be. But how perfectly absurd is the reason they would give for it! 'You are to do this, because most people use a certain word to denote conduct such as this.' 'You are to say the thing which is not, because most people call it lying.' That is an argument just as good!— My dear sirs, what we want to know from you as ethical teachers, is not how people use a word; it is not even, what kind of actions they approve, which the use of this word 'good' may certainly imply: what we want to know is simply what *is* good. We may indeed agree that what most people do think good, is actually so; we shall at all events be glad to know their opinions: but when we say their opinions about what *is* good, we do mean what we say; we do not care whether they call that thing which they mean 'horse' or 'table' or 'chair,' 'gut' or 'bon' or 'ἀγαθός'; we want to know what it is that they so call. When they say 'Pleasure is good,' we cannot believe that they merely mean 'Pleasure is pleasure' and nothing more than that.

12. Suppose a man says 'I am pleased'; and suppose that is not a lie or a mistake but the truth. Well, if it is true, what does that mean? It means that his mind, a certain definite mind, distinguished by certain definite marks from all others, has at this moment a certain definite feeling called pleasure. 'Pleased' *means* nothing but having pleasure, and though we may be more pleased or less pleased, and even, we may admit for the present, have one or another kind of pleasure; yet in so far as it is pleasure we have, whether there be more or less of it, and whether it be of one kind or another, what we have is one definite thing, absolutely indefinable, some one thing that is the same in all the various degrees and all the various kinds of it that there may be. We may be able to say how it is related to other things: that, for example, it is in the mind, that it causes desire, that we are conscious of it, etc., etc. We can, I say, describe its relations to other things, but define it we can *not*. And if anybody tried to define pleasure for us as being any other natural object; if anybody were to say, for instance, that pleasure *means* the sensation of red, and were to proceed to deduce from that that pleasure is a colour, we should be entitled to laugh at him and to distrust his future statements about pleasure. Well, that would be the same fallacy which I have called the naturalistic fallacy. That 'pleased' does not mean 'having the sensation of red,' or anything else whatever, does not prevent us from understanding what it does mean. It is enough for us to know that 'pleased' does mean 'having the sensation of pleasure,' and though pleasure is absolutely indefinable, though pleasure is pleasure and nothing else whatever, yet we feel no difficulty in saying that we are pleased. The reason is, of course, that when I say 'I am pleased,' I do *not* mean that 'I' am the

same thing as 'having pleasure.' And similarly no difficulty need be found in my saying that 'pleasure is good' and yet not meaning that 'pleasure' is the same thing as 'good,' that pleasure *means* good, and that good *means* pleasure. If I were to imagine that when I said 'I am pleased,' I meant that I was exactly the same thing as 'pleased,' I should not indeed call that a naturalistic fallacy, although it would be the same fallacy as I have called naturalistic with reference to Ethics. The reason of this is obvious enough. When a man confuses two natural objects with one another, defining the one by the other, if for instance, he confuses himself, who is one natural object, with 'pleased' or with 'pleasure' which are others, then there is no reason to call the fallacy naturalistic. But if he confuses 'good,' which is not in the same sense a natural object, with any natural object whatever, then there is a reason for calling that a naturalistic fallacy; its being made with regard to 'good' marks it as something quite specific, and this specific mistake deserves a name because it is so common. As for the reasons why good is not to be considered a natural object, they may be reserved for discussion in another place. But, for the present, it is sufficient to notice this: Even if it were a natural object, that would not alter the nature of the fallacy nor diminish its importance one whit. All that I have said about it would remain quite equally true: only the name which I have called it would not be so appropriate as I think it is. And I do not care about the name: what I do care about is the fallacy. It does not matter what we call it, provided we recognise it when we meet with it. It is to be met with in almost every book on Ethics; and yet it is not recognised: and that is why it is necessary to multiply illustrations of it, and convenient to give it a name. It is a very simple fallacy indeed. When we say that an orange is yellow, we do not think our statement binds us to hold that 'orange' means nothing else than 'yellow,' or that nothing can be yellow but an orange. Supposing the orange is also sweet! Does that bind us to say that 'sweet' is exactly the same thing as 'yellow,' that 'sweet' must be defined as 'yellow'? And supposing it be recognised that 'yellow' just means 'yellow' and nothing else whatever, does that make it any more difficult to hold that oranges are yellow? Most certainly it does not: on the contrary, it would be absolutely meaningless to say that oranges were yellow, unless yellow did in the end mean just 'yellow' and nothing else whatever—unless it was absolutely indefinable. We should not get any very clear notion about things, which are yellow—we should not get very far with our science, if we were bound to hold that everything which was yellow, *meant* exactly the same thing as yellow. We should find we had to hold that an orange was exactly the same thing as a stool, a piece of paper, a lemon, anything you like. We could prove any number of absurdities; but should we be the nearer to the truth? Why, then, should it be different with 'good'? Why, if good is good and indefinable, should I be held to deny that pleasure is good? Is there any difficulty in holding both to be true at once? On the contrary, there is no meaning in saying that pleasure is good, unless good is something different from pleasure. It is absolutely useless, as far as Ethics is concerned, to prove, as Mr Spencer tries to do, that increase of pleasure coincides with increase of life, unless good *means* something different from either life or pleasure. He might just as well try to prove that an orange is yellow by shewing that it always is wrapped up in paper.

13. In fact, if it is not the case that 'good' denotes something simple and indefinable, only two alternatives are possible: either it is a complex, a given whole, about the correct analysis of which there may be disagreement; or else it means nothing at all, and there is no such subject as Ethics. In general, however, ethical philosophers have attempted to define good, without recognising what such an attempt must mean. They actually use arguments which involve one or both of the absurdities considered in §11. We are, therefore, justified in concluding that the attempt to define good is chiefly due to want of clearness as to the possible nature of definition. There are, in fact, only two serious alternatives to be considered, in order to establish the conclusion that 'good' does denote a simple and indefinable notion. It might possibly denote a complex, as 'horse' does; or it might have no meaning at all. Neither of these possibilities has, however, been clearly conceived and seriously maintained, as such, by those who presume to define good; and both may be dismissed by a simple appeal to facts.

(1) The hypothesis that disagreement about the meaning of good is disagreement with regard to the correct analysis of a given whole, may be most plainly seen to be incorrect by consideration of the fact that, whatever definition be offered, it may be always asked, with significance, of the complex so defined, whether it is itself good. To take, for instance, one of the more plausible, because one of the more complicated, of such proposed definitions, it may easily be thought, at first sight, that to be good may mean to be that which we desire to desire. Thus if we apply this definition to a particular instance and say 'When we think that A is good, we are thinking that A is one of the things which we desire to desire,' our proposition may seem quite plausible. But, if we carry the investigation further, and ask ourselves 'Is it good to desire to desire A?' it is apparent, on a little reflection, that this question is itself as intelligible, as the original question 'Is A good?'—that we are in fact, now asking for exactly the same information about the desire to desire A, for which we formerly asked with regard to A itself. But it is also apparent that the meaning of this second question cannot be correctly analysed into 'Is the desire to desire A one of the things which we desire to desire?': we have not before our minds anything so complicated as the question 'Do we desire to desire to desire to desire A?' Moreover any one can easily convince himself by inspection that the predicate of this proposition—'good'—is positively different from the notion of 'desiring to desire' which enters into its subject: 'That we should desire to desire A is good' is *not* merely equivalent to 'That A should be good is good.' It may indeed be true that what we desire to desire is always also good; perhaps, even the converse may be true: but it is very doubtful whether this is the case, and the mere fact that we understand very well what is meant by doubting it, shews clearly that we have two different notions before our minds.

(2) And the same consideration is sufficient to dismiss the hypothesis that 'good' has no meaning whatsoever. It is very natural to make the mistake of supposing that what is universally true is of such a nature that its negation

would be self-contradictory: the importance which has been assigned to analytic propositions in the history of philosophy shews how easy such a mistake is. And thus it is very easy to conclude that what seems to be a universal ethical principle is in fact an identical proposition; that, if, for example, whatever is called 'good' seems to be pleasant, the proposition 'Pleasure is the good' does not assert a connection between two different notions, but involves only one, that of pleasure, which is easily recognised as a distinct entity. But whoever will attentively consider with himself what is actually before his mind when he asks the question 'Is pleasure (or whatever it may be) after all good?' can easily satisfy himself that he is not merely wondering whether pleasure is pleasant. And if he will try this experiment with each suggested definition in succession, he may become expert enough to recognise that in every case he has before his mind a unique object, with regard to the connection of which with any other object, a distinct question may be asked. Every one does in fact understand the question 'Is this good?' When he thinks of it, his state of mind is different from what it would be, were he asked 'Is this pleasant, or desired, or approved?' It has a distinct meaning for him, even though he may not recognise in what respect it is distinct. Whenever he thinks of 'intrinsic value,' or 'intrinsic worth,' or says that a thing 'ought to exist,' he has before his mind the unique object—the unique property of things—which I mean by 'good.' Everybody is constantly aware of this notion, although he may never become aware at all that it is different from other notions of which he is also aware. But, for correct ethical reasoning, it is extremely important that he should become aware of this fact; and, as soon as the nature of the problem is clearly understood, there should be little difficulty in advancing so far in analysis.

• • •

10

The Emotive Theory of Ethics

A. J. AYER

Alfred Jules Ayer (1910–1989) taught for many years at the University of London and at Oxford University. His book Language, Truth, and Logic, *first published in 1936, introduced the English-speaking world to the movement known as logical positivism. Ayer's other works include* Foundations of Empirical Knowledge, Philosophical Essays, *and* The Problem of Knowledge.

In this selection, from Language, Truth, and Logic, *Chapter 6, Ayer argues that ethical utterances are not attempts to state facts, and so are not capable of being either true or false. Since they thus lack cognitive meaning, they must play some other role. In Ayer's view, their function is roughly like that of cheers and boos. When we say something like "lying is wrong," we are merely expressing our disapproval of lying and thus attempting to discourage others from lying.*

Why does Ayer hold that ethical utterances lack cognitive meaning? The lynchpin of his argument is his "verifiability principle." This principle asserts that any statement that is neither true by definition nor verifiable through the five senses is meaningless. Like Moore (reading 9), Ayer argues that "good" (and related terms such as "right") cannot be defined. But Ayer rejects Moore's alternative view that goodness is simple and indefinable. Moreover, he argues that claims to "see" or "intuit" what is good or right, such as those advanced by Ross in reading 29, cannot be verified by sense-observation. Thus, Ayer concludes that ethical utterances are, in the specified sense, meaningless.

There is still one objection to be met before we can claim to have justified our view that all synthetic propositions are empirical hypotheses. This objection is based on the common supposition that our speculative knowledge is of two distinct kinds—that which relates to questions of empirical fact, and that which relates to questions of value. It will be said that "statements of value" are genuine synthetic propositions, but that they cannot with any show of justice be represented as hypotheses, which are used to predict the course of our sensations; and, accordingly, that the existence of ethics and aesthetics as branches of speculative knowledge presents an insuperable objection to our radical empiricist thesis.

In face of this objection, it is our business to give an account of "judgments of value" which is both satisfactory in itself and consistent with our general empiricist principles. We shall set ourselves to show that in so far as statements of value are significant, they are ordinary "scientific" statements, and that in so far as they are not scientific, they are not in the literal sense significant, but are simply expressions of emotion which can be neither true nor false. In maintaining this view, we may confine ourselves for the present to the case of ethical statements. What is said about them will be found to apply, *mutatis mutandis*, to the case of aesthetic statements also.

The ordinary system of ethics, as elaborated in the works of ethical philosophers, is very far from being a homogeneous whole. Not only is it apt to contain pieces of metaphysics, and analyses of non-ethical concepts: its actual ethical contents are themselves of very different kinds. We may divide them, indeed, into four main classes. There are, first of all, propositions which express definitions of ethical terms, or judgements about the legitimacy or possibility of certain definitions. Secondly, there are propositions describing the phenomena of moral experience, and their causes. Thirdly, there are exhortations to moral virtue. And, lastly, there are actual ethical judgements. It is unfortunately the case that the distinction between these four classes, plain as it is, is commonly ignored by ethical philosophers; with the result that it is often very difficult to tell from their works what it is that they are seeking to discover or prove.

In fact, it is easy to see that only the first of our four classes, namely that which comprises the propositions relating to the definitions of ethical terms, can be said to constitute ethical philosophy. The propositions which describe the phenomena of moral experience, and their causes, must be assigned to the science of psychology, or sociology. The exhortations to moral virtue are not propositions at all, but ejaculations or commands which are designed to provoke the reader to action of a certain sort. Accordingly, they do not belong to any branch of philosophy or science. As for the expressions of ethical judgements, we have not yet determined how they should be classified. But inasmuch as they are certainly neither definitions nor comments upon definitions, nor quotations, we may say decisively that they do not belong to ethical philosophy. A strictly philosophical treatise on ethics should therefore make no ethical pronouncements. But it should, by giving an analysis of ethical terms, show what is the category to which all such pronouncements belong. And this is what we are now about to do.

A question which is often discussed by ethical philosophers is whether it is possible to find definitions which would reduce all ethical terms to one or two fundamental terms. But this question, though it undeniably belongs to ethical philosophy, is not relevant to our present enquiry. We are not now concerned to discover which term, within the sphere of ethical terms, is to be taken as fundamental; whether, for example, "good" can be defined in terms of "right" or "right" in terms of "good," or both in terms of "value." What we are interested in is the possibility of reducing the whole sphere of ethical terms to non-ethical terms. We are enquiring whether statements of ethical value can be translated into statements of empirical fact.

That they can be so translated is the contention of those ethical philosophers who are commonly called subjectivists, and of those who are known as utilitarians. For the utilitarian defines the rightness of actions, and the goodness of ends, in terms of the pleasure, or happiness, or satisfaction, to which they give rise; the subjectivist, in terms of the feelings of approval which a certain person, or group of people, has towards them. Each of these types of definition makes moral judgements into a sub-class of psychological or sociological judgements; and for this reason they are very attractive to us. For, if either was correct, it would follow that ethical assertions were not generically different from the factual assertions which are ordinarily contrasted with them; and the account which we have already given of empirical hypotheses would apply to them also.

Nevertheless we shall not adopt either a subjectivist or a utilitarian analysis of ethical terms. We reject the subjectivist view that to call an action right, or a thing good, is to say that it is generally approved of, because it is not self-contradictory to assert that some actions which are generally approved of are not right, or that some things which are generally approved of are not good. And we reject the alternative subjectivist view that a man who asserts that a certain action is right, or that a certain thing is good, is saying that he himself approves of it, on the ground that a man who confessed that he sometimes approved of what was bad or wrong would not be contradicting himself. And a similar argument is fatal to utilitarianism. We cannot agree that to call an action right is to say that of all the actions possible in the circumstances it would cause, or be likely to cause, the greatest happiness, or the greatest balance of pleasure over pain, or the greatest balance of satisfied over unsatisfied desire, because we find that it is not self-contradictory to say that it is sometimes wrong to perform the action which would actually or probably cause the greatest happiness, or the greatest balance of pleasure over pain, or of satisfied over unsatisfied desire. And since it is not self-contradictory to say that some pleasant things are not good, or that some bad things are desired, it cannot be the case that the sentence "x is good" is equivalent to "x is pleasant," or to "x is desired." And to every other variant of utilitarianism with which I am acquainted the same objection can be made. And therefore we should, I think, conclude that the validity of ethical judgements is not determined by the felicific tendencies of actions, any more than by the nature of people's feelings; but that it must be regarded as "absolute" or "intrinsic," and not empirically calculable.

If we say this, we are not, of course, denying that it is possible to invent a language in which all ethical symbols are definable in non-ethical terms, or even that it is desirable to invent such a language and adopt it in place of our own; what we are denying is that the suggested reduction of ethical to non-ethical statements is consistent with the conventions of our actual language. That is, we reject utilitarianism and subjectivism, not as proposals to replace our existing ethical notions by new ones, but as analyses of our existing ethical notions. Our contention is simply that, in our language, sentences which contain normative ethical symbols are not equivalent to sentences which express psychological propositions, or indeed empirical propositions of any kind.

It is advisable here to make it plain that it is only normative ethical symbols, and not descriptive ethical symbols, that are held by us to be indefinable in factual terms. There is a danger of confusing these two types of symbols, because they are commonly constituted by signs of the same sensible form. Thus a complex sign of the form "*x* is wrong" may constitute a sentence which expresses a moral judgement concerning a certain type of conduct, or it may constitute a sentence which states that a certain type of conduct is repugnant to the moral sense of a particular society. In the latter case, the symbol "wrong" is a descriptive ethical symbol, and the sentence in which it occurs expresses an ordinary sociological proposition; in the former case, the symbol "wrong" is a normative ethical symbol, and the sentence in which it occurs does not, we maintain, express an empirical proposition at all. It is only with normative ethics that we are at present concerned; so that whenever ethical symbols are used in the course of this argument without qualification, they are always to be interpreted as symbols of the normative type.

In admitting that normative ethical concepts are irreducible to empirical concepts, we seem to be leaving the way clear for the "absolutist" view of ethics—that is, the view that statements of value are not controlled by observation, as ordinary empirical propositions are, but only by a mysterious "intellectual intuition." A feature of this theory, which is seldom recognized by its advocates, is that it makes statements of value unverifiable. For it is notorious that what seems intuitively certain to one person may seem doubtful, or even false, to another. So that unless it is possible to provide some criterion by which one may decide between conflicting intuitions, a mere appeal to intuition is worthless as a test of a proposition's validity. But in the case of moral judgements, no such criterion can be given. Some moralists claim to settle the matter by saying that they "know" that their own moral judgements are correct. But such an assertion is of purely psychological interest, and has not the slightest tendency to prove the validity of any moral judgement. For dissentient moralists may equally well "know" that their ethical views are correct. And, as far as subjective certainty goes, there will be nothing to choose between them. When such differences of opinion arise in connection with an ordinary empirical proposition, one may attempt to resolve them by referring to, or actually carrying out, some relevant empirical test. But with regard to ethical statements, there is, on the "absolutist" or "intuitionist" theory, no relevant empirical test. We are therefore justified in saying that on this theory ethical statements are held to be unverifiable. They are, of course, also held to be genuine synthetic propositions.

Considering the use which we have made of the principle that a synthetic proposition is significant only if it is empirically verifiable, it is clear that the acceptance of an "absolutist" theory of ethics would undermine the whole of our main argument. And as we have already rejected the "naturalistic" theories which are commonly supposed to provide the only alternative to "absolutism" in ethics, we seem to have reached a difficult position. We shall meet the difficulty by showing that the correct treatment of ethical statements is afforded by a third theory, which is wholly compatible with our radical empiricism.

We begin by admitting that the fundamental ethical concepts are unanalysable, inasmuch as there is no criterion by which one can test the validity of the judgements in which they occur. So far we are in agreement with the absolutists.

But, unlike the absolutists, we are able to give an explanation of this fact about ethical concepts. We say that the reason why they are unanalysable is that they are mere pseudo-concepts. The presence of an ethical symbol in a proposition adds nothing to its factual content. Thus if I say to someone, "You acted wrongly in stealing that money," I am not stating anything more than if I had simply said, "You stole that money." In addition that this action is wrong I am not making any further statement about it. I am simply evincing my moral disapproval of it. It is as if I had said, "You stole that money," in a peculiar tone of horror, or written it with the addition of some special exclamation marks. The tone, or the exclamation marks, adds nothing to the literal meaning of the sentence. It merely serves to show that the expression of it is attended by certain feelings in the speaker.

If now I generalise my previous statement and say, "Stealing money is wrong," I produce a sentence which has no factual meaning—that is, expresses no proposition which can be either true or false. It is as if I had written "Stealing money!!"—where the shape and thickness of the exclamation marks show, by a suitable convention, that a special sort of moral disapproval is the feeling which is being expressed. It is clear that there is nothing said here which can be true or false. Another man may disagree with me about the wrongness of stealing, in the sense that he may not have the same feelings about stealing as I have, and he may quarrel with me on account of my moral sentiments. But he cannot, strictly speaking, contradict me. For in saying that a certain type of action is right or wrong, I am not making any factual statement, not even a statement about my own state of mind. I am merely expressing certain moral sentiments. And the man who is ostensibly contradicting me is merely expressing his moral sentiments. So that there is plainly no sense in asking which of us is in the right. For neither of us is asserting a genuine proposition.

What we have just been saying about the symbol "wrong" applies to all normative ethical symbols. Sometimes they occur in sentences which record ordinary empirical facts besides expressing ethical feeling about those facts: sometimes they occur in sentences which simply express ethical feeling about a certain type of action, or situation, without making any statement of fact. But in every case in which one would commonly be said to be making an ethical judgement, the function of the relevant ethical word is purely "emotive." It is used to express feeling about certain objects, but not to make any assertion about them.

It is worth mentioning that ethical terms do not serve only to express feeling. They are calculated also to arouse feeling, and so to stimulate action. Indeed some of them are used in such a way as to give the sentences in which they occur the effect of commands. Thus the sentence "It is your duty to tell the truth" may be regarded both as the expression of a certain sort of ethical feeling about truthfulness and as the expression of the command "Tell the truth." The sentence "You ought to tell the truth" also involves the command "Tell the truth," but here the tone of the command is less emphatic. In the sentence "It is good to tell the truth" the command has become little more than a suggestion. And thus the "meaning" of the word "good," in its ethical usage, is differentiated from that of the word "duty" or the word "ought." In fact we may define the meaning of the various ethical words in terms both of the different feelings they are ordinarily taken to express, and also the different responses which they are calculated to provoke.

We can now see why it is impossible to find a criterion for determining the validity of ethical judgements. It is not because they have an "absolute" validity which is mysteriously independent of ordinary sense-experience, but because they have no objective validity whatsoever. If a sentence makes no statement at all, there is obviously no sense in asking whether what it says is true or false. And we have seen that sentences which simply express moral judgements do not say anything. They are pure expressions of feeling and as such do not come under the category of truth and falsehood. They are unverifiable for the same reason as a cry of pain or a word of command is unverifiable—because they do not express genuine propositions.

Thus, although our theory of ethics might fairly be said to be radically subjectivist, it differs in a very important respect from the orthodox subjectivist theory. For the orthodox subjectivist does not deny, as we do, that the sentences of a moralizer express genuine propositions. All he denies is that they express propositions of a unique non-empirical character. His own view is that they express propositions about the speaker's feelings. If this were so, ethical judgements clearly would be capable of being true or false. They would be true if the speaker had the relevant feelings, and false if he had not. And this is a matter which is, in principle, empirically verifiable. Furthermore they could be significantly contradicted. For if I say, "Tolerance is a virtue," and someone answers, "You don't approve of it," he would, on the ordinary subjectivist theory, be contradicting me. On our theory, he would not be contradicting me, because, in saying that tolerance was a virtue, I should not be making any statement about my own feelings or about anything else. I should simply be evincing my feelings, which is not at all the same thing as saying that I have them.

The distinction between the expression of feeling and the assertion of feeling is complicated by the fact that the assertion that one has a certain feeling often accompanies the expression of that feeling, and is then, indeed, a factor in the expression of that feeling. Thus I may simultaneously express boredom and say that I am bored, and in that case my utterance of the words, "I am bored," is one of the circumstances which make it true to say that I am expressing or evincing boredom. But I can express boredom without actually saying that I am bored. I can express it by my tone and gestures, while making a statement about something wholly unconnected with it, or by an ejaculation, or without uttering any words at all. So that even if the assertion that one has a certain feeling always involves the expression of that feeling, the expression of a feeling assuredly does not always involve the assertion that one has it. And this is the important point to grasp in considering the distinction between our theory and the ordinary subjectivist theory. For whereas the subjectivist holds that ethical statements actually assert the existence of certain feelings, we hold that ethical statements are expressions and excitants of feeling which do not necessarily involve any assertions.

We have already remarked that the main objection to the ordinary subjectivist theory is that the validity of ethical judgements is not determined by the nature of their author's feelings. And this is an objection which our theory escapes. For it does not imply that the existence of any feelings is a necessary and sufficient condition of the validity of an ethical judgement. It implies, on the contrary, that ethical judgements have no validity.

There is, however, a celebrated argument against subjectivist theories which our theory does not escape. It has been pointed out by Moore that if ethical statements were simply statements about the speaker's feelings, it would be impossible to argue about questions of value. To take a typical example: if a man said that thrift was a virtue, and another replied that it was a vice, they would not, on this theory, be disputing with one another. One would be saying that he approved of thrift, and the other that *he* didn't; and there is no reason why both these statements should not be true. Now Moore held it to be obvious that we do dispute about questions of value, and accordingly concluded that the particular form of subjectivism which he was discussing was false.

It is plain that the conclusion that it is impossible to dispute about questions of value follows from our theory also. For as we hold that such sentences as "Thrift is a virtue" and "Thrift is a vice" do not express propositions at all, we clearly cannot hold that they express incompatible propositions. We must therefore admit that if Moore's argument really refutes the ordinary subjectivist theory, it also refutes ours. But, in fact, we deny that it does refute even the ordinary subjectivist theory. For we hold that one really never does dispute about questions of value.

This may seem, at first sight, to be a very paradoxical assertion. For we certainly do engage in disputes which are ordinarily regarded as disputes about questions of value. But, in all such cases, we find, if we consider the matter closely, that the dispute is not really about a question of value, but about a question of fact. When someone disagrees with us about the moral value of a certain action or type of action, we do admittedly resort to argument in order to win him over to our way of thinking. But we do not attempt to show by our arguments that he has the "wrong" ethical feeling towards a situation whose nature he has correctly apprehended. What we attempt to show is that he is mistaken about the facts of the case. We argue that he has misconceived the agent's motive: or that he has misjudged the effects of the action, or its probable effects in view of the agent's knowledge; or that he has failed to take into account the special circumstances in which the agent was placed. Or else we employ more general arguments about the effects which actions of a certain type tend to produce, or the qualities which are usually manifested in their performance. We do this in the hope that we have only to get our opponent to agree with us about the nature of the empirical facts for him to adopt the same moral attitude towards them as we do. And as the people with whom we argue have generally received the same moral education as ourselves, and live in the same social order, our expectation is usually justified. But if our opponent happens to have undergone a different process of moral "conditioning" from ourselves, so that, even when he acknowledges all the facts, he still disagrees with us about the moral value of the actions under discussion, then we abandon the attempt to convince him by argument. We say that it is impossible to argue with him because he has a distorted or undeveloped moral sense; which signifies merely that he employs a different set of values from our own. We feel that our own system of values is superior, and therefore speak in such derogatory terms of his. But we cannot bring forward any arguments to show that our system is superior. For our judgement that it is so is itself a judgement of value, and accordingly outside the scope of argument. It is because argument fails us when we come to deal with pure questions of value, as distinct from questions of fact, that we finally resort to mere abuse.

In short, we find that argument is possible on moral questions only if some system of values is presupposed. If our opponent concurs with us in expressing moral disapproval of all actions of a given type t, then we may get him to condemn a particular action A, by bringing forward arguments to show that A is of type t. For the question whether A does or does not belong to that type is a plain question of fact. Given that a man has certain moral principles, we argue that he must, in order to be consistent, react morally to certain things in a certain way. What we do not and cannot argue about is the validity of these moral principles. We merely praise or condemn them in the light of our own feelings.

If anyone doubts the accuracy of this account of moral disputes, let him try to construct even an imaginary argument on a question of value which does not reduce itself to an argument about a question of logic or about an empirical matter of fact. I am confident that he will not succeed in producing a single example. And if that is the case, he must allow that its involving the impossibility of purely ethical arguments is not, as Moore thought, a ground of objection to our theory, but rather a point of favour of it.

Having upheld our theory against the only criticism which appeared to threaten it, we may now use it to define the nature of all ethical enquiries. We find that ethical philosophy consists simply in saying that ethical concepts are pseudo-concepts and therefore unanalysable. The further task of describing the different feelings that the different ethical terms are used to express, and the different reactions that they customarily provoke, is a task for the psychologist. There cannot be such a thing as ethical science, if by ethical science one means the elaboration of a "true" system of morals. For we have seen that, as ethical judgements are mere expressions of feeling, there can be no way of determining the validity of any ethical system, and, indeed, no sense in asking whether any such system is true. All that one may legitimately enquire in this connection is, What are the moral habits of a given person or group of people, and what causes them to have precisely those habits and feelings? And this enquiry falls wholly within the scope of the existing social sciences.

It appears, then, that ethics, as a branch of knowledge, is nothing more than a department of psychology and sociology. And in case anyone thinks that we are overlooking the existence of casuistry, we may remark that casuistry is not a science, but is a purely analytical investigation of the structure of a given moral system. In other words, it is an exercise in formal logic.

When one comes to pursue the psychological enquiries which constitute ethical science, one is immediately enabled to account for the Kantian and hedonistic theories of morals. For one finds that one of the chief causes of moral behaviour is fear, both conscious and unconscious, of a god's displeasure, and fear of the enmity of society. And this, indeed, is the reason why moral precepts present themselves to some people as "categorical" commands. And one finds, also, that the moral code of a society is partly determined by the beliefs of that society concerning the conditions of its own happiness—or, in other words, that a society tends to encourage or discourage a given type of conduct by the use of moral sanctions according as it appears to promote or detract from the contentment of the society as a whole. And this is the reason why altruism is recommended in most moral codes and egotism condemned. It is from the observation of this connection between morality and happiness that hedonistic or eudaemonistic theories of morals ultimately spring, just as the moral theory of Kant is based on the fact, previously explained, that moral precepts have for some people the force of inexorable commands. As each of these theories ignores the fact which lies at the root of the other, both may be criticized as being one-sided; but this is not the main objection to either of them. Their essential defect is that they treat propositions which refer to the causes and attributes of our ethical feelings as if they were definitions of ethical concepts. And thus they fail to recognize that ethical concepts are pseudo-concepts and consequently indefinable.

11

Freedom and Reason

R. M. HARE

R. M. Hare (b. 1919) is Professor of Philosophy emeritus at the University of Florida. Previously he was White's Professor of Moral Philosophy at Corpus Christi College, Oxford University. He has done important work both in moral theory and in the application of moral theory to practical problems. His major works include The Language of Morals, Freedom and Reason, *and* Moral Thinking.

In Hare's view, every moral judgment involves two elements. When someone judges that he morally ought to do something, he commits himself to doing it and also extends his principle of action to anyone else in a similar position. As Hare puts it, all moral judgments are both prescriptive and universalizable.

In this selection from Freedom and Reason, *Chapter 6, Hare argues that these rules place important constraints on our moral thought. To show this, he proposes a simple example. Suppose that A owes B money, and B owes C money. Suppose further that B is considering imprisoning A for nonpayment. Given the universalizability requirement, accepting this judgment would force B to judge that C ought to imprison him for not paying. But B does not want to go to jail, and so cannot prescribe that C imprison him. Thus, B must withdraw his judgment that he ought to imprison A. Moreover, he must withdraw this judgment even if his creditor C is not real, but only imagined.*

Could B escape this conclusion? As Hare recognizes, he might try. For one thing B might either reject Hare's definition of morality or refuse to think in moral terms. Failing that, he might look for differences between himself and A. Or he might simply accept the prescription that he too be sent to jail. In the later part of the selection, Hare considers such maneuvers. His conclusion is that few if any are effective.

The rules of moral reasoning are, basically, two, corresponding to the two features of moral judgements which I argued for in the first half of this book, prescriptivity and universalizability. When we are trying, in a concrete case, to decide what we ought to do, what we are looking for (as I have already said) is an action to which we can commit ourselves (prescriptivity) but which we are at the same time prepared to accept as exemplifying a principle of action to be prescribed for others in like circumstances (universalizability). If, when we consider some proposed action, we find that, when universalized, it yields prescriptions which we cannot accept, we reject this action as a solution to our moral problem—if we cannot universalize the prescription, it cannot become an 'ought'.

•   •   •

I will now try to exhibit the bare bones of the theory of moral reasoning that I wish to advocate by considering a very simple (indeed over-simplified) example. As we shall see, even this very simple case generates the most baffling complexities; and so we may be pardoned for not attempting anything more difficult to start with.

This example is adapted from a well-known parable.[1] *A* owes money to *B*, and *B* owes money to *C*, and it is the law that creditors may exact their debts by putting their debtors into prison. *B* asks himself, 'Can I say that I ought to take this measure against *A* in order to make him pay? He is no doubt *inclined* to do this, or *wants* to do it. Therefore, if there were no question of universaliz-ing his prescriptions, he would assent readily to the *singular* prescription 'Let me put *A* into prison' (4.3). But when he seeks to turn this prescription into a moral judgement, and say, 'I *ought* to put *A* into prison because he will not pay me what he owes', he reflects that this would involve accepting the principle 'Anyone who is in my position ought to put his debtor into prison if he does not pay'. But then he reflects that *C* is in the same position of unpaid creditor with regard to himself (*B*), and that the cases are otherwise identical; and that if anyone in this position ought to put his debtors into prison, then so ought *C* to put him (*B*) into prison. And to accept the moral prescription '*C* ought to put me into prison' would commit him (since, as we have seen, he must be using the word 'ought' prescriptively) to accepting the singular prescription 'Let *C* put me into prison'; and this he is not ready to accept. But if he is not, then neither can he accept the original judgement that he (*B*) ought to put *A* into prison for debt. Notice that the whole of this argument would break down if 'ought' were not being used both universalizably *and prescriptively;* for if it were not being used prescriptively, the step from '*C* ought to put me into prison' to 'Let *C* put me into prison' would not be valid.

The structure and ingredients of this argument must now be examined. We must first notice an analogy between it and the Popperian theory of scientific method. What has happened is that a provisional or suggested moral principle has been rejected because one of its particular consequences proved unaccept-able. But an important difference between the two kinds of reasoning must also be noted; it is what we should expect, given that the data of scientific observation are recorded in descriptive statements, whereas we are here dealing with prescriptions. What knocks out a suggested hypothesis, on Popper's the-ory, is a singular statement of fact: the hypothesis has the consequence that *p*; but not-*p*. Here the logic is just the same, except that in place of the observation-statements '*p*' and 'not-*p*' we have the singular *prescriptions* 'Let *C* put *B* into

[1] Matt. 18:23.

prison for debt' and its contradictory. Nevertheless, given that *B* is disposed to reject the first of these prescriptions, the argument against him is just as cogent as in the scientific case.

We may carry the parallel further. Just as science, seriously pursued, is the search for hypotheses and the testing of them by the attempt to falsify their particular consequences, so morals, as a serious endeavour, consists in the search for principles and the testing of them against particular cases. Any rational activity has its discipline, and this is the discipline of moral thought: to test the moral principles that suggest themselves to us by following out their consequences and seeing whether we can accept *them*.

No argument, however, starts from nothing. We must therefore ask what we have to have before moral arguments of the sort of which I have given a simple example can proceed. The first requisite is that the facts of the case should be given; for all moral discussion is about some particular set of facts, whether actual or supposed. Secondly we have the logical framework provided by the meaning of the word 'ought' (i.e., prescriptivity and universalizability, both of which we saw to be necessary). Because moral judgements have to be universalizable, *B* cannot say that he ought to put *A* into prison for debt without committing himself to the view that *C*, who is *ex hypothesi* in the same position *vis-à-vis* himself, ought to put *him* into prison; and because moral judgements are prescriptive, this would be, in effect, prescribing to *C* to put him into prison; and this he is unwilling to do, since he has a strong inclination not to go to prison. This inclination gives us the third necessary ingredient in the argument: if *B* were a completely apathetic person, who literally did not mind what happened to himself or to anybody else, the argument would not touch him. The three necessary ingredients which we have noticed, then, are (1) facts; (2) logic; (3) inclinations. These ingredients enable us, not indeed to arrive at an evaluative conclusion, but to *reject* an evaluative proposition. We shall see later that these are not, in all cases, the only necessary ingredients.

In the example which we have been using, the position was deliberately made simpler by supposing that *B* actually stood to some other person in exactly the same relation as *A* does to him. Such cases are unlikely to arise in practice. But it is not necessary for the force of the argument that *B* should *in fact* stand in this relation to anyone; it is sufficient that he should consider hypothetically such a case, and see what would be the consequences in it of those moral principles between whose acceptance and rejection he has to decide. Here we have an important point of difference from the parallel scientific argument, in that the crucial case which leads to rejection of the principle can itself be a supposed, not an observed, one. That hypothetical cases will do as well as actual ones is important, since it enables us to guard against a possible misinterpretation of the argument which I have outlined. It might be thought that what moves *B* is the *fear* that *C* will actually do to him as he does to *A*— as happens in the gospel parable. But this fear is not only irrelevant to the moral argument; it does not even provide a particularly strong non-moral motive unless the circumstances are somewhat exceptional. *C* may, after all, not find out what *B* has done to *A*; or *C*'s moral principles may be different from *B*'s, and independent of them, so that what moral principle *B* accepts makes no difference to the moral principles on which *C* acts.

Even, therefore, if *C* did not exist, it would be no answer to the argument for *B* to say 'But in my case there is no fear that anybody will ever be in a position to do to me what I am proposing to do to *A*'. For the argument does not rest on any such fear. All that is essential to it is that *B* should disregard the fact that he plays the particular role in the situation which he does, without disregarding the inclinations which people have in situations of this sort. In other words, he must be prepared to give weight to *A*'s inclinations and interests as if they were his own. This is what turns selfish prudential reasoning into moral reasoning. It is much easier, psychologically, for *B* to do this if he is actually placed in a situation like *A*'s *vis-à-vis* somebody else; but this is not necessary, provided that he has sufficient imagination to envisage what it is like to be *A*. For our first example, a case was deliberately chosen in which little imagination was necessary; but in most normal cases a certain power of imagination and readiness to use it is a fourth necessary ingredient in moral arguments, alongside those already mentioned, viz. logic (in the shape of universalizability and prescriptivity), the facts, and the inclinations or interests of the people concerned.

It must be pointed out that the absence of even one of these ingredients may render the rest ineffective. For example, impartiality by itself is not enough. If, in becoming impartial, *B* became also completely dispassionate and apathetic, and moved as little by other people's interests as by his own, then, as we have seen, there would be nothing to make him accept or reject one moral principle rather than another. That is why those who, like Adam Smith and Professor Kneale, advocate what have been called 'Ideal Observer Theories' of ethics, sometimes postulate as their imaginary ideal observer not merely an impartial spectator, but an impartially *sympathetic* spectator.[2] To take another example, if the person who faces the moral decision has no imagination, then even the fact that someone can do the very same thing to him may pass him by. If, again, he lacks the readiness to universalize, then the vivid imagination of the sufferings which he is inflicting on others may only spur him on to intensify them, to increase his own vindictive enjoyment. And if he is ignorant of the material facts (for example about what is likely to happen to a person if one takes out a writ against him), then there is nothing to tie the moral argument to particular choices.

---

[2] It will be plain that there are affinities, though there are also differences, between this type of theory and my own. For such theories see W. C. Kneale, *Philosophy*, xxv (1950), 162; R. Firth and R. B. Brandt, *Philosophy and Phenomenological Research*, xii (1951/2), 317, and xv (1954/5), 407, 414, 422; and J. Harrison, *Aristotelian Society*, supp. vol. xxviii (1954), 132. Firth, unlike Kneale, says that the observer must be 'dispassionate', but see Brandt, op. cit., p. 411 n. For a shorter discussion see Brandt, *Ethical Theory*, p. 173. Since for many Christians God occupies the role of 'ideal observer', the moral judgements which they make may be expected to coincide with those arrived at by the method of reasoning which I am advocating.

The best way of testing the argument which we have outlined will be to consider various ways in which somebody in *B*'s position might seek to escape from it. There are indeed a number of ways; and all of them may be successful, at a price. It is important to understand what the price is in each case. We may classify these manœuvres which are open to *B* into two kinds. There are first of all the moves which depend on his using the moral words in a different way from that on which the argument relied. We saw that for the success of the argument it was necessary that 'ought' should be used universalizably and prescriptively. If *B* uses it in a way that is either not prescriptive or not universalizable, then he can escape the force of the argument, at the cost of resigning from the kind of discussion that we thought we were having with him. We shall discuss these two possibilities separately. Secondly, there are moves which can still be made by *B*, even though he is using the moral words in the same way as we are. We shall examine three different sub-classes of these.

Before dealing with what I shall call the *verbal* manœuvres in detail, it may be helpful to make a general remark. Suppose that we are having a simple mathematical argument with somebody, and he admits, for example, that there are five eggs in this basket, and six in the other, but maintains that there are a dozen eggs in the two baskets taken together; and suppose that this is because he is using the expression 'a dozen' to mean 'eleven'. It is obvious that we cannot compel him logically to admit that there are not a dozen eggs, in *his* sense of 'dozen'. But it is equally obvious that this should not disturb us. For such a man only appears to be dissenting from us. His dissent is only apparent, because the proposition which his words express is actually consistent with the conclusion which we wish to draw; he says 'There are a dozen eggs'; but he *means* what we should express by saying 'There are eleven eggs'; and this we are not disputing. It is important to remember that in the moral case also the dissent may be only apparent, if the words are being used in different ways, and that it is no defect in a method of argument if it does not make it possible to prove a conclusion to a person when he is using words in such a way that the conclusion does not follow.

It must be pointed out, further (since this is a common source of confusion), that in this argument nothing whatever hangs upon our *actual* use of words in common speech, any more than it does in the arithmetical case. That we use the sound 'dozen' to express the meaning that we customarily do use it to express is of no consequence for the argument about the eggs; and the same may be said of the sound 'ought'. There is, however, something which I, at any rate, customarily express by the sound 'ought', whose character is correctly described by saying that it is a universal or universalizable prescription. I hope that what I customarily express by the sound 'ought' is the same as what most people customarily express by it; but if I am mistaken in this assumption, I shall still have given a correct account, so far as I am able, of that which I express by this sound.[3] Nevertheless, this account will interest other people

3 Cf. Moore, *Principia Ethica*, p. 6.

mainly in so far as my hope that they understand the same thing as I do by 'ought' is fulfilled; and since I am moderately sure that this is indeed the case with many people, I hope that I may be of use to them in elucidating the logical properties of the concept which they thus express.

At this point, however, it is of the utmost importance to stress that the fact that two people express the same thing by 'ought' does not entail that they share the same moral opinions. For the formal, logical properties of the word 'ought' (those which are determined by its *meaning*) are only one of the four factors (listed earlier) whose combination governs a man's moral opinion on a given matter. Thus ethics, the study of the logical properties of the moral words, remains morally neutral (its conclusions neither are substantial moral judgements, nor entail them, even in conjunction with factual premisses); its bearing upon moral questions lies in this, that it makes logically impossible certain combinations of moral and other prescriptions. Two people who are using the word 'ought' in the same way may yet disagree about what ought to be done in a certain situation, either because they differ about the facts, or because one or other of them lacks imagination, or because their different inclinations make one reject some singular prescription which the other can accept. For all that, ethics (i.e. the logic of moral language) is an immensely powerful engine for producing moral agreement; for if two people are willing to use the moral word 'ought', and to use it in the same way (viz. the way that I have been describing), the other possible sources of moral disagreement are all eliminable. People's inclinations about most of the important matters in life tend to be the same (very few people, for example, like being starved or run over by motor-cars); and, even when they are not, there is a way of generalizing the argument, to be described in the next chapter, which enables us to make allowance for differences in inclinations. The facts are often, given sufficient patience, ascertainable. Imagination can be cultivated. If these three factors are looked after, as they can be, agreement on the use of 'ought' is the only other necessary condition for producing moral agreement, at any rate in typical cases. And, if I am not mistaken, this agreement in use is already there in the discourse of anybody with whom we are at all likely to find ourselves arguing; all that is needed is to think clearly, and so make it evident.

After this methodological digression, let us consider what is to be done with the man who professes to be using 'ought' in some different way from that which I have described—because he is not using it prescriptively, or not universalizably. For the reasons that I have given, if he takes either of these courses, he is no longer in substantial moral disagreement with us. Our apparent moral disagreement is really only verbal; for although, as we shall see shortly, there may be a residuum of substantial disagreement, this cannot be moral. It cannot even be an evaluative disagreement, in the sense of 'evaluative' above defined.

Let us take first the man who is using the word 'ought' prescriptively, but not universalizably. He can say that he ought to put his debtor into prison, although he is not prepared to agree that his creditor ought to put *him* into prison. We, on the other hand, since we are not prepared to admit that our creditors in these circumstances ought to put us into prison, cannot say that we ought to put our debtors into prison. So there is an appearance of substantial moral disagreement, which is intensified by the fact that, since we are both using the word 'ought' prescriptively, our respective views will lead to different particular actions. Different *singular* prescriptions about what to do are (since both our judgements are prescriptive) derivable from what we are respectively saying. But this is not enough to constitute a moral disagreement. For there to be a moral disagreement, or even an evaluative one of any kind, we must differ, not only about what *is* to be done in some particular case, but about some universal principle concerning what *ought* to be done in cases of a certain sort; and since B is (on the hypothesis considered) advocating no such universal principle, he is saying nothing with which we can be in moral or evaluative disagreement. Considered purely as prescriptions, indeed, our two views are in substantial disagreement; but the moral, evaluative (i.e. the *universal* pre-scriptive) disagreement is only verbal, because, when the expression of B's view is understood as he means it, the view turns out not to be a view about the morality of the action at all. So B, by this manœuvre, can go on prescribing to himself to put A into prison, but has to abandon the claim that he is justifying the action morally, as we understand the word 'morally'. One may, of course, use any word as one pleases, at a price. But he can no longer claim to be giving that sort of justification of his action for which, as I think, the common expression is 'moral justification'.

I need not deal at length with the second way in which B might be differing from us in his use of 'ought', viz. by not using it prescriptively. If he were not using it prescriptively, it will be remembered, he could assent to the singular prescription 'Let not C put me into prison for debt', and yet assent also to the non-prescriptive moral judgement 'C ought to put me into prison for debt'. And so his disinclination to be put into prison for debt by C would furnish no obstacle to his saying that he (B) ought to put A into prison for debt. And thus he could carry out his own inclination to put A into prison with apparent moral justification. The justification would be, however, only apparent. For if B is using the word 'ought' non-prescriptively, then 'I ought to put A into pri-son for debt' does not entail the singular prescription 'Let me put A into prison for debt'; the 'moral' judgement becomes quite irrelevant to the choice of what to do. There would also be the same lack of substantial moral disagreement as we noticed in the preceding case. B would not be disagreeing with us other than verbally, so far as the moral question is concerned (though there might be points of *factual* disagreement between us, arising from the *descriptive* meaning of our judgements). The 'moral' disagreement could be only verbal, because whereas we should be dissenting from the universalizable prescription 'B ought to put A into prison for debt', *this* would not be what B was expressing, though the words he would be using would be the same. For B would not, by these words, be expressing a prescription at all.

So much for the ways (of which my list may well be incomplete) in which B can escape from our argument by using the word 'ought' in a different way from us. The remaining ways of escape are open to him even if he is using 'ought' in the same way as we are, viz. to express a universalizable prescription.

We must first consider that class of escape-routes whose distinguishing feature is that *B*, while using the moral words in the same way as we are, refuses to make positive moral judgements at all in certain cases. There are two main variations of this manœuvre. *B* may either say that it is indifferent, morally, whether he imprisons *A* or not; or he may refuse to make any moral judgement at all, even one of indifference, about the case. It will be obvious that if he adopts either of these moves, he can evade the argument as so far set out. For that argument only forced him to *reject* the moral judgement 'I ought to imprison *A* for debt'. It did not force him to assent to any moral judgement; in particular, he remained free to assent, either to the judgement that he ought not to imprison *A* for debt (which is the one that we want him to accept) or to the judgement that it is neither the case that he ought, nor the case that he ought not (that it is, in short, indifferent); and he remained free, also, to say 'I am just not making any moral judgements at all about this case'.

We have not yet, however, exhausted the arguments generated by the demand for universalizability, provided that the moral words are being used in a way which allows this demand. For it is evident that these manœuvres could, in principle, be practised in any case whatever in which the morality of an act is in question. And this enables us to place *B* in a dilemma. Either he practises this manœuvre in *every* situation in which he is faced with a moral decision; or else he practises it only *sometimes*. The first alternative, however, has to be sub-divided; for 'every situation' might mean 'every situation in which he himself has to face a moral decision regarding one of his own actions', or it might mean 'every situation in which a moral question arises for him, whether about his own actions or about somebody else's.' So there are three courses that he can adopt: (1) He either refrains altogether from making moral judgements, or makes none except judgements of indifference (that is to say, he either observes a complete moral silence, or says 'Nothing matters morally'; either of these two positions might be called a sort of amoralism); (2) He makes moral judgements in the normal way about other people's actions, but adopts one or other of the kinds of amoralism, just mentioned, with regard to his own; (3) He expresses moral indifference, or will make no moral judgement at all, with regard to *some* of his own actions and those of other people, but makes moral judgements in the normal way about others.

Now it will be obvious that in the first case there is nothing that we can do, and that this should not disturb us. Just as one cannot win a game of chess against an opponent who will not make any moves—and just as one cannot argue mathematically with a person who will not commit himself to any mathematical statements—so moral argument is impossible with a man who will make no moral judgements at all, or—which for practical purposes comes to the same thing—makes only judgements of indifference. Such a person is not entering the arena of moral dispute, and therefore it is impossible to contest with him. He is compelled also—and this is important—to abjure the protection of morality for his own interests.

In the other two cases, however, we have an argument left. If a man is prepared to make positive moral judgements about other people's actions, but not about his own, or if he is prepared to make them about some of his own decisions, but not about others, then we can ask him on what principle he makes the distinction between these various cases. This is a particular application of the demand for universalizability. He will still have left to him the ways of escape from this demand which are available in all its applications, and which we shall consider later. But there is no way of escape which is available in this application, but not in others. He must either produce (or at least admit the existence of) some principle which makes him hold different moral opinions about apparently similar cases, or else admit that the judgements he is making are not moral ones. But in the latter case, he is in the same position, in the present dispute, as the man who will not make any moral judgements at all; he has resigned from the contest.

In the particular example which we have been considering, we supposed that the cases of B and of C, his own creditor, were identical. The demand for universalization therefore compels B to make the same moral judgement, whatever it is, about both cases. He had therefore, unless he is going to give up the claim to be arguing morally, either to say that neither he nor C ought to exercise their legal rights to imprison their debtors; or that both ought (a possibility to which we shall recur in the next section); or that it is indifferent whether they do. But the last alternative leaves it open to B and C to do what they like in the matter; and we may suppose that, though B himself would like to have this freedom, he will be unwilling to allow it to C. It is as unlikely that he will *permit* C to put him (B) into prison as that he will *prescribe* it. We may say, therefore, that while move (1), described above, constitutes an abandonment of the dispute, moves (2) and (3) really add nothing new to it.

We must next consider a way of escape which may seem much more respectable than those which I have so far mentioned. Let us suppose that B is a firm believer in the rights of property and the sanctity of contracts. In this case he may say roundly that debtors ought to be imprisoned by their creditors whoever they are, and that, specifically, C ought to imprison him (B), and he (B) ought to imprison A. And he may, unlike the superficially similar person described earlier, be meaning by 'ought' just what we usually mean by it—i.e., he may be using the word prescriptively, realizing that in saying that C ought to put him into prison, he is prescribing that C put him in prison. B, in this case, is perfectly ready to go to prison for his principles, in order that the sanctity of contracts may be enforced. In real life, B would be much more likely to take this line if the situation in which he himself played the role of debtor were not actual but only hypothetical; but this, as we saw earlier, ought not to make any difference to the argument.

We are not yet, however, in a position to deal with this escape-route. All we can do is to say why we cannot now deal with it, and leave this loose end to be picked up later. B, if he is sincere in holding the principle about the sanctity of contracts (or any other universal moral principle which has the same effect in this particular case), may have two sorts of grounds for it. He may hold it on utilitarian grounds, thinking that, unless contracts are rigorously enforced, the results will be so disastrous as to outweigh any benefit that A, or *B* himself, may get from being let off. This could, in certain circumstances, be a good argument. But we cannot tell whether it is, until we have generalized the type of moral argument which has been set out in this chapter, to cover cases in which the interests of more than two parties are involved. As we saw, it is only the interests of *A* and *B* that come into the argument as so far considered (the interests of the third party, *C*, do not need separate consideration, since *C* was introduced only in order to show *B*, if necessary fictionally, a situation in which the roles were reversed; therefore *C*'s interests, being a mere replica of *B*'s, will vanish, as a separate factor, once the *A/B* situation, and the moral judgements made on it, are universalized). But if utilitarian grounds of the sort suggested are to be adduced, they will bring with them a reference to all the other people whose interests would be harmed by laxity in the enforcement of contracts. This escape-route, therefore, if this is its basis, introduces considerations which cannot be assessed until we have generalized our form of argument to cover 'multilateral' moral situations. At present, it can only be said that if *B* can show that leniency in the enforcement of contracts would really have the results he claims for the community at large, he might be justified in taking the severer course. This will be apparent after we have considered in some detail an example (that of the judge and the criminal) which brings out these considerations even more clearly.

On the other hand, *B* might have a quite different, non-utilitarian kind of reason for adhering to his principle. He might be moved, not by any weight which he might attach to the interests of other people, but by the thought that to enforce contracts of this sort is necessary in order to conform to some moral or other *ideal* that he has espoused. Such ideals might be of various sorts. He might be moved, for example, by an ideal of abstract justice, of the *fiat justitia, ruat caelum* variety. We have to distinguish such an ideal of justice, which pays no regard to people's interests, from that which is concerned merely to do justice *between* people's interests. It is very important, if considerations of justice are introduced into a moral argument, to know of which sort they are. Justice of the second kind can perhaps be accommodated within a moral view which it is not misleading to call utilitarian. But this is not true of an ideal of the first kind. It is characteristic of this sort of non-utilitarian ideals that, when they are introduced into moral arguments, they render ineffective the appeal to universalized self-interest which is the foundation of the argument that we have been considering. This is because the person who has whole-heartedly espoused such an ideal (we shall call him the 'fanatic') does not mind if people's interests—even his own—are harmed in the pursuit of it.

It need not be justice which provides the basis of such an escape-route as we are considering. Any moral ideal would do, provided that it were pursued regardless of other people's interests. For example, *B* might be a believer in the survival of the fittest, and think that, in order to promote this, he (and everyone else) ought to pursue their own interests by all means in their power and regardless of everyone else's interests. This ideal might lead him, in this particular case, to put *A* in prison, and he might agree that *C* ought to do the same to him, if he were not clever enough to avoid this fate. He might think that universal obedience to such a principle would maximize the production of supermen and so make the world a better place. If these were his grounds, it is possible that we might argue with him factually, showing that the universal observance of the principle would not have the results he claimed. But we might be defeated in this factual argument if he had an ideal which made him call the world 'a better place' when the jungle law prevailed; he could then agree to our factual statements, but still maintain that the condition of the world described by us as resulting from the observance of his principle would be better than its present condition. In this case, the argument might take two courses. If we could get him to imagine himself in the position of the weak, who went to the wall in such a state of the world, we might bring him to realize that to hold his principle involved prescribing that things should be done to him, in hypothetical situations, which he could not sincerely prescribe. If so, then the argument would be on the rails again, and could proceed on lines which we have already sketched. But he might stick to his principle and say "If I were weak, then I ought to go to the wall." If he did this, he would be putting himself beyond the reach of what we shall call 'golden rule' or 'utilitarian' arguments by becoming what we shall call a 'fanatic'. Since a great part of the rest of this book will be concerned with people who take this sort of line, it is unnecessary to pursue their case further at this point.

The remaining manœuvre that B might seek to practise is probably the commonest. It is certainly the one which is most frequently brought up in philosophical controversies on this topic. This consists in a fresh appeal to the facts—i.e. in asserting that there are in fact morally relevant differences between his case and that of others. In the example which we have been considering, we have artificially ruled out this way of escape by assuming that the case of B and C is exactly similar to that of A and B; from this it follows *a fortiori* that there are no morally relevant differences. Since the B/C case may be a hypothetical one, this condition of exact similarity can always be fulfilled, and therefore this manœuvre is based on a misconception of the type of argument against which it is directed. Nevertheless it may be useful, since this objection is so commonly raised, to deal with it at this point, although nothing further will be added thereby to what has been said already.

It may be claimed that no two actual cases would ever be exactly similar; there would always be some differences, and B might allege that some of these were morally relevant. He might allege, for example, that, whereas his family would starve if C put him into prison, this would not be the case if he put A into prison, because A's family would be looked after by A's relatives. If such a difference existed, there might be nothing logically disreputable in calling it morally relevant, and such arguments are in fact often put forward and accepted.

The difficulty, however, lies in drawing the line between those arguments of this sort which are legitimate, and those which are not. Suppose that B alleges that the fact that A has a hooked nose or a black skin entitles him, B, to put him in prison, but that C ought not to do the same thing to him, B, because his nose is straight and his skin white. Is this an argument of equal logical respectability? Can I say that the fact that I have a mole in a particular place on my chin entitles me to further my own interests at others' expense, but that they are forbidden to do this by the fact that they lack this mark of natural pre-eminence?

The answer to this manœuvre is implicit in what has been said already about the relevance, in moral arguments, of hypothetical as well as actual cases. The fact that no two actual cases are ever identical has no bearing on the problem. For all we have to do is to imagine an identical case in which the roles are reversed. Suppose that my mole disappears, and that my neighbor grows one in the very same spot on his chin. Or, to use our other example, what does *B* say about a hypothetical case in which he has a black skin or a hooked nose, and *A* and *C* are both straight-nosed and white-skinned? Since this is the same argument, in essentials, as we used at the very beginning, it need not be repeated here. *B* is in fact faced with a dilemma. Either the property of his own case, which he claims to be morally relevant, is a properly universal property (i.e. one describable without reference to individuals), or it is not. If it is a universal property, then, because of the meaning of the word 'universal', it is a property which might be possessed by another case in which he played a different role (though in fact it may not be); and we can therefore ask him to ignore the fact that it is he himself who plays the role which he does in this case. This will force him to count as morally relevant only those properties which he is prepared to allow to be relevant even when other people have them. And this rules out all the attractive kinds of special pleading. On the other hand, if the property in question is not a properly universal one, then he has not met the demand for universalizability, and cannot claim to be putting forward a moral argument at all.

It is necessary, in order to avoid misunderstanding, to add two notes to the foregoing discussion. The misunderstanding arises through a too literal interpretation of the common forms of expression—which constantly recur in arguments of this type—'How would you like it if . . .?' and 'Do as you would be done by'. Though I shall later, for convenience, refer to the type of arguments here discussed as 'golden-rule' arguments, we must not be misled by these forms of expression.

First of all, we shall make the nature of the argument clearer if, when we are asking *B* to imagine himself in the position of his victim, we phrase our question, never in the form 'What *would* you say, or feel, or think, or how *would* you like it, if you were he?', but always in the form 'What *do* you say (*in propria persona*) about a hypothetical case in which you are in your victim's position?' The importance of this way of phrasing the question is that, if the question were put in the first way, *B* might reply 'Well, of course, if anybody did this to me I should resent it very much and make all sorts of adverse moral judgements about the act; but this has absolutely no bearing on the validity of the moral opinion which I am *now* expressing'. To involve him in contradiction, we have to show that he *now* holds an opinion about the hypothetical case which is inconsistent with his opinion about the actual case.

The second thing which has to be noticed is that the argument, as set out, does not involve any sort of deduction of a moral judgement, or even of the negation of a moral judgement, from a factual statement about people's inclinations, interests, &c. We are not saying to B 'You are as a matter of fact averse to this being done to you in a hypothetical case; and from this it follows logically that you ought not to do it to another'. Such a deduction would be a breach of Hume's Law ('No "ought" from an "is" '), to which I have repeatedly declared my adherence. The point is, rather, that because of his aversion to its being done to him in the hypothetical case, he cannot accept the singular *prescription* that in the hypothetical case it should be done to him; and this, because of the logic of 'ought', precludes him from accepting the moral judgement that he ought to do likewise to another in the actual case. It is not a question of a factual statement about a person's inclinations being inconsistent with a moral judgement; rather, his inclinations being what they are, he cannot assent sincerely to a certain singular prescription, and if he cannot do this, he cannot assent to a certain universal prescription which entails it, when conjoined with factual statements about the circumstances whose truth he admits. Because of this entailment, if he assented to the factual statements and to the universal prescription, but refused (as he must, his inclinations being what they are) to assent to the singular prescription, he would be guilty of a logical inconsistency.

If it be asked what the relation is between his aversion to being put in prison in the hypothetical case, and his inability to accept the hypothetical singular prescription that if he were in such a situation he should be put into prison, it would seem that the relation is not unlike that between a belief that the cat is on the mat, and an inability to accept the proposition that the cat is not on the mat. Further attention to this parallel will perhaps make the position clearer. Suppose that somebody advances the hypothesis that cats never sit on mats, and that we refute him by pointing to a cat on a mat. The logic of our refutation proceeds in two stages. Of these, the second is: 'Here is a cat sitting on a mat, so it is not the case that cats never sit on mats'. This is a piece of logical deduction; and to it, in the moral case, corresponds the step from 'Let this not be done to me' to 'It is not the case that I ought to do it to another in similar circumstances'. But in both cases there is a first stage whose nature is more obscure, and different in the two cases, though there is an analogy between them.

In the 'cat' case, it is logically possible for a man to look straight at the cat on the mat, and yet believe that there is no cat on the mat. But if a person with normal eyesight and no psychological aberrations does this, we say that he does not understand the meaning of the words, 'The cat is on the mat'. And even if he does not have normal eyesight, or suffers from some psychological aberration (such as a phobia of cats, say, that he just *cannot* admit to himself that he is face to face with one), yet, if we can convince him that everyone else can see a cat there, he will have to admit that there *is* a cat there, or be accused of misusing the language.

If, on the other hand, a man says 'But I *want* to be put in prison, if ever I am in that situation', we can, indeed, get as far as accusing him of having eccentric desires; but we cannot, when we have proved to him that nobody else has such a desire, face him with the choice of either saying, with the rest, 'Let this not be done to me', or else being open to the accusation of not understanding what he is saying. For it is not an incorrect use of words to want eccentric things. Logic does not prevent me wanting to be put in a gas chamber if a Jew. It is perhaps true that I logically cannot want for its own sake an experience which I think of as *unpleasant;* for to say that I think of it as unpleasant may be logically inconsistent with saying that I want it for its own sake. If this is so, it is because 'unpleasant' is a prescriptive expression. But 'to be put in prison' and 'to be put in a gas chamber if a Jew', are not prescriptive expressions; and therefore these things can be wanted without offence to logic. It is, indeed, in the logical possibility of wanting *anything* (neutrally described) that the 'freedom' which is alluded to in my title essentially consists. And it is this, as we shall see, that lets by the person whom I shall call the 'fanatic'.

There is not, then, a complete analogy between the man who says 'There is no cat on the mat' when there is, and the man who wants things which others do not. But there is a partial analogy, which, having noticed this difference, we may be able to isolate. The analogy is between two relations: the relations between, in both cases, the 'mental state' of these men and what they say. If I believe that there is a cat on the mat I cannot sincerely say that there is not; and, if I want not to be put into prison more than I want anything else, I cannot sincerely say 'Let me be put into prison'. When, therefore, I said above 'His inclinations being what they are, he cannot assent sincerely to a certain singular prescription', I was making an analytic statement (although the 'cannot' is not a logical 'cannot'); for if he were to assent sincerely to the prescription, that would entail *ex vi terminorum* that his inclinations had changed— in the very same way that it is analytically true that, if the other man were to say sincerely that there was a cat on the mat, when before he had sincerely denied this, he must have changed his belief.

If, however, instead of writing 'His inclinations being what they are, he cannot . . .', we leave out the first clause and write simply 'He cannot . . .', the statement is no longer analytic; we are making a statement about his psychology which might be false. For it is logically possible for inclinations to change; hence it is possible for a man to come sincerely to hold an ideal which requires that he himself should be sent to a gas chamber if a Jew. That is the price we have to pay for our freedom. But, as we shall see, in order for reason to have a place in morals it is not necessary for us to close this way of escape by means of a logical barrier; it is sufficient that, men and the world being what they are, we can be very sure that hardly anybody is going to take it with his eyes open. And when we are arguing with one of the vast majority who are not going to take it, the reply that somebody else *might* take it does not help his case against us. In this respect, all moral arguments are *ad hominem.*

12

Moral Judgment and the Acceptance of Norms*

ALLAN GIBBARD

Allan Gibbard (b. 1942) is Professor of Philosophy at the University of Michigan. His book Wise Choices, Apt Feelings *is an important contemporary work of meta-ethics. This selection first appeared in* Ethics *(October 1985).*

Like A. J. Ayer (reading 10), Gibbard is a non-cognitivist—that is, someone who believes that ethical utterances do not attempt to state facts, and so are neither true nor false. However, unlike Ayer, Gibbard wants to develop a theory that situates morality within a larger account of human psychology and motivation. To do so, he first equates calling an act (or belief or feeling) rational with expressing acceptance of a norm that permits it. Next, he defines moral rightness and wrongness in terms of standards associated with certain sorts of norms. Very roughly, the idea is that if an agent accepts a norm that calls for him to feel guilty, and for others to condemn him, when he violates certain standards, then he acts wrongly when he fails to conform to those standards despite the absence of extenuating circumstances. To elucidate the crucial notion of accepting a norm, Gibbard appeals to the role of language in allowing us to "work out together reactions to an absent situation" and so develop "complex schemes of interpersonal cooperation." While much of Gibbard's discussion is highly programmatic, it opens up new possibilities for understanding how morality and rationality are related and the role that each plays in our lives.

In recent years, various ethical theorists have turned to considering the nature of rationality.[1] How, after all, might we best seek out a promising

---

* Much of this article is drawn from work done while I was a Fellow of the Center for Advanced Study in the Behavioral Sciences, with support from a National Endowment for the Humanities Fellowship for Independent Study and Research and from the Andrew W. Mellon Foundation.

1 I have in mind, among other people, Richard Brandt and aspects of recent work by R. M. Hare and John Rawls. See R. B. Brandt, *A Theory of the Good and the Right* (Oxford: Oxford University Press, 1979); R. M. Hare, *Moral Thinking: Its Levels, Method, and Point* (Oxford: Oxford University Press, 1981), esp. pt. 3; and John Rawls, "Kantian Constructivism in Moral Theory," *Journal of Philosophy* 77 (1980): 515–572.

line of approach to fundamental moral questions? A possible strategem is to ask first why moral questions matter. The chief reasons must surely lie in what their answers can tell us how to live—and in this response may lie hints of a way to proceed. Look for what, in a general prescription for living, plays the role of morality and take that itself to constitute morality. Deciding how to live, after all, is in effect deciding how it is rational to live. Begin, then, by developing a theory of rational conduct, and then in that theory, see if there is anything that fits our ordinary, vague picture of the demands of morality. If there is, call that morality—for whether or not it is what we initially conceived morality to be, it is what we can rationally treat in much the way we initially treated morality in our thinking.

This broad approach evidently requires a theory of rational conduct. What does it mean for something to be "rational"? To call a thing "rational" is to endorse it in some sense, and that in turn suggests a scheme for eliciting the meaning of 'rational'. Instead of seeking to define a property, "rationality," by giving the conditions under which a thing would have that property or lack it, start with the use of the term. Fix on the dictum "To call a thing rational is to endorse it" and search for a sense of the term 'endorse' for which the dictum holds true.

The word 'rational' has a learned flavor, but the concept I am tracking is familiar enough. It is the one we use when we talk about "what it makes sense" to do or to believe, or when we speak of actions as "reasonable" or "unreasonable," or when we search for the "best thing to do" in a way that does not presuppose that we are searching for the morally best thing to do. There does seem to be a common notion involved in all these turns of phrase; one test is that to affirm one of an action while denying another would be to invite puzzlement, not to invoke a distinction we could expect the audience to grasp antecedently. When we use the more learned term 'rational,' it is often this notion we are trying to apply.

I try in this article to give some inkling of a larger project. What I say will thus be sketchy and incomplete, but I hope it will suggest directions for thought. I begin by laying out some characteristics of rationality as it appears in ordinary thought, suitably refined. These are characteristics we might want an analysis of the term 'rational' to capture. I then turn to the relation of morality to rationality and develop a proposal that stems from Mill. Questions of morality, on this proposal, are questions concerning the rationality of certain specifically moral emotions: guilt and resentment. Only after this do I return to the concept of rationality and broach the analysis I want to combine with Mill's proposal. Cryptically put, the analysis is that to call something rational is to express one's acceptance of norms that permit it. That leaves much to be explained: among other things, what it is for a person to accept a norm. In the last part of the article I speculate on the psychological nature of the acceptance of norms. I sketch how the psychic mechanisms involved might be explained naturalistically; they can be understood, I suggest, as devices for interpersonal coordination. Normative discussion coordinates emotions and actions, and in the life of a social animal such coordination can be vital.

The analysis I broach is noncognitivistic, in the narrow sense that on the analysis, to call a thing "rational" is not straightforwardly to attribute a property to it, but to do something else. I have argued elsewhere that leading cognitivistic accounts of what 'rational' means fail; the same kinds of arguments as G. E. Moore used to discredit "naturalistic" definitions of moral terms apply to 'rational' as well.[2] I shall not repeat these arguments here, but I should say at the outset that what I say here presupposes that attempts to treat rationality as a straightforward property fail. They miss a crucial element of endorsement that the term connotes.

My analysis is not meant to capture a substantive view on the nature of rationality; rather it is meant to capture the common element in dispute when people disagree on the nature of rationality. It is supposed to tell us what it is to debate what is rational and to wonder what is rational. If I am right, deciding what sorts of things are rational is in effect deciding what norms to accept for a given domain of appraisal.

I. WHAT IS APPRAISED AS RATIONAL OR IRRATIONAL

In everyday life we appraise a wide variety of human attributes as "rational" or "irrational." Not only can a person act rationally or irrationally, but he can also believe rationally or irrationally, and he can be angry or grateful or envious rationally or irrationally. It is irrational, for example, to be angry at the messenger who brings bad tidings but rational to be angry at the miscreant who deliberately wrongs one. Or at least this, I take it, is what we tend to think in the normal course of life. If the word "rational" seems overly learned here, I suggest close substitutes with a more homely flavor: "It doesn't make sense" to be angry at the person who brings bad news he had no part in making. You "shouldn't be grateful" to someone who benefited you only inadvertently in seeking his own gain.

It is this family of appraisals I seek to interpret. Do they make genuine sense, and if so, how are they to be understood? If the term 'rational' can be applied intelligibly to as wide a range of human attributes as we seem to think, does it have the same meaning in all these contexts?

It might be thought that for something to be rational is for it to be desirable or advantageous. Such a crude pragmatism, though, would leave ordinary thought about rationality mysterious: it fits actions, perhaps, but not beliefs and attitudes. Take the stock example of the man who has some evidence his wife is unfaithful. Whether it is still *rational* for him to believe her faithful depends on his evidence, and on his evidence alone. Whether it is *desirable* for him to believe her faithful, and whether his believing her faithful is *good for him*, depend as well on how his beliefs would affect his feelings toward her. The rationality of a belief and its desirability, then, are different, if ordinary

---

2 See my "A Non-Cognitivistic Analysis of Rationality in Action," *Social Theory and Practice* 9 (1984): 199–221, esp. 200–206.

thought is to be trusted. Likewise, it might be disadvantageous for one of Cleopatra's courtiers to be angry at her, even if she ordered an execution unjustly, and it thus "made sense" to be angry at her. For the courtier might want to ingratiate himself with her, and he might rightly fear that anger would cloud his countenance and spoil his charm. In that case, he would have every reason to want not to be angry, and still, we seem to think, it would make sense for him to be angry. It made no like sense for Cleopatra to be angry at the slave who brought news of Anthony's defeat—however therapeutic or palliative her anger might have been. For anger to make sense is not for it to be advantageous.

In all this we must distinguish saying that it makes sense for a person *to be* angry from saying that it makes sense *that* the person *is* angry. If I have had a bad day and now face a new disappointment, it "makes sense that I am angry"—we can expect me to be angry in the circumstances, for reasons we understand—even if it doesn't "make sense for me to be angry" because the new disappointment is no one's fault. Likewise, it makes sense that Cleopatra was angry at the messenger, but it made no sense *for* her to be angry at him. Misdirected anger in the circumstances was to be expected, but the bad news was not the messenger's fault.

Are these ordinary distinctions truly intelligible? Can we really distinguish anger's making sense from anger's being desirable? If we understood the word 'rational,' we could put the distinction as follows. In the case of the courtier and the queen, even though it is rational for him to be angry with her for ordering an execution unjustly, it may also be rational for him to want to ingratiate himself with her, for his own good or for that of her subjects. If anger would prevent that, then it may be rational for him to *want* not to be angry with her. Thus in such a case, it is rational *to be angry* but also rational *to want not to be angry*. This pattern applies not only to emotion but also to belief. Take the stock case of a deceived husband: his evidence may make it rational for him *to believe* his wife unfaithful, but the way the belief would affect his feelings toward her may make it rational for him *to want to believe* her faithful. Rationally *feeling* or *believing* something is distinct from rationally *wanting* to feel or believe it.

Talk of emotions as "rational" or "irrational" will strike many readers as dubious. True, we may say the kinds of things I have been claiming we say: that it "makes sense to be angry" in certain cases and "it makes no sense to be angry" in others. It may still be asked, though, whether these judgments can bear scrutiny. It may well seem that we can appraise as rational or irrational only what is under a person's voluntary control. Emotions fail this test, since they are not under a person's direct voluntary control. True, they can be nurtured or repressed, but a person cannot simply be angry at will, or grateful at will. Nor can a person refrain from any of these things simply at will. What can be appraised as rational or irrational is not an emotion itself, it may be said, but taking measures to nurture or repress it.

Now I accept, of course, that emotions cannot be had or cast off at will. What I deny is the dictum "Only the voluntary can be appraised as rational or irrational." Beliefs seem prime examples of what we can appraise as rational or irrational, but beliefs, like emotions, cannot be had or cast off at will. We may be able to "make believe" at will, but that is not the same as really believing at will.

None of this is to say that when we call an act, belief, or emotion "rational" we are saying something intelligible; that remains to be seen. I am saying that we talk and think as if such appraisals are intelligible. It may be worthwhile, then, to see if we can interpret them as intelligible.

II. RATIONALITY AND MORALITY

Before I proceed to hunt for an account of what 'rational' means, I turn to morality and its relation to rationality. In what follows, I shall naively suppose that we know what 'rational' means; only later will I be broaching an analysis of the term.

In the history of moral philosophy, there seem to be at least two sharply different conceptions of what morality is. On what I shall call the "broad" conception, morality is simply practical rationality in the fullest sense: to say that an act is morally right is to say that it is rational. Kant and Sidgwick are prime exponents of this broad conception, which is shared by many current writers. On this conception, it makes no sense to ask, "Is it always rational to do what is morally right?" for 'the morally right' simply means "the rational." On a "narrow" conception of morality, in contrast, moral considerations are just some of the considerations that bear on what it makes sense to do. Nonmoral considerations matter too. On the narrow conception, for instance, it is normally wrong to injure others, to steal, or to break one's word. It would normally not be morally wrong, though, to fritter away a day for which one had planned an enjoyable hike—however irrational that might be. On the broad conception of morality, morally right action simply is action that is truly rational, whereas on the narrow conception, an act may be truly irrational without being morally wrong.

In chapter 5 of *Utilitarianism,* John Stuart Mill uses the term 'morality' in this narrow sense and offers an account of what is distinctive about "morality" so taken. "Morality," he says, "pertains to what is wrong or not wrong, and to say that an act is wrong is to say that there ought to be a sanction against it, a sanction of law, of public opinion, or of conscience." The 'ought' here, Mill proposes, should be judged by the standards of the greatest happiness principle—but that is part of Mill's normative theory, not his theory of meanings. What I propose to do is to take over Mill's analysis of what "morality" is in the narrow sense, with various interpretations and modifications.[3]

When Mill says there "ought" to be a sanction, let us read him as saying that a sanction is rational—or, perhaps, rationally required. Let us also drop

---

[3] It was David Lyons who brought Mill's theory to current philosophical attention in a series of articles. See esp. his "Mill's Theory of Morality," *Nous* 10 (1976): 101–120.

talk of legal sanctions. Suppose, say, we think that people who overpark at parking meters ought to be fined, but that they ought not to feel guilty and ought not to be resented by others for overparking. In that case, it seems to me, we do not think overparking morally wrong; we merely think that a price should be charged. That leaves sanctions of conscience and of public opinion: sanctions of guilt and remorse, on the one hand, and of blame, resentment, and moral outrage, on the other. Thus as the proposal now stands, what a person does is *morally wrong* if and only if it is rational for him to feel guilty for doing it, and for others to resent him for doing it.

As it stands, the analysis is more plausible for 'blameworthy' than for 'morally wrong.' The term 'wrong,' it is often said, has two distinct moral senses, the objective and the subjective. The difference between the two is displayed through stories like this: Yesterday, I had the brakes of my car checked. Today, I drive a friend to the supermarket, but on the way, my brakes fail and I kill a pedestrian. Driving my car, then, has turned out to be wrong in the "objective" sense, but not in the "subjective" sense—since I had every reason to think my brakes reliable, and my friend needed to get to the store. Thus an act is wrong in the objective sense if it is wrong in light of all the facts, knowable and unknowable, whereas it is wrong in the subjective sense if it is wrong in light of what the agent had good reason to believe. More precisely, an act is wrong in the subjective sense if it is wrong in light of the degrees of plausibility (or "subjective probabilities") the agent has reason to ascribe to relevant propositions.

Now the analysis I have proposed will clearly not work for 'wrong' in the objective sense. In the story, my driving my car turns out to be wrong in the objective sense, but it would not make sense for me to feel guilty over it, or for others to resent me for it. What about the subjective sense? It is this sense that really matters, for a theory for the subjective sense can offer moral guidance: even when we know we are ignorant of the relevant facts, we can use the theory, together with what we think we do know, to decide what acts to avoid on moral grounds.[4] Might the analysis I have proposed work, then, for 'wrong' in the subjective sense? Might an act be wrong in the subjective sense if and only if it is rational for the agent to feel guilty over the act and for others to resent him for it?

I think not. Wrongness, even in the subjective sense, is not the same as blameworthiness, and when the two diverge, the proposal seems most apt as an analysis of 'blameworthiness.'[5] Imagine that, in a paroxysm of grief, I speak rudely to a friend who offers condolences and so hurt his feelings. My rudeness is unprovoked but understandable in the circumstances. I have thus acted wrongly, but because of my agitated state, it may not make sense to blame

---

4 This is argued in my "Act-Utilitarian Agreements," in *Values and Morals,* eds. Alvin I. Goldman and Jaegwon Kim (Dordrecht: D. Reidel Publishing Co., 1978), pp. 95–96.

5 R. B. Brandt, in *Ethical Theory* (Englewood Cliffs, NJ: Prentice-Hall, 1959), argues that 'reprehensible' cannot be defined in terms of 'moral obligation' (p. 458) and then offers a definition of 'reprehensible' that is quite close, in some respects, to the one I am offering.

me. If it does not, then my act is wrong in the subjective sense, but not blameworthy. An act is *blameworthy*, we might say, if and only if it makes sense for the agent to feel guilty over it, and for others to resent him for it— but we still need to ask what it means to call an act "morally wrong."

Why, then, should we need a distinct concept of "wrong" in the subjective sense, as opposed to "blameworthy"? The answer seems to be that the concepts of "right" and "wrong" are forward looking in a way that the concept of blameworthiness is not. The morally conscientious agent is one who asks himself which of the acts open to him are right and which are wrong and then rules out any act he judges wrong. That means, among other things, that the rightness or wrongness of an alternative does not depend on the agent's motives. Rather, conscientious motivation consists in trying to confine one's actions to what is right. Blame, in contrast, attaches to the agent in retrospect; the agent is blamed for acting with insufficient morally desirable motivation. Rightness is prospective; blame is retrospective.

What, then, might it mean to call an act wrong? Roughly, we might say, the standards of right and wrong are the standards we demand an agent use to rule out certain alternatives. In assessing blame, we apply two kinds of tests. First, we ask whether the agent's level of morally desirable motivation was satisfactory. If not, we ask whether there are extenuating circumstances that render the agent not fully responsible. Standards of right and wrong pertain to the first part: an agent's motives are morally acceptable if he is sufficiently motivated to avoid wrong acts. Standards for wrongness, then, are the standards such that an agent is prima facie blameworthy if he does not use them to rule out acts that violate them. The reason the blameworthiness is only prima facie is that facts about the person's motivational state may be extenuating. Blame thus depends both on standards of wrongness in the subjective sense and on standards for responsibility. Formally put, then, the definitions I propose are these: an act is *wrong* if and only if it violates standards for ruling out actions, such that if an agent in a normal frame of mind violated those standards because he was not substantially motivated to conform to them, he would be to blame. To say that he would *be to blame*, here, is to say that it would be rational for him to feel guilty and for others to resent him.

What I have done in my discussion so far is to suppose that we know what 'rational' means and to propose a way of interpreting the relation between rationality, on the one hand, and concepts that are "moral" in the narrow sense. In the next section, I propose in rough terms an analysis of 'rational' and plug it into the analyses I have given these moral concepts.

III. AN ANALYSIS OF
'RATIONAL' APPLIED TO MORAL TERMS

What does it mean to call something "rational"? One way of tackling such a question is to psychologize it. What, we may ask, is the psychological state of regarding something as rational, of taking it to be rational, of believing it rational? The answer I want to give is noncognitivistic. To call an action, belief, or attitude "rational," if I am on the right track, is not to express a proposition; it is to do something else. What that "something else" is I shall try to explain psychologistically, by saying what it is to think something rational.

Put cryptically, the hypothesis I shall develop is this: that to *think something rational* is to accept norms that permit it. This rough analysis needs much elucidation and refinement, and I will not be able to say here nearly all I think should be said. I do hope to give you some intimation of what I hope can be done along the lines I am suggesting.

Take first my use of the word 'norm.' By a "norm" here, I mean a possible rule or prescription, either general or specific. The prescription need not actually be made by anyone, or accepted by anyone, to count as a "norm" as I am using the term; I am thus using the term as a short way of saying "possible norm." The main thing to be explained, then, is not what a "norm" is, but what "accepting a norm" is—or more precisely, what it is for something to be permitted or required by "the norms" a person "accepts." I mean these latter notions to be psychological: they are meant to figure in an explanatory theory of human experience and action.

Consider next some schematic illustrations. Delilah, let us suppose, is pondering whether various of Samson's acts, beliefs, and emotions are rational. What is it, on the proposal, for her to conclude that one of Samson's acts, beliefs, or emotions indeed is rational? It is for her to accept norms that, as applied to Samson's situation as she thinks it to be, permit that act, belief, or emotion. Thus when Samson destroys the Philistine temple, Delilah considers the act rational if and only if she accepts norms that permit—for Samson's situation as she takes it to be—destroying the temple. She might, for instance, accept the norm, "When in the hands of one's enemies with no hope of escape, kill as many of them as possible, even if you must kill yourself in the process." Then if she believes that Samson is in the hands of his enemies with no hope of escape and that destroying the temple will kill as many of his enemies as possible, then she considers his action rational. Earlier, Samson believed Delilah loyal to him. Delilah, then, thinks this belief to have been rational if and only if she accepts norms for belief that, for Samson's situation at the time as she now conceives it, permit believing one's woman loyal to one. Samson hates the Philistines, and Delilah considers his hatred rational if and only if she accepts norms that, for his situation, permit such hatred.

Nothing I have said here, I stress, speaks to whether Samson's actions, beliefs, and emotions really were rational. My hypothesis is not that a person's action, belief, or emotion really is rational if someone—be it I, or the person in question, or a commentator—accepts norms that prescribe it for that person's circumstances. It is not directly a hypothesis about what it is for something to be rational at all. It is a hypothesis about what it is to *think* or *believe* something rational, to *regard* it as rational, to *consider* it rational. An observer believes an action, belief, or emotion A of mine to be rational, the hypothesis is, if and only if he accepts norms that permit A for my circumstances. It follows that, if we want to decide what really is rational, we shall have to decide what norms to accept ourselves—for that is what it is to form an opinion as to the rationality of something.

To believe something rational, I have said, is to accept norms that permit it. In this cryptic form, the proposal says very little, and even what little it says will need to be refined and modified in various ways. Many of its problems I shall not be able to address here. I will, though, try to say a little about two sets of problems: first, what a norm is and what it is to accept one, and second, what distinguishes norms of rationality from other kinds of norms, such as norms of morality, norms of etiquette, and aesthetic norms.

I turn first to moral norms, and the narrowly moral notions, "blameworthy" and "wrong." In analyzing these notions in the previous section, I took the term 'rational' as understood. If we now combine these analyses with our rough analysis of 'rational,' we can derive an account of the distinction between moral norms and norms of rationality. All norms, we can say, are norms of rationality, but moral norms in particular are norms for guilt and resentment. Consider first what it is for an action to be "blameworthy." The analyses given so far tell us this: (1) An observer thinks an act blameworthy, or morally reprehensible, if and only if he thinks it rational for the agent to feel guilty over the act, and for others to resent the agent for it. (2) To think something 'rational' is to accept norms that prescribe it. Therefore, we may conclude, to think an act morally reprehensible is to accept norms that prescribe, for such a situation, guilt on the part of the agent and resentment on the part of others.

Next consider the term 'morally wrong' (in the subjective sense). The standards for whether an act is wrong, we have said, are the standards such that guilt and resentment are prima facie rational if the agent is not disposed to rule out alternatives that violate them. Thus to *think* an act *wrong* is to accept norms for guilt and resentment that, prima facie, would sanction guilt and resentment if the act were preformed. 'Prima facie' here means before questions of the psychological peculiarities of the agent are raised—the psychological peculiarities, that is, that bear on whether the agent is to be considered fully responsible. Norms for wrongness are thus explained in terms of norms for guilt and resentment.

This proposal as it stands smacks of circularity; the terms 'prima facie blameworthy' and 'responsible' seem to be defined in terms of each other. The psychic makeup of the agent, after all, has some bearing not only on whether the agent is responsible, but on what acts open to him are wrong. Suppose, for instance, that an act is the only one that is eligible, in the sense that all alternatives to it would leave the agent desperately unhappy. That fact may, in our opinion, tend to justify the act morally: it might be that even though the act would otherwise be wrong, this consideration renders it right. A moral adviser, after all, might sincerely advise the agent not to regard the action he was contemplating as wrong, even though it is of a kind that would normally be wrong, and do so precisely because of the psychological effects the alternatives would have on the agent. That, in any case, is what we might well think, and an analysis should allow for the possibility. In what ways, then, are we saying that the "psychological peculiarities" of an agent bear on his degree of moral responsibility, as opposed to the rightness and wrongness of the acts open to him? So far, there is no clear answer. Standards for responsibility, I have said, are standards for when an agent is to blame for acting on prima facie blameworthy motivations. Prima facie blameworthy motivations are motives for which an agent is to blame if he is fully responsible. Hence although 'blameworthy' itself has been defined independently, the terms 'prima facie blameworthy' and 'responsible' have been defined only in terms of each other.

This circularity, I think, can be eliminated as follows: consider an agent who has various psychological peculiarities, and an act for which I would consider the agent to blame if I thought him normal. Our problem, recall, is to untangle whether, because of his psychological peculiarities, I regard the act as right, or whether, rather, I consider the act to be wrong but excusable. The test I propose is this. Imagine the agent for the moment rendered normal but expecting to reacquire his "psychological peculiarities" once he had decided how to act on this occasion. He thus must take these psychological peculiarities into account in deciding what to do, though he is not presently subject to them apart from his belief that he has them. Whether I consider the act to be wrong, then, is a matter of whether I accept norms that would sanction guilt and resentment if the agent, while temporarily rendered normal, were to perform that act.

A moral norm forbidding an action, I have proposed, is a norm of rationality governing guilt and resentment. We might likewise speculate that all norms are primarily norms of rationality, and the various different kinds of norms governing, say, a given action—moral norms, aesthetic norms, norms of propriety—are each norms for the rationality of some one kind of attitude one can have toward an action. Just as moral norms are norms for the rationality of guilt and resentment, the aesthetic norms that apply to an action might be norms for the rationality of kinds of aesthetic appreciation of actions, and norms of propriety might be norms for the rationality of shock at an action. Norms of moral praiseworthiness, we can say, are norms for the rationality of an emotion of moral approbation. To call an action praiseworthy, on this proposal, is to say that it would make sense to feel moral approbation of the agent for having performed it. To say that, in turn, is to express one's acceptance of norms that permit that feeling, given the facts of the situation as one takes them to be.

IV. ACCEPTING A NORM AND BEING IN ITS GRIP

To think something rational, I have been proposing, is to accept norms that permit that thing. This is cryptic and incomplete in many ways, and I shall be able to take up just one central respect in which it is incomplete. The analysis as I have stated it gives the meaning of 'rational' in terms of another notion that has so far been left unexplained—in terms of a person's "accepting norms." This places great demands on the notion of accepting a norm.

The most straightforward way to elucidate the "acceptance of norms" would be further analysis: we might look for an analysis of what it means to say things like "Mary accepts the following norms: . . ." I doubt, though, that such an analysis is possible. Instead of trying for an analysis, I shall engage in incipient psychological theorizing. "Accepting a norm," I want to suggest, is a significant kind of psychological state that we are far from entirely understanding. What we can hope to do is not define this state precisely but to point to it.

Start by considering a case of "weakness of will." Suppose I "can't get myself to stop" eating nuts at a party. What is happening? One commonsense description is this: I think it "makes sense" to stop eating the nuts—indeed that it doesn't "make sense" to go on eating them—but I nevertheless go on. In this case, it seems, I accept a norm that prescribes eating no more nuts but go on eating them even so.

In this commonsense account, it is assumed that the acceptance of a norm is motivating, at least to a degree: believing I ought to stop tends to make me stop. On this occasion, though, the motivation that stems from my accepting a norm is "overpowered" by motivation of another kind: my craving or appetite for nuts. The craving is not itself a matter of my accepting norms; indeed such cravings are sometimes referred to as "animal": we think that they are motivations of a kind we share with beasts.

This is a picture of two motivational systems in conflict. One system is of a kind we think peculiar to human beings; it works through a person's accepting norms. We might call this kind of motivation *normative* motivation, and the putative psychological faculty involved the *normative control system*. The other putative system we might call the *animal control system*, since it, we think, is the part of our motivational system that we share with the beasts. Let us treat this picture as a vague psychological hypothesis.

"Weakness of will" involves conflict, and so far in my discussion, the conflict has been one between the norms a person accepts and an appetite. Many apparent cases of "weakness of will," though, are not of this kind. Often what we experience is not a conflict between the norms we accept and a bodily appetite but a conflict between our "better judgment" and powerful social motivations. We are paralyzed by embarrassment, or a desire to ingratiate, or some other motivation that is peculiarly social. Examples abound: I may be unable to get myself to walk out of a lecture, even though it is important for me to be somewhere else. I may find myself unable to say something that will be painful to my listener, even though I think it needs to be said. My discussion of "normative control" seems not to have addressed cases like these.

An especially powerful demonstration of the kind of conflict I have in mind lies in Milgram's series of experiments on compliance. Subjects of his experiments were told to administer electric shocks—shocks that were increasingly painful and eventually lethal—to another subject (who in fact was not being shocked but was acting as a confederate of the experimenter). Roughly two-thirds of the subjects eventually did all they were ordered to do, although they were upset and protested vigorously.[6]

---

6 Stanley Milgram, *Obedience to Authority* (New York: Harper & Row, 1974). A fascinating discussion of these experiments and their implications is to be found in John Sabini and Maury Silver, *Moralities of Everyday Life* (Oxford: Oxford University Press, 1982), esp. chaps. 3–5, 9–11.

Now when we read about these experiments, we are appalled by what the subjects did. Their actions violate norms that we accept. The near uniformity with which the subjects substantially acquiesced, however, should suggest to each of us, "Had I been a subject in one of these experiments before I first read or heard of them, I too would have cooperated with the experimenter—perhaps fully, and almost certainly more than I would like to acknowledge. I would have felt immensely disturbed about the situation in which I found myself, and I would have protested vigorously and regarded the experimenter as a madman. Nevertheless, I probably would have complied."

A typical subject in one of these experiments clearly experiences conflict of some sort; that is shown by his protests and his extreme agitation. The conflict, though, is not between a norm he accepts and a bodily appetite. It seems rather to be a conflict between one norm and another. The subject accepts the norm against intentional harm in terms of which we ourselves, as we read about the experiment, condemn his behavior. Nevertheless, he obeys an experimenter who tells him to violate that norm, and he does so, it would appear, because he is strongly motivated to be polite and cooperative—because to refuse, having originally agreed to participate in the experiment, would be uncooperative and insulting to the experimenter. The conflict, we might therefore say, is between opposing norms: a norm of nonharm, on the one hand, and norms of politeness and cooperativeness, on the other.

What is the role of norms here? The conflict is between one set of norms and another, true enough, but that suggests a symmetry that is specious. The two sets of norms play different psychological roles. The norm of noninfliction of harm prevails in the judgments of detached observers, whereas the norms of cooperativeness and politeness control the agent in the heat of social encounter. Ordinary language has devices that come close to labeling this contrast. We, as judges, accept a norm against infliction of harm and accept that this norm, in the situation of Milgram's subjects, overrides those norms of politeness and cooperativeness that we also accept. The subjects, on the other hand, do not genuinely accept that, in their situation, norms of politeness and cooperativeness override all other norms. Rather, we might say, they are *in the grip* of these norms. In common language, then, the contrast is between *accepting* a norm (or, more precisely, *accepting* that one set of norms outweighs another in a given situation) with *being in the grip* of a norm.

Now presumably, whatever happens when I am "in the grip" of a norm that I do not "accept" happens also, much of the time, when I do accept a norm. Take again our ordinary norms of politeness and cooperativeness. In my usual dealings with people, I not only accept these norms as having some weight; I accept them as having enough weight to override any conflicting norms that apply to my situation. I normally give people directions when asked, even if I am in a slight hurry, and this I do not out of weakness of will, but because I accept that it makes sense to help people who need it when the cost is small. In these cases, we would not say that I am "in the grip" of the norms of politeness and cooperativeness that guide my conduct, since I accept them as reasonably controlling in the situation. It may well be, though, that these norms would control my behavior even if I did not accept them or did not accept them as having greatest weight in my situation. In this respect, my psychological state is like the state of being in the grip of a norm.

We need, then, some term for what is common to situations in which I am "in the grip" of a norm and situations of the more usual kind: situations in which I accept a norm as rightly controlling on balance but would be in its grip if I did not. I propose the colorless, rather technical term *internalizing* a norm.

I have pointed to three sources of motivation that can be teased out of commonsense accounts of weakness of will: appetites, the internalization of norms, and the acceptance of norms. If there are distinctions of this kind to be drawn, how are they tied to ascriptions of rationality? I proposed that rationality has something to do with norms: to call something rational is to express one's acceptance of norms that, on balance, permit it. Once "accepting" a norm has been distinguished from "internalizing" it, we need to ask which of the two belongs in the analysis of 'rational.' Now in the examples, the answer seems clear: it is "accepting" norms that matters here, not "internalizing" them. What, after all, does a subject in one of Milgram's compliance experiments think it rational to do? If his plight is genuinely one of "weakness of will," that is presumably because he thinks that it makes no sense to cooperate but finds himself cooperating nevertheless. In other words, he does what he thinks irrational. Now what he actually does, in this case, is a matter of the norms that have him "in their grip"—norms of politeness and cooperativeness that he has internalized. What he thinks it "rational" to do, on the other hand, is what is required by norms against inflicting pain and danger—and these are the norms he "accepts" as having most weight in his situation. Thinking something rational or irrational thus seems to be a matter not of internalizing norms but of accepting them.

V. THE NATURE OF ACCEPTANCE

How might we explain the acceptance of norms as a psychological phenomenon? I shall only be able to give the briefest sketch of some lines for investigation that strike me as promising.

In the first place, I have distinguished "accepting" a norm from "internalizing" a norm, and so let me say briefly how I think we should understand internalizing a norm. The capacity to do so, I suggest, is one we share with other mammals, especially those who live in groups. Two dogs meeting on neutral ground will engage in elaborate "rituals," and this anthropomorphic language suggests that something akin to humans' internalizing norms may be in play. As in the human case, these animal interactions follow certain regular patterns, and the patterns seem, in a way, to have a rationale. They presumably constitute adaptations; that is to say, they are the result of natural selection favoring these patterns. Internalizing a norm, I suggest, involves tendencies toward action and emotion, tendencies that are coordinated with the tendencies of others in ways that constitute matched biological adaptations, or are the results of matched adaptations. We share the capacity to internalize norms with other animals, although the greater complexity of human social life may well mean that our capacities to internalize norms are more refined than those of any other animal.[7]

If that is what it is to "internalize" a norm, what is it to "accept" one? To understand acceptance, I suggest, we should look to language. Think of what language has to do with motivation, apart from simply making us aware of the states of affairs we confront. Although the most obvious function of language is to convey information, much of language is more than merely informative. Language is used to exhort, to criticize, and to summon up emotions. Language influences actions and emotions not only by conveying information that prompts those actions or emotions but in many other ways as well.

A central way in which language affects human motivation is by enabling people to share a picture of an absent situation. Reactions can then be shared— not only reactions to the immediate situation but to past, future, and hypothetical situations as well. Various kinds of reactions can be expressed in various ways: emotional responses can be shared simply by evincing them. Hypothetical decisions—decisions on what to do in the place of someone who is in the situation being discussed—can be expressed in language. Emotionally laden words can be used to label actions and characters. Explicit precepts can be formulated. Discussion, then, allows for shared evaluation.

A capacity for shared evaluation would be biologically fitness-enhancing in a species with a complex social life. Those who can work out together reactions to an absent situation—what to do and what to feel—are ready for similar situations. They are better prepared than they would otherwise be to do what is advantageous in a new situation, and they can rely on complex schemes of interpersonal coordination. On general evolutionary grounds, then, we might expect shared evaluation to figure centrally in a complex social life.

Working out, in community, what to do, what to think, and how to feel in absent situations, if it has these biological functions, must presumably influence what we do, think, and feel when faced with like situations. It is in such control of action, belief, and emotion, I suggest, that we can find a place for phenomena that constitute acceptance of norms, as opposed merely to internalizing them. When we work out at a distance, in community, what to do or think or feel in a situation we are discussing, we come to accept norms for the situation. This is the tentative hypothesis I want to propose; I shall be calling the discussion involved "normative discussion."

We evaluate in community, but part of what goes on is individual. Groups do, to be sure, reach normative consensus in many situations, but sometimes

---

7 The classic discussion of coordination in the broad sense I have in mind is Thomas Schelling, *The Strategy of Conflict* (Cambridge, MA: Harvard University Press, 1960), chap. 2. It is, of course, a theme that runs through the political theories of Hobbes and Hume. Matched adaptations are treated in John Maynard Smith's theory of "evolutionarily stable strategies" (see "The Evolution of Behavior," *Scientific American* 239 [1978]: 136–145, and *Evolution and the Theory of Games* [Cambridge: Cambridge University Press, 1982]).

they do not. Even when consensus is reached, it may well emerge from individuals' taking positions and then, to some degree, persuading each other. Acceptance of norms is tied not only to a consensus that emerges from normative discussion but also to individuals' taking positions in normative discussion. This taking of normative positions I shall call "normative avowal." By 'avowal' here I mean to include a wide range of kinds of expression we might count as taking a position in normative discussion—in the discussion of absent states of affairs. The simplest kind might simply be the evincing of an emotion toward an absent situation. Other kinds of avowal are linguistically more explicit: we may express a hypothetical decision in words or label an action in emotively charged words. To understand acceptance of norms, we need to look to such avowal—the kind of avowal from which consensus emerges when it does and which may persist even without approach to consensus.

What is the connection of avowal to acceptance? As a first approximation, we might say that to accept a norm is to be prepared to avow it in normative discussion—at least when the discussion is reasonably unconstrained, so that the avowal would be spontaneous rather than calculated. Acceptance, though, involves more than this; it involves a response to demands for consistency. Normative discussion consists of taking positions; even a conversational groan stakes out a position. Consensus may then be reached by a mechanism that is incipiently Socratic. Discussants hold each other to consistency in their positions and thus force each other to shift positions by exposing inconsistency. A person, then, must take positions in order to engage in normative discussion responsibly, and in doing so, he exposes himself to pressures toward consistency. To accept a norm, we might say, is to be disposed to avow it in unconstrained normative discussion, as a result of the workings of demands for consistency in the positions one takes in normative discussion.

To prepare oneself to meet demands for consistency requires a strong imaginative life. A person will engage in imaginative rehearsal for actual normative discussion; he practices by holding himself to consistency. I do not mean to suggest that the pressure for consistency will be as strong as it is in good philosophical discussion, but there will be some demand for consistency, and it may exert a significant pressure. From this imaginative rehearsal, a kind of imaginative persona may emerge, an "I" who develops a consistent position to take in normative discussion. It is then, perhaps, that we can speak more clearly of what the person accepts; he then has a worked out normative position to take in unconstrained contexts.

Why expose oneself to these demands for consistency? We do so naturally, but what selection pressures might have shaped us to do so? The answer should be clear from what I have said. The demands for consistency are reciprocal, and the system of mutual demands is part of a coordinating device. It is partly because of these mutual demands that there is any hope of reaching consensus in normative discussion. A person who refuses these demands must therefore be a poor candidate for cooperation of any kind—and in human life, cooperation is vital. It is fitness enhancing, then, to stand ready to engage in normative discussion and so to accept the demands for consistency that involves.

In the picture I have sketched, the difference between accepting a norm and internalizing it is this. Accepting a norm is something that we do primarily in the context of normative discussion, actual and imaginary. We take positions and thereby expose ourselves to demands for consistency. Normative discussion of a situation influences action and emotion in like situations. It is then that we can speak of norms as "governing" action and emotion, and it is through this governance that normative discussion serves to coordinate. The state of accepting a norm, then, is a syndrome of tendencies toward action and avowal—a syndrome produced by the language-infused system of coordination peculiar to human beings. The system works through discussion of absent situations, and it allows for the delicate adjustments of coordination that human social life requires. Internalizing a norm is also a matter of coordinating propensities, but propensities of a different kind: these propensities work independently of normative discussion.

VI. CONCLUDING REMARKS

There remains much to be done before the kind of analysis I am proposing could stand much chance of seeming plausible. To call something rational, I have proposed, is to express one's acceptance of a system of norms that permits that thing. I have speculated on the psychological nature of accepting norms, in an attempt to lend plausibility to my claim that there is such a state and that it plays an important part in human life. Many other things I have not discussed. I have not talked about what it is to express a state of mind—be it belief in a straightforwardly factual proposition or acceptance of a system of norms. I have not said how we can give the meaning of a term by talking about the state of mind a speaker expresses when he uses that term.

Other problems will no doubt leap to mind. An observer may accept many different norms that apply to a situation, and some of these norms may weigh in opposing directions. Norms of rationality apply to a person's subjective situation, in that facts a person has no way of knowing do not affect whether an action, belief, or attitude of his is rational. A person who contemplates the rationality of another person's acts, beliefs, or emotions normally does not take himself to know everything about the other person's situation. An explanation of what it is to think an act rational does not automatically yield an account of what is involved in thinking more complicated things about rationality, such as "Samson would never do anything so irrational as *that!*" Handling these considerations will require not only elucidation of the analysis but also elaboration and revision.

Moreover, I have said nothing here about a central problem for any theory of rationality: what constitutes the "objectivity" we sometimes want to attribute to judgments of rationality. Much of what is involved in claims of objectivity for normative judgments, I think, can be explained in terms of conversational demands in normative discussion. Normative discussion, as I have pictured it, is a communal activity: we subject ourselves to mutual influence and form a partial community of judgment. To put a judgment forth as objective, I want to say, is to make an appropriate response a requirement for membership in one's community of judgment—or at least this gives as much of ordinary claims to objectivity as is tenable.

All this, however, is for other occasions. What I have done here is to sketch part of a program. Moral judgments, I have suggested, concern the rationality of certain specifically moral emotions. To judge something rational is to accept a system of norms that permits it, in the circumstances as one thinks them to be. The psychological state of accepting a norm is partly to be understood in terms of the ways it underlies normative discussion. In biological terms, the capacities that underlie normative discussion are coordinating devices; they allow for the kinds of flexible, complex coordination that is peculiar to human social life. That is the rough hypothesis I have sketched in this paper, and I hope it is worth further exploration.

13

The Form and Content of Moral Judgments

DAVID BRINK

David Brink (b. 1958) is Associate Professor of Philosophy at the University of California at San Diego. This selection is from Chapter 2 of his book Moral Realism and the Foundations of Ethics.

Brink's target is the non-cognitivist view that ethical utterances are merely expressions of approval or disapproval or attempts to elicit behavior. A simple version of this view is advanced by A. J. Ayer in reading 10. Against it, Brink points out that one can perfectly well make a moral judgment without either expressing one's own feelings or trying to influence others. He also points out that expressive accounts do not work well when moral phrases are embedded in larger contexts. As an example, he cites the use of "wrong" in the sentence "one can be held responsible only for actions one could have known were wrong." If "wrong" is always used expressively, then an action's wrongness is not something that can be known. Hence, a non-cognitivist cannot take this sentence to assert that knowledge of the wrongness of one's acts is a necessary condition for responsibility. Instead, he must interpret it in some other way—for example, as "prescribing that people be held responsible only for actions against which they could have sincerely prescribed." But, according to Brink, neither this nor any other expressive rendering preserves the intent of the original. For these reasons, and also because expressive accounts leave no room for moral mistakes, Brink rejects Ayer's version of non-cognitivism. Whether his criticism also applies to more sophisticated versions such as Gibbard's (reading 12) is left for the reader to consider.

Moral realism and other cognitivist theories derive support from the form and content of our moral judgments. As many have observed, moral discourse is typically declarative or assertive in form. We say things like 'The government's tax plan is unfair', 'Waldo is just', 'It would be wrong to work for that cause', and 'My obligation to Maurice is greater than my obligation to Malcolm'. This language is putatively fact-stating (because it is declarative in form) and certainly seems to ascribe moral properties to persons, actions, policies, and so forth.

Our moral judgments not only have fact-stating and property-ascribing *form;* they have cognitivist *content* as well. Many common moral judgments themselves make reference to moral properties, moral facts, or moral knowledge. For instance, it is often claimed that one should not be held responsible for actions one could not have *known were wrong,* that *goodness* deserves reward, that the *turpitude* of a crime should determine the severity of punishment, and that *good* intentions do not always excuse. In making such moral judgments, we (or at least those who make them) certainly seem to presuppose the existence of moral facts and properties and the possibility of moral knowledge. The form and content of our moral judgments, therefore, presuppose cognitivism.

The form and content of our moral judgments also tell against those versions of moral relativism that claim that moral truth for someone is constituted by something like her sincere moral beliefs. We do not say that murder is wrong for Spike, unless by this we mean to imply only the nonrelativistic claim that Spike believes murder is wrong or the equally nonrelativistic claim that it is wrong for someone in Spike's circumstances to commit murder. Nor do we say that Spike should be held responsible only for those actions he could have known were wrong for him, unless, again, we mean by this only the nonrelativisitic claim that Spike should be held responsible only for those actions he could have known were wrong for someone in his circumstances.

If we reject moral realism (or any other antinoncognitivist and antirelativist metaethical view), it seems we must regard the form of our moral judgments as misleading and inappropriate. We can retain the declarative form of moral judgments only by treating these putative assertions of moral fact as something like disguised imperatives, prescriptions, or expressions of approval. We must treat putative assertions of moral fact, such as '*x* is wrong', as disguised expressions of the appraiser's disapproval of *x* or as disguised prescriptions to avoid *x*.

But it seems an open question whether the noncognitivist can account for the form and content of our moral judgments in this way. First, it seems that one can make moral judgments with no intention of expressing one's feelings and with no intention or even hope of influencing others' conduct. If asked about my own moral views, for example, I can reveal them by expressing moral judgments without, it seems, necessarily intending to express my approval or influence others. Someone might reply that if I really only intend to inform others what my moral views are in saying '*x* is wrong', then my claim reports only a nonmoral fact about what my moral views are and does not express a genuine moral judgment. But this seems to confuse what J. L. Austin distinguished as illocutionary and perlocutionary speech acts; the fact that I may hope to inform you of my moral views (and succeed in so informing you) by asserting '*x* is wrong' does not show that my assertion fails to express a moral judgment. Also, it seems we can conceive of the amoralist, that is, someone who recognizes certain considerations as moral considerations and yet remains unmoved by them and sees no reason to act on them.[1] An amoralist makes moral judgments with no intention of expressing his attitudes or of influencing the conduct of others. These noncognitivist paraphrases, therefore, seem inadequate to these actual and possible contexts in which people make moral judgments.

Second, it is still more difficult to see how the noncognitivist is going to account for the references to moral facts, moral properties, and moral knowledge embedded within many of our moral judgments. Can someone who denies the existence of moral properties, moral facts, and hence the possibility of moral knowledge continue to assert or even understand moral claims such as 'One can be held responsible only for actions one could have *known were wrong*' or 'The *turpitude* of a crime should determine the severity of punishment'? The noncognitivist might conclude that no one is ever responsible for her actions and that it is impossible to determine the severity of punishment appropriate to different crimes. I assume, however, that the noncognitivist will instead attempt to paraphrase or reconstruct these common moral judgments. But I have doubts about the adequacy, or at least the equivalence, of the reconstructions the noncognitivist can offer.

The noncognitivist might suggest that she who judges that the turpitude of a crime should determine the severity of punishment is, say, prescribing to others that the severity of punishment for a certain activity should be determined by the intensity with which she prescribes against engaging in that activity. But I am not sure how to gauge the intensity of a prescription, and I doubt that the intensity with which we prescribe against a particular kind of conduct should determine how severely we punish that conduct, if for no other reason than that we think that our own moral views might be mistaken and we think that punishment should track the actual turpitude of the crime and not our beliefs or attitudes to the crime (should these diverge).

Concerning our other example, deriving from the M'Naghten Rule, the noncognitivist may suggest that because moral knowledge is, strictly speaking, impossible, she who judges that one can be held responsible only for actions one could have known were wrong is really doing something like prescribing that people be held accountable only for actions against which they could have sincerely prescribed. (The relevant sense of 'possibility' or 'capacity' in both the original and reconstructed claims is, of course, a kind of psychological possibility or capacity.) But I doubt that the capacity to prescribe against an action is, as I do think the cognitive capacity to know that an action is wrong is, a necessary condition for responsibility or culpability, if only because this reconstruction would allow amoralists to avoid responsibility. At any rate, the original claim and reconstructed claim are not equivalent, as the case of the amoralist shows. Or suppose the noncognitivist suggests we reinterpret the original claim as the claim that we should not hold people responsible for actions unless they could have known that their actions had those nonmoral

---

1 Noncognitivists deny, explicitly or implicitly, the existence of the amoralist. But this is a defect, not a defense, of noncognitivism.

characteristics by virtue of which we think such actions wrong. But this won't do either. Consider Zenobia's case. The actions Zenobia thinks are wrong (i.e., prescribes against) all have nonmoral characteristic C, and she thinks them wrong because they have C. Can Zenobia's claim that people should be held responsible only for things they could have known were wrong really be analyzed as the claim that people should be held responsible only for actions that they could have seen possessed C? One reason this won't do is that people might be able to recognize C but not (be able to) recognize C as a wrong-making characteristic (this is true of certain psychopaths), and although the original claim absolves them of responsibility (although they may still require detention and treatment), the reconstructed claim does not. The noncognitivist might avoid this inequivalence by understanding Zenobia's claim as follows: People are to be held responsible only for actions that they could have seen were C *and* that they could or would have prescribed against. But this reintroduces the inequivalence between the original and reconstructed claims that the amoralist's case demonstrates. Moreover, there is still the problem that this ties the content of the reconstructed principle to Zenobia's criteria of wrong-making in a way in which the original claim does not. Zenobia would want to allow that her moral views might be mistaken and that there are wrong-making characteristics different from, or in addition to, C and that people should be held responsible only if they could have known that their actions were in fact wrong and not merely believed by Zenobia to be wrong (should these diverge). In this way the reconstructed claim will absolve some people whom the original claim would not have absolved (i.e., those who hold correct moral views, contrary to those of the person holding or asserting the reconstructed moral claim).

Hence I find it hard to believe in the adequacy of noncognitivist reconstructions of the apparent cognitive character of the form and content of moral judgments; they seem unable to capture the actual content of our moral judgments. If so, then it is not clear that noncognitivists can make (all of) the moral judgments contained in commonsense moral thinking and available to the moral realist. Perhaps the form and content of our moral judgments are systematically misleading in some way, but this claim should be accepted only as the conclusion of a compelling philosophical argument.

THE EXISTENCE OF RIGHT ANSWERS IN ETHICS

Commonsense moral thinking also supports moral realism insofar as we act as if there are moral facts. This is true in both intrapersonal and interpersonal contexts. We often *recognize* the existence of moral requirements that constrain our conduct in certain ways. And when we are uncertain about moral issues, we often *deliberate* as if there were a right answer to the issue before us. At other times, we disagree and argue with others as if there were right answers to the moral issues about which we disagree. About some moral issues, of course, we are unsure what to think, and sometimes, when we do have moral views, we do not hold them all that confidently. But about many moral issues we have fairly firm views. We can and do argue with others about these issues. We examine the moral and nonmoral beliefs that underlie our disagreement. If our dispute is genuine and we see no reason to give up our position, we regard the other parties to the dispute as mistaken. If our dispute is not the result of nonmoral disagreement, we regard our opponents as *morally mistaken*. Indeed, the possibility of moral mistakes is explained by a thesis often taken to have antirealist implications, namely, the is/ought thesis. I shall discuss the is/ought thesis at greater length in Chapter 6. But one of the ideas originally behind it is that there can be disagreement between persons and the possibility of error even once all the nonmoral facts are in or agreed on.

If moral mistakes are possible, then moral argument and deliberation are intellectual activities that, at least in principle, always make sense. This is so even if there are good reasons for terminating argument or deliberation, say, because we regard further argument as unprofitable or unfriendly.

Noncognitivist theories such as emotivism or prescriptivism underplay the possibilities for moral mistakes and so for moral argument and deliberation. Of course, noncognitivist theories allow room for deliberation about moral issues. According to the noncognitivist, we can argue about those nonmoral matters upon which, as a matter of psychological fact, our moral attitudes and commitments depend, and we can deliberate about the logical consistency and coherence of our attitudes and commitments. But the point of *moral* argument, as opposed to argument about what is sometimes called "logic or the (nonmoral) facts," according to these views, is to change the attitudes or commitments of one's interlocutor, not to establish truth. No sense can be made of being wrong in one's consistent and informed attitudes or commitments.

Noncognitivists do sometimes try to allow for the possibility of mistaken attitudes. The suggestion is usually that an individual's attitude or set of attitudes, say, the set consisting of an aversion to poetry and an affinity for push-pin, is mistaken (1) if the individual actually possesses a second-order attitude, say, the desire to cultivate intellectual attitudes, which conflicts with this set of first-order attitudes, or (2) if the individual would come to possess such a second-order attitude were she to acquire more nonmoral information (e.g., more experience reading difficult poetry). We might wonder why either condition should be taken to show that the first-order attitude or set of attitudes is *mistaken*. Why doesn't (1) simply establish conflict within the individual's attitudes, and, if it must be taken to reveal mistaken attitudes, why not conclude that the second-order attitude is the mistaken one? Does (2) establish anything more than that the individual's first-order attitudes are revisable? In any case, neither condition (1) nor condition (2) adds anything to the picture of mistaken attitudes that I have not already conceded; (1) reveals inconsistent attitudes, and (2) reveals insufficiently informed attitudes. The noncognitivist still has no explanation of how fully informed and consistent, yet mistaken (perhaps monstrously mistaken), attitudes are possible. If one's moral judgments express a consistent and well informed set of attitudes or commitments, then, according to the noncognitivist, the question of the correctness of those attitudes or commitments does not arise and no sense can be attached to moral deliberation. But we do think that some actual and possible sets of attitudes are fully informed (as to the nonmoral facts) and consistent, yet wrong, and we do sometimes want to know which attitude or commitment of those we could (in consistency) have is the correct one or the one worth having.

14

Euthyphro

PLATO

For biographical information about Plato, see reading 2.

In this dialogue, Plato discusses the relation between morality and the gods. The topic is important because many believe that God is the source of moral principles. As Hare observes in reading 11, moral principles are prescriptive and thus resemble laws or commands. Hence it is tempting to trace them to some commander or lawgiver. But no ordinary person has the authority to issue binding moral commands. Thus it is natural to suppose that the moral lawgiver is divine.

But Plato's argument implies that this cannot be correct. Through his spokesman Socrates, Plato examines the beliefs of Euthyphro, who intends to proscecute his own father for killing a servant. In defense of this, Euthyphro insists that prosecuting murderers is pious because such actions are loved by the gods. But Socrates goes further and asks why the gods love the actions that they do. If they have no reasons, then their love is arbitrary. Yet if they do have reasons, then the actions are not pious because they are loved by the gods. Instead, the acts are loved by the gods because they are pious. If this argument is successful, a similar argument will show that acts are not made right simply by God's commands.

EUTHYPHRO: What's new, Socrates, to make you leave your usual haunts in the Lyceum and spend your time here by the king-archon's court. Surely you are not prosecuting any one before the king archon as I am?

SOCRATES: The Athenians do not call this a prosecution but an indictment, Euthyphro.

E: What is this you say? Someone must have indicted you, for you are not going to tell me that you have indicted someone else.

S: No indeed.

E: But someone else has indicted you?

S: Quite so.

E: Who is he?

S: I do not really know myself, Euthyphro. He is apparently young and unknown. They call him Meletus, I believe. He belongs to the Pitthean deme, if you know anyone from that deme called Meletus, with long hair, not much of a beard, and a rather acquiline nose.

E: I don't know him, Socrates. What charge does he bring against you?

S: What charge? A not ignoble one I think, for it is no small thing for a young man to have knowledge of such an important subject. He says he knows how our young men are corrupted and who corrupts them. He is likely to be wise, and when he sees my ignorance corrupting his contemporaries, he proceeds to accuse me to the city as to their mother. I think he is the only one of our public men to start out the right way, for it is right to care first that the young should be as good as possible, just as a good farmer is likely to take care of the young plants first, and of the others later. So, too, Meletus first gets rid of us who corrupt the growth of the young, as he says, and then afterwards he will obviously take care of the older and become a source of great blessings for the city, as seems likely to happen to one who started out this way.

E: I could wish this were true, Socrates, but I fear the opposite may happen. He seems to me to start out by harming the very heart of the city by attempting to wrong you. Tell me, what does he say you do to corrupt the young?

S: Strange things, to hear him tell it, for he says that I am a maker of gods, that I create new gods while not believing in the old gods, and he has indicted me for this very reason, as he puts it.

E: I understand, Socrates. This is because you say that the divine sign keeps coming to you. So he has written this indictment against you as one who makes innovations in religious matters, and he comes to court to slander you, knowing that such things are easily misrepresented to the crowd. The same is true in my case. Whenever I speak of divine matters in the assembly and foretell the future, they laugh me down as if I were crazy; and yet I have foretold nothing that did not happen. Nevertheless, they envy all of us who do this. One need not give them any thought, but carry on just the same.

S: My dear Euthyphro, to be laughed at does not matter perhaps, for the Athenians do not mind anyone they think clever, as long as he does not teach his own wisdom, but if they think that he makes others to be like himself they get angry, whether through envy, as you say, or for some other reason.

E: I have certainly no desire to test their feelings toward me in this matter.

S: Perhaps you seem to make yourself but rarely available, and not to be willing to teach your own wisdom, but my liking for people makes them think that I pour out to anybody anything I have to say, not only without charging a fee but appearing glad to reward anyone who is willing to listen. If then they were intending to laugh at me, as you say they laugh at you, there would be nothing unpleasant in their spending their time in court laughing and jesting, but if they are going to be serious, the outcome is not clear except to you prophets.

E: Perhaps it will come to nothing, Socrates, and you will fight your case as you think best, as I think I will mine.

S: What is your case, Euthyphro? Are you the defendant or the prosecutor?

E: The prosecutor.

s: Whom do you prosecute?

E: One whom I am thought crazy to prosecute.

s: Are you pursuing someone who will easily escape you?

E: Far from it, for he is quite old.

s: Who is it?

E: My father.

s: My dear sir! Your own father?

E: Certainly.

s: What is the charge? What is the case about?

E: Murder, Socrates.

s: Good heavens! Certainly, Euthyphro, most men would not know how they could do this and be right. It is not the part of anyone to do this, but of one who is far advanced in wisdom.

E: Yes by Zeus, Socrates, that is so.

s: Is then the man your father killed one of your relatives? Or is that obvious, for you would not prosecute your father for the murder of a stranger.

E: It is ridiculous, Socrates, for you to think that it makes any difference whether the victim is a stranger or a relative. One should only watch whether the killer acted justly or not; if he acted justly, let him go, but if not, one should prosecute, even if the killer shares your hearth and table. The pollution is the same if you knowingly keep company with such a man and do not cleanse yourself and him by bringing him to justice. The victim was a dependent of mine, and when we were farming in Naxos he was a servant of ours. He killed one of our household slaves in drunken anger, so my father bound him hand and foot and threw him in a ditch, and then sent a man here to enquire from the priest what should be done. During that time he gave no thought or care to the bound man, as being a killer, and it was no matter if he died, which he did. Hunger and cold and his bonds caused his death before the messenger came back from the seer. Both my father and my other relatives are angry that I am prosecuting my father for murder on behalf of a murderer, as he did not even kill him. They say that such a victim does not deserve a thought and that it is impious for a son to prosecute his father for murder. But their ideas of the divine attitude to piety and impiety are wrong, Socrates.

s: Whereas, by Zeus, Euthyphro, you think that your knowledge of the divine, and of piety and impiety, is so accurate that, when those things happened as you say, you have no fear of having acted impiously in bringing your father to trial?

E: I should be of no use, Socrates, and Euthyphro would not be superior to the majority of men, if I did not have accurate knowledge of all such things.

s: It is indeed most important, my admirable Euthyphro, that I should become your pupil, and as regards this indictment challenge Meletus about these very things and say to him: that in the past too I considered knowledge about the divine to be most important, and that now that he says that I improvise and innovate about the gods I have become your pupil. I would say to him: "If, Meletus, you agree that Euthyphro is wise in these matters, consider me, too, to have the right beliefs and do not bring me to trial. If you do not think so, then prosecute that teacher of mine for corrupting the older men, me and his own father, by teaching me and by exhorting and punishing him." If he is not convinced, does not discharge me, or indicts you instead of me, I shall repeat the same challenge in court.

E: Yes by Zeus, Socrates, and, if he should try to indict me, I think I would find his weak spots and the talk in court would be about him rather than about me.

S: It is because I realize this that I am eager to become your pupil, my dear friend. I know that other people as well as this Meletus do not even seem to notice you, whereas he sees me so sharply and clearly that he indicts me for ungodliness. So tell me now, by Zeus, what you just now maintained you clearly knew: what kind of thing do you say that godliness and ungodliness are, both as regards murder and other things; or is the pious not the same and alike in every action, and the impious the opposite of all that is pious and like itself, and everything is to be impious presents us with one form or appearance in so far as it is impious.

E: Most certainly, Socrates.

S: Tell me then, what is the pious, and what the impious, do you say?

E: I say that the pious is to do what I am doing now, to prosecute the wrongdoer, be it about murder or temple robbery or anything else, whether the wrongdoer is your father or your mother or anyone else; not to prosecute is impious. And observe, Socrates, that I can quote the law as a great proof that this is so. I have already said to others that such actions are right, not to favour the ungodly, whoever they are. These people themselves believe that Zeus is the best and most just of the gods, yet they agree that he bound his father because he unjustly swallowed his sons, and that he in turn castrated his father for similar reasons. But they are angry with me because I am prosecuting my father for his wrongdoing. They contradict themselves in what they say about the gods and about me.

S: Indeed, Euthyphro, this is the reason why I am a defendant in the case, because I find it hard to accept things like that being said about the gods, and it is likely to be the reason why I shall be told I do wrong. Now, however, if you, who have full knowledge of such things, share their opinions, then we must agree with them, too, it would seem. For what are we to say, we who agree that we ourselves have no knowledge? Tell me, by the god of friendship, do you really believe these things are true?

E: Yes, Socrates, and so are even more surprising things, of which the majority has no knowledge.

S: And do you believe that there really is war among the gods, and terrible emmities and battles, and other such things as are told by the poets, and other sacred stories such as are embroidered by good writers and by representations of which the robe of the goddess is adorned when it is carried up to the Acropolis? Are we to say these things are true, Euthyphro?

E: Not only these, Socrates, but, as I was saying just now, I will, if you wish, relate many other things about the gods which I know will amaze you.

s : I should not be surprised, but you will tell me these at leisure some other time. For now, try to tell me more clearly what I was asking just now, for, my friend, you did not teach me adequately when I asked you what the pious was, but you told me that what you are doing now, to prosecute your father for murder, is pious.

E : And I told the truth, Socrates.

s : Perhaps. You agree, however, that there are many other pious actions.

E : There are.

s : Bear in mind then that I did not bid you tell me one or two of the many pious actions but that form itself that makes all pious actions pious, for you agreed that all impious actions are impious and all pious actions pious through one form, or don't you remember?

E : I do.

s : Tell me then what form itself is, so that I may look upon it, and using it as a model, say that any action of yours or another's that is of that kind is pious, and if it is not that it is not.

E : If that is how you want it, Socrates, that is how I will tell you.

s : That is what I want.

E : Well then, what is dear to the gods is pious, what is not is impious.

s : Splendid, Euthyphro! You have now answered in the way I wanted. Whether your answer is true I do not know yet, but you will obviously show me that what you say is true.

E : Certainly.

s : Come then, let us examine what we mean. An action or a man dear to the gods is pious, but an action or a man hated by the gods is impious. They are not the same, but opposites, the pious and the impious. Is that not so?

E : It is indeed.

s : And that seems to be a good statement?

E : I think so, Socrates.

s : We have also stated that the gods are in a state of discord, that they are at odds with each other, Euthyphro, and that they are at enmity with each other. That too has been said.

E : It has.

s : What are the subjects of difference that cause hatred and anger? Let us look at it this way. If you and I were to differ about numbers as to which is the greater, would this difference make us enemies and angry with each other, or would we proceed to count and soon resolve our difference about this?

E : We would certainly do so.

s : Again, if we differed about the larger and the smaller, we would turn to measurement and soon cease to differ.

E : That is so.

s : And about the heavier and the lighter, we would resort to weighing and be reconciled.

E : Of course.

s: What subject of difference would make us angry and hostile to each other if we were unable to come to a decision? Perhaps you do not have an answer ready, but examine as I tell you whether these subjects are the just and the unjust, the beautiful and the ugly, the good and the bad. Are these not the subjects of difference about which, when we are unable to come to a satisfactory decision, you and I and other men become hostile to each other whenever we do.

e: That is the difference, Socrates, about those subjects.

s: What about the gods, Euthyphro? If indeed they have differences, will it not be about these same subjects?

e: It certainly must be so.

s: Then according to your argument, my good Euthyphro, different gods consider different things to be just, beautiful, ugly, good and bad, for they would not be at odds with one another unless they differed about these subjects, would they?

e: You are right.

s: And they like what each of them considers beautiful, good, and just, and hate the opposites of these?

e: Certainly.

s: But you say that the same things are considered just by some gods and unjust by others, and as they dispute about these things they are at odds and at war with each other. Is that not so?

e: It is.

s: The same things then are loved by the gods and hated by the gods, both god-loved and god-hated.

e: It seems likely.

s: And the same things would be both pious and impious, according to this argument?

e: I'm afraid so.

s: So you did not answer my question, you surprising man. I did not ask you what same thing is both pious and impious, and it appears that what is loved by the gods is also hated by them. So it is in no way surprising if your present action, namely punishing your father, may be pleasing to Zeus but displeasing to Kronos and Ouranos, pleasing to Hephaestus but displeasing to Hera, and so with any other gods who differ from each other on this subject.

e: I think, Socrates, that on this subject no gods would differ from one another, that whoever has killed anyone unjustly should pay the penalty.

s: Well now, Euthyphro, have you ever heard any man maintaining that one who has killed or done anything else unjustly should not pay the penalty?

e: They never cease to dispute on this subject, both elsewhere and in the courts, for when they have committed many wrongs they do and say anything to avoid the penalty.

s: Do they agree they have done wrong, Euthyphro, and in spite of so agreeing do they nevertheless say they should not be punished?

e: No, they do not agree on that point.

s: So they do not say or do anything. For they do not venture to say this, or dispute that they must not pay the penalty if they have done wrong, but I think they deny doing wrong. Is that not so?

e: That is true.

s: Then they do not dispute that the wrongdoer must be punished, but they may disagree as to who the wrongdoer is, what he did and when.

e: You are right.

s: Do not the gods have the same experience, if indeed they are at odds with each other about the just and the unjust, as your argument maintains? Some assert that they wrong one another, while others deny it, but no one among gods or men ventures to say that the wrongdoer must not be punished.

e: Yes, that is true, Socrates, as to the main point.

s: And those who disagree, whether men or gods, dispute about each action, if indeed the gods disagree. Some say it is done justly, others unjustly. Is that not so?

e: Yes indeed.

s: Come now, my dear Euthyphro, tell me, too, that I may become wiser, what proof you have that all the gods consider that man to have been killed unjustly who became a murderer while in your service, was bound by the master of his victim, and died in his bonds before the one who bound him found out from the seers what was to be done with him, and that it is right for a son to denounce and to prosecute his father on behalf of such a man. Come, try to show me a clear sign that all the gods definitely believe this action to be right. If you can give me adequate proof of this, I shall never cease to extol your wisdom.

e: This is perhaps no light task, Socrates, though I could show you very clearly.

s: I understand that you think me more dull-witted than the jury, as you will obviously show them that these actions were unjust and that all the gods hate such actions.

e: I will show it to them clearly, Socrates, if only they will listen to me.

s: They will listen if they think you show them well. But this thought came to me as I was speaking, and I am examining it, saying to myself: "If Euthyphro shows me conclusively that all the gods consider such a death unjust, to what greater extent have I learned from him the nature of piety and impiety? This action would then, it seems, be hated by the gods, but the pious and the impious were not thereby now defined, for what is hated by the gods has also been shown to be loved by them." So I will not insist on this point; let us assume, if you wish, that all the gods consider this unjust and that they all hate it. However, is this the correction we are making in our discussion, that what all the gods hate is impious, and what they all love is pious, and that what some gods love and others hate is neither or both? Is that how you now wish us to define piety and impiety?

e: What prevents us from doing so, Socrates?

s: For my part nothing, Euthyphro, but you look whether on your part this proposal will enable you to teach me most easily what you promised.

E: I would certainly say that the pious is what all the gods love, and the opposite, which all the gods hate, is the impious.

S: Then let us again examine whether that is a sound statement, or do we let it pass, and if one of us, or someone else, merely says that this is so, do we accept that it is so? Or should we examine what the speaker means?

E: We must examine it, but I certainly think that this is now a fine statement.

S: We shall soon know better whether it is. Consider this: Is the pious loved by the gods because it is pious, or is it pious because it is loved by the gods?

E: I don't know what you mean, Socrates.

S: I shall try to explain more clearly; we speak of something being carried and something carrying, of something being led and something leading, of something being seen and something seeing, and you understand that these things are all different from one another and how they differ?

E: I think I do.

S: So there is something being loved and something loving, and the loving is a different thing.

E: Of course.

S: Tell me then whether that which is (said to be) being carried is being carried because someone carries it or for some other reason.

E: No, that is the reason.

S: And that which is being led is so because someone leads it, and that which is being seen because someone sees it?

E: Certainly.

S: It is not seen by someone because it is being seen but on the contrary it is being seen because someone sees it, nor is it because it is being led that someone leads it but because someone leads it that it is being led; nor does someone carry an object because it is being carried, but it is being carried because someone carries it. Is what I want to say clear, Euthyphro? I want to say this, namely, that if anything comes to be, or is affected, it does not come to be because it is coming to be, but it is coming to be because it comes to be; nor is it affected because it is being affected but because something affects it. Or do you not agree?

E: I do.

S: What is being loved is either something that comes to be or something that is affected by something?

E: Certainly.

S: So it is in the same case as the things just mentioned; it is not loved by those who love it because it is being loved, but it is being loved because they love it?

E: Necessarily.

S: What then do we say about the pious, Euthyphro? Surely that is loved by all the gods, according to what you say?

E: Yes.

S: Is it loved because it is pious, or for some other reason?

E: For no other reason.

S: It is loved then because it is pious, but it is not pious because it is loved.

E: Apparently.

S: And because it is loved by the gods it is being loved and is dear to the gods?

E: Of course.

S: The god-beloved is then not the same as the pious, Euthyphro, nor the pious the same as the god-beloved, as you say it is, but one differs from the other.

E: How so, Socrates?

S: Because we agree that the pious is beloved for the reason that it is pious, but it is not pious because it is loved. Is that not so?

E: Yes.

S: And that the god-beloved, on the other hand, is so because it is loved by the gods, by the very fact of being loved, but it is not loved because it is god-beloved.

E: True.

S: But if the god-beloved and the pious were the same, my dear Euthyphro, and the pious were loved because it was pious, then the god-beloved would be loved because it was god-beloved, and if the god-beloved was god-beloved because it was loved by the gods, then the pious would also be pious because it was loved by the gods; but now you see that they are in opposite cases as being altogether different from each other: the one is of a nature to be loved because it is loved, the other is loved because it is of a nature to be loved. I'm afraid, Euthyphro, that when you were asked what piety is, you did not wish to make its nature clear to me, but you told me an affect or quality of it, that the pious has the quality of being loved by all the gods, but you have not yet told me what the pious is. Now, if you will, do not hide things from me but tell me again from the beginning what piety is, whether loved by the gods or having some other quality—we shall not quarrel about that—but be keen to tell me what the pious and the impious are.

E: But Socrates, I have no way of telling you what I have in mind, for whatever proposition we put forward goes around and refuses to stay put where we establish it.

S: Your statements, Euthyphro, seem to belong to my ancestor, Daedalus. If I were stating them and putting them forward, you would perhaps be making fun of me and say that because of my kinship with him my conclusions in discussion run away and will not stay where one puts them. As these propositions are yours, however, we need some other jest, for they will not stay put for you, as you say yourself.

E: I think the same jest will do for our discussion, Socrates, for I am not the one who makes them go round and not remain in the same place; it is you who are the Daedalus; for as far as I am concerned they would remain as they were.

S: It looks as if I was cleverer than Daedalus in using my skill, my friend, in so far as he could only cause to move the things he made himself, but I can make other people's move as well as my own. And the smartest part of my skill is that I am clever without wanting to be, for I would rather have my arguments remain unmoved than possess the wealth of Tantalus as well as the cleverness of Daedalus. But enough of this. Since I think you are making unnecessary difficulties, I am as eager as you are to find a way to teach me about piety, and do not give up before you do. See whether you think all that is pious is of necessity just.

E: I think so.

S: And is then all that is just pious? Or is all that is pious just, but not all that is just pious, but some of it is and some is not?

E: I do not follow what you are saying, Socrates.

S: Yet you are younger than I by as much as you are wiser. As I say, you are making difficulties because of your wealth of wisdom. Pull yourself together, my dear sir, what I am saying is not difficult to grasp. I am saying the opposite of what the poet said who wrote:

> You do not wish to name Zeus, who had done it, and who made all things grow, for where there is fear there is also shame.

I disagree with the poet. Shall I tell you why?

E: Please do.

S: I do not think that "where there is fear there is also shame," for I think that many people who fear disease and poverty and many other such things feel fear, but are not ashamed of the things they fear. Do you not think so?

E: I do indeed.

S: But where there is shame there is also fear. Does anyone feel shame at something who is not also afraid at the same time of a reputation for wickedness?

E: He is certainly afraid.

S: It is then not right to say "where there is fear there is also shame," but that where there is shame there is also fear, for fear covers a larger area than shame. Shame is a part of fear just as odd is a part of number, with the result that it is not true that where there is number there is also oddness, but that where there is oddness there is also number. Do you follow me?

E: Surely.

S: This is the kind of thing I was asking before, whether where there is piety there is also justice, but where there is justice there is not always piety, for the pious is a part of justice. Shall we say that, or do you think otherwise?

E: No, but like that, for what you say appears to be right.

S: See what comes next; if the pious is a part of the just, we must, it seems, find out what part of the just it is. Now if you asked me something of what we mentioned just now, such as what part of number is the even, and what number that is, I would say it is the number that is divisible into two equal, not unequal, parts. Or do you not think so?

E: I do.

S: Try in this way to tell me what part of the just the pious is, in order to tell Meletus not to wrong us any more and not to indict me for ungodliness, since I have learned from you sufficiently what is godly and pious and what is not.

E: I think, Socrates, that the godly and pious is the part of the just that is concerned with the care of the gods, while that concerned with the care of men is the remaining part of justice.

S: You seem to me to put that very well, but I still need a bit of information. I do not know yet what you mean by care, for you do not mean it in the sense as the care of other things, as, for example, not everyone knows how to care for horses, but the horse breeder does.

E: Yes, I do mean it that way.

S: So horse breeding is care of horses.

E: Yes.

S: Nor does everyone know how to care for dogs, but the hunter does.

E: That is so.

S: So hunting is the care of dogs.

E: Yes.

S: And cattle raising is the care of cattle.

E: Quite so.

S: While piety and godliness is the care of the gods, Euthyphro. Is that what you mean?

E: It is.

S: Now care in each case has the same effect; it aims at the good and the benefit of the object cared for, as you can see that horses cared for by horse breeders are benefited and become better. Or do you not think so?

E: I do.

S: So dogs are benefited by dog breeding, cattle by cattle raising, and so with all the others. Or do you think that care aims to harm the object of its care?

E: By Zeus, no.

S: It aims to benefit the object of its care.

E: Of course.

S: Is piety then, which is the care of the gods, also to benefit the gods and make them better? Would you agree that when you do something pious you make some one of the gods better?

E: By Zeus, no.

S: Nor do I think that this is what you mean—far from it—but that is why I asked you what you meant by the care of gods, because I did not believe you meant this kind of care.

E: Quite right, Socrates, that is not the kind of care I mean.

S: Very well, but what kind of care of the gods would piety be?

E: The kind of care, Socrates, that slaves take of their masters.

S: I understand. It is likely to be the service of the gods.

E: Quite so.

S: Could you tell me to the achievement of what goal service to doctors tends? Is it not, do you think to achieving health?

E: I think so.

S: What about service to shipbuilders? To what achievement is it directed?

E: Clearly, Socrates, to the building of a ship.

S: And service to housebuilders to the building of a house?

E: Yes.

S: Tell me then, my good sir, to the achievement of what aim does service to the gods tend? You obviously know since you say that you, of all men, have the best knowledge of the divine.

E: And I am telling the truth, Socrates.

S: Tell me then, by Zeus, what is that excellent aim that the gods achieve, using us as their servants?

E: Many fine things, Socrates.

S: So do generals, my friend. Nevertheless you could tell me their main concern, which is to achieve victory in war, is it not?

E: Of course.

S: The farmers too, I think, achieve many fine things, but the main point of their efforts is to produce food from the earth.

E: Quite so.

S: Well then, how would you sum up the many fine things that the gods achieve?

E: I told you a short while ago, Socrates, that it is a considerable task to acquire any precise knowledge of these things, but, to put it simply, I say that if a man knows how to say and do what is pleasing to the gods at prayer and sacrifice, those are pious actions such as preserve both private houses and public affairs of state. The opposite of these pleasing actions are impious and overturn and destroy everything.

S: You could tell me in far fewer words, if you were willing, the sum of what I asked, Euthyphro, but you are not keen to teach me, that is clear. You were on the point of doing so, but you turned away. If you had given that answer, I should now have acquired from you sufficient knowledge of the nature of piety. As it is, the lover of inquiry must follow it wherever it may lead him. Once more then, what do you say that piety and the pious are, and also impiety? Are they a knowledge of how to sacrifice and pray?

E: They are.

S: To sacrifice is to make a gift to the gods, whereas to pray is to beg from the gods?

E: Definitely, Socrates.

S: It would follow from this statement that piety would be a knowledge of how to give to, and beg from, the gods.

E: You understood what I said very well, Socrates.

S: That is because I am so desirous of your wisdom, and I concentrate my mind on it, so that no word of yours may fall to the ground. But tell me, what is this service to the gods? You say it is to beg from them and to give to them?

E: I do.

S: And to beg correctly would be to ask from them things that we need?

E: What else?

S: And to give correctly is to give them what they need from us, for it would not be skillful to bring gifts to anyone that are in no way needed.

E: True, Socrates.

s: Piety would then be a sort of trading skill between gods and men?

e: Trading yes, if you prefer to call it that.

s: I prefer nothing, unless it is true. But tell me, what benefit do the gods derive from the gifts they receive from us? What they give us is obvious to all. There is for us no good that we do not receive from them, but how are they benefited by what they receive from us? Or do we have such an advantage over them in the trade that we receive all our blessings from them and they receive nothing from us?

e: Do you suppose, Socrates, that the gods are benefited by what they receive from us?

s: What could those gifts from us to the gods be, Euthyphro?

e: What else, you think, than honour, reverence, and what I mentioned before, gratitude.

s: The pious is then, Euthyphro, pleasing to the gods, but not beneficial or dear to them?

e: I think it is of all things most dear to them.

s: So the pious is once again what is dear to the gods.

e: Most certainly.

s: When you say this, will you be surprised if your arguments seem to move about instead of staying put? And will you accuse me of being Daedalus who makes them move, though you are yourself much more skillful than Daedalus and make them go round in a circle? Or do you not realize that our argument has moved around and come again to the same place? You surely remember that earlier the pious and the god-beloved were shown not to be the same but different from each other. Or do you not remember?

e: I do.

s: Do you then not realize that when you say now that that what is dear to the gods is the pious? Is this not the same as the god-beloved? Or is it not?

e: It certainly is.

s: Either we were wrong when we agreed before, or, if we were right then, we are wrong now.

e: That seems to be so.

s: So we must investigate again from the beginning what piety is, as I shall not willingly give up before I learn this. Do not think me unworthy, but concentrate your attention and tell the truth. For you know it, if any man does, and I must not let you go, like Proteus, before you tell me. If you had no clear knowledge of piety and impiety you would never have ventured to prosecute your old father for murder on behalf of a servant. For fear of the gods you would have been afraid to take the risk lest you should not be acting rightly, and would have been ashamed before men, but now I know well that you believe you have clear knowledge of piety and impiety. So tell me, my good Euthyphro, and do not hide what you believe.

e: Some other time, Socrates, for I am in a hurry now, and it is time for me to go.

s: What a thing to do, my friend! By going you have cast me down from a great hope I had, that I would learn from you the nature of the pious and the impious and so escape Meletus' indictment by showing that I had acquired wisdom in divine matters from Euthyphro, and my ignorance would no longer cause me to be careless and inventive about such things, and that I would be better for the rest of my life.

15

A New Divine
Command Theory

ROBERT MERRIHEW ADAMS

Robert M. Adams (b. 1937) is Professor of Philosophy at Yale University. Previously he taught at the University of California at Los Angeles. His books include Leibniz: Determinist, Theist, Idealist *and* The Virtue of Faith and Other Essays in Philosophical Theology. *This selection first appeared in* The Journal of Religious Ethics *(1979).*

According to one version of the divine command theory, "right" simply means "commanded by God." Understood in this way, the theory invites the objection that many who use the word "right" do not even believe in God. But in the current selection, Adams develops a kind of divine command theory that is not vulnerable to this objection. Drawing on recent work in metaphysics and the philosophy of language, he presents the theory not as a definition of "right," but rather as a hypothesis about what the term refers to.

The lynchpin of his discussion is an influential recent account of reference. On the traditional view, if a term like water *is defined through a list of characteristics—for example, as a liquid that is transparent and tasteless—then the term would always refer to anything that had those characteristics. By contrast, according to the new account,* water *refers to just the stuff, H_2O, that actually has those characteristics now. If by some accident H_2O ceased to be transparent or tasteless,* water *would still refer to it. Applying similar reasoning, Adams first proposes a number of characteristics of moral rightness—for example, that it provides reasons for acting and is determined by a standard "that has a sanctity that is greater than that of any merely human will"—and then proposes that what have these characteristics are just actions commanded by a loving God. If Adams is correct, then "right" necessarily refers to what a loving God commands. Thus, Adams's theory provides a clear answer to Plato's question (reading 14) of whether acts are right because commanded by God or commanded by God because they are right.*

In a recent issue of *The Journal of Religious Ethics,* Jeffrey Stout (1978) has written about an earlier paper of mine (Adams, 1973) urging development and modification of the very point on which, as it happens, my own metaethical views have changed most. My thoughts have been moving in a rather different direction from his, however.[1] For that reason, and because of his paper's interesting and perceptive linkage of metaethical issues with the most fundamental questions in the theory of meaning I would like to respond to him.

I. MY OLD POSITION

My modified divine command theory was proposed as a partial analysis of the *meaning* of '(ethically) wrong.' Recognizing that it would be most implausible as an analysis of the sense in which the expression is used by many speakers (for instance, by atheists), I proposed the theory only as an analysis of the meaning of 'wrong' in the discourse of some Jewish and Christian believers. In the theory that I now prefer, as we shall see, the identification of wrongness with contrariety to God's commands is neither presented as a meaning analysis nor relativized to a group of believers. According to the old theory, however, it is part of the meaning of '(ethically) wrong' for at least some believers that

(1) (for any action X) X is ethically wrong if and only if X is contrary to God's commands,
    but also that
(2) 'X is wrong' normally expresses opposition or certain other negative attitudes toward X.

The meaning of 'wrong' seems to be overdetermined by (1) and (2). Conflicts could arise. Suppose God commanded me to practice cruelty for its own sake. (More precisely, suppose he commanded me to make it my chief end in life to inflict suffering on other human beings, for no other reason than that he commanded it.) I cannot summon up the relevant sort of opposition or negative attitude toward disobedience to such a command, and I will not say that it would be wrong to disobey it.

Such conflicts within the religious ethical belief system are prevented by various background beliefs, which are *presupposed* by (1). Particularly important is the belief that

(3) God is loving, and therefore does not and will not command such things as (e.g.) the practice of cruelty for its own sake.

But (3) is contingent. It is allowed by the theory to be logically possible for God to command cruelty for its own sake, although the believer is confident he will not do such a thing. Were the believer to come to think (3) false, however, I suggested that his concept of ethical wrongness would "break down." It would not function as it now does, because he would not be prepared to use it to say that any action is wrong (Adams, 1973:322–324). Because of the interplay and tension of the various considerations involved in it, this picture of the meaning of '(ethically) wrong' is (as I acknowledged) somewhat "untidy." But its untidiness should not obscure the fact that I meant it quite definitely to follow from the theory that the following are necessary truths:

(4) If X is wrong, then X is contrary to the commands of God.

(5) If X is obligatory, then X is required by the commands of God.

(6) If X is ethically permitted, then X is permitted by the commands of God.

(7) If there is not a *loving* God, then nothing is ethically wrong or obligatory or permitted.

These four theses are still taken to be necessary truths in my present divine command theory.

• • •

III. THE SEPARATION OF NECESSITY AND NATURES FROM ANALYTICITY AND CONCEPTS

An important group of recent papers (especially Donnellan, 1966 and 1972; Kripke, 1972; and Putnam, 1975:196–290)[2] has made a persuasive case for a view that there are necessary truths that are neither analytic nor knowable *a priori*. Among these are truths about the nature of many properties. And I am now inclined to believe that the truth about the nature of ethical wrongness is of this sort.

A case of individual identity or non-identity provides a first example of a truth that is necessary but empirical. In the Gospels according to Mark (2:14) and Luke (5:27–29) there is a story about a tax collector named 'Levi,' who left his business to follow Jesus. There is a tradition, supported by the relevant texts in Matthew (9:9 and 10:3) and by some important manuscripts of Mark (2:14), that this man was the Matthew who appears in the lists of the twelve apostles. This belief is naturally expressed by saying that Levi was Matthew, or that Levi and Matthew were the same man. But perhaps they were not; none of us really knows.

Suppose they were in fact two different men. That is a truth that is in principle knowable, but only empirically knowable. It is certainly not an analytic truth, which could be discovered by analyzing our concepts of Levi and Matthew. But there is a compelling argument for believing it to be necessary truth if it is true at all. For suppose it were a contingent truth. Then the actual world, w_1, would be one in which Matthew the apostle and Levi the tax collector are not identical, but a world, w_2, in which they would be identical would also be possible. Since identity is a transitive relation, however, and since Levi in w_1, is identical with Levi in w_2, and Levi in w_2 is identical with Matthew in w_2, and Matthew in w_2 with Matthew in w_1, it follows that Levi in w_1 is identical with Matthew in w_1. Thus the hypothesis that the non-identity of Matthew and Levi is contingent leads to a contradiction. This argument is not completely uncontroversial in its assumptions about trans-world identity, but it seems to me to be correct. A similar argument can be given for holding that if Levi and Matthew were in fact identical, that is a necessary truth, although it is not *a priori*.

It should be emphasized that 'possible' is not being used in its *epistemic* sense here. Both worlds in which Matthew and Levi are identical and worlds in which they are distinct are epistemically possible; that is, either sort may be actual for all we know. But whichever sort is actual, the other sort lacks broadly logical possibility, or "metaphysical possibility" as it is often called by those who hold the views I am exploring here.

Another interesting feature of this example is that there is a property which our understanding of the meaning of 'Matthew' and 'Levi' in this context tells us Matthew and Levi must have had if they (or he) existed, but which is a property that they (or he) possessed contingently. By 'Matthew' we mean the individual who stands in a certain historical relation (not yet spelled out in a very detailed way by philosophers of language) to the use of 'Matthew' (on certain occasions known to us) as a name of a man believed to have been one of the disciples of Jesus. It is epistemically possible that Matthew was named 'Levi' and not 'Matthew,' or that he was not one of the twelve apostles but got counted as one by mistake. But no one who does not stand in an appropriate historical relation to the relevant uses of 'Matthew' counts as Matthew; that is what is settled by the meaning with which we use 'Matthew.' Standing in this relation to these uses of 'Matthew' is surely a contingent property of Matthew, however. Matthew could have existed in a world in which he was never called 'Matthew' during or after his life, or in a world in which Jesus never had any disciples and the relevant uses of 'Matthew' never occurred.

Similar considerations apply to theories about the natures of properties or of kinds of things. Hilary Putnam uses the theory that the nature of water is to be H_2O as an example in arguing that such theories, if true, are commonly necessary truths but not *a priori* (see also Kripke, 1972:314–331). (As it happens, this example was given a somewhat different treatment, hereby superseded, in Adams, 1973:345.)

Suppose a vessel from outer space landed, carrying a group of intelligent creatures that brought with them, and drank, a transparent, colorless, odorless, tasteless liquid that dissolved sugar and salt and other things that normally dissolve in water. Even if we non-chemists could not distinguish it from water, we might intelligibly (and prudently) ask whether this substance really is water. Our question would be answered, in the negative, by a laboratory analysis showing that the beverage from outer space was not H_2O but a different liquid whose long and complicated chemical formula may be abbreviated as XYZ (see Putnam, 1975:223).

Why is it right to say that this XYZ would not be water? I take it to be Putnam's view that it is not an analytic truth that water is H_2O. What is true analytically, by virtue of what every competent user of the word 'water' must know about its meaning, is rather that if most of the stuff that we (our linguistic community) have been calling 'water' is of a single nature, water is liquid that is of the same nature as *that*.

This view enables Putnam to maintain against Quine that substantial change and development in scientific theories is possible without change in meaning (although he agrees with Quine "that meaning change and theory change cannot be sharply separated," and that *some* possible changes in scientific theory would change the meaning of crucial terms—see Putnam 1975:255f.). "Thus, the fact that an English speaker in 1750 might have called *XYZ* 'water,' while he or his successors would not have called *XYZ* water in 1800 or 1850 does not mean that the 'meaning' of 'water' changed for the average speaker in the interval" (Putnam, 1975:225). This claim is plausible. Had the visitors from outer space arrived with their clear, tasteless liquid in England in 1750, the English of that time might wisely have wondered whether the stuff was really water, even if it satisfied all the tests they yet knew for being water. And the correct answer to *their* question too would have been negative, if the liquid was *XYZ* and not H_2O.

Although it is not an *a priori* but an empirical truth that water is H_2O, Putnam thinks it is metaphysically necessary. Suppose there is a possible world, w_3, in which there is no H_2O but *XYZ* fills the ecological and cultural role that belongs to H_2O in the actual world. *XYZ* looks, tastes, etc. like H_2O, and is even called 'water' by English speakers in w_3. In such a case, Putnam (1975:231) maintains, the *XYZ* in w_3 is *not* water, for in order to be water a liquid in *any* possible world must be the same liquid (must have the same nature, I would say) as the stuff that we actually call 'water'—which is H_2O. We may say, on this view, that the property of being water *is* the property of being H_2O, so that nothing could have the one property without having the other, or lack one without lacking the other.

It should also be noted that on this view the property ascribed to water by the description that expresses the *concept* of water, or what every competent user of 'water' knows, is not a property that belongs to water necessarily. The description is 'liquid of the same nature as most of the stuff that we have been calling "water." ' But it is only contingent that water is called 'water.' Water could perfectly well have existed if no one had given it a name at all, or if the English had called it 'yoof.'

This view of the relation between the nature of water and the meaning of 'water' seems to me plausible. And if we think it is correct, that will enhance the plausibility of an analogous treatment of the nature of right and wrong. But even if Putnam's claims about 'water' are mistaken, we certainly *could* use an expression as he says we use 'water,' and it would be worth considering whether 'right' and 'wrong' are used in something like that way.

IV. THE NATURE OF WRONGNESS AND THE MEANING OF 'WRONG'

I do not think that every competent user of 'wrong' in its ethical sense must know what the nature of wrongness is. The word is used—with the same meaning, I would now say—by people who have different views, or none at all, about the nature of wrongness. As I remarked in my earlier paper, "There is probably much less agreement about the most basic issues in moral theory than there is about many ethical issues of less generality" (Adams, 1973:343). That people can use an expression to signify an ethical property, knowing it is a property they seek (or shun, as the case may be), but not knowing what its nature is, was realized by Plato when he characterized the good as

> That which every soul pursues, doing everything for the sake of it, divining that it is something, but perplexed and unable to grasp adequately what it is or to have such a stable belief as about other things (*Republic* 505D–E).

What every competent user of 'wrong' must know about wrongness is first of all, that wrongness is a property of actions (perhaps also of intentions and of various attitudes, but certainly of actions); and second that people are generally opposed to actions they regard as wrong, and count wrongness as a reason (often a conclusive reason) for opposing an action. In addition I think the competent user must have some opinion about what actions have this property, and some fairly settled disposition as to what he will count as reasons for and against regarding an action as wrong. There is an important measure of agreement among competent users in these opinions and dispositions—not complete agreement, nor universal agreement on some points and disagreement on others, but overlapping agreements of one person with another on some points and with still others on other points. "To call an action 'wrong' is, among other things, to classify it with certain other actions," as having a common property, "and there is considerable agreement . . . as to what actions those are" (Adams, 1973:344). Torturing children for fun is one of them in virtually everyone's opinion.

Analysis of the concept or understanding with which the word 'wrong' is used is not sufficient to determine what wrongness is. What it can tell us about the nature of wrongness, I think, is that wrongness will be the property of actions (if there is one) that best fills the role assigned to wrongness by the concept. My theory is that contrariety to the command of a loving God is that property; but we will come to that in section V. Meanwhile I will try to say something about what is involved in being the property that *best* fills the relevant role, though I do not claim to be giving an adequate set of individually necessary and jointly sufficient conditions.

(i) We normally speak of actions being right and wrong as of facts that obtain objectively, independently of whether we think they do. 'Wrong' has the syntax of an ordinary predicate, and we worry that we may be mistaken in our ethical judgments. This feature of ethical concepts gives emotivism and prescriptivism in metaethics much of their initial implausibility. If possible, therefore, the property to be identified with ethical wrongness should be one that actions have or lack objectively.

(ii) The property that is wrongness should belong to those types of action that are thought to be wrong—or at least it should belong to an important central group of them. It would be unreasonable to expect a theory of the nature of wrongness to yield results that agree perfectly with pre-theoretical opinion. One of the purposes a metaethical theory may serve is to give guidance in revising one's particular ethical opinions. But there is a limit to how far those opinions may be revised without changing the subject entirely; and we are bound to take it as a major test of the acceptability of a theory of the nature of wrongness that it should in some sense account for the wrongness of a major portion of the types of action we have believed to be wrong.

(iii) Wrongness should be a property that not only belongs to the most important types of action that are thought to be wrong, but also plays a causal role (or a role as object of perception) in their coming to be regarded as wrong. It should not be connected in a merely fortuitous way with our classification of actions as wrong and not wrong.[3]

(iv) Understanding the nature of wrongness should give one more rather than less reason to oppose wrong actions as such. Even if it were discovered (as it surely will not be) that there is a certain sensory pleasure produced by all and only wrong actions, it would be absurd to say that wrongness *is* the property of producing that pleasure. For the property of producing such a pleasure, in itself, gives us no reason whatever to oppose an action that has the property.

(v) The best theory about the nature of wrongness should satisfy other intuitions about wrongness as far as possible. One intuition that is rather widely held and is relevant to theological metaethics is that rightness and wrongness are determined by a law or standard that has a sanctity that is greater than that of any merely human will or institution.

We are left, on this view, with a concept of wrongness that has both objective and subjective aspects. The best theory of the nature of wrongness, I think, will be one that identifies wrongness with some property that actions have or lack objectively. But we do not have a fully objective procedure for determining which theory of the nature of wrongness is the best, and therefore which property is wrongness.

For example, the property that is wrongness should belong to the most important types of action that are believed to be wrong. But the concept possessed by every competent user of 'wrong' does not dictate exactly which types of action those are. A sufficiently eccentric classification of types of action as right or wrong would not fit the concept. But there is still room for much difference of opinion. In testing theories of the nature of wrongness by their implications about what types of action are wrong, I will be guided by my own classification of types of action as right and wrong, and by my own sense of which parts of the classification are most important.

Similarly, in considering whether identifying wrongness with a given property, *P,* makes wrongness more or less of a reason for opposing an action, I will decide partly on the basis of how *P* weighs with me. And in general I think that this much is right about prescriptivist intuitions in metaethics: to identify a property with ethical wrongness is in part to assign it a certain complex role in my life (and, for my part, in the life of society); in deciding to do that I will (quite reasonably) be influenced by what attracts and repels me personally. But it does not follow that the theory I should choose is not one that identifies wrongness with a property that actions would have or lack regardless of how I felt about them.

V. A NEW DIVINE COMMAND THEORY

The account I have given of the concept of wrongness that every competent user of 'wrong' must have is consistent with many different theories about the nature of wrongness—for example, with the view that wrongness is the property of failing to maximize human happiness, and with a Marxist theory that wrongness is the property of being contrary to the objective interests of the progressive class or classes. But given typical Christian beliefs about God, it seems to me most plausible to identify wrongness with the property of being contrary to the commands of loving God. (i) This is a property that actions have or lack objectively, regardless of whether we think they do. (I assume the theory can be filled out with a satisfactory account of what love consists in here.) (ii) The property of being contrary to the commands of a loving God is certainly believed by Christians to belong to all and only wrong actions. (iii) It also plays a causal role in our classification of actions as wrong, in so far as God has created our moral faculties to reflect his commands. (iv) Because of what is believed about God's actions, purposes, character, and power, he inspires such devotion and/or fear that contrariness to his commands is seen as a supremely weighty reason for opposing an action. Indeed, (v) God's commands constitute a law or standard that seems to believers to have sanctity that is not possessed by any merely human will or institution.

My new divine command theory of the nature of ethical wrongness, then, is that ethical wrongness *is* (i.e., is identical with) the property of being contrary to the commands of a loving God. I regard this as a metaphysically necessary, but not an analytic or *a priori* truth. Because it is not conceptual analysis, this claim is not relative to a religious sub-community of the larger linguistic community. It purports to be the correct theory of the nature of the ethical wrongness that *everybody* (or almost everybody) is talking about.

Further explanation is in order, first about the notion of a divine *command*, and second about the *necessity* that is claimed here. On the first point I can only indicate here the character of the explanation that is needed; for it amounts to nothing less than a theory of revelation. Theists sometimes speak of wrong action as action contrary to the "will" of God, but that way of speaking ignores some important distinctions. One is the distinction between the absolute will of God (his "good pleasure") and his revealed will. Any Christian theology will grant that God in his godly pleasure sometimes decides, for reasons that may be mysterious to us, not to do everything he could to prevent a wrong action. According to some theologies nothing at all can happen contrary to God's good pleasure. It is difficult, therefore, to suppose that all wrong actions are unqualified, contrary to God's will in the sense of his good pleasure. It is God's *revealed* will—not what he wants or plans to have happen, but what he has told us to do—that is thought to determine the rightness and wrongness of human actions. Roman Catholic theology has made a further distinction, within God's revealed will, between his commands, which it would be wrong not to follow, and "counsels (of perfection)," which it would be better to follow but not wrong not to follow. It is best, therefore, in our metaethical theory, to say that wrongness is contrariety to God's *commands;* and commands must have been issued, promulgated, or somehow revealed.

The notion of the issuance of a divine command requires a theory of revelation for its adequate development. The first such theory that comes to mind may be a Biblical literalism that takes divine commands to be just what is written in the Bible as commanded by God. But there will also be Roman Catholic theories involving the *magisterium* of the Church, a Quaker theory about "the inner light," theories about "general revelation" through the moral feelings and intuitions of unbelievers as well as believers—and other theories as well. To develop these theories and choose among them is far too large a task for the present essay.

The thesis that wrongness is (identical with) contrariety to a loving God's commands must be *metaphysically necessary* if it is true. That is, it cannot be false in any possible world if it is true in the actual world. For if it were false in some possible world, then wrongness would be non-identical with contrariety to God's commands in the actual world as well, by the transitivity of identity, just as Matthew and Levi must be non-identical in all worlds if they are non-identical in any.

This argument establishes the metaphysical necessity of property identities in general; and that leads me to identify wrongness with contrariety to the commands of a *loving* God, rather than simply with contrariety to the commands of God. Most theists believe that both of those properties are in fact possessed by all and only wrong actions. But if wrongness is simply contrariety to the commands of God, it is necessarily so, which implies that it would be wrong to disobey God even if he were so unloving as to command the practice of cruelty for its own sake. That consequence is unacceptable. I am not prepared to adopt the negative attitude toward possible disobedience in that situation that would be involved in identifying wrongness simply with contrariety to God's commands. The loving character of the God who issues them seems to me therefore to be a metaethically relevant feature of divine commands. (I assume that in deciding what property is wrongness, and therefore would be wrongness in all possible worlds, we are to rely on our own actual moral feelings and convictions, rather than on those that we or others would have in other possible worlds.)

If it is necessary that ethical wrongness is contrariety to a loving God's commands, it follows that no actions would be ethically wrong if there were not a loving God. This consequence will seem (at least initially) implausible to many, but I will try to dispel as much as I can of the air of paradox. It should be emphasized, first of all, that my theory does not imply what would ordinarily be meant by saying that no actions *are* ethically wrong if there *is* no loving God. If there is no loving God, then the theological part of my theory is false; but the more general part presented in section IV above, implies that in that case ethical wrongness is the property with which it is identified by the best remaining alternative theory.

Similarly, if there is in fact a loving God, and if ethical wrongness is the property of being contrary to the commands of a loving God, there is still, I suppose, a possible world, w_4, in which there would not be a loving God but there would be people to whom w_4 would seem much as the actual world seems to us, and who would use the world 'wrong' much as we use it. We may say that they would associate it with the same *concept* as we do although the property it would signify in their mouths is not wrongness. The actions they call 'wrong' would not be wrong—that is, they would not have the property that actually is wrongness (the property of being contrary to the commands of a loving God). But that is not to say that they would be mistaken whenever they predicated 'is wrong' of an action. For 'wrong' in their speech would signify the property (if any) that is assigned to it by the metaethical theory that would be the best in relation to an accurate knowledge of their situation in w_4. We can even say that they would believe, as we do, that cruelty is wrong, if by that we mean, not that the property they would ascribe to cruelty by calling it 'wrong' is the same as the property that we so ascribe, but that the subjective psychological state that they would express by the ascription is that same that we express.

Readers who think that I have not sufficiently dispelled the air of paradox may wish to consider a slightly different divine command theory, according to which it is a contingent truth that contrariety to God's commands constitutes the nature of wrongness. Instead of saying that wrongness is the property that in the actual world best fills a certain role, we could say that wrongness is the property of having whatever property best fills that role in whatever possible world is in question. On the latter view it would be reasonable to say that the property that best fills the role constitutes the nature of wrongness, but that the nature of wrongness may differ in different possible worlds. The theist could still hold that the nature of wrongness in the actual world is constituted by contrariety to the commands of God (or of a loving God—it does not make as much difference which we say, on this view, since the theist believes God is loving in the actual world anyway). But it might be constituted by other properties in some other possible worlds. This theory does not imply that no action would be wrong if there were no loving God; and that may still seem to be an advantage. On the other hand I think there is also an air of paradox about the idea that wrongness may have different natures in different possible worlds; and if a loving God does issue commands, actual wrongness has a very different character from anything that could occur in a world without a loving God.

The difference between this alternative theory and the one I have endorsed should not be exaggerated. On both theories the nature of wrongness is actually constituted by contrariety to the commands of (a loving) God. And on both theories there may be other possible worlds in which other properties best fill the role by which contrariety to a loving God's commands is linked in the actual world to our concept of wrongness.

NOTES

1. The metaethical position to be presented here was briefly indicated in Adams (1979). Though not all the arguments given there in favor of the theory are repeated here, the position is much more fully expounded in the present essay.

2. I have selected from these papers points that are relevant to my theory. I do not claim to give a comprehensive account of their aims and contents. I am also indebted here to David Kaplan and Bernard Kobes, for discussion and for the opportunity of reading unpublished papers of theirs.

3. Cf. Putnam (1975:290): "I would apply a generally causal account of reference also to moral terms . . . " I do not know how similar the metaethical views at which Putnam hints are to those that are developed in section IV of the present paper.

4. I follow Putnam in this use of 'concept.' I have avoided committing myself as to whether English speakers in w_4 would use 'wrong' with the same *meaning* as we do. See Putnam, 1975:234.

REFERENCES

Adams, Robert Merrihew
1973   "A modified divine command theory of ethical wrongness." Pp. 318–347 in Gene Outka and John P. Reeder, Jr. (eds.), *Religion and Morality.* Garden City: Anchor.
1979   "Moral arguments for theistic belief." In C. F. Delaney (ed.), *Rationality and Religious Belief.* Notre Dame, In: University of Notre Dame Press.

Donnellan, Keith
1965   "Reference and definite descriptions." *The Philosophical Review* 75:281–304.
1972   "Proper names and identifying descriptions." Pp. 356–379 in Donald Davidson and Gilbert Harman (eds.), *The Semantics of Natural Languages.* Dordrecht and Boston: Reidel.

Kripke, Paul A.
1972   "Naming and necessity." Pp. 253–355 and 763–769 in Donald Davidson and Gilbert Harman (eds.), *The Semantics of Natural Languages.* Dordrecht and Boston: Reidel.

Putnam, Hilary
1975   *Mind, Language and Reality: Philosophical Papers,* Vol. 2. Cambridge: Cambridge University Press.

Quine, Willard Van Orman
1963   *From a Logical Point of View: 9 Logico-Philosophical Essays,* 2nd ed. New York and Evanston: Harper Torchbooks.
1966   *The Ways of Paradox and Other Essays.* New York: Random House.

Stout, Jeffrey L.
1978   "Metaethics and the death of meaning: Adams' tantalizing closing." *The Journal of Religious Ethics* (Spring) 6:1–18.

III

OBJECTIVITY AND KNOWLEDGE

Noncognitivism, discussed in the readings in section two, challenges the objectivity of morality by denying that ethical utterances attempt to say anything true. But other challenges focus on reality instead of language. Some deny that the world contains the sorts of facts that would *make* ethical utterances true, while others deny that we could know about such facts if they did exist. Because moral facts have received more attention than moral knowledge, we will focus mainly on them.

One common argument takes as its point of departure the absence of moral agreement. If there are objective truths about what is right or good, then it may seem that even people of widely differing backgrounds should agree about what they are. However, anthropological data suggest that different cultures hold widely divergent values and norms. This has led some to hold that what one ought to do is just what is approved of or commanded by one's society. On this view, often referred to as *cultural relativism*, the members of societies that condone polygamy or ritual murder, for example, are morally permitted to practice these activities; but because our own society forbids such acts, we are not. According to cultural relativism, there is no deeper truth about how everyone ought to act.

As we just saw, it is customary to defend cultural relativism by appealing to anthropological evidence. Yet as James Rachels argues in reading 16, it is not clear that this evidence proves that societies disagree about the most basic values. It may be, instead, that most, or all, societies accept the same ultimate principles, but that differences of history, belief, and economic and geographic circumstance have led societies to embrace different secondary codes. More-over, even if societies do hold differing ultimate principles, Rachels argues that this by itself does not establish cultural relativism. Nor, we may add, do we clearly avoid commitment to independent moral facts by saying that what each person ought to do is what his society commands or approves.

Should we then agree that such facts exist? As both Gilbert Harman and J. L. Mackie argue, there may simply be no good reason to do so. In reading 17, Harman argues that although we need to postulate scientific facts to explain our observations of the world, we may not need to postulate moral facts to explain our moral observations or beliefs. When someone observes that an act such as setting a cat on fire for fun is wrong, the explanation may lie solely in his psychological conditioning and other nonmoral facts. Although Harman ultimately defends a version of relativism, and so holds that moral facts can be reduced to natural facts, his position here is that introducing independent moral facts may be unreasonable. And to this Mackie adds, in reading 19, that various "patterns of objectification" would lead us to believe that the world contained objective moral values whether or not it really did. For example, all communities impose demands on their members for the common good; and these (merely social) demands are easily confused with the demands of an objective morality. Mackie also argues that independently existing moral val-ues—what others call moral facts—would be such strange entities that their existence is implausible and that the variation among moral codes is most easily explained if we abandon objectivism. For these and other reasons, Mackie denies that there are objective values.

Can objectivists respond to these arguments? In reading 18, Nicholas Stur-geon carefully criticizes Harman's position. As we have seen, Harman contends that moral facts do not appear to play any role in explaining our observations. To establish this, he must assume, for purposes of argument, that moral facts exist. But Sturgeon argues that once we assume this, we find that moral facts "*do* appear relevant, by perfectly ordinary standards, to the explanation of moral beliefs and of a good deal else besides." If we discount their explanatory role, we must also discount the role of tables and chairs in explaining our observations of the world. Thus, Sturgeon concludes that the only remaining arguments against moral facts are general skeptical arguments.

Although Sturgeon rejects Harman's conclusion, he does not deny that the question of moral objectivity turns on the explanatory role of moral facts. But other philosophers place greater stress on the practical nature of morality, and so conceive the question differently. Thus, Thomas Nagel writes in reading 20 that "just as realism about the facts leads us to seek a detached point of view from which reality can be discerned and appearance corrected, so realism about values leads us to seek a detached point of view from which it will be possible to correct inclination and to discern what we really should do, or want." In Nagel's view, an objective value would be a source of reasons that are indepen-dent of any agent's particular stake in the situation. Moreover, according to Nagel, such values do exist: Some reasons are "agent-neutral" in the sense that they apply even to persons who are not themselves affected or involved. For example, if *A* is in pain, then not only *A*, but also *B*, has a reason to want, and try to bring about, *A*'s relief from pain. Thus, Nagel implies that we can sometimes make the transition from "*X* is good for *A*" to "*X* is good in itself." Although Nagel's main example involves relief from pain, he does not believe either that people want only pleasure and the absence of pain or that all agent-neutral reasons are reasons to promote what someone desires. Rather, he holds that such reasons can take a variety of forms.

The idea that moral objectivity must reflect the practical nature of morality is pressed even harder by John Rawls. Although Nagel insists that "the view that values are real is not the view that they are real occult entities or properties, but that they are real *values*," he also allows that "claims about value and about what people have reason to do may be *true* or *false* independently of our beliefs and inclinations." By contrast, in reading 21 Rawls argues for an approach within which "the idea of approximating to moral truth has no place." For Rawls, there simply is no independent moral realm. Instead, the principles of right and justice must be *constructed* by persons pursuing their highest-order interests. Only actions which conform to such principles can be autonomous in the Kantian sense (see reading 30). In his book *A Theory of Justice*, excerpted in reading 34, Rawls elaborates both his conception of the person and his view of the principles that appropriately situated persons would choose. Here, however, his aim is only to suggest that "objectivity is to be understood by reference to a suitably constructed social point of view."

How, on Rawls's account, can we know when a point of view is "suitably constructed"? And how, on the other accounts of objectivity, can we know which moral beliefs are true? In reading 22, Norman Daniels elaborates Rawls's view that justifying a moral belief consists of testing it against one's other beliefs. By moving back and forth, and by making whatever adjustments seem appropriate, we try to arrive at a (temporarily) stable set of beliefs, or "reflective equilibrium." Achieving such an equilibrium requires more than testing principles against intuitions about particular cases: in addition, we must consider both judgments from other areas of morality and a broad range of nonmoral beliefs. By employing this method of *wide reflective equilibrium*, Daniels argues, we may replace intractable problems with more tractable ones, and so "recast and resolve some traditional worries about objectivity in ethics."

16

The Challenge of
Cultural Relativism

JAMES RACHELS

James Rachels (b. 1941) is Professor of Philosophy at the University of Alabama at Birmingham. He is the author of many articles on ethics, and his books include The End of Life: Euthanasia and Morality *and* Created from Animals: The Moral Implications of Darwinism. *This selection is chapter 2 of his book* The Elements of Moral Philosophy.

Many people take the diversity of moral codes to constitute a serious challenge to the objectivity of ethics. They argue that because different societies disagree about the rightness of so many types of behavior, no moral standards apply at all times and places, and there is no basis upon which to judge that any society's moral code is better than any other's. These and a number of related views represent a position that is often called cultural relativism. *But, according to Rachels, the case for cultural relativism is far from compelling. He points out that in many other contexts—for example, when we consider the shape of the earth—we do not take disagreement to show that there is no fact of the matter. He also points out that if societies could not be judged by standards other than their own, we would have no basis upon which to criticize Nazis or slaveholders. For these and other reasons, Rachels rejects many (though not all) of the claims of cultural relativists. For a partially contrasting view, see reading 19, by J. L. Mackie.*

> "MORALITY DIFFERS IN EVERY SOCIETY, AND IS A CONVENIENT TERM FOR SOCIALLY APPROVED HABITS."
>
> *Ruth Benedict, Patterns of Culture (1934)*

HOW DIFFERENT CULTURES
HAVE DIFFERENT MORAL CODES

Darius, a king of ancient Persia, was intrigued by the variety of cultures he encountered in his travels. He had found, for example, that the Callatians (a tribe of Indians) customarily ate the bodies of their dead fathers. The Greeks, of course, did not do that—the Greeks practiced cremation and regarded the funeral pyre as the natural and fitting way to dispose of the dead. Darius thought that a sophisticated understanding of the world must include an appreciation of such differences between cultures. One day, to teach this lesson, he summoned some Greeks who happened to be present at his court and asked them what they would take to eat the bodies of their dead fathers. They were shocked, as Darius knew they would be, and replied that no amount of money would persuade them to do such a thing. Then Darius called in some Callatians, and while the Greeks listened asked them what they would take to burn their dead fathers' bodies. The Callatians were horrified and told Darius not even to mention such a dreadful thing.

This story, recounted by Herodotus in his *History,* illustrates a recurring theme in the literature of social science: different cultures have different moral codes. What is thought right within one group may be utterly abhorrent to the members of another group, and vice versa. Should we eat the bodies of the dead or burn them? If you were a Greek, one answer would seem obviously correct; but if you were a Callatian, the opposite would seem equally certain.

It is easy to give additional examples of the same kind. Consider the Eskimos. They are a remote and inaccessible people. Numbering only about 25,000, they live in small, isolated settlements scattered mostly along the northern fringes of North America and Greenland. Until the beginning of this century, the outside world knew little about them. Then explorers began to bring back strange tales.

Eskimo customs turned out to be very different from our own. The men often had more than one wife, and they would share their wives with guests, lending them for the night as a sign of hospitality. Moreover, within a community, a dominant male might demand—and get—regular sexual access to other men's wives. The women, however, were free to break these arrangements simply by leaving their husbands and taking up with new partners—free, that is, so long as their former husbands chose not to make trouble. All in all, the Eskimo practice was a volatile scheme that bore little resemblance to what we call marriage.

But it was not only their marriage and sexual practices that were different. The Eskimos also seemed to have less regard for human life. Infanticide, for example, was common. Knud Rasmussen, one of the most famous early explorers, reported that he met one woman who had born twenty children but had killed ten of them at birth. Female babies, he found, were especially liable to be destroyed, and this was permitted simply at the parents' discretion, with no social stigma attached to it. Old people also, when they became too feeble to contribute to the family, were left out in the snow to die. So there seemed to be, in this society, remarkably little respect for life.

To the general public, these were disturbing revelations. Our own way of living seems so natural and right that for many of us it is hard to conceive of others living so differently. And when we do hear of such things, we tend immediately to categorize those other peoples as "backward" or "primitive."

But to anthropologists and sociologists, there was nothing particularly surprising about the Eskimos. Since the time of Herodotus, enlightened observers have been accustomed to the idea that conceptions of right and wrong differ from culture to culture. If we assume that *our* ideas of right and wrong will be shared by all peoples at all times, we are merely naive.

CULTURAL RELATIVISM

To many thinkers, this observation—"Different cultures have different moral codes"—has seemed to be the key to understanding morality. The idea of universal truth in ethics, they say, is a myth. The customs of different societies are all that exist. These customs cannot be said to be "correct" or "incorrect," for that implies we have an independent standard of right and wrong by which they may be judged. But there is no such independent standard; every standard is culture-bound. The great pioneering sociologist William Graham Sumner, writing in 1906, put the point like this:

> The "right" way is the way which the ancestors used and which has been handed down. The tradition is its own warrant. It is not held subject to verification by experience. The notion of right is in the folkways. It is not outside of them, of independent origin, and brought to test them. In the folkways, whatever is, is right. This is because they are traditional, and therefore contain in themselves the authority of the ancestral ghosts. When we come to the folkways we are at the end of our analysis.

This line of thought has probably persuaded more people to be skeptical about ethics than any other single thing. *Cultural Relativism*, as it has been called, challenges our ordinary belief in the objectivity and universality of moral truth. It says, in effect, that there is no such thing as universal truth in ethics; there are only the various cultural codes, and nothing more. Moreover, our own code has no special status; it is merely one among many.

As we shall see, this basic idea is really a compound of several different thoughts. It is important to separate the various elements of the theory because, on analysis, some parts of the theory turn out to be correct, whereas others seem to be mistaken. As a beginning, we may distinguish the following claims, all of which have been made by cultural relativists:

1. Different societies have different moral codes.
2. There is no objective standard that can be used to judge one societal code better than another.
3. The moral code of our own society has no special status; it is merely one among many.
4. There is no "universal truth" in ethics—that is, there are no moral truths that hold for all peoples at all times.

5. The moral code of a society determines what is right within that society; that is, if the moral code of a society says that a certain action is right, then that action *is* right, at least within that society.
6. It is mere arrogance for us to try to judge the conduct of other peoples. We should adopt an attitude of tolerance toward the practices of other cultures.

Although it may seem that these six propositions go naturally together, they are independent of one another, in the sense that some of them might be true even if others are false. In what follows, we will try to identify what is correct in Cultural Relativism, but we will also be concerned to expose what is mistaken about it.

THE CULTURAL DIFFERENCES ARGUMENT

Cultural Relavitism is a theory about the nature of morality. At first blush it seems quite plausible. However, like all such theories, it may be evaluated by subjecting it to rational analysis; and when we analyze Cultural Relativism we find that it is not so plausible as it first appears to be.

The first thing we need to notice is that at the heart of Cultural Relativism there is a certain *form of argument*. The strategy used by cultural relativists is to argue from facts about the differences between cultural outlooks to a conclusion about the status of morality. Thus we are invited to accept this reasoning:

(1) The Greeks believed it was wrong to eat the dead, whereas the Callatians believed it was right to eat the dead.
(2) Therefore, eating the dead is neither objectively right nor objectively wrong. It is merely a matter of opinion, which varies from culture to culture.

Or, alternatively:

(1) The Eskimos see nothing wrong with infanticide, whereas Americans believe infanticide is immoral.
(2) Therefore, infanticide is neither objectively right nor objectively wrong. It is merely a matter of opinion, which varies from culture to culture.

Clearly, these arguments are variations of one fundamental idea. They are both special cases of a more general argument, which says:

(1) Different cultures have different moral codes.
(2) Therefore, there is no objective "truth" in morality. Right and wrong are only matters of opinion, and opinions vary from culture to culture.

We may call this the *Cultural Differences Argument*. To many people, it is very persuasive. But from a logical point of view, is it a *sound* argument?

It is not sound. The trouble is that the conclusion does not really follow from the premise—that is, even if the premise is true, the conclusion still might be false. The premise concerns what people *believe:* in some societies, people believe one thing; in other societies, people believe differently. The conclusion, however, concerns *what really is the case.* The trouble is that this sort of conclusion does not follow logically from this sort of premise.

Consider again the example of the Greeks and Callatians. The Greeks believed it was wrong to eat the dead; the Callatians believed it was right. Does it follow, *from the mere fact that they disagreed,* that there is no objective truth in the matter? No, it does not follow; for it *could* be that the practice was objectively right (or wrong) and that one or the other of them was simply mistaken.

To make the point clearer, consider a very different matter. In some societies, people believe the earth is flat. In other societies, such as our own, people believe the earth is (roughly) spherical. Does it follow, *from the mere fact that they disagree,* that there is no "objective truth" in geography? Of course not; we would never draw such a conclusion because we realize that, in their beliefs about the world, the members of some societies might simply be wrong. There is no reason to think that if the world is round everyone must know it. Similarly, there is no reason to think that if there is moral truth everyone must know it. The fundamental mistake in the Cultural Differences Argument is that it attempts to derive a substantive conclusion about a subject (morality) from the mere fact that people disagree about it.

It is important to understand the nature of the point that is being made here. We are *not* saying (not yet, anyway) that the conclusion of the argument is false. Insofar as anything being said here is concerned, it is still an open question whether the conclusion is true. We *are* making a purely logical point and saying that the conclusion does not *follow from* the premise. This is important, because in order to determine whether the conclusion is true, we need arguments in its support. Cultural Relativism proposes this argument, but unfortunately the argument turns out to be fallacious. So it proves nothing.

THE CONSEQUENCES OF TAKING CULTURAL RELATIVISM SERIOUSLY

Even if the Cultural Differences Argument is invalid, Cultural Relativism might still be true. What would it be like if it were true?

In the passage quoted above, William Graham Sumner summarizes the essence of Cultural Relativism. He says that there is no measure of right and wrong other than the standards of one's society: "The notion of right is in the folkways. It is not outside of them, of independent origin, and brought to test them. In the folkways, whatever is, is right."

Suppose we took this seriously. What would be some of the consequences?

1. *We could no longer say that the customs of other societies are morally inferior to our own.* This, of course, is one of the main points stressed by

Cultural Relativism. We would have to stop condemning other societies merely because they are "different." So long as we concentrate on certain examples, such as the funerary practices of the Greeks and Callatians, this may seem to be a sophisticated, enlightened attitude.

However, we would also be stopped from criticizing other, less benign practices. Suppose a society waged war on its neighbors for the purpose of taking slaves. Or suppose a society was violently anti-Semitic and its leaders set out to destroy the Jews. Cultural Relativism would preclude us from saying that either of these practices was wrong. We would not even be able to say that a society tolerant of Jews is *better* than the anti-Semitic society, for that would imply some sort of transcultural standard of comparison. The failure to condemn *these* practices does not seem "enlightened"; on the contrary, slavery and anti-Semitism seem wrong *wherever* they occur. Nevertheless, if we took Cultural Relativism seriously, we would have to admit that these social practices also are immune from criticism.

2. *We could decide whether actions are right or wrong just by consulting the standards of our society.* Cultural Relativism suggests a simple test for determining what is right and what is wrong: all one has to do is ask whether the action is in accordance with the code of one's society. Suppose a resident of South Africa is wondering whether his country's [former] policy of *apartheid*—rigid racial segregation—is morally correct. All he has to do is ask whether this policy conforms to his society's moral code. If it does, there is nothing to worry about, at least from a moral point of view.

This implication of Cultural Relativism is disturbing because few of us think that our society's code is perfect—we can think of ways it might be improved. Yet Cultural Relativism would not only forbid us from criticizing the codes of *other* societies; it would stop us from criticizing our *own*. After all, if right and wrong are relative to culture, this must be true for our own culture just as much as for others.

3. *The idea of moral progress is called into doubt.* Usually, we think that at least some changes in our society have been for the better. (Some, of course, may have been changes for the worse.) Consider this example: Throughout most of Western history the place of women in society was very narrowly circumscribed. They could not own property; they could not vote or hold political office; with a few exceptions, they were not permitted to have paying jobs; and generally they were under the almost absolute control of their husbands. Recently much of this has changed, and most people think of it as progress.

If Cultural Relativism is correct, can we legitimately think of this as progress? Progress means replacing a way of doing things with a *better* way. But by what standard do we judge the new ways as better? If the old ways were in accordance with the social standards of their time, then Cultural Relativism would say it is a mistake to judge them by the standards of a different time. Eighteenth-century society was, in effect, a different society from the one we have now. To say that we have made progress implies a judgment that present-day society is better, and that is just the sort of transcultural judgment that, according to Cultural Relativism, is impermissible.

Our idea of social *reform* will also have to be reconsidered. A reformer such as Martin Luther King, Jr., seeks to change his society for the better. Within the constraints imposed by Cultural Relativism, there is one way this might be done. If a society is not living up to its own ideals, the reformer may be regarded as acting for the best: the ideals of the society are the standard by which we judge his or her proposals as worthwhile. But the "reformer" may not challenge the ideals themselves, for those ideals are by definition correct. According to Cultural Relativism, then, the idea of social reform makes sense only in this very limited way.

These three consequences of Cultural Relativism have led many thinkers to reject it as implausible on its face. It does make sense, they say, to condemn some practices, such as slavery and anti-Semitism, wherever they occur. It makes sense to think that our own society has made some moral progress, while admitting that it is still imperfect and in need of reform. Because Cultural Relativism says that these judgments make no sense, the argument goes, it cannot be right.

WHY THERE IS LESS DISAGREEMENT
THAN IT SEEMS

The original impetus for Cultural Relativism comes from the observation that cultures differ dramatically in their views of right and wrong. But just how much do they differ? It is true that there are differences. However, it is easy to overestimate the extent of those differences. Often, when we examine what *seems* to be a dramatic difference, we find that the cultures do not differ nearly as much as it appears.

Consider a culture in which people believe it is wrong to eat cows. This may even be a poor culture, in which there is not enough food; still, the cows are not to be touched. Such a society would *appear* to have values very different from our own. But does it? We have not yet asked why these people will not eat cows. Suppose it is because they believe that after death the souls of humans inhabit the bodies of animals, especially cows, so that a cow may be someone's grandmother. Now do we want to say that their values are different from ours? No; the difference lies elsewhere. The difference is in our belief systems, not in our values. We agree that we shouldn't eat Grandma; we simply disagree about whether the cow *is* (or could be) Grandma.

The general point is this. Many factors work together to produce the customs of a society. The society's values are only one of them. Other matters, such as the religious and factual beliefs held by its members and the physical circumstances in which they must live, are also important. We cannot conclude, then, merely because customs differ, that there is a disagreement about *values*. The difference in customs may be attributable to some other aspect of social life. Thus there may be less disagreement about values than there appears to be.

Consider the Eskimos again. They often kill perfectly normal infants, especially girls. We do not approve of this at all; a parent who did this in our society would be locked up. Thus there appears to be a great difference in the values of our two cultures. But suppose we ask *why* the Eskimos do this. The explanation is not that they have less affection for their children or less respect for human life. An Eskimo family will always protect its babies if conditions permit. But they live in a harsh environment, where food is often in short supply. A fundamental postulate of Eskimo thought is: "Life is hard, and the margin of safety small." A family may want to nourish its babies but be unable to do so.

As in many "primitive" societies, Eskimo mothers will nurse their infants over a much longer period of time than mothers in our culture. The child will take nourishment from its mother's breast for four years, perhaps even longer. So even in the best of times there are limits to the number of infants that one mother can sustain. Moreover, the Eskimos are a nomadic people—unable to farm, they must move about in search of food. Infants must be carried, and a mother can carry only one baby in her parka as she travels and goes about her outdoor work. Other family members can help, but this is not always possible.

Infant girls are more readily disposed of because, first, in this society the males are the primary food providers—they are the hunters, according to the traditional division of labor—and it is obviously important to maintain a sufficient number of food gatherers. But there is an important second reason as well. Because the hunters suffer a high casualty rate, the adult men who die prematurely far outnumber the women who die early. Thus if male and female infants survived in equal numbers, the female adult population would greatly outnumber the male adult population. Examining the available statistics, one writer concluded that "were it not for female infanticide . . . there would be approximately one-and-a-half times as many females in the average Eskimo local group as there are food-producing males."

So among the Eskimos, infanticide does not signal a fundamentally different attitude toward children. Instead, it is a recognition that drastic measures are sometimes needed to ensure the family's survival. Even then, however, killing the baby is not the first option considered. Adoption is common; childless couples are especially happy to take a more fertile couple's "surplus." Killing is only the last resort. I emphasize this in order to show that the raw data of the anthropologists can be misleading; it can make the differences in values between cultures appear greater than they are. The Eskimos' values are not all that different from our values. It is only that life forces upon them choices that we do not have to make.

HOW ALL CULTURES HAVE SOME VALUES IN COMMON

It should not be surprising that, despite appearances, the Eskimos are protective of their children. How could it be otherwise? How could a group survive that did *not* value its young? This suggests a certain argument, one which shows that all cultural groups must be protective of their infants:

(1) Human infants are helpless and cannot survive if they are not given extensive care for a period of years.
(2) Therefore, if a group did not care for its young, the young would not survive, and the older members of the group would not be replaced. After a while the group would die out.
(3) Therefore, any cultural group that continues to exist must care for its young. Infants that are *not* cared for must be the exception rather than the rule.

Similar reasoning shows that other values must be more or less universal. Imagine what it would be like for a society to place no value at all on truth telling. When one person spoke to another, there would be no presumption at all that he was telling the truth—for he could just as easily be speaking falsely. Within that society, there would be no reason to pay attention to what anyone says. (I ask you what time it is, and you say "Four o'clock." But there is no presumption that you are speaking truly; you could just as easily have said the first thing that came into your head. So I have no reason to pay attention to your answer—in fact, there was no point in my asking you in the first place!) Communication would then be extremely difficult, if not impossible. And because complex societies cannot exist without regular communication among their members, society would become impossible. It follows that in any complex society there *must* be a presumption in favor of truthfulness. There may of course be exceptions to this rule: there may be situations in which it is thought to be permissible to lie. Nevertheless, these will be exceptions to a rule that *is* in force in the society.

Let me give one further example of the same type. Could a society exist in which there was no prohibition on murder? What would this be like? Suppose people were free to kill other people at will, and no one thought there was anything wrong with it. In such a "society," no one could feel secure. Everyone would have to be constantly on guard. People who wanted to survive would have to avoid other people as much as possible. This would inevitably result in individuals trying to become as self-sufficient as possible—after all, associating with others would be dangerous. Society on any large scale would collapse. Of course, people might band together in smaller groups with others that they *could* trust not to harm them. But notice what this means: they would be forming smaller societies that *did* acknowledge a rule against murder. The prohibition of murder, then, is a necessary feature of all societies.

There is a general theoretical point here, namely, that *there are some moral rules that all societies will have in common, because those rules are necessary for society to exist.* The rules against lying and murder are two examples. And in fact, we do find these rules in force in all viable cultures. Cultures may differ in what they regard as legitimate exceptions to the rules, but this disagreement exists against a background of agreement on the larger issues. Therefore, it is a mistake to overestimate the amount of difference between cultures. Not *every* moral rule can vary from society to society.

WHAT CAN BE LEARNED FROM CULTURAL RELATIVISM

At the outset, I said that we were going to identify both what is right and what is wrong in Cultural Relativism. Thus far I have mentioned only its mistakes: I have said that it rests on an invalid argument, that it has consequences that make it implausible on its face, and that the extent of cultural disagreement is far less than it implies. This all adds up to a pretty thorough repudiation of the theory. Nevertheless, it is still a very appealing idea, and the reader may have the feeling that all this is a little unfair. The theory *must* have something going for it, or else why has it been so influential? In fact, I think there *is* something right about Cultural Relativism, and now I want to say what that is. There are two lessons we should learn from the theory, even if we ultimately reject it.

1. Cultural Relativism warns us, quite rightly, about the danger of assuming that all our preferences are based on some absolute rational standard. They are not. Many (but not all) of our practices are merely peculiar to our society, and it is easy to lose sight of that fact. In reminding us of it, the theory does a service.

Funerary practices are one example. The Callatians, according to Herodotus, were "men who eat their fathers"—a shocking idea, to us at least. But eating the flesh of the dead could be understood as a sign of respect. It could be taken as a symbolic act that says: We wish this person's spirit to dwell within us. Perhaps this was the understanding of the Callatians. On such a way of thinking, burying the dead could be seen as an act of rejection, and burning the corpse as positively scornful. If this is hard to imagine, then we may need to have our imaginations stretched. Of course we may feel a visceral repugnance at the idea of eating human flesh in any circumstances. But what of it? This repugnance may be, as the relativists say, only a matter of what is customary in our particular society.

There are many other matters that we tend to think of in terms of objective right and wrong, but that are really nothing more than social conventions. Should women cover their breasts? A publicly exposed breast is scandalous in our society, whereas in other cultures it is unremarkable. Objectively speaking, it is neither right nor wrong—there is no objective reason why either custom is better. Cultural Relativism begins with the valuable insight that many of our practices are like this—they are only cultural products. Then it goes wrong by concluding that, because *some* practices are like this, *all* must be.

2. The second lesson has to do with keeping an open mind. In the course of growing up, each of us has acquired some strong feelings: we have learned to think of some types of conduct as acceptable, and others we have learned to regard as simply unacceptable. Occasionally, we may find those feelings challenged. We may encounter someone who claims that our feelings are mistaken. For example, we may have been taught that homosexuality is immoral, and we may feel quite uncomfortable around gay people and see them as alien

and "different." Now someone suggests that this may be a mere prejudice; that there is nothing evil about homosexuality; that gay people are just people, like anyone else, who happen, through no choice of their own, to be attracted to others of the same sex. But because we feel so strongly about the matter, we may find it hard to take this seriously. Even after we listen to the arguments, we may still have the unshakable feeling that homosexuals *must*, somehow, be an unsavory lot.

Cultural Relativism, by stressing that our moral views can reflect the prejudices of our society, provides an antidote for this kind of dogmatism. When he tells the story of the Greeks and Callatians, Herodotus adds:

> For if anyone, no matter who, were given the opportunity of choosing from amongst all the nations of the world the set of beliefs which he thought best, he would inevitably, after careful consideration of their relative merits, choose that of his own country. Everyone without exception believes his own native customs, and the religion he was brought up in, to be the best.

Realizing this can result in our having more open minds. We can come to understand that our feelings are not necessarily perceptions of the truth—they may be nothing more than the result of cultural conditioning. Thus when we hear it suggested that some element of our social code is *not* really the best and we find ourselves instinctively resisting the suggestion, we might stop and remember this. Then we may be more open to discovering the truth, whatever that might be.

We can understand the appeal of Cultural Relativism, then, even though the theory has serious shortcomings. It is an attractive theory because it is based on a genuine insight—that many of the practices and attitudes we think so natural are really only cultural products. Moreover, keeping this insight firmly in view is important if we want to avoid arrogance and have open minds. These are important points, not to be taken lightly. But we can accept these points without going on to accept the whole theory.

17

Ethics and Observation

GILBERT HARMAN

Gilbert Harman (b. 1938) is Professor of Philosophy at Princeton University. In addition to his work in ethics, he has made major contributions in the theory of knowledge. He is the author of Thought, The Nature of Morality, Change in View, *and many articles.*

In this selection from chapter 1 of The Nature of Morality, *Harman compares the principles of ethics to those of science. He argues that while observation and experiment can make it reasonable to accept or reject scientific principles, the principles of ethics do not appear similarly confirmable or testable. At first glance, his reason for saying this may seem to be simply that observation can tell us what happens, but cannot tell us whether what happens is right or wrong. But this is not quite Harman's position. On his account, an observation is any opinion that is formed as a direct result of perception without conscious inference. Because a given perception (say of some children setting fire to a cat) may directly cause us to believe that what is happening is wrong, Harman believes that there can be moral observation.*

If moral observations are possible, why should we doubt that they can confirm moral principles as labortory observations confirm scientific principles? The answer, according to Harman, lies in the explanatory role of what is observed. When a physicist sees a vapor trail in a cloud chamber and directly forms the opinion that he is confronted with a proton, the best explanation of his forming this opinion will include a reference to the fact that he has been confronted with a proton. By contrast, when a moralist sees a child torturing a cat and directly forms the opinion that the child's activity is wrong, the best explanation of his forming this opinion seems to include no *reference to the torture's wrongness. Instead, it appears to include only references to the moralist's upbringing, conditioning, and so on. Because moral facts do not seem to be needed to explain moral observations, those observations do not appear to confirm moral principles. This is not Harman's final position, but it is one he regards as worthy of serious consideration.*

THE BASIC ISSUE

Can moral principles be tested and confirmed in the way scientific principles can? Consider the principle that, if you are given a choice between five people alive and one dead or five people dead and one alive, you should always choose to have five people alive and one dead rather than the other way round. We can easily imagine examples that appear to confirm this principle. Here is one:

> You are a doctor in a hospital's emergency room when six accident victims are brought in. All six are in danger of dying but one is much worse off than the others. You can just barely save that person if you devote all of your resources to him and let the others die. Alternatively, you can save the other five if you are willing to ignore the most seriously injured person.

It would seem that in this case you, the doctor, would be right to save the five and let the other person die. So this example, taken by itself, confirms the principle under consideration. Next, consider the following case.

> You have five patients in the hospital who are dying, each in need of a separate organ. One needs a kidney, another a lung, a third a heart, and so forth. You can save all five if you take a single healthy person and remove his heart, lungs, kidneys, and so forth, to distribute to these five patients. Just such a healthy person is in room 306. He is in the hospital for routine tests. Having seen his test results, you know that he is perfectly healthy and of the right tissue compatibility. If you do nothing, he will survive without incident; the other patients will die, however. The other five patients can be saved only if the person in Room 306 is cut up and his organs distributed. In that case, there would be one dead but five saved.

The principle in question tells us that you should cut up the patient in Room 306. But in this case, surely you must not sacrifice this innocent bystander, even to save the five other patients. Here a moral principle has been tested and disconfirmed in what may seem to be a surprising way.

This, of course, was a "thought experiment." We did not really compare a hypothesis with the world. We compared an explicit principle with our feelings about certain imagined examples. In the same way, a physicist performs thought experiments in order to compare explicit hypotheses with his "sense" of what should happen in certain situations, a "sense" that he has acquired as a result of his long working familiarity with current theory. But scientific hypotheses can also be tested in real experiments, out in the world.

Can moral principles be tested in the same way, out in the world? You can observe someone do something, but can you ever perceive the rightness or wrongness of what he does? If you round a corner and see a group of young hoodlums pour gasoline on a cat and ignite it, you do not need to *conclude* that what they are doing is wrong; you do not need to figure anything out; you can *see* that it is wrong. But is your reaction due to the actual wrongness of what you see or is it simply a reflection of your moral "sense," a "sense" that you have acquired perhaps as a result of your moral upbringing?

OBSERVATION

The issue is complicated. There are no pure observations. Observations are always "theory laden." What you perceive depends to some extent on the theory you hold, consciously or unconsciously. You see some children pour gasoline on a cat and ignite it. To really see that, you have to possess a great deal of knowledge, know about a considerable number of objects, know about people: that people pass through the life stages infant, baby, child, adolescent, adult. You must know what flesh and blood animals are, and in particular, cats. You must have some idea of life. You must know what gasoline is, what burning is, and much more. In one sense, what you "see" is a pattern of light on your retina, a shifting array of splotches, although, even that is theory, and you could never adequately describe what you see in that sense. In another sense, you see what you do because of the theories you hold. Change those theories and you would see something else, given the same pattern of light.

Similarly, if you hold a moral view, whether it is held consciously or unconsciously, you will be able to perceive rightness or wrongness, goodness or badness, justice or injustice. There is no difference in this respect between moral propositions and other theoretical propositions. If there is a difference, it must be found elsewhere.

Observation depends on theory because perception involves forming a belief as a fairly direct result of observing something; you can form a belief only if you understand the relevant concepts and a concept is what it is by virtue of its role in some theory or system of beliefs. To recognize a child as a child is to employ, consciously or unconsciously, a concept that is defined by its place in a framework of the stages of human life. Similarly, burning is an empty concept apart from its theoretical connections to the concepts of heat, destruction, smoke, and fire.

Moral concepts—Right and Wrong, Good and Bad, Justice and Injustice—also have a place in your theory or system of beliefs and are the concepts they are because of their context. If we say that observation has occurred whenever an opinion is a direct result of perception, we must allow that there is moral observation, because such an opinion can be a moral opinion as easily as any other sort. In this sense, observation may be used to confirm or disconfirm moral theories. The observational opinions that, in this sense, you find yourself with can be in either agreement or conflict with your consciously explicit moral principles. When they are in conflict, you must choose between your explicit theory and observation. In ethics, as in science, you sometimes opt for theory, and say that you made an error in observation or were biased or whatever, or you sometimes opt for observation, and modify your theory.

In other words, in both science and ethics, general principles are invoked to explain particular cases and, therefore, in both science and ethics, the general principles you accept can be tested by appealing to particular judgments that certain things are right or wrong, just or unjust, and so forth; and these judgments are analogous to direct perceptual judgments about facts.

OBSERVATIONAL EVIDENCE

Nevertheless, observation plays a role in science that it does not seem to play in ethics. The difference is that you need to make assumptions about certain physical facts to explain the occurrence of the observations that support a scientific theory, but you do not seem to need to make assumptions about any moral facts to explain the occurrence of the so-called moral observations I have been talking about. In the moral case, it would seem that you need only make assumptions about the psychology or moral sensibility of the person making the moral observation. In the scientific case, theory is tested against the world.

The point is subtle but important. Consider a physicist making an observation to test a scientific theory. Seeing a vapor trail in a cloud chamber, he thinks, "There goes a proton." Let us suppose that this is an observation in the relevant sense, namely, an immediate judgment made in response to the situation without any conscious reasoning having taken place. Let us also suppose that his observation confirms his theory, a theory that helps give meaning to the very term "proton" as it occurs in his observational judgment. Such a confirmation rests on inferring an explanation. He can count his making the observation as confirming evidence for his theory only to the extent that it is reasonable to explain his making the observation by assuming that, not only is he in a certain psychological "set," given the theory he accepts and his beliefs about the experimental apparatus, but furthermore, there really was a proton going through the cloud chamber, causing the vapor trail, which he saw as a proton. (This is evidence for the theory to the extent that the theory can explain the proton's being there better than competing theories can.) But, if his having made that observation could have been equally well explained by his psychological set alone, without the need for any assumption about a proton, then the observation would not have been evidence for the existence of that proton and therefore would not have been evidence for the theory. His making the observation supports the theory only because, in order to explain his making the observation, it is reasonable to assume something about the world over and above the assumptions made about the observer's psychology. In particular, it is reasonable to assume that there was a proton going through the cloud chamber, causing the vapor trail.

Compare this case with one in which you make a moral judgment immediately and without conscious reasoning, say, that the children are wrong to set the cat on fire or that the doctor would be wrong to cut up one healthy patient to save five dying patients. In order to explain your making the first of these judgments, it would be reasonable to assume, perhaps, that the children really are pouring gasoline on a cat and you are seeing them do it. But, in neither case is there any obvious reason to assume anything about "moral facts," such as that it really is wrong to set the cat on fire or to cut up the patient in Room 306. Indeed, an assumption about moral facts would seem to be totally irrelevant to the explanation of your making the judgment you make. It would seem that all we need assume is that you have certain more or less well articulated moral principles that are reflected in the judgments you make, based on your moral sensibility. It seems to be completely irrelevant to our explanation whether your intuitive immediate judgment is true or false.

The observation of an event can provide observational evidence for or against a scientific theory in the sense that the truth of that observation can be relevant to a reasonable explanation of why that observation was made. A moral observation does not seem, in the same sense, to be observational evidence for or against any moral theory, since the truth or falsity of the moral observation seems to be completely irrelevant to any reasonable explanation of why that observation was made. The fact that an observation of an event was made at the time it was made is evidence not only about the observer but also about the physical facts. The fact that you made a particular moral observation when you did does not seem to be evidence about moral facts, only evidence about you and your moral sensibility. Facts about protons can affect what you observe, since a proton passing through the cloud chamber can cause a vapor trail that reflects light to your eye in a way that, given your scientific training and psychological set, leads you to judge that what you see is a proton. But there does not seem to be any way in which the actual rightness or wrongness of a given situation can have any effect on your perceptual apparatus. In this respect, ethics seems to differ from science.

In considering whether moral principles can help explain observations, it is therefore important to note an ambiguity in the word "observation." You see the children set the cat on fire and immediately think, "That's wrong." In one sense, your observation is that what the children are doing is wrong. In another sense, your observation is your thinking that thought. Moral observations might explain observations in the first sense but not in the second sense. Certain moral principles might help to explain why it was *wrong* of the children to set the cat on fire, but moral principles seem to be of no help in explaining *your thinking* that that is wrong. In the first sense of "observation," moral principles can be tested by observation—"That this act is wrong is evidence that causing unnecessary suffering is wrong." But in the second sense of "observation," moral principles cannot clearly be tested by observation, since they do not appear to help explain observations in this second sense of "observation." Moral principles do not seem to help explain your observing what you observe.

Of course, if you are already given the moral principle that it is wrong to cause unnecessary suffering, you can take your seeing the children setting the cat on fire as observational evidence that they are doing something wrong. Similarly, you can suppose that your seeing the vapor trail is observational evidence that a proton is going through the cloud chamber, if you are given the relevant physical theory. But there is an important apparent difference between the two cases. In the scientific case, your making that observation is itself evidence for the physical theory because the physical theory explains the proton, which explains the trail, which explains your observation. In the moral case, your making your observation does not seem to be evidence for the relevant moral principle because that principle does not seem to help explain your observation. The explanatory chain from principle to observation seems to be broken in morality. The moral principle may "explain" why it is wrong for the children to set the cat on fire. But the wrongness of that act does not appear to help explain the act, which you observe, itself. The explanatory chain appears to be broken in such a way that neither the moral principle nor the wrongness of the act can help explain why you observe what you observe.

A qualification may seem to be needed here. Perhaps the children perversely set the cat on fire simply "because it is wrong." Here it may seem at first that the actual wrongness of the act does help explain why they do it and therefore indirectly helps explain why you observe what you observe just as a physical theory, by explaining why the proton is producing a vapor trail, indirectly helps explain why the observer observes what he observes. But on reflection we must agree that this is probably an illusion. What explains the children's act is not clearly the actual wrongness of the act but, rather, their belief that the act is wrong. The actual rightness or wrongness of their act seems to have nothing to do with why they do it.

Observational evidence plays a part in science it does not appear to play in ethics, because scientific principles can be justified ultimately by their role in explaining observations, in the second sense of observation—by their explanatory role. Apparently, moral principles cannot be justified in the same way. It appears to be true that there can be no explanatory chain between moral principles and particular observings in the way that there can be such a chain between scientific principles and particular observings. Conceived as an explanatory theory, morality, unlike science, seems to be cut off from observation.

Not that every legitimate scientific hypothesis is susceptible to direct observational testing. Certain hypotheses about "black holes" in space cannot be directly tested, for example, because no signal is emitted from within a black hole. The connection with observation in such a case is indirect. And there are many similar examples. Nevertheless, seen in the large, there is the apparent difference between science and ethics we have noted. The scientific realm is accessible to observation in a way the moral realm is not.

ETHICS AND MATHEMATICS

Perhaps ethics is to be compared, not with physics, but with mathematics. Perhaps such a moral principle as "You ought to keep your promises" is confirmed or disconfirmed in the way (whatever it is) in which such a mathematical principle as "5 + 7 = 12" is. Observation does not seem to play the role in mathematics it plays in physics. We do not and cannot perceive numbers, for example, since we cannot be in causal contact with them. We do not even understand what it would be like to be in causal contact with the number 12, say. Relations among numbers cannot have any more of an effect on our perceptual apparatus than moral facts can.

Observation, however, *is* relevant to mathematics. In explaining the observations that support a physical theory, scientists typically appeal to mathematical principles. On the other hand, one never seems to need to appeal in this way to moral principles. Since an observation is evidence for what best explains it, and since mathematics often figures in the explanations of scientific observations, there is indirect observational evidence for mathematics. There does not seem to be observational evidence, even indirectly, for basic moral principles. In explaining why certain observations have been made, we never seem to use purely moral assumptions. In this respect, then, ethics appears to differ not only from physics but also from mathematics.

•   •   •

18

Moral Explanations

NICHOLAS STURGEON

Nicholas Sturgeon (b. 1942) is Professor of Philosophy at Cornell University. He has published a number of articles on moral philosophy. This selection originally appeared in Morality, Reason, and Truth: New Essays on the Foundations of Ethics, *edited by David Copp and David Zimmerman.*

Sturgeon's topic is a problem raised by Gilbert Harman. In reading 17, Harman notes that morality seems importantly different from science. Unlike scientific facts, moral facts appear to play no role in explaining our observations (or anything else). But Sturgeon argues that this has not been established. In his view, a plausible explanation of behavior such as that of Adolf Hitler makes reference to the (moral) fact that Hitler was depraved. Of course, anyone with exactly Hitler's psychology would have acted just as Hitler did. But in Sturgeon's view, to have Hitler's psychology is to be depraved. It is thus impossible to explain Hitler's behavior without appealing to moral facts.

We might, of course, be wrong in holding that persons with that psychology are depraved. Despite the evidence, the moral theory in which this belief is embedded might be mistaken. But, just so, we might, despite all the evidence, be mistaken in holding our theories of subatomic physics or of the external world. Thus construed, Harman's argument is a special case of a much wider skepticism. For this reason, Sturgeon argues, it poses no special threat to ethics.

There is one argument for moral skepticism that I respect even though I remain unconvinced. It has sometimes been called the argument from moral diversity or relativity, but that is somewhat misleading, for the problem arises not from the diversity of moral views, but from the apparent difficulty of *settling* moral disagreements, or even of knowing what would be required to settle them, a difficulty thought to be noticeably greater than any found in settling disagreements that arise in, for example, the sciences. This provides an argument for moral skepticism because one obviously possible explanation of our difficulty in settling moral disagreements is that they are really unsettleable, that there is no way of justifying one rather than another competing view on these issues; and a possible further explanation for the unsettleability of moral disagreements, in turn, is moral nihilism, the view that on these issues there just is no fact of the matter, that the impossibility of discovering and establishing moral truths is due to there not being any.

I am, as I say, unconvinced: partly because I think this argument exaggerates the difficulty we actually find in settling moral disagreements, partly because there are alternative explanations to be considered for the difficulty we do find. Under the latter heading, for example, it certainly matters to what extent moral disagreements depend on disagreements about other questions which, however, disputed they may be, are nevertheless regarded as having objective answers: questions such as which, if any, religion is true, which account of human psychology, which theory of human society. And it also matters to what extent consideration of moral questions is in practice skewed by distorting factors such as personal interest and social ideology. These are large issues. Although it is possible to say some useful things to put them in perspective,[1] it appears impossible to settle them quickly or in any a priori way. Consideration of them is likely to have to be piecemeal and, in the short run at least, frustratingly indecisive.

These large issues are not my topic here. But I mention them, and the difficulty of settling them, to show why it is natural that moral skeptics have hoped to find some quicker way of establishing their thesis. I doubt that any exist, but some have of course been proposed. Verificationist attacks on ethics should no doubt be seen in this light, and J. L. Mackie's recent "argument from queerness" is a clear instance.[2] The quicker response on which I shall concentrate, however, is neither of these, but instead an argument by Gilbert Harman designed to bring out the "basic problem" about morality, which in his view is "its apparent immunity from observational testing" and "the seeming irrelevance of observational evidence."[3] The argument is that reference to moral facts appears unnecessary for the *explanation* of our moral observations and beliefs.

Harman's view, I should say at once, is not in the end a skeptical one, and he does not view the argument I shall discuss as a decisive defense of moral skepticism or moral nihilism. Someone else might easily so regard it, however. For Harman himself regards it as creating a strong *prima facie* case for skepticism and nihilism, strong enough to justify calling it "the problem with ethics."[4] And he believes it shows that the only recourse for someone who wishes to avoid moral skepticism is to find defensible reductive definitions for ethical terms; so skepticism would be the obvious conclusion to draw for anyone who doubted the possibility of such definitions. I believe, however, that Harman is

---

1 As, for example, in Alan Gewirth, "Positive 'Ethics' and Normative 'Science' ", *The Philosophical Review* 69 (1960), pp. 311–330, in which there are some useful remarks about the first of them.

2 J. L. Mackie, *Ethics: Inventing Right and Wrong* (Harmondsworth, England: Penguin, 1977), pp. 38–42.

3 Gilbert Harman, *The Nature of Morality: An Introduction to Ethics* (New York: Oxford University Press, 1977), pp. vii, viii. Parenthetical page references are to this work.

4 Harman's title for the entire first section of his book.

mistaken on both counts. I shall show that his argument for skepticism either rests on claims that most people would find quite implausible (and so cannot be what constitutes, for *them*, the problem with ethics); or else becomes just the application to ethics of a familiar *general* skeptical strategy, one which, if it works for ethics, will work equally well for unobservable theoretical entities, or for other minds, or for an external world (and so, again, can hardly be what constitutes the distinctive problem with *ethics*). I have argued elsewhere,[5] moreover, that one can in any case be a moral realist, and indeed an ethical naturalist, without believing that we are now or ever will be in possession of reductive naturalistic definitions for ethical terms.

I. THE PROBLEM WITH ETHICS

Moral theories are often tested in thought experiments, against imagined examples; and, as Harman notes, trained researchers often test scientific theories in the same way. The problem, though, is that scientific theories can also be tested against the world, by observations or real experiments; and, Harman asks, "can moral principles be tested in the same way, out in the world?"

This would not be a very interesting or impressive challenge, of course, if it were merely a resurrection of standard verificationist worries about whether moral assertions and theories have any testable empirical implications, implications statable in some relatively austere "observational" vocabulary. One problem with that form of the challenge, as Harman points out, is that there are no "pure" observations, and in consequence no purely observational vocabulary either. But there is also a deeper problem that Harman does not mention, one that remains even if we shelve worries about "pure" observations and, at least for the sake of argument, grant the verificationist his observational language, pretty much as it was usually conceived: that is, as lacking at the very least any obviously theoretical terminology from any recognized science, and of course as lacking any moral terminology. For then the difficulty is that moral principles fare just as well (or just as badly) against the verificationist challenge as do typical scientific principles. For it is by now a familiar point about scientific principles—principles such as Newton's law of universal gravitation or Darwin's theory of evolution—that they are entirely devoid of empirical implications when considered in isolation.[6] We do of course base observational predictions on such theories and so test them against experience, but that is because we do *not* consider them in isolation. For we can derive these predictions only by relying at the same time on a large background of additional

5 In the longer article of which this is an abridgement.

6 This point is generally credited to Pierre Duhem; see *The Aim and Structure of Physical Theory*, trans. Philip P. Wiener (Princeton, NJ: Princeton University Press, 1954). It is a prominent theme in the influential writings of W. V. O. Quine. For an especially clear application of it, see Hilary Putnam, "The 'Corroboration' of Theories," in *Mathematics, Matter and Method: Philosophical Papers, Volume I*, second ed. (Cambridge: Cambridge University Press, 1977), pp. 250–269.

assumptions, many of which are equally theoretical and equally incapable of being tested in isolation.

A less familiar point, because less often spelled out, is that the relation of moral principles to observation is similar in *both* these respects. Candidate moral principles—for example, that an action is wrong just in case there is something else the agent could have done that would have produced a greater balance of pleasure over pain—lack empirical implications when considered in isolation. But it is easy to derive empirical consequences from them, and thus to test them against experience, if we allow ourselves, as we do in the scientific case, to rely on a background of other assumptions of comparable status. Thus, if we conjoin the act-utilitarian principle I just cited with the further view, also untestable in isolation, that it is always wrong deliberately to kill a human being, we can deduce from these two premises together the consequence that deliberately killing a human being always produces a lesser balance of pleasure over pain than some available alternative act; and this claim is one any positivist would have conceded we know, in principle at least, how to test. If we found it to be false, moreover, then we would be forced by this empirical test to abandon at least one of the moral claims from which we derived it.

It might be thought a worrisome feature of this example, however, and a further opening for skepticism, that there could be controversy about which moral premise to abandon, and that we have not explained how our empirical test can provide an answer to *this* question. And this may be a problem. It should be a familiar problem, however, because the Duhemian commentary includes a precisely corresponding point about the scientific case: that if we are at all cautious in characterizing what we observe, then the requirement that our theories merely be *consistent* with observation is a very weak one. There are always many, perhaps indefinitely many, different mutually inconsistent ways to adjust our views to meet this constraint. Of course, in practice we are often confident of how to do it: if you are a freshman chemistry student, you do not conclude from your failure to obtain the predicted value in an experiment that it is all over for the atomic theory of gases. And the decision can be equally easy, one should note, in a moral case. Consider two examples. From the surprising moral thesis that Adolf Hitler was a morally admirable person, together with a modest piece of moral theory to the effect that no morally admirable person would, for example, instigate and oversee the degradation and death of millions of persons, one can derive the testable consequence that Hitler did not do this. But he did, so we must give up one of our premises; and the choice of which to abandon is neither difficult nor controversial.

Or, to take a less monumental example, contrived around one of Harman's own, suppose you have been thinking yourself lucky enough to live in a neighborhood in which no one would do anything wrong, at least not in public; and that the modest piece of theory you accept, this time, is that malicious cruelty, just for the hell of it, is wrong. Then, as in Harman's example, "you round a corner and see a group of young hoodlums pour gasoline on a cat and ignite it." At this point, either your confidence in the neighborhood or your principle about cruelty has got to give way. But the choice is easy, if dispiriting, so easy as hardly to require thought. As Harman says, "You do not need to *conclude* that what they are doing is wrong; you do not need to figure anything out; you can *see* that it is wrong" (p. 4). But a skeptic can still wonder whether this practical confidence, or this "seeing," rests in either sort of case on anything more than deeply ingrained conventions of thought— respect for scientific experts, say, and for certain moral traditions—as opposed to anything answerable to the facts of the matter, any reliable strategy for getting it right about the world.

Now, Harman's challenge is interesting partly because it does not rest on these verificationist doubts about whether moral beliefs have observational implications, but even more because what it does rest on is a partial answer to the kind of general skepticism to which, as we have seen, reflection on the verificationist picture can lead. Many of our beliefs are justified, in Harman's view, by their providing or helping to provide a reasonable *explanation* of our observing what we do. It would be consistent with your failure, as a beginning student, to obtain the experimental result predicted by the gas laws, that the laws are mistaken. But a better explanation, in light of your inexperience and the general success experts have had in confirming and applying these laws, is that you made some mistake in running the experiment. So our scientific beliefs can be justified by their explanatory role; and so too, in Harman's view, can mathematical beliefs and many commonsense beliefs about the world.

Not so, however, moral beliefs: they appear to have no such explanatory role. That is "the problem with ethics." Harman spells out his version of this contrast:

> You need to make assumptions about certain physical facts to explain the occur- rence of the observations that support a scientific theory, but you do not seem to need to make assumptions about any moral facts to explain the occurrence of the so-called moral observations I have been talking about. In the moral case, it would seem that you need only make assumptions about the psychology or moral sensibility of the person making the moral observation (p. 6)

More precisely, and applied to his own example, it might be reasonable, in order to explain your judging that the hoodlums are wrong to set the cat on fire, to assume "that the children really are pouring gasoline on a cat and you are seeing them do it." But there is no

> obvious reason to assume anything about "moral facts," such as that it is really wrong to set the cat on fire. . . . Indeed, an assumption about moral facts would seem to be totally irrelevant to the explanation of your making the judgment you make. It would seem that all we need assume is that you have certain more or less well articulated moral principles that are reflected in the judgments you make, based on your moral sensibility. (p. 7)

And Harman thinks that if we accept this conclusion, suitably generalized, then, subject to one possible qualification concerning reduction that I have discussed elsewhere,[7] we must conclude that moral theories cannot be tested against the world as scientific theories can, and that we have no reason to believe that moral facts are part of the order of nature or that there is any moral knowledge (pp. 23, 35).

My own view is that Harman is quite wrong, not in thinking that the explanatory role of our beliefs is important to their justification, but in thinking that moral beliefs play no such role.[8] I shall have to say something about the initial plausibility of Harman's thesis as applied to his own example, but part of my reason for dissenting should be apparent from the other example I just gave. We find it easy (and so does Harman [p. 108]) to conclude from the evidence not just that Hitler was not morally admirable, but that he was morally depraved. But isn't it plausible that Hitler's moral depravity—the fact of his really having been morally depraved—forms part of a reasonable explanation of why we believe he was depraved? I think so, and I shall argue concerning this and other examples that moral beliefs very commonly play the explanatory role Harman denies them. Before I can press my case, however, I need to clear up several preliminary points about just what Harman is claiming and just how his argument is intended to work.

II. OBSERVATION AND EXPLANATION

(1) For there are several ways in which Harman's argument invites misunderstanding. One results from his focusing at the start on the question of whether there can be moral *observations*.[9] But this question turns out to be a side issue, in no way central to his argument that moral principles cannot be tested against the world. There are a couple of reasons for this, of which the more important[10] by far is that Harman does not really require of moral facts,

---

7 See note 5.

8 Harman is careful always to say only that moral beliefs *appear* to play no such role, and since he eventually concludes that there *are* moral facts (p. 132), this caution may be more than stylistic. I shall argue that this more cautious claim, too, is mistaken (indeed, that is my central thesis). But to avoid issues about Harman's intent, I shall simply mean by "Harman's argument" the skeptical argument of his first two chapters, whether or not he means to endorse all of it. This argument surely deserves discussion in its own right in either case, especially since Harman never explains what is wrong with it.

9 He asks: "Can moral principles be tested in the same way [as scientific hypotheses can], out in the world? You can observe someone do something, but can you ever perceive the rightness or wrongness of what he does?" (p. 4).

10 The other is that Harman appears to use "observe" (and "perceive" and "see") in a surprising way. One would normally take observing (or perceiving, or seeing) something to involve *knowing* it was the case. But Harman apparently takes an observation to be *any* opinion arrived at as "a direct result of perception" (p. 5) or, at any rate (see next footnote), "immediately and without conscious reasoning" (p. 7). This means that observations need not even be true, much less known to be true. A consequence is that the existence of moral observations, in Harman's sense, would not be sufficient to show that there is moral knowledge, although this *would* be sufficient if "observe" were being used in a more standard sense. What I argue in the text is that the existence of moral observations (in either Harman's or the standard sense) is not *necessary* for showing that there is moral knowledge, either.

if belief in them is to be justified, that they figure in the explanation of moral observations. It would be enough, on the one hand, if they were needed for the explanation of moral beliefs that are not in any interesting sense observations. For example, Harman thinks belief in moral facts would be vindicated if they were needed to explain our drawing the moral conclusions we do when we reflect on hypothetical cases, but I think there is no illumination in calling these conclusions observations.[11] It would also be enough, on the other hand, if moral facts were needed for the explanation of what were clearly observations, but not moral observations. Harman thinks mathematical beliefs are justified, but he does not suggest that there are mathematical observations; it is rather that appeal to mathematical truths helps to explain why we make the physical observations we do (p. 10). Moral beliefs would surely be justified, too, if they played such a role, whether or not there are any moral observations.

So the claim is that moral facts are not needed to explain our having any of the moral beliefs we do, whether or not those beliefs are observations, and are equally unneeded to explain any of the observations we make, whether or not those observations are moral. In fact, Harman's view appears to be that moral facts aren't needed to explain anything at all: though it would perhaps be question-begging for him to begin with this strong a claim, since he grants that if there were any moral facts, then appeal to other moral facts—more general ones, for example—might be needed to explain *them* (p. 8). But he is certainly claiming, at the very least, that moral facts aren't needed to explain any nonmoral facts we have any reason to believe in.

(2) Other possible misunderstandings concern what is meant in asking whether reference to moral facts is *needed* to explain moral beliefs. One warning about this question I have dealt with in my discussion of reduction elsewhere;[12]

11 This sort of case does not meet Harman's characterization of an observation as an opinion that is "a direct result of perception" (p. 5), but he is surely right that moral facts would be as well vindicated if they were needed to explain our drawing conclusions about hypothetical cases as they would be if they were needed to explain observations in the narrower sense. To be sure, Harman is still confining his attention to cases in which we draw the moral conclusion from our thought experiment "immediately and without conscious reasoning" (p. 7), and it is no doubt the existence of such cases that gives purchase to talk of a "moral sense." But this feature, again, can hardly matter to the argument: would belief in moral facts be less justified if they were needed only to explain the instances in which we draw the moral conclusion *slowly?* Nor can it make any difference for that matter whether the case we are reflecting on is hypothetical: so my example in which we, quickly or slowly, draw a moral conclusion about Hitler from what we know of him, is surely relevant.

12 In the longer paper from which this one is abridged. The salient point is that there are two very *different* reasons one might have for thinking that no reference to moral facts is needed in the explanation of moral beliefs. One—Harman's reason, and my target in this essay—is that no moral explanations even *seem* plausible, that reference to moral facts always strikes us as "completely irrelevant" to the explanation of moral beliefs. This claim, if true, would tend to support moral skepticism. The other, which might appeal to a "reductive" naturalist in ethics, is that any moral explanations that *do* seem plausible can be paraphrased without explanatory loss in entirely nonmoral terms. I doubt this view, too, and I argue in the longer version of this paper that no ethical naturalist need hold it. But anyone tempted by it should note that it is anyway no version of moral skepticism: for what it says is that we know so *much* about ethics that we are always able to say, in entirely nonmoral terms, exactly which natural properties the moral terms in any plausible moral explanations refer to—that's why the moral expressions are dispensable. These two reasons should not be confused with one another.

but another, about what Harman is clearly *not* asking, and about what sort of answer I can attempt to defend to the question he is asking, I can spell out here. For Harman's question is clearly not just whether there is *an* explanation of our moral beliefs that does not mention moral facts. Almost surely there is. Equally surely, however, there is *an* explanation of our commonsense nonmoral beliefs that does not mention an external world: one which cites only our sensory experience, for example, together with whatever needs to be said about our psychology to explain why with that history of experience we would form just the beliefs we do. Harman means to be asking a question that will lead to skepticism about moral facts, but not to skepticism about the existence of material bodies or about well-established scientific theories of the world.

Harman illustrates the kind of question he is asking, and the kind of answer he is seeking, with an example from physics that it will be useful to keep in mind. A physicist sees a vapor trail in a cloud chamber and thinks, "There goes a proton." What explains his thinking this? Partly, of course, his psychological set, which largely depends on his beliefs about the apparatus and all the theory he has learned; but partly also, perhaps, the hypothesis that "there really was a proton going through the cloud chamber, causing the vapor trail, which he saw as a proton." We will *not* need this latter assumption, however, "if his having made that observation could have been equally well explained by his psychological set alone, without the need for any assumption about a proton" (p. 6).[13] So for reference to moral facts to be *needed* in the explanation of our beliefs and observations, is for this reference to be required for an explanation that is somehow *better* than competing explanations. Correspondingly, reference to moral facts will be unnecessary to an explanation, in Harman's view, not just because we can find some explanation that does not appeal to them, but because *no* explanation that appeals to them is any better than some competing explanation that does not.

Now, fine discriminations among competing explanations of almost anything are likely to be difficult, controversial, and provisional. Fortunately, however, my discussion of Harman's argument will not require any fine discriminations. This is because Harman's thesis, as we have seen, is *not* that moral explanations lose out by a small margin; nor is it that moral explanations, though sometimes initially promising, always turn out on further examination to be inferior to nonmoral ones. It is, rather, that reference to moral facts always looks, right from the start, to be "completely irrelevant" to the explanation of any of our observations and beliefs. And my argument will be that this is mistaken: that many moral explanations appear to be good explanations,

---

13 It is surprising that Harman does not mention the obvious intermediate possibility, which would occur to any instrumentalist: to cite the physicist's psychological set *and* the vapor trail, but say nothing about protons or other unobservables. It is *this* explanation, as I emphasize below, that is most closely parallel to an explanation of beliefs about an external world in terms of sensory experience and psychological makeup, or of moral beliefs in terms of nonmoral facts together with our "moral sensibility."

or components in good explanations, that are not obviously undermined by anything else that we know. My suspicion, in fact, is that moral facts are needed in the sense explained, that they will turn out to belong in our best overall explanatory picture of the world, even in the long run, but I shall not attempt to establish that here. Indeed, it should be clear why I could not pretend to do so. For I have explicitly put to one side the issue (which I regard as incapable in any case of quick resolution) of whether and to what extent actual moral disagreements can be settled satisfactorily; but I assume it would count as a defect in any sort of explanation to rely on claims about which rational agreement proved unattainable. So I concede that it *could* turn out, for anything I say here, that moral explanations are all defective and should be discarded. What I shall try to show is merely that many moral explanations look reasonable enough to be in the running; and, more specifically, that nothing Harman says provides any reason for thinking they are not. This claim is surely strong enough (and controversial enough) to be worth defending.

(3) It is implicit in this statement of my project, but worth noting separately, that I take Harman to be proposing an *independent* skeptical argument— independent not merely of the argument from the difficulty of settling disputed moral questions, but also of other standard arguments for moral skepticism. Otherwise his argument is not worth separate discussion. For *any* of these more familiar skeptical arguments will of course imply that moral explanations are defective, on the reasonable assumption that it would be a defect in any explanation to rely on claims as doubtful as these arguments attempt to show all moral claims to be. But if *that* is why there is a problem with moral explanations, one should surely just cite the relevant skeptical argument, rather than this derivative difficulty about moral explanations, as the basic "problem with ethics," and it is that argument we should discuss. So I take Harman's interesting suggestion to be that there is a *different* difficulty that remains even if we put other arguments for moral skepticism aside and *assume*, for the sake of argument, that there are moral facts (for example, that what the children in his example are doing is really wrong): namely, that these assumed facts *still* seem to play no explanatory role.

This understanding of Harman's thesis crucially affects my argumentative strategy in a way to which I should alert the reader in advance. For it should be clear that assessment of this thesis not merely permits, but *requires,* that we provisionally assume the existence of moral facts. I can see no way of evaluating the claim that *even if* we assumed the existence of moral facts they would still appear explanatorily irrelevant, without assuming the existence of some, to see how they would look. So I do freely assume this in each of the examples I discuss in the next section. (I have tried to choose plausible examples, moreover, moral facts most of us would be inclined to believe in if we did believe in moral facts, since those are the easiest to think about; but the precise examples don't matter, and anyone who would prefer others should feel free to substitute her own.) I grant, furthermore, that if Harman were right about the outcome of this thought experiment—that even after we assumed these facts they still looked irrelevant to the explanation of our moral beliefs and other nonmoral facts—then we might conclude with him that there were, after all, no such facts. But I claim he is wrong: that once we have provisionally assumed the existence of moral facts they *do* appear relevant, by perfectly ordinary standards, to the explanation of moral beliefs and of a good deal else besides. Does this prove that there *are* such facts? Well of course it helps support that view, but here I carefully make no claim to have shown so much. What I *show* is that any remaining reservations about the existence of moral facts must be based on those *other* skeptical arguments, of which Harman's argument is independent. In short, there may still be a "problem with ethics," but it has *nothing* special to do with moral explanations.

III. MORAL EXPLANATIONS

Now that I have explained how I understand Harman's thesis, I turn to my arguments against it. I shall first add to my example of Hitler's moral character several more in which it seems plausible to cite moral facts as part of an explanation of nonmoral facts, and in particular of people's forming the moral opinions they do. I shall then argue that Harman gives us no plausible reason to reject or ignore these explanations; I shall claim, in fact, that the same is true for his own example of the children igniting the cat. I shall conclude, finally, by attempting to diagnose the source of the disagreement between Harman and me on these issues.

My Hitler example suggests a whole range of extremely common cases that appear not to have occurred to Harman, cases in which we cite someone's moral character as part of an explanation of his or her deeds, and in which that whole story is then available as a plausible further explanation of someone's arriving at a correct assessment of that moral character. Take just one other example. Bernard DeVoto, in *The Year of Decision: 1846*, describes the efforts of American emigrants already in California to rescue another party of emigrants, the Donner Party, trapped by snows in the High Sierras, once their plight became known. At a meeting in Yerba Buena (now San Francisco), the relief efforts were put under the direction of a recent arrival, Passed Midshipman Selim Woodworth, described by a previous acquaintance as "a great busybody and ambitious of taking a command among the emigrants."[14] But Woodworth not only failed to lead rescue parties into the mountains himself, where other rescuers were counting on him (leaving children to be picked up by him, for example), but had to be "shamed, threatened and bullied" even into organizing the efforts of others willing to take the risk; he spent time arranging comforts

14 Bernard DeVoto, *The Year of Decision: 1846* (Boston: Houghton Mifflin, 1942), p. 426; a quotation from the notebooks of Francis Parkman. The account of the entire rescue effort is on pp. 424–444.

for himself in camp, preening himself on the importance of his position; and as a predictable result of his cowardice and his exercises in vainglory, many died who might have been saved, including four known still to be alive when he turned back for the last time in mid-March.

DeVoto concludes: "Passed Midshipman Woodworth was just no damned good" (1942, p. 442). I cite this case partly because it has so clearly the structure of an inference to a reasonable explanation. One can think of competing explanations, but the evidence points against them. It isn't, for example, that Woodworth was a basically decent person who simply proved too weak when thrust into a situation that placed heroic demands on him. He volunteered, he put no serious effort even into tasks that required no heroism, and it seems clear that concern for his own position and reputation played a much larger role in his motivation than did any concern for the people he was expected to save. If DeVoto is right about this evidence, moreover, it seems reasonable that part of the explanation of his believing that Woodworth was no damned good is just that Woodworth *was* no damned good.

DeVoto writes of course with more moral intensity (and with more of a flourish) than academic historians usually permit themselves, but it would be difficult to find a serious work of biography, for example, in which actions are not explained by appeal to moral character: sometimes by appeal to specific virtues and vices, but often enough also by appeal to a more general assessment. A different question, and perhaps a more difficult one, concerns the sort of example on which Harman concentrates, the explanation of judgments of right and wrong. Here again he appears just to have overlooked explanations in terms of moral character: a judge's thinking that it would be wrong to sentence a particular offender to the maximum prison term the law allows, for example, may be due in part to her decency and fairmindedness, which I take to be moral properties if any are. But do moral features of the action or institution being judged ever play an explanatory role? Here is an example in which they appear to. An interesting historical question is why vigorous and reasonably widespread moral opposition to slavery arose for the first time in the eighteenth and nineteenth centuries, even though slavery was a very old institution; and why this opposition arose primarily in Britain, France, and in French- and English-speaking North America, even though slavery existed throughout the New World.[15] There is a standard answer to this question. It is that chattel slavery in British and French America, and then in the United States, was much *worse* than previous forms of slavery, and much worse than slavery in Latin America. This is, I should add, a controversial explanation. But as is often the case with historical explanations, its proponents do not claim it is the whole story, and many of its opponents grant that there may be some truth in these

---

15 What is being explained, of course, is not just why people came to think slavery wrong, but why people who were not themselves slaves or in danger of being enslaved came to think it so seriously wrong as to be intolerable. There is a much larger and longer history of people who thought it wrong but tolerable and an even longer one of people who appear not to have gotten past the thought that the world would be a better place without it. See David Brion Davis, *The Problem of Slavery in Western Culture* (Ithaca, NY: Cornell University Press, 1966).

comparisons, and that they may after all form a small part of a larger explanation.[16] This latter concession is all I require for my example. Equally good for my purpose would be the more limited thesis which explains the growth of antislavery sentiment in the United States, between the Revolution and the Civil War, in part by saying that slavery in the United States became a more oppressive institution during that time. The appeal in these standard explanations is straightforwardly to moral facts.

What is supposed to be wrong with all these explanations? Harman says that assumptions about moral facts seem "completely irrelevant" in explaining moral observations and moral beliefs (p. 7), but on its more natural reading that claim seems pretty obviously mistaken about these examples. For it is natural to think that if a particular assumption is completely irrelevant to the explanation of a certain fact, then that fact would have obtained, and we could have explained it just as well, even if the assumption had been false.[17] But I do not believe that Hitler would have done all he did if he had not been morally depraved, nor, on the assumption that he was not depraved, can I think of any plausible explanation for his doing those things. Nor is it plausible that we would all have believed he was morally depraved even if he hadn't been. Granted, there is a tendency for writers who do not attach much weight to fascism as a social movement to want to blame its evils on a single maniacal leader, so perhaps some of them would have painted Hitler as a moral monster even if he had not been one. But this is only a tendency, and one for which many people know how to discount, so I doubt that our moral belief really is overdetermined in this way. Nor, similarly, do I believe that Woodworth's actions were overdetermined, so that he would have done just as he did even if he had been a more admirable person. I suppose one could have doubts about DeVoto's objectivity and reliability; it is obvious he dislikes Woodworth, so perhaps he would have thought him a moral loss and convinced his readers of this no matter what the man was really like. But it is more plausible that the dislike is mostly based on the same evidence that supports DeVoto's moral view of him, and that very different evidence, at any rate, would have produced a different verdict. If so, then Woodworth's moral character is part of the explanation of DeVoto's belief about his moral character.

It is more plausible of course that serious moral opposition to slavery would have emerged in Britain, France, and the United States even if slavery hadn't been worse in the modern period than before, and worse in the United States than in Latin America, and that the American antislavery movement would have grown even if slavery had not become more oppressive as the nineteenth century progressed. But that is because these moral facts are offered as at best a partial explanation of these developments in moral opinion. And if they

16 For a version of what I am calling the standard view of slavery in the Americas, see Frank Tannenbaum, *Slave and Citizen* (New York: Alfred A. Knopf, 1947). For an argument against both halves of the standard view, see Davis, *The Problem of Slavery*, esp. pp. 60–61, 223–225, 262–263.

17 This counterfactual test requires qualification to be exactly right, but none of the plausible qualifications matters to my examples. See the longer version of this paper.

really *are* part of the explanation, as seems plausible, then it is also plausible that whatever effect they produced was not entirely overdetermined; that, for example, the growth of the antislavery movement in the United States would at least have been somewhat slower if slavery had been and remained less bad an institution. Here again it hardly seems "completely irrelevant" to the explanation whether or not these moral facts obtained.

It is more puzzling, I grant, to consider Harman's own example in which you see the children igniting a cat and react immediately with the thought that this is wrong. Is it true, as Harman claims, that the assumption that the children are really doing something wrong is "totally irrelevant" to any reasonable explanation of your making that judgment? Would you, for example, have reacted in just the same way, with the thought that the action is wrong, even if what they were doing *hadn't* been wrong, and could we explain your reaction equally well on this assumption? Now, there is more than one way to understand this counterfactual question, and I shall return below to a reading of it that might appear favorable to Harman's view. What I wish to point out for now is merely that there is a natural way of taking it, parallel to the way in which I have been understanding similar counterfactual questions about my own examples, on which the answer to it has to be simply: it depends. For to answer the question, I take it,[18] we must consider a situation in which what the children are doing is not wrong, but which is otherwise as much like the actual situation as possible, and then decide what your reaction would be in that situation. But since what makes their action wrong, what its wrongness *consists* in, is presumably something like its being an act of gratuitous cruelty (or, perhaps we should add, of intense cruelty, and to a helpless victim), to imagine them not doing something wrong we are going to have to imagine their action different in this respect. More cautiously and more generally, if what they are actually doing is wrong, and if moral properties are, as many writers have held, supervenient on natural ones,[19] then in order to imagine them not doing something wrong we are going to have to suppose their action different from the actual one in some of its natural features as well. So our question becomes: Even if the children had been doing something else,

---

18 Following, informally, Stalnaker and Lewis on counterfactuals. See Robert Stalnaker, "A Theory of Conditionals," in Nicholas Rescher, ed., *Studies in Logical Theory*, APQ Monograph No. 2 (Oxford: Basil Blackwell, 1968); and David Lewis, *Counterfactuals* (Cambridge, MA: Harvard University Press, 1973).

19 What would be generally granted is just that *if* there are moral properties they supervene on natural properties. But, remember, we are assuming for the sake of argument that there are.

I think moral properties *are* natural properties; and from this view it of course follows trivially that they supervene on natural properties: that, necessarily, nothing could differ in its moral properties without differing in some natural respect. But I also accept the more interesting thesis usually intended by the claim about supervenience—that there are more basic natural features such that, necessarily, once they are fixed, so are the moral properties. (In supervening on more basic natural facts of some sort, moral facts are like *most* natural facts. Social facts like unemployment, for example, supervene on complex histories of many individuals and their relations; and facts about the existence and properties of macroscopic physical objects—colliding billiard balls, say—clearly supervene on the microphysical constitution of the situations that include them.)

something just different enough not to be wrong, would you have taken them even so to be doing something wrong?

Surely there is no one answer to this question. It depends on a lot about you, including your moral views and how good you are at seeing at a glance what some children are doing. It probably depends also on a debatable moral issue; namely, just *how* different the children's action would have to be in order not to be wrong. (Is unkindness to animals, for example, also wrong?) I believe we can see how, in a case in which the answer was clearly affirmative, we might be tempted to agree with Harman that the wrongness of the action was no part of the explanation of your reaction. For suppose you are like this. You hate children. What you especially hate, moreover, is the sight of children enjoying themselves; so much so that whenever you see children having fun, you immediately assume they are up to no good. The more they seem to be enjoying themselves, furthermore, the readier you are to fasten on any pretext for thinking them engaged in real wickedness. Then it is true that even if the children had been engaged in some robust but innocent fun, you would have thought they were doing something wrong; and Harman is perhaps right[20] about you that the actual wrongness of the action you see is irrelevant to your thinking it wrong. This is because your reaction is due to a feature of the action that coincides only very accidentally with the ones that make it wrong.[21] But, of course, and fortunately, many people aren't like this (nor does Harman argue that they are). It isn't true of them, in general, that if the children had been doing something similar, although different enough not to be wrong, they would still have thought the children were doing something wrong. And it isn't true either, therefore, that the wrongness of the action is irrelevant to the explanation of why they think it wrong.

Now, one might have the sense from my discussion of all these examples, but perhaps especially from my discussion of this last one, Harman's own, that I have perversely been refusing to understand his claim about the explanatory irrelevance of moral facts in the way he intends. And perhaps I have not been understanding it as he wishes. In any case, I agree, I have certainly not been understanding the crucial counterfactual question, of whether we would have

---

20 Not *certainly* right, because there is still the possibility that your reaction is to some extent overdetermined, and is to be explained partly by your sympathy for the cat and your dislike of cruelty, as well as by your hatred for children (although this last alone would have been sufficient to produce it).

We could of course rule out this possibility by making you an even less attractive character, indifferent to the suffering of animals and not offended by cruelty. But it may then be hard to imagine that such a person (whom I shall cease calling "you") could retain enough of a grip on moral thought for us to be willing to say he thought the action *wrong*, as opposed to saying that he merely pretended to do so. This difficulty is perhaps not insuperable, but it is revealing. Harman says that the actual wrongness of the action is "completely irrelevant" to the explanation of the observer's reaction. Notice that what is in fact true, however, is that it is *very hard* to imagine someone who reacts in the way Harman describes, but whose reaction is *not* due, at least in part, to the actual wrongness of the action.

21 Perhaps deliberate cruelty is worse the more one enjoys it (a standard counterexample to hedonism). If so, the fact that the children are enjoying themselves makes their action worse, but presumably isn't what makes it wrong to begin with.

drawn the same moral conclusion even if the moral facts had been different, in the way he must intend. But I am not being perverse. I believe, as I have said, that my way of taking the question is the more natural one. And, more importantly: although there is, I grant, a reading of that question on which it will always yield the answer Harman wants—namely, that a difference in the moral facts would *not* have made a difference in our judgment—I do not believe this reading can support his argument. I must now explain why.

It will help if I contrast my general approach with his. I am approaching questions about the justification of belief in the spirit of what Quine has called "epistemology naturalized."[22] I take this to mean that we have in general no a priori way of knowing which strategies for forming and refining our beliefs are likely to take us closer to the truth. The only way we have of proceeding is to assume the approximate truth of what seems to us the best overall theory we already have of what we are like and what the world is like, and to decide in the light of *that* what strategies of research and reasoning are likely to be reliable in producing a more nearly true overall theory. One result of applying these procedures, in turn, is likely to be the refinement or perhaps even the abandonment of parts of the tentative theory with which we began.

I take Harman's approach, too, to be an instance of this one. He says we are justified in believing in those facts that we need to assume to explain why we observe what we do. But he does not think that our knowledge of this principle about justification is a priori. Furthermore, as he knows, we cannot decide whether one explanation is better than another without relying on beliefs we already have about the world. Is it really a better explanation of the vapor trail the physicist sees in the cloud chamber to suppose that a proton caused it, as Harman suggests in his example, rather than some other charged particle? Would there, for example, have been no vapor trail in the absence of that proton? There is obviously no hope of answering such questions without assuming at least the approximate truth of some quite far-reaching microphysical theory, and our knowledge of such theories is not a priori.

But my approach differs from Harman's in one crucial way. For among the beliefs in which I have enough confidence to rely on in evaluating explanations, at least at the outset, are some moral beliefs. And I have been relying on them in the following way.[23] Harman's thesis implies that the supposed moral fact of Hitler's being morally depraved is irrelevant to the explanation of Hitler's doing what he did. (For we may suppose that if it explains his doing what he

---

22 W. V. O. Quine, "Epistemology Naturalized," in *Ontological Relativity and Other Essays* (New York: Columbia University Press, 1969), pp. 69–90. In the same volume, see also "Natural Kinds," pp. 114–138.

23 Harman of course allows us to assume the moral facts whose explanatory relevance is being assessed: that Hitler was depraved, or that what the children in his example are doing is wrong. But I have been assuming something more—something about what depravity *is,* and about what *makes* the children's action wrong. (At a minimum, in the more cautious version of my argument, I have been assuming that *something* about its more basic features makes it wrong, so that it could not have differed in its moral quality without differing in those other features as well.)

did, it also helps explain, at greater remove, Harman's belief and mine in his moral depravity.) To assess this claim, we need to conceive a situation in which Hitler was *not* morally depraved and consider the question whether in that situation he would still have done what he did. My answer is that he would not, and this answer relies on a (not very controversial) moral view: that in any world at all like the actual one, only a morally depraved person could have initiated a world war, ordered the "final solution," and done any number of other things Hitler did. That is why I believe that, if Hitler hadn't been morally depraved, he wouldn't have done those things, and hence that the fact of his moral depravity is relevant to an explanation of what he did.

Harman, however, cannot want us to rely on any such moral views in answering this counterfactual question. This comes out most clearly if we return to his example of the children igniting the cat. He claims that the wrongness of this act is irrelevant to an explanation of your thinking it wrong, that you would have *thought* it wrong even if it wasn't. My reply was that in order for the action not to be wrong it would have had to lack the feature of deliberate, intense, pointless cruelty, and that if it had differed in this way you might very well *not* have thought it wrong. I also suggested a more cautious version of this reply: that since the action is in fact wrong, and since moral properties supervene on more basic natural ones, it would have had to be different in *some* further natural respect in order not to be wrong; and that we do not know whether if it had so differed you would still have thought it wrong. Both of these replies, again, rely on moral views, the latter merely on the view that there is *something* about the natural features of the action in Harman's example that makes it wrong, the former on a more specific view as to which of these features do this.

But Harman, it is fairly clear, intends for us *not* to rely on any such moral views in evaluating his counterfactual claim. His claim is not that if the action had not been one of deliberate cruelty (or had otherwise differed in whatever way would be required to remove its wrongness), you would still have thought it wrong. It is, instead, that if the action were one of deliberate, pointless cruelty, but this *did not make it wrong,* you would still have thought it was wrong. And to return to the example of Hitler's moral character, the counterfactual claim that Harman will need in order to defend a comparable conclusion about that case is not that if Hitler had been, for example, humane and fairminded, free of nationalistic pride and racial hatred, he would still have done exactly as he did. It is, rather, that if Hitler's psychology, and anything else about his situation that could strike us as morally relevant, had been exactly as it in fact was, but this had *not constituted moral depravity,* he would still have done exactly what he did.

Now the antecedents of these two conditionals are puzzling. For one thing, both are, I believe, necessarily false. I am fairly confident, for example, that Hitler really was morally depraved;[24] and since I also accept the view that

---

24 And anyway, remember, this is the sort of fact Harman allows us to assume in order to see whether, if we assume it, it will look explanatory.

moral features supervene on more basic natural properties,[25] I take this to imply that there is no possible world in which Hitler has just the personality he in fact did, in just the situation he was in, but is not morally depraved. Any attempt to describe such a situation, moreover, will surely run up against the limits of our moral concepts—what Harman calls our "moral sensibility"—and this is no accident. For what Harman is asking us to do, in general, is to consider cases in which absolutely *everything* about the nonmoral facts that could seem morally relevant to us, in light of whatever moral theory we accept and of the concepts required for understanding that theory, is held fixed, but in which the moral judgment that our theory yields about the case is nevertheless mistaken. So it is hardly surprising that, using that theory and those concepts, we should find it difficult to conceive in any detail what such a situation would be like. It is especially not surprising when the cases in question are as paradigmatic in light of the moral outlook we in fact have as is Harman's example or is, even more so, mine of Hitler's moral character. The only way we could be wrong about this latter case (assuming we have the nonmoral facts right) would be for our whole theory to be hopelessly wrong, so radically mistaken that there could be no hope of straightening it out through adjustments from within.

But I do not believe we should conclude, as we might be tempted to,[26] that we therefore know a priori that this is not so, or that we cannot understand these conditionals that are crucial to Harman's argument. Rather, now that we have seen how we have to understand them, we should grant that they are true: that if our moral theory were somehow hopelessly mistaken, but all the nonmoral facts remained exactly as they in fact are, then, since we do *accept* that moral theory, we would still draw exactly the moral conclusions we in

---

25 It is about here that I have several times encountered the objection: but surely *supervenient* properties aren't needed to explain anything. It is a little hard, however, to see just what this objection is supposed to come to. If it includes endorsement of the conditional I here attribute to Harman, then I believe the remainder of my discussion is an adequate reply to it. If it is the claim that, because moral properties are supervenient, we can always exploit the insights in any moral explanations, however plausible, without resort to moral *language,* then I have already dealt with it in my discussion of reductionism (see note 10, above): the claim is probably false, but even if it is true it is no support for Harman's view, which is not that moral explanations are plausible but reducible, but that they are totally implausible. And doubts about the causal efficacy of supervenient facts seem misplaced in any case, as attention to my earlier examples (note 17) illustrates. High unemployment causes widespread hardship, and can also bring down the rate of inflation. The masses and velocities and two colliding billiard balls causally influence the subsequent trajectories of the two balls. There is no doubt some sense in which these facts are causally efficacious *in virtue of* the way they supervene on—that is, are constituted out of, or causally realized by—more basic facts, but this hardly shows them *inefficacious.* (Nor does Harman appear to think it does: for his *favored* explanation of your moral belief about the burning cat, recall, appeals to psychological facts [about your moral sensibility], a biological fact [that it's a cat], and macrophysical facts [that it's on fire]—supervenient facts all, on his physicalist view and mine.) If anyone does hold to a general suspicion of causation by supervenient facts and properties, however, as Jaegwon Kim appears to (see "Causality, Identity, and Supervenience in the Mind-Body Problem," *Midwest Studies in Philosophy* 4 [1979], pp. 31–49), it is enough to note that this suspicion cannot diagnose any special difficulty with *moral* explanations, any distinctive "problem with ethics." The "problem," arguably, will be with every discipline but fundamental physics.

26 And as I take it Philippa Foot, for example, is still prepared to do, at least about paradigmatic cases. See her *Moral Relativism* (Lawrence: The University of Kansas, 1978).

fact do. But we should deny that any skeptical conclusion follows from this. In particular, we should deny that it follows that moral facts play no role in explaining our moral judgments.

For consider what follows from the parallel claim about microphysics, in particular about Harman's example in which a physicist concludes from his observation of a vapor trail in a cloud chamber, and from the microphysical theory he accepts, that a free proton has passed through the chamber. The parallel claim, notice, is *not* just that if the proton had not been there the physicist would still have thought it was. This claim is implausible, for we may assume that the physicist's theory is generally correct, and it follows from that theory that if there hadn't been a proton there, then there wouldn't have been a vapor trail. But in a perfectly similar way it is implausible that if Hitler hadn't been morally depraved we would still have thought he was: for we may assume that our moral theory also is at least roughly correct, and it follows from the most central features of that theory that if Hitler hadn't been morally depraved, he wouldn't have done what he did. The *parallel* claim about the microphysical example is, instead, that if there hadn't been a proton there, but there *had* been a vapor trail, the physicist would still have concluded that a proton was present. More precisely, to maintain a perfect parallel with Harman's claims about the moral cases, the antecedent must specify that although no proton is present, absolutely *all* the non-microphysical facts that the physicist, in light of his theory, might take to be relevant to the question of whether or not a proton is present, are exactly as in the actual case. (These macrophysical facts, as we may for convenience call them, surely include everything one would normally think of as an observable fact.) Of course, we shall be unable to imagine this without imagining that the physicist's theory is pretty badly mistaken;[27] but I believe we should grant that, *if* the physicist's theory were somehow this badly mistaken, but all the macrophysical facts (including all the

---

27 If we imagine the physicist *regularly* mistaken in this way, moreover, we will have to imagine his theory not just mistaken but hopelessly so. And we can easily reproduce the other notable feature of Harman's claims about the moral cases, that what we are imagining is *necessarily* false, if we suppose that one of the physicist's (or better, chemist's) conclusions is about the microstructure of some common substance, such as water. For I agree with Saul Kripke that whatever microstructure water has is essential to it, that it has this structure in every possible world in which it exists (Saul Kripke, *Naming and Necessity* [Cambridge, MA: Harvard University Press, 1980]). If we are right (as we have every reason to suppose) in thinking that water is actually H_2O, therefore, the conditional, "If water were not H_2O, but all the observable, macrophysical facts were just as they actually are, chemists would still have come to *think* it was H_2O," has a necessarily false antecedent; just as, if we are right (as we also have good reason to suppose) in thinking that Hitler was actually morally depraved, the conditional, "If Hitler were just as he was in all natural respects, but not morally depraved, we would still have *thought* he was depraved," has a necessarily false antecedent. Of course, I am not suggesting that in either case our knowledge that the antecedent is false is a priori.

These counterfactuals, because of their impossible antecedents, will have to be interpreted over worlds that are (at best) only "epistemically" possible; and, as Richard Boyd has pointed out to me, this helps to explain why anyone who accepts a causal theory of knowledge (or any theory according to which the justification of our belief depends on what explains our holding them) will find their truth irrelevant to the question of how much we know, either in chemistry or in morals. For although there certainly are counterfactuals that are relevant to questions about what causes what (and, hence, about what explains what), these have to be counterfactuals about real possibilities, not merely epistemic ones.

observable facts) were held fixed, then the physicist, since he does accept that theory, would still draw all the same conclusions that he actually does. That is, this conditional claim, like Harman's parallel claim about the moral cases, is true.

But no skeptical conclusions follow; nor can Harman, since he does not intend to be a skeptic about physics, think that they do. It does not follow, in the first place, that we have any reason to think the physicist's theory *is* generally mistaken. Nor does it follow, furthermore, that the hypothesis that a proton really did pass through the cloud chamber is not part of a good explanation of the vapor trail, and hence of the physicist's thinking this has happened. This looks like a reasonable explanation, of course, only on the assumption that the physicist's theory is at least roughly true, for it is this theory that tells us, for example, what happens when charged particles pass through a supersaturated atmosphere, what other causes (if any) there might be for a similar phenomenon, and so on. But, as I say, we have not been provided with any reason for not trusting the theory to this extent.

Similarly, I conclude, we should draw no skeptical conclusions from Harman's claims about the moral cases. It is true that if our moral theory were seriously mistaken, but we still believed it, and the nonmoral facts were held fixed, we would still make just the moral judgments we do. But *this* fact by itself provides us with no reason for thinking that our moral theory *is* generally mistaken. Nor, again, does it imply that the fact of Hitler's really having been morally depraved forms no part of a good explanation of his doing what he did and hence, at greater remove, of our thinking him depraved. This explanation will appear reasonable, of course, only on the assumption that our accepted moral theory is at least roughly correct, for it is this theory that assures us that only a depraved person could have thought, felt, and acted as Hitler did. But, as I say, Harman's argument has provided us with no reason for not trusting our moral views to this extent, and hence with no reason for doubting that it is sometimes moral facts that explain our moral judgments.

I conclude with three comments about my argument.

(1) I have tried to show that Harman's claim—that we would have held the particular moral beliefs we do even if those beliefs were untrue—admits of two readings, one of which makes it implausible, and the other of which reduces it to an application of a general skeptical strategy, a strategy which could as easily be used to produce doubt about microphysical as about moral facts. The general strategy is this. Consider any conclusion *C* we arrive at by relying both on some distinguishable "theory" *T* and on some body of evidence not being challenged, and ask whether we would have believed *C* even if it had been false. The plausible answer, *if* we are allowed to rely on *T*, will often be no: for if *C* had been false, then (according to *T*) the evidence would have had to be different, and in that case we wouldn't have believed *C*. (I have illustrated the plausibility of this sort of reply for all my moral examples, as well as for the microphysical one.) But the skeptic of course intends us *not* to rely on *T* in this way, and so rephrases the question: Would we have believed *C* even if it were false *but* all the evidence had been exactly as it in fact was?

Now the answer has to be yes; and the skeptic concludes that C is doubtful. (It should be obvious how to extend this strategy to belief in other minds, or in an external world.) I am of course not convinced: I do not think answers to the rephrased question show anything interesting about what we know or justifiably believe. But it is enough for my purposes here that no such *general* skeptical strategy could pretend to reveal any problems peculiar to belief in *moral* facts.

(2) My conclusion about Harman's argument, although it is not exactly the same as, is nevertheless similar to and very much in the spirit of the Duhemian point I invoked earlier against verificationism. There the question was whether typical moral assertions have testable implications, and the answer was that they do, so long as you include additional moral assumptions of the right sort among the background theories on which you rely in evaluating these assertions. Harman's more important question is whether we should ever regard moral facts as relevant to the explanation of nonmoral facts, and in particular of our having the moral beliefs we do. But the answer, again, is that we should, so long as we are willing to hold the right sorts of *other* moral assumptions fixed in answering counterfactual questions. Neither answer shows morality to be on any shakier ground than, say, physics, for typical microphysical hypotheses, too, have testable implications, and appear relevant to explanations, only if we are willing to assume at least the approximate truth of an elaborate microphysical theory and to hold this assumption fixed in answering counterfactual questions.

(3) Of course, this picture of how explanations depend on background theories, and moral explanations in particular on moral background theories, does show why someone already tempted toward moral skepticism on other grounds (such as those I mentioned at the beginning of this essay) might find Harman's claim about moral explanations plausible. To the extent that you already have pervasive doubts about moral theories, you will also find moral facts nonexplanatory. So I grant that Harman has located a natural symptom of moral skepticism; but I am sure he has neither traced this skepticism to its roots nor provided any independent argument for it. His claim (p. 22) that we do not *in fact* cite moral facts in explanation of moral beliefs and observations cannot provide such an argument, for that claim is false. So, too, is the claim that assumptions about moral facts seem irrelevant to such explanations, for many do not. The claim that we *should* not rely on such assumptions because they *are* irrelevant, on the other hand, unless it is supported by some independent argument for moral skepticism, will just be question-begging: for the principal test of whether they are relevant, in any situation in which it appears they might be, is a counterfactual question about what would have happened if the moral fact had not obtained, and how we answer that question depends precisely upon whether we *do* rely on moral assumptions in answering it.

My own view I stated at the outset: that the only argument for moral skepticism with any independent weight is the argument from the difficulty of settling disputed moral questions. I have shown that anyone who finds Harman's claim about moral explanations plausible must already have been tempted toward skepticism by some other considerations, and I suspect that the other considerations will typically be the ones I sketched. So that is where discussion should focus. I also suggested that those considerations may provide less support for moral skepticism than is sometimes supposed, but I must reserve a thorough defense of that thesis for another occasion.[28]

[28] This essay has benefited from helpful discussion of earlier versions read at the University of Virginia, Cornell University, Franklin and Marshall College, Wayne State University, and the University of Michigan. I have been aided by a useful correspondence with Gilbert Harman; and I am grateful also for specific comments from Richard Boyd, David Brink, David Copp, Stephen Darwall, Terence Irwin, Norman Kretzmann, Ronald Nash, Peter Railton, Bruce Russell, Sydney Shoemaker, and Judith Slein.

19

The Subjectivity
of Values

J. L. MACKIE

J. L. Mackie (1917–1981) taught philosophy at various universities, most recently at Oxford. He was a philosopher of impressive breadth. His works include The Cement of the Universe, the Miracle of Theism, Problems from Locke, *and* Ethics: Inventing Right and Wrong.

In this selection, taken from Ethics: Inventing Right and Wrong, *chapter 1, Mackie argues that there are no objective values. He begins by distinguishing his thesis from a number of others. For example, unlike A. J. Ayer (reading 10) Mackie is not maintaining that ethical utterances lack cognitive meaning. He is, instead, contending that such utterances are meaningful but false. In his view, the basic question is whether the world contains items such as values—entities at once external to persons and authoritative over their bahavior. According to Mackie, it does not.*

Why does Mackie take this position? Although he says more than can easily be summarized, his main arguments include appeals to variations in actual moral codes and to the "queerness" of the entities that objectivists must postulate. (For relevant discussion, see, respectively, James Rachels, reading 16, and Gilbert Harman, reading 17.) In addition, Mackie tries to show how people could come to believe in objective values even if none existed. Taken together, his arguments constitute a formidable challenge to the objectivity of value.

1. MORAL SCEPTICISM

There are no objective values. This is a bald statement of the thesis of this chapter, but before arguing for it I shall try to clarify and restrict it in ways that may meet some objections and prevent some misunderstanding.

The statement of this thesis is liable to provoke one of three very different reactions. Some will think it not merely false but pernicious; they will see it as a threat to morality and to everything else that is worthwhile, and they will find the presenting of such a thesis in what purports to be a book on ethics paradoxical or even outrageous. Others will regard it as a trivial truth, almost too obvious to be worth mentioning, and certainly too plain to be worth much argument. Others again will say that it is meaningless or empty, that no real issue is raised by the question whether values are or are not part of the fabric of the world. But, precisely because there can be these three different reactions, much more needs to be said.

The claim that values are not objective, are not part of the fabric of the world, is meant to include not only moral goodness, which might be most naturally equated with moral value, but also other things that could be more loosely called moral values or disvalues—rightness or wrongness, duty, obligation, an action's being rotten and contemptible, and so on. It also includes non-moral values, notably aesthetic ones, beauty and various kinds of artistic merit. I shall not discuss these explicitly, but clearly much the same considerations apply to aesthetic and to moral values, and there would be at least some initial implausibility in a view that gave the one a different status from the other.

Since it is with moral values that I am primarily concerned, the view I am adopting may be called moral scepticism. But this name is likely to be misunderstood: 'moral scepticism' might also be used as a name for either of two first order views, or perhaps for an incoherent mixture of the two. A moral sceptic might be the sort of person who says 'All this talk of morality is tripe,' who rejects morality and will take no notice of it. Such a person may be literally rejecting all moral judgements; he is more likely to be making moral judgements of his own, expressing a positive moral condemnation of all that conventionally passes for morality; or he may be confusing these two logically incompatible views, and saying that he rejects all morality, while he is in fact rejecting only a particular morality that is current in the society in which he has grown up. But I am not at present concerned with the merits or faults of such a position. These are first order moral views, positive or negative: the person who adopts either of them is taking a certain practical, normative, stand. By contrast, what I am discussing is a second order view, a view about the status of moral values and the nature of moral valuing, about where and how they fit into the world. These first and second order views are not merely distinct but completely independent: one could be a second order moral sceptic without being a first order one, or again the other way round. A man could hold strong moral views, and indeed ones whose content was thoroughly conventional, while believing that they were simply attitudes and policies with regard to conduct that he and other people held. Conversely, a man could reject all established morality while believing it to be an objective truth that it was evil or corrupt.

With another sort of misunderstanding moral scepticism would seem not so much pernicious as absurd. How could anyone deny that there is a difference between a kind action and a cruel one, or that a coward and a brave man behave differently in the face of danger? Of course, this is undeniable; but it is not to the point. The kinds of behaviour to which moral values and disvalues are ascribed are indeed part of the furniture of the world, and so are the natural, descriptive, differences between them; but not, perhaps, their differences in value. It is a hard fact that cruel actions differ from kind ones, and hence that we can learn, as in fact we all do, to distinguish them fairly well in practice, and to use the words 'cruel' and 'kind' with fairly clear descriptive meanings;

but is it an equally hard fact that actions which are cruel in such a descriptive sense are to be condemned? The present issue is with regard to the objectivity specifically of value, not with regard to the objectivity of those natural, factual, differences on the basis of which differing values are assigned.

2. SUBJECTIVISM

Another name often used, as an alternative to 'moral scepticism', for the view I am discussing is 'subjectivism'. But this too has more than one meaning. Moral subjectivism too could be a first order, normative, view, namely that everyone really ought to do whatever he thinks he should. This plainly is a (systematic) first order view; on examination it soon ceases to be plausible, but that is beside the point, for it is quite independent of the second order thesis at present under consideration. What is more confusing is that different second order views compete for the name 'subjectivism'. Several of these are doctrines about the meaning of moral terms and moral statements. What is often called moral subjectivism is the doctrine that, for example, 'This action is right' *means* 'I approve of this action', or more generally that moral judgements are equivalent to reports of the speaker's own feelings or attitudes. But the view I am now discussing is to be distinguished in two vital respects from any such doctrine as this. First, what I have called moral scepticism is a negative doctrine, not a positive one: it says what there isn't, not what there is. It says that there do not exist entities or relations of a certain kind, objective values or requirements, which many people have believed to exist. Of course, the moral sceptic cannot leave it at that. If his position is to be at all plausible, he must give some account of how other people have fallen into what he regards as an error, and this account will have to include some positive suggestions about how values fail to be objective, about what has been mistaken for, or has led to false beliefs about, objective values. But this will be a development of his theory, not its core: its core is the negation. Secondly, what I have called moral scepticism is an ontological thesis, not a linguistic or conceptual one. It is not, like the other doctrine often called moral subjectivism, a view about the meanings of moral statements. Again, no doubt, if it is to be at all plausible, it will have to give some account of their meanings, and I shall say something about this in Section 7 of this chapter and again in Chapters 2, 3, and 4. But this too will be a development of the theory, not its core.

It is true that those who have accepted the moral subjectivism which is the doctrine that moral judgements are equivalent to reports of the speaker's own feelings or attitudes have usually presupposed what I am calling moral scepticism. It is because they have assumed that there are no objective values, that they have looked elsewhere for an analysis of what moral statements might mean, and have settled upon subjective reports. Indeed, if all our moral statements were such subjective reports, it would follow that, at least so far as we are aware, there are no objective moral values. If we were aware of them, we would say something about them. In this sense this sort of subjectivism entails moral scepticism. But the converse entailment does not hold. The denial that there are objective values does not commit one to any particular view about what moral statements mean, and certainly not to the view that they are equivalent to subjective reports. No doubt if moral values are not objective they are in some very broad sense subjective, and for this reason I would accept 'moral subjectivism' as an alternative name to 'moral scepticism'. But subjectivism in this broad sense must be distinguished from the specific doctrine about meaning referred to above. Neither name is altogether satisfactory: we simply have to guard against the (different) misinterpretations which each may suggest.

3. THE MULTIPLICITY OF SECOND ORDER QUESTIONS

The distinctions drawn in the last two sections rest not only on the well-known and generally recognized difference between first and second order questions, but also on the more controversial claim that there are several kinds of second order moral questions. Those most often mentioned are questions about the meaning and use of ethical terms, or the analysis of ethical concepts. With these go questions about the logic of moral statements: there may be special patterns of moral argument, licensed, perhaps, by aspects of the meanings of moral terms—for example, it may be part of the meaning of moral statements that they are universalizable. But there are also ontological, as contrasted with linguistic or conceptual, questions about the nature and status of goodness or rightness or whatever it is that first order moral statements are distinctively about. These are questions of factual rather than conceptual analysis: the problem of what goodness is cannot be settled conclusively or exhaustively by finding out what the word 'good' means, or what it is conventionally used to say or to do.

Recent philosophy, biased as it has been towards various kinds of linguistic inquiry, has tended to doubt this, but the distinction between conceptual and factual analysis in ethics can be supported by analogies with other areas. The question of what perception is, what goes on when someone perceives something, is not adequately answered by finding out what words like 'see' and 'hear' mean, or what someone is doing in saying 'I perceive . . . ', by analysing, however fully and accurately, any established concept of perception. There is a still closer analogy with colours. Robert Boyle and John Locke called colours 'secondary qualities', meaning that colours as they occur in material things consist simply in patterns of arrangement and movement of minute particles on the surfaces of objects, which make them, as we would now say, reflect light of some frequencies better than others, and so enable these objects to produce colour sensations in us, but that colours as we see them do not literally belong to the surfaces of material things. Whether Boyle and Locke were right about this cannot be settled by finding out how we use colour words and what we mean in using them. Naïve realism about colours might be a correct analysis not only of our pre-scientific colour concepts but also of the conventional meanings of colour words, and even of the meanings with which scientifically sophisticated people use them when they are off their guard, and yet it might not be a correct account of the status of colours.

Error could well result, then, from a failure to distinguish factual from conceptual analysis with regard to colours, from taking an account of the meanings of statements as a full account of what there is. There is a similar and in practice even greater risk of error in moral philosophy. There is another reason, too, why it would be a mistake to concentrate second order ethical discussions on questions of meaning. The more work philosophers have done on meaning, both in ethics and elsewhere, the more complications have come to light. It is by now pretty plain that no simple account of the meanings of first order moral statements will be correct, will cover adequately even the standard, conventional, senses of the main moral terms; I think, none the less, that there is a relatively clear-cut issue about the objectivity of moral values which is in danger of being lost among the complications of meaning.

4. IS OBJECTIVITY A REAL ISSUE?

It has, however, been doubted whether there is a real issue here. I must concede that it is a rather old-fashioned one. I do not mean merely that it was raised by Hume, who argued that 'The vice entirely escapes you . . . till you turn your reflexion into your own breast,' and before him by Hobbes, and long before that by some of the Greek sophists. I mean rather that it was discussed vigorously in the nineteen thirties and forties, but since then has received much less attention. This is not because it has been solved or because agreement has been reached: instead it seems to have been politely shelved.

But was there ever a genuine problem? R. M. Hare has said that he does not understand what is meant by 'the objectivity of values', and that he has not met anyone who does. We all know how to recognize the activity called 'saying, thinking it to be so, that some act is wrong', and he thinks that it is to this activity that the subjectivist and the objectivist are both alluding, though one calls it 'an attitude of disapproval' and the other 'a moral intuition': these are only different names for the same thing. It is true that if one person says that a certain act is wrong and another that it is not wrong the objectivist will say that they are contradicting one another; but this yields no significant discrimination between objectivism and subjectivism, because the subjectivist too will concede that the second person is negating what the first has said, and Hare sees no difference between contradicting and negating. Again, the objectivist will say that one of the two must be wrong; but Hare argues that to say that the judgement that a certain act is wrong is itself wrong is merely to negate that judgement, and the subjectivist too must negate one or other of the two judgements, so that still no clear difference between objectivism and subjectivism has emerged. He sums up his case thus: 'Think of one world into whose fabric values are objectively built; and think of another in which those values have been annihilated. And remember that in both worlds the people in them go on being concerned about the same things—there is no difference in the "subjective" concern which people have for things, only in their "objective" value. Now I ask, "What is the difference between the states of affairs in these two worlds?" Can any answer be given except "None whatever"?'

Now it is quite true that it is logically possible that the subjective concern, the activity of valuing or of thinking things wrong, should go on in just the same way whether there are objective values or not. But to say this is only to reiterate that there is a logical distinction between first and second order ethics: first order judgements are not necessarily affected by the truth or falsity of a second order view. But it does not follow, and it is not true, that there is no difference whatever between these two worlds. In the one there is something that backs up and validates some of the subjective concern which people have for things, in the other there is not. Hare's argument is similar to the positivist claim that there is no difference between a phenomenalist or Berkeleian world in which there are only minds and their ideas and the commonsense realist one in which there are also material things, because it is logically possible that people should have the same experiences in both. If we reject the positivism that would make the dispute between realists and phenomenalists a pseudo-question, we can reject Hare's similarly supported dismissal of the issue of the objectivity of values.

In any case, Hare has minimized the difference between his two worlds by considering only the situation where people already have just such subjective concern; further differences come to light if we consider how subjective concern is acquired or changed. If there were something in the fabric of the world that validated certain kinds of concern, then it would be possible to acquire these merely by finding something out, by letting one's thinking be controlled by how things were. But in the world in which objective values have been annihilated the acquiring of some new subjective concern means the development of something new on the emotive side by the person who acquires it, something that eighteenth-century writers would put under the head of passion or sentiment.

The issue of the objectivity of values needs, however, to be distinguished from others with which it might be confused. To say that there are objective values would not be to say merely that there are some things which are valued by everyone, nor does it entail this. There could be agreement in valuing even if valuing is just something that people do, even if this activity is not further validated. Subjective agreement would give intersubjective values, but intersubjectivity is not objectivity. Nor is objectivity simply universalizability: someone might well be prepared to universalize his prescriptive judgements or approvals—that is, to prescribe and approve in just the same ways in all relevantly similar cases, even ones in which he was involved differently or not at all—and yet he could recognize that such prescribing and approving were his activities, nothing more. Of course if there were objective values they would presumably belong to *kinds* of things or actions or states of affairs, so that the judgements that reported them would be universalizable; but the converse does not hold.

A more subtle distinction needs to be made between objectivism and descriptivism. Descriptivism is again a doctrine about the meanings of ethical terms and statements, namely that their meanings are purely descriptive rather than even partly prescriptive or emotive or evaluative, or that it is not an essential feature of the conventional meaning of moral statements that they have some special illocutionary force, say of commending rather than asserting. It contrasts with the view that commendation is in principle distinguishable from description (however difficult they may be to separate in practice) and that moral statements have it as at least part of their meaning that they are commendatory and hence in some uses intrinsically action-guiding. But descriptive meaning neither entails nor is entailed by objectivity. Berkeley's subjective idealism about material objects would be quite compatible with the admission that material object statements have purely descriptive meaning. Conversely, the main tradition of European moral philosophy from Plato onwards has combined the view that moral values are objective with the recognition that moral judgements are partly prescriptive or directive or action-guiding. Values themselves have been seen as at once prescriptive and objective. In Plato's theory the Forms, and in particular the Form of the Good, are eternal, extra-mental, realities. They are a very central structural element in the fabric of the world. But it is held also that just knowing them or 'seeing' them will not merely tell men what to do but will ensure that they do it, overruling any contrary inclinations. The philosopher-kings in the *Republic* can, Plato thinks, be trusted with unchecked power because their education will have given them knowledge of the Forms. Being acquainted with the Forms of the Good and Justice and Beauty and the rest they will, by this knowledge alone, without any further motivation, be impelled to pursue and promote these ideals. Similarly, Kant believes that pure reason can by itself be practical, though he does not pretend to be able to explain how it can be so. Again, Sidgwick argues that if there is to be a science of ethics—and he assumes that there can be, indeed he defines ethics as 'the science of conduct'—what ought to be 'must in another sense have objective existence: it must be an object of knowledge and as such the same for all minds'; but he says that the affirmations of this science 'are also precepts', and he speaks of happiness as 'an end *absolutely* prescribed by reason'. Since many philosophers have thus held that values are objectively prescriptive, it is clear that the ontological doctrine of objectivism must be distinguished from descriptivism, a theory about meaning.

But perhaps when Hare says that he does not understand what is meant by 'the objectivity of values' he means that he cannot understand how values could be objective, he cannot frame for himself any clear, detailed, picture of what it would be like for values to be part of the fabric of the world. This would be a much more plausible claim; as we have seen, even Kant hints at a similar difficulty. Indeed, even Plato warns us that it is only through difficult studies spread over many years that one can approach the knowledge of the Forms. The difficulty of seeing how values could be objective is a fairly strong reason for thinking that they are not so; . . . but it is not a good reason for saying that this is not a real issue.

I believe that as well as being a real issue it is an important one. It clearly matters for general philosophy. It would make a radical difference to our metaphysics if we had to find room for objective values—perhaps something like Plato's Forms—somewhere in our picture of the world. It would similarly make a difference to our epistemology if it had to explain how such objective values are or can be known, and to our philosophical psychology if we had to allow such knowledge, or Kant's pure practical reason, to direct choices and actions. Less obviously, how this issue is settled will affect the possibility of certain kinds of moral argument. For example, Sidgwick considers a discussion between an egoist and a utilitarian, and points out that if the egoist claims that his happiness or pleasure is objectively desirable or good, the utilitarian can argue that the egoist's happiness 'cannot be more objectively desirable or more a good than the similar happiness of any other person: the mere fact . . . that *he is he* can have nothing to do with its objective desirability or goodness'. In other words, if ethics is built on the concept of objective goodness, then egoism as a first order system or method of ethics can be refuted, whereas if it is assumed that goodness is only subjective it cannot. But Sidgwick correctly stresses what a number of other philosophers have missed, that this argument against egoism would require the objectivity specifically of goodness: the objectivity of what ought to be or of what it is rational to do would not be enough. If the egoist claimed that it was objectively rational, or obligatory upon him, to seek his own happiness, a similar argument about the irrelevance of the fact that he is he would lead only to the conclusion that it was objectively rational or obligatory for each other person to seek *his* own happiness, that is, to a universalized form of egoism, not to the refutation of egoism. And of course insisting on the universalizability of moral judgements, as opposed to the objectivity of goodness, would yield only the same result.

5. STANDARDS OF EVALUATION

One way of stating the thesis that there are no objective values is to say that value statements cannot be either true or false. But this formulation, too, lends itself to misinterpretation. For there are certain kinds of value statements which undoubtedly can be true or false, even if, in the sense I intend, there are no objective values. Evaluations of many sorts are commonly made in relation to agreed and assumed standards. The classing of wool, the grading of apples, the awarding of prizes at sheepdog trials, flower shows, skating and diving championships, and even the marking of examination papers are carried out in relation to standards of quality or merit which are peculiar to each particular subject-matter or type of contest, which may be explicitly laid down but which, even if they are nowhere explicitly stated, are fairly well understood and agreed by those who are recognized as judges or experts in each particular field. Given any sufficiently determinate standards, it will be an objective issue, a matter of truth and falsehood, how well any particular specimen measures up to those standards. Comparative judgements in particular will be capable of truth and falsehood: it will be a factual question whether this sheepdog has performed better than that one.

The subjectivist about values, then, is not denying that there can be objective evaluations relative to standards, and these are as possible in the aesthetic and moral fields as in any of those just mentioned. More than this, there is an objective distinction which applies in many such fields, and yet would itself be regarded as a peculiarly moral one: the distinction between justice and injustice. In one important sense of the word it is a paradigm case of injustice if a court declares someone to be guilty of an offence of which it knows him to be innocent. More generally, a finding is unjust if it is at variance with what the relevant law and the facts together require, and particularly if it is known by the court to be so. More generally still, any award of marks, prizes, or the like is unjust if it is at variance with the agreed standards for the contest in question: if one diver's performance in fact measures up better to the accepted standards for diving than another's, it will be injust if the latter is awarded higher marks or the prize. In this way the justice or injustice of decisions relative to standards can be a thoroughly objective matter, though there may still be a subjective element in the interpretation or application of standards. But the statement that a certain decision is thus just or unjust will not be objectively prescriptive: in so far as it can be simply true it leaves open the question whether there is an objective requirement to do what is just and to refrain from what is unjust, and equally leaves open the practical decision to act in either way.

Recognizing the objectivity of justice in relation to standards, and of evaluative judgements relative to standards, then, merely shifts the question of the objectivity of values back to the standards themselves. The subjectivist may try to make his point by insisting that there is no objective validity about the choice of standards. Yet he would clearly be wrong if he said that the choice of even the most basic standards in any field was completely arbitrary. The standards used in sheepdog trials clearly bear some relation to the work that sheepdogs are kept to do, the standards for grading apples bear some relation to what people generally want in or like about apples, and so on. On the other hand, standards are not as a rule strictly validated by such purposes. The appropriateness of standards is neither fully determinate nor totally indeterminate in relation to independently specifiable aims or desires. But however determinate it is, the objective appropriateness of standards in relation to aims or desires is no more of a threat to the denial of objective values than is the objectivity of evaluation relative to standards. In fact it is logically no different from the objectivity of goodness relative to desires. Something may be called good simply in so far as it satisfies or is such as to satisfy a certain desire; but the objectivity of such relations of satisfaction does not constitute in our sense an objective value.

6. HYPOTHETICAL AND CATEGORICAL IMPERATIVES

We may make this issue clearer by referring to Kant's distinction between hypothetical and categorical imperatives, though what he called imperatives are more naturally expressed as 'ought'-statements than in the imperative mood. 'If you want X, do Y' (or 'You ought to do Y') will be a hypothetical imperative if it is based on the supposed fact that Y is, in the circumstances, the only (or the best) available means to X, that is, on a causal relation between Y and X. The reason for doing Y lies in its causal connection with the desired end, X; the oughtness is contingent upon the desire. But 'You ought to do Y' will be a categorical imperative if you ought to do Y irrespective of any such desire for any end to which Y would contribute, if the oughtness is not thus contingent upon any desire. But this distinction needs to be handled with some care. An 'ought'-statement is not in this sense hypothetical merely because it incorporates a conditional clause. 'If you promised to do Y, you ought to do Y' is not a hypothetical imperative merely on account of the stated if-clause; what is meant may be either a hypothetical or a categorical imperative, depending upon the implied reason for keeping the supposed promise. If this rests upon some such further unstated conditional as 'If you want to be trusted another time', then it is a hypothetical imperative; if not, it is categorical. Even a desire of the agent's can figure in the antecedent of what, though conditional in grammatical form, is still in Kant's sense of a categorical imperative. 'If you are strongly attracted sexually to young children you ought not to go in for school teaching' is not, in virtue of what it explicitly says, a hypothetical imperative: the avoidance of school teaching is not being offered as a means to the satisfaction of the desires in question. Of course, it could still be a hypothetical imperative, if the implied reason were a prudential one; but it could also be a categorical imperative, a moral requirement where the reason for the recommended action (strictly, avoidance) does not rest upon that action's being a means to the satisfaction of any desire that the agent is supposed to have. Not every conditional ought-statement or command, then, is a hypothetical imperative; equally, not every non-conditional one is a categorical imperative. An appropriate if-clause may be left unstated. Indeed, a simple command in the imperative mood, say a parade-ground order, which might seem most literally to qualify for the title of a categorical imperative, will hardly ever be one in the sense we need here. The implied reason for complying with such an order will almost always be some desire of the person addressed, perhaps simply the desire to keep out of trouble. If so, such an apparently categorical order will be in our sense a hypothetical imperative. Again, an imperative remains hypothetical even if we change the 'if' to 'since': the fact that the desire for X is actually present does not alter the fact that the reason for doing Y is contingent upon the desire for X by way of Y's being a means to X. In Kant's own treatment, while imperatives of skill relate to desires which an agent may or may not have, imperatives of prudence relate to the desire for happiness which, Kant assumes, everyone has. So construed, imperatives of prudence are no less hypothetical than imperatives of skill, no less contingent upon desires that the agent has at the time the imperatives are addressed to him. But if we think rather of a counsel of prudence as being related to the agent's future welfare, to the satisfaction of desires that he does not yet have— not even to a present desire that his future desires should be satisfied—then a counsel of prudence is a categorical imperative, different indeed from a moral one, but analogous to it.

A categorical imperative, then, would express a reason for acting which was unconditional in the sense of not being contingent upon any present desire of the agent to whose satisfaction the recommended action would contribute as a means—or more directly: 'You ought to dance', if the implied reason is just that you want to dance or like dancing, is still a hypothetical imperative. Now Kant himself held that moral judgements are categorical imperatives, or perhaps are all applications of one categorical imperative, and it can plausibly be maintained at least that many moral judgements contain a categorically imperative element. So far as ethics is concerned, my thesis that there are no objective values is specifically the denial that any such categorically imperative element is objectively valid. The objective values which I am denying would be action-directing absolutely, not contingently (in the way indicated) upon the agent's desires and inclinations.

Another way of trying to clarify this issue is to refer to moral reasoning or moral arguments. In practice, of course, such reasoning is seldom fully explicit: but let us suppose that we could make explicit the reasoning that supports some evaluative conclusion, where this conclusion has some action-guiding force that is not contingent upon desires or purposes or chosen ends. Then what I am saying is that somewhere in the input to this argument—perhaps in one or more of the premisses, perhaps in some part of the form of the argument—there will be something which cannot be objectively validated—some premiss which is not capable of being simply true, or some form of argument which is not valid as a matter of general logic, whose authority or cogency is not objective, but is constituted by our choosing or deciding to think in a certain way.

7. THE CLAIM TO OBJECTIVITY

If I have succeeded in specifying precisely enough the moral values whose objectivity I am denying, my thesis may now seem to be trivially true. Of course, some will say, valuing, preferring, choosing, recommending, rejecting, condemning, and so on, are human activities, and there is no need to look for values that are prior to and logically independent of all such activities. There may be widespread agreement in valuing, and particular value-judgements are not in general arbitrary or isolated: they typically cohere with others, or can be criticized if they do not, reasons can be given for them, and so on: but if all that the subjectivist is maintaining is that desires, ends, purposes, and the like figure somewhere in the system of reasons, and that no ends or purposes are objective as opposed to being merely intersubjective, then this may be conceded without much fuss.

But I do not think that this should be conceded so easily. As I have said, the main tradition of European moral philosophy includes the contrary claim, that there are objective values of just the sort I have denied. I have referred already to Plato, Kant, and Sidgwick. Kant in particular holds that the categorical imperative is not only categorical and imperative but objectively so: though a rational being gives the moral law to himself, the law that he thus makes is determinate and necessary. Aristotle begins the *Nicomachean Ethics* by saying that the good is that at which all things aim, and that ethics is part of a science which he calls 'politics', whose goal is not knowledge but practice; yet he does not doubt that there can be *knowledge* of what is the good for man, nor, once he has identified this as well-being or happiness, *eudaimonia*, that it can be known, rationally determined, in what happiness consists; and it is plain that he thinks that this happiness is intrinsically desirable, not good simply because it is desired. The rationalist Samuel Clarke holds that

> these eternal and necessary differences of things make it *fit and reasonable* for creatures so to act . . . even separate from the consideration of these rules being the *positive will* or *command of God;* and also antecedent to any respect or regard, expectation, or apprehension, of any *particular private and personal advantage or disadvantage, reward or punishment,* either present or future . . .

Even the sentimentalist Hutcheson defines moral goodness as 'some quality apprehended in actions, which procures approbation . . . ', while saying that the moral sense by which we perceive virtue and vice has been given to us (by the Author of nature) to direct our actions. Hume indeed was on the other side, but he is still a witness to the dominance of the objectivist tradition, since he claims that when we 'see that the distinction of vice and virtue is not founded merely on the relations of objects, nor is perceiv'd by reason', this 'wou'd subvert all the vulgar systems of morality'. And Richard Price insists that right and wrong are 'real characters of actions', not 'qualities of our minds', and are perceived by the understanding; he criticizes the notion of moral sense on the ground that it would make virtue an affair of taste, and moral right and wrong 'nothing in the objects themselves'; he rejects Hutcheson's view because (perhaps mistakenly) he sees it as collapsing into Hume's.

But this objectivism about values is not only a feature of the philosophical tradition. It has also a firm basis in ordinary thought, and even in the meanings of moral terms. No doubt it was an extravagance for Moore to say that 'good' is the name of a non-natural quality, but it would not be so far wrong to say that in moral contexts it is used as if it were the name of a supposed non-natural quality, where the description 'non-natural' leaves room for the peculiar evaluative, prescriptive, intrinsically action-guiding aspects of this supposed quality. This point can be illustrated by reflection on the conflicts and swings of opinion in recent years between non-cognitivist and naturalist views about the central, basic, meanings of ethical terms. If we reject the view that it is the function of such terms to introduce objective values into discourse about conduct and choices of action, there seem to be two main alternative types of account. One (which has importantly different subdivisions) is that they conventionally express either attitudes which the speaker purports to adopt towards whatever it is that he characterizes morally, or prescriptions or recommendations, subject perhaps to the logical constraint of universalizability. Different views of this type share the central thesis that ethical terms have, at least partly and primarily, some sort of non-cognitive, non-descriptive, meaning. Views of the other type hold that they are descriptive in meaning, but descriptive of natural features, partly of such features as everyone, even the non-cognitivist, would recognize as distinguishing kind actions from cruel ones, courage from cowardice, politeness from rudeness, and so on, and partly (though these two overlap) of relations between the actions and some human wants, satisfactions, and the like, I believe that views of both these types capture part of the truth. Each approach can account for the fact that moral judgements are action-guiding or practical. Yet each gains much of its plausibility from the felt inadequacy of the other. It is a very natural reaction to any non-cognitive analysis of ethical terms to protest that there is more to ethics than this, something more external to the maker of moral judgements, more authoritative over both him and those of or to whom he speaks, and this reaction is likely to persist even when full allowance has been made for the logical, formal, constraints of full-blooded prescriptivity and universalizability. Ethics, we are inclined to believe, is more a matter of knowledge and less a matter of decision than any non-cognitive analysis allows. And of course naturalism satisfies this demand. It will not be a matter of choice or decision whether an action is cruel or unjust or imprudent or whether it is likely to produce more distress than pleasure. But in satisfying this demand, it introduces a converse deficiency. On a naturalist analysis, moral judgements can be practical, but their practicality is wholly relative to desires or possible satisfactions of the person or persons whose actions are to be guided; but moral judgements seem to say more than this. This view leaves out the categorical quality of moral requirements. In fact both naturalist and non-cognitive analyses leave out the apparent authority of ethics, the one by excluding the categorically imperative aspect, the other the claim to objective validity or truth. The ordinary user of moral language means to say something about whatever it is that he characterizes morally, for example a possible action, as it is in itself, or would be if it were realized, and not about, or even simply expressive of, his, or anyone else's, attitude or relation to it. But the something he wants to say is not purely descriptive, certainly not inert, but something that involves a call for action or for the refraining from action, and one that is absolute, not contingent upon any desire or preference or policy or choice, his own or anyone else's. Someone in a state of moral perplexity, wondering whether it would be wrong for him to engage, say, in research related to bacteriological warfare, wants to arrive at some judgement about this concrete case, his doing this work at this time in these actual circumstances; his relevant characteristics will be part of the subject of the judgement, but no relation between him and the proposed action will be part of the predicate. The question is not, for example, whether he really wants to do this work, whether it will satisfy or dissatisfy him, whether he will in the long run have a pro-attitude towards it, or even whether this is an action of a sort that he can happily and sincerely recommend in all relevantly similar cases. Nor is he even wondering just whether to recommend such action in all relevantly similar cases. He wants to know whether this course of action would be wrong in itself. Something like this is the everyday objectivist concept of which talk about non-natural qualities is a philosopher's reconstruction.

The prevalence of this tendency to objectify values—and not only moral ones—is confirmed by a pattern of thinking that we find in existentialists and those influenced by them. The denial of objective values can carry with it an extreme emotional reaction, a feeling that nothing matters at all, that life has lost its purpose. Of course this does not follow; the lack of objective values is not a good reason for abandoning subjective concern or for ceasing to want anything. But the abandonment of a belief in objective values can cause, at least temporarily, a decay of subjective concern and sense of purpose. That it does so is evidence that the people in whom this reaction occurs have been tending to objectify their concerns and purposes, have been giving them a fictitious external authority. A claim to objectivity has been so strongly associated with their subjective concerns and purposes that the collapse of the former seems to undermine the latter as well.

This view, that conceptual analysis would reveal a claim to objectivity, is sometimes dramatically confirmed by philosophers who are officially on the other side. Bertrand Russell, for example, says that 'ethical propositions should be expressed in the optative mood, not in the indicative'; he defends himself effectively against the charge of inconsistency in both holding ultimate ethical valuations to be subjective and expressing emphatic opinions on ethical questions. Yet at the end he admits:

> Certainly there *seems* to be something more. Suppose, for example, that some one were to advocate the introduction of bull-fighting in this country. In opposing the proposal, I should *feel*, not only that I was expressing my desires, but that my desires in the matter are *right*, whatever that may mean. As a matter of argument, I can, I think, show that I am not guilty of any logical inconsistency in holding to the above interpretation of ethics and at the same time expressing strong ethical preferences. But in feeling I am not satisfied.

But he concludes, reasonably enough, with the remark: 'I can only say that, while my own opinions as to ethics do not satisfy me, other people's satisfy me still less.'

I conclude, then, that ordinary moral judgements include a claim to objectivity, an assumption that there are objective values in just the sense in which I am concerned to deny this. And I do not think it is going too far to say that this assumption has been incorporated in the basic, conventional, meanings of moral terms. Any analysis of the meanings of moral terms which omits this claim to objective, intrinsic, prescriptivity is to that extent incomplete; and this is true of any non-cognitive analysis, any naturalist one, and any combination of the two.

If second order ethics were confined, then, to linguistic and conceptual analysis, it ought to conclude that moral values at least are objective: that they are so is part of what our ordinary moral statements mean: the traditional moral concepts of the ordinary man as well as of the main line of western philosophers are concepts of objective value. But it is precisely for this reason that linguistic and conceptual analysis is not enough. The claim to objectivity, however ingrained in our language and thought, is not self-validating. It can and should be questioned. But the denial of objective values will have to be put forward not as the result of an analytic approach, but as an 'error theory', a theory that although most people in making moral judgements implicitly claim, among other things, to be pointing to something objectively prescriptive, these claims are all false. It is this that makes the name 'moral scepticism' appropriate.

But since this is an error theory, since it goes against assumptions ingrained in our thought and built into some of the ways in which language is used, since it conflicts with what is sometimes called common sense, it needs very solid support. It is not something we can accept lightly or casually and then quietly pass on. If we are to adopt this view, we must argue explicitly for it. Traditionally it has been supported by arguments of two main kinds, which I shall call the argument from relativity and the argument from queerness, but these can, as I shall show, be supplemented in several ways.

8. THE ARGUMENT FROM RELATIVITY

The argument from relativity has at its premiss the well-known variation in moral codes from one society to another and from one period to another, and also the differences in moral beliefs between different groups and classes within a complex community. Such variation is in itself merely a truth of descriptive morality, a fact of anthropology which entails neither first order nor second order ethical views. Yet it may indirectly support second order subjectivism: radical differences between first order moral judgements make it difficult to treat those judgements as apprehensions of objective truths. But it is not the mere occurrence of disagreements that tells against the objectivity of values. Disagreement on questions in history or biology or cosmology does not show that there are no objective issues in these fields for investigators to disagree about. But such scientific disagreement results from speculative inferences or explanatory hypotheses based on inadequate evidence, and it is hardly plausible to interpret moral disagreement in the same way. Disagreement about moral codes seems to reflect people's adherence to and participation in different ways of life. The causal connection seems to be mainly that way round: it is that people approve of monogamy because they participate in a monogamous way of life rather than that they participate in a monogamous way of life because they approve of monogamy. Of course, the standards may be an idealization of the way of life from which they arise: the monogamy in which people participate may be less complete, less rigid, than that of which it leads them to approve. This is not to say that moral judgements are purely conventional. Of course there have been and are moral heretics and moral reformers, people who have turned against the established rules and practices of their own communities for moral reasons, and often for moral reasons that we would endorse. But this can usually be understood as the extension, in ways which, though new and unconventional, seemed to them to be required for consistency, of rules to which they already adhered as arising out of an existing way of life. In short, the argument from relativity has some force simply because the actual variations in the moral codes are more readily explained by the hypothesis that they reflect ways of life than by the hypothesis that they express perceptions, most of them seriously inadequate and badly distorted, of objective values.

But there is a well-known counter to this argument from relativity, namely to say that the items for which objective validity is in the first place to be claimed are not specific moral rules or codes but very general basic principles which are recognized at least implicitly to some extent in all society—such principles as provide the foundations of what Sidgwick has called different methods of ethics: the principle of universalizability, perhaps, or the rule that one ought to conform to the specific rules of any way of life in which one takes part, from which one profits, and on which one relies, or some utilitarian principle of doing what tends, or seems likely, to promote the general happiness. It is easy to show that such general principles, married with differing concrete circumstances, different existing social patterns or different preferences, will beget different specific moral rules; and there is some plausibility in the claim that the specific rules thus generated will vary from community to community or from group to group in close agreement with the actual variations in accepted codes.

The argument from relativity can be only partly countered in this way. To take this line the moral objectivist has to say that it is only in these principles that the objective moral character attaches immediately to its descriptively specified ground or subject: other moral judgements are objectively valid or true, but only derivatively and contingently—if things had been otherwise, quite different sorts of actions would have been right. And despite the prominence in recent philosophical ethics of universalization, utilitarian principles, and the like, these are very far from constituting the whole of what is actually affirmed as basic in ordinary moral thought. Much of this is concerned rather with what Hare calls 'ideals' or, less kindly, 'fanaticism'. That is, people judge that some things are good or right, and others are bad or wrong, not because—or at any rate not only because—they exemplify some general principle for which widespread implicit acceptance could be claimed, but because something about those things arouses certain responses immediately in them, though they would arouse radically and irresolvably different responses in others. 'Moral sense' or 'intuition' is an initially more plausible description of what supplies many of our basic moral judgements than 'reason'. With regard to all these starting points of moral thinking the argument from relativity remains in full force.

9. THE ARGUMENT FROM QUEERNESS

Even more important, however, and certainly more generally applicable, is the argument from queerness. This has two parts, one metaphysical, the other epistemological. If there were objective values, then they would be entities or qualities or relations of a very strange sort, utterly different from anything else in the universe. Correspondingly, if we were aware of them, it would have to be by some special faculty of moral perception or intuition, utterly different from our ordinary ways of knowing everything else. These points were recognized by Moore when he spoke of non-natural qualities, and by the intuitionists in their talk about a 'faculty of moral intuition'. Intuitionism has long been out of favour, and it is indeed easy to point out its implausibilities. What is not so often stressed, but is more important, is that the central thesis of intuitionism is one to which any objectivist view of values is in the end committed: intuitionism merely makes unpalatably plain what other forms of objectivism wrap up. Of course the suggestion that moral judgements are made or moral problems solved by just sitting down and having an ethical intuition is a travesty of actual moral thinking. But, however complex the real process, it will require (if it is to yield authoritatively prescriptive conclusions) some input of this distinctive sort, either premises or forms of argument or both. When we ask the awkward question, how we can be aware of this authoritative prescriptivity, of the truth of these distinctively ethical premises or of the cogency of this distinctively ethical pattern of reasoning, none of our ordinary accounts of sensory perception or introspection or the framing and confirming of explanatory hypotheses or inference or logical construction or conceptual analysis, or any combination of these, will provide a satisfactory answer; 'a special sort of intuition' is a lame answer, but it is the one to which the clear-headed objectivist is compelled to resort.

Indeed, the best move for the moral objectivist is not to evade this issue, but to look for companions in guilt. For example, Richard Price argues that it is not moral knowledge alone that such an empiricism as those of Locke and Hume is unable to account for, but also our knowledge and even our ideas of essence, number, identity, diversity, solidity, inertia, substance, the necessary existence and infinite extension of time and space, necessity and possibility in general, power, and causation. If the understanding, which Price defines as the faculty within us that discerns truth, is also a source of new simple ideas of so many other sorts, may it not also be a power of immediately perceiving right and wrong, which yet are real characters of action?

This is an important counter to the argument from queerness. The only adequate reply to it would be to show how, on empiricist foundations, we can construct an account of the ideas and beliefs and knowledge that we have of all these matters. I cannot even begin to do that here, though I have undertaken some parts of the task elsewhere. I can only state my belief that satisfactory accounts of most of these can be given in empirical terms. If some supposed metaphysical necessities or essences resist such treatment, then they too should be included, along with objective values, among the targets of the argument from queerness.

This queerness does not consist simply in the fact that ethical statements are 'unverifiable'. Although logical positivism with its verifiability theory of descriptive meaning gave an impetus to non-cognitive accounts of ethics, it is not only logical positivists but also empiricists of a much more liberal sort who should find objective values hard to accommodate. Indeed, I would not only reject the verifiability principle but also deny the conclusion commonly drawn from it, that moral judgements lack descriptive meaning. The assertion that there are objective values or intrinsically prescriptive entities or features of some kind, which ordinary moral judgements presuppose, is, I hold, not meaningless but false.

Plato's Forms give a dramatic picture of what objective values would have to be. The Form of the Good is such that knowledge of it provides the knower with both a direction and an overriding motive; something's being good both tells the person who knows this to pursue it and makes him pursue it. An objective good would be sought by anyone who was acquainted with it, not because of any contingent fact that this person, or every person, is so constituted that he desires this end, but just because the end has to-be-pursuedness somehow built into it. Similarly, if there were objective principles of right and wrong, any wrong (possible) course of action would have not-to-be-doneness somehow built into it. Or we should have something like Clarke's necessary relations of fitness between situations and actions, so that a situation would have a demand for such-and-such and action somehow built into it.

The need for an argument of this sort can be brought out by reflection on Hume's argument that 'reason'—in which at this stage he includes all sorts of knowing as well as reasoning—can never be an 'influencing motive of the will'. Someone might object that Hume has argued unfairly from the lack of influencing power (not contingent upon desires) in ordinary objects of knowledge and ordinary reasoning, and might maintain that values differ from natural objects precisely in their power, when known, automatically to influence the will. To this Hume could, and would need to, reply that this objection involves the postulating of value-entities or value-features of quite a different order from anything else with which we are acquainted, and of a corresponding faculty with which to detect them. That is, he would have to supplement his explicit argument with what I have called the argument from queerness.

Another way of bringing out this queerness is to ask, about anything that is supposed to have some objective moral quality, how this is linked with its natural features. What is the connection between the natural fact that an action is a piece of deliberate cruelty—say, causing pain just for fun—and the moral fact that it is wrong? It cannot be an entailment, a logical or semantic necessity. Yet it is not merely that the two features occur together. The wrongness must somehow be 'consequential' or 'supervenient'; it is wrong because it is a piece of deliberate cruelty. But just what *in the world* is signified by this 'because'? And how do we know the relation that it signifies, if this is something more than such actions being socially condemned, and condemned by us too, perhaps through our having absorbed attitudes from our social environment? It is not even sufficient to postulate a faculty which 'sees' the wrongness: something must be postulated which can see at once the natural features that constitute the cruelty, and the wrongness, and the mysterious consequential link between the two. Alternatively, the intuition required might be the perception that wrongness is a higher order property belonging to certain natural properties;

but what is this belonging of properties to other properties, and how can we discern it? How much simpler and more comprehensible the situation would be if we could replace the moral quality with some sort of subjective response which could be causally related to the detection of the natural features on which the supposed quality is said to be consequential.

It may be thought that the argument from queerness is given an unfair start if we thus relate it to what are admittedly among the wilder products of philosophical fancy—Platonic Forms, non-natural qualities, self-evident relations of fitness, faculties of intuition, and the like. Is it equally forceful if applied to the terms in which everyday moral judgements are more likely to be expressed—though still, as has been argued in Section 7, with a claim to objectivity—'you must do this', 'you can't do that', 'obligation', 'unjust', 'rotten', 'disgraceful', 'mean', or talk about good reasons for or against possible actions? Admittedly not; but that is because the objective prescriptivity, the element a claim for whose authoritativeness is embedded in ordinary moral thought and language, is not yet isolated in these forms of speech, but is presented along with relations to desires and feelings, reasoning about the means to desired ends, interpersonal demands, the injustice which consists in the violation of what are in the context the accepted standards of merit, the psychological constituents of meanness, and so on. There is nothing queer about any of these, and under cover of them the claim for moral authority may pass unnoticed. But if I am right in arguing that it is ordinarily there, and is therefore very likely to be incorporated almost automatically in philosophical accounts of ethics which systematize our ordinary thought even in such apparently innocent terms as these, it needs to be examined, and for this purpose it needs to be isolated and exposed as it is by the less cautious philosophical reconstructions.

10. PATTERNS OF OBJECTIFICATION

Considerations of these kinds suggest that it is in the end less paradoxical to reject than to retain the common-sense belief in the objectivity of moral values, provided that we can explain how this belief, if it is false, has become established and is so resistant to criticisms. This proviso is not difficult to satisfy.

On a subjectivist view, the supposedly objective values will be based in fact upon attitudes which the person has who takes himself to be recognizing and responding to those values. If we admit what Hume calls the mind's 'propensity to spread itself on external objects', we can understand the supposed objectivity of moral qualities as arising from what we can call the projection or objectification of moral attitudes. This would be analogous to what is called the 'pathetic fallacy', the tendency to read our feelings into their objects. If a fungus, say, fills us with disgust, we may be inclined to ascribe to the fungus itself a non-natural quality of foulness. But in moral contexts there is more than this propensity at work. Moral attitudes themselves are at least partly social in origin: socially established—and socially necessary—patterns of behaviour put pressure on individuals, and each individual tends to internalize these pressures and to join in requiring these patterns of behaviour of himself and of others. The attitudes that are objectified into moral values have indeed an external source, though not the one assigned to them by the belief in their absolute authority. Moreover, there are motives that would support objectification. We need morality to regulate interpersonal relations, to control some of the ways in which people behave towards one another, often in opposition to contrary inclinations. We therefore want our moral judgements to be authoritative for other agents as well as for ourselves: objective validity would give them the authority required. Aesthetic values are logically in the same position as moral ones; much the same metaphysical and epistemological considerations apply to them. But aesthetic values are less strongly objectified than moral ones; their subjective status, and an 'error theory' with regard to such claims to objectivity as are incorporated in aesthetic judgements, will be more readily accepted, just because the motives for their objectification are less compelling.

But it would be misleading to think of the objectification of moral values as primarily the projection of feelings, as in the pathetic fallacy. More important are wants and demands. As Hobbes says, 'whatsoever is the object of any man's Appetite or Desire, that is it, which he for his part called *Good*'; and certainly both the adjective 'good' and the noun 'goods' are used in non-moral contexts of things because they are such as to satisfy desires. We get the notion of something's being objectively good, or having intrinsic value, by reversing the direction of dependence here, by making the desire depend upon the goodness, instead of the goodness on the desire. And this is aided by the fact that the desired thing will indeed have features that make it desired, that enable it to arouse a desire or that make it such as to satisfy some desire that is already there. It is fairly easy to confuse the way in which a thing's desirability is indeed objective with its having in our sense objective value. The fact that the word 'good' serves as one of our main moral terms is a trace of this pattern of objectification.

Similarly related uses of words are covered by the distinction between hypothetical and categorical imperatives. The statement that someone 'ought to' or, more strongly, 'must' do such-and-such may be backed up explicitly or implicitly by reference to what he wants or to what his purposes and objects are. Again, there may be a reference to the purposes of someone else, perhaps the speaker: 'You must do this'—'Why?'—'Because I want such-and-such'. The moral categorical imperative which could be expressed in the same words can be seen as resulting from the suppression of the conditional clause in a hypothetical imperative without its being replaced by any such reference to the speaker's wants. The action in question is still required in something like the way in which it would be if it were appropriately related to a want, but it is no longer admitted that there is any contingent want upon which is being required depends. Again this move can be understood when we remember that at least our central and basic moral judgements represent social demands, where the source of the demand is indeterminate and diffuse. Whose demands or wants are in question, the agent's, or the speaker's, or those of an indefinite multitude of other people? All of these in a way, but there are advantages in not specifying them precisely. The speaker is expressing demands which he makes as a member of a community, which he has developed in and by participation in a joint way of life; also, what is required of this particular agent would be required of any other in a relevantly similar situation; but the agent too is expected to have internalized the relevant demands, to act as if the ends for which the action is required were his own. By suppressing any explicit reference to demands and making the imperatives categorical we facilitate conceptual moves from one such demand relation to another. The moral uses of such words as 'must' and 'ought' and 'should', all of which are used also to express hypothetical imperatives, are traces of this pattern of objectification.

It may be objected that this explanation links normative ethics too closely with descriptive morality, with the mores or socially enforced patterns of behaviour that anthropologists record. But it can hardly be denied that moral thinking starts from the enforcement of social codes. Of course it is not confined to that. But even when moral judgements are detached from the mores of any actual society they are liable to be framed with reference to an ideal community of moral agents, such as Kant's kingdom of ends, which but for the need to give God a special place in it would have been better called a commonwealth of ends.

Another way of explaining the objectification of moral values is to say that ethics is a system of law from which the legislator has been removed. This might have been derived either from the positive law of a state or from a supposed system of divine law. There can be no doubt that some features of modern European moral concepts are traceable to the theological ethics of Christianity. The stress on quasi-imperative notions, on what ought to be done or on what is wrong in a sense that is close to that of 'forbidden', are surely relics of divine commands. Admittedly, the central ethical concepts for Plato and Aristotle also are in a broad sense prescriptive or intrinsically action-guiding, but in concentrating rather on 'good' than on 'ought' they show that their moral thought is an objectification of the desired and the satisfying rather than of the commanded. Elizabeth Anscombe has argued that modern, non-Aristotelian, concepts of *moral* obligation, *moral* duty, of what is *morally* right and wrong, and of the *moral* sense of 'ought' are survivals outside the framework of thought that made them really intelligible, namely the belief in divine law. She infers that 'ought' has 'become a word of mere mesmeric force', with only a 'delusive appearance of content', and that we would do better to discard such terms and concepts altogether, and go back to Aristotelian ones.

There is much to be said for this view. But while we can explain some distinctive features of modern moral philosophy in this way, it would be a mistake to see the whole problem of the claim to objective prescriptivity as merely local and unnecessary, as a post-operative complication of a society from which a dominant system of theistic belief has recently been rather hastily excised. As Cudworth and Clarke and Price, for example, show, even those who still admit divine commands, or the positive law of God, may believe moral values to have an independent objective but still action-guiding authority.

Responding to Plato's *Euthyphro* dilemma, they believe that God commands what he commands because it is in itself good or right, not that it is good or right merely because and in that he commands it. Otherwise God himself could not be called good. Price asks, 'What can be more preposterous, than to make the Deity nothing but will; and to exalt this on the ruins of all his attributes?' The apparent objectivity of moral value is a widespread phenomenon which has more than one source: the persistence of a belief in something like divine law when the belief in the divine legislator has faded out is only one factor among others. There are several different patterns of objectification, all of which have left characteristic traces in our actual moral concepts and moral language.

11. THE GENERAL GOAL OF HUMAN LIFE

The argument of the preceding sections is meant to apply quite generally to moral thought, but the terms in which it has been stated are largely those of the Kantian and post-Kantian tradition of English moral philosophy. To those who are more familiar with another tradition, which runs through Aristotle and Aquinas, it may seem wide of the mark. For them, the fundamental notion is that of the good for man, or the general end or goal of human life, or perhaps of a set of basic goods or primary human purposes. Moral reasoning consists partly in achieving a more adequate understanding of this basic goal (or set of goals), partly in working out the best way of pursuing and realizing it. But this approach is open to two radically different interpretations. According to one, to say that something is the good for man or the general goal of human life is just to say that this is what men in fact pursue or will find ultimately satisfying, or perhaps that it is something which, if postulated as an implicit goal, enables us to make sense of actual human strivings and to detect a coherent pattern in what would otherwise seem to be a chaotic jumble of conflicting purposes. According to the other interpretation, to say that something is the good for man or the general goal of human life is to say that this is man's proper end, that this is what he ought to be striving after, whether he in fact is or not. On the first interpretation we have a descriptive statement, on the second a normative or evaluative or prescriptive one. But this approach tends to combine the two interpretations, or to slide from one to the other, and to borrow support for what are in effect claims of the second sort from the plausibility of statements of the first sort.

I have no quarrel with this notion interpreted in the first way. I would only insert a warning that there may well be more diversity even of fundamental purposes, more variation in what different human beings will find ultimately satisfying, than the terminology of '*the* good for man' would suggest. Nor indeed, have I any quarrel with the second, prescriptive, interpretation, provided that it is recognized as subjectively prescriptive, that the speaker is here putting forward his own demands or proposals, or those of some movement that he represents, though no doubt linking these demands or proposals with what he takes to be already in the first, descriptive, sense fundamental human goals. In fact, I shall myself make use of the notion of the good for man, interpreted in both these ways, when I try in Chapter 8 to sketch a positive moral system. But if it is claimed that something is objectively the right or proper goal of human life, then this is tantamount to the assertion of something that is objectively categorically imperative, and comes fairly within the scope of our previous arguments. Indeed, the running together of what I have here called the two interpretations is yet another pattern of objectification: a claim to objective prescriptivity is constructed by combining the normative element in the second interpretation with the objectivity allowed by the first, by the statement that such and such are fundamentally pursued or ultimately satisfying human goals. The argument from relativity still applies: the radical diversity of the goals that men actually pursue and find satisfying makes it implausible to construe such pursuits as resulting from an imperfect grasp of a unitary true good. So too does the argument from queerness; we can still ask what this objectively prescriptive rightness of the true goal can be, and how this is linked on the one hand with the descriptive features of this goal and on the other with the fact that it is *to some extent* an actual goal of human striving.

To meet these difficulties, the objectivist may have recourse to the purpose of God: the true purpose of human life is fixed by what God intended (or, intends) men to do and to be. Actual human strivings and satisfactions have some relation to this true end because God made men for this end and made them such as to pursue it—but only *some* relation, because of the inevitable imperfection of created beings.

I concede that if the requisite theological doctrine could be defended, a kind of objective ethical prescriptivity could be thus introduced. Since I think that theism cannot be defended, I do not regard this as any threat to my argument. But I shall take up the question of relations between morality and religion again in Chapter 10. Those who wish to keep theism as a live option can read the arguments of the intervening chapters hypothetically, as a discussion of what we can make of morality without recourse to God, and hence of what we can say about morality if, in the end, we dispense with religious belief.

12. CONCLUSION

I have maintained that there is a real issue about the status of values, including moral values. Moral scepticism, the denial of objective moral values, is not to be confused with any one of several first order normative views, or with any linguistic or conceptual analysis. Indeed, ordinary moral judgements involve a claim to objectivity which both non-cognitive and naturalist analyses fail to capture. Moral scepticism must, therefore, take the form of an error theory, admitting that a belief in objective values is built into ordinary moral thought and language, but holding that this ingrained belief is false. As such, it needs arguments to support it against 'common sense'. But solid arguments can be found. The considerations that favour moral scepticism are: first, the relativity or variability of some important starting points of moral thinking and their apparent dependence on actual ways of life; secondly, the metaphysical peculiarity of the supposed objective values, in that they would have to be intrinsically action-guiding and motivating; thirdly, the problem of how such values could be consequential or supervenient upon natural features; fourthly, the corresponding epistemological difficulty of accounting for our knowledge of value entities or features and of their links with the features on which they would be consequential; fifthly, the possibility of explaining, in terms of several different patterns of objectification, traces of which remain in moral language and moral concepts, how even if there were no such objective values people not only might have come to suppose that there are but also might persist firmly in that belief. These five points sum up the case for moral scepticism; but of almost equal importance are the preliminary removal of misunderstandings that often prevent this thesis from being considered fairly and explicitly, and the isolation of those items about which the moral sceptic is sceptical from many associated qualities and relations whose objective status is not in dispute.

•　•　•

20

Value   — an analysis of types of reason

THOMAS NAGEL

Thomas Nagel (b. 1937) taught philosophy at Princeton University and now teaches at New York University. He is the author of several important works including The Possibility of Altruism, The View from Nowhere, *and, most recently,* Equality and Partiality. *This selection is excerpted from* The Tanner Lectures in Human Values, Vol. 1 *(1980).*

In the selection, Nagel discusses one version of the question of whether values are objective. In his view, an objective value is one that provides reasons for acting that do not depend on anyone's particular situation or perspective. These reasons can be recognized even by persons who are not interested parties. Although Nagel warns that we must not "elevate personal tastes and prejudices into cosmic views," his position is that there are objective values that provide all persons with reasons for acting. For example, the awfulness of physical pain is a reason for even nonsufferers to want it to disappear. Just as my pain is a reason for me to take an aspirin, so too is it a reason for you to want me to take an aspirin.

The view that values are objective has been criticized by many philosophers, among them Gilbert Harman and J. L. Mackie (readings 17 and 19). However, Nagel tries to show that arguments like theirs are inconclusive. In addition, he draws several interesting distinctions between different types of objective values. On these and other matters, his views require, and reward, careful study.

1. Whether values can be objective depends on whether an interpretation of objectivity can be found that allows us to advance our knowledge of what to do, what to want, and what things provide reasons for and against action. Last week I argued that the physical conception of objectivity was not able to provide an understanding of the mind, but that another conception was available which allowed external understanding of at least some *aspects* of mental phenomena. A still different conception is required to make sense of the objectivity of values, for values are neither physical nor mental. And even if we find a conception, it must be applied with care. Not all values are likely to prove to be objective in any sense.

Let me say in advance that my discussion of values and reasons in this lecture and the next will be quite general. I shall be talking largely about what determines whether something has value, or whether someone has a reason to do or want something. I shall say nothing about how we pass from the identification of values and reasons to a conclusion as to what should be *done*. That is of course what makes reasons important; but I shall just assume that values do often provide the basis for such conclusions, without trying to describe even in outline how the full process of practical reasoning works. I am concerned here only with the general question, whether values have an objective foundation at all.

In general, as I said last time, objectivity is advanced when we step back, detach from our earlier point of view toward something, and arrive at a new view of the whole that is formed by including ourselves and our earlier viewpoint in what is to be understood.

In theoretical reasoning this is done by forming a new conception of reality that includes ourselves as components. This involves an alteration, or at least an extension, of our beliefs. Whether the effort to detach will actually result in an increase of understanding depends on the creative capacity to form objective ideas which is called into action when we add ourselves to the world and start over.

In the sphere of values or practical reasoning, the problem is somewhat different. As in the theoretical case, in order to pursue objectivity we must take up a new, comprehensive viewpoint after stepping back and including our former perspective in what is to be understood. But in this case the new view point will be *not* a new set of *beliefs*, but a new, or extended, set of *values*. If objectivity means anything here, it will mean that when we detach from our individual perspective and the values and reasons that seem acceptable from within it, we can sometimes arrive at a new conception which may endorse some of the original reasons but will reject some as subjective appearances and add others. This is what is usually meant by an objective, disinterested view of a practical question.

The basic step of placing ourselves and our attitudes within the world to be considered is familiar, but the form of the result—a new set of values, reasons, and motives—is different. In order to discover whether there are any objective values or reasons we must try to arrive at *normative* judgments, with *motivational content*, from an impersonal standpoint; a standpoint outside of our lives. We cannot use a *non-normative* criterion of objectivity: for *if* any values are objective, they are objective *values*, not objective anything else.

2. There are many opinions about whether what we have reason to do or want can be determined from a detached standpoint toward ourselves and the world. They range all the way from the view that objectivity has *no* place in this domain except what is inherited from the objectivity of those theoretical and factual elements that play a role in practical reasoning, to the view that objectivity applies here, but with a nihilistic result: i.e., that nothing is objectively right or wrong because objectively nothing matters. In between are many positive objectifying views which claim to get some definite results from a

detached standpoint. Each of them is criticized by adherents of opposing views either for trying to force too much into a single objective framework or for according too much or too little respect to divergent subjective points of view.

Here as elsewhere there is a direct connection between the goal of objectivity and the belief in *realism*. The most basic idea of practical objectivity is arrived at by a practical analogue of the rejection of solipsism or idealism in the theoretical domain. Just as realism about the facts leads us to seek a detached point of view from which reality can be discerned and appearance corrected, so realism about values leads us to seek a detached point of view from which it will be possible to correct inclination and to discern what we really should do, or want. Practical objectivity means that practical reason can be understood and even engaged in by the objective self.

This assumption, though powerful, is not yet an ethical position. It merely marks the place which an ethical position will occupy if we can make any sense of the subject. It says that the world of reasons, including my reasons, does not exist only from my point of view. I am in a world whose properties are to a certain extent independent of what I think, and if I have reasons to act it is because the person who I am has those reasons, in virtue of his condition and circumstances. One would expect those reasons to be understandable from outside. Here as elsewhere objectivity is a form of understanding not necessarily available for all of reality. But it is reasonable at least to look for such understanding over as wide an area as possible.

3. It is important not to lose sight of the dangers of *false* objectification, which too easily elevate personal tastes and prejudices into cosmic values. But initially, at least, it is natural to look for some objective account of those reasons that appear from one's own point of view.

In fact those reasons usually present themselves with some pretensions of objectivity to begin with, just as perceptual appearances do. When two things look the same size to me, they look at least initially as if they *are* the same size. And when I want to take aspirin because it will cure my headache, I believe at least initially that this *is* a reason for me to take aspirin, that it can be recognized as a reason from outside, and that if I failed to take it into account, that would be a mistake, and others could recognize this.

The ordinary process of deliberation, aimed at finding out what I have reason to do, assumes that the question has an answer. And in difficult cases especially, deliberation is often accompanied by the belief that I may not *arrive* at that answer. I do not assume that the correct answer is just whatever will result or has resulted from consistent application of deliberative methods— even assuming perfect information about the facts. In deliberation we are trying to arrive at conclusions that are correct in virtue of something *independent* of our arriving at them. If we arrive at a conclusion, we believe that it would have been correct even if we *hadn't* arrived at it. And we can also acknowledge that we might be *wrong*, since the process of reasoning doesn't guarantee the correctness of the result. So the pursuit of an objective account of practical reasons has its basis in the realist claims of ordinary practical reasoning. In accordance with pretheoretical judgment we adopt the working hypothesis that there are reasons which may diverge from actual motivation even under conditions of perfect information—as reality can diverge from appearance—and then consider what form these reasons take. I shall say more about the general issue of realism later on. But first I want to concentrate on the process of thought by which, against a realist background, one might try to arrive at objective conclusions about reasons for action. In other words, if there really are values, how is objective knowledge of them possible?

In this inquiry no particular hypothesis occupies a privileged position, and it is certain that some of our starting points will be abandoned as we proceed. However, one condition on reasons obviously presents itself for consideration: a condition of generality. This is the condition that if something provides a reason for a particular individual to do something, then there is a general form of that reason which applies to anyone else in comparable circumstances. What count as comparable circumstances depends on the general form of the reason. This condition is not tautological. It is a rather strong condition which may be false, or true only for some kinds of reasons. But the search for generality is a natural beginning.

4. There is more than one type of generality, and no reason to assume that a single form will apply to every kind of reason or value. In fact I think that the choice among types of generality defines some of the central issues of contemporary moral theory.

One respect in which reasons may vary is in their *breadth*. A general principle may apply to everyone but be quite specific in content, and it is an open question to what extent narrower principles of practical reasons (don't lie; develop your talents) can be subsumed under broader ones (don't hurt others; consider your long-term interests), or even at the limit under a single widest principle from which all the rest derive. Reasons may be general, in other words, without forming a unified system that always provides a method for arriving at determinate conclusions about what one should do.

A second respect in which reasons vary is in their *relativity to the agent*, the person for whom they are reasons. The distinction between reasons that are relative to the agent and reasons that are not is an extremely important one. I shall follow Derek Parfit in using the terms 'agent-relative' and 'agent-neutral' to mark this distinction. (Formerly I used the terms 'subjective' and 'objective,' but those terms are here reserved for other purposes.)

If a reason can be given a general form which does *not* include an essential reference to the person to whom it applies, it is an *agent-neutral* reason. For example, if it is a reason for *anyone* to do or want something that it would reduce the amount of wretchedness in the world, then that is an agent-neutral reason.

If on the other hand the general form of a reason *does* include an essential reference to the person to whom it applies, it is an *agent-relative* reason. For example, if it is a reason for anyone to do or want something that it would be in *his* interest, then that is an agent-relative reason. In such a case, if something were in Jones's interest but contrary to Smith's, Jones would have reason to want it to happen and Smith would have the *same* reason to want it *not* to happen. (Both agent-relative and agent-neutral reasons are objective, since both can be understood from outside the viewpoint of the individual who has them.)

A third way in which reasons may vary is in their degree of externality, or independence of the interests of sentient beings. Most of the apparent reasons that initially present themselves to us are intimately connected with interests and desires, our own or those of others, and often with experiential satisfaction. But it is conceivable that some of these interests give evidence that their objects have intrinsic value independent of the satisfaction that anyone may derive from them or of the fact that anyone wants them—independent even of the existence of beings who can take an interest in them. I shall call a reason *internal* if it depends on the existence of an interest or desire in someone, and *external* if it does not. External reasons were believed to exist by Plato, and more recently by G. E. Moore, who believed that aesthetic value provided candidates for this kind of externality.

These three types of variation cut across one another. Formally, a reason may be narrow, external, and agent-relative (don't eat pork, keep your promises), or broad, internal, and agent-neutral (promote happiness), or internal and agent-relative (promote your own happiness). There may be other significant dimensions of variation. I want to concentrate on these because they locate the main controversies about what ethics is. Reasons and values that can be described in these terms provide the material for objective judgments. If one looks at human action and its conditions from outside and considers whether some normative principles are plausible, these are the forms they will take.

The actual *acceptance* of a general normative judgment will have motivational implications, for it will commit you under some circumstances to the acceptance of reasons to want and do things *yourself*.

This is most clear when the objective judgment is that something has *agent-neutral* value. That means *anyone* has reason to want it to happen—*and that includes someone considering the world in detachment from the perspective of any particular person within it*. Such a judgment has motivational content even before it is brought back down to the particular perspective of the individual who has accepted it objectively.

Agent-relative reasons are different. An objective judgment that some kind of thing has *agent-relative* value commits us only to believing that someone has reason to want and pursue it if it is related to him in the right way (being in *his* interest, for example). Someone who accepts this judgment is not committed to wanting it to *be the case* that people in general are influenced by such reasons. The judgment commits him to wanting something only when its implications are drawn *for the individual person he happens to be*. With regard to others, the content of the objective judgment concerns only what *they* should do or want.

I believe that judgments of both these kinds, as well as others, are evoked from us when we take up an objective standpoint. And I believe such judgments can be just as true and compelling as objective factual judgments about the real world that contains us.

5. When we take the step to objectivity in practical reasoning by detaching from our own point of view, the question we must ask ourselves is this: What reasons for action can be said to apply to people when we regard them from a standpoint detached from the values of any particular person?

The simplest answer, and one that some people would give, is "None." But that is not the only option. The suggested classification of types of generality provides a range of alternative hypotheses. It also provides some flexibility of response, for with regard to any reason that may appear to a particular individual to exist subjectively, the corresponding objective judgment may be that it does not exist at all, or that it corresponds to an agent-neutral, external value, or anything in between.

The choice among these hypotheses, plus others not yet imagined, is difficult, and there is no general method of making it any more than there is a general method of selecting the most plausible objective account of the facts on the basis of the appearances. The only 'method,' here or elsewhere, is to try to generate hypotheses and then to consider which of them seems most reasonable, in light of everything else one is fairly confident of.

This is not quite empty, for it means at least that logic alone can settle nothing. We do not have to be shown that the denial of some kind of objective values is *self-contradictory* in order to be reasonably led to accept their existence. There is no constraint to pick the weakest or narrowest or most economical principle consistent with the initial data that arise from individual perspectives. Our admission of reasons beyond these is determined *not* by logical entailment, but by what we cannot help believing, or at least finding most plausible among the alternatives.

In this respect it is no different from anything else: theoretical knowledge does not arise by deductive inference from the appearances either. The main difference is that our objective thinking about practical reasons is very primitive, and has difficulty taking even the first step. Philosophical skepticism and idealism about values are much more popular than their metaphysical counterparts. Nevertheless I believe they are no more correct. I shall argue that although no *single* objective principle of practical reason like egoism or utilitarianism covers everything, the acceptance of some objective values is unavoidable—not because the alternative is inconsistent but because it is not *credible*. Someone who, as in Hume's example, prefers the destruction of the whole world to the scratching of his finger, may not be involved in a *contradiction* or in any false *expectations*, but he is unreasonable nonetheless (to put it mildly), and anyone else not in the grip of an overly narrow conception of what reasoning is would regard his preference as objectively wrong.

6. But even if it is unreasonable to deny that anyone ever objectively has a reason to do anything, it is not easy to find positive objective principles that *are* reasonable. I am going to attempt to defend a few in the rest of this lecture

and the next. But I want to acknowledge in advance that it is not easy to follow the objectifying impulse without distorting individual life and personal relations. We want to be able to understand and accept the way we live from outside, but it may not always follow that we should control our lives from inside by the terms of that external understanding. Often the objective viewpoint will not be suitable as a replacement for the subjective, but will coexist with it, setting a standard with which the subjective is constrained not to clash. In deciding what to do, for example, we should not reach a result different from what we could decide objectively that that *person* should do—but we need not arrive at the result in the same way from the two standpoints.

Sometimes, also, the objective standpoint will allow us to judge how people should *be* or should *live*, without permitting us to translate this into a judgment about what they have *reasons* to do. For in some respects it is better to live and act not for reasons, but because we cannot help it. This is especially true of close personal relations. Here the objective standpoint cannot be brought into the perspective of *action* without destroying precisely what it affirms the value of. Nevertheless the possibility of this objective affirmation is important. We should be *able* to view our lives from outside without extreme dissociation or distaste, and the extent to which we should live without *considering* the objective point of view or even any reasons *at all* is itself *determined* largely from that point of view.

It is also possible that some idiosyncratic individual grounds of action, or the values of strange communities, will prove objectively inaccessible. To take an example in our midst: I didn't think that people who want to be able to run twenty-six miles without stopping are irrational, but their reasons can be understood only from the perspective of a value system that is completely alien to me, and will I hope remain so. A correct objective view will have to allow for such pockets of unassimilable subjectivity, which need not clash with objective principles but won't be affirmed by them either. Many aspects of personal taste will come in this category, if, as I think, they cannot all be brought under a general hedonistic principle.

But the most difficult and interesting problems of accommodation appear where objectivity *can* be employed as a standard, but we have to decide *how*. Some of the problems are these: To what extent should an objective view admit *external* values? To what extent should it admit *internal* but *agent-neutral* values? To what extent should the reasons to respect the interests of *others* take an *agent-relative* form? To what extent is it legitimate for each person to give priority to his own interests? These are all questions about the proper form of generality for different kinds of practical reasoning, and the proper relation between objective principles and the deliberations of individual agents. I shall return to some of them later, but there is a great deal that I shall not get to.

I shall not, for example, discuss the question of external values, i.e., values which may be *revealed* to us by the attractiveness of certain things, but whose existence is independent of the existence of any interests or desires. I am not sure whether there are any such values, though the objectifying tendency produces a strong impulse to believe that there are, especially in aesthetics where the object of interest is external and the interest seems perpetually capable of criticism in light of further attention to the object.

What I shall discuss is the proper form of *internal* values or reasons—those which depend on interests or desires. They can be objectified in more than one way, and I believe different forms of objectification are appropriate for different cases.

7. I plan to take up some of these complications in the next lecture. Let me begin, however, with a case for which I think the solution is simple: that of pleasure and pain. I am not an ethical hedonist, but I think pleasure and pain are very important, and they have a kind of neutrality that makes them fit easily into ethical thinking—unlike preferences or desires, for example, which I shall discuss later on.

I mean the kinds of pleasure and pain that do not depend on activities or desires which *themselves* raise questions of justification and value. Many pleasures and pains are just sensory experiences in relation to which we are fairly passive, but toward which we feel involuntary desire or aversion. Almost everyone takes the avoidance of his own pain and the promotion of his own pleasure as subjective reasons for action in a fairly simple way; they are not backed up by any further reasons. On the other hand if someone pursues pain or avoids pleasure, these idiosyncrasies usually *are* backed up by further reasons, like guilt or sexual masochism. The question is, what sort of general value, if any, ought to be assigned to pleasure and pain when we consider these facts from an objective standpoint?

It seems to me that the least plausible hypothesis is the zero position, that pleasure and pain have no value of any kind that can be objectively recognized. That would mean that looking at it from outside, you couldn't even say that someone had a reason not to put his hand on a hot stove. Try looking at it from the outside and see whether you can manage to withhold that judgment.

But I want to leave this position aside, because what really interests me is the choice between two other hypotheses, both of which admit that people have reason to avoid their own pain and pursue their own pleasure. They are the fairly obvious general hypotheses formed by assigning (a) agent-relative or (b) agent-neutral value to those experiences. If the avoidance of pain has only agent-relative value, then people have reason to avoid their own pain, but not to avoid the pain of others (unless other kinds of reasons come into play). If the avoidance of pain has agent-neutral value as well, then *anyone* has a reason to want *any* pain to stop, whether or not it is his. From an objective standpoint, which of these hypotheses is more plausible? Is the value of sensory pleasure and pain agent-relative or agent-neutral?

I believe it is agent-neutral, at least in part. That is, I believe pleasure is a good thing and pain is a bad thing, and that the most reasonable objective principle which admits that each of us has reason to pursue his own pleasure and avoid his own pain will acknowledge that these are not the only reasons present. This is a normative claim. Unreasonable, as I have said, does not mean inconsistent.

In arguing for this claim, I am somewhat handicapped by the fact that I find it self-evident. It is therefore difficult for me to find something still more certain with which to back it up. But I shall try to say what is wrong with rejecting it, and with the reasons that may lie behind its rejection. What would it be to really *accept* the alternative hypothesis that pleasure and pain are not impersonally good or bad? If I accept this hypothesis, assuming at the same time that each person has reason to seek pleasure and avoid pain for *himself*, then when I regard the matter objectively the result is very peculiar. I will have to believe that I have a reason to take aspirin for a headache, but that there *is no reason* for me to *have* an aspirin. And I will have to believe the same about anyone else. From an objective standpoint I must judge that everyone has reason to pursue a type of result that is *impersonally valueless*, that has value only to *him*.

This needs to be explained. If agent-neutral reasons are not ruled out of consideration from the start (and one would need reasons for that), why do we not have evidence of them here? The avoidance of pain is not an individual project, expressing the agent's personal values. The desire to make pain stop is simply *evoked* in the person who feels it. He may decide for various reasons not to stop it, but in the first instance he doesn't have to *decide* to want it to stop: he just does. He wants it to go away because it's *bad*: it is not *made* bad by his deciding that he wants it to go away. And I believe that when we think about it objectively, concentrating on what pain is *like*, and ask ourselves whether it is (a) not bad at all, (b) bad only for its possessor, or (c) bad *period*, the third answer is the one that needs to be argued *against*, not the one that needs to be argued *for*. The philosophical problem here is to get rid of the obstacles to the admission of the obvious. But first they have to be identified.

Consider how *strange* is the question posed by someone who wants a justification for altruism about such a basic matter as this. Suppose he and some other people have been admitted to a hospital with severe burns after being rescued from a fire. "I understand how *my* pain provides *me* with a reason to take an analgesic," he says, "and I understand how my groaning neighbor's pain gives *him* a reason to take an analgesic; but how does *his* pain give *me* any reason to want him to be given an analgesic? How can *his* pain give *me* or anyone else looking at it from outside a reason?"

This question is *crazy*. As an expression of puzzlement, it has that characteristic philosophical craziness which indicates that something very fundamental has gone wrong. This shows up in the fact that the *answer* to the question is *obvious*, so obvious that to ask the question is obviously a philosophical act. The answer is that pain is *awful*. The pain of the man groaning in the next bed is just as awful as yours. That's your reason to want him to have an analgesic.

Yet to many philosophers, when they think about the matter theoretically, this answer seems not to be available. The pain of the person in the next bed is thought to need major external help before it can provide me with a reason for wanting or doing anything: otherwise it can't get its hooks into me. Since most of these people are perfectly aware of the force such considerations actually have for them, justifications of some kind are usually found. But they take the form of working *outward* from the desires and interests of the individual for whom reasons are being sought. The burden of proof is thought always to be on the claim that he has reason to care about anything that is not *already* an object of his interest.

These justifications are unnecessary. They plainly falsify the real nature of the case. My reason for wanting my neighbor's pain to cease is just that it's awful, and I know it.

8. What is responsible for this demand for justification with its special flavor of philosophical madness? I believe it is something rather deep, which doesn't surface in the ordinary course of life: an inappropriate sense of the burden of proof. Basically, we are being asked for a demonstration of the *possibility* of real impersonal values, on the assumption that they are *not* possible unless such a general proof can be given.

But I think this is wrong. We can already *conceive* of such a possibility, and once we take the step of thinking about what reality, if any, there is in the domain of practical reason, it becomes a possibility we are bound to consider, that we cannot help considering. If there really are *reasons*, not just motivational pushes and pulls, and if agent-neutral reasons are among the kinds we can conceive of, then it becomes an obvious possibility that physical pain is simply bad: that even from an impersonal standpoint there is reason to want it to stop. When we view the matter objectively, this is one of the general positions that naturally suggests itself.

And once this is seen as a *possibility*, it becomes difficult *not* to accept it. It becomes a hypothesis that has to be *dislodged* by anyone who wishes to claim, for example, that all reasons are agent-relative. The question is, what are the alternatives, once we take up the objective standpoint? We must think *something*. If there is room in the realistic conception of reasons for agent-neutral values, then it is unnatural *not* to ascribe agent-neutral badness to burn pains. That is the natural conclusion from the fact that anyone who has a burn pain and is therefore closest to it wants acutely to be rid of it, and requires no indoctrination or training to want this. This evidence does not *entail* that burn pains are impersonally bad. It is logically conceivable that there is nothing bad about them at all, or that they provide only agent-relative reasons to their possessors to want them to go away. But to take such hypotheses seriously we would need justifications of a kind that seem totally unavailable in this case.

What could possibly show us that acute physical pain, which everyone finds horrible, is in reality not impersonally bad at all, so that except from the point of view of the sufferer it doesn't in itself matter? Only a very remarkable and farfetched picture of the value of a cosmic order beyond our immediate grasp, in which pain played an essential part which made it good or at least neutral— or else a demonstration that there can *be* no agent-neutral values. But I take it that neither of these is available: the first because the Problem of Evil has not been solved, the second because the absence of a logical demonstration that there *are* agent-neutral values is not a demonstration that there are *not* agent-neutral values.

My position is this. No demonstration is necessary in order to allow us to *consider* the possibility of agent-neutral reasons: the possibility simply *occurs* to us once we take up an objective stance. And there is no mystery about how an individual could have a reason to want something independently of its relation to his particular interests or point of view, because beings like ourselves are not *limited* to the particular point of view that goes with their personal position inside the world. They are also, as I have put it earlier, *objective selves:* they cannot *help* forming an objective conception of the world with themselves in it; they cannot help trying to arrive at judgments of *value* from that standpoint; they cannot help asking whether, from that standpoint, in abstraction from who in the world they are, they have any reason to want anything to be the case or not—any reason to want anything to happen or not.

Agent-neutral reasons do not have to find a miraculous source in our personal lives, because we are not *merely* personal beings: we are also importantly and essentially viewers of the world *from nowhere within it*—and in this capacity we remain open to judgments of value, both general and particular. The possibility of agent-neutral values is evident as soon as we begin to think from this standpoint about the reality of any reasons whatever. If we acknowledge the possibility of realism, then we cannot rule out agent-neutral values in advance.

Realism is therefore the fundamental issue. If there really are values and reasons, then it should be possible to expand our understanding of them by objective investigation, and there is no reason to rule out the natural and compelling objective judgment that pain is impersonally bad and pleasure impersonally good. So let me turn now to the abstract issue of realism about values.

9. Like the presumption that things exist in an external world, the presumption that there are real values and reasons can be defeated in individual cases, if a purely subjective account of the appearances is more plausible. And like the presumption of an external world, its complete falsity is not self-contradictory. The reality of values, agent-neutral or otherwise, is not *entailed* by the totality of appearances any more than the reality of a physical universe is. But if either of them is recognized as a possibility, then its reality in detail can be confirmed by appearances, at least to the extent of being rendered more plausible than the alternatives. So a lot depends on whether the possibility of realism is admitted in the first place.

It is very difficult to argue for such a possibility. Sometimes there will be arguments against it, which one can try to refute. Berkeley's argument against the conceivability of a world independent of experience is an example. But what is the result when such an argument is refuted? Is the possibility in a stronger position? I believe so: in general, there is no way to prove the possibility of realism; one can only refute impossibility arguments, and the more often one does this the more confidence one may have in the realist alternative. So to consider the merits of an admission of realism about value, we have to

[handwritten marginalia: "Anti-Realism 3 variations"]

consider the reasons against it. I shall discuss three. They have been picked for their apparent capacity to convince people.

The first argument depends on the question-begging assumption that if values are real, they must be real objects of some other kind. John Mackie, for example, in his recent book *Ethics*, denies the objectivity of values by saying that they are not part of the fabric of the world, and that if they were, they would have to be "entities or qualities or relations of a very strange sort, utterly different from anything else in the universe."[1] Apparently he has a very definite picture of what the universe is like, and assumes that realism about value would require crowding it with extra entities, qualities, or relations—things like Platonic Forms or Moore's non-natural qualities. But this assumption is not correct. The impersonal badness of pain is not some mysterious further property that all pains have, but just the fact that there is reason for anyone capable of viewing the world objectively to want it to *stop*, whether it is his or someone else's. The view that values are real is not the view that they are real occult entities or properties, but that they are real *values*: that our claims about value and about what people have reason to do may be *true* or *false* independently of our beliefs and inclinations. No *other* kinds of truths are involved. Indeed, no other kinds of truths *could* imply the reality of values.[2]

[handwritten marginalia, left margin: "Values are real. Not truly ungradated change but real values."]

The second argument I want to consider is not, like the first, based on a misinterpretation of moral objectivity. Instead, it tries to represent the unreality of values as an objective *discovery*. The argument is that if claims of value have to be objectively correct or incorrect, and if they are not reducible to any *other* kind of objective claim, then we can just *see* that all positive value claims must be false. Nothing has any objective value, because objectively nothing matters at all. If we push the claims of objective detachment to their logical conclusion, and survey the world from a standpoint completely detached from all interests, we discover that there is *nothing*—no values left of any kind: things can be said to matter at all only to individuals within the world. The result is objective nihilism.

I don't deny that the objective standpoint tempts one in this direction. But I believe this can seem like the required conclusion only if one makes the mistake of assuming that objective judgments of value must emerge from the detached standpoint *alone*. It is true that with nothing to go on but a conception of the world from nowhere, one would have no way of telling whether anything

---

1 J. L. Mackie, *Ethics* (Harmondsworth, Middlesex: Penguin Books, 1977), p. 38.

2 In discussion, Mackie claimed that I had misrepresented him, and that his disbelief in the reality of values and reasons does not depend on the assumption that to be real they must be strange *entities* or *properties*. As he says in his book, it applies directly to reasons themselves. For whatever they are they are not needed to explain anything that happens, and there is consequently no reason to believe in their existence. But I would reply that this raises the same issue. It begs the question to assume that *explanatory* necessity is the test of reality in this area. The claim that certain reasons exist is a normative claim, not a claim about the best explanation of anything. To assume that only what has to be included in the best explanatory picture of the world is real, is to assume that there are no irreducibly normative truths.

There is much more to be said on both sides of this issue, and I hope I have not misrepresented Mackie in this short footnote.

had value. But an objective view has more to go on, for its data include the appearance of value to individuals with particular perspectives, including oneself. In this respect practical reason is no different from anything else. Starting from a pure idea of a possible reality and a very impure set of appearances, we try to fill in the idea of reality so as to make some partial sense of the appearances, using objectivity as a method. To find out what the world is like from outside we have to approach it from within: it is no wonder that the same is true for ethics. And indeed, when we take up the objective standpoint, the problem is not that values seem to disappear but that there seem to be too many of them, coming from every life and drowning out those that arise from our own. It is just as easy to form desires from an objective standpoint as it is to form beliefs. Probably easier. Like beliefs, these desires and evaluations must be criticized and justified partly in *terms* of the appearances. But they are not just further appearances, any more than the beliefs about the world which arise from an impersonal standpoint are just further appearances.

The third type of argument against the objective reality of values is an empirical argument. It is also perhaps the most common. It is intended not to rule out the possibility of real values from the start, but rather to demonstrate that even if their *possibility* is admitted, we have no reason to believe that there are any. The claim is that if we consider the wide cultural variation in normative beliefs, the importance of social pressure and other psychological influences to their formation, and the difficulty of settling moral disagreements, it becomes highly implausible that they are anything but pure appearances.

Anyone offering this argument must admit that not every psychological factor in the explanation of an appearance shows that the appearance corresponds to nothing real. Visual capacities and elaborate training play a part in explaining the physicist's perception of a cloud-chamber track, or a student's coming to believe a proposition of geometry, but the path of the particle and the truth of the proposition also play an essential part in these explanations. So far as I know, no one has produced a general account of the kinds of psychological explanation that discredit an appearance. But some skeptics about ethics feel that because of the way we acquire moral beliefs and other impressions of value, there are grounds for confidence that no real, objective values play a part in the explanation.

I find the popularity of this argument surprising. The fact that morality is socially inculcated and that there is radical disagreement about it across cultures, over time, and even within cultures at a time is a poor reason to conclude that values have no objective reality. Even where there is truth, it is not always easy to discover. Other areas of knowledge are taught by social pressure, many truths as well as falsehoods are believed without rational grounds, and there is wide disagreement about scientific and social facts, especially where strong interests are involved which will be affected by different answers to a disputed question. This last factor is present throughout ethics to a uniquely high degree: it is an area in which one would expect extreme variation of belief and radical disagreement however objectively real the subject actually was. For comparably motivated disagreements about matters of fact, one has to go to the heliocentric theory, the theory of evolution, the Dreyfus case, the Hiss case, and the genetic contribution to racial differences in I.Q.

Although the methods of ethical reasoning are rather primitive, the degree to which agreement can be achieved and social prejudices transcended in the face of strong pressures suggests that something real is being investigated, and that part of the explanation of the appearances, both at simple and at complex levels, is that we perceive, often inaccurately, that certain reasons for action exist, and go on to infer, often erroneously, the general form of the principles that best accounts for those reasons.

The controlling conception that supports these efforts at understanding, in ethics as in science, is realism, or the possibility of realism. Without being sure that we will find one, we look for an account of what reasons there really are, an account that can be objectively understood.

I have not discussed all the possible arguments against realism about values, but I have tried to give general reasons for skepticism about such arguments. It seems to me that they tend to be supported by a narrow preconception of what there *is*, and that this is essentially question-begging.

•   •   •

21

Construction and Objectivity

JOHN RAWLS

John Rawls (b. 1921) is Professor of Philosophy Emeritus at Harvard University. He is among the leading moral and political theorists of the twentieth century. His books include the classic A Theory of Justice *and, more recently,* Political Liberalism. *This essay is one of a series of Dewey Lectures whose overall title was "Kantian Constructivism in Moral Theory." They were published in* The Journal of Philosophy *(September 1980).*

Here Rawls contests the view that objectivity in ethics consists of correspondence to moral facts. This assumption is common both to many who accept the objectivity of ethics (for example, W. D. Ross, readings 29 and 48) and to many who reject it (for example, J. L. Mackie, reading 19). However, as an alternative, Rawls suggests that moral principles may be constructed rather than discovered. Their objectivity may reside, not in their fidelity to any independent moral reality, but rather in the fact that they are chosen by suitably situated persons.

To flesh out this view, Rawls must specify when persons are suitably situated. That depends, he suggests, on what ideal of the person we favor. If we accept an ideal of persons as free and equal, and as moved by certain "highest-order interests," then the relevant features of our ideal will be modeled by the "original position" that is central to Rawls's own theory of justice (see reading 34). Moreover, according to Rawls, this ideal is "the conception of the person most likely to be held, at least implicitly, in a modern democratic society." Thus, Rawls's constructivism is connected at a deep level to his substantive views about justice.

In the preceding lectures I sketched the main idea of Kantian constructivism, which is to establish a connection between the first principles of justice and the conception of moral persons as free and equal. These first principles are used to settle the appropriate understanding of freedom and equality for a modern democratic society. The requisite connection is provided by a procedure of construction in which rationally autonomous agents subject to reasonable conditions agree to public principles of justice. With the sketch of these ideas behind us, I consider in this final lecture how a Kantian doctrine interprets the notion of objectivity in terms of a suitably constructed social point of view that is authoritative with respect to all individual and associational points of view. This rendering of objectivity implies that, rather than think of the principles of justice as true, it is better to say that they are the principles most reasonable for us, given our conception of persons as free and equal, and fully cooperating members of a democratic society. [Here 'reasonable' is used, as explained later, in contrast with 'true' as understood in rational intuitionism, and not, as previously, with 'rational', as in the notion of rational autonomy.]

I

To fix ideas, let's look back roughly a hundred years to Henry Sidgwick. *The Methods of Ethics* (first edition 1874) is, I believe, the outstanding achievement in modern moral theory.[1] By "moral theory" I mean the systematic and comparative study of moral conceptions, starting with those which historically and by current estimation seem to be the most important. Moral philosophy includes moral theory, but takes as its main question justification and how it is to be conceived and resolved; for example, whether it is to be conceived as an epistemological problem (as in rational intuitionism) or as a practical problem (as in Kantian constructivism). Sidgwick's *Methods* is the first truly academic work in moral theory, modern in both method and spirit. Treating ethics as a discipline to be studied like any other branch of knowledge, it defines and carries out in exemplary fashion, if not for the first time, some of the comprehensive comparisons that constitute moral theory. By pulling together the work of previous writers, and through its influence on G. E. Moore and others, this work defined much of the framework of subsequent moral philosophy. Sidgwick's originality lies in his conception and mode of presentation of the subject and in his recognition of the significance of moral theory for moral philosophy.

It is natural, then, that the limitations of *Methods* have been as important as its merits. Of these limitations I wish to mention two. First, Sidgwick gives relatively little attention to the conception of the person and the social role of morality as main parts of a moral doctrine. He starts with the idea of a method of ethics as a method specified by certain first principles, principles by which we are to arrive at a judgment about what we ought to do. He takes for granted that these methods aim at reaching true judgments that hold for all rational minds. Of course, he thinks it is best to approach the problem of justification only when a broad understanding of moral theory has been achieved. In the preface of the first edition of *Methods* he explains that he wants to resist the natural urgency to discover the true method of ascertaining what it is right to do. He wishes instead to expound, from a neutral position and as impartially

---

1 On Sidgwick now, see the comprehensive work by J. B. Schneewind, *Sidgwick's Ethics and Modern Victorian Moral Philosophy* (New York: Oxford, 1977).

as possible, the different methods found in the moral consciousness of human-kind and worked into familiar historical systems.[2] But these detailed exposi-tions—necessary as they are—are merely preparation for comparing the various methods and evaluating them by criteria that any rational method that aims at truth must satisfy.

But a consequence of starting with methods of ethics defined as methods that seek truth is not only that it interprets justification as an epistemological problem, but also that it is likely to restrict attention to the first principles of moral conceptions and how they can be known. First principles are however only one element of a moral conception; of equal importance are its conception of the person and its view of the social role of morality. Until these other elements are clearly recognized, the ingredients of a constructivist doctrine are not at hand. It is characteristic of Sidgwick's *Methods* that the social role of morality and the conception of the person receive little notice. And so the possibility of constructivism was closed to him.

Sidgwick overlooked this possibility because of a second limitation: he failed to recognize that Kant's doctrine (and perfectionism also for that matter) is a distinctive method of ethics. He regarded the categorical imperative as a purely formal principle, or what he called "the principle of equity": whatever is right for one person is right for all similar persons in relevantly similar circumstances. This principle Sidgwick accepts, but, since it is plainly not a sufficient basis for a moral view, Kant's doctrine could not be counted a substantive method. This formal reading of Kant, together with the dismissal of perfectionism, led Sidgwick to reduce the traditional moral conceptions essentially to three main methods: regional egoism, (pluralistic) intuitionism, and classical utilitarianism. Surely he was right to restrict himself to a few conceptions so that each could be explored in considerable detail. Only in this way can depth of understanding be achieved. But rational egoism, which he accepted as a method of ethics, is really not a moral conception at all, but rather a challenge to all such concep-tions, although no less interesting for that. Left with only (pluralistic) intuition-ism and classical utilitarianism as methods of ethics in the usual sense, it is no surprise that utilitarianism seemed superior to Sidgwick, given his desire for unity and system in a moral doctrine.

Since Kant's view is the leading historical example of a constructivist doc-trine, the result once again is that constructivism finds no place in *Methods*. Nor is the situation altered if we include another leading representative work, F. H. Bradley's *Ethical Studies* (first edition 1876); following Hegel, Bradley likewise regarded Kant's ethics as purely formal and lacking in content and, therefore, to be assigned to an early stage of the dialectic as an inadequate view.[3] The result of these formal interpretations of Kant is that constructivism was not recognized as a moral conception to be studied and assimilated into moral theory. Nor was this lack made good in the first half of this century;

---

2 *The Methods of Ethics* (London: Macmillan 1907), 7th ed., pp. v–vi; parenthetical page references to Sidgwick are to this book, this edition.

3 See Essay IV: "Duty for Duty's Sake," 2nd ed. (New York: Oxford, 1927).

for in this period, beginning with Moore's *Principia Ethica* (1903), interest centered mainly on philosophical analysis and its bearing on justification regarded as an epistemological problem and on the question whether its conclusions support or deny the notion of moral truth. During this time, however, utilitarianism and intuitionism made important advances. A proper understanding of Kantian constructivism, on a par with our grasp of these views, is still to be achieved.

II

Let us now try to deepen our understanding of Kantian constructivism by contrasting it with what I shall call *rational intuitionism*. This doctrine has, of course, been expressed in various ways; but in one form or another it dominated moral philosophy from Plato and Aristotle onwards until it was challenged by Hobbes and Hume, and, I believe, in a very different way by Kant. To simplify matters, I take rational intuitionism to be the view exemplified in the English tradition by Clarke and Price, Sidgwick and Moore, and formulated in its minimum essentials by W. D. Ross.[4] With qualifications, it was accepted by Leibniz and Wolff in the guise of perfectionism, and Kant knows of it in this form.

For our purposes here, rational intuitionism may be summed up by two theses: first, the basic moral concepts of the right and the good, and the moral worth of persons, are not analyzable in terms of nonmoral concepts (although possibly analyzable in terms of one another); and, second, first principles of morals (whether one or many), when correctly stated, are self-evident propositions about what kinds of considerations are good grounds for applying one of the three basic moral concepts, that is, for asserting that something is (intrinsically) good, or that a certain action is the right thing to do, or that a certain trait of character has moral worth. These two theses imply that the agreement in judgment which is so essential for an effective conception of justice is founded on the recognition of self-evident truths about good reasons. And what these reasons are is fixed by a moral order that is prior to and independent of our conception of the person and the social role of morality. This order is given by the nature of things and is known, not by sense, but by rational intuition. It is with this idea of moral truth that the idea of first principles as reasonable will be contrasted.

It should be observed that rational intuitionism is compatible with a variety of contents for the first principles of a moral conception. Even classical utilitarianism, which Sidgwick was strongly inclined to favor (although he could not see how to eliminate rational egoism as a rival) was sometimes viewed by him

---

4 See *The Right and the Good* (Oxford: The Clarendon Press, 1930), esp. chs. 1–2. I shall adopt Ross's characterization of rational intuitionism, adjusted to allow for any number of first principles and, thus, as fitting either single-principle or pluralistic intuitionism. I should add that, for my purposes here, I interpret Aristotle's view as combining teleological and metaphysical perfectionism. Although this may not be a sound interpretation in the light of contemporary scholarship, it suits well enough how Aristotle was interpreted up to Kant's time.

as following from three principles each self-evident in its own right.[5] In brief, these three propositions were: the principle of equity so-called: that it cannot be right to treat two different persons differently merely on the ground of their being numerically different individuals; a principle of rational prudence: that mere difference of position in time is not by itself a reasonable ground for giving more regard to well-being at one moment than to well-being at another; and a principle of rational benevolence: the good of one person is of no more importance from the point of view of the universe than the good of any other person. These three principles, when combined with the principle that, as reasonable beings, we are bound to aim at good generally and not at any particular part of it, Sidgwick thought yielded the principle of utility: namely, to maximize the net balance of happiness. And this principle, like those from which it followed, he was tempted to hold as self-evident.

Of all recent versions of rational intuitionism, the appeal to self-evidence is perhaps most striking in Moore's so-called "ideal utilitarianism" in *Principia Ethica* (1903). A consequence of Moore's principle of organic unity is that his view is extremely pluralistic; there are few if any useful first principles, and distinct kinds of cases are to be decided by intuition as they arise. Moore held a kind of Platonic atomism:[6] moral concepts (along with other concepts) are subsisting and independent entities grasped by the mind. That pleasure and beauty are good, and that different combinations of them alone or together with other good things are also good, and to what degree, are truths known by intuition: by seeing with the mind's eye how these separate and distinct objects (universals) are (timelessly) related. This picture is even more vivid in the early philosophy of mathematics of Bertrand Russell, who talks of searching for the indefinable concepts of mathematics with a mental telescope (as one might look for a planet).[7]

Now my aim in recalling these matters is to point out that rational intuitionism, as illustrated by Sidgwick, Moore, and Ross, is sharply opposed to a constructivist conception along Kantian lines. That Kant would have rejected Hume's psychological naturalism as heteronomous is clear.[8] I believe that the contrast with rational intuitionism, no matter what the content of the view

---

5 *Methods*, Book III, ch. 13, pp. 379–389. See Schneewind's discussion, ch. 10, pp. 286–309.

6 I borrow this expression from Peter Hylton's discussion, *The Origins of Analytic Philosophy*, ch. 3 (Dissertation: Harvard University, 1978).

7 See *The Principles of Mathematics* (London: Allen & Unwin, 1937), 2nd ed. (1st ed. 1903), pp. xv–xvi. The analogy of the mental telescope is Russell's.

8 Because it formulates definitions of the basic moral concepts in terms of nonmoral concepts, this being the mode of identifying those facts which are to count as good reasons in applying the basic moral concepts, naturalism is a form of heteronomy from the Kantian standpoint. The various definitions, presumably arrived at by the analysis of concepts, convert moral judgments into statements about the world on all fours with those of science and common sense. Therefore, these definitions, combined with the natural order itself, now come to constitute the moral order, which is prior to and independent from our conception of ourselves as free and equal moral persons. If time permitted, this could be substantiated by setting out, for example, the details of Hume's view (as often interpreted) and of Bentham's hedonistic utilitarianism, at least once these views are expressed in the requisite naturalistic format. (Rational intuitionism tries to secure a kind of independence of the moral order from the order of nature.)

(whether utilitarian, perfectionist, or pluralist) is even more instructive. It is less obvious that for Kant rational intuitionism is also heteronomous. The reason is that from the first thesis of rational intuitionism, the basic moral concepts are conceptually independent of natural concepts, and first principles are independent of the natural world and, as grasped by rational intuition, are regarded as synthetic a priori. This may seem to make these principles not heteronomous. Yet it suffices for heteronomy that these principles obtain in virtue of relations among objects the nature of which is not affected or determined by the conception of the person. Kant's idea of autonomy requires that there exist no such order of given objects determining the first principles of right and justice among free and equal moral persons. Heteronomy obtains not only when first principles are fixed by the special psychological constitution of human nature, as in Hume, but also when they are fixed by an order of universals or concepts grasped by rational intuition, as in Plato's realm of forms or in Leibniz's hierarchy of perfections.[9] Perhaps I should add, to prevent misunderstanding, that a Kantian doctrine of autonomy need not deny that the procedures by which first principles are selected are synthetic a priori. This thesis, however, must be properly interpreted. The essential idea is that such procedures must be suitably founded on practical reason, or, more exactly, on notions which characterize persons as reasonable and rational and which are incorporated into the way in which, as such persons, they represent to themselves their free and equal moral personality. Put another way, first principles of justice must issue from a conception of the person through a suitable representation of that conception as illustrated by the procedure of construction in justice as fairness.

Thus in a Kantian doctrine a relatively complex conception of the person plays a central role. By contrast, rational intuitionism requires but a sparse notion of the person, founded on the self as knower. This is because the content of first principles is already fixed, and the only requirements on the self are to be able to know what these principles are and to be moved by this knowledge. A basic assumption is that the recognition of first principles as true and self-evident gives rise, in a being capable of rationally intuiting these principles, to a desire to act from them for their own sake. Moral motivation is defined by reference to desires that have a special kind of cause, namely, the intuitive grasp of first principles.[10] This sparse conception of the person joined with its moral psychology characterizes the rational intuitionism of Sidgwick, Moore, and Ross, although there is nothing that forces rational intuitionism to so thin

---

9 This fundamental contention is unfortunately obscured by the fact that although in the *Grundlegung* Kant classifies the view of Leibniz and Wolff as a form of heteronomy, his criticism of it is that it is circular and therefore empty. See Academy Edition, p. 443. Much the same happens in the *Second Critique*, Academy Edition, p. 41, where Kant argues that the notion of perfection in practical reasoning means fitness for any given ends and therefore is again empty until these ends are specified independently. These arguments give the erroneous impression that, if perfectionism had sufficient content, it would be compatible with autonomy.

10 See, for example, *Methods*, pp. 23–28, 34–37, 39ff., read together with the discussion of the self-evident basis of the principle of utility, cited in fn 5 above.

a notion. The point is rather that, in rational intuitionism in contrast to a Kantian view, since the content of first principles is already given, a more complex conception of the person, of a kind adequate to determine the content of these principles, together with a suitable moral psychology, is simply unnecessary.

III

Having contrasted Kantian constructivism to rational intuitionism with respect to the idea of a moral order that is prior to and independent from our conception of the person, I now consider a second contrast, namely, how each regards the inevitable limitations that constrain our moral deliberations. The constructionist view accepts from the start that a moral conception can establish but a loose framework for deliberation which must rely very considerably on our powers of reflection and judgment. These powers are not fixed once and for all, but are developed by a shared public culture and hence shaped by that culture. In justice as fairness this means that the principles adopted by the parties in the original position are designed by them to achieve a public and workable agreement on matters of social justice which suffices for effective and fair social cooperation. From the standpoint of the parties as agents of construction, the first principles of justice are not thought to represent, or to be true of, an already given moral order, as rational intuitionism supposes. The essential point is that a conception of justice fulfills its social role provided that citizens equally conscientious and sharing roughly the same beliefs find that, by affirming the framework of deliberation set up by it, they are normally led to a sufficient convergence of opinion. Thus a conception of justice is framed to meet the practical requirements of social life and to yield a public basis in the light of which citizens can justify to one another their common institutions. Such a conception need be only precise enough to achieve this result.

On the constructivist view, the limitations that constrain our moral deliberations affect the requirements of publicity and support the use of priority rules. These limitations also lead us to take the basic structure of a well-ordered society as the first subject of justice and to adopt the primary goods as the basis of interpersonal comparison. To begin with publicity: at the end of the preceding lecture I mentioned why in a constructivist view first principles are to satisfy the requirements of publicity. The moral conception is to have a wide social role as a part of public culture and is to enable citizens to appreciate and accept the conception of the person as free and equal. Now if it is to play this wide role, a conception's first principles cannot be so complex that they cannot be generally understood and followed in the more important cases. Thus, it is desirable that knowing whether these principles are satisfied, at least with reference to fundamental liberties and basic institutions, should not depend on information difficult to obtain or hard to evaluate. To incorporate these desiderata in a constructivist view, the parties are assumed to take these considerations into account and to prefer (other things equal) principles that are easy to understand and simple to apply. The gain in compliance and willing acceptance by citizens more than makes up for the rough and ready nature of the guiding framework that results and its neglect of certain distinctions and differences. In effect, the parties agree to rule out certain facts as irrelevant in questions of justice concerning the basic structure, even though they recognize that in regard to other cases it may be appropriate to appeal to them. From the standpoint of the original position, eliminating these facts as reasons of social justice sufficiently increases the capacity of the conception to fulfill its social role. Of course, we should keep in mind that the exclusion of such facts as reasons of social justice does not alone entail that they are not reasons in other kinds of situation where different moral notions apply. Indeed, it is not even ruled out that the account of some notions should be constructivist, whereas the account of others is not.

It is evident, then, why a constructivist view such as justice as fairness incorporates into the framework of moral deliberation a number of schematic and practical distinctions as ways that enable us to deal with the inevitable limitations of our moral capacities and the complexity of our social circumstances. The need for such distinctions supports and helps to account for the use of certain priority rules to settle the relative weight of particular kinds of grounds in extremely important cases. Two such rules in justice as fairness are: first, the priority of justice over efficiency (in the sense of Pareto) and the net balance of advantages (summed over all individuals in society), and second, the priority of the principle of equal liberty (understood in terms of certain enumerated basic liberties) over the second principle of justice.[11] These rules are introduced to handle the complexity of the many prima facie reasons we are ready to cite in everyday life; and their plausibility depends in large part on the first principles to which they are adjoined. But although these rules are intended to narrow the scope of judgment in certain fundamental questions of justice, this scope can never be entirely eliminated, and for many other questions sharp and definite conclusions cannot usually be derived. Sharp and definite conclusions are not needed, however, if sufficient agreement is still forthcoming (TJ 44/5).*

Similar considerations apply in beginning with the basic structure of a well-ordered society as the first subject of justice and trying to develop a conception of justice for this case alone. The idea is that this structure plays a very special role in society by establishing what we may call *background justice;* and if we can find suitable first principles of background justice, we may be able to exclude enough other considerations as irrelevant for this case, so as to develop a reasonably simple and workable conception of justice for the basic structure. The further complexities of everyday cases that cannot be ignored in a more

---

11 For a statement of these principles and priority rules, see TJ, pp. 60–62, 250, 302–303.

* TJ is Rawls's abbreviation for his book *A Theory of Justice* (Cambridge, MA: Harvard University Press, 1971).—Ed.

complete moral conception may be dealt with later in the less general situations that occur within the various associations regulated by the basic structure, and in that sense subordinate to it.[12]

Finally, parallel observations hold in finding a feasible basis for interpersonal comparisons of well-being relevant for questions of justice that arise in regard to the basic structure. These comparisons are to be made in terms of primary goods (as defined in the first lecture), which are, so far as possible, certain public features of social institutions and of people's situations with respect to them, such as their rights, liberties, and opportunities, and their income and wealth, broadly understood. This has the consequence that the comparison of citizens' shares in the benefits of social cooperation is greatly simplified and put on a footing less open to dispute.

Thus the reason why a constructivist view uses the schematic or practical distinctions we have just noted is that such distinctions are necessary if a workable conception of justice is to be achieved. These distinctions are incorporated into justice as fairness through the description of the parties as agents of construction and the account of how they are to deliberate. Charged with the task of agreeing to a workable conception of justice designed to achieve a sufficient convergence of opinion, the parties can find no better way in which to carry out this task. They accept the limitations of human life and recognize that at best a conception of justice can establish but a guiding framework for deliberation.

A comparison with classical utilitarianism will highlight what is involved here. On that view, whether stated as a form of rational intuitionism (Sidgwick) or as a form of naturalism (Bentham), every question of right and justice has an answer: whether an institution or action is right depends upon whether it will produce the greatest net balance of satisfaction. We may never be in a position to know the answer, or even to come very near to it, but, granting that a suitable measure of satisfaction exists, there is an answer: a fact of the matter. Of course, utilitarianism recognizes the needs of practice: working precepts and secondary rules are necessary to guide deliberation and coordinate our actions. These norms may be thought of as devised to bring our actions as close as possible to those which would maximize utility, so far as this is feasible. But of course, such rules and precepts are not first principles; they are at best directives that when followed make the results of our conduct approximate to what the principle of utility enjoins. In this sense, our working norms are approximations to something given.

By contrast, justice as fairness, as a constructivist view, holds that not all the moral questions we are prompted to ask in everyday life have answers. Indeed, perhaps only a few of them can be settled by any moral conception that we can understand and apply. Practical limitations impose a more modest aim upon a reasonable conception of justice, namely, to identify the most fundamental questions of justice that can be dealt with, in the hope that, once

---

12 See "The Basic Structure As Subject," in A. I. Goldman and Jaegwon Kim, eds., *Values and Morals* (Boston: Reidel, 1978), especially secs. iv–v, pp. 52–57.

this is done and just basic institutions established, the remaining conflicts of opinion will not be so deep or widespread that they cannot be compromised. To accept the basic structure as the first subject of justice together with the account of primary goods is a step toward achieving this more modest goal. But in addition, the idea of approximating to moral truth has no place in a constructivist doctrine: the parties in the original position do not recognize any principles of justice as true or correct and so as antecedently given; their aim is simply to select the conception most rational for them, given their circumstances. This conception is not regarded as a workable approximation to the moral facts: there are no such moral facts to which the principles adopted could approximate.

As we have just seen, the differences between constructivism and classical utilitarianism are especially sharp in view of the content of the principle of utility: it always yields an answer that we can at least verbally describe. With the rational (pluralistic) intuitionism of Ross, however, the contrast is less obvious, since Ross's list of self-evident prima facie principles that identify good reasons also specifies but a loose guiding framework of moral deliberation which shares a number of the features of the framework provided by construct-ivism. But though these resemblances are real, the underlying idea of Ross's view is still essentially different from constructivism. His pluralistic intuitionism rejects utilitarianism (even an ideal utilitarianism) as oversimplifying the given moral facts, especially those concerning the correct weight of special duties and obligations. The complexity of the moral facts in particular kinds of cases is said to force us to recognize that no family of first principles that we can formulate characterizes these facts sufficiently accurately to lead to a definite conclusion. Decision and judgment are almost always to some degree uncertain and must rest with "perception,"[13] that is, with our intuitive estimate of where the greatest balance of prima facie reasons lies in each kind of case. And this perception is that of a balance of reasons each of which is given by an independent moral order known by intuition. The essential contrast with constructivism remains.

IV

Having examined several contrasts between Kantian constructivism and rational intuitionism, we are now in a position to take up a fundamental point suggested by the discussion so far: an essential feature of a constructivist view, as illustrated by justice as fairness, is that its first principles single out what facts citizens in a well-ordered society are to count as reasons of justice. Apart from the procedure of constructing these principles, there are no reasons of justice. Put in another way, whether certain facts are to count as reasons of justice and what their relative force is to be can be ascertained only on the

---

13 See *The Right and the Good,* pp. 41–42. Ross refers to Aristotle's remark: "The decision rests with perception" (*Nicomachean Ethics* 1109 b 23, 1126 b 4).

basis of the principles that result from the construction. This connects with the use of pure procedural justice at the highest level. It is, therefore, up to the parties in the original position to decide how simple or complex the moral facts are to be, that is, to decide on the number and complexity of the principles that identify which facts are to be accepted as reasons of justice by citizens in society (see TJ 45). There is nothing parallel to this in rational intuitionism.

This essential feature of constructivism may be obscured by the fact that in justice as fairness the first principles of justice depend upon those general beliefs about human nature and how society works which are allowed to the parties in the original position. First principles are not, in a constructivist view, independent of such beliefs, nor, as some forms of rational intuitionism hold, true in all possible worlds. In particular, they depend on the rather specific features and limitations of human life that give rise to the circumstances of justice.[14] Now, given the way the original position is set up, we can allow, in theory, that, as the relevant general beliefs change, the beliefs we attribute to the parties likewise change, and conceivably also the first principles that would be agreed to. We can say, if we like that *the* (most reasonable) principles of justice are those which would be adopted if the parties possessed all relevant general information and if they were properly to take account of all the practical desiderata required for a workable public conception of justice. Though these principles have a certain preeminence, they are still the outcome of construction. Furthermore, it is important to notice here that no assumptions have been made about a theory of truth. A constructivist view does not require an idealist or a verificationist, as opposed to a realist, account of truth. Whatever the nature of truth in the case of general beliefs about human nature and how society works, a constructivist moral doctrine requires a distinct procedure of construction to identify the first principles of justice. To the extent that Kant's moral doctrine depends upon what to some may appear to be a constructivist account of truth in the *First Critique* (I don't mean to imply that such an interpretation is correct), justice as fairness departs from that aspect of Kant's view and seeks to preserve the over-all structure of his moral conception apart from that background.

In the preceding paragraph I said that the way justice as fairness is set up allows the possibility that, as the general beliefs ascribed to the parties in the original position change, the first principles of justice may also change. But I regard this as a mere possibility noted in order to explain the nature of a constructivist view. To elaborate: at the end of the first lecture I distinguished between the roles of a conception of the person and of a theory of human nature, and I remarked that in justice as fairness these are distinct elements and enter at different places. I said that a conception of the person is a companion moral ideal paired with the ideal of a well-ordered society. A theory of human nature and a view of the requirements of social life tell us whether these ideals are feasible, whether it is possible to realize them under normally favorable conditions of human life. Changes in the theory of human nature or

---

14 See Lecture II, section I.

in social theory generally which do not affect the feasibility of the ideals of the person and of a well-ordered society do not affect the agreement of the parties in the original position. It is hard to imagine realistically any new knowledge that should convince us that these ideals are not feasible, given what we know about the general nature of the world, as opposed to our particular social and historical circumstances. In fact, the relevant information on these matters must go back a long time and is available to the common sense of any thoughtful and reflective person. Thus such advances in our knowledge of human nature and society as may take place do not affect our moral conception, but rather may be used to implement the application of its first principles of justice and suggest to us institutions and policies better designed to realize them in practice.[15]

In justice as fairness, then, the main ideals of the conception of justice are embedded in the two model-conceptions of the person and of a well-ordered society. And, granting that these ideals are allowed by the theory of human nature and so in that sense feasible, the first principles of justice to which they lead, via the constructivist procedure of the original position, determine the long-term aim of social change. These principles are not, as in rational intuitionism, given by a moral order prior to and independent from our conception of the person and the social role of morality; nor are they, as in some naturalist doctrines, to be derived from the truths of science and adjusted in accordance with advances in human psychology and social theory. (These remarks are admittedly too brief, but we must return to the main line of discussion.)

V

The rational intuitionist may object that an essential feature of constructivism—the view that the facts to count as reasons of justice are singled out by the parties in the original position as agents of construction and that, apart from such construction, there are no reasons of justice—is simply incoherent.[16] This view is incompatible not only with the notion of truth as given by a prior and independent moral order, but also with the notions of reasonableness and objectivity, neither of which refer to what can be settled simply by agreement, much less by choice. A constructivist view, the objection continues, depends

---

15 Therefore these advances in our knowledge of human psychology and social theory might be relevant at the constitutional, legislative, and judicial stages in the application of the principles of justice, as opposed to the adoption of principles in the original position. For a brief account of these stages, see TJ, §31.

16 For this and other objections to what I call "constructivism" in this lecture, see the review of TJ by Marcus Singer, *Philosophy of Science*, XLIV, 4 (December 1977): 594–618, pp. 612–615. I am grateful to him for raising this objection, which I here try to meet. Singer's criticism starts from the passage on page 45 of TJ. It should not be assumed that Singer's own position is that of rational intuitionism. I simply suppose that a rational intuitionist would make this objection.

on the idea of adopting or choosing first principles, and such principles are not the kind of thing concerning which it makes sense to say that their status depends on their being chosen or adopted. We cannot "choose" them; what we can do is choose whether to follow them in our actions or to be guided by them in our reasoning, just as we can choose whether to honor our duties, but not what our duties are.

In reply, one must distinguish the three points of view that we noted at the end of the first lecture: that of the parties in the original position, that of the citizens in a well-ordered society, and that of you and me who are examining justice as fairness to serve as a basis for a conception that may yield a suitable understanding of freedom and equality. It is, of course, the parties in the original position whose agreement singles out the facts to count as reasons. But their agreement is subject to all the conditions of the original position which represent the Reasonable and the Rational. And the facts singled out by the first principles count as reasons not for the parties, since they are moved by their highest-order interests, but for the citizens of a well-ordered society in matters of social justice. As citizens in society we are indeed bound by first principles and by what our duties are, and must act in the light of reasons of justice. Constructivism is certain to seem incoherent unless we carefully distinguish these points of view.

The parties in the original position do not agree on what the moral facts are, as if there already were such facts. It is not that, being situated impartially, they have a clear and undistorted view of a prior and independent moral order. Rather (for constructivism), there is no such order, and therefore no such facts apart from the procedure of construction as a whole; the facts are identified by the principles that result. Thus the rational intuitionists' objection, properly expressed, must be that no hypothetical agreement by rationally autonomous agents, no matter how circumscribed by reasonable conditions in a procedure of construction, can determine the reasons that settle what we as citizens should consider just and unjust; right and wrong are not, even in that way, constructed. But this is merely to deny what constructivism asserts. If, on the other hand, such a construction does yield the first principles of a conception of justice that matches more accurately than other views our considered convictions in general and wide reflective equilibrium, then constructivism would seem to provide a suitable basis for objectivity.

The agreement of the parties in the original position is not a so-called "radical" choice: that is, a choice not based on reasons, a choice that simply fixes, by sheer fiat, as it were, the scheme of reasons that we, as citizens, are to recognize, at least until another such choice is made. The notion of radical choice, commonly associated with Nietzsche and the existentialists, finds no place in justice as fairness. The parties in the original position are moved by their preference for primary goods, which preference in turn is rooted in their highest-order interests in developing and exercising their moral powers. More-over, the agreement of the parties takes place subject to constraints that express reasonable conditions.

In the model-conception of a well-ordered society, citizens affirm their public conception of justice because it matches their considered convictions and coheres with the kind of persons they, on due reflection, want to be. Again, this affirmation is not radical choice. The ideals of the person and of social cooperation embedded in the two model-conceptions mediated by the original position are not ideals that, at some moment in life, citizens are said simply to choose. One is to imagine that, for the most part, they find on examination that they hold these ideals, that they have taken them in part from the culture of their society.

The preceding paragraph ties in with what I said at the beginning of the first lecture, except that there I was talking about us and not about a well-ordered society. Recall that a Kantian view, in addressing the public culture of a democratic society, hopes to bring to awareness a conception of the person and of social cooperation conjectured to be implicit in that culture, or at least congenial to its deepest tendencies when properly expressed and presented. Our society is not well-ordered: the public conception of justice and its understanding of freedom and equality are in dispute. Therefore, for us—you and me—a basis of public justification is still to be achieved. In considering the conception of justice as fairness we have to ask whether the ideals embedded in its model-conceptions are sufficiently congenial to our considered convictions to be affirmed as a practicable basis of public justification. Such an affirmation would not be radical choice (if choice at all); nor should it be confused with the adoption of principles of justice by the parties in the original position. To the contrary, it would be rooted in the fact that this Kantian doctrine as a whole, more fully than other views available to us, organized our considered convictions.

Given the various contrasts between Kantian constructivism and rational intuitionism, it seems better to say that in constructivism first principles are reasonable (or unreasonable) than that they are true (or false)—better still, that they are most reasonable for those who conceive of their person as it is represented in the procedure of construction. And here 'reasonable' is used instead of 'true' not because of some alternative theory of truth, but simply in order to keep to terms that indicate the constructivist standpoint as opposed to rational intuitionism. This usage, however, does not imply that there are no natural uses for the notion of truth in moral reasoning. To the contrary, for example, particular judgments and secondary norms may be considered true when they follow from, or are sound applications of, reasonable first principles. These first principles may be said to be true in the sense that they would be agreed to if the parties in the original position were provided with all the relevant true general beliefs.

Nor does justice as fairness exclude the possibility of there being a fact of the matter as to whether there is a single most reasonable conception. For it seems quite likely that there are only a few viable conceptions of the person both sufficiently general to be part of a moral doctrine and congruent with the ways in which people are to regard themselves in a democratic society. And only one of these conceptions may have a representation in a procedure of construction that issues in acceptable and workable principles, given the relevant general beliefs.[17] Of course, this is conjecture, intended only to indicate that constructivism is compatible with there being, in fact, only one most reasonable conception of justice, and therefore that constructivism is compatible with objectivism in this sense. However, constructivism does not presuppose that this is the case, and it may turn out that, for us, there exists no reasonable and workable conception of justice at all. This would mean that the practical task of political philosophy is doomed to failure.

VI

My account of Kantian constructivism in moral theory (as illustrated by justice as fairness) is now concluded. I should stress, however, that for all I have said it is still open to the rational intuitionist to reply that I have not shown that rational intuitionism is false or that it is not a possible basis for the necessary agreement in our judgments of justice. It has been my intention to describe constructivism by contrast and not to defend it, much less to argue that rational intuitionism is mistaken. In any case, Kantian constructivism, as I would state it, aims to establish only that the rational intuitionist notion of objectivity is unnecessary for objectivity. Of course, it is always possible to say, if we ever do reach general and wide reflective equilibrium, that now at last we intuit the moral truths fixed by a given moral order; but the constructivist will say instead that our conception of justice, by all the criteria we can think of to apply, is now the most reasonable for us.

We have arrived at the idea that objectivity is not given by "the point of view of the universe," to use Sidgwick's phrase. Objectivity is to be understood by reference to a suitably constructed social point of view, an example of which is the framework provided by the procedure of the original position. This point of view is social in several respects. It is the publicly shared point of view of citizens in a well-ordered society, and the principles that issue from it are accepted by them as authoritative with regard to the claims of individuals and associations. Moreover, these principles regulate the basic structure of society within which the activities of individuals and associations take place. Finally, by representing the person as a free and equal citizen of a well-ordered society, the constructivist procedure yields principles that further everyone's highest-order interests and define the fair terms of social cooperation among persons so understood. When citizens invoke these principles they speak as members of a political community and appeal to its shared point of view either in their own behalf or in that of others. Thus, the essential agreement in judgments of justice arises not from the recognition of a prior and independent moral order, but from everyone's affirmation of the same authoritative social perspective.

The central place of the conception of the person in these lectures prompts me to conclude with a note of warning, addressed as much to me as to anyone

---

17 I am indebted to Samuel Scheffler for valuable discussion on this point.

else: ever since the notion of the person assumed a central place in moral philosophy in the latter part of the eighteenth century, as seen in Rousseau and Kant and the philosophy of idealism, its use has suffered from excessive vagueness and ambiguity. And so it is essential to devise an approach that disciplines our thought and suitably limits these defects. I view the three model-conceptions that underlie justice as fairness as having this purpose.

To elucidate: suppose we define the concept of a person as that of a human being capable of taking full part in social cooperation, honoring its ties and relationships over a complete life. There are plainly many specifications of this capacity, depending, for example, on how social cooperation or a complete life is understood; and each such specification yields another conception of the person falling under the concept. Moreover, such conceptions must be distinguished from specifications of the concept of the self as knower, used in epistemology and metaphysics, or the concept of the self as the continuant carrier of psychological states: the self as substance, or soul. These are prima facie distinct notions, and questions of identity, say, may well be different for each; for these notions arise in connection with different problems. This much is perhaps obvious. The consequence is that there are numerous conceptions of the person as the basic unit of agency and responsibility in social life, and of its requisite intellectual, moral, and active powers. The specification of these conceptions by philosophical analysis alone, apart from any background theoretical structure or general requirements, is likely to prove fruitless. In isolation these notions play no role that fixes or limits their use, and so their features remain vague and indeterminate.

One purpose of a model-conception like that of the original position is that, by setting up a definite framework within which a binding agreement on principles must be made, it serves to fix ideas. We are faced with a specific problem that must be solved, and we are forced to describe the parties and their mutual relations in the process of construction so that appropriate principles of justice result. The context of the problem guides us in removing vagueness and ambiguity in the conception of the person, and tells us how precise we need to be. There is no such thing as absolute clarity or exactness; we have to be only clear or exact enough for the task at hand. Thus the structure defined by the original position may enable us to crystallize our otherwise amorphous notion of the person and to identify with sufficient sharpness the appropriate characterization of free and equal moral personality.

The constructivist view also enables us to exploit the flexibility and power of the idea of rational choice subject to appropriate constraints. The rational deliberations of the parties in the original position serve as a way to select among traditional or other promising conceptions of justice. So understood, the original position is not an axiomatic (or deductive) basis from which principles are derived but a procedure for singling out principles most fitting to the conception of the person most likely to be held, at least implicitly, in a modern democratic society. To exaggerate, we compute via the deliberations of the parties and in this way hope to achieve sufficient rigor and clarity in moral theory. Indeed, it is hard to see how there could be any more direct connection between the conception of free and equal moral persons and first principles of justice than this construction allows. For here persons so conceived and moved by their highest-order interests are themselves, in their rationally autonomous deliberations, the agents who select the principles that are to govern the basic structure of their social life. What connection could be more intimate than this?

Finally, if we ask, what is clarity and exactness enough? the answer is: enough to find an understanding of freedom and equality that achieves workable public agreement on the weight of their respective claims. With this we return to the current impasse in the understanding of freedom and equality which troubles our democratic tradition and from which we started. Finding a way out of this impasse defines the immediate practical task of political philosophy. Having come full circle, I bring these lectures to a close.

22

Wide Reflective Equilibrium and Theory Acceptance in Ethics*

NORMAN DANIELS

Norman Daniels (b. 1942) is Professor of Philosophy at Tufts University. His research interests include ethical theory and bioethics. He is the author of many articles and books including Just Health Care *and* Am I My Parents' Keeper? *This selection is the first half of an article that appeared in* The Journal of Philosophy *(May 1979).*

Daniels's topic is the justification of moral principles. According to one influential view, advanced by John Rawls in A Theory of Justice *(reading 34), justifying a principle involves adjusting it in light of one's other beliefs while simultaneously adjusting them in light of it. But which other beliefs are relevant? On one version of the view, we need test moral principles only against our intuitions about the cases to which they apply. However, as Daniels notes, those intuitions "may only reflect class or cultural background, self-interest, or historical accident." For this and other reasons, we must also test principles against a variety of background theories, some of which are themselves moral. Applied to Rawls's own theory of justice, this means testing the design of the original position against "a theory of the person, a theory of procedural justice, general social theory, and a theory of the role of morality in society." It also means testing the principles that emerge against the body of social theory that determines whether their realization is "feasible." When one's principles have survived this exacting test, one has achieved what Daniels, following Rawls, calls wide, as opposed to narrow, reflective equilibrium.*

There is a widely held view that a moral theory consists of a set of moral judgments plus a set of principles that account for or generate them.

* I am indebted to Richard Boyd, Arthur Caplan, Christopher Cherniak, C. A. J. Coady, Josh Cohen, Daniel Dennett, Jane English, Paul Horwich, Allan Garfinkel, William Lycan, Miles Morgan, John Rawls, Amelie Rorty, George Smith, and M. B. E. Smith for helpful comments on ideas contained in this paper. The research was supported by an NEH Fellowship for 1977–1978.

This two-tiered view of moral theories has helped make the problem of theory acceptance or justification[1] in ethics intractable, unless, that is, one is willing to grant privileged epistemological status to the moral judgments (calling them "intuitions") or to the moral principles (calling them "self-evident" or otherwise a priori). Neither alternative is attractive. Nor, given this view of moral theory, do we get very far with a simple coherence view of justification. To be sure, appeal to elementary coherence (here, consistency) constraints between principles and judgments sometimes allows us to clarify our moral views or to make progress in moral argument. But there must be more to moral justification of both judgments and principles than such simple coherence considerations, especially in the face of the many plausible bases for rejecting moral judgments; e.g., the judgments may only reflect class or cultural background, self-interest, or historical accident.

I shall argue that a version of what John Rawls has called the *method of wide reflective equilibrium*[2] reveals a greater complexity in the structure of moral theories than the traditional view. Consequently, it may render theory acceptance in ethics a more tractable problem. If it does, it may permit us to recast and resolve some traditional worries about objectivity in ethics. To make this suggestion at all plausible, I shall have to defend reflective equilibrium against various charges that it is really a disguised form of moral intuitionism and therefore "subjectivist." First, however, I must explain what wide equilibrium is and show why seeking it may increase our ability to choose among competing moral conceptions.

1. WIDE REFLECTIVE EQUILIBRIUM

The method of wide reflective equilibrium is an attempt to produce coherence in an ordered triple of sets of beliefs held by a particular person, namely, (a) a set of considered moral judgments, (b) a set of moral principles, and (c) a set of relevant background theories. We begin by collecting the person's initial moral judgments and filter them to include only those of which he is relatively

---

1 Since the notion of justification is broadly used in philosophy, it is worth forestalling a confusion right at the outset. The problem I address in this paper is strictly analogous to the general and abstract problem of theory acceptance or justification posed in the philosophy of science with regard to nonmoral theories. I am not directly concerned with explaining when a particular individual is justified in, or can be held accountable for, holding a particular moral belief or performing a particular action. So, too, the philosopher of science, interested in how theory acceptance depends on the relation of one theory to another, is not directly concerned to determine whether or not a given individual is justified in believing some feature of one of the theories. Just how relevant my account of theory acceptance is to the question, Is so-and-so justified in believing P or in doing A on evidence E in conditions C (vary P,A,E)? would require a detailed examination of particular cases. I am indebted to Miles Morgan and John Rawls for discussion of this point.

2 The distinction between narrow and wide reflective equilibria is implicit in *A Theory of Justice* (Cambridge, MA: Harvard, 1971), p. 49, and is explicit in "The Independence of Moral Theory," *Proceedings and Addresses of the American Philosophical Association*, XLVII (1974–1975): 5–22, p. 8.

confident and which have been made under conditions conducive to avoiding errors of judgment. For example, the person is calm and has adequate information about cases being judged.[3] We then propose alternative sets of moral principles that have varying degrees of "fit" with the moral judgments. We do *not* simply settle for the best fit of principles with judgments, however, which would give us only a narrow equilibrium.[4] Instead, we advance philosophical arguments intended to bring out the relative strengths and weaknesses of the alternative sets of principles (or competing moral conceptions). These arguments can be construed as inferences from some set of relevant background theories (I use the term loosely). Assume that some particular set of arguments wins and that the moral agent is persuaded that some set of principles is more acceptable than the others (and, perhaps, than the conception that might have emerged in narrow equilibrium). We can imagine the agent working back and forth, making adjustments to his considered judgments, his moral principles, and his background theories. In this way he arrives at an equilibrium point that consists of the ordered triple (a), (b), (c).[5]

We need to find more structure here. The background theories in (c) should show that the moral principles in (b) are more acceptable than alternative principles on grounds to some degree independent of (b)'s match with relevant considered moral judgments in (a). If they are not in this way independently supported, then there seems to be no gain over the support the principles would have had in a corresponding narrow equilibrium, where there never was any appeal to (c). Another way to raise this point is to ask how we can be sure that the moral principles that systematize the considered moral judgments are not just "accidental generalizations" of the "moral facts," analogous to accidental generalizations which we want to distinguish from real scientific laws. In science, we have evidence that we are not dealing with accidental

---

3 Though Rawls's earlier formulations of the notion [in his "Outline for a Decision Procedure for Ethics," *Philosophical Review*, LX, 2 (April 1951): 177–197, esp. pp. 182–183] restricts considered judgments to moral judgments about particular cases, his later formulations drop the restriction, so they can be of any level of generality. Cf. Rawls, "Independence of Moral Theory," p. 8. These "ideal" conditions may have drawbacks, as Allan Garfinkel has pointed out to me. Sometimes anger or (moral) indignation may lead to morally better actions and judgments than "calm"; also, the formulation fails to correct for divergence between stated beliefs and beliefs revealed in action.

4 Narrow reflective equilibrium might be construed as the moral analogue of solving the projection problem for syntactic competence: the principles are the moral analogue of a grammar. This analogy is not extendable to wide equilibrium, as I show in "Some Methods of Ethics and Linguistics," *Philosophical Studies*, 37, 1 (January 1980), pp. 21–23. Narrow equilibrium leaves us with the traditional two-tiered view of moral theories and is particularly ill suited to provide a basis for a justificational argument. It does not offer a special epistemological claim about the considered moral judgments (other than the rather weak claim that they are filtered to avoid some obvious sources of error), nor are there constraints on the acceptability of moral principles beyond their good "fit" with the initial considered judgments. If we have reason to suspect that the initial judgments are the product of bias, historical accident, or ideology, then these elementary coherence considerations alone give us little basis for comfort, since they provide inadequate pressure to correct for them. Cf. Rawls, *A Theory of Justice*, p. 49.

5 The fact that I describe wide equilibrium as being built up out of judgments, principles, and relevant background theories does not mean that this represents an order of epistemic priority or a natural sequence in the genesis of theories. Arthur Caplan reminded me of this point.

generalizations if we can derive the purported laws from a body of interconnected theories, provided these theories reach, in a diverse and interesting way, beyond the "facts" that the principle generalizes.

This analogy suggests one way to achieve independent support for the principles in (b) and to rule out their being mere accidental generalizations of the considered judgments. We should require that the background theories in (c) be more than reformulations of the same set of considered moral judgments involved when the principles are matched to moral judgments. The background theories should have a scope reaching beyond the range of the considered moral judgments used to "test" the moral principles. Some interesting, nontrivial portions of the set of considered moral judgments that constrains the background theories and of the set that constrains the moral principles should be disjoint.

Suppose that some set of considered *moral* judgments (a') plays a role in constraining the background theories in (c). It is important to note that the acceptability of (c) may thus in part depend on some *moral* judgments, which means we are not in general assuming that (c) constitutes a reduction of the moral [in (b) and (a)] to the nonmoral. Then, our *independence constraint* amounts to the requirement that (a') and (a) be to some significant degree disjoint.[6] The background theories might, for example, not incorporate the same type of moral notions as are employed by the principles and those considered judgments relevant to "testing" the principles.

It will help to have an example of a wide equilibrium clearly in mind. Consider Rawls's theory of justice.[7] We are led by philosophical argument, Rawls believes, to accept the contract and its various constraints as a reasonable device for selecting between competing conceptions of justice (or right). These arguments, however, can be viewed as inferences from a number of relevant background theories, in particular, from a theory of the person, a theory of procedural justice, general social theory, and a theory of the role of morality in society (including the ideal of a well-ordered society). These *level* III theories, as I shall call them, are what persuade us to adopt the contract apparatus, with all its constraints (call it the *level* II apparatus). Principles chosen at level II are subject to two constraints: (i) they must match our considered moral judgments in (partial) reflective equilibrium; and (ii) they must yield a feasible, stable, well-ordered society. I will call *level* I the *partial* reflective equilibrium that holds between the moral principles and the relevant set of considered moral judgments. *Level* IV contains the body of social theory relevant to testing level I principles (and level III theories) for "feasibility."

---

6 My formulation is not adequate as it stands, since there will even be trivial truth-functional counterexamples to it unless some specification of 'interesting' and 'nontrivial' is given, to say nothing of providing a measure for the "scope" of a theory. This is a standing problem in philosophy of science [cf. Michael Friedman's attempt to handle the related question of unifying theories in "Explanation and Scientific Understanding," *The Journal of Philosophy*, LXXI, 1 (Jan. 17, 1974): 5–19, esp. 15 ff.]. I will assume that this difficulty can be overcome, though doing so might require dropping the loose talk about theories. I am indebted to George Smith for helpful discussion of this point.

7 I draw here on my "Reflective Equilibrium and Archimedean Points," *Canadian Journal of Philosophy*, X, 1 (March 1980), pp. 83–103.

The independence constraint previously defined for wide equilibrium in general applies in this way: the considered moral judgments [call them (a′)] which may act to constrain level III theory acceptability must to a significant extent be disjoint from the considered moral judgments [call them (a)] which act to constrain level I partial equilibrium. I argue elsewhere that Rawls's construction appears to satisfy this independence constraint, since his central level III theories of the person and of the role of morality in society are probably not just recharacterizations or systematizations of level I moral judgments.[8] If I am right, then (supposing soundness of Rawls's arguments!), the detour of deriving the principles from the contract adds justificatory force to them, justification not found simply in the level I matching of principles and judgments. Notice that this advantage is exactly what would be lost if the contract and its defining conditions were "rigged" just to yield the best level I equilibrium.[9] The other side of this coin is that the level II apparatus will not be acceptable if competing theories of the person or of the role of morality in society are preferable to the theories Rawls advances. Rawls's Archimedean point is fixed only against the acceptability of particular level III theories.

This argument suggests that we abstract from the details of the Rawlsian example to find quite general features of the structure of moral theories in wide equilibrium. Alternatives to justice as fairness are likely to contain some level II device for principle selection other than the contract (say a souped-up impartial spectator). Such variation would reflect variation in the level III theories, especially the presence of alternative theories of the person or of the role of morality. Finally, developed alternatives to justice as fairness would still be likely to contain some version of the level I and level IV constraints, though the details of how these constraints function will reflect the content of component theories at the different levels.

By revealing this structural complexity, the search for wide equilibrium can benefit moral inquiry in several ways. First, philosophers have often suggested that many apparently "moral" disagreements rest on other, nonmoral disagreements. Usually these are lumped together as the "facts" of the situation. Wide equilibrium may reveal a more systematic, if complex, structure to these sources of disagreement, and, just as important, to sources of agreement as well.

[8] In particular, Rawls's level III theories rest on no considered moral judgments about rights and entitlements: all such considered judgments are segregated into level I, so that level III theories provide a foundation for our notions of rights and entitlements without themselves appealing to such notions (though they appeal to other moral notions, such as fairness and various claims about persons). Rawls seems attracted to this view of his project [cf. his "Reply to Alexander and Musgrave," *Quarterly Journal of Economics,* LXXXCII, 4 (November 1974), p. 634]. In contrast, Ronald Dworkin argues that a background right to equal respect is needed at what I call "level III." [Cf. his "The Original Position," *University of Chicago Law Review,* XL, 3 (Spring 1973): 500–533; reprinted in my anthology, *Reading Rawls* (New York: Basic Books, 1975), pp. 16–53, esp. pp. 45, 50 ff.]. For an argument that Dworkin is wrong to posit such a level III right, see my "Reflective Equilibrium and Archimedean Points."

[9] Rawls leaves himself open to the accusation of "rigging" when he says, e.g., "We want to define the original position so that we get the desired solution" (*A Theory of Justice,* p. 141). Critics have had a field day using this and similar remarks to show that the contract can have no justificational role.

Second, aside from worries about universalizability and generalizability, philosophers have not helped us to understand what factors *actually do* constrain the considerations people cite as reasons, or treat as "relevant" and "important," in moral reasoning and argument. A likely suggestion is that these features of moral reasoning depend on the *content* of underlying level III theories and level II principle selectors, or on properties of the level I and IV constraints. An adequate moral psychology, in other words, would have to incorporate features of what I am calling "wide equilibrium." Understanding these features of moral argument more clearly might lead to a better grasp of what constitutes evidence for and against moral judgments and principles. This result should not be surprising: as in science, judgments about the plausibility and acceptability of various claims are the complex result of the whole system of interconnected theories already found acceptable. My guess—I cannot undertake to confirm it here—is that the type of coherence constraint that operates in the moral and nonmoral cases functions to produce many similarities: we should find methodological conservatism in both; we will find that "simplicity" judgments in both really depend on determining how little we have to change in the interconnected background theories already accepted (not on more formal measures of simplicity); and we will find in both that apparently "intuitive" judgments about how "interesting," "important," and "relevant" puzzles or facts are, are really guided by underlying theory.[10]

A third possible benefit of wide equilibrium is that level III disagreements about theories may be more tractable than disagreements about moral judgments and principles. Consequently, if the moral disagreements can be traced to disagreements about theory, greater moral agreement may result.

Some examples may perhaps make this claim more plausible. A traditional form of criticism against utilitarianism consists in deriving unacceptable moral judgments about punishment, desert, or distributive justice from a general utilitarian principle. Some utilitarians then may bite the bullet and reject reliance on these "pretheoretical" intuitions. Rawls has suggested an explanation for the class of examples involving distributive justice. He suggests that the utilitarian has imported into social contexts, where we distribute goods between persons, a principle acceptable only for distributing goods between life-stages of one person. Derek Parfit urges a different explanation: the utilitarian, perhaps supported by evidence from the philosophy of mind, uses a weaker criterion of personal identity than that presupposed by, say, Rawls's account of life plans. Accordingly, he treats interpersonal boundaries as metaphysically less deep and morally less important. The problem between the utilitarian and the contractarian thus becomes the (possibly) more manageable problem of determining the acceptability of competing theories of the person, and only

---

10 We know relatively little about these features of theory acceptance in either domain, a fact traceable to the same empiricist and positivist legacy: too narrow an account of the relation between theory and "data," be it laws-plus-observation or principles-plus-judgments.

one of many constraints on that task is the connection of the theory of the person to the resulting moral principles.[11]

A second example derives from a suggestion of Bernard Williams.[12] He argues that there may be a large discrepancy between the dictates of utilitarian theory in a particular case and what a person will be inclined to do given that he has been raised to have virtues (e.g., beneficence) that in general optimize his chances of doing utilitarian things. We may generalize Williams's point: suppose any moral conception can be paired with an *optimal* set of virtues, those which make their bearer most likely to do what is right according to the given conception. Moral conceptions may differ significantly in the degree to which acts produced by their optimal virtues tend to differ from acts they deem right. Level III and IV theories of moral psychology and development would be needed to determine the facts here. Since we want to reduce such discrepancies (at least according to some level III and IV theories), we may have an important scale against which to compare moral conceptions.

•   •   •

---

[11] Compare Derek Parfit, "Later Selves and Moral Principles," in Alan Montefiore, ed., *Philosophy and Personal Relations* (London: Routledge & Kegan Paul, 1973), pp. 149–160. See Rawls's reply in "Independence of Moral Theory," pp. 17 ff. The degree to which a theory of the person constrains moral-theory acceptance, and conversely, the degree to which moral theory constrains theories of the person are discussed in my "Moral Theory and the Plasticity of Persons," *The Monist*, LXII, 3 (July 1979), pp. 265–287. The Marxist worry that there is no non-class-relative notion of the person substantial enough to found a moral theory on thus appears as an argument about level III theory acceptability.

[12] Utilitarianism and Moral Self-Indulgence" in H. D. Lewis, *Contemporary British Philosophy*, IVth Series (New York: Humanities, 1976), pp. 306–321.

IV

NORMATIVE ETHICS: CONSEQUENTIALISM

We all praise many different actions as admirable and upright and condemn many others as despicable. Moreover, in planning our own activities, we reject many possible acts because they are wrong, and decide on others because they are morally required. On what underlying principles are these judgments and decisions based? And, whatever our actual principles, why accept these and not others? In posing such questions, we are asking which moral norms should govern our lives. We are thus seeking a theory of *normative ethics*.

In general, substantive normative principles can take two forms; for they may tell us to perform acts either because they produce good consequences or for some other reason. A principle of the first type is called *consequentialist*. Because there are different views about what is good—these are explored in the readings in Part VII—there are also different consequentialist principles. But by far the most popular is the *principle of utility*, which tells us to do what produces the greatest amount of pleasure, happiness, or satisfaction of desire. Versions of this principle are set forth by Jeremy Bentham in reading 43 and by John Stuart Mill in reading 23. Those who accept it are called *utilitarians*.

Utilitarianism offers many advantages. Because it considers each person's happiness equally, it displays the impartiality that many take to characterize morality. Also, because every act produces some determinate amount of happiness, utilitarianism allows us to compare the rightness of any two acts. With enough information, utilitarians can always tell us which acts to perform. Of course, in the actual world, we rarely can foresee all the effects of any possible act. Yet just because of this, the utilitarian can plausibly explain our commitment to such apparently nonutilitarian principles as "Do not harm others," "Treat people fairly," and "Do not kill." As Mill argues, these commonsense principles may serve as guides to the maximization of happiness when we must act under conditions of incomplete information. Given the circumstances of ordinary life, we may produce the best results by not considering happiness every time we act.

This ability to account for commonsense moral beliefs is a point in favor of utilitarianism. But in another way, these same beliefs may work *against* utilitarianism. For if the only reason not to steal or kill is that such acts generally fail to maximize happiness, then we will lack a reason not to steal or kill when such acts clearly *would* maximize happiness. For example, if we can best promote utility by killing a rich miser and redistributing his money, the utilitarian principle must endorse this act. As Thomas Nagel argues in reading 55 while discussing the rules of war, utilitarianism seems incapable of limiting the means we may use to promote worthwhile ends. Also, because it considers only consequences, utilitarianism may fail to capture the moral importance of the distinction between what a person does and what he merely allows. Thus, as Bernard Williams argues in reading 27, a consistent utilitarian must hold someone just as responsible for harms that he fails to prevent—including harms inflicted by others—as for harms that he inflicts himself. But, Williams points out, in order to prevent persons from harming others, we sometimes have to do things that violate our own integrity. Moreover, as Williams adds in reading 39, someone who consistently tries to maximize utility may have little room to pursue the projects that give his own life meaning.

In reading 26, John Rawls proposes a general diagnosis of what is wrong with utilitarianism. According to Rawls, the basic problem is a false analogy between society and the individual. It is rational for individuals to try to maximize the sum of their satisfactions because their sacrifices are offset by their own later gains. For example, a person may rationally endure pain at the dentist's office to avoid worse pain later. But, Rawls argues, it is not similarly rational for society to try to maximize the sum of its members' satisfactions; for those whose interests are sacrificed are not compensated by the greater gains of others. There is no larger entity within whose life these gains and losses can be balanced. Because it fails to recognize this, utilitarianism is said not to take seriously the distinctness of persons.

Utilitarians, naturally, disagree, and they have displayed considerable ingenuity in responding to these challenges. Thus, in reading 24, R. M. Hare defends consequentialism in general, and utilitarianism in particular, by drawing out their implications concerning slavery. Just as critics charge that utilitarians must condone murder when it brings better consequences than its alternatives, they charge that utilitarians must sometimes condone slavery. However, Hare replies that a utility-maximizing slave system is not a realistic possibility. When we try to fill in the details, we find that the laws of psychology and other features of the human situation would almost always prevent a slave system from maximizing utility. Hence, a moral education aimed at promoting utility in the world as it is must include psychological conditioning that leads people to find all slavery repugnant. According to Hare, it is this utilitarian conditioning, and not an intuitive awareness that slavery is inherently evil, that accounts for the near universal abhorrence of the practice. And similar conditioning accounts for all the other intuitions that specific types of acts or practices are inherently wrong.

Other utilitarians respond to the challenges differently. They note that the principle of utility can be brought to bear on individual acts in either of two ways. On one account, an act is right if and only if performing *it* will bring about at least as much utility as the performance of any alternative act. On another account, the question is whether the act conforms to a set of rules which *if generally accepted* would bring about at least as much utility as any alternative set. Of the two forms of utilitarianism, the first is known as *act-utilitarianism*, while the second is known as *rule-utilitarianism*. Because rule-utilitarianism asserts that we should *always* follow the rules whose general adoption would maximize utility, it implies that we should follow these rules even when we could promote more utility by violating them. Thus, because a utility-maximizing set of rules would presumably forbid acts like killing a miser to redistribute his money, a rule-utilitarian can explain why murder and theft remain wrong even when they do maximize utility. In reading 25, Richard Brandt presents a careful and detailed statement of the rule-utilitarian approach.

Although Hare and Brandt advance quite different accounts, each in his own way seeks to reconcile utilitarianism with commonsense morality. But other utilitarians, such as Shelly Kagan (reading 28), opt for confrontation rather than accommodation. According to Kagan, the familiar arguments for imposing constraints on the maximization of utility all fail. For example, when philosophers like Bernard Williams characterize the killing of one person to prevent the killing of several others as a violation of the agent's moral integrity (reading 27), Kagan contends that they illegitimately suppose that such killing is not morally justified. If it were justified, then it would not compromise anyone's integrity. However, the point of defending a constraint against such killing is precisely to *show* that the killing is not justified, so Kagan concludes that this argument begs the question.

23

Utilitarianism

JOHN STUART MILL

John Stuart Mill (1806–1873) was among the most important British thinkers of the nineteenth century. A philosopher in the Empiricist tradition, he published works on logic, scientific method, and epistemology, as well as on ethics and social and political philosophy. His books include A System of Logic, On Liberty, *and* The Subjection of Women. *This section is from his* Utilitarianism, *chapters 2 and 4.*

Utilitarianism, the view defended here, asserts that the ultimate principle of morality is "Strive to produce as much overall happiness as possible." Mill was taught this approach by his father, James Mill, who in turn learned it from the philosopher and social reformer Jeremy Bentham. However, whereas Bentham makes no distinctions among types of pleasures (see reading 43), Mill believes that some forms of happiness are more worthwhile than others. He argues that the pleasures of a Socrates are more valuable than those we share with animals because anyone who was "competently acquainted" with both would choose the former.

In whatever form we favor, utilitarianism offers many advantages. As Mill notes, it provides a ready-made answer to the question of what to do when obligations conflict. For example, suppose you have promised to meet a friend for lunch. On the way there, you encounter someone drowning in a lake. If no single moral principle dominates, you will have no principled way of deciding between your conflicting obligations to provide aid and to keep your promise. However, if you are a utilitarian, you will perform whichever act brings more happiness—in this case, rescuing the drowning person. Moreover, besides adjudicating moral conflicts, utilitarianism explains why we accept the conflicting principles, and why we ought to accept them. In Mill's view, we generally ought to help others and keep our promises, because doing these things brings great social benefits. Our familiar principles are like signposts that reflect collective past experience about what maximizes happiness.

One further aspect of Mill's account deserves brief mention. Toward the end of this selection, Mill offers a famous argument for the principle of utility. He argues that whatever is desired is desirable, and that in the last analysis people desire happiness and nothing else. Therefore, happiness is the only truly desirable thing, and it should be maximized. This argument offers a number of opportunities for careful reflection and analysis. You may find it helpful to refer to Feinberg's discussion of psychological egoism (reading 1) as you weigh Mill's argument.

WHAT UTILITARIANISM IS

• • •

The creed which accepts as the foundation of morals "utility" or the "greatest happiness principle" holds that actions are right in proportion as they tend to promote happiness; wrong as they tend to produce the reverse of happiness. By happiness is intended pleasure and the absence of pain; by unhappiness, pain and the privation of pleasure. To give a clear view of the moral standard set up by the theory, much more requires to be said; in particular, what things it includes in the ideas of pain and pleasure, and to what extent this is left an open question. But these supplementary explanations do not affect the theory of life on which this theory of morality is grounded— namely, that pleasure and freedom from pain are the only things desirable as ends; and that all desirable things (which are as numerous in the utilitarian as in any other scheme) are desirable either for pleasure inherent in themselves or as means to the promotion of pleasure and the prevention of pain.

Now such a theory of life excites in many minds, and among them in some of the most estimable in feeling and purpose, inveterate dislike. To suppose that life has (as they express it) no higher end than pleasure—no better and nobler object of desire and pursuit—they designate as utterly mean and groveling, as a doctrine worthy only of swine, to whom the followers of Epicurus were, at a very early period, contemptuously likened; and modern holders of the doctrine are occasionally made the subject of equally polite comparisons by its German, French, and English assailants.

When thus attacked, the Epicureans have always answered that it is not they, but their accusers, who represent human nature in a degrading light, since the accusation supposes human beings to be capable of no pleasures except those of which swine are capable. If this supposition were true, the charge could not be gainsaid, but would then be no longer an imputation; for if the sources of pleasure were precisely the same to human beings and to swine, the rule of life which is good enough for the one would be good enough for the other. The comparison of the Epicurean life to that of beasts is felt as degrading, precisely because a beast's pleasures do not satisfy a human being's conceptions of happiness. Human beings have faculties more elevated than the animal appetites and, when once made conscious of them, do not regard anything as happiness which does not include their gratification. I do not indeed, consider the Epicureans to have been by any means faultless in drawing out their scheme of consequences from the utilitarian principle. To do this in any sufficient manner, many Stoic, as well as Christian, elements require to be included. But there is no known Epicurean theory of life which does not assign to the pleasures of the intellect, of the feelings and imagination, and of the moral sentiments a much higher value as pleasures than to those of mere sensation. It must be admitted, however, that utilitarian writers in general have placed the superiority of mental over bodily pleasures chiefly in the greater permanency, safety, uncostliness, etc., of the former—that is, in their circumstantial advantages rather than in their intrinsic nature. And on all these points utilitarians have fully proved their case; but they might have taken the other and, as it may be called, higher ground with entire consistency. It is quite compatible with the principle of utility to recognize the fact that some kinds of pleasure are more desirable and more valuable than others. It would be absurd that, while in estimating all other things quality is considered as well as quantity, the estimation of pleasure should be supposed to depend on quantity alone.

If I am asked what I mean by difference of quality in pleasures, or what makes one pleasure more valuable than another, merely as a pleasure, except its being greater in amount, there is but one possible answer. Of two pleasures, if there be one to which all or almost all who have experience of both give a decided preference, irrespective of any feeling of moral obligation to prefer it, that is the most desirable pleasure. If one of the two is, by those who are competently acquainted with both, placed so far above the other that they prefer it, even though knowing it to be attended with a greater amount of discontent, and would not resign it for any quantity of the other pleasure which their nature is capable of, we are justified in ascribing to the preferred enjoyment a superiority in quality so far outweighing quantity as to render it, in comparison, of small account.

Now it is an unquestionable fact that those who are equally acquainted with and equally capable of appreciating and enjoying both do give a most marked preference to the manner of existence which employs their higher faculties. Few human creatures would consent to be changed into any of the lower animals for a promise of the fullest allowance of a beast's pleasures; no intelligent human being would consent to be a fool, no instructed person would be an ignoramus, no person of feeling and conscience would be selfish and base, even though they should be persuaded that the fool, the dunce, or the rascal is better satisfied with his lot than they are with theirs. They would not resign what they possess more than he for the most complete satisfaction of all the desires which they have in common with him. If they ever fancy they would, it is only in cases of unhappiness so extreme that to escape from it they would exchange their lot for almost any other, however undesirable in their own eyes. A being of higher faculties requires more to make him happy, is capable probably of more acute suffering, and certainly accessible to it at more points, than one of an inferior type; but in spite of these liabilities, he can never really wish to sink into what he feels to be a lower grade of existence. We may give what explanation we please of this unwillingness; we may attribute it to pride, a name which is given indiscriminately to some of the most and to some of the least estimable feelings of which mankind are capable; we may refer it to the love of liberty and personal independence, an appeal to which was with the Stoics one of the most effective means for the inculcation of it; to the love of power or to the love of excitement, both of which do really enter into and contribute to it; but its most appropriate appellation is a sense of dignity, which all human beings possess in one form or other, and in some, though by no means in exact, proportion to their higher faculties, and which is so essential a part of the happiness of those in whom it is strong that nothing which conflicts with it could be otherwise than momentarily an object of desire to them. Whoever supposes that this preference takes place at a sacrifice of happiness—that the superior being, in anything like equal circumstances, is not happier than the inferior—confounds the two very different ideas of happiness and content. It is indisputable that the being whose capacities of enjoyment are low has the greatest chance of having them fully satisfied; and a highly endowed being will always feel that any happiness which he can look for, as the world is constituted, is imperfect. But he can learn to bear its imperfections, if they are at all bearable; and they will not make him envy the being who is indeed unconscious of the imperfections, but only because he feels not at all the good which those imperfections qualify. It is better to be a human being dissatisfied than a pig satisfied; better to be Socrates dissatisfied than a fool satisfied. And if the fool, or the pig, are of a different opinion, it is because they only know their own side of the question. The other party to the comparison knows both sides.

It may be objected that many who are capable of the higher pleasures occasionally, under the influence of temptation, postpone them to the lower. But this is quite compatible with a full appreciation of the intrinsic superiority of the higher. Men often, from infirmity of character, make their election for the nearer good, though they know it to be the less valuable; and this no less when the choice is between two bodily pleasures than when it is between bodily and mental. They pursue sensual indulgences to the injury of health, though perfectly aware that health is the greater good. It may be further objected that many who begin with youthful enthusiasm for everything noble, as they advance in years, sink into indolence and selfishness. But I do not believe that those who undergo this very common change voluntarily choose the lower description of pleasures in preference to the higher. I believe that, before they devote themselves exclusively to the one, they have already become incapable of the other. Capacity for the nobler feelings is in most natures a very tender plant, easily killed, not only by hostile influences, but by mere want of sustenance; and in the majority of young persons it speedily dies away if the occupations to which their position in life has devoted them, and the society into which it has thrown them, are not favorable to keeping that higher capacity in exercise. Men lose their high aspirations as they lose their intellectual tastes, because they have not time or opportunity for indulging them; and they addict themselves to inferior pleasures, not because they deliberately prefer them, but because they are either the only ones to which they have access or the only ones which they are any longer capable of enjoying. It may be questioned whether anyone who has remained equally susceptible to both classes of pleasures ever knowingly and calmly preferred the lower, though many, in all ages, have broken down in an ineffectual attempt to combine both.

From this verdict of the only competent judges, I apprehend there can be no appeal. On a question which is the best worth having of two pleasures, or which of two modes of existence is the most grateful to the feelings, apart from its moral attributes and from its consequences, the judgment of these who are qualified by knowledge of both, or, if they differ, that of the majority among them, must be admitted as final. And there needs be the less hesitation to accept this judgment respecting the quality of pleasures, since there is no other tribunal to be referred to even on the question of quantity. What means are there of determining which is the acutest of two pains, or the interest of two pleasurable sensations, except the general suffrage of those who are familiar with both? Neither pains nor pleasures are homogeneous, and pain is always heterogeneous with pleasure. What is there to decide whether a particular pleasure is worth purchasing at the cost of a particular pain, except the feelings and judgment of the experienced? When, therefore, those feelings and judgment declare the pleasures derived from the higher faculties to be preferable *in kind,* apart from the question of intensity, to those of which the animal nature, disjoined from the higher faculties, is susceptible, they are entitled on this subject to the same regard.

• • •

I must again repeat what the assailants of utilitarianism seldom have the justice to acknowledge, that the happiness which forms the utilitarian standard of what is right in conduct is not the agent's own happiness but that of all concerned. As between his own happiness and that of others, utilitarianism requires him to be as strictly impartial as a disinterested and benevolent spectator. In the golden rule of Jesus of Nazareth, we read the complete spirit of the ethics of utility. "To do as you would be done by," and "to love your neighbor as yourself," constitute the ideal perfection of utilitarian morality. As the means of making the nearest approach to this ideal, utility would enjoin, first, that laws and social arrangements should place the happiness or (as, speaking practically, it may be called) the interest of every individual as nearly as possible in harmony with the interest of the whole; and, secondly, that education and opinion, which have so vast a power over human character, should so use that power as to establish in the mind of every individual an indissoluble association between his own happiness and the good of the whole, especially between his own happiness and the practice of such modes of conduct, negative and positive, as regard for the universal happiness prescribes; so that not only he may be unable to conceive the possibility of happiness to himself, consistently with conduct opposed to the general good, but also that a direct impulse to promote the general good may be in every individual one of the habitual motives of action, and the sentiments connected therewith may fill a large and prominent place in every human being's sentient existence. If the impugners of the utilitarian morality represented it to their own minds in this its true character, I know not what recommendation possessed by any other morality they could possibly affirm to be wanting to it; what more beautiful or more exalted developments of human nature any other ethical system can be supposed to foster, or what springs of action, not accessible to the utilitarian, such systems rely on for giving effect to their mandates.

The objectors to utilitarianism cannot always be charged with representing it in a discreditable light. On the contrary, those among them who entertain anything like a just idea of its disinterested character sometimes find fault with its standard as being too high for humanity. They say it is exacting too much to require that people shall always act from the inducement of promoting the general interest of society. But this is to mistake the very meaning of a standard of morals and confound the rule of action with the motive of it. It is the business of ethics to tell us what are our duties, or by what test we may know them; but no system of ethics requires that the sole motive of all we do shall be a feeling of duty; on the contrary, ninety-nine hundredths of all our actions are done from other motives, and rightly so done if the rule of duty does not condemn them. It is the more unjust to utilitarianism that this particular misapprehension should be made a ground of objection to it, inasmuch as utilitarian moralists have gone beyond almost all others in affirming that the motive has nothing to do with the morality of the action, though much with the worth of the agent. He who saves a fellow creature from drowning does what is morally right, whether his motive be duty or the hope of being paid for his trouble; he who betrays the friend that trusts him is guilty of a crime, even if his object be to serve another friend to whom he is under greater obligation.[1] But to speak only of actions done from the motive or duty, and in direct obedience to principle: it is a misapprehension of the utilitarian mode of thought to conceive it as implying that people should fix their minds upon so wide a generality as the world, or society at large. The great majority of good actions are intended not for the benefit of the world, but for that of individuals, of which the good of the world is made up; and the thoughts of the most virtuous man need not on these occasions travel beyond the particular persons concerned, except so far as is necessary to assure himself that in

---

1 An opponent, whose intellectual and moral fairness it is a pleasure to acknowledge (the Rev. J. Llewellyn Davies), has objected to this passage, saying, "Surely the rightness or wrongness of saving a man from drowning does depend very much upon the motive with which it is done. Suppose that a tyrant, when his enemy jumped into the sea to escape from him, saved him from drowning simply in order that he might inflict upon him more exquisite tortures, would it tend to clearness to speak of that rescue as 'a morally right action'? Or suppose again, according to one of the stock illustrations of ethical inquiries, that a man betrayed a trust received from a friend, because the discharge of it would fatally injure that friend himself or someone belonging to him, would utilitarianism compel one to call the betrayal 'a crime' as much as if it had been done from the meanest motive?"

I submit that he who saves another from drowning in order to kill him by torture afterwards does not differ only in motive from him who does the same thing from duty or benevolence; the act itself is different. The rescue of the man is, in the case supposed, only the necessary first step of an act far more atrocious than leaving him to drown would have been. Had Mr. Davies said, "The rightness or wrongness of saving a man from drowning does depend very much"—not upon the motive, but—"upon the *intention*," no utilitarian would have differed from him. Mr. Davies, by an oversight too common not to be quite venial, has in this case confounded the very different ideas of Motive and Intention. There is no point which utilitarian thinkers (and Bentham pre-eminently) have taken more pains to illustrate than this. The morality of the action depends entirely upon the intention—that is, upon what the agent *wills to do*. But the motive, that is, the feeling which makes him will so to do, if it makes no difference in the act, makes none in the morality: though it makes a great difference in our moral estimation of the agent, especially if it indicates a good or a bad habitual *disposition*—a bent of character from which useful, or from which hurtful actions are likely to arise.

benefiting them he is not violating the rights, that is, the legitimate and author-
ized expectations, of anyone else. The multiplication of happiness is, according
to the utilitarian ethics, the object of virtue: the occasions on which any person
(except one in a thousand) has it in his power to do this on an extended scale—
in other words, to be a public benefactor—are but exceptional; and on these
occasions alone is he called on to consider public utility; in every other case,
private utility, the interest or happiness of some few persons, is all he has to
attend to. Those alone the influence of whose actions extends to society in
general need concern themselves habitually about so large an object. In the
case of abstinences indeed—of things which people forbear to do from moral
considerations, though the consequences in the particular case might be beneficial—it would be unworthy of an intelligent agent not to be consciously aware
that the action is of a class which, if practiced generally, would be generally
injurious, and that this is the ground of the obligation to abstain from it. The
amount of regard for the public interest implied in this recognition is no greater
than is demanded by every system of morals, for they all enjoin to abstain
from whatever is manifestly pernicious to society.

The same considerations dispose of another reproach against the doctrine
of utility, founded on a still grosser misconception of the purpose of a standard
of morality and of the very meaning of the words "right" and "wrong." It is
often affirmed that utilitarianism renders men cold and unsympathizing; that
it chills their moral feelings toward individuals; that it makes them regard only
the dry and hard consideration of the consequences of actions, not taking into
their moral estimate the qualities from which those actions emanate. If the
assertion means that they do not allow their judgment respecting the rightness
or wrongness of an action to be influenced by their opinion of the qualities of
the person who does it, this is a complaint not against utilitarianism, but
against any standard or morality at all; for certainly no known ethical standard
decides an action to be good or bad because it is done by a good or bad man,
still less because done by an amiable, a brave, or a benevolent man, or the
contrary. These considerations are relevant, not to the estimation of actions,
but of persons; and there is nothing in the utilitarian theory inconsistent with
the fact that there are other things which interest us in persons besides the
rightness and wrongness of their actions. The Stoics, indeed, with the paradoxical misuse of language which was part of their system, and by which they
strove to raise themselves above all concern about anything but virtue, were
fond of saying that he who has that has everything; that he, and only he, is
rich, is beautiful, is a king. But no claim of this description is made for the
virtuous man by the utilitarian doctrine. Utilitarians are quite aware that there
are other desirable possessions and qualities besides virtue, and are perfectly
willing to allow to all of them their full worth. They are also aware that a
right action does not necessarily indicate a virtuous character, and that actions
which are blamable often proceed from qualities entitled to praise. When this
is apparent in any particular case, it modifies their estimation, not certainly of
the act, but of the agent. I grant that they are, notwithstanding, of opinion

that in the long run the best proof of a good character is good actions; and resolutely refuse to consider any mental disposition as good of which the predominant tendency is to produce bad conduct. This makes them unpopular with many people, but it is an unpopularity which they must share with everyone who regards the distinction between right and wrong in a serious light; and the reproach is not one which a conscientious utilitarian need be anxious to repel.

• • •

Again, utility is often summarily stigmatized as an immoral doctrine by giving it the name of "expediency," and taking advantage of the popular use of that term to contrast it with principle. But the expedient, in the sense in which it is opposed to the right, generally means that which is expedient for the particular interest of the agent himself; as when a minister sacrifices the interests of his country to keep himself in place. When it means anything better than this, it means that which is expedient for some immediate object, some temporary purpose, but which violates a rule whose observance is expedient in a much higher degree. The expedient, in this sense, instead of being the same thing with the useful, is a branch of the hurtful. Thus it would often be expedient, for the purpose of getting over some momentary embarrassment, or attaining some object immediately useful to ourselves or others, to tell a lie. But inasmuch as the cultivation in ourselves of a sensitive feeling on the subject of veracity is one of the most useful, and the enfeeblement of that feeling one of the most hurtful, things to which our conduct can be instrumental; and inasmuch as any, even unintentional, deviation from truth does that much toward weakening the trustworthiness of human assertion, which is not only the principal support of all present social well-being, but the insufficiency of which does more than any one thing that can be named to keep back civilization, virtue, everything on which human happiness on the largest scale depends— we feel that the violation, for a present advantage, of a rule of such transcendent expediency is not expedient, and that he who, for the sake of convenience to himself or to some other individual, does what depends on him to deprive mankind of the good, and inflict upon them the evil, involved in the greater or less reliance which they can place in each other's words, acts the part of one of their worst enemies. Yet that even this rule, sacred as it is, admits of possible exceptions is acknowledged by all moralists; the chief of which is when the withholding of some fact (as of information from a malefactor, or of bad news from a person dangerously ill) would save an individual (especially an individual other than oneself) from great and unmerited evil, and when the withholding can only be effected by denial. But in order that the exception may not extend itself beyond the need, and may have the least possible effect in weakening reliance on veracity, it ought to be recognized and, if possible, its limits defined; and, if the principle of utility is good for anything, it must be good for weighing these conflicting utilities against one another and marking out the region within which one or the other preponderates.

Again, defenders of utility often find themselves called upon to reply to such objections as this—that there is not time, previous to action, for calculating and weighing the effects of any line of conduct on the general happiness. This is exactly as if anyone were to say that it is impossible to guide our conduct by Christianity because there is not time, on every occasion on which anything has to be done, to read through the Old and New Testaments. The answer to the objection is that there has been ample time, namely, the whole past duration of the human species. During all that time mankind have been learning by experience the tendencies of actions; on which experience all the prudence as well as all the morality of life are dependent. People talk as if the commencement of this course of experience had hitherto been put off, and as if, at the moment when some man feels tempted to meddle with the property or life of another, he had to begin considering for the first time whether murder and theft are injurious to human happiness. Even then I do not think that he would find the question very puzzling; but, at all events, the matter is now done to his hand. It is truly a whimsical supposition that, if mankind were agreed in considering utility to be the test of morality, they would remain without any agreement as to what *is* useful, and would take no measures for having their notions on the subject taught to the young and enforced by law and opinion. There is no difficulty in proving any ethical standard whatever to work ill if we suppose universal idiocy to be conjoined with it; but on any hypothesis short of that, mankind must by this time have acquired positive beliefs as to the effects of some actions on their happiness; and the beliefs which have thus come down are the rules of morality for the multitude, and for the philosopher until he has succeeded in finding better. That philosophers might easily do this, even now, on many subjects; that the received code of ethics is by no means of divine right; and that mankind have still much to learn as to the effects of actions on the general happiness, I admit or rather earnestly maintain. The corollaries from the principle of utility, like the precepts of every practical art, admit of indefinite improvement, and, in a progressive state of the human mind, their improvement is perpetually going on. But to consider the rules of morality as improvable is one thing; to pass over the intermediate generalization entirely and endeavor to test each individual action directly by the first principle is another. It is a strange notion that the acknowledgment of a first principle is inconsistent with the admission of secondary ones. To inform a traveler respecting the place of his ultimate destination is not to forbid the use of landmarks and direction-posts on the way. The proposition that happiness is the end and aim of morality does not mean that no road ought to be laid down to that goal, or that persons going thither should not be advised to take one direction rather than another. Men really ought to leave off talking a kind of nonsense on this subject, which they would neither talk nor listen to on other matters of practical concernment. Nobody argues that the art of navigation is not founded on astronomy because sailors cannot wait to calculate the Nautical Almanac. Being rational creatures, they go to sea with it ready calculated; and all rational creatures go out upon the sea of life with their minds made up on the common questions of right and wrong, as well as on many of the far more difficult questions of wise and foolish. And this, as long as foresight is a human quality, it is to be presumed they will continue to do. Whatever we adopt as the fundamental principle of morality, we require subordinate principles to apply it by; the impossibility of doing without them, being common to all systems, can afford no argument against any one in particular; but gravely to argue as if no such secondary principles could be had, and as if mankind had remained till now, and always must remain, without drawing any general conclusions from the experience of human life is as high a pitch, I think, as absurdity has ever reached in philosophical controversy.

The remainder of the stock arguments against utilitarianism mostly consist in laying to its charge the common infirmities of human nature, and the general difficulties which embarrass conscientious persons in shaping their course through life. We are told that a utilitarian will be apt to make his own particular case an exception to moral rules, and, when under temptation, will see a utility in the breach of a rule, greater than he will see in its observance. But is utility the only creed which is able to furnish us with excuses for evil-doing and means of cheating our own conscience? They are afforded in abundance by all doctrines which recognize as a fact in morals the existence of conflicting considerations, which all doctrines do that have been believed by sane persons. It is not the fault of any creed, but of the complicated nature of human affairs, that rules of conduct cannot be so framed as to require no exceptions, and that hardly any kind of action can safely be laid down as either always obligatory or always condemnable. There is no ethical creed which does not temper the rigidity of its laws by giving a certain latitude, under the moral responsibility of the agent, for accommodation to peculiarities of circumstances; and under every creed, at the opening thus made, self-deception and dishonest casuistry get in. There exists no moral system under which there do not arise unequivocal cases of conflicting obligation. These are the real difficulties, the knotty points both in the theory of ethics and in the conscientious guidance of personal conduct. They are overcome practically, with greater or with less success, according to the intellect and virtue of the individual; but it can hardly be pretended that anyone will be the less qualified for dealing with them, from possessing an ultimate standard to which conflicting rights and duties can be referred. If utility is the ultimate source of moral obligations, utility may be invoked to decide between them when their demands are incompatible. Though the application of the standard may be difficult, it is better than none at all; while in other systems, the moral laws all claiming independent authority, there is no common umpire entitled to interfere between them; their claims to precedence one over another rest on little better than sophistry, and, unless determined, as they generally are, by the unacknowledged influence of consideration of utility, afford a free scope for the action of personal desires and partialities. We must remember that only in these cases of conflict between secondary principles is it requisite that first principles should be appealed to. There is no case of moral obligation in which some secondary principle is not involved; and if only one, there can seldom be any real doubt which one it is, in the mind of any person by whom the principle itself is recognized.

OF WHAT SORT OF PROOF
THE PRINCIPLE OF UTILITY IS SUSCEPTIBLE

It has already been remarked that questions of ultimate ends do not admit of proof, in the ordinary acceptation of the term. To be incapable of proof by reasoning is common to all first principles, to the first premises of our knowledge, as well as to those of our conduct. But the former, being matters of fact, may be the subject of a direct appeal to the faculties which judge of fact—namely, our senses and our internal consciousness. Can an appeal be made to the same faculties on questions of practical ends? Or by what other faculty is cognizance taken of them?

Questions about ends are, in other words, questions of what things are desirable. The utilitarian doctrine is that happiness is desirable, and the only thing desirable, as an end; all other things being only desirable as means to that end. What ought to be required of this doctrine, what conditions is it requisite that the doctrine should fulfill—to make good its claim to be believed?

The only proof capable of being given that an object is visible is that people actually see it. The only proof that a sound is audible is that people hear it; and so of the other sources of our experience. In like manner, I apprehend, the sole evidence it is possible to produce that anything is desirable is that people do actually desire it. If the end which the utilitarian doctrine proposes to itself were not, in theory and in practice, acknowledged to be an end, nothing could ever convince any person that it was so. No reason can be given why the general happiness is desirable, except that each person, so far as he believes it to be attainable, desires his own happiness. This, however, being a fact, we have not only all the proof which the case admits of, but all which it is possible to require, that happiness is a good, that each person's happiness is a good to that person, and the general happiness, therefore, a good to the aggregate of all persons. Happiness has made out its title as *one* of the ends of conduct and, consequently, one of the criteria of morality.

But it has not, by this alone, proved itself to be the sole criterion. To do that, it would seem, by the same rule, necessary to show, not only that people desire happiness, but that they never desire anything else. Now it is palpable that they do desire things which, in common language, are decidedly distinguished from happiness. They desire, for example, virtue and the absence of vice no less really than pleasure and the absence of pain. The desire of virtue is not as universal, but it is as authentic a fact as the desire of happiness. And hence the opponents of the utilitarian standard deem that they have a right to infer that there are other ends of human action besides happiness, and that happiness is not the standard of approbation and disapprobation.

But does the utilitarian doctrine deny that people desire virtue, or maintain that virtue is not a thing to be desired? The very reverse. It maintains not only that virtue is to be desired, but that it is to be desired disinterestedly, for itself. Whatever may be the opinion of utilitarian moralists as to the original conditions by which virtue is made virtue, however they may believe (as they do) that actions and dispositions are only virtuous because they promote another end than virtue, yet this being granted, and it having been decided, from considerations of this description, what *is* virtuous, they not only place virtue at the very head of the things which are good as means to the ultimate end, but they also recognize as a psychological fact the possibility of its being, to the individual, a good in itself, without looking to any end beyond it; and hold that the mind is not in a right state, not in a state conformable to utility, not in the state most conducive to the general happiness, unless it does love virtue in this manner—as a thing desirable in itself, even although, in the individual instance, it should not produce those other desirable consequences which it tends to produce, and on account of which it is held to be virtue. This opinion is not, in the smallest degree, a departure from the happiness principle. The ingredients of happiness are very various, and each of them is desirable in itself, and not merely when considered as swelling an aggregate. The principle of utility does not mean that any given pleasure, as music, for instance, or any given exemption from pain, as for example health, is to be looked upon as means to a collective something termed happiness, and to be desired on that account. They are desired and desirable in and for themselves; besides being means, they are a part of the end. Virtue, according to the utilitarian doctrine, is not naturally and originally part of the end, but it is capable of becoming so; and in those who live it disinterestedly it has become so, and is desired and cherished, not as a means to happiness, but as part of their happiness.

To illustrate this further, we may remember that virtue is not the only thing originally a means, and which if it were not a means to anything else would be and remain indifferent, but which by association with what it is a means to comes to be desired for itself, and that too with the utmost intensity. What, for example, shall we say of the love of money? There is nothing originally more desirable about money than about any heap of glittering pebbles. Its worth is solely that of the things which it will buy; the desires for other things than itself, which it is a means of gratifying. Yet the love of money is not only one of the strongest moving forces of human life, but money is, in many cases, desired in and for itself; the desire to possess it is often stronger than the desire to use it, and goes on increasing when all the desires which point to ends beyond it, to be compassed by it, are falling off. It may, then, be said truly that money is desired not for the sake of an end, but as part of the end. From being a means to happiness, it has come to be itself a principal ingredient of the individual's conception of happiness. The same may be said of the majority of the great objects of human life: power, for example, or fame, except that to each of these there is a certain amount of immediate pleasure annexed, which has at least the semblance of being naturally inherent in them—a thing which cannot be said of money. Still, however, the strongest natural attraction, both of power and of fame, is the immense aid they give to the attainment of our other wishes; and it is the strong association thus generated between them and all our objects of desire which gives to the direct desire of them the intensity it often assumes, so as in some characters to surpass in strength all other desires. In these cases the means have become a part of the end, and a more important part of it than any of the things which they are means to. What was once desired as an instrument for the attainment of happiness has come to be desired for its own sake. In being desired for its own sake it is, however, desired as *part* of happiness. The person is made, or thinks he would be made, happy by its mere possession; and is made unhappy by failure to obtain it. The desire of it is not a different thing from the desire of happiness any more than the love of music or the desire of health. They are included in happiness. They are some of the elements of which the desire of happiness is made up. Happiness is not an abstract idea but a concrete whole; and these are some of its parts. And the utilitarian standard sanctions and approves their being so. Life would be a poor thing, very ill provided with sources of happiness, if there were not this provision of nature by which things originally indifferent, but conducive to, or otherwise associated with, the satisfaction of our primitive desires, become in themselves sources of pleasure more valuable than the primitive pleasures, both in permanency, in the space of human existence that they are capable of covering, and even in intensity.

Virtue, according to the utilitarian conception is a good of this description. There was no original desire of it, or motive to it, save its conduciveness to pleasure, and especially to protection from pain. But through the association thus formed it may be felt a good in itself, and desired as such with as great intensity as any other good; and with this difference between it and the love of money, of power, or of fame—that all of these may, and often do, render the individual noxious to the other members of the society to which he belongs, whereas there is nothing which makes him so much a blessing to them as the cultivation of the disinterested love of virtue. And consequently, the utilitarian standard, while it tolerates and approves those other acquired desires, up to the point beyond which they would be more injurious to the general happiness than promotive of it, enjoins and requires the cultivation of the love of virtue up to the greatest strength possible, as being above all things important to the general happiness.

It results from the preceding considerations that there is in reality nothing desired except happiness. Whatever is desired otherwise than as a means to some end beyond itself, and ultimately to happiness, is desired as itself a part of happiness, and is not desired for itself until it has become so. Those who desire virtue for its own sake desire it either because the consciousness of it is a pleasure, or because the consciousness of being without it is a pain, or for both reasons united; as in truth the pleasure and pain seldom exist separately, but almost always together—the same person feeling pleasure in the degree of virtue attained, and pain in not having attained more. If one of these gave him no pleasure, and the other no pain, he would not love or desire virtue, or would desire it only for the other benefits which it might produce to himself or to persons whom he cared for.

We have now, then, an answer to the question, of what sort of proof the principle of utility is susceptible. If the opinion which I have now stated is psychologically true—if human nature is so constituted as to desire nothing which is not either a part of happiness or a means of happiness—we can have no other proof, and we require no other, that these are the only things desirable.

If so, happiness is the sole end of human action, and the promotion of it the test by which to judge of all human conduct; from whence it necessarily follows that it must be the criterion of morality, since a part is included in the whole.

And now to decide whether this is really so, whether mankind do desire nothing for itself but that which is a pleasure to them, or of which the absence is a pain, we have evidently arrived at a question of fact and experience, dependent, like all similar questions, upon evidence. It can only be determined by practiced self-consciousness and self-observation, assisted by observation of others. I believe that these sources of evidence, impartially consulted, will declare that desiring a thing and finding it pleasant, aversion to it and thinking of it as painful, are phenomena entirely inseparable or, rather, two parts of the same phenomenon—in strictness of language, two different modes of naming the same psychological fact; that to think of an object as desirable (unless for the sake of its consequences) and to think of it as pleasant are one and the same thing; and that to desire anything except in proportion as the idea of it is pleasant is a physical and metaphysical impossibility.

So obvious does this appear to me that I expect it will hardly be disputed; and the objection made will be, not that desire can possibly be directed to anything ultimately except pleasure and exemption from pain, but that the will is a different thing from desire; that a person of confirmed virtue or any other person whose purposes are fixed carries out his purposes without any thought of the pleasure he has in contemplating them or expects to derive from their fulfillment, and persists in acting on them, even though these pleasures are much diminished by changes in his character or decay of his passive sensibilities, or are outweighed by the pains which the pursuit of the purposes may bring upon him. All this I fully admit and have stated it elsewhere as positively and emphatically as anyone. Will, the active phenomenon, is a different thing from desire, the state of passive sensibility, and, though originally an offshoot from it, may in time take root and detach itself from the parent stock, so much so that in the case of a habitual purpose, instead of willing the thing because we desire it, we often desire it only because we will it. This, however, is but an instance of that familiar fact, the power of habit, and is nowise confined to the case of virtuous actions. Many indifferent things which men originally did from a motive of some sort they continue to do from habit. Sometimes this is done unconsciously, the consciousness coming only after the action; at other times with conscious volition, but volition which has become habitual and is put in operation by the force of habit, in opposition perhaps to the deliberate preference, as often happens with those who have contracted habits of vicious or hurtful indulgence. Third and last comes the case in which the habitual act of will in the individual instance is not in contradiction to the general intention prevailing as other times, but in fulfillment of it, as in the case of the person of confirmed virtue and of all who pursue deliberately and consistently any determinate end. The distinction between will and desire thus understood is an authentic and highly important psychological fact; but the fact consists solely in this—that will, like all other parts of our constitution, is amenable to habit, and that we may will from habit what we no longer desire for itself, or desire only because we will it. It is not the less true that will, in the beginning, is entirely produced by desire, including in that term the repelling influence of pain as well as the attractive one of pleasure. Let us take into consideration no longer the person who has a confirmed will to do right, but him in whom that virtuous will is still feeble, conquerable by temptation, and not to be fully relied on; by what means can it be strengthened? How can the will to be virtuous, where it does not exist in sufficient force, be implanted or awakened? Only by making the person *desire* virtue—by making him think of it in a pleasurable light, or of its absence in a painful one. It is by associating the doing right with pleasure, or the wrong with pain, or by eliciting and impressing and bringing home to the person's experience the pleasure naturally involved in the one or the pain in the other, that it is possible to call forth that will to be virtuous which, when confirmed, acts without any thought of either pleasure or pain. Will is the child of desire, and passes out of the dominion of its parent only to come under that of habit. That which is the result of habit affords no presumption of being intrinsically good; and there would be no reason for wishing that the purpose of virtue should become independent of pleasure and pain were it not that the influence of the pleasurable and painful associations which prompt to virtue is not sufficiently to be depended on for unerring constancy of action until it has acquired the support of habit. Both in feeling and in conduct, habit is the only thing which imparts certainty; and it is because of the importance to others of being able to rely absolutely on one's feelings and conduct, and to oneself of being able to rely on one's own, that the will to do right ought to be cultivated into this habitual independence. In other words, this state of the will is a means to good, not intrinsically a good; and does not contradict the doctrine that nothing is a good to human beings but in so far as it is either itself pleasurable or a means of attaining pleasure or averting pain.

But if this doctrine be true, the principle of utility is proved. Whether it is so or not must now be left to the consideration of the thoughtful reader.

24

What Is Wrong
with Slavery

R. M. HARE

*For biographical information on R. M. Hare, see reading 11. This selection
first appeared in* Philosophy and Public Affairs *(Winter 1979).*

*In the selection, Hare invokes the utility principle to evaluate the
practice of slavery. Slavery is morally important, not because anyone
seriously recommends it, but because it is often thought to be an
embarrassment to utilitarians. As critics note, we can imagine cases in
which tolerating slavery would maximize utility. Because slavery still seems
wrong, the critics conclude that utilitarianism has unacceptable
implications.*

*But Hare rejects this conclusion. To show that it does not follow, he
asks why we feel that slavery is wrong. The answer, he contends, is itself
provided by utilitarianism. In most if not all actual situations, slavery has
brought far more misery than happiness. Realizing this, we have
internalized principles that strongly condemn slavery. Since these principles
were designed to apply in the actual world, it does not matter that they fail
to fit unrealistic imaginary cases. But, given what we know about people
and the ways they would react to slavery, all cases in which slavery
maximizes utility are unrealistic. Thus, such cases do not damage
utilitarianism.*

Nearly everybody would agree that slavery is wrong; and I can say
this perhaps with greater feeling than most, having in a manner of speaking *been*
a slave. However, there are dangers in just taking for granted that something is
wrong; for we may then assume that it is obvious that it is wrong and indeed
obvious why it is wrong; and this leads to a prevalence of very bad arguments
with quite silly conclusions, all based on the so-called absolute value of human
freedom. If we could see more clearly what *is* valuable about freedom, and
why it is valuable, then we might be protected against the rhetoric of those
who, the moment anything happens that is disadvantageous or distasteful to
them, start complaining loudly about some supposed infringement of their
liberty, without telling us why it is wrong that they should be prevented from
doing what they would like to do. It may well *be* wrong in many such cases;

but until we have some way of judging when it is and when it is not, we shall be at the mercy of every kind of demagogy.

This is but one example of the widespread abuse of the appeal to human rights. We may even be tempted to think that our politics would be more healthy if rights had never been heard of; but that would be going too far. It is the unthinking appeal to ill-defined rights, unsupported by argument, that does the harm. There is no doubt that arguments justifying some of these appeals are possible; but since the forms of such arguments are seldom understood even by philosophers, it is not surprising that many quite unjustified claims of this sort go unquestioned, and thus in the end bring any sort of appeal to human rights into disrepute. It is a tragedy that this happens, because there really are rights that ought to be defended with all the devotion we can command. Things are being done the world over which can properly be condemned as infringements of human rights; but so long as rights are used so loosely as an all-purpose political weapon, often in support of very questionable causes, our protests against such infringements will be deprived of most of their force.

Another hazard of the appeal to rights is that it is seldom that such an appeal by one side cannot be countered with an appeal to some conflicting right by the opposite side. The controversies which led finally to the abolition of slavery provide an excellent example of this, with one side appealing to rights of liberty and the other to rights of property. But we do not have to go so far back in history to find examples of this sort of thing. We have only to think of the disputes about distributive justice between the defenders of equality and of individual liberty; or of similar arguments about education. I have written about both these disputes elsewhere, in the attempt to substitute for intuitions some more solid basis for argument.[1] I have the same general motive in raising the topic of slavery, and also a more particular motive. Being a utilitarian, I need to be able to answer the following attack frequently advanced by opponents of utilitarianism. It is often said that utilitarianism must be an objectionable creed because it could in certain circumstances condone or even commend slavery, given that circumstances can be envisaged in which utility would be maximized by preserving a slave-owning society and not abolishing slavery. The objectors thus seek to smear utilitarians with the taint of all the atrocious things that were done by slave-traders and slave-owners. The objection, as I hope to show, does not stand up; but in order to see through this rhetoric we shall have to achieve a quite deep understanding of some rather difficult issues in moral philosophy; and this, too, adds to the importance and interest of the topic.

First, we have to ask what this thing, slavery, is, about whose wrongness we are arguing. As soon as we ask this question we see at once, if we have any knowledge of history, that it is, in common use, an extremely ill-defined concept.

---

1 'Justice and Equality', in J. Arthur and W. H. Shaw, eds., *Justice and Economic Distribution* (Englewood Cliffs, NJ: Prentice-Hall, 1978); 'Opportunity for What?: Some Remarks on Current Disputes About Equality in Education', *Oxford Review of Education* 3 (1977).

Even if we leave out of account such admittedly extended uses of 'wage-slave' in the writings of Marxists, it is clear that the word 'slave' and its near-equivalents such as '*servus*' and '*doulos*' have meant slightly different things in different cultures; for slavery is, primarily, a *legal* status, defined by the disabilities or the liabilities which are imposed by the law on those called slaves; and obviously these may vary from one jurisdiction to another. Familiar logical difficulties arise about how we are to decide, of a word in a foreign language, that it means the same as the English word 'slave.' Do the relevant laws in the country where the language is spoken have to be identical with those which held in English-speaking countries before slavery was abolished? Obviously not; because it would be impossible for them to be identical with the laws of all such countries at all periods, since these did not remain the same. Probably we have a rough idea of the kind of laws which have to hold in a country before we can say that that country has an institution properly called 'slavery'; but it is pretty rough.

It would be possible to pursue at some length, with the aid of legal, historical and anthropological books on slavery in different cultures and jurisdictions, the different shades of meaning of the word 'slave'. But since my purpose is philosophical, I shall limit myself to asking what is essential to the notion of slavery in common use. The essential features are, I think, to be divided under two heads: slavery is, first, a *status* in society, and secondly, a *relation* to a master. The slave is so called first of all because he occupies a certain place in society, lacking certain rights and privileges secured by the law to others, and subject to certain liabilities from which others are free. And secondly, he is the slave *of* another person or body (which might be the state itself). The first head is not enough to distinguish slavery from other legal disabilities; for example the lower castes in some societies are as lacking in legal rights as slaves in some others, or more so, but are not called slaves because they are not the slaves *of* anybody.

The *status* of a slave was defined quite early by the Greeks in terms of four freedoms which the slave lacks. These are: a legally recognized position in the community, conferring a right of access to the courts; protection from illegal seizure and detention and other personal violence; the privilege of going where he wants to go; and that of working as he pleases. The first three of these features are present in a manumission document from Macedonia dated about 235 B.C.; the last is added in the series of manumission documents from Delphi which begins about thirty years later.[2] The state could to some extent regulate by law the treatment of slaves without making us want to stop calling them slaves, so that the last three features are a bit wobbly at the edges. But we are seeking only a rough characterization of slavery, and shall have to put up with this indefiniteness of the concept.

The *relation* of the slave to a master is also to some extent indefinite. It might seem that we could tie it up tight by saying that a slave has to be the *property* of an *owner*; but a moment's reflection will show what unsafe ground

---

2 See W. L. Westermann, *The Slave Systems of Greek and Roman Antiquity* (Philadelphia: American Philosophical Society, 1955), p. 35.

this is. So-called property-owners do not need to be reminded that legal restrictions upon the use and enjoyment of property can become so onerous as to make it almost a joke to call it property at all. I am referring not only to such recent inventions as zoning and other planning laws (though actually they are not so recent, having been anticipated even in ancient times), and to rent acts, building regulations, clean air acts and the like, but also to the ancient restrictions placed by the common law on uses of one's property which might be offensive to one's neighbours. In relation to slavery, it is also instructive to think of the cruelty-to-animals legislation which now rightly forbids one to do what one likes to one's own dog or cow which one has legally purchased. Legislation of just this kind was passed in the days before abolition, and was even to some extent enforced, though not always effectively. The laws forbidding the slave trade were, of course, the outstanding example of such legislation preventing people from doing what they wanted with their own property.

However, as before, we are seeking only a general and rough characterization of slavery, and shall therefore have to put up with the open texture of the concept of property. This, like slavery itself, is defined by the particular rights and obligations which are conferred or imposed by a particular legal system, and these may vary from one such system to another. It will be enough to have a general idea of what would stop us calling a person the slave of another—how far the law would have to go in assigning rights to slaves before we stopped using that word of them. I have gone into these difficulties in such detail as space has allowed only because I am now going on to describe, for the purposes of our moral discussion, certain conditions of life about which I shall invite the reader's judgment, and I do not want anybody to say that what I am describing *is* not really slavery. The case I shall sketch is admittedly to some extent fantastic; and this, as we shall later see, is very important when we come to assess the philosophical arguments that have been based on similar cases. But although it is extremely unlikely that what I describe should actually occur, I wish to maintain that *if* it occurred, we should still call it slavery, so that *if* imaginary cases are allowed to be brought into the arguments, this case will have to be admitted.

It may be helpful if, before leaving the question of what slavery is, I list a few conditions of life which have to be *distinguished* from slavery proper. The first of these is *serfdom* (a term which, like 'slavery' itself, has a wide range of meaning). A serf is normally tied, not directly to a master, but to a certain area of land; the rights to his services pass with the land if it changes hands. This very distinction, however, separates the English villein in gross, who approximates to a slave although enjoying certain legal rights, from the villein regardant, whose serfdom arises through his feudal tenure of land. Those who unsuccessfully tried to persuade Lord Mansfield in Sommersett's case that slavery could exist in England attempted to show that the defendant was a villein in gross.[3] Secondly, one is not a slave merely because one belongs to a

---

3 Summing up for defence and judgement of Lord Mansfield in Sommersett's case, King's Bench, 12 George III, 1771–1772, *Howell's State Trials* 20, pp. 1 ff.

caste which has an inferior legal status, even if it has pretty well no rights; as I have said, the slave has to be the slave *of* some owner. Thirdly, slavery has to be distinguished from *indenture,* which is a form of contract. Apprentices in former times, and football players even now, are bound by contract, entered into by themselves or, in the case of children, by their parents, to serve employers for a fixed term under fixed conditions, which were in some cases extremely harsh (so that the actual sufferings of indentured people could be as bad as those of slaves).[4] The difference lies in the voluntariness of the contract and in its fixed term. We must note however that in some societies (Athens before Solon for example) one could *choose* to become a slave by selling one's person to escape debt;[5] and it might be possible to sell one's children as well, as the Greeks sometimes did, so that even the hereditability of the slave status does not serve to make definite the rather fuzzy boundary between slavery and indenture.

We ought perhaps to notice two other conditions which approximate to slavery but are not called slavery. The first is a compulsory *military* or *naval service* and, indeed, other forced labour. The impressed sailors of Nelson's navy no doubt endured conditions as bad as many slaves; Dr. Johnson remarked that nobody would choose to be a sailor if he had the alternative of being put in prison.[6] But they were not called slaves, because their status as free men was only in abeyance and returned to them on discharge. By contrast, the galley slaves of the Mediterranean powers in earlier times really were slaves. Secondly, although the term 'penal servitude' was once in use, *imprisonment* for crime is not usually called slavery. This is another fuzzy boundary, because in ancient times it was possible for a person to lose his rights as a citizen and become a slave by sentence of a court for some crime;[7] though when something very like this happened recently in South Africa, it was not *called* slavery, officially.[8] Again, prisoners of war and other captives and bondsmen are not always called slaves, however grim their conditions, although in ancient times capture in war was a way of becoming a slave, if one was not fortunate enough to be ransomed.[9] I have myself, as a prisoner of war, worked on the Burma railway in conditions not *at the time* distinguishable from slavery; but because my status was temporary I can claim to have been a slave only 'in a manner of speaking'.

I shall put my philosophical argument, to which we have now come, in terms of an imaginary example, to which I shall give as much verisimilitude as I can. It will be seen, however, that quite unreal assumptions have to be made in

---

4 See O. Patterson, *The Sociology of Slavery* (London: MacGibbon and Kee, 1967), p. 74; A. Sampson, *Drum* (London: Collins, 1956), chap. 3.

5 See Westermann, *Slave Systems,* p. 4.

6 Boswell, *Life of Johnson,* ed. G. B. Hill and L. F. Powell (Oxford: Oxford University Press, 1934), vol. 1, p. 348, 16 March 1759.

7 See Westermann, *Slave Systems,* p. 81. In pre-revolutionary France one could be sentenced to the galleys.

8 See Sampson, *Drum,* p. 241.

9 See Westermann, *Slave Systems,* pp. 2, 5–7, 29.

order to get the example going—and this is very important for the argument between the utilitarians and their opponents. It must also be noted that to play its role in the argument the example will have to meet certain requirements. It is intended as a fleshed-out substitute for the rather jejune examples often to be found in anti-utilitarian writers. To serve its purpose it will have to be a case in which to abolish slavery really and clearly would diminish utility. This means, first, that the slavery to be abolished must really be slavery, and, secondly, that it must have a total utility clearly, but not enormously, greater than the total utility of the kind of regime which would be, in that situation, a practical alternative to slavery.

If it were not *clearly* greater, utilitarians could argue that, since all judgements of this sort are only probable, caution would require them to stick to a well-tried principle favouring liberty, the principle itself being justified on utilitarian grounds (see below); and thus the example would cease to divide them from their opponents, and would become inapposite.

If, on the other hand, the utility of slavery were *enormously* greater, anti-utilitarians might complain that their own view was being made too strong; for many anti-utilitarians are pluralists and hold that among the principles of morality a principle requiring beneficence is to be included. Therefore, if the advantages of retaining slavery are made sufficiently great, a non-utilitarian with a principle of beneficence in his repertory could agree that it ought to be retained—that is, that *in this case* the principle of beneficence has greater weight than that favouring liberty. Thus there would again be no difference, in this case, between the verdicts of the utilitarians and their opponents, and the example would be inapposite.

There is also another dimension in which the example has to be carefully placed. An anti-utilitarian might claim that the example I shall give makes the difference between the conditions of the slaves and those of the free in the supposed society too small, and the number of slaves too great. If, he might claim, I had made the number of slaves small and the difference between the miseries of the slaves and the pleasures of the slave-owners much greater, then the society might have the same total utility as mine (that is, greater than that of the free society with which I compare it), but it would be less plausible for me to maintain that if such a comparison had to be made in real life, we ought to follow the utilitarians and prefer the slave society.[10]

I cannot yet answer this objection without anticipating my argument; I shall merely indicate briefly how I would answer it. The answer is that the objection rests on an appeal to our ordinary intuitions; but that these are designed to deal with ordinary cases. They give no reliable guide to what we ought to say in highly unusual cases. But, further, the case desiderated is never likely to

---

10 I am grateful to the Editors for pressing this objection. I deal with it only so far as it concerns slavery such as might occur in the world as we know it. Brave New World situations in which people are conditioned from birth to be obedient slaves and given disagreeable or dangerous tasks require separate treatment which is beyond the scope of this paper, though anti-utilitarian arguments based on them meet the same defence, namely the requirement to assess realistically what the consequences of such practises would actually be.

occur. How could it come about that the existence of a small number of slaves was necessary in order to preserve the happiness of the rest? I find it impossible to think of any technological factors (say, in agriculture or in transport by land or sea) which would make the preservation of slavery for a small class necessary to satisfy the interests of the majority. It is quite true that in the past there have been *large* slave populations supporting the higher standard of living of *small* minorities. But in that case it is hard to argue that slavery has more utility than its abolition, if the difference in happiness between slaves and slave-owners is great. Yet if, in order to produce a case in which the retention of slavery really would be optimal, we reduce the number of slaves relative to slave-owners, it becomes hard to say how the existence of this relatively small number of slaves is necessary for the happiness of the large number of free men. What on earth are the slaves doing that could not be more efficiently done by paid labour? And is not the abolition (perhaps not too abrupt) of slavery likely to promote those very mechanical changes which are necessary to enable the society to do without it?

The crux of the matter, as we shall see, is that in order to use an appeal to our ordinary intuitions as an argument, the opponents of utilitarianism have to produce cases which are not too far removed from the sort of cases with which our intuitions are designed to deal, namely the ordinary run of cases. If the cases they use fall outside this class, then the fact that our common intuitions give a different verdict from utilitarianism has no bearing on the argument; our intuitions could well be wrong about such cases, and be none the worse for that, because they will never have to deal with them in practise.

We may also notice, while we are sifting possible examples, that cases of *individual* slave-owners who are kind to their slaves will not do. The issue is one of whether slavery is an institution protected by law should be preserved; and if it is preserved, though there may be individuals who do not take advantage of it to maltreat their slaves, there will no doubt be many others who do.

Let us imagine, then, that the battle of Waterloo, that 'damned nice thing, the nearest run thing you ever saw in your life',[11] as Wellington called it, went differently from the way it actually did go, in two respects. The first was that the British and Prussians lost the battle; the last attack of the French Guard proved too much for them, the Guard's morale having been restored by Napoleon who in person led the advance instead of handing it over to Ney. But secondly, having exposed himself to fire as Wellington habitually did, but lacking Wellington's amazing good fortune, Napoleon was struck by a cannon ball and killed instantly. This so disorganized the French, who had no other commanders of such ability, that Wellington was able to rally his forces and conduct one of those holding operations at which he was so adept, basing himself on the Channel ports and their intricate surrounding waterways; the result was a cross between the Lines of Torres Vedras and the trench warfare

11 For references, see E. Longford, *Wellington, The Years of the Sword* (London: Weidenfeld and Nicholson, 1969), p. 489.

of the first World War. After a year or two of this, with Napoleon out of the way and the war party discredited in England, liberal (that is, neither revolutionary nor reactionary) regimes came into power in both countries, and the Congress of Vienna reconvened in a very different spirit, with the French represented on equal terms.

We have to consider these events only as they affected two adjacent islands in the Caribbean which I am going to call Juba and Camaica. I need not relate what happened in the rest of the world, because the combined European powers could at that time command absolute supremacy at sea, and the Caribbean could therefore be effectively isolated from world politics by the agreement which they reached to take that area out of the imperial war game. All naval and other forces were withdrawn from it except for a couple of bases on small islands for the suppression of the slave trade, which, in keeping with their liberal principles, the parties agreed to prohibit (those that had not already done so). The islands were declared independent and their white inhabitants, very naturally, all departed in a hurry, leaving the government in the hands of local black leaders, some of whom were of the calibre of Toussaint l'Ouverture and others of whom were very much the reverse.

On Juba, a former Spanish colony, at the end of the colonial period there had been formed, under pressure of military need, a militia composed of slaves under white officers, with conditions of service much preferable to those of the plantation slaves, and forming a kind of elite. The senior serjeant-major of this force found himself, after the white officers fled, in a position of unassailable power, and, being a man of great political intelligence and ability, shaped the new regime in a way that made Juba the envy of its neighbours.

What he did was to retain the institution of slavery but to remedy its evils. The plantations were split up into smaller units, still under overseers, responsible to the state instead of to the former owners. The slaves were given rights to improved conditions of work; the wage they had already received as a concession in colonial times was secured to them and increased; all cruel punishments were prohibited. However, it is still right to call them slaves, because the state retained the power to direct their labour and their place of residence and to enforce these directions by sanctions no more severe than are customary in countries without slavery, such as fines and imprisonment. The Juban government, influenced by early communist ideas (though Marx had not yet come on the scene) kept the plantations in its own hands; but private persons were also allowed to own a limited number of slaves under conditions at least as protective to the slaves as on the state-owned plantations.

The island became very prosperous, and the slaves in it enjoyed a life far preferable in every way to that of the free inhabitants of the neighbouring island of Camaica. In Camaica there had been no such focus of power in the early days. The slaves threw off their bonds and each seized what land he could get hold of. Though law and order were restored after a fashion, and democracy of a sort prevailed, the economy was chaotic, and this, coupled with a population explosion, led to widespread starvation and misery. Camaica lacked what Juba had: a government with the will *and the instrument, in the shape of the institution of slavery,* to control the economy and the population, and so make its slave-citizens, as I said, the envy of their neighbours. The flood of people in fishing boats seeking to emigrate from free Camaica and insinuate themselves as slaves into the plantations of Juba became so great that the Juban government had to employ large numbers of coastguards (slaves of course) to stop it.

That, perhaps, will do for our imaginary example. Now for the philosophical argument. It is commonly alleged that utilitarianism could condone or commend slavery. In the situation described, utility would have been lessened and not increased if the Juban government had abolished slavery and if as a result the economy of Juba had deteriorated to the level of that of Camaica. So, it might be argued, a utilitarian would have had to oppose the abolition. But everyone agrees, it might be held, that slavery is wrong; so the utilitarians are convicted of maintaining a thesis which has consequences repugnant to universally accepted moral convictions.

What could they reply to this attack? There are, basically, two lines they could take. These lines are not incompatible but complementary; indeed, the defence of utilitarianism could be put in the form of a dilemma. Either the defender of utilitarianism is allowed to question the imagined facts of the example, or he is not. First let us suppose that he is not. He might then try, as a first move, saying that in the situation *as portrayed* it would indeed be wrong to abolish slavery. If the argument descends to details, the anti-utilitarians may be permitted to insert any amount of extra details (barring the actual abolition of slavery itself) in order to make sure that its retention really does maximize utility. But then the utilitarian sticks to his guns and maintains that in that case it *would* be wrong to abolish slavery, and that, further, most ordinary people, if they could be got to consider the case on its merits and not allow their judgements to be confused by association with more detestable forms of slavery, would agree with this verdict. The principle of liberty which forbids slavery is a prima facie principle admitting of exceptions, and this imaginary case is one of the exceptions. If the utilitarians could sustain this line of defence, they would win the case; but perhaps not everyone would agree that it is sustainable.

So let us allow the utilitarian another slightly more sophisticated move, still staying, however, perched on the first horn of the dilemma. He might admit that not everyone would agree on the merits of this case, but explain this by pointing to the fantastic and unusual nature of the case, which, he might claim, would be unlikely to occur in real life. *If* he is not allowed to question the facts of the case, he has to admit that abolition would be wrong; but ordinary people, he might say, cannot see this because the principles of political and social morality which we have all of us *now* absorbed (as contrasted with our eighteenth-century ancestors), and with which we are deeply imbued, prevent us from considering the case on its merits. The principles are framed to cope with the cases of slavery which actually occur (all of which are to a greater or less degree harmful). Though they are the best principles for us to have when confronting the actual world, they give the wrong answer when presented with this fantastic case. But all the same, the world being as it is, we should be morally worse people if we did not have these principles; for then we might be tempted, whether through ignorance or by self-interest, to condone slavery in cases in which, though actually harmful, it could be colourably represented as being beneficial. Suppose, it might be argued, that an example of this sort had been used in anti-abolitionist writings in, say 1830 or thereabouts. Might it not have persuaded many people that slavery *could* be an admirable thing, and thus have secured their votes against abolition; and would this not have been very harmful? For the miseries caused by the *actual* institution of slavery in the Caribbean and elsewhere were so great that it was desirable from a utilitarian point of view that people should hold and act on moral convictions which condemned slavery as such and without qualification, because this would lead them to vote for its abolition.

If utilitarians take this slightly more sophisticated line, they are left saying at one and the same time that it would have been wrong to abolish slavery in the imagined circumstances, *and* that it is a good thing that nearly everyone, if asked about it, would say that it was right. Is this paradoxical? Not, I think, to anybody who understands the realities of the human situation. What resolves the paradox is that the example *is* imaginary and that therefore people are not going to have to pronounce, as a practical issue, on what the laws of Juba are to be. In deciding what principles it is good that people have, it is not necessary or even desirable to take into account such imaginary cases. It does not really matter, from a practical point of view, what judgements people reach about imaginary cases, provided that this does not have an adverse effect upon their judgements about real cases. From a practical point of view, the principles which it is best for them to have are those which will lead them to make the highest proportion of right decisions in actual cases where their decisions make a difference to what happens—weighted, of course, for the importance of the cases, that is, the amount of difference the decisions make to the resulting good or harm.

It is therefore perfectly acceptable that we should at one and the same time feel a strong moral conviction that even the Juban slave system, however beneficial, is wrong, *and* confess, when we reflect on the features of this imagined system, that we cannot see anything specifically wrong about it, but rather a great deal to commend. This is bound to be the experience of anybody who has acquired the sort of moral convictions that one ought to acquire, and at the same time is able to reflect rationally on the features of some unusual imagined situation. I have myself constantly had this experience when confronted with the sort of anti-utilitarian examples which are the stock-in-trade of philosophers like Bernard Williams. One is led to think, on reflection, that *if* such cases were to occur, one ought to do what is for the best in the circumstances (as even Williams himself appears to contemplate in one of his cases);[12] but one is bound also to find this conclusion repugnant to one's deepest

---

[12] See Williams, 'A Critique of Utilitarianism', in J. J. C. Smart and B. Williams, *Utilitarianism: For and Against* (Cambridge: Cambridge University Press, 1973), p. 99.

convictions; if it is not, one's convictions are not the best convictions one could have.

Against this, it might be objected that if one's deep moral convictions yield the wrong answer even in imaginary or unusual cases, they are *not* the best one could have. Could we not succeed, it might be asked, in inculcating into ourselves convictions of a more accommodating sort? Could we not, that is to say, absorb principles which had written into them either exceptions to deal with awkward cases like that in my example, or even provision for writing in exceptions ad hoc when the awkward cases arose? Up to a point this is a sensible suggestion; but beyond that point (a point which will vary with the temperament of the person whose principles they are to be) it becomes psychologically unsound. There are some simple souls, no doubt, who really cannot keep themselves in the straight and narrow way unless they cling fanatically and in the face of what most of us would call reason to extremely simple and narrow principles. And there are others who manage to have very complicated principles with many exceptions written into them (only 'written' is the wrong word, because the principles of such people defy formulation). Most of us come somewhere in between. It is also possible to have fairly simple principles but to attach to them a rubric which allows us to depart from them, either when one conflicts with another in a particular case, or where the case is such an unusual one that we find ourselves doubting whether the principles were designed to deal with it. In these cases we may apply utilitarian reasoning directly; but it is most unwise to do this in more normal cases, for those are precisely the cases (the great majority) which our principles *are* designed to deal with, since they were chosen to give the best results in the general run of cases. In normal cases, therefore, we are more likely to achieve the right decision (even from the utilitarian point of view) by sticking to these principles than by engaging in utilitarian reasoning about the particular case, with all its temptations to special pleading.

I have dealt with these issues at length elsewhere.[13] Here all I need to say is that there is a psychological limit to the complexity and to the flexibility of the moral principles that we can wisely seek to build deeply, as moral convictions, into our character; and the person who tries to go beyond this limit will end up as (what he will be called) an unprincipled person, and will not in fact do the best he could with his life, even by the test of utility. This may explain why I would always vote for the abolition of slavery, even though I can admit that cases could be *imagined* in which slavery would do more good than harm, and even though I am a utilitarian.

So much, then, for the first horn of the dilemma. Before we come to the second horn, on which the utilitarian is allowed to object to his opponents' argument on the ground that their example would not in the actual world be realized, I wish to make a methodological remark which may help us to find our bearings in this rather complex dispute. Utilitarianism, like any other theory of moral

---

13 See my 'Ethical Theory and Utilitarianism', in H. D. Lewis, ed., *Contemporary British Philosophy 4* (London: Allen and Unwin, 1976), and the references given there.

reasoning that gets anywhere near adequacy, consists of two parts, one formal and one substantial. The formal part is no more than a rephrasing of the requirement that moral prescriptions be universalizable: this has the consequence that equal interests of all are to be given equal weight in our reasoning: everybody to count for one and nobody for more than one. One should not expect such a formal requirement to generate, by itself, any substantial conclusions even about the actual world, let alone about all logically possible worlds. But there is also a substantial element in the theory. This is contributed by factual beliefs about what interests people in the real world actually have (which depends on what they actually want or like or dislike, and on what they would want or like or dislike under given conditions); and also about the actual effects on these interests of different actions in the real world. Given the truth of these beliefs, we can reason morally and shall come to certain moral conclusions. But the conclusions are not generated by the formal part of the theory alone.

Utilitarianism therefore, unlike some other theories, is *exposed* to the facts. The utilitarian cannot reason a priori that *whatever* the facts about the world and human nature, slavery is wrong. He has to show that it is wrong by showing, through a study of history and other factual observation, that slavery does have the effects (namely the production of misery) which make it wrong. This, though it may at first sight appear a weakness in the doctrine, is in fact its strength. A doctrine, like some kinds of intuitionism, according to which we can think up examples as fantastic as we please and the doctrine will still come up with the same old answers, is really showing that it has lost contact with the actual world with which the intuitions it relies on were designed to cope. Intuitionists think they can face the world armed with nothing but their inbred intuitions; utilitarians know that they have to look at what actually goes on in the world and see if the intuitions are really the best ones to have in that sort of world.

I come now to the second horn of the dilemma, on which the utilitarian is allowed to say, 'Your example won't do: it would never happen that way'. He may admit that Waterloo and the Congress of Vienna could have turned out differently—after all it was a damned nice thing, and high commanders were in those days often killed on the battlefield (it was really a miracle that Wellington was not), and there were liberal movements in both countries. But when we come to the Caribbean, things begin to look shakier. Is it really likely that there would have been such a contrast between the economies of Juba and Camaica? I do not believe that the influence of particular national leaders is ever so powerful, or that such perfectly wise leaders are ever forthcoming. And I do not believe that in the Caribbean or anywhere else a system of nationalized slavery could be made to run so smoothly. I should, rather, expect the system to deteriorate very rapidly. I base these expectations on general beliefs about human nature, and in particular upon the belief that people in the power of other people will be exploited, whatever the good intentions of those who founded the system.

Alternatively, if there really had been leaders of such amazing statesmanship, could they not have done better by abolishing slavery and substituting a free but disciplined society? In the example, they gave the slaves some legal rights; what was to prevent them giving others, such as the right to change residences and jobs, subject of course to an overall system of land-use and economic planning such as exists in many free countries? Did the retention of *slavery* in particular contribute very much to the prosperity of Juba that could not have been achieved by other means? And likewise, need the government of Camaica have been so incompetent? Could it not without reintroducing slavery, have kept the economy on the rails by such controls as are compatible with a free society? In short, did not the optimum solution lie somewhere *between* the systems adopted in Juba and Camaica, but on the free side of the boundary between slavery and liberty?

These factual speculations, however, are rather more superficial than I can be content with. The facts that it is really important to draw attention to are rather deep facts about human nature which must always, or nearly always, make slavery an intolerable condition.[14] I have mentioned already a fact about slave ownership; that ordinary, even good, human beings will nearly always exploit those over whom they have absolute power. We have only to read the actual history of slavery in all centuries and cultures to see that. There is also the effect on the characters of the exploiters themselves. I had this brought home to me recently when, staying in Jamaica, I happened to pick up a history book[15] written there at the very beginning of the nineteenth century, before abolition, whose writer had added at the end an appendix giving his views on the abolition controversy, which was then at its height. Although obviously a kindly man with liberal leanings, he argues against abolition; and one of his arguments struck me very forcibly. He argues that although slavery can be a cruel fate, things are much better in Jamaica now: there is actually a law that a slave on a plantation may not be given more than thirty-six lashes by the foreman without running him up in front of the overseer. The contrast between the niceness of the man and what he says here does perhaps more than any philosophical argument to make the point that our moral principles have to be designed for human nature as it is.

The most fundamental point is one about the human nature of the slave which makes ownership by another more intolerable for him than for, say, a horse (not that we should condone cruelty to horses). Men are different from other animals in that they can look a long way ahead, and therefore can become an object of deterrent punishment. Other animals, we may suppose, can only be the object of Skinnerian reinforcement and Pavlovian conditioning. These methods carry with them, no doubt, their own possibilities of cruelty; but they fall short of the peculiar cruelty of human slavery. One can utter to a man

---

14 For the effects of slavery on slaves and slave-owners, see O. Patterson, *Sociology of Slavery*; and S. M. Elkins, *Slavery* (Chicago: University of Chicago Press, 1959).

15 R. C. Dallas, *The History of the Maroons* (London: Longman and Rees, 1803; reprinted by Frank Cass, 1968). I have not been able to obtain the book again to verify this reference.

threats of punishment in the quite distant future which he can understand. A piece of human property, therefore, unlike a piece of inanimate property or even a brute animal in a man's possession, can be subjected to a sort of terror from which other kinds of property are immune; and, human owners being what they are, many will inevitably take advantage of this fact. That is the reason for the atrocious punishments that have usually be inflicted on slaves; there would have been no point in inflicting them on animals. A slave is the only being that is *both* able to be held responsible in this way, *and* has no escape from, or even redress against, the power that this ability to threaten confers upon his oppressor. If he were a free citizen, he would have rights which would restrain the exercise of the threat; if he were a horse or a piece of furniture, the threat would be valueless to his owner because it would not be understood. By being subjected to the threat of legal and other punishment, but at the same time deprived of legal defences against its abuse (since he has no say in what the laws are to be, nor much ability to avail himself of such laws as there are) the slave becomes, or is likely to become if his master is an ordinary human, the most miserable of all creatures.

No doubt there are other facts I could have adduced. But I will end by reiterating the general point I have been trying to illustrate. The wrongness of slavery, like the wrongness of anything else, has to be shown in the world as it actually is. We can do this by first reaching an understanding of the meaning of this and the other moral words, which brings with it certain rules of moral reasoning, as I have tried to show in other places.[16] One of the most important of these rules is a formal requirement reflected in the Golden Rule: the requirement that what we say we ought to do to others we have to be able to say ought to be done to ourselves were we in precisely their situation with their interests. And this leads to a way of moral reasoning (utilitarianism) which treats the equal interests of all as having equal weight. Then we have to apply this reasoning to the world as it actually is, which will mean ascertaining what will actually be the result of adopting certain principles and policies, and how this will actually impinge upon the interests of ourselves and others. Only so can we achieve a morality suited for use in real life; and nobody who goes through this reasoning in real life will adopt principles which permit slavery, because of the miseries which in real life it causes. Utilitarianism can thus show what is wrong with slavery; and so far as I can see it is the kind of moral reasoning best able to show this, as opposed to merely *protesting* that slavery is wrong.

---

16 See fn. 13 above, and my *Freedom and Reason* (Oxford: Oxford University Press, 1963), especially chap. 6.

This is a revised version of a lecture given in 1978 in the Underwood Memorial Series, Wesleyan University, Middletown, Connecticut.

25

Toward a Credible
Form of Utilitarianism

RICHARD BRANDT

*Richard Brandt (b. 1910) has taught philosophy at Swarthmore College
and, more recently, at the University of Michigan. He has published many
articles on ethics and the philosophy of mind. His books include* Hopi
Ethics, Ethical Theory, *and* A Theory of the Good and the Right. *This
selection originally appeared in* Morality and the Language of Conduct,
edited by Hector-Neri Castañeda and George Nakhnikian.

*In the selection, Brandt tries to formulate a version of rule-utilitarianism
that is not open to decisive objections. Rule-utilitarianism says that we
should apply the principle of utility ("do what will produce the best
results") to choices among rules or systems of rules rather than to
individual acts. But how, exactly, should we do this? Should we ask what
would happen if everyone followed a given set of rules? What would
happen if the rules were learned and accepted by a society of people of
average consciousness? What would happen if the rules were learned and
accepted by all actual members of the agent's society? In posing the
question, should we consider members of other societies? And how, in any
case, can we formulate systems of rules to resolve potential conflicts within
those systems? As Brandt proceeds, he offers detailed and careful answers
to these questions. By working through these answers, we learn much
about the resources of rule-utilitarianism.*

INTRODUCTION

This paper is an attempt to formulate, in a tolerably precise way, a
type of utilitarian ethical theory which is not open to obvious and catastrophic
objections. It is not my aim especially to advocate the kind of view finally
stated, although I do believe it is more acceptable than any other type of
utilitarianism.

• • •

The view to be discussed is a form of "rule-utilitarianism." This terminology
must be explained. I call a utilitarianism "act-utilitarianism" if it holds that
the rightness of an act is fixed by the utility of *its* consequences, as compared

with those of other acts the agent might perform instead. Act-utilitarianism is hence an atomistic theory: the value of the effects of a single act on the world is decisive for its rightness. "Rule-utilitarianism," in contrast, applies to views according to which the rightness of an act is not fixed by *its* relative utility, but by conformity with general rules or principles; the utilitarian feature of these theories consists in the fact that the correctness of these rules or principles is fixed in some way by the utility of their general acceptance. In contrast with the atomism of act-utilitarianism, rule-utilitarianism is in a sense an organic theory: the rightness of individual acts can be ascertained only by assessing a whole social policy.

Neither form of utilitarianism is necessarily committed on the subject of what counts as "utility": not on the meaning or function of such phrases as "maximize intrinsic good," and not on the identity of intrinsic goods—whether enjoyments, or states of persons, or states of affairs, such as equality of distribution.

In recent years, types of rule-utilitarianism have been the object of much interest. And for good reason. Act-utilitarianism, at least given the assumptions about what is valuable which utilitarians commonly make, has implications which it is difficult to accept. It implies that if you have employed a boy to mow your lawn and he has finished the job and asks for his pay, you should pay him what you promised only if you cannot find a better use for your money. It implies that when you bring home your monthly pay-check you should use it to support your family and yourself only if it cannot be used more effectively to supply the needs of others. It implies that if your father is ill and has no prospect of good in his life, and maintaining him is a drain on the energy and enjoyments of others, then, if you can end his life without provoking any public scandal or setting a bad example, it is your positive duty to take matters into your own hands and bring his life to a close. A virtue of rule-utilitarianism, in at least some of its forms, is that it avoids at least some of such objectionable implications.

In the present paper I wish to arrive at a more precise formulation of a rule-utilitarian type of theory which is different from act-utilitarianism and which is not subject to obvious and catastrophic difficulties. To this end I shall, after an important preliminary discussion, begin by considering two formulations, both supported by distinguished philosophers, which, as I shall show, lead us in the wrong direction. This discussion will lead to a new formulation devised to avoid the consequences of the first theories. I shall then describe three problems which the new theory seems to face, and consider how—by amendments or otherwise—these difficulties may be met.

1. UTILITARIANISM AS A THEORY ABOUT THE OBJECTIVELY RIGHT

Before we can proceed there is a preliminary issue to be settled. It is generally agreed that utilitarianism is a proposal about which acts are *right* or *wrong*.

Unfortunately it is also widely held—although this is a matter of dispute—that these terms are used in several senses. Hence, in order to state the utilitarian thesis clearly, we must identify which sense of these words (if there is more than one) we have in mind. Utilitarianism may be clearly false in all of its forms if it is construed as a universal statement about which acts are right or wrong, in some of the senses in which these words are, or at least are supposed to be, used.

It is plausible to say that "wrong" is sometimes used in a sense equivalent to "morally blameworthy" or "reprehensible," in a sense which implies the propriety of disapproval of the agent for his deed. Now, if utilitarianism is understood as a theory about right and wrong actions in this sense, I believe it is an indefensible theory in all its forms. For we have good reason to think that whether an act is wrong in this sense depends in part on such things as whether the agent sincerely believed he was doing his duty, whether the temptation to do what he did was so strong that only a person of very unusual firmness of will would have succeeded in withstanding it, and whether the agent's action was impulsive and provoked, or deliberate and unprovoked. If whether an act is wrong depends in part on any one of these factors, then it is difficult to see how the utilitarian thesis that rightness or wrongness is in some sense a function of utility can be correct.

We can, however, construe utilitarianism as a thesis about which acts are right or wrong in some other sense. It may, for instance, be taken as a theory about which acts are right or wrong in a forward-looking sense, which I shall call the "objective" sense. But what is this sense?

• • •

If we . . . say that "duty" is sometimes used in a sense such that whether something is one's duty depends on what the facts really are, then we are conceding that the word (and, presumably, "right" and "wrong" *and* "moral obligation") is sometimes used in an "objective" sense—the sense in which G. E. Moore thought it was sometimes used when he wrote *Ethics and Principia Ethica*. And if so, it is not entirely stupid to propose, as Moore did, that furthermore, an act is right, in that objective sense of "right," if and only if its *actual* consequences, whether foreseeable at the time or not, are such that the performance of the act produces at least as much intrinsic good as could be produced by any other act the agent could perform instead. It is this sense of these terms—the sense in which duty (etc.) depends on what the facts really are and not on what the agent thinks about them—which I am terming the "objective" sense. I shall construe utilitarianism as a proposal about which acts are right or wrong in this objective sense.

It would be foolish, however, . . . to affirm without doubt that there is a sense of "duty" in which duty depends on what the facts are and not on what the agent thinks they are—and much more foolish to affirm without doubt that there is *no* sense of "duty" in which duty depends, not on the facts, but on what the agent thinks the facts are, at least after properly careful investigation.

Philosophers who think these words have no "objective" sense at all, or who at least think there is still a third sense of these terms, over and above the two I have sketched, probably can mostly be said to think that these words are used in what we may call the "subjective" sense—and either that this is their only sense or that it is one ordinary sense. They do not agree among themselves about what this sense is. Some of them hold that "right" (etc.) is sometimes so used that—if I may identify their conception by my own terminology, which, of course, some of them would not accept—an act is right in that sense if and only if it would have been right in my objective sense, if the facts had really been what the agent thought they were, or at least would have thought they were if he had investigated properly. What is one's duty, on this view, depends on what the agent thinks about the facts—or would think if he investigated properly—not on what the facts really are. Naturally, if one has this (alleged) sense of "duty" or "right" in mind when formulating the principle of utilitarianism, one will say the principle is that an act is right if and only if the agent *thinks*—or would think, if he investigated properly—it will maximize utility (or have some such relation to utility). Or, perhaps, the principle will say that an act is right if and only if it will maximize expectable utility, or something of the sort.

The question whether there is an objective sense, or a subjective sense, or perhaps both such senses, is a difficult one. Although I think it plausible to suppose there is an "objective" sense, I do feel doubt about the matter. I propose, nevertheless, to discuss utilitarianism as a theory about right and wrong in this sense. I do so for several reasons. First, there are many philosophers who think there is such a sense, and an examination of utilitarianism construed in this way "speaks to their condition."[1] Second, even if there were no such ordinary sense of "right," we could define such a sense by reference to the "subjective" sense of "right" (assuming there is one); and it so happens that we could say all the things that we have occasion to say in ethics by using this defined "objective" sense of "right" and also terms like "blameworthy" and "reprehensible." We could say "all we have occasion to say" in the sense that any statement we make, and think important, could be put in terms of this vocabulary. Third, it is important to see how types of rule-utilitarian theory fare if they are construed as theories about which acts are right or wrong in this sense. Doubtless sometimes writers on this topic have not kept clearly in mind just which sense of "right" they were talking about; it is useful to see what difficulties arise *if* they are to be taken as talking of what is right or wrong in the objective sense. Finally, an assessment of utilitarianisms as theories about which acts are objectively right will enable us to make at least some assessment of utilitarianisms as theories about which acts are subjectively

---

1 Notice that such philosophers are not refuted by the mere consideration that sometimes we say "is right" and not "is probably right" even when we know we lack evidence about some facts that might be relevant to what is right in the objective sense. It would be a mistake to infer from such usage that we are not employing "right" in the objective sense. For, in general, we are entitled to make any assertion roundly without the qualifying word "probable" if we know of no definite grounds for questioning the truth of the assertion.

right, in view of the logical connection indicated above between "right" in the objective sense and "right" in the subjective sense.

2. ACCEPTED RULES VS. JUSTIFIABLE RULES AS THE TEST OF RIGHTNESS

It is convenient to begin by taking as our text some statements drawn from an interesting article by J. O. Urmson. In this paper, Urmson suggested that John Stuart Mill should be interpreted as a rule-utilitarian; and Urmson's opinion was that Mill's view would be more plausible if he were so interpreted. Urmson summarized the possible rule-utilization interpretation of Mill in four propositions, of which I quote the first two:

A. A particular action is justified as being right [in the sense of being morally obligatory] by showing that it is in accord with [is required by] some moral rule. It is shown to be wrong by showing that it transgresses some moral rule.

B. A moral rule is shown to be correct by showing that the recognition of that rule promotes the ultimate end.[2]

Urmson's first proposition could be taken in either of two ways. When it speaks of a "moral rule," it may refer to an *accepted* moral rule, presumably one accepted in the society of the agent. Alternatively, it may refer to a *correct* moral rule, presumably one the recognition of which promotes the ultimate end. If we ask in which way the proposed theory should be taken, in order to arrive at a defensible theory, part of the answer is that qualifications are going to be required, whichever way we take it. I think it more worthwhile and promising, however, to try to develop it in the second interpretation.

•   •   •

For a start, we might summarize the gist of Urmson's proposal, construed in the second way, as follows: "An act is right if and only if it conforms with that set of moral rules, the recognition of which would have significantly desirable consequences." A somewhat modified version of this is what I shall be urging.

One minor amendment I wish to make immediately. I think we should replace the second clause by the expression, "the recognition of which would have the *best* consequences." This amendment may be criticized on the ground that the business of moral rules is with commanding or prohibiting actions whose performance or omission would be quite harmful if practiced widely, but not to require actions which just maximize benefits, especially if the benefit concerns only the agent. It may be said, then, that the amendment I propose is possibly a clue to *perfect* behavior but not to right behavior. But this objection

---

2 J. O. Urmson, "The Interpretation of the Moral Philosophy of J. S. Mill," *Philosophical Quarterly*, Vol. III (1953), 33–39.

overlooks an important point. We must remember that it is a serious matter to have a moral rule at all, for moral rules take conduct out of the realm of preference and free decision. So, for the recognition of a certain moral rule to have good consequences, the benefits of recognition must outweigh the costliness of restricting freedom. Therefore, to recognize a moral rule restricting self-regarding behavior will rarely have the best consequences; rules of prudence should normally not be moral rules. Again, my proposal implies that moral rules will regard services for other people only when it is better to have such services performed from a sense of obligation than not performed at all; so the amendment does not commit us to saying that it is morally obligatory to perform minor altruistic services for others.

But why insist on the amendment? The reason is that the original, as I stated it (but not necessarily as Urmson intended it), is insufficiently comparative in form. The implication is that a rule is acceptable so long as it is significantly better than no regulation at all. But the effect of this is tolerantly to accept a great many rules which we should hardly regard as morally acceptable. Consider promises. There are various possible rules about when promises must be kept. One such possible rule is to require keeping *all* promises, absolutely irrespective of unforeseeable and uncontemplated hardships on the promisee. Recognition of this rule might have good consequences as compared with no rule at all. Therefore it seems to satisfy the unamended formula. Many similar rules would satisfy it. But we know of another rule—the one we recognize—with specifications about allowable exceptions, which would have much better consequences. If we are utilitarian in spirit, we shall want to endorse such a rule but not both of these rules; and the second one is much closer to our view about what our obligations are. The amendment in general endorses as correct many rules which command our support for parallel reasons, and refuses to endorse many others which we reject for parallel reasons.

3. A SPECIOUS RULE-UTILITARIANISM

I shall now digress briefly, in order to bring out the importance of avoiding a form of rule-utilitarianism which seems to differ only insignificantly from our above initial suggestion, and which at first seems most attractive. It is worthwhile doing so, partly because two very interesting and important papers developing a rule-utilitarian theory may be construed as falling into the trap I shall describe.[3] I say only that they "may be" so construed because their authors are possibly using somewhat different concepts and, in particular, may not be thinking of utilitarianism as a thesis about right and wrong in the objective sense.

---

[3] These articles are: J. Harrison, "Utilitarianism, Universalisation, and Our Duty to Be Just," *Proceedings of the Aristotelian Society*, Vol. LIII (1952–1953), pp. 105–134; and R. F. Harrod, "Utilitarianism Revised," *Mind*, n.s. XLV (1936), 137–156.

Suppose that we wrote, instead of the above suggested formulation, the following: "An act is right if and only if it conforms with that set of moral rules, general conformity with which would have best consequences." This phrasing is a bit vague, however, so let us expand it to this: "An act is right if and only if it conforms with that set of general prescriptions for action such that, if everyone always did, from among all the things which he could do on a given occasion, what conformed with these prescriptions, then at least as much intrinsic good would be produced as by conformity with any other set of general prescriptions." This sounds very like our above formulation. It is, however, different in a very important way: for its test of whether an act is right, or a general rule correct, is what would happen if people *really all did act* in a certain way. The test is not the consequences of recognizing a rule, or of acting with such a rule in mind; the test as stated does not require that people do, or even can, think of or formulate, much less apply the rule of a moral code. What is being said is simply that a rule is correct, and corresponding conduct right, if it would have the best consequences for everyone actually to act, for whatever reason, in accordance with the rule. Of course, one of the consequences to be taken into account may be the fact that expectations of conduct according to the rule might be built up, and that people could count on conforming behavior.

This theory is initially attractive. We seem to be appealing to it in our moral reasoning when we say, "You oughtn't to do so-and-so, because if everybody in your circumstances did this, the consequences would be bad."

Nevertheless, the fact is that this theory—however hard it may be to see that it does—has identically the same consequences for behavior as does act-utilitarianism. And since it does, it is a mistake to advocate it as a theory preferable to act-utilitarianism, as some philosophers may have done. Let us see how this is.

Let us ask ourselves: What would a set of moral prescriptions be like, such that general conformity with it, in the sense intended, would have the best consequences? The answer is that the set would contain just one rule, the prescription of the *act-utilitarians:* "Perform an act, among those open to you, which will have at least as good consequences as any other." There cannot be a moral rule, conformity with which could have better consequences than this one. If it really is true that doing a certain thing will have the very best consequences in the long run, everything considered, of all the things I can do, then there is nothing better I can do than this. If everyone always did the very best thing it was possible for him to do, the total intrinsic value produced would be at a maximum. Any act which deviated from this principle would produce less good than some other act which might have been performed. It is clear, then, that the moral rule general conformity with which would produce most good is a rule corresponding to the principle of act-utilitarianism. The two theories, then, have identical consequences for behavior. I am, of course, not at all suggesting that everyone *trying* to produce the best consequences will have the same consequences as everyone *trying* to follow some different set of rules—or that everyone trying to follow some different set of rules may not have better consequences than everyone trying just to produce the best consequences. Far from it. What I am saying is that *succeeding* in producing the best consequences is a kind of success which cannot be improved upon. And it is this which is in question, when we are examining the formula we are now looking at.

To say that succeeding in producing the best consequences cannot be improved upon is consistent with admitting that what will in fact have the best consequences, in view of what other people in fact have done or will do, may be different from what would have had the best consequences if other people were to behave differently from the way in which they did or will do. The behavior of others is part of the context relevant for determining the effects of a given act of any agent.

It may be thought that this reasoning is unfair to this rule-utilitarian view. For what this theory has in mind, it may be said, is rules forbidding classes of actions described in ways other than by reference to their utility—rules forbidding actions like lies, adultery, theft, etc. So, it may be said, the principle of act-utilitarianism is not even a competitor for the position of one of the rules admitted by this theory.

My reply to this objection is twofold. In the first place, it would be rather foolish to suppose that any system of moral rules could omit rules about doing good, rules about doing what will maximize utility. Surely we do wish to include among our rules one roughly to the effect that, if we have the opportunity to do a great deal of good for others at little cost, we should do it. And also a rule to the effect that we should avoid harming others. It is no accident that W. D. Ross's list of seven prima facie obligations contains four which refer to doing good, in one way or another. But the point would still stand even if we ignore this fact. For suppose we set about to describe a set of rules, none of which is explicitly to prescribe *doing good*, but general conformity with which will maximize utility. Now obviously, the set of rules in question will be that set which prescribes, by descriptions which make no reference to having good consequences, exactly that very class of actions which would also be prescribed by the act-utilitarian principle. And one can find a set of rules which will prescribe exactly this class of acts without referring to utility. We can find such a set, because every member of the class of acts prescribed by the act-utilitarian principle will have some other property *on account of which* it will maximize utility in the circumstances. Every act, that is to say, which maximizes utility does so because of some doubtless very complex property that it has. As a result, we can set up a system of prescriptions for action which refer to these complex properties, such that our system of rules will prescribe exactly the set of acts prescribed by the act-utilitarian principle. The set of rules may be enormously long and enormously complex. But this set of rules will have the property of being that set, general conformity with which will maximize utility. And the acts prescribed will be identical with the acts prescribed by the act-utilitarian principle. So, again, the prescriptions for conduct of this form of rule-utilitarianism are identical with those of the act-utilitarian theory.

4. RULE-UTILITARIANISM: A SECOND APPROXIMATION

The whole point of the preceding remarks has been to focus attention on the point that a rule-utilitarianism like Urmson's is different from act-utilitarianism only when it speaks of something like "*recognition* of a rule having the best consequences" instead of something like "*conformity* with a certain rule having the best consequences." With this in mind, we can see clearly one of the virtues of Urmson's proposal, which we interpreted as being: "An act is right if and only if it conforms with that set of moral rules, *the recognition of which* would have the best consequences."

But, having viewed the difficulties of a view verbally very similar to the above, we are now alert to the fact that the formulation we have suggested is itself open to interpretations that may lead to problems. How may we construe Urmson's proposal, so that it is both unambiguous and credible? Of course we do not wish to go to the opposite extreme and take "recognition of" to mean merely "doffing the hat to" without attempt to practice. But how shall we take it?

I suggest the following as a second approximation.

First, let us speak of a set of moral rules as being "learnable" if people of ordinary intelligence are able to learn or absorb its provisions, so as to believe the moral propositions in question in the ordinary sense of "believe" for such contexts.[4] Next, let us speak of "the adoption" of a moral code by a person as meaning "the learning and belief of its provisions (in the above sense) and conformity of behavior to these to the extent we may expect people of ordinary conscientiousness to conform their behavior to rules they believe are principles about right or obligatory behavior." Finally, let us, purely arbitrarily and for the sake of brevity, use the phrase "maximizes intrinsic value" to mean "would produce at least as much intrinsic good as would be produced by any relevant alternative action." With these stipulations, we can now propose, as a somewhat more precise formulation of Urmson's proposal, the following rule-utilitarian thesis: "An act is right if and only if it conforms with that learnable set of rules, the adoption of which by everyone would maximize intrinsic value."

This principle does not at all imply that the rightness or wrongness of an act is contingent upon the agent's having *thought about* all the complex business of the identity of a set of ideal moral rules; it asserts, rather, that an act is right if and only if it *conforms* to such a set of rules, regardless of what the agent may think. Therefore the principle is not disqualified from being a correct principle about what is objectively right or wrong, in Moore's sense; for it makes rightness and wrongness a matter of the facts, and totally independent of what the agent thinks is right, or of what the agent thinks about the facts,

---

4 To say that a moral code can be learned by a person is not to say he can learn to *recite* it. It is enough if he learns it well enough to recall the relevant rule when stimulated by being in a context to which it is relevant. Learning a moral code is thus like learning a complex route into a large city: we may not be able to draw it or explain to others what it is, but when we drive it and have the landmarks before us, we remember each turn we are to make.

or of the evidence the agent may have, or of what is probably the case on the basis of this evidence.

An obvious merit of this principle is that it gives expression to at least part of our practice or procedure in trying to find out what is right or wrong. For when we are in doubt about such matters, we often try to think out how it would work in practice to have a moral code which prohibited or permitted various actions we are considering. We do not, of course, ordinarily do anything as complicated as try to think out the *complete* ideal moral code; we are content with considering whether certain specific injunctions relevant to the problem we are considering might be included in a good and workable code. Nevertheless, we are prepared to admit that the whole ideal code is relevant. For if someone shows us that a specific injunction which we think would be an acceptable part of a moral code clearly would not work out in view of other provisions necessary to an ideal code, we should agree that a telling point had been made and revise our thinking accordingly.

In order to get a clearer idea of the kind of "set of rules" (with which right actions must conform) which could satisfy the conditions this rule-utilitarian principle lays down, let us note some general features such a set presumably would have. First, it would contain rules giving directions for recurrent situations which involve conflicts of human interests. Presumably, then, it would contain rules rather similar to W. D. Ross's list of prima facie obligations: rules about the keeping of promises and contracts, rules about debts of gratitude such as we may owe to our parents, and, of course, rules about not injuring other persons and about promoting the welfare of others where this does not work a comparable hardship on us. Second, such a set of rules would not include petty restrictions; nor, at least for the most part, would it contain purely prudential rules. Third, the rules would not be very numerous; an upper limit on quantity is set by the ability of ordinary people to learn them. Fourth, such a set of rules would not include unbearable demands; for their inclusion would only serve to bring moral obligation into discredit. Fifth, the set of rules adoption of which would have the best consequences could not leave too much to discretion. It would make concessions to the fact that ordinary people are not capable of perfectly fine discriminations, and to the fact that, not being morally perfect, people of ordinary conscientiousness will have a tendency to abuse a moral rule where it suits their interest. We must remember that a college dormitory rule like "Don't play music at such times or in such a way as to disturb the study or sleep of others" would be ideally flexible if people were perfect; since they aren't, we have to settle for a rule like "No music after 10 P.M." The same thing is true for a moral code. The best moral code has to allow for the fact that people are what they are; it has to be less flexible and less efficient than a moral code that was to be adopted by perfectly wise and perfectly conscientious people could be.

Should we think of such a moral code as containing only prescriptions for situations likely to arise in *everyone's* life—rules like "If you have made a promise, then . . ." or "If you have a parent living, then treat him thus-and-so"? Or should we think of it as containing distinct sets of prescriptions for *different roles or statuses,* such as "If you are a policeman, then . . ." or "If you are a physician, then . . ."? And if the ideal code is to contain different prescriptions for different roles and statuses, would it not be so complex that it could not be learned by people of ordinary intelligence? The answer to these questions is that the rule-utilitarian is not committed, by his theory, to the necessity of such special codes, although I believe he may well admit their desirability—admit, for instance, that it is a good thing for a physician to carry a rule in his mental kit, specially designed to answer the question, "Shall I treat a patient who does not pay his bill?" In any case, our rule-utilitarian theory can *allow* for such special rules. Nor is there a difficulty in the fact that people of normal intelligence could hardly learn all these special sets of rules. For we can mean, by saying that a code can be "learned" by people of ordinary intelligence, that any person can learn all the rules relevant to the problem *he* will face. A rule-utilitarian will not, of course, have in mind a moral code which in some part is secret—for instance, lawyers having a moral code known only to themselves, a code which it would be harmful for others to know about. For surely in the long run it could not have best consequences for a society to have a moral code, perhaps granting special privileges to some groups, which could not stand the light of public knowledge.

5. FIRST PROBLEM:
MORAL CODES FOR AN IMPERFECT SOCIETY

Our "second approximation" to a rule-utilitarian principle has proposed that an act is right if and only if it conforms with the requirements of a learnable moral code, the adoption of which by *everyone* would maximize utility—and meaning by "adoption of a code" the learning and belief that the code lays down the requirements for moral behavior, and conformity to it to the extent we may expect from people of *ordinary conscientiousness.*

The italicized words in the preceding paragraph indicate two respects in which the proposed test of rightness in a sense departs from reality. In actuality moral codes are not subscribed to by everybody in all particulars: there is virtual unanimity on some items of what we call "the code of the community" (such as the prohibition of murder and incest), but on other matters there is less unanimity (in the United States, the "code" permits artificial birth-control measures despite disapproval by many Catholics), and it is a somewhat arbitrary matter to decide when the disagreement has become so general that we ought not to speak of something as part of the code of the community at all. There is probably some measure of disagreement on many or most moral matters in most modern communities (and, surely, in at least many primitive communities). Furthermore, our proposal, in an effort to be definite about the degree of commitment involved in the "adoption" of a code, spoke of an "ordinary conscientiousness." This again departs from reality. Ordinary conscientiousness may be the exception: many people are extremely, perhaps even overly, conscientious; at the other extreme, some people act as if they have developed no such thing as a conscience at all. It is characteristic of actual communities that there is a wide range in degrees of conscientiousness.

As a result of these departures from reality, our test for rightness savors a bit of the utopian. We are invited to think of different worlds, each populated by people of "ordinary conscientiousness," all of whom are inoculated with a standard moral code. We are to decide whether given types of action are right or wrong by considering which of these hypothetical communities would realize a maximum of value.

There is force in the proposal. In fact, if we are thinking of sponsoring some ideal, this conception is a useful one for appraising whatever ideal we are considering. Just as we might ask whether large military establishments or a capitalist economy would be suitable for the ideal community of the future, so we can ask whether certain features of our present moral code would be suitable in such a community. It may be that such a conception should play a large role in deciding what ultimate ideals we should espouse.

Nevertheless, this conception may, from its very framework, necessarily be unsuitable for deciding the rightness of actions in the real world. It appears that, in fact, this is the case with both of the features mentioned above.

First, the proposal is to test rightness by the desirability of a rule in a moral code among people of ordinary conscientiousness. Now, in a community composed of people of ordinary conscientiousness we do not have to provide for the contingency of either saints or great sinners. In particular, we do not have to provide for the occurrence of people like Adolf Hitler. In such a community, presumably, we could get along with a minimal police force, perhaps an unarmed police force. Similarly, it would seem there would be no value in a moral prescription like "Resist evil men." In the community envisaged, problems of a certain sort would presumably not arise, and therefore the moral code need not have features designed to meet those problems. Very likely, for instance, a moral code near to that of extreme pacifism would work at least as well as a code differing in its nonpacifism.

More serious is the flaw in the other feature: that the test of rightness is to be compatibility with the requirements of the moral code, adoption of which *by everyone* would maximize utility. The trouble with this is that it permits behavior which really would be desirable if everyone agreed, but which might be objectionable and undesirable if not everyone agreed. For instance, it may well be that it would have the best consequences if the children are regarded as responsible for an elderly parent who is ill or needy; but it would be most unfortunate if the members of a Hopi man's native household—primarily his sisters and their families—decided that their presently recognized obligation had no standing on this account, since the result would be that as things now stand, no one at all would take the responsibility. Again, if everyone recognized an obligation to share in duties pertaining to national defense, it would be morally acceptable to require this legally; but it would hardly be morally acceptable to do so if there are pacifists who on moral grounds are ready to die rather than bear arms. And similarly for other matters about which there are existing and pronounced moral convictions.

It seems clear that some modification must be made if our rule-utilitarian proposal is to have implications consistent with the moral convictions of thoughtful people. Unfortunately it is not clear just what the modification should be. The one I am inclined to adopt is as follows. First, we must drop that part of our conception which assumes that people in our hypothetical societies are of ordinary conscientiousness. We want to allow for the existence of both saints and sinners and to have a moral code to cope with them. In order to do this, we had better move closer to Urmson's original suggestion. We had better drop the notion of "adoption" and replace it by his term "recognition," meaning by "recognition by all" simply "belief by all that the rules formulate moral requirements." Second, we must avoid the conception of the acceptance of all the rules of a given moral code by *everybody* and replace it by something short of this, something which does not rule out the problems created by actual convictions about morals. Doing so means a rather uneasy compromise, because we cannot sacrifice the central feature of the rule-utilitarian view, which is that the rightness of an act is to be tested by whether it conforms with rules the (somehow) general acceptance of which would maximize utility. The compromise I propose is this: that the test whether an act is right is whether it is compatible with that set of rules which, were it to replace the moral commitments of members of the *actual society* at the time, *except where there are already fairly decided moral convictions,* would maximize utility.

The modified theory, then, is this: "An act is right if and only if it conforms with that learnable set of rules, the recognition of which as morally binding, roughly at the time of the act, by all actual people insofar as these rules are not incompatible with existing fairly decided moral commitments, would maximize intrinsic value."[5]

The modification has the effect that whether an act is right depends to some extent on such things as (1) how large a proportion of the actual population is conscientious and (2) what are the existing fairly decided moral beliefs at the time. This result is not obviously a mistake.

6. SECOND PROBLEM: CONFLICTS OF RULES

The objection is sure to be raised against any rule-utilitarian theory of the general sort we are considering that the whole conception is radically misconceived. For the theory proposes that what makes an act right is its

---

[5] This formulation is rather similar in effect to one suggested to me by Wilfrid Sellars. (I have no idea whether he now inclines toward it, or whether he ever did lean toward it strongly.) This is: "An act is right if and only if it conforms with that set of rules the *teaching of which* to the society of the agent, at the time of the action, would maximize welfare." This formulation is simpler, but it has its own problems. Teaching to which and how many individuals? By whom? With what skill and means? We should remember that it may be unwise to teach children the rules that are best for adults and that it may sometimes be desirable to teach ideals which are more extreme than we want people actually to live by, e.g., those of the Sermon on the Mount.

conformity to the set of rules, recognition of which would maximize utility; and it is proposed that if we are in serious doubt whether an action would be right, we should ask ourselves whether it would conform with a utility-maximizing set of rules. Now, the objection will run, the very conception of such a set of rules evaporates, or else appears to involve contradictions, when we try to get it in sharp focus. The very idea of a set of rules simple enough to be learned and different from act-utilitarianism, and at the same time sufficiently comprehensive and precise to yield directions for conduct in every situation which may arise, is an impossible dream.

The reason is that moral problems are often quite complex. There are pros and cons—obligations and counter-obligations—which have to be weighed delicately. For instance, a promise that has been made to do something is normally a point in favor of saying that doing it is obligatory; but just how much force the promise will have depends on various circumstances, such as when it was made, how solemnly it was made, whether it was fully understood by both parties, etc. The force of these circumstances cannot be stated and weighed by any set of rules. There is a moral to be drawn, it may be said, from W. D. Ross's theory of prima facie obligations: Ross could provide no general direction for what to do when prima facie obligations conflict; he had to leave the resolution of such conflicts to conscience or intuition. So, in general, no code simple enough to be written down and learned (and different from act-utilitarianism) can prescribe what is right in complex cases.

The difficulty is obviously a serious one. If the very concept of a complete code, the recognition of which would maximize utility, cannot be explained in detail, then the proposal that the rightness of every action is fixed by its conformity with the provisions of such a code must be abandoned.

What must be done to meet this charge? Of course, it cannot be demanded that we actually produce the ideal moral code for our society, or even a complete code of which the correct code might be supposed to be a variation. What can be fairly demanded is that we describe classes of rules or elements which may be expected in the ideal code, and that we make clear, in the course of this description, that the rules constituting the classes are simple enough to be learned, and that a person who had learned the rules of the several classes would be in a position to give an answer to all moral questions—or at least as definite an answer as can reasonably be expected. We may suppose that, if the theory is to be plausible, these classes of rules will be familiar—that they will be rules which thoughtful people do use in deciding moral issues. Let us see what can be said.

It is clear that a complete moral code must contain rules or principles of more than one level. The lowest level will consist of rules devised to cover familiar recurrent situations, presumably rather like those proposed by Ross in his formulation of prima facie obligations. Thus, it will contain rules like "Do not injure conscious beings," "Do what you have promised to do," etc. On reflection, we can see that such rules must be qualified in two ways. First, each of them must conclude with an exceptive clause something like "except as otherwise provided in this code." But second, they must be more complex than our samples; as Ross well knew, such simple rules do not state accurately what we think are our prima facie obligations—and presumably such rules are not the rules it would maximize welfare to have recognized as first-order rules. Consider, for instance the rule I have suggested about promises. It is too simple, for we do not seriously believe that *all* promises have even a prima facie claim to be fulfilled; nor would it be a good thing for people to think they ought. For instance, we think there is no obligation at all to keep a promise made on the basis of deliberate misrepresentation by the promisee; and it is to the public interest that we should think as we do. Just as the law of contracts lists various types of contracts which it is against the public interest for the courts to enforce, so there are types of promises the fulfillment of which we do not think obligatory, and a moral requirement to fulfill them would be contrary to the public interest. The lowest-level group of rules, then, will include one about promise-keeping which will state explicitly which types of promises must be kept except when some more stringent obligation intervenes. And the same for the other basic moral rules.

I do not know if anyone would contend that it would be impossible to write down an exact statement formulating our total prima facie obligations—the kinds of considerations which to some extent make a moral claim on agents. I do not know if anyone would say that in principle we cannot state exactly the list of prima facie obligations it would maximize utility for everyone to feel. Whether or not anyone does say that a list of exact prima facie obligations cannot be stated, I know of no solid argument which can be put forward to show that this is the case. I do not believe a satisfactory list *has* been provided (Ross's statement being quite abbreviated), but I know of no sound reason for thinking that it cannot be. It would not, I think, be an impossible inquiry to determine what is the total set of distinct fundamental prima facie obligations people in fact do recognize in their moral thinking.

A set of first-level rules, however, is not enough. For moral perplexities arise most often where there are conflicts of prima facie obligations, where there would be conflicts of the first-level moral rules. If the rule-utilitarian theory is to work, it must provide for the resolution of such perplexities. How can this be done?

The problem can be partially met by supposing that a complete moral code will contain second-level rules specifically prescribing for conflicts of the basic rules. One second-level rule might be: "Do not injure anyone solely in order to produce something good, unless the good achieved be substantially greater than the injury." In fact we already learn and believe rules roughly of this kind. For instance, Ross suggested in *The Right and the Good* that we think there is normally a stronger obligation to avoid injury to others than to do good or to keep one's promises. A moral code can contain some such second-order rules without intolerable complexity.

But such rules will hardly be numerous enough to solve all the problems. And the rule we stated was not precise: it used the vague phrase "substantially greater," which is clear enough, in context, to decide for many situations, but it is by no means precise enough to legislate for all. I think, therefore, that if the very conception of a set of rules simple enough to be learned and adequate to adjudicate all possible cases is to be intelligible, it must be possible to formulate a consistent and plausible "remainder-rule," that is, a top-level rule giving adequate directions for all cases for which the lower-level rules do not prescribe definitely enough or for which their prescriptions are conflicting. We are not here called upon to identify the correct remainder-rule—although we know that the rule-utilitarian theory is that the correct one is the one the recognition of which (etc.) would do most good. What we are called upon to do is to sketch out what such a rule might well be like.

It is worthwhile to mention two possibilities for a remainder-rule.[6] First, such a rule might specify that all cases not legislated for by other clauses in the code be decided simply on the basis of comparative utility of consequences. For such cases, then, the remainder-rule would prescribe exactly what the act-utilitarian principle prescribes. Second (and I think this possibility the more interesting), the remainder-rule might be: "One is obligated to perform an action if and only if a person who knew the relevant facts and had them vividly in mind, had been carefully taught the other rules of this code, and was uninfluenced by interests beyond those arising from learning the code, would feel obligated to perform that action." Such a rule could decide cases not legislated for by the remainder of the code only if the explicit rules were taught so as to be connected with different degrees of *felt obligation*. In some cases such an association could be established by the very content of the rule, for instance, in the case of a rule stating that there is an obligation not to injure others, and that the obligation increases in strength with the amount of injury involved. Another example is that of second-level rules about the priorities of first-level rules. In other cases the association might be fixed simply by the relative insistence or firmness of the teachers, with respect to the rule in question. As a result of the rules being taught in this way, conscientious people would have established in them hesitations, of different degrees of strengths, to do certain sorts of things—in other words, a sense of obligation to do or avoid certain things, the sense having different force for different things. Therefore, when persons so trained were faced with a situation in which lower-order rules gave conflicting directions (and where no higher-order rule assigned an explicit priority), they would hesitate to resolve the problem in various ways because of the built-in sense of obligation. Now, the proposed remainder-rule would in effect be a somewhat qualified prescription to take whatever course of action would leave morally well-trained people least dissatisfied. (I imagine that something like this is what Ross had in mind when he said that in complex situations one must rely on one's intuition.) The rule-utilitarian proposal is, of course, that the correct degree of felt obligation to be associated with a rule is, like the order of priorities expressed in the second-level rules, fixed by the

---

6 It will probably be clear why the remainder-rule cannot simply be the rule-utilitarian principle itself. For the rule-utilitarian principle states that an act is right if and only if it conforms with the rules of a certain kind of code. If one of the rules of the code were the rule-utilitarian principle, it would contain reference to a code which presumably would itself contain again the rule-utilitarian principle, and so on ad infinitum.

relative utilities of the various possible arrangements—partly the utilities of the adjudications of complex cases by the remainder-rule.

It is after all possible, then, for a moral code different from act-utilitarianism to be simple enough to be learned and still able to decide for all problems which may arise.

7. THIRD PROBLEM:
RELATIVITY TO THE AGENT'S SOCIETY

One final complication may be needed in the rule-utilitarian proposal. In place of saying that the rightness of an act is fixed by conformity with the prescriptions of the moral code, the recognition of which as morally binding by people (etc.) *everywhere* would maximize intrinsic good, we might say that the rightness of an act is fixed by conformity with the prescriptions of that moral code, the recognition of which as morally binding by people *in the agent's society* would maximize intrinsic good. This kind of complication should be avoided if possible, because it is difficult to assign a definite meaning to the phrase "in the agent's society." We should notice, incidentally, that it is *not* suggested that the test be the maximizing of intrinsic good only in the agent's society; such a thesis would promise quite dubious consequences.

A modification of this sort would admit a kind of relativism into ethics. For, while it is consistent with the rule-utilitarian principle itself being correct for everyone, it has the consequence that an act might be right in one society which would be wrong in another society. For instance, it might be a moral obligation for a man to support his elderly father in one society, but not his obligation in another society. Most philosophers, however, would probably view this kind of relativism as innocuous, since such differences in obligation could occur only when conditions in the two societies were different in such a way that recognition of one rule by one society would have best consequences, and recognition of a different rule by another society would also have best consequences.

But is there any reason for adopting this complicating feature? Why not say that, if a moral code is valid for anybody it is valid for everybody? Surely, it will be said, *some* moral rules are universally valid—perhaps, for instance, a rule forbidding a person from causing another pain merely in order to give himself pleasure. And if so, perhaps we can go on, with Ross, to say that the fundamental principles of obligation are universally true, although their application in special circumstances may give rise to an *appearance* of society-bound rules. For instance, Ross would say that "Keep your promises" is universally a true and important first-level rule. But in some places a thing is promised with certain mutually-understood but not explicitly stated conditions, while in other places the implicit conditions are different. As a result, the conduct required, in view of the explicit promise, by the universally valid principle is different in different societies. Or again, "Thou shalt not steal" or "Thou shalt not commit adultery" might be construed as universally valid injunctions, the first being not to take property which, according to the institutions of the society, is recognized as belonging to another, and the second, not to have sexual relations with any person if either party is, according to the custom of the society, the marriage partner of another. All fundamental moral principles, then, may be thought to have intersocietal validity; only the specific conduct enjoined or prohibited may vary from one society to another because of local conditions.

This view, however, faces serious difficulties. In order to bring these into focus, let us consider an example: the obligations of a father to his children. In the United States, I believe, it is thought that a father should see to it—within the limits of his financial capacities—that his children receive a good education, enjoy physical and mental health, and have some security against unforeseeable catastrophes. Contrast this with a society, like that of the Hopi, in which responsibility for children falls primarily on a household, "household" being defined primarily by blood-ties with the mother. In this situation, responsibility for children is primarily a problem for the mother and her blood relatives. (The factual accuracy of these assertions is not, I believe, a material consideration.) In the United States, the father is generally charged with responsibility for bringing the welfare, or prospects of welfare, of his children up to a certain rough minimum; in the Hopi society this responsibility falls roughly on other persons, although the father may share in it as far as affection dictates. Correspondingly, in the United States grown children have responsibility for their father, whereas among the Hopi the responsibility for the father belongs elsewhere—not on a man's own children but on the household of the father, the one to which he belongs through blood-ties with his mother and siblings.

I take it nobody is going to argue that fathers in the United States do not have the obligations they are generally thought to have, or that Hopi fathers do have obligations which are generally thought to fall elsewhere. (There may be some exceptions to this.) Therefore, if there is to be a *universal* moral rule locating obligations for the welfare of children, it will be one which roughly places it, at least for the present, where it is recognized to be in these societies. What kind of rule might this be? It is hard to say. Very possibly there is uniformity of assignment of such responsibilities in societies with a certain kind of social structure, and hence one could conceivably state a general rule prescribing that fathers do certain things in societies of a specified sociological description. It is doubtful, however, whether such a rule is simple enough to be learned. Moreover, social structures may be too much organic wholes to permit even such generalizations; if so, in respect of some kinds of conduct there can be no general, intersocietally valid moral rule at all.

There is another way of putting much the same point. Instead of asking whether we can frame a general rule which will have implications for particular societies coincident with what we should want to say are the actual locations of responsibilities in these societies, we might ask whether any universal rules can be framed, recognition of which as morally binding would have consequences comparably as good as local rules, devised on the basis of examination of individual institutional structures as a whole. Is the universality of moral rules to be so sacrosanct that we shall not recognize a moral rule as binding on a given society unless it can be viewed as a special case of some universally valid rule? A person who wishes to make utility the test of moral rules will, I think, wish to make the utility of local rules his test.

It may be supposed that the example of family obligations is untypically complex. But to do so would be a mistake. The responsibilities of physicians and teachers—or professional men in general—to the individuals whom they serve pose similar difficulties. So do the ethics of borrowing and the charging of interest. It is possible that the broad outlines of prohibited and required behavior will be rather similar in all societies. But when we come to the fine points—the exceptions, the qualifications, the priorities—we are in for difficulties if we must defend the view that statable universal rules are the best ones for everybody to feel bound by, or that they conform to serious opinions about the location of obligations in various types of society. This, I think, has been the conclusion of various "self-realizationist" philosophers like A. MacBeath and C. A. Campbell.

Let us then consider (without necessarily insisting that it be adopted) the view that the rightness of an act is fixed by conformity with the prescriptions of that moral code, the recognition of which as morally binding by people (etc.) *in the agent's society* would maximize intrinsic good. Can we propose a meaning of "in the agent's society" sufficiently definite that we can say the proposal is at least a clear one?

How shall we identify "the society" of the agent? This question could have been answered fairly simply in much earlier times when all societies were rather clearly demarcated atomic units, although when we remember the relationships of the *kula* reported by Malinowski, we can see that matters were not always so simple even among primitive peoples. The question is difficult in a modern civilization. What is a Columbia University professor who lives in the suburbs to count as his "society"? The faculty club? His suburb? New York City? The state of New York? Any choice seems a bit arbitrary. Or suppose Khrushchev makes a promise to Eisenhower. What society should we bear in mind as the one the utility of a set of rules in which sets the standard of right and wrong?

Very tentatively, I am inclined to suggest that we understand the "society of an agent" in the following way. An individual, I suggest, may live in several "moral worlds," and the rules for these several moral worlds may be different. For one thing, he is a member of a succession of local groups, each one more inclusive than the last: the local community, the metropolitan area, etc. Now a good part of one's life is lived as a resident, a neighbor, a citizen. Insofar as moral problems arise as part of one's life in this capacity, the problem is to be settled by reference to the rules best for the geographical community. How wide a geographical community should we pick? The best answer seems to be: the largest area over which common rules can be adopted without loss of utility. If it were costly in utility to apply to a borough the rules which were the best for the metropolitan area, then we had better consider our case in the light of rules useful for the smaller group. But a person has other roles besides that of citizen and neighbor. One may be a member of groups which transcend the local community—perhaps nation-wide associations, class, or caste. Most important, perhaps, are transactions resulting from the institutional involvement of the participants; for example, business transactions involving corporations or unions, or the affairs of the church, or educational affairs, or the activities of the press or radio. In these cases a segment of the life-relations of the individuals involved consists in their interactions with others who have the same role or who participate in the same institution. In such cases, I suggest that the moral rules governing behavior should be the rules adoption of which by the relevant group (for example, the group participating in a given institution) would be best, as governing the transactions of that group. It may be, of course, that we do not need some of these complications, that there is no need to distinguish the rules for businessmen in dealing with each other or with a union from the ones properly followed in one's relations with wife and neighbor.[7]

8. CONCLUDING REMARKS

The principle with which we end is this: "An act is right if and only if it conforms with that learnable set of rules the recognition of which as morally binding—roughly at the time of the act—by everyone in the society of the agent, except for the retention by individuals of already formed and decided moral convictions, would maximize intrinsic value."[8]

I wish to make three final comments on this principle.

First, one may ask whether a set of moral roles which would maximize intrinsic value in the way described would necessarily be a *just* set of rules. Surely, if the rules are not just, conformity with them will by no means guarantee that an action is right. A further inquiry must be made about whether additional requirements are needed to assure that moral rules are just. It may be that, as I have suggested elsewhere, none is called for if equality of some sort is an intrinsic good.

Second, if the proposed principle is correct, we can give at least a partial answer to a person who asks *why* he ought to perform actions he is obligated to perform, if they conflict with his self-interest. Perhaps a person who asks such a question is merely confused, and his query not worth our attention. But we can say to him that one reason for meeting his obligation is that by doing so he plays the game of living according to the rules which will maximize welfare. And this will be, at least partially, a satisfying answer to a man who is activated by love or sympathy or respect directed at other sentient beings generally.

---

[7] The above discussion shows that the theory that what is right is behavior conforming with the *accepted* rules of the agent's society has complications which have not been adequately discussed.

[8] As the principle now stands, a given individual might have to learn several codes, corresponding to his several roles in society.

Finally, some reflections on the employment of the principle. It is, perhaps, obvious that it is not necessary to advocate that everyone always bear the rule-utilitarian principle in mind in deciding what he ought to do. Not that it would be harmful—beyond the waste of time—to do so; for it is obvious that the clear moral obligations are prescribed by the principle. For example, only an instant's thought is required to see that it is socially useful to recognize the rule that solemn promises should be kept—doubtless with some qualifications. The rule's employment is important, however, in analyzing more difficult cases, in making clear whether a given moral rule should be qualified in a certain way. Of course, it would be foolish to suggest that application of the principle is an easy road to the resolution of moral problems. It may very often be that after most careful reflection along the lines suggested, the most that can be said is that a given action is probably the one which the principle requires. If so, if we accept the principle, we can go on to say that this action is probably the right one.

26

Classical
Utilitarianism

JOHN RAWLS

For biographical information about John Rawls, see reading 21.

In this selection, taken from A Theory of Justice, *chapter 1, Rawls elaborates and criticizes what he views as the intuitive basis of utilitarianism. He argues that utilitarianism draws its plausibility from an analogy between the individual and society. Just as a rational individual tries to maximize his satisfactions over time, so too will a rational society try to maximize the satisfactions of all its members. Thus understood, the principle of utility has a basis that is plausible and elegant.*

Yet that basis also raises problems. When individuals sacrifice for their own future welfare, they themselves are the ultimate beneficiaries. But when a society burdens some for the greater benefit of others, the losers and gainers are different persons. This leads Rawls to end by remarking that "utilitarianism does not take seriously the distinction between persons."

There are many forms of utilitarianism, and the development of the theory has continued in recent years. I shall not survey these forms here, nor take account of the numerous refinements found in contemporary discussions. My aim is to work out a theory of justice that represents an alternative to utilitarian thought generally and so to all of these different versions of it. I believe that the contrast between the contract view and utilitarianism remains essentially the same in all these cases. Therefore I shall compare justice as fairness with familiar variants of intuitionism, perfectionism, and utilitarianism in order to bring out the underlying differences in the simplest way. With this end in mind, the kind of utilitarianism I shall describe here is the strict classical doctrine which receives perhaps its clearest and most accessible formulation in Sidgwick. The main idea is that society is rightly ordered, and therefore just, when its major institutions are arranged so as to achieve the greatest net balance of satisfaction summed over all the individuals belonging to it.[1]

---

1 I shall take Henry Sidgwick's *The Methods of Ethics*, 7th ed. (London, 1907), as summarizing the development of utilitarian moral theory. Book III of his *Principles of Political Economy* (London, 1883) applies this doctrine to questions of economic and social justice, and is a precursor of A. C. Pigou, *The Economics of Welfare* (London, Macmillan, 1920). Sidgwick's

We may note first that there is, indeed, a way of thinking of society which makes it easy to suppose that the most radical conception of justice is utilitarian. For consider: each man in realizing his own interests is certainly free to balance his own losses against his own gains. We may impose a sacrifice on ourselves now for the sake of a greater advantage later. A person quite properly acts, at least when others are not affected, to achieve his own greatest good, to advance his rational ends as far as possible. Now why should not a society act on precisely the same principle applied to the group and therefore regard that which is rational for one man as right for an association of men? Just as the well-being of a person is constructed from the series of satisfactions that are experienced at different moments in the course of his life, so in very much the same way the well-being of society is to be constructed from the fulfillment of the systems of desires of the many individuals who belong to it. Since the principle for an individual is to advance as far as possible his own welfare, his own system of desires, the principle for society is to advance as far as possible the welfare of the group, to realize to the greatest extent the comprehensive system of desire arrived at from the desire of its members. Just as an individual balances present and future gains against present and future losses, so a society may balance satisfactions and dissatisfactions between different individuals. And so by these reflections one reaches the principle of utility in a natural way: a society is properly arranged when its institutions maximize the net balance of satisfaction. The principle of choice for an association of men is interpreted as an extension of the principle of choice for one man. Social justice is the

Outlines of the History of Ethics, 5th ed. (London, 1902), contains a brief history of the utilitarian tradition. We may follow him in assuming, somewhat arbitrarily, that it begins with Shaftesbury's *An Inquiry Concerning Virtue and Merit* (1711) and Hutcheson's *An Inquiry Concerning Moral Good and Evil* (1725). Hutcheson seems to have been the first to state clearly the principle of utility. He says in *Inquiry*, sec. III, §8, that "that action is best, which procures the greatest happiness for the greatest numbers; and that, worst, which, in like manner, occasions misery." Other major eighteenth century works are Hume's *A Treatise of Human Nature* (1739), and *An Enquiry Concerning the Principles of Morals* (1751); Adam Smith's *A Theory of the Moral Sentiments* (1759); and Bentham's *The Principles of Morals and Legislation* (1789). To these we must add the writings of J. S. Mill represented by *Utilitarianism* (1863) and F. Y. Edgeworth's *Mathematical Psychics* (London, 1888).

The discussion of utilitarianism has taken a different turn in recent years by focusing on what we may call the coordination problem and related questions of publicity. This development stems from the essays of R. F. Harrod, "Utilitarianism Revised," *Mind*, vol. 45 (1936); J. D. Mabbott, "Punishment," *Mind*, vol. 48 (1939); Jonathan Harrison, "Utilitarianism, Universalisation, and Our Duty to Be Just," *Proceedings of the Aristotelian Society*, vol. 53 (1952–1953); and J. O. Urmson, "The Interpretation of the Philosophy of J. S. Mill," *Philosophical Quarterly*, vol. 3 (1953). See also J. J. C. Smart, "Extreme and Restricted Utilitarianism," *Philosophical Quarterly*, vol. 6 (1956), and his *An Outline of a System of Utilitarian Ethics* (Cambridge, The University Press, 1961). For an account of these matters, see David Lyons, *Forms and Limits of Utilitarianism* (Oxford, The Clarendon Press, 1965); and Allan Gibbard, "Utilitarianisms and Coordination" (dissertation, Harvard University, 1971). The problems raised by these works, as important as they are, I shall leave aside as not bearing directly on the more elementary question of distribution which I wish to discuss.

Finally, we should note here the essays of J. C. Harsanyi, in particular, "Cardinal Utility in Welfare Economics and in the Theory of Risk-Taking," *Journal of Political Economy*, 1953, and "Cardinal Welfare, Individualistic Ethics, and Interpersonal Comparisons of Utility," *Journal of Political Economy*, 1955; and R. B. Brandt, "Some Merits of One Form of Rule-Utilitarianism," *University of Colorado Studies* (Boulder, Colorado, 1967).

principle of rational prudence applied to an aggregative conception of the welfare of the group (§30).[2]

This idea is made all the more attractive by a further consideration. The two main concepts of ethics are those of the right and the good; the concept of a morally worthy person is, I believe, derived from them. The structure of an ethical theory is, then, largely determined by how it defines and connects these two basic notions. Now it seems that the simplest way of relating them is taken by teleological theories: the good is defined independently from the right, and then the right is defined as that which maximizes the good.[3] More precisely, those institutions and acts are right which of the available alternatives produce the most good, or at least as much good as any of the other institutions and acts open as real possibilities (a rider needed when the maximal class is not a singleton). Teleological theories have a deep intuitive appeal since they seem to embody the idea of rationality. It is natural to think that rationality is maximizing something and that in morals it must be maximizing the good. Indeed, it is tempting to suppose that it is self-evident that things should be arranged so as to lead to the most good.

It is essential to keep in mind that in a teleological theory the good is defined independently from the right. This means two things. First, the theory accounts for our considered judgments as to which things are good (our judgments of value) as a separate class of judgments intuitively distinguishable by common sense, and then proposes the hypothesis that the right is maximizing the good as already specified. Second, the theory enables one to judge the goodness of things without referring to what is right. For example, if pleasure is said to be the sole good, then presumably pleasures can be recognized and ranked in value by criteria that do not presuppose any standards of right, or what we would normally think of as such. Whereas if the distribution of goods is also counted as a good, perhaps a higher order one, and the theory directs us to produce the most good (including the good of distribution among others), we no longer have a teleological view in the classical sense. The problem of distribution falls under the concept of right as one intuitively understands it, and so the theory lacks an independent definition of the good. The clarity and simplicity of classical teleological theories derives largely from the fact that they factor our moral judgments into two classes, the one being characterized separately while the other is then connected with it by a maximizing principle.

---

2 On this point see also D. P. Gauthier, *Practical Reasoning* (Oxford, Clarendon Press, 1963), pp. 126f. The text elaborates the suggestion found in "Constitutional Liberty and the Concept of Justice," *Nomos VI: Justice,* ed. C. J. Friedrich and J. W. Chapman (New York, Atherton Press, 1963), pp. 124f, which in turn is related to the idea of justice as a higher-order administrative decision. See "Justice As Fairness," *Philosophical Review,* 1958, pp. 185–187. . . . That the principle of social integration is distinct from the principle of personal integration is stated by R. B. Perry, *General Theory of Value* (New York, Longmans, Green, and Company, 1926) pp. 674–677. He attributes the error of overlooking this fact to Émile Durkheim and others with similar views. His conception of social integration is that brought about by a shared and dominant benevolent purpose.

3 Here I adopt W. K. Frankena's definition of teleological theories in *Ethics* (Englewood Cliffs, NJ: Prentice Hall, Inc., 1963), p. 13.

Teleological doctrines differ, pretty clearly, according to how the conception of the good is specified. If it is taken as the realization of human excellence in the various forms of culture, we have what may be called perfectionism. This notion is found in Aristotle and Nietzsche, among others. If the good is defined as pleasure, we have hedonism; if as happiness, eudaimonism, and so on. I shall understand the principle of utility in its classical form as defining the good as the satisfaction of desire, or perhaps better, as the satisfaction of rational desire. This accords with the view in all essentials and provides, I believe, a fair interpretation of it. The appropriate terms of social cooperation are settled by whatever in the circumstances will achieve the greatest sum of satisfaction of the rational desires of individuals. It is impossible to deny the initial plausibility and attractiveness of this conception.

The striking feature of the utilitarian view of justice is that it does not matter, except indirectly, how this sum of satisfactions is distributed among individuals any more than it matters, except indirectly, how one man distributes his satisfactions over time. The correct distribution in either case is that which yields the maximum fulfillment. Society must allocate its means of satisfaction whatever these are, rights and duties, opportunities and privileges, and various forms of wealth, so as to achieve this maximum if it can. But in itself no distribution of satisfaction is better than another except that the more equal distribution is to be preferred to break ties.[4] It is true that certain common sense precepts of justice, particularly those which concern the protection of liberties and rights, or which express the claims of desert, seem to contradict this contention. But from a utilitarian standpoint the explanation of these precepts and of their seemingly stringent character is that they are those precepts which experience shows should be strictly respected and departed from only under exceptional circumstances if the sum of advantages is to be maximized.[5] Yet, as with all other precepts, those of justice are derivative from the one end of attaining the greatest balance of satisfaction. Thus there is no reason in principle why the greater gains of some should not compensate for the lesser losses of others; or more importantly, why the violation of the liberty of a few might not be made right by the greater good shared by many. It simply happens that under most conditions, at least in a reasonably advanced stage of civilization, the greatest sum of advantages is not attained in this way. No doubt the strictness of common sense precepts of justice has a certain usefulness in limiting men's propensities to injustice and to socially injurious actions, but the utilitarian believes that to affirm this strictness as a first principle of morals is a mistake. For just as it is rational for one man to maximize the fulfillment of his system of desires, it is right for a society to maximize the net balance of satisfaction taken over all of its members.

The most natural way, then, of arriving at utilitarianism (although not, of course, the only way of doing so) is to adopt for society as a whole the principle of rational choice for one man. Once this is recognized, the place of the impartial

4 On this point see Sidgwick, *The Methods of Ethics*, pp. 416f.

5 See J. S. Mill, *Utilitarianism*, ch. V, last two pars.

spectator and the emphasis on sympathy in the history of utilitarian thought is readily understood. For it is by the conception of the impartial spectator and the use of sympathetic identification in guiding our imagination that the principle for one man is applied to society. It is this spectator who is conceived as carrying out the required organization of the desires of all persons into one coherent system of desire; it is by this construction that many persons are fused into one. Endowed with ideal powers of sympathy and imagination, the impartial spectator is the perfectly rational individual who identifies with and experiences the desires of others as if these desires were his own. In this way he ascertains the intensity of these desires and assigns them their appropriate weight in the one system of desire the satisfaction of which the ideal legislator then tries to maximize by adjusting the rules of the social system. On this conception of society separate individuals are thought of as so many different lines along which rights and duties are to be assigned and scarce means of satisfaction allocated in accordance with rules so as to give the greatest fulfill-ment of wants. The nature of the decision made by the ideal legislator is not, therefore, materially different from that of an entrepreneur deciding how to maximize his profits by producing this or that commodity, or that of a consumer deciding how to maximize his satisfaction by the purchase of this or that collection of goods. In each case there is a single person whose system of desires determines the best allocation of limited means. The correct decision is essentially a question of efficient administration. This view of social coopera-tion is the consequence of extending to society the principle of choice for one man, and then, to make this extension work, conflating all persons into one through the imaginative acts of the impartial sympathetic spectator. Utilitarian-ism does not take seriously the distinction between persons.

27

A Critique of
Utilitarianism

BERNARD WILLIAMS

Bernard Williams (b. 1929) is Knightsbridge Professor of Philosophy at Cambridge University. He has made important contributions to ethics and the philosophy of mind. His books include Problems of the Self, Ethics and the Limits of Philosophy *and, most recently,* Shame and Necessity. *This selection is excerpted from his contribution to* Utilitarianism: For and Against, *coauthored by J. J. C. Smart.*

Williams presents two well-chosen examples to show that utilitarianism distorts various aspects of our moral thought. For one thing, because it focuses exclusively on the outcomes of actions, utilitarianism is said to imply that we are just as responsible for failing to prevent another person from causing harm as we are for actively causing the same amount of harm ourselves. This is inconsistent with the commonly held belief that "each of us is specially responsible for what he does, rather than what other people do." Also, because utilitarianism requires that we abandon our own commitments whenever doing so will maximize utility, it alienates a person "from the projects and attitudes with which he is most closely identified." In this way, utilitarianism is said to undermine an agent's integrity. Because pursuing a project typically involves acting and not merely allowing things to happen, Williams's two objections to utilitarianism are closely linked.

Consequentialism is basically indifferent to whether a state of affairs consists in what I do, or is produced by what I do, where that notion is itself wide enough to include, for instance, situations in which other people do things which I have made them do, or allowed them to do, or encouraged them to do, or given them a chance to do. All that consequentialism is interested in is the idea of these doings being *consequences* of what I do, and that is a relation broad enough to include the relations just mentioned, and many others.

Just what the relation is, is a different question, and at least as obscure as the nature of its relative, cause and effect. It is not a question I shall try to pursue; I will rely on cases where I suppose that any consequentialist would be bound to regard the situations in question as consequences of what the agent does. There are cases where the supposed consequences stand in a rather remote relation to the action, which are sometimes difficult to assess from a practical point of view, but which raise no very interesting question for the present enquiry. The more interesting points about consequentialism lie rather elsewhere. There are certain situations in which the causation of the situation, the relation it has to what I do, is in no way remote or problematic in itself, and entirely justifies the claim that the situation is a consequence of what I do: for instance, it is quite clear, or reasonably clear, that if I do a certain thing, this situation will come about, and if I do not, it will not. So from a consequentialist point of view it goes into the calculation of consequences along with any other state of affairs accessible to me. Yet from some, at least, non-consequentialist points of view, there is a vital difference between some such situations and others: namely, that in some a vital link in the production of the eventual outcome is provided by *someone else's* doing something. But for consequentialism, all causal connexions are on the same level, and it makes no difference, so far as that goes, whether the causation of a given state of affairs lies through another agent, or not.

Correspondingly, there is no relevant difference which consists *just* in one state of affairs being brought about by me, without intervention of other agents, and another being brought about through the intervention of other agents; although some genuinely causal differences involving a difference of value may correspond to that (as when, for instance, the other agents derive pleasure or pain from the transaction), that kind of difference will already be included in the specification of the state of affairs to be produced. Granted that the states of affairs have been adequately described in causally and evaluatively relevant terms, it makes no further comprehensible difference who produces them. It is because consequentialism attaches value ultimately to states of affairs, and its concern is with what states of affairs the world contains, that it essentially involves the notion of *negative responsibility:* that if I am ever responsible for anything, then I must be just as much responsible for things that I allow or fail to prevent, as I am for things that I myself, in the more everyday restricted sense, bring about. Those things also must enter my deliberations, as a responsible moral agent, on the same footing. What matters is what states of affairs the world contains, and so what matters with respect to a given action is what comes about if it is done, and what comes about if it is not done, and those are questions not intrinsically affected by the nature of the causal linkage, in particular by whether the outcome is partly produced by other agents.

The strong doctrine of negative responsibility flows directly from consequentialism's assignment of ultimate value to states of affairs. Looked at from another point of view, it can be seen also as a special application of something that is favoured in many moral outlooks not themselves consequentialist— something which, indeed, some thinkers have been disposed to regard as the essence of morality itself: a principle of impartiality. Such a principle will claim that there can be no relevant difference from a moral point of view which consists just in the fact, not further explicable in general terms, that benefits or harms accrue to one person rather than to another—'it's me' can never in itself be a morally comprehensible reason.[1] This principle, familiar with regard to the reception of harms and benefits, we can see consequentialism as extending to their production: from the moral point of view, there is no comprehensible difference which consists just in my bringing about a certain outcome rather than someone else's producing it. That the doctrine of negative responsibility represents in this way the extreme of impartiality, and abstracts from the identity of the agent, leaving just a locus of causal intervention in the world— that fact is not merely a surface paradox. It helps to explain why consequentialism can seem to some to express a more serious attitude than non-consequentialist views, why part of its appeal is to a certain kind of high-mindedness. Indeed, that is part of what is wrong with it.

For a lot of the time so far we have been operating at an exceedingly abstract level. This has been necessary in order to get clearer in general terms about the differences between consequentialist and other outlooks, an aim which is important if we want to know what features of them lead to what results for our thought. Now, however, let us look more concretely at two examples, to see what utilitarianism might say about them, what we might say about utilitarianism and, most importantly of all, what would be implied by certain ways of thinking about the situations. The examples are inevitably schematized, and they are open to the objection that they beg as many questions as they illuminate. There are two ways in particular in which examples in moral philosophy tend to beg important questions. One is that, as presented, they arbitrarily cut off and restrict the range of alternative courses of action—this objection might particularly be made against the first of my two examples. The second is that they inevitably present one with the situation as a going concern, and cut off questions about how the agent got into it, and correspondingly about moral considerations which might flow from that: this objection might perhaps specially arise with regard to the second of my two situations. These difficulties, however, just have to be accepted, and if anyone finds these examples cripplingly defective in this sort of respect, then he must in his own thought rework them in richer and less question-begging form. If he feels that no presentation of any imagined situation can ever be other than misleading in morality, and that there can never be any substitute for the concrete experienced complexity of actual moral situations, then this discussion, with him, must certainly grind to a halt: but then one may legitimately wonder whether every discussion with him about conduct will not grind to a halt, including any discussion about the actual situations, since discussion about how one would think and feel about situations somewhat different from the actual (that is to say, situations to that extent imaginary) plays an important role in discussion of the actual.

(1) George, who has just taken his Ph.D. in chemistry, finds it extremely difficult to get a job. He is not very robust in health, which cuts down the

---

1 There is a tendency in some writers to suggest that it is not a comprehensible reason at all. But this, I suspect, is due to the overwhelming importance those writers ascribe to the moral point of view.

number of jobs he might be able to do satisfactorily. His wife has to go out to work to keep them, which itself causes a great deal of strain, since they have small children and there are severe problems about looking after them. The results of all this, especially on the children, are damaging. An older chemist, who knows about this situation, says that he can get George a decently paid job in a certain laboratory, which pursues research into chemical and biological warfare. George says that he cannot accept this, since he is opposed to chemical and biological warfare. The older man replies that he is not too keen on it himself, come to that, but after all George's refusal is not going to make the job or the laboratory go away; what is more, he happens to know that if George refuses the job, it will certainly go to a contemporary of George's who is not inhibited by any such scruples and is likely if appointed to push along the research with greater zeal than George would. Indeed, it is not merely concern for George and his family, but (to speak frankly and in confidence) some alarm about this other man's excess of zeal, which has led the older man to offer to use his influence to get George the job. . . . George's wife, to whom he is deeply attached, has views (the details of which need not concern us) from which it follows that at least there is nothing particularly wrong with research into CBW. What should he do?

(2)   Jim finds himself in the central square of a small South American town. Tied up against the wall are a row of twenty Indians, most terrified, a few defiant, in front of them several armed men in uniform. A heavy man in a sweat-stained khaki shirt turns out to be the captain in charge and, after a good deal of questioning of Jim which establishes that he got there by accident while on a botanical expedition, explains that the Indians are a random group of the inhabitants who, after recent acts of protest against the government, are just about to be killed to remind other possible protestors of the advantages of not protesting. However, since Jim is an honoured visitor from another land, the captain is happy to offer him a guest's privilege of killing one of the Indians himself. If Jim accepts, then as a special mark of the occasion, the other Indians will be let off. Of course, if Jim refuses, then there is no special occasion, and Pedro here will do what he was about to do when Jim arrived, and kill them all. Jim, with some desperate recollection of schoolboy fiction, wonders whether if he got hold of a gun, he could hold the captain, Pedro and the rest of the soldiers to threat, but it is quite clear from the set-up that nothing of that kind is going to work: any attempt at that sort of thing will mean that all the Indians will be killed, and himself. The men against the wall, and the other villagers, understand the situation, and are obviously begging him to accept. What should he do?

To these dilemmas, it seems to me that utilitarianism replies, in the first case, that George should accept the job, and in the second, that Jim should kill the Indian. Not only does utilitarianism give these answers but, if the situations are essentially as described and there are no further special factors, it regards them, it seems to me, as *obviously* the right answers. But many of us would certainly wonder whether, in (1), that could possibly be the right answer at all; and in the case of (2), even one who came to think that perhaps that was the answer, might well wonder whether it was obviously the answer. Nor is it just a question of the rightness or obviousness of these answers. It is also a question of what sort of considerations come into finding the answer. A feature of utilitarianism is that it cuts out a kind of consideration which for some others makes a difference to what they feel about such cases: a consideration involving the idea, as we might first and very simply put it, that each of us is specially responsible for what *he* does, rather than for what other people do. This is an idea closely connected with the value of integrity. It is often suspected that utilitarianism, at least in its direct forms, makes integrity as a value more or less unintelligible. I shall try to show that this suspicion is correct. Of course, even if that is correct, it would not necessarily follow that we should reject utilitarianism; perhaps, as utilitarians sometimes suggest, we should just forget about integrity, in favour of such things as a concern for the general good. However, if I am right, we cannot merely do that, since the reason why utilitarianism cannot understand integrity is that it cannot coherently describe the relations between a man's projects and his actions.

TWO KINDS OF REMOTER EFFECTS

A lot of what we have to say about this question will be about the relations between my projects and other people's projects. But before we get on to that, we should first ask whether we are assuming too hastily what the utilitarian answers to the dilemmas will be. In terms of more direct effects of the possible decisions, there does not indeed seem much doubt about the answer in either case; but it might be said that in terms of more remote or less evident effects counterweights might be found to enter the utilitarian scales. Thus the effect on George of a decision to take the job might be invoked, or its effect on others who might know of his decision. The possibility of there being more beneficent labours in the future from which he might be barred or disqualified, might be mentioned; and so forth. Such effects—in particular, possible effects on the agent's character, and effects on the public at large—are often invoked by utilitarian writers dealing with problems about lying or promise-breaking, and some similar considerations might be invoked here.

There is one very general remark that is worth making about arguments of this sort. The certainty that attaches to these hypotheses about possible effects is usually pretty low; in some cases, indeed, the hypothesis invoked is so implausible that it would scarcely pass if it were not being used to deliver the respectable moral answer, as in the standard fantasy that one of the effects of one's telling a particular lie is to weaken the disposition of the world at large to tell the truth. The demands on the certainty or probability of these beliefs as beliefs about particular actions are much milder than they would be on beliefs favouring the unconventional course. It may be said that this is as it should be, since the presumption must be in favour of the conventional course: but that scarcely seems a *utilitarian* answer, unless utilitarianism has already taken off in the direction of not applying the consequences to the particular act at all.

Leaving aside that very general point, I want to consider now two types of effect that are often invoked by utilitarians, and which might be invoked in connexion with these imaginary cases. The attitude or tone involved in invoking these effects may sometimes seem peculiar; but that sort of peculiarity soon becomes familiar in utilitarian discussions, and indeed it can be something of an achievement to retain a sense of it.

First, there is the psychological effect on the agent. Our descriptions of these situations have not so far taken account of how George or Jim will be after they have taken the one course or the other; and it might be said that if they take the course which seemed at first the utilitarian one, the effects on them will be in fact bad enough and extensive enough to cancel out the initial utilitarian advantages of that course. Now there is one version of this effect in which, for a utilitarian, some confusion must be involved, namely that in which the agent feels bad, his subsequent conduct and relations are crippled and so on, *because he thinks that he has done the wrong thing*—for if the balance of outcomes was as it appeared to be *before* invoking this effect, then he has not (from the utilitarian point of view) done the wrong thing. So that version of the effect, for a rational and utilitarian agent, could not possibly make any difference to the assessment of right and wrong. However, perhaps he is not a thoroughly rational agent, and is disposed to have bad feelings, whichever he decided to do. Now such feelings, which are from a strictly utilitarian point of view irrational—nothing, a utilitarian can point out, is advanced by having them—cannot, consistently, have any great weight in a utilitarian calculation. I shall consider in a moment an argument to suggest that they should have no weight at all in it. But short of that, the utilitarian could reasonably say that such feelings should not be encouraged, even if we accept their existence, and that to give them a lot of weight is to encourage them. Or, at the very best, even if they are straightforwardly and without any discount to be put into the calculation, their weight must be small: they are after all (and at best) one man's feelings.

•   •   •

If, then, one is really going to regard one's feelings from a strictly utilitarian point of view, Jim should give very little weight at all to his; it seems almost indecent, in fact, once one has taken that point of view, to suppose that he should give any at all. In George's case one might feel that things were slightly different. It is interesting, though, that one reason why one might think that— namely that one person principally affected is his wife—is very dubiously available to a utilitarian. George's wife has some reason to be interested in George's integrity and his sense of it; the Indians, quite properly, have no interest in Jim's. But it is not at all clear how utilitarianism would describe that difference.

There is an argument, and a strong one, that a strict utilitarian should give not merely small extra weight, in calculations of right and wrong, to feelings of this kind, but that he should give absolutely no weight to them at all. This is based on the point, which we have already seen, that if a course of action is, before taking these sorts of feelings into account, utilitarianly preferable, then bad feelings about that kind of action will be from a utilitarian point of view irrational. Now it might be thought that even if that is so, it would not mean that in a utilitarian calculation such feelings should not be taken into account; it is after all a well-known boast of utilitarianism that it is a realistic outlook which seeks the best in the world as it is, and takes any form of happiness or unhappiness into account. While a utilitarian will no doubt seek to diminish the incidence of feelings which are utilitarianly irrational—or at least of disagreeable feelings which are so—he might be expected to take them into account while they exist. This is without doubt classical utilitarian doctrine, but there is good reason to think that utilitarianism cannot stick to it without embracing results which are startlingly unacceptable and perhaps self-defeating.

Suppose that there is in a certain society a racial minority. Considering merely the ordinary interests of the other citizens, as opposed to their sentiments, this minority does no particular harm; we may suppose that it does not confer any very great benefits either. Its presence is in those terms neutral or mildly beneficial. However, the other citizens have such prejudices that they find the sight of this group, even the knowledge of its presence, very disagreeable. Proposals are made for removing in some way this minority. If we assume various quite plausible things (as that programmes to change the majority sentiment are likely to be protracted and ineffective) then even if the removal would be unpleasant for the minority, a utilitarian calculation might well end up favouring this step, especially if the minority were a rather small minority and the majority were very severely prejudiced, that is to say, were made very severely uncomfortable by the presence of the minority.

A utilitarian might find that conclusion embarrassing; and not merely because of its nature, but because of the grounds on which it is reached. While a utilitarian might be expected to take into account certain other sorts of consequences of the prejudice, as that a majority prejudice is likely to be displayed in conduct disagreeable to the minority, and so forth, he might be made to wonder whether the unpleasant experiences of the prejudiced people should be allowed, *merely as such,* to count. If he does count them, merely as such, then he has once more separated himself from a body of ordinary moral thought which he might have hoped to accommodate; he may also have started on the path of defeating his own view of things. For one feature of these sentiments is that they are from the utilitarian point of view itself irrational, and a thoroughly utilitarian person would either not have them, or if he found that he did tend to have them, would himself seek to discount them. Since the sentiments in question are such that a rational utilitarian would discount them in himself, it is reasonable to suppose that he should discount them in his calculations about society; it does seem quite unreasonable for him to give just as much weight to feelings—considered just in themselves, one must recall, as experiences of those that have them—which are essentially based on views which are from a utilitarian point of view irrational, as to those which accord with utilitarian principles. Granted this idea, it seems reasonable for him to rejoin a body of moral thought in other respects congenial to him, and discount those sentiments, just considered in themselves, totally, on the principle that no pains or discomforts are to count in the utilitarian sum which their subjects have just because they hold views which are by utilitarian standards irrational. But if he accepts that, then in the cases we are at present considering no extra weight at all can be put in for bad feelings of George or Jim about their choices, if those choices are, leaving out those feelings, on the first round utilitarianly rational.

The psychological effect on the agent was the first of two general effects considered by utilitarians, which had to be discussed. The second is in general a more substantial item, but it need not take so long, since it is both clearer and has little application to the present cases. This is the *precedent effect*. As Burke rightly emphasized, this effect can be important: that one morally *can* do what someone has actually done, is a psychologically effective principle, if not a deontically valid one. For the effect to operate, obviously some conditions must hold on the publicity of the act and on such things as the status of the agent (such considerations weighed importantly with Sir Thomas More); what these may be will vary evidently with circumstances.

In order for the precedent effect to make a difference to a utilitarian calculation, it must be based upon a confusion. For suppose that there is an act which would be the best in the circumstances, except that doing it will encourage by precedent other people to do things which will not be the best things to do. Then the situation of those other people must be relevantly different from that of the original agent; if it were not, then in doing the same as what would be the best course for the original agent, they would necessarily do the best thing themselves. But if the situations are in this way relevantly different, it must be a confused perception which takes the first situation, and the agent's course in it, as an adequate precedent for the second.

However, the fact that the precedent effect, if it really makes a difference, is in this sense based on a confusion, does not mean that it is not perfectly real, or that it is to be discounted: social effects are by their nature confused in this sort of way. What it does emphasize is that calculations of the precedent effect have got to be realistic, involving considerations of how people are actually likely to be influenced. In the present examples, however, it is very implausible to think that the precedent effect could be invoked to make any difference to the calculation. Jim's case is extraordinary enough, and it is hard to imagine who the recipients of the effect might be supposed to be; while George is not in a sufficiently public situation or role for the question to arise in that form, and in any case one might suppose that the motivations of others on such an issue were quite likely to be fixed one way or another already.

No appeal, then, to these other effects is going to make a difference to what the utilitarian will decide about our examples. Let us now look more closely at the structure of those decisions.

INTEGRITY

The situations have in common that if the agent does not do a certain disagreeable thing, someone else will, and in Jim's situation at least the result, the state of affairs after the other man has acted, if he does, will be worse than after Jim has acted, if Jim does. The same, on a smaller scale, is true of George's case. I have already suggested that it is inherent in consequentialism that it offers a strong doctrine of negative responsibility: if I know that if I do X, O_1 will eventuate, and if I refrain from doing X, O_2 will, and that O_2 is worse than O_1, then I am responsible for O_2 if I refrain voluntarily from doing X. 'You could have prevented it', as will be said, and truly, to Jim, if he refuses, by the relatives of the other Indians. (I shall leave the important question, which is to the side of the present issue, of the obligations, if any, that nest around the word 'know': how far does one, under utilitarianism, have to research into the possibilities of maximally beneficent action, including prevention?)

In the present cases, the situation of O_2 includes another agent bringing about results worse than O_1. So far as O_2 has been identified up to this point—merely as the worse outcome which will eventuate if I refrain from doing X—we might equally have said that what that other brings about is O_2; but that would be to underdescribe the situation. For what occurs if Jim refrains from action is not solely twenty Indians dead, but *Pedro's killing twenty Indians,* and that is not a result which Pedro brings about, though the death of the Indians is. We can say: what one does is not included in the outcome of what one does, while what another does can be included in the outcome of what one does. For that to be so, as the terms are now being used, only a very weak condition has to be satisfied: for Pedro's killing the Indians to be the outcome of Jim's refusal, it only has to be causally true that if Jim had not refused, Pedro would not have done it.

That may be enough for us to speak, in some sense, of Jim's responsibility for that outcome, if it occurs; but it is certainly not enough, it is worth noticing, for us to speak of Jim's *making* those things happen. For granted this way of their coming about, he could have made them happen only by making Pedro shoot, and there is no acceptable sense in which his refusal makes Pedro shoot. If the captain had said on Jim's refusal, 'you leave me with no alternative', he would have been lying, like most who use that phrase. While the deaths, and the killing, may be the outcome of Jim's refusal, it is misleading to think in such a case, of Jim having an *effect* on the world through the medium (as it happens) of Pedro's acts; for this is to leave Pedro out of the picture in his essential role of one who has intentions and projects, projects for realizing which Jim's refusal would leave an opportunity. Instead of thinking in terms of supposed effects of Jim's projects on Pedro, it is more revealing to think in terms of the effects of Pedro's projects on Jim's decision.

•   •   •

Let us now go back to the agent as utilitarian, and his higher-order project of maximizing desirable outcomes. At this level, he is committed only to that: what the outcome will actually consist of will depend entirely on the facts, on what persons with what projects and what potential satisfactions there are within calculable reach of the causal levers near which he finds himself. His own substantial projects and commitments come into it, but only as one lot among others—they potentially provide one set of satisfactions among those which he may be able to assist from where he happens to be. He is the agent of the satisfaction system who happens to be at a particular point at a particular time: in Jim's case, our man in South America. His own decisions as a utilitarian agent are a function of all the satisfactions which he can affect from where he is: and this means that the projects of others, to an indeterminately great extent, determine his decision.

This may be so either positively or negatively. It will be so positively if agents within the causal field of his decision have projects which are at any rate harmless, and so should be assisted. It will equally be so, but negatively, if there is an agent within the causal field whose projects are harmful, and have to be frustrated to maximize desirable outcomes. So it is with Jim and the soldier Pedro. On the utilitarian view, the undesirable projects of other people as much determine, in this negative way, one's decisions as the desirable ones do positively: if those people were not there, or had different projects, the causal nexus would be different, and it is the actual state of the causal nexus which determines the decision. The determination to an indefinite degree of my decisions by other people's projects is just another aspect of my unlimited responsibility to act for the best in a causal framework formed to a considerable extent by their projects.

The decision so determined is, for utilitarianism, the right decision. But what if it conflicts with some project of mine? This, the utilitarian will say, has already been dealt with: the satisfaction to you of fulfilling your project, and any satisfactions to others of your so doing, have already been through the calculating device and have been found inadequate. Now in the case of many sorts of projects, that is a perfectly reasonable sort of answer. But in the case of projects of the sort I have called 'commitments', those with which one is more deeply and extensively involved and identified, this cannot just by itself be an adequate answer, and there may be no adequate answer at all. For, to take the extreme sort of case, how can a man, as a utilitarian agent, come to regard as one satisfaction among others, and a dispensable one, a project or attitude round which he has built his life, just because someone else's projects have so structured the causal scene that that is how the utilitarian sum comes out?

The point here is not, as utilitarians may hasten to say, that if the project or attitude is that central to his life, then to abandon it will be very disagreeable to him and great loss of utility will be involved. I have already argued . . . that it is not like that; on the contrary, once he is prepared to look at it like that, the argument in any serious case is over anyway. The point is that he is identified with his actions as flowing from projects and attitudes which in some cases he takes seriously at the deepest level, as what his life is about (or, in some cases, this section of his life—seriously is not necessarily the same as persistence). It is absurd to demand of such a man, when the sums come in from the utility network which the projects of others have in part determined, that he should just step aside from his own project and decision and acknowledge the decision which utilitarian calculation requires. It is to alienate him in a real sense from his actions and the source of his action in his own convictions. It is to make him into a channel between the input of everyone's projects, including his own, and an output of optimific decision; but this is to neglect the extent to which *his* actions and *his* decisions have to be seen as the actions and decisions which flow from the projects and attitudes with which he is most closely identified. It is thus, in the most literal sense, an attack on his integrity.[2]

These sorts of considerations do not in themselves give solutions to practical dilemmas such as those provided by our examples; but I hope they help to provide other ways of thinking about them. In fact, it is not hard to see that in George's case, viewed from this perspective, the utilitarian solution would be wrong. Jim's case is different, and harder. But if (as I suppose) the utilitarian is probably right in this case, that is not to be found out just by asking the utilitarian's questions. Discussions of it—and I am not going to try to carry it further here—will have to take seriously the distinction between my killing someone, and its coming about because of what I do that someone else kills them: a distinction based, not so much on the distinction between action and inaction, as on the distinction between my projects and someone else's projects. At least it will have to start by taking that seriously, as utilitarianism does not; but then it will have to build out from there by asking why that distinction seems to have less, or a different, force in this case than it has in George's. One question here would be how far one's powerful objection to killing people just is, in fact, an application of a powerful objection to their being killed. Another dimension of that is the issue of how much it matters that the people at risk are actual, and there, as opposed to hypothetical, or future, or merely elsewhere.[3]

There are many other considerations that could come into such a question, but the immediate point of all this is to draw one particular contrast with utilitarianism: that to reach a grounded decision in such a case should not be regarded as a matter of just discounting one's reactions, impulses and deeply held projects in the face of the pattern of utilities, nor yet merely adding them in—but in the first instance of trying to understand them.

---

2 Interestingly related to these notions is the Socratic idea that courage is a virtue particularly connected with keeping a clear sense of what one regards as most important. They also centrally raise questions about the value of pride. Humility, as something beyond the real demand of correct self-appraisal, was specially a Christian virtue because it involved subservience to God. In a secular context it can only represent subservience to other men and their projects.

3 For a more general discussion of this issue see Charles Fried, *An Anatomy of Values* (Cambridge, MA: Harvard University Press, 1970), Part Three.

28

Constraints

SHELLY KAGAN

Shelly Kagan is Professor of Philosophy at Yale University. This selection is from his book The Limits of Morality, *chapter 1.*

According to commonsense morality, there are constraints on what we may do to maximize utility. For example, even if we could prevent two people from being killed by killing one ourselves, commonsense morality says that we should not kill. However, unlike Bernard Williams and Thomas Nagel (readings 27 and 55), Kagan regards such constraints as indefensible. He examines a number of ways of defending them—for example, by arguing that someone who kills another sacrifices his own integrity, or that he fails to respect the other as a person—but finds each argument wanting. Thus, Kagan concludes that the uncompromising utilitarian, or "extremist," has a stronger position than the "moderate" who accepts ordinary morality.

Although we could discuss in a perfectly general fashion the difficulties of arguing for any sort of constraint, our primary interest in the question is motivated by the moderate's need to block various unacceptable options that would otherwise be supported by the appeal to cost. For example, the moderate needs to provide an overriding reason why I must not kill uncle Albert. Now cases involving the doing of harm may not be the only ones where the moderate would find an option unacceptable, but they are probably the most important such cases. In any event, if the moderate is to retain his use of the appeal to cost, then blocking or overriding that appeal in cases involving the doing of harm will certainly be essential to the moderate's defense of ordinary morality. So let us focus the discussion by examining the constraint against doing harm—and more specifically, the constraint against killing. (A discussion of constraints other than the constraint against harming would, of course, require corresponding alterations in the arguments about to be considered; in the case of certain special obligations, these alterations might be rather extensive. Still, the arguments given below are typical of those moderates offer in defense of constraints.)

In principle, our investigation could proceed by considering an example of what is doubtless the most common kind of case, i.e., one in which the best outcome will *not* be brought about by violating the constraint against killing. In such cases, of course, the moderate and the extremist are in agreement that the constraint must not be violated. But such agreement masks the deeper disagreement between the two as to the *reason* why the given act of killing should not be performed. The extremist believes the act in question to be forbidden because, by hypothesis, it would not lead to the best outcome overall. The moderate, however, believes that this answer fails to bring out the distinct and far more important reason why the given act of killing is forbidden, a reason so compelling that it grounds a *constraint* against such acts. In principle, it should be possible for the moderate to isolate that reason even in the typical cases in which the moderate and the extremist have no dispute over whether the killing is permitted.

Nonetheless, there is a clear danger of confusion if we focus on a case in which violating the constraint will not bring about the best outcome. We run the risk of misdiagnosing the source of the moral prohibition against killing in such cases. In the attempt to isolate a reason capable of grounding a constraint against killing, we may mistakenly produce instead variants on the already-noted fact that the given act of killing will not lead to the best outcome available. (And *this* consideration, obviously, cannot justify a constraint against killing, which would prohibit such acts even when they *would* lead to the best outcome.) At the very least, by focusing instead on cases in which the extremist and the moderate disagree about the permissibility of killing, we may hope to bring the grounds for constraints more sharply into relief, better enabling the moderate to articulate and defend his belief.

Let us, therefore, imagine a case in which it *would* promote the good to kill. Imagine that by killing one innocent person I can prevent the murders of two other innocent persons. That is, by violating the constraint against killing, I prevent two other violations of the same constraint, and this is the only way to promote this desirable outcome. In short, if I kill the one, I save the two.[1]

Several features of this case deserve comment. Most importantly, the description is obviously schematic; I have deliberately neglected filling in most of the details of the case. This is not because such details cannot have any moral significance. On the contrary, it is quite possible that filling in a concrete example would introduce a variety of *additional* morally relevant considerations. That is the very reason why I have left the case schematic. If the moderate is going to justify a constraint against killing, it will not help to have our attention distracted by accidental features that may muddy the moral waters. This is true regardless of whether the additional factors would happen to make the given act of killing even worse, or serve to make it somewhat more acceptable in the given case. It may, therefore, help us to focus on the constraint against killing, if we simply stipulate that in the case we are considering there

---

[1] Since the present discussion is meant to be neutral between a constraint against doing harm and a constraint against intending harm, it may be best to assume explicitly that, in the case being described, my killing the one is an essential means to (and not a mere side-effect of) my saving the two.

are no other morally relevant factors (no mitigating side-effects, no more desirable course of action open to me, and so on).

What the case does involve, of course, is a situation in which, by hypothesis, a greater amount of good will be done by killing than by refraining from killing. This description assumes, obviously, that it is worse—all other things being equal—if two innocent people die than if only one innocent person dies. But it would be hard to deny this claim. (Matters might be different if one or more of the three people were morally culpable, or somehow responsible for being in the situation; that is the reason for imagining all three to be innocent. Of course, many other differences in the individuals might be relevant as well; but let us assume that the three are, in the relevant respects, similar.) However, since we are leaving open the possibility that a pluralist account of the good should be accepted, we cannot assume that the loss of innocent life is the only factor relevant to the goodness of the two possible outcomes.

On some accounts, for example, it might be suggested that the existence of an act of murder makes the world bad above and beyond the badness of the resulting loss of innocent life. On such a view, even if killing the one were the only way to save the two from dying of natural causes, we could not automatically assume that killing the one would result in the greater amount of good overall. For the choice would be between, on the one hand, the badness of two innocent deaths and, on the other hand, the badness of one innocent death *plus* the additional badness of an act of murder. It would be possible that the contribution that an act of murder makes to the badness of outcomes is so great that murdering the one so as to save the two from dying of natural causes would not actually promote the greater good.

I do not propose to examine the plausibility of such views. In fact, I have deliberately described our case in such a way as to sidestep the difficulty. We are not imagining that, by killing the one, I am merely saving the two from death by natural causes. Rather, I prevent the two from being murdered themselves, let us say, by two other potential murderers. Even if the existence of an act of murder makes outcomes bad in its own right, since my act of murder prevents two other acts of murder, it will remain true that by killing the one I bring about the better outcome overall. (Similar remarks, or minor variations in the case, could handle other versions of the objection.)

We are imagining, then, a situation in which it is genuinely the case that killing the one so as to save two others promotes the best available outcome. I do not mean to suggest that such cases are especially common. On the other hand, I also do not mean to concede that such cases never arise. (In point of fact, I believe that they do sometimes arise.) For our purposes it should not matter whether such cases actually occur or not. The moderate needs to defend a constraint against killing. Such a constraint would rule out killing even in cases where it would lead to the best consequences overall, so it should rule out killing the one to save the two. And this is just as the moderate would have it. He believes that it *is* morally forbidden for me to kill the one, even though this is the only way to save the two. But the moderate needs to defend this belief.

If I kill the one, I save the two. What reason can the moderate give for prohibiting me from doing this?[2]

1. Moderates typically try to defend the constraint against killing by stressing what a horrible thing I am doing to the victim if I kill him. And it is indeed a horrible thing to be killed. But it does not seem that emphasizing this point brings the moderate any closer to justifying the constraint. The death of my victim is a horrible thing to happen to him; but the deaths of the two other potential victims are obviously horrible things to happen to *them*. My victim is uncompensated—but the two others would be uncompensated too. If my victim's death is a bad thing, then the deaths of the two would, together, be worse. Why should I be forbidden to minimize the badness?

As long as the moderate sticks to what happens to a person when the constraint is violated he gets no closer to justifying the constraint. Talk of the value of an individual's being able to shape his own life, the disvalue of a life being violated, and the like—none of this helps explain why a constraint against killing should be erected; it only supports the extremist's view that it is permissible to inflict one such harm in order that a greater number of such harms—a greater overall amount of badness—may be avoided. The barrier to promoting the best outcome created by a constraint is inexplicable in terms of the badness of what happens to the victims.

2. The inadequacy of stressing the badness of what *happens* to the person when the constraint is violated may suggest shifting the focus of the moderate's argument to the *relationship* which obtains between the agent and his victim. Moderates have often emphasized the quality or character of the acts they wish to constrain—as distinct from merely noting their outcomes. If I kill my victim, I stand in a particular relationship to him—and moderates have stressed how horrible it is for that relationship to obtain. In killing my victim, even for a good end, I am degrading him, violating his integrity as a person, treating him as a means, breaching our common humanity, and the like. Presumably I do not stand in these horrible relationships with all those whom I merely allow harm to befall.

Once again, however, the moderate's argument fails to bring him any closer to justifying the constraint. For however horrible the interpersonal relationship in which I stand to my victim, the relationships between the two would-be murderers and their victims would be equally horrible. Violating the constraint may put me in a horrible relationship with my victim, but if it prevents a greater number of violations then the moderate has as yet no reason to forbid it.

So far the moderate has concentrated on badness—the badness of what happens, and the badness of relations—but it seems clear that such an approach cannot justify a constraint against killing. For *badness* relates to the objective

---

2 If the arguments criticized in this section appear to be straw men, the blame should fall upon the moderates themselves, for they have made quite a poor showing at defending their views. Most moderates are unusually vague or sloppy about the basis of constraints (even by the standards of moral philosophy); even when they are not, there is rarely much offered by way of *justification* of their views. Often they merely present their particular moderate position, at best appealing to intuition for support. . . .

value of the outcomes. The extremist wants to promote the most valuable outcome open to him. Considerations of the disvalue of this or that can only affect judgments about what *is* the best outcome—but it can't possibly justify creating a barrier to promoting the best outcome once we determine what that is. Constraints cannot be erected on considerations of badness.

Perhaps when the moderate says how horrible it is to kill, we misunderstand him if we take him to be arguing for a constraint on the basis of the objective disvalue of killings. It may be so clear that considerations of disvalue are not sufficient justification for constraints, that it is unfair to read the moderate in this way. Perhaps his saying that it is bad to kill is simply a way of saying that it is *wrong* to kill—that killing is forbidden. But this, of course, is simply to state the claim, not to justify it; and surely, the moderate thought he was offering *reasons* for his view. So let us ask again: why is there a constraint against doing harm even when this is necessary to prevent greater harm?

3. We soon come to a fundamental intuition for the moderate. He feels there is something deeply wrong about the extremist's willingness to do evil in order to prevent it. Somehow it seems utterly against the spirit of morality to be flirting with evil in the name of the good. The extremist, of course, may bemoan the fact that he was forced to do evil at all; but the moderate's intuition is that we have *misconceived* our relation to evil, if we will enter into partnership with it for whatever purpose. It is the nature of evil that we should *avoid* it. It is the nature of evil that we should simply never turn our mind to bringing any about.

No doubt all of us have felt the force of this view. Indeed it is embedded in our language, making it all the harder to recognize it as an assumption which needs to be questioned. We may find ourselves being reassured by the thought that if it is *evil* to perform some act, then clearly one cannot perform that act. One cannot do an act which is itself evil—a fortiori one cannot do the evil act for some desirable end. Hence one cannot do evil—even that good may come of it. But such thoughts conceal a non sequitur: we cannot move without argument from 'one cannot do what is forbidden' to 'one cannot do harm'. The non sequitur is covered by the fact that both claims can be expressed as 'one cannot do evil'—and the ambiguity is doubtless due to the belief of ordinary morality that doing harm *is* forbidden, even for good ends. But the moderate must *show* that it is evil (forbidden) to do evil (harm). The extremist believes that although we cannot eliminate suffering from the world, we should at least do what we can to minimize it. To the moderate, this attitude is fundamentally misguided. But whatever the force of his intuition, the moderate still needs to justify it.

4. The moderate may return to the nature of the relation between me and my victim. He may suggest that to deliberately harm another degrades not only the victim of the harm, but the *agent* of the harm. It is hard to escape metaphor here: when I kill another, I become *polluted*. (Even those who believe in thresholds for constraints will feel soiled and profaned if forced to do harm in order to prevent some catastrophe.) The constraint against killing—the moderate argues—respects the agent's need to preserve his moral integrity.

It seems, however, that a concern with the moral integrity of the agent cannot provide a justification for having a *constraint* against doing harm. At the very best it could only help ground an option to refrain from harming others in pursuit of the good; but if an agent were willing to sacrifice his moral integrity in order to promote the greater good, the moderate has given no reason to prohibit his doing so. If I am *willing* to kill the one out of my concern for the two, then the moderate still needs to provide a reason to forbid the killing.

The moderate might reply that even if this objection is sound—and a concern with the moral integrity of the agent cannot justify a constraint—the extremist has been defeated nonetheless. Granted, some other argument will be needed to establish constraints; and granted, the moderate ultimately hopes to establish a far broader range of options than the mere option to refrain from doing harm; but still: if the appeal to moral integrity is indeed sufficient to ground even this limited option, then the extremist has been refuted, since he denies the existence of any options at all.

The extremist, however, has a compelling response. It is clear that no argument based on the loss of moral integrity can succeed—regardless of whether it is meant to establish a constraint or an option—unless killing the one does actually involve a sacrifice of the agent's integrity. But if killing the one to save the two is justified—as the extremist believes—then it is no sacrifice of moral integrity for the agent to do so. What this means is that the moderate's appeal to moral integrity simply begs the question against the extremist. The moderate believes that killing the one is morally forbidden, but he has still given no reason to accept this claim.

5. The moderate may return to the relation between agent and victim once again, and suggest that if I kill the one to save the two, I am failing to respect the one as a person. As a member of the moral community, each person deserves to be treated in accordance with his standing *as* a person; that is, I must treat other individuals as the persons that they are. But to deliberately harm an individual, even for a desired end, is to reduce that individual to a mere means in my treatment of him, and to fail to accord to him the respect due him as a person. A person must be treated as an end, not a means—and so I am forbidden to kill the one.

The general tenor of this argument is, of course, a familiar one. The concept of treating an individual as a person (or an end) is often used to try to bridge the gaps which have bothered the extremist. But the concept won't do the job. The extremist will certainly want to agree that each person deserves to be given the sort of treatment befitting the valuable type of being that he is. But the moderate is too hasty in assuming that the appropriate sort of treatment rules out harming one person to prevent harm to others—for this is the very claim that he needs to establish. The moderate hasn't shown that treating a person with the respect that is due him requires something *different* from taking his well-being equally into account in weighing the objective value of an outcome and promoting the best outcome overall. To kill without justification is undoubtedly to fail to treat the person with respect, and the moderate *claims* that to kill one in order to save two is *not* adequate justification; but he has given no reason to think so.

The cataloguing of attempts by the moderate to establish the existence of a constraint against killing could go on; but I know of none that succeed. What is striking about all of these arguments is that they suffer not from failures of detail, but from failure to get off the ground altogether. The moderate's belief in constraints may well be backed by intuition, but I have argued that this is not sufficient to justify the belief if it cannot be supported by a coherent explanation. Not only has the moderate failed to give an adequate explanation; he has failed to give even the beginnings of one.

V

NORMATIVE ETHICS: DEONTOLOGY

The readings in the previous section discussed consequentialism, which tells us to perform whichever acts bring the best consequences. In this section, we will take up the alternative view that some acts are required or forbidden simply because of the kinds of acts they are. This view is often known as *deontology* (although that term can also be used more broadly to refer to any theory that is not consequentialist).

Ordinary thought has both consequentialist and deontological elements. Most people believe that we ought to promote good consequences when we can do so without undue cost or risk to ourselves; but most also believe that many *methods* of promoting good consequences are morally off-limits because of the kinds of acts they involve. Impressed by both facts, W. D. Ross argues in reading 29 that no single moral principle is basic. Instead, we have a basic duty to promote good consequences, but equally basic duties to avoid dishonesty, ingratitude, and injustice. Because these basic duties may yield conflicting directives—because promoting the best consequences may require being dishonest and being just may mean ignoring debts of gratitude—we need some way of resolving these conflicts. According to Ross, there is no simple formula or mechanical method of deciding which duties take precedence. We must use our judgment about each situation as it arises.

Viewed as a description of our actual practice, Ross's view seems accurate enough. But what are we doing when we judge that one duty takes priority over another if not appealing to some implicit ordering principle? If no such principles exist, then what makes one judgment better than another? Moved by these questions, many deontologists reject Ross's pluralism in favor of a more unified approach.

By far the most famous unified deontological theory is that of Immanuel Kant. In reading 30, Kant defends several versions of a single basic principle— a "Categorical Imperative"—that he thinks should regulate all behavior. One way of putting Kant's principle is "Act only according to that maxim [i.e., that rule of conduct] by which you can at the same time will that it should become a universal law." Another formulation asserts "Act so that you treat humanity, whether in your own person or in that of another, always as an end and never as a means only." In either formulation, Kant's basic principle rules out various types of acts—for example, making promises that cannot be kept. If everyone made such promises, then no promises would be credible and so the institution of promising itself would disappear. Hence, the maxim "make promises you cannot keep" cannot be a universal law. Also, when we make a promise we cannot keep, we treat the person to whom we make it as a mere means, and thus do not treat all humanity as an end.

Because Kant's prohibition against deceptive promises is independent of their consequences, his theory is clearly deontological. Indeed, Kant argues that consequences are irrelevant in two respects. They are irrelevant, first, because an act's anticipated consequences cannot determine whether one ought to perform it, and, second, because its actual consequences cannot affect its moral worth when it *is* performed. Even an unsuccessful attempt to do the right thing would "sparkle like a jewel in its own right." In saying this, Kant gives voice to the common belief that we are only responsible for what we can control. However, as Thomas Nagel notes in reading 33, Kant thereby rejects the equally common belief that results sometimes *do* matter. For example, we believe that reckless driving that causes death is worse than reckless driving that does not, yet "whether a reckless driver hits a pedestrian depends on the presence of the pedestrian at the point where he recklessly passes the red light."

Because Kant's theory is exceptionally rich, the relations among its elements are not always easy to see. However, in reading 31, William Nelson provides a helpful overview and interpretation of the theory. Among the topics he discusses are Kant's idea that duty alone can move us to act, the role of reason in Kant's theory, the meaning of Kant's universalization requirement, and the relation between Kant's different formulations of the Categorical Imperative. This last topic is also discussed by Christine Korsgaard in reading 32. She argues that the different versions of the Categorical Imperative sometimes tell us to do different things. For example, suppose a murderer tells you what you know to be a lie in order to get you to reveal the location of his intended victim. According to Korsgaard, the principle "act only on maxims you can universalize" permits you to lie to the murderer in return, but the principle "treat humanity only as an end in itself" forbids all lies. To square the discrepancy, Korsgaard suggests that we take the treatment-as-ends formula to apply under ideal conditions and the universalization formula to apply when we must deal with evil—that is, in the imperfect actual world. In this way, she argues, we can rescue Kant's theory from the implausible implication that one may not lie even to prevent a murder.

According to Kant, each person gives himself the moral law. We do this by acting as though our decisions will create the laws that we and all other members of a society of rational beings—a "realm of ends"—are bound to obey. As Kant frames the point, "the rational being must regard himself always as legislative in a realm of ends possible through the freedom of the will, whether he belongs to it as member or as sovereign." In reading 34, John Rawls proposes a theory which provides a possible model for Kant's realm of ends. According to Rawls, we may think of that realm as composed of persons who must decide on principles to regulate their common affairs without knowing the particulars of their actual lives. Because these persons do not know their race, sex, class, degree of wealth, talents, or likes and dislikes—because all of these facts are concealed by a "veil of ignorance"—their choices cannot be biased by any merely contingent facts. Hence, "by acting from these principles persons express their nature as free and equal rational beings."

Because Rawls's main concern is not the rightness of individual acts, but rather the justice of social institutions such as the legal and economic system, his primary aim is to develop principles to govern the design of such institutions. In his view, a just set of social institutions is one that allows all citizens the greatest possible amount of equal liberty and also maximizes the economic position of society's worst-off group. Of these two requirements, the first takes precedence over the second. No increase in economic well-being—even for the worst-off—may be achieved at the cost of any sacrifice of basic liberties. By construing the principles of justice as stemming from a constrained agreement among all the affected parties, and by suggesting that a similar agreement may yield principles of individual action, Rawls adds an important dimension to the deontological approach.

29

What Makes Right Acts Right?

W. D. ROSS

Sir William David Ross (1877–1971) was Provost of Oriel College, Oxford University. His views on ethics, set forth in The Right and the Good *and* Foundations of Ethics, *continue to command widespread attention. He also published influential translations of, and commentaries upon, the works of Aristotle. This selection is from* The Right and the Good, *chapter 2.*

Ross's view about what makes acts right incorporates elements of both utilitarianism and Kantianism. He rejects the utilitarian assumptions that happiness is the only good thing and that our only duty is to maximize what is good. However, he agrees that our duties include the promotion of happiness (and other goods) as well as keeping promises, promoting justice, and developing our talents. Because an act that satisfies one of these duties will often not satisfy another, Ross calls all such duties prima facie. We have a prima facie duty to perform an act when the act "would be a duty proper if it were not at the same time of another kind which is morally significant." By contrast, our duty proper in a particular situation is what we should do, all things considered.

How do we know our prima facie and all-things-considered duties? According to Ross, we know that the keeping of promises, gratitude, and the production of happiness are among our prima facie duties through a kind of direct apprehension. It is simply self-evident that these features always count in favor of acts. But what we should do in any particular situation is not self-evident. To ascertain this, we must carefully weigh all the relevant factors. For example, if telling someone the truth would pain him, we must balance our prima facie duty of fidelity against our prima facie duty not to do harm. This requires the conscientious exercise of judgment.

As many critics have noted, Ross's account gives little guidance about how to exercise judgment in particular cases. Yet even if we are dissatisfied with this, we may remain attracted to his views about which considerations are relevant. In claiming that there is a variety of irreducibly different moral duties, Ross captures the considered belief of many thoughtful people.

The real point at issue between hedonism and utilitarianism on the one hand and their opponents on the other is not whether 'right' means 'productive of so and so'; for it cannot with any plausibility be maintained that it does. The point at issue is that to which we now pass, viz. whether there is any general character which makes right acts right, and if so, what it is. Among the main historical attempts to state a single characteristic of all right actions which is the foundation of their rightness are those made by egoism and utilitarianism. But I do not propose to discuss these, not because the subject is unimportant, but because it has been dealt with so often and so well already, and because there has come to be so much agreement among moral philosophers that neither of these theories is satisfactory. A much more attractive theory has been put forward by Professor Moore: that what makes actions right is that they are productive of more *good* than could have been produced by any other action open to the agent.

This theory is in fact the culmination of all the attempts to base rightness on productivity of some sort of result. The first form this attempt takes is the attempt to base rightness on conduciveness to the advantage or pleasure of the agent. This theory comes to grief over the fact, which stares us in the face, that a great part of duty consists in an observance of the rights and a furtherance of the interests of others, whatever the cost to ourselves may be. Plato and others may be right in holding that a regard for the rights of others never in the long run involves a loss of happiness for the agent, that 'the just life profits a man'. But this, even if true, is irrelevant to the rightness of the act. As soon as a man does an action *because* he thinks he will promote his own interests thereby, he is acting not from a sense of its rightness but from self-interest.

To the egoistic theory hedonistic utilitarianism supplies a much-needed amendment. It points out correctly that the fact that a certain pleasure will be enjoyed by the agent is no reason why he *ought* to bring it into being rather than an equal or greater pleasure to be enjoyed by another, though, human nature being what it is, it makes it not unlikely that he *will* try to bring it into being. But hedonistic utilitarianism in its turn needs a correction. On reflection it seems clear that pleasure is not the only thing in life that we think good in itself, that for instance we think the possession of a good character, or an intelligent understanding of the world, as good or better. A great advance is made by the substitution of 'productive of the greatest good' for 'productive of the greater pleasure'.

Not only is this theory more attractive than hedonistic utilitarianism, but its logical relation to that theory is such that the latter could not be true unless *it* were true, while it might be true though hedonistic utilitarianism were not. It is in fact one of the logical bases of hedonistic utilitarianism. For the view that what produces the maximum pleasure is right has for its bases the views (1) that what produces the maximum good is right, and (2) that pleasure is the only thing good in itself. If they were not assuming that what produces the maximum *good* is right, the utilitarians' attempt to show that pleasure is the only thing good in itself, which is in fact the point they take most pains to establish, would have been quite irrelevant to their attempt to prove that only what produces the maximum *pleasure* is right. If, therefore, it can be shown that productivity of the maximum good is not what makes all right actions right, we shall *a fortiori* have refuted hedonistic utilitarianism.

When a plain man fulfills a promise because he thinks he ought to do so, it seems clear that he does so with no thought of its total consequences, still less with any opinion that these are likely to be the best possible. He thinks in fact much more of the past than of the future. What makes him think it right to act in a certain way is the fact that he has promised to do so— that and, usually, nothing more. That his act will produce the best possible consequences is not his reason for calling it right. What lends colour to the theory we are examining, then, is not the actions (which form probably a great majority of our actions) in which some reflection as 'I have promised' is the only reason we give ourselves for thinking a certain action right, but the exceptional cases in which the consequences of fulfilling a promise (for instance) would be so disastrous to others that we judge it right not to do so. It must of course be admitted that such cases exist. If I have promised to meet a friend at a particular time for some trivial purpose, I should certainly think myself justified in breaking my engagement if by doing so I could prevent a serious accident or bring relief to the victims of one. And the supporters of the view we are examining hold that my thinking so is due to my thinking that I shall bring more good into existence by the one action than by the other. A different account may, however, be given of the matter, an account which will, I believe, show itself to be the true one. It may be said that besides the duty of fulfilling promises I have and recognize a duty of relieving distress, and that when I think it right to do the latter at the cost of not doing the former, it is not because I think I shall produce more good thereby but because I think it the duty which is in the circumstances more of a duty. This account surely corresponds much more closely with what we really think in such a situation. If, so far as I can see, I could bring equal amounts of good into being by fulfilling my promise and by helping some one to whom I had made no promise, I should not hesitate to regard the former as my duty. Yet on the view that what is right is right because it is productive of the most good I should not so regard it.

There are two theories, each in its way simple, that offer a solution of such cases of conscience. One is the view of Kant, that there are certain duties of perfect obligation, such as those of fulfilling promises, of paying debts, of telling the truth, which admit of no exception whatever in favour of duties of imperfect obligation, such as that of relieving distress. The other is the view of, for instance, Professor Moore and Dr. Rashdall, that there is only the duty of producing good, and that all 'conflicts of duties' should be resolved by asking 'by which action will most good be produced?' But it is more important that our theory fit the facts than that it be simple, and the account we have given above corresponds (it seems to me) better than either of the simpler theories with what we really think, viz. that normally promise-keeping, for example, should come before benevolence, but that when and only when the good to be produced by the benevolent act is very great and the promise comparatively trivial, the act of benevolence becomes our duty.

In fact the theory of 'ideal utilitarianism', if I may for brevity refer so to the theory of Professor Moore, seems to simplify unduly our relations to our fellows. It says, in effect, that the only morally significant relation in which my neighbours stand to me is that of being possible beneficiaries by my action. They do stand in this relation to me, and this relation is morally significant. But they may also stand to me in the relation of promisee to promiser, of creditor to debtor, of wife to husband, of child to parent, of friend to friend, of fellow countryman to fellow countryman, and the like; and each of these relations is the foundation of a *prima facie* duty, which is more or less incumbent on me according to the circumstances of the case. When I am in a situation, as perhaps I always am, in which more than one of these *prima facie* duties is incumbent on me, what I have to do is to study the situations as fully as I can until I form the considered opinion (it is never more) that in the circumstances one of them is more incumbent than any other; then I am bound to think that to do this *prima facie* duty is my duty *sans phrase* in the situation.

I suggest '*prima facie* duty' or 'conditional duty' as a brief way of referring to the characteristic (quite distinct from that of being a duty proper) which an act has, in virtue of being of a certain kind (e.g., the keeping of a promise), of being an act which would be a duty proper if it were not at the same time of another kind which is morally significant. Whether an act is a duty proper or actual duty depends on *all* the morally significant kinds it is an instance of. The phrase '*prima facie* duty' must be apologized for, since (1) it suggests that what we are speaking of is a certain kind of duty, whereas it is in fact not a duty, but something related in a special way to duty. Strictly speaking, we want not a phrase in which duty is qualified by an adjective, but a separate noun. (2) '*Prima*' *facie* suggests that one is speaking only of an appearance which a moral situation presents at first sight, and which may turn out to be illusory; whereas what I am speaking of is an objective fact involved in the nature of the situation, or more strictly in an element of its nature, though not, as duty proper does, arising from its *whole* nature. . . .

There is nothing arbitrary about these *prima facie* duties. Each rests on a definite circumstance which cannot seriously be held to be without moral significance. Of *prima facie* duties I suggest, without claiming completeness or finality for it, the following division.

(1) Some duties rest on previous acts of my own. These duties seem to include two kinds, (*a*) those resting on a promise or what may fairly be called an implicit promise, such as the implicit undertaking not to tell lies which seems to be implied in the act of entering into conversation (at any rate by civilized men), or of writing books that purport to be history and not fiction. These may be called the duties of fidelity. (*b*) Those resting on a previous wrongful act. These may be called the duties of reparation. (2) Some rest on previous acts of other men, i.e., services done by them to me. These may be loosely described as the duties of gratitude. (3) Some rest on the fact or possibility of a distribution of pleasure or happiness (or of the means thereto) which is not in accordance with the merit of the persons concerned; in such cases there arises a duty to upset or prevent such a distribution. These are the duties of justice. (4) Some rest on the mere fact that there are other beings in the world

whose conditions we can make better in respect of virtue, or of intelligence, or of pleasure. These are the duties of beneficence. (5) Some rest on the fact that we can improve our own condition in respect of virtue or of intelligence. These are the duties of self-improvement. (6) I think that we should distinguish from (4) the duties that may be summed up under the title of 'not injuring others'. No doubt to injure others is incidentally to fail to do them good; but it seems to me clear that nonmaleficence is apprehended as a duty distinct from that of beneficence, and as a duty of a more stringent character. . . . We should not in general consider it justifiable to kill one person in order to keep another alive, or to steal from one in order to give alms to another.

The essential defect of the 'ideal utilitarian' theory is that it ignores, or at least does not do full justice to, the highly personal character of duty. If the only duty is to produce the maximum of good, the question who is to have the good—whether it is myself, or my benefactor, or a person to whom I have made a promise to confer that good on him, or a mere fellow man to whom I stand in no such special relation—should make no difference to my having a duty to produce that good. But we are all in fact sure that it makes a vast difference.

•   •   •

If the objection be made, that this catalogue of the main types of duty is an unsystematic one resting on no logical principle, it may be replied, first, that it makes no claim to being ultimate. It is a *prima facie* classification of the duties which reflection on our moral convictions seems actually to reveal. And if these convictions are, as I would claim that they are, of the nature of knowledge, and if I have not misstated them, the list will be a list of authentic conditional duties, correct as far as it goes though not necessarily complete. The list of *goods* put forward by the rival theory is reached by exactly the same method—the only sound one in the circumstances—viz. that of direct reflection on what we really think. Loyalty to the facts is worth more than a symmetrical architectonic or a hastily reached simplicity. If further reflection discovers a perfect logical basis for this or for a better classification, so much the better.

It may, again, be objected that our theory that there are these various and often conflicting types of *prima facie* duty leaves us with no principle upon which to discern what is our actual duty in particular circumstances. But this objection is not one which the rival theory is in a position to bring forward. For when we have to choose between the production of two heterogeneous goods, say knowledge and pleasure, the 'ideal utilitarian' theory can only fall back on an opinion, for which no logical basis can be offered, that one of the goods is the greater; and this is no better than a similar opinion that one of two duties is the more urgent. And again, when we consider the infinite variety of the effects of our actions in the way of pleasure, it must surely be admitted that the claim which *hedonism* sometimes makes, that it offers a readily applicable criterion of right conduct, is quite illusory.

I am unwilling, however, to content myself with an *argumentum ad homi-nem*, and I would contend that in principle there is no reason to anticipate that every act that is our duty is so for one and the same reason. Why should two sets of circumstances, or one set of circumstances, *not* possess different characteristics, any one of which makes a certain act our *prima facie* duty? When I ask what it is that makes me in certain cases sure that I have a *prima facie* duty to do so and so, I find that it lies in the fact that I have made a promise; when I ask the same question in another case, I find the answer lies in the fact that I have done a wrong. And if on reflection I find (as I think I do) that neither of these reasons is reducible to the other, I must not on any *a priori* ground assume that such a reduction is possible.

● ● ●

The duty of justice is particularly complicated, and the word is used to cover things which are really very different—things such as the payment of debts, the reparation of injuries done by oneself to another, and the bringing about of a distribution of happiness between other people in proportion to merit. I use the word to denote only the last of these three. [Elsewhere] I shall try to show that besides the three (comparatively) simple goods, virtue, knowledge, and pleasure, there is a more complex good, not reducible to these, consisting in the proportionment of happiness to virtue. The bringing of this about is a duty which we owe to all men alike, though it may be reinforced by special responsibilities that we have undertaken to particular men. This, therefore, with beneficence and self-improvement, comes under the general principle that we should produce as much good as possible, though the good here involved is different in kind from any other.

But besides this general obligation, there are special obligations. These may arise, in the first place, incidentally, from acts which were not essentially meant to create such an obligation, but which nevertheless create it. From the nature of the case such acts may be of two kinds—the infliction of injuries on others, and the acceptance of benefits from them. It seems clear that these put us under a special obligation to other men, and that only these acts can do so incidentally. From these arise the twin duties of reparation and gratitude.

And finally there are special obligations arising from acts the very intention of which, when they were done, was to put us under such an obligation. The name for such acts is 'promises'; the name is wide enough if we are willing to include under it implicit promises, i.e., modes of behaviour in which without explicit verbal promise we intentionally create an expectation that we can be counted on to behave in a certain way in the interest of another person.

These seem to be, in principle, all the ways in which *prima facie* duties arise. In actual experience they are compounded together in highly complex ways. Thus, for example, the duty of obeying the laws of one's country arises partly (as Socrates contends in the *Crito*) from the duty of gratitude for the benefits one has received from it; partly from the implicit promise to obey which seems to be involved in permanent residence in a country whose laws we know we are *expected* to obey, and still more clearly involved when we ourselves invoke the protection of its laws (this is the truth underlying the doctrine of the social contract); and partly (if we are fortunate in our country) from the fact that its laws are potent instruments for the general good.

Or again, the sense of a general obligation to bring about (so far as we can) a just apportionment of happiness to merit is often greatly reinforced by the fact that many of the existing injustices are due to a social and economic system which we have, not indeed created, but taken part in and assented to; the duty of justice is then reinforced by the duty of reparation.

It is necessary to say something by way of clearing up the relation between *prima facie* duties and the actual or absolute duty to do one particular act in particular circumstances. If, as almost all moralists except Kant are agreed, and as most plain men think, it is sometimes right to tell a lie or to break a promise, it must be maintained that there is a difference between *prima facie* duty and actual or absolute duty. When we think ourselves justified in breaking, and indeed morally obliged to break, a promise in order to relieve some one's distress, we do not for a moment cease to recognize a *prima facie* duty to keep our promise, and this leads us to feel, not indeed shame or repentance, but certainly compunction, for behaving as we do; we recognize, further, that it is our duty to make up somehow to the promisee for the breaking of the promise. We have to distinguish from the characteristic of being our duty that of tending to our duty. Any act that we do contains various elements in virtue of which it falls under various categories. In virtue of being the breaking of a promise, for instance, it tends to be wrong; in virtue of being an instance of relieving distress it tends to be right. . . .

Another instance of the same distinction may be found in the operation of natural laws. *Qua* subject to the force of gravitation towards some other body, each body tends to move in a particular direction with a particular velocity; but its actual movement depends on *all* the forces to which it is subject. It is only by recognizing this distinction that we can preserve the absoluteness of laws of nature, and only by recognizing a corresponding distinction that we can preserve the absoluteness of the general principles of morality. But an important difference between the two cases must be pointed out. When we say that in virtue of gravitation a body tends to move in a certain way, we are referring to a causal influence actually exercised on it by another body or other bodies. When we say that in virtue of being deliberately untrue a certain remark tends to be wrong, we are referring to no causal relation, to no relation that involves succession in time, but to such a relation as connects the various attributes of a mathematical figure. And if the word 'tendency' is thought to suggest too much a causal relation, it is better to talk of certain types of act as being *prima facie* right or wrong (or of different persons as having different and possibly conflicting claims upon us), than of their tending to be right or wrong.

Something should be said of the relation between our apprehension of the *prima facie* rightness of certain types of act and our mental attitude towards particular acts. It is proper to use the word 'apprehension' in the former case and not in the latter. That an act, *qua* fulfilling a promise, or *qua* effecting a just distribution of good, or *qua* returning services rendered, or *qua* promoting the good of others, or *qua* promoting the virtue or insight of the agent, is *prima facie* right, is self-evident; not in the sense that it is evident from the beginning of our lives, or as soon as we attend to the proposition for the first time, but in the sense that when we have reached sufficient mental maturity and have given sufficient attention to the proposition it is evident without any need of proof, or of evidence beyond itself. It is self-evident just as a mathematical axiom, or the validity of a form of inference, is evident. The moral order expressed in these propositions is just as much part of the fundamental nature of the universe (and, we may add, of any possible universe in which there were moral agents at all) as is the spatial or numerical structure expressed in the axioms of geometry or arithmetic. In our confidence that these propositions are true there is involved the same trust in our reason that is involved in our confidence in mathematics; and we should have no justification for trusting it in the latter sphere and distrusting it in the former. In both cases we are dealing with propositions that cannot be proved, but that just as certainly need no proof.

•   •   •

Our judgements about our actual duty in concrete situations have none of the certainty that attaches to our recognition of the general principles of duty. A statement is certain, i.e., is an expression of knowledge, only in one or other of two cases: when it is either self-evident, or a valid conclusion from self-evident premises. And our judgements about our particular duties have neither of these characters. (1) They are not self-evident. Where a possible act is seen to have two characteristics, in virtue of one of which it is *prima facie* right, and in virtue of the other *prima facie* wrong, we are (I think) well aware that we are not certain whether we ought or ought not to do it; that whether we do it or not, we are taking a moral risk. We come in the long run, after consideration, to think one duty more pressing than the other, but we do not feel certain that it is so. And though we do not always recognize that a possible act has two such characteristics, and though there *may* be cases in which it has not, we are never certain that any particular possible act has not, and therefore never certain that it is right, nor certain that it is wrong. For, to go no further in the analysis, it is enough to point out that any particular act will in all probability in the course of time contribute to the bringing about of good or of evil for many human beings, and thus have a *prima facie* rightness or wrongness of which we know nothing. (2) Again, our judgements about our particular duties are not logical conclusions from self-evident premises. The only possible premises would be the general principles stating their *prima facie* rightness or wrongness *qua* having the different characteristics they do have; and even if we could (as we cannot) apprehend the extent to which an act will tend on the one hand, for example, to bring out advantages for our benefactors, and on the other hand to bring about disadvantages for fellow men who are not our benefactors, there is no principle by which we can draw the conclusion that it is on the whole right or on the whole wrong. In this respect the judgement as to the rightness of a particular act is just like the judgement as to the beauty of a particular natural object or work of art. A poem is, for instance, in respect of certain qualities beautiful and in respect of certain others not beautiful; and our judgement as to the degree of beauty it possesses on the whole is never reached by logical reasoning from the apprehension of its particular beauties or particular defects. Both in this and in the moral case we have more or less probable opinions which are not logically justified conclusions from the general principles that are recognized as self-evident.

There is therefore much truth in the description of the right act as a fortunate act. If we cannot be certain that it is right, it is our good fortune if the act we do is the right act. This consideration does not, however, make the doing of our duty a mere matter of chance. There is a parallel here between the doing of duty and the doing of what will be to our personal advantage. We never *know* what act will in the long run be to our advantage. Yet it is certain that we are more likely in general to secure our advantage if we estimate to the best of our ability the probable tendencies of our actions in this respect, than if we act on caprice. And similarly we are more likely to do our duty if we reflect to the best of our ability on the *prima facie* rightness or wrongness of various possible acts in virtue of the characteristics we perceive them to have, than if we act without reflection. With this greater likelihood we must be content.

Many people would be inclined to say that the right act for me is not that whose general nature I have been describing, viz. that which if I were omniscient I should see to be my duty, but that which on all the evidence available to me I should think to be my duty. But suppose that from the state of partial knowledge in which I think act *A* to be my duty, I could pass to a state of perfect knowledge in which I saw act *B* to be my duty, should I not say 'act *B* was the right act for me to do'? I should no doubt add 'though I am not to be blamed for doing act *A*'. . . .

It might seem absurd to suggest that it could be right for any one to do an act which would produce consequences less good than those which would be produced by some other act in his power. Yet a little thought will convince us that this is not absurd. The type of case in which it is easiest to see that this is so is, perhaps, that in which one has made a promise. In such a case we all think that *prima facie* it is our duty to fulfill the promise irrespective of the precise goodness of the total consequences. And though we do not think it is necessarily our actual or absolute duty to do so, we are far from thinking that any, even the slightest, gain in the value of the total consequences will necessarily justify us in doing something else instead. Suppose, to simplify the case by abstraction, that the fulfillment of a promise to *A* would produce 1,000 units of good for him, but that by doing some other act I would produce 1,001 units of good for *B*, to whom I have made no promise, the other consequences of the two acts being of equal value; should we really think it self-evident that it was our duty to do the second act and not the first? I think not. We should, I fancy, hold that only a much greater disparity of value between the total consequences would justify us in failing to discharge our *prima facie* duty to A. After all, a promise is a promise, and is not to be treated so lightly as the theory we are examining would imply. What, exactly, a promise is, is not so easy to determine, but we are surely agreed that it constitutes a serious moral limitation to our freedom of action. To produce the 1,001 units of goods for B rather than fulfill our promise to A would be to take, not perhaps our duty as philanthropists too seriously, but certainly our duty as makers of promises too lightly.

• • •

I conclude that the attributes 'right' and 'optimific'* are not identical, and that we do not know either by intuition, by deduction, or by induction that they coincide in their application, still less that the latter is the foundation of the former. It must be added, however, that if we are ever under no special obligation such as that of fidelity to a promisee or of gratitude to a benefactor, we ought to do what will produce most good; and that even when we are under a special obligation the tendency of acts to promote general good is one of the main factors in determining whether they are right.

In what has preceded, a good deal of use has been made of 'what we really think' about moral questions; a certain theory has been rejected because it does not agree with what we really think. It might be said that this is in principle wrong; that we should not be content to expound what our present moral consciousness tells us but should aim at a criticism of our existing moral consciousness in the light of theory. Now I do not doubt that the moral consciousness of men has in detail undergone a good deal of modification as regards the things we think right, at the hands of moral theory. But if we are told, for instance, that we should give up our view that there is a special obligatoriness attaching to the keeping of promises because it is self-evident that the only duty is to produce as much good as possible, we have to ask ourselves whether we really, when we reflect, *are* convinced that this is self-evident, and whether we really *can* get rid of our view that promise-keeping has a bindingness independent of productiveness of maximum good. In my own experience I find that I cannot, in spite of a very genuine attempt to do so; and I venture to think that most people will find the same, and that just because they cannot lose the sense of special obligation, they cannot accept as self-evident, or even as true, the theory which would require them to do so. In fact it seems, on reflection, self-evident that a promise, simply as such, is something that *prima facie* ought to be kept, and it does *not*, on reflection, seem self-evident that production of maximum good is the only thing that makes an act obligatory. And to ask us to give up at the bidding of a theory our actual apprehension of what is right and what is wrong seems like asking people to repudiate their actual experience of beauty, at the bidding of a theory

---

* Productive of the most possible good.

which says 'only that which satisfies such and such conditions can be beautiful'. If what I have called our actual apprehension is (as I would maintain that it is) truly an apprehension, i.e., an instance of knowledge, the request is nothing less than absurd.

I would maintain, in fact, that what we are apt to describe as 'what we think' about moral questions contains a considerable amount that we do not think but know, and that this forms the standard by reference to which the truth of any moral theory has to be tested, instead of having itself to be tested by reference to any theory. I hope that I have in what precedes indicated what in my view these elements of knowledge are that are involved in our ordinary moral consciousness.

It would be a mistake to found a natural science on 'what we really think', i.e., on what reasonably thoughtful and well-educated people think about the subjects of the science before they have studied them scientifically. For such opinions are interpretations, and often misinterpretations, of sense-experience; and the man of science must appeal from these to sense-experience itself, which furnishes his real data. In ethics no such appeal is possible. We have no more direct way of access to the facts about rightness and goodness and about what things are right or good, than by thinking about them; the moral convictions of thoughtful and well-educated people are the data of ethics just as sense-perceptions are the data of a natural science. Just as some of the latter have to be rejected as illusory, so have some of the former; but as the latter are rejected only when they are in conflict with other more accurate sense-perceptions, the former are rejected only when they are in conflict with convictions which stand better the test of reflection. The existing body of moral convictions of the best people is the cumulative product of the moral reflection of many generations, which has developed an extremely delicate power of appreciation of moral distinctions; and this the theorist cannot afford to treat with anything other than the greatest respect. The verdicts of the moral consciousness of the best people are the foundation on which we must build; though he must first compare them with one another and eliminate any contradictions they may contain.

30

Morality and Rationality

IMMANUEL KANT

Any shortlist of the greatest philosophers in Western thought will include Immanuel Kant (1724–1804). Kant made major contributions to most of the central areas of philosophy: ethics, political philosophy, epistemology, metaphysics, philosophy of art, philosophy of mind, and philosophy of religion. His two most important works are The Critique of Pure Reason *(1781) and* The Foundations of the Metaphysics of Morals *(1785).*

The Foundations of the Metaphysics of Morals, excerpted here, has had a profound influence on the development of ethical thought. Kant's theory is extremely difficult to understand, and the reader must be prepared to exert considerable intellectual effort to come to grips with this very important perspective on ethics. Because Kant's approach is superficially rather puzzling, this introduction provides a roadmap that points out some of the major landmarks in Kant's theory. The text has also been divided into sections, and descriptive titles have been provided for different parts of Kant's long argument.

In a sense, the true starting places for Kant's essays are his reflections on the need for philosophy in ethical thinking (see section D in the reading). Kant believes that the ordinary person knows perfectly well which actions are right and which actions are wrong. (As we read, we will see why Kant has such faith in the average person.) Therefore, the role of philosophy is not to tell people what is right or wrong, but to enable them to defend their ordinary moral views when attacked by a skeptic. Kant's work in this reading falls into two halves. First, he will try to provide an illuminating description of our ordinary moral views; second, he will try to show how those common moral views may be defended.

Kant describes our common moral views in the two passages we have called "The Good Will" and "Acting from the Motive of Duty." His point in "The Good Will" is that we usually do not consider the consequences when evaluating the moral worth of an action, but rather the intention with which the act was done. If the intention was good—if the agent had a good will—then the action is good. Kant expands upon this theme in the section on duty. He claims that we believe that an agent deserves moral praise for an action, not simply because he or she has in fact done the right thing, but because the agent was motivated by the intention to do the right thing. The agent was motivated by a sense of duty.

How do we decide what our duties are? Kant believes that persons, unlike animals, are capable of formulating laws of conduct for themselves

*and of acting on those laws (section E). The fundamental law of conduct—
the "moral law"—is that one should perform an act only if one would will
that anyone in similar circumstances do the same thing. That is, one should
will to perform an act only if one would will that behavior of that type be
a law of human conduct. Kant believes that it is a fundamental fact about
human reason that whenever we think about performing a particular act,
we always think about that act from a more general standpoint. We always
ask: Should that be a universal law governing human action? This is why
Kant believes that the ordinary person can always tell right from wrong.
When considering an action, the ordinary person, possessed of reason, will
always ask: Should it be a universal law of conduct that people do this
action? Immorality arises when we flout the moral law. Even though we
would not want a particular type of behavior to be the law, we selfishly
make an exception in our own case and allow ourselves to engage in the
behavior anyway.*

*In section G, Kant draws out a startling consequence of his theory of
morality. According to that theory, persons themselves are the ultimate
source of morality. Hence, Kant claims that all persons have ultimate and
intrinsic worth. No "market value" can be placed on any individual
person. This leads Kant to restate the moral law in a different way: we
must always treat persons with respect and never as a mere means to some
goal. Finally, in section H, Kant tries to illuminate the moral law from yet
another standpoint. He suggests that when acting we must always think of
ourselves as belonging to a community of persons, each of whom creates
the laws governing this realm by his or her own actions.*

[A. THE GOOD WILL]

Nothing in the world—indeed nothing even beyond the world—can
possibly be conceived which could be called good without qualification except
a *good will.* Intelligence, wit, judgment, and the other talents of the mind,
however they may be named, or courage, resoluteness, and perseverance as
qualities of temperament, are doubtless in many respects good and desirable.
But they can become extremely bad and harmful if the will, which is to make
use of these gifts of nature and which in its special constitution is called
character, is not good. It is the same with the gifts of fortune, power, riches,
honor, even health, general well-being, and the contentment with one's condition which is called happiness, make for pride and even arrogance if there is
not a good will to correct their influence on the mind and on its principles of
action so as to make it universally conformable to its end. It need hardly be
mentioned that the sight of a being adorned with no feature of a pure and
good will, yet enjoying uninterrupted prosperity, can never give pleasure to a
rational impartial observer. Thus the good will seems to constitute the indispensable condition even of worthiness to be happy.

Some qualities seem to be conducive to this good will and can facilitate its
action, but, in spite of that, they have no intrinsic unconditional worth. They

rather presuppose a good will, which limits the high esteem which one otherwise rightly has for them and prevents their being held to be absolutely good. Moderation in emotions and passions, self-control, and calm deliberation not only are good in many respects but even seem to constitute a part of the inner worth of the person. But however unconditionally they were esteemed by the ancients, they are far from being good without qualification. For without the principle of a good will they can become extremely bad, and the coolness of a villain makes him not only far more dangerous but also more directly abominable in our eyes than he would have seemed without it.

The good will is not good because of what it effects or accomplishes or because of its adequacy to achieve some proposed end; it is good only because of its willing, i.e., it is good of itself. And, regarded for itself, it is to be esteemed incomparably higher than anything which could be brought about by it in favor of any inclination or even of the sum total of all inclinations. Even if it should happen that, by a particularly unfortunate fate or by the niggardly provision of a stepmotherly nature, this will should be wholly lacking in power to accomplish its purpose, and if even the greatest effort should not avail it to achieve anything of its end, and if there remained only the good will (not as a mere wish but as the summoning of all the means in our power), it would sparkle like a jewel in its own right, as something that had its full worth in itself. Usefulness or fruitlessness can neither diminish nor augment this worth. Its usefulness would be only its setting, as it were, so as to enable us to handle it more conveniently in commerce or to attract the attention of those who are not yet connoisseurs, but not to recommend it to those who are experts or to determine its worth.

But there is something so strange in this idea of the absolute worth of the will alone, in which no account is taken of any use, that, notwithstanding the agreement even of common sense, the suspicion must arise that perhaps only high-flown fancy is its hidden basis, and that we may have misunderstood the purpose of nature in its appointment of reason as the ruler of our will. We shall therefore examine this idea from this point of view.

In the natural constitution of an organized being, i.e., one suitably adapted to life, we assume as an axiom that no organ will be found for any purpose which is not the fittest and best adapted to that purpose. Now if its preservation, its welfare—in a word, its happiness—were the real end of nature in a being having reason and will, then nature would have hit upon a very poor arrangement in appointing the reason of the creature to be the executor of this purpose. For all the actions which the creature has to perform with this intention, and the entire rule of its conduct, would be dictated much more exactly by instinct, and that end would be far more certainly attained by instinct than it ever could be by reason. And if, over and above this, reason should have been granted to the favored creature, it would have served only to let it contemplate the happy constitution of its nature, to admire it, to rejoice in it, and to be grateful for it to its beneficent cause. But reason would not have been given in order that the being should subject its faculty of desire to that weak and delusive guidance and to meddle with the purpose of nature. In a word, nature would have taken care that reason did not break forth into practical use nor have the presumption, with its weak insight, to think out for itself the plan of happiness and the means of attaining it. Nature would have taken over not only the choice of ends but also that of the means, and with wise foresight she would have entrusted both to instinct alone.

And, in fact, we find that the more a cultivated reason deliberately devotes itself to the enjoyment of life and happiness, the more the man falls short of true contentment. From this fact there arises in many persons, if only they are candid enough to admit it, a certain degree of misology, hatred of reason. This is particularly the case with those who are most experienced in its use. After counting all the advantages which they draw—I will not say from the invention of the arts of common luxury—from the sciences (which in the end seem to them to be also a luxury of the understanding), they nevertheless find that they have actually brought more trouble on their shoulders instead of gaining in happiness; they finally envy, rather than despise, the common run of men who are better guided by mere natural instinct and who do not permit their reason much influence on their conduct. And we must at least admit that a morose attitude or ingratitude to the goodness with which the world is governed is by no means found always among those who temper or refute the boasting eulogies which are given of the advantages of happiness and contentment with which reason is supposed to supply us. Rather their judgment is based on the idea of another and far more worthy purpose of their existence for which, instead of happiness, their reason is properly intended, this purpose, therefore, being the supreme condition to which the private purposes of men must for the most part defer.

Reason is not, however, competent to guide the will safely with regard to its objects and the satisfaction of all our needs (which it in part multiplies), and to this end an innate instinct would have led with far more certainty. But reason is given to us as a practical faculty, i.e., one which is meant to have an influence on the will. As nature has elsewhere distributed capacities suitable to the functions they are to perform, reason's proper function must be to produce a will good in itself and not one good merely as a means, for to the former reason is absolutely essential. This will must indeed not be the sole and complete good but the highest good and the condition of all others, even of the desire for happiness. In this case it is entirely compatible with the wisdom of nature that the cultivation of reason, which is required for the former unconditional purpose, at least in this life restricts in many ways—indeed can reduce to less than nothing—the achievement of the latter conditional purpose, happiness. For one perceives that nature here does not proceed unsuitably to its purpose, because reason, which recognizes its highest practical vocation in the establishment of a good will, is capable only of a contentment of its own kind, i.e., one that springs from the attainment of a purpose which is determined by reason, even though this injures the ends of inclination.

We have, then, to develop the concept of a will which is to be esteemed as good of itself without regard to anything else. It dwells already in the natural sound understanding and does not need so much to be taught as only to be brought to light. In the estimation of the total worth of our actions it always takes first place and is the condition of everything else. In order to show this, we shall take the concept of duty. It contains that of a good will, though with certain subjective restrictions and hindrances; but these are far from concealing it and making it unrecognizable, for they rather bring it out by contrast and make it shine forth all the brighter.

[B. ACTING FROM THE MOTIVE OF DUTY]

I here omit all actions which are recognized as opposed to duty, even though they may be useful in one respect or another, for with these the question does not arise at all as to whether they may be carried out *from* duty, since they conflict with it. I also pass over the actions which are really in accordance with duty and to which one has no direct inclination, rather executing them because impelled to do so by another inclination. For it is easily decided whether an action in accord with duty is performed from duty or for some selfish purpose. It is far more difficult to note this difference when the action is in accordance with duty and, in addition, the subject has a direct inclination to do it. For example, it is in fact in accordance with duty that a dealer should not overcharge an inexperienced customer, and wherever there is much business the prudent merchant does not do so, having a fixed price for everyone, so that a child may buy of him as cheaply as any other. Thus the customer is honestly served. But this is far from sufficient to justify the belief that the merchant has behaved in this way from duty and principles of honesty. His own advantage required this behavior; but it cannot be assumed that over and above that he had a direct inclination to the purchaser and that, out of love, as it were, he gave none an advantage in price over another. Therefore the action was done neither from duty nor from direct inclination but only for a selfish purpose.

On the other hand, it is a duty to preserve one's life, and moreover everyone has a direct inclination to do so. But for that reason the often anxious care which most men take of it has no intrinsic worth, and the maxim of doing so has no moral import. They preserve their lives according to duty, but not from duty. But if adversities and hopeless sorrow completely take away the relish for life, if an unfortunate man, strong in soul, is indignant rather than despondent or dejected over his fate and wishes for death, and yet preserves his life without loving it and from neither inclination nor fear but from duty—then his maxim has a moral import.

To be kind where one can is duty, and there are, moreover, many persons so sympathetically constituted that without any motive of vanity or selfishness they find an inner satisfaction in spreading joy, and rejoice in the contentment of others which they have made possible. But I say that, however dutiful and amiable it may be, that kind of action has no true moral worth. It is on a level with [actions arising from] other inclinations, such as the inclination to honor, which, if fortunately directed to what in fact accords with duty and is generally useful and thus honorable, deserve praise and encouragement but no esteem.

For the maxim lacks the moral import of an action done not from inclination but from duty. But assume that the mind of that friend to mankind was clouded by a sorrow of his own which extinguished all sympathy with the lot of others and that he still had the power to benefit others in distress, but that their need left him untouched because he was preoccupied with his own need. And now supposed him to tear himself, unsolicited by inclination, out of this dead insensibility and to perform this action only from duty and without any inclination—then for the first time his action has genuine moral worth. Furthermore, if nature has put little sympathy in the heart of a man, and if he, though an honest man, is by temperament cold and indifferent to the sufferings of others, perhaps because he is provided with special gifts of patience and fortitude and expects or even requires that others should have the same—and such a man would certainly not be the meanest product of nature—would not he find in himself a source from which to give himself a far higher worth than he could have got by having a good-natured temperament? This is unquestionably true even though nature did not make him philanthropic, for it is just here that the worth of the character is brought out, which is morally and incomparably the highest of all: he is beneficent not from inclination but from duty.

To secure one's own happiness is at least indirectly a duty, for discontent with one's condition under pressure from many cares and amid unsatisfied wants could easily become a great temptation to transgress duties. But without any view to duty all men have the strongest and deepest inclination to happiness, because in this idea all inclinations are summed up. But the precept of happiness is often so formulated that it definitely thwarts some inclinations, and men can make no definite and certain concept of the sum of satisfaction of all inclinations which goes under the name of happiness. It is not to be wondered at, therefore, that a single inclination, definite as to what it promises and as to the time at which it can be satisfied, can outweigh a fluctuating idea, and that, for example, a man with the gout can choose to enjoy what he likes and to suffer what he may, because according to his calculations at least on this occasion he has not sacrificed the enjoyment of the present moment to a perhaps groundless expectation of a happiness supposed to lie in health. But even in this case, if the universal inclination to happiness did not determine his will, and if health were not at least for him a necessary factor in these calculations, there yet would remain, as in all other cases, a law that he ought to promote his happiness, not from inclination but from duty. Only from this law would his conduct have true moral worth.

It is in this way, undoubtedly, that we should understand those passages of Scripture which command us to love our neighbor and even our enemy, for love as an inclination cannot be commanded. But beneficence from duty, when no inclination impels it and even when it is opposed by a natural and unconquerable aversion, is practical love, not pathological love; it resides in the will and not in the propensities of feeling, in principles of action and not in tender sympathy; and it alone can be commanded.

[Thus the first proposition of morality is that to have moral worth an action must be done from duty.] The second proposition is: An action performed from duty does not have its moral worth in the purpose which is to be achieved through it but in the maxim by which it is determined. Its moral value, therefore, does not depend on the realization of the object of the action but merely on the principle of volition by which the action is done, without any regard to the objects of the faculty of desire. From the preceding discussion it is clear that the purposes we may have for our actions and their effects as ends and incentives of the will cannot give the actions any unconditional and moral worth. Wherein, then, can this worth lie, if it is not in the will in relation to its hoped-for effect? It can lie nowhere else than in the principle of the will, irrespective of the ends which can be realized by such action. For the will stands, as it were, at the crossroads halfway between its a priori principle which is formal and its a posteriori incentive which is material. Since it must be determined by something, if it is done from duty it must be determined by the formal principle of volition as such since every material principle has been withdrawn from it.

The third principle, as a consequence of the two preceding, I would express as follows: Duty is the necessity of an action executed from respect for law. I can certainly have an inclination to the object as an effect of the proposed action, but I can never have respect for it precisely because it is a mere effect and not an activity of a will. Similarly, I can have no respect for any inclination whatsoever, whether my own or that of another; in the former case I can at most approve of it and in the latter I can even love it, i.e., see it as favorable to my own advantage. But that which is connected with my will merely as ground and not as consequence, that which does not serve my inclination but overpowers it or at least excludes it from being considered in making a choice— in a word, law itself—can be an object of respect and thus a command. Now as an act from duty wholly excludes the influence of inclination and therewith every object of the will, nothing remains which can determine the will objectively except the law, and nothing subjectively except pure respect for this practical law. This subjective element is the maxim[1] that I ought to follow such a law even if it thwarts all my inclinations.

Thus the moral worth of an action does not lie in the effect which is expected from it or in any principle of action which has to borrow its motive from this expected effect. For all these effects (agreeableness of my own condition, indeed even the promotion of the happiness of others) could be brought about through other causes and would not require the will of a rational being, while the highest and unconditional good can be found only in such a will. Therefore, the preeminent good can consist only in the conception of the law in itself (which can be present only in a rational being) so far as this conception and not the hoped-for effect is the determining ground of the will. This pre-eminent good, which we call moral, is already present in the person who acts

---

1 A maxim is the subjective principle of volition. The objective principle (i.e., that which would serve all rational beings also subjectively as a practical principle if reason had full power over the faculty of desire) is the practical law.

according to this conception, and we do not have to look for it first in the result.[2]

[C. THE MORAL LAW]

But what kind of a law can that be, the conception of which must determine the will without reference to the expected result? Under this condition alone the will can be called absolutely good without qualification. Since I have robbed the will of all impulses which could come to it from obedience to any law, nothing remains to serve as a principle of the will except universal conformity of its action to law as such. That is, I should never act in such a way that I could not also will that my maxim should be a universal law. Mere conformity to law as such (without assuming any particular law applicable to certain actions) serves as the principle of the will, and it must serve as such a principle if duty is not to be a vain delusion and chimerical concept. The common reason of mankind in its practical judgments is in perfect agreement with this and has this principle constantly in view.

Let the question, for example, be: May I, when in distress, make a promise with the intention not to keep it? I easily distinguish the two meanings which the question can have, viz., whether it is prudent to make a false promise, or whether it conforms to my duty. Undoubtedly the former can often be the case, though I do see clearly that it is not sufficient merely to escape from the present difficulty by this expedient, but that I must consider whether inconveniences much greater than the present one may not later spring from this lie. Even with all my supposed cunning, the consequences cannot be so easily foreseen. Loss of credit might be far more disadvantageous than the misfortune I now seek to avoid, and it is hard to tell whether it might not be more prudent to act according to a universal maxim and to make it a habit not to promise

2 It might be objected that I seek to take refuge in an obscure feeling behind the word "respect," instead of clearly resolving the question with a concept of reason. But though respect is a feeling, it is not one received through any [outer] influence but is self-wrought by a rational concept; thus it differs specifically from all feelings of the former kind which may be referred to inclination or fear. What I recognize directly as a law for myself I recognize with respect, which means merely the consciousness of the submission of my will to a law without the intervention of other influences on my mind. The direct determination of the will by the law and the consciousness of this determination is respect; thus respect can be regarded as the effect of the law on the subject and not as the cause of the law. Respect is properly the conception of a worth which thwarts my self-love. Thus it is regarded as an object neither of inclination nor of fear, though it has something analogous to both. The only object of respect is the law, and indeed only the law which we impose on ourselves and yet recognize as necessary in itself. As a law, we are subject to it without consulting self-love; as imposed on us by ourselves, it is a consequence of our will. In the former respect it is analogous to fear and in the latter to inclination. All respect for a person is only respect for the law (of righteousness, etc.) of which the person provides an example. Because we see the improvement of our talents as a duty, we think of a person of talents as the example of a law, as it were (the law that we should by practice become like him in his talents), and that constitutes our respect. All so-called moral interest consists solely in respect for the law.

anything without intending to fulfill it. But it is soon clear to me that such a maxim is based only on an apprehensive concern with consequences.

To be truthful from duty, however, is an entirely different thing from being truthful out of fear of disadvantageous consequences, for in the former case the concept of the action itself contains a law for me, while in the latter I must first look about to see what results for me may be connected with it. For to deviate from the principle of duty is certainly bad, but to be unfaithful to my maxim of prudence can sometimes be very advantageous to me, though it is certainly safe to abide by it. The shortest but most infallible way to find the answer to the question as to whether a deceitful promise is consistent with duty is to ask myself: Would I be content that my maxim (of extricating myself from difficulty by a false promise) should hold as a universal law for myself as well as for others? And could I say to myself that everyone may make a false promise when he is in a difficulty from which he otherwise cannot escape? I immediately see that I could will the lie but not a universal law to lie. For with such a law there would be no promises at all, inasmuch as it would be futile to make a pretense of my intention in regard to future actions to those who would not believe this pretense or—if they overhastily did so—who would pay me back in my own coin. Thus my maxim would necessarily destroy itself as soon as it was made a universal law.

[D. COMMON MORALITY
AND THE NEED FOR PHILOSOPHY]

I do not, therefore, need any penetrating acuteness in order to discern what I have to do in order that my volition may be morally good. Inexperienced in the course of the world, incapable of being prepared for all its contingencies, I ask myself only: Can I will that my maxim become a universal law? If not, it must be rejected, not because of any disadvantage accruing to myself or even to others, but because it cannot enter as a principle into a possible universal legislation, and reason extorts from me an immediate respect for such legislation. I do not as yet discern on what it is grounded (a question the philosopher may investigate), but I at least understand that it is an estimation of the worth which far outweighs all the worth of whatever is recommended by the inclinations, and that the necessity of my actions from pure respect for the practical law constitutes duty. To duty every other motive must give place, because duty is the condition of a will good in itself, whose worth transcends everything.

Thus within the moral knowledge of common human reason we have attained its principle. To be sure, common human reason does not think of it abstractly in such a universal form, but it always has it in view and uses it as the standard of its judgments. It would be easy to show how common human reason, with this compass, knows well how to distinguish what is good, what is bad, and what is consistent or inconsistent with duty. Without in the least teaching common reason anything new, we need only to draw its attention to its own principle, in the manner of Socrates, thus showing that neither science nor philosophy is needed in order to know what one has to do in order to be honest and good, and even wise and virtuous. We might have conjectured beforehand that the knowledge of what everyone is obliged to do and thus also to know would be within the reach of everyone, even the most ordinary man. Here we cannot but admire the great advantages which the practical faculty of judgment has over the theoretical in ordinary human understanding. In the theoretical, if ordinary reason ventures to go beyond the laws of experience and perceptions of the senses, it falls into sheer inconceivabilities and self-contradictions, or at least into a chaos of uncertainty, obscurity, and instability. In the practical, on the other hand, the power of judgment first shows itself to advantage when common understanding excludes all sensuous incentives from practical laws. It then becomes even subtle, quibbling with its own conscience or with other claims to what should be called right, or wishing to determine correctly for its own instruction the worth of certain actions. But the most remarkable thing about ordinary reason in its practical concern is that it may have as much hope as any philosopher of hitting the mark. In fact, it is almost more certain to do so than the philosopher, because he has no principle which the common understanding lacks, while his judgment is easily confused by a mass of irrelevant considerations, so that it easily turns aside from the correct way. Would it not, therefore, be wiser in moral matters to acquiesce in the common rational judgment, or at most to call in philosophy in order to make the system of morals more complete and comprehensible and its rules more convenient for use (especially in disputation) than to steer the common understanding from its happy simplicity in practical matters and to lead it through philosophy into a new path of inquiry and instruction?

Innocence is indeed a glorious thing, but, on the other hand, it is very sad that it cannot well maintain itself, being easily led astray. For this reason, even wisdom—which consists more in acting than in knowing—needs science, not to learn from it but to secure admission and permanence to its precepts. Man feels in himself a powerful counterpoise against all commands of duty which reason presents to him as so deserving of respect; this counterpoise is his needs and inclinations, the complete satisfaction of which he sums up under the name of happiness. Now reason issues inexorable commands without promising anything to the inclinations. It disregards, as it were, and holds in contempt those claims which are so impetuous and yet so plausible, and which will not allow themselves to be abolished by any command. From this a natural dialectic arises, i.e., a propensity to argue against the stern laws of duty and their validity, or at least to place their purity and strictness in doubt and, where possible, to make them more accordant with our wishes and inclinations. This is equivalent to corrupting them in their very foundations and destroying their dignity—a thing which even common practical reason cannot ultimately call good.

In this way common human reason is impelled to go outside its sphere and to take a step into the field of practical philosophy. But it is forced to do so not by any speculative need, which never occurs to it so long as it is satisfied to remain merely healthy reason; rather, it is so impelled on practical grounds in order to obtain information and clear instruction respecting the source of its principle and the correct determination of this principle in its opposition to the maxims which are based on need and inclination. It seeks this information in order to escape from the perplexity of opposing claims and to avoid the danger of losing all genuine moral principles through the equivocation in which it is easily involved. Thus, when practical common reason cultivates itself, a dialectic surreptitiously ensues which forces it to seek aid in philosophy, just as the same thing happens in the theoretical use of reason. In this case, as in the theoretical, it will find rest only in a thorough critical examination of our reason.

* * *

[E. ACTING ACCORDING TO THE CONCEPT OF LAW]

In this study we do not advance merely from the common moral judgment (which here is very worthy of respect) to the philosophical, as this has already been done, but we advance by natural stages from a popular philosophy (which goes no further than it can grope by means of examples) to metaphysics (which is not held back by anything empirical and which, as it must measure out the entire scope of rational knowledge of this kind, reaches even Ideas, where examples fail us). In order to make this advance, we must follow and clearly present the practical faculty of reason from its universal rules of determination to the point where the concept of duty arises from it.

Everything in nature works according to laws. Only a rational being has the capacity of acting according to the conception of laws, i.e., according to principles. This capacity is will. Since reason is required for the derivation of actions from laws, will is nothing else than practical reason. If reason infallibly determines the will, the actions which such a being recognizes as objectively necessary are also subjectively necessary. That is, the will is a faculty of choosing only that which reason, independently of inclination, recognizes as practically necessary, i.e., as good. But if reason of itself does not sufficiently determine the will, and if the will is subjugated to subjective conditions (certain incentives) which do not always agree with objective conditions; in a word, if the will is not of itself in complete accord with reason (the actual case of men), then the actions which are recognized as objectively necessary are subjectively contingent, and the determination of such a will according to objective laws is constraint. That is, the relation of objective laws to a will which is not completely good is conceived as the determination of the will of a rational being by principles of reason to which this will is not by nature necessarily obedient.

The conception of an objective principle, so far as it constrains a will, is a command (of reason), and the formula of this command is called an *imperative*.

All imperatives are expressed by an "ought" and thereby indicate the relation of an objective law of reason to a will which is not in its subjective constitution necessarily determined by this law. This relation is that of constraint. Imperatives say that it would be good to do or to refrain from doing something, but they say it to a will which does not always do something simply because it is presented as a good thing to do. Practical good is what determines the will by means of the conception of reason and hence not by subjective causes but, rather, objectively, i.e., on grounds which are valid for every rational being as such. It is distinguished from the pleasant as that which has an influence on the will only by means of a sensation from merely subjective causes, which hold only for the senses of this or that person and not as a principle of reason which holds for everyone.

A perfectly good will, therefore, would be equally subject to objective laws (of the good), but it could not be conceived as constrained by them to act in accord with them, because, according to its own subjective constitution, it can be determined to act only through the conception of the good. Thus no imperatives hold for the divine will or, more generally, for a holy will. The "ought" is here out of place, for the volition of itself is necessarily in unison with the law. Therefore imperatives are only formulas expressing the relation of objective laws of volition in general to the subjective imperfection of the will of this or that rational being, e.g., the human will.

All imperatives command either hypothetically or categorically. The former present the practical necessity of a possible action as a means to achieving something else which one desires (or which one may possibly desire). The categorical imperative would be one which presented an action as of itself objectively necessary, without regard to any other end.

Since every practical law presents a possible action as good and thus as necessary for a subject practically determinable by reason, all imperatives are formulas of the determination of action which is necessary by the principle of a will which is in any way good. If the action is good only as a means to something else, the imperative is hypothetical; but if it is thought of as good in itself, and hence as necessary in a will which of itself conforms to reason as the principle of this will, the imperative is categorical.

The imperative thus says what action possible to me would be good, and it presents the practical rule in relation to a will which does not forthwith perform an action simply because it is good, in part because the subject does not always know that the action is good and in part (when he does know it) because his maxims can still be opposed to the objective principles of practical reason.

The hypothetical imperative, therefore, says only that the action is good to some purpose, possible or actual. In the former case it is a problematical, in the latter an assertorical, practical principle. The categorical imperative, which declares the action to be of itself objectively necessary without making any reference to a purpose, i.e., without having any other end, holds as an apodictical (practical) principle.

•   •   •

[F. HOW IS THE CATEGORICAL IMPERATIVE POSSIBLE?]

In attacking this problem, we will first inquire whether the mere concept of a categorical imperative does not also furnish the formula containing the proposition which alone can be a categorical imperative. For even when we know the formula of the imperative, to learn how such an absolute law is possible will require difficult and special labors which we shall postpone to the last section.

If I think of a hypothetical imperative as such, I do not know what it will contain until the condition is stated [under which it is an imperative]. But if I think of a categorical imperative, I know immediately what it contains. For since the imperative contains besides the law only the necessity that the maxim should accord with this law, while the law contains no condition to which it is restricted, there is nothing remaining in it except the universality of law as such to which the maxim of the action should conform; and in effect this conformity alone is represented as necessary by the imperative.

There is, therefore, only one categorical imperative. It is: Act only according to that maxim by which you can at the same time will that it should become a universal law.

Now if all imperatives of duty can be derived from this one imperative as a principle, we can at least show what we understand by the concept of duty and what it means, even though it remain undecided whether that which is called duty is an empty concept or not.

The universality of law according to which effects are produced constitutes what is properly called nature in the most general sense (as to form), i.e., the existence of things so far as it is determined by universal laws. [By analogy], then, the universal imperative of duty can be expressed as follows: Act as though the maxim of your action were by your will to become a universal law of nature.

We shall now enumerate some duties, adopting the usual division of them into duties to ourselves and to others and into perfect and imperfect duties.

1. A man who is reduced to despair by a series of evils feels a weariness with life but is still in possession of his reason sufficiently to ask whether it would not be contrary to his duty to himself to take his own life. Now he asks whether the maxim of his action could become a universal law of nature. His maxim, however, is: For love of myself, I make it my principle to shorten my life when by a longer duration it threatens more evil than satisfaction. But it is questionable whether this principle of self-love could become a universal law of nature. One immediately sees a contradiction in a system of nature whose law would be to destroy life by the feeling whose special office is to impel the improvement of life. In this case it would not exist as nature; hence that maxim cannot obtain as a law of nature, and thus it wholly contradicts the supreme principle of all duty.

2. Another man finds himself forced by need to borrow money. He well knows that he will not be able to repay it, but he also sees that nothing will

be loaned him if he does not firmly promise to repay it at a certain time. He desires to make such a promise, but he has enough conscience to ask himself whether it is not improper and opposed to duty to relieve his distress in such a way. Now, assuming he does decide to do so, the maxim of his action would be as follows: When I believe myself to be in need of money, I will borrow money and promise to repay it, although I know I shall never do so. Now this principle of self-love or of his own benefit may very well be compatible with his whole future welfare, but the question is whether it is right. He changes the pretension of self-love into a universal law and then puts the question: How would it be if my maxim became a universal law? He immediately sees that it could never hold as a universal law of nature and be consistent with itself; rather it must necessarily contradict itself. For the universality of a law which says that anyone who believes himself to be in need could promise what he pleased with the intention of not fulfilling it would make the promise itself and the end to be accomplished by it impossible; no one would believe what was promised to him but would only laugh at any such assertion as vain pretense.

3. A third finds in himself a talent which could, by means of some cultivation, make him in many respects a useful man. But he finds himself in comfortable circumstances and prefers indulgence in pleasure to troubling himself with broadening and improving his fortunate natural gifts. Now, however, let him ask whether his maxim of neglecting his gifts, besides agreeing with his propensity to idle amusement, agrees also with what is called duty. He sees that a system of nature could indeed exist in accordance with such a law, even though man (like the inhabitants of the South Sea Islands) should let his talents rust and resolve to devote his life merely to idleness, indulgence, and propagation—in a word, to pleasure. But he cannot possibly will that this should become a universal law of nature or that it should be implanted in us by a natural instinct. For, as a rational being, he necessarily wills that all his faculties should be developed, inasmuch as they are given to him for all sorts of possible purposes.

4. A fourth man, for whom things are going well, sees that others (whom he could help) have to struggle with great hardships, and he asks, "What concern of mine is it? Let each one be as happy as heaven wills, or as he can make himself; I will not take anything from him or even envy him; but to his welfare or to his assistance in time of need I have no desire to contribute." If such a way of thinking were a universal law of nature, certainly the human race could exist, and without doubt even better than in a state where everyone talks of sympathy and good will, or even exerts himself occasionally to practice them while, on the other hand, he cheats when he can and betrays or otherwise violates the rights of man. Now although it is possible that a universal law of nature according to that maxim could exist, it is nevertheless impossible to will that such a principle should hold everywhere as a law of nature. For a will which resolved this would conflict with itself, since instances can often arise in which he would need the love and sympathy of others, and in which he would have robbed himself, by such a law of nature springing from his own will, of all hope of the aid he desires.

The foregoing are a few of the many actual duties, or at least of duties we hold to be actual, whose derivation from the one stated principle is clear. We must be able to will that a maxim of our action become a universal law; this is the canon of the moral estimation of our action generally. Some actions are of such a nature that their maxim cannot even be *thought* as a universal law of nature without contradiction, far from it being possible that one could will that it should be such. In others this internal impossibility is not found, though it is still impossible to *will* that their maxim should be raised to the universality of a law of nature, because such a will would contradict itself. We easily see that the former maxim conflicts with the stricter or narrower (imprescriptible) duty, the latter with broader (meritorious) duty. Thus all duties, so far as the kind of obligation (not the object of their action) is concerned, have been completely exhibited by these examples in their dependence on the one principle.

When we observe ourselves in any transgression of a duty, we find that we do not actually will that our maxim should become a universal law. That is impossible for us; rather, the contrary of this maxim should remain as a law generally, and we only take the liberty of making an exception to it for ourselves or for the sake of our inclination, and for this one occasion. Consequently, if we weighed everything from one and the same standpoint, namely, reason, we would come upon a contradiction in our own will, viz., that a certain principle is objectively necessary as a universal law and yet subjectively does not hold universally but rather admits exceptions. However, since we regard our action at one time from the point of view of a will wholly conformable to reason and then from that of a will affected by inclinations, there is actually no contradiction, but rather an opposition of inclination to the precept of reason (*antagonismus*). In this the universality of the principle (*universalitas*) is changed into mere generality (*generalitas*), whereby the practical principle of reason meets the maxim halfway. Although this cannot be justified in our own impartial judgment, it does show that we actually acknowledge the validity of the categorical imperative and allow ourselves (with all respect to it) only a few exceptions which seem to us to be unimportant and forced upon us.

We have thus at least established that if duty is a concept which is to have significance and actual legislation for our actions, it can be expressed only in categorical imperatives and not at all in hypothetical ones. For every application of it we have also clearly exhibited the content of the categorical imperative which must contain the principle of all duty (if there is such). This is itself very much. But we are not yet advanced far enough to prove a priori that that kind of imperative really exists, that there is a practical law which of itself commands absolutely and without any incentives, and that obedience to this law is duty.

[G. THE ULTIMATE WORTH OF PERSONS]

[*We must now inquire how such a categorical imperative is possible.*]
With a view to attaining this, it is extremely important to remember that we must not let ourselves think that the reality of this principle can be derived

from the particular constitution of human nature. For duty is practical unconditional necessity of action; it must, therefore, hold for all rational beings (to which alone an imperative can apply), and only for that reason can it be a law for all human wills. Whatever is derived from the particular natural situation of man as such, or from certain feelings and propensities, or even from a particular tendency of the human reason which might not hold necessarily for the will of every rational being (if such a tendency is possible), can give a maxim valid for us but not a law; that is, it can give a subjective principle by which we might act only if we have the propensity and inclination, but not an objective principle by which we would be directed to act even if all our propensity, inclination, and natural tendency were opposed to it. This is so far the case that the sublimity and intrinsic worth of the command is the better shown in a duty the fewer subjective causes there are for it and the more there are against it; the latter do not weaken the constraint of the law or diminish its validity.

Here we see philosophy brought to what is, in fact, a precarious position, which should be made fast even though it is supported by nothing in either heaven or earth. Here philosophy must show its purity as the absolute sustainer of its laws, and not as the herald of those which an implanted sense or who knows what tutelary nature whispers to it. Those may be better than no laws at all, but they can never afford fundamental principles, which reason alone dictates. These fundamental principles must originate entirely a priori and thereby obtain their commanding authority; they can expect nothing from the inclination of men but everything from the supremacy of the law and due respect for it. Otherwise they condemn man to self-contempt and inner abhorrence.

Thus everything empirical is not only wholly unworthy to be an ingredient in the principle of morality but is even highly prejudicial to the purity of moral practices themselves. For, in morals, the proper and inestimable worth of an absolutely good will consists precisely in the freedom of the principle of action from all influences from contingent grounds which only experience can furnish. We cannot too much or too often warn against the lax or even base manner of thought which seeks principles among empirical motives and laws, for human reason in its weariness is glad to rest on this pillow. In a dream of sweet illusions (in which it embraces not Juno but a cloud), it substitutes for morality a bastard patched up from limbs of very different parentage, which looks like anything one wishes to see in it, but not like virtue to anyone who has ever beheld her in her true form.

The question then is: Is it a necessary law for all rational beings that they should always judge their actions by such maxims as they themselves could will to serve as universal laws? If it is such a law, it must be connected (wholly a priori) with the concept of the will of a rational being as such. But in order to discover this connection we must, however reluctantly, take a step into metaphysics, although into a region of it different from speculative philosophy, i.e., into metaphysics of morals. In a practical philosophy it is not a question of assuming grounds for what happens but of assuming laws of what ought to happen even though it may never happen—that is to say, objective, practical laws. Hence in practical philosophy we need not inquire into the reasons why something pleases or displeases, how the pleasure of mere feeling differs from taste, and whether this is distinct from a general satisfaction of reason. Nor need we ask on what the feeling of pleasure or displeasure rests, how desires and inclinations arise, and how, finally, maxims arise from desires and inclination under the co-operation of reason. For all these matters belong to an empirical psychology, which would be the second part of physics if we consider it as philosophy of nature so far as it rests on empirical laws. But here it is a question of objectively practical laws and thus of the relation of a will to itself so far as it determines itself only by reason; for everything which has a relation to the empirical automatically falls away, because if reason of itself alone determines conduct it must necessarily do so a priori. The possibility of reason thus determining conduct must now be investigated.

The will is thought of as a faculty of determining itself to action in accordance with the conception of certain laws. Such a faculty can be found only in rational beings. That which serves the will as the objective ground of its self-determination is an end, and, if it is given by reason alone, it must hold alike for all rational beings. On the other hand, that which contains the ground of the possibility of the action, whose result is an end, is called the means. The subjective ground of desire is the incentive, while the objective ground of volition is the motive. Thus arises the distinction between subjective ends, which rest on incentives, and objective ends, which depend on motives valid for every rational being. Practical principles are formal when they disregard all subjective ends; they are material when they have subjective ends, and thus certain incentives, as their basis. The ends which a rational being arbitrarily proposes to himself as consequences of his action are material ends and are without exception only relative, for only their relation to a particularly constituted faculty of desire in the subject gives them their worth. And this worth cannot, therefore, afford any universal principles for all rational beings or valid and necessary principles for every volition. That is, they cannot give rise to any practical laws. All these relative ends, therefore, are grounds for hypothetical imperatives only.

But suppose that there were something the existence of which in itself had absolute worth, something which, as an end in itself, could be a ground of definite laws. In it and only in it could lie the ground of a possible categorical imperative, i.e., of a practical law.

Now, I say, man and, in general, every rational being exists as an end in himself and not merely as a means to be arbitrarily used by this or that will. In all his actions, whether they are directed to himself or to other rational beings, he must always be regarded at the same time as an end. All objects of inclinations have only a conditional worth, for if the inclinations and the needs founded on them did not exist, their object would be without worth. The inclinations themselves as the sources of needs, however, are so lacking in absolute worth that the universal wish of every rational being must be indeed to free himself completely from them. Therefore, the worth of any objects to be obtained by our actions is at all times conditional. Beings whose existence does not depend on our will but on nature, if they are not rational beings, have only a relative worth as means and are therefore called "things"; on the other hand, rational beings are designated "persons" because their nature indicates that they are ends in themselves, i.e., things which may not be used merely as means. Such a being is thus an object of respect and, so far, restricts all [arbitrary] choice. Such beings are not merely subjective ends whose existence as a result of our action has a worth for us, but are objective ends, i.e., beings whose existence in itself is an end. Such an end is one for which no other end can be substituted, to which these beings should serve merely as means. For, without them, nothing of absolute worth could be found, and if all worth is conditional and thus contingent, no supreme practical principle for reason could be found anywhere.

Thus if there is to be a supreme practical principle and a categorical imperative for the human will, it must be one that forms an objective principle of the will from the conception of that which is necessarily an end for everyone because it is an end in itself. Hence this objective principle can serve as a universal practical law. The ground of this principle is: rational nature exists as an end in itself. Man necessarily thinks of his own existence in this way; thus far it is a subjective principle of human actions. Also every other rational being thinks of his existence by means of the same rational ground which holds also for myself; thus it is at the same time an objective principle from which, as a supreme practical ground, it must be possible to derive all laws of the will. The practical imperative, therefore, is the following: Act so that you treat humanity, whether in your own person or in that of another, always as an end and never as a means only.

● ● ●

[H. MORAL AGENTS AS LAW-GIVERS TO THEMSELVES]

If we now look back upon all previous attempts which have ever been undertaken to discover the principle of morality, it is not to be wondered at that they all had to fail. Man was seen to be bound to laws by his duty, but it was not seen that he is subject only to his own, yet universal, legislation, and that he is only bound to act in accordance with his own will, which is, however, designed by nature to be a will giving universal laws. For if one thought of him as subject only to a law (whatever it may be), this necessarily implied some interest as a stimulus or compulsion to obedience because the law did not arise from his will. Rather, his will was constrained by something else according to a law to act in a certain way. By this strictly necessary consequence, however, all the labor of finding a supreme ground for duty was irrevocably lost, and one never arrived at duty but only at the necessity of action from a certain interest. This might be his own interest or that of another, but in either case the imperative always had to be conditional and could not at all serve as a moral command. This principle I will call the principle of *autonomy* of the will in contrast to all other principles which I accordingly count under heteronomy.

The concept of each rational being as a being that must regard itself as giving universal law through all the maxims of its will, so that it may judge itself and its actions from this standpoint, leads to a very fruitful concept, namely, that of a *realm of ends.*

By "realm" I understand the systematic union of different rational beings through common laws. Because laws determine ends with regard to their universal validity, if we abstract from the personal difference of rational beings and thus from all content of their private ends, we can think of a whole of all ends in systematic connection, a whole of rational beings as ends in themselves as well as of the particular ends which each may set for himself. This is a realm of ends, which is possible on the aforesaid principles. For all rational beings stand under the law that each of them should treat himself and all others never merely as means but in every case also as an end in himself. Thus there arises a systematic union of rational beings through common objective laws. This is a realm which may be called a realm of ends (certainly only an ideal), because what these laws have in view is just the relation of these beings to each other as ends and means.

A rational being belongs to the realm of ends as a member when he gives universal laws in it while also himself subject to these laws. He belongs to it as sovereign when he, as legislating, is subject to the will of no other. The rational being must regard himself always as legislative in a realm of ends possible through the freedom of the will, whether he belongs to it as member or as sovereign. He cannot maintain the latter position merely through the maxims of his will but only when he is a completely independent being without need and with power adequate to his will.

Morality, therefore, consists in the relation of every action to that legislation through which alone a realm of ends is possible. This legislation, however, must be found in every rational being. It must be able to arise from his will, whose principle then is to take no action according to any maxim which would be inconsistent with its being a universal law and thus to act only so that the will through its maxims could regard itself at the same time as universally lawgiving. If now the maxims do not by their nature already necessarily conform to this objective principle of rational beings as universally lawgiving, the necessity of acting according to that principle is called practical constraint, i.e., duty. Duty pertains not to the sovereign in the realm of ends, but rather to each member, and to each in the same degree.

The practical necessity of acting according to this principle, i.e., duty, does not rest at all on feelings, impulses, and inclinations; it rests merely on the relation of rational beings to one another, in which the will of a rational being must always be regarded as legislative, for otherwise it could not be thought of as an end in itself. Reason, therefore, relates every maxim of the will as giving universal laws to every other will and also to every action toward itself;

it does so not for the sake of any other practical motive or future advantage but rather from the idea of the dignity of a rational being who obeys no law except that which he himself also gives.

In the realm of ends everything has either a *price* or a *dignity*. Whatever has a price can be replaced by something else as its equivalent; on the other hand, whatever is above all price, and therefore admits of no equivalent, has a dignity.

That which is related to general human inclinations and needs has a *market price*. That which, without presupposing any need, accords with a certain taste, i.e., with pleasure in the mere purposeless play of our faculties, has an *affective price*. But that which constituted the condition under which alone something can be an end in itself does not have mere relative worth, i.e., a price, but an intrinsic worth, i.e., *dignity*.

Now morality is the condition under which alone a rational being can be an end in itself, because only through it is it possible to be a legislative member in the realm of ends. Thus morality and humanity, so far as it is capable of morality, alone have dignity. Skill and diligence in work have a market value; wit, lively imagination, and humor have an affective price; but fidelity in promises and benevolence on principle (not from instinct) have intrinsic worth. Nature and likewise art contain nothing which could replace their lack, for their worth consists not in effects which flow from them, nor in advantage and utility which they procure; it consists only in intentions, i.e., maxims of the will which are ready to reveal themselves in this manner through actions even though success does not favor them. These actions need no recommendation from any subjective disposition or taste in order that they may be looked upon with immediate favor and satisfaction, nor do they have need of any immediate propensity or feeling directed to them. They exhibit the will which performs them as the object of an immediate respect, since nothing but reason is required in order to impose them on the will. The will is not to be cajoled into them, for this, in the case of duties, would be a contradiction. This esteem lets the worth of such a turn of mind be recognized as dignity and puts it infinitely beyond any price, with which it cannot in the least be brought into competition or comparison without, as it were, violating its holiness.

And what is it that justifies the morally good disposition or virtue in making such lofty claims? Is it nothing less than the participation it affords the rational being in giving universal laws. He is thus fitted to be a member in a possible realm of ends to which his own nature already destined him. For, as an end in himself, he is destined to be legislative in the realm of ends, free from all laws of nature and obedient only to those which he himself gives. Accordingly, his maxims can belong to a universal legislation to which he is at the same time also subject. A thing has no worth other than that determined for it by the law. The legislation which determines all worth must therefore have a dignity, i.e., unconditional and incomparable worth. For the esteem which a rational being must have for it, only the word "respect" is a suitable expression. Autonomy is thus the basis of the dignity of both human nature and every rational nature.

The three aforementioned ways of presenting the principle of morality are fundamentally only so many formulas of the very same law, and each of them unites the others in itself.

• • •

31

Kant's Moral Philosophy

WILLIAM NELSON

William Nelson (b. 1945) is Professor of Philosophy at the University of Houston. He is the author of On Justifying Democracy. *This selection is from his book* Morality: What's in It for Me?, *chapter 3.*

In the selection, Nelson summarizes and interprets Kant's moral theory. He focuses on two aspects of the theory that are especially important and controversial. The first is Kant's view that the laws of morality must be categorical—that is, that their demands must be independent of our desires or "inclinations." As Nelson points out, this Kantian view provides one way of capturing the familiar distinction between acts that merely conform to moral requirements and acts that are morally praiseworthy. It allows us to say that a morally praiseworthy act is one whose motivation is independent of desire. However, as Nelson also points out, this is not the only way of capturing the distinction. An alternative, suggested by Aristotle (see reading 35) is that a morally praiseworthy action is motivated by a particular sort of desire—namely, a settled disposition to do what is right.

The other Kantian theme that Nelson explores is universality. The moral point of view is often said to be impartial, and a version of Kant's categorical imperative—roughly, act only on maxims that you can will to be universal laws—is one important way of understanding this idea. However, Nelson again argues that it is not the only way. One alternative is the utilitarian view that each person's happiness counts as much as another's; and there are further alternatives too. To understand fully the impartiality requirement, we must choose among these competing interpretations.

In the preface to the *Grounding for the Metaphysics of Morals*,[1] Kant speaks of morality in terms of moral *laws*. He wishes to work out a "pure moral philosophy," a moral philosophy that makes sense of "the common idea of duty and of moral laws." According to this common idea, he thinks, a law

---

[1] Immanuel Kant, *Grounding for the Metaphysics of Morals*, 1785, trans. James W. Ellington (Indianapolis: Hackett, 1981). I rely on this translation, but my page references will be to the standard Prussian Academy edition of Kant's works. These appear in the margins of Ellington's edition and of most other scholarly editions of Kant's work.

that is morally valid "must carry with it absolute necessity" and must apply to all rational beings [389]. Yet these laws are to be distinguished from laws of nature, that is, laws of the kind the natural sciences discover. The latter are laws "according to which everything does happen," while moral laws, which he also calls "laws of freedom," are laws "according to which everything ought to happen" [387–388]. Kant begins his investigation of morality in the first section, however, not by discussing moral laws directly but by discussing the nature of morally good *action*.

According to Kant, nothing in the world is "good without qualification," except for "a *good will*." Other "talents of the mind" and "qualities of tempera-ment" of the kind Aristotle and Epictetus valued (Kant mentions wit, judgment, courage, moderation in emotions and passions, and self-control, among others) are good in some respects, he says, but they have no "unconditional worth." Only a good will has that [393–394]. As I understand Kant, he thinks of these judgments as judgments his readers will find perfectly natural. They are a fundamental part of the moral outlook he shares with his readers. What he believes is that when we look carefully at what a good will is, at what acting with a good will involves, we will be led to understand the essential nature of morality. What, then, is it like to act with a good will?

When *we* speak of a man of goodwill, we probably think of someone who is kind and generous, charitable in his judgments of others and anxious to cooperate. But Kant does not think of a morally good will in these terms. In order to understand what it is like to have or to act from a good will, Kant says, we must begin with the concept of "duty" [397]. The idea, evidently, is that when people act with a good will, they act *from duty*. But what does acting from duty amount to? When people act from duty, they do what morality requires (refrain from cheating customers, help others in need), but they do not do it because they think it will promote some further goal they seek. They do not even act from a direct inclination, like a direct benevolent concern for the welfare of others [397–398]. People who act with a good will act "not from inclination, but from duty" [399]. Acting with a good will then, is inconsis-tent with acting from any inclination.

In addition, Kant says, acting with a good will is good in itself, regardless of whether one actually succeeds in achieving the purpose one intended to achieve [399, cf. 394]. Thus, while acting with a good will is acting from duty, acting from duty is not a matter of actually achieving some purpose (like successfully alleviating the distress of someone in need). Instead, acting from duty is (just) a matter of acting in a way necessitated by respect for the moral law [400–401]. We might put it this way: A person who acts with a good will, a person whose actions have unconditional worth, is a person who endeavors to do what is right, *just* because it is required by the moral law. Such people act, as we might say, purely on principle and not as a result of any desire.

Both parts of this are important. A person who acts, say, on the principle of not telling a lie, but who acts on this principle because she hopes to gain the trust of others, is acting on an inclination and so is not acting from duty. Indeed, even someone who has the virtue of truthfulness, as Aristotle might understand it—a person who has acquired an aversion to lying itself and so has a desire not to lie and acts on it—is not acting with a good will as Kant understands this. A person who acts with a good will acts on a moral law, but on *no* inclination, not even a direct one.

This idea creates a puzzle for Kant:

> What sort of law can that be the thought of which must determine the will without reference to any expected effect, so that the will can be called absolutely good without qualification? Since I have deprived the will of every impulse that might arise for it from obeying any particular law, there is nothing left to serve the will as principle except the universal conformity of its actions to law as such, i.e., I should never act except in such a way that I can also will that my maxim should become a universal law. [402]

When we act with a good will, Kant is saying, the only motive for our action, the only explanation for what we do, is that the act is required by a moral principle. But how can that fact by itself explain our acting as we do? Kant apparently thinks that any ordinary moral principle, like "don't lie" or "treat people fairly," cannot in itself be a person's only reason for acting. If that is one's principle, then one must be acting on it in part because one also has some inclination, direct or indirect, that leads one to care about acting on the principle. What he concludes, in the above passage, is that there is only one principle that can motivate an action independent of any inclination. That principle says one must always act in such a way that one can will one's maxim (the specific principle on which one acts) to be a universal law.

I will call this principle the "Universalization Principle." In my judgment, Kant fails to show that, in fact, this is the only principle one could be acting on if one is acting with a good will. (He does not propose or consider alternatives.) However, I will put this objection to one side. The Universalization Principle is philosophically interesting in its own right. For one thing, it seems to embody an interesting conception of the distinctive standpoint of morality, and I will have a good deal to say about it subsequently. For the moment, however, I shall focus on the main line of Kant's argument. For, *if* Kant had indeed shown that the Universalization Principle is the principle on which one must be acting if one acts with a good will, and *if* he were right that acting morally is acting with a good will, he would have shown that anyone who ever acts morally acts on this principle.

There are two big "ifs" here; but assuming for the moment that Kant is right, further consequences follow. One consequence is that it is very difficult ever to *know* whether someone is acting with a morally good will: "We meet frequent and—as we ourselves admit—justified complaints that there cannot be cited a single certain example of the disposition to act from pure duty" [406]. "It is indeed sometimes the case ... that we can find nothing except the moral ground of duty that could have been strong enough to move us to this or that good action ... [b]ut there cannot with certainty be at all inferred from this that some secret impulse of self-love, merely appearing as the idea of duty, was not the actual determining cause of the will" [407].

If Kant is right, an essential part of our idea of morality is that people act morally—with a good will—only when their actions are not based on any desire or inclination. They must be acting *simply* in obedience to some law and *just* because that law requires them so to act. But since it is hard to know whether some inclination plays even a small role in a decision to act, we never know for sure whether a person acts with a good will.

In order to sharpen and clarify this point, Kant formulates a distinction between two different kinds of law that apply to people. Human beings, like other things in nature, are subject to laws. Some laws, like the law of gravity, we "obey" automatically. No one bothers to say that we *ought* to obey this law. We just do. Laws of physics, chemistry, and biology determine what we do because we are physical bodies. We are not, however, *just* physical bodies. We also have a rational nature, and how we behave is determined partly by the laws of reason. As Kant sees it, laws of reason, which include laws of logic (good reasoning) and also moral laws and laws of rational choice and action generally, govern the behavior of rational creatures just as laws of physics or chemistry govern the behavior of physical bodies.

Though we are rational creatures, and so tend to behave as reason requires, we are not perfectly rational. While laws of reason sometimes help determine how we behave—while they sometimes explain what we do—the forces of reason are not always sufficiently strong to guarantee that we think or act rationally. Laws like laws of reason or morality, the consciousness of which can determine how we act but which do not do so automatically, Kant calls "imperatives." And imperatives, he says, are expressed by the term "ought" [412–413]. While we don't say that people *ought* to obey laws of gravity, we do say that they *ought* to be moral or that they *ought* to reason validly.

There are, Kant goes on to say, two kinds of imperative: hypothetical imperatives and categorical imperatives. What is the difference? Hypothetical imperatives "represent the practical necessity of a possible action as a means for attaining something else that one wants (or may possibly want). The categorical imperative would be one that represented an action as objectively necessary in itself, without reference to another end" [414]. To put it another way, hypothetical imperatives tell us how to behave rationally in the pursuit of some independently given end or goal; categorical imperatives tell us what is rationally required, whatever goals we have or do not have.

Imperatives are expressed by the word "ought." When an imperative applies to someone, we say there is something the person ought to do. Part of what Kant means when he says that some ought-judgments are hypothetical and some categorical is that what makes hypothetical oughts true or false is different from what makes categorical oughts true or false. Suppose I say to my daughter that she ought to take out the garbage. Is it true that she ought to do so? Well, if the imperative is (merely) hypothetical, then it is true that she ought to take out the garbage *only if her doing so is necessary for her because of something she wants*. (Perhaps she will get her allowance only if she takes out the garbage.) If it turns out she does not want her allowance or that she can get it without taking out the garbage, then the hypothetical ought-judgment would be false.

If the imperative is categorical, on the other hand, then it is true *even if her taking out the garbage satisfies no desire or inclination she has.* Categorical imperatives, when they are true, are true regardless of the desires or inclinations of those to whom they apply. Hypothetical imperatives, as Kant says later, are "contingent." They "can always be ignored once the purpose is abandoned" [420]. Categorical imperatives, by contrast, are *inescapable.*

The laws and imperatives of morality must be categorical, if Kant is correct. It is easy to see why he has to believe this, given the rest of his theory. According to Kant, when one acts morally, with a good will, one acts on a moral law but not on a desire or inclination. But notice that if one were acting on a mere hypothetical imperative, an essential part of one's reason for acting *would* be some desire or inclination. That is because hypothetical imperatives apply to people only when they have a desire that is satisfied by acting on the imperative. Hence, moral laws must apply categorically, not hypothetically. And on this point many modern philosophers, even when they reject the rest of what Kant says, agree. It is almost a commonplace that, if a moral judgment is true—if it is true, for example, that we morally ought not to steal or cheat—it is true regardless of whether we *want* something that we get by obeying these rules.

Having formulated the distinction between hypothetical and categorical imperatives, Kant next asks how categorical imperatives are *possible* [419]. This is a hard question for Kant because, as he understands the idea of a categorical imperative, it is not just an imperative that is true, regardless of the agent's desires. It is also an imperative that the agent is not free to ignore: If a categorical imperative applies to me, then I must have an inescapable reason to do what it requires, and this reason must also be the kind of reason that motivates me to act and could serve to explain how I act as I do. What concerns Kant is how there could be imperatives, or laws, that explain, all by themselves, a person's acting a certain way. The real question is how moral *action,* understood as action motivated by a categorical imperative, is possible. How can a categorical moral law be a motivating reason for a person's action in the same way that the law of gravity is the reason for an object's falling to earth?

When we explain an action, the explanation usually has at least two parts. Why did Alfred put money in the soft drink machine? Because he wanted a cold drink *and* because he thought that, if one wants a cold drink, one ought to put money in a soft drink machine. If he hadn't believed this, or something like it, then no matter how thirsty he was, that wouldn't have explained putting the money in the machine. Thirst, by itself, doesn't explain putting quarters in slots. The hypothetical imperative, "if one wants a soft drink, one ought to . . . ," is part of the explanation, too. But then, this imperative cannot explain the action all by itself, either. The general rule helps explain the action only if there is also a desire for a cold drink. That, again, is why hypothetical imperatives cannot be the basis for *moral* action, as Kant understands it; for moral action is not even partly based on desires.

The problem Kant means to address when he asks how categorical imperatives are possible is the problem of explaining how some imperatives—the categorical ones—can explain action all by themselves. How is it possible that someone does something, for example, helps someone in need or refrains from cheating on a test, and does it *just* because the moral law requires it, and not because he or she has an independent desire to do it?

This is equivalent to the question of whether anyone ever *could* act with a good will. As Kant himself says in a passage I quoted, we cannot find out whether such action is possible by observing others or even ourselves. Someone may appear to be motivated solely by a categorical demand of morality, but it is always possible that there is some independent desire or inclination, hidden perhaps even from the agent himself.

Kant's own idea (which he does not justify independently) is that the categorical imperatives of morality apply to us because they are requirements of reason. Like rules of logic, they tell us what we need to do to be rational. Since all categorical imperatives derive from one basic one, the one he formulated as the Universalization Principle, and since this principle is a principle of reason, he concludes that we must follow this principle if we are to be rational. But since we are naturally rational creatures in part, we are to some extent motivated naturally to do what this and other principles of reason require. If we were purely rational creatures, we would follow laws of reason as automatically as we "follow" the law of gravity. (They wouldn't be imperatives, or "oughts," for us.) We aren't perfectly rational, though, and so we don't always act rationally (or morally). Still, when we do so, we are following our rational nature. Reason is in charge.

Acting on categorical imperatives is possible, then, according to Kant, because these imperatives are laws of reason and because, as rational creatures, it is natural for us to follow such laws. And this leads Kant to a further interesting idea. He thinks of our rational nature as our *real* nature, our essential nature, and he proposes that we act *freely* only when we act according to our real nature. But we act fully rationally only when we follow all laws of reason, and we do this only when we follow moral laws. Hence, we are fully free only when we act morally. Thus, to be free, we must rise above our nature as creatures of inclination and let our behavior be determined by rational and moral principles. The laws of morality, as he says in the preface, are laws of freedom. By acting morally, we realize our nature as free and rational beings. (Here Kant echoes, in an interesting way, the Stoic idea, found in the work of Epictetus, that the ethical life is a life of freedom. By following Stoic teachings, we avoid being dominated either by external events or by our own emotions. We *choose* how we will respond to events.)

Moral action is possible, as Kant conceives it, only if it is possible that we sometimes act as we do just *because reason requires it.* Is this possible? Does reason ever explain our conduct? It has been said, most notoriously by the Scottish philosopher David Hume (1711–1776), that reason alone has no power to influence conduct. "Reason," Hume said, "is, and ought only to be the slave of the passions."[2] Remember the example of Alfred and the soft drink machine. Reason tells us what we have to do to get a drink, but it leads us to

---

2 David Hume, *A Treatise of Human Nature,* 1739, 1740, ed. L. A. Selby-Bigge (Oxford: Oxford University Press, 1888): 415.

put money in the machine only if we are also thirsty. According to Hume, all explanations of action involve a desire in this way.

But there is reason to disagree with Hume. It seems to me perfectly clear that reason can play an explanatory role in our lives. It can certainly explain mental activity like coming to believe, or not to believe, something. We think, for example, that we can explain a person's abandoning a certain belief simply by discovering that it is inconsistent with his or her other beliefs. Similarly, we explain someone's adopting a belief simply on the ground that it follows logically from other beliefs he or she has. The "mere" fact that laws of logic require a belief, given other beliefs, explains someone's having that belief. And though philosophers like Hume tend to emphasize the idea that reason *alone* never explains action, the other side of their theory is that laws of reason play a significant role in motivating and explaining our action, too. People follow rational strategies in deciding what to do. They seem to be influenced, for example, by variations in probabilities and in the size of possible gains and losses in choosing investments or in selecting plays in games like football. In short, in our ordinary thinking about people, we assume they are rational creatures whose actions and beliefs are to be explained at least in part by laws of reason. They tend to follow rules of consistency, of logical inference, and of rational choice.

Suppose we are rational, in the sense that reason at least plays a role in determining our behavior. Does that mean that Kant's problem is solved? Does it show that moral action is possible—that there are categorical imperatives of morality and that people actually act on them, uninfluenced by prior inclinations? Hardly. Perhaps it points in the direction of a solution, but it does not provide one. In the preceding paragraph I assumed, without argument, that requirements of consistency, for example, are requirements of reason. Perhaps it is hard to disagree with that, but it cannot be assumed, without argument, that what we, or Kant, consider to be ordinary rules of morality are also requirements of reason. Kant happens to believe that these ordinary rules can be derived from his general Universalization Principle, so, if that is a principle of reason, the other moral rules are too. But is the Universalization Principle a principle of reason in the same way that the laws of logic are? Philosophers have tried to show that it is, but whether they have succeeded is controversial, to say the least. And even if it is, there would remain the question of whether it is ever sufficient to motivate action.

Before we conclude this section, it is worth considering what bearing these ideas might have on the underlying question of this book. On the one hand, if Kant is right, then it is no part of the point of morality to promote the satisfaction of our independent desires. If we understand the question "why be moral?" as "what's in it for me?" then the most natural answer is "nothing." On the other hand, though, it is Kant's whole idea that if there is such a thing as morality, then we all have a kind of reason to be moral; for the requirements of morality just *are* the requirements of reason. Indeed, in the picture Kant paints, by acting morally we not only choose to be rational, but we also achieve the only genuine freedom. We allow our lives to be governed by reason instead of by nonrational inclinations. And, if this does not mean that we live more happily by living morally, it at least puts morality in what must seem, to many, an attractive light.

KANT'S ARGUMENT CRITICIZED

Kant presents us with an elaborate and exciting system of interrelated ideas. He attempts to show that if we begin with a very simple and, in his view, obvious idea about the nature of morally good action, we can show that moral laws must be categorical laws of reason, that being moral and realizing our nature as free and rational beings are identical, and even that the basic principle of morality must be some version of his Universalization Principle. He does not think he has *proved* that there actually are moral laws or that anyone actually does act morally. What he thinks he has shown is what morality must be like, what must be true about it, if there is such a thing. But he is mistaken, even in this conditional conclusion.

The whole argument depends crucially on assumptions Kant makes very early, when he gives his account of the nature of morally good action. He begins, you will recall, with the idea that there is a difference between morally good or praiseworthy action—what he calls acting with a good will—and action that is correct, that accords with moral requirements, but is not done with a good will. Now most people do agree that there is such a difference. Certainly Aristotle agrees. Aristotle also thinks that a person could do what a virtuous person would do without doing it *as* a virtuous person would—that is, without having the virtues. People can tell the truth, for example, only out of fear of being caught, not because they have come to care about the truth and to choose it for its own sake. A truthful person, on the other hand, has a fixed and firm desire to tell the truth, takes pleasure in doing so, and so chooses the truth for its own sake.

Aristotle then, like Kant, accepts the distinction between good and merely correct action. But he makes the distinction in a different way. Hence, we also can accept the distinction without drawing it in the same way Kant does. For Aristotle, the person who has the virtues and acts virtuously is a person who has acquired certain desires and who acts on them. The generous or truthful person, as Aristotle describes him, has what Kant would call a "direct inclination" to share or to tell the truth. For Kant, though, one who acts with a good will acts on no inclination, not even a direct one. This is a crucial difference. For Aristotle, being moral is, in part, a matter of having the *right* inclinations; for Kant, it is a matter of rising *above* inclination, a matter of reason's taking control over our affective nature.

Suppose we agree with *Kant* that morally good or praiseworthy action is different from action that is not morally good, but suppose we adopt something more like *Aristotle's* account of what makes action morally good: People act with a good will when they take a direct interest in doing the right thing, choosing it for its own sake. In that case, a person who acts with a good will is not a person who acts without inclination. But then, we also are not forced to conclude that moral laws are categorical, that they are based on reason alone, or that their motivating force is the force of rationality alone. Finally, even if the Universalization Principle is the only principle that can "determine the will" independent of any prior inclination, we are not forced to conclude that it must be the principle of morality.

It follows that Kant has not demonstrated, on the basis of assumptions that are essential to our very idea of moral action, the main conclusions he wanted to demonstrate concerning the nature of morality. That does not mean these conclusions are false. Perhaps they are true, but for different reasons. I will examine this possibility further in the next section. Here, though, I want to consider the question of *why* Kant makes the assumptions about the good will with which he begins. Why does he assume that people who act with a good will act on no inclination?

Any answer must be, to some extent, speculative; but I suspect Kant came to view the good will as he did for two reasons. First, he makes the assumption, noted at the beginning of this chapter, that the moral standpoint is different from the standpoint of self-interest and, in particular, that moral action is not self-interested action. Second, he believes that any time one acts on an inclination, any time one acts on one of one's own desires, one is acting out of self-interest. Only when we do what reason demands, just because reason demands it and independent of any prior inclination, do we act in a nonself-interested way. Hence, given that morality and self-interest are incompatible, only when we act on *no* inclination do we act morally. How good is this reasoning?

The idea that the ethical life involves some limits on the direct pursuit of immediate self-interest is, in fact, an idea that almost all moral philosophers have accepted. On this point, Kant does not depart from tradition. Indeed, it seems to me clear that Epictetus and Aristotle, though each saw ethics as the study of how one should live in order to have a good life for oneself, both thought that one had to control selfish impulses; and Aristotle in particular thought one had to develop a direct concern for, for example, truth and justice. They saw the fundamental point of morality as the promotion of one's own good, but they thought this required that individual actions *not* be self-interested. As Kant sees it, though, even someone who has and acts out of a direct inclination to do what justice requires is "really" just acting out of self-interest. After all, he is really *just doing what he wants*. Hence, he is not really acting morally.

Who is right here? Should we say that the Aristotelian virtuous person is acting morally since he acts out of a direct desire to do justice and not out of a desire to benefit himself? Or should we say that he really is acting selfishly since he is doing what he wants? Kant's way of thinking about self-interest is very common in contemporary culture. Jeremy Bentham and John Stuart Mill . . . both accept it. Indeed, most modern economists accept it, and accept it for a reason like Kant's: They think that people tend to do *what they want*, and they conclude from this that people always act out of self-interest. But, since most modern theorists have rejected Kant's idea that we ever act out of reason alone, they conclude that people can only act out of self-interest. Still, are they right?

What we need, if we are to resolve this dispute, is a clear definition of what it means to act out of self-interest. [Elsewhere I] examine a definition offered by Joseph Butler, together with his argument that it is impossible to act *solely* out of self-interest and that it certainly is possible to act for reasons entirely other than self-interest. What is significant about Butler's account of selfish and unselfish action is that the distinction does not depend on whether one acts on inclination or not. Thus, one could be acting on inclination but still not out of self-interest. Hence, if Butler is right, Kant is wrong, and that means that someone with the Aristotelian virtues would be acting in a moral (i.e., nonself-interested) way. Moreover, it also opens the way for an account of the nature and basis of morality quite different from Kant's, in which the distinction between the moral and nonmoral depends not on reason but on sentiment or emotion. An account like this was offered in the eighteenth century by Hume.

THE CATEGORICAL IMPERATIVE REVISITED

Based on his assumption that people act with a good will only when they act on no inclination, Kant concludes that moral imperatives must be categorical and, also, that there is only one *basic* categorical moral law, namely, the Universalization Principle. This law (which Kant formulates in several different ways) is often called *the* categorical imperative. Kant claims that it is the only law capable of determining the will independent of any prior inclination, though he also thinks additional, more specific imperatives, like the requirement that one not break a promise, can be derived from it. When people act with a good will, they may be directly following specific requirements, like the requirement not to lie. But, if their action is fully moral, they will be acting on that requirement because, in turn, they see that the maxim of not lying is a maxim they can will to be a universal law. Their most basic reason—the reason that "determines the will"—is the Universalization Principle.

If I am correct, Kant is wrong in his original assumption. Acting with a good will does not require acting on no inclination. Therefore, Kant has not shown that moral imperatives must be categorical nor that *the* categorical imperative is the basic principle of morality. However, even if Kant has not *shown* it, it might still be true that this is the basic principle of morality. Some ethical questions, I have claimed, need to be addressed and answered from a standpoint different from the standpoint of any particular individual. These include, most obviously, questions about what rights people have against other people, what obligations people have to other people, or, more generally, what people must do or refrain from doing when there is a conflict of interest among them. Questions about the extent and limits of property rights, about the fair distribution of the tax burden, about rights to health care, and about the rights and duties of patients and health care professionals are only a few examples. What most philosophers now would say is that, to answer these questions, we need to employ some procedure that is *impartial* among the different persons or interests that are involved. What is interesting is that Kant's Universalization Principle looks, to many people, like the very embodiment of a kind of moral impartiality. So, perhaps it is the principle we ought to employ, even if it is not necessary for the reasons Kant offers.

When we apply the universalization test to a proposed course of action, what we are asking, in effect, is whether we would be prepared to make it a law that anyone faced with similar circumstances act as we propose to act. If we would be unwilling to accept the consequences of others acting as we propose to, we should not do so ourselves. Thus, for example, if we care about some goal or project and if we need the cooperation of others to gain it, the categorical imperative tells us that we cannot exempt ourselves from the requirement of cooperating. It tells us not to demand of others more than we are willing to demand of ourselves. In that sense, it tells us to treat others equally with ourselves. If we would want others to treat us a certain way, it requires that we treat them the same way. Thus, it seems to rule out both certain kinds of "free-riding" and also things like deception, discrimination, and physical violence.

Should we then conclude that Kant's principle is the right principle to use in making moral decisions? There are at least two reasons to resist this conclusion. First, though it appears on first examination that the principle has quite definite consequences and, indeed, that its consequences coincide with obvious moral requirements, under more careful scrutiny it is not clear that it has any definite consequences at all. Second, though it might appear that the principle captures the very essence of the idea of impartiality, it turns out that impartiality can be interpreted in a variety of ways. Kant's principle is not the only impartial principle. Let me explain each of these objections in more detail.

The first objection is that Kant's principle does not, in fact, settle interesting moral questions. Why not? The Universalization Principle is a lot like The Golden Rule, and the problem should really be familiar to anyone who has thought seriously about how this rule is supposed to work. Suppose that a member of my family, someone I love, is suffering from a terminal illness and is no longer able to make decisions rationally or even to understand the real nature of her condition. There is no doubt that she will live a month at most. She is quite uncomfortable and is no longer able to interact socially with friends and family. She can die a quick and peaceful death if certain treatments are stopped. The doctor offers to stop them. Should I agree?

I could ask Kant's question, namely, could I will that everyone act as I propose to act? But just how do I describe my act? If we withdraw the treatment, we kill an innocent person. Could I will that everyone with the opportunity to kill an innocent person do so? On the other hand, if we withdraw treatment, we end the suffering of a dying person and we help her to die more peacefully. Surely, I can will that, in cases like this, we should help dying people to die peacefully. (I would want it for myself.) But now it seems that Kant's test leads to a different answer depending on how we describe the action we are considering. Both descriptions are true, so which should we choose? Nothing in

Kant's theory tells us how to answer this question, and without an answer we cannot use his principle to resolve ethical dilemmas like this one.

Now consider the second objection. Even if we could give an unambiguous interpretation to Kant's principle, it could still be objected that it is not impartial among people *in the right way*. The Universalization Principle requires that we demand the same of ourselves that we demand of others. It requires a kind of consistency. We shouldn't, for example, demand sacrifices of others unless we would demand them of ourselves. But is this the only kind of impartiality that morality requires? Suppose we *would* be willing that others act a certain way. Is this enough to justify our acting in that way? What if we would be willing to have them act that way toward us, but they are not willing that anyone act that way toward them?

The kind of impartiality implicit in the Universalization Principle seems to amount just to a kind of consistency, consistency in the application of our own ideals or preferences to the evaluation of everyone's conduct. If we apply certain standards to the evaluation of what others do, it says that we must apply the same standards to the evaluation of our own conduct. Immorality, in this view, is a kind of hypocrisy. A different idea of impartiality is that, before we decide what to do, we must put ourselves in the position of others. We do not just view our conduct, consistently, from the standpoint of our own values and interests; we consider it from the standpoint of the values and interests of others as well.

Consider an example. I support a variety of environmental causes. I value clean air and clean water; I care about protecting endangered species and unspoiled wilderness. As a result, I want people to make certain sacrifices, to accept limits on their liberty to pollute and otherwise to exploit the land in ways that might be profitable and productive. Applying Kant's Universalization Principle to the evaluation of my own conduct, I accept similar restrictions on my liberty. I try to refrain from activities that pollute, for example, because I would not will that others pollute. I consistently demand from myself the same sacrifices I want from others. (Indeed, I do this, even though I realize that if I *alone* polluted, it would do no noticeable damage. My reasoning is not based on consequences alone, but on something like the notion that burdens should be shared fairly.)

Now, imagine someone else who does not care about preserving natural beauty, but who likes, say, riding his motorcycle through fragile mountain meadows. May he do so? If he asks Kant's question, that is, whether he would will that everyone do as he proposes to do, the answer might well be "yes." He has no interest in preserving the meadows. So, for him, it is permissible to destroy them. Is this a reasonable moral conclusion? Perhaps so. Perhaps what is permissible for him is not permissible for me. Perhaps what is permissible for each of us depends on our own commitments and ideals. (Since we all share *some* interests, like an interest in not being maimed or injured, some things are permissible for no one.) But some people might disagree with this conclusion. They might say that morality demands more of the motorcyclist than consistent adherence to his own values. He needs to ask not just what

logically possible

he, with his commitments, could will that everyone do, but instead what other people, with their commitments, could accept, too.

The moral ideal of impartiality, then, might be understood to require more than consistent avoidance of hypocrisy. It might be understood to require that we in some way take account of the interests, values, or viewpoints of others. If morality requires that we act from an impartial standpoint, but there is more than one kind of impartiality, then mere appeal to the idea of impartiality itself does not determine what we must do. As I have said, much of modern moral philosophy consists of disputes about just what kind of impartiality morality demands and about the relative merits of different conceptions of this notion. Utilitarianism . . . can be understood as a systematic development of one particular ideal of impartiality. Before we turn to utilitarianism, however, it is important to recall that Kant himself formulates the categorical imperative, the basic principle of morality, in more than one way; and though he believes that they are all equivalent, they actually, at the very least, convey rather different images of moral reasoning.

I will focus on two formulations. In the second section of the *Grounding,* Kant formulates the imperative as follows: "Act in such a way that you treat humanity, whether in your own person or in the person of another, always at the same time as an end and never simply as a means" [429]. This, Kant says, is the "supreme limiting condition of every man's freedom of action" [431]. Moral people not only limit their actions to those they are willing that others do as well, they also refrain from using others as means to their own ends. Moreover, Kant makes clear at this point, morality is not a matter of just avoiding what one cannot will universally; it is a matter of following obligatory *laws,* but laws one wills oneself as universal laws consistent with the demands of reason, including the "supreme limiting condition" [431]. People are both creators of the moral law (when they "legislate" in accordance with the requirements of reason) and they are also the people to whom the laws apply. This thought leads Kant to the further idea of what he calls "a kingdom of ends," "a systematic union of rational beings through common objective laws" [433].

could not will

Admittedly, it is hard to know just what to make of these rather heady ideas, but one possible interpretation is this: People act morally when and only when they obey laws or rules, in their dealings with one another, which *all* of them would be willing to accept as universally binding. In obeying these laws that all could will, they would each be acting as both sovereign and subject. Each would act in a way consistent with rules he or she would be willing to have universally followed, and since each would also be following laws the *others* would be willing to accept, each could be said to be treating the others as ends, not merely as means. What any one does can be justified *to* the others for it is consistent with rules each can agree to. Morality, viewed this way, is a kind of agreement, though an ideal or hypothetical agreement, not an actual one.

It needs to be emphasized that this is not something Kant says explicitly in the *Grounding.* I claim only to have drawn a picture of an idea of morality suggested by Kant's remarks. Regardless of whether Kant would endorse this idea, however, it is an intriguing one and one that many twentieth-century philosophers in the so-called "social contract" tradition have found attractive. There are a number of versions of this idea, and this is not the place to try to describe the different possibilities. . . . I mention it now for two reasons. First, if the moral standpoint is the impartial standpoint, one interpretation of this idea is that it requires us to act in a way that can be justified to everyone in terms of principles each can accept. This idea contrasts, I will later argue, with the idea of impartiality implicit in the moral philosophy of utilitarianism. Second, in its emphasis on what is justifiable *to each*, it embodies a possible interpretation of the Kantian injunction to treat everyone as an end, and so it can be said to be inspired by Kant.

32

The Right to Lie: Kant on Dealing with Evil

CHRISTINE M. KORSGAARD

Christine Korsgaard (b. 1952) has done important work on Kantian moral philosophy and other topics in ethics. She is Professor of Philosophy at Harvard University. This essay first appeared in Philosophy and Public Affairs *(Fall 1986).*

    Korsgaard discusses two problems about Kantian ethics. The first is that unwavering obedience to moral law can put us at a severe disadvantage in our dealings with evil or immoral people. For example, if a murderer lies to find out where his intended victim is, it should be acceptable to lie to him in return. However, an absolute prohibition against lying, of the sort that is often attributed to Kant, would rule this out. The second problem is that Kant's different formulations of his categorical imperative seem to have different implications about how to deal with the murderer. As Korsgaard interprets them, the formulation that tells us to act only on maxims that we can will to be universal laws does permit us to lie to him, but a second formulation—treat humanity exclusively as an end—does not.

    Korsgaard offers a single solution to both problems. She suggests that an adequate moral theory needs two components, one of which tells us what a perfectly moral world would be like, while the other tells us how to deal with evil in light of this ideal. In the case of Kant's theory, the Formula of Humanity can be viewed as the ideal component, the Formula of Universal Law as the nonideal component. By adopting this reading, Korsgaard provides explanations both of how Kant's theory can deal with evil and of how his two formulations of the categorical imperative may fit together.

    This paper was delivered as the Randall Harris Lecture at Harvard University in October, 1985. Versions of the paper have been presented at the University of Illinois at Urbana–Champaign, the University of Wisconsin at Milwaukee, the University of Michigan, and to the Seminar on Contemporary Social and Political Theory in Chicago. I owe a great deal to the discussions on these occasions. I want to thank the following people for their comments: Margaret Atherton, Charles Chastain, David Copp, Stephen Darwall, Michael Davis, Gerald Dworkin, Alan Gewirth, David Greenstone, John Koethe, Richard Kraut, Richard Strier, and Manley Thompson. And I owe special thanks to Peter Hylton and Andrews Reath for extensive and useful comments on the early versions of the paper.

One of the great difficulties with Kant's moral philosophy is that it seems to imply that our moral obligations leave us powerless in the face of evil. Kant's theory sets a high ideal of conduct and tells us to live up to that ideal regardless of what other persons are doing. The results may be very bad. But Kant says that the law "remains in full force, because it commands categorically" (G, 438–39/57).[1] The most well-known example of this "rigorism," as it is sometimes called, concerns Kant's views on our duty to tell the truth.

In two passages in his ethical writings, Kant seems to endorse the following pair of claims about this duty: first, one must never under any circumstances or for any purpose tell a lie; second, if one does tell a lie one is responsible for all the consequences that ensue, even if they were completely unforeseeable.

One of the two passages appears in the *Metaphysical Principles of Virtue*. There Kant classifies lying as a violation of a perfect duty to oneself. In one of the casuistical questions, a servant, under instructions, tells a visitor the lie that his master is not at home. His master, meanwhile, sneaks off and commits a crime, which would have been prevented by the watchman sent to arrest him. Kant says:

> Upon whom . . . does the blame fall? To be sure, also upon the servant, who here violated a duty to himself by lying, the consequence of which will now be imputed to him by his own conscience. (*MMV*, 431/93)

The other passage is the infamous one about the murderer at the door from the essay, "On a Supposed Right to Lie from Altruistic Motives." Here Kant's claims are more extreme, for he says that the liar may be held legally as well

---

[1] Where I cite or refer to any of Kant's works more than once, I have inserted the reference into the text. The following abbreviations are used:

G: *Foundations of the Metaphysics of Morals* (1785). The first page number is that of the Prussian Academy Edition Volume IV; the second is that of the translation by Lewis White Beck (Indianapolis: Bobbs-Merrill Library of Liberal Arts, 1959).

C_2: *Critique of Practical Reason* (1788). Prussian Academy Volume V; Lewish White Beck's translation (Indianapolis: Bobbs-Merrill Library of Liberal Arts, 1956).

MMV: *The Metaphysical Principles of Virtue* (1797). Prussian Academy Volume VI; James Ellington's translation in *Immanuel Kant: Ethical Philosophy* (Indianapolis: Hackett, 1983).

MMJ: *The Metaphysical Elements of Justice* (1797). Prussian Academy Volume VI; John Ladd's translation (Indianapolis: Bobbs-Merrill Library of Liberal Arts, 1965).

PP: *Perpetual Peace* (1795). Prussian Academy Volume VIII, translation by Lewis White Beck in *On History*, edited by Lewis White Beck (Indianapolis: Bobbs-Merrill Library of Liberal Arts, 1963).

SRL: "On a Supposed Right to Lie from Altruistic Motives" (1797). Prussian Academy Volume VIII; translation by Lewis White Beck in *Immanuel Kant: Critique of Practical Reason and Other Writings in Moral Philosophy* (Chicago: University of Chicago Press, 1949; reprint, New York: Garland Publishing Company, 1976).

LE: *Lectures on Ethics* (1775–1780). Edited by Paul Menzer from the notes of Theodor Friedrich Brauer, using the notes of Gottlieb Kutzner and Christian Mrongovius; translated by Louis Infield (London: Methuen & Co., Ltd., 1930; reprint, New York: Harper Torchbooks, 1963; current reprint, Indianapolis: Hackett Publishing Co., 1980).

as ethically responsible for the consequences, and the series of coincidences he imagines is even more fantastic:

> After you have honestly answered the murderer's question as to whether his intended victim is at home, it may be that he has slipped out so that he does not come in the way of the murderer, and thus that the murder may not be committed. But if you had lied and said he was not at home when he had really gone out without your knowing it, and if the murderer had then met him as he went away and murdered him, you might justly be accused as the cause of his death. For if you had told the truth as far as you knew it, perhaps the murderer might have been apprehended by the neighbors while he searched the house and thus the deed might have been prevented. (SRL, 427/348)

Kant's readers differ about whether Kant's moral philosophy commits him to the claims he makes in these passages. Unsympathetic readers are inclined to take them as evidence of the horrifying conclusions to which Kant was led by his notion that the necessity in duty is rational necessity—as if Kant were clinging to a logical point in the teeth of moral decency. Such readers take these conclusions as a defeat for Kant's ethics, or for ethical rationalism generally; or they take Kant to have confused principles which are merely general in their application and *prima facie* in their truth with absolute and universal laws. Sympathetic readers are likely to argue that Kant here mistook the implications of his own theory, and to try to show that, by careful construction and accurate testing of the maxim on which this liar acts, Kant's conclusions can be blocked by his own procedures.

Sympathetic and unsympathetic readers alike have focused their attention on the implications of the first formulation of the categorical imperative, the Formula of Universal Law. The *Foundations of the Metaphysics of Morals* contains two other sets of terms in which the categorical imperative is formulated: the treatment of humanity as an end in itself, and autonomy, or legislative membership in a Kingdom of Ends. My treatment of the issue falls into three parts. First, I want to argue that Kant's defenders are right in thinking that, when the case is treated under the Formula of Universal Law, this particular lie can be shown to be permissible. Second, I want to argue that when the case is treated from the perspective provided by the Formulas of Humanity and the Kingdom of Ends, it becomes clear why Kant is committed to the view that lying is wrong in every case. But from this perspective we see that Kant's rigorism about lying is not the result of a misplaced love of consistency or legalistic thinking. Instead, it comes from an attractive ideal of human relations which is the basis of his ethical system. If Kant is wrong in his conclusion about lying to the murderer at the door, it is for the interesting and important reason that morality itself sometimes allows or even requires us to do something that from an ideal perspective is wrong. The case does not impugn Kant's ethics as an *ideal* system. Instead, it shows that we need special principles for dealing with evil. My third aim is to discuss the structure that an ethical system must have in order to accommodate such special principles.

UNIVERSAL LAW

The Formula of Universal Law tells us never to act on a maxim that we could not at the same time will to be a universal law. A maxim which cannot even be conceived as a universal law without contradiction is in violation of a strict and perfect duty, one which assigns us a particular action or omission. A maxim which cannot be willed as universal law without contradicting the will is in violation of a broad and imperfect duty, one which assigns us an end, but does not tell us what or how much we should do toward it. Maxims of lying are violations of perfect duty, and so are supposed to be the kind that cannot be conceived without contradiction when universalized.

The sense in which the universalization of an immoral maxim is supposed to "contradict" itself is a matter of controversy. On my reading, which I will not defend here, the contradiction in question is a "practical" one: the universalized maxim contradicts itself when the efficacy of the action as a method of achieving its purpose would be undermined by its universal practice.[2] So, to use Kant's example, the point against false promising as a method of getting ready cash is that if everyone attempted to use false promising as a method of getting ready cash, false promising would no longer *work* as a method of getting ready cash, since, as Kant says, "no one would believe what was promised to him but would only laugh at any such assertion as vain pretense" (*G*, 422/40).

Thus the test question will be: could this action be the universal method of achieving this purpose? Now when we consider lying in general, it looks as if it could not be the universal method of doing anything. For lies are usually efficacious in achieving their purposes because they deceive, but if they were universally practiced they would not deceive. We believe what is said to us in a given context because most of the time people in that context say what they really think or intend. In contexts in which people usually say false things— for example, when telling stories that are jokes—we are not deceived. If a story that is a joke and is false counts as a lie, we can say that a lie in this case is not wrong, because the universal practice of lying in the context of jokes does not interfere with the *purpose* of jokes, which is to amuse and does not depend on deception. But in most cases lying falls squarely into the category of the sort of action Kant considers wrong: actions whose efficacy depends upon the fact that most people do not engage in them, and which therefore can only be performed by someone who makes an exception of himself (*G*, 424/42).

When we try to apply this test to the case of the murderer at the door, however, we run into a difficulty. The difficulty derives from the fact that there is probably already deception in the case. If murderers standardly came to the door and said: "I wish to murder your friend—is he here in your house?" then

---

2 I defend it in "Kant's Formula of Universal Law," *Pacific Philosophical Quarterly* 66, nos. 1 & 2 (January/April 1986): 24–47.

perhaps the universal practice of lying in order to keep a murderer from his victim would not work. If everyone lied in these circumstances the murderer would be aware of that fact and would not be deceived by your answer. But the murderer is not likely to do this, or, in any event, this is not how I shall imagine the case. A murderer who expects to conduct his business by asking questions must suppose that you do not know who he is and what he has in mind.[3] If these are the circumstances, and we try to ascertain whether there could be a universal practice of lying in these circumstances, the answer appears to be yes. The lie will be efficacious even if universally practiced. But the reason it will be efficacious is rather odd: it is because the murderer supposes you do not know what circumstances you are in—that is, that you do not know you are addressing a murderer—and so does not conclude from the fact that people in those circumstances always lie that *you* will lie.

The same point can be made readily using Kant's publicity criterion (*PP*, 381–83/129–31). Can we announce in advance our intention of lying to murderers without, as Kant says, vitiating our own purposes by publishing our maxims (*PP*, 383/131)? Again the answer is yes. It does not matter if you say publicly that you will lie in such a situation, for the murderer supposes that you do not know you are in that situation.[4]

These reflections might lead us to believe, then, that Kant was wrong in thinking that it is never all right to lie. It is permissible to lie to deceivers in order to counteract the intended results of their deceptions, for the maxim of lying to a deceiver is universalizable. The deceiver has, so to speak, placed

---

[3] I am relying here on the assumption that when people ask us questions, they give us some account of themselves and of the context in which the questions are asked. Or, if they don't, it is because they are relying on a context that is assumed. If someone comes to your door looking for someone, you assume that there is a family emergency or some such thing. I am prepared to count such reliance as deception if the questioner knows about it and uses it, thinking that we would refuse to answer his questions if we knew the real context to be otherwise. Sometimes people ask me, "Suppose the murderer just asks whether his friend is in your house, without saying anything about why he wants to know?" I think that, in our culture anyway, people do not *just ask* questions of each other about anything except the time of day and directions for getting places. After all, the reason why refusal to answer is an unsatisfactory way of dealing with this case is that it will almost inevitably give rise to suspicion of the truth, and this is because people normally answer such questions. Perhaps if we did live in a culture in which people regularly *just asked* questions in the way suggested, refusal to answer would be commonplace and would not give rise to suspicion; it would not even be considered odd or rude. Otherwise there would be no way to maintain privacy.

[4] In fact, it will now be the case that if the murderer supposes that you suspect him, he is not going to ask you, knowing that you will answer so as to deceive him. Since we must avoid the silly problem about the murderer being able to deduce the truth from his knowledge that you will speak falsely, what you announce is that you will say whatever is necessary in order to conceal the truth. There is no reason to suppose that you will be mechanical about this. You are not going to be a reliable source of information. The murderer will therefore seek some other way to locate his victim.

On the other hand, suppose that the murderer does, contrary to my supposition, announce his real intentions. Then the arguments that I have given do not apply. In this case, I believe your only recourse is refusal to answer (whether or not the victim is in your house, or you know his whereabouts). If an answer is extorted from you by force you may lie, according to the argument I will give later in this article.

himself in a morally unprotected position by his own deception. He has created a situation which universalization cannot reach.

HUMANITY

When we apply the Formula of Humanity, however, the argument against lying that results applies to any lie whatever. The formula runs:

> Act so that you treat humanity, whether in your own person or in that of another, always as an end and never as a means only. (G, 429/47)

In order to use this formula for casuistical purposes, we need to specify what counts as treating humanity as an end. "Humanity" is used by Kant specifically to refer to the capacity to determine ends through rational choice (G, 437/56; MMV, 392/50). Imperfect duties arise from the obligation to make the exercise, preservation, and development of this capacity itself an end. The perfect duties—that is, the duties of justice, and, in the realm of ethics, the duties of respect—arise from the obligation to make each human being's capacity for autonomous choice the condition of the value of every other end.

In his treatment of the lying promise case under the Formula of Humanity, Kant makes the following comments:

> For he whom I want to use for my own purposes by means of such a promise cannot possibly assent to my mode of acting against him and cannot contain the end of this action in himself . . . he who transgresses the rights of men intends to make use of the persons of others merely as means, without considering that as rational beings, they must always be esteemed at the same time as ends, i.e., only as beings who must be able to contain in themselves the end of the very same action. (G, 429–30/48)

In these passages, Kant uses two expressions that are the key to understanding the derivation of perfect duties to others from the Formula of Humanity. One is that the other person "cannot possibly assent to my mode of acting toward him" and the second is that the other person cannot "contain the end of this action in himself." These phrases provide us with a test for perfect duties to others: an action is contrary to perfect duty if it is not possible for the other to assent to it or to hold its end.

It is important to see that these phrases do not mean simply that the other person *does not* or *would not* assent to the transaction or that she does not happen to have the same end I do, but strictly that she *cannot* do so: that something makes it impossible. If what we cannot assent to means merely what we are likely to be annoyed by, the test will be subjective and the claim that the person does not assent to being used as a means will sometimes be false. The object you steal from me may be the gift I intended for you, and we may both have been motivated by the desire that you should have it. And I may care about you too much or too little to be annoyed by the theft. For all that, this must be a clear case of your using me as a mere means.[5]

So it must not be merely that your victim will not like the way you propose to act, that this is psychologically unlikely, but that something makes it impossible for her to assent to it. Similarly, it must be argued that something makes it impossible for her to hold the end of the very same action. Kant never spells out why it is impossible, but it is not difficult to see what he has in mind.

People cannot *assent* to a way of acting when they are given no chance to do so. The most obvious instance of this is when coercion is used. But it is also true of deception: the victim of the false promise cannot assent to it because he doesn't know it is what he is being offered. But even when the victim of such conduct does happen to know what is going on, there is a sense in which he cannot assent to it. Suppose, for example, that you come to me and ask to borrow some money, falsely promising to pay it back next week, and suppose that by some chance I know perfectly well that your promise is a lie. Suppose also that I have the same end you do, in the sense that I want you to have the money, so that I turn the money over to you anyway. Now here I have the same end that you do, and I tolerate your attempts to deceive me to the extent that they do not prevent my giving you the money. Even in this case I cannot really assent to the transaction *you* propose. We can imagine the case in a number of different ways. If I call your bluff openly and say "never mind that nonsense, just take this money" then what I am doing is not accepting a false promise, but giving you a handout, and scorning your promise. The nature of the transaction is changed: now it is not a promise but a handout. If I don't call you on it, but keep my own counsel, it is still the same. I am not accepting a false promise. In this case what I am doing is *pretending* to accept your false promise. But there is all the difference in the world between actually doing something and pretending to do it. In neither of these cases can I be described as accepting a false promise, for in both cases I fix it so that it is something else that is happening. My knowledge of what is going on makes it *impossible* for me to accept the deceitful promise in the ordinary way.

The question whether another can assent to your way of acting can serve as a criterion for judging whether you are treating her as a mere means. We will say that knowledge of what is going on and some power over the proceedings are the conditions of possible assent; without these, the concept of assent does not apply. This gives us another way to formulate the test for treating someone as a mere means: suppose it is the case that if the other person knows what you are trying to do and has the power to stop you, then what you are trying to do cannot be what is really happening. If this is the case, the action is one that by its very nature is impossible for the other to assent to. You

---

5 Kant himself takes notice of this sort of problem in a footnote to this passage in which he criticizes Golden-Rule type principles for, among other things, the sort of subjectivity in question: such principles cannot establish the duty of beneficence, for instance, because "many a man would gladly consent that others should not benefit him, provided only that he might be excused from showing benevolence to them" (*G*, 430n./48n.).

cannot wrest from me what I freely give to you; and if I have the power to stop you from wresting something from me and do not use it, I am in a sense freely giving it to you. This is of course not intended as a legal point: the point is that any action which depends for its nature and efficacy on the other's ignorance or powerlessness fails this test. Lying clearly falls into this category of action: it only deceives when the other does not know that it is a lie.[6]

A similar analysis can be given of the possibility of holding the end of the very same action. In cases of violation of perfect duty, lying included, the other person is unable to hold the end of the very same action because the way that you act prevents her from *choosing* whether to contribute to the realization of that end or not. Again, this is obviously true when someone is forced to contribute to an end, but it is also true in cases of deception. If you give a lying promise to get some money, the other person is invited to think that the end she is contributing to is your temporary possession of the money: in fact, it is your permanent possession of it. It doesn't matter whether that would be all right with her if she knew about it. What matters is that she never gets a chance to choose the end, not knowing that it is to be the consequence of her action.[7]

According to the Formula of Humanity, coercion and deception are the most fundamental forms of wrongdoing to others—the roots of all evil. Coercion and deception violate the conditions of possible assent, and all actions which depend for their nature and efficacy on their coercive or deceptive character are ones that others cannot assent to. Coercion and deception also make it impossible for others to choose to contribute to our ends. This in turn makes it impossible, according to Kant's value theory, for the ends of such actions to be good. For on Kant's view "what we call good must be, in the judgment of every reasonable man, an object of the faculty of desire" (C_2, 60/62–63). If your end is one that others cannot choose—not because of what they want, but because they are not in a position to choose—it cannot, as the end of that action, be good. This means that in any cooperative project—whenever you need the decisions and actions of others in order to bring about your end—everyone who is to contribute must be in a position to *choose* to contribute to the end.

The sense in which a good end is an object for everyone is that a good end is in effect one that everyone, in principle, and especially everyone who contributes to it, gets to cast a vote on. This voting, or legislation, is the

---

6 Sometimes it is objected that someone could assent to being lied to in advance of the actual occasion of the lie, and that in such a case the deception might still succeed. One can therefore agree to be deceived. I think it depends what circumstances are envisioned. I can certainly agree to remain uninformed about something, but this is not the same as agreeing to be deceived. For example, I could say to my doctor: "Don't tell me if I am fatally ill, even if I ask." But if I then do ask the doctor whether I am fatally ill, I cannot be certain whether she will answer me truthfully. Perhaps what's being envisioned is that I simply agree to be lied to, but not about anything in particular. Will I then trust the person with whom I have made this odd agreement?

7 A similar conclusion about the way in which the Formula of Humanity makes coercion and deception wrong is reached by Onora O'Neill in "Between Consenting Adults," *Philosophy & Public Affairs* 14, no. 3 (Summer 1985): 252–77.

prerogative of rational beings; and the ideal of a world in which this prerogative is realized is the Kingdom of Ends.

THE KINGDOM OF ENDS

The Kingdom of Ends is represented by the kingdom of nature; we determine moral laws by considering their viability as natural laws. On Kant's view, the will is a kind of causality (*G*, 446/64). A person, an end in itself, is a free cause, which is to say a first cause. By contrast, a thing, a means, is a merely mediate cause, a link in the chain. A first cause is, obviously, the initiator of a causal chain, hence a real determiner of what will happen. The idea of deciding for yourself whether you will contribute to a given end can be represented as a decision whether to initiate that causal chain which constitutes your contribution. Any action which prevents or diverts you from making this initiating decision is one that treats you as a mediate rather than a first cause; hence as a mere means, a thing, a tool. Coercion and deception both do this. And deception treats you as a mediate cause in a specific way: it treats your reason as a mediate cause. The false promiser thinks: if I tell her I will pay her back next week, then she will choose to give me the money. Your reason is worked, like a machine: the deceiver tries to determine what levers to pull to get the desired results from you. Physical coercion treats someone's person as a tool; lying treats someone's *reason* as a tool. This is why Kant finds it so horrifying; it is a direct violation of autonomy.

We may say that a tool has two essential characteristics: it is there to be used, and it does not control itself—its nature is to be directed by something else. To treat someone as a mere means is to treat her as if these things were true of her. Kant's treatment of our duties to others in the *Metaphysical Principles of Virtue* is sensitive to *both* characteristics. We are not only forbidden to use another as a mere means to our private purposes. We are also forbidden to take attitudes toward her which involve regarding her as not in control of herself, which is to say, as not using her reason.

This latter is the basis of the duties of respect. Respect is violated by the vices of calumny and mockery (*MMV*, 466–68/131–33): we owe to others not only a practical generosity toward their plans and projects—a duty of aid— but also a generosity of attitude toward their thoughts and motives. To treat another with respect is to treat him as if he were using his reason and as far as possible as if he were using it well. Even in a case where someone evidently *is* wrong or mistaken, we ought to suppose he must have what he takes to be good reasons for what he believes or what he does. This is not because, as a matter of fact, he probably does have good reasons. Rather, this attitude is something that we *owe* to him, something that is his right. And he cannot forfeit it. Kant is explicit about this:

> Hereupon is founded a duty to respect man even in the logical use of his reason:
> not to censure someone's errors under the name of absurdity, inept judgment,

and the like, but rather to suppose that in such an inept judgment there must be something true, and to seek it out. . . . Thus it is also with the reproach of vice, which must never burst out in complete contempt or deny the wrongdoer all moral worth, because on that hypothesis he could never be improved either— and this latter is incompatible with the idea of man, who as such (as a moral being) can never lose all predisposition to good. (*MMV*, 463–64/128–29)

To treat others as ends in themselves is always to address and deal with them as rational beings. Every rational being gets to reason out, for herself, what she is to think, choose, or do. So if you need someone's contribution to your end, you must put the facts before her and ask for her contribution. If you think she is doing something wrong, you may try to convince her by argument but you may not resort to tricks or force. The Kingdom of Ends is a democratic ideal, and poor judgment does not disqualify anyone for citizenship. In the *Critique of Pure Reason*, Kant says:

> Reason depends on this freedom for its very existence. For reason has no dictatorial authority; its verdict is always simply the agreement of free citizens, of whom each one must be permitted to express, without let or hindrance, his objections or even his veto.[8]

This means that there cannot be a good reason for taking a decision out of someone else's hands. It is a rational being's prerogative, as a first cause, to have a share in determining the destiny of things.

This shows us in another way why lying is for Kant a paradigm case of treating someone as a mere means. Any attempt to control the actions and reactions of another by any means except an appeal to reason treats her as a mere means, because it attempts to reduce her to a mediate cause. This includes much more than the utterance of falsehoods. In the *Lectures on Ethics*, Kant says "whatever militates against frankness lowers the dignity of man" (*LE*, 231).[9] It is an everyday temptation, even (or perhaps especially) in our dealings with those close to us, to withhold something, or to tidy up an anecdote, or to embellish a story, or even just to place a certain emphasis, in order to be sure of getting the reaction we want.[10] Kant holds the Socratic view that any sort of persuasion that is aimed at distracting its listener's attention from either

---

8 *Immanuel Kant's "Critique of Pure Reason,"* translated by Norman Kemp Smith (New York: St. Martin's Press, 1965) A738–39/B766–67, p. 593.

9 It is perhaps also relevant that in Kant's discussion of perfect moral friendship the emphasis is not on good will toward one another, but on complete confidence and openness. See *MMV*, 471–72/138–39.

10 Some evidence that Kant is concerned with this sort of thing may be found in the fact that he identifies two meanings of the word "prudence" (*Klugheit*); "The former sense means the skill of a man in having an influence on others so as to use them for his own purposes. The latter is the ability to unite all these purposes to his own lasting advantage" (*G.* 416n./33n.). A similar remark is found in *Anthropology from a Pragmatic Point of View* (1798). See the translation by Mary J. Gregor (The Hague: Martinus Nijhoff, 1974), p. 183; Prussian Academy Edition Volume VII, p. 322.

the reasons that she ought to use or the reasons the speaker thinks she will use is wrong.[11]

In light of this account it is possible to explain why Kant says what he does about the liar's responsibility. In a Kantian theory our responsibility has definite boundaries: each person as a first cause exerts some influence on what happens, and it is your part that is up to you. If you make a straightforward appeal to the reason of another person, your responsibility ends there and the other's responsibility begins. But the liar tries to take the consequences out of the hands of others; he, and not they, will determine what form their contribution to destiny will take. By refusing to share with others the determination of events, the liar takes the world into his own hands, and makes the events his own. The results, good or bad, are imputable to him, at least in his own conscience. It does not follow from *this*, of course, that this is a risk one will never want to take.

HUMANITY AND UNIVERSAL LAW

If the foregoing casuistical analyses are correct, then applying the Formula of Universal Law and the Formula of Humanity lead to different answers in the case of lying to the murderer at the door. The former seems to say that this lie is permissible, but the latter says that coercion and deception are the most fundamental forms of wrongdoing. In a Kingdom of Ends coercive and deceptive methods can never be used.

This result impugns Kant's belief that the formulas are equivalent. But it is not necessary to conclude that the formulas flatly say different things, and are unrelated except for a wide range of coincidence in their results. For one thing, lying to the murderer at the door was not shown to be permissible in a straightforward manner: the maxim did not so much pass as evade universalization. For another, the two formulas can be shown to be expressions of the same basic theory of justification. Suppose that your maxim is in violation of the Formula of Universal Law. You are making an exception of yourself, doing something that everyone in your circumstances could not do. What this means is that you are treating the reason *you* have for the action as if it were stronger, had more justifying force, than anyone else's exactly similar reason. You are

11 I call this view Socratic because of Socrates' concern with the differences between reason and persuasion and, in particular, because in the *Apology*, he makes a case for the categorical duty of straightforwardness. Socrates and Plato are also concerned with a troublesome feature of this moral view that Kant neglects. An argument must come packaged in some sort of presentation, and one may well object that it is impossible to make a straightforward presentation of a case to someone who is close to or admires you, without emphasis, without style, without taking some sort of advantage of whatever it is about you that has your listener's attention in the first place. So how can we avoid the nonrational influence of others? I take it that most obviously in the *Symposium*, but also in other dialogues concerned with the relation of love and teaching such as the *Phaedrus*, Plato is at work on the question whether you can use your sex appeal to draw another's attention to the reasons he has for believing or doing things, rather than as a distraction that aids your case illicitly.

then acting as if the fact that it was in particular *your* reason, and not just the reason of a human being, gave it special weight and force. This is an obvious violation of the idea that it is your humanity—your power of rational choice—which is the condition of all value and which therefore gives your needs and desires the justifying force of *reasons*. Thus, any violation of the Formula of Universal Law is also a violation of the Formula of Humanity. This argument, of course, only goes in one direction: it does not show that the two formulas are equivalent. The Formula of Humanity is stricter than the Formula of Universal Law—but both are expressions of the same basic theory of value: that your rational nature is the source of justifying power of your reasons, and so of the goodness of your ends.

And although the Formula of Humanity gives us reason to think that all lies are wrong, we can still give an account in the terms it provides of what vindicates lying to a liar. The liar tries to use your reason as a means—your honesty as a tool. You do not have to passively submit to being used as a means. In the *Lectures on Ethics,* this is the line that Kant takes. He says:

> If we were to be at all times punctiliously truthful we might often become victims of the wickedness of others who were ready to abuse our truthfulness. If all men were well-intentioned it would not only be a duty not to lie, but no one would do so because there would be no point in it. But as men are malicious, it cannot be denied that to be punctiliously truthful is often dangerous . . . if I cannot save myself by maintaining silence, then my lie is a weapon of defence. (*LE,* 228)

The common thought that lying to a liar is a form of self-defense, that you can resist lies with lies as you can resist force with force, is according to this analysis correct.[12] This should not be surprising, for we have seen that deception and coercion are parallel. Lying and the use of force are attempts to undercut the two conditions of possible assent to actions and of autonomous choice of ends, namely, knowledge and power. So, although the Formula of Universal Law and the Formula of Humanity give us different results, this does not show that they simply express different moral outlooks. The relation between them is more complex than that.

---

12 Of course you may also resist force with lies, if resisting it with force is not an option for you. This gives rise to a question about whether these options are on a footing with each other. In many cases, lying will be the better option. This is because when you use coercion you risk doing injury to the person you coerce. Injuring people unnecessarily is wrong, a wrong that should be distinguished from the use of coercion. When you lie you do not risk doing this extra wrong. But Kant thinks that lying is in itself worse than coercion, because of the peculiarly direct way in which it violates autonomy. So it should follow that if you can deal with the murderer by coercion, this is a *better* option than lying. Others seem to share this intuition. Cardinal John Henry Newman, responding to Samuel Johnson's claim that he would lie to a murderer who asked which way his victim had gone, suggests that the appropriate thing to do is "to knock the man down, and to call out for the police" (*Apoligia Pro Vita Sua: Being a History of His Religious Opinions* [London: Longmans, Green & Co., 1880], p. 361. I am quoting from Sissela Bok, *Lying* [New York: Vintage Books, 1979], p. 42). If you can do it without seriously hurting the murderer, it is, so to speak, cleaner just to kick him off the front porch than to lie. This treats the *murderer himself* more like a human being than lying to him does.

TWO CASUISTICAL PROBLEMS

Before I discuss this relation, however, I must take up two casuistical problems arising from the view I have presented so far. First, I have argued that we *may* lie to the murderer at the door. But most people think something stronger: that we ought to lie to the murderer—that we will have done something wrong if we do not. Second, I have argued that it is permissible to lie to a deceiver in order to counter the deception. But what if someone lies to you for a good end, and, as it happens, you know about it? The fact that the murderer's *end* is evil has played no direct role in the arguments I have given so far. We have a right to resist liars and those who try to use force because of their methods, not because of their purposes. In one respect this is a virtue of my argument. It does not license us to lie or to use violence against persons *just* because we think their purposes are bad. But it looks as if it may license us to lie to liars whose purposes are good. Here is a case: suppose someone comes to your door and pretends to be taking a survey of some sort.[13] In fact, this person is a philanthropist who wants to give his money to people who meet certain criteria, and this is his way of discovering appropriate objects for his beneficence. As it happens, you know what is up. By lying, you could get some money, although you do not in fact meet his criteria. The argument that I derived from the Formula of Universal Law about lying to the murderer applies here. Universalizing the lie to the philanthropist will not destroy its efficacy. Even if it is a universal law that everyone will lie in these circumstances, the philanthropist thinks you do not know you are in these circumstances. By my argument, it is permissible to lie in this case. The philanthropist, like the murderer, has placed himself in a morally unprotected position by his own deception.

Start with the first casuistical problem. There are two reasons to lie to the murderer at the door. First, we have a duty of mutual aid. This is an imperfect duty of virtue, since the law does not say exactly what or how much we must do along these lines. This duty gives us *a* reason to tell the lie. Whether it makes the lie imperative depends on how one understands the duty of mutual aid, on how one understands the "wideness" of imperfect duties.[14] It may be that on such an urgent occasion, the lie is imperative. Notice that if the lie were impermissible, this duty would have no force. Imperfect duties are always secondary to perfect ones. But if the lie is permissible, this duty will provide a reason, whether or not an imperative one, to tell the lie.

The second reason is one of self-respect. The murderer wants to make you a tool of evil; he regards your integrity as a useful sort of predictability. He is trying to use you, and your good will, as a means to an evil end. You owe it to humanity in your own person not to allow your honesty to be used as a resource for evil. I think this would be a perfect duty of virtue; Kant does not

---

13 I owe this example to John Koethe.

14 For a discussion of this question see Barbara Herman, "Mutual Aid and Respect for Persons," *Ethics* 94 (July 1984): 577–602.

say this specifically, but in his discussion of servility (the avoidance of which is a perfect duty of virtue) he says "Do not suffer your rights to be trampled underfoot by others with impunity" (*MMV*, 436/99).

Both of these reasons spring from duties of virtue. A person with a good character will tell the lie. Not to tell it is morally bad. But there is no duty of justice to tell the lie. If we do not tell it, we cannot be punished, or, say, treated as an accessory to the murder. Kant would insist that even if the lie ought to be told this does not mean that the punctiliously truthful person who does not tell it is somehow implicated in the murder. It is the murderer, not the truthful person, who commits this crime. Telling the truth cannot be part of the crime. On Kant's view, persons are not supposed to be responsible for managing each other's conduct. If the lie were a duty of justice, we would be responsible for that.

These reflections will help us to think about the second casuistical problem, the lie to the philanthropist. I think it does follow from the line of argument I have taken that the lie cannot be shown to be impermissible. Although the philanthropist can hardly be called evil, he is doing something tricky and underhanded, which on Kant's view is wrong. He should not use this method of getting the information he wants. This is especially true if the reason he does not use a more straightforward method is that he assumes that if he does, people will lie to him. We are not supposed to base our actions on the assumption that other people will behave badly. Assuming this does not occur in an institutional context, and you have not sworn that your remarks were true, the philanthropist will have no recourse to justice if you lie to him.[15] But the reasons that favor telling the lie that exist in the first case do not exist here. According to Kant, you do not have a duty to promote your own happiness. Nor would anyone perform such an action out of self-respect. This is, in a very trivial way, a case of dealing with evil. But you can best deal with it by telling the philanthropist that you know what he is up to, perhaps even that you find it sneaky. This is *because* the ideal that makes his action a bad one is an ideal of straightforwardness in human relations. This would also be the best way to deal with the murderer, if it *were* a way to deal with a murderer. But of course it is not.

IDEAL AND NONIDEAL THEORY

I now turn to the question of what structure an ethical theory must have in order to accommodate this way of thinking. In *A Theory of Justice*, John Rawls proposes a division of moral philosophy into ideal and nonideal theory.[16]

---

15 In the *Lectures on Ethics*, Kant takes the position that you may lie to someone who lies to or bullies you as long as you don't say specifically that your words will be true. He claims this is not lying, because such a person should not expect you to tell the truth. (*LE*, 227, 229)

16 John Rawls, *A Theory of Justice* (Cambridge, MA: Harvard University Press, 1971). Section and page numbers referring to this work will appear in the text.

In that work, the task of ideal theory is to determine "what a perfectly just society would be like," while nonideal theory deals with punishment, war, opposition to unjust regimes, and compensatory justice (Sec. 2, pp. 8–9). Since I wish to use this feature of Rawls's theory for a model, I am going to sketch his strategy for what I will call a double-level theory.

Rawls identifies two conceptions of justice, which he calls the general conception and the special conception (Secs. 11, 26, 39, 46). The general conception tells us that all goods distributed by society, including liberty and opportunity, are to be distributed equally unless an unequal distribution is to the advantage of everyone, and especially those who fall on the low side of the inequality (Sec. 13). Injustice, according to the general conception, occurs whenever there are inequalities that are not to the benefit of everyone (Sec. 11, p. 62). The special conception in its most developed form removes liberty and opportunity from the scope of this principle and says they must be distributed equally, forbidding tradeoffs of these goods for economic gains. It also introduces a number of priority rules, for example, the priority of liberty over all other considerations, and the priority of equal opportunity over economic considerations (Secs. 11, 46, 82).

Ideal theory is worked out under certain assumptions. One is strict compliance: it is assumed that everyone will act justly. The other, a little harder to specify, is that historical, economic, and natural conditions are such that realization of the ideal is feasible. Our conduct toward those who do not comply, or in circumstances which make the immediate realization of a just state of affairs impossible, is governed by the principles of nonideal theory. Certain ongoing natural conditions which may always prevent the full realization of the ideal state of affairs also belong to nonideal theory: the problems of dealing with the seriously ill or mentally disturbed, for instance, belong in this category. For purposes of constructing ideal theory, we assume that everyone is "rational and able to manage their own affairs" (Sec. 39, p. 248). We also assume in ideal theory that there are no massive historic injustices, such as the oppression of blacks and women, to be corrected. The point is to work out our ideal view of justice on the assumption that people, nature, and history will behave themselves so that the ideal can be realized, and then to determine— in light of that ideal—what is to be done in actual circumstances when they do not. The special conception is not applied without regard to circumstances. Special principles will be used in nonideal conditions.

Nonideal conditions exist when, or to the extent that, the special conception of justice cannot be realized effectively. In these circumstances our conduct is to be determined in the following way: the special conception becomes a goal, rather than an ideal to live up to; we are to work toward the conditions in which it is feasible. For instance, suppose there is a case like this: widespread poverty or ignorance due to the level of economic development is such that the legal establishment of equal liberties makes no real difference to the lot of the disadvantaged members of society. It is an empty formality. On the other hand, some inequality, temporarily instituted, would actually tend to foster conditions in which equal liberty could become a reality for everyone. In these circumstances, Rawls's double-level theory allows for the temporary inequality (Secs. 11, 39). The priority rules give us guidance as to which features of the special conception are most urgent. These are the ones that we should be striving to achieve as soon as possible. For example, if formal equal opportunity for blacks and women is ineffective, affirmative action measures may be in order. If some people claim that this causes inefficiency at first, it is neither here nor there, since equality of opportunity has priority over efficiency. The special conception may also tell us which of our nonideal options is least bad, closest to ideal conduct. For instance, civil disobedience is better than resorting to violence not only because violence is bad in itself, but because of the way in which civil disobedience expresses the democratic principles of the just society it aspires to bring about (Sec. 59). Finally, the general conception of justice commands categorically. In sufficiently bad circumstances none of the characteristic features of the special conception may be realizable. But there is no excuse *ever* for violation of the general conception. If inequalities are not benefiting those on the lower end of them in some way, they are simply oppression. The general conception, then, represents the point at which justice becomes uncompromising.[17]

A double-level theory can be contrasted to two types of single-level theory, both of which in a sense fail to distinguish the way we should behave in ideal and nonideal conditions, but which are at opposite extremes. A consequentialist theory such as utilitarianism does not really distinguish ideal from nonideal conditions. Of course, the utilitarian can see the difference between a state of affairs in which everyone can be made reasonably happy and a state of affairs in which the utilitarian choice must be for the "lesser of evils," but it is still really a matter of degree. In principle we do not know what counts as a state in which everyone is "as happy as possible" absolutely. Instead, the utilitarian wants to make everyone as happy as possible relative to the circumstances, and pursues this goal regardless of how friendly the circumstances are to human happiness. The difference is not between ideal and nonideal states of affairs but simply between better and worse states of affairs.

Kant's theory as he understood it represents the other extreme of single-level theory. The standard of conduct he sets for us is designed for an ideal state of affairs: we are always to act as if we were living in a Kingdom of Ends, regardless of possible disastrous results. Kant is by no means dismissive toward the distressing problems caused by the evil conduct of other human beings and the unfriendliness of nature to human ideals, but his solution to these problems is different. He finds in them grounds for a morally motivated religious faith

---

17 In a nonideal case, one's actions may be guided by a more instrumental style of reasoning than in ideal theory. But nonideal theory is not a form of consequentialism. There are two reasons for this. One is that the goal set by the ideal is not just one of good consequences, but of a just state of affairs. If a consequentialist view is one that defines right action entirely in terms of good consequences (which are not themselves defined in terms of considerations of rightness or justice), then nonideal theory is not consequentialist. The second reason is that the ideal will also guide our choice among nonideal alternatives, importing criteria for this choice other than effectiveness. I would like to thank Alan Gewirth for prompting me to clarify my thoughts on this matter, and David Greenstone for helping me to do so.

in God.[18] Our rational motive for belief in a moral author of the world derives from our rational need for grounds for hope that these problems will be resolved. Such an author would have designed the laws of nature so that, in ways that are not apparent to us, our moral actions and efforts do tend to further the realization of an actual Kingdom of Ends. With faith in God, we can trust that a Kingdom of Ends will be the consequence of our actions as well as the ideal that guides them.

In his *Critique of Utilitarianism*, Bernard Williams spells out some of the unfortunate consequences of what I am calling single-level theories.[19] According to Williams, the consequentialist's commitment to doing whatever is necessary to secure the best outcome may lead to violations of what we would ordinarily think of as integrity. There is no kind of action that is so mean or so savage that it can *never* lead to a better outcome than the alternatives. A commitment to always securing the best outcome never allows you to say "bad consequences or not, this is not the sort of thing I do; I am not that sort of person." And no matter how mean or how savage the act required to secure the best outcome is, the utilitarian thinks that you will be irrational to regret that you did it, for you will have done what is in the straightforward sense the right thing.[20] A Kantian approach, by defining a determinate *ideal* of conduct to live up to rather than setting a *goal* of action to strive for, solves the problem about integrity, but with a high price. The advantage of the Kantian approach is the definite sphere of responsibility. Your share of the responsibility for the way the world is is well-defined and limited, and if you act as you ought, bad outcomes are not your responsibility. The trouble is that in cases such as that of the murderer at the door it seems grotesque simply to say that I have done my part by telling the truth and the bad results are not my responsibility.

The point of a double-level theory is to give us both a definite and well-defined sphere of responsibility for everyday life and some guidance, at least, about when we may or must take the responsibility of violating ideal standards. The common-sense approach to this problem uses an intuitive quantitative measure: we depart from our ordinary rules and standards of conduct when the consequences of following them would be "very bad." This is unhelpful for two reasons. First, it leaves us on our own about determining *how* bad. Second, the attempt to justify it leads down a familiar consequentialist slippery slope: if very bad consequences justify a departure from ordinary norms, why do not slightly bad consequences justify such a departure? A double-level theory substitutes something better than this rough quantitative measure. In Rawls's theory, for example, a departure from equal liberty cannot be justified by the fact that the consequences of liberty are "very bad" in terms of mere efficiency.

---

18 See the "Dialectic of Pure Practical Reason" of the *Critique of Practical Reason*, and the *Critique of Teleological Judgment*, sec. 87.

19 Bernard Williams, in *Utilitarianism For and Against*, by J. J. C. Smart and Bernard Williams (Cambridge: Cambridge University Press, 1973), pp. 75–150.

20 Williams also takes this issue up in "Ethical Consistency," originally published in the Supplementary Volumes to the *Proceedings of the Aristotelian Society* XXXIX, 1965, and reprinted in his collection, *Problems of the Self* (Cambridge: Cambridge University Press, 1973), pp. 166–86.

This does not mean that an endless amount of inefficiency will be tolerated, because presumably at some point the inefficiency may interfere with the effectiveness of liberty. One might put the point this way: the measure of "very bad" is not entirely intuitive but rather, bad enough to interfere with the reality of liberty. Of course this is not an algorithmic criterion and cannot be applied without judgment, but it is not as inexact as a wholly intuitive quantitative measure, and, importantly, does not lead to a consequentialist slippery slope.

Another advantage of a double-level theory is the explanation it offers of the other phenomenon Williams is concerned about: that of regret for doing a certain kind of action even if in the circumstances it was the "right" thing. A double-level theory offers an account of at least some of the occasions for this kind of regret. We will regret having to depart from the ideal standard of conduct, for we identify with this standard and think of our autonomy in terms of it. Regret for an action we would not do under ideal circumstances seems appropriate even if we have done what is clearly the right thing.[21]

KANTIAN NONIDEAL THEORY

Rawls's special conception of justice is a stricter version of the egalitarian ideal embodied in his general conception. In the same way, it can be argued that the Formula of Universal Law and the Formula of Humanity are expressions of the same idea—that humanity is the source of value, and of the justifying force of reason. But the Formula of Humanity is stricter, and gives implausible answers when we are dealing with the misconduct of others and the recalcitrance of nature. This comparison gives rise to the idea of using the two formulas and the relation between them to construct a Kantian double-level theory of individual morality, with the advantages of that sort of account. The Formulas of Humanity and the Kingdom of Ends will provide the ideal which governs our daily conduct. When dealing with evil circumstances we may depart from this ideal. In such cases, we can say that the Formula of Humanity is inapplicable because it is not designed for use when dealing with evil. But it can still guide our conduct. It defines the goal toward which we are working, and if we can generate priority rules we will know which features of it are most important. It gives us guidance about which of the measures we may take is the least objectionable.

Lying to deceivers is not the only case in which the Formula of Humanity seems to set a more ideal standard than the Formula of Universal Law. The

---

21 It is important here to distinguish two kinds of exceptions. As Rawls points out in "Two Conceptions of Rules" (*The Philosophical Review* 64 [January 1965]), a practice such as promising may have certain exceptions built into it. Everyone who has learned the practice understands that the obligation to keep the promise is cancelled if one of these obtains. When one breaks a promise because this sort of exception obtains, regret would be inappropriate and obsessive. And these sorts of exceptions may occur even in "ideal" circumstances. The kind of exception one makes when dealing with evil should be distinguished from exceptions built into practices.

arguments made about lying can all be made about the use of coercion to deal with evildoers. Another very difficult case in which the two formulas give different results, as I think, is suicide. Kant gives an argument against suicide under the Formula of Universal Law, but that argument does not work.[22] Yet under the Formula of Humanity we can give a clear and compelling argument against suicide: nothing is of any value unless the human person is so, and it is a great crime, as well as a kind of incoherence, to act in a way that denies and eradicates the source of all values. Thus it might be possible to say that suicide is wrong from an ideal point of view, though justifiable in circumstances of very great natural or moral evil.

There is also another, rather different sense of "rigorism" in which the Formula of Humanity seems to be more rigorous than that of Universal Law. It concerns the question whether Kant's theory allows for the category of merely permissible ends and actions, or whether we must always be doing something that is morally worthy: that is, whether we should *always* pursue the obligatory ends of our own perfection and the happiness of others, when no other duty is in the case.

The Formula of Universal Law clearly allows for the category of the permissible. Indeed, the first contradiction test is a test for permissibility. But in the *Metaphysical Principles of Virtue,* there are passages which have sometimes been taken to imply that Kant holds the view that our conduct should always be informed by morally worthy ends (*MMV,* 390/48). The textual evidence is not decisive. But the tendency in Kant's thought is certainly there. For complete moral worth is only realized when our actions are not merely in accordance with duty but from duty, or, to say the same thing a different way, perfect autonomy is only realized when our actions and ends are completely determined by reason, and this seems to be the case only when our ends are chosen as instantiations of the obligatory ends.

Using the Formula of Humanity it is possible to argue for the more "rigorous" interpretation. First, the obligatory ends can be derived more straightforwardly from Humanity than from Universal Law. Kant does derive the obligatory ends from the Formula of Universal Law, but he does it by a curiously roundabout procedure in which someone is imagined formulating a maxim of rejecting them and then finding it to be impermissible. This argument does not show that there would be a moral failing if the agent merely unthinkingly neglected rather than rejected these ends. The point about the pervasiveness of these ends in the moral life is a more complicated one, one that follows from their adoption by this route: among the obligatory ends is our own moral perfection. Pursuing ends that are determined by reason, rather than merely

---

22 Kant's argument depends on a teleological claim: that the instinct whose office is to impel the improvement of life cannot universally be used to destroy life without contradiction (*G,* 422/40). But as I understand the contradiction in conception test, teleological claims have no real place in it. What matters is not whether nature assigns a certain purpose to a certain motive or instinct, but whether everyone with the same motive or instinct could act in the way proposed and still achieve their purpose. There is simply no argument to show that everyone suffering from acute misery could not commit suicide and still achieve their purpose: ending that misery.

acceptable to it, cultivates one's moral perfection in the required way (*MMV*, 380–81/37–38; 444–47/108–111).

It is important to point out that even if this is the correct way to understand Kant's ideal theory, it does not imply that Kantian ethics commands a life of conventional moral "good deeds." The obligatory ends are one's own perfection and the happiness of others; to be governed by them is to choose instantiations of these larger categories as the aim of your vocation and other everyday activities. It is worth keeping in mind that natural perfection is a large category, including all the activities that cultivate body and mind. Kant's point is not to introduce a strenuous moralism but to find a place for the values of perfectionism in his theory. But this perfectionism will be a part of ideal theory if the argument for it is based on the Formula of Humanity and cannot be derived from that of Universal Law. This seems to me a desirable outcome. People in stultifying economic or educational conditions cannot really be expected to devote all their spare time to the cultivation of perfectionist values. But they can be expected not to do what is impermissible, not to violate the Formula of Universal Law. Here again, the Formula of Humanity sheds light on the situation even if it is not directly applied: it tells us why it is morally as well as in other ways regrettable that people should be in such conditions.

CONCLUSION

If the account I have given is correct, the resources of a double-level theory may be available to the Kantian. The Formula of Humanity and its corollary, the vision of a Kingdom of Ends, provide an ideal to live up to in daily life as well as a long-term political and moral goal for humanity. But it is not feasible always to live up to this ideal, and where the attempt to live up to it would make you a tool of evil, you should not do so. In evil circumstances, but only then, the Kingdom of Ends can become a goal to seek rather than an ideal to live up to, and this will provide us with some guidance. The Kantian priorities— of justice over the pursuit of obligatory ends, and of respect over benevolence— still help us to see what matters most. And even in the worst circumstances, there is always the Formula of Universal Law, telling us what we must not in any case do. For whatever bad circumstances may drive us to do, we cannot possibly be justified in doing something which others in those same circumstances could not also do. The Formula of Universal Law provides the point at which morality becomes uncompromising.

Let me close with some reflections about the extent to which Kant himself might have agreed with this modification of his views. Throughout this essay, I have portrayed Kant as an uncompromising idealist, and there is much to support this view. But in the historical and political writings, as well as in the *Lectures on Ethics*, we find a somewhat different attitude. This seems to me to be especially important. Kant believes that the Kingdom of Ends on earth, the highest political good, can only be realized in a condition of peace (*MMJ*, 354–55/127–29). But he does not think that this commits a nation to a simple pacifism that would make it the easy victim of its enemies. Instead, he draws up laws of war in which peace functions not as an uncompromising ideal to be lived up to in the present, but as a long-range goal which guides our conduct even when war is necessary (*PP,* 343–48/85–91; *MMJ,* 343–51/114–25). If a Kantian can hold such a view for the conduct of nations, why not for that of individuals? If this is right, the task of Kantian moral philosophy is to draw up for individuals something analogous to Kant's laws of war: special principles to use when dealing with evil.

33

Moral Luck

THOMAS NAGEL

For biographical information about Thomas Nagel, see reading 20. This selection is from his collection of essays, Mortal Questions.

Nagel's topic here is a tension within our attitudes toward moral responsibility. On the one hand, it seems that persons are not responsible for what they cannot control. As Kant asserts in reading 30, a good will appears to retain its moral worth even when it achieves nothing or actually brings bad results. Yet as Nagel notes, this is not the way we actually think. We consider it worse to run a red light and kill a pedestrian than to run a red light and not harm anyone. But a pedestrian's unforeseen presence is not within the driver's control. Hence, how wrongly the driver turns out to have acted depends on his "moral luck."

Other factors have similar effects. A person has no control over his basic character traits, nor does he have control over the opportunities and temptations he encounters, yet these also influence our evaluation of him. In fact, when we strip away everything a person cannot control, very little, if anything, remains. This leads some to say that persons can be blamed and held responsible even for things they could not control.

But Nagel argues that this response is inadequate. To come to grips with the problem, we must understand its source. According to Nagel, this is the need to view ourselves as both components of an objective world and subjective initiators of action. For a contrasting attempt to draw moral conclusions from facts about agency, see reading 5 by Alan Gewirth.

Kant believed that good or bad luck should influence neither our moral judgment of a person and his actions, nor his moral assessment of himself.

The good will is not good because of what it effects or accomplishes or because of its adequacy to achieve some proposed end; it is good only because of its willing, i.e., it is good of itself. And, regarded for itself, it is to be esteemed incomparably higher than anything which could be brought about by it in favor of any inclination or even of the sum total of all inclinations. Even if it should happen that, by a particular unfortunate fate or by the niggardly provision of a stepmotherly nature, this will should be wholly lacking in power to accomplish its purpose, and if even the greatest effort should not avail it to achieve anything of its end, and if there remained only the good will (not as a mere wish but as the summoning of all the means in our power), it would sparkle like a jewel in its own right, as something that had its full worth in itself. Usefulness or fruitlessness can neither diminish nor augment this worth.[1]

He would presumably have said the same about a bad will: whether it accomplishes its evil purposes is morally irrelevant. And a course of action that would be condemned if it had a bad outcome cannot be vindicated if by luck it turns out well. There cannot be moral risk. This view seems to be wrong, but it arises in response to a fundamental problem about moral responsibility to which we possess no satisfactory solution.

The problem develops out of the ordinary conditions of moral judgment. Prior to reflection it is intuitively plausible that people cannot be morally assessed for what is not their fault, or for what is due to factors beyond their control. Such judgment is different from the evaluation of something as a good or bad thing, or state of affairs. The latter may be present in addition to moral judgment, but when we blame someone for his actions we are not merely saying it is bad that they happened, or bad that he exists: we are judging *him*, saying he is bad, which is different from his being a bad thing. This kind of judgment takes only a certain kind of object. Without being able to explain exactly why, we feel that the appropriateness of moral assessment is easily undermined by the discovery that the act or attribute, no matter how good or bad, is not under the person's control. While other evaluations remain, this one seems to lose its footing. So a clear absence of control, produced by involuntary movement, physical force, or ignorance of the circumstances, excuses what is done from moral judgment. But what we do depends in many more ways than these on what is not under our control—what is not produced by a good or a bad will, in Kant's phrase. And external influences in this broader range are not usually thought to excuse what is done from moral judgment, positive or negative.

Let me give a few examples, beginning with the type of case Kant has in mind. Whether we succeed or fail in what we try to do nearly always depends to some extent on factors beyond our control. This is true of murder, altruism, revolution, the sacrifice of certain interests for the sake of others—almost any morally important act. What has been done, and what is morally judged, is partly determined by external factors. However jewel-like the good will may be in its own right, there is a morally significant difference between rescuing someone from a burning building and dropping him from a twelfth-story window while trying to rescue him. Similarly, there is a morally significant difference between reckless driving and manslaughter. But whether a reckless driver hits a pedestrian depends on the presence of the pedestrian at the point where he recklessly passes a red light. What we do is also limited by the opportunities and choices with which we are faced, and these are largely determined by factors beyond our control. Someone who was an officer in a concentration camp might have led a quiet and harmless life if the Nazis had never come to power in Germany. And someone who led a quiet and harmless life in Argentina might have become an officer in a concentration camp if he had not left Germany for business reasons in 1930.

---

[1] *Foundations of the Metaphysics of Morals*, first section, third paragraph.

I shall say more later about these and other examples. I introduce them here to illustrate a general point. Where a significant aspect of what someone does depends on factors beyond his control, yet we continue to treat him in that respect as an object of moral judgment, it can be called moral luck. Such luck can be good or bad. And the problem posed by this phenomenon, which led Kant to deny its possibility, is that the broad range of external influences here identified seems on close examination to undermine moral assessment as surely as does the narrower range of familiar excusing conditions. If the condition of control is consistently applied, it threatens to erode most of the moral assessments we find it natural to make. The things for which people are morally judged are determined in more ways than we at first realize by what is beyond their control. And when the seemingly natural requirement of fault or responsibility is applied in light of these facts, it leaves few pre-reflective moral judgments intact. Ultimately, nothing or almost nothing about what a person does seems to be under his control.

Why not conclude, then, that the condition of control is false—that it is an initially plausible hypothesis refuted by clear counter-examples? One could in that case look instead for a more refined condition which picked out the *kinds* of lack of control that really undermine certain moral judgments, without yielding the unacceptable conclusion derived from the broader condition, that most or all ordinary moral judgments are illegitimate.

What rules out this escape is that we are dealing not with a theoretical conjecture but with a philosophical problem. The condition of control does not suggest itself merely as a generalization from certain clear cases. It seems *correct* in the further cases to which it is extended beyond the original set. When we undermine moral assessment by considering new ways in which control is absent, we are not just discovering what *would* follow given the general hypothesis, but are actually being persuaded that in itself the absence of control is relevant in these cases too. The erosion of moral judgment emerges not as the absurd consequence of an over-simple theory, but as a natural consequence of the ordinary idea of moral assessment, when it is applied in view of a more complete and precise account of the facts. It would therefore be a mistake to argue from the unacceptability of the conclusions to the need for a different account of the conditions of moral responsibility. The view that moral luck is paradoxical is not a *mistake,* ethical or logical, but a perception of one of the ways in which the intuitively acceptable conditions of moral judgment threaten to undermine it all.

It resembles the situation in another area of philosophy, the theory of knowledge. There too conditions which seem perfectly natural, and which grow out of the ordinary procedures for challenging and defending claims to knowledge, threaten to undermine all such claims if consistently applied. Most skeptical arguments have this quality: they do not depend on the imposition of arbitrarily stringent standards of knowledge, arrived at by misunderstanding, but appear to grow inevitably from the consistent application of ordinary standards.[2]

---

2 See Thompson Clark, 'The Legacy of Skepticism', *Journal of Philosophy,* LXIX, no. 20 (November 9, 1972), 754–69.

There is a substantive parallel as well, for epistemological skepticism arises from consideration of the respects in which our beliefs and their relation to reality depend on factors beyond our control. External and internal causes produce our beliefs. We may subject these processes to scrutiny in an effort to avoid error, but our conclusions at this next level also result, in part, from influences which we do not control directly. The same will be true no matter how far we carry the investigation. Our beliefs are always, ultimately, due to factors outside our control, and the impossibility of encompassing those factors without being at the mercy of others leads us to doubt whether we know anything. It looks as though, if any of our beliefs are true, it is pure biological luck rather than knowledge.

Moral luck is like this because while there are various respects in which the natural objects of moral assessment are out of our control or influenced by what is out of our control, we cannot reflect on these facts without losing our grip on the judgments.

There are roughly four ways in which the natural objects of moral assessment are disturbingly subject to luck. One is the phenomenon of constitutive luck—the kind of person you are, where this is not just a question of what you deliberately do, but of your inclinations, capacities, and temperament. Another category is luck in one's circumstances—the kind of problems and situations one faces. The other two have to do with the causes and effects of action: luck is how one is determined by antecedent circumstances, and luck in the way one's actions and projects turn out. All of them present a common problem. They are all opposed by the idea that one cannot be more culpable or estimable for anything than one is for that fraction of it which is under one's control. It seems irrational to take or dispense credit or blame for matters over which a person has no control, or for their influence on results over which he has partial control. Such things may create the conditions for action, but action can be judged only to the extent that it goes beyond these conditions and does not just result from them.

Let us first consider luck, good and bad, in the way things turn out. Kant, in the above-quoted passage, has one example of this in mind, but the category covers a wide range. It includes the truck driver who accidentally runs over a child, the artist who abandons his wife and five children to devote himself to painting,[3] and other cases in which the possibilities of success and failure are even greater. The driver, if he is entirely without fault, will feel terrible about

---

3 Such a case, modelled on the life of Gauguin, is discussed by Bernard Williams in 'Moral Luck,' *Proceedings of the Aristotelian Society,* supplementary vol. L (1976), 115–35 (to which the original version of this essay was a reply). He points out that though success or failure cannot be predicted in advance, Gauguin's most basic retrospective feelings about the decision will be determined by the development of his talent. My disagreement with Williams is that his account fails to explain why such retrospective attitudes can be called moral. If success does not permit Gauguin to justify himself to others, but still determines his most basic feelings, that shows only that his most basic feelings need not be moral. It does not show that morality is subject to luck. If the retrospective judgment were moral, it would imply the truth of a hypothetical judgment made in advance, of the form 'If I leave my family and become a great painter, I will be justified by success; if I don't become a great painter, the act will be unforgivable.'

his role in the event, but will not have to reproach himself. Therefore this example of agent-regret[4] is not yet a case of *moral* bad luck. However, if the driver was guilty of even a minor degree of negligence—failing to have his brakes checked recently, for example—then if that negligence contributes to the death of the child, he will not merely feel terrible. He will blame himself for the death. And what makes this an example of moral luck is that he would have to blame himself only slightly for the negligence itself if no situation arose which required him to brake suddenly and violently to avoid hitting a child. Yet the *negligence* is the same in both cases, and the driver has no control over whether a child will run into his path.

The same is true at higher levels of negligence. If someone has had too much to drink and his car swerves onto the sidewalk, he can count himself morally lucky if there are no pedestrians in its path. If there were, he would be to blame for their deaths, and would probably be prosecuted for manslaughter. But if he hurts no one, although his recklessness is exactly the same, he is guilty of a far less serious legal offense and will certainly reproach himself and be reproached by others much less severely. To take another legal example, the penalty for attempted murder is less than that for successful murder—however similar the intentions and motives of the assailant may be in the two cases. His degree of culpability can depend, it would seem, on whether the victim happened to be wearing a bullet-proof vest, or whether a bird flew into the path of the bullet—matters beyond his control.

Finally, there are cases of decision under uncertainty—common in public and in private life. Anna Karenina goes off with Vronsky, Gauguin leaves his family, Chamberlain signs the Munich agreement, the Decembrists persuade the troops under their command to revolt against the czar, the American colonies declare their independence from Britain, you introduce two people in an attempt at match-making. It is tempting in all such cases to feel that some decision must be possible, in the light of what is known at the time, which will make reproach unsuitable no matter how things turn out. But this is not true; when someone acts in such ways he takes his life, or his moral position, into his hands, because how things turn out determines what he has done. It is possible *also* to assess the decision from the point of view of what could be known at the time, but this is not the end of the story. If the Decembrists had succeeded in overthrowing Nicholas I in 1825 and establishing a constitutional regime, they would be heroes. As it is, not only did they fail and pay for it, but they bore some responsibility for the terrible punishments meted out to the troops who had been persuaded to follow them. If the American Revolution had been a bloody failure resulting in greater repression, then Jefferson, Franklin and Washington would still have made a noble attempt, and might not even have regretted it on their way to the scaffold, but they would also have had to blame themselves for what they had helped to bring on their compatriots. (Perhaps peaceful efforts at reform would eventually have succeeded.) If Hitler had not overrun Europe and exterminated millions, but instead had died of a

---

4 Williams' term (*ibid.*).

heart attack after occupying the Sudetenland, Chamberlain's action at Munich would still have utterly betrayed the Czechs, but it would not be the great moral disaster that has made his name a household word.[5]

In many cases of difficult choice the outcome cannot be foreseen with certainty. One kind of assessment of the choice is possible in advance, but another kind must await the outcome, because the outcome determines what has been done. The same degree of culpability or estimability in intention, motive, or concern is compatible with a wide range of judgments, positive or negative, depending on what happened beyond the point of decision. The *mens rea* which could have existed in the absence of any consequences does not exhaust the grounds of moral judgment. Actual results influence culpability or esteem in a large class of unquestionably ethical cases ranging from negligence through political choice.

That these are genuine moral judgments rather than expressions of temporary attitude is evident from the fact that one can say *in advance* how the moral verdict will depend on the results. If one negligently leaves the bath running with the baby in it, one will realize, as one bounds up the stairs toward the bathroom, that if the baby has drowned one has done something awful, whereas if it has not one has merely been careless. Someone who launches a violent revolution against an authoritarian regime knows that if he fails he will be responsible for much suffering that is in vain, but if he succeeds he will be justified by the outcome. I do not mean that *any* action can be retroactively justified by history. Certain things are so bad in themselves, or so risky, that no results can make them all right. Nevertheless, when moral judgment does depend on the outcome, it is objective and timeless and not dependent on a change of standpoint produced by success or failure. The judgment after the fact follows from an hypothetical judgment that can be made beforehand, and it can be made as easily by someone else as by the agent.

From the point of view which makes responsibility dependent on control, all this seems absurd. How is it possible to be more or less culpable depending on whether a child gets into the path of one's car, or a bird into the path of one's bullet? Perhaps it is true that what is done depends on more than the agent's state of mind or intention. The problem then is, why is it not irrational to base moral assessment on what people do, in this broad sense? It amounts to holding them responsible for the contributions of fate as well as for their own—provided they have made some contributions to begin with. If we look at cases of negligence or attempt, the pattern seems to be that overall culpability corresponds to the product of mental or intentional fault and the seriousness of the outcome. Cases of decision under uncertainty are less easily explained in this way, for it seems that the overall judgment can even shift from positive to negative depending on the outcome. But here too it seems rational to subtract the effects of occurrences subsequent to the choice, that were merely possible

---

[5] For a fascinating but morally repellent discussion of the topic of justification by history, see Maurice Merleau-Ponty, *Humanisme et Terreur* (Paris: Gallimard, 1947), translated as *Humanism and Terror* (Boston: Beacon Press, 1969).

at the time, and concentrate moral assessment on the actual decision in light of the probabilities. If the object of moral judgment is the *person*, then to hold him accountable for what he has done in the broader sense is akin to strict liability, which may have its legal uses but seems irrational as a moral position.

The result of such a line of thought is to pare down each act to its morally essential core, an inner act of pure will assessed by motive and intention. Adam Smith advocates such a position in *The Theory of Moral Sentiments*, but notes that it runs contrary to our actual judgments.

> But how well soever we may seem to be persuaded of the truth of this equitable maxim, when we consider it after this manner, in abstract, yet when we come to particular cases, the actual consequences which happen to proceed from any action, have a very great effect upon our sentiments concerning its merit or demerit, and almost always either enhance or diminish our sense of both. Scarce, in any one instance, perhaps, will our sentiments be found, after examination, to be entirely regulated by this rule, which we all acknowledge ought entirely to regulate them.[6]

Joel Feinberg points out further that restricting the domain of moral responsibility to the inner world will not immunize it to luck. Factors beyond the agent's control, like a coughing fit, can interfere with his decisions as surely as they can with the path of a bullet from his gun.[7] Nevertheless the tendency to cut down the scope of moral assessment is pervasive, and does not limit itself to the influence of effects. It attempts to isolate the will from the other direction, so to speak, by separating out constitutive luck. Let us consider that next.

Kant was particularly insistent on the moral irrelevance of qualities of temperament and personality that are not under the control of the will. Such qualities as sympathy or coldness might provide the background against which obedience to moral requirements is more or less difficult, but they could not be objects of moral assessment themselves, and might well interfere with confident assessment of its proper object—the determination of the will by the motive of duty. This rules out moral judgment of many of the virtues and vices, which are states of character that influence choice but are certainly not exhausted by dispositions to act deliberately in certain ways. A person may be greedy, envious, cowardly, cold, ungenerous, unkind, vain, or conceited, but *behave* perfectly by a monumental effort of will. To possess these vices is to be unable to help having certain feelings under certain circumstances, and to have strong spontaneous impulses to act badly. Even if one controls the impulses, one still has the vice. An envious person hates the greater success of others. He can be morally condemned as envious even if he congratulates them cordially and does nothing to denigrate or spoil their success. Conceit, likewise, need not be displayed. It is fully present in someone who cannot help dwelling with secret

---

6 Pt II, sect. 3, Introduction, para. 5.

7 'Problematic Responsibility in Law and Morals', in Joel Feinberg, *Doing and Deserving* (Princeton, NJ: Princeton University Press, 1970).

satisfaction on the superiority of his own achievements, talents, beauty, intelligence, or virtue. To some extent such a quality may be the product of earlier choices; to some extent it may be amenable to change by current actions. But it is largely a matter of constitutive bad fortune. Yet people are morally condemned for such qualities, and esteemed for others equally beyond control of the will: they are assessed for what they are *like.*

To Kant this seems incoherent because virtue is enjoined on everyone and therefore must in principle be possible for everyone. It may be easier for some than for others, but it must be possible to achieve it by making the right choices, against whatever temperamental background.[8] One may want to have a generous spirit, or regret not having one, but it makes no sense to condemn oneself or anyone else for a quality which is not within the control of the will. Condemnation implies that you should not be like that, not that it is unfortunate that you are.

Nevertheless, Kant's conclusion remains intuitively unacceptable. We may be persuaded that these moral judgments are irrational, but they reappear involuntarily as soon as the argument is over. This is the pattern throughout the subject.

The third category to consider is luck in one's circumstances, and I shall mention it briefly. The things we are called upon to do, the moral tests we face, are importantly determined by factors beyond our control. It may be true of someone that in a dangerous situation he would behave in a cowardly or heroic fashion, but if the situation never arises, he will never have the chance to distinguish or disgrace himself in this way, and his moral record will be different.[9]

A conspicuous example of this is political. Ordinary citizens of Nazi Germany had an opportunity to behave heroically by opposing the regime. They also had an opportunity to behave badly, and most of them are culpable for having failed this test. But it is a test to which the citizens of other countries were not subjected, with the result that even if they, or some of them, would have behaved as badly as the Germans in like circumstances, they simply did not and therefore are not similarly culpable. Here again one is morally at the mercy of fate, and it may seem irrational upon reflection, but our ordinary

---

[8] 'If nature has put little sympathy in the heart of a man, and if he, though an honest man, is by temperament cold and indifferent to the sufferings of others, perhaps because he is provided with special gifts of patience and fortitude and expects or even requires that others should have the same—and such a man would certainly not be the meanest product of nature—would not he find in himself a source from which to give himself a far higher worth than he could have got by having a good-natured temperament?' (*Foundations of the Metaphysics of Morals,* first section, eleventh paragraph).

[9] Cf. Thomas Gray, 'Elegy Written in a Country Churchyard':
　　Some mute inglorious Milton here may rest,
　　Some Cromwell, guiltless of his country's blood.
An unusual example of circumstantial moral luck is provided by the kind of moral dilemma with which someone can be faced through no fault of his own, but which leaves him with nothing to do which is not wrong. . . . Bernard Williams, 'Ethical Consistency', *Proceedings of the Aristotelian Society,* supplementary vol. xxxix (1965), reprinted in *Problems of the Self* (Cambridge: Cambridge University Press, 1973), pp. 166–86.

moral attitudes would be unrecognizable without it. We judge people for what they actually do or fail to do, not just for what they would have done if circumstances had been different.[10]

This form of moral determination by the actual is also paradoxical, but we can begin to see how deep in the concept of responsibility the paradox is embedded. A person can be morally responsible only for what he does; but what he does results from a great deal that he does not do; therefore he is not morally responsible for what he is and is not responsible for. (This is not a contradiction, but it is a paradox.)

It should be obvious that there is a connection between these problems about responsibility and control and an even more familiar problem, that of freedom of the will. That is the last type of moral luck I want to take up, though I can do no more within the scope of this essay than indicate its connection with the other types.

If one cannot be responsible for consequences of one's acts due to factors beyond one's control, or for antecedents of one's acts that are properties of temperament not subject to one's will, or for the circumstances that pose one's moral choices, then how can one be responsible even for the stripped-down acts of the will itself, if *they* are the product of antecedent circumstances outside of the will's control?

The area of genuine agency, and therefore of legitimate moral judgment, seems to shrink under this scrutiny to an extensionless point. Everything seems to result from the combined influence of factors, antecedent and posterior to action, that are not within the agent's control. Since he cannot be responsible for them, he cannot be responsible for their results—though it may remain possible to take up the aesthetic or other evaluative analogues of the moral attitudes that are thus displaced.

It is also possible, of course, to brazen it out and refuse to accept the results, which indeed seem unacceptable as soon as we stop thinking about the arguments. Admittedly, if certain surrounding circumstances had been different, then no unfortunate consequences would have followed from a wicked intention, and no seriously culpable act would have been performed; but since the circumstances were *not* different, and the agent *in fact* succeeded in perpetrating a particularly cruel murder, *that* is what he did, and that is what he is responsible for. Similarly, we may admit that if certain antecedent circumstances had been different, the agent would never have developed into the sort of person who would do such a thing; but since he *did* develop (as

---

10 Circumstantial luck can extend to aspects of the situation other than individual behavior. For example, during the Vietnam War even U.S. citizens who had opposed their country's actions vigorously from the start often felt compromised by its crimes. Here they were not even responsible; there was probably nothing they could do to stop what was happening, so the feeling of being implicated may seem unintelligible. But it is nearly impossible to view the crimes of one's own country in the same way that one views the crimes of another country, no matter how equal one's lack of power to stop them in the two cases. One *is* a citizen of one of them, and has a connection with its actions (even if only through taxes that cannot be withheld)—that one does not have with the other's. This makes it possible to be ashamed of one's country, and to feel a victim of moral bad luck that one was an American in the 1960s.

the inevitable result of those antecedent circumstances) into the sort of swine he is, and into the person who committed such a murder, *that* is what he is blameable for. In both cases one is responsible for what one actually does— even if what one actually does depends in important ways on what is not within one's control. This compatibilist account of our moral judgments would leave room for the ordinary conditions of responsibility—the absence of coercion, ignorance, or involuntary movement—as part of the determination of what someone has done—but it is understood not to exclude the influence of a great deal that he has not done.[11]

The only thing wrong with this solution is its failure to explain how skeptical problems arise. For they arise not from the imposition of an arbitrary external requirement, but from the nature of moral judgment itself. Something in the ordinary idea of what someone does must explain how it can seem necessary to subtract from it anything that merely happens—even though the ultimate consequence of such subtraction is that nothing remains. And something in the ordinary idea of knowledge must explain why it seems to be undermined by any influences on belief not within the control of the subject—so that knowledge seems impossible without an impossible foundation in autonomous reason. But let us leave epistemology aside and concentrate on action, character, and moral assessment.

The problem arises, I believe, because the self which acts and is the object of moral judgment is threatened with dissolution by the absorption of its acts and impulses into the class of events. Moral judgment of a person is a judgment not of what happens to him, but of him. It does not say merely that a certain event or state of affairs is fortunate or unfortunate or even terrible. It is not an evaluation of a state of the world, or of an individual as part of the world. We are not thinking just that it would be better if he were different, or did not exist, or had not done some of the things he has done. We are judging *him,* rather than his existence or characteristics. The effect of concentrating on the influence of what is not under his control is to make this responsible self seem to disappear, swallowed up by the order of mere events.

What, however, do we have in mind that a person must *be* to be the object of these moral attitudes? While the concept of agency is easily undermined, it is very difficult to give it a positive characterization. That is familiar from the literature on Free Will.

I believe that in a sense the problem has no solution, because something in the idea of agency is incompatible with actions being events, or people being things. But as the external determinants of what someone has done are gradually exposed, in their effect on consequences, character, and choice itself, it becomes gradually clear that actions are events and people things. Eventually nothing remains which can be ascribed to the responsible self, and we are left with

11 The corresponding position in epistemology would be that knowledge consists of true beliefs formed in certain ways, and that it does not require all aspects of the process to be under the knower's control, actually or potentially. Both the correctness of these beliefs and the process by which they are arrived at would therefore be importantly subject to luck. The Nobel Prize is not awarded to people who turn out to be wrong, no matter how brilliant their reasoning.

nothing but a portion of the larger sequence of events, which can be deplored or celebrated, but not blamed or praised.

Though I cannot define the idea of the active self that is thus undermined, it is possible to say something about its sources. There is a close connection between our feelings about ourselves and our feelings about others. Guilt and indignation, shame and contempt, pride and admiration are internal and external sides of the same moral attitudes. We are unable to view ourselves simply as portions of the world, and from inside we have a rough idea of the boundary between what is us and what is not, what we do and what happens to us, what is our personality and what is an accidental handicap. We apply the same essentially internal conception of the self to others. About ourselves we feel pride, shame, guilt, remorse—and agent-regret. We do not regard our actions and our characters merely as fortunate or unfortunate episodes— though they may also be that. We cannot *simply* take an external evaluative view of ourselves—of what we most essentially are and what we do. And this remains true even when we have seen that we are not responsible for our own existence, or our nature, or the choices we have to make, or the circumstances that give our acts the consequences they have. Those acts remain ours and we remain ourselves, despite the persuasiveness of the reasons that seem to argue us out of existence.

It is this internal view that we extend to others in moral judgment—when we judge *them* rather than their desirability or utility. We extend to others the refusal to limit ourselves to external evaluation, and we accord to them selves like our own. But in both cases this comes up against the brutal inclusion of humans and everything about them in a world from which they cannot be separated and of which they are nothing but contents. The external view forces itself on us at the same time that we resist it. One way this occurs is through the gradual erosion of what we do by the subtraction of what happens.[12]

The inclusion of consequences in the conception of what we have done is an acknowledgment that we are parts of the world, but the paradoxical character of moral luck which emerges from this acknowledgment shows that we are unable to operate with such a view, for it leaves us with no one to be. The same thing is revealed in the appearance that determinism obliterates responsibility. Once we see an aspect of what we or someone else does as something that happens, we lose our grip on the idea that it has been done and that we can judge the doer and not just the happening. This explains why the absence of determinism is no more hospitable to the concept of agency than is its presence—a point that has been noticed often. Either way the act is viewed externally, as part of the course of events.

The problem of moral luck cannot be understood without an account of the internal conception of agency and its special connection with the moral

12 See P. F. Strawson's discussion of the conflict between the objective attitude and personal reactive attitudes in 'Freedom and Resentment', *Proceedings of the British Academy*, 1962, reprinted in *Studies in the Philosophy of Thought and Action*, ed. P. F. Strawson (London: Oxford University Press, 1968), and in P. F. Strawson, *Freedom and Resentment and Other Essays* (London: Methuen, 1974).

attitudes as opposed to other types of value. I do not have such an account. The degree to which the problem has a solution can be determined only by seeing whether in some degree the incompatibility between this conception and the various ways in which we do not control what we do is only apparent. I have nothing to offer on that topic either. But it is not enough to say merely that our basic moral attitudes toward ourselves and others are determined by what is actual; for they are also threatened by the sources of that actuality, and by the external view of action which forces itself on us when we see how everything we do belongs to a world that we have not created.

34

A Theory of Justice

JOHN RAWLS

For biographical information about John Rawls, see reading 21.

In this selection, taken from his book A Theory of Justice, *Rawls argues that social arrangements are just, and actions are right, when they conform to principles arising out of certain choices. These choices are not actual, but rather are choices that* would *be made by ideally situated persons. Such persons would know only the most general facts about the world. They would not know their own race, sex, degree of wealth, or natural abilities. Being ignorant of these things, they could not tailor principles to their own advantage. Because they would not even know their actual preferences and psychological tendencies, they would want only "primary goods"—goods that it is rational to want whatever else one wants. According to Rawls, such goods include rights and liberties, powers and opportunities, wealth and income, and the social bases of self-respect.*

What principles would persons who are behind this "veil of ignorance" choose? To structure basic social institutions, such as the political constitution and economic system, they would choose that "each person have a right to the most extensive basic liberty compatible with a similar liberty for others." However, they would tolerate some social and economic inequalities provided that (a) they did not restrict equality of opportunity, and (b) they raised the position of even the worst-off (for example, by providing the better-off with incentives that raised productivity). Because such inequalities help both the worse-off and the better-off, it would be irrational not to accept them. Because Rawls is more concerned with social justice than individual action, he says far less about the choice of principles regulating personal behavior. However, he believes that persons in his "original position" would choose principles imposing such familiar duties and obligations as fidelity, mutual aid, mutual respect, and noninfliction of harm.

Because Rawls does not equate justice or rightness with the maximization of benefit, his theory is a deep and systematic alternative to utilitarianism (readings 23, 24, and 25). In this and other respects, the theory resembles Kant's (reading 30). For illuminating discussion of the parallels, see Rawls's own "Kantian interpretation" of his theory at the selection's end.

THE MAIN IDEA OF THE THEORY OF JUSTICE

My aim is to present a conception of justice which generalizes and carries to a higher level of abstraction the familiar theory of the social contract as found, say, in Locke, Rousseau, and Kant.[1] In order to do this we are not to think of the original contract as one to enter a particular society or to set up a particular form of government. Rather, the guiding idea is that the principles of justice for the basic structure of society are the object of the original agreement. They are the principles that free and rational persons concerned to further their own interests would accept in an initial position of equality as defining the fundamental terms of their association. These principles are to regulate all further agreements; they specify the kinds of social cooperation that can be entered into and the forms of government that can be established. This way of regarding the principles of justice I shall call justice as fairness.

Thus we are to imagine that those who engage in social cooperation choose together, in one joint act, the principles which are to assign basic rights and duties and to determine the division of social benefits. Men are to decide in advance how they are to regulate their claims against one another and what is to be the foundation charter of their society. Just as each person must decide by rational reflection what constitutes his good, that is, the system of ends which it is rational for him to pursue, so a group of persons must decide once and for all what is to count among them as just and unjust. The choice which rational men would make in this hypothetical situation of equal liberty, assuming for the present that this choice problem has a solution, determines the principles of justice.

In justice as fairness the original position of equality corresponds to the state of nature in the traditional theory of the social contract. This original position is not, of course, thought of as an actual historical state of affairs, much less as a primitive condition of culture. It is understood as a purely hypothetical situation characterized so as to lead to a certain conception of justice.[2] Among the essential features of this situation is that no one knows his place in society, his class position or social status, nor does any one know

---

[1] As the text suggests, I shall regard Locke's *Second Treatise of Government*, Rousseau's *The Social Contract*, and Kant's ethical works beginning with *The Foundations of the Metaphysics of Morals* as definitive of the contract tradition. For all of its greatness, Hobbes's *Leviathan* raises special problems. A general historical survey is provided by J. W. Gough, *The Social Contract*, 2nd ed. (Oxford, The Clarendon Press, 1957), and Otto Gierke, *Natural Law and the Theory of Society*, trans. with an introduction by Ernest Barker (Cambridge, The University Press, 1934). A presentation of the contract view as primarily an ethical theory is to be found in G. R. Grice, *The Grounds of Moral Judgment* (Cambridge, The University Press, 1967). See also §19, note 30.

[2] Kant is clear that the original agreement is hypothetical. See *The Metaphysics of Morals*, pt. I (*Rechtslehre*), especially §§47, 52; and pt. II of the essay "Concerning the Common Saying: This May Be True in Theory but It Does Not Apply in Practice," in *Kant's Political Writings*, ed. Hans Reiss and trans. by H. B. Nisber (Cambridge, The University Press, 1970), pp. 73–87. See Georges Vlachos, *La Pensée politique de Kant* (Paris, Presses Universitaires de France, 1962), pp. 326–335; and J. G. Murphy, *Kant: The Philosophy of Right* (London, Macmillan, 1970), pp. 109–112, 133–136, for a further discussion.

his fortune in the distribution of natural assets and abilities, his intelligence, strength, and the like. I shall even assume that the parties do not know their conceptions of the good or their special psychological propensities. The principles of justice are chosen behind a veil of ignorance. This ensures that no one is advantaged or disadvantaged in the choice of principles by the outcome of natural chance or the contingency of social circumstances. Since all are similarly situated and no one is able to design principles to favor his particular condition, the principles of justice are the result of a fair agreement or bargain. For given the circumstances of the original position, the symmetry of everyone's relations to each other, this initial situation is fair between individuals as moral persons, that is, as rational beings with their own ends and capable, I shall assume, of a sense of justice. The original position is, one might say, the appropriate initial status quo, and thus the fundamental agreements reached in it are fair. This explains the propriety of the name "justice as fairness": it conveys the idea that the principles of justice are agreed to in an initial situation that is fair. The name does not mean that the concepts of justice and fairness are the same, any more than the phrase "poetry as metaphor" means that the concepts of poetry and metaphor are the same.

Justice as fairness begins, as I have said, with one of the most general of all choices which persons might make together, namely, with the choice of the first principles of a conception of justice which is to regulate all subsequent criticism and reform of institutions. Then, having chosen a conception of justice, we can suppose that they are to choose a constitution and a legislature to enact laws, and so on, all in accordance with the principles of justice initially agreed upon. Our social situation is just if it is such that by this sequence of hypothetical agreements we would have contracted into the general system of rules which defines it. Moreover, assuming that the original position does determine a set of principles (that is, that a particular conception of justice would be chosen), it will then be true that whenever social institutions satisfy these principles those engaged in them can say to one another that they are cooperating on terms on which they would agree if they were free and equal persons whose relations with respect to one another were fair. They could all view their arrangements as meeting the stipulations which they would acknowledge in an initial situation that embodies widely accepted and reasonable constraints on the choice of principles. The general recognition of this fact would provide the basis for a public acceptance of the corresponding principles of justice. No society can, of course, be a scheme of cooperation which men enter voluntarily in a literal sense; each person finds himself placed at birth in some particular position in some particular society, and the nature of this position materially affects his life prospects. Yet a society satisfying the principles of justice as fairness comes as close as a society can to being a voluntary scheme, for it meets the principles which free and equal persons would assent to under circumstances that are fair. In this sense its members are autonomous and the obligations they recognize self-imposed.

One feature of justice as fairness is to think of the parties in the initial situation as rational and mutually disinterested. This does not mean that the parties are egoists, that is, individuals with only certain kinds of interests, say in wealth, prestige, and domination. But they are conceived as not taking an interest in one another's interests. They are to presume that even their spiritual aims may be opposed, in the way that the aims of those of different religions may be opposed. Moreover, the concept of rationality must be interpreted as far as possible in the narrow sense, standard in economic theory, of taking the most effective means to given ends. I shall modify this concept to some extent, as explained later, but one must try to avoid introducing into it any controversial ethical elements. The initial situation must be characterized by stipulations that are widely accepted.

In working out the conception of justice as fairness one main task clearly is to determine which principles of justice would be chosen in the original position. To do this we must describe this situation in some detail and formulate with care the problem of choice which it presents. These matters I shall take up in the immediately succeeding chapters. It may be observed, however, that once the principles of justice are thought of as arising from an original agreement in a situation of equality, it is an open question whether the principle of utility would be acknowledged. Offhand it hardly seems likely that persons who view themselves as equals, entitled to press their claims upon one another, would agree to a principle which may require lesser life prospects for some simply for the sake of a greater sum of advantages enjoyed by others. Since each desires to protect his interests, his capacity to advance his conception of the good, no one has a reason to acquiesce in an enduring loss for himself in order to bring about a greater net balance of satisfaction. In the absence of strong and lasting benevolent impulses, a rational man would not accept a basic structure merely because it maximized the algebraic sum of advantages irrespective of its permanent effects on his own basic rights and interests. Thus it seems that the principle of utility is incompatible with the conception of social cooperation among equals for mutual advantage. It appears to be inconsistent with the idea of reciprocity implicit in the notion of a well-ordered society. Or, at any rate, so I shall argue.

I shall maintain instead that the persons in the initial situation would choose two rather different principles: the first requires equality in the assignment of basic rights and duties, while the second holds that social and economic inequalities, for example, inequalities of wealth and authority, are just only if they result in compensating benefits for everyone, and in particular for the least advantaged members of society. These principles rule out justifying institutions on the grounds that the hardships of some are offset by a greater good in the aggregate. It may be expedient but it is not just that some should have less in order that others may prosper. But there is no injustice in the greater benefits earned by a few provided that the situation of persons not so fortunate is thereby improved. The intuitive idea is that since everyone's well-being depends upon a scheme of cooperation without which no one could have a satisfactory life, the division of advantages should be such as to draw forth the willing cooperation of everyone taking part in it, including those less well situated. Yet this can be expected only if reasonable terms are proposed. The two principles mentioned seem to be a fair agreement on the basis of which those better endowed, or more fortunate in their social position, neither of which we can be said to deserve, could expect the willing cooperation of others when some workable scheme is a necessary condition of the welfare of all.[3] Once we decide to look for a conception of justice that nullifies the accidents of natural endowment and the contingencies of social circumstance as counters in quest for political and economic advantage, we are led to these principles. They express the result of leaving aside those aspects of the social world that seem arbitrary from a moral point of view.

The problem of the choice of principles, however, is extremely difficult. I do not expect the answer I shall suggest to be convincing to everyone. It is, therefore, worth noting from the outset that justice as fairness, like other contract views, consists of two parts: (1) an interpretation of the initial situation and of the problem of choice posed there, and (2) a set of principles which, it is argued, would be agreed to. One may accept the first part of the theory (or some variant thereof), but not the other, and conversely. The concept of the initial contractual situation may seem reasonable although the particular principles proposed are rejected. To be sure, I want to maintain that the most appropriate conception of this situation does lead to principles of justice contrary to utilitarianism and perfectionism, and therefore that the contract doctrine provides an alternative to these views. Still, one may dispute this contention even though one grants that the contractarian method is a useful way of studying ethical theories and of setting forth their underlying assumptions.

• • •

A final remark. Justice as fairness is not a complete contract theory. For it is clear that the contractarian idea can be extended to the choice of more or less an entire ethical system, that is, to a system including principles for all the virtues and not only for justice. Now for the most part I shall consider only principles of justice and others closely related to them; I make no attempt to discuss the virtues in a systematic way. Obviously if justice as fairness succeeds reasonably well, a next step would be to study the more general view suggested by the name "rightness as fairness." But even this wider theory fails to embrace all moral relationships, since it would seem to include only our relations with other persons and to leave out of account how we are to conduct ourselves toward animals and the rest of nature. I do not contend that the contract notion offers a way to approach these questions which are certainly of the first importance; and I shall have to put them aside. We must recognize the limited scope of justice as fairness and of the general type of view that it exemplifies. How far its conclusions must be revised once these other matters are understood cannot be decided in advance.

---

3 For the formulation of this intuitive idea I am indebted to Allan Gibbard.

THE ORIGINAL POSITION AND JUSTIFICATION

I have said that the original position is the appropriate initial status quo which ensures that the fundamental agreements reached in it are fair. This fact yields the name "justice as fairness." It is clear, then, that I want to say that one conception of justice is more reasonable than another, or justifiable with respect to it, if rational persons in the initial situation would choose its principles over those of the other for the role of justice. Conceptions of justice are to be ranked by their acceptability to persons so circumstanced. Understood in this way the question of justification is settled by working out a problem of deliberation: we have to ascertain which principles it would be rational to adopt given the contractual situation. This connects the theory of justice with the theory of rational choice.

If this view of the problem of justification is to succeed, we must, of course, describe in some detail the nature of this choice problem. A problem of rational decision has a definite answer only if we know the beliefs and interests of the parties, their relations with respect to one another, the alternatives between which they are to choose, the procedure whereby they make up their minds, and so on. As the circumstances are presented in different ways, correspondingly different principles are accepted. The concept of the original position, as I shall refer to it, is that of the most philosophically favored interpretation of this initial choice situation for the purposes of a theory of justice.

But how are we to decide what is the most favored interpretation? I assume, for one thing, that there is a broad measure of agreement that principles of justice should be chosen under certain conditions. To justify a particular description of the initial situation one shows that it incorporates these commonly shared presumptions. One argues from widely accepted but weak premises to more specific conclusions. Each of the presumptions should by itself be natural and plausible; some of them may seem innocuous or even trivial. The aim of the contract approach is to establish that taken together they impose significant bounds on acceptable principles of justice. The ideal outcome would be that these conditions determine a unique set of principles; but I shall be satisfied if they suffice to rank the main traditional conceptions of social justice.

One should not be misled, then, by the somewhat unusual conditions which characterize the original position. The idea here is simply to make vivid to ourselves the restrictions that it seems reasonable to impose on arguments for principles of justice, and therefore on these principles themselves. Thus it seems reasonable and generally acceptable that no one should be advantaged or disadvantaged by natural fortune or social circumstances in the choice of principles. It also seems widely agreed that it should be impossible to tailor principles to the circumstances of one's own case. We should ensure further that particular inclinations and aspirations and persons' conceptions of their good do not affect the principles adopted. The aim is to rule out those principles that it would be rational to propose for acceptance, however little the chance of success, only if one knew certain things that are irrelevant from the standpoint of justice. For example, if a man knew that he was wealthy, he might find it rational to advance the principle that various taxes for welfare measures be counted unjust; if he knew that he was poor, he would most likely propose the contrary principle. To represent the desired restrictions one imagines a situation in which everyone is deprived of this sort of information. One excludes the knowledge of those contingencies which sets men at odds and allows them to be guided by their prejudices. In this manner the veil of ignorance is arrived at in a natural way. This concept should cause no difficulty if we keep in mind the constraints on arguments that it is meant to express. At any time we can enter the original position, so to speak, simply by following a certain procedure, namely, by arguing for principles of justice in accordance with these restrictions.

It seems reasonable to suppose that the parties in the original position are equal. That is, all have the same rights in the procedure for choosing principles; each can make proposals, submit reasons for their acceptance, and so on. Obviously the purpose of these conditions is to represent equality between human beings as moral persons, as creatures having a conception of their good and capable of a sense of justice. The basis of equality is taken to be similarity in these two respects. Systems of ends are not ranked in value; and each man is presumed to have the requisite ability to understand and to act upon whatever principles are adopted. Together with the veil of ignorance, these conditions define the principles of justice as those which rational persons concerned to advance their interests would consent to as equals when none are known to be advantaged or disadvantaged by social and natural contingencies.

There is, however, another side to justifying a particular description of the original position. This is to see if the principles which would be chosen match our considered convictions of justice or extend them in an acceptable way. We can note whether applying these principles would lead us to make the same judgments about the basic structure of society which we now make intuitively and in which we have the greatest confidence; or whether, in cases where our present judgments are in doubt and given with hesitation, these principles offer a resolution which we can affirm on reflection. There are questions which we feel sure must be answered in a certain way. For example, we are confident that religious intolerance and racial discrimination are unjust. We think that we have examined these things with care and have reached what we believe is an impartial judgment not likely to be distorted by an excessive attention to our own interests. These convictions are provisional fixed points which we presume any conception of justice must fit. But we have much less assurance as to what is the correct distribution of wealth and authority. Here we may be looking for a way to remove our doubts. We can check an interpretation of the initial situation, then, by the capacity of its principles to accommodate our firmest convictions and to provide guidance where guidance is needed.

In searching for the most favored description of this situation we work from both ends. We begin by describing it so that it represents generally shared and preferably weak conditions. We then see if these conditions are strong enough to yield a significant set of principles. If not, we look for further premises equally reasonable. But if so, and these principles match our considered convictions of justice, then so far well and good. But presumably there will be discrepancies.

In this case we have a choice. We can either modify the account of the initial situation or we can revise our existing judgments, for even the judgments we take provisionally as fixed points are liable to revision. By going back and forth, sometimes altering the conditions of the contractual circumstances, at others withdrawing our judgments and conforming them to principle, I assume that eventually we shall find a description of the initial situation that both expresses reasonable conditions and yields principles which match our considered judgments duly pruned and adjusted. This state of affairs I refer to as reflective equilibrium.[4] It is an equilibrium because at last our principles and judgments coincide; and it is reflective since we know to what principles our judgments conform and the premises of their derivation. At the moment everything is in order. But this equilibrium is not necessarily stable. It is liable to be upset by further examination of the conditions which should be imposed on the contractual situation and by particular cases which may lead us to revise our judgments. Yet for the time being we have done what we can to render coherent and to justify our convictions of social justice. We have reached a conception of the original position.

● ● ●

TWO PRINCIPLES OF JUSTICE

I shall now state in a provisional form the two principles of justice that I believe would be chosen in the original position. In this section I wish to make only the most general comments, and therefore the first formulation of these principles is tentative. As we go on I shall run through several formulations and approximate step by step the final statement to be given much later. I believe that doing this allows the exposition to proceed in a natural way.

The first statement of the two principles reads as follows.

> First: each person is to have an equal right to the most extensive basic liberty compatible with a similar liberty for others.
> Second: social and economic inequalities are to be arranged so that they are both (a) reasonably expected to be to everyone's advantage, and (b) attached to positions and offices open to all.

There are two ambiguous phrases in the second principle, namely "everyone's advantage" and "open to all." . . .

By way of general comment, these principles primarily apply, as I have said, to the basic structure of society. They are to govern the assignment of rights and duties and to regulate the distribution of social and economic advantages.

---

[4] The process of mutual adjustment of principles and considered judgments is not peculiar to moral philosophy. See Nelson Goodman, *Fact, Fiction, and Forecast* (Cambridge, MA, Harvard University Press, 1955), pp. 65–68, for parallel remarks concerning the justification of the principles of deductive and inductive inference.

As their formulation suggests, these principles presuppose that the social structure can be divided into two more or less distinct parts, the first principle applying to the one, the second to the other. They distinguish between those aspects of the social system that define and secure the equal liberties of citizenship and those that specify and establish social and economic inequalities. The basic liberties of citizens are, roughly speaking, political liberty (the right to vote and to be eligible for public office) together with freedom of speech and assembly; liberty of conscience and freedom of thought; freedom of the person along with the right to hold (personal) property; and freedom from arbitrary arrest and seizure as defined by the concept of the rule of law. These liberties are all required to be equal by the first principle, since citizens of a just society are to have the same basic rights.

The second principle applies, in the first approximation, to the distribution of income and wealth and to the design of organizations that make use of differences in authority and responsibility, or chains of command. While the distribution of wealth and income need not be equal, it must be to everyone's advantage, and at the same time, positions of authority and offices of command must be accessible to all. One applies the second principle by holding positions open, and then, subject to this constraint, arranges social and economic inequalities so that everyone benefits.

These principles are to be arranged in a serial order with the first principle prior to the second. This ordering means that a departure from the institutions of equal liberty required by the first principle cannot be justified by, or compensated for, by greater social and economic advantages. The distribution of wealth and income, and the hierarchies of authority, must be consistent with both the liberties of equal citizenship and equality of opportunity.

It is clear that these principles are rather specific in their content, and their acceptance rests on certain assumptions that I must eventually try to explain and justify. A theory of justice depends upon a theory of society in ways that will become evident as we proceed. For the present, it should be observed that the two principles (and this holds for all formulations) are a special case of a more general conception of justice that can be expressed as follows.

> All social values—liberty and opportunity, income and wealth, and the bases of self-respect—are to be distributed equally unless an unequal distribution of any, or all, of these values is to everyone's advantage.

Injustice, then, is simply inequalities that are not to the benefit of all. Of course, this conception is extremely vague and requires interpretation.

As a first step, suppose that the basic structure of society distributes certain primary goods, that is, things that every rational man is presumed to want. These goods normally have a use whatever a person's rational plan of life. For simplicity, assume that the chief primary goods at the disposition of society are rights and liberties, powers and opportunities, income and wealth. (Later on in Part Three the primary good of self-respect has a central place.) These are the social primary goods. Other primary goods such as health and vigor, intelligence and imagination, are natural goods; although their possession is influenced by the basic structure, they are not so directly under its control. Imagine, then, a hypothetical initial arrangement in which all the social primary goods are equally distributed: everyone has similar rights and duties, and income and wealth are evenly shared. This state of affairs provides a benchmark for judging improvements. If certain inequalities of wealth and organizational powers would make everyone better off than in this hypothetical starting situation, then they accord with the general conception.

Now it is possible, at least theoretically, that by giving up some of their fundamental liberties men are sufficiently compensated by the resulting social and economic gains. The general conception of justice imposes no restrictions on what sort of inequalities are permissible; it only requires that everyone's position be improved. We need not suppose anything so drastic as consenting to a condition of slavery. Imagine instead that men forego certain political rights when the economic returns are significant and their capacity to influence the course of policy by the exercise of these rights would be marginal in any case. It is this kind of exchange which the two principles as stated rule out; being arranged in serial order they do not permit exchanges between basic liberties and economic and social gains. The serial ordering of principles expresses an underlying preference among primary social goods. When this preference is rational so likewise is the choice of these principles in this order.

In developing justice as fairness I shall, for the most part, leave aside the general conception of justice and examine instead the special case of the two principles in serial order. The advantage of this procedure is that from the first the matter of priorities is recognized and an effort made to find principles to deal with it. One is led to attend throughout to the conditions under which the acknowledgment of the absolute weight of liberty with respect to social and economic advantages, as defined by the lexical order of the two principles, would be reasonable. Offhand, this ranking appears extreme and too special a case to be of much interest; but there is more justification for it than would appear at first sight. Or at any rate, so I shall maintain. Furthermore, the distinction between fundamental rights and liberties and economic and social benefits marks a difference among primary social goods that one should try to exploit. It suggests an important division in the social system. Of course, the distinctions drawn and the ordering proposed are bound to be at best only approximations. There are surely circumstances in which they fail. But it is essential to depict clearly the main lines of a reasonable conception of justice; and under many conditions anyway, the two principles in serial order may serve well enough. When necessary we can fall back on the more general conception.

The fact that the two principles apply to institutions has certain consequences. Several points illustrate this. First of all, the rights and liberties referred to by these principles are those which are defined by the public rules of the basic structure. Whether men are free is determined by the rights and duties established by the major institutions of society. Liberty is a certain pattern of social forms. The first principle simply requires that certain sorts of rules, those defining basic liberties, apply to everyone equally and that they allow the most extensive liberty compatible with a like liberty for all. The only reason for circumscribing the rights defining liberty and making men's freedom less extensive than it might otherwise be is that these equal rights as institutionally defined would interfere with one another.

Another thing to bear in mind is that when principles mention persons, or require that everyone gains from an inequality, the reference is to representative persons holding the various social positions, or offices, or whatever, established by the basic structure. Thus in applying the second principle I assume that it is possible to assign an expectation of well-being to representative individuals holding these positions. This expectation indicates their life prospects as viewed from their social station. In general, the expectations of representative persons depend on the distribution of rights and duties throughout the basic structure. When this changes, expectations change. I assume, then, that expectations are connected: by raising the prospects of the representative man in one position we presumably increase or decrease the prospects of representative men in other positions. Since it applies to institutional forms, the second principle (or rather the first part of it) refers to the expectations of representative individuals. As I shall discuss below, neither principle applies to distributions of particular goods to particular individuals who may be identified by their proper names. The situation where someone is considering how to allocate certain commodities to needy persons who are known to him is not within the scope of the principles. They are meant to regulate basic institutional arrangements. We must not assume that there is much similarity from the standpoint of justice between an administrative allotment of goods to specific persons and the appropriate design of society. Our common sense intuitions for the former may be a poor guide to the latter.

Now the second principle insists that each person benefit from permissible inequalities in the basic structure. This means that it must be reasonable for each relevant representative man defined by this structure, when he views it as a going concern, to prefer his prospects with the inequality to his prospects without it. One is not allowed to justify differences in income or organizational powers on the ground that the disadvantages of those in one position are outweighed by the greater advantages of those in another. Much less can infringements of liberty be counterbalanced in this way. Applied to the basic structure, the principle of utility would have us maximize the sum of expectations of representative men (weighed by the number of persons they represent, on the classical view); and this would permit us to compensate for the losses of some by the gains of others. Instead, the two principles require that everyone benefit from economic and social inequalities.

●　●　●

PRINCIPLES FOR INDIVIDUALS: THE PRINCIPLE OF FAIRNESS

In the discussion so far I have considered the principles which apply to institutions or, more exactly, to the basic structure of society. It is clear, however, that principles of another kind must also be chosen, since a complete theory of right includes principles for individuals as well.

•   •   •

Now the order in which principles are chosen raises a number of questions which I shall skip over. The important thing is that the various principles are to be adopted in a definite sequence and the reasons for this ordering are connected with the more difficult parts of the theory of justice. To illustrate: while it would be possible to choose many of the natural duties before those for the basic structure without changing the principles in any substantial way, the sequence in either case reflects the fact that obligations presuppose principles for social forms. And some natural duties also presuppose such principles, for example, the duty to support just institutions. For this reason it seems simpler to adopt all principles for individuals after those for the basic structure. That principles for institutions are chosen first shows the social nature of the virtue of justice, its intimate connection with social practices so often noted by idealists. When Bradley says that the individual is a bare abstraction, he can be interpreted to say, without too much distortion, that a person's obligations and duties presuppose a moral conception of institutions and therefore that the content of just institutions must be defined before the requirements for individuals can be set out.[5] And this is to say that, in most cases, the principles for obligations and duties should be settled upon after those for the basic structure.

Therefore, to establish a complete conception of right, the parties in the original position are to choose in a definite order not only a conception of justice but also principles to go with each major concept falling under the concept of right. These concepts are I assume relatively few in number and have a determinate relation to each other. Thus, in addition to principles for institutions there must be an agreement on principles for such notions as fairness and fidelity, mutual respect and beneficence as these apply to individuals, as well as on principles for the conduct of states. The intuitive idea is this: the concept of something's being right is the same as, or better, may be replaced by, the concept of its being in accordance with the principles that in the original position would be acknowledged to apply to things of its kind. I do not interpret this concept of right as providing an analysis of the meaning of the term "right" as normally used in moral contexts. It is not meant as an analysis of the concept of right in the traditional sense. Rather, the broader notion of rightness as fairness is to be understood as a replacement for existing conceptions. There is no necessity to say that sameness of meaning holds between the word "right" (and its relatives) in its ordinary use and the more elaborate locutions needed to express this ideal contractarian concept of right. For our purposes here I accept the view that a sound analysis is best understood as providing a satisfactory substitute, one that meets certain desiderata while avoiding certain obscurities and confusions. In other words, explication is elimination: we start with

5 See F. H. Bradley, *Ethical Studies*, 2nd ed. (Oxford, The Clarendon Press, 1927), pp. 163–189.

a concept the expression for which is somehow troublesome; but it serves certain ends that cannot be given up. An explication achieves these ends in other ways that are relatively free of difficulty.[6] Thus if the theory of justice as fairness, or more generally of rightness as fairness, fits our considered judgments in reflective equilibrium, and if it enables us to say all that on due examination we want to say, then it provides a way of eliminating customary phrases in favor of other expressions. So understood one may think of justice as fairness and rightness as fairness as providing a definition or explication of the concepts of justice and right.

●   ●   ●

THE REASONING LEADING
TO THE TWO PRINCIPLES OF JUSTICE

●   ●   ●

It seems clear . . . that the two principles are at least a plausible conception of justice. The question, though, is how one is to argue for them more systematically. Now there are several things to do. One can work out their consequences for institutions and note their implications for fundamental social policy. In this way they are tested by a comparison with our considered judgments of justice. Part II is devoted to this. But one can also try to find arguments in their favor that are decisive from the standpoint of the original position. In order to see how this might be done, it is useful as a heuristic device to think of the two principles as the maximin solution to the problem of social justice. There is an analogy between the two principles and the maximin rule for choice under uncertainty.[7] This is evident from the fact that the two principles are those a person would choose for the design of a society in which his enemy is to assign him his place. The maximin rule tells us to rank alternatives by their worst possible outcomes: we are to adopt the alternative the worst outcome of which is superior to the worst outcomes of the others. The persons in the original position do not, of course, assume that their initial place in society is decided by a malevolent opponent. As I note below, they should not reason from false premises. The veil of ignorance does not violate this idea, since an absence of information is not misinformation. But that the two principles of justice would be chosen if the parties were forced to protect themselves against

---

6 See W. V. Quine, *Word and Object* (Cambridge, MA, M.I.T. Press, 1960), pp. 257–262, whom I follow here.

7 An accessible discussion of this and other rules of choice under uncertainty can be found in W. J. Baumol, *Economic Theory and Operations Analysis,* 2nd ed. (Englewood Cliffs, NJ, Prentice-Hall, Inc., 1965), ch. 24. Baumol gives a geometric interpretation of these rules, including the diagram used in §13 to illustrate the difference principle. See pp. 558–562. See also R. D. Luce and Howard Raiffa, *Games and Decisions* (New York, John Wiley and Sons, Inc., 1957), ch. XIII, for a fuller account.

such a contingency explains the sense in which this conception is the maximin solution. And this analogy suggests that if the original position has been described so that it is rational for the parties to adopt the conservative attitude expressed by this rule, a conclusive argument can indeed be constructed for these principles. Clearly the maximin rule is not, in general, a suitable guide for choices under uncertainty. But it is attractive in situations marked by certain special features. My aim, then, is to show that a good case can be made for the two principles based on the fact that the original position manifests these features to the fullest possible degree, carrying them to the limit, so to speak.

· · ·

Now there appear to be three chief features of situations that give plausibility to this unusual rule.[8] First, since the rule takes no account of the likelihoods of the possible circumstances, there must be some reason for sharply discounting estimates of these probabilities. Offhand, the most natural rule of choice would seem to be to compute the expectation of monetary gain for each decision and then to adopt the course of action with the highest prospect. (This expectation is defined as follows: let us suppose that g_{ij} represent the numbers in the gain-and-loss table, where i is the row index and j is the column index; and let p_j, $j = 1, 2, 3$, be the likelihoods of the circumstances, with $\Sigma p_j = 1$. Then the expectation for the ith decision is equal to $\Sigma p_j g_{ij}$.) Thus it must be, for example, that the situation is one in which a knowledge of likelihoods is impossible, or at best extremely insecure. In this case it is unreasonable not to be skeptical of probabilistic calculations unless there is no other way out, particularly if the decision is a fundamental one that needs to be justified to others.

The second feature that suggests the maximin rule is the following: the person choosing has a conception of the good such that he cares very little, if anything, for what he might gain above the minimum stipend that he can, in fact, be sure of by following the maximin rule. It is not worthwhile for him to take a chance for the sake of a further advantage, especially when it may turn out that he loses much that is important to him. This last provision brings in the third feature, namely, that the rejected alternatives have outcomes that one can hardly accept. The situation involves grave risks. Of course these features work most effectively in combination. The paradigm situation for following the maximin rule is when all three features are realized to the highest degree. This rule does not, then, generally apply, nor of course is it self-evident. Rather, it is a maxim, a rule of thumb, that comes into its own in special circumstances. Its application depends upon the qualitative structure of the possible gains and losses in relation to one's conception of the good, all this against a background in which it is reasonable to discount conjectural estimates of likelihoods.

· · ·

---

8 Here I borrow from William Fellner, *Probability and Profit* (Homewood, IL, R. D. Irwin, Inc., 1965), pp. 140–142, where these features are noted.

Now, as I have suggested, the original position has been defined so that it is a situation in which the maximin rule applies. In order to see this, let us review briefly the nature of this situation with these three special features in mind. To begin with, the veil of ignorance excludes all but the vaguest knowledge of likelihoods. The parties have no basis for determining the probable nature of their society, or their place in it. Thus they have strong reasons for being wary of probability calculations if any other course is open to them. They must also take in account the fact that their choice of principles should seem reasonable to others, in particular their descendants, whose rights will be deeply affected by it. There are further grounds for discounting that I shall mention as we go along. For the present it suffices to note that these considerations are strengthened by the fact that the parties know very little about the gain-and-loss table. Not only are they unable to conjecture the likelihood of the various possible circumstances, they cannot say much about what the possible circumstances are, much less enumerate them and foresee the outcome of each alternative available. Those deciding are much more in the dark than the illustration by a numerical table suggests. It is for this reason that I have spoken of an analogy with the maximin rule.

Several kinds of arguments for the two principles of justice illustrate the second feature. Thus, if we can maintain that these principles provide a workable theory of social justice, and that they are compatible with reasonable demands of efficiency, then this conception guarantees a satisfactory minimum. There may be, on reflection, little reason for trying to do better. Thus much of the argument . . . is to show, by their application to the main questions of social justice, that the two principles are a satisfactory conception. These details have a philosophical purpose. Moreover, this line of thought is practically decisive if we can establish the priority of liberty, the lexical ordering of the two principles. For this priority implies that the persons in the original position have no desire to try for greater gains at the expense of the equal liberties. The minimum assured by the two principles in lexical order is not one that the parties wish to jeopardize for the sake of greater economic and social advantages. . . .

Finally, the third feature holds if we can assume that other conceptions of justice may lead to institutions that the parties would find intolerable. For example, it has sometimes been held that under some conditions the utility principle (in either form) justifies, if not slavery or serfdom, at any rate serious infractions of liberty for the sake of greater social benefits. We need not consider here the truth of this claim, or the likelihood that the requisite conditions obtain. For the moment, this contention is only to illustrate the way in which conceptions of justice may allow for outcomes which the parties may not be able to accept. And having the ready alternative of the two principles of justice which secure a satisfactory minimum, it seems unwise, if not irrational, for them to take a chance that these outcomes are not realized.

•   •   •

THE KANTIAN INTERPRETATION OF JUSTICE AS FAIRNESS

For the most part I have considered the content of the principle of equal liberty and the meaning of the priority of the rights that it defines. It seems appropriate at this point to note that there is a Kantian interpretation of the conception of justice from which this principle derives. This interpretation is based upon Kant's notion of autonomy. It is a mistake, I believe, to emphasize the place of generality and universality in Kant's ethics. That moral principles are general and universal is hardly new with him; and as we have seen these conditions do not in any case take us very far. It is impossible to construct a moral theory on so slender a basis, and therefore to limit the discussion of Kant's doctrine to these notions is to reduce it to triviality. The real force of his view lies elsewhere.[9]

For one thing, he begins with the idea that moral principles are the object of rational choice. They define the moral law that men can rationally will to govern their conduct in an ethical commonwealth. Moral philosophy becomes the study of the conception and outcome of a suitably defined rational decision. This idea has immediate consequences. For once we think of moral principles as legislation for a kingdom of ends, it is clear that these principles must not only be acceptable to all but public as well. Finally Kant supposes that this moral legislation is to be agreed to under conditions that characterize men as free and equal rational beings. The description of the original position is an attempt to interpret this conception. I do not wish to argue here for this interpretation on the basis of Kant's text. Certainly some will want to read him differently. Perhaps the remarks to follow are best taken as suggestions for relating justice as fairness to the high point of the contractarian tradition in Kant and Rousseau.

Kant held, I believe, that a person is acting autonomously when the principles of his action are chosen by him as the most adequate possible expression of his nature as a free and equal rational being. The principles he acts upon are not adopted because of his social position or natural endowments, or in view of the particular kind of society in which he lives or the specific things that he happens to want. To act on such principles is to act heteronomously. Now

---

[9] To be avoided at all costs is the idea that Kant's doctrine simply provides the general, or formal, elements for a utilitarian (or indeed for any other) theory. See, for example, R. M. Hare, *Freedom and Reason* (Oxford, The Clarendon Press, 1963), pp. 123f. One must not lose sight of the full scope of his view, one must take the later works into consideration. Unfortunately, there is no commentary on Kant's moral theory as a whole; perhaps it would prove impossible to write. But the standard works of H. J. Paron, *The Categorical Imperative* (Chicago, University of Chicago Press, 1948), and L. W. Beck, *A Commentary on Kant's Critique of Practical Reason* (Chicago, University of Chicago Press, 1960), and others need to be further complemented by studies of the other writings. See here M. J. Gregor's *Laws of Freedom* (Oxford, Basil Blackwell, 1963), an account of *The Metaphysics of Morals*, and J. G. Murphy's brief *Kant: The Philosophy of Right* (London, Macmillan, 1970). Beyond this, *The Critique of Judgment, Religion Within the Limits of Reason*, and the political writings cannot be neglected without distorting his doctrine. For the last, see *Kant's Political Writings*, ed. Hans Reiss and trans. H. B. Nisbet (Cambridge, The University Press, 1970).

the veil of ignorance deprives the persons in the original position of the knowledge that would enable them to choose heteronomous principles. The parties arrive at their choice together as free and equal rational persons knowing only that those circumstances obtain which give rise to the need for principles of justice.

To be sure, the argument for these principles does add in various ways to Kant's conception. For example, it adds the feature that the principles chosen are to apply to the basic structure of society; and premises characterizing this structure are used in deriving the principles of justice. But I believe that this and other additions are natural enough and remain fairly close to Kant's doctrine, at least when all of his ethical writings are viewed together. Assuming, then, that the reasoning in favor of the principles of justice is correct, we can say that when persons act on these principles they are acting in accordance with principles that they would choose as rational and independent persons in an original position of equality. The principles of their actions do not depend upon social or natural contingencies, nor do they reflect the bias of the particulars of their plan of life or the aspirations that motivate them. By acting from these principles persons express their nature as free and equal rational beings subject to the general conditions of human life. For to express one's nature as a being of a particular kind is to act on the principles that would be chosen if this nature were the decisive determining element. Of course, the choice of the parties in the original position is subject to the restrictions of that situation. But when we knowingly act on the principles of justice in the ordinary course of events, we deliberately assume the limitations of the original position. One reason for doing this, for persons who can do so and want to, is to give expression to one's nature.

The principles of justice are also categorical imperatives in Kant's sense. For by a categorical imperative Kant understands a principle of conduct that applies to a person in virtue of his nature as a free and equal rational being. The validity of the principle does not presuppose that one has a particular desire or aim. Whereas a hypothetical imperative by contrast does assume this: it directs us to take certain steps as effective means to achieve a specific end. Whether the desire is for a particular thing, or whether it is for something more general, such as certain kinds of agreeable feelings or pleasures, the corresponding imperative is hypothetical. Its applicability depends upon one's having an aim which one need not have as a condition of being a rational human individual. The argument for the two principles of justice does not assume that the parties have particular ends, but only that they desire certain primary goods. These are things that it is rational to want whatever else one wants. Thus given human nature, wanting them is part of being rational; and while each is presumed to have some conception of the good, nothing is known about his final ends. The preference for primary goods is derived, then, from only the most general assumptions about rationality and the conditions of human life. To act from the principles of justice is to act from categorical imperatives in the sense that they apply to us whatever in particular our aims are. This simply reflects the fact that no such contingencies appear as premises in their derivation.

We may note also that the motivational assumption of mutual disinterest accords with Kant's notion of autonomy, and gives another reason for this condition. So far this assumption has been used to characterize the circumstances of justice and to provide a clear conception to guide the reasoning of the parties. We have also seen that the concept of benevolence, being a second-order notion, would not work out well. Now we can add that the assumption of mutual disinterest is to allow for freedom in the choice of a system of final ends.[10] Liberty in adopting a conception of the good is limited only by principles that are deduced from a doctrine which imposes no prior constraints on these conceptions. Presuming mutual disinterest in the original position carries out this idea. We postulate that the parties have opposing claims in a suitably general sense. If their ends were restricted in some specific way, this would appear at the outset as an arbitrary restriction on freedom. Moreover, if the parties were conceived as altruists, or as pursuing certain kinds of pleasures, then the principles chosen would apply, as far as the argument would have shown, only to persons whose freedom was restricted to choices compatible with altruism or hedonism. As the argument now runs, the principles of justice cover all persons with rational plans of life, whatever their content, and these principles represent the appropriate restrictions on freedom. Thus it is possible to say that the constraints on conceptions of the good are the result of an interpretation of the contractual situation that puts no prior limitations on what men may desire. There are a variety of reasons, then, for the motivational premise of mutual disinterest. This premise is not only a matter of realism about the circumstances of justice or a way to make the theory manageable. It also connects up with the Kantian idea of autonomy.

There is, however, a difficulty that should be clarified. It is well expressed by Sidgwick.[11] He remarks that nothing in Kant's ethics is more striking than the idea that a man realizes his true self when he acts from the moral law, whereas if he permits his actions to be determined by sensuous desires or contingent aims, he becomes subject to the law of nature. Yet in Sidgwick's opinion this idea comes to naught. It seems to him that on Kant's view the lives of the saint and the scoundrel are equally the outcome of a free choice (on the part of the noumenal self) and equally the subject of causal laws (as a phenomenal self). Kant never explains why the scoundrel does not express in a bad life his characteristic and freely chosen selfhood in the same way that a saint expresses his characteristic and freely chosen selfhood in a good one. Sidgwick's objection is decisive, I think, as long as one assumes, as Kant's exposition may seem to allow, both that the noumenal self can choose any

---

10 For this point I am indebted to Charles Fried.

11 See *The Methods of Ethics*, 7th ed. (London, Macmillan, 1907), Appendix, "The Kantian Conception of Free Will" (reprinted from *Mind*, vol. 13, 1888), pp. 511–516, esp. p. 516.

consistent set of principles and that acting from such principles, whatever they are, is sufficient to express one's choice as that of a free and equal rational being. Kant's reply must be that though acting on any consistent set of principles could be the outcome of a decision on the part of the noumenal self, not all such action by the phenomenal self expresses this decision as that of a free and equal rational being. Thus if a person realizes his true self by expressing it in his actions, and if he desires above all else to realize this self, then he will choose to act from principles that manifest his nature as a free and equal rational being. The missing part of the argument concerns the concept of expression. Kant did not show that acting from the moral law expresses our nature in identifiable ways that acting from contrary principles does not.

This defect is made good, I believe, by the conception of the original position. The essential point is that we need an argument showing which principles, if any, free and equal rational persons would choose and these principles must be applicable in practice. A definite answer to this question is required to meet Sidgwick's objection. My suggestion is that we think of the original position as the point of view from which noumenal selves see the world. The parties qua noumenal selves have complete freedom to choose whatever principles they wish; but they also have a desire to express their nature as rational and equal members of the intelligible realm with precisely this liberty to choose, that is, as beings who can look at the world in this way and express this perspective in their life as members of society. They must decide, then, which principles when consciously followed and acted upon in everyday life will best manifest this freedom in their community, most fully reveal their independence from natural contingencies and social accident. Now if the argument of the contract doctrine is correct, these principles are indeed those defining the moral law, or more exactly, the principles of justice for institutions and individuals. The description of the original position interprets the point of view of noumenal selves, of what it means to be a free and equal rational being. Our nature as such beings is displayed when we act from the principles we would choose when this nature is reflected in the conditions determining the choice. Thus men exhibit their freedom, their independence from the contingencies of nature and society, by acting in ways they would acknowledge in the original position.

Properly understood, then, the desire to act justly derives in part from the desire to express most fully what we are or can be, namely free and equal rational beings with a liberty to choose. It is for this reason, I believe, that Kant speaks of the failure to act on the moral law as giving rise to shame and not to feelings of guilt. And this is appropriate, since for him acting unjustly is acting in a manner that fails to express our nature as a free and equal rational being. Such actions therefore strike at our self-respect, our sense of our own worth, and the experience of this loss is shame. We have acted as though we belonged to a lower order, as though we were a creature whose first principles are decided by natural contingencies. Those who think of Kant's moral doctrine as one of law and guilt badly misunderstand him. Kant's main aim is to deepen and to justify Rousseau's idea that liberty is acting in accordance with a law that we give to ourselves. And this leads not to a morality of austere command but to an ethic of mutual respect and self-esteem.[12]

The original position may be viewed, then, as a procedural interpretation of Kant's conception of autonomy and the categorical imperative. The principles regulative of the kingdom of ends are those that would be chosen in this position, and the description of this situation enables us to explain the sense in which acting from these principles expresses our nature as free and equal rational persons. No longer are these notions purely transcendent and lacking explicable connections with human conduct, for the procedural conception of the original position allows us to make these ties. It is true that I have departed from Kant's views in several respects. I shall not discuss these matters here; but two points should be noted. The person's choice as a noumenal self I have assumed to be a collective one. The force of the self's being equal is that the principles chosen must be acceptable to other selves. Since all are similarly free and rational, each must have an equal say in adopting the public principles of the ethical commonwealth. This means that as noumenal selves, everyone is to consent to these principles. Unless the scoundrel's principles would be chosen, they cannot express this free choice, however much a single self might be of a mind to opt for them. Later I shall try to define a clear sense in which this unanimous agreement is best expressive of the nature of even a single self. It in no way overrides a person's interests as the collective nature of the choice might seem to imply. But I leave this aside for the present.

Secondly, I have assumed all along that the parties know that they are subject to the conditions of human life. Being in the circumstances of justice, they are situated in the world with other men who likewise face limitations of moderate scarcity and competing claims. Human freedom is to be regulated by principles chosen in the light of these natural restrictions. Thus justice as fairness is a theory of human justice and among its premises are the elementary facts about persons and their place in nature. The freedom of pure intelligences not subject to these constraints, and the freedom of God, is outside the scope of the theory. It might appear that Kant meant his doctrine to apply to all rational beings as such and therefore to God and the angels as well. Men's social situation in the world may seem to have no role in his theory in determining the first principles of justice. I do not believe that Kant held this view, but I cannot discuss this question here. It suffices to say that if I am mistaken, the Kantian interpretation of justice as fairness is less faithful to Kant's intentions than I am presently inclined to suppose.

12 See B. A. O. Williams, "The Idea of Equality," in *Philosophy, Politics and Society*, Second Series, ed. Peter Laslett and W. G. Runciman (Oxford, Basil Blackwell, 1962), pp. 115f. For confirmation of this interpretation, see Kant's remarks on moral education in *The Critique of Practical Reason*, pt. II. See also Beck, *Commentary on Kant's Critique of Practical Reason*, pp. 233–236.

VI

VIRTUE

While deontologists and consequentialists disagree about when acts are morally right, they agree that questions of rightness are fundamental to ethics. But another important approach takes as its fundamental question not "What is the right way for me to act?" but "What sort of person should I be?" Because this approach focuses on enduring dispositions rather than behavior—because it emphasizes character rather than action—it is often known as *virtue ethics*.

The most influential figure in this tradition is Aristotle, represented here in reading 35. Like the other ancient Greeks, Aristotle saw ethics as the study of the good life. He argued that human flourishing requires both a variety of intellectual skills and various desirable character traits. These traits include, but are not exhausted by, justice, truthfulness, courage, generosity, and temperance. Each virtue, Aristotle argued, is a mean between two extremes. For example, the courageous person is neither inordinately fearful nor rash and foolhardy: He experiences fear or boldness "at the right times on the right occasions toward the right people for the right motive and in the right way." According to Aristotle, we acquire the virtues in the same way that we acquire any other habits—namely, through repeated performance of the relevant acts. In his view, we learn to be good precisely *by* being good.

One obvious question about any such theory is *why* the favored traits are better than others. In readings 36 and 38, Martha Nussbaum and Alasdair MacIntyre offer contrasting answers to this question. According to Nussbaum, the virtues have an objective basis in certain fixed features of human life. As she reads Aristotle, his starting point is the fact that every human being must deal with such issues as fear of danger and death, bodily appetites, the management of personal property, and various aspects of social interaction. In each case, we can abstractly identify as a virtue "whatever it is that being disposed to choose and respond well consists in, in that sphere." We can also examine and compare different ways of filling in each abstract specification. This, Nussbaum argues, is both Aristotle's view and a view that we would do well to adopt.

MacIntyre's answer is different. He argues that we cannot make sense of our lives without regarding them as ongoing stories or narratives. This means that we must understand the traditions and social institutions in which those stories are embedded. As MacIntyre notes, even a simple activity like gardening "may be part of the history both of the cycle of household activity and of [one's] marriage, two histories which happen to intersect." Because our lives are intelligible only as narratives, what is good for someone is what will bring his life—his story—to a satisfactory conclusion. And because each person is a citizen, son or daughter, member of a profession, and occupant of other roles, each person's "moral starting point" is a variety of "debts, inheritances, rightful expectations, and obligations" derived from those roles. To appreciate how these factors shape our good, we must overcome dangers, temptations, and distractions. We must also exercise judgment in carrying on and developing our traditions. Hence, the virtues that allow us to do these things are also part of our good.

Despite their differences, Nussbaun and MacIntyre are both broadly in sympathy with Aristotle. They also both offer lists of virtues that are recognizable and familiar. But Friedrich Nietzsche (reading 37) does not believe that what are commonly called virtues are desirable traits. He argues that the prevailing attitudes merely codify the fears of the weak and mediocre. In his view, the highest value attaches to the emergence of a *new* type of person— one who is powerful, joyous, unafraid, and without the crippling inhibitions of "civilization."

Nietzsche's theory, clearly, is at odds with traditional morality. But even views that are far less radical raise questions about how virtue and morality are related. According to many moral theories, we are only permitted to do what morality allows. As Alan Gewirth (reading 5) points out, the demands of morality are often regarded as overriding. But in reading 39, Bernard Williams contests this ordering. He points out that certain goals are so central to each agent's character that it is unrealistic to expect him to subordinate them. When these goals conflict with moral principles, it may well be the moral principles that ought to give way. Williams also points out that our personal relationships may demand a kind of partiality that rules out the impersonal perspective of morality. For example, our devotion to our children may require that we favor them over others. In a similar vein, Susan Wolf argues in reading 40 that nonmoral values and ideals provide reasons that are just as compelling, and just as valid, as moral reasons. If Williams and Wolf are right, then those who always assign the highest priority to moral duty may be alienated from other worthwhile goals and relationships.

Carol Gilligan (reading 41) approaches the relation between moral principles and personal relationships from a different angle. Gilligan, a psychologist, draws on her empirical studies to argue that men and women display different patterns of moral development. She contends that from an early age boys tend to construe morality in abstract, impersonal terms while girls tend to be more personal and more attuned to context and the requirements of specific others. If morality has been understood only in the former terms, it is because the "different voice" of women has not been heard. Although Gilligan does not explicitly say so, her description of the female voice displays some striking similarities to the theoretical suggestions of Williams, Wolf, and others.

But George Sher contends in reading 42 that Gilligan's contrasts are over-drawn. He argues that moral philosophers have long acknowledged the opposi-tions between the concrete and the abstract, general principle and particular cases, the personal and the impersonal, duty and care, and rights and responsi-bilities. He argues, further, that various familiar theories contain the resources to reconcile these oppositions. For example, if someone regards moral principles as justified when they would be chosen behind a "veil of ignorance" (see John Rawls, reading 34), he may well hold that a reasonable set of moral principles would itself acknowledge special duties to husbands, wives, children, and friends. Thus, Sher concludes that "Gilligan's findings may edge us in certain theoretical directions, . . . but [take] us nowhere near the boundaries of the known territories."

35

The Nature of
Moral Virtue

ARISTOTLE

*Aristotle (384–322 B.C.) systematically explored virtually every branch of
what is now thought of as philosophy. In addition, he did pioneering work
in rhetoric, politics, astronomy, physics, biology, and other areas. The
selection included here is from his* Nicomachean Ethics, Books 2 and 7.

*In the first part of this selection, Aristotle discusses the way people
acquire a virtuous disposition. One possible answer is that they are taught
the correct principles or reasons for acting. However, Aristotle objects that
merely theoretical knowledge of what is right makes us like invalids "who
listen carefully to all the doctor says but do not carry out a single one of
his orders." He proposes, instead, that we best learn virtue by actually
practicing it. If we continually do what is right, we will eventually acquire
the appropriate habits. These habits will enable us to strike the proper
balance between extremes. Thus, the virtuous person is neither rash nor
cowardly but brave, neither obsequious nor surly but friendly, and so on.*

*In the selection's second part, Aristotle addresses the difficult topic of
incontinence, or weakness of will. Here the problem is whether, and how, a
person who knows what he ought to do can nevertheless do something
else. Aristotle rejects the straightforward Socratic view that all who act
wrongly do so through ignorance. In its stead, he offers a number of subtle
distinctions among types of incontinence and ways of lacking full
knowledge.*

FROM *NICOMACHEAN ETHICS,* BOOK TWO

Chapter I

Virtue, then, is of two kinds, intellectual and moral. Of these the
intellectual is in the main indebted to teaching for its production and growth,
and this calls for time and experience. Moral goodness, on the other hand, is
the child of habit, from which it has got its very name, ethics being derived
from *ethos,* 'habit,' by a slight alteration in the quantity of the *e.* This is an
indication that none of the moral virtues is implanted in us by nature, since
nothing that nature creates can be taught by habit to change the direction of
its development. For instance a stone, the natural tendency of which is to fall

down, could never, however often you threw it up in the air, be trained to go in that direction. No more can you train fire to burn downwards. Nothing in fact, if the law of its being is to behave in one way, can be habituated to behave in another. The moral virtues, then, are produced in us neither *by* Nature nor *against* Nature. Nature, indeed, prepares in us the ground for their reception, but their complete formation is the product of habit.

Consider again these powers or faculties with which Nature endows us. We acquire the ability to use them before we do use them. The senses provide us with a good illustration of this truth. We have not acquired the sense of sight from repeated acts of seeing, or the sense of hearing from repeated acts of hearing. It is the other way round. We had these senses before we used them, we did not acquire them as a result of using them. But the moral virtues we do acquire by first exercising them. The same is true of the arts and crafts in general. The craftsman has to learn how to make things, but he learns in the process of making them. So men become builders by building, harp players by playing the harp. By a similar process we become just by performing just actions, temperate by performing temperate actions, brave by performing brave actions. Look at what happens in political societies—it confirms our view. We find legislators seeking to make good men of their fellows by making good behaviour habitual with them. That is the aim of every lawgiver, and when he is unable to carry it out effectively, he is a failure; nay, success or failure in this is what makes the difference between a good constitution and a bad.

Again, the creation and the destruction of any virtue are effected by identical causes and identical means; and this may be said, too, of every art. It is as a result of playing the harp that harpers become good or bad in their art. The same is true of builders and all other craftsmen. Men will become good builders as a result of building well, and bad builders as a result of building badly. Otherwise what would be the use of having anyone to teach a trade? Craftsmen would all be born either good or bad. Now this holds also of the virtues. It is in the course of our dealings with our fellow-men that we become just or unjust. It is our behaviour in a crisis and our habitual reactions to danger that make us brave or cowardly, as it may be. So with our desires and passions. Some men are made temperate and gentle, others profligate and passionate, the former by conducting themselves in one way, the latter by conducting themselves in another, in situations in which their feelings are involved. We may sum it all up in the generalization, 'Like activities produce like dispositions.' This makes it our duty to see that our activities have the right character, since the differences of quality in them are repeated in the dispositions that follow in their train. So it is a matter of real importance whether our early education confirms us in one set of habits or another. It would be nearer the truth to say that it makes a very great difference indeed, in fact all the difference in the world.

Chapter II

Since the branch of philosophy on which we are at present engaged differs from the others in not being a subject of merely intellectual interest—I mean we are not concerned to know what goodness essentially is, but how we are to become good men, for this alone gives the study its practical value—we must apply our minds to the solution of the problems of conduct. For, as I remarked, it is our actions that determine our dispositions.

Now that when we act we should do so according to the right principle, is common ground and I propose to take it as a basis of discussion.[1] But we must begin with the admission that any theory of conduct must be content with an outline without much precision in details. We noted this when I said at the beginning of our discussion of this part of our subject that the measure of exactness of statement in any field of study must be determined by the nature of the matter studied. Now matters of conduct and considerations of what is to our advantage have no fixity about them any more than matters affecting our health. And if this be true of moral philosophy as a whole, it is still more true that the discussion of particular problems in ethics admits of no exactitude. For they do not fall under any science or professional tradition, but those who are following some line of conduct are forced in every collocation of circumstances to think out for themselves what is suited to these circumstances, just as doctors and navigators have to do in their different *métiers*. We can do no more than give our arguments, inexact as they necessarily are, such support as is available.

Let us begin with the following observation. It is in the nature of moral qualities that they can be destroyed by deficiency on the one hand and excess on the other. We can see this in the instances of bodily health and strength.[2] Physical strength is destroyed by too much and also by too little exercise. Similarly health is ruined by eating and drinking either too much or too little, while it is produced, increased and preserved by taking the right quantity of drink and victuals. Well, it is the same with temperance, courage, and the other virtues. The man who shuns and fears everything and can stand up to nothing becomes a coward. The man who is afraid of nothing at all, but marches up to every danger, becomes foolhardy. In the same way the man who indulges in every pleasure without refraining from a single one becomes incontinent. If, on the other hand, a man behaves like the Boor in comedy and turns his back on every pleasure, he will find his sensibilities becoming blunted. So also temperance and courage are destroyed both by excess and deficiency, and they are kept alive by observance of the mean.

Let us go back to our statement that the virtues are produced and fostered as a result, and by the agency, of actions of the same quality as effect their destruction. It is also true that after the virtues have been formed they find expression in actions of that kind. We may see this in a concrete instance—bodily strength. It results from taking plenty of nourishment and going in for hard training, and it is the strong man who is best fitted to cope with such conditions. So with the virtues. It is by refraining from pleasures that we

---

1 There will be an opportunity later of considering what is meant by this formula, in particular what is meant by 'the right principle' and how, in its ethical aspect, it is related to the moral virtues.

2 If we are to illustrate the material, it must be by concrete images.

become temperate, and it is when we have become temperate that we are most able to abstain from pleasures. Or take courage. It is by habituating ourselves to make light of alarming situations and to confront them that we become brave, and it is when we have become brave that we shall be most able to face an alarming situation.

Chapter III

We may use the pleasure (or pain) that accompanies the exercise of our dispositions as an index of how far they have established themselves. A man is temperate who abstaining from bodily pleasures finds this abstinence pleasant; if he finds it irksome, he is intemperate. Again, it is the man who encounters danger gladly, or at least without painful sensations, who is brave; the man who has these sensations is a coward. In a word, moral virtue has to do with pains and pleasures. There are a number of reasons for believing this. (1) Pleasure has a way of making us do what is disgraceful; pain deters us from doing what is right and fine. Hence the importance—I quote Plato—of having been brought up to find pleasure and pain in the right things. True education is just such a training. (2) The virtues operate with actions and emotions, each of which is accompanied by pleasure or pain. This is only another way of saying that virtue has to do with pleasures and pains. (3) Pain is used as an instrument of punishment. For in her remedies Nature works by opposites, and pain can be remedial. (4) When any disposition finds its complete expression it is, as we noted, in dealing with just those things by which it is its nature to be made better or worse, and which constitute the sphere of its operations. Now when men become bad it is under the influence of pleasures and pains when they seek the wrong ones among them, or seek them at the wrong time, or in the wrong manner, or in any of the wrong forms which such offences may take; and in seeking the wrong pleasures and pains they shun the right. This has led some thinkers to identify the moral virtues with conditions of the soul in which passion is eliminated or reduced to a minimum. But this is to make too absolute a statement—it needs to be qualified by adding that such a condition must be attained 'in the right manner and at the right time' together with the other modifying circumstances.

So far, then, we have got this result. Moral goodness is a quality disposing us to act in the best way when we are dealing with pleasures and pains, while vice is one which leads us to act in the worst way when we deal with them.

The point may be brought out more clearly by some other considerations. There are three kinds of things that determine our choice in all our actions—the morally fine, the expedient, the pleasant; and three that we shun—the base, the harmful, the painful. Now in his dealings with all of these it is the good man who is most likely to go right, and the bad man who tends to go wrong, and that most notably in the matter of pleasure. The sensation of pleasure is felt by us in common with all animals, accompanying everything we choose, for even the fine and the expedient have a pleasurable effect upon us. (6) The capacity for experiencing pleasure has grown in us from infancy as part of our general development, and human life, being dyed in grain with it, receives therefrom a colour hard to scrape off. (7) Pleasure and pain are also the standards by which with greater or less strictness we regulate our considered actions. Since to feel pleasure and pain rightly or wrongly is an important factor in human behaviour, it follows that we are primarily concerned with these sensations. (8) Heraclitus says it is hard to fight against anger, but it is harder still to fight against pleasure. Yet to grapple with the harder has always been the business, as of art, so of goodness, success in a task being proportionate to its difficulty. This gives us another reason for believing that morality and statesmanship must concentrate on pleasures and pains, seeing it is the man who deals rightly with them who will be good, and the man who deals with them wrongly who will be bad.

Here, then, are our conclusions. (a) Virtue is concerned with pains and pleasures. (b) The actions which produce virtue are identical in character with those which increase it. (c) These actions differently performed destroy it. (d) The actions which produced it are identical with those in which it finds expression.

Chapter IV

A difficulty, however, may be raised as to what we mean when we say that we must perform just actions if we are to become just, and temperate actions if we are to be temperate. It may be argued that, if I do what is just and temperate, I am just and temperate already, exactly as, if I spell words or play music correctly, I must already be literate or musical. This I take to be a false analogy, even in the arts. It is possible to spell a word right by accident or because somebody tips you the answer. But you will be a scholar only if your spelling is done as a scholar does it, that is thanks to the scholarship in your own mind. Nor will the suggested analogy with the arts bear scrutiny. A work of art is good or bad in itself—let it possess a certain quality, and that is all we ask of it. But virtuous actions are not done in a virtuous—a just or temperate—way merely because *they* have the appropriate quality. The *doer* must be in a certain frame of mind when he does them. Three conditions are involved. (1) The agent must act in full consciousness of what he is doing. (2) He must 'will' his action, and will it for its own sake. (3) The act must proceed from a fixed and unchangeable disposition. Now these requirements, if we expect mere knowledge, are not counted among the necessary qualifications of an artist. For the acquisition of virtue, on the other hand, knowledge is of little or no value, but the other requirements are of immense, of sovran, importance, since it is the repeated performance of just and temperate actions that produces virtue. Actions, to be sure, are *called* just and temperate when they are such as a just or temperate man would do. But the doer is just or temperate not because he does such things but when he does them in the way of just and temperate persons. It is therefore quite fair to say that a man becomes just by the performance of just, and temperate by the performance of temperate, actions; nor is there the smallest likelihood of a man's becoming good by any other course of conduct. It is not, however, a popular line to take, most men preferring theory to practice under the impression that arguing about morals proves them to be philosophers, and that in this way they will turn out to be fine characters. Herein they resemble invalids, who listen carefully to all the doctor says but do not carry out a single one of his orders. The bodies of such people will never respond to treatment—nor will the souls of such 'philosophers.'

Chapter V

We now come to the formal definition of virtue. Note first, however, that the human soul is conditioned in three ways. It may have (1) feelings, (2) capacities, (3) dispositions; so virtue must be one of these three. By 'feelings' I mean a desire, anger, fear, daring, envy, gratification, friendliness, hatred, longing, jealousy, pity and in general all states of mind that are attended by pleasure or pain. By 'capacities' I mean those faculties in virtue of which we may be described as capable of the feelings in question—anger, for instance, or pain, or pity. By 'dispositions' I mean states of mind in virtue of which we are well or ill disposed in respect of the feelings concerned. We have, for instance, a bad disposition where angry feelings are concerned if we are disposed to become excessively or insufficiently angry, and a good disposition in this respect if we consistently feel the due amount of anger, which comes between these extremes. So with the other feelings.

Now, neither the virtues nor the vices are feelings. We are not spoken of as good or bad in respect of our feelings but of our virtues and vices. Neither are we praised or blamed for the way we feel. A man is not praised for being frightened or angry, nor is he blamed just for being angry; it is for being angry in a particular way. But we *are* praised and blamed for our virtues and vices. Again, feeling angry or frightened is something we can't help, but our virtues are in a manner expressions of our will; at any rate there is an element of will in their formation. Finally, we are said to be 'moved' when our feelings are affected, but when it is a question of moral goodness or badness we are not said to be 'moved' but to be 'disposed' in a particular way. A similar line of reasoning will prove that the virtues and vices are not capacities either. We are not spoken of as good or bad, nor are we praised or blamed, merely because we are *capable* of feeling. Again, what capacities we have, we have by nature; but it is not nature that makes us good or bad. . . . So, if the virtues are neither feelings nor capacities, it remains that they must be dispositions. . . .

Chapter VI

It is not, however, enough to give this account of the *genus* of virtue—that it is a disposition; we must describe its *species*. Let us begin, then, with this proposition. Excellence of whatever kind affects that of which it is the excellence in two ways. (1) It produces a good state in it. (2) It enables it to perform its function well. Take eyesight. The goodness of your eye is not only that which makes your eye good, it is also that which makes it function well. Or take the case of a horse. The goodness of a horse makes him a good horse, but it also makes him good at running, carrying a rider and facing the enemy. Our proposition, then, seems to be true, and it enables us to say that virtue in a man will be the disposition which (a) makes him a good man, (b) enables him to perform his function well. We have already touched on this point, but more light will be thrown upon it if we consider what is the specific nature of virtue.

In anything continuous and divisible it is possible to take the half, or more than the half, or less than the half. Now these parts may be larger, smaller and equal either in relation to the thing divided or in relation to us. The equal part may be described as a mean between too much and too little. By the mean of the thing I understand a point equidistant from the extremes; and this is one and the same for everybody. Let me give an illustration. Ten, let us say, is 'many' and two is 'few' of something. We get the mean of the thing if we take six;[3] that is, six exceeds and is exceeded by an equal number. This is the rule which gives us the arithmetical mean. But such a method will not give us the mean in relation to ourselves. Let ten pounds of food be a large, and two pounds a small, allowance for an athlete. It does not follow that the trainer will prescribe six pounds. That might be a large or it might be a small allowance for the particular athlete who is to get it. It would be little for Milo but a lot for a man who has just begun his training.[4] It is the same in all walks of life. The man who knows his business avoids both too much and too little. It is the mean he seeks and adopts—not the mean of the thing but the relative mean.

Every form, then, of applied knowledge, when it performs its function well, looks to the mean and works to the standard set by that. It is because people feel this that they apply the *cliché*, 'You couldn't add anything to it or take anything from it' to an artistic masterpiece, the implication being that too much and too little alike destroy perfection, while the mean preserves it. Now if this be so, and if it be true, as we say, that good craftsmen work to the standard of the mean, then, since goodness like nature is more exact and of a higher character than any art, it follows that goodness is the quality that hits the mean. By 'goodness' I mean goodness of moral character, since it is moral goodness that deals with feelings and actions, and it is in them that we find excess, deficiency and a mean. It is possible, for example, to experience fear, boldness, desire, anger, pity, and pleasures and pains generally, too much or too little or to the right amount. If we feel them too much or too little, we are wrong. But to have these feelings at the right times on the right occasions towards the right people for the right motive and in the right way is to have them in the right measure, that is somewhere between the extremes; and this is what characterizes goodness. The same may be said of the mean and extremes in actions. Now it is in the field of actions and feelings that goodness operates; in them we find excess, deficiency and, between them, the mean, the first two

---

3 $6-2 = 10-6$.

4 What applies to gymnastics applies also to running and wrestling.

being wrong, the mean right and praised as such.[5] Goodness, then, is a mean condition in the sense that it aims at and hits the mean.

Consider, too, that it is possible to go wrong in more ways than one. (In Pythagorean terminology evil is a form of the Unlimited, good of the Limited.) But there is only one way of being right. That is why going wrong is easy, and going right difficult; it is easy to miss the bull's-eye and difficult to hit it. Here, then, is another explanation of why the too much and the too little are connected with evil and the mean with good. As the poet says,

> Goodness is one, evil is multiform.

We may now define virtue as a disposition of the soul in which, when it has to choose among actions and feelings, it observes the mean relative to us, this being determined by such a rule or principle as would take shape in the mind of a man of sense or practical wisdom. We call it a mean condition as lying between two forms of badness, one being excess and the other deficiency; and also for this reason, that, whereas badness either falls short of or exceeds the right measure in feelings and actions, virtue discovers the mean and deliberately chooses it. Thus, looked at from the point of view of its essence as embodied in its definition, virtue no doubt is a mean; judged by the standard of what is right and best, it is an extreme.

But choice of a mean is not possible in every action or every feeling. The very names of some have an immediate connotation of evil. Such are malice, shamelessness, envy among feelings, and among actions adultery, theft, murder. All these and more like them have a bad name as being evil in themselves; it is not merely the excess or deficiency of them that we censure. In their case, then it is impossible to act rightly; whatever we do is wrong. Nor do circumstances make any difference in the rightness or wrongness of them. When a man commits adultery there is no point in asking whether it is with the right woman or at the right time or in the right way, for to do anything like that is simply wrong. It would amount to claiming that there is a mean and excess and defect in unjust or cowardly or intemperate actions. If such a thing were possible, we should find ourselves with a mean quantity of excess, a mean of deficiency, an excess of excess and a deficiency of deficiency. But just as in temperance and justice there can be no mean or excess or deficiency, because the mean in a sense *is* an extreme, so there can be no mean or excess or deficiency in those vicious actions—however done, they are wrong. Putting the matter into general language, we may say that there is no mean in the extremes, and no extreme in the mean, to be observed by anybody.

Chapter VII

But a generalization of this kind is not enough; we must show that our definition fits particular cases. When we are discussing actions particular statements come nearer the heart of the matter, though general statements cover a

---

5 Being right or successful and being praised are both indicative of excellence.

wider field. The reason is that human behaviour consists in the performance of particular acts, and our theories must be brought into harmony with them.

You see here a diagram of the virtues. Let us take our particular instances from that.

In the section confined to the feelings inspired by danger you will observe that the mean state is 'courage.' Of those who go to extremes in one direction or the other the man who shows an excess of fearlessness has no name to describe him, the man who exceeds in confidence or daring is called 'rash' or 'foolhardy,' the man who shows an excess of fear and a deficiency of confidence is called a 'coward.' In the pleasures and pains—though not all pleasures and pains, especially pains—the virtue which observes the mean is 'temperance,' the excess is the vice of 'intemperance.' Persons defective in the power to enjoy pleasures are a somewhat rare class, and so have not had a name assigned to them: suppose we call them 'unimpressionable.' Coming to the giving and acquiring of money, we find that the mean is 'liberality,' the excess 'prodigality,' the deficiency 'meanness.' But here we meet a complication. The prodigal man and the mean man exceed and fall short in opposite ways. The prodigal exceeds in giving and falls short in getting money, whereas the mean man exceeds in getting and falls short in giving it away. Of course this is but a summary account of the matter—a bare outline. But it meets our immediate requirements. Later on these types of character will be more accurately delineated.

• • •

Chapter IX

I have said enough to show that moral excellence is a mean, and I have shown in what sense it is so. It is, namely, a mean between two forms of badness, one of excess and the other of defect, and is so described because it aims at hitting the mean point in feelings and in actions. This makes virtue hard of achievement, because finding the middle point is never easy. It is not everybody, for instance, who can find the centre of a circle—that calls for a geometrician. Thus, too, it is easy to fly into a passion—anybody can do that—but to be angry with the right person and to the right extent and at the right time and with the right object and in the right way—that is not easy, and it is not everyone who can do it. This is equally true of giving or spending money. Hence we infer that to do these things properly is rare, laudable and fine.

In view of this we shall find it useful when aiming at the mean to observe these rules (1) *Keep away from that extreme which is the more opposed to the mean.* It is Calypso's advice:

'Swing round the ship clear of this surf and surge.'

For one of the extremes is always a more dangerous error than the other; and—since it is hard to hit the bull's-eye—we must take the next best course and choose the least of the evils. And it will be easiest for us to do this if we follow the rule I have suggested. (2) *Note the errors into which we personally are most liable to fall.* (Each of us has his natural bias in one direction or another.) We shall find out what ours are by noting what gives us pleasure and pain. After that we must drag ourselves in the opposite direction. For our best way of reaching the middle is by giving a wide berth to our darling sin. It is the method used by a carpenter when he is straightening a warped board. (3) *Always be particularly on your guard against pleasure and pleasant things.* When Pleasure is at the bar the jury is not impartial. So it will be best for us if we feel towards her as the Trojan elders felt towards Helen, and regularly apply their words to her. If we are for packing her off, as they were with Helen, we shall be the less likely to go wrong.

To sum up. These are the rules by observation of which we have the best chance of hitting the mean. But of course difficulties spring up, especially when we are confronted with an exceptional case. For example, it is not easy to say precisely what is the right way to be angry and with whom and on what grounds and for how long. In fact we are inconsistent on this point, sometimes praising people who are deficient in the capacity for anger and calling them 'gentle,' sometimes praising the choleric and calling them 'stout fellows.' To be sure we are not hard on a man who goes off the straight path in the direction of too much or too little, if he goes off only a little way. We reserve our censure for the man who swerves widely from the course, because then we are bound to notice it. Yet it is not easy to find a formula by which we may determine how far and up to what point a man may go wrong before he incurs blame. But this difficulty of definition is inherent in every object of perception; such questions of degree are bound up with the circumstances of the individual case, where our only criterion *is* the perception.

So much, then, has become clear. In all our conduct it is the mean state that is to be praised. But one should lean sometimes in the direction of the more, sometimes in that of the less, because that is the readiest way of attaining to goodness and the mean.

FROM *NICOMACHEAN ETHICS*, BOOK SEVEN

Chapter I

• • •

I cannot, however, omit here some account of incontinence and softness of luxuriousness, as well as of continence and fortitude or endurance. We should not think of either of these dispositions—the good and the bad—as identical with virtue and vice respectively. Neither must we think of them as different in kind.

The true method for us to follow, here and elsewhere, is to set forth the views which are held on the subject and then, after discussing the problems involved in these, to indicate what truth lies in all or—if that proves impossible—in the greatest in number and importance of the beliefs generally entertained about these states of mind. I am convinced that, if the difficulties can be resolved and we are left with certain of these beliefs—those, namely, which have stood our test—we shall have reached as satisfactory a conclusion as is possible in cases of the kind. In the present case the general beliefs are these. (*a*) Continence and endurance are good and commendable qualities, whereas their opposites, incontinence and softness, are bad and blameworthy. (*b*) The continent man has the characteristic of sticking by the conclusions he has been led to draw, whereas the incontinent man tends to give his up. (*c*) The incontinent or morally weak man does wrong, knowing it to be wrong, because he cannot control his passions, whereas the continent man, knowing that his lusts are evil, refuses to follow them, because his principles forbid it. (*d*) The temperate man is always continent and enduring, though whether the continent man is always temperate is an open question, some asserting and others denying that it is so, the former distinguishing between the intemperate and the incontinent man, the latter confounding all distinction between them. (*e*) It is sometimes maintained that it is impossible for the prudent man to be incontinent, sometimes that *some* prudent and clever men are guilty of incontinence. (*f*) Some men are described as 'incontinent' in their anger and in their pursuit of honour or gain.—Such are the views that have found expression.

Chapter II

Now for the difficulties that may be raised. To take the third (*c*) of our opinions first, how can a man be said to show incontinence, if he has a correct apprehension of the fact that he is acting wrongly? Some thinkers maintain that he cannot, if he has full knowledge that the action is wrong. It is, as Socrates thought, hard to believe that, if a man really *knows,* and has this knowledge in his soul, it should be mastered by something else which, in Plato's phrase, 'hauls it about like a slave.' Socrates to be sure was out and out opposed to the view we are now criticizing, on the ground that there is no such thing as this moral weakness we call 'incontinence.' For, said he, nobody acts in opposition to what is best—and the best is the goal of all our endeavours—if he has a clear idea of what he is doing. He can only go wrong out of ignorance. This reasoning, however, is in glaring contrast with notorious facts; and that obliges us to look more closely into the frame of mind on which it is based. Conceding that ignorance is the cause of moral weakness, let us consider what form of ignorance. For it is clear that the man who succumbs to temptation is not ignorant of the wrongness of his action *before* he is involved in the temptation.

• • •

Chapter III

We have then to consider these points. (1) When men show moral weakness (or incontinence) do they or do they not know the wrongness of their actions? If they know it, in what sense do they know it? (2) What are we to posit as the objects to which continence and incontinence are directed? I mean, are they concerned with every kind of pleasures and pains or only with a special division of them? (3) Is continence the same or not the same as endurance? (4) Other questions germane to the subject.

We may begin our enquiry by asking whether it is the objects or the dispositions of the continent and incontinent man that enter into the definition of these types as their differentiating qualities. Put it this way. Is a man to be described as incontinent merely because he cannot restrain his desires for certain things, or is it because he has a certain disposition, or do both causes operate? Here is a second question. Can incontinence and continence be exercised towards everything? Yes or no? One is aware that when a man is described as "incontinent" without further qualification it is not implied that he is incontinent in everything, but only in those things in which a man can show intemperance; nor is it implied merely that he is concerned with those things,[6] but that he is concerned with them in a certain way. The intemperate man deliberately chooses to follow in the train of his lusts from a belief that he ought always to pursue the pleasure of the moment. The incontinent man pursues it too, but has no such belief.

(1) The theory that when men behave incontinently they are not acting against knowledge but against true opinion contributes nothing of value to our discussion. It never occurs to some people to question the truth of their opinions; indeed, they do not regard them as opinions but as ascertained truths. Consequently, if we base an argument on lack of conviction in some men, and say that this is the reason why those who shall be found to act against their conception of what is right must be said to have an opinion rather than knowledge, the difference between opinion and knowledge will vanish. For some men are just as sure of the truth of their opinions as are others of what they know. Heraclitus alone proves that. And if we say a man 'knows' something, we may be using the word in one of two senses. We may mean that he has the knowledge and acts upon it, or that he has the knowledge but makes no use of it. This being so, it will make a difference whether a man who is doing wrong knows that what he is doing is wrong but has this knowledge only in a latent or subconscious form, or whether, having the knowledge, he has it in an active form. If the latter, his doing wrong may well surprise us; but it will not, if his knowledge is not fully realized.

(2) When logical reasoning is applied to actions, the premises will assume two forms.[7] Now a man who is acting against knowledge may very well know both premises, yet put into practice only his knowledge of the universal or major premise and not his knowledge of the particular or minor premise. Yet it is this minor premise that is decisive for action, because acts are particulars. We have also to note that in reasoning about actions there are two universals involved. One is predicated of the *man,* the other of the *thing.* For example, he may know, and be in a position to act on the knowledge, that (*a*) dry food

---

6 For if that were so, incontinence would be identical with intemperance.

7 In other words the application of a 'practical syllogism' involves two syllogisms.

is good for all men,[8] and (b) he is himself a man. But he may not know, or may not be prepared to act on his knowledge, whether the particular food before him is that sort of food. It will be found then that there is an immeasurable distance between these two ways of knowing, so that we cannot think it odd that the incontinent man should know in one and not the other. The truly strange thing would be if he *did* know in the other.

(3) Moreover, it is possible for men to have knowledge—I use the word without prejudice—in another way besides those described. We have noted the distinction between actual and potential knowledge. But even in the second case, which is a condition of having knowledge without allowing it to operate, we can see a distinction. For there is a sense in which a man can both have and not have knowledge—he might, for instance, be asleep or out of his mind, or drunk. And what better are people when their feelings are too much for them? Doesn't everybody know that rage and lust and some other passions actually produce physiological changes, in some cases even insanity? It is evident then that, if we must say that the incontinent have knowledge, it can only be like that possessed by the persons to whom I have referred. The moral weakling may *say* he has knowledge, but that is no proof that he has it. People suffering from the disabilities I have mentioned will repeat to you the proof of some problem in geometry or a passage from Empedocles. In the same way people who have begun the study of a subject reel off a string of propositions which they do not as yet understand. For knowledge must be worked into the living texture of the mind, and this takes time. So we should think of incontinent men as like actors—mouthpieces of the sentiments of other people.

(4) It is also possible to study the cause of incontinence from the point of view of the scientist. This involves what we call the practical syllogism. In this the major premise is an opinion, while the minor premise is a statement about particulars, the objects of sense-perception. When the two premises are combined to form the syllogism, we have a result analogous to what we have in pure ratiocination. As in the latter the mind is forced to *affirm* the conclusion, so in the practical syllogism we are forced straight-way to *do* it. Suppose you have these premises: 'All sweet things ought to be tasted,' and 'That thing is sweet.'[9] When these premises are brought into relation you are bound, if nothing prevents you and you can do it, to go and taste the thing. Now there may be simultaneously present in the mind two universal judgments, one saying, 'You must not taste,' the other, 'Every sweet thing is pleasant.' When this happens, and then the minor premise, 'That thing is sweet,' presents itself,[10] while at the same time desire is present, then in spite of the fact that the first universal bids you avoid the thing in question, the desire leads you to it.[11] It is therefore,

---

8 We may even know that such and such a food is dry.

9 Here the minor premise is a particular instance of the class of things about which the major premise makes a general statement.

10 Remember that it is the minor premise that introduces the possibility of action.

11 This is because only desire can set the various limbs in motion—the body corresponding to the potential major premise, and the desire to the active minor.

we conclude, to some extent an intellectual principle or opinion which influences the incontinent man to behave as he does—an opinion not in itself contradictory of the right principle but only opposed to it by an accidental conjunction of circumstances.[12] This is the reason why the lower animals are not incontinent. They are incapable of understanding a generalization; all they have is mental images and the memory of particular objects.

We may ask how the ignorance of the incontinent man is overcome and knowledge restored to him. The explanation which accounts for the so-called knowledge of the drunk or sleeping man will serve in this case also; it applies to more than continence. But on this point it is for the physiologist to instruct us.

There are then these points to be considered. (a) The last—that is the minor—premise, that which can influence action, is an opinion which is related to some object of sense-perception. (b) This opinion the incontinent man, when he abandons himself to his emotions, does not possess or possesses only in such a way as does not entitle it to be regarded as knowledge, but only enables him to quote its tenor as a drunk man quotes Empedocles. (c) The ultimate term—that is the particular proposition which forms the minor premise—is not a universal and is not regarded as an object of knowledge in the way that a universal judgment is. Since these three statements are evidently true, it does appear that our conclusions must be that which Socrates directed his questions to prove. For the knowledge which accompanies the collapse of moral resistance is not what is thought to be knowledge properly speaking. Neither is it true knowledge that is dragged about by passion, but only such as can be supplied by the senses. . . .

Chapter VII

• • •

Opposed to incontinence is continence, opposed to softness is hardness or endurance. The difference between endurance and continence is this. Endurance consists in holding out, continence in preserving mastery. They are two very different things, as different as the avoidance of defeat from victory. We are bound therefore to prefer continence. A man who fails to withstand such pains as most people can and do support is soft or luxury-loving; for luxury is a kind of softness. He is the sort of man to let his cloak trail on the ground rather than have the bother of lifting it, or to affect the languor of sickness without reflecting that an assumed distress is a real distress. It is much the same with continence and incontinence. If a man gives way to violent or excessive pleasure or pain, that can surprise nobody. Indeed, he may be forgiven for succumbing, if he does not do it without a struggle. One thinks of Philoctetes when he is bitten by the viper in the play of Theodectes, or of Cercyon in the *Alope* of Carcinus. Or—to take an example of resistance to pleasure—think of a man trying his best to hold in a laugh who bursts out at last into a

---

12 It is the desire, not the opinion, that is the true opposite.

stentorian guffaw.[13] But it does surprise us to see a man give way to pleasures and pains which most of us are capable of withstanding. It is different of course if his weakness is due to disease or some hereditary taint, such as the congenital impotence of the Scythian royal family, or the less hardy constitution of the female, as compared with the male, sex.

It is a popular notion that a love of amusement is a sign of intemperance. In reality it is a sign of softness. For amusement is a way of enjoying one's leisure by relaxation. You may say, then, that the devotee of amusement indulges too much in relaxation. But relaxation is not pleasure, and it is the man who is insatiable in his pursuit of pleasure that is intemperate.

Incontinence is found in two forms, which we may call (a) impulsiveness and (b) weakness. The weak do form a resolution, but they are prevented by their sensibilities from keeping to it. The impulsive or headstrong are carried away by their feelings, because they have not thought about the matter that excites them at all. If they had, their behaviour might be different. For some people can hold out against strong emotion, whether painful or pleasurable, if they feel or see it coming and have time to rouse themselves—by which I mean their reasoning faculty—beforehand, just as a man can't tickle you if you have tickled him first. It is high-strung and excitable people who are most prone to the impulsive form of incontinence. The high-strung are too hasty, and the excitable too vehement, to wait for reason, since they instinctively follow the suggestions of their own imaginations.

Chapter VIII

It is different with the intemperate man, who, as I said, does not repent or feel remorse, since he abides by his choice. The incontinent man on the other hand is always capable of remorse. Consequently the objection we mentioned— that the intemperate man might be cured—is refuted by the fact. It is just the intemperate man who is incurable; the incontinent man is not. Vice such as is shown by the intemperate man is like dropsy or tuberculosis, whereas incontinence is like epilepsy. For vice is a chronic, incontinence an intermittent, ill. More than that, vice and incontinence are totally different in kind. The vicious man does not realize that he is vicious, but the incontinent man is aware of his incontinence.

With regard to the incontinent themselves, the impulsive among them are morally superior to the weak, who are in possession of the right principle but do not hold fast to it. These are worse, because they yield to a feebler impulse and after deliberation. Such men resemble dipsomaniacs, who get drunk quickly and on a small amount of wine or less than most people. It is obvious in fact that incontinence is not a vice, at least in the strict sense of that word. For vice is deliberate, and incontinence is not. Yet there is a similarity in the actions which result from them. Something of the kind is noted in the epigram of Demodocus upon the citizens of Miletus.

13 This actually happened to Xenophantus.

Milesians are no fools, you'd swear,
And yet they act as if they were.

To parody Demodocus: The incontinent are not bad, but they act badly.

To resume. While pursuing bodily pleasures of an excessive kind and contrary to right principle, the incontinent man is so constituted that he pursues them without the conviction that he is right, whereas the intemperate man has this conviction, which he has come to feel because it is now second nature with him to seek these gratifications. Hence the incontinent man can readily be persuaded to change his mode of behaviour—but not the other. For virtue preserves, while vice destroys, that intuitive perception of the true end of life which is the starting point in conduct. We may compare the propositions which the geometer sets out to prove and which are *his* starting-point. In moral as in mathematical science the knowledge of its first principles is not reached by a process of reasoning. The good man has it in virtue of his goodness, whether innate or acquired by the habit of thinking rightly about the first principle. Such a man is temperate, while the man who does not know the primary assumptions of all ethics is intemperate. But there is another type—the man who is driven from his considered course of action by a flood of emotion contrary to right principle. He is prevented by overmastering passion from acting in accordance with that principle, yet not so completely as to make him the kind of man to believe that it is right to abandon himself to such pleasures as he seeks. Such is the incontinent man. He is morally superior to the intemperate man and is not to be called bad without qualification, for he preserves his noblest element—that conviction on which all morality is founded. Different and at the opposite pole from him is the man who having made his choice holds fast by that, unshaken by the storms of passion. These considerations prove that continence is a good, and incontinence a bad, quality.

36

Non-Relative Virtues: An Aristotelian Approach

MARTHA NUSSBAUM

Martha Nussbaum (b. 1947) is University Professor of Philosophy, Classics, and Contemporary Literature, at Brown University. She has done important work in ancient philosophy, moral philosophy, and the philosophy of literature. Her books include The Fragility of Goodness, Love's Knowledge, *and, most recently,* The Therapy of Desire. *This essay first appeared in* Midwest Studies in Philosophy *(1983).*

One important tendency in recent ethical thought has been to stress the notion of virtue and to deemphasize duty. According to those who take this approach, the fundamental question is not "Which actions must I perform?" but "What sort of person should I be?" Because different societies have different conceptions of virtue, this approach is often associated with relativism (see reading 16). But, according to Nussbaum, it need not be.

Nussbaum's point of departure is the theory of Aristotle (reading 35). As she interprets him, Aristotle grounded his list of virtues in certain basic and inescapable features of human life: for example, the facts that we die, are vulnerable, have limited resources, and need to live with others. These facts are human universals, and so pose problems that all societies must address. Moreover, while different societies respond differently to each fact, there is room for rational debate about which responses are best.

As Nussbaum realizes, this approach is open to challenge. She considers three objections: first, that there may be no best approach to the problematic facts; second, that what is problematic about them may itself be socially constructed; and, third, that if the conditions of human life were to change drastically enough, the terms of the discussion might entirely shift. Although she finds some merit in each objection, Nussbaum concludes that none compels us to abandon the Aristotelian approach.

"ALL GREEKS USED TO GO AROUND ARMED WITH SWORDS."

Thucydides, *History of the Peloponnesian War*

"THE CUSTOMS OF FORMER TIMES MIGHT BE SAID TO BE TOO SIMPLE AND BARBARIC. FOR GREEKS USED TO GO AROUND ARMED WITH SWORDS; AND THEY USED TO BUY WIVES FROM ONE ANOTHER, AND THERE ARE SURELY OTHER ANCIENT CUSTOMS THAT ARE EXTREMELY STUPID. (FOR EXAMPLE, IN CYME THERE IS A LAW ABOUT HOMICIDE, THAT IF A MAN PROSECUTING A CHARGE CAN PRODUCE A CERTAIN NUMBER OF WITNESSES FROM AMONG HIS OWN RELATIONS, THE DEFENDANT WILL AUTOMATICALLY BE CONVICTED OF MURDER.) IN GENERAL, ALL HUMAN BEINGS SEEK NOT THE WAY OF THEIR ANCESTORS, BUT THE GOOD."

Aristotle, *Politics* 1268a39 ff.

"ONE MAY ALSO OBSERVE IN ONE'S TRAVELS TO DISTANT COUNTRIES THE FEELINGS OF RECOGNITION AND AFFILIATION THAT LINK EVERY HUMAN BEING TO EVERY OTHER HUMAN BEING."

Aristotle, *Nicomachean Ethics* 1155a21–22

I

The virtues are attracting increasing interest in contemporary philosophical debate. From many different sides one hears of a dissatisfaction with ethical theories that are remote from concrete human experience. Whether this remoteness results from the utilitarian's interest in arriving at a universal calculus of satisfactions or from a Kantian concern with universal principles of broad generality, in which the names of particular contexts, histories, and persons do not occur, remoteness is now being seen by an increasing number of moral philosophers as a defect in an approach to ethical questions. In the search for an alternative approach, the concept of virtue is playing a prominent role. So, too, is the work of Aristotle, the greatest defender of an ethical approach based on the concept of virtue. For Aristotle's work seems, appealingly, to combine rigor with concreteness, theoretical power with sensitivity to the actual circumstances of human life and choice in all their multiplicity, variety, and mutability.

But on one central point there is a striking divergence between Aristotle and contemporary virtue theory. To many current defenders of an ethical approach based on the virtues, the return to the virtues is connected with a turn toward relativism—toward, that is, the view that the only appropriate criteria of ethical goodness are local ones, internal to the traditions and practices of each local society or group that asks itself questions about the good. The rejection of general algorithms and abstract rules in favor of an account of the good life based on specific modes of virtuous action is taken, by writers as otherwise diverse as Alasdair MacIntyre, Bernard Williams, and Philippa Foot,[1] to be connected with the abandonment of the project of rationally justifying a single norm of flourishing life for and to all human beings and with a reliance, instead, on norms that are local both in origin and in application.

The positions of all of these writers, where relativism is concerned, are complex; none unequivocally endorses a relativist view. But all connect virtue ethics with a relativist denial that ethics, correctly understood, offers any trans-cultural norms, justifiable with reference to reasons of universal human validity, with reference to which we may appropriately criticize different local conceptions of the good. And all suggest that the insights we gain by pursuing ethical questions in the Aristotelian virtue-based way lend support to relativism.

For this reason it is easy for those who are interested in supporting the rational criticism of local traditions and in articulating an idea of ethical progress to feel that the ethics of virtue can give them little help. If the position of women, as established by local traditions in many parts of the world, is to be improved, if traditions of slave holding and racial inequality, if religious intolerance, if aggressive and warlike conceptions of manliness, if unequal norms of material distribution are to be criticized in the name of practical reason, this criticizing (one might easily suppose) will have to be done from a Kantian or utilitarian viewpoint, not through the Aristotelian approach.

This is an odd result, where Aristotle is concerned. For it is obvious that he was not only the defender of an ethical theory based on the virtues, but also the defender of a single objective account of the human good, or human flourishing. This account is supposed to be objective in the sense that it is justifiable with reference to reasons that do not derive merely from local traditions and practices, but rather from features of humanness that lie beneath all local traditions and are there to be seen whether or not they are in fact recognized in local traditions. And one of Aristotle's most obvious concerns is the criticism of existing moral traditions, in his own city and in others, as unjust or repressive, or in other ways incompatible with human flourishing. He uses his account of the virtues as a basis for this criticism of local traditions: prominently, for example, in Book II of the *Politics,* where he frequently argues against existing social forms by pointing to ways in which they neglect or hinder the development of some important human virtue.[2] Aristotle evidently believes that there is no incompatibility between basing an ethical theory on the virtues and defending the singleness and objectivity of the human good. Indeed, he seems to believe that these two aims are mutually supportive.

---

1 A. MacIntyre, *After Virtue* (Notre Dame, IN, 1981); P. Foot, *Virtues and Vices* (Los Angeles, 1978); B. Williams, *Ethics and the Limits of Philosophy* (Cambridge, MA, 1985) and Tanner Lectures, Harvard, 1983. See also M. Walzer, *Spheres of Justice* (New York, 1983) and Tanner Lectures, Harvard, 1985.

2 For examples of this, see Nussbaum, "Nature, Function, and Capability: Aristotle on Political Distribution," circulated as a WIDER working paper, and in *Oxford Studies in Ancient Philosophy,* 1988, and also, in an expanded version, in the Proceedings of the 12th Symposium Aristotelicum.

Now the fact that Aristotle believes something does not make it true. (Though I have sometimes been accused of holding that position!) But it does, on the whole, make that something a plausible *candidate* for the truth, one deserving our most serious scrutiny. In this case, it would be odd indeed if he had connected two elements in ethical thought that are self-evidently incompatible, or in favor of whose connectedness and compatibility there is nothing interesting to be said. The purpose of this paper is to establish that Aristotle does indeed have an interesting way of connecting the virtues with a search for ethical objectivity and with the criticism of existing local norms, a way that deserves our serious consideration as we work on these questions. Having described the general shape of the Aristotelian approach, we can then begin to understand some of the objections that might be brought against such a non-relative account of the virtues, and to imagine how the Aristotelian could respond to those objections.

II

The relativist, looking at different societies, is impressed by the variety and the apparent non-comparability in the lists of virtues she encounters. Examining the different lists, and observing the complex connections between each list and a concrete form of life and a concrete history, she may well feel that any list of virtues must be simply a reflection of local traditions and values, and that, virtues being (unlike Kantian principles or utilitarian algorithms) concrete and closely tied to forms of life, there can in fact be no list of virtues that will serve as normative for all these varied societies. It is not only that the specific forms of behavior recommended in connection with the virtues differ greatly over time and place, it is also that the very areas that are singled out as spheres of virtue, and the manner in which they are individuated from other areas, vary so greatly. For someone who thinks this way, it is easy to feel that Aristotle's own list, despite its pretensions to universality and objectivity, must be similarly restricted, merely a reflection of one particular society's perceptions of salience and ways of distinguishing. At this point, relativist writers are likely to quote Aristotle's description of the "great-souled" person, the *megalopsuchos,* which certainly contains many concrete local features and sounds very much like the portrait of a certain sort of Greek gentleman, in order to show that Aristotle's list is just as culture-bound as any other.[3]

But if we probe further into the way in which Aristotle in fact enumerates and individuates the virtues, we begin to notice things that cast doubt upon the suggestion that he has simply described what is admired in his own society. First of all, we notice that a rather large number of virtues and vices (vices especially) are nameless, and that, among the ones that are not nameless, a

---

3 See, for example, Williams, *Ethics and the Limits,* 34–36; Stuart Hampshire, *Morality and Conflict* (Cambridge, MA, 1983), 150 ff.

good many are given, by Aristotle's own account, names that are somewhat arbitrarily chosen by Aristotle, and do not perfectly fit the behavior he is trying to describe.[4] Of such modes of conduct he writes, "Most of these are nameless, but we must try . . . to give them names in order to make our account clear and easy to follow" (NE 1108a16–19). This does not sound like the procedure of someone who is simply studying local traditions and singling out the virtue names that figure most prominently in those traditions.

What *is* going on becomes clearer when we examine the way in which he does, in fact, introduce his list. For he does so, in the *Nicomachean Ethics*,[5] by a device whose very straightforwardness and simplicity has caused it to escape the notice of most writers on this topic. What he does, in each case, is to isolate a sphere of human experience that figures in more or less any human life, and in which more or less any human being will have to make *some* choices rather than others, and act in *some* way rather than some other. The introductory chapter enumerating the virtues and vices begins from an enumeration of these spheres (NE 2.7); and each chapter on a virtue in the more detailed account that follows begins with "Concerning X . . . " or words to this effect, where "X" names a sphere of life with which all human beings regularly and more or less necessarily have dealings.[6] Aristotle then asks: What is it to choose and respond well within that sphere? What is it, on the other hand, to choose defectively? The "thin account" of each virtue is that it is whatever it is to be stably disposed to act appropriately in that sphere. There may be, and usually are, various competing specifications of what acting well, in each case, in fact comes to. Aristotle goes on to defend in each case some concrete specifications, producing, at the end, a full or "thick" definition of the virtue.

Here are the most important spheres of experience recognized by Aristotle, along with the names of their corresponding virtues:[7]

---

4 For "nameless" virtues and vices, see NE 1107b1–2, 1107b8, 1107b30–31, 1108a17, 1119a10–11, 1126b20, 1127a12, 1127a14; for recognition of the unsatisfactoriness of names given, see 1107b8, 1108a5–6, 1108a20 ff. The two categories are largely overlapping, on account of the general principles enunciated at 1108a16–19, that where there is no name a name should be given, unsatisfactory or not.

5 It should be noted that this emphasis on spheres of experience is not present in the *Eudemian Ethics*, which begins with a list of virtues and vices. This seems to me a sign that that treatise expresses a more primitive stage of Aristotle's thought on the virtues—whether earlier or not.

6 For statements with *peri*, connecting virtues with spheres of life, see 1115a6–7, 1117a29–30, 1117b25, 27, 1119b23, 1122a19, 1122b34, 1125b26, 1126b13; and NE 2.7 throughout. See also the related usages at 1126b11, 1127b32.

7 My list here inserts justice in a place of prominence. (In the NE it is treated separately, after all the other virtues, and the introductory list defers it for that later examination.) I have also added at the end of the list categories corresponding to the various intellectual virtues discussed in NE 6, and also to *phronesis* or practical wisdom, discussed in 6 as well. Otherwise the order and wording of my list closely follows 2.7, which gives the program for the more detailed analyses of 3.5–4.

SPHERE	VIRTUE
1. Fear of important damages, esp. death	courage
2. Bodily appetites and their pleasures	moderation
3. Distribution of limited resources	justice
4. Management of one's personal property, where others are concerned	generosity
5. Management of personal property, where hospitality is concerned	expansive hospitality
6. Attitudes and actions with respect to one's own worth	greatness of soul
7. Attitude to slights and damages	mildness of temper
8. "Association and living together and the fellowship of words and actions"	
a. truthfulness in speech	truthfulness
b. social association of a playful kind	easy grace (contrasted with coarseness, rudeness, insensitivity)
c. social association more generally	nameless, but a kind of friendliness (contrasted with irritability and grumpiness)
9. Attitude to the good and ill fortune of others	proper judgment (contrasted with enviousness, spitefulness, etc.)
10. Intellectual life	the various intellectual virtues (such as perceptiveness, knowledge, etc.)
11. The planning of one's life and conduct	practical wisdom

There is, of course, much more to be said about this list, its specific members, and the names Aristotle chooses for the virtue in each case, some of which are indeed culture bound. What I want, however, to insist is the care with which Aristotle articulates his general approach, beginning from a characterization of a sphere of universal experience and choice, and introducing the virtue name as the name (as yet undefined) of whatever it is to choose appropriately in that area of experience. On this approach, it does not seem possible to say, as the relativist wishes to, that a given society does not contain anything that corresponds to a given virtue. Nor does it seem to be an open question, in the case of a particular agent, whether a certain virtue should or should not be included in his or her life—except in the sense that she can always choose to pursue the corresponding deficiency instead. The point is that everyone makes some choices and acts somehow or other in these spheres: if not properly, then improperly. Everyone has *some* attitude and behavior toward her own death; toward her bodily appetites and their management; toward her property and its use; toward the distribution of social goods; toward telling the truth; toward being kindly or not kindly to others; toward cultivating or not cultivating a sense of play and delight; and so on. No matter where one lives one cannot escape these questions, so long as one is living a human life. But then this means that one's behavior falls, willy nilly, within the sphere of the Aristotelian virtue, in each case. If it is not appropriate, it is inappropriate; it cannot be off the map altogether. People will of course disagree about what the appropriate ways of acting and reacting in fact *are*. But in that case, as Aristotle has set things up, they are arguing about the same thing, and advancing competing specifications of the same virtue. The reference of the virtue term in each case is fixed by the sphere of experience—by what we shall from now on call the "grounding experiences." The thin or "nominal definition" of the virtue will be, in each case, that it is whatever it is that being disposed to choose and respond well consists in, in that sphere. The job of ethical theory will be to search for the best further specification corresponding to this nominal definition, and to produce a full definition.

III

We have begun to introduce considerations from the philosophy of language. We can now make the direction of the Aristotelian account clearer by considering his own account of linguistic indicating (referring) and defining, which guides his treatment of both scientific and ethical terms, and of the idea of progress in both areas.[8]

Aristotle's general picture is as follows. We begin with some experiences—not necessarily our own, but those of members of our linguistic community, broadly construed.[9] On the basis of these experiences, a word enters the language of the group, indicating (referring to) whatever it is that is the content of those experiences. Aristotle gives the example of thunder.[10] People hear a noise in the clouds, and they then refer to it, using the word "thunder." At this point, it may be that nobody has any concrete account of the noise or any idea about what it really is. But the experience fixes a subject for further inquiry. From now on, we can refer to thunder, ask "What is thunder?" and advance and assess competing theories. The thin or, we might say, "nominal

---

8 For a longer account of this, with references to the literature and to related philosophical discussions, see Nussbaum, *The Fragility of Goodness* (Cambridge, MA, 1986), chap. 8.

9 Aristotle does not worry about questions of translation in articulating this idea; for some worries about this, and an Aristotelian response, see below sections IV and VI.

10 *Posterior Analytics*, 2.8, 93a21 ff.; see *Fragility*, chap. 8.

definition" of thunder is "That noise in the clouds, whatever it is." The competing explanatory theories are rival candidates for correct full or thick definition.
So the explanation story citing Zeus' activities in the clouds is a false account
of the very same thing of which the best scientific explanation is a true account.
There is just one debate here, with a single subject.

So too, Aristotle suggests, with our ethical terms. Heraclitus, long before
him, already had the essential idea, saying, "They would not have known the
name of justice, if these things did not take place."[11] "These things," our source
for the fragment informs us, are experiences of injustice—presumably of harm,
deprivation, inequality. These experiences fix the reference of the corresponding
virtue word. Aristotle proceeds along similar lines. In the *Politics* he insists
that only human beings, and not either animals or gods, will have our basic
ethical terms and concepts (such as just and unjust, noble and base, good and
bad), because the beasts are unable to form the concepts, and gods lack the
experiences of limit and finitude that give a concept such as justice its point.[12]
In the *Nicomachean Ethics* enumeration of the virtues, he carries the line of
thought further, suggesting that the reference of the virtue terms is fixed by
spheres of choice, frequently connected with our finitude and limitation, that
we encounter in virtue of shared conditions of human existence.[13] The question
about virtue usually arises in areas in which human choice is both non-optional
and somewhat problematic. (Thus, he stresses, there is no virtue involving the
regulation of listening to attractive sounds or seeing pleasing sights.) Each
family of virtue and vice or deficiency words attaches to some such sphere.
And we can understand progress in ethics, like progress in scientific understanding, to be progress in finding the correct fuller specification of a virtue, isolated
by its thin or "nominal" definition. This progress is aided by a perspicuous
mapping of the sphere of the grounding experiences. When we understand
more precisely what problems human beings encounter in their lives with one
another, what circumstances they face in which choice of some sort is required,
we will have a way of assessing competing responses to those problems, and
we will begin to understand what it might be to act well in the face of them.

Aristotle's ethical and political writings provide many examples of how such
progress (or, more generally, such a rational debate) might go. We find argument against Platonic asceticism, as the proper specification of moderation
(appropriate choice and response vis-à-vis the bodily appetites) and the consequent proneness to anger over slights, that was prevalent in Greek ideals of
maleness and in Greek behavior, together with a defense of a more limited

---

11 Heraclitus, fragment DK B23; see Nussbaum, "*Psuche* in Heraclitus, II," *Phronesis* 17
(1972): 153–70.

12 See *Politics* 1.2. 1253a1–18; that discussion does not deny the virtues to gods explicitly, but
this denial is explicit at *NE* 1145a25–7 and 1178b10 ff.

13 Aristotle does not make the connection with his account of language explicit, but his project
is one of defining the virtues, and we would expect him to keep his general view of defining
in mind in this context. A similar idea about the virtues, and experience of a certain sort as a
possible basis for a non-relative account, is developed, without reference to Aristotle, in a
review of P. Foot's *Virtues and Vices* by N. Sturgeon, *Journal of Philosophy* 81 (1984): 326–33.

and controlled expression of anger, as the proper specification of the virtue that Aristotle calls "mildness of temper." (Here Aristotle evinces some discomfort with the virtue term he has chosen, and he is right to do so, since it certainly loads the dice heavily in favor of his concrete specification and against the traditional one.)[14] And so on for all the virtues.

In an important section of *Politics* II, part of which forms one of the epigraphs to this paper, Aristotle defends the proposition that laws should be revisable and not fixed by pointing to evidence that there is progress toward greater correctness in our ethical conceptions, as also in the arts and sciences. Greeks used to think that courage was a matter of waving swords around; now they have (the *Ethics* informs us) a more inward and a more civic and communally attuned understanding of proper behavior toward the possibility of death. Women used to be regarded as property, bought and sold; now this would be thought barbaric. And in the case of justice as well we have, the *Politics* passage claims, advanced toward a more adequate understanding of what is fair and appropriate. Aristotle gives the example of an existing homicide law that convicts the defendant automatically on the evidence of the prosecutor's relatives (whether they actually witnessed anything or not, apparently). This, Aristotle says, is clearly a stupid and unjust law; and yet it once seemed appropriate—and, to a tradition-bound community, must still be so. To hold tradition fixed is then to prevent ethical progress. What human beings want and seek is not conformity with the past, it is the good. So our systems of law should make it possible for them to progress beyond the past, when they have agreed that a change is good. (They should not, however, make change too easy, since it is no easy matter to see one's way to the good, and tradition is frequently a sounder guide than current fashion.)

In keeping with these ideas, the *Politics* as a whole presents the beliefs of the many different societies it investigates not as unrelated local norms, but as competing answers to questions of justice and courage (and so on) with which all the societies (being human) are concerned, and in response to which they are all trying to find what is good. Aristotle's analysis of the virtues gives him an appropriate framework for these comparisons, which seem perfectly appropriate inquiries into the ways in which different societies have solved common human problems.

In the Aristotelian approach it is obviously of the first importance to distinguish two stages of the inquiry: the initial demarcation of the sphere of choice, of the "grounding experiences" that fix the reference of the virtue term; and the ensuing more concrete inquiry into what appropriate choice, in that sphere, *is*. Aristotle does not always do this carefully, and the language he has to work with is often not helpful to him. We do not have much difficulty with terms like "moderation" and "justice" and even "courage," which seem vaguely normative but relatively empty, so far, of concrete moral content. As the

---

[14] 1108a5, where Aristotle says that the virtues and the corresponding person are "pretty much nameless," and says "Let us call ..." when he introduces the names. See also 1125b29, 1126a3–4.

approach requires, they can serve as extension-fixing labels under which many competing specifications may be investigated. But we have already noticed the problem with "mildness of temper," which seems to rule out by fiat a prominent contender for the appropriate disposition concerning anger. And much the same thing certainly seems to be true of the relativists' favorite target, *megalopsuchia*, which implies in its very name an attitude to one's own worth that is more Greek than universal. (For example, a Christian will feel that the proper attitude to one's own worth requires understanding one's lowness, frailty, and sinfulness. The virtue of humility requires considering oneself *small*, not great.) What we ought to get at this point in the inquiry is a word for the proper behavior toward anger and offense and a word for the proper behavior toward one's worth that are more truly neutral among the competing specifications, referring only to the sphere of experience within which we wish to determine what is appropriate. Then we could regard the competing conceptions as rival accounts of one and the same thing, so that, for example, Christian humility would be a rival specification of the same virtue whose Greek specification is given in Aristotle's account of *megalopsuchia*, namely, the proper way to behave toward the question of one's own worth.

And in fact, oddly enough, if one examines the evolution in the use of this word from Aristotle through the Stoics to the Christian fathers, one can see that this is more or less what happened, as "greatness of soul" became associated, first, with Stoic emphasis on the supremacy of virtue and the worthlessness of externals, including the body, and, through this, with the Christian denial of the body and of the worth of earthly life.[15] So even in this apparently unpromising case, history shows that the Aristotelian approach not only provided the materials for a single debate but actually succeeded in organizing such a debate, across enormous differences of both place and time.

Here, then, is a sketch for an objective human morality based upon the idea of virtuous action—that is, of appropriate functioning in each human sphere. The Aristotelian claim is that, further developed, it will retain virtue morality's immersed attention to actual human experiences, while gaining the ability to criticize local and traditional moralities in the name of a more inclusive account of the circumstances of human life, and of the needs for human functioning that these circumstances call forth.

IV

The proposal will encounter many objections. The concluding sections of this paper will present three of the most serious and will sketch the lines along which the Aristotelian conception might proceed in formulating a reply. To a great extent these objections are not imagined or confronted by Aristotle himself, but his position seems capable of confronting them.

---

15 See John Procope, *Magnanimity* (1987); also R.-A. Gauthier, *Magnanimité* (Paris, 1951).

The first objection concerns the relationship between singleness of problem and singleness of solution. Let us grant for the moment that the Aristotelian approach has succeeded in coherently isolating and describing areas of human experience and choice that form, so to speak, the *terrain* of the virtues, and in giving thin definitions of each of the virtues as whatever it is that consists in choosing and responding well within that sphere. Let us suppose that the approach succeeds in doing this in a way that embraces many times and places, bringing disparate cultures together into a single debate about the good human being and the good human life. Different cultural accounts of good choice within the sphere in question in each case are now seen not as untranslatably different forms of life, but as competing answers to a single general question about a set of shared human experiences. Still, it might be argued, what has been achieved is, at best, a single discourse or debate about virtue. It has not been shown that this debate will have, as Aristotle believes, a single answer. Indeed, it has not even been shown that the discourse we have set up will have the form of a *debate* at all, rather than that of a plurality of culturally specific narratives, each giving the thick definition of a virtue that corresponds to the experience and traditions of a particular group. There is an important disanalogy with the case of thunder, on which the Aristotelian so much relies in arguing that our questions will have a single answer. For in that case what is given in experience is the definiendum itself, so that experiences establish a rough extension, to which any good definition must respond. In the case of the virtues, things are more indirect. What is given in experience across groups is only the *ground* of virtuous action, the circumstances of life to which virtuous action is an appropriate response. Even if these grounding experiences are shared, that does not tell us that there will be a shared appropriate response.

In the case of thunder, furthermore, the conflicting theories are clearly put forward as competing candidates for the truth; the behavior of those involved in the discourse suggests that they are indeed, as Aristotle says, searching "not for the way of their ancestors, but for the good." And it seems reasonable in that case for them to do so. It is far less clear, where the virtues are concerned (the objector continues) that a unified practical solution is either sought by the actual participants or a desideratum for them. The Aristotelian proposal makes it possible to conceive of a way in which the virtues might be non-relative. It does not, by itself, answer the question of relativism.

The second objection goes deeper. For it questions the notion of spheres of shared human experience that lies at the heart of the Aristotelian approach. The approach, says this objector, seems to treat the experiences that ground the virtues as in some way primitive, given, and free from the cultural variation that we find in the plurality of normative conceptions of virtue. Ideas of proper courage may vary, but the fear of death is shared by all human beings. Ideas of moderation may vary, but the experiences of hunger, thirst, and sexual desire are (so the Aristotelian seems to claim) invariant. Normative conceptions introduce an element of cultural interpretation that is not present in the grounding experiences, which are, for that very reason, the Aristotelian's starting point.

But, the objector continues, such assumptions are naive. They will not stand up either to our best account of experience or to a close examination of the ways in which these so-called grounding experiences have in fact been differently constructed by different cultures. In general, first of all, our best accounts of the nature of experience, even perceptual experience, inform us that there is no such thing as an "innocent eye" that receives an uninterpreted "given." Even sense-perception is interpretive, heavily influenced by belief, teaching, language, and in general by social and contextual features. There is a very real sense in which members of different societies do not see the same sun and stars, encounter the same plants and animals, hear the same thunder.

But if this seems to be true of human experience of nature, which was the allegedly unproblematic starting point for Aristotle's account of naming, it is all the more plainly true, the objector claims, in the area of the human good. Here it is only a very naive and historically insensitive moral philosopher who would say that the experience of the fear of death or the experience of bodily appetites is a human constant. Recent anthropological work on the social construction of the emotions,[16] for example, has shown to what extent the experience of fear has learned and culturally variant elements. When we add that the object of the fear in which the Aristotelian takes an interest is death, which has been so variously interpreted and understood by human beings at different times and in different places, the conclusion that the "grounding experience" is an irreducible plurality of experiences, highly various and in each case deeply infused with cultural interpretation, becomes even more inescapable.

Nor is the case different with the apparently less complicated experience of the bodily appetites. Most philosophers who have written about the appetites have treated hunger, thirst, and sexual desire as human universals, stemming from our shared animal nature. Aristotle himself was already more sophisticated, since he insisted that the object of appetite is "the apparent good" and that appetite is therefore something interpretive and selective, a kind of intentional awareness.[17] But he does not seem to have reflected much about the ways in which historical and cultural differences could shape that awareness. The Hellenistic philosophers who immediately followed him did so reflect, arguing that the experience of sexual desire and of many forms of the desire for food and drink are, at least in part, social constructs, built up over time on the basis of a social teaching about value that is external to start with, but that enters so deeply into the perceptions of the individual that it actually forms and transforms the experience of desire.[18] Let us take two Epicurean

---

16 See, for example, *The Social Construction of the Emotions,* edited by Rom Harré (Oxford, 1986).

17 See Nussbaum, *Aristotle's De Motu Animalium* (Princeton, NJ, 1976), notes on chap. 6, and *Fragility,* chap. 9.

18 A detailed study of the treatment of these ideas in the three major Hellenistic schools was presented in Nussbaum, *The Therapy of Desire: Theory and Practice in Hellenistic Ethics,* The Martin Classical Lectures 1986, and forthcoming.

examples. People are taught that to be well fed they require luxurious fish and meat, that a simple vegetarian diet is not enough. Over time, the combination of teaching with habit produces an appetite for meat, shaping the individual's perceptions of the objects before him. Again, people are taught that what sexual relations are all about is a romantic union or fusion with an object who is seen as exalted in value, or even as perfect. Over time, this teaching shapes sexual behavior and the experience of desire, so that sexual arousal itself responds to this culturally learned scenario.[19]

This work of social criticism has recently been carried further by Michel Foucault in his *History of Sexuality*.[20] This work has certain gaps as a history of Greek thought on this topic, but it does succeed in establishing that the Greeks saw the problem of the appetites and their management in an extremely different way from the way of twentieth-century Westerners. To summarize two salient conclusions of his complex argument, the Greeks did not single out the sexual appetite for special treatment; they treated it alongside hunger and thirst, as a drive that needed to be mastered and kept within bounds. Their central concern was with self-mastery, and they saw the appetites in the light of this concern. Furthermore, where the sexual appetite is concerned, they did not regard the gender of the partner as particularly important in assessing the moral value of the act. Nor did they identify or treat as morally salient a stable disposition to prefer partners of one sex rather than the other. Instead, they focused on the general issue of activity and passivity, connecting it in complex ways with the issue of self-mastery.

Work like Foucault's—and there is a lot of it in various areas, some of it very good—shows very convincingly that the experience of bodily desire, and of the body itself, has elements that vary with cultural and historical change. The names that people call their desires and themselves as subjects of desire, the fabric of belief and discourse into which they integrate their ideas of desiring, all this influences, it is clear, not only their reflection about desire, but also their experience of desire itself. Thus, for example, it is naive to treat our modern debates about homosexuality as continuations of the very same debate about sexual activity that went on in the Greek world.[21] In a very real sense there was no "homosexual experience" in a culture that did not contain our emphasis on the gender of the object, our emphasis on the subjectivity of inclination and the permanence of appetitive disposition, our particular ways of problematizing certain forms of behavior.

If we suppose that we can get underneath this variety and this constructive power of social discourse in at least one case—namely, with the universal experience of bodily pain as a bad thing—even here we find subtle arguments

---

19   The relevant texts are discussed in Nussbaum, *The Therapy*, chaps. 4–6. See also Nussbaum, "Therapeutic Arguments: Epicurus and Aristotle," in *The Norms of Nature*, edited by M. Schofield and G. Striker (Cambridge, 1986), 31–74.

20   M. Foucault, *Histoire de la sexualité*, vols. 2 and 3 (Paris, 1984).

21   See the papers by D. Halperin and J. Winkler in *Before Sexuality*, edited by D. Halperin, J. Winkler, and F. Zeitlin, forthcoming (Princeton).

against us. For the experience of pain seems to be embedded in a cultural discourse as surely as the closely related experiences of the appetites; and significant variations can be alleged here as well. The Stoics already made this claim against the Aristotelian virtues. In order to establish that bodily pain is not bad by its very nature, but only by cultural tradition, the Stoics had to provide some explanation for the ubiquity of the belief that pain is bad and of the tendency to shun it. This explanation would have to show that the reaction was learned rather than natural, and to explain why, in the light of this fact, it is learned so widely. This they did by pointing to certain features in the very early treatment of infants. As soon as an infant is born, it cries. Adults, assuming that the crying is a response to its pain at the unaccustomed coldness and harshness of the place where it finds itself, hasten to comfort it. This behavior, often repeated, teaches the infant to regard its pain as a bad thing—or, better, teaches it the concept of pain, which includes the notion of badness, and teaches it the forms of life its society shares concerning pain. It is all social teaching, they claim, though this usually escapes our notice because of the early and non-linguistic nature of the teaching.[22]

These and related arguments, the objector concludes, show that the Aristotelian idea that there is a single non-relative discourse about human experiences such as mortality or desire is a naive idea. There is no such bedrock of shared experience, and thus no single sphere of choice within which the virtue is the disposition to choose well. So the Aristotelian project cannot even get off the ground.

Now the Aristotelian confronts a third objector, who attacks from a rather different direction. Like the second, she charges that the Aristotelian has taken for a universal and necessary feature of human life an experience that is contingent on certain non-necessary historical conditions. Like the second, she argues that human experience is much more profoundly shaped by non-necessary social features than the Aristotelian has allowed. But her purpose is not simply, like second objector's, to point to the great variety of ways in which the "grounding experiences" corresponding to the virtues are actually understood and lived by human beings. It is more radical still. It is to point out that we could imagine a form of human life that does not contain these experiences— or some of them—at all, in any form. Thus the virtue that consists in acting well in that sphere need not be included in an account of the human good. In some cases, the experience may even be a sign of *bad* human life, and the corresponding virtue, therefore, no better than a form of non-ideal adaptation to a bad state of affairs. The really good human life, in such a case, would contain neither the grounding deficiency nor the remedial virtue.

This point is forcefully raised by some of Aristotle's own remarks about the virtue of generosity. One of his points against societies that eliminate private ownership is that they have thereby done away with the opportunity for generous action, which requires having possessions of one's own to give to others.[23]

---

22 The evidence for this part of the Stoic view is discussed in Nussbaum, *The Therapy*.

23 *Politics* 1263b11 ff.

This sort of remark is tailor-made for the objector, who will immediately say that generosity, if it really rests upon the experience of private possession, is a dubious candidate indeed for inclusion in a purportedly non-relative account of the human virtues. If it rests upon a "grounding experience" that is non-necessary and is capable of being evaluated in different ways, and of being either included or eliminated in accordance with that evaluation, then it is not the universal the Aristotelian said it was.

Some objectors of the third kind will stop at this point, or use such observations to support the second objector's relativism. But in another prominent form this argument takes a non-relativist direction. It asks us to assess the "grounding experiences" against an account of human flourishing, produced in some independent manner. If we do so, the objector urges, we will discover that some of the experiences are remediable deficiencies. The objection to Aristotelian virtue ethics will then be that it limits our social aspirations, getting us to regard as permanent and necessary what we might in fact improve to the benefit of all human life. This is the direction in which the third objection to the virtues was pressed by Karl Marx, its most famous proponent.[24] According to Marx's argument, a number of the leading bourgeois virtues are responses to defective relations of production. Bourgeois justice, generosity, etc. presuppose conditions and structures that are non-ideal and that will be eliminated when communism is achieved. And it is not only the current *specification* of these virtues that will be superceded with the removal of deficiency. It is the virtues themselves. It is in this sense that communism leads human beings beyond ethics.

Thus the Aristotelian is urged to inquire into the basic structures of human life with the daring of a radical political imagination. It is claimed that when she does so she will see that human life contains more possibilities than are dreamed of in her list of virtues.

V

Each of these objections is profound. To answer any one of them adequately would require a treatise. But we can still do something at this point to map out an Aristotelian response to each one, pointing the direction in which a fuller reply might go.

The first objector is right to insist on the distinction between singleness of framework and singleness of answer, and right, again, to stress that in constructing a debate about the virtues based on the demarcation of certain spheres of experience we have not yet answered any of the "What is X?" questions that this debate will confront. We have not even said very much about the structure of the debate itself, beyond its beginnings—about how it will both use and

24 For a discussion of the relevant passages, see S. Lukes, *Marxism and Morality* (Oxford, 1987). For an acute discussion of these issues I am indebted to an exchange between Alan Ryan and Stephen Lukes at the Oxford Philosophical Society, March 1987.

criticize traditional beliefs, how it will deal with conflicting beliefs, how it will move critically from the "way of one's ancestors" to the "good"—in short, about whose judgments it will trust. I have addressed some of these issues, again with reference to Aristotle, in two other papers,[25] but much more remains to be done. At this point, however, we can make four observations to indicate how the Aristotelian might deal with some of the objector's concerns here. First, the Aristotelian position that I wish to defend need not insist, in every case, on a single answer to the request for a specification of a virtue. The answer might well turn out to be a disjunction. The process of comparative and critical debate will, I imagine, eliminate numerous contenders—for example, the view of justice that prevailed in Cyme. But what remains might well be a (probably small) plurality of acceptable accounts. These accounts may or may not be capable of being subsumed under a single account of greater generality. Success in the eliminative task will still be no trivial accomplishment. For example, if we should succeed in ruling out conceptions of the proper attitude to one's own human worth that are based on a notion of original sin, this would be moral work of enormous significance, even if we got no further than that in specifying the positive account.

Second, the general answer to a "What is X?" question in any sphere may well be susceptible of several or even of many concrete specifications, in connection with other local practices and local conditions. For example, the normative account where friendship and hospitality are concerned is likely to be extremely general, admitting of many concrete "fillings." Friends in England will have different customs, where regular social visiting is concerned, from friends in ancient Athens. And yet both sets of customs can count as further specifications of a general account of friendship that mentions, for example, the Aristotelian criteria of mutual benefit and well-wishing, mutual enjoyment, mutual awareness, a shared conception of the good, and some form of "living together."[26] Sometimes we may want to view such concrete accounts as optional alternative specifications, to be chosen by a society on the basis of reasons of ease and convenience. Sometimes, on the other hand, we may want to insist that this account gives the only legitimate specification of the virtue in question for that concrete context; in that case, the concrete account could be viewed as a part of a longer or fuller version of the single normative account. The decision between these two ways of regarding it will depend upon our assessment of its degree of non-arbitrariness for its context (both physical and historical), its relationship to other non-arbitrary features of the moral conception of that context, and so forth.

Third, whether we have one or several general accounts of a virtue, and whether this account or these accounts do or do not admit of more concrete specifications relative to ongoing cultural contexts, the particular choices that

---

25 *Fragility,* chap. 8, and "Internal Criticism and Indian Rationalist Traditions," the latter co-authored with Amartya Sen, in *Relativism,* edited by M. Krausz (Notre Dame, IN, 1988) and a WIDER Working Paper.

26 See *Fragility,* chap. 12.

the virtuous person, under this conception, makes will always be a matter of being keenly responsive to the local features of his or her concrete context. So in this respect, again, the instructions the Aristotelian gives to the person of virtue do not differ from one part of what a relativist would recommend. The Aristotelian virtues involve a delicate balancing between general rules and the keen awareness of particulars, in which process, as Aristotle stresses, the perception of the particular takes priority. It takes priority in the sense that a good rule is a good summary of wise particular choices and not a court of last resort. Like rules in medicine and in navigation, ethical rules should be held open to modification in the light of new circumstances; and the good agent must therefore cultivate the ability to perceive and correctly describe his or her situation finely and truly, including in this perceptual grasp even those features of the situation that are not covered under the existing rule.

I have written a good deal elsewhere on this idea of the "priority of the particular," exactly what it does and does not imply, in exactly what ways the particular perception is and is not prior to the general rule. Those who want clarification on this central topic will have to turn to those writings.[27]

What I want to stress here is that Aristotelian particularism is fully compatible with Aristotelian objectivity. The fact that a good and virtuous decision is context-sensitive does not imply that it is right only *relative to,* or *inside,* a limited context, any more than the fact that a good navigational judgment is sensitive to particular weather conditions shows that it is correct only in a local or relational sense. It is right absolutely, objectively, from anywhere in the human world, to attend to the particular features of one's context; and the person who so attends and who chooses accordingly is making, according to Aristotle, the humanly correct decision, period. If another situation ever should arise with all the same morally relevant features, including contextual features, the same decision would again be absolutely right.[28]

Thus the virtue-based morality can capture a great deal of what the relativist is after and still lay claim to objectivity. In fact, we might say that the Aristotelian virtues do better than the relativist virtues in explaining what people are actually doing when they scrutinize the features of their context carefully, looking at both the shared and the non-shared features with an eye to what is best. For as Aristotle says, people who do this are usually searching for the good, not just for the way of their ancestors. They are prepared to defend their decisions as good or right, and to think of those who advocate a different course as disagreeing about what is right, not just narrating a different tradition.

---

27 *Fragility,* chap. 10, "The Discernment of Perception," *Proceedings of the Boston Area Colloquium in Ancient Philosophy* 1 (1985): 151–201; "Finely Aware and Richly Responsible: Moral Awareness and the Moral Task of Literature," *Journal of Philosophy* 82 (1985): 516–29, reprinted in expanded form in *Philosophy and the Question of Literature,* edited by A. Cascardi (Baltimore, 1987).

28 I believe, however, that some morally relevant features, in the Aristotelian view, may be features that are not, even in principle, replicable in another context. See "The Discernment," and *Fragility,* chap. 10.

Finally, we should point out that the Aristotelian virtues, and the deliberations they guide, unlike some systems of moral rules, remain always open to revision in the light of new circumstances and new evidence. In this way, again, they contain the flexibility to local conditions that the relativist would desire, but, again, without sacrificing objectivity. Sometimes the new circumstances may simply give rise to a new concrete specification of the virtue as previously defined; in some cases it may cause us to change our view about what the virtue itself is. All general accounts are held provisionally, as summaries of correct decisions and as guides to new ones. This flexibility, built into the Aristotelian procedure, will again help the Aristotelian account to answer the questions of the relativist, without relativism.

VI

We must now turn to the second objection. Here, I believe, is the really serious threat to the Aristotelian position. Past writers on virtue, including Aristotle himself, have lacked sensitivity to the ways in which different traditions of discourse, different conceptual schemes, articulate the world, and also to the profound connections between the structure of discourse and the structure of experience itself. Any contemporary defense of the Aristotelian position must display this sensitivity, responding somehow to the data that the relativist historian or anthropologist brings forward.

The Aristotelian should begin, it seems to me, by granting that with respect to any complex matter of deep human importance there is no "innocent eye"— no way of seeing the world that is entirely neutral and free of cultural shaping. The work of philosophers such as Putnam, Goodman, and Davidson[29]—following, one must point out, from the arguments of Kant and, I believe, from those Aristotle himself[30]—have shown convincingly that even where sense-perception is concerned, the human mind is an active and interpretive instrument and that its interpretations are a function of its history and its concepts, as well as of its innate structure. The Aristotelian should also grant, it seems to me, that the nature of human world-interpretations is holistic and that the criticism of them must, equally well, be holistic. Conceptual schemes, like languages, hang together as whole structures, and we should realize, too, that a change in any single element is likely to have implications for the system as a whole.

But these two facts do not imply, as some relativists in literary theory and in anthropology tend to assume, that all world interpretations are equally valid

---

[29] See H. Putnam, *Reason, Truth, and History* (Cambridge, 1981); *The Many Faces of Realism*, The Carus Lectures, forthcoming; and *Meaning and the Moral Sciences* (London, 1979); N. Goodman, *Languages of Art* (Indianapolis, 1968) and *Ways of World-Making* (Indianapolis, 1978); D. Davidson, *Inquiries into Truth and Interpretation* (Oxford, 1984).

[30] On his debt to Kant, see Putnam, *The Many Faces;* on Aristotle's "internal realism," see Nussbaum, *Fragility*, chap. 8.

and altogether non-comparable, that there are no good standards of assessment and "anything goes." The rejection of the idea of ethical truth as correspondence to an altogether uninterpreted reality does not imply that the whole idea of searching for the truth is an old-fashioned error. Certain ways in which people see the world can still be criticized exactly as Aristotle criticized them: as stupid, pernicious, and false. The standards used in such criticisms must come from inside human life. (Frequently they will come from the society in question itself, from its own rationalist and critical traditions.) And the inquirer must attempt, prior to criticism, to develop an inclusive understanding of the conceptual scheme being criticized, seeing what motivates each of its parts and how they hang together. But there is so far no reason to think that the critic will not be able to reject the institution of slavery or the homicide law of Cyme as out of line with the conception of virtue that emerges from reflection on the variety of different ways in which human cultures have had the experiences that ground the virtues.

The "grounding experiences" will not, the Aristotelian should concede, provide precisely a single language—neutral bedrock on which an account of virtue can be straightforwardly and unproblematically based. The description and assessment of the ways in which different cultures have constructed these experiences will become one of the central tasks of Aristotelian philosophical criticism. But the relativist has, so far, shown no reasons why we could not, at the end of the day, say that certain ways of conceptualizing death are more in keeping with the totality of our evidence and with the totality of our wishes for flourishing life than others; that certain ways of experiencing appetitive desire are for similar reasons more promising than others.

Relativists tend, furthermore, to understate the amount of attunement, recognition, and overlap that actually obtains across cultures, particularly in the areas of the grounding experiences. The Aristotelian in developing her conception in a culturally sensitive way, should insist, as Aristotle himself does, upon the evidence of such attunement and recognition. Despite the evident differences in the specific cultural shaping of the grounding experiences, we do recognize the experiences of people in other cultures as similar to our own. We do converse with them about matters of deep importance, understand them, allow ourselves to be moved by them. When we read Sophocles' *Antigone*, we see a good deal that seems strange to us; and we have not read the play well if we do not notice how far its conceptions of death, womanhood, and so on differ from our own. But it is still possible for us to be moved by the drama, to care about its people, to regard their debates as reflections upon virtue that speak to our own experience, and their choices as choices in spheres of conduct in which we too must choose. Again, when one sits down at a table with people from other parts of the world and debates with them concerning hunger or just distribution or in general the quality of human life, one does find, in spite of evident conceptual differences, that it is possible to proceed as if we are all talking about the same human problem; and it is usually only in a context in which one or more of the parties is intellectually committed to a theoretical relativist position that this discourse proves impossible to sustain.

This sense of community and overlap seems to be especially strong in the areas that we have called the areas of the grounding experiences. And this, it seems, supports the Aristotelian claim that those experiences can be a good starting point for ethical debate.

Furthermore, it is necessary to stress that hardly any cultural group today is as focused upon its own internal traditions and as isolated from other cultures as the relativist argument presupposes. Cross-cultural communication and debate are ubiquitous facts of contemporary life. Our experience of cultural interaction indicates that in general the inhabitants of different conceptual schemes do tend to view their interaction in the Aristotelian and not the relativist way. A traditional society, confronted with new technologies and sciences, and the conceptions that go with them, does not, in fact, simply fail to understand them or regard them as totally alien incursions upon a hermetically sealed way of life. Instead, it assesses the new item as a possible contributor to flourishing life, making it comprehensible to itself and incorporating elements that promise to solve problems of flourishing. Examples of such assimilation, and the debate that surrounds it,[31] suggest that the parties do, in fact, recognize common problems and that the traditional society is perfectly capable of viewing an external innovation as a device to solve a problem that it shares with the innovating society. The parties do, in fact, search for the good, not the way of their ancestors; only traditionalist anthropologists insist, nostalgically, on the absolute preservation of the ancestral.

And this is so even when cross-cultural discourse reveals a difference at the level of the conceptualization of the grounding experiences. Frequently the effect of work like Foucault's, which reminds us of the non-necessary and non-universal character of one's own ways of seeing in some such area, is precisely to prompt a critical debate in search of the human good. It is difficult, for example, to read Foucault's observations about the history of our sexual ideas without coming to feel that certain ways in which the Western contemporary debate on these matters has been organized, as a result of some combination of Christian morality with nineteenth-century pseudo-science, are especially silly, arbitrary, and limiting, inimical to a human search for flourishing. Foucault's moving account of Greek culture, as he himself insists in a preface,[32] provides not only a sign that someone once thought differently, but also evidence that it is possible for *us* to think differently. Foucault announced that the purpose of his book was to "free thought" so that it could think differently, imagining new and more fruitful possibilities. And close analysis of spheres of cultural discourse, which stresses cultural differences in the spheres of the grounding experiences, is being combined, increasingly, in current debates about sexuality and related matters, with the critique of existing social

---

31 C. Abeysekera, paper presented at Value and Technology Conference, WIDER 1986.

32 Foucault, *Histoire*, vol. 2, preface.

arrangements and attitudes, and with the elaboration of a new norm of human flourishing. There is no reason to think this combination incoherent.[33]

As we pursue these possibilities, the basic spheres of experience identified in the Aristotelian approach will no longer, we have said, be seen as spheres of *uninterpreted* experience. But we have also insisted that there is much family relatedness and much overlap among societies. And certain areas of relatively greater universality can be specified here, on which we should insist as we proceed to areas that are more varied in their cultural expression. Not without a sensitive awareness that we are speaking of something that is experienced differently in different contexts, we can nonetheless identify certain features of our common humanity, closely related to Aristotle's original list, from which our debate might proceed.

1. *Mortality.* No matter how death is understood, all human beings face it and (after a certain age) know that they face it. This fact shapes every aspect of more or less every human life.

2. *The Body.* Prior to any concrete cultural shaping, we are born with human bodies, whose possibilities and vulnerabilities do not as such belong to one culture rather than any other. Any given human being might have belonged to any culture. The experience of the body is culturally influenced; but the body itself, prior to such experience, provides limits and parameters that ensure a great deal of overlap in what is going to be experienced, where hunger, thirst, desire, the five senses are concerned. It is all very well to point to the cultural component in these experiences. But when one spends time considering issues of hunger and scarcity, and in general of human misery, such differences appear relatively small and refined, and one cannot fail to acknowledge that "there are no known ethnic differences in human physiology with respect to metabolism of nutrients. Africans and Asians do not burn their dietary calories or use their dietary protein any differently from Europeans and Americans. It follows then that dietary requirements cannot vary widely as between different races."[34] This and similar facts should surely be focal points for debate about appropriate human behavior in this sphere. And by beginning with the body, rather than with the subjective experience of desire, we get, furthermore, an opportunity to criticize the situation of people who are so persistently deprived that their *desire* for good things has actually decreased. This is a further advantage of the Aristotelian

---

[33] This paragraph expands remarks made in a commentary on papers by D. Halperin and J. Winkler at the conference on "Homosexuality in History and Culture" at Brown University, February 1987. The combination of historically sensitive analysis with cultural criticism was forcefully developed at the same conference in Henry Abelove's "Is Gay History Possible?," forthcoming.

[34] C. Gopalan, "Undernutrition: Measurement and Implications," paper prepared for the WIDER Conference on Poverty, Undernutrition, and Living Standards, Helsinki, 27–31 July 1987, and forthcoming in the volume of Proceedings, edited by S. Osmani.

approach, when contrasted with approaches to choice that stop with subjective expressions of preference.

3. *Pleasure and pain.* In every culture, there is a conception of pain; and these conceptions, which overlap very largely with one another, can be plausibly seen as grounded in universal and pre-cultural experience. The Stoic story of infant development is highly implausible; the negative response to bodily pain is surely primitive and universal, rather than learned and optional, however much its specific "grammar" may be shaped by later learning.

4. *Cognitive capability.* Aristotle's famous claim that "all human beings by nature reach out for understanding"[35] seems to stand up to the most refined anthropological analysis. It points to an element in our common humanity that is plausibly seen, again, as grounded independently of particular acculturation, however much it is later shaped by acculturation.

5. *Practical reason.* All human beings, whatever their culture, participate (or try to) in the planning and managing of their lives, asking and answering questions about how one should live and act. This capability expresses itself differently in different societies, but a being who altogether lacked it would not be likely to be acknowledged as a human being, in any culture.[36]

6. *Early infant development.* Prior to the greatest part of specific cultural shaping, though perhaps not free from all shaping, are certain areas of human experiences and development that are broadly shared and of great importance for the Aristotelian virtues: experiences of desire, pleasure, loss, one's own finitude, perhaps also of envy, grief, gratitude. One may argue about the merits of one or another psychoanalytical account of infancy. But it seems difficult to deny that the work of Freud on infant desire and of Klein on grief, loss, and other more complex emotional attitudes has identified spheres of human experience that are to a large extent common to all humans, regardless of their particular society. All humans begin as hungry babies, perceiving their own helplessness, their alternating closeness to and distance from those on whom they depend, and so forth. Melanie Klein records a conversation with an anthropologist in which an event that at first looked (to Western eyes) bizarre was interpreted by Klein as the expression of a universal pattern of mourning. The anthropologist accepted her interpretation.[37]

7. *Affiliation.* Aristotle's claim that human beings as such feel a sense of fellowship with other human beings, and that we are by nature social

---

35 *Metaphysics* 1.1.

36 See Nussbaum, "Nature, Function, and Capability," where this Aristotelian view is compared with Marx's views on human functioning.

37 M. Klein, in Postscript to "Our Adult World and Its Roots in Infancy," in *Envy, Gratitude and Other Works 1946–1963* (London, 1984), 247–63.

animals, is an empirical claim, but it seems to be a sound one. However varied our specific conceptions of friendship and love are, there is a great point in seeing them as overlapping expressions of the same family of shared human needs and desires.

8. *Humor*. There is nothing more culturally varied than humor, and yet, as Aristotle insists, some space for humor and play seems to be a need of any human life. The human being was not called the "laughing animal" for nothing; it is certainly one of our salient differences from almost all animals, and (in some form or other) a shared feature, I somewhat boldly assert, of any life that is going to be counted as fully human.

This is just a list of suggestions, closely related to Aristotle's list of common experiences. One could subtract some of these items and/or add others. But it seems plausible to claim that in all these areas we have a basis for further work on the human good. We do not have a bedrock of completely uninterpreted "given" data, but we do have nuclei of experience around which the construction of different societies proceed. There is no Archimedean point here, and no pure access to unsullied "nature"—even, here, human nature—as it is in and of itself. There is just human life as it is lived. But in life as it is lived, we do find a family of experiences, clustering around certain foci, which can provide reasonable starting points for cross-cultural reflection.

VII

The third objection raises, at bottom, a profound conceptual question: What is it to inquire about the *human* good? What circumstances of existence go to define what it is to live the life of a *human being*, and not some other life? Aristotle likes to point out that an inquiry into the human good cannot, on pain of incoherence, end up describing the good of some other being, say a god, a good, that on account of our circumstances, it is impossible for us to attain (cf. *NE* 1159a10–12, 1166a18–23). Which circumstances then? The virtues are defined relatively to certain problems and limitations, and also to certain endowments. Which ones are sufficiently central that their removal would make us into different beings, and open up a wholly new and different debate about the good? This question is itself part of the ethical debate we propose. For there is no way to answer it but ask ourselves which elements of our experience seem to us so important that they count, for us, as part of who we are. I discuss Aristotle's attitude to this question elsewhere, and I shall simply summarize here.[38] It seems clear, first of all, that our mortality is an essential feature of our circumstances as human beings. An immortal being

---

[38] "Aristotle on Human Nature and the Foundations of Ethics," forthcoming in a volume of essays on the work of Bernard Williams, edited by R. Harrison and J. Altham (Cambridge). This paper will be a WIDER Working Paper.

would have such a different form of life, and such different values and virtues, that it does not seem to make sense to regard that being as part of the same search for good. Essential, too, will be our dependence upon the world outside of us: some sort of need for food, drink, the help of others. On the side of abilities, we would want to include cognitive functioning and the activity of practical reasoning as elements of any life that we would regard as human. Aristotle argues, plausibly, that we would want to include sociability as well, some sensitivity to the needs of and pleasure in the company of other beings similar to ourselves.

But it seems to me that the Marxian question remains, as a deep question about human forms of life and the search for the human good. For one certainly can imagine forms of human life that do not contain the holding of private property—and, therefore, not those virtues that have to do with its proper management. And this means that it remains an open question whether these virtues ought to be regarded as virtues, and kept upon our list. Marx wished to go much further, arguing that communism would remove the need for justice, courage, and most of the bourgeois virtues. I think we might be skeptical here. Aristotle's general attitude to such transformations of life is to suggest that they usually have a tragic dimension. If we remove one sort of problem— say, by removing private property—we frequently do so by introducing an- other—say, the absence of a certain sort of freedom of choice, the freedom that makes it possible to do fine and generous actions for others. If things are complex even in the case of generosity, where we can rather easily imagine the transformation that removes the virtue, they are surely far more so in the cases of justice and courage. And we would need a far more detailed description than Marx ever gives us of the form of life under communism, before we would be able even to begin to see whether this form of life has in fact transformed things where these virtues are concerned, and whether it has or has not intro- duced new problems and limitations in their place.

In general it seems that all forms of life, including the imagined life of a god, contain boundaries and limits.[39] All structures, even that of putative limitlessness, are closed to something, cut off from something—say, in that case, from the specific value and beauty inherent in the struggle against limita- tion. Thus it does not appear that we will so easily get beyond the virtues. Nor does it seem to be so clearly a good thing for human life that we should.

VIII

The best conclusion to this sketch of an Aristotelian program for virtue ethics was written by Aristotle himself, at the end of his discussion of human nature in *Nicomachean Ethics* I:

---

39 See *Fragility,* chap. 11.

So much for our outline sketch for the good. For it looks as if we have to draw an outline first, and fill it in later. It would seem to be open to anyone to take things further and to articulate the good parts of the sketch. And time is a good discoverer or ally in such things. That's how the sciences have progressed as well: it is open to anyone to supply what is lacking. (*NE* 1098a20–26)[40]

[40] This paper was motivated by questions discussed at the WIDER conference on Value and Technology, summer 1986, Helsinki. I would like to thank Steve and Frédérique Marglin for provoking some of these arguments, with hardly any of which they will agree. I also thank Dan Brock for his helpful comments, and Amartya Sen for many discussions of these issues.

37

Beyond Morality

FRIEDRICH NIETZSCHE

*The dark and cryptic writings of German philosopher Friedrich Nietzsche
(1844–1900) have had a strong impact on twentieth-century intellectual
movements. Nietzsche's many books contain important discussions of
aesthetics and epistemology as well as moral philosophy. This selection
contains excerpts from* Human, All Too Human; Beyond Good and Evil;
Genealogy of Morals; *and* Thus Spoke Zarathustra.

*Unlike most philosophers, Nietzsche does not present his views in the
form of extended arguments. Rather, he tends to write in aphorisms—terse
and often witty pronouncements. This selection brings together some of his
typically provocative reflections on ethics. In it, he contends that the
traditional demands of morality grow out of civilization's need to suppress
our more primal impulses. When our moral standards call for benevolence
and self-sacrifice, they do not reflect any authoritative requirements.
Instead, they represent only the desire of the weak to protect themselves
from the strong. This is especially true of the requirement proposed by the
British utilitarians—to produce the greatest happiness for the greatest
number. (For discussion see readings 23, 24, and 25.) If these claims do not
seem obvious, Nietzsche believes it is only because we have forgotten how
morality developed.*

*If traditional values represent only the fears of the timid, then what, if
anything, should replace them? According to Nietzsche, what is required is
a "revaluation of values." He anticipates the development of a new kind of
person—an "overman"—who disdains the familiar values of happiness,
justice, and pity. Powerful in will and spirit, this "overman" will create
new values by giving new expression to ancient instincts. In so doing, he
will exemplify what is best about humanity.*

FROM *HUMAN, ALL TOO HUMAN*

38

How beneficial. Let us table the question, then, of whether psychological observation brings more advantage or harm upon men. What is certain is
that it is necessary, for science cannot do without it. Science, however, takes
as little consideration of final purposes as does nature; just as nature sometimes

brings about the most useful things without having wanted to, so too true science, *which is the imitation of nature in concepts,* will sometimes, nay often, further man's benefit and welfare and achieve what is useful—but likewise *without having wanted to.* Whoever feels too wintry in the breeze of this kind of observation has perhaps too little fire in him. Let him look around meanwhile, and he will perceive diseases which require cold poultices, and men who are so "moulded" out of glowing spirit that they have great trouble in finding an atmosphere cold and biting enough for them anywhere. Moreover, as all overly earnest individuals and peoples have a need for frivolity; as others, who are overly excitable and unstable, occasionally need heavy, oppressive burdens for their health's sake; so should not *we*—the *more* intellectual men in an age that is visibly being set aflame more and more—reach for all quenching and cooling means available to remain at least as steady, harmless, and moderate as we now are and thus render service to this age at some future time as a mirror and self-reflection of itself?

39

The fable of intelligible freedom.[1] The history of those feelings, by virtue of which we consider a person responsible, the so-called moral feelings, is divided into the following main phases. At first we call particular acts good or evil without any consideration of their motives, but simply on the basis of their beneficial or harmful consequences. Soon, however, we forget the origin of these terms and imagine that the quality "good" or "evil" is inherent in the actions themselves, without consideration of their consequences; this is the same error language makes when calling the stone itself hard, the tree itself green—that is, we take the effect to be the cause. Then we assign the goodness or evil to the motives, and regard the acts themselves as morally ambiguous. We go even further and cease to give to the particular motive the predicate good or evil, but give it rather to the whole nature of a man; the motive grows out of him as a plant grows out of the earth. So we make man responsible in turn for the effects of his actions, then for his actions, then for his motives and finally for his nature. Ultimately we discover that his nature cannot be responsible either, in that it is itself an inevitable consequence, an outgrowth of the elements and influences of past and present things; that is, man cannot be made responsible for anything, neither for his nature, nor his motives, nor his actions, nor the effects of his actions. And thus we come to understand that the history of moral feelings is the history of an error, an error called "responsibility," which in turn rests on an error called "freedom of the will."

---

[1] In ancient Greece, Plato's world of ideas—as a model for the sensual world—was referred to as the "intelligible world." "Intelligible freedom" is the pure form of freedom, the idea of freedom. See *The World as Will and Idea,* bk. 4, par. 55. —TRANS.

41

The unchangeable character. In the strict sense, it is not true that one's character is unchangeable; rather, this popular tenet[2] means only that during a man's short lifetime the motives affecting him cannot normally cut deeply enough to destroy the imprinted writing of many millennia. If a man eighty thousand years old were conceivable, his character would in fact be absolutely variable, so that out of him little by little an abundance of different individuals would develop. The brevity of human life misleads us to many an erroneous assertion about the qualities of man.

42

Morality and the ordering of the good. The accepted hierarchy of the good, based on how a low, higher, or a most high egoism desires that thing or the other, decides today about morality or immorality. To prefer a low good (sensual pleasure, for example) to one esteemed higher (health, for example) is taken for immoral, likewise to prefer comfort to freedom. The hierarchy of the good, however, is not fixed and identical at all times. If someone prefers revenge to justice, he is moral by the standard of an earlier culture, yet by the standard of the present culture he is immoral. "Immoral" then indicates that someone has not felt, or not felt strongly enough, the higher, finer, more spiritual motives which the new culture of the time has brought with it. It indicates a backward nature, but only in degree.

The hierarchy itself is not established or changed from the point of view of morality; nevertheless an action is judged moral or immoral according to the prevailing determination.

45

Double prehistory of good and evil. The concept of good and evil has a double prehistory: namely, first of all, in the soul of the ruling clans and castes. The man who has the power to requite goodness with goodness, evil with evil, and really does practice requital by being grateful and vengeful, is called "good." The man who is unpowerful and cannot requite is taken for bad. As a good man, one belongs to the "good," a community that has a communal feeling, because all the individuals are entwined together by their feeling for requital. As a bad man, one belongs to the "bad," to a mass of abject, powerless men who have no communal feeling. The good men are a caste; the bad men are a multitude, like particles of dust. Good and bad are for a time equivalent to noble and base, master and slave. Conversely, one does not regard the enemy as evil: he can requite. In Homer, both the Trojan and the Greek are good. Not the man who inflicts harm on us, but the man who is contemptible, is

---

2 Cf. Aristotle, *Nichomachean Ethics,* 6.13.1: "The several kinds of character are bestowed by nature," or Heraclitus: "Character is destiny." —TRANS.

bad. In the community of the good, goodness is hereditary; it is impossible for a bad man to grow out of such good soil. Should one of the good men nevertheless do something unworthy of good men, one resorts to excuses; one blames God, for example, saying that he struck the good man with blindness and madness.

Then, in the souls of oppressed, powerless men, every *other* man is taken for hostile, inconsiderate, exploitative, cruel, sly, whether he be noble or base. Evil is their epithet for man, indeed for every possible living being, even, for example, for a god; "human," "divine" mean the same as "devilish," "evil." Signs of goodness, helpfulness, pity are taken anxiously for malice, the prelude to a terrible outcome, bewilderment, and deception, in short, for refined evil. With such a state of mind in the individual, a community can scarcely come about at all—or at most in the crudest form; so that wherever this concept of good and evil predominates, the downfall of individuals, their clans and races, is near at hand.

Our present morality has grown up on the ground of the *ruling* clans and castes.[3]

92

Origin of justice. Justice (fairness) originates among approximately *equal powers,* as Thucydides (in the horrifying conversation between the Athenian and Melian envoys)[4] rightly understood. When there is no clearly recognizable supreme power and a battle would lead to fruitless and mutual injury, one begins to think of reaching an understanding and negotiating the claims on both sides: the initial character of justice is *barter.* Each satisfies the other in that each gets what he values more than the other. Each man gives the other what he wants, to keep henceforth, and receives in turn what which he wishes. Thus, justice is requital and exchange on the assumption of approximately equal positions of strength. For this reason, revenge belongs initially to the realm of justice: it is an exchange. Likewise gratitude.

Justice naturally goes back to the viewpoint of an insightful self-preservation, that is, to the egoism of this consideration: "Why should I uselessly injure myself and perhaps not reach my goal anyway?"

So much about the *origin* of justice. Because men, in line with their intellectual habits, have *forgotten* the original purpose of so-called just, fair actions, and particularly because children have been taught for centuries to admire and imitate such actions, it has gradually come to appear that a just action is a selfless one. The high esteem of these actions rests upon this appearance, an esteem which, like all estimations, is also always in a state of growth: for men strive after, imitate, and reproduce with their own sacrifices that which is highly esteemed, and it grows because its worth is increased by the worth of the effort and exertion made by each individual.

---

3 Cf. *On the Genealogy of Morals* (1887), first essay. —TRANS.

4 In Bk. 5, 85–113, Thucydides recounts the surrender of Melos in 416 B.C. —TRANS.

How slight the morality of the world would seem without forgetfulness! A poet could say that God had stationed forgetfulness as a guardian at the door to the temple of human dignity.

93

The right of the weaker. If one party, a city under siege, for example, submits under certain conditions to a greater power, its reciprocal condition is that this first party can destroy itself, burn the city, and thus make the power suffer a great loss. Thus there is a kind of *equalization,* on the basis of which rights can be established. Preservation is to the enemy's advantage.

Rights exist between slaves and masters to the same extent, exactly insofar as the possession of his slave is profitable and important to the master. The *right* originally extends *as far* as the one *appears* to the other to be valuable, essential, permanent, invincible, and the like. In this regard even the weaker of the two has rights, though they are more modest. Thus the famous dictum: "unusquisque tantum juris habet, quantum potenti valet"[5] (or, more exactly, "quantum potentia valere creditur").[6]

94

The three phases of morality until now. The first sign that an animal has become human is that his behavior is no longer directed to his momentary comfort, but rather to his enduring comfort, that is, when man becomes useful, *expedient:* then for the first time the free rule of reason bursts forth. A still higher state is reached when man acts according to the principle of *honor,* by means of which he finds his place in society, submitting to commonly held feelings; that raises him high above the phase in which he is guided only by personal usefulness. Now he shows—and wants to be shown—respect; that is, he understands his advantage as dependent on his opinion of others and their opinion of him. Finally, at the highest stage of morality *until now,* he acts according to *his* standard of things and men; he himself determines for himself and others what is honorable, what is profitable. He has become the lawgiver of opinions, in accordance with the ever more refined concept of usefulness and honor. Knowledge enables him to prefer what is most useful, that is, general usefulness to personal usefulness, and the respectful recognition of what has common, enduring value to things of momentary value. He lives and acts as a collective-individual.

95

Morality of the mature individual. Until now man has taken the true sign of a moral act to be its impersonal nature; and it has been shown that in the

---

5 "Each has as much right as his power is worth." Spinoza, *Tractatus Politicus*, vol. 2, par. 8. —TRANS.

6 "as his power is assessed to be" —TRANS.

beginning all impersonal acts were praised and distinguished in respect to the common good. Might not a significant transformation of these views be at hand, now when we see with ever greater clarity that precisely in the most *personal* respect the common good is also greatest; so that now it is precisely the strictly personal action which corresponds to the current concept of morality (as a common profit)? To make a whole *person* of oneself and keep in mind that person's *greatest good* in everything one does—this takes us further than any pitying impulses and actions for the sake of others. To be sure, we all still suffer from too slight a regard for our own personal needs; it has been poorly developed. Let us admit that our mind has instead been forcibly diverted from it and offered in sacrifice to the state, to science, to the needy, as if it were something bad which had to be sacrificed. Now too we wish to work for our fellow men, but only insofar as we find our own highest advantage in this work; no more, no less. It depends only on what one understands by his *advantage*. The immature, undeveloped, crude individual will also understand it most crudely.

96

Mores and morality. To be moral, correct, ethical means to obey an age-old law or tradition. Whether one submits to it gladly or with difficulty makes no difference; enough that one submits. We call "good" the man who does the moral thing as if by nature, after a long history of inheritance—that is, easily, and gladly, whatever it is (he will, for example, practice revenge when that is considered moral, as in the older Greek culture). He is called good because he is good "for" something. But because, as mores changed, goodwill, pity, and the like were always felt to be "good for" something, useful, it is primarily the man of goodwill, the helpful man, who is called "good." To be evil is to be "not moral" (immoral), to practice bad habits, go against tradition, however reasonable or stupid it may be. To harm one's fellow, however, has been felt primarily as injurious in all moral codes of different times, so that when we hear the word "bad" now, we think particularly of voluntary injury to one's fellow. When men determine between moral and immoral, good and evil, the basic opposition is not "egoism" and "selflessness," but rather adherence to a tradition or law, and release from it. The *origin* of the tradition makes no difference, at least concerning good and evil, or an immanent categorical imperative; but is rather above all for the purpose of maintaining *a community*, a people. Every superstitious custom, originating in a coincidence that is interpreted falsely, forces a tradition that it is moral to follow. To release oneself from it is dangerous, even more injurious for the *community* than for the individual (because the divinity punishes the whole community for sacrilege and violation of its rights, and the individual only as a part of that community). Now, each tradition grows more venerable the farther its origin lies in the past, the more it is forgotten; the respect paid to the tradition accumulates from generation to generation; finally the origin becomes sacred and awakens awe; and thus the morality of piety is in any case much older than that morality which requires selfless acts.

FROM *BEYOND GOOD AND EVIL*

186

The moral sentiment in Europe today is as refined, old, diverse, irritable, and subtle, as the "science of morals" that accompanies it is still young, raw, clumsy, and butterfingered—an attractive contrast that occasionally even becomes visible and incarnate in the person of a moralist. Even the term "science of morals" is much too arrogant considering what it designates, and offends *good* taste—which always prefers more modest terms.

One should own up in all strictness to what is still necessary here for a long time to come, to what alone is justified so far: to collect material, to conceptualize and arrange a vast realm of subtle feelings of value and differences of value which are alive, grow, beget, and perish—and perhaps attempts to present vividly some of the more frequent and recurring forms of such living crystallizations—all to prepare a *typology* of morals.

To be sure, so far one has not been so modest. With a stiff seriousness that inspires laughter, all our philosophers demanded something far more exalted, presumptuous, and solemn from themselves as soon as they approached the study of morality: they wanted to supply a *rational foundation* for morality—and every philosopher so far has believed that he has provided such a foundation. Morality itself, however, was accepted as "given." How remote from their clumsy pride was that task which they considered insignificant and left in dust and must—the task of description—although the subtlest fingers and senses can scarcely be subtle enough for it.

Just because our moral philosophers knew the facts of morality only very approximately in arbitrary extracts or in accidental epitomes—for example, as the morality of their environment, their class, their church, the spirit of their time, their climate and part of the world—just because they were poorly informed and not even very curious about different peoples, times, and past ages—they never laid eyes on the real problems of morality; for these emerge only when we compare *many* moralities. In all "science of morals" so far one thing was *lacking,* strange as it may sound: the problem of morality itself; what was lacking was any suspicion that there was something problematic here. What the philosophers called "a rational foundation for morality" and tried to supply was, seen in the right light, merely a scholarly variation of the common *faith* in the prevalent morality; a new means of *expression* for this faith; and thus just another fact within a particular morality; indeed, in the last analysis a kind of denial that this morality might ever be considered problematic—certainly the very opposite of an examination, analysis, questioning, and vivisection of this very faith.

• • •

198

All these moralities that address themselves to the individual, for the sake of his "happiness," as one says—what are they but counsels for behavior in relation to the degree of *dangerousness* in which the individual lives with himself; recipes against his passions, his good and bad inclinations insofar as they have the will to power and want to play the master; little and great prudences and artifices that exude the nook odor of old nostrums and of the wisdom of old women; all of them baroque and unreasonable in form—because they address themselves to "all," because they generalize where one must not generalize. All of them speak unconditionally, take themselves for unconditional, all of them flavored with more than one grain of salt and tolerable only— at times even seductive—when they begin to smell over-spiced and dangerous, especially "of the other world." All of it is, measured intellectually, worth very little and not by a long shot "science," much less "wisdom," but rather, to say it once more, three times more, prudence, prudence, prudence, mixed with stupidity, stupidity, stupidity—whether it be that indifference and statue coldness against the hot-headed folly of the affects which the Stoics advised and administered; or that laughing-no-more and weeping-no-more of Spinoza, his so naïvely advocated destruction of the affects through their analysis and vivisection; or that tuning down of the affects to a harmless mean according to which they may be satisfied, the Aristotelianism of morals; even morality as enjoyment of the affects in a deliberate thinness and spiritualization by means of the symbolism of art, say, as music, or as love of God and of man for God's sake—for in religion the passions enjoy the rights of citizens again, assuming that—; finally even that accommodating and playful surrender to the affects, as Hafiz and Goethe taught it, that bold dropping of the reins, that spiritual-physical *licentia morum*[7] in the exceptional case of wise old owls and sots for whom it "no longer holds much danger." This, too, for the chapter "Morality as Timidity."

199

Inasmuch as at all times, as long as there have been human beings, there have also been herds of men (clans, communities, tribes, peoples, states, churches) and always a great many people who obeyed, compared with the small number of those commanding—considering, then, that nothing has been exercised and cultivated better and longer among men so far than obedience— it may fairly be assumed that the need for it is now innate in the average man, as a kind of *formal conscience* that commands: "thou shalt unconditionally do something, unconditionally not do something else," in short, "thou shalt."

---

[7] Moral license. —TRANS.

This need seeks to satisfy itself and to fill its form with some content. According to its strength, impatience, and tension, it seizes upon things as a rude appetite, rather indiscriminately, and accepts whatever is shouted into its ears by someone who issues commands—parents, teachers, laws, class prejudices, public opinions.

The strange limits of human development, the way it hesitates, takes so long, often turns back, and moves in circles, is due to the fact that the herd instinct of obedience is inherited best, and at the expense of the art of commanding. If we imagine this instinct progressing for once to its ultimate excesses, then those who command and are independent would eventually be lacking altogether; or they would secretly suffer from a bad conscience and would find it necessary to deceive themselves before they could command—as if they, too, merely obeyed. This state is actually encountered in Europe today: I call it the moral hypocrisy of those commanding. They know no other way to protect themselves against their bad conscience than to pose as the executors of more ancient or higher commands (of ancestors, the constitution, of right, the laws, or even of God). Or they even borrow herd maxims from the herd's way of thinking, such as "first servants of their people" or "instruments of the common weal."

On the other side, the herd man in Europe today gives himself the appearance of being the only permissible kind of man, and glorifies his attributes, which make him tame, easy to get along with, and useful to the herd, as if they were the truly human virtues: namely, public spirit, benevolence, consideration, industriousness, moderation, modesty, indulgence, and pity. In those cases, however, where one considers leaders and bellwethers indispensable, people today make one attempt after another to add together clever herd men by way of replacing commanders: all parliamentary constitutions, for example, have this origin. Nevertheless, the appearance of one who commands unconditionally strikes these herd-animal Europeans as an immense comfort and salvation from a gradually intolerable pressure, as was last attested in a major way by the effect of Napoleon's appearance. The history of Napoleon's reception is almost the history of the higher happiness attained by this whole century in its most valuable human beings and moments.

201

As long as the utility reigning in moral value judgments is solely the utility of the herd, as long as one considers only the preservation of the community, and immorality is sought exactly and exclusively in what seems dangerous to the survival of the community—there can be no morality of "neighbor love." Supposing that even then there was a constant little exercise of consideration, pity, fairness, mildness, reciprocity of assistance; supposing that even in that state of society all those drives are active that later receive the honorary designation of "virtues" and eventually almost coincide with the concept of "morality"—in that period they do not yet at all belong in the realm of moral valuations; they are still *extra-moral*. An act of pity, for example, was not considered either good or bad, moral or immoral, in the best period of the Romans; and even when it was praised, such praise was perfectly compatible with a kind of disgruntled disdain as soon as it was juxtaposed with an action that served the welfare of the whole, of the *res publica*.[8]

In the last analysis, "love of the neighbor" is always something secondary, partly conventional and arbitrary-illusory in relation to *fear of the neighbor*. After the structure of society is fixed on the whole and seems secure against external dangers, it is this fear of the neighbor that again creates new perspectives of moral valuation. Certain strong and dangerous drives, like an enterprising spirit, foolhardiness, vengefulness, craftiness, rapacity, and the lust to rule, which had so far not merely been honored insofar as they were socially useful— under different names, to be sure, from those chosen here—but had to be trained and cultivated to make them great (because one constantly needed them in view of the dangers to the whole community, against the enemies of the community), are now experienced as doubly dangerous, since the channels to divert them are lacking, and, step upon step, they are branded as immoral and abandoned to slander.

Now the opposite drives and inclinations receive moral honors; step upon step, the herd instinct draws its conclusions. How much or how little is dangerous to the community, dangerous to equality, in an opinion, in a state or affect, in a will, in a talent—that now constitutes the moral perspective: here, too, fear is again the mother of morals.

The highest and strongest drives, when they break out passionately and drive the individual far above the average and the flats of the herd conscience, wreck the self-confidence of the community, its faith in itself, and it is as if its spine snapped. Hence just these drives are branded and slandered most. High and independent spirituality, the will to stand alone, even a powerful reason are experienced as dangers; everything that elevates an individual above the herd and intimidates the neighbor is henceforth called *evil;* and the fair, modest, submissive, conforming mentality, the *mediocrity* of desires attains moral designations and honors. Eventually, under very peaceful conditions, the opportunity and necessity for educating one's feelings to severity and hardness is lacking more and more; and every severity, even in justice, begins to disturb the conscience; any high and hard nobility and self-reliance is almost felt to be an insult and arouses mistrust; the "lamb," even more than the "sheep," gains in respect.

There is a point in the history of society when it becomes so pathologically soft and tender that among other things it sides even with those who harm it, criminals, and does this quite seriously and honestly. Punishing somehow seems unfair to it, and it is certain that imagining "punishment" and "being supposed to punish" hurts it, arouses fear in it. "Is it not enough to render him *undangerous?* Why still punish? Punishing itself is terrible." With this question, herd morality, the morality of timidity, draws its ultimate consequence. Supposing that one could altogether abolish danger, the reason for fear, this morality

---

8 Commonwealth. —TRANS.

would be abolished, too, *eo ispo:* it would no longer be needed, it would no longer *consider itself* necessary.

Whoever examines the conscience of the European today will have to pull the same imperative out of a thousand moral folds and hideouts—the imperative of herd timidity: "we want that some day there should be *nothing any more to be afraid of!*" Some day—throughout Europe, the will and way to this day is now called "progress."

202

Let us immediately say once more what we have already said a hundred times, for today's ears resist such truths—*our* truths. We know well enough how insulting it sounds when anybody counts man, unadorned and without metaphor, among the animals; but it will be charged against us as almost a *guilt* that precisely for the men of "modern ideas" we constantly employ such expressions as "herd," "herd instincts," and so forth. What can be done about it? We cannot do anything else; for here exactly lies our novel insight. We have found that in all major moral judgments Europe is now of one mind, including even the countries dominated by the influence of Europe: plainly, one now *knows* in Europe what Socrates thought he did not know and what that famous old serpent once promised to teach—today one "knows" what is good and evil.

Now it must sound harsh and cannot be heard easily when we keep insisting: that which here believes it knows, that which here glorifies itself with its praises and reproaches, calling itself good, that is the instinct of the herd animal, man, which has scored a breakthrough and attained prevalence and predominance over other instincts—and this development is continuing in accordance with the growing physiological approximation and assimilation of which it is the symptom. *Morality in Europe today is herd animal morality*—in other words, as we understand it, merely *one* type of human morality beside which, before which, and after which many other types, above all *higher* moralities, are, or ought to be, possible. But this morality resists such a "possibility," such an "ought" with all its power: it says stubbornly and inexorably, "I am morality itself, and nothing besides is morality." Indeed, with the help of a religion which indulged and flattered the most sublime herd-animal desires, we have reached the point where we find even in political and social institutions an ever more visible expression of this morality: the *democratic* movement is the heir of the Christian movement.

•   •   •

203

•   •   •

Toward *new philosophers;* there is no choice; toward spirits strong and original enough to provide the stimuli for opposite valuations and to revalue and invert "eternal values"; toward forerunners, toward men of the future who in the present tie the knot and constraint that forces the will of millennia upon *new* tracks. To teach man the future of man as his *will*, as dependent on a human will, and to prepare great ventures and over-all attempts of discipline and cultivation by way of putting an end to that gruesome dominion of nonsense and accident that has so far been called "history"—the nonsense of the "greatest number" is merely its ultimate form: at some time new types of philosophers and commanders will be necessary for that, and whatever has existed on earth of concealed, terrible, and benevolent spirits, will look pale and dwarfed by comparison. It is the image of such leaders that *we* envisage: may I say this out loud, you free spirits? The conditions that one would have partly to create and partly to exploit for their genesis; the probable ways and tests that would enable a soul to grow to such a height and force that it would feel the *compulsion* for such tasks; a revaluation of values under whose new pressure and hammer a conscience would be steeled, a heart turned to bronze, in order to endure the weight of such responsibility; on the other hand, the necessity of such leaders, the frightened danger that they might fail to appear or that they might turn out badly or degenerate—these are *our* real worries and gloom—do you know that, you free spirits?—these are the heavy distant thoughts and storms that pass over the sky of *our* life.

· · ·

228

May I be forgiven the discovery that all moral philosophy so far has been boring and was a soporific and that "virtue" has been impaired more for me by its *boring* advocates than by anything else, though I am not denying their general utility. It is important that as few people as possible should think about morality; hence it is *very* important that morality should not one day become interesting. But there is no reason for worry. Things still stand today as they have always stood: I see nobody in Europe who has (let alone, *promotes*) any awareness that thinking about morality could become dangerous, captious, seductive—that there might be any *calamity* involved.

Consider, for example, the indefatigable, inevitable British utilitarians, how they walk clumsily and honorably in Bentham's footsteps, walking along (a Homeric simile says it more plainly), even as he himself had already walked in the footsteps of the honorable Helvétius[9] (no, he was no dangerous person, this Helvétius, *ce sénateur Pococurante*,[10] to speak with Galiani). Not a new idea, no trace of a subtler version or twist of an old idea, not even a real

---

9 Claude Adrien Helvétius (1715–1771) was a French philosopher whose ancestors had borne the name of Schweitzer. He was a materialist and utilitarian. —TRANS.

10 *Poco*: little; *curante*: careful, caring; *pococurante*: easygoing. —TRANS.

history of what had been thought before: altogether an *impossible* literature, unless one knows how to flavor it with some malice.

For into these moralists, too (one simply has to read them with ulterior thoughts, if one *has* to read them), that old English vice has crept which is called *cant* and consists in *moral Tartuffery;* only this time it hides in a new, scientific, form. A secret fight against a bad conscience is not lacking either, as it is only fair that a race of former Puritans will have a bad conscience whenever it tries to deal with morality scientifically. (Isn't a moral philosopher opposite of a Puritan? Namely, insofar as he is a thinker who considers morality questionable, as calling for questions marks, in short as a problem? Should moralizing not be—immoral?)

Ultimately they all want *English* morality to be proved right—because this serves humanity best, or "the general utility," or "the happiness of the greatest number"—no, the happiness of *England*. With all their powers they want to prove to themselves that the striving for *English* happiness—I mean for comfort and fashion[11] (and at best a seat in Parliament)—is at the same time also the right way to virtue; indeed that whatever virtue has existed in the world so far must have consisted in such striving.

None of these ponderous herd animals with their unquiet consciences (who undertake to advocate the cause of egoism as the cause of the general welfare) wants to know or even sense that "the general welfare" is no ideal, no goal, no remotely intelligible concept, but only an emetic—that what is fair for one *cannot* by any means for that reason alone also be fair for others; that the demand of one morality for all is detrimental for the higher men; in short, that there is an order of rank between man and man, hence also between morality and morality. They are a modest and thoroughly mediocre type of man, these utilitarian Englishmen, and, as said above, insofar as they are boring one cannot think highly enough of their utility. They should even be *encouraged:* the following rhymes represent an effort in this direction.

> Hail, dear drudge and patient fretter!
> "More drawn out is always better,"
> Stiffness grows in head and knee,
> No enthusiast and no joker,
> Indestructibly mediocre,
> *Sans génie et sans esprit!*

FROM *GENEALOGY OF MORALS*

16

At this point I can no longer avoid giving a first, provisional statement of my own hypothesis concerning the origin of the "bad conscience": it may

---

11 Nietzsche uses the English words "comfort" and "fashion." —Trans.

sound rather strange and needs to be pondered, lived with, and slept on for a long time. I regard the bad conscience as the serious illness that man was bound to contract under the stress of the most fundamental change he ever experienced—that change which occurred when he found himself finally enclosed within the walls of society and of peace. The situation that faced sea animals when they were compelled to become land animals or perish was the same as that which faced these semi-animals, well adapted to the wilderness, to war, to prowling, to adventure: suddenly all their instincts were disvalued and "suspended." From now on they had to walk on their feet and "bear themselves" whereas hitherto they had been borne by the water: a dreadful heaviness lay upon them. They felt unable to cope with the simplest undertakings; in this new world they no longer possessed their former guides, their regulating, unconscious and infallible drives: they were reduced to thinking, inferring, reckoning, co-ordinating cause and effect, these unfortunate creatures; they were reduced to their "consciousness," their weakest and most fallible organ! I believe there has never been such a feeling of misery on earth, such a leaden discomfort—and at the same time the old instincts had not suddenly ceased to make their usual demands Only it was hardly or rarely possible to humor them: as a rule they had to seek new and, as it were, subterranean gratifications.

All instincts that do not discharge themselves outwardly *turn inward*—this is what I call the *internalization* of man: thus it was that man first developed what was later called his "soul." The entire inner world, originally as thin as if it were stretched between two membranes, expanded and extended itself, acquired depth, breadth, and height, in the same measure as outward discharge was *inhibited*. Those fearful bulwarks with which the political organization protected itself against the old instincts of freedom—punishments belong among these bulwarks—brought about that all those instincts of wild, free, prowling man turned backward *against man himself*. Hostility, cruelty, joy in persecuting, in attacking, in change, in destruction—all this turned against the possessors of such instincts: *that* is the origin of the "bad conscience."

The man who, from lack of external enemies and resistances and forcibly confined to the oppressive narrowness and punctiliousness of custom, impatiently lacerated, persecuted, gnawed at, assaulted, and maltreated himself; this animal that rubbed itself raw against the bars of its cage as one tried to "tame" it; this deprived creature, racked with homesickness for the wild, who had to turn himself into an adventure, a torture chamber, an uncertain and dangerous wilderness—this fool, this yearning and desperate prisoner became the inventor of the "bad conscience." But thus began the gravest and uncanniest illness, from which humanity has not yet recovered, man's suffering *of man, of himself*—the result of a forcible sundering from his animal past, as it were a leap and plunge into new surroundings and conditions of existence, a declaration of war against the old instincts upon which his strength, joy, and terribleness had rested hitherto.

· · ·

FROM *THUS SPOKE ZARATHUSTRA*

And Zarathustra spoke thus to the people:

"*I teach you the overman.* Man is something that shall be overcome. What have you done to overcome him?

"All beings so far have created something beyond themselves; and do you want to be the ebb of this great flood and even go back to the beasts rather than overcome man? What is the ape to man? A laughingstock or a painful embarrassment. And man shall be just that for the overman: a laughingstock or a painful embarrassment. You have made your way from worm to man, and much in you is still worm. Once you were apes, and even now, too, man is more ape than any ape.

"Whoever is the wisest among you is also a mere conflict and cross between plant and ghost. But do I bid you become ghosts or plants?

"Behold, I teach you the overman. The overman is the meaning of the earth. Let your will say: the overman *shall be* the meaning of the earth! I beseech you, my brothers, *remain faithful to the earth,* and do not believe those who speak to you of otherwordly hopes! Poison mixers are they, whether they know it or not. Despisers of life are they, decaying and poisoning themselves of whom the earth is weary: so let them go.

"Once the sin against God was the greatest sin; but God died, and these sinners died with him. To sin against the earth is now the most dreadful thing, and to esteem the entrails of the unknowable higher than the meaning of the earth.

"Once the soul looked contemptuously upon the body, and then this contempt was the highest: she wanted the body meager, ghastly, and starved. Thus she hoped to escape it and the earth. Oh, this soul herself was still meager, ghastly, and starved: and cruelty was the lust of this soul. But you, too, my brothers, tell me: what does your body proclaim of your soul? Is not your soul poverty and filth and wretched contentment?

"Verily, a polluted stream is man. One must be a sea to be able to receive a polluted stream without becoming unclean. Behold, I teach you the overman: he is this sea; in him your great contempt can go under.

"What is the greatest experience you can have? It is the hour of the great contempt. The hour in which your happiness, too, arouses your disgust, and even your reason and your virtue.

"The hour when you say, 'What matters my happiness? It is poverty and filth and wretched contentment. But my happiness ought to justify existence itself.'

"The hour when you say, 'What matters my reason? Does it crave knowledge as the lion his food? It is poverty and filth and wretched contentment.'

"The hour when you say, 'What matters my virtue? As yet it has not made me rage. How weary I am of my good and my evil! All that is poverty and filth and wretched contentment.'

"The hour when you say, 'What matters my justice? I do not see that I am flames and fuel. But the just are flames and fuel.'

"The hour when you say, 'What matters my pity? Is not pity the cross on which he is nailed who loves man? But my pity is no crucifixion.'

"Have you yet spoken thus? Have you yet cried thus? Oh, that I might have heard you cry thus!

"Not your sin but your thrift cries to heaven; your meanness even in your sin cries to heaven.

"Where is the lightning to lick you with its tongue? Where is the frenzy with which you should be inoculated?

"Behold, I teach you the overman: he is this lightning, he is this frenzy."

• • •

"Man is a rope, tied between beast and overman—a rope over an abyss. A dangerous across, a dangerous on-the-way, a dangerous looking-back, a dangerous shuddering and stopping.

"What is great in man is that he is a bridge and not an end: what can be loved in man is that he is an *overture* and a *going under*.

• • •

38

The Virtues,
the Unity of a
Human Life,
and the Concept of
a Tradition

ALASDAIR MacINTYRE

Alasdair MacIntyre (b. 1929) has taught philosophy at a number of colleges and universities and is currently Professor of Philosophy at the University of Notre Dame. His books include A Short History of Ethics, After Virtue, Whose Justice? Which Rationality?, *and* Three Rival Versions of Moral Enquiry.

In this selection, taken from After Virtue, *chapter 15, MacIntyre traces the moral importance of the concept of narrative. While many philosophers have concentrated on isolated actions, MacIntyre argues that such actions are intelligible only as parts of the larger stories that agents tell about themselves. To understand these stories, we must appreciate both the agents' intentions and the concepts that those intentions presuppose. We must also appreciate that each storyteller is himself a character in the stories of others. So central is our status as protagonists of narratives that personal identity itself must be understood in these terms.*

What bearing does all of this have on morality? According to MacIntyre, there are a number of connections. If the unity of a life depends on its narrative structure, then a person's good is the way he "might live out that unity and bring it to completion." More generally, the "good for man" is whatever the goods of all individual persons have in common. And the virtues are dispositions that, among other things, enable us to pursue the quest for the good. Since the good is illuminated by the notion of narrative, and narratives in turn are illuminated by traditions and social practices, the good must also have a social and historical dimension. Thus, views like Kant's, which regard morality as ahistorical (see reading 30), are bound to fail.

Any contemporary attempt to envisage each human life as a whole, as a unity, whose character provides the virtues with an adequate *telos* encounters two different kinds of obstacle, one social and one philosophical. The social obstacles derive from the way in which modernity partitions each human life into a variety of segments, each with its own norms and modes of behaviour. So work is divided from leisure, private life from public, the corporate from the personal. So both childhood and old age have been wrenched away from the rest of human life and made over into distinct realms. And all these separations have been achieved so that it is the distinctiveness of each and not the unity of the life of the individual who passes through those parts in terms of which we are taught to think and to feel.

The philosophical obstacles derive from two distinct tendencies, one chiefly, though not only, domesticated in analytical philosophy and one at home in both sociological theory and in existentialism. The former is the tendency to think atomistically about human action and to analyse complex actions and transactions in terms of simple components. Hence the recurrence in more than one context of the notion of 'a basic action'. That particular actions derive their character as parts of larger wholes is a point of view alien to our dominant ways of thinking and yet one which it is necessary at least to consider if we are to begin to understand how a life may be more than a sequence of individual actions and episodes.

Equally the unity of a human life becomes invisible to us when a sharp separation is made between the individual and the roles that he or she plays—a separation characteristic not only of Sartre's existentialism, but also of the sociological theory of Ralf Dahrendorf—or between the different role- and quasi-role—enactments of an individual life so that life comes to appear as nothing but a series of unconnected episodes—a liquidation of the self characteristic, as I noticed earlier, of Goffman's sociological theory. I already also suggested in Chapter 3 that both the Sartrian and the Goffmanesque conceptions of selfhood are highly characteristic of the modes of thought and practice of modernity. It is perhaps therefore unsurprising to realise that the self as thus conceived cannot be envisaged as a bearer of the Aristotelian virtues.

For a self separated from its roles in the Sartrian mode loses that arena of social relationships in which the Aristotelian virtues function if they function at all. The patterns of a virtuous life would fall under those condemnations of conventionality which Sartre put into the mouth of Antoine Roquentin in *La Nausée* and which he uttered in his own person in *L'Être et le néant*. Indeed the self's refusal of the inauthenticity of conventionalised social relationships becomes what integrity is diminished into in Sartre's account.

At the same time the liquidation of the self into a set of demarcated areas of role-playing allows no scope for the exercise of dispositions which could genuinely be accounted virtues in any sense remotely Aristotelian. For a virtue is not a disposition that makes for success only in some one particular type of situation. What are spoken of as the virtues of a good committee man or of a good administrator or of a gambler or a pool hustler are professional skills professionally deployed in those situations where they can be effective, not virtues. Someone who genuinely possesses a virtue can be expected to manifest it in very different types of situation, many of them situations where the practice of a virtue cannot be expected to be effective in the way that we expect a professional skill to be. Hector exhibited one and the same courage in his parting from Andromache and on the battlefield with Achilles; Eleanor Marx exhibited one and the same compassion in her relationship with her father, in her work with trade unionists and in her entanglement with Aveling. And the unity of a virtue in someone's life is intelligible only as a characteristic of a unitary life, a life that can be conceived and evaluated as a whole. Hence just as in the discussion of the changes in and fragmentation of morality which accompanied the rise of modernity in the earlier parts of this book, each stage in the emergence of the characteristically modern views of the moral judgment was accompanied by a corresponding stage in the emergence of the characteristically modern conceptions of selfhood; so now, in defining the particular premodern concept of the virtues with which I have been preoccupied, it has become necessary to say something of the concomitant concept of selfhood, a concept of a self whose unity resides in the unity of a narrative which links birth to life to death as narrative beginning to middle to end.

Such a conception of the self is perhaps less unfamiliar than it may appear at first sight. Just because it has played a key part in the cultures which are historically the predecessors of our own, it would not be surprising if it turned out to be still an unacknowledged presence in many of our ways of thinking and acting. Hence it is not inappropriate to begin by scrutinising some of our most taken-for-granted, but clearly correct conceptual insights about human actions and selfhood in order to show how natural it is to think of the self in a narrative mode.

It is a conceptual commonplace, both for philosophers and for ordinary agents, that one and the same segment of human behaviour may be correctly characterised in a number of different ways. To the question 'What is he doing?' the answers may with equal truth and appropriateness be 'Digging', 'Gardening', 'Taking exercise', 'Preparing for winter' or 'Pleasing his wife'. Some of these answers will characterise the agent's intentions, others unintended consequences of his actions, and of these unintended consequences some may be such that the agent is aware of them and others not. What is important to notice immediately is that any answer to the questions of how we are to understand or to explain a given segment of behaviour will presuppose some prior answer to the question of how these different correct answers to the question 'What is he doing?' are related to each other. For if someone's primary intention is to put the garden in order before the winter and it is only incidentally the case that in so doing he is making exercise and pleasing his wife, we have one type of behaviour to be explained; but if the agent's primary intention is to please his wife by taking exercise, we have quite another type of behaviour to be explained and we will have to look in a different direction for understanding and explanation.

In the first place the episode has been situated in an annual cycle of domestic activity, and the behaviour embodies an intention which presupposes a particular type of household-cum-garden setting with the peculiar narrative history of that setting in which this segment of behaviour now becomes an episode. In the second instance the episode has been situated in the narrative history of a marriage, a very different, even if related, social setting. We cannot, that is to say, characterise behaviour independently of intentions, and we cannot characterise intentions independently of the settings which make those intentions intelligible both to agents themselves and to others.

I use the word 'setting' here as a relatively inclusive term. A social setting may be an institution, it may be what I have called a practice, or it may be a milieu of some other human kind. But it is central to the notion of a setting as I am going to understand it that a setting has a history, a history within which the histories of individual agents not only are, but have to be, situated, just because without the setting and its changes through time the history of the individual agent and his changes through time will be unintelligible. Of course one and the same piece of behaviour may belong to more than one setting. There are at least two different ways in which this may be so.

In my earlier example the agent's activity may be part of the history both of the cycle of household activity and of his marriage, two histories which have happened to intersect. The household may have its own history stretching back through hundreds of years, as do the histories of some European farms, where the farm has had a life of its own, even though different families have in different periods inhabited it; and the marriage will certainly have its own history, a history which itself presupposes that a particular point has been reached in the history of the institution of marriage. If we are to relate some particular segment of behaviour in any precise way to an agent's intentions and thus to the settings which that agent inhabits, we shall have to understand in a precise way how the variety of correct characterisations of the agent's behaviour relate to each other first by identifying which characteristics refer us to an intention and which do not and then by classifying further the items in both categories.

Where intentions are concerned, we need to know which intention or intentions were primary, that is to say, of which it is the case that, had the agent intended otherwise, he would not have performed that action. Thus if we know that a man is gardening with the self-avowed purposes of healthful exercise and of pleasing his wife, we do not yet know how to understand what he is doing until we know the answer to such questions as whether he would continue gardening if he continued to believe that gardening was healthful exercise, but discovered that his gardening no longer pleased his wife, *and* whether he would continue gardening, if he ceased to believe that gardening was healthful exercise, but continued to believe that it pleased his wife, *and* whether he would continue gardening if he changed his beliefs on both points. That is to say, we need to know both what certain of his beliefs are and which of them are causally effective; and, that is to say, we need to know whether certain contrary-to-fact hypothetical statements are true or false. And until we know this, we shall not know how to characterise correctly what the agent is doing.

Consider another equally trivial example of a set of compatibly correct answers to the question 'What is he doing?' 'Writing a sentence'; 'Finishing his book'; 'Contributing to the debate on the theory of action'; 'Trying to get tenure'. Here the intentions can be ordered in terms of the stretch of time to which reference is made. Each of the shorter-term intentions is, and can only be made, intelligible by reference to some longer-term intentions; and the characterisation of the behaviour in terms of the longer-term intentions can only be correct if some of the characterisations in terms of shorter-term intentions are also correct. Hence the behaviour is only characterised adequately when we know what the longer and longest-term intentions invoked are and how the shorter-term intentions are related to the longer. Once again we are involved in writing a narrative history.

Intentions thus need to be ordered both causally and temporally and both orderings will make references to settings, references already made obliquely by such elementary terms as 'gardening', 'wife', 'book' and 'tenure'. Moreover the correct identification of the agent's beliefs will be an essential constituent of this task; failure at this point would mean failure in the whole enterprise. . . .

Consider what the argument so far implies about the interrelationships of the intentional, the social and the historical. We identify a particular action only by invoking two kinds of context, implicitly if not explicitly. We place the agent's intentions, I have suggested, in causal and temporal order with reference to their role in his or her history; and we also place them with reference to their role in the history of the setting or settings to which they belong. In doing this, in determining what causal efficacy the agent's intentions had in one or more directions, and how his short-term intentions succeeded or failed to be constitutive of long-term intentions, we ourselves write a further part of these histories. Narrative history of a certain kind turns out to be the basic and essential genre for the characterisation of human actions.

It is important to be clear how different the standpoint presupposed by the argument so far is from that of those analytical philosophers who have constructed accounts of human actions which make central the notion of 'a' human action. A course of human events is then seen as a complex sequence of individual actions, and a natural question is: How do we individuate human actions? Now there are contexts in which such notions are at home. In the recipes of a cookery book for instance actions are individuated in just the way that some analytical philosophers have supposed to be possible of all actions. 'Take six eggs. Then break them into a bowl. Add flour, salt, sugar, etc.' But the point about such sequences is that each element in them is intelligible as an action only as a-possible-element-in-a-sequence. Moreover even such a sequence requires a context to be intelligible. If in the middle of my lecture on Kant's ethics I suddenly broke six eggs into a bowl and added flour and sugar, proceeding all the while with my Kantian exegesis, I have *not,* simply in virtue of the fact that I was following a sequence prescribed by Fanny Farmer, performed an intelligible action.

•   •   •

The most familiar type of context in and by reference to which speech-acts and purposes are rendered intelligible is the conversation. Conversation is so all-pervasive a feature of the human world that it tends to escape philosophical attention. Yet remove conversation from human life and what would be left? Consider then what is involved in following a conversation and finding it intelligible or unintelligible. (To find a conversation intelligible is not the same as to understand it; for a conversation which I overhear may be intelligible, but I may fail to understand it.) If I listen to a conversation between two other people my ability to grasp the thread of the conversation will involve an ability to bring it under some one out of a set of descriptions in which the degree and kind of coherence in the conversation is brought out: 'a drunken, rambling quarrel', 'a serious intellectual disagreement', 'a tragic misunderstanding of each other', 'a comic, even farcical misconstrual of each other's motives', 'a penetrating interchange of views', 'a struggle to dominate each other', 'a trivial exchange of gossip.'

The use of words such as 'tragic', 'comic', and 'farcical' is not marginal to such evaluations. We allocate conversations to genres, just as we do literary narratives. Indeed a conversation is a dramatic work, even if a very short one, in which the participants are not only the actors, but also the joint authors, working out in agreement or disagreement the mode of their production. For it is not just that conversations belong to genres in just the way that plays and novels do; but they have beginnings, middles and endings just as do literary works. They embody reversals and recognitions; they move towards and away from climaxes. There may within a longer conversation be digressions and subplots, indeed digressions within digressions and subplots within subplots.

But if this is true of conversations, it is true also *mutatis mutandis* of battles, chess games, courtships, philosophy seminars, families at the dinner table, businessmen negotiating contracts—that is, of human transactions in general. For conversation, understood widely enough, is the form of human transactions in general. Conversational behaviour is not a special sort or aspect of human behaviour, even though the forms of language-using and of human life are such that the deeds of others speak for them as much as do their words. For that is possible only because they are the deeds of those who have words.

I am presenting both conversations in particular then and human actions in general as enacted narratives. Narrative is not the work of poets, dramatists and novelists reflecting upon events which had no narrative order before one was imposed by the singer or the writer; narrative form is neither disguise nor decoration. Barbara Hardy has written that 'we dream in narrative, daydream in narrative, remember, anticipate, hope, despair, believe, doubt, plan, revise, criticise, construct, gossip, learn, hate and love by narrative' in arguing the same point.[1]

At the beginning of this chapter I argued that in successfully identifying and understanding what someone else is doing we always move towards placing a particular episode in the context of a set of narrative histories, histories both of the individuals concerned and of the settings in which they act and suffer. It is now becoming clear that we render the actions of others intelligible in

---

[1] Barbara Hardy, "Towards a Poetics of Fiction: An Approach Through Narrative," *Novel* 2 (1968), p. 5.

this way because action itself has a basically historical character. It is because we all live our narratives in our lives and because we understand our own lives in terms of the narratives that we live out that the form of narrative is appropriate for understanding the actions of others. Stories are lived before they are told—except in the case of fiction.

This has of course been denied in recent debates. Louis O. Mink, quarrelling with Barbara Hardy's view, has asserted: 'Stories are not lived but told. Life has no beginnings, middles, or ends; there are meetings, but the start of an affair belongs to the story we tell ourselves later, and there are partings, but final partings only in the story. There are hopes, plans, battles and ideas, but only in retrospective stories are hopes unfulfilled, plans miscarried, battles decisive, and ideas seminal. Only in the story as it America which Columbus discovers and only in the story is the kingdom lost for want of a nail.'[2]

What are we to say to this? Certainly we must agree that it is only retrospectively that hopes can be characterised as unfulfilled or battles as decisive and so on. But we so characterise them in life as much as in art. And to someone who says that in life there are no endings, or that final partings take place only in stories, one is tempted to reply, 'But have you never heard of death?' Homer did not have to tell the tale of Hector before Andromache could lament unfulfilled hope and final parting. There are countless Hectors and countless Andromaches whose lives embodied the form of their Homeric namesakes, but who never came to the attention of any poet. What is true is that in taking an event as a beginning or an ending we bestow a significance upon it which may be debatable. Did the Roman republic end with the death of Julius Caesar, or at Philippi, or with the founding of the principate? The answer is surely that, like Charles II, it was a long time a-dying; but this answer implies the reality of its ending as much as do any of the former. There is a crucial sense in which the principate of Augustus, or the taking of the oath in the tennis court, or the decision to construct an atomic bomb at Los Alamos constitute beginnings, the peace of 404 B.C., the abolition of the Scottish Parliament and the battle of Waterloo equally constitute endings; while there are many events which are both endings and beginnings.

As with beginnings, middles and endings, so also with genres and with the phenomenon of embedding. Consider the question of to what genre the life of Thomas Becket belongs, a question which has to be asked and answered before we can decide how it is to be written. (On Mink's paradoxical view this question could not be asked until *after* the life had been written.) In some of the medieval versions, Thomas's career is presented in terms of the canons of medieval hagiography. In the Icelandic *Thomas Saga* he is presented as a saga hero. In Dom David Knowles's modern biography the story is a tragedy, the tragic relationship of Thomas and Henry II, each of whom satisfies Aristotle's demand that the hero be a great man with a fatal flaw. Now it clearly makes sense to ask who is right, if anyone: the monk William of Canterbury, the

---

2 Louis O. Mink, "History and Fiction as Modes of Comprehension," *New Literary History*, 1 (1970), pp. 557–58.

author of the saga, or the Cambridge Regius Professor Emeritus? The answer appears to be clearly the last. The true genre of the life is neither hagiography nor saga, but tragedy. So of such modern narrative subjects as the life of Trotsky or that of Lenin, of the history of the Soviet Communist Party or the American presidency, we may also ask: To what genre does their history belong? And this is the same question as: What type of account of their history will be both true and intelligible?

• • •

I spoke earlier of the agent as not only an actor, but an author. Now I must emphasize that what the agent is able to do and say intelligibly as an actor is deeply affected by the fact that we are never more (and sometimes less) than the co-authors of our own narratives. Only in fantasy do we live what story we please. In life, as both Aristotle and Engels noted, we are always under certain constraints. We enter upon a stage which we did not design and we find ourselves part of an action that was not of our making. Each of us being a main character in his own drama plays subordinate parts in the dramas of others, and each drama constrains the others. In my drama, perhaps, I am Hamlet or Iago or at least the swineherd who may yet become a prince, but to you I am only A Gentleman or at best Second Murderer, while you are my Polonius or my Gravedigger, but your own hero. Each of our dramas exerts constraints on each other's, making the whole different from the parts, but still dramatic.

It is considerations as complex as these which are involved in making the notion of intelligibility the conceptual connecting link between the notion of action and that of narrative. Once we have understood its importance the claim that the concept of an action is secondary to that of an intelligible action will perhaps appear less bizarre and so too will the claim that the notion of 'an' action, while of the highest practical importance, is always a potentially misleading abstraction. An action is a moment in a possible or actual history or in a number of such histories. The notion of a history is as fundamental a notion as the notion of an action. Each requires the other. . . .

A central thesis then begins to emerge: man is in his actions and practice, as well as in his fictions, essentially a story-telling animal. He is not essentially, but becomes through his history, a teller of stories that aspire to truth. But the key question for men is not about their own authorship; I can only answer the question 'What am I to do?' if I can answer the prior question 'Of what story or stories do I find myself a part?' We enter human society, that is, with one or more imputed characters—roles into which we have been drafted—and we have to learn what they are in order to be able to understand how others respond to us and how our responses to them are apt to be construed. It is through hearing stories about wicked stepmothers, lost children, good but misguided kings, wolves that suckle twin boys, youngest sons who receive no inheritance but must make their own way in the world and eldest sons who waste their inheritance on riotous living and go into exile to live with the swine, that children learn or mislearn both what a child and what a parent is, what the cast of characters may be in the drama into which they have been born and what the ways of the world are. Deprive children of stories and you leave them unscripted, anxious stutterers in their actions as in their words. Hence there is no way to give us an understanding of any society, including our own, except through the stock of stories which constitute its initial dramatic resources. Mythology, in its original sense, is at the heart of things. Vico was right and so was Joyce. And so too of course is that moral tradition from heroic society to its medieval heirs according to which the telling of stories has a key part in educating us into the virtues.

I suggested earlier that 'an' action is always an episode in a possible history: I would now like to make a related suggestion about another concept, that of personal identity. Derek Parfit and others have recently drawn our attention to the contrast between the criteria of strict identity, which is an all-or-nothing matter (*either* the Tichborne claimant *is* the last Tichborne heir; *either* all the properties of the last heir belong to the claimant *or* the claimant is not the heir—Leibniz's Law applies) and the psychological continuities of personality which are a matter of more or less. (Am I the same man at fifty as I was at forty in respect of memory, intellectual powers, critical responses? More or less.) But what is crucial to human beings as characters in enacted narratives is that, possessing only the resources of psychological continuity, we have to be able to respond to the imputation of strict identity. I am forever whatever I have been at any time for others—and I may at any time be called upon to answer for it—no matter how changed I may be now. There is no way of *founding* my identity—or lack of it—on the psychological continuity or discontinuity of the self. The self inhabits a character whose unity is given as the unity of a character. Once again there is a crucial disagreement with empiricist or analytical philosophers on the one hand and with existentialists on the other.

Empiricists, such as Locke or Hume, tried to give an account of personal identity solely in terms of psychological states or events. Analytical philosophers, in so many ways their heirs as well as their critics, have wrestled with the connection between those states and events and strict identity understood in terms of Leibniz's Law. Both have failed to see that a background has been omitted, the lack of which makes the problems insoluble. That background is provided by the concept of a story and of that kind of unity of character which a story requires. Just as a history is not a sequence of actions, but the concept of an action is that of a moment in an actual or possible history abstracted for some purpose from that history, so the characters in a history are not a collection of persons, but the concept of a person is that of a character abstracted from a history.

What the narrative concept of selfhood requires is thus twofold. On the one hand, I am what I may justifiably be taken by others to be in the course of living out a story that runs from my birth to my death; I am the *subject* of a history that is my own and no one else's, that has its own peculiar meaning. When someone complains—as do some of those who attempt or commit suicide—that his or her life is meaningless, he or she is often and perhaps characteristically complaining that the narrative of their life has become unintelligible to them, that it lacks any point, any movement towards a climax or a *telos*. Hence the point of doing any one thing rather than another at crucial junctures in their lives seems to such a person to have been lost.

To be the subject of a narrative that runs from one's birth to one's death is, I remarked earlier, to be accountable for the actions and experiences which compose a narratable life. It is, that is, to be open to being asked to give a certain kind of account of what one did or what happened to one or what one witnessed at any earlier point in one's life the time at which the question is posed. Of course someone may have forgotten or suffered brain damage or simply not attended sufficiently at the relevant times to be able to give the relevant account. But to say of someone under some one description ('The prisoner of the Chateau d'If') that he is the same person as someone character- ised quite differently ('The Count of Monte Cristo') is precisely to say that it makes sense to ask him to give an intelligible narrative account enabling us to understand how he could at different times and different places be one and the same person and yet be so differently characterised. Thus personal identity is just that identity presupposed by the unity of the character which the unity of a narrative requires. Without such unity there would not be subjects of whom stories could be told.

The other aspect of narrative selfhood is correlative: I am not only account- able, I am one who can always ask others for an account, who can put others to the question. I am part of their story, as they are part of mine. The narrative of any one life is part of an interlocking set of narratives. Moreover this asking for and giving of accounts itself plays an important part in constituting narratives. Asking you what you did and why, saying what I did and why, pondering the differences between your account of what I did and my account of what I did, and *vice versa,* these are essential constituents of all but the very simplest and barest of narratives. Thus without the accountability of the self those trains of events that constitute all but the simplest and barest of narratives could not occur; and without that same accountability narratives would lack that continuity required to make both them and the actions that constitute them intelligible.

It is important to notice that I am not arguing that the concepts of narrative or of intelligibility or of accountability are *more* fundamental than that of personal identity. The concepts of narrative, intelligibility and accountability presuppose the applicability of the concept of personal identity, just as it presupposes their applicability and just as indeed each of these three presup- poses the applicability of the two others. The relationship is one of mutual presupposition. It does follow of course that all attempts to elucidate the notion of personal identity independently of and in isolation from the notions of narrative, intelligibility and accountability are bound to fail. As all such at- tempts have.

It is now possible to return to the question from which this enquiry into the nature of human action and identity started: In what does the unity of an individual life consist? The answer is that its unity is the unity of a narrative embodied in a single life. To ask 'What is the good for me?' is to ask how best

I might live out that unity and bring it to completion. To ask 'What is the good for man?' is to ask what all answers to the former question must have in common. But now it is important to emphasise that it is the systematic asking of these two questions and the attempt to answer them in deed as well as in word which provide the moral life with its unity. The unity of a human life is the unity of a narrative quest. Quests sometimes fail, are frustrated, abandoned or dissipitated into distractions; and human lives may in all these ways also fail. But the only criteria for success or failure in a human life as a whole are the criteria of success or failure in a narrated or to-be-narrated quest. A quest for what?

Two key features of the medieval conception of a quest need to be recalled. The first is that without some at least partly determinate conception of the final *telos* there could not be any beginning to a quest. Some conception of the good for man is required. Whence is such a conception to be drawn? Precisely from those questions which led us to attempt to transcend that limited conception of the virtues which is available in and through practices. It is in looking for a conception of *the* good which will enable us to order other goods, for a conception of *the* good which will enable us to extend our understanding of the purpose and content of the virtues, or a conception of *the* good which will enable us to understand the place of integrity and constancy of life, that we initially define the kind of life which is a quest for the good. But secondly it is clear the medieval conception of a quest is not at all that of a search for something already adequately characterised, as miners search for gold or geologists for oil. It is in the course of the quest and only through encountering and coping with the various particular harms, dangers, temptations and distractions which provide any quest with its episodes and incidents that the goal of the quest is finally to be understood. A quest is always an education both as to the character of that which is sought and in self-knowledge.

The virtues therefore are to be understood as those dispositions which will not only sustain practices and enable us to achieve the goods internal to practices, but which will also sustain us in the relevant kind of quest for the good, by enabling us to overcome the harms, dangers, temptations and distractions which we encounter, and which will furnish us with increasing self-knowledge and increasing knowledge of the good. The catalogue of the virtues will therefore include the virtues required to sustain the kind of households and the kind of political communities in which men and women can seek for the good together and the virtues necessary for philosophical enquiry about the character of the good. We have then arrived at a provisional conclusion about the good life for man: the good life for man is the life spent in seeking for the good life for man, and the virtues necessary for the seeking are those which will enable us to understand what more and what else the good life for man is. We have also completed the second stage in our account of the virtues, by situating them in relation to the good life for man and not only in relation to practices. But our enquiry requires a third stage.

For I am never able to seek for the good or exercise the virtues only *qua* individual. This is partly because what it is to live the good life concretely varies from circumstance to circumstance even when it is one and the same conception of the good life and one and the same set of virtues which are being embodied in a human life. What the good life is for a fifth-century Athenian general will not be the same as what it was for a medieval nun or a seventeenth-century farmer. But it is not just that different individuals live in different social circumstances; it is also that we all approach our own circumstances as bearers of a particular social identity. I am someone's son or daughter, someone else's cousin or uncle; I am a citizen of this or that city, a member of this or that guild or profession; I belong to this clan, that tribe, this nation. Hence what is good for me has to be the good for one who inhabits these roles. As such, I inherit from the past of my family, my city, my tribe, my nation, a variety of debts, inheritances, rightful expectations and obligations. These constitute the given of my life, my moral starting point. This is in part what gives my life its own moral particularity.

This thought is likely to appear alien and even surprising from the standpoint of modern individualism. From the standpoint of individualism I am what I myself choose to be. I can always, if I wish to, put in question what are taken to be the merely contingent social features of my existence. I may biologically be my father's son; but I cannot be held responsible for what he did unless I choose implicitly or explicitly to assume such responsibility. I may legally be a citizen of a certain country; but I cannot be held responsible for what my country does or has done unless I choose implicitly or explicitly to assume such responsibility. Such individualism is expressed by those modern Americans who deny any responsibility for the effects of slavery upon black Americans, saying 'I never owned any slaves'. It is more subtly the standpoint of those other modern Americans who accept a nicely calculated responsibility for such effects measured precisely by the benefits they themselves as individuals have indirectly received from slavery. In both cases 'being an American' is not in itself taken to be part of the moral identity of the individual. And of course there is nothing peculiar to modern Americans in this attitude: the Englishman who says, 'I never did any wrong to Ireland; why bring up that old history as though it had something to do with *me?*' or the young German who believes that being born after 1945 means that what Nazis did to Jews has no moral relevance to his relationship to his Jewish contemporaries, exhibit the same attitude, that according to which the self is detachable from its social and historical roles and statuses. And the self so detached is of course a self very much at home in either Sartre's or Goffman's perspective, a self that can have no history. The contrast with the narrative view of the self is clear. For the story of my life is always embedded in those communities from which I derive my identity. I am born with a past; and to try to cut myself off from that past, in the individualist mode, is to deform my present relationships. The possession of an historical identity and the possession of a social identity coincide. Notice that rebellion against my identity is always one possible mode of expressing it.

Notice also that the fact that the self has to find its moral identity in and through its membership in communities such as those of the family, the neighbourhood, the city and the tribe does not entail that the self has to accept the moral *limitations* of the particularity of those forms of community. Without those moral particularities to begin from there would never be anywhere to begin; but it is in moving forward from such particularity that the search for the good, for the universal, consists. Yet particularity can never be simply left behind or obliterated. The notion of escaping from it into a realm of entirely universal maxims which belong to man as such, whether in its eighteenth-century Kantian form or in the presentation of some modern analytical moral philosophies, is an illusion and an illusion with painful consequences. When men and women identify what are in fact their partial and particular causes too easily and too completely with the cause of some universal principle, they usually behave worse than they would otherwise do.

What I am, therefore, is in key part what I inherit, a specific past that is present to some degree in my present. I find myself part of a history and that is generally to say, whether I like it or not, whether I recognise it or not, one of the bearers of a tradition. It was important when I characterised the concept of a practice to notice that practices always have histories and that at any given moment what a practice is depends on a mode of understanding it which has been transmitted often through many generations. And thus, insofar as the virtues sustain the relationships required for practices, they have to sustain relationships to the past—and to the future—as well as in the present. But the traditions through which particular practices are transmitted and reshaped never exist in isolation for larger social traditions. What constitutes such traditions?

We are apt to be misled here by the ideological uses to which the concept of a tradition has been put by conservative political theorists. Characteristically such theorists have followed Burke in contrasting tradition with reason and the stability of tradition with conflict. Both contrasts obfuscate. For all reasoning takes place within the context of some traditional mode of thought, transcending through criticism and invention the limitations of what had hitherto been reasoned in that tradition; this is as true of modern physics as of medieval logic. Moreover when a tradition is in good order it is always partially constituted by an argument about the goods the pursuit of which gives to that tradition its particular point and purpose.

So when an institution—a university, say, or a farm, or a hospital—is the bearer of a tradition of practice or practices, its common life will be partly, but in a centrally important way, constituted by a continuous argument as to what a university is and ought to be or what good farming is or what good medicine is. Traditions, when vital, embody continuities of conflict. Indeed when a tradition becomes Burkean, it is always dying or dead.

The individualism of modernity could of course find no use for the notion of tradition within its own conceptual scheme except as an adversary notion; it therefore all to willingly abandoned it to the Burkeans, who, faithful to Burke's own allegiance, tried to combine adherence in politics to a conception of tradition which would vindicate the oligarchical revolution of property of 1688 and adherence in economics to the doctrine and institutions of the free market. The theoretical incoherence of this mismatch did not deprive it of ideological usefulness. But the outcome has been that modern conservatives are for the most part engaged in conserving only older rather than later versions of liberal individualism. Their own core doctrine is as liberal and as individualist as that of self-avowed liberals.

A living tradition then is an historically extended, socially embodied argument, and an argument precisely in part about the goods which constitute that tradition. Within a tradition the pursuit of goods extends through generations, sometimes through many generations. Hence the individual's search for his or her good is generally and characteristically conducted within a context defined by those traditions of which the individual's life is a part, and this is true both of those goods which are internal to practices and of the goods of a single life. Once again the narrative phenomenon of embedding is crucial: the history of a practice in our time is generally and characteristically embedded in and made intelligible in terms of the larger and longer history of the tradition through which the practice in its present form was conveyed to us; the history of each of our own lives is generally and characteristically embedded in and made intelligible in terms of the larger and longer histories of a number of traditions. I have to say 'generally and characteristically' rather than 'always', for traditions decay, disintegrate and disappear. What then sustains and strengthens traditions? What weakens and destroys them?

The answer in key part is: the exercise or the lack of exercise of the relevant virtues. The virtues find their point and purpose not only in sustaining those relationships necessary if the variety of goods internal to practices are to be achieved and not only in sustaining the form of an individual life in which that individual may seek out his or her good as the good of his or her whole life, but also in sustaining those traditions which provide both practices and individual lives with their necessary historical context. Lack of justice, lack of truthfulness, lack of courage, lack of the relevant intellectual virtues—these corrupt traditions, just as they do those institutions and practices which derive their life from the traditions of which they are the contemporary embodiments. To recognise this is of course also to recognise the existence of an additional virtue, one whose importance is perhaps most obvious when it is least present, the virtue of having an adequate sense of the traditions to which one belongs or which confront one. This virtue is not to be confused with any form of conservative antiquarianism; I am not praising those who choose the conventional conservative role of *laudator temporis acti*. It is rather the case that an adequate sense of tradition manifests itself in a grasp of those future possibilities which the past has made available to the present. Living traditions, just because they continue a not-yet-completed narrative, confront a future whose determinate and determinable character, so far as it possesses any, derives from the past.

In practical reasoning the possession of this virtue is not manifested so much in the knowledge of a set of generalisations or maxims which may provide our practical inferences with major premises; its presence or absence rather appears on the kind of capacity for judgment which the agent possesses in knowing how to select among the relevant stack of maxims and how to apply them in particular situations. Cardinal Pole possessed it, Mary Tudor did not; Montrose possessed it, Charles I did not. What Cardinal Pole and the Marquis of Montrose possessed were in fact those virtues which enable their possessors to pursue both their own good and the good of the tradition of which they are the bearers even in situations defined by the necessity of tragic, dilemmatic choice. Such choices, understood in the context of the tradition of the virtues, are very different from those which face the modern adherents of rival and incommensurable moral premises in the debates about which I wrote in Chapter 2. Wherein does the difference lie?

It has often been suggested—by J. L. Austin, for example—that *either* we can admit the existence of rival and contingently incompatible goods which make incompatible claims to our practical allegiance *or* we can believe in some determinate conception of *the* good life for man, but that these are mutually exclusive alternatives. No one can consistently hold both these views. What this contention is blind to is that there may be better or worse ways for individuals to live through the tragic confrontation of good with good. And that to know what the good life for man is may require knowing what are the better and what are the worse ways of living in and through such situations. Nothing a priori rules out this possibility; and this suggests that within a view such as Austin's there is concealed an unacknowledged empirical premise about the character of tragic situations.

One way in which the choice between rival goods in a tragic situation differs from the modern choice between incommensurable moral premises is that *both* of the alternative courses of action which confront the individual have to be recognised as leading to some authentic and substantial good. By choosing one I do nothing to diminish or derogate from the claims upon me of the other; and therefore, whatever I do, I shall have left undone what I ought to have done. The tragic protagonist, unlike the moral agent as depicted by Sartre or Hare, is not choosing between allegiance to one moral principle rather than another, nor is he or she deciding upon some principle of priority between moral principles. Hence the 'ought' involved has a different meaning and force from that of the 'ought' in moral principles understood in a modern way. For the tragic protagonist cannot do everything that he or she ought to do. This 'ought', unlike Kant's, does not imply 'can'. Moreover any attempt to map the logic of such 'ought' assertions on to some modal calculus so as to produce a version of deontic logic has to fail.[3]

Yet it is clear that the moral task of the tragic protagonist may be performed better or worse, independently of the choice between alternatives that he or she makes—*ex hypothesi* he or she has no *right* choice to make. The tragic protagonist may behave heroically or unheroically, generously or ungenerously, gracefully or gracelessly, prudently or imprudently. To perform his or her task better rather than worse will be to do both what is better for him or her *qua* individual or *qua* parent or child or *qua* citizen or member of a profession, or perhaps *qua* some or all of these. The existence of tragic dilemmas casts no

---

3 See, from a very different point of view, Bas C. Van Fraasen, "Values and the Heart's Command," *The Journal of Philosophy*, 70 (1973), pp. 5–19.

doubt upon and provides no counter-examples to the thesis that assertions of the form 'To do this in this way would be better for X and/or for his or her family, city or profession' are susceptible of objective truth and falsity, any more than the existence of alternative and contingently incompatible forms of medical treatment casts doubt on the thesis that assertions of the form 'To undergo this medical treatment in this way would be better for X and/or his or her family' are susceptible of objective truth and falsity.[4]

The presupposition of this objectivity is of course that we can understand the notion of 'good for X' and cognate notions in terms of some conception of the unity of X's life. What is better or worse for X depends upon the character of that intelligible narrative which provides X's life with its unity. Unsurprisingly it is the lack of any such unifying conception of a human life which underlies modern denials of the factual character of moral judgments and more especially of those judgments which ascribe virtues or vices to individuals.

---

[4] See, from a different point of view, the illuminating discussion in Samuel Guttenplan, "Moral Realism and Moral Dilemmas," *Proceedings of the Aristotelian Society* (1979–1980), pp. 61–81.

39

Persons, Character, and Morality

BERNARD WILLIAMS

For biographical information about Bernard Williams, see reading 27.

    In this essay, taken from his collection Moral Luck, *Williams mounts an important criticism of two very familiar moral theories, utilitarianism and Kantianism. (For presentation of these theories, see readings 23 and 30.) Although the two theories differ in many respects, Williams argues that they share an overly abstract conception of the person. More particularly, they both tend to ignore the basic commitments that are central to people's characters. These commitments, or "ground projects," may range from artistic endeavors to attempts to bring social justice. They give meaning to people's lives and provide reasons for wanting to continue to live. In Williams's view, inattention to the commitments has led some utilitarians to underestimate the strength of the connections between the different stages of people's lives. In addition, inattention to the demands of personal relationships has led both utilitarians and Kantians to overestimate the force of impersonal morality. According to Williams, impartial principles provide neither the only nor the ultimate reason for acting.*

I

    Much of the most interesting recent work in moral philosophy has been of basically Kantian inspiration; Rawls' own work[1] and those to varying degrees influenced by him such as Richards[2] and Nagel[3] are very evidently in the debt of Kant, while it is interesting that a writer such as Fried[4] who gives evident signs of being pulled away from some characteristic features of this way of looking at morality nevertheless, I shall suggest later, tends to get pulled back into it. This is not of course a very pure Kantianism, and still less is it an expository or subservient one. It differs from Kant among other things in

---

1 John Rawls, *A Theory of Justice* (Oxford, 1972).

2 D. A. J. Richards, *A Theory of Reasons for Action* (Oxford, 1971).

3 Thomas Nagel, *The Possibility of Altruism* (Oxford, 1970).

4 Charles Fried, *An Anatomy of Values* (Cambridge, MA, 1970).

making no demands on a theory of noumenal freedom, and also, importantly, in admitting considerations of a general empirical character in determining fundamental moral demands, which Kant at least supposed himself not to be doing. But allowing for those and many other important differences, the inspiration is there and the similarities both significant and acknowledged. They extend far beyond the evident point that both the extent and the nature of opposition to Utilitarianism resembles Kant's: though it is interesting that in this respect they are more Kantian than a philosophy which bears an obvious but superficial formal resemblance to Kantianism, namely Hare's. Indeed, Hare now supposes that when a substantial moral theory is elicited from his philosophical premises, it turns out to be a version of Utilitarianism. This is not merely because the universal and prescriptive character of moral judgments lays on the agent, according to Hare, a requirement of hypothetical identification with each person affected by a given decision— so much is a purely Kantian element. It is rather that each identification is treated just as yielding 'acceptance' or 'rejection' of a certain prescription, and they in turn are construed solely in terms of satisfactions, so that the outputs of the various identifications can, under the usual Utilitarian assumptions, be regarded additively.

Among Kantian elements in these outlooks are, in particular, these: that the moral point of view is basically different from a non-moral, and in particular self-interested, point of view, and by a difference of kind; that the moral point of view is specially characterized by its impartiality and its indifference to any particular relations to particular persons, and that moral thought requires abstraction from particular circumstances and particular characteristics of the parties, including the agent, except in so far as these can be treated as universal features of any morally similar situation; and that the motivations of a moral agent, correspondingly, involve a rational application of impartial principle and are thus different in kind from the sorts of motivations that he might have for treating some particular persons (for instance, though not exclusively, himself) differently because he happened to have some particular interest towards them. Of course, it is not intended that these demands should exclude other and more intimate relations not prevent someone from acting in ways demanded by and appropriate to them: that is a matter of the relations of the moral point of view to other points of view. But I think it is fair to say that included among the similarities of these views to Kant's is the point that like his they do not make the question of the relations between those points of view at all easy to answer. The deeply disparate character of moral and of non-moral motivation, together with the special dignity or supremacy attached to the moral, make it very difficult to assign to those other relations and motivations the significance or structural importance in life which some of them are capable of processing.

It is worth remarking that this detachment of moral motivations and the moral point of view from the level of particular relations to particular persons, and more generally from the level of all motivations and perceptions other than those of an impartial character, obtains even when the moral point of view is itself explained in terms of the self-interest under conditions of ignorance of some abstractly conceived contracting parties, as it is by Rawls, and by Richards, who is particularly concerned with applying directly to the characterization of the moral interest, the structure used by Rawls chiefly to characterize social justice. For while the contracting parties are pictured as making some kind of self-interested or prudential choice of a set of rules, they are entirely abstract persons making this choice in ignorance of their own particular properties, tastes, and so forth; and the self-interested choice of an abstract agent is intended to model precisely the moral choice of a concrete agent, by representing what he would choose granted that he made just the kinds of abstraction from his actual personality, situation and relations which the Kantian picture of moral experience requires.

Some elements in this very general picture serve already to distinguish the outlook in question from Utilitarianism. Choices made in deliberate abstraction from empirical information which actually exists are necessarily from a Utilitarian point of view irrational, and to that extent the formal structure of the outlook, even allowing the admission of *general* empirical information, is counter-Utilitarian. There is a further point of difference with Utilitarianism, which comes out if one starts from the fact that there is one respect at least in which Utilitarianism itself requires a notable abstraction in moral thought, an abstraction which in this respect goes even further than the Kantians': if Kantianism abstracts in moral thought from the identity of persons, Utilitarianism strikingly abstracts from their separateness. This is true in more than one way. First, as the Kantian theories have themselves emphasized, persons lose their separateness as beneficiaries of the Utilitarian provisions, since in the form which maximizes total utility, and even in that which maximizes average utility, there is an agglomeration of satisfactions which is basically indifferent to the separateness of those who have the satisfactions; this is evidently so in the total maximization system, and it is only superficially not so in the average maximization system, where the agglomeration occurs before the division. Richards,[5] following Rawls, has suggested that the device of the ideal observer serves to model the agglomeration of these satisfactions: equivalent to the world could be one person, with an indefinite capacity for happiness and pain. The Kantian view stands opposed to this; the idea of the contractual element, even between these shadowy and abstract participants, is in part to make the point that there are limitations built in at the bottom to permissible trade-offs between the satisfactions of individuals.

A second aspect of the Utilitarian abstraction from separateness involves agency.[6] It turns on the point that the basic bearer of value for Utilitarianism is the *state of affairs,* and hence, when the relevant causal differences have been allowed for, it cannot make any further difference who produces a given

---

5 Richards, op. cit., p. 87 al; cf. Rawls, op. cit., p. 27; also Nagel, op. cit., p. 134. This is not the only, nor perhaps historically the soundest, interpretation of the device: cf. Derek Parfit, 'Later Selves and Moral Principles', in A. Montefiore, ed., *Philosophy and Personal Relations* (London, 1973), pp. 149–50 and nn. 30–4.

6 For a more detailed account, see 'A Critique of Utilitarianism', in J. J. C. Smart and B. Williams, *Utilitarianism: For and Against* (Cambridge, 1973).

state of affairs: if S1 consists of my doing something, together with consequences, and S2 consists of someone else doing something, with consequences,
and S2 comes about just in case S1 does not, and S1 is better than S2, then I
should bring about S1, however *prima facie* nasty S1 is. Thus, unsurprisingly,
the doctrine of negative responsibility has its roots at the foundation of Utilitarianism; and whatever projects, desires, ideals, or whatever I may have as a
particular individual, as a Utilitarian agent my action has to be the output of
all relevant causal items bearing on the situation, including all projects and
desires within causal reach, my own and others. As a Utilitarian agent, I am
just the representative of the satisfaction system who happens to be near certain
causal levers at a certain time. At this level, there is abstraction not merely
from the identity of agents, but once more, from their separateness, since a
conceivable extension or restriction of the causal powers of a given agent could
always replace the activities of some other agent, so far as Utilitarian outcomes
are concerned, and an outcome allocated to two agents as things are could
equivalently be the product of one agent, or three, under a conceivable redistribution of causal powers.

In this latter respect also the Kantian outlook can be expected to disagree.
For since we are concerned not just with outcomes, but at a basic level with
actions and policies, *who* acts in a given situation makes a difference, and in
particular I have a particular responsibility for *my* actions. Thus in more than
one way the Kantian outlook emphasizes something like the separateness of
agents, and in that sense makes less of an abstraction than Utilitarianism does
(though, as we have seen, there are other respects, with regard to causally
relevant empirical facts, in which its abstraction is greater). But now the question arises, of whether the honourable instincts of Kantianism to defend the
individuality of individuals against the agglomerative indifference of Utilitarianism can in fact be effective granted the impoverished and abstract character
of persons as moral agents which the Kantian view seems to impose. Findlay
has said 'the separateness of persons . . . is . . . the basic fact for morals',[7]
and Richards hopes to have respected that fact.[8] Similarly Rawls claims that
impartiality does not mean impersonality.[9] But it is a real question, whether
the conception of the individual provided by the Kantian theories is in fact
enough to yield what is wanted, even by the Kantians; let alone enough for
others who, while equally rejecting Utilitarianism, want to allow more room
than Kantianism can allow for the importance of individual character and
personal relations in moral experience.

II

I am going to take up two aspects of this large subject. They both involve
the idea that an individual person has a set of desires, concerns or, as I shall

---

[7] Findlay, *Values and Intentions* (London, 1961), pp. 235–36.

[8] Richards, op. cit., p. 87.

[9] Rawls, op. cit., p. 190.

often call them, projects, which help to constitute a *character*. The first issue concerns the connection between that fact and the man's having a reason for living at all. I approach this through a discussion of some work by Derek Parfit; though I touch on a variety of points in this, my overriding aim is to emphasize the basic importance for our thought of the ordinary idea of a self or person which undergoes changes of character, as opposed to an approach which, even if only metaphorically, would dissolve the person, under changes of character, into a series of 'selves'.

In this section I am concerned just with the point that each person has a character, not with the point that different people have different characters. That latter point comes more to the fore on the second issue, which I take up in part III, and which concerns personal relations. Both issues suggest that the Kantian view contains an important misrepresentation.

First, then, I should like to comment on some arguments of Parfit which explore connections between moral issues and a certain view of personal identity: a view which, he thinks, might offer, among other things, '*some* defence'[10] of the Utilitarian neglect of the separateness of persons. This view Parfit calls the 'Complex View'. This view takes seriously the idea that relations of psychological connectedness (such as memory and persistence of character and motivation) are what really matter with regard to most questions which have been discussed in relation to personal identity. The suggestion is that morality should take this seriously as well, and that there is more than one way of its doing so. Psychological connectedness (unlike the surface logic of personal identity) admits of degrees. Let us call the relevant properties and relations which admit of degrees, *scalar* items. One of Parfit's aims is to make moral thought reflect more directly the scalar character of phenomena which underlie personal identity. In particular, in those cases in which the scalar relations hold in reduced degree, this fact should receive recognition in moral thought.

Another, and more general, consequence of taking the Complex View is that the matter of personal identity may appear altogether less deep, as Parfit puts it, than if one takes the Simple View, as he calls that alternative view which sees as basically significant the all-or-nothing logic of personal identity. If the master of personal identity appears less deep, the *separateness* of persons, also, may come to seem less an ultimate and specially significant consideration for morality. The connection between those two thoughts is not direct, but there is more than one indirect connection between them.[11]

So far as the problems of *agency* are concerned, Parfit's treatment is not going to help Utilitarianism. His loosening of identity is diachronic, by reference to the weakening of psychological connectedness over time: where there is such weakening to a sufficient degree, he is prepared to speak of 'successive selves', though this is intended only as a *façon de parler*.[12] But the problems that face

10 Parfit, op. cit., p. 160, his emphasis. In what follows and elsewhere in this chapter I am grateful to Parfit for valuable criticisms of an earlier draft.

11 Parfit develops one such connection in the matter of distributive justice: pp. 148ff. In general it can be said that one very natural correlate of being impressed by the separateness of several persons' lives is being impressed by the particular unity of one person's life.

12 Ibid., n. 14, pp. 161–62.

Utilitarianism about agency can arise with any agent whose projects stretch over enough time, and are sufficiently grounded in character, to be in any substantial sense *his* projects, and that condition will be satisfied by something that is, for Parfit, even *one* self. Thus there is nothing in this degree of dissolution of the traditional self which can help over agency.

In discussing the issues involved in making moral thought reflect more directly the scalar nature of what underlies personal identity, it is important to keep in mind that the talk of 'past selves', 'future selves' and generally 'several selves' is only a convenient fiction. Neglect of this may make the transpositions in moral thought required by the Complex View seem simpler and perhaps more inviting than they are, since they may glide along on what seems to be a mere multiplication, in the case of these new 'selves', of familiar interpersonal relations. We must concentrate on the scalar facts. But many moral notions show a notable resistance to reflecting the scalar: or, rather, to reflecting it in the right way. We may take the case of promising, which Parfit has discussed.[13] Suppose that I promise to A that I will help him in certain ways in three years time. In three years time a person appears, let us say A*, whose memories, character etc., bear some, but a rather low, degree of connectedness to A's. How am I to mirror these scalar facts in my thought about whether, or how, I am to carry out my promise?

Something, first, should be said about the promise itself. '*You*' was the expression it used: 'I will help *you*', and it used that expression in such a way that it covered both the recipient of these words and the potential recipient of the help. This was not a promise that could be carried out (or, more generally, honoured) by helping anyone else, or indeed by doing anything except helping that person I addressed when I said 'you'—thus the situation is not like that with some promises to the dead (those where there is still something one can do about it).[14] If there is to be any action of mine which is to count as honouring the promise, it will have to be action which consists in now helping A*. How am I to mirror, in my action and my thought about it, A*'s scalar relations to A?

There seem to be only three ways in which they could be so mirrored, and none seems satisfactory. First, the action promised might itself have some significant scalar dimension, and it might be suggested that this should vary with my sense of the proximity or remoteness of A* from A. But this will not do: it is clearly a lunatic idea that if I promised to pay A a sum of money, then my obligation is to pay A* some money, but a smaller sum. A more serious suggestion would be that what varies with the degree of connectedness of A* to A is the degree of stringency of the obligation to do what was promised. While less evidently dotty, it is still, on reflection, dotty; thus, to take a perhaps unfair example, it seems hard to believe that if someone had promised to marry A, they would have an obligation to marry A*, only an obligation which came lower down the queue.

13 Ibid., pp. 144ff.
14 Ibid., p. 144 fin.

What, in contrast, is an entirely familiar sort of thought is, last of all, one that embodies degrees of doubt or obscurity whether a given obligation (of fixed stringency) applies or not. Thus a secret agent might think that he was obliged to kill the man in front of him if and only if that man was Martin Bormann; and be in doubt whether he should kill this man, because he was in doubt whether it was Bormann. (Contrast the two analogously dotty types of solution to this case: that, at any rate, he is obliged to wound him; or, that he is obliged to kill him, but it has a lower priority than it would have otherwise.) But this type of thought is familiar at the cost of not really embodying the scalar facts; it is a style of thought appropriate to uncertainty about a matter of all-or-nothing and so embodies in effect what Parfit calls the Simple View, that which does not take seriously the scalar facts to which the Complex View addresses itself.

These considerations do not, of course show that there are no ways of mirroring the Complex View in these areas of moral thought, but they do suggest that the displacements required are fairly radical. It is significant that by far the easiest place to which to find the influence of the scalar considerations is in certain *sentiments,* which themselves have a scalar dimension—here we can see a place where the Complex View and Utilitarianism easily fit together. But the structure of such sentiments is not adequate to produce the structure of all moral thought. The rest of it will have to be more radically adapted, or abandoned, if the Complex View is really to have its effect.

One vitally important item which is in part (though only in part) scalar is a man's concern for (what commonsense would call) his own future. That a man should have some interest now in what he will do or undergo later, requires that he have some desires or projects or concerns now which relate to those doings or happenings later; or, as a special case of that, that some very general desire or project or concern of his now relate to desires or projects which he will have then. The limiting case, at the basic physical level, is that in which he is merely concerned with future pain, and it may be that that concern can properly reach through any degree of psychological discontinuity.[15] But even if so, it is not our present concern, since the mere desire to avoid physical pain is not adequate to constitute a character. We are here concerned with more distinctive and structured patterns of desire and project, and there are possible psychological changes in these which could be predicted for a person and which would put his future after such changes beyond his present interest. Such a future would be, so to speak, over the horizon of his interest, though of course if the future picture could be filled in as a *series* of changes leading from here to there, he might recapture an interest in the outcome.

● ● ●

It might be wondered why, unless we believe in a possibly hostile after-life, or else are in a muddle which the Epicureans claimed to expose, we should

15 Cf. 'The Self and the Future', in *Problems of the Self* (Cambridge, 1973).

regard death as an evil.[16] One answer to that is that we desire certain things: if one desires something, then to that extent one has reason to resist the happening of anything which prevents one getting it, and death certainly does that, for a large range of desires. Some desires are admittedly contingent on the prospect of one's being alive, but not all desires can be in that sense conditional, since it is possible to imagine a person rationally contemplating suicide, in the face of some predicted evil, and if he decides to go on in life, then he is propelled forward into it by some desire (however general or inchoate) which cannot operate conditionally on his being alive, since it settles the question of whether he is going to be alive. Such a desire we may call a categorical desire. Most people have many categorical desires, which do not depend on the assumption of the person's existence, since they serve to prevent that assumption's being questioned, or to answer the question if it is raised. Thus one's pattern of interests, desires and projects not only provide the reason for an interest in what happens within the horizon of one's future, but also constitute the conditions of there being such a future at all.

Here, once more, to deal in terms of later selves who were like descendants would be to misplace the heart of the problem. Whether to commit suicide, and whether to leave descendants, are two separate decisions: one can produce children before committing suicide. A person might even choose deliberately to do that, for comprehensible sorts of reasons; or again one could be deterred, as by the thought that one would not be there to look after them. Later selves, however, evade all these thoughts by having the strange property that while they come into existence only with the death of their ancestor, the physical death of their ancestor will abort them entirely. The analogy seems unhelpfully strained, when we are forced to the conclusion that the failure of all my projects, and my consequent suicide, would take with me all my 'descendants', although they are in any case a kind of descendants who arise only with my ceasing to exist. More than unhelpfully, it runs together what are two quite different questions: whether my projects having failed, I should cease to exist, and whether I shall have descendants whose projects may be quite different from mine and are in any case largely unknown. The analogy makes every question of the first kind involve a question of the second kind, and thus obscures the peculiar significance of the first question to the theory of the self. If, on the other hand, a man's future self is not another self, but the future of his self, then it is unproblematic why it should be eliminated with the failure of that which might propel him into it. The primacy of one's ordinary self is given, once more, by the thought that it is precisely what will not be in the world if one commits suicide.

The language of 'later selves', too literally taken, could exaggerate in one direction the degree to which my relation to some of my own projects resembles my relation to the projects of others. The Kantian emphasis on moral impartiality exaggerates it in quite another, by providing ultimately too slim a sense in which any projects are mine at all. This point once more involves the idea that

---

16 The argument is developed in more detail in *Problems of the Self*, pp. 82ff.

my present projects are the condition of my existence,[17] in the sense that unless I am propelled forward by the conatus of desire, project and interest, it is unclear why I should go on at all: the world, certainly, as a kingdom of moral agents, has no particular claim on my presence or, indeed, interest in it. (That kingdom, like others, has to respect the natural right to emigration.) Now the categorical desires which propel one on do not have to be even very evident to consciousness, let alone grand or large; one good testimony to one's existence having a point is that the question of its point does not arise, and the propelling concerns may be of a relatively everyday kind such as certainly provide the ground of many sorts of happiness. Equally, while these projects may present *some* conflicts with the demands of morality, as Kantianly conceived, these conflicts may be fairly minor; after all—and I do not want to deny or forget it—these projects, in a normally socialized individual, have in good part been formed within, and formed by, dispositions which constitute a commitment to morality. But, on the other hand, the possibility of radical conflict is also there. A man may have, for a lot of his life or even just for some part of it, a *ground* project or set of projects which are closely related to his existence and which to a significant degree give a meaning to his life.

I do not mean by that they provide him with a life-plan, in Rawls' sense. On the contrary, Rawls' conception, and the conception of practical rationality, shared by Nagel, which goes with it, seems to me rather to imply an external view of one's own life, as something like a given rectangle that has to be optimally filled in.[18] This perspective omits the vital consideration already mentioned, that the continuation and size of this rectangle is up to me; so, slightly less drastically, is the question of how much of it I care to cultivate. The correct perspective on one's life is *from now*. The consequences of that for practical reasoning (particularly with regard to the relevance of proximity or remoteness in time of one's objective), is a large question which cannot be pursued here; here we need only the idea of a man's ground projects providing the motive force which propels him into the future, and gives him a reason for living.

For a project to play this ground role, it does not have to be true that if it were frustrated or in any of various ways he lost it, he would have to commit suicide, nor does he have to think that. Other things, or the mere hope of other things, may keep him going. But he may feel in those circumstances that he

---

17 We can note the consequence that present projects are the condition of future ones. This view stands in opposition to Nagel's: as do the formulations used above, [p. 10]. But while, as Nagel says, taking a rational interest in preparing for the realization of my later projects does not require that they be my present projects, it seems nevertheless true that it presupposes my having some present projects which directly or indirectly reach out to a time when those later projects will be my projects.

18 It is of course a separate question what the criteria of optimality are, but it is not surprising that a view which presupposes that no risks are taken with the useful area of the rectangle should also favour a very low risk strategy in filling it: cf. Rawls (on prudential rationality in general), op. cit., p. 422: 'we have the guiding principle that a rational individual is always to act so that he need never blame himself no matter how things finally transpire.' Cf. also the passages cited in Rawls' footnote. . . .

might as well have died. Of course, in general a man does not have one separable project which plays this ground role: rather, there is a nexus of projects, related to his conditions of life, and it would be the loss of all or most of them that would remove meaning.

Ground projects do not have to be selfish, in the sense that they are just concerned with things for the agent. Nor do they have to be self-centred, in the sense that the creative projects of a Romantic artist could be considered self-centred (where it has to be *him,* but not *for* him). They may certainly be altruistic, and in a very evident sense moral, projects; thus he may be working for reform, or justice, or general improvement. There is no contradiction in the idea of a man's dying for a ground project—quite the reverse, since if death really is necessary for the project, then to live would be to live with it unsatisfied, something which, if it really is his ground project, he has no reason to do.

That a man's projects were altruistic or moral would not make them immune to conflict with impartial morality, any more than the artist's projects are immune. Admittedly *some* conflicts are ruled out by the projects sincerely being *those* projects; thus a man devoted to the cause of curing injustice in a certain place, cannot just insist on his plan for doing that over others', if convinced that theirs will be as effective as his (something it may be hard to convince him of). For if he does insist on that, then we learn that his concern is not merely that injustice be removed, but that *he* remove it—not necessarily a dishonourable concern, but a different one. Thus some conflicts are ruled out by the project being not self-centred. But not all conflicts: thus his selfless concern for justice may do havoc to quite other commitments.

A man who has such a ground project will be required by Utilitarianism to give up what it requires in a given case just if that conflicts with what he is required to do as an impersonal utility-maximizer when all the causally relevant considerations are in. That is a quite absurd requirement.[19] But the Kantian, who can do rather better than that, still cannot do well enough. For impartial morality, if the conflict really does arise, must be required to win; and that cannot necessarily be a reasonable demand on the agent. There can come a point at which it is quite unreasonable for a man to give up, in the name of the impartial good ordering of the world of moral agents, something which is a condition of his having any interest in being around in that world at all. Once one thinks about what is involved in having a character, one can see that the Kantians' omission of character is a condition of their ultimate insistence on the demands of impartial morality, just as it is a reason for finding inadequate their account of the individual.

III

All this argument depends on the idea of one person's having a character, in the sense of having projects and categorical desires with which that person

---

[19] Cf. 'A Critique of Utilitarianism', sections 3–5.

is identified; nothing has yet been said about different persons having different characters. It is perhaps important, in order to avoid misunderstanding, to make clear a way in which difference of character does *not* come into the previous argument. It does not come in by way of the man's thinking that only if he affirms these projects will they be affirmed, while (by contrast) the aims of Kantian morality can be affirmed by anyone. Though that thought could be present in some cases, it is not the point of the argument. The man is not pictured as thinking that he will have earned his place in the world, if his project is affirmed: that a distinctive contribution to the world will have been made, if his distinctive project is carried forward. The point is that he wants these things, finds his life bound up with them, and that they propel him forward, and thus they give him a reason for living his life. But that is compatible with these drives, and this life, being much like others'. They give him, distinctively, a reason for living this life, in the sense that he has no desire to give up and make room for others, but they do not require him to lead a *distinctive* life. While this is so, and the point has some importance, nevertheless the interest and substance of most of the discussion depends on its in fact being the case that people have dissimilar characters and projects. Our *general* view of these matters, and the significance given to individuality in our own and others' lives, would certainly change if there were not between persons indefinitely many differences which are important to us. The level of description is of course also vital for determining what is the same or different. A similar description can be given of two people's dispositions, but the concrete detail be perceived very differently—and it is a feature of our experience of persons that we can perceive and be conscious of an indefinitely fine degree of difference in concrete detail (though it is only in certain connections and certain cultures that one spends much time rehearsing it).

One area in which *difference* of character directly plays a role in the concept of moral individuality is that of personal relations, and I shall close with some remarks in this connection. Differences of character give substance to the idea that individuals are not inter-substitutable. As I have just argued, a particular man so long as he is propelled forward does not need to assure himself that he is unlike others, in order not to feel substitutable, but in his personal relations to others the idea of difference can certainly make a contribution, in more than one way. To the thought that his friend cannot just be equivalently replaced by another friend, is added both the thought that he cannot just be replaced himself, and also the thought that he and his friend are different from each other. This last thought is important to us as part of our view of friendship, a view thus set apart from Aristotle's opinion that a good man's friend was a duplication of himself. This I suspect to have been an Aristotelian, and not generally a Greek, opinion. It is connected with another feature of his views which seems even stranger to us, at least with regard to any deeply committed friendship, namely that friendship for him has to be minimally *risky*—one of his problems is indeed to reconcile the role of friendship with his unappetizing ideal of self-sufficiency. Once one agrees that a three-dimensional mirror would not represent the ideal of friendship, one can begin to see both how some degree of difference can play an essential role, and, also, how a commitment or involvement with a particular other person might be one of the kinds of project which figured basically in a man's life in the ways already sketched— something which would be mysterious or even sinister on an Aristotelian account.

For Kantians, personal relations at least presuppose moral relations, and some are rather disposed to go further and regard them as a *species* of moral relations, as in the richly moralistic account given by Richards[20] of one of the four main principles of supererogation which would be accepted in 'the Original Position' (that is to say, adopted as a moral limitation):

> a principle of mutual love requiring that people should not show personal affection and love to others on the basis of arbitrary physical characteristics alone, but rather on the basis of traits of personality and character related to acting on moral principles.

This righteous absurdity is no doubt to be traced to a feeling that love, even love based on 'arbitrary physical characteristics', is something which has enough power and even authority to conflict badly with morality unless it can be brought within it from the beginning, and evidently that is a sound feeling, though it is an optimistic Kantian who thinks that much will be done about that by the adoption of this principle in the Original Position. The weaker view, that love and similar relations presuppose moral relations, in the sense that one could love someone only if one also had to them the moral relations one has to all people, is less absurd, but also wrong. It is of course true that loving someone involves some relations of the kind that morality requires or imports more generally, but it does not follow from that that one cannot have them in a particular case unless one has them generally in the way the moral person does. Someone might be concerned about the interests of someone else, and even about carrying out promises he made to that person, while not very concerned about these things with other persons. To the extent (whatever it may be) that loving someone involves showing some of the same concerns in relation to them that the moral person shows, or at least thinks he ought to show, elsewhere, the lover's relations will be examples of moral relations, or at least resemble them, but this does not have to be because they are *applications to this case* of relations which the lover, *qua* moral person, more generally enters into. (That might not be the best description of the situation even if he *is* a moral person who enters into such relations more generally.)

However, once morality is there, and also personal relations to be taken seriously, so is the possibility of conflict. This of course does not mean that if there is some friendship with which his life is much involved, then a man must prefer any possible demand of that over other, impartial, moral demands. That would be absurd, and also a pathological kind of friendship, since both parties exist in the world and it is part of the sense of their friendship that it exists

20 Richards, op. cit., p. 94.

in the world. But the possibility of conflict with substantial moral claims of others is there, and it is not only in the outcome. There can also be conflict with moral demands on how the outcome is arrived at: the situation may not have been subjected to an impartial process of resolution, and this fact itself may cause unease to the impartial moral consciousness. There is an example of such unease in a passage by Fried. After an illuminating discussion of the question why, if at all, we should give priority of resources to actual and present sufferers over absent or future ones, he writes:[21]

> surely it would be absurd to insist that if a man could, at no risk or cost to himself, save one or two persons in equal peril, and one of those in peril was, say, his wife, he must treat both equally, perhaps by flipping a coin. One answer is that where the potential rescuer occupies no office such as that of captain of a ship, public health official or the like, the occurrence of the accident may itself stand as a sufficient randomizing event to meet the dictates of fairness, so he may prefer his friend, or loved one. Where the rescuer does occupy an official position, the argument that he must overlook personal ties is not unacceptable.

The most striking feature of this passage is the direction in which Fried implicitly places the onus of proof: the fact that coin-flipping would be inappropriate raises some question to which an 'answer' is required, while the resolution of the question by the rescuer's occupying an official position is met with what sounds like relief (though it remains unclear what that rescuer does when he 'overlooks personal ties'—does *he* flip a coin?). The thought here seems to be that it is unfair to the second victim that, the first being the rescuer's wife, they never even get a chance of being rescued; and the answer (as I read the reference to the 'sufficient randomizing event') is that at another level it is sufficiently fair—although in this disaster this rescuer has a special reason for saving the other person, it might have been another disaster in which another rescuer had a special reason for saving them. But, apart from anything else, that 'might have been' is far too slim to sustain a reintroduction of the notion of fairness. The 'random' element in such events, as in certain events of tragedy, should be seen not so much as affording a justification, in terms of an appropriate application of a lottery, as being a reminder that some situations lie beyond justifications.

But has anything yet shown that? For even if we leave behind thoughts of higher-order randomization, surely *this* is a justification on behalf of the rescuer, that the person he chose to rescue was his wife? It depends on how much weight is carried by 'justification': the consideration that it was his wife is certainly, for instance, an explanation which should silence comment. But something more ambitious than this is usually intended, essentially involving the idea that moral principle can legitimate his preference, yielding the conclusion that in situations of this kind it is at least all right (morally permissible)

---

21 Fried, op. cit., p. 227 [Note 1981]. Fried has perhaps now modified the view criticised here. He has himself used the idea of friendship as creating special moral relations, but in a connexion where, it seems to me, it is out of place. . . .

to save one's wife. (This could be combined with a variety of higher-order thoughts to give it a rationale: rule-Utilitarians might favour the idea that in matters of this kind it is best for each to look after his own, like house insurance.) But this construction provides the agent with one thought too many: it might have been hoped by some (for instance, by his wife) that his motivating thought, fully spelled out, would be the thought that it was his wife, not that it was his wife and that in situations of this kind it is permissible to save one's wife.

Perhaps others will have other feelings about this case. But the point is that somewhere (and if not in this case, where?) one reaches the necessity that such things as deep attachments to other persons will express themselves in the world in ways which cannot at the same time embody the impartial view, and that they also run the risk of offending against it.

They run that risk if they exist at all; yet unless such things exist, there will not be enough substance or conviction in a man's life to compel his allegiance to life itself. Life has to have substance if anything is to have sense, including adherence to the impartial system; but if it has substance, then it cannot grant supreme importance to the impartial system, and that system's hold on it will be, at the limit, insecure.

It follows that moral philosophy's habit, particularly in its Kantian forms, of treating persons in abstraction from character is not so much a legitimate device for dealing with one aspect of thought, but is rather a misrepresentation, since it leaves out what both limits and helps to define that aspect of thought. Nor can it be judged solely as a theoretical device: this is one of the areas in which one's conception of the self, and of oneself, most importantly meet.

40

Moral Saints

SUSAN WOLF*

*Susan Wolf (b. 1952) is Professor of Philosophy at the University of
Maryland. She is the author of* Freedom Within Reason. *This selection first
appeared in* The Journal of Philosophy *(August 1979).*

*In the selection, Wolf asks whether moral perfection is a desirable ideal
toward which to strive. Although many would answer affirmatively, Wolf
does not agree. Instead, she contends that a perfectly moral person—a
"moral saint"—would be deficient in important ways. Such a person would
be bland and uninteresting. More importantly, being always committed to
furthering the good of others, this person could not be deeply interested in
intellectual inquiry, sports, art, or the other activities that enrich human
life. If one is wholeheartedly committed to some such activity, one cannot
be fully responsive to the needs of others. Thus, we must choose between
moral and nonmoral ideals.*

*This may not seem surprising. It has always been clear that being moral
requires restrictions on self-interested action. But Wolf's insight is that it
requires more. The moral person must forego aspects of life that are of
genuine value, even apart from the perspective of the agent. Moreover,
Wolf argues that this problem is raised not only by the inchoate moral
ideals of common sense, but also by such more formal theories as
utilitarianism and Kantianism. Like Bernard Williams (reading 39), she
denies that morality is the highest source of ideals or reasons for acting.
But if morality does not dominate, then neither do ideals of personal
perfection. At some point, we must "raise normative questions from a
perspective that is unattached to a commitment to any particular well-
ordered system of values."*

I don't know whether there are any moral saints. But if there are, I
am glad that neither I nor those about whom I care most are among them. By
moral saint I mean a person whose every action is as morally good as possible,
a person, that is, who is as morally worthy as can be. Though I shall in a
moment acknowledge the variety of types of person that might be thought

* I have benefited from the comments of many people who have heard or read an earlier draft
of this paper. I wish particularly to thank Douglas MacLean, Robert Nozick, Martha Nussbaum,
and the Society for Ethics and Legal Philosophy.

to satisfy this description, it seems to me that none of these types serve as unequivocally compelling personal ideals. In other words, I believe that moral perfection, in the sense of moral saintliness, does not constitute a model of personal well-being toward which it would be particularly rational or good or desirable for a human being to strive.

Outside the context of moral discussion, this will strike many as an obvious point. But, within that context, the point, if it be granted, will be granted with some discomfort. For within that context it is generally assumed that one ought to be as morally good as possible and that what limits there are to morality's hold on us are set by features of human nature of which we ought not to be proud. If, as I believe, the ideals that are derivable from common sense and philosophically popular moral theories do not support these assumptions, then something has to change. Either we must change our moral theories in ways that will make them yield more palatable ideals, or, as I shall argue, we must change our conception of what is involved in affirming a moral theory.

In this paper, I wish to examine the notion of a moral saint, first, to understand what a moral saint would be like and why such a being would be unattractive, and second, to raise some questions about the significance of this paradoxical figure for moral philosophy. I shall look first at the model(s) of moral sainthood that might be extrapolated from the morality or moralities of common sense. Then I shall consider what relations these have to conclusions that can be drawn from utilitarian and Kantian moral theories. Finally, I shall speculate on the implications of these considerations for moral philosophy.

MORAL SAINTS AND COMMON SENSE

Consider first what, pretheoretically, would count for us—contemporary members of Western culture—as a moral saint. A necessary condition of moral sainthood would be that one's life be dominated by a commitment to improving the welfare of others or of society as a whole. As to what role this commitment must play in the individual's motivational system, two contrasting accounts suggest themselves to me which might equally be thought to qualify a person for moral sainthood.

First, a moral saint might be someone whose concern for others plays the role that is played in most of our lives by more selfish, or, at any rate, less morally worthy concerns. For the moral saint, the promotion of the welfare of others might play the role that is played for most of us by the enjoyment of material comforts, the opportunity to engage in the intellectual and physical activities of our choice, and the love, respect, and companionship of people whom we love, respect, and enjoy. The happiness of the moral saint, then, would truly lie in the happiness of others, and so he would devote himself to others gladly, and with a whole and open heart.

On the other hand, a moral saint might be someone for whom the basic ingredients of happiness are not unlike those of most of the rest of us. What makes him a moral saint is rather that he pays little or no attention to his own happiness in light of the overriding importance he gives to the wider concerns of morality. In other words, this person sacrifices his own interests to the interests of others, and feels the sacrifice as such.

Roughly, these two models may be distinguished according to whether one thinks of the moral saint as being a saint out of love or one thinks of the moral saint as being a saint out of duty (or some other intellectual appreciation and recognition of moral principles). We may refer to the first model as the model of the Loving Saint; to the second, as the model of the Rational Saint.

The two models differ considerably with respect to the qualities of the motives of the individuals who conform to them. But this difference would have limited effect on the saints' respective public personalities. The shared content of what these individuals are motivated to be—namely, as morally good as possible—would play the dominant role in the determination of their characters. Of course, just as a variety of large-scale projects, from tending the sick to political campaigning, may be equally and maximally morally worthy, so a variety of characters are compatible with the ideal of moral sainthood. One moral saint may be more or less jovial, more or less garrulous, more or less athletic than another. But above all, a moral saint must have and cultivate those qualities which are apt to allow him to treat others as justly and kindly as possible. He will have the standard moral virtues to a nonstandard degree. He will be patient, considerate, even-tempered, hospitable, charitable in thought as well as in deed. He will be very reluctant to make negative judgments of other people. He will be careful not to favor some people over others on the basis of properties they could not help but have.

Perhaps what I have already said is enough to make some people begin to regard the absence of moral saints in their lives as a blessing. For there comes a point in the listing of virtues that a moral saint is likely to have where one might naturally begin to wonder whether the moral saint isn't after all, too good—if not too good for his own good, at least too good for his own well-being. For the moral virtues, given that they are, by hypothesis, *all* present in the same individual, and to an extreme degree, are apt to crowd out the non-moral virtues, as well as many of the interests and personal characteristics that we generally think contribute to a healthy, well-rounded, richly developed character.

In other words, if the moral saint is devoting all his time to feeding the hungry or healing the sick or raising money for Oxfam, then necessarily he is not reading Victorian novels, playing the oboe, or improving his backhand. Although no one of the interests or tastes in the category containing these latter activities could be claimed to be a necessary element in a life well lived, a life in which *none* of these possible aspects of character are developed may seem to be a life strangely barren.

The reasons why a moral saint cannot, in general, encourage the discovery and development of significant nonmoral interests and skills are not logical but practical reasons. There are, in addition, a class of nonmoral characteristics that a moral saint cannot encourage in himself for reasons that are not just practical. There is a more substantial tension between having any of these qualities unashamedly and being a moral saint. These qualities might be described as going against the moral grain. For example, a cynical or sarcastic wit, or a sense of humor that appreciates this kind of wit in others, requires that one take an attitude of resignation and pessimism toward the flaws and vices to be found in the world. A moral saint, on the other hand, has reason to take an attitude in opposition to this—he should try to look for the best in people, give them the benefit of the doubt as long as possible, try to improve regrettable situations as long as there is any hope of success. This suggests that, although a moral saint might well enjoy a good episode of *Father Knows Best,* he may not in good conscience be able to laugh at a Marx Brothers movie or enjoy a play by George Bernard Shaw.

An interest in something like gourmet cooking will be, for different reasons, difficult for a moral saint to rest easy with. For it seems to me that no plausible argument can justify the use of human resources involved in producing a *paté de canard en croute* against possible alternative beneficent ends to which these resources might be put. If there is a justification for the institution of haute cuisine, it is one which rests on the decision *not* to justify every activity against morally beneficial alternatives, and this is a decision a moral saint will never make. Presumably, an interest in high fashion or interior design will face much the same, as will, very possibly, a cultivation of the finer arts as well.

A moral saint will have to be very, very nice. It is important that he may not be offensive. The worry is that, as a result, he will have to be dull-witted or humorless or bland.

This worry is confirmed when we consider what sorts of characters, taken and refined both from life and from fiction, typically form our ideals. One would hope they would be figures who are morally good—and by this I mean more than just not morally bad—but one would hope, too, that they are not *just* morally good, but talented or accomplished or attractive in nonmoral ways as well. We may make ideals out of athletes, scholars, artists—more frivolously, out of cowboys, private eyes, and rock stars. We may strive for Katharine Hepburn's grace, Paul Newman's "cool"; we are attracted to the high-spirited passionate nature of Natasha Rostov; we admire the keen perceptiveness of Lambert Strether. Though there is certainly nothing immoral about the ideal characters or traits I have in mind, they cannot be superimposed upon the ideal of a moral saint. For although it is a part of many of these ideals that the characters set high, and not merely acceptable, moral standards for themselves, it is also essential to their power and attractiveness that the moral strengths go, so to speak, alongside of specific independently admirable, nonmoral ground projects and dominant personal traits.

When one does finally turn one's eyes toward lives that are dominated by explicitly moral commitments, moreover, one finds oneself relieved at the discovery of idiosyncrasies or eccentricities not quite in line with the picture of moral perfection. One prefers the blunt, tactless, and opinionated Betsy Trotwood to the unfailingly kind and patient Agnes Copperfield; one prefers the mischievousness and the sense of irony in Chesterton's Father Brown to the innocence and undiscriminating love of St. Francis.

It seems that, as we look in our ideals for people who achieve nonmoral varieties of personal excellence in conjunction with or colored by some version of high moral tone, we look in our paragons of moral excellence for people whose moral achievements occur in conjunction with or colored by some interests or traits that have low moral tone. In other words, there seems to be a limit on how much morality we can stand.

One might suspect that the essence of the problem is simply that there is a limit to how much of *any* single value, or any single type of value, we can stand. Our objection then would not be specific to a life in which one's dominant concern is morality, but would apply to any life that can be so completely characterized by an extraordinarily dominant concern. The objection in that case would reduce to the recognition that such a life is incompatible with well-roundedness. If that were the objection, one could fairly reply that well-roundedness is no more supreme a virtue than the totality of moral virtues embodied by the ideal it is being used to criticize. But I think this misidentifies the objection. For the way in which a concern for morality may dominate a life, or, more to the point, the way in which it may dominate an ideal of life, is not easily imagined by analogy to the dominance an aspiration to become an Olympic swimmer or a concert pianist might have.

A person who is passionately committed to one of these latter concerns might decide that her attachment to it is strong enough to be worth the sacrifice of her ability to maintain and pursue a significant portion of what else life might offer which a proper devotion of her dominant passion would require. But a desire to be as morally good as possible is not likely to take the form of one desire among others which, because of its peculiar psychological strength, requires one to forego the pursuit of other weaker and separately less demanding desires. Rather, the desire to be as morally good as possible is apt to have the character not just of a stronger, but of a higher desire, which does not merely successfully compete with one's other desires but which rather subsumes or demotes them. The sacrifice of other interests for the interest in morality, then, will have the character, not of a choice, but of an imperative.

Moreover, there is something odd about the idea of morality itself, or moral goodness, serving as the object of a dominant passion in the way that a more concrete and specific vision of a goal (even a concrete *moral* goal) might be imagined to serve. Morality itself does not seem to be a suitable object of passion. Thus, when one reflects, for example, on the Loving Saint easily and gladly giving up his fishing trip or his stereo or his hot fudge sundae at the drop of the moral hat, one is apt to wonder not at how much he loves morality, but at how little he loves these other things. One thinks that, if he can give these up so easily, he does not know what it *is* to truly love them. There seems, in other words, to be a kind of joy which the Loving Saint, either by nature or by practice, is incapable of experiencing. The Rational Saint, on the other hand, might retain strong nonmoral and concrete desires—he simply denies himself the opportunity to act on them. But this is no less troubling. The Loving Saint one might suspect of missing a piece of perceptual machinery, of being blind to some of what the world has to offer. The Rational Saint, who sees it but forgoes it, one suspects of having a different problem—a pathological fear of damnation, perhaps, or an extreme form of self-hatred that interferes with his ability to enjoy the enjoyable in life.

In other words, the ideal of a life of moral sainthood disturbs not simply because it is an ideal of a life in which morality unduly dominates. The normal person's direct and specific desires for objects, activities, and events that conflict with the attainment of moral perfection are not simply sacrificed but removed, suppressed, or subsumed. The way in which morality, unlike other possible goals, is apt to dominate is particularly disturbing, for it seems to require either the lack or the denial of the existence of an identifiable, personal self.

This distinctively troubling feature is not, I think, absolutely unique to the ideal of the moral saint, as I have been using that phrase. It is shared by the conception of the pure aesthete, by a certain kind of religious ideal, and, somewhat paradoxically, by the model of the thorough-going self-conscious egoist. It is not a coincidence that the ways of comprehending the world of which these ideals are the extreme embodiments are sometimes described as "moralities" themselves. At any rate, they compete with what we ordinarily mean by 'morality'. Nor is it a coincidence that these ideals are naturally described as fanatical. But it is easy to see that these other types of perfection cannot serve as satisfactory personal ideals; for the realization of these ideals would be straightforwardly immoral. It may come as a surprise to some that there may in addition be such a thing as a *moral* fanatic.

Some will object that I am being unfair to "common-sense morality"—that it does not really require a moral saint to be either a disgusting goody-goody or an obsessive ascetic. Admittedly, there is no logical inconsistency between having any of the personal characteristics I have mentioned and being a moral saint. It is not morally wrong to notice the faults and shortcomings of others or to recognize and appreciate nonmoral talents and skills. Nor is it immoral to be an avid Celtics fan or to have a passion for caviar or to be an excellent cellist. With enough imagination, we can always contrive a suitable history and set of circumstances that will embrace such characteristics in one or another specific fictional story of a perfect moral saint.

If one turned onto the path of moral sainthood relatively late in life, one may have already developed interests that can be turned to moral purposes. It may be that a good golf game is just what is needed to secure that big donation to Oxfam. Perhaps the cultivation of one's exceptional artistic talent will turn out to be the way one can make one's greatest contribution to society. Furthermore, one might stumble upon joys and skills in the very service of morality. If, because the children are short a ninth player for the team, one's generous offer to serve reveals a natural fielding arm or if one's part in the campaign against nuclear power requires accepting a lobbyist's invitation to lunch et Le Lion d'Or, there is no moral gain in denying the satisfaction one gets from these activities. The moral saint, then, may, by happy accident, find himself with nonmoral virtues on which he can capitalize morally or which make psychological demands to which he has no choice but to attend. The point is that, for a moral saint, the existence of these interests and skills can be given at best the status of happy accidents—they cannot be encouraged for their own sakes as distinct, independent aspects of the realization of human good.

It must be remembered that from the fact that there is a tension between having any of these qualities and being a moral saint it does not follow that having any of these qualities is immoral. For it is not part of common-sense morality that one ought to be a moral saint. Still, if someone just happened to want to be a moral saint, he or she would not have or encourage these qualities, and, on the basis of our common-sense values, this counts as a reason *not* to want to be a moral saint.

One might still wonder what kind of reason this is, and what kind of conclusion this properly allows us to draw. For the fact that the models of moral saints are unattractive does not necessarily mean that they are unsuitable ideals. Perhaps they are unattractive because they make us feel uncomfortable— they highlight our own weaknesses, vices, and flaws. If so, the fault lies not in the characters of the saints, but in those of our unsaintly selves.

To be sure, some of the reasons behind the disaffection we feel for the model of moral sainthood have to do with a reluctance to criticize ourselves and a reluctance to committing ourselves to trying to give up activities and interests that we heartily enjoy. These considerations might provide an *excuse* for the fact that we are not moral saints, but they do not provide a basis for criticizing sainthood as a possible ideal. Since these considerations rely on an appeal to the egoistic, hedonistic side of our natures, to use them as a basis for criticizing the ideal of the moral saint would be at best to beg the question and at worst to glorify features of ourselves that ought to be condemned.

The fact that the moral saint would be without qualities which we have and which, indeed, we like to have, does not in itself provide reason to condemn the ideal of the moral saint. The fact that some of these qualities are good qualities, however, and that they are qualities we *ought* to like, does provide reason to discourage this ideal and to offer other ideals in its place. In other words, some of the qualities the moral saint necessarily lacks are virtues, albeit nonmoral virtues, in the unsaintly characters who have them. The feats of Groucho Marx, Reggie Jackson, and the head chef at *Lutèce* are impressive accomplishments that it is not only permissible but positively appropriate to recognize as such. In general, the admiration of and striving toward achieving any of a great variety of forms of personal excellence are character traits it is valuable and desirable for people to have. In advocating the development of these varieties of excellence, we advocate nonmoral reasons for acting, and in thinking that it is good for a person to strive for an ideal that gives a substantial role to the interests and values that correspond to these virtues, we implicitly acknowledge the goodness of ideals incompatible with that of the moral saint. Finally, if we think that it is *as* good, or even better for a person to strive for one of these ideals than it is for him or her to strive for and realize the ideal of the moral saint, we express a conviction that it is good not to be a moral saint.

MORAL SAINTS AND MORAL THEORIES

I have tried so far to paint a picture—or rather, two pictures—of what a moral saint might be like, drawing on what I take to be the attitudes and beliefs about morality prevalent in contemporary, common-sense thought. To my suggestion that common-sense morality generates conceptions of moral saints that are unattractive or otherwise unacceptable, it is open to someone to reply, "so much the worse for common-sense morality." After all, it is often claimed that the goal of moral philosophy is to correct and improve upon common-sense morality, and I have as yet given no attention to the question of what conceptions of moral sainthood, if any, are generated from the leading moral theories of our time.

A quick, breezy reading of utilitarian and Kantian writings will suggest the images, respectively, of the Loving Saint and the Rational Saint. A utilitarian, with his emphasis on happiness, will certainly prefer the Loving Saint to the Rational one, since the Loving Saint will himself be a happier person than the Rational Saint. A Kantian, with his emphasis on reason, on the other hand, will find at least as much to praise in the latter as in the former. Still, both models, drawn as they are from common sense, appeal to an impure mixture of utilitarian and Kantian intuitions. A more careful examination of these moral theories raises questions about whether either model of moral sainthood would really be advocated by a believer in the explicit doctrines associated with either of these views.

Certainly, the utilitarian in no way denies the value of self-realization. He in no way disparages the development of interests, talents, and other personally attractive traits that I have claimed the moral saint would be without. Indeed, since just these features enhance the happiness both of the individuals who possess them and of those with whom they associate, the ability to promote these features both in oneself and in others will have considerable positive weight in utilitarian calculations.

This implies that the utilitarian would not support moral sainthood as a universal ideal. A world in which everyone, or even a large number of people, achieved moral sainthood—even a world in which they *strove* to achieve it— would probably contain less happiness than a world in which people realized a diversity of ideals involving a variety of personal and perfectionist values. More pragmatic considerations also suggest that, if the utilitarian wants to influence more people to achieve more good, then he would do better to encourage them to pursue happiness-producing goals that are more attractive and more within a normal person's reach.

These considerations still leave open, however, the question of what kind of an ideal the committed utilitarian should privately aspire to himself. Utilitarianism requires him to want to achieve the greatest general happiness, and this would seem to commit him to the ideal of the moral saint.

One might try to use the claims I made earlier as a basis for an argument that a utilitarian should choose to give up utilitarianism. If, as I have said, a moral saint would be a less happy person both to be and to be around than many other possible ideals, perhaps one could create more total happiness by not trying too hard to promote the total happiness. But this argument is simply unconvincing in light of the empirical circumstances of our world. The gain in happiness that would accrue to oneself and one's neighbors by a more well-rounded, richer life than that of the moral saint would be pathetically small in comparison to the amount by which one could increase the general happiness if one devoted oneself explicitly to the care of the sick, the downtrodden, the starving, and the homeless. Of course, there may be psychological limits to the extent to which a person can devote himself to such things without going crazy. But the utilitarian's individual limitations would not thereby become a positive feature of his personal ideals.

The unattractiveness of the moral saint, then, ought not rationally convince the utilitarian to abandon his utilitarianism. It may, however, convince him to take efforts not to wear his saintly moral aspirations on his sleeve. If it is not too difficult, the utilitarian will try not to make those around him uncomfortable. He will not want to appear "holier than thou"; he will not want to inhibit others' ability to enjoy themselves. In practice, this might make the perfect utilitarian a less nauseating companion than the moral saint I earlier portrayed. But insofar as this kind of reasoning produces a more bearable public personality, it is at the cost of giving him a personality that must be evaluated as hypocritical and condescending when his private thoughts and attitudes are taken into account.

Still, the criticisms I have raised against the saint of common-sense morality should make some difference to the utilitarian's conception of an ideal which neither requires him to abandon his utilitarian principles nor forces him to fake an interest he does not have or a judgment he does not make. For it may be that a limited and carefully monitored allotment of time and energy to be devoted to the pursuit of some nonmoral interests or to the development of some nonmoral talents would make a person a better contributor to the general welfare than he would be if he allowed himself no indulgences of this sort. The enjoyment of such activities in no way compromises a commitment to utilitarian principles as long as the involvement with these activities is conditioned by a willingness to give them up whenever it is recognized that they cease to be in the general interest.

This will go some way in mitigating the picture of the loving saint that an understanding of utilitarianism will on first impression suggest. But I think it will not go very far. For the limitations on time and energy will have to be rather severe, and the need to monitor will restrict not only the extent but also the quality of one's attachment to these interests and traits. They are only weak and somewhat peculiar sorts of passions to which one can consciously remain so conditionally committed. Moreover, the way in which the utilitarian can enjoy these "extra-curricular" aspects of his life is simply not the way in which these aspects are to be enjoyed insofar as they figure into our less saintly ideals.

The problem is not exactly that the utilitarian values these aspects of his life only as a means to an end, for the enjoyment he and others get from these aspects are not a means to, but a part of, the general happiness. Nonetheless, he values these things only because of and insofar as they *are* a part of the general happiness. He values them, as it were, under the description 'a contribution to the general happiness'. This is to be contrasted with the various ways in which these aspects of life may be valued by nonutilitarians. A person might love literature because of the insights into human nature literature affords. Another might love the cultivation of roses because roses are things of great beauty and delicacy. It may be true that these features of the respective activities also explain why these activities are happiness-producing. But, to the nonutilitarian, this may not be to the point. For if one values these activities in these more direct ways, one may not be willing to exchange them for others that produce an equal, or even a greater amount of happiness. From that point of view, it is not because they produce happiness that these activities are valuable; it is because these activities are valuable in more direct and specific ways that they produce happiness.

To adopt a phrase of Bernard Williams', the utilitarian's manner of valuing the not explicitly moral aspects of his life "provides (him) with one thought too many".[1] The requirement that the utilitarian have this thought—periodically, at least—is indicative of not only a weakness but a shallowness in his appreciation of the aspects in question. Thus, the ideals toward which a utilitarian could acceptably strive would remain too close to the model of the common-sense moral saint to escape the criticisms of that model which I earlier suggested. Whether a Kantian would be similarly committed to so restrictive and unattractive a range of possible ideals is a somewhat more difficult question.

The Kantian believes that being morally worthy consists in always acting from maxims that one could will to be universal law, and doing this not out of any pathological desire but out of reverence for the moral law as such. Or, to take a different formulation of the categorical imperative, the Kantian believes that moral action consists in treating other persons always as ends and never as means only. Presumably, and according to Kant himself, the Kantian thereby commits himself to some degree of benevolence as well as to the rules of fair play. But we surely would not will that *every* person become a moral saint, and treating others as ends hardly requires bending over backwards to protect and promote their interests. On one interpretation of Kantian doctrine, then, moral perfection would be achieved simply by unerring obedience to a limited set of side-constraints. On this interpretation, Kantian theory simply does not yield an ideal conception of a person of any fullness comparable to that of the moral saints I have so far been portraying.

On the other hand, Kant does say explicitly that we have a duty of benevolence, a duty not only to allow others to pursue their ends, but to take up their ends as our own. In addition, we have positive duties to ourselves, duties to increase our natural as well as our moral perfection. These duties are unlimited in the degree to which they *may* dominate a life. If action in accordance with

---

1 "Persons, Character and Morality" in Amelie Rorty, ed., *The Identities of Persons* (Berkeley: Univ. of California Press, 1976), p. 214.

and motivated by the thought of these duties is considered virtuous, it is natural to assume that the more one performs such actions, the more virtuous one is. Moreover, of virtue in general Kant says, "it is an ideal which is unattainable while yet our duty is constantly to approximate to it".[2] On this interpretation, then, the Kantian moral saint, like the other moral saints I have been considering, is dominated by the motivation to be moral.

Which of these interpretations of Kant one prefers will depend on the interpretation and the importance one gives to the role of the imperfect duties in Kant's over-all system. Rather than choose between them here, I shall consider each briefly in turn.

On the second interpretation of Kant, the Kantian moral saint is, not surprisingly, subject to many of the same objections I have been raising against other versions of moral sainthood. Though the Kantian saint may differ from the utilitarian saint as to *which* actions he is bound to perform and which he is bound to refrain from performing, I suspect that the range of activities acceptable to the Kantian saint will remain objectionably restrictive. Moreover, the manner in which the Kantian saint must think about and justify the activities he pursues and the character traits he develops will strike us, as it did with the utilitarian saint, as containing "one thought too many." As the utilitarian could value his activities and character traits only insofar as they fell under the description of 'contributions to the general happiness', the Kantian would have to value his activities and character traits insofar as they were manifestations of respect for the moral law. If the development of our powers to achieve physical, intellectual, or artistic excellence, or the activities directed toward making others happy are to have any moral worth, they must arise from a reverence for the dignity that members of our species have as a result of being endowed with pure practical reason. This is a good and noble motivation, to be sure. But it is hardly what one expects to be dominantly behind a person's aspirations to dance as well as Fred Astaire, to paint as well as Picasso, or to solve some outstanding problem in abstract algebra, and it is hardly what one hopes to find lying dominantly behind a father's action on behalf of his son or a lover's on behalf of her beloved.

Since the basic problem with any of the models of moral sainthood we have been considering is that they are dominated by a single, all-important value under which all other possible values must be subsumed, it may seem that the alternative interpretation of Kant, as providing a stringent but finite set of obligations and constraints, might provide a more acceptable morality. According to this interpretation of Kant, one is as morally good as can be so long as one devotes some limited portion of one's energies toward altruism and the maintenance of one's physical and spiritual health, and otherwise pursues one's independently motivated interests and values in such a way as to avoid overstepping certain bounds. Certainly, if it be a requirement of an acceptable moral theory that perfect obedience to its laws and maximal devotion to its

---

2 Immanuel Kant, *The Doctrine of Virtue*, Mary J. Gregor, trans. (New York: Harper & Row, 1964), p. 71.

interests and concerns be something we can wholeheartedly strive for in ourselves and wish for in those around us, it will count in favor of this brand of Kantianism that its commands can be fulfilled without swallowing up the perfect moral agent's entire personality.

Even this more limited understanding of morality, if its connection to Kant's views is to be taken at all seriously, is not likely to give an unqualified seal of approval to the nonmorally directed ideals I have been advocating. For Kant is explicit about what he calls "duties of apathy and self-mastery" (69/70)— duties to ensure that our passions are never so strong as to interfere with calm, practical deliberation, or so deep as to wrest control from the more disinterested, rational part of ourselves. The tight and self-conscious rein we are thus obliged to keep on our commitments to specific individuals and causes will doubtless restrict our value in these things, assigning them a necessarily attenuated place.

A more interesting objection to this brand of Kantianism, however, comes when we consider the implications of placing the kind of upper bound on moral worthiness which seemed to count in favor of this conception of morality. For to put such a limit on one's capacity to be moral is effectively to deny, not just the moral necessity, but the moral goodness of a devotion to benevolence and the maintenance of justice that passes beyond a certain, required point. It is to deny the possibility of going morally above and beyond the call of a restricted set of duties. Despite my claim that all-consuming moral saintliness is not a particularly healthy and desirable ideal, it seems perverse to insist that, were moral saints to exist, they would not, in their way, be remarkably noble and admirable figures. Despite my conviction that it is as rational and as good for a person to take Katharine Hepburn or Jane Austen as her role model instead of Mother Theresa, it would be absurd to deny that Mother Theresa is a morally better person.

I can think of two ways of viewing morality as having an upper bound. First, we can think that altruism and impartiality are indeed positive moral interests, but that they are moral only if the degree to which these interests are actively pursued remains within certain fixed limits. Second, we can think that these positive interests are only incidentally related to morality and that the essence of morality lies elsewhere, in, say, an implicit social contract or in the recognition of our own dignified rationality. According to the first conception of morality, there is a cut-off line to the amount of altruism or to the extent of devotion to justice and fairness that is worthy of moral praise. But to draw this line earlier than the line that brings the altruist in question to a worse-off position than all those to whom he devotes himself seems unacceptably artificial and gratuitous. According to the second conception, these positive interests are not essentially related to morality at all. But then we are unable to regard a more affectionate and generous expression of good will toward others as a natural and reasonable extension of morality, and we encourage a cold and unduly self-centered approach to the development and evaluation of our motivations and concerns.

A moral theory that does not contain the seeds of an all-consuming ideal of moral sainthood thus seems to place false and unnatural limits on our opportunity to do moral good and our potential to deserve moral praise. Yet the main thrust of the arguments of this paper has been leading to the conclusion that when such ideals are present, they are not ideals to which it is particularly reasonable or healthy or desirable for human beings to aspire. These claims, taken together, have the appearance of a dilemma from which there is no obvious escape. In a moment, I shall argue that, despite appearances, these claims should not be understood as constituting a dilemma. But, before I do, let me briefly describe another path which those who are convinced by my above remarks may feel inclined to take.

If the above remarks are understood to be implicitly critical of the views on the content of morality which seem more popular today, an alternative that naturally suggests itself is that we revise our views about the content of morality. More specifically, my remarks may be taken to support a more Aristotelian, or even a more Nietzschean, approach to moral philosophy. Such a change in approach involves substantially broadening or replacing our contemporary intuitions about which character traits constitute moral virtues and vices and which interests constitute moral interests. If, for example, we include personal bearing, or creativity, or sense of style, as features that contribute to one's *moral* personality, then we can create moral ideals which are incompatible with and probably more attractive than the Kantian and utilitarian ideals I have discussed. Given such an alteration of our conception of morality, the figures with which I have been concerned above might, far from being considered to be moral saints, be seen as morally inferior to other more appealing or more interesting models of individuals.

This approach seems unlikely to succeed, if for no other reason, because it is doubtful that any single, or even any reasonably small number of substantial personal ideals could capture the full range of possible ways of realizing human potential or achieving human good which deserve encouragement and praise. Even if we could provide a sufficiently broad characterization of the range of positive ways for human beings to live, however, I think there are strong reasons not to want to incorporate such a characterization more centrally into the framework of morality itself. For, in claiming that a character trait or activity is morally good, one claims that there is a certain kind of reason for developing that trait or engaging in that activity. Yet, lying behind our criticism of more conventional conceptions of moral sainthood, there seems to be a recognition that among the immensely valuable traits and activities that a human life might positively embrace are some of which we hope that, if a person does embrace them, he does so *not* for moral reasons. In other words, no matter how flexible we make the guide to conduct which we choose to label "morality," no matter how rich we make the life in which perfect obedience to this guide would result, we will have reason to hope that a person does not wholly rule and direct his life by the abstract and impersonal consideration that such a life would be morally good.

Once it is recognized that morality itself should not serve as a comprehensive guide to conduct, moreover, we can see reasons to retain the admittedly vague contemporary intuitions about what the classification of moral and nonmoral virtues, interests, and the like should be. That is, there seem to be important differences between the aspects of a person's life which are currently considered appropriate objects of moral evaluation and the aspects that might be included under the altered conception of morality we are now considering, which the latter approach would tend wrongly to blur or to neglect. Moral evaluation now is focused primarily on features of a person's life over which that person has control; it is largely restricted to aspects of his life which are likely to have considerable effect on other people. These restrictions seem as they should be. Even if responsible people could reach agreement as to what constituted good taste or a healthy degree of well-roundedness, for example, it seems wrong to insist that everyone try to achieve these things or to blame someone who fails or refuses to conform.

If we are not to respond to the unattractiveness of the moral ideals that contemporary theories yield either by offering alternative theories with more palatable ideals or by understanding these theories in such a way as to prevent them from yielding ideals at all, how, then, are we to respond? Simply, I think, by admitting that moral ideals do not, and need not, make the best personal ideals. Earlier, I mentioned one of the consequences of regarding as a test of an adequate moral theory that perfect obedience to its laws and maximal devotion to its interests be something we can wholeheartedly strive for in ourselves and wish for in those around us. Drawing out the consequences somewhat further should, I think, make us more doubtful of the proposed test than of the theories which, on this test, would fail. Given the empirical circumstances of our world, it seems to be an ethical fact that we have unlimited potential to be morally good, and endless opportunity to promote moral interests. But this is not incompatible with the not-so-ethical fact that we have sound, compelling, and not particularly selfish reasons to choose or to devote ourselves univocally to realizing this potential or to taking up this opportunity.

Thus, in one sense at least, I am not really criticizing either Kantianism or utilitarianism. Insofar as the point of view I am offering bears directly on recent work in moral philosophy, in fact, it bears on critics of these theories who, in a spirit not unlike the spirit of most of this paper, point out that the perfect utilitarian would be flawed in this way or the perfect Kantian flawed in that.[3] The assumption lying behind these claims, implicitly or explicitly, has been that the recognition of these flaws shows us something wrong with utilitarianism, as opposed to Kantianism, or something wrong with Kantianism as opposed to utilitarianism, or something wrong with both of these theories as opposed to some nameless third alternative. The claims of this paper suggest, however,

---

[3] See, e.g., Williams, op. cit. and J. J. C. Smart and Bernard Williams, *Utilitarianism: For and Against* (New York: Cambridge, 1973). Also, Michael Stocker, "The Schizophrenia of Modern Ethical Theories," *The Journal of Philosophy*, LXIII, 14 (Aug. 12, 1976): 453–466.

that this assumption is unwarranted. The flaws of a perfect master of a moral theory need not reflect flaws in the intramoral content of the theory itself.

MORAL SAINTS AND MORAL PHILOSOPHY

In pointing out the regrettable features and the necessary absence of some desirable features in a moral saint, I have not meant to condemn the moral saint or the person who aspires to become one. Rather, I have meant to insist that the ideal of moral sainthood should not be held as a standard against which any other ideal must be judged or justified, and that the posture we take in response to the recognition that our lives are not as morally good as they might be need not be defensive.[4] It is misleading to insist that one is *permitted* to live a life in which the goals, relationships, activities, and interests that one pursues are not maximally morally good. For our lives are not so comprehensively subject to the requirement that we apply for permission, and our nonmoral reasons for the goals we set ourselves are not excuses, but may rather be positive, good reasons which do not exist *despite* any reasons that might threaten to outweigh them. In other words, a person may be *perfectly wonderful* without being *perfectly moral*.

Recognizing this requires a perspective which contemporary moral philosophy has generally ignored. This perspective yields judgments of a type that is neither moral nor egoistic. Like moral judgments, judgments about what it would be good for a person to be are made from a point of view outside the limits set by the values, interests, and desires that the person might actually have. And, like moral judgments, these judgments claim for themselves a kind of objectivity or a grounding in a perspective which any rational and perceptive being can take up. Unlike moral judgments, however, the good with which these judgments are concerned is not the good of anyone or any group other than the individual himself.

Nonetheless, it would be equally misleading to say that these judgments are made for the sake of the individual himself. For these judgments are not concerned with what kind of life it is in a person's interest to lead, but with what kind of interests it would be good for a person to have, and it need not be in a person's interest that he acquire or maintain objectively good interests. Indeed, the model of the Loving Saint, whose interests are identified with the interests of morality, is a model of a person for whom the dictates of rational self-interest and the dictates of morality coincide. Yet, I have urged that we

4 George Orwell makes a similar point in "Reflections on Gandhi," in *A Collection of Essays by George Orwell* (New York: Harcourt Brace Jovanovich, 1945), p. 176: "sainthood is . . . a thing that human beings must avoid. . . . It is too readily assumed that . . . the ordinary man only rejects it because it is too difficult; in other words, that the average human being is a failed saint. It is doubtful whether this is true. Many people genuinely do not wish to be saints, and it is probable that some who achieve or aspire to sainthood have never felt much temptation to be human beings."

have reason not to aspire to this ideal and that some of us would have reason to be sorry if our children aspired to and achieved it.

The moral point of view, we might say, is the point of view one takes up insofar as one takes the recognition of the fact that one is just one person among others equally real and deserving of the good things in life as a fact with practical consequences, a fact the recognition of which demands expression in one's actions and in the form of one's practical deliberations. Competing moral theories offer alternative answers to the question of what the most correct or the best way to express this fact is. In doing so, they offer alternative ways to evaluate and to compare the variety of actions, states of affairs, and so on that appear good and bad to agents from other, nonmoral points of view. But it seems that alternative interpretations of the moral point of view do not exhaust the ways in which our actions, characters, and their consequences can be comprehensively and objectively evaluated. Let us call the point of view from which we consider what kinds of lives are good lives, and what kinds of persons it would be good for ourselves and others to be, the *point of view of individual perfection.*

Since either point of view provides a way of comprehensively evaluating a person's life, each point of view takes account of, and, in a sense, subsumes the other. From the moral point of view, the perfection of an individual life will have some, but limited, value—for each individual remains, after all, just one person among others. From the perfectionist point of view, the moral worth of an individual's relation to his world will likewise have some, but limited, value—for, as I have argued, the (perfectionist) goodness of an individual's life does not vary proportionally with the degree to which it exemplifies moral goodness.

It may not be the case that the perfectionist point of view is like the moral point of view in being a point of view we are ever *obliged* to take up and express in our actions. Nonetheless, it provides us with reasons that are independent of moral reasons for wanting ourselves and others to develop our characters and live our lives in certain ways. When we take up this point of view and ask how much it would be good for an individual to act from the moral point of view, we do not find an obvious answer.[5]

The considerations of this paper suggest, at any rate, that the answer is not "as much as possible." This has implications both for the continued development of moral theories and for the development of metamoral views and for our conception of moral philosophy more generally. From the moral point of view, we have reasons to want people to live lives that seem good from outside that point of view. If, as I have argued, this means that we have reason to

---

5 A similar view, which has strongly influenced mine, is expressed by Thomas Nagel in "The Fragmentation of Value," in *Mortal Questions* (New York: Cambridge, 1979), pp. 128–141. Nagel focuses on the difficulties such apparently incommensurable points of view create for specific, isolable practical decisions that must be made both by individuals and by societies. In focusing on the way in which these points of view figure into the development of individual personal ideals, the questions with which I am concerned are more likely to lurk in the background of any individual's life.

want people to live lives that are not morally perfect, then any plausible moral theory must make use of some conception of supererogation.[6]

If moral philosophers are to address themselves at the most basic level to the question of how people should live, however, they must do more than adjust the content of their moral theories in ways that leave room for the affirmation of nonmoral values. They must examine explicitly the range and nature of these nonmoral values, and, in light of this examination, they must ask how the acceptance of a moral theory is to be understood and acted upon. For the claims of this paper do not so much conflict with the content of any particular currently popular moral theory as they call into question a metamoral assumption that implicitly surrounds discussions of moral theory more generally. Specifically, they call into question the assumption that it is always better to be morally better.

The role morality plays in the development of our characters and the shape of our practical deliberations need be neither that of a universal medium into which all other values must be translated nor that of an ever-present filter through which all other values must pass. This is not to say that moral value should not be an important, even the most important, kind of value we attend to in evaluating and improving ourselves and our world. It is to say that our values cannot be fully comprehended on the model of a hierarchical system with morality at the top.

The philosophical temperament will naturally incline, at this point, toward asking, "What, then, *is* at the top—or, if there is no top, how *are* we to decide when and how much to be moral?" In other words, there is a temptation to seek a metamoral—though not, in the standard sense, metaethical—theory that will give us principles, or, at least, informal directives on the basis of which we can develop and evaluate more comprehensive personal ideals. Perhaps a theory that distinguishes among the various roles a person is expected to play within a life—as professional, as citizen, as friend, and so on—might give us some rules that would offer us, if nothing else, a better framework in which to think about and discuss these questions. I am pessimistic, however, about the chances of such a theory to yield substantial and satisfying results. For I do not see how a metamoral theory could be constructed which would not be subject to considerations parallel to those which seem inherently to limit the appropriateness of regarding moral theories as ultimate comprehensive guides for action.

6 The variety of forms that a conception of supererogation might take, however, has not generally been noticed. Moral theories that make use of this notion typically do so by identifying some specific set of principles as universal moral requirements and supplement this list with a further set of directives which it is morally praiseworthy but not required for an agent to follow. [See, e.g., Charles Fried, *Right and Wrong* (Cambridge, MA: Harvard, 1979).] But it is possible that the ability to live a morally blameless life cannot be so easily or definitely secured as this type of theory would suggest. The fact that there are some situations in which an agent is morally required to do something and other situations in which it would be good but not required for an agent to do something does not imply that there are specific principles such that, in any situation, an agent is required to act in accordance with these principles and other specific principles such that, in any situation, it would be good but not required for an agent to act in accordance with those principles.

This suggests that, at some point, both in our philosophizing and in our lives, we must be willing to raise normative questions from a perspective that is unattached to a commitment to any particular well-ordered system of values. It must be admitted that, in doing so, we run the risk of finding normative answers that diverge from the answers given by whatever moral theory one accepts. This, I take it, is the grain of truth in G. E. Moore's "open question" argument. In the background of this paper, then, there lurks a commitment to what seems to me to be a healthy form of intuitionism. It is a form of intuitionism which is not intended to take the place of more rigorous, systematically developed, moral theories—rather, it is intended to put these more rigorous and systematic moral theories in their place.

41

In a Different Voice

CAROL GILLIGAN

Carol Gilligan (b. 1936) is Professor of Education at Harvard University. She has done groundbreaking work on the moral development of women. This selection is from her book In a Different Voice, *chapters 1 and 2.*

In the selection, Gilligan argues that women and men approach morality very differently. Men generally think in terms of fairness, rights, and abstract principles, whereas women emphasize responsibility for others and bonds of affection and care. These differences, Gilligan suggests, show that it is a mistake to equate moral development with progress toward a sense of abstract fairness. Another equally valid model stresses increased responsiveness to the needs of others and sensitivity to competing claims. Although Gilligan is a psychologist, her work has also been influential among philosophers: Following her lead, some recent theorists have elaborated a moral theory built on the notions of care and responsibility to others.

"It is obvious," Virginia Woolf says, "that the values of women differ very often from the values which have been made by the other sex."[1] Yet, she adds, "it is the masculine values that prevail." As a result, women come to question the normality of their feelings and to alter their judgments in deference to the opinion of others. In the nineteenth century novels written by women, Woolf sees at work "a mind which was slightly pulled from the straight and made to alter its clear vision in deference to external authority." The same deference to the values and opinions of others can be seen in the judgments of twentieth century women. The difficulty women experience in finding or speaking publicly in their own voices emerges repeatedly in the form of qualification and self-doubt, but also in intimations of a divided judgment, a public assessment and private assessment which are fundamentally at odds.

Yet the deference and confusion that Woolf criticizes in women derive from the values she sees as their strength. Women's deference is rooted not only in their social subordination but also in the substance of their moral concern. Sensitivity to the needs of others and the assumption of responsibility for taking care lead women to attend to voices other than their own and to include in

---

1 Virginia Woolf, *A Room of One's Own* (New York: Harcourt, Bruce and World, 1929), p. 76.

their judgment other points of view. Women's moral weakness, manifest in an apparent diffusion and confusion of judgment, is thus inseparable from women's moral strength, an overriding concern with relationships and responsibilities. The reluctance to judge may itself be indicative of the care and concern for others that infuse the psychology of women's development and are responsible for what is generally seen as problematic in its nature.

Thus women not only define themselves in a context of human relationship but also judge themselves in terms of their ability to care. Women's place in man's life cycle has been that of nurturer, caretaker, and helpmaker, the weaver of those networks of relationships on which she in turn relies. But while women have thus taken care of men, men have, in their theories of psychological development, as in their economic arrangements, tended to assume or devalue that care. When the focus on individuation and individual achievement extends into adulthood and maturity is equated with personal autonomy, concern with relationships appears as a weakness of women rather than as a human strength.

The discrepancy between womanhood and adulthood is nowhere more evident than in the studies on sex-role stereotypes reported by Broverman, Vogel, Broverman, Clarkson, and Rosenkrantz. The repeated finding of these studies is that the qualities deemed necessary for adulthood—the capacity for autonomous thinking, clear decision-making, and responsible action—are those associated with masculinity and considered undesirable as attributes of the feminine self. The stereotypes suggest a splitting of love and work that relegates expressive capacities to women while placing instrumental abilities in the masculine domain. Yet looked at from a different perspective, these stereotypes reflect a conception of adulthood that is itself out of balance, favoring the separateness of the individual self over connection to others, and leaning more toward an autonomous life of work than toward the interdependence of love and care.

The discovery now being celebrated by men in mid-life of the importance of intimacy, relationships, and care is something that women have known from the beginning. However, because that knowledge in women has been considered "intuitive" or "instinctive," a function of anatomy coupled with destiny, psychologists have neglected to describe its development. In my research, I have found that women's moral development centers on the elaboration of that knowledge and thus delineates a critical line of psychological development in the lives of both of the sexes. The subject of moral development not only provides the final illustration of the reiterative pattern in the observation and assessment of sex differences in the literature on human development, but also indicates more particularly why the nature and significance of women's development has been for so long obscured and shrouded in mystery.

The criticism that Freud makes of women's sense of justice, seeing it as compromised in its refusal of blind impartiality, reappears not only in the work of Piaget but also in that of Kohlberg. While in Piaget's account of the moral judgment of the child, girls are an aside, a curiosity to whom he devotes four brief entries in an index that omits "boys" altogether because "the child" is assumed to be male, in the research from which Kohlberg derives his theory, females simply do not exist. Kohlberg's six stages that describe the development of moral judgment from childhood to adulthood are based empirically on a study of eighty-four boys whose development Kohlberg has followed for a period of over twenty years. Although Kohlberg claims universality for his stage sequence, those groups not included in his original sample rarely reach his higher stages. Prominent among those who thus appear to be deficient in moral development when measured by Kohlberg's scale are women, whose judgments seem to exemplify the third stage of his six-stage sequence. At this stage morality is conceived in interpersonal terms and goodness is equated with helping and pleasing others. This conception of goodness is considered by Kohlberg and Kramer to be functional in the lives of mature women insofar as their lives take place in the home. Kohlberg and Kramer imply that only if women enter the traditional arena of male activity will they recognize the inadequacy of this moral perspective and progress like men toward higher stages where relationships are subordinated to rules (stage four) and rules to universal principles of justice (stages five and six).

Yet herein lies a paradox, for the very traits that traditionally have defined the "goodness" of women, their care for and sensitivity to the needs of others, are those that mark them as deficient in moral development. In this version of moral development, however, the conception of maturity is derived from the study of men's lives and reflects the importance of individuation in their development. Piaget, challenging the common impression that a developmental theory is built like a pyramid from its base in infancy, points out that a conception of development instead hangs from its vertex of maturity, the point toward which progress is traced. Thus, a change in the definition of maturity does not simply alter the description of the highest stage but recasts the understanding of development, changing the entire account.

When one begins with the study of women and derives developmental constructs from their lives, the outline of a moral conception different from that described by Freud, Piaget, or Kohlberg begins to emerge and informs a different description of development. In this conception, the moral problem arises from conflicting responsibilities rather than from competing rights and requires for its resolution a mode of thinking that is contextual and narrative rather than formal and abstract. This conception of morality as concerned with the activity of care centers moral development around the understanding of responsibility and relationships, just as the conception of morality as fairness ties moral development to the understanding of rights and rules.

This different construction of the moral problem by women may be seen as the critical reason for their failure to develop within the constraints of Kohlberg's system. Regarding all constructions of responsibility as evidence of a conventional moral understanding, Kohlberg defines the highest stages of moral development as deriving from a reflective understanding of human rights. That the morality of rights differs from the morality of responsibility in its emphasis on separation rather than connection, in its consideration of the

individual rather than the relationship as primary, is illustrated by two responses to interview questions about the nature of morality. The first comes
from a twenty-five-year-old man, one of the participants in Kohlberg's study:

> [*What does the word morality mean to you?*] Nobody in the world knows the
> answer. I think it is recognizing the right of the individual, the rights of other
> individuals, not interfering with those rights. Act as fairly as you would have
> them treat you. I think it is basically to preserve the human being's right to
> existence. I think that is the most important. Secondly, the human being's right
> to do as he pleases, again without interfering with somebody else's rights.

> [*How have your views on morality changed since the last interview?*] I think I
> am more aware of an individual's rights now. I used to be looking at it strictly
> from my point of view, just for me. Now I think I am more aware of what the
> individual has a right to.

Kohlberg cites this man's response as illustrative of the principled conception
of human rights that exemplifies his fifth and sixth stages. Commenting on the
response, Kohlberg says: "Moving to a perspective outside of that of his society,
he identifies morality with justice (fairness, rights, the Golden Rule), with
recognition of the rights of others as these are defined naturally or intrinsically.
The human being's right to do as he pleases without interfering with somebody
else's rights is a formula defining rights prior to social legislation."[2]

The second response comes from a woman who participated in the rights
and responsibilities study. She also was twenty-five and, at the time, a third-
year law student.

> [*Is there really some correct solution to moral problems, or is everybody's opinion
> equally right?*] No, I don't think everybody's opinion is equally right. I think that
> in some situations there may be opinions that are equally valid, and one could
> conscientiously adopt one of several courses of action. But there are other situa-
> tions in which I think there are right and wrong answers, that sort of inhere in
> the nature of existence, of all individuals here who need to live with each other
> to live. We need to depend on each other, and hopefully it is not only a physical
> need but a need of fulfillment in ourselves, that a person's life is enriched by
> cooperating with other people and striving to live in harmony with everybody
> else, and to that end, there are right and wrong, there are things which promote
> that end and that move away from it, and in that way it is possible to choose in
> certain cases among different courses of action that obviously promote or harm
> that goal.

> [*Is there a time in the past when you would have thought about these things
> differently?*] Oh, yeah, I think that I went through a time when I thought that
> things were pretty relative, that I can't tell you what to do and you can't tell me
> what to do, because you've got your conscience and I've got mine.

2 Lawrence Kohlberg, "Continuities and Discontinuities in Childhood and Adult Moral Development Revisited," in *Collected Papers on Moral Development and Moral Education* (Cambridge,
MA: Moral Education Research Foundation, Harvard University, 1973), pp. 29–30.

[*When was that?*] When I was in high school. I guess that it just sort of dawned on me that my own ideas changed, and because my own judgment changed, I felt I couldn't judge another person's judgment. But now I think even when it is only the person himself who is going to be affected, I say it is wrong to the extent it doesn't cohere with what I know about human nature and what I know about you, and just from what I think is true about the operation of the universe, I could say I think you are making a mistake.

[*What led you to change, do you think?*] Just seeing more of life, just recognizing that there are an awful lot of things that are common among people. There are certain things that you come to learn promote a better life and better relationships and more personal fulfillment than other things that in general tend to do the opposite, and the things that promote these things, you would call morally right.

This response also represents a personal reconstruction of morality following a period of questioning and doubt, but the reconstruction of moral understanding is based not on the primacy and universality of individual rights, but rather on what she describes as a "very strong sense of being responsible to the world." Within this construction, the moral dilemma changes from how to exercise one's rights without interfering with the rights of others to how "to lead a moral life which includes obligations to myself and my family and people in general." The problem then becomes one of limiting responsibilities without abandoning moral concern. When asked to describe herself, this woman says that she values "having other people that I am tied to, and also having people that I am responsible to. I have a very strong sense of being responsible to the world, that I can't just live for my enjoyment, but just the fact of being in the world gives me an obligation to do what I can to make the world a better place to live in, no matter how small a scale that may be on." Thus while Kohlberg's subject worries about people interfering with each other's rights, this woman worries about "the possibility of omission, of your not helping others when you could help them."

The issue that this woman raises is addressed by Jane Loevinger's fifth "autonomous" stage of ego development, where autonomy, placed in a context of relationships, is defined as modulating an excessive sense of responsibility through the recognition that other people have responsibility for their own destiny. The autonomous stage in Loevinger's account witnesses a relinquishing of moral dichotomies and their replacement with "a feeling for the complexity and multifaceted character of real people and real situations."[3] Whereas the rights conception of morality that informs Kohlberg's principled level (stages five and six) is geared to arriving at an objectively fair or just resolution to moral dilemmas upon which all rational persons could agree, the responsibility conception focuses instead on the limitations of any particular resolution and describes the conflicts that remain.

Thus it becomes clear why a morality of rights and noninterference may appear frightening to women in its potential justification of indifference and

---

3 Jane Loevinger and Ruth Wessler, *Measuring Ego Development* (San Francisco: Jossey-Bass, 1970), p. 6.

unconcern. At the same time, it becomes clear why, from a male perspective, a morality of responsibility appears inconclusive and diffuse, given its insistent contextual relativism. Women's moral judgments thus elucidate the pattern observed in the description of the developmental differences between the sexes, but they also provide an alternative conception of maturity by which these differences can be assessed and their implications traced. The psychology of women that has consistently been described as distinctive in its greater orientation toward relationships and interdependence implies a more contextual model of judgment and a different moral understanding. Given the differences in women's conceptions of self and morality, women bring to the life cycle a different point of view and order human experience in terms of different priorities.

● ● ●

In 1914, with his essay "On Narcissism," Freud swallows his distaste at the thought of "abandoning observation for barren theoretical controversy" and extends his map of the psychological domain. Tracing the development of the capacity to love, which he equates with maturity and psychic health, he locates its origins in the contrast between love for the mother and love for the self. But in thus dividing the world of love into narcissism and "object" relationships, he finds that while men's development becomes clearer, women's becomes increasingly opaque. The problem arises because the contrast between mother and self yields two different images of relationships. Relying on the imagery of men's lives in charting the course of human growth, Freud is unable to trace in women the development of relationships, morality, or a clear sense of self. This difficulty in fitting the logic of his theory to women's experience leads him in the end to set women apart, marking their relationships, like their sexual life, as "a 'dark continent' for psychology."

Thus the problem of interpretation that shadows the understanding of women's development arises from the differences observed in their experience of relationships. To Freud, though living surrounded by women and otherwise seeing so much and so well, women's relationships seemed increasingly mysterious, difficult to discern, and hard to describe. While this mystery indicates how theory can blind observation, it also suggests that development in women is masked by a particular conception of human relationships. Since the imagery of relationships shapes the narrative of human development the inclusion of women, by changing that imagery, implies a change in the entire account.

The shift in imagery that creates the problem in interpreting women's development is elucidated by the moral judgments of two eleven-year-old children, a boy and a girl, who see, in the same dilemma, two very different moral problems. While current theory brightly illuminates the line and the logic of the boy's thought, it casts scant light on that of the girl. The choice of a girl whose moral judgments elude existing categories of developmental assessment is meant to highlight the issue of interpretation rather than to exemplify sex differences per se. Adding a new line of interpretation, based on the imagery of the girl's thought, makes it possible not only to see development where previously development was not discerned but also to consider differences in the understanding of relationships without scaling these differences from better to worse.

The two children were in the same sixth-grade class at school and were participants in the rights and responsibilities study, designed to explore different conceptions of morality and self. The sample selected for this study was chosen to focus the variables of gender and age while maximizing developmental potential by holding constant, at a high level, the factors of intelligence, education, and social class that have been associated with moral development, at least as measured by existing scales. The two children in question, Amy and Jake, were both bright and articulate and, at least in their eleven-year-old aspirations, resisted easy categories of sex-role stereotyping, since Amy aspired to become a scientist while Jake preferred English to math. Yet their moral judgments seemed initially to confirm familiar notions about differences between the sexes, suggesting that the edge girls have on moral development during the early school years gives way at puberty with the ascendance of formal logical thought in boys.

The dilemma that these eleven-year-olds were asked to resolve was one in the series devised by Kohlberg to measure moral development in adolescence by presenting a conflict between moral norms and exploring the logic of its resolution. In this particular dilemma, a man named Heinz considers whether or not to steal a drug, which he cannot afford to buy in order to save the life of his wife. In the standard format of Kohlberg's interviewing procedure, the description of the dilemma itself—Heinz's predicament, the wife's disease, the druggist's refusal to lower his price—is followed by the question, "Should Heinz steal the drug?" The reasons for and against stealing are then explored through a series of questions that vary and extend the parameters of the dilemma in a way designed to reveal the underlying structure of moral thought.

Jake, at eleven, is clear from the outset that Heinz should steal the drug. Constructing the dilemma, as Kohlberg did, as a conflict between the values of property and life, he discerns the logical priority of life and uses that logic to justify his choice:

> For one thing, a human life is worth more than money, and if the druggist only makes $1,000, he is still going to live, but if Heinz doesn't steal the drug, his wife is going to die. (*Why is life worth more than money?*) Because the druggist can get a thousand dollars later from rich people with cancer, but Heinz can't get his wife again. (*Why not?*) Because people are all different and so you couldn't get Heinz's wife again.

Asked whether Heinz should steal the drug if he does not love his wife, Jake replies that he should, saying that not only is there "a difference between hating and killing," but also, if Heinz were caught, "the judge would probably think it was the right thing to do." Asked about the fact that, in stealing, Heinz would be breaking the law, he says that "the laws have mistakes, and you can't go writing up a law for everything that you can imagine."

Thus, while taking the law into account and recognizing its function in maintaining social order (the judge, Jake says, "should give Heinz the lightest possible sentence"), he also sees the law as man-made and therefore subject to error and change. Yet his judgment that Heinz should steal the drug, like his view of the law as having mistakes, rests on the assumption of agreement, a societal consensus around moral values that allows one to know and expect others to recognize what is "the right thing to do."

Fascinated by the power of logic, this eleven-year-old boy locates truth in math, which, he says, is "the only thing that is totally logical." Considering the moral dilemma to be "sort of like a math problem with humans," he sets it up as an equation and proceeds to work out the solution. Since his solution is rationally derived, he assumes that anyone following reason would arrive at the same conclusion and thus that a judge would also consider stealing to be the right thing for Heinz to do. Yet he is also aware of the limits of logic. Asked whether there is a right answer to moral problems, Jake replied that "there can only be right and wrong in judgment," since the parameters of action are variable and complex. Illustrating how actions undertaken with the best of intentions can eventuate in the most disastrous of consequences, he says, "like if you give an old lady your seat on the trolley, if you are in a trolley crash and that seat goes through the window, it might be that reason that the old lady dies."

Theories of developmental psychology illuminate well the position of this child, standing at the juncture of childhood and adolescence, at what Piaget describes as the pinnacle of childhood intelligence, and beginning through thought to discover a wider universe of possibility. The moment of preadolescence is caught by the conjunction of formal operational thought with a description of self still anchored in the factual parameters of his childhood world—his age, his town, his father's occupation, the substance of his likes, dislikes, and beliefs. Yet as his self-description radiates the self-confidence of a child who has arrived, in Erikson's terms, at a favorable balance of industry over inferiority—competent, sure of himself, and knowing well the rules of the game—so his emergent capacity for formal thought, his ability to think about thinking and to reason things out in a logical way, frees him from dependence on authority and allows him to find solutions to problems by himself.

This emergent autonomy follows the trajectory that Kohlberg's six stages of moral development trace, a three-level progression from an egocentric understanding of fairness based on individual need (stages one and two), to a conception of fairness anchored in the shared conventions of societal agreement (stages three and four), and finally to a principled understanding of fairness that rests on the free-standing logic of equality and reciprocity (stages five and six). While the boy's judgments at eleven are scored as conventional on Kohlberg's scale, a mixture of stages three and four, his ability to bring deductive logic to bear on the solution of moral dilemmas, to differentiate morality from law, and to see how laws can be considered to have mistakes points toward the principled conception of justice that Kohlberg equates with moral maturity.

In contrast, Amy's response to the dilemma conveys a very different impression, an image of development stunted by a failure of logic, an inability to think for herself. Asked if Heinz should steal the drug, she replies in a way that seems evasive and unsure:

> Well, I don't think so. I think there might be other ways besides stealing it, like if he could borrow the money or make a loan or something, but he really shouldn't steal the drug—but his wife shouldn't die either.

Asked why he should not steal the drug, she considers neither property nor law but rather the effect that theft could have on the relationship between Heinz and his wife:

> If he stole the drug, he might save his wife then, but if he did, he might have to go to jail, and then his wife might get sicker again, and he couldn't get more of the drug, and it might not be good. So, they should really just talk it out and find some other way to make the money.

Seeing in the dilemma not a math problem with humans but a narrative of relationships that extends over time, Amy envisions the wife's continuing need for her husband and the husband's continuing concern for his wife and seeks to respond to the druggist's need in a way that would sustain rather than sever connection. Just as she ties the wife's survival to the preservation of relationships, so she considers the value of the wife's life in a context of relationships, saying that it would be wrong to let her die because, "if she died, it hurts a lot of people and it hurts her." Since Amy's moral judgment is grounded in the belief that, "if somebody has something that would keep somebody alive, then it's not right not to give it to them," she considers the problem in the dilemma to arise not from the druggist's assertion of rights but from his failure of response.

As the interviewer proceeds with the series of questions that follow from Kohlberg's construction of the dilemma, Amy's answers remain essentially unchanged, the various probes serving neither to elucidate nor to modify her initial response. Whether or not Heinz loves his wife, he still shouldn't steal or let her die; if it were a stranger dying instead, Amy says that "if the stranger didn't have anybody near or anyone she knew," then Heinz should try to save her life, but he should not steal the drug. But as the interviewer conveys through the repetition of questions that the answers she gave were not heard or not right, Amy's confidence begins to diminish, and her replies become more constrained and unsure. Asked again why Heinz should not steal the drug, she simply repeats, "Because it's not right." Asked again to explain why, she states again that theft would not be a good solution, adding lamely, "if he took it, he might not know how to give it to his wife, and so his wife might still die." Failing to see the dilemma as a self-contained problem in moral logic, she does not discern the internal structure of its resolution; as she constructs the problem differently herself, Kohlberg's conception completely evades her.

Instead, seeing a world comprised of relationships rather than of people standing alone, a world that coheres through human connection rather than through systems of rules, she finds the puzzle in the dilemma to lie in the failure of the druggist to respond to the wife. Saying that "it is not right for someone to die when their life could be saved," she assumes that if the druggist were to see the consequences of his refusal to lower his price, he would realize that "he should just give it to the wife and then have the husband pay back the money later." Thus she considers the solution to the dilemma to lie in making the wife's condition more salient to the druggist or, that failing, in appealing to others who are in a position to help.

Just as Jake is confident the judge would agree that stealing is the right thing for Heinz to do, so Amy is confident that, "if Heinz and the druggest had talked it out long enough, they could reach something besides stealing." As he considers the law to "have mistakes," so she sees this drama as a mistake, believing that "the world should just share things more and then people wouldn't have to steal." Both children thus recognize the need for agreement but see it as mediated in different ways—he impersonally through systems of logic and law, she personally through communication in relationship. Just as he relies on the conventions of logic to deduce the solution to this dilemma, assuming these conventions to be shared, so she relies on a process of communication, assuming connection and believing that her voice will be heard. Yet while his assumptions about agreement are confirmed by the convergence in logic between his answers and the questions posed, her assumptions are belied by the failure of communication, the interviewer's inability to understand her response.

Although the frustration of the interview with Amy is apparent in the repetition of questions and its ultimate circularity, the problem of interpretation is focused by the assessment of her response. When considered in the light of Kohlberg's definition of the stages and sequences of moral development, her moral judgments appear to be a full stage lower in maturity than those of the boy. Scored as a mixture of stages two and three, her responses seem to reveal a feeling of powerlessness in the world, an inability to think systematically about the concepts of morality or law, a reluctance to challenge authority or to examine the logic of received moral truths, a failure even to conceive of acting directly to save a life or to consider that such action, if taken, could possibly have an effect. As her reliance on relationships seems to reveal a continuing dependence and vulnerability, so her belief in communication as the mode through which to resolve moral dilemmas appears naive and cognitively immature.

Yet Amy's description of herself conveys a markedly different impression. Once again, the hallmarks of the preadolescent child depict a child secure in her sense of herself, confident in the substance of her beliefs, and sure of her ability to do something of value in the world. Describing herself at eleven as "growing and changing," she says that she "sees some things differently now, just because I know myself really well now, and I know a lot more about the world." Yet the world she knows is a different world from that refracted by Kohlberg's construction of Heinz's dilemma. Her world is a world of relationships and psychological truths where an awareness of the connection between people gives rise to a recognition of responsibility for one another, a perception of the need for response. Seen in this light, her understanding of morality as arising from the recognition of relationship, her belief in communication as the mode of conflict resolution, and her conviction that the solution to the dilemma will follow from its compelling representation seem far from naive or cognitively immature. Instead, Amy's judgments contain the insights central to an ethic of care, just as Jake's judgments reflect the logic of the justice approach. Her incipient awareness of the "method of truth," the central tenet of nonviolent conflict resolution, and her belief in the restorative activity of care, lead her to see the actors in the dilemma arrayed not as opponents in a contest of rights but as members of a network of relationships on whose continuation they all depend. Consequently her solution to the dilemma lies in activating the network by communication, securing the inclusion of the wife by strengthening rather than severing connections.

But the different logic of Amy's response calls attention to the interpretation of the interview itself. Conceived as an interrogation, it appears instead as a dialogue, which takes on moral dimensions of its own, pertaining to the interviewer's uses of power and to the manifestations of respect. With this shift in the conception of the interview, it immediately becomes clear that the interviewer's problem in understanding Amy's response stems from the fact that Amy is answering a different question from the one the interviewer thought had been posed. Amy is considering not *whether* Heinz should act in this situation ("*should* Heinz steal the drug?") but rather *how* Heinz should act in response to his awareness of his wife's need ("Should Heinz *steal* the drug?"). The interviewer takes the mode of action for granted, presuming it to be a matter of fact; Amy assumes the necessity for action and considers what form it should take. In the interviewer's failure to imagine a response not dreamt of in Kohlberg's moral philosophy lies the failure to hear Amy's question and to see the logic in her response, to discern that what appears, from one perspective, to be an evasion of the dilemma signifies in other terms a recognition of the problem and a search for a more adequate solution.

Thus in Heinz's dilemma these two children see two very different moral problems—Jake a conflict between life and property that can be resolved by logical deduction, Amy a fracture of human relationship that must be mended with its own thread. Asking different questions that arise from different conceptions of the moral domain, the children arrive at answers that fundamentally diverge, and the arrangement of these answers as successive stages on a scale of increasing moral maturity calibrated by the logic of the boy's response misses the different truth revealed in the judgment of the girl. To the question, "What does he see that she does not?" Kohlberg's theory provides a ready response, manifest in the scoring of Jake's judgments a full stage higher than Amy's in moral maturity; to the question, "What does she see that he does not?"

Kohlberg's theory has nothing to say. Since most of her responses fall through the sieve of Kohlberg's scoring system, her responses appear from his perspective to lie outside the moral domain.

Yet just as Jake reveals a sophisticated understanding of the logic of justification, so Amy is equally sophisticated in her understanding of the nature of choice. Recognizing that "if both the roads went in totally separate ways, if you pick one, you'll never know what would happen if you went the other way," she explains that "that's the chance you have to take, and like I said, it's just really a guess." To illustrate her point "in a simple way," she describes her choice to spend the summer at camp:

> I will never know what would have happened if I had stayed here, and if something goes wrong at camp, I'll never know if I stayed here if it would have been better. There's really no way around it because there's no way you can do both at once, so you've got to decide, but you'll never know.

In this way, these two eleven-year-old children, both highly intelligent and perceptive about life, though in different ways, display different modes of moral understanding, different ways of thinking about conflict and choice. In resolving Heinz's dilemma, Jake relies on theft to avoid confrontation and turns to the law to mediate the dispute. Transposing a hierarchy of power into a hierarchy of values, he defuses a potentially explosive conflict between people by casting it as an impersonal conflict of claims. In this way, he abstracts the moral problem from the interpersonal situation, finding in the logic of fairness an objective way to decide who will win the dispute. But this hierarchical ordering, with its imagery of winning and losing and the potential for violence which it contains, gives way to Amy's construction of the dilemma to a network of connection, a web of relationships that is sustained by a process of communication. With this shift, the moral problem changes from one of unfair domination, the imposition of property over life, to one of unnecessary exclusion, the failure of the druggist to respond to the wife.

42

Other Voices, Other Rooms? Women's Psychology and Moral Theory

GEORGE SHER

George Sher (b. 1942) is Herbert S. Autrey Professor of Philosophy at Rice University. He is the author of Desert *and numerous articles on moral and political philosophy. This essay first appeared in Eva Kittay and Diana Meyers, eds.,* Women and Moral Theory.

Its topic is the relation between Carol Gilligan's research on the psychology of women and the traditional problems of moral philosophy. Gilligan's work, excerpted in reading 41, has been said to point the way to a new approach to moral theory. Although that approach can be developed in various ways, its distinguishing features include a new emphasis on the particular, the concrete, and the personal. But Sher argues that attention to these factors is not novel at all. He argues, for example, that every moral theory must direct us to pay attention to the specifics of our situation, but must also require that we distinguish what is relevant from what is irrelevant. He argues, too, that the distinction between care and impersonal principle is overdrawn. Some versions of the principle of utility, for example, are said to be rooted precisely in the agent's sympathetic identification with each person whom his action will affect. For these and other reasons, Gilligan's findings "seem neither to undermine nor decisively to adjudicate among the familiar options of moral theory."

Of all the reasons for the recent surge of interest in Carol Gilligan's work, not the least is the idea that her findings may have important implications for moral theory. Although this idea is not always made explicit, its overall thrust is clear enough. By showing that women and men construe moral problems differently, and by demonstrating that their moral development traverses different stages, Gilligan is thought to have uncovered an imbalance in existing moral theories. She is thought to have shown that their standard categories and questions embody a subtle bias—a male bias—and thus to have opened our eyes to alternative possibilities.[1] Here I want to register some skepticism about this idea. Despite their undeniable importance, I believe Gilligan's findings open few new doors for moral theory. Women's moral judgments may be expressed in a different voice, but that voice echoes through some quite familiar rooms.

For an initial sense of what is at stake, let us briefly review Gilligan's reconstruction of women's moral thought. Her conception of the prevailing paradigms, and her views about how women deviate from them, are interwoven with her discussion of the three empirical studies around which her book[2] is built. Thus, I shall begin by citing a few representative passages:

> Claire's inability to articulate her moral position stems in part from the fact that hers is a contextual judgment, bound to the particulars of time and place, contingent always on "that mother" and that "unborn child" and thus resisting a categorical formulation. To her the possibilities of imagination outstrip the capacity for generalization [pp. 58–59].

> Hypothetical dilemmas, in the abstraction of their presentation, divest moral actors from the history and psychology of their individual lives and separate the moral problem from the social contingencies of its possible occurrence. In doing so, these dilemmas are useful for the distillation and refinement of objective principles of justice and for measuring the formal logic of equality and reciprocity. However, the reconstruction of the dilemma in its contextual particularity allows the understanding of cause and consequence which engages the compassion and tolerance repeatedly noted to distinguish the moral judgments of women [p. 100].

> Seeing in the dilemma not a math problem with humans but a narrative of relationships that extends over time, Amy envisions the wife's continuing need for her husband and the husband's continuing concern for his wife and seeks to respond to the druggist's need in a way that would sustain rather than sever connection. Just as she ties the wife's survival to the preservation of relationships, so she considers the value of the wife's life in a context of relationships [p. 28].

> Women's construction of the moral problem as a problem of care and responsibility in relationships rather than as one of rights and rules ties the development of their moral thinking to changes in their understanding of responsibility and relationships, just as the conception of morality as justice ties development to the logic of equality and reciprocity [p. 73].

> Thus it becomes clear why a morality of rights and noninterference may appear frightening to women in its potential justification of indifference and unconcern. At the same time, it becomes clear why, from a male perspective, a morality of responsibility appears inconclusive and diffuse given its insistent contextual relativism [p. 22].

---

[1] Thus, for example, Linda J. Nicholson writes, in an issue of *Social Research* devoted to Gilligan's work, that "many feminists have responded that the masculinity of the authors has affected the very content of the theory itself. . . . I agree with the feminist argument" (Linda J. Nicholson, "Women, Morality and History," *Social Research,* 50, 3 (Autumn 1983), p. 514). I do not mean to imply that either Nicholson or the other contributors to that issue subscribe to the specific views I criticize below.

[2] Carol Gilligan, *In a Different Voice* (Cambridge, MA: Harvard University Press, 1982). All page references in the text are to this volume.

In these and many similar passages, Gilligan elaborates her conception of women's distinctive moral "voice" through a series of oppositions. She can be read as saying that women's morality is concrete and contextual rather than abstract; that it is nonprincipled rather than principled; that it is personal rather than impersonal; that it motivates through care rather than through awareness of duty; and that it is structured around responsibilities rather than rights. There is room for debate over which of these claims Gilligan regards as fundamental, and, indeed, over which she is committed to at all. But if our question is whether any aspect (or plausible extension) of Gilligan's findings can lead to a recasting of moral theory, then we will do well to examine each opposition.

Thus, consider first the suggestion that women's moral decisions are concrete and contextual rather than abstract. Taken literally, the opposition here seems spurious, for at least *prima facie,* it is hard to see either how all contextual features could ever be *irrelevant* to a moral decision, or how they all could be *relevant* to it. Even the most unbending absolutist, who believes that (say) no promises should ever be broken, must allow moral agents to pay enough attention to context to ascertain whether a particular act *would* break a promise, and additional attention to context is required by the notorious problem of conflict of duty. Yet, on the other hand, even the most ardent proponent of "situation ethics" must acknowledge that moral decision-making requires some selectivity of attention, and thus too, some abstraction from total context. The woman who agonizes over an abortion may be influenced by a myriad of "particulars of time and place"; but given the uncountable number of such particulars, she plainly cannot consider them all. *A fortiori,* she cannot assign them all weight. Thus, the proper question is not so much *whether* context is relevant, but rather how many, and which aspects of it are pertinent to our moral decisions, and how these interact to generate moral duties. But when the role of context is thus tamed,[3] it no longer represents a new discovery for moral theory. Instead, the questions it raises are the very stuff of orthodox normative ethics.[4]

---

3 That it must be so tamed is one of the few points of agreement between Owen Flanagan and Lawrence Kohlberg in their interchange on moral development. See Owen J. Flanagan, "Virtue, Sex, and Gender: Some Philosophical Reflections on the Moral Psychology Debate," *Ethics* 92 (April 1982), pp. 499–512; and Lawrence Kohlberg, "A Reply to Owen Flanagan and Some Comments on the Puka-Goodpaster Exchange," *Ethics,* 92 (April 1982), pp. 513–28.

4 Moral philosophers have proposed a variety of approaches to the question of which aspects of one's context are morally relevant. Some focus exclusively on a single factor, such as the happiness or preference-satisfaction that available acts would produce. See, for instance, John Stuart Mill, *Utilitarianism* (Indianapolis, IN: Hackett Publishing Company, 1979). Others hold that more than one factor is relevant, but that some factors take priority over others. This approach is exemplified by John Rawls' "lexical ordering" of his principles of justice; see his *A Theory of Justice* (Cambridge, MA: Harvard University Press, 1971). Still others say that more than one factor is relevant, and that there are no priority rules to adjudicate conflicts. See, for example, W. D. Ross, *The Right and the Good* (Oxford: Oxford University Press, 1973), and William Frankena, *Ethics,* 2nd Edition (Englewood Cliffs, NJ: Prentice-Hall, 1973). Again, R. M. Hare has argued that a factor's moral relevance for an agent depends on his willingness to universalize a principle in which it appears; see his *Freedom and Reason* (Oxford: Oxford University Press, 1963).

Not surprisingly, these *a priori* remarks are borne out by the reports of Gilligan's own subjects. Despite Gilligan's claim that these women make moral decisions contextually and concretely, their words often evidence a well developed sense of differential relevance. Moreover, this sense emerges not only in their responses to Kohlberg's hypothetical dilemmas, but also in their formulations of dilemmas from their actual lives. Thus, for example, Claire, whose doubts about her activities as an abortion counselor were the occasion for the first passage quoted, remarks that "yes, life is sacred, but the quality of life is also important, and it has to be the determining thing in this particular case" (p. 58). One might quarrel with Claire's characterization of life as "sacred" when she takes its value to be overridden by other considerations; but she is undeniably trying both to isolate the relevant features of her situation and to impose an order upon them.

This is, of course, not to deny that women may in general be more attuned than men to context; nor is it to deny that such receptivity may be extremely important in shaping women's moral assessments. Certainly genetic or environmental factors may have conspired to make women especially sensitive to what their acts really mean to the persons they affect. It is also conceivable that women may care more than men about this. Indeed, given Gilligan's data, such differences seem far more than mere possibilities. Furthermore, any reasonable theory will acknowledge that both the rightness of one's acts and one's moral goodness are heavily influenced by how accurately and fully one assesses one's situation and the possibilities for action within it. For a deontologist, one's attentiveness to context determines how well one appreciates the nature, and so too the right-making characteristics of the available acts; for a consequentialist, it determines how well one appreciates those acts' potential consequences. Yet even taken together, these concessions imply at most that women may be better than men at one aspect of a multifaceted common enterprise. They surely do not imply that women operate within a "morality of context" while men do not. If Kohlberg's "masculine" stage-sequence construes moral development only as movement toward greater abstraction, and ignores the possibility that persons may also develop in sensitivity to context, then so much the worse for its pretensions to measure all aspects of moral progress. So much the worse, too, for its claim to capture all that is importantly common among traditional competing theories.

This way of dismissing the contextual/abstract distinction may seem too quick. Even if we agree that every moral decision requires both sensitivity to context and abstraction from it, we need not agree about the form such abstraction must take. More specifically, even if persons cannot make moral decisions without selectively focusing on some features of their situations, there remains a question about whether the selected features can license decisions all by themselves, or whether they can do so only in concert with more general moral principles. It is a commonplace of most moral theories that if a given constellation of facts is to be a good reason for a person X to do A, then a similar constellation must be equally good reason for another person Y, or for the same person X at a different time.[5] Putting the point slightly differently, most theories agree that all moral justification involves at least tacit appeal to principle. Yet Gilligan can be read as taking her findings to show that women's decisions are often *not* backed by universal principles.[6] Hence, her results may seem to point the way to a new view of what constitutes a moral reason.

With this, we have shifted from the first to the second of our contrasts. Underlying the opposition between the contextual and the abstract, we have found a further opposition between the principled and the nonprincipled. This second opposition is, for us, the more interesting; for the role of principle in moral thought is far less clear than the mere need for abstraction. There have, of course, been many attempts to show that nonprincipled decisions are irrational, or in other ways deficient. But when pitted against these, Gilligan's findings may seem to carry considerable weight. For if women commonly do make nonprincipled decisions, then to reject such decisions as unacceptable would be to dismiss the standard moral *modus operandi* of half the world's population.

It is, in fact, a nice question of metatheory how heavily such empirical findings should weigh against other, more nearly *a priori* arguments about standards of rationality. To philosophers sympathetic to naturalism, who operate in the spirit of Nelson Goodman's suggestion that "[t]he process of justification is the delicate one of making mutual adjustments between rules and accepted inferences,"[7] the empirical findings will presumably matter a lot. To others, more a prioristically inclined, they will presumably matter less. But in fact, and fortunately, we need not resolve the general problem of method here. For, despite appearances to the contrary, Gilligan's results show very little about the role of principle in women's decisions.

To see why, we must keep our attention firmly fixed on what acting on principle is. As we saw, to act on principle is just to act for reasons that one takes (or perhaps would take) to apply with similar force to any others who were similarly situated. But, given the counterfactual element of this formulation, the mere fact that women's responses are rarely *couched* in terms of principle provides little evidence about the underlying structure of their decisions. Even persons who fail to mention principles in reconstructing their deliberations, and indeed even persons who explicitly disavow them, may well have decided on principled grounds. Their omissions or disavowals may reflect, not a lack

---

5 For two of the many statements of this view, see Henry Sidgwick, *Methods of Ethics*, 7th Edition (London; Macmillan, 1922), Book III, Chap. I; and J. L. Mackie, *Ethics: Inventing Right and Wrong* (Harmondsworth, England: Penguin, 1977), chap. 4.

6 As the editors of this volume have suggested to me, Gilligan's point may be not that women's decisions are nonprincipled, but only that their principles tend not to be couched in such terms as fairness and justice. I agree that this interpretation is available, but continue to regard the stronger interpretation as at least as plausible. More importantly, even if Gilligan herself does not hold the stronger view, the questions of its tenability and relation to her data remain worth discussing.

7 Nelson Goodman, *Fact, Fiction, and Forecast* (Indianapolis, IN: Bobbs-Merrill, 1965), p. 64.

of commitment to principles, but rather an imperfect appreciation of what such commitment amounts to. Whether one acts on principle depends not just on what one says about principles, but rather on what one does or would say (or do) about a variety of other matters. There are, of course, difficult problems here—problems about which questions would best elicit a person's considered views, about what distinguishes deviations from principles from lack of commitment to them, and about which acts or assertions would best show that persons regard their reasons as fully general. However, given our purposes, we need not resolve these problems. Instead, we need only note that *whatever* resolution one adopts, no one can establish the role of principle in a subject's deliberations without some focused and directive counterfactual inquiry. Since Gilligan's questions do not take this form, the responses she elicits do not show that women's decisions are generally nonprincipled (or even that they are less often principled than men's.

This is, I think, not quite to say that Gilligan's data provide *no* evidence for such a conclusion. Since that conclusion is one possible explanation of women's reluctance to appeal explicitly to principles, it does draw some confirmation from Gilligan's data. But because the same data can be explained in many other ways, the degree of confirmation is minimal. Of the plausible competing explanations, one—that Gilligan's subjects lack the somewhat recondite understanding of principled action that figures in philosophical debates—has already been noted. But there are also others. Women's principles may be hedged with more qualifications than men's, and so may be more difficult to articulate, and thus less ready at hand. Women, being more attuned to the need for qualification, may be more aware of the inadequacies of the principles that first come to mind, and so more hesitant to assert them. Women may attach comparatively less importance to the generality of their reasons, and comparatively more to the reasons' complete specification. Given these and other possibilities, the fact that women seldom explicitly invoke moral principles implies little about whether their actual decisions are principled.

This is still not the end of the story. A further aspect of Gilligan's account is that women's moral decisions tend in two ways to be more personal than men's. For one thing, her female subjects often represent moral dilemmas as problems in balancing the needs of specific individuals (who sometimes, but not always, include themselves). For another, they often represent the proper resolutions to these dilemmas as stemming not from impersonal duty, but rather from personal sympathy and care. Since there is at least a *prima facie* tension between the duty to implement an impersonal principle and the concern that stems from a personal relationship, these findings may seem to lend further (if indirect) support to the view that women's decisions are nonprincipled. In addition, they may seem to add further dimension to the claim that women approach problems of conflicting interests differently than men. If these things are true, then our earlier question of how heavily to count actual practice in establishing standards of moral reasonableness will return with a vengeance.

Yet before concluding this, we must look more closely at the tension between personal relationship and impersonal principle, and at the prospects for resolving it within something like the traditional framework. Let us begin by asking why that tension should be thought to exist at all. Although there are surely many contributing factors, one obvious reason is the unique and unrepeatable nature of personal relationships. Because such relationships are rooted in particular histories of transactions between particular persons, any demands they impose must apply to those persons alone. Even if other persons are similarly situated, their different histories will insure that they are not subject to similar demands. Moreover, if personal relationships do impose demands, then those demands must apparently not just differ from, but also sometimes conflict with, the demands of impersonal principle. In particular, such conflict must arise whenever relationship and principle call for incompatible acts.

Thus interpreted, the opposition between the personal and the impersonal is at least *prima facie* plausible. Yet on this account, its challenge to the familiar body of theory invites at least two objections. Most obviously, even if historically rooted relationships do raise questions about the hegemony of a morality of principle, they cannot possibly provide a comprehensive alternative to it; for many pressing moral choices affect only persons with whom the agent *has* no personal relationship. This may be obscured by the prominence of parents, husbands, and lovers in the reports of Gilligan's subjects; but it emerges as soon as we scrutinize the "relationships" between newly pregnant women and the fetuses they carry. It emerges yet more clearly when we consider such cases as that of Hilary, who as a trial lawyer has discovered that the opposing counsel has

> overlooked a document that provided critical support for his client's "meritorious claim." Deliberating whether or not to tell her opponent . . . Hilary realized that the adversary system of justice impedes not only "the supposed search for truth" but also the expression of concern for the person on the other side. Choosing in the end to adhere to the system, in part because of the vulnerability of her own professional position, she sees herself as having failed to live up to her standard of personal integrity as well as to her moral ideal of self-sacrifice [p. 135].

Whatever Hilary's compromised ideal amounts to, it is plainly *not* an ideal of responsiveness to personal relationships; for no such relationships here exist.[8]

Of course, even if decisions like Hilary's cannot be guided by the demands of personal relationships, they may still be motivated and guided by care and sympathy for all the affected parties. That this is part of what Gilligan takes Hilary to have sacrificed is suggested by her observation that the adversary system impedes "the expression of concern for the person on the other side." Yet as soon as care and concern are detached from the demands of unique and historically rooted relationships—as soon as they are said to be elicited

8 In a recent public presentation, Gilligan has distinguished between the view that care rests on attachment, and the view that care rests on knowledge gained through attachment. If she holds that personal relationships are important primarily because they provide a sort of knowledge that can guide and inform our dealings even with strangers, her view is of course not vulnerable to the objections just mounted. It is, however, then vulnerable to the objection to follow.

merely by the affected parties' common humanity, or by the fact that those parties all have interests, or all can suffer—the care and concern are once again viewed as appropriate responses to shared and repeatable characteristics. By so regarding them, we completely lose the contrast between the particularity of relationship and the generality of principle. Having lost it, we seem to be left with an approach that seeks to resolve moral dilemmas through sympathetic identification with all the affected parties. Yet far from being novel, this approach—which is at least closely related to that of the familiar impartial and benevolent observer—is central to the existing tradition.[9]

There is also a deeper difficulty with the suggestion that a morality that is sensitive to the demands of relationship must be incompatible with a morality of duty and principle. As I have reconstructed it, the incompatibility arises when the demands of relationship and principle conflict. Yet the assumption that such conflict is inevitable should itself not go unquestioned. Even if we concede that relationships impose demands which *differ* from the demands of moral principles—and I think we ought to concede this—it remains possible that each set of demands might be adjusted to, and might be bounded by, the other. It is, on the one hand, not at all farfetched that friendship might never demand that one betray the trust of another, or that one do anything else that is seriously wrong. It is also not farfetched that the demands of some impersonal moral principles might be contingent on the prior demands of personal relationships. For one thing, we may sometimes be morally permitted, or even required, to give our friends and loved ones preference over others. For another, even where we are not forced to choose whom to help, we may be morally required to produce just the responses that our relationships demand. Such a convergence of demand upon a single action would be no more anomalous than the convergence that occurs when a given act is demanded both by (say) an obligation one has incurred by undertaking a public position and one's natural duty to support just institutions. In general, the demands of relationship and principle may be so interwoven that there is no theoretical bar to our being fully responsive to both.

Needless to say, there are many questions here. It is one thing to suggest that the demands of relationships and impersonal principle might be reconciled, and quite another to tell a plausible detailed story about how this would work. Of all the problems facing such an account, perhaps the most familiar is the objection that the motive of duty is in some sense alienating, and that persons who act merely on principle are *ipso facto* not displaying the affection and care appropriate to personal relationships. Bernard Williams has put this worry well in his influential discussion of the suggestion that a moral principle might license a decision to save one's wife rather than a stranger when only one can be saved. Williams remarks that "this construction provides the agent with

9 Two classical representatives of this approach are: David Hume, *Treatise of Human Nature*, L. A. Selby-Bigge, ed. (Oxford: Oxford University Press, 1960), bk. III, pt. III, sec. 1; and Adam Smith, *The Theory of Moral Sentiments*, in L. A. Selby-Bigge, *The British Moralists* Vol. 1 (Oxford: Oxford University Press, 1897), pp. 257–77. For a more recent treatment, see R. M. Hare, *Moral Thinking* (Oxford: Oxford University Press, 1981), part II.

one thought too many: it might have been hoped by some (for instance, by his wife) that his motivating thought, fully spelled out, would be the thought that it was his wife, not that it was his wife and, that in situations of this kind, it is permissible to save one's wife."[10] Yet Williams' worry, though provocative, is far from decisive. In an interesting recent essay, Marcia Baron has argued that the worry draws its apparent force partly from our tendency to associate acting from duty with motives that really are inimical to care and affection, but that have no intrinsic connection with duty, and partly from a failure to see that moral principles may operate not as independent sources of motivating force, but rather as filters through which other motives must pass.[11] Since I find Baron's diagnosis convincing, I shall not discuss this problem further. Instead, I shall briefly take up another, less familiar problem that the reconciliationist project faces.

In a nutshell, the further problem is that of justification. It is the problem of finding, within the standard repertoire of justificatory approaches, resources sufficient to ground not merely principles of impartial morality, but also principles licensing the sort of partiality that reconciliationism requires. Put (too) briefly, the difficulty here is that both deontologists and consequentialists have standardly tried to justify their favored principles from some abstract and general perspective. For this reason, the impersonality of their starting points may itself seem to guarantee the rejection of any principles which acknowledge the demands of personal relationships. As Williams notes, this point seems to obtain

> even when the moral point of view is itself explained under conditions of ignorance of some abstractly conceived contracting parties. . . . For while the contracting parties are pictured as making some kind of self-interested or prudential choice of a set of rules, they are entirely abstract persons making this choice in ignorance of their own particular properties, tastes, and so forth.[12]

If this is right, and if Gilligan is right to say that women often resolve dilemmas precisely by responding to the demands of personal relationships, then we will indeed be forced to choose between denying that women's decisions are made on moral grounds and radically altering our conceptions of what counts as well grounded morality.

But *does* impersonality of the familiar justificatory approaches rule out the justification of principles that accommodate the demands of personal relationships? Although we obviously cannot examine all the possibilities, it will be worth our while to look more closely at one familiar strategy. Since the Rawlsian

---

10 Bernard Williams, "Persons, Character, and Morality," in Amelie Rorty, ed., *The Identities of Persons* (Berkeley: University of California Press, 1976), pp. 214–15.

11 Marcia Baron, "The Alleged Moral Repugnance of Acting from Duty," *The Journal of Philosophy* LXXXI, 4 (April 1984), pp. 197–220. For related discussion, see Peter Railton, "Alienation, Consequentialism, and the Demands of Morality," *Philosophy and Public Affairs*, 13, 2 (Spring 1984), pp. 134–171.

12 Williams, "Persons, Character, and Morality," pp. 198–99. The approach to which Williams alludes is of course that developed by Rawls in *A Theory of Justice*.

approach has already been mentioned, I shall stick with it. In this approach, a principle is justified if it would be chosen by rational and self-interested persons who were ignorant of the particulars of their situations, and thus were prevented from making biased choices. Although I am no particular friend of hypothetical contractarianism, I cannot see that its difficulties lie where Williams say they do. It is true that Rawls himself says little about personal relationships, and true also that Richards' adaptation of his framework leads to such "righteous absurdities" as that persons should not base their relationships on "arbitrary physical characteristics alone."[13] But none of this implies that Rawlsian contractors could not, in fact, agree on more sensible principles concerning relationships. It does not imply that they could not agree on principles that prescribe compliance with the demands of personal relationships under certain conditions, or that permit or require some partiality to friends and loved ones. In particular, the choice of such principles seems plainly *not* to be ruled out merely by the ignorance of the contracting parties. The contractors' ignorance does rule out the choice of principles that name either specific agents who are allowed or required to be partial or the specific recipients of their partiality. However, this is irrelevant; for the question is not whether any *given* person may or should display partiality to any other, but rather whether *all* persons may or should be partial to their wives, husbands, or friends. The relevant principles, even if licensing or dictating partiality, must do so impartially. Hence, there is no obvious reason why such principles could not be chosen even by contractors ignorant of the particulars of their lives.

Can we go further? Is there any positive reason for rational, self-interested, but ignorant Rawlsian contractors to opt for principles that adjust duties and obligations to the demands of personal relationships? To answer this question fully, we would have to say far more about the demands of relationships than can be said here. But given present purposes, which are merely dialectical, there is indeed something to be said. Our question about the Rawlsian contractors has arisen because their failure to choose principles adjusted to the demands of relationships would support the broader claim that *all* impersonal justificatory strategies yield principles that sometimes conflict with the demands of relationships. This, in turn, would combine with Gilligan's findings to suggest a reconceptualization of the moral point of view in more personal and relationship-oriented terms. But this last move will only be plausible if the demands of personal relationships are in themselves sufficiently compelling to warrant description as moral demands. Hence, for us, the question is not what the Rawlsian contractors would choose *simpliciter*, but rather what they would choose *on the assumption that the demands of relationships are this compelling.*

When the issue is framed in these terms, I think the Rawlsian contractors might well have good reason to choose principles that conflicted as little as

---

13 David A. J. Richards, *A Theory of Reasons for Action* (Oxford: Oxford University Press, 1971), p. 94. The apt phrase "righteous absurdity" is used by Williams in "Persons, Character, and Morality," p. 212.

possible with the demands of personal relationships. To see why, consider what the demands of relationships would have to be like to be compelling enough to qualify as moral demands. At a minimum, they would have to be so urgent that persons could not violate them without at the same time violating their own integrity. The demands would have to grow out of the kind of deep personal commitment that, as Williams puts it, "compels . . . allegiance to life itself."[14] In addition, when viewed from the perspective of the other parties to relationships, the demands would have to dictate responses that were not merely optional, but were in some sense owed. The demands' nonfulfillment would have to be real grounds for complaint. Just how relationships can generate such demands is of course a large part of the mystery about them. But if they can—and I believe they not only can but often do—then the satisfaction of those demands, when they arise, must itself be a good that transcends mere personal preference. Like liberty and other Rawlsian primary goods, a general ability both to give and to receive such satisfaction must be something it is rational to want whatever else one wants. But if so, then rational contractors endowed with full general information about human psychology could hardly avoid wanting to protect this ability. Since protecting it requires choosing principles whose prescriptions are adjusted to the demands of important relationships, I conclude that they would indeed be motivated to choose such principles.

This conclusion might be challenged through appeal to the last of Gilligan's oppositions. As derived, the conclusion rests on the premise that morality is fundamentally a matter of what persons owe to others. It thus appears to presuppose that any genuinely moral principle must specify people's *rights*. Yet one of Gilligan's most persistent themes is that a preoccupation with rights rather than responsibilities is itself a typically male construction. As she often notes, her female subjects think less about what they are entitled to than about what they are responsible for providing. Thus, it may seem illegitimate for us to say that only demands that specify responses that are owed can qualify as moral. For, if we do say this, we may seem to beg the question against those who see Gilligan's work as prefiguring a new vision of morality.

Yet, here again, the worry is overdrawn. Let us simply grant that women, at least in the earlier stages of their development, think more readily of what they are responsible for providing than of what they are entitled to receive. Even so, nothing follows about the status of the responsibilities they acknowledge. Indeed, one very reasonable suggestion is that they regard themselves as responsible for providing sympathy, care, and help to others precisely *because* they regard themselves as owing these things. Putting the point in terms of rights, and ignoring the complexities and differing interpretations of that notion, we can say that nothing rules out the possibility that women regard others as having a *right* to their sympathy, care, and help. To suppose otherwise would be to conflate the well supported claim that women are less concerned

---

14 Williams, "Persons, Character, and Morality," p. 215.

than men with the protection of *their* rights with the quite different claim that women are less inclined than men to think that people *have* rights (or to hold views functionally equivalent to this).

All things considered, Gilligan's findings seem neither to undermine nor decisively to adjudicate among the familiar options of moral theory. They may edge us in certain theoretical directions, but the movement they compel takes us nowhere near the boundaries of the known territories. This is not to deny that the findings suggest that women are, in some respects, better equipped than men to reach morally adequate decisions; but it is to deny that that result requires any exotic recasting of our familiar understanding of "morally adequate." To all of this, the still-hopeful revisionist might finally complain that I have interpreted the received body of theory so broadly that it is not clear what *could* show that it needs radical revision. But this, though true, is precisely the point I want to make. The oppositions of concrete and abstract, personal and impersonal, duty and care are not recent empirical discoveries, but generic determinants of the moral problematic. We have always known that an adequate theory must assign each its proper place. What we have not known, and what Gilligan's findings bring us little closer to knowing, is what those places are.

VII
VALUE

The two main concepts of ethics are the right and the good. We ask ourselves what is right when we try to discover which acts we ought to perform. We ask ourselves what is good when we try to discover which things, or states of affairs, have value. Because many theories of right hold that our duties include the production of good consequences, these questions must be connected. But we cannot promote the good without knowing what it is, so the two questions remain distinct.

The simplest answer to the question "What is good?" is "pleasant sensation." The view that pleasure, and only pleasure, has intrinsic value is known as *hedonism*, and it is defended by Jeremy Bentham in reading 43. According to Bentham, something other than pleasure can be good only in the sense that it will *cause* pleasure. Even virtuous motives, which Kant took to have moral worth in themselves (see reading 30) are good only for this reason. If Bentham is correct, the best way to live is to experience as much pleasure as possible. Thus, it is important to find out which lives *are* most pleasurable. In reading 45, the ancient Greek philosopher Epicurus proposes one influential answer. Epicurus argues that we maximize our pleasures not by living luxuriously, but by cultivating simple tastes that are easily satisfied. As he points out, "plain savours bring us pleasure equal to a luxurious diet, when all the pain due to want is removed; and bread and water produce the highest pleasure when one who needs them puts them to his lips." By training ourselves not to want what is expensive or hard to acquire, we lose nothing in the quality of our sensations, and gain security from frustration and disappointment.

Assuming that pleasure is at least one of life's goods, exactly *why* is it good? One answer, of course, is that its goodness is a basic feature that cannot be further explained. But another answer is that pleasure is valuable because we all want and prefer it. Certainly pleasure would seem far less valuable if we did not care whether we experienced it. If pleasure owes its value to the fact that we want it, then anything else we want will presumably be valuable too. Thus, anyone who accepts this explanation will espouse a *desire-satisfaction theory* of value.

Can a desire-satisfaction theorist say, with Bentham, that *only* pleasure is good in itself? To do so, he must hold that pleasure is the only thing anyone wants for its own sake. This view, known as *psychological hedonism*, is defended in reading 23 by John Stuart Mill. However, the view is vulnerable to serious objections, some of which are advanced by Joel Feinberg in reading 1. Also, as Robert Nozick points out in reading 35, anyone to whom pleasure alone mattered would have good reason to be connected to an "experience machine"—that is, a machine that would cause him to enjoy his favorite pleasures while he floated in a tank with electrodes attached to his brain. But most of us would refuse to be attached to such a machine. Thus, what matters to us appears to include not only the passive experience of pleasure, but also various activities that *bring* us pleasure. If a desire-satisfaction theorist rejects psychological hedonism, he must hold that much in addition to pleasure is valuable.

Desire-satisfaction theories can take various forms. Some attach value only to the satisfaction of *current* desires, others also to the satisfaction of past or future desires. Some count even very specific desires, others only desires to live in certain broad ways. Some focus on actual desires, others on the desires that agents *would* have if they were rational or fully informed. In reading 49, Derek Parfit discusses a number of these complexities while comparing desire-satisfaction theories to other views of the good.

The role of information is also discussed by Richard Brandt and Don Loeb. In reading 46, Brandt defines a rational desire as one that could not be altered by exposure to any further information. He argues that we should equate a person's good with the satisfaction of his rational desires. By this criterion, many actual desires are not relevant to a person's good. For example, suppose I was bitten by a dog as a child and consequently want to avoid dogs now. If repeatedly being told that most dogs do not bite would cause my fear of dogs to diminish, then Brandt would deny that avoiding dogs is any part of my present good. But Don Loeb argues in reading 47 that information can affect desire in ways that are *not* relevant to one's good. For example, immature people will respond to information in immature ways, while "insane people sometimes have insane motivations, and often would have them no matter what they knew." For these and other reasons, Loeb denies that a person's good consists of the satisfaction of his informed desires.

So far, we have considered only theories that trace goodness to subjective states like pleasure or desire. But as Parfit notes, there are also theories which assert that certain states, activities, or characteristics are good, or good for people, for reasons *independent* of any subjective states. Because these theories often supply lists of intrinsic goods, Parfit calls them *objective list theories*. One such theory is put forth by W. D. Ross in reading 48. Whereas Bentham held that virtue is good only because virtuous acts tend to produce pleasure, Ross contends that even apart from these effects, it is better to be virtuous than vicious. Ross also argues that knowledge and the matching of happiness to virtue are intrinsically valuable. As Parfit points out, other objective lists have included such entries as rational activity, aesthetic appreciation, and the development of one's abilities.

One objection to objective list theories is that they provide no common denominator for the comparison of goods. If two activities both owe their value to the fact that they produce pleasure, then we can establish which one is more valuable by finding out which one produces *more* pleasure. But if two activities are good for reasons *independent* of pleasure or desire, then the procedure for establishing which one is better will be far less clear. For this reason, many philosophers have sought a unified account of value.

But Charles Taylor argues that their quest for unity distorts much that is relevant. He points out in reading 50 that we commonly make "qualitative distinctions . . . between different actions, or feelings, or modes of life, as being in some way morally higher or lower, noble or base, admirable or contemptible." For example, some think it crucial to display integrity and to remain true to one's deepest convictions. Others embrace the Christian ideal of associating oneself with God's love for mankind. As these examples suggest, our moral ideals are couched in a variety of distinct vocabularies which resist reduction to any single set of terms. Thus, according to Taylor, "the really important question may turn out to be how we combine in our lives two or three or four different goals, or virtues, or standards, which we feel we cannot repudiate but which seem to demand incompatible things of us."

43
Pleasure as the Good

JEREMY BENTHAM

Jeremy Bentham (1748–1832) was a British utilitarian and legal reformer. His writings include An Introduction to the Principles of Morals and Legislation, *from which this selection is taken.*

In the selection, Bentham argues that pleasure and the absence of pain are the only things that ultimately have value. If anything else is said to be good, it is only because it promotes pleasure or prevents pain. Even agents' motives are good (or bad) only for these reasons. Other things being equal, a pleasure of longer duration or greater intensity is better than a pleasure that is shorter or less intense.

Bentham's view of the good has the virtue of simplicity. If correct, it provides a common denominator to compare the value of different states and the acts that produce them. But the view also raises questions. Do all pleasant experiences really involve a single kind of feeling? Even if they do, is the capacity to produce that feeling really all that is valuable about friendship, knowledge, and human excellence? Are even malice, envy, and cruelty good insofar as they produce the feeling? If the answers to these questions are negative, then Bentham's view will require modification.

VALUE OF A LOT OF
PLEASURE OR PAIN, HOW TO BE MEASURED

I. Pleasures then, and the avoidance of pains, are the *ends* which the legislator has in view: it behooves him therefore to understand their *value*. Pleasures and pains are the *instruments* he has to work with: it behooves him therefore to understand their force, which is again, in other words, their value.

II. To a person considered *by himself*, the value of a pleasure or pain considered *by itself*, will be greater or less, according to the four following circumstances.[1]

---

[1] These circumstances have since been denominated *elements* or *dimensions of value* in a pleasure or a pain.

Not long after the publication of the first edition, the following memoriter verses were framed, in the view of lodging more effectually, in the memory, these points, on which the whole fabric of morals and legislation may be seen to rest:

1. Its *intensity.*
2. Its *duration.*

3. Its *certainty* or *uncertainty.*
4. Its *propinquity* or *remoteness.*

III. These are the circumstances which are to be considered in estimating a pleasure or a pain considered each of them by itself. But when the value of any pleasure or pain is considered for the purpose of estimating the tendency of any *act* by which it is produced, there are two other circumstances to be taken into the account; these are,

5. Its *fecundity,* or the chance it has of being followed by sensations of the *same* kind: that is, pleasures, if it be a pleasure: pains, if it be a pain.

6. Its *purity,* or the chance it has of *not* being followed by sensations of the *opposite* kind: that is, pains, if it be a pleasure: pleasures, if it be a pain.

These two last, however, are in strictness scarcely to be deemed properties of the pleasures or the pain itself; they are not, therefore, in strictness to be taken into the account of the value of that pleasure or that pain. They are in strictness to be deemed properties only of the act, or other event, by which such pleasure or pain has been produced; and accordingly are only to be taken into the account of the tendency of such act or such event.

IV. To a *number* of persons, with reference to each of whom the value of a pleasure or a pain is considered, it will be greater or less, according to seven circumstances: to wit, the six preceding ones; *viz.*

1. Its *intensity.*
2. Its *duration.*
3. Its *certainty* or *uncertainty.*

4. Its *propinquity* or *remoteness.*
5. Its *fecundity.*
6. Its *purity.*

And one other; to wit:

7. Its *extent;* that is, the number of persons to whom it *extends;* or (in other words) who are affected by it.

V. To take an exact account then of the general tendency of any act, by which the interests of a community are affected, proceed as follows. Begin with any one person of those whose interests seem most immediately to be affected by it: and take an account.

1. Of the value of each distinguishable *pleasure* which appears to be produced by it in the *first* instance.

2. Of the value of each *pain* which appears to be produced by it in the *first* instance.

Intense, long, certain, speedy, fruitful, pure—
Such marks in *pleasures* and in *pains* endure.
Such pleasures seek, if *private* be thy end:
If it be *public,* wide let them *extend.*
Such *pains* avoid, whichever be thy view:
If pains *must* come, let them *extend* to few.

3. Of the value of each pleasure which appears to be produced by it *after* the first. This constitutes the *fecundity* of the first *pleasure* and the *impurity* of the first *pain*.

4. Of the value of each *pain* which appears to be produced by it after the first. This constitutes the *fecundity* of the first *pain*, and the *impurity* of the first pleasure.

5. Sum up all the values of all the *pleasures* on the one side, and those of all the pains on the other. The balance, if it be on the side of pleasure, will give the *good* tendency of the act upon the whole, with respect to the interests of that *individual* person; if on the side of pain, the *bad* tendency of it upon the whole.

6. Take an account of the *number* of persons whose interests appear to be concerned; and repeat the above process with respect to each. *Sum up* the numbers expressive of the degrees of *good* tendency, which the act has, with respect to each individual, in regard to whom the tendency of it is *good* upon the whole: do this again with respect to each individual, in regard to whom the tendency of it is *bad* upon the whole. Take the *balance;* which, if on the side of *pleasure,* will give the general *good tendency* of the act, with respect to the total number of community of individuals concerned; if on the side of pain the general *evil tendency,* with respect to the same community.

VI. It is not to be expected that this process should be strictly pursued previously to every moral judgment, or to every legislative or judicial operation. It may, however, be always kept in view: and as near as the process actually pursued on these occasions approached to it, so near will such process approach to the character of an exact one.

VII. The same process is alike applicable to pleasure and pain in whatever shape they appear: and by whatever denomination they are distinguished: to pleasure, whether it be called *good* (which is properly the cause or instrument of pleasure), or *profit* (which is distant pleasure, or the cause or instrument of distant pleasure), or *convenience,* or *advantage, benefit, emolument, happiness,* and so forth: to pain, whether it be called *evil* (which corresponds to *good*), or *mischief,* or *inconvenience,* or *disadvantage,* or *loss,* or *unhappiness,* and so forth.

VIII. Nor is this a novel and unwarranted, any more than it is a useless theory. In all this there is nothing but what the practice of mankind, wheresoever they have a clear view of their own interest, is perfectly comformable to. An article of property, an estate in land, for instance, is valuable, on what account? On account of the pleasures of all kinds which it enables a man to produce, and what comes to the same thing, the pains of all kinds which it enables him to avert. But the value of such an article of property is universally understood to rise or fall according to the length or shortness of the time which a man has in it: the certainty or uncertainty of its coming into possession: and the nearness or remoteness of the time at which, if at all, it is to come into possession. As to the *intensity* of the pleasures which a man may derive from it, this is never thought of, because it depends upon the use which each particular person may come to make of it; which cannot be estimated till the particular pleasures he may come to derive from it, or the particular pains he may come to exclude by means of it, are brought to view. For the same reason, neither does he think of the *fecundity* or *purity* of those pleasures.

• • •

NO MOTIVES EITHER
CONSTANTLY GOOD, OR CONSTANTLY BAD

IX. In all this chain of motives, the principal or original link seems to be the last internal motive in prospect; it is to this that all the other motives in prospect owe their materiality; and the immediately acting motive its existence. This motive in prospect, we see, is always some pleasure, or some pain; some pleasure, which the act in question is expected to be a means of continuing or producing: some pain which it is expected to be a means of discontinuing or preventing. A motive is substantially nothing more than pleasure or pain, operating in a certain manner.

X. Now, pleasure is in *itself* a good: nay, even setting aside immunity from pain, the only good: pain is in itself an evil; and, indeed, without exception, the only evil; or else the words good and evil have no meaning. And this is alike true of every sort of pain, and of every sort of pleasure. It follows, therefore, immediately and incontestably, that *there is no such thing as any sort of motive that is in itself a bad one.*[2]

XI. It is common, however, to speak of actions as proceeding from *good* or *bad* motives: in which case the motives meant are such as are internal. The expression is far from being an accurate one; and as it is apt to occur in the consideration of almost every kind of offence, it will be requisite to settle the precise meaning of it, and observe how far it quadrates with the truth of things.

XII. With respect to goodness and badness, as it is with everything else that is not itself either pain or pleasure, so is it with motives. If they are good or bad, it is only on account of their effects: good, on account of their tendency to produce pleasure, or avert pain: bad, on account of their tendency to produce pain, or avert pleasure. Now the case is, that from one and the same motive, and from every kind of motive, may proceed actions that are good, others that are bad, and others that are indifferent. This we shall proceed to show with respect to all the different kinds of motives, as determined by the various kinds of pleasures and pains.

• • •

---

2 Let a man's motive be ill-will; call it even malice, envy, cruelty; it is still a kind of pleasure that is his motive: the pleasure he takes at the thought of the pain which he sees, or expects to see, his adversary undergo. Now even this wretched pleasure, taken by itself, is good: it may be faint; it may be short: it must at any rate be impure: yet while it lasts, and before any bad consequences arrive, it is good as any other that is not more intense.

44

The Experience Machine

ROBERT NOZICK

Robert Nozick (b. 1938) is Professor of Philosophy at Harvard University. His books include Anarchy, State, and Utopia; Philosophical Explanations; *and* The Nature of Rationality.

In this selection from Anarchy, State, and Utopia, *chapter 3, Nozick argues against the view that pleasure, and only pleasure, matters to us. If that were correct, we would have overwhelming reason to want to be hooked up to a machine that would cause all our favorite sensations. But Nozick argues that few would allow themselves to be connected to such an "experience machine." Their reasons for refusing, he speculates, would include desires to act in certain ways, desires to be certain sorts of people, and desires to be in contact with reality. But if so, then these things must matter to people for reasons that are independent of the pleasure they bring.*

Although Nozick does not say so, his conclusion may have an important bearing on the view defended by Bentham in reading 43. According to Bentham, pleasure is the only good. But in the eyes of many, the fact that something matters to people is part of what makes it good. If so, and if pleasure is not all that matters to people, then pleasure is not the only good.

There are also substantial puzzles when we ask what matters other than how *people's* experiences feel "from the inside." Suppose there were an experience machine that would give you any experience you desired. Super-duper neuropsychologists could stimulate your brain so that you would think and feel you were writing a great novel, or making a friend, or reading an interesting book. All the time you would be floating in a tank, with electrodes attached to your brain. Should you plug into this machine for life, preprogramming your life's experiences? If you are worried about missing out on desirable experiences, we can suppose that business enterprises have researched thoroughly the lives of many others. You can pick and choose from their large library or smorgasbord of such experiences, selecting your life's experiences for, say, the next two years. After two years have passed, you will have ten minutes or ten hours out of the tank, to select the experiences of your *next* two years. Of course, while in the tank you won't know that you're there; you'll think it's all actually happening. Others can also plug in to have the experiences they want, so there's no need to stay unplugged to serve them. (Ignore problems such as who will service the machines if everyone plugs in.) Would you plug in? *What else can matter to us, other than how our lives feel from the inside?* Nor should you refrain because of the few moments of distress between the moment you've decided and the moment you're plugged. What's a few moments of distress compared to a lifetime of bliss (if that's what you choose), and why feel any distress at all if your decision *is* the best one?

What does matter to us in addition to our experiences? First, we want to *do* certain things, and not just have the experience of doing them. In the case of certain experiences, it is only because first we want to do the actions that we want the experiences of doing them or thinking we've done them. (But *why* do we want to do the activities rather than merely to experience them?) A second reason for not plugging in is that we want to *be* a certain way, to be a certain sort of person. Someone floating in a tank is an indeterminate blob. There is no answer to the question of what a person is like who has long been in the tank. Is he courageous, kind, intelligent, witty, loving? It's not merely that it's difficult to tell; there's no way he is. Plugging into the machine is a kind of suicide. It will seem to some, trapped by a picture, that nothing about what we are like can matter except as it gets reflected in our experiences. But should it be surprising that what *we are* is important to us? Why should we be concerned only with how our time is filled, but not with what we are?

Thirdly, plugging into an experience machine limits us to a man-made reality, to a world no deeper or more important than that which people can construct. There is no *actual* contact with any deeper reality, though the experience of it can be simulated. Many persons desire to leave themselves open to such contact and to a plumbing of deeper significance.[1] This clarifies the intensity of the conflict over psychoactive drugs, which some view as mere local experience machines, and others view as avenues to a deeper reality; what some view as equivalent to surrender to the experience machine, others view as following one of the reasons *not* to surrender!

We learn that something matters to us in addition to experience by imagining an experience machine and then realizing that we would not use it. We can continue to imagine a sequence of machines each designed to fill lacks suggested for the earlier machines. For example, since the experience machine doesn't meet our desire to *be* a certain way, imagine a transformation machine which transforms us into whatever sort of person we'd like to be (compatible with our staying us). Surely one would not use the transformation machine to

---

1 Traditional religious views differ on the *point* of contact with a transcendent reality. Some say that contact yields eternal bliss or Nirvana, but they have not distinguished this sufficiently from merely a *very* long run on the experience machine. Others think it is intrinsically desirable to do the will of a higher being which created us all, though presumably no one would think this if we discovered we had been created as an object of amusement by some superpowerful child from another galaxy or dimension. Still others imagine an eventual merging with a higher reality, leaving unclear its desirability, or where that merging leaves *us*.

become as one would wish, and thereupon plug into the experience machine![2] So something matters in addition to one's experiences *and* what one is like. Nor is the reason merely that one's experiences are unconnected with what one is like. For the experience machine might be limited to provide only experiences possible to the sort of person plugged in. Is it that we want to make a difference in the world? Consider then the result machine, which produces in the world any result you would produce and injects your vector input into any joint activity. We shall not pursue here the fascinating details of these or other machines. What is most disturbing about them is their living of our lives for us. Is it misguided to search for *particular* additional functions beyond the competence of machines to do for us? Perhaps what we desire is to live (an active web) ourselves, in contact with reality. (And this, machines cannot do *for* us.) Without elaborating on the implications of this, which I believe connect surprisingly with issues about free will and causal accounts of knowledge, we need merely note the intricacy of the question of what matters *for people* other than their experiences. Until one finds a satisfactory answer, and determines that this answer does not *also* apply to animals, one cannot reasonably claim that only the felt experiences of animals limit what we may do to them.

---

2 Some wouldn't use the transformation machine at all; it seems like *cheating*. But the one-time use of the transformation machine would not remove all challenges; there would still be obstacles for the new us to overcome, a new plateau from which to strive even higher. And is this plateau any the less earned or deserved than that provided by genetic endowment and early childhood environment? But if the transformation machine could be used indefinitely often, so that we could accomplish anything by pushing a button to transform ourselves into someone who could do it easily, there would remain no limits we *need* to strain against or try to transcend. Would there be anything left *to do?* Do some theological views place God outside of time because an omniscient omnipotent being couldn't fill up his days?

45

The Good Life

EPICURUS

Epicurus (341–271 B.C.) was a Greek thinker and teacher. He spent much of his life in Athens. Though few of his writings survive, the selections that follow contain the main elements of his views.

Like Bentham (reading 43), Epicurus identified the good with whatever is pleasant. In addition, he held specific views about which lives are pleasant. Such lives, he argued, are not spent at voluptuous or extravagant pursuits. These pursuits bring pain and disappointment and so should be avoided. In their place, we should be content with simpler pleasures, notably including those of friendship. Since acquiring and maintaining these pleasures requires neither power nor wealth, they are within the grasp of everyone.

Although Epicurus's main concern was personal happiness, his views on this had implications about other topics. Of these, two warrant special mention. First, Epicurus regarded happiness as closely bound up with justice. In his view, to live a life that is truly pleasant, we must be honorable and just as well as prudent. And, second, since he viewed only sensations as good or bad, Epicurus believed that death is not to be feared. Since the dead lack sensation, their condition is not an evil.

LETTER TO MENOECEUS

Let no one when young delay to study philosophy, nor when he is old grow weary of his study. For no one can come too early or too late to secure the health of his soul. And the man who says that the age for philosophy has either not yet come or has gone by is like the man who says that the age for happiness is not yet come to him, or has passed away. Wherefore both when young and old a man must study philosophy, that as he grows old he may be young in blessings through the grateful recollection of what has been, and that in youth he may be old as well, since he will know no fear of what is to come. We must then meditate on the things that make our happiness, seeing that when that is with us we have all, but when it is absent we do all to win it.

The things which I used unceasingly to commend to you, these do and practise, considering them to be the first principles of the good life. First of all believe that god is a being immortal and blessed, even as the common idea of

615

a god is engraved on men's minds, and do not assign to him anything alien to his immortality or illsuited to his blessedness: but believe about him everything that can uphold his blessedness and immortality. For gods there are, since the knowledge of them is by clear vision. But there are not such as the many believe them to be: for indeed they do not consistently represent them as they believe them to be. And the impious man is not he who denies the gods of the many, but he who attaches to the gods the beliefs of the many. For the statements of the many about the gods are not conceptions derived from sensation, but false suppositions, according to which the greatest misfortunes befall the wicked and the greatest blessings the good by the gift of the gods. For men being accustomed always to their own virtues welcome those like themselves, but regard all that is not of their nature as alien.

Become accustomed to the belief that death is nothing to us. For all good and evil consists in sensation, but death is deprivation of sensation. And therefore a right understanding that death is nothing to us makes the mortality of life enjoyable, not because it adds to it an infinite span of time, but because it takes away the craving for immortality. For there is nothing terrible in life for the man who has truly comprehended that there is nothing terrible in not living. So that the man speaks but idly who says that he fears death not because it will be painful when it comes, but because it is painful in anticipation. For that which gives no trouble when it comes, is but an empty pain in anticipation. So death, the most terrifying of ills, is nothing to us, since so long as we exist, death is not with us; but when death comes, then we do not exist. It does not then concern either the living or the dead, since for the former it is not, and the latter are no more.

But the many at one moment shun death as the greatest of evils, at another yearn for it as a respite from the evils in life. But the wise man neither seeks to escape life nor fears the cessation of life, for neither does life offend him nor does the absence of life seem to be any evil. And just as with food he does not seek simply the larger share and nothing else, but rather the most pleasant, so he seeks to enjoy not the longest period of time, but the most pleasant.

And he who counsels the young man to live well, but the old man to make a good end, is foolish, not merely because of the desirability of life, but also because it is the same training which teaches to live well and to die well. Yet much worse still is the man who says it is good not to be born, but

'once born make haste to pass the gates of Death'.

For if he says this from conviction why does he not pass away out of life? For it is open to him to do so, if he had firmly made up his mind to this. But if he speaks in jest, his words are idle among men who cannot receive them.

We must then bear in mind that the future is neither ours, nor yet wholly not ours, so that we may not altogether expect it as sure to come, nor abandon hope of it, as if it will certainly not come.

We must consider that of desires some are natural, others vain, and of the natural some are necessary and others merely natural; and of the necessary some are necessary for happiness, others for the repose of the body, and others for very life. The right understanding of these facts enables us to refer all choice and avoidance to the health of the body and the soul's freedom from disturbance, since this is the aim of the life of blessedness. For it is to obtain this end that we always act, namely, to avoid pain and fear. And when this is once secured for us, all the tempest of the soul is dispersed, since the living creature has not to wander as though in search of something that is missing, and to look for some other thing by which he can fulfil the good of the soul and the good of the body. For it is then that we have need of pleasure, when we feel pain owing to the absence of pleasure; but when we do not feel pain, we no longer need pleasure. And for this cause we call pleasure the beginning and end of the blessed life. For we recognize pleasure as the first good innate in us, and from pleasure we begin every act of choice and avoidance, and to pleasure we return again, using the feeling as the standard by which we judge every good.

And since pleasure is the first good and natural to us, for this very reason we do not choose every pleasure, but sometimes we pass over many pleasures, when greater discomfort accrues to us as the result of them: and similarly we think many pains better than pleasures, since a greater pleasure comes to us when we have endured pains for a long time. Every pleasure then because of its natural kinship to us is good, yet not every pleasure is to be chosen: even as every pain also is an evil, yet not all are always of a nature to be avoided. Yet by a scale of comparison and by the consideration of advantages and disadvantages we must form our judgement on all these matters. For the good on certain occasions we treat as bad, and conversely the bad as good.

And again independence of desire we think a great good—not that we may at all times enjoy but a few things, but that, if we do not possess many, we may enjoy the few in the genuine persuasion that those have the sweetest pleasure in luxury who least need it, and that all that is natural is easy to be obtained, but that which is superfluous is hard. And so plain savours bring us pleasure equal to a luxurious diet, when all the pain due to want is removed; and bread and water produce the highest pleasure, when one who needs them puts them to his lips. To grow accustomed therefore to simple and not luxurious diet gives us health to the full, and makes a man alert for the needful employments of life, and when after long intervals we approach luxuries, disposes us better towards them, and fits us to be fearless of fortune.

When, therefore, we maintain that pleasure is the end, we do not mean the pleasures of profligates and those that consist in sensuality, as is supposed by some who are either ignorant or disagree with us or do not understand, but freedom from pain in the body and from trouble in the mind. For it is not continuous drinkings and revellings, nor the satisfaction of lusts, nor the enjoyment of fish and other luxuries of the wealthy table, which produce a pleasant life, but sober reasoning, searching out the motives for all choice and avoidance, and banishing mere opinions, to which are due the greatest disturbance of the spirit.

Of all this the beginning and the greatest good is prudence. Wherefore prudence is a more precious thing even than philosophy: far from prudence are sprung all the other virtues, and it teaches us that it is not possible to live pleasantly without living prudently and honourably and justly, nor, again, to live a life of prudence, honour, and justice without living pleasantly. For the virtues are by nature bound up with the pleasant life, and the pleasant life is inseparable from them. For indeed who, think you, is a better man than he who holds reverent opinions concerning the gods, and is at all times free from fear of death, and has reasoned out the end ordained by nature? He understands that the limit of good things is easy to fulfil and easy to attain, whereas the course of ills is either short in time or slight in pain: he laughs at destiny, whom some have introduced as the mistress of all things. He thinks that with us lies the chief power in determining events, some of which happen by necessity and some by chance, and some are within our control; for while necessity cannot be called to account, he sees that chance is inconstant, but that which is in our control is subject to no master, and to it are naturally attached praise and blame. For, indeed, it were better to follow the myths about the gods than to become a slave to the destiny of the natural philosophers: for the former suggests a hope of placating the gods by worship, whereas the latter involves a necessity which knows no placation. As to chance, he does not regard it as a god as most men do (for in a god's acts there is no disorder), nor as an uncertain cause of all things: for he does not believe that good and evil are given by chance to man for the framing of a blessed life, but that opportunities for great good and great evil are afforded by it. He therefore thinks it better to be unfortunate in reasonable action than to prosper in unreason. For it is better in a man's actions that what is well chosen should fail, rather than that what is ill chosen should be successful owing to chance.

Meditate therefore on these things and things akin to them night and day by yourself, and with a companion like to yourself, and never shall you be disturbed waking or asleep, but you shall live like a god among men. For a man who lives among immortal blessings is not like to a mortal being.

PRINCIPAL DOCTRINES

I. The blessed and immortal nature knows no trouble itself nor causes trouble to any other, so that it is never constrained by anger or favour. For all such things exist only in the weak.

II. Death is nothing to us: for that which is dissolved is without sensation; and that which lacks sensation is nothing to us.

III. The limit of quantity in pleasures is the removal of all that is painful. Wherever pleasure is present, as long as it is there, there is neither pain of body nor of mind, nor of both at once.

IV. Pain does not last continuously in the flesh, but the acutest pain is there for a very short time, and even that which just exceeds the pleasure in the flesh does not continue for many days at once. But chronic illnesses permit a predominance of pleasure over pain in the flesh.

V. It is not possible to live pleasantly without living prudently and honoura-bly and justly, nor again to live a life of prudence, honour, and justice without living pleasantly. And the man who does not possess the pleasant life, is not living prudently and honourably and justly, and the man who does not possess the virtuous life, cannot possibly live pleasantly.

VI. To secure protection from men anything is a natural good, by which you may be able to attain this end.

VII. Some men wished to become famous and conspicuous, thinking that they would thus win for themselves safety from other men. Wherefore if the life of such men is safe, they have obtained the good which nature craves; but if it is not safe, they do not possess that for which they strove at first by the instinct of nature.

VIII. No pleasure is a bad thing in itself: but the means which produce some pleasures bring with them disturbances many times greater than the pleasures.

IX. If every pleasure could be intensified so that it lasted and influenced the whole organism or the most essential parts of our nature, pleasures would never differ from one another.

X. If the things that produce the pleasures of profligates could dispel the fears of the mind about the phenomena of the sky and death and its pains, and also teach the limits of desires and of pains, we should never have cause to blame them: for they would be filling themselves full with pleasures from every source and never have pain of body or mind, which is the evil of life.

XI. If we were not troubled by our suspicions of the phenomena of the sky and about death, fearing that it concerns us, and also by our failure to grasp the limits of pains and desires, we should have no need of natural science.

XII. A man cannot dispel his fear about the most important matters if he does not know what is the nature of the universe but suspects the truth of some mythical story. So that without natural science it is not possible to attain our pleasures unalloyed.

XIII. There is no profit in securing protection in relation to men, if things above and things beneath the earth and indeed all in the boundless universe remain matters of suspicion.

XIV. The most unalloyed source of protection from men, which is secured to some extent by a certain force of expulsion, is in fact the immunity which results from a quiet life and the retirement from the world.

XV. The wealth demanded by nature is both limited and easily procured; that demanded by idle imaginings stretches on to infinity.

XVI. In but few things chance hinders a wise man, but the greatest and most important matters reason has ordained and throughout the whole period of life does and will ordain.

XVII. The just man is most free from trouble, the unjust most full of trouble.

XVIII. The pleasure in the flesh is not increased, when once the pain due to want is removed, but is only varied: and the limit as regards pleasure in the mind is begotten by the reasoned understanding of these very pleasures and of the emotions akin to them, which used to cause the greatest fear to the mind.

XIX. Infinite time contains no greater pleasure than limited time, if one measures by reason the limits of pleasure.

XX. The flesh perceives the limits of pleasure as unlimited and unlimited time is required to supply it. But the mind, having attained a reasoned understanding of the ultimate good of the flesh and its limits and having dissipated the fears concerning the time to come, supplies us with the complete life, and we have no further need of infinite time: but neither does the mind shun pleasure, nor, when circumstances begin to bring about the departure from life, does it approach its end as though it fell short in any way of the best life.

XXI. He who has learned the limits of life knows that that which removes the pain due to want and makes the whole of life complete is easy to obtain; so that there is no need of actions which involve competition.

XXII. We must consider both the real purpose and all the evidence of direct perception, to which we always refer the conclusions of opinion; otherwise, all will be full of doubt and confusion.

XXIII. If you fight against all sensations, you will have no standard by which to judge even those of them which you say are false.

XXIV. If you reject any single sensation and fail to distinguish between the conclusion of opinion as to the appearance awaiting confirmation and that which is actually given by the sensation or feeling, or each intuitive apprehension of the mind, you will confound all other sensations as well with the same groundless opinion, so that you will reject every standard of judgement. And if among the mental images created by your opinion you affirm both that which awaits confirmation and that which does not, you will not escape error, since you will have preserved the whole cause of doubt in every judgement between what is right and what is wrong.

XXV. If on each occasion instead of referring your actions to the end of nature, you turn to some other nearer standard when you are making a choice or an avoidance, your actions will not be consistent with your principles.

XXVI. Of desires, all that do not lead to a sense of pain, if they are not satisfied, are not necessary, but involve a craving which is easily dispelled, when the object is hard to procure or they seem likely to produce harm.

XXVII. Of all the things which wisdom acquires to produce the blessedness of the complete life, far the greatest is the possession of friendship.

XXVIII. The same conviction which has given us confidence that there is nothing terrible that lasts for ever or even for long, has also seen the protection of friendship most fully completed in the limited evils of this life.

XXIX. Among desires some are natural and necessary, some natural but not necessary, and others neither natural nor necessary, but due to idle imagination.

XXX. Wherever in the case of desires which are physical, but do not lead to a sense of pain, if they are not fulfilled, the effort is intense, such pleasures are due to idle imagination, and it is not owing to their own nature that they fail to be dispelled, but owing to the empty imaginings of the man.

XXXI. The justice which arises from nature is a pledge of mutual advantage to restrain men from harming one another and save them from being harmed.

XXXII. For all living things which have not been able to make compacts not to harm one another or be harmed, nothing ever is either just or unjust; and likewise too for all tribes of men which have been unable or unwilling to make compacts not to harm or be harmed.

XXXIII. Justice never is anything in itself, but in the dealings of men with one another in any place whatever and at any time it is a kind of compact not to harm or be harmed.

XXXIV. Injustice is not an evil in itself, but only in consequence of the fear which attaches to the apprehension of being unable to escape those appointed to punish such actions.

XXXV. It is not possible for one who acts in secret contravention of the terms of the compact not to harm or be harmed, to be confident that he will escape detection, even if at present he escapes a thousand times. For up to the time of death it cannot be certain that he will indeed escape.

XXXVI. In its general aspect justice is the same for all, for it is a kind of mutual advantage in the dealings of men with one another: but with reference to the individual peculiarities of a country or any other circumstances the same thing does not turn out to be just for all.

XXXVII. Among actions which are sanctioned as just by law, that which is proved on examination to be of advantage in the requirements of men's dealings with one another, has the guarantee of justice, whether it is the same for all or not. But if a man makes a law and it does not turn out to lead to advantage in men's dealings with each other, then it no longer has the essential nature of justice. And even if the advantage in the matter of justice shifts from one side to the other, but for a while accords with the general concept, it is none the less just for that period in the eyes of those who do not confound themselves with empty sounds but look to the actual facts.

XXXVIII. Where, provided the circumstances have not been altered, actions which were considered just, have been shown not to accord with the general concept in actual practice, then they are not just. But where, when circumstances have changed, the same actions which were sanctioned as just no longer lead to advantage, there they were just at the time when they were of advantage for the dealings of fellow-citizens with one another; but subsequently they are no longer just, when no longer of advantage.

XXXIX. The man who has best ordered the element of disquiet arising from external circumstances has made those things that he could akin to himself and the rest at least not alien: but with all to which he could not do even this, he has refrained from mixing, and has expelled from his life all which it was of advantage to treat thus.

XL. As many as possess the power to procure complete immunity from their neighbours, these also live most pleasantly with one another, since they have the most certain pledge of security, and after they have enjoyed the fullest intimacy, they do not lament the previous departure of a dead friend, as though he were to be pitied.

46

Goodness as the Satisfaction of Informed Desire

RICHARD BRANDT

For biographical information about Richard Brandt, see reading 25. This selection is from chapter 6 of his book A Theory of the Good and the Right.

According to one influential account of value, what is good for any person is just the satisfaction of his desires. But which desires are relevant? Are all desires on an equal footing, or do some have more authority than others?

In this reading, Brandt proposes a version of the second answer. His point is not merely that some desires cannot be satisfied unless more, or more intensely held, others are frustrated. Instead, the crucial question is whether a desire could survive exposure to repeated and vivid presentations of all available information—that is, current scientific knowledge and whatever can be inferred from it. If a desire would not persist under these conditions—if it would be extinguished by "cognitive psychotherapy"— then it is what Brandt calls an irrational *desire.*

What sorts of desires might not persist? Among Brandt's examples are desires that depend on false beliefs, desires that were shaped by the attitudes of parents, teachers, and respected others, and desires that were caused by childhood deprivation. To the extent that these desires would be extinguished by full exposure to facts and logic, a rational person would not wish to pursue them. Hence, their satisfaction is no part of a person's good.

The general project of the first part of this book has been to see how far logic and evidence can take us in criticizing actions, pleasures, and desires. We have already discussed how far they can take us in criticizing actions to a first approximation, that is, while ignoring the question whether the desires or aversions involved in action can themselves be criticized on the basis of information. We now consider how we can appraise actions to a second approximation by providing a critique of desires and aversions.

This critique, based on the theory of the genesis of pleasures and desires, will tell us which things a fully rational—roughly, a fully informed—person would want or enjoy. I shall show that certain and only certain kinds of things would be rationally desired by certain kinds of persons or in certain kinds of situation, and in some cases that a certain kind of thing would be enjoyed or desired by *every* rational person.

Most philosophers have supposed that such a critique of desires and pleasures is impossible; it is thought that facts and logic cannot show, say, that an intrinsic desire is mistaken. Hume, it is supposed, had the last word:

> . . . it is only in two senses that any affection can be called unreasonable. First, when a passion such as hope or fear, grief or joy, despair or security, is founded on the supposition of the existence of objects, which really do not exist. Secondly, when in exerting any passion in action, we choose means insufficient for the designed end, and deceive ourselves in our judgment of causes and effects. Where a passion is neither founded on false suppositions, nor chooses means insufficient for the end, the understanding can neither justify nor condemn it. It is not contrary to reason to prefer the destruction of the whole world to the scratching of my finger. It is not contrary to reason for me to choose my total ruin, to prevent the least uneasiness of an Indian, or person wholly unknown to me. It is as little contrary to reason to prefer even my own acknowledged lesser good to my greater, and have a more ardent affection for the former than the latter. A trivial good may, from certain circumstances, produce a desire superior to what arises from the greatest and most valuable enjoyment. . . .[1]

Of course, we are here concerned only with at least partly intrinsic desires and aversions—desires for some outcome at least partly *for itself*, not just because it is in some way a means to something else that is desired.

Earlier conclusions have already shown that some desires or aversions are in a sense mistaken. For they show that a rational person, with his desires just as they are, had sometimes better undertake psychological treatment to *remove* a certain desire. A member of Congress might find that the whole set of outcomes he most wants can be realized only if he gives up drinking excessive amounts of alcohol. So the drinking has to go. And, if that has to go, the desire had also better be changed; removal of the desire will make him more comfortable. So, if he is rational, he will see to the removal of the desire. Such reflections do not show, however, that there is anything wrong with a desire for alcohol itself. All that is shown is the relation between this desire and the satisfaction of a large set of other desires. In what follows, however, I shall show something very different from this: that there is something mistaken about certain desires or aversions, just in themselves, or at least in their occurring with an intensity beyond a certain point.

The critique to come will show that some desires, aversions, or pleasures would be present (or absent) in some persons if their total motivational machinery were fully suffused by available information; and will show how to identify such desires, aversions, or pleasures for a given person. Less metaphorically, the aim is to show that some intrinsic desires and aversions would be present

---

1 David Hume, *Treatise of Human Nature* (1740), Bk. II, Pt. III, Sec. 3.

in some persons if relevant available information registered fully, that is, if the persons repeatedly represented to themselves, in an ideally vivid way, and at an appropriate time, the available information which is relevant in the sense that it would make a difference to desires and aversions if they thought of it. By 'ideally vivid way' I mean that the person gets the information at the focus of attention, with maximal vividness and detail, and with no hesitation or doubt about its truth. I mean by 'available information' . . . relevant beliefs which are a part of the 'scientific knowledge' of the day, or which are justified on the basis of publicly available evidence in accordance with the canons of inductive or deductive logic, or justified on the basis of evidence which could now be obtained by procedures known to science.

We need to restrict further the kind of information that qualifies as 'relevant', in order to guarantee that the effectiveness of the information is a function of its content. If every time I thought of having a martini, I made myself go through multiplication tables for five minutes, the valence of a martini might well decline. But obviously the desire for a martini is not misdirected simply if it fails to survive confrontation with the multiplication table in this way. Any desire would be discouraged by this procedure. We want to say that a thought is functioning properly in the criticism of desires only if its effect is not one its occurrence would have on any desire, and only if its effect is a function of its content. It must be a thought in some fairly restricted way about the thing desired; for instance, a thought about the expectable effects of the thing, or about the kind of thing it is, or about how well one would like it if it happened, and so on.

The claim is that relevant available information, if confronted on repeated occasions, affects our desires. But how often is 'repeated'? We cannot be, and need not be, precise on this. If several representations have no effect, we can reasonably infer that more of them would do no better. But if several representations have some effect, the question arises what would happen if there were more? Presumably what we are after is the asymptote: what desires, aversions, and pleasures a person would have if the number of representations increased without limit, if the reflection had maximal impact by representation as often as you like.

Finally, I have said that the self-stimulation by representation of relevant information should come at 'an appropriate time'. When is that? Obviously, when the effect will maximize counterconditioning, inhibition, or relevant discrimination. For instance, the appropriate times for a smoker to reflect on the bad consequences of his habit are (1) just after inhaling, when the reflection may destroy any pleasure he ordinarily takes in the cigarette; (2) when he wants or is thinking about lighting a cigarette, when the reflection will tend (a) to set up an association between the idea of the state of affairs and contrary motivation, or (b) to make it clear that the total outcome will in fact not be pleasant with the inhibiting effect of that reflection; and (3) when he is having thoughts or images which tend to make the idea of smoking exciting, so that the reflection will associate these mental occurrences with a less glamorous image. But it is not clear that such reflections will be fruitless on any occasion when one is thinking about an outcome.

This whole process of confronting desires with relevant information, by repeatedly representing it, in an ideally vivid way, and at an appropriate time, I call *cognitive psychotherapy*. I call it so because the process relies simply upon reflection on available information, without influence by prestige of someone, use of evaluative language, extrinsic reward or punishment, or use of artificially induced feeling-states like relaxation. It is *value-free reflection*.

I shall call a person's desire, aversion, or pleasure 'rational' if it would survive or be produced by careful 'cognitive psychotherapy' for that person. I shall call a desire 'irrational' if it cannot survive compatibly with clear and repeated judgements about established facts. What this means is that rational desire (etc.) can confront, or will even be produced by, awareness of the truth; irrational desire cannot. It is obvious, of course, that desires do not logically follow from the awareness which supports them; the relation is causal and sometimes involves other desires, aversions, or pleasures.[2]

One implication of our definitions may be surprising. It arises from the fact that some valences, or dispositions to enjoy something, may resist extinction by inhibition and anything else, since they have been so firmly learned at an early age. By my definition these qualify as rational. For I use 'rational' as the contradictory of 'irrational' and have defined an 'irrational' desire (etc.) as one that would extinguish after cognitive psychotherapy. If a desire will not extinguish, then it is not irrational. This result is consistent with the general view that a desire (etc.) is rational if it has been influenced by facts and logic as much as possible. Unextinguishable desires meet this condition.

What reason do we have for thinking that optimal exposure to certain information, such as contemplated in cognitive psychotherapy, will affect desires/aversions in specified ways? First there is theoretical reason. In the examples to follow I shall in each case present first a theory of the genesis of the relevant desires/aversions. In some cases this will be obvious, hardly open to controversy; in other cases I shall cite evidence to show that certain desires in fact have developed in a certain way. Then I shall show that desires/aversions produced in these ways are bound to extinguish by repeated self-stimulation by information, given the facts about how desires (etc.) extinguish as described in the preceding chapter. The procedure will therefore be deductive; it will be like showing how a physical particle of a given description must move under specified conditions, given what we know of gravitational attraction, electromagnetism, and the theory of motion under forces.

There is also empirical support from the clinical reports of psychotherapists for the view that exposure to relevant information will affect desires/aversions in the ways to be suggested. There is less of this kind of support than we would like and one reason for this is probably that psychotherapists aim primarily

---

2 If a desire required to support another desire, the rationality of which is being assessed, is itself irrational, we must say that the desire being appraised is irrational.

to help the patient, at least mostly in the direction in which the patient himself asks for help, and not to help the patient find his ideal value-system. Usually the therapist is more engaged in reducing anxieties than he is in changing desires, or finding rational desires; and he uses whatever devices, from cognitive self-stimulations to electric shocks, will reach the intended goal. Nevertheless, many therapists have had a good deal of success in changing desires through patient self-stimulation by true statements—for example, making excessive alcohol consumption aversive, reducing the craving for the approval of other people, mitigating the aversiveness of being alone, reducing the aversiveness of being self-assertive in relation to one's spouse or employer, reducing the intensity of the desire to achieve in all situations, and reducing the desire to smoke. So we have fairly direct observational evidence that self-stimulation can change desires (etc.) in the anticipated way. In fact, we hardly need to turn to therapists to know that reflections can change intrinsic desires and pleasures. What woman does not know that repeating to herself the facts that a beloved male is inflexible, selfish, unloving, not very bright, and wholly concerned with success in business, will over time reduce her emotional commitment to him, and make her enjoy his company less?

I. SOME TYPES OF 'MISTAKEN' DESIRES, AVERSIONS, OR PLEASURES

Let us now look at some types of likes/dislikes, or desires/aversions and see how it is that we must view them as irrational. The various types are neither exhaustive nor mutually exclusive. They are to be viewed as collections of examples, and should be used as a guide in thinking about cases of particular concern.

i. First Mistake: Dependence on False Beliefs.

It is obvious that persons often desire outcomes now as a result of having (falsely) thought them means to ends already wanted or enjoyed: associating the means with the end or with the thought of the end, or associating the thought of the means with the liked end or the thought of the liked end. For instance, a student may have begun to work for a Ph.D. and an academic profession because he thought his parents (themselves professors) would be disappointed in him if he did not; and now he wants an academic life for itself (but not because he has found it satisfying). Or, a person may have developed an aversion to the taste of a certain food because he thought it made him ill. A person may now feel uncomfortable about enjoying himself because he thought God (or his parents) wanted him to work hard and eschew indulgences; and he wanted to please God (or his parents).

Let us suppose (as often happens) that the relevant beliefs are false. Parents wish a child only to be happy, not to enter an academic life; certain foods do not make one ill; there may be no God, or if there is one, he may not disapprove of personal indulgence. Assuming that there are no other facts, not involved in the genesis, reflection upon which supports the desire, a desire with such a genesis will extinguish in cognitive psychotherapy. Why?

Extinction will occur primarily through inhibition. If the person repeats to himself the fact that he will not achieve the goals involved in instituting the desire by doing a certain thing, the intrinsic desire for doing that thing will diminish. Consider the parallel with the salivation of Pavlov's dogs. The thought of the instrumental outcome (the Ph.D.) is like the sound of the buzzer; the desire for it to occur is like the salivation; the pleasant thought that its occurrence would please parents is like being offered the food. Then, as the dogs stopped salivating at the sound of the buzzer when the food was regularly omitted, so the student will stop being motivated to go for the Ph.D. when he regularly reminds himself that doing so will not please his parents. (Of course, the desire to get the Ph.D. will not extinguish if by this time the student has other reasons—for instance, finds academic work inherently satisfying.) Counterconditioning can presumably also play some role: if the student reminds himself that a Ph.D. is for him very hard work, that he was not cut out to be an academic, and so on.

ii. Second Mistake: Artificial Desire-Arousal in Culture-Transmission.

An important factor in the genesis of desires, aversions, likes, dislikes, is a child's observation of the attitudes and values of other persons—parents, teachers, or peers, not to mention films and television—producing ambition perhaps to own a powerful sports car, aspiration (to belong to a prestige occupation) or aversion (to belonging to a low-prestige one).

How does the observation of the attitudes of others produce these likes and dislikes, desires and aversions? In part the process is one of direct conditioning: the child feels anxiety when another child is the target of the critical attitudes of others . . . ; and this anxiety becomes attached by conditioning to the idea of the situation for which the other child is criticized. Alternatively, the process may be one of those roughly classified as 'desire acquisition by identification'. . . .

Still again, there may be beliefs essentially involved. For instance, the statements of parents may make the child believe there are unspecified unpleasant consequences of being in a certain situation, from which the child will infer that the situation itself must be unpleasant in some way. Given any of these cases, an *intrinsic* aversion (desire, etc.) is produced after conditioning has done its work.

The production of these intrinsic desires/aversions is artificial if they could not have been brought about by experience with actual situations which the desires are for and the aversions against. Take, for instance, a non-prestige occupation like garbage collection, or marriage to a person of another race, religion or nationality. Actual experience with these situations could be highly satisfying (and there is no reason to suppose it would be aversive), and would not produce an intrinsic aversion. So, naturally produced desires/aversions would not coincide with those produced in these artificial ways. I shall call a desire/aversion artificial if it could not have been produced naturally. (A desire/aversion which could be produced naturally may be called 'authentic'.)

These attitudes do derive from the realities of the situation in one sense, for the firm attitudes of others are real facts with which people have to deal. But intense concern with the attitudes of other people is itself founded on error—the false belief that the attitudes of others are crucially important for an adult, especially if the attitudes in question are those of one's own parents only. An independent adult need not fear the sanctions his parents might try to impose; for, realistically, a person will not lose the affection of his parents through doing some of the things of which they disapprove. Of course, if a person wishes not to upset his parents, then their reaction is a fact to be taken into account like any other; just as, if all one's friends strongly dislike someone one is considering for marriage, that fact is one to be taken into account too. The situation arising from favourable or unfavourable attitudes of others is complex, but on the whole the attitudes of others hardly serve by themselves to render a desire realistic.

All artificial desires are prime candidates for extinction or diminution, by cognitive psychotherapy, through inhibition or counterconditioning, or both. Why? Partly because the usually essential supporting beliefs are false; and in so far as they are, the attitude will tend to extinguish for reasons already explained. Partly also because any anxiety conditioned through the attitudes of others will tend to extinguish by inhibition after a review of the relative unimportance of such attitudes for the mature adult. And partly by counterconditioning: through reflection on the fact that one's aversion is preventing one from having some potentially very satisfying experiences or relationships, or that one's desire is leading one into experiences or relationships one simply does not like. For instance, a person might want, as a result of these artificial processes, to be in the academic profession; but he might have good reason also to believe—if he thought about it—that he would be bored by the scholarly work involved, that he would not be effective as a teacher and therefore would dislike teaching, and that he would not like the limited financial prospects of the academic life. If he did reflect on these things, he would tend to establish an aversion which would be incompatible with his ambition to hold an academic post.

Since such 'artificial' desires/aversions would extinguish by this kind of reflection, in 'cognitive psychotherapy', they are irrational.

Let us pause and apply our results so far to a desire which has received more attention in the psychological literature than any other, except perhaps sex: the desire for achievement. Unfortunately, when we say that a person has a strong desire to achieve, it is not clear precisely what we mean. Psychologists seem to agree on a rather broad but vague definition. Desire to achieve is said to be desire for 'success in competition with some standards of excellence.'[3]

---

[3] J. W. Atkinson, ed., *Motives in Fantasy, Action, and Society* (New York: D. Van Nostrand, 1958), p. 181; also pp. 76, 324, 497, 516–17.

But a comparative notion gives us a more interesting conception. On this conception, the desire to achieve is not just a desire to do difficult things well, or make some important contribution in life, or reach some long-term professional goal. It is a desire to be, and to appear, superior in many areas in which one is emotionally involved—such as tennis, argument, doing well professionally, and so on.

Where might this general desire come from? It could come from native satisfaction from doing difficult things. Children take pleasure in learning to stand or turn over; they enjoy exploring the environment, constructing things, solving puzzles. In summary, they enjoy learning skills which enable effective interaction with their environment. Insofar as a desire to achieve is a desire just to do difficult things well, it derives from native liking, and is not artificial; but some persons desire achievement in my explained sense because they think it brings respect if not affection—a belief which is partially false, since achievement is apt to produce irritation; or, they think that achievement will lead to satisfaction of various sorts. Empirical studies suggest that the desire comes from early experiences, especially from demands made by, and rewards given by, parents who are anxious about the performance of their children. A middle-class family, concerned for the child's later success, is apt to welcome any sign of precocity with delight and praise, and to be uncomfortably rejecting if the child fails to do well. One study has shown that children high in achievement motivation had mothers who (1) made demands on them for mastery of various forms of behaviour at a relatively early age (going outside to play, knowing their way about the city, doing well in competition), (2) gave more physically expressed affection for success, and (3) set relatively fewer restrictions on behaviour (such as forbidding sloppiness at the table, leaving clothes about, or failing in school).

If the desire for achievement must be explained in this way—primarily by the congratulations, rejections, and training practices of concerned parents—is it authentic and rational? Consider motivation to be superior in tennis. Could it have been produced realistically by contact with the costs and satisfactions to which such motivation leads? The motivation to be superior may lead to a determination to win (which can put off partners or opponents who merely want to enjoy the game), or to a choice of partners and opponents who are at least one's equal in competence (to the irritation of the others). Hence, being so motivated may be a loss. On the other hand, a reputation for competence will bring invitations to play from abler players and one will enjoy more exciting competition. This is a gain. Such losses and gains have their analogues in professional or business life. Only here there are further costs: of encompassing absorption in getting ahead, which diminishes other benefits of living; of disappointment, because of the difficulty of being superior to everyone. Achievement motivation in this sense is very different from the desire just to work well, or to make a contribution to social life. In reviewing his motivation, a person must ask himself in detail where the total activity is leading. If, when he does this, his fever diminishes, his desire is shown to be at too high a pitch. At that level it is irrational.

Some business firms have thought it worthwhile to encourage achievement motivation (in some sense) among their executives, and they have employed psychologists to bring about that motivation, apparently with some success. The reported methods raise some doubts about the rationality of the heightened motivation. The new level of motivation is neither authentic nor rational if it can be reached only by a mixture of threats, misinformation, and good company.

iii. Third Mistake: Generalization from Untypical Examples.

Some further values which would extinguish in cognitive psychotherapy are neither artificial attitudes, nor based on mistaken beliefs. Rather, they are attitudes which have developed from familiarity with samples of liked/disliked situations but from *untypical* samples, or in an untypical context. For instance, I may dislike dogs because in childhood one attacked me; or I may feel uncomfortable inside public school buildings because in my childhood I was punished or wholly bored there; or, on a simpler level, as a small boy I may refuse a serving of any kind of fish because I have eaten a piece of cod (my first and only experience of fish) and disliked it heartily, saying now, 'I can't stand fish.'

How do such attitudes come about? All learning involves some generalization. Much to our advantage we do not learn a response only to stimuli exactly like those in the original learning situation, but to a *range* of stimuli more or less like the originals. Thus, if I acquire a conditioned like or dislike (etc.) because of one or more experiences, the attitude will be directed towards some *type* of object, and this type may be much broader than the kind of example which was the source of that attitude. If I am attacked by a dog, I could develop an attitude towards all dogs or all mammals, or at least all mammals outside my house.

It is obvious that attitudes which are the result of wild generalizations from a narrow set of experiences—say an aversion to all dogs as a result of being bitten by a terrier which I had provoked—will extinguish in cognitive psychotherapy. Why will they? Partly by counterconditioning because, say, interaction with a friendly well-behaved intelligent poodle will elicit warm attitudes towards dogs of this type, incompatible with my aversion towards *all* dogs. But partly it will diminish by inhibition, since the aversion to all dogs will receive little or no support from further experience with dogs. As we broaden the set of samples of interaction with dogs, the conditioned disliking response will rarely be given new support by another unfortunate experience. So much is clear.[4]

But not all attitudes resulting from generalization are irrational. Let us try to state more exactly which such attitudes would extinguish in psychotherapy and which would not. It is plausible to suppose that an attitude towards

---

[4] One might ask why, then, seriously disabling aversions based on early unrepeated traumatic experiences do not extinguish readily. Part of the answer to this is that the early experience produces avoidance behaviour so that there are no further experiences which could reduce the impact of the original.

something which has its genesis in an experience not likely to repeat itself would extinguish. This generalization can be more precisely formulated if we define the notion of a 'typical experience' as one producing an attitude which would not extinguish if the agent reflected on the percentage of experiences which could rationally be expected with things of that sort over the course of his lifetime. Take my aversion towards dogs because of being bitten by a terrier which I had provoked by tramping on its nose. Suppose the aversion would extinguish after repeated reflection on the fact that only .0001 per cent of terriers will attack me if I do not provoke them. Or suppose that only .0001 per cent of St. Bernards will attack me even if I do step on both nose and tail, and reflection on this would extinguish my terrier-based aversion to St. Bernards. Then my actual aversion to all dogs is based on untypical experiences.[5] If we adopt this definition, then we can say of the attitudes based on generalization, only those which are untypical will extinguish in cognitive psychotherapy and hence are irrational.[6]

J. S. Mill stated in *Utilitarianism* that power, fame, and money come to be wanted for themselves and indeed come to be part of one's 'happiness' (one really does like them for themselves and would be unhappy in their absence), because of associations with the good things to which they lead. Let us suppose he is right in this. Are the valence and liking irrational? To answer, we must first determine as best we can (on the basis of available information) the frequency and consistency with which money will provide us with the things we already like. Then, we must see if a clear awareness of these facts will extinguish our desire for money. Money does buy a good many things, and absence of it can have unpleasant consequences. But how much can it buy, and how universally does a merely modest income have unpleasant consequences? When we get the answer to these questions firmly in mind we shall be well on the way to knowing whether a desire for money is irrational.

Some critics might say that any desire for money *for itself* is irrational. It is obviously irrational to want money for any other reason than for what it buys. Our theory need not lead to this consequence; at least it does not if it is just a fact of human nature that we learn to like (want) for themselves things which reliably lead to other things we already like (want). But this consequence need not be dismaying; for we can discriminate various situations involving money, and our theory certainly does not imply that it is rational to prefer money to various other goods in life with which it might be in competition—quite the contrary.

---

5 There is a kind of person-relativism here: what would count as an untypical experience for an Oxford don (meeting a rattlesnake) might be typical for a Navajo Indian.

6 A related point is that our likes and desires are sometimes fixed not by untypical *experiences* but by *memory-traces* which may be unrepresentative of the experiences. If I have selectively forgotten the aversive aspects of some experience, my present attitude may be more positive than is rational. So my attitudes to sea-voyages may be more positive than the actual past combination of fun and nausea would lead one to expect. Presumably they would change after firm and repeated reminders of how things typically were and are.

iv. Fourth Mistake: Exaggerated Valences Produced by Early Deprivation.

Some people, especially children, appear to have a virtually insatiable craving for attention. And there are abnormally high desires for commendation or admiration from others, or for the company of others. Sometimes these desires seem similar to the condition of persons who literally do not know when they have had enough to eat or drink, although the physiology cannot be parallel.[7]

Similarly there are abnormal aversions, say to spending money except for necessities, like that noted in the following letter to a columnist:

> Dear Abby: My husband grew up fatherless during the depression. Now, at age 50, his net worth is around the half-million dollar mark. He is a professor with tenure, and has an excellent retirement and insurance program. Yet he buys second-hand clothes, day-old bread, and refuses to spend any money on a decent car, vacations or travel.
>
> The reason? He wants to be sure he has enough money for his old age. What could be the matter with him?
>
> HIS WIFE.

This case is extreme, but in milder forms the syndrome is not infrequent. It appears among rats. Rats which have been deprived of food, especially shortly after the time of weaning, respond to restriction of food intake for a week or more, by massive hoarding when food becomes abundant, acquiring and storing as many as several hundred pellets an hour as compared with the normal practice of storing half-a-dozen pellets.

There is testimony that the absence of affection and warm cuddling early in a child's life can lead to insatiable demands for attention.

These cases suggest a syndrome whereby an early and prolonged deprivation of something wanted—enough for discomfort and anxiety to be involved—results in an abnormally high development of desire for that thing in later years. It looks as if anxiety gets associated with its absence or with the expectation, even quite small, of its absence. The anxiety then drives the person to relieve it, by securing the object the absence of which arouses it. Thus a child who has been deprived of affection and esteem may, even very shortly after a friendly compliment, become anxious about the attitudes of others and can be made unanxious only by a steady stream of attention or praise. Or, a man who has been economically deprived during childhood will experience conditioned anxiety with the thought of absence of economic means, so that expenditure of money is a threatening experience. We may recall McClelland's point that the experience of deprivation is apt to be very emotionally disturbing at an

---

[7] The desires to eat and drink arise partly from the activation of sensing devices in the brain, by the content of the blood. Eating or drinking does not bring the content of the blood up to standard for some period of time, but a person stops eating or drinking long before elapse of such a period. Hence we know there is a system of signalling which renders the sensing device temporarily impervious to the relevant deficiency in the blood and thereby shuts off the desire for food or water—say a signal from a wet throat, or from a full stomach. If this system of signals does not work properly, the person may continue to feel like eating or drinking, and enjoy eating or drinking, almost indefinitely.

early age, when the child does not have any clear expectation about when the deprivation will end.

It is not suggested that all 'insatiable' desires derive from early deprivation.

It seems that such abnormally strong desires would extinguish in cognitive psychotherapy. Such traditional psychoanalysts would say that if a person brought to consciousness the connection of early deprivation with his intense desire (= insight), the abnormally strong desire would abate. On the theory of learning and conditioning adopted earlier, the question is whether cognitive procedures can extinguish the connection between anxiety and the thought of the absence, or possible absence, of something. The answer is that if a person repeatedly reminds himself when he feels rejected, that others warmly accept him and will continue to do so in the foreseeable future, his anxiety in the absence of an expression of affection will diminish by inhibition. (One might also say that the thoughts will produce pleasant relaxation, so that the anxiety tends to be extinguished by counterconditioning.) Of course, the extinction process may take time. So, in so far as the suggested theory about these abnormal desires is correct, vivid repeated representation of knowable facts should bring about a reduction in intensity. We must conclude that a desire of this abnormal sort is 'irrational'.

What sorts of desires might be related to anxiety in this way? It would seem that desire for any situation thought to help secure the presence of an object of which one was once deprived might be a result. So, if the deprivation was of affection or acceptance, the desire might be to conform with conventional proprieties (others dislike unconventionality), to work for financial security (money buys affection), or to achieve in professional work (achievement buys love).[8]

The whole issue whether some desires or pleasures can be identified as irrational may seem purely theoretical. It may be thought that important decisions are so complex that, even if we became convinced that some desire was irrational, the discovery could make no significant difference to the decision process. This view, however, is a profound mistake. Very often difficult decisions are difficult because, although a great many pros point in one direction, and almost all cons can be overmatched by pros, there is one consideration which remains a serious matter. For instance, suppose a Harvard professor is offered a position in Los Angeles, and is tempted to take it: his salary will be better, the research facilities equal, the graduate students and colleagues equal,

---

8 Could a rational person desire a logically impossible state of affairs (for example, to prove that π is a rational number), or a state of affairs describable only in meaningless language (for example, his being reincarnated 100 years from now), or a causally impossible state of affairs (for example, the past being different)? Desire is an 'intentional attitude' and can occur when its object is unreal or even impossible. Obviously people do desire such things. But would they if they were rational in my sense? And if not, why not? Obviously people do not stop desiring such things the instant they see the states of affairs are impossible—a man in love may know full well that his heart's desire is something that cannot be.

In my view, a rational person would not desire these things, but because the desire would disappear in cognitive psychotherapy—by inhibition, or counterconditioning after repeated reminders that the situation cannot possibly obtain. There is no simpler reason for thinking that such desires are irrational.

the climate appealing, and he likes surfing. There is one difficulty: he is appalled by the thought of detaching himself from Harvard. Not that he thinks his stature in his profession would be diminished if he were to move; he knows that this is not the case. But he 'identifies' with Harvard; he feels himself part of a great tradition, the historically most important educational institution in the United States. Furthermore, his father would have wanted him to be at Harvard. Now undoubtedly most persons have very good reasons for hesitating to leave Harvard, but it could well be that *his* reason, his 'identification' with Harvard, is just irrational. However that may be, the point is that if he found that his basic reason for preferring to stay at Harvard is irrational, his practical problem would be resolved. For a decision to move had been blocked by one particular concern. And, when he identifies this concern as irrational, he will be clear that the rational thing is to make the move. Thus the identification of a single desire as irrational may have profound importance for a large personal decision.

2. RATIONAL DESIRES AND THE CONCEPT OF THE INTRINSICALLY GOOD

We now have before us the concept of an irrational desire or aversion: one that would not survive cognitive psychotherapy, at least with its present strength. And we have the concept of a rational desire or aversion: one that is not irrational. How nearly does the notion of the rationally desired approximate to the concept of the *good?*

One might say that it makes no difference how close it is. For, if we want to desire and act with reason, we want to know what is a rational desire—one that is maximally criticized by facts and logic. When we have identified a rational desire, we have that: a desire in which all the changes confrontation with available information will bring have been wrought. If we are dedicated to rational desiring and acting, we have what we want. If the term 'good' does not refer to what is rationally desired, so much the worse for the concept of the 'good'.

Even so, it is of interest whether the term 'rationally desired', or some longer phrase incorporating it, means the same as 'good', or if not, would be a useful replacement for that term. If so, it might be wise to conduct primary education so as to give a new meaning to 'good'—in terms of 'rationally desired'.

The word 'good', of course, appears in many different constructions, and the meaning or use of the term in these several constructions is not identical. Consider, for instance: 'a good car', 'a good father', 'good at swimming', 'good for making jelly'. Historically, philosophers have been most concerned with its use in such sentences as 'Knowledge is intrinsically good.'

Recently, some philosophers have thought that no expression in which no value word occurs is either exactly or even approximately synonymous with 'good', at least in its important uses. In contrast, many other philosophers, from Aristotle to Sidgwick and Rawls, have thought that there are expressions approximately synonymous with 'good' in its important uses, or at least functionally good replacements for it. In particular, some have thought that for something to be intrinsically good is just for somebody, or everybody, to like it or want it for itself. On this view, if fame were what someone or everyone wants, it would be good. Others have thought that for something to be intrinsically good is for it to be wanted or liked by persons (or perhaps some individual person) with certain qualifications, perhaps knowledge or virtue. Obviously the proposal I have been making belongs with this latter group. We should notice, however, that the altruistic or at least non-self-interested desires pose a problem, for while something may be a good thing if it is the object of a rational altruistic desire, we should clearly hesitate to say that the object of someone's rational altruistic desire is necessarily something good for him, something that is a part of the person's welfare or well-being. This problem will arise again later.

We need not deliberate whether 'rationally desired' in my sense is exactly or approximately synonymous with 'intrinsically good' in its ordinary meaning. I have not argued that it is: in fact I think it is not. Whether it is a useful replacement I shall not debate at this juncture. . . .

I wish now, however, to put forward two claims on behalf of the conception of rational desire and its utility.

The first is that there is no sentence in which the word 'good' appears, at least in that core complex of uses which have been important for philosophy, which makes an identifiable point which cannot be made by a sentence containing 'rationally desired', doubtless in some complex clause but in which no 'value-word' is present. The claim is a large one. I shall not try to support it further, but merely offer two examples to make clear what claim is being made. Take: 'The Oldsmobile Cutlass is a good car for turnpike driving.' The meaning of this could be quite well construed as 'The Cutlass has a relatively large proportion of those qualities a fully rational person planning on turnpike driving would seek in a car.' In fact, this construction may be an over-kill. It would seem we may not need to appeal to a *fully* rational person in the sense which involves cognitive psychotherapy (and hence goes beyond rationality to a first approximation) unless it is to exclude desires to drive at speeds of 150 m.p.h. Or take: 'Knowledge is good in itself.' The meaning of this could be construed as 'Knowledge is something any fully rational person would want for himself, for no further reason.'

The second claim is that there are various things we want to say, on reflection, which can be said by talk of 'rational desire', but which cannot be said by 'good' or 'intrinsically good' in the ordinary use of these terms.

Suppose I ask myself whether, if I were fully rational, I would want fame for myself, or my own enjoyment. This seems a perfectly good and sensible question for anyone to raise. Yet how is one to raise it if one must do so with the terminology of 'good' in some of its constructions? It has been widely held that when we say that something is intrinsically good, we are committed to saying that anything just like it in respect of abstract properties is also good. As W. K. Frankena has said, 'A particular value judgement, however, is always implicitly general: when one says that X is good, one must be prepared to say that anything just like it is good and good in the same degree. Also, we must be prepared to give reasons why it is good, and this can only be done in the light of more general value judgements about what is good or at least prima facie good.'[9] But, if this is what 'good' implies, then we are in trouble with our original question whether I would want fame or enjoyment for myself, if I were fully rational. For I was not asking about everybody's fame or enjoyment. In fact, if I want fame for myself, what I precisely do not want, usually, is for everyone else to be famous. (What would fame be if everyone were famous?) Suppose I do want fame for myself but not for others, even after cognitive psychotherapy. What then am I to say, if I want to express the situation by 'good'? Not that fame is a good thing, which suggests it is good for everybody. Not that my being famous is a good thing, but not the fame of others. How about that my fame is a good thing for me? This sounds odd: it suggests that my fame would benefit my health, or promote my other interests. It is possible that some apt phrasing can be found, but it is doubtful.

It might be replied that if a question about what would be desired by a rational person cannot well be put in a familiar phrase involving 'good', then so much the worse for the importance of the question. It is true that 'good' is an old word, and that we might expect that phrases involving it would have developed meanings to permit us to make all the appraisive statements we want to make. But this seems not to be the case. 'Good' seems to be not flexible enough, in its standard English uses, for us to be able to raise the important questions we want to raise about desires.

---

[9] William Frankena, *Ethics* (Englewood Cliffs, NJ: Prentice-Hall, 1963), p. 64.

47

Full–Information Theories of Individual Good

DON LOEB*

Don Loeb (b. 1956) is Assistant Professor of Philosophy at the University of Vermont. He has published essays in metaethics. This essay first appeared in Social Theory and Practice *(Spring 1995).*

Loeb criticizes the view that a person's good consists of getting what he would want if he were fully informed. He traces the appeal of this view to two attractive ideas: first, that a person's good should bear some important relation to his actual motivational tendencies (the internalist intuition), and, second, that informed desires are more authoritative than uninformed ones (the epistemic intuition). However, Loeb argues that the effects of acquiring information depend on many factors, such as the manner and order of its presentation, which have nothing to do with its content. Some full-information theorists, such as Richard Brandt (reading 46), offer no principled reason to discount these effects, so their views violate the epistemic intuition. By contrast, others imagine the fully informed person as having greatly enhanced cognitive and imaginative powers. These theorists may do somewhat better at filtering out irrelevant effects. However, because they postulate vast changes in the person himself, they imply that his informed desires would have little connection to his actual motivational tendencies. In this way, their theories violate the internalist intuition. Because the epistemic and internalist intuitions pull us in different directions, and because no informed-desire theory can fully satisfy the epistemic intuition, Loeb concludes that we should abandon the full-information approach.

Our motivations often change as we become better informed, and it seems obvious that these changes are for the better. Thirsty though I am, I

---

* Richard Brandt and Peter Railton served as models of good philosophical thinking during my years in graduate school. I am grateful to them for inspiring me to continue working in ethics. As usual, my colleagues at the University of Vermont generously provided a great deal of very helpful discussion, commentary, and criticism. I am especially indebted to Sin Yee Chan, David Christensen, Hilary Kornblith, Arthur Kuflik, William Mann, and Derk Pereboom. A number of anonymous referees also helped me to improve the paper. I am grateful to them as well.

This paper is dedicated to the memory of William Frankena.

would no longer wish to drink the liquid in that glass were I to learn that it is poison and not water. My desire to see that man hanged would vanish upon my learning that he is the defense attorney and not the accused. And my desire to give up my career as a philosopher and become a lifeguard would diminish if I were to learn that lifeguards earn even less than philosophers. In each of these cases, the latter desire seems to reflect progress over the former, and the fuller information seems responsible for that progress.

Considerations like these have played a central role in a number of theories of rational desire and action, individual good and morality. Prominent among these are the enormously popular *full-information* theories of individual good. For example, Peter Railton holds that "an individual's good consists in what he would want himself to want, or to pursue, were he to contemplate his present situation from a standpoint fully and vividly informed about himself and his circumstances, and entirely free of cognitive error or lapses of instrumental rationality," and he uses this account of nonmoral goodness to build up his account of moral rightness.[1] Similarly, Richard Brandt proposes that we treat as rational all and only those desires which would survive a process of "cognitive psychotherapy"—roughly, "maximal criticism and correction by facts and logic." He then suggests that we treat as rational those actions which a person with such desires would perform if fully informed, and that we replace the phrase 'the best thing to do' with 'the rational thing to do,' since "the latter expression contains all that is clear in the former."[2]

Despite a good deal of criticism,[3] much of it involving clever and appealing counterexamples, full-information theories of individual good have shown remarkable resilience. In part, their resilience is due to the fact that the theories

---

1 Peter Railton, "Facts and Values," XIV *Philosophical Topics* No. 2 (Fall 1986), p. 16. See also "Moral Realism," *Philosophical Review,* XCV, No. 2 (April 1986) pp. 173–78, 190.

2 R. B. Brandt, *A Theory of the Good and the Right* (Oxford: Clarendon Press, 1979), pp. 10, 15. Among those who have accepted similar views are Stephen Darwall, *Impartial Reason* (Ithaca, NY: Cornell University Press, 1983), pp. 85–100, esp. pp. 96–98; Richard Hare, *Moral Thinking* (Oxford: Clarendon Press, 1981), pp. 101–106, 214–16; John Harsanyi, "Morality and the Theory of Rational Behaviour," in Amartya Sen and Bernard Williams, eds., *Utilitarianism and Beyond* (Cambridge: Cambridge University Press, 1982), pp. 55–56; John Rawls, *A Theory of Justice* (Cambridge: Harvard University Press, 1971), pp. 407–24; and Henry Sidgwick, *The Methods of Ethics,* 7th ed. (Indianapolis, IN: Hackett, 1981), pp. 109–13. For a related, but importantly different view, see David Lewis, "Dispositional Theories of Value," (symposium) *Proceedings of the Aristotlelian Society,* supp. vol. 63 (1989), pp. 112–38.

3 See, for example, Elizabeth Anderson, *Value in Ethics and Economics* (Cambridge: Harvard University Press, 1993), pp. 129–40; Norman Daniels, "Can Cognitive Psychotherapy Reconcile Reason and Desire?" *Ethics* 93 (July 1983) pp. 772–85; Gilbert Harman, "Critical Review," *Philosophical Studies* 42 (1982), pp. 119–39; Connie Rosati, "Naturalism, Normativity, and the Open Question Argument" (forthcoming in *Nous*); and David Sobel, "Full Information Accounts of Well-Being," *Ethics* 104 (July 1994), pp. 784–810.

  Particularly powerful objections are raised by J. David Velleman in "Brandt's Definition of 'Good'," XCVII *The Philosophical Review* (July 1988). Velleman directs two main criticisms against Brandt: that his definition of "good" alters the ordinary meaning of "good" in indefensible ways, and that it leaves questions about what is good empirically indeterminable. Although I am sympathetic with much of what Velleman has to say, I take issue with him on a few important points, and argue that some of his claims make sense only if we understand certain more fundamental problems with the full-information view. For the most part, however, my criticisms take a different approach than his.

have a strong intuitive appeal of their own: They appear to accommodate two very powerful intuitions, one motivational and the other epistemological, about the nature of the values they seek to define. Bringing these intuitive underpinnings into focus will help us to get beyond the counterexamples, and to see both why full-information theories continue to hang on and why they should ultimately be rejected. In what follows I argue, in part, that no single theory can adequately accommodate both intuitions. Although I focus mainly on the theories of Brandt and Railton, much of what I say will apply to other approaches in the neighborhood. Brandt and Railton are among the most thoughtful proponents of the full-information line of thinking, and their theories offer an interesting contrast, representing alternative ways of accommodating the intuitions that underlie the approach. Understanding how their theories go wrong may help us to see how we might better approach the questions to which they are addressed.[4]

THE APPEAL OF FULL-INFORMATION THEORIES

Full-information theories appeal to us because of the way they appear to accommodate two powerful intuitions. The first is motivational. The theories typically embrace a version of *internalism*. They characterize a person's good (or reasons for action, etc.) in terms of her motivations. The motivations in question need not be actual. Dispositions to be motivated would suffice. Likewise, the circumstances in which the person is disposed to be motivated need only be hypothetical. Although no one reasonably expects to be fully informed, we can still ask about the motivations a fully informed person would have. The important thing is that it is *her* motivations that count, however unlikely or idealized the circumstances in which they would come into play.

The attractiveness of the internalist link between a person's motivations and her good is undeniable. It is appealing to think that one's good depends on something in *oneself*. And there may be other advantages to internalism, beyond this raw intuitive appeal. For example, it may help us to avoid a problem of alienation faced by externalist approaches. Why take an interest in one's good, if it need not be connected to one's motivations? Internalism may also help us to explain why people normally *do* take an interest in their own good. Of course an externalist can attempt to explain this phenomenon as well, by positing a desire to pursue one's good, whatever it may be. But that merely relocates the worry about alienation. Why have such a desire, when one's good might have nothing to do with one's (actual or potential) motivations.[5] Finally,

---

4 These issues are of interest in other contexts as well. For example, many are tempted by the method of wide reflective equilibrium as an approach to moral reasoning. But it is worth asking how informed an equilibrium we should be seeking, and an evaluation of full-information theories may help us to answer this question.

5 See Stephen Darwall, *Impartial Reason* (Ithaca, NY: Cornell University Press, 1983) p. 57. For a related point, see Bernard Williams, "Internal and External Reasons," in *Moral Luck* (Cambridge: Cambridge University Press, 1981) pp. 101–13.

we might think that there is no good alternative to maintaining the internalist connection between value and motivation. As one recent discussion suggests, "[I]t may be a strength of 'idealized response' views that there seems nothing for value to be, on deepest reflection, wholly apart from what moves, or could move, valuers—agents for whom something can matter."[6]

The second intuition is that our fully informed motivations are improvements over our uninformed ones. Call this the *epistemic* intuition. As plausible as it seems to treat a person's good as linked to her motivations, it does not seem plausible to link it with just *any* motivations she might have. The epistemic intuition urges us to put aside the motivations we have when laboring under a mistaken or incomplete apprehension of the facts, and look instead to those we would have in ideal epistemic conditions.

Full-information theories bring these intuitions together, yielding an approach with tremendous surface appeal. It can reconcile the very plausible Humean idea that only beliefs are directly subject to rational criticism with the equally plausible Kantian idea that some of our motivations nevertheless *are* irrational. Since at least some of these motivations depend causally on beliefs, we can criticize them indirectly by criticizing the beliefs on which they depend. At a deeper level, the approach appeals to a sense that our cognitive and motivational sides are separate and importantly different from one another. We *identify* with our motivational natures in a way that we do not identify with our cognitive natures. Cognitively perfect people, we might think, would be cognitively identical to one another. Motivationally, on the other hand, we are individuals. Thus we can imagine ourselves epistemically perfected, but with our underlying motivational natures intact. And doing so appears to generate a perspective that is of special relevance to us as ordinary people contemplating our goods.

Despite their great appeal, however, full-information theories are untenable. Why that is so depends in part on how the theories get cashed out. In what follows, I begin by examining Brandt's and Railton's approaches in turn, arguing that each fails to accommodate one of the intuitions which underlie the full-information approach. While Brandt's approach fails adequately to accommodate the epistemic intuition, I argue, Railton's does better in this regard, but only by employing an idealization which undermines his internalism. In any case, I go on to argue, all such theories ultimately fail to accommodate the epistemic intuition, because of their causal approach to the questions they purport to answer. Finally, I argue that the intuitions on which the full-information approach is based are not really as attractive as they might have

---

6 Stephen Darwall, Allan Gibbard, and Peter Railton, "Toward *Fin de siècle* Ethics: Some Trends," *The Philosophical Review*, CL (January 1992), pp. 176–77. See also "Facts and Values," p. 9. This point of view is often connected with philosophical naturalism. See *Impartial Reason,* pp. 55–56 and "Facts and Values," pp. 25–29. For a naturalist who rejects internalism about value, however, see David Brink, *Moral Realism and the Foundations of Ethics* (Cambridge: Cambridge University Press, 1989) pp. 217–36.

seemed, and that in view of all these problems, the approach should be abandoned.

MANNER OF PRESENTATION
AND THE EPISTEMIC INTUITION

In this and the following section I develop the objection that Brandt's account fails adequately to accommodate the epistemic intuition—that a person's informed desires are improvements over his uninformed ones. This happens in two ways. First, his proposals about the manner in which information is to be presented go beyond anything that could be justified by that intuition. On the other hand, his proposals about how much information the subject is to get do not go as far as they should. In this section, I develop the first of these claims.[7]

Information can be presented in a variety of ways, and the manner of presentation may have a significant impact on the motivational outputs we can expect. For example, information may be more or less vivid, and more vivid information will often affect us differently than less. Take, for example, Mel's motivation to exercise. Suppose Mel reads a newspaper article which momentarily reminds him of the benefits of regular aerobic exercise. Such a reminder might well motivate him to begin a training program. But watching a well-done documentary (especially one with stories about particular people) is likely to have a far more significant motivational impact than any mere recitation of the facts, no matter how detailed.[8] Similarly, repetition can have an impact on motivation. Mel's motivation to exercise may at first increase along with the number of occasions on which he views the documentary. Of course, if he sees too much, he may start to lose the motivation again. We should not expect the trajectories of these impacts to be linear.

How should full-information theorists respond to these differences in presentation? For two reasons, they must not offer result-driven answers to questions about the appropriate manner of presentation. The first has to do with their internalism. It would defeat that internalism to hold, for example, that Mel is fully informed if and only if he has watched the documentary often enough to be motivated to begin exercising, but not so often as to lose that motivation. We might as well appeal to the outcome directly, dispensing with Mel's role

---

7 For interesting criticisms of Brandt's approach (along mostly different lines) see Allan Gibbard, *Wise Choices, Apt Feelings* (Cambridge: Harvard University Press, 1990), pp. 18–19; and Nicholas L. Sturgeon, "Brandt's Moral Empiricism," *The Philosophical Review*, XCI, No. 3 (July 1982), pp. 389–422.

8 Richard Nisbett and Lee Ross, *Human Inference: Strategies and Shortcomings of Social Judgment* (Englewood Cliffs, NJ: Prentice-Hall, 1980), pp. 47–49. Partly, of course, the change may be due to Mel's coming to understand facts of which he was previously unaware (such as the fact that a particular person appeared vigorous and healthy after a few months of moderate exercise) or focusing on previously known facts for a longer period of time. Partly, however, it results from his confronting the same facts, but presented in a way that makes them come alive for him (such as they might if he were to see pictures of the vigorous specimen).

altogether.[9] The second reason is that understanding is an epistemic notion, not a motivational one, even if understanding sometimes has an impact on motivation. Although Mel might be motivated to exercise if he only understood the potential benefits, it is also possible that he understands them perfectly well, but nevertheless lacks the motivation to do anything. While having certain motivations might sometimes be *evidence* of fuller understanding, it is always possible for a person to understand fully, but fail to be motivated in the way we have in mind.

Still, vividness and repetition can have an impact on how well informed a person is. A more vivid presentation, for example, may penetrate a subject's awareness more deeply than a dim one. Thus, even if a dim awareness would pass some minimal threshold for knowledge, a fuller awareness would represent epistemic progress. Similarly, repeatedly confronting the same information might better allow it to "sink in," and once again, this seems to represent an epistemic improvement. Perhaps for this reason, Brandt imagines his subjects confronting maximally vivid information, repeated until further repetitions would no longer affect their motivations.[10] After all, if some repetitions (or increases in vividness) would bring some improvement, shouldn't maximal repetitions (or increases) bring maximal improvement, allowing the information, as Brandt says, to "register" fully? Despite its initial allure, however, this maximizing approach to repetitions and vividness faces serious problems, because it cannot be justified by the epistemic intuition.

Repetitions

Look first at repetitions. One advantage of these is that they may increase the chances that information will be stored in long-term memory. Perhaps some of our short-term beliefs count as knowledge, but more stable knowledge clearly represents an epistemic advance. Another advantage has to do with *degree* of awareness, and repetitions can improve that as well. For example, they may help to make some beliefs more accessible than others, or to bring them closer to the focus of attention. They may also improve the subject's degree of confidence. The epistemic intuition applies to all of these dimensions of knowledge, and a full-information theorist should take them into account. Increasing the number of repetitions is one way to begin doing so.

[9] On this point, see Darwall, "Internalism and Agency," in 6 *Philosophical Perspectives, Ethics* (Atascadero, CA: Ridgeview Publishing, 1992), p. 165. Brink makes a similar point in a related context. Arguing that what he calls "counterfactual desire-satisfaction theories of value" will sometimes have counterintuitive implications, he notes that it is always possible to avoid these implications by introducing additional constraints on the subjects' capacities. But, he argues, such constraints are incompatible with the theories' internalism—his term is "subjectivism" (*Moral Realism and the Foundations of Ethics*, p. 230). While Brink is right that severe result-driven constraints would undermine these theories' internalism, he overlooks the possibility that less severe constraints could do the trick, while still leaving some constitutive role for the subject's motivations. (Whether such constraints could be well motivated is, of course, another question.)

[10] *A Theory of the Good and the Right*, pp. 111–12.

In spite of the epistemic advantages which sometimes flow from repetitions, however, the epistemic intuition does not justify maximizing them, since motivational impact does not always signal epistemic improvement. No doubt one's motivations will often change as one becomes more and more fully aware. But there is a limit to how much epistemic improvement can result from continued repetitions, and there is no guarantee that the motivational changes will cease when that limit is reached. In the example given above, Mel was first more, then less, inclined to begin exercising, upon confronting repeated representations of the same facts. But it would be a mistake to hold that he did not fully apprehend these facts until his motivations stopped changing and he no longer had a strong motivation to exercise. As we saw, the later repetitions may simply have made him indifferent to those benefits, without further improving his understanding at all.[11] If so, then the motivations to which they gave rise ought to be treated as irrelevant from the standpoint of the theory. No doubt it is difficult to specify when further repetitions would cease to produce epistemic improvements, and the answer will differ from case to case. But to maximize repetitions merely in order to avoid this difficulty is to buy a clear criterion at the expense of a coherent rationale.[12]

Brandt, of course, is not concerned with repetitions merely for the sake of epistemic improvement. He wants to allow the information to have some effect on motivations. (If a subject had taken a pill which somehow disconnected his motivations from any influence of new information, there would be no point to his undergoing cognitive psychotherapy.) In an ordinary person, repetitions would sometimes have the effect of achieving this connection between the subject's motivations and the information he receives. But, even so, a similar problem arises. There does not seem to be any nonarbitrary way of specifying how much or what sort of a connection between information and motivation cognitive psychotherapy should aim for. Drawing the line at maximal repetitions merely papers over the problem.[13]

---

11 It is possible, in fact, that the later repetitions had the effect of *worsening* his epistemic position. Suppose the reason for his indifference is that, in view of his comparatively unhealthy condition, he can no longer bear to attend fully to the information. (Think of the way people sometimes respond to advertisements about world hunger.) Such a failure of attention hardly represents epistemic progress, and the theory should not require repetitions which would bring it about. On the other hand, there is no reason to think that his indifference *must* be the product of such a failure.

12 For the view that Brandt's criterion was chosen with an eye toward empirical determinability, see "Brandt's Definition of 'Good,' " pp. 364–65. Railton distinguishes the question of determinability (whether we can know the truth values of the counterfactuals about what fully informed people would choose) from the question of determinacy (whether they have determinate truth values at all), and argues that indeterminability would not undermine a theory of value. It may be that there are facts about what is good for a person, but that they are beyond our epistemic reach ("Facts and Values," pp. 23–24). But there could be a more significant problem here. If the standards of epistemic optimality are themselves indeterminate, then counterfactuals about what people would choose in epistemically optimal circumstances will be indeterminate as well.

13 The objection here was raised by an anonymous referee.

Vividness

A second requirement Brandt puts forward is that information be maximally vivid. And it is plausible to think that a gain in vividness can sometimes result in epistemic progress. Consider, for example, Darwall's case of Otto, who is considering whether to take an unpleasant tasting hangover preventative before going to bed.[14] Otto's decision to eschew the medicine stems from his inability vividly to imagine how bad he will feel in the morning if he fails to take it, together with his vivid awareness of how bad it would taste now. Were he vividly to imagine both, he would choose to take the medicine, and his motivation for doing so would flow from his fuller awareness of the situation— precisely the sort of response to epistemic improvement the full-information theorist is looking for.

On the other hand, it is not entirely clear what 'vividness' is supposed to mean. As in Otto's case, a more vivid presentation will often enable a subject to know how certain experiences would feel. But there is more to vividness than that. Likewise, a more vivid presentation will often convey more information (or more detailed information) than a pale one. But there may be more to vividness than mere quantity or detail as well. One thing that *is* clear is that vividness is a function of both the information and the perceiver.[15] What is vivid to you may be less so to me. That suggests that vividness has something to do with the capacity of a given presentation to affect the perceiver. Thus, it might be tempting to identify vividness with degree of motivational impact.[16]

A problem with this approach is that when changes in motivation follow a nonlinear trajectory, it will not be clear which impact is greatest. (Which showed the greater impact: Mel's motivation to exercise, or his later motivation not to?) More importantly, requiring maximal vividness, defined in this way, would raise a problem analogous to the one raised by requiring maximal repetitions. The motivational impact of a presentation is not always a product of epistemic improvement. (Laughing at Mel's potbelly might motivate him to begin exercising, but not because he would come to understand anything better than he did before.) A full-information theorist should be interested in vividness only insofar as it will bring about epistemic improvement. Thus, if he defines vividness in this way, then he should not require maximally vivid presentations.[17]

---

[14] *Impartial Reason,* pp. 89–91, 94–96.

[15] On this point, see Railton, "Facts and Values," p. 22.

[16] An alternative would be to define it in a way that ties it to epistemic improvement. For example, Shelly Kagan thinks it possible that vividness *is* just a matter of detail (*The Limits of Morality* [Oxford: Clarendon Press, 1989], p. 284). Since Kagan views vividness as a property of beliefs, every gain in vividness is, on this suggestion, an epistemic gain, and there is no gap between the maximally vivid presentation (for a given fact/subject pairing) and the ideally vivid one. On this view, however, vividness turns out not to be a separate desideratum after all.

[17] Velleman argues that the motivational impact of exposure to the facts is empirically indeterminable, since the *kind* of impact will depend on which of various vivid presentations the subject confronts. If it were true, however, that the presentations had only one kind of effect, which

The maximizing approach to repetitions (and perhaps to vividness) fails because it goes beyond the justification provided by the epistemic intuition. That intuition supports calling for repetitions and vividness only insofar as they would produce epistemic improvements. But this is not the only way Brandt's account fails to accommodate the epistemic intuition. In another respect, it does not go far enough. The problem has to do with the question of how fully informed the subject is expected to be. I turn to that next.

HOW MUCH INFORMATION?

Strictly speaking, Brandt's theory is not a *full*-information approach at all. "Cognitive psychotherapy" involves confronting "all *available* information," by which Brandt means, "the propositions accepted by the science of the agent's day, plus factual propositions justified by publicly accessible evidence (including testimony of others about themselves) and the principles of logic."[18] Although that is an immense quantity of information, it is still less than all.

In taking this approach, Brandt chooses a position intermediate between two others. On the one hand, he rejects the proposal that we treat desires as rational only if they would survive confrontation "with the factual beliefs an agent would have had at the time of action, if his beliefs had been fixed by *his* total observational evidence and the principles of logic . . . ."[19] Brandt does not say why he rejects this proposal (except to say that his alternative "seems more useful"), but presumably he wants to give more weight to the epistemic intuition—that information improves desires. Moreover, he uses his notion of rational desire to build up his account of rational action, and recommends that we substitute questions about what it is rational for an agent to do for questions about what it is best for him to do. What is best in this sense should not depend on the limitations of the agent's experience.

On the other hand, Brandt also rejects the proposal that we treat desires as rational only if they would survive confrontation with the information that would be available to an omniscient being. He rejects *this* proposal because he wants his theory to be a useful tool for evaluating desires. No matter how much we would like to have it, some information is beyond our reach, and thus cannot be used to criticize desires. Brandt recognizes that even information that is available in his more moderate sense might be "intolerably expensive

differed only in degree, then perhaps "fully confronting the facts would require undergoing that effect to the fullest extent, which would in turn require confronting the most vivid representation" ("Brandt's Definition of 'Good'," pp. 367–68). But even this concedes too much. Why should we be interested in the fullest motivational impact, regardless of whether that impact reflects any cognitive improvement?

18 *A Theory of the Good and the Right*, p. 13 (emphasis added).

19 Ibid. (emphasis added).

[for the subject] to get, so that trying to get it might itself be irrational."[20] But, he thinks, it is still possible for *others* to criticize desires on the basis of such information, even if the subject himself is in no position to do so.[21] Of course, it might be irrational for *anyone* to get the information. So, if utility were the only concern, the limitation would have to be extended to exclude information which, although technically available, is practically unavailable.

Regardless of how we interpret this limitation, however, the utility gained by it is purchased at too high a price. For one thing, the epistemic intuition is just as strong for unavailable information as it is for available information. Suppose the liquid in the glass in front of me contains a powerful carcinogen undetectable by the methods of current science. My desire to drink it is no less objectionable than it would be if the carcinogen were familiar. Of course, in the first case I could not learn of my precarious situation, even by consulting the experts. But, as we have seen, what makes my desire objectionable does not depend on my failure to get the information, since I do not always have a responsibility to do so. It depends on the existence of facts which, were I aware of them, would cause the desire to change. Why should it matter whether these facts are publicly available?

Furthermore, given Brandt's suggestion that we substitute questions about what it is rational for an agent to want for questions about what it is best for the agent to do, his approach leads to an unacceptable relativization. If the carcinogen were suddenly to come to the attention of the scientific community, then by Brandt's criterion, drinking the liquid would suddenly become a bad thing for me to do. But whether or not drinking it is good to do should not depend on what modern science, unbeknownst to me, has or has not discovered. Similarly, it should not depend on the period in which I happen to live. It is not plausible that smoking a pipe was a good thing for Freud to do, merely because he lived at a time in which tobacco's carcinogenic properties could not have been discovered.[22]

Finally, desires affected by *false* information need not be improvements over those held before confronting it. But the propositions accepted by the science of one's day might not be true. And even if they are, true information can still lead to false beliefs. An unscrupulous prosector can secure a conviction by presenting incriminating evidence and withholding exculpatory evidence. But so can one who is simply unaware of the exculpatory evidence. In either case, the information which is presented causes the jury to draw a mistaken inference.

---

20 Ibid.

21 Thus we should not be misled by his use of the phrase "rational desire." Sometimes we think of rationality as making the most one can out of the information one already has. But Brandt has something else in mind, since he distinguishes between objective and subjective senses of "rational." Desires which can be criticized only in light of information practically unavailable to the agent (but "available" in Brandt's more general sense) are objectively irrational, but subjectively rational (ibid., pp. 72–73). When Brandt suggests that we substitute "the rational thing to do" for "the best thing to do," he intends the objective sense of "rational."

22 Brandt, of course, intends his definition as a *reform*. But a reform can sometimes take us *too* far away from what we set out to characterize.

With respect to the issue of guilt or innocence, they were better off before they learned the incriminating facts. Similarly, a subject informed of all that the science of his day has to offer may sometimes be led to draw reasonable, but false, conclusions. And once again the motivational changes which flow from these false conclusions need not be changes for the better.[23]

There is another important respect in which Brandt's subjects would end up less than fully informed. Any normal person has substantial cognitive limitations, and thus could never really come to know all of the information the account treats as relevant. The consequence is that on his approach, a person's good is relativized not only to the science of her day, but to her cognitive abilities as well. For some people, even the most vivid presentations, repeated "as often as you like," would not suffice to achieve maximum cognitive penetration of certain information. Paradoxically, on Brandt's account, these people's desires are immune to criticism in light of that information, since they would not be affected by cognitive psychotherapy, but the desires of more cognitively able individuals are not immune to criticism in light of the very same information. To put it crudely, the smarter you are, the more exposed to criticism are your desires; the less intelligent you are, the less they are. A person's good should not be tied to her intellectual capabilities in this way.[24]

AN ALTERNATIVE

The obvious solution to these problems is to imagine subjects with improved cognitive abilities, and exposed to all of the facts. And that is precisely what Railton does. Instead of treating as relevant only information available to contemporary science, Railton treats all information as relevant. And instead of asking about the motivations of ordinary people repeatedly confronted with this information, Railton asks what their idealized counterparts—people with "unqualified cognitive and imaginative powers"—would want their less-informed counterparts to pursue. These idealized counterparts would know everything there is to know. They would "not want any more information," because, "there is no more to be had. . . ."[25]

In the next section, I will argue that this idealization leads to serious problems. But it is worth noting first how it may help to solve another problem faced by full-information views—the problem of order of presentation. As Railton himself notes, differences in order of presentation will sometimes carry different motivational impacts. If so, then there might be no determinate answer

---

23 Even without leading to a mistaken inference, partial information may provoke a motivation that would alter on a fuller view. If I hear something bad about a person, I may wish him ill, even if I would wish him well if I were more fully informed. But the original motivation need not have been based on any inference about his overall character.

24 Daniels makes a related point in "Can Cognitive Psychotherapy Reconcile Reason and Desire?" p. 776.

25 "Moral Realism," pp. 173–74.

to the question of what the counterpart would choose for his less-informed self, since that could depend on the order in which the counterpart considers the information. On the other hand, favoring any particular order of presentation would achieve determinacy only at the expense of arbitrariness.

In response to this worry, Railton argues that the differential effects are likely to be diluted upon receipt of more and more information.[26] Furthermore, he says, a fully informed person would be aware of her susceptibility to these differential impacts, and this awareness would diminish their actual effects to insignificant levels.[27] But this response is inadequate. In the analogous context of "belief perseverance" there is evidence that our tendency to make mistaken inferences based on order of presentation may *sometimes* diminish upon receipt of information about that very phenomenon. But, as Railton himself notes, there is also evidence that our beliefs are often quite resistant to change. In fact, this resistance persists even when subjects are informed about the phenomenon of belief perseverance itself.[28] Analogously, "motivation perseverance" might be similarly resistant to undermining through more complete information.

Although Railton's response is inadequate, it might be possible to exploit his idealization in order to avoid the indeterminacy that threatens his account. Of course it would not do to make demands on the subject's motivational *responses,* requiring, for example, that she have the same response no matter what the order of presentation. That would undermine the account's internalism. Instead what is needed is an adjustment in the subject's *cognitive* apparatus. As things stand, we can only keep a few "chunks" of information in mind at any given time. And, presumably, these will have a disproportionate effect on motivation, compared with that of previously considered data. But if we imagine short-term memory and attentive capabilities expanded to the point where all information can be considered simultaneously, then we might achieve determinacy without modifying the subject's motivational dispositions.[29]

WHY IDEALIZATION THREATENS INTERNALISM

As we have seen, Railton's criterion looks to the choices, not of ordinary people, but of their idealized counterparts—beings capable of knowing everything perfectly. But beings with "unqualified cognitive and imaginative powers" would have to be vastly different from ordinary people. Railton does not say

---

26 "Facts and Values," p. 21.

27 Railton responds similarly to worries about the differential effects of alternate, but equally vivid, modes of presentation (ibid., pp. 21–22).

28 *Human Inference: Strategies and Shortcomings of Social Judgment,* pp. 175–79.

29 Idealization might also eliminate the need for repetitions, since idealized subjects would (presumably) not need them. And it might help with the problems about vividness as well. Perhaps we can imagine subjects so perceptive that even a pale presentation would be sufficient to inform them perfectly.

what sort of powers he has in mind. But it seems likely that, in addition to greatly improved short-term memory, they would require massively expanded long-term memory as well, in order to store all of the data they would be receiving. And merely storing and recalling the information are not sufficient, since memorizing facts does not guarantee that one fully grasps them and sees their interconnections. A fully informed person would require a far greater capacity for *comprehension* than that of an ordinary person. But even that is not enough. Informing oneself takes time, and *fully* informing oneself would take more than a lifetime for any ordinary person. A fully informed person would have to be able to process information very rapidly indeed if her preferences were to appear within a reasonable amount of time.

So far, I have focused only on changes in intellectual capabilities. But more than intellect is required if one is to become fully informed. Changes in the subject's imaginative faculties would be necessary as well, especially in light of the kinds of things a fully informed person would have to know. Much of what there is to know has to do with what it would be like to have certain experiences. And surely this sort of knowledge is relevant from the standpoint of the theory. Mill's confidence that it is "better to be Socrates dissatisfied than a fool satisfied" was justified, he thought, on the grounds that he (unlike the fool) knew both sides of the question. But that knowledge was, in part, knowledge of what the pleasures of each sort of life *feel* like, and Mill acquired it, if he did, by experiencing both.[30] Similarly, a person who has sampled a variety of Chinese dishes is better informed than one whose experience is limited to Chop Suey and Egg Foo Young.

Since the changes in preference which result from these experiences (such as the desire to incorporate more Chinese food into one's diet) seem to represent improvements in just the same way as changes due to greater knowledge of other kinds, we should treat as fully informed only someone who has the knowledge she would have after a full range of such experiences. But *actually* having all of these experiences is impossible for ordinary people. The idealization gives us a way around this problem, for we can envision our subjects as having imaginative powers far beyond those of ordinary human beings. One aspect of imagination that would have to be significantly enhanced is the capacity for empathetic identification. In order for Emily to make a fully informed decision about whether to make a donation to charity, for example, she would have to know exactly how it feels to suffer in the way that each of her potential beneficiaries is suffering, and how it would feel for each of them to be benefitted in the ways her donation would make possible.[31] Even an

---

30 John Stuart Mill, *Utilitarianism*, in Samuel Gorovitz, ed., *Utilitarianism with Critical Essays* (Indianapolis: Bobbs-Merrill, 1971), p. 20. Mill may have been exaggerating when he claimed to know the fool's side of the question.

31 Railton distinguishes an individual's good, which can include his ideally informed concerns about the well-being of others, from his *welfare*, which can not ("Facts and Values," p. 30, n. 9). Similarly, Brandt draws a distinction between "the best thing for me to do" and "the best thing for me to do from the standpoint of my own welfare" (*A Theory of the Good and the Right*, p. 16).

extraordinarily sensitive person would require enormous improvements in this regard.

Finally, for ordinary people, capacity for learning depends on certain features of our affective and conative lives as well. First, the subject must have a *desire* to learn. And she must be psychologically prepared in many other ways as well. Stress, depression, elation, boredom, nervousness, and infatuation are just a few of the emotional factors which can interfere with the ability to learn and understand new information fully. No matter how vivid the presentation or how often she confronts it, Emily might be too despondent ever really to see how much good her contribution would do. Or too much in love. And just as these factors can cause interference, so can personal interest. It might be difficult for Emily to see just how much good her money can do for others, while at the same time aware of what it can do for her.[32] A fully informed person would have to be free of these sources of interference, or immune to their effects on his cognitive abilities.

Even if slightly different changes would do the trick, the severity of the idealization spells trouble for the *internalist* character of the full-information approach. Whatever normative force was supposed to come from holding a person's good to depend on his own motivations appears to be vitiated by the drastic changes the idealization would involve. A subject's counterpart would be so different from that subject that it is hard to see how his motivations—even his motivations for the subject—could be relevant to the subject's good or to the rationality of his desires.

The answer the full-information theorist must give is that although the counterpart is *cognitively* very different from the subject, he is *motivationally* identical. That being so, the argument could continue, the worry about internalism is misguided; the counterpart is in this respect a perfect surrogate for the subject. After all, the argument would go, everyone has a certain basic motivational nature—a set of dispositions to be motivated in various ways under various circumstances. Among these circumstances are those in which one's mental capacities are radically modified. What is changed is not this basic motivational nature, but only the *actual* motivations one ends up having. And the full-information theorist need not be bothered by these changes, any more than he should be bothered by the changes in motivation that occur when an ordinary person becomes better informed. It was in expectation of such changes that the full-information view got off the ground in the first place.

But there is a more significant problem here. Given the aims of his approach, the full-information theorist should not be interested in motivational changes which would come about merely as a result of the idealization *itself*. He is

---

32 Darwall argues that attention to *subjective considerations* (roughly, facts whose expressions make reference to oneself) inhibits vivid awareness of *objective considerations*—whose expressions do not (*Impartial Reason*, pp. 134–36). But it would be an exaggeration to claim that such inhibitions *always* accompany attention to subjective considerations. And we should not overlook the many other ways in which attention to one set of consideration can inhibit vivid awareness of others. A very generous person may not be able fully to grasp how much her contribution will cost her, as long as she thinks about how much it will benefit others.

concerned to find the motivations that would flow from the subject's *being* better informed—not from being the sort of person who could be. And some aspects of the idealization seem very likely to result in changes in motivation, regardless of whether the subject gets fuller information. A more empathetic Emily, for example, might be more inclined than her real-life self to choose a career as a social worker, even without the knowledge which her enhanced empathy would make possible. The same is true for emotional changes. If the only way to inform George is to cure his depression, then it seems likely that his informed motivations will trace, in part, to the curing of the depression, and not just to the epistemic improvements he is now in a position to realize.[33] Most worrisome of all are the cases in which we cannot fully inform a person without first changing her motivations themselves. Perhaps Sally could not fully understand the options before her unless she cared more about the people who would be affected by her choices. If so, and if the changes are made, then we should not be surprised if they have an impact on her ensuing motivations.[34] Since, in all of these cases, idealization appears to change the subjects' basic motivational *natures,* theories which idealize in these ways fail to capture the internalist intuition in a satisfactory way. There is no justification within the full-information approach for treating the subjects' new motivational natures as relevant to their goods.[35]

Railton might be tempted to respond that we are overlooking the second-order feature of his view.[36] After all, a subject's good is not what her idealized counterpart would want for *herself,* but what the counterpart would want for *the subject* to want or pursue. Perhaps Mary's counterpart could not become

33 Even apart from the idealization, problems stemming from the dependency of motivations on mood are sure to crop up, and they spell trouble for the determinacy of the counterfactual. George may not be too depressed to become fully informed, but when he is depressed he may be less generous than when he is happy. In asking for the single motivational response to full information, the theory assumes too simple a picture of human motivation. In real life our motivations are quite variable. Yet stipulating in favor of one sort of mood seems arbitrary.

34 In fact, the changes in her cognitive abilities might themselves produce motivational changes. Since that depends on how these cognitive changes would be accomplished, and we have no way of knowing that, we cannot be sure that the unwelcome changes could be avoided.

35 Recognizing the possibility of motivational changes which trace to the idealization itself can help us to understand a point that might have been unclear in Velleman's arguments against Brandt. Velleman focuses, in part, on the question of empirical determinability—whether we could discover what our fully informed motivations would be. But in a footnote he addresses the question of determinacy as well, claiming that if there are a number of different ways in which a person could be changed in order to effectuate her being fully informed, then counterfactuals about what her counterpart would choose will have indeterminate truth values ("Brandt's Definition of 'Good'," pp. 368–69). But that is true only if the resulting motivations would vary depending on how she is changed. And that can only happen if the changes themselves would have an impact on her motivations. What I say above shows why we can expect that they would, and why that is a problem even if the new motivations would *not* vary. To whatever extent these new motivations result from the idealization itself, they are impurities from the standpoint of the theory, and taking them into account would undermine the theory's internalism.

36 For an early criticism of Rawls's first-order approach, see Robert K. Shope, "The Conditional Fallacy in Contemporary Philosophy," *The Journal of Philosophy,* LLXXV, No. 8 (August 1978), pp. 397–413.

fully informed without a stronger desire to learn. But surely this would not affect the counterpart's desires *for Mary*. The counterpart would know that, unlike her, Mary does *not* love learning. Likewise, Emily's counterpart may be more empathetic than Emily, but surely she would not want Emily to follow preferences that stem from that empathy alone (and not from the enhanced knowledge which the empathy makes possible), since the counterpart would be aware that Emily herself still lacks it.

This reply would miss the point of the objection. If Mary's counterpart's love of learning is strong enough, she might want Mary to pursue learning in *spite* of Mary's indifference to it. And insofar as this desire is attributable to the idealization, the connection between Mary and her counterpart is weakened. Likewise, Emily's lack of empathy is part of her basic motivational nature. Eliminate it, and you wind up with a person whose basic motivational nature is different than Emily's. No doubt many would think the counterparts' basic motivational natures represent improvements over those of the original subjects. But the internalist intuition requires that we leave the subjects' own basic motivational natures intact.

THE EPISTEMIC INTUITION REVISITED

In the preceding sections, I argued that a more moderate view like Brandt's fails, in various ways, to accommodate the epistemic intuition. Idealizing the subjects appeared to give the full-information theorist a way out, but only by undermining the internalism. Either way 'full-information' is interpreted, I argued, one of the intuitions cannot be accommodated fully.

But there is another problem with the full-information approach, and it is common to both versions. With or without the idealization, these theories are unable to stay within the parameters of the epistemic intuition after all. The problem stems from the fact that they are *causal* theories. They seek the *effects* on motivations of full information. And just as the idealization necessary for fully informing people can have unwelcome effects on their basic motivational natures, so the circumstances of informing them can have unwelcome effects on their actual motivations. Given the causal nature of the approach, there is no way to avoid winding up with motivations which are tainted by the influence of factors other than information itself, and hence not made relevant by the epistemic intuition.

The reason is that getting information is *itself* a causal process. As such, it can have impacts on motivation quite apart from the impacts of the fuller information alone. Earlier we saw that maximizing repetitions (and perhaps vividness) is inconsistent with the aims of the full-information approach, since these factors may have effects on motivation even after all epistemic improvements have taken place. But if these factors can affect motivations when they do not produce epistemic improvements, then they can affect motivations even when they do produce such improvements. Yet the epistemic intuition gives us no reason to seek the motivations which trace to these factors, but only those which reflect the information itself.[37]

In fact, repetitions and vividness are not the only noninformational factors which can affect motivations. If information is to be confronted, it must be confronted in some circumstance or other, and the nature of the circumstances may have an impact on the resulting motivations. Mel's counterpart might be more inclined to want Mel to exercise if he hears the facts from a man with a loud voice or while sitting on a hard stool than he would if he hears them from a woman with a soft voice or while sitting in a comfortable chair. And that is true even if exactly the same information is conveyed and the counterpart believes it completely. Thus, there will not always be a single motivational response to the information itself, but only to the information *in the circumstances in which it is presented.* A different set of circumstances might well have a different effect.[38] But although the epistemic intuition makes the effects of the information itself relevant, it does not make relevant effects on motivation that trace, even in part, to the circumstances in which that information is acquired. Thus actual confrontations will sometimes have impacts with which the theory ought not be concerned.

Full-information theorists might respond that although it is impossible to prevent these influences as a causal matter, we can nevertheless distinguish them as a theoretical matter. Thus, a sophisticated full-information theorist could ask, not what a person would want herself to want if she had gone through a process of becoming fully informed, but if, *per* (nomologically) *impossible,* she had been influenced by nothing but the fuller information itself. As Railton argues in another context, "In general, it is not an objection to a

---

37 Brandt recognizes that the confrontation itself may sometimes affect our desires independently of the information conveyed: "If every time I thought of having a martini, I made myself go through the multiplication tables for five minutes, the valence of a martini might well decline." His response is to hold that "a thought is functioning properly in the criticism of desires only if its effect is not one its occurrence would have on any desire, and only if its effect is a function of its content" (*A Theory of the Good and the Right,* p. 112). But this response is inadequate. The diminution in Mel's motivation to exercise may be due precisely to his thinking further about exercise, even though his doing so is no longer helping him to become better informed.

38 Velleman has something like this in mind when he argues that there are an infinite number of ways in which the same facts may be presented, and that there is no justification for favoring one mode of presentation over another. He argues that this possibility of multiple modes of presentation undermines the empirical determinability of counterfactuals about how subjects would respond to full information, since there is no empirical method for discovering all of the possible modes of presentation, and hence what people's fully informed motivations would be. He appears to concede, however, that these counterfactuals have determinate truth values, on the grounds that, for each person, there is a fact about how that person would be motivated after confronting *all* possible presentations ("Brandt's Definition of 'Good'," pp. 365–71). He credits this suggestion to Railton.

But, if there are *infinitely* many possible modes of presentation, why should we think that there *are* determinate answers to our questions about how people would respond to them all? And even if there are, these are not the questions full-information theorists should be asking. The *reason* the various individual presentations have differing effects is that the circumstances or modes of presentation themselves, and not just the information, can affect the subjects' motivations. But only the information is relevant—not these other factors. Confronting all possible presentations would only compound the problem.

counterfactual that it involves hypothesizing circumstances that are, in the actual course of things, nomologically impossible."[39]

It would be ironic for a theory which makes questions of value depend on a causal matter (and which is presented in the spirit of naturalism) to take refuge in imagining massive alterations in the laws of nature. But irony is no guarantee of incorrectness. Still, it is not at all clear that such massively impossible counterfactuals *have* determinate truth values. Counterfactuals about what people would want in causally impossible circumstances are still causal counterfactuals. As such, they depend on causal laws—in particular, laws of psychology. But the laws of psychology would have to be vastly different from the actual laws if they were to rule out all of the unwelcome influences I have pointed out. And since these are the very laws that support the counterfactuals, it is not at all clear that enough is left of them to ensure that the counterfactuals have determinate truth values.[40]

It is also not clear that the full-information approach would be *plausible* if it required that we imagine such wide-scale changes in the laws of psychology. We know too little to be confident of that. Perhaps my counterpart would no longer wish for me to shun the poison liquid in a world in which he would react no differently to yelling than to whispering, and in which one's motivations would not be influenced by massive alterations in one's cognitive capabilities alone. Without knowing how the laws of psychology would be altered, we are in no position to judge whether the approach maintains whatever plausibility it initially appeared to have.

RETHINKING THE INTUITIONS

Even if it were possible to eliminate the unwelcome effects on motivation of factors other than the information itself, the full-information approach would still face serious objections. For one thing, information *itself* may have effects which ought to be unwelcome from the standpoint of any adequate account of value. To see this, we need only look at the range of information a *fully* informed person would have to know.

What sorts of things would such a person be vividly aware of? He would have to be thoroughly acquainted with every kind of pain imaginable: what it is like to be burned at the stake, what it is like to be burned in an oven, what it is like to be eaten by sharks, what it is like to drown, and for that matter, what it is like to be eaten by sharks *while* drowning. But it is possible that this knowledge would scar him, and leave him no longer caring about anything but avoiding these horrible experiences, or preventing his counterpart from having them. And these are merely physical pains. He would have to possess a vivid appreciation of all psychological pains as well. He would have

---

[39] "Facts and Values," p. 24.

[40] *A fortiori*, it is not clear that these counterfactuals would have truth values which are empirically *determinable*.

to know unspeakable loneliness, sadness, and self-doubt. But this knowledge might leave him too depressed to care about his own or his counterpart's welfare. He would have to know what it would feel like to believe that everyone hated him, or pitied him, or felt revulsion at the very sight of him. But this knowledge might make him wish he or his counterpart were dead. Granted, he would also know (*if* it were true) that he will not suffer horribly and that others do not really despise him, but there is no reason to think that this knowledge would always prevent these sorts of unwelcome effects on his motivations. Likewise, he would know all manner of pleasures, but there is no reason to think that this knowledge would somehow counterbalance that of the pains. On the contrary, it might have unwelcome effects of its own. Perhaps once he is fully aware of the pleasures, he would be seduced by them, and wish for himself or his counterpart to pursue them at the expense of everything else. But if he would, surely we need not treat his informed desires as the final word on his or his counterpart's good.

And we have still barely scratched the surface. So far I have emphasized knowledge of what it is like to have certain kinds of experiences. But full information would encompass much more than that. What remains would be staggering in its own right, and might well have effects which should also be treated as unwelcome. For example many people are suffering, and our fully informed subject would have to know each of their stories in every detail, even if this knowledge would make him feel so bad about being better off that he would no longer want any enjoyments for himself or his counterpart. Meanwhile other people are experiencing pleasures, and our subject would know that he and his counterpart will never experience most of these pleasures.[41] But he would have to know of them just the same—once again, in every detail. He would have to know just how cruel some people can be, even if this knowledge would jade him and leave him wishing that he or his counterpart never pursue contact with others again. He would know everyone's thoughts, including their thoughts about him. He would know exactly how and when he and everyone else will die, and how everyone in history died too. Why should we think that the motivational changes which would flow from such knowledge would always be changes for the better?

In fact they would not. The idea that perfect information would *always* improve desires is *not* plausible, and the approach which relies on it is bound to have implications which are profoundly counterintuitive. For one thing, information which appears irrelevant to certain motivations could nevertheless have an influence on them. Although the knowledge of what it would feel like to be tickled for two years straight might seem relevant to my preferences about whether to be tickled, it does not seem relevant to my preferences regarding whether to be a lifeguard. But there is nothing to stop it from having

41 Similar cases are discussed in Harman, "Critical Review," p. 128; and Mark Johnston, "Dispositional Theories of Value," p. 152. Among the many others who have described cases in which
fuller information seems to lead one away from one's good are Gibbard, *Wise Choices, Apt
Feelings,* pp. 20–22, 183–88; James Griffin, *Well Being* (Oxford: Clarendon Press, 1986), pp.
12–13; and Derek Parfit, *Reasons and Persons* (Oxford: Clarendon Press, 1984), pp. 117–26.

such an influence if I, as a psychological matter, am so put together as to no longer care what I or my counterpart does for a living after learning what this would feel like. Second, even information that does seem relevant could cause someone to have motivations which have nothing plausibly to do with the sorts of value the approach aims to characterize. Knowledge of the suffering of others might cause her to despair. Knowledge of pleasures unavailable to her might drive her insane with jealousy. But the motivations of a despairing or insane person—even her motivations for her less-informed (and noninsane) counterpart—hardly seem relevant to these question of value, much less conclusive.

Can counterintuitive implications like these be avoided? It would not be appropriate to build further psychological changes into the idealization in order to do so. Imagining subjects to have psychological properties which, unlike their actual properties, would make them immune to effects such as these would once again undermine the internalism. Perhaps, instead, the counterintuitive implications can be explained away. As Railton suggests:

> We can explain a good deal of our objection to certain desires—for example, those involving cruelty—by saying that they are not *morally* good; others—for example, those of a philistine nature—by saying that they are not *aesthetically* valuable; and so on. . . . People, or at least some people, might be put together in a way that makes some not-very-appetizing things essential to their flourishing, and we do not want to be guilty of wishful thinking on this score.[42]

No doubt this reply will help with some of the counterintuitive cases that have been offered in the critical literature. But we ourselves would be guilty of wishful thinking if we were to assume that it will help with all or even most of the cases we can imagine. Surely much of what is counterintuitive in these cases has nothing to do with these other sorts of value. If Jack's counterpart reacts to the fact that others do not like Jack as much as Jack had hoped by wishing for Jack to die in the most painful way imaginable, the problem with his desire is not just that it is immoral or unaesthetic. It simply has nothing to do with Jack's good.

The full-information approach might have seemed plausible for certain very simple cases: Railton's Lonnie is a dehydrated traveler whose fully informed counterpart would wish for him to drink clear liquids instead of milk, since he would know that the clear liquids make Lonnie feel better, while milk would make him feel worse.[43] But the difference between Lonnie's beliefs and those of his counterpart is relatively minor, and involves information Lonnie would have wanted to know anyway. As we have seen, a *fully* informed person would have to possess a far greater range of information than this. When we even begin to consider what that would involve, we can see the implausibility of holding a subject's good to depend on his, or his counterpart's, response to full information.

42 "Moral Realism," p. 177, n. 20.

43 Ibid., pp. 174–75.

Earlier we saw that restricting the scope of relevant information to the science of the subject's day would lead to an implausibly relativized account of individual good. Now it appears that treating all information as relevant would lead to equally implausible results. It might be tempting to try to split the difference, and find a criterion somewhere in between. But to do so would miss the point. Even the more moderate approach is susceptible to counterexamples like those mentioned above. Information about how people feel about Jack or about the suffering and pleasure of others is well within the grasp of social science, and so would be treated as relevant by even the more moderate approach. The real problem is that it is not always true that full information—even full available information—would improve desires. The most we seem able to say is that *sometimes* it would and sometimes it would not. Thus, our initial read on the epistemic intuition was too coarse. Our more reflective intuitions are much more fine-grained.

Perhaps what is needed is a theory which incorporates these more fine-grained intuitions, and asks for our *well* informed motivations, instead of our fully informed ones. But it is hard to imagine a criterion which could capture what we are looking for here, especially one that would constitute a satisfactory reduction, of the sort Railton, at least, has in mind. And even if we could come up with such a criterion, a serious problem would remain. In many cases, the reason that informing a person does not improve her motivations has nothing to do with the information itself, but instead lies in her motivational nature itself. There are undoubtedly people whose motivations, no matter what their epistemic position, would have nothing to do with their goods or with what it is best for them to want or to do.[44] My four year old, for example, has *immature* motivations, and the immaturity would not vanish if he were suddenly to become fully informed. But if he can have immature motivations, then so can anyone. Likewise, insane people sometimes have insane motivations, and often would have them no matter what they knew. The problem in these cases is not that people have been exposed to the wrong information or too much of it. The problem lies in their motivational natures. If so, then at least in these cases, the internalist intuition seems to go too far as well. Once again, an idea that seemed plausible in certain core cases seems quite implausible once we get beyond those cases.

CONCLUSION

Full-information theories fail, in part, because fully informing people would change their motivations in ways that have nothing to do with the information itself. But they also fail in different ways, depending on how strictly they interpret "full information." More moderate versions, like Brandt's, fail because they interpret it in a way that does not take the epistemic intuition

---

44 Brink makes a similar charge against the theories of value he calls subjectivist (*Moral Realism and the Foundations of Ethics*, pp. 229–30).

seriously enough. More extreme versions, like Railton's, fail because in taking that intuition further, they cannot do justice to its internalist counterpart. And these intuitions go too far anyway. Our fully informed motivations would not always be improvements over our less informed ones; sometimes they would be far worse than the ones with which we started. In some cases that is because the information would cause people to have motivations which do not reflect their goods. In others it is because there is something wrong with their motivational natures themselves.

Still, the intuitions which lie behind the full-information approach have a core of plausibility. Perhaps information would not always improve desires, but often it would. And perhaps our motivational natures are not always bound up with our goods in the ways the theory claims. But surely they are relevant. Whether we can find an account which preserves what is right in these intuitions is a question worth pursuing. In the meantime, however, we should put the full-information theory to rest.

48

What Things
Are Good?

W. D. ROSS

*For biographical information about W. D. Ross, see reading 29. This
selection is from* The Right and the Good, *chapter 5.*

    *In reading 29, Ross argues that we have a variety of moral duties. Here
he argues that a variety of things are intrinsically good. Among the objects
of value, he includes virtue, pleasure, the matching of pleasure to virtue,
and knowledge. To show that each item belongs on the list, he compares
imaginary states of the world that differ only by that item's presence or
absence. For example, he imagines two states that differ only in quantity of
pleasure. Because the state containing the greater amount of pleasure seems
better, Ross concludes that pleasure is intrinsically good.*

    *If so, then how can.the pleasures of the vicious be bad? To
accommodate this, Ross must complicate his theory. Instead of saying that
all pleasures are good, he says that the presence of pleasure always creates
a presumption of goodness. In some cases, this presumption is outweighed
by other aspects of the situation. In this respect, goodness resembles prima
facie rightness, which provides a reason for acting that is sometimes
outweighed by stronger contrary reasons.*

    Our next step is to inquire what kinds of thing are intrinsically good.
(1) The first thing for which I would claim that it is intrinsically good is
virtuous disposition and action, i.e., action, or disposition to act, from any
one of certain motives, of which at all events the most notable are the desire
to do one's duty, the desire to bring into being something that is good, and
the desire to give pleasure or save pain to others. It seems clear that we regard
all such actions and dispositions as having value in themselves apart from any
consequence. And if any one is inclined to doubt this and to think that, say,
pleasure alone is intrinsically good, it seems to me enough to ask the question
whether, of two states of the universe holding equal amounts of pleasure, we
should really think no better of one in which the actions and dispositions of
all the persons in it were thoroughly virtuous than of one in which they were
highly vicious. To this there can be only one answer. Most hedonists would
shrink from giving the plainly false answer which their theory requires, and
would take refuge in saying that the question rests on a false abstraction. Since

virtue, as they conceive it, is a disposition to do just the acts which will produce most pleasure, a universe full of virtuous persons would be bound, they might say, to contain more pleasure than a universe full of vicious persons. To this two answers may be made. (*a*) Much pleasure, and much pain, do not spring from virtuous or vicious actions at all but from the operation of natural laws. Thus even if a universe filled with virtuous persons were bound to contain more of the pleasure and less of the pain that springs from human action than a universe filled with vicious persons would, that inequality of pleasantness might easily be supposed to be precisely counteracted by, for instance, a much greater incidence of disease. The two states of affairs would then, on balance, be equally pleasant; would they be equally good? And (*b*) even if we could not imagine any circumstances in which two states of the universe equal in pleasantness but unequal in virtue could exist, the supposition is a legitimate one, since it is only intended to bring before us in a vivid way what is really self-evident, that virtue is good apart from its consequences.

(2) It seems at first sight equally clear that pleasure is good in itself. Some will perhaps be helped to realize this if they make the corresponding supposition to that we have just made; if they suppose two states of the universe including equal amounts of virtue but the one including also widespread and intense pleasure and the other widespread and intense pain. Here too it might be objected that the supposition is an impossible one, since virtue always tends to promote general pleasure, and vice to promote general misery. But this objection may be answered just as we have answered the corresponding objection above.

Apart from this, however, there are two ways in which even the most austere moralists and the most anti-hedonistic philosophers are apt to betray the conviction that pleasure is good in itself. (*a*) One is the attitude which they, like all other normal human beings, take towards kindness and towards cruelty. If the desire to give pleasure to others is approved, and the desire to inflict pain on others condemned, this seems to imply the conviction that pleasure is good and pain bad. Some may think, no doubt, that the mere thought that a certain state of affairs would be *painful* for another person is enough to account for our conviction that the desire to produce it is bad. But I am inclined to think that there is involved the further thought that a state of affairs in virtue of being painful is *prima facie* (i.e., where other considerations do not enter into the case) one that a rational spectator would not approve, i.e., is *bad;* and that similarly our attitude towards kindness involves the thought that pleasure is good. (*b*) The other is the insistence, which we find in the most austere moralists as in other people, on the conception of merit. If virtue deserves to be rewarded by happiness (whether or not vice also deserves to be rewarded by unhappiness), this seems at first sight to imply that happiness and unhappiness are not in themselves things indifferent, but are good and bad respectively.

Kant's view on this question is not as clear as might be wished. He points out that the Latin *bonum* covers two notions, distinguished in German as *das Gute* (the good) and *das Wohl* (well-being, i.e., pleasure or happiness); and he speaks of 'good' as being properly supplied only to actions, i.e., he treats 'good' as equivalent to 'morally good', and by implication denies that pleasure (even deserved pleasure) is good. It might seem then that when he speaks of the union of virtue with the happiness it deserves as the *bonum consummatum* he is not thinking of deserved happiness as good but only as *das Wohl,* a source of satisfaction to the person who has it. But if this exhausted his meaning, he would have no right to speak of virtue, as he repeatedly does, as *das oberste Gut;* he should call it simply *das Gute,* and happiness *das Wohl.* Further, he describes the union of virtue with happiness not merely as 'the object of the desires of rational finite beings', but adds that it approves itself 'even in the judgement of an impartial reason' as 'the whole and perfect good', rather than virtue alone. And he adds that 'happiness, while it is pleasant to the possessor of it, is not of itself absolutely and in all respects good, but always presupposes morally right behaviour as its condition'; which implies that *when* that condition is fulfilled, happiness *is* good. All this seems to point to the conclusion that in the end he had to recognize that while virtue alone is morally good, deserved happiness also is not merely a source of satisfaction to its possessor, but objectively good.

But reflection on the conception of merit does not support the view that pleasure is always good in itself and pain always bad in itself. For while this conception implies the conviction that pleasure when deserved is good, and pain when undeserved bad, it also suggests strongly that pleasure when undeserved is bad and pain when deserved good.

There is also another set of facts which casts doubt on the view that pleasure is always good and pain always bad. We have a decided conviction that there are bad pleasures and (though this is less obvious) that there are good pains. We think that the pleasure taken either by the agent or by a spectator in, for instance, a lustful or cruel action is bad; and we think it a good thing that people should be pained rather than pleased by contemplating vice or misery.

Thus the view that pleasure is always good and pain always bad, while it seems to be strongly supported by some of our convictions, seems to be equally strongly opposed by others. The difficulty can, I think, be removed by ceasing to speak simply of pleasure and pain as good or bad, and by asking more carefully what it is that we mean. Consideration of the question is aided if we adopt the view (tentatively adopted already) that what is good or bad is always something properly expressed by a that-clause, i.e., an objective, or as I should prefer to call it, a *fact.* If we look at the matter thus, I think we can agree that the fact that a sentient being is in a state of pleasure is always in itself good, and the fact that a sentient being is in a state of pain always in itself bad, when this fact is not an element in a more complex fact having some other characteristic relevant to goodness or badness. And where considerations of desert or of moral good or evil do not enter, i.e., in the case of animals, the fact that a sentient being is feeling pleasure or pain is the whole fact (or the fact sufficiently described to enable us to judge of its goodness or badness), and we need not hesitate to say that the pleasure of animals is always good, and the pain of animals always bad, in itself and apart from its consequences. But when a moral being is feeling a pleasure or pain that is deserved or undeserved, or a pleasure or pain that implies a good or a bad disposition, the total fact is quite inadequately described if we say 'a sentient being is feeling pleasure, or pain'. The total fact may be that 'a sentient and moral being is feeling a pleasure that is undeserved, or that is the realization of a vicious disposition', and though the fact included in this, that 'a sentient being is feeling pleasure' would be good if it stood alone, that creates only a presumption that the total fact is good, and a presumption that is outweighed by the other element in the total fact.

Pleasure seems, indeed, to have a property analogous to that which we have previously recognized under the name of conditional or *prima facie* rightness. An act of promise-keeping has the property, not necessarily of being right but of being something that is right if the act has no other morally significant characteristic (such as that of causing much pain to another person). And similarly a state of pleasure has the property, not necessarily of being good, but of being something that is good if the state has no other characteristic that prevents it from being good. The two characteristics that may interfere with its being good are (*a*) that of being contrary to desert, and (*b*) that of being a state which is the realization of a bad disposition. Thus the pleasures of which we can say without doubt that they are good are (i) the pleasures of non-moral beings (animals), (ii) the pleasures of moral beings that are deserved and are either realizations of good moral dispositions or realizations of neutral capacities (such as the pleasures of the senses).

In so far as the goodness or badness of a particular pleasure depends on its being the realization of a virtuous or vicious disposition, this has been allowed for by our recognition of virtue as a thing good in itself. But the mere recognition of virtue as a thing good in itself, and of pleasure as a thing *prima facie* good in itself, does not do justice to the conception of merit. If we compare two imaginary states of the universe, alike in the total amounts of virtue and vice and of pleasure and pain present in the two, but in one of which the virtuous were all happy and the vicious miserable, while in the other the virtuous were miserable and the vicious happy, very few people would hesitate to say that the first was a much better state of the universe than the second. It would seem then that, besides virtue and pleasure, we must recognize (3), as a third independent good, the apportionment of pleasure and pain to the virtuous and the vicious respectively. And it is on the recognition of this as a separate good that the recognition of the duty of justice, in distinction from fidelity to promises on the one hand and from beneficence on the other, rests.

(4) It seems clear that knowledge, and in a less degree what we may for the present call 'right opinion', are states of mind good in themselves. Here too we may, if we please, help ourselves to realize the fact by supposing two states of the universe equal in respect of virtue and of pleasure and of the allocation of pleasure to the virtuous, but such that the persons in the one had a far greater understanding of the nature and laws of the universe than those in the other. Can any one doubt that the first would be a better state of the universe?

From one point of view it seems doubtful whether knowledge and right opinion, no matter what it is of or about, should be considered good. Knowledge of mere matters of fact (say of the number of stories in a building), without knowledge of their relation to other facts, might seem to be worthless; it certainly seems to be worth much less than the knowledge of general principles, or of facts as depending on general principles—what we might call insight or understanding as opposed to mere knowledge. But on reflection it seems clear that even about matters of fact right opinion is in itself a better state of mind to be in than wrong, and knowledge than right opinion.

There is another objection which may naturally be made to the view that knowledge is as such good. There are many pieces of knowledge which we in fact think it well for people *not* to have; e.g., we may think it a bad thing for a sick man to know how ill he is, or for a vicious man to know how he may most conveniently indulge his vicious tendencies. But it seems that in such cases it is not the knowledge but the consequences in the way of pain or of vicious action that we think bad.

It might perhaps be objected that knowledge is not a better state than right opinion, but merely a source of greater satisfaction to its possessor. It no doubt is a source of greater satisfaction. Curiosity is the desire to *know*, and is never really satisfied by mere opinion. Yet there are two facts which seem to show that this is not the whole truth. (*a*) While opinion recognized to be such is never thoroughly satisfactory to its possessor, there is another state of mind which is not knowledge—which may even be mistaken—yet which through lack of reflection is not distinguished from knowledge by its possessor, the state of mind which Professor Cook Wilson has called 'that of being under the impression that so-and-so is the case'.[1] Such a state of mind may be as great a source of satisfaction to its possessor as knowledge, yet we should all think it to be an inferior state of mind to knowledge. This surely points to a recognition by us that knowledge has a worth other than that of being a source of satisfaction to its possessor. (*b*) Wrong opinion, so long as its wrongness is not discovered, may be as great a source of satisfaction as right. Yet we should agree that it is an inferior state of mind, because it is to a less extent founded on knowledge and is itself a less close approximation to knowledge; which again seems to point to our recognizing knowledge as something good in itself.

Four things, then, seem to be intrinsically good—virtue, pleasure, the allocation of pleasure to the virtuous, and knowledge (and in a less degree right opinion). And I am unable to discover anything that is intrinsically good, which is not either one of these or a combination of two or more of them. And while this list of goods has been arrived at on its own merits, by reflection on what we really think to be good, it perhaps derives some support from the fact that it harmonizes with a widely accepted classification of the elements in the life of the soul. It is usual to enumerate these as cognition, feeling, and conation. Now knowledge is the ideal state of the mind, and right opinion an approximation to the ideal, on the cognitive or intellectual side; pleasure is its ideal state on the side of feeling; and virtue is its ideal state on the side of conation; while the allocation of happiness to virtue is a good which we recognize when we reflect on the ideal relation between the conative side and the side of feeling. It might of course be objected that there are or may be intrinsic goods that

---

1 *Statement and Inference*, i, 113.

are not states of mind or relations between states of mind at all, but in this suggestion I can find no plausibility. Contemplate any imaginary universe from which you suppose mind entirely absent, and you will fail to find anything in it that you can call good in itself. That is not to say, of course, that the existence of a material universe may not be a necessary condition for the existence of many things that are good in themselves. Our knowledge and our true opinions are to a large extent about the material world, and to that extent could not exist unless it existed. Our pleasures are to a large extent derived from material objects. Virtue owes many of its opportunities to the existence of material conditions of good and material hindrances to good. But the value of material things appears to be purely instrumental, not intrinsic.

Of the three elements virtue, knowledge, and pleasure are compounded all the complex states of mind that we think good in themselves. Aesthetic enjoyment, for example, seems to be a blend of pleasure with insight into the nature of the object that inspires it. Mutual love seems to be a blend of virtuous disposition of two minds towards each other, with the knowledge which each has of the character and disposition of the other, and with the pleasure which arises from such disposition and knowledge. And a similar analysis may probably be applied to all other complex goods.

49

What Makes
Someone's Life
Go Best?

DEREK PARFIT

Derek Parfit is Research Fellow of All Souls College, Oxford. His book
Reasons and Persons *is an important and highly original contribution to
moral philosophy. This selection appeared in that book as Appendix I.*

*Parfit compares three ways of understanding a person's good. One type
of theory, known as hedonism, identifies a person's good with his
happiness. A theory of this sort is advanced by Jeremy Bentham in reading
43. A second class of theories, which Parfit calls "desire-fulfillment
theories," focus instead on the satisfaction of the agent's actual or possible
desires; for an example, see Richard Brandt's discussion in reading 46. A
third class of theories, which Parfit calls "objective list theories," asserts
that certain things—for example, knowledge, rational activity, and
awareness of beauty—are good for persons whether or not they are wanted
or enjoyed. A theory of this type is presented by W. D. Ross in reading 48.*

*Although Parfit does not try to choose among the three approaches, he
does survey the strengths and weaknesses of each. In so doing, he
introduces a number of useful distinctions. For example, he points out that
a person's life does not seem to be improved by the satisfaction of his long-
forgotten desire that a casual acquaintance be cured of a disease. To avoid
such implications, Parfit suggests that desire-satisfaction theories count only
desires directed at the agent's own life. In this and other ways, Parfit
deepens our understanding of the available options.*

What would be best for someone, or would be most in this person's
interests, or would make this person's life go, for him, as well as possible?
Answers to this question I call *theories about self-interest.* There are three
kinds of theory. On *Hedonistic Theories,* what would be best for someone is
what would make his life happiest. On *Desire-Fulfillment Theories,* what would
be best for someone is what, throughout his life, would best fulfil his desires.
On *Objective List Theories,* certain things are good or bad for us, whether or
not we want to have the good things, or to avoid the bad things.

Narrow Hedonists assume, falsely, that pleasure and pain are two distinctive
kinds of experience. Compare the pleasures of satisfying an intense thirst or

lust, listening to music, solving an intellectual problem, reading a tragedy, and knowing that one's child is happy. These various experiences do not contain any distinctive common quality.

What pains and pleasures have in common are their relations to our desires. On the use of 'pain' which has rational and moral significance, all pains are when experienced unwanted, and a pain is worse or greater the more it is unwanted. Similarly, all pleasures are when experienced wanted, and they are better or greater the more they are wanted. These are the claims of *Preference-Hedonism*. On this view, one of two experiences is more pleasant if it is preferred.

This theory need not follow the ordinary uses of the words 'pain' and 'pleasure'. Suppose that I could go to a party to enjoy the various pleasures of eating, drinking, laughing, dancing, and talking to my friends. I could instead stay at home and read *King Lear*. Knowing what both alternatives would be like, I prefer to read *King Lear*. It extends the ordinary use to say that this would give me more pleasure. But on Preference-Hedonism, if we add some further assumptions given below, reading *King Lear* would give me a better evening. Griffin cites a more extreme case. Near the end of his life Freud refused pain-killing drugs, preferring to think in torment than to be confusedly euphoric. Of these two mental states, euphoria is more pleasant. But on Preference-Hedonism thinking in torment was, for Freud, a better mental state. It is clearer here not to stretch the meaning of the word 'pleasant'. A Preference-Hedonist should merely claim that, since Freud preferred to think clearly though in torment, his life went better if it went as he preferred.

Consider next Desire-Fulfillment Theories. The simplest is the *Unrestricted Theory*. This claims that what is best for someone is what would best fulfil *all* of his desires, throughout his life. Suppose that I meet a stranger who has what is believed to be a fatal disease. My sympathy is aroused, and I strongly want this stranger to be cured. Much later, when I have forgotten our meeting, the stranger is cured. On the Unrestricted Desire-Fulfillment Theory, this event is good for me, and makes my life go better. This is not plausible. We should reject this theory.

Another theory appeals only to someone's desires about his own life. I call this the *Success Theory*. This theory differs from Preference-Hedonism in only one way. The Success Theory appeals to all of our preferences about our own lives. A Preference-Hedonist appeals only to preferences about those present features of our lives that are introspectively discernible. Suppose that I strongly want not to be deceived by other people. On Preference-Hedonism it would be better for me if I believe that I am not being deceived. It would be irrelevant if my belief is false, since this makes no difference to my state of mind. On the Success Theory, it would be worse for me if my belief is false. I have a strong desire about my own life—that I should not be deceived in this way. It is bad for me if this desire is not fulfilled, even if I falsely believe that it is.

When this theory appeals only to desires that are about our own lives, it may be unclear what this excludes. Suppose that I want my life to be such that all of my desires, whatever their objects, are fulfilled. This may seem to make the Success Theory, when applied to me, coincide with the Unrestricted Desire-Fulfillment Theory. But a Success Theorist should claim that this desire is not really about my own life. This is like the distinction between a real change in some object, and a so-called *Cambridge-change*. An object undergoes a Cambridge-change if there is any change in the true statements that can be made about this object. Suppose that I cut my cheek while shaving. This causes a real change in me. It also causes a change in Confucius. It becomes true, of Confucius, that he lived on a planet in which later one more cheek was cut. This is merely a Cambridge-change.

Suppose that I am an exile, and cannot communicate with my children. I want their lives to go well. I might claim that I want to live the life of someone whose children's lives go well. A Success Theorist should again claim that this is not really a desire about my own life. If unknown to me one of my children is killed by an avalanche, this is not bad for me, and does not make my life go worse.

A Success Theorist *would* count some similar desires. Suppose that I try to give my children a good start in life. I try to give them the right education, good habits, and psychological strength. Once again, I am now an exile, and will never be able to learn what happens to my children. Suppose that, unknown to me, my children's lives go badly. One finds that the education that I gave him makes him unemployable, another has a mental breakdown, another becomes a petty thief. If my children's lives fail in these ways, and these failures are in part the result of mistakes I made as their parent, these failures in my children's lives would be judged to be bad for me on the Success Theory. One of my strongest desires was to be a successful parent. What is now happening to my children, though it is unknown to me, shows that this desire is not fulfilled. My life failed in one of the ways in which I most wanted it to succeed. Though I do not know this fact, it is bad for me, and makes it true that I have had a worse life. This is like the case where I strongly want not to be deceived. Even if I never know, it is bad for me both if I am deceived and if I turn out to be an unsuccessful parent. These are not introspectively discernible differences in my conscious life. On Preference-Hedonism, these events are not bad for me. On the Success Theory, they are.

Because they are thought by some to need special treatment, I mention next the desires that people have about what happens after they are dead. For a Preference-Hedonist, once I am dead, nothing bad can happen to me. A Success Theorist should deny this. Return to the case where all my children have wretched lives, because of the mistakes I made as their parent. Suppose that my children's lives all go badly only after I am dead. My life turns out to have been a failure, in the one of the ways I cared about most. A Success Theorist should claim that, here too, this makes it true that I had a worse life.

Some Success Theorists would reject this claim. Their theory ignores the desires of the dead. I believe this theory to be indefensible. Suppose that I was asked, 'Do you want it to be true that you were a successful parent even after you are dead?' I would answer 'Yes'. It is irrelevant to my desire whether it is fulfilled before or after I am dead. These Success Theorists count it as bad for me if my desire is not fulfilled, even if, because I am an exile, I never know this. How then can it matter whether, when my desire is not fulfilled, I am dead? All that my death does is to *ensure* that I will never know this. If we think it irrelevant that I never know about the non-fulfillment of my desire, we cannot defensibly claim that my death makes a difference.

I turn now to questions and objections which arise for both Preference-Hedonism and the Success Theory.

Should we appeal only to the desires and preferences that someone actually has? Return to my choice between going to a party or staying at home to read *King Lear*. Suppose that, knowing what both alternatives would be like, I choose to stay at home. And suppose that I never later regret this choice. On one theory, this shows that staying at home to read *King Lear* gave me a better evening. This is a mistake. It might be true that, if I had chosen to go to the party, I would never have regretted that choice. According to this theory, this would have shown that going to the party gave me a better evening. This theory thus implies that each alternative would have been better than the other. Since this theory implies such contradictions, it must be revised. The obvious revision is to appeal not only to my actual preferences, in the alternative I choose, but also to the preferences that I would have had if I had chosen otherwise.

In this example, whichever alternative I choose, I would never regret this choice. If this is true, can we still claim that one of the alternatives would give me a better evening? On some theories, when in two alternatives I would have such contrary preferences, neither alternative is better or worse for me. This is not plausible when one of my contrary preferences would have been much stronger. Suppose that, if I choose to go to the party, I shall be only mildly glad that I made this choice, but that, if I choose to stay and read *King Lear*, I shall be extremely glad. If this is true, reading *King Lear* gives me a better evening.

Whether we appeal to Preference-Hedonism or the Success Theory, we should not appeal only to the desires or preferences that I actually have. We should also appeal to the desires and preferences that I would have had, in the various alternatives that were, at different times, open to me. One of these alternatives would be best for me if it is the one in which I would have the strongest desires and preferences fulfilled. This allows us to claim that some alternative life would have been better for me, even if throughout my actual life I am glad that I chose this life rather than this alternative.

There is another distinction which applies both to Preference-Hedonism and to the Success Theory. These theories are *Summative* if they appeal to all of someone's desires, actual and hypothetical, about his own life. In deciding which alternative would produce the greatest total net sum of desire-fulfillment, we assign some positive number to each desire that is fulfilled, and some negative number to each desire that is not fulfilled. How great these numbers are depends on the intensity of the desires in question. (In the case of the Success Theory, which appeals to past desires, it may also depend on how long these desires were had. [. . .] this may be a weakness in this theory. The issue does not arise for Preference-Hedonism, which appeals only to desires about one's present state of mind.) The total net sum of desire-fulfillment is the sum of the positive numbers minus the negative numbers. Provided that we can compare the relative strength of different desires, this calculation could in theory be performed. The choice of a unit for the numbers makes no difference to the result.

Another version of both theories does not appeal, in this way, to all of a person's desires and preferences about his own life. It appeals only to *global* rather than *local* desires and preferences. A preference is global if it is about some part of one's life considered as a whole, or is about one's whole life. The *Global* versions of these theories I believe to be more plausible.

Consider this example. Knowing that you accept a Summative theory, I tell you that I am about to make your life go better. I shall inject you with an addictive drug. From now on, you will wake each morning with an extremely strong desire to have another injection of this drug. Having this desire will be in itself neither pleasant nor painful, but if the desire is not fulfilled within an hour it would then become extremely painful. This is no cause for concern, since I shall give you ample supplies of this drug. Every morning, you will be able at once to fulfil this desire. The injection, and its after-effects, would also be neither pleasant nor painful. You will spend the rest of your days as you do now.

What would the Summative theories imply about this case? We can plausibly suppose that you would not welcome my proposal. You would prefer not to become addicted to this drug, even though I assure you that you will never lack supplies. We can also plausibly suppose that, if I go ahead, you will always regret that you became addicted to this drug. But it is likely that your initial desire not to become addicted, and your later regrets that you did, would not be as strong as the desires you have each morning for another injection. Given the facts as I described them, your reason to prefer not to become addicted would not be very strong. You might dislike the thought of being addicted to anything. And you would regret the minor inconvenience that would be involved in remembering always to carry with you, like a diabetic, sufficient supplies. But these desires might be far weaker than the desires you would have each morning for a fresh injection.

On the Summative Theories, if I make you an addict, I would be increasing the sum-total of your desire-fulfillment. I would be causing one of your desires not to be fulfilled: your desire not to become an addict, which, after my act, becomes a desire to be cured. But I would also be giving you an indefinite series of extremely strong desires, one each morning, all of which you can fulfil. The fulfillment of all these desires would outweigh the non-fulfillment of your desires not to become an addict, and to be cured. On the Summative Theories, by making you an addict, I would be benefiting you—making your life go better.

This conclusion is not plausible. Having these desires, and having them fulfilled, are neither pleasant nor painful. We need not be Hedonists to believe, more plausibly, that it is in no way better for you to have and to fulfil this series of strong desires.

Could the Summative Theories be revised, so as to meet this objection? Is there some feature of the addictive desires which would justify the claim that we should ignore them when we calculate the sum total of your desire-fulfillment? We might claim that they can be ignored because they are desires that you would prefer not to have. But this is not an acceptable revision. Suppose that you are in great pain. You now have a very strong desire not to be in the state that you are in. On our revised theory, a desire does not count if you would prefer not to have this desire. This must apply to your intense desire not to be in the state you are in. You would prefer not to have this desire. If you did not dislike the state you are in, it would not be painful. Since our revised theory does not count desires that you would prefer not to have, it implies, absurdly, that it cannot be bad for you to be in great pain.

There may be other revisions which could meet these objections. But it is simpler to appeal to the Global versions of both Preference-Hedonism and the Success Theory. These appeal only to someone's desires about some part of his life, considered as a whole, or about his whole life. The Global Theories give us the right answer in the case where I make you an addict. You would prefer not to become addicted, and you would later prefer to cease to be addicted. These are the only preferences to which the Global Theories appeal. They ignore your particular desires each morning for a fresh injection. This is because you have yourself taken these desires into account in forming your global preference.

This imagined case of addiction is in its essentials similar to countless other cases. There are countless cases in which it is true both (1) that, if someone's life goes in one of two ways, this would increase the sum total of his local desire-fulfillment, but (2) that the other alternative is what he would globally prefer, *whichever* way his actual life goes.

Rather than describing another of the countless actual cases, I shall mention an imaginary case. . . . Suppose that I could either have fifty of years of life of an extremely high quality, or an indefinite number of years that are barely worth living. In the first alternative, my fifty years would, on any theory, go extremely well. I would be very happy, would achieve great things, do much good, and love and be loved by many people. In the second alternative my life would always be, though not by much, worth living. There would be nothing bad about this life, and it would each day contain a few small pleasures.

On the Summative Theories, if the second life was long enough, it would be better for me. In each day within this life I have some desires about my life that are fulfilled. In the fifty years of the first alternative, there would be a very great sum of local desire-fulfillment. But this would be a finite sum, and in the end it would be outweighed by the sum of desire-fulfillment in my indefinitely long second alternative. A simpler way to put this point is this. The first alternative would be good. In the second alternative, since my life is worth living, living each extra day is good for me. If we merely add together whatever is good for me, some number of these extra days would produce the greatest total sum.

I do not believe that the second alternative would give me a better life. I therefore reject the Summative Theories. It is likely that, in both alternatives, I would globally prefer the first. Since the Global Theories would then imply that the first alternative gives me a better life, these theories seem to me more plausible.

Turn now to the third kind of Theory that I mentioned: the Objective List Theory. According to this theory, certain things are good or bad for people, whether or not these people would want to have the good things, or to avoid the bad things. The good things might include moral goodness, rational activity, the development of one's abilities, having children and being a good parent, knowledge, and the awareness of true beauty. The bad things might include being betrayed, manipulated, slandered, deceived, being deprived of liberty or dignity, and enjoying either sadistic pleasure, or aesthetic pleasure in what is in fact ugly.

An Objective List Theorist might claim that his theory coincides with the Global version of the Success Theory. On this theory, what would make my life go best depends on what I would prefer, now and in the various alternatives, if I knew all of the relevant facts about these alternatives. An Objective List Theorist might say that the most relevant facts are what his theory claims— what would in fact be good or bad for me. And he might claim that anyone who knew these facts would want what is truly good for him, and want to avoid what would be bad for him.

If this was true, though the Objective List Theory would coincide with the Success Theory, the two theories would remain distinct. A Success Theorist would reject this description of the coincidence. On his theory, nothing is good or bad for people, whatever their preferences are. Something is bad for someone only if, knowing the facts, he wants to avoid it. And the relevant facts do not include the alleged facts cited by the Objective List Theorist. On the Success Theory it is, for instance, bad for someone to be deceived if and because this is not what he wants. The Objective List Theorist makes the reverse claim. People want not to be deceived because this is bad for them.

As these remarks imply, there is one important difference between on the one hand Preference-Hedonism and the Success Theory, and on the other hand the Objective List Theory. The first two kinds of theory give an account of self-interest which is entirely factual, or which does not appeal to facts about value. The account appeals to what a person does and would prefer, given full knowledge of the purely non-evaluative facts about the alternatives. In contrast, the Objective List Theory appeals directly to facts about value.

In choosing between these theories, we must decide how much weight to give to imagined cases in which someone's fully informed preferences would be bizarre. If we can appeal to these cases, they cast doubt on both Preference-Hedonism and the Success Theory. Consider the man that Rawls imagined who wants to spend his life counting the numbers of blades of grass in different lawns. Suppose that this man knows that he could achieve great progress if instead he worked in some especially useful part of Applied Mathematics. Though he could achieve such significant results, he prefers to go on counting blades of grass. On the Success Theory, if we allow this theory to cover all imaginable cases, it could be better for this person if he counts his blades of grass rather than achieves great and beneficial results in Mathematics.

The counter-example might be more offensive. Suppose that what someone would most prefer, knowing the alternatives, is a life in which, without being detected, he causes as much pain as he can to other people. On the Success Theory, such a life would be what is best for this person.

We may be unable to accept these conclusions. Ought we therefore to abandon this theory? This is what Sidgwick did, though those who quote him seldom notice this. He suggests that 'a man's future good on the whole is what he would now desire and seek on the whole if all the consequences of all the different lines of conduct open to him were accurately foreseen and adequately realised in imagination at the present point of time'. As he comments: 'The notion of "Good" thus attained has an ideal element: it is something that *is* not always actually desired and aimed at by human beings: but the ideal element is entirely interpretable in terms of *fact*, actual or hypothetical, and does not introduce any judgement of value'. Sidgwick then rejects this account, claiming that what is ultimately good for someone is what this person *would* desire if his desires were in harmony with reason. This last phrase is needed, Sidgwick thought, to exclude the cases where someone's desires are irrational. He assumes that there are some things that we have good reason to desire, and others that we have good reason not to desire. These might be the things which are held to be good or bad for us by Objective List Theories.

Suppose we agree that, in some imagined cases, what someone would most want both now and later, fully knowing about the alternatives, would *not* be what would be best for him. If we accept this conclusion, it may seem that we must reject both Preference-Hedonism and the Success Theory. Perhaps, like Sidgwick, we must put constraints on what can be rationally desired.

It might be claimed instead that we can dismiss the appeal to such imagined cases. It might be claimed that what people would in fact prefer, if they knew the relevant facts, would always be something that we could accept as what is really good for them. Is this a good reply? If we agree that in the imagined cases what someone would prefer might be something that is bad for him, in these cases we have abandoned our theory. If this is so, can we defend our theory by saying that, in the actual cases, it would not go astray? I believe that this is not an adequate defence. But I shall not pursue this question here.

This objection may apply with less force to Preference-Hedonism. On this theory, what can be good or bad for someone can only be discernible features of his conscious life. These are the features that, at the time, he either wants or does not want. I asked above whether it is bad for people to be deceived because they prefer not to be, or whether they prefer not to be deceived because this is bad for them. Consider the comparable question with respect to pain.

Some have claimed that pain is intrinsically bad, and that this is why we dislike it. As I have suggested, I doubt this claim. After taking certain kinds of drug, people claim that the quality of their sensations has not altered, but they no longer dislike these sensations. We would regard such drugs as effective analgesics. This suggests that the badness of a pain consists in its being disliked, and that it is not disliked because it is bad. The disagreement between these views would need much more discussion. But, if the second view is better, it is more plausible to claim that whatever someone wants or does not want to experience—however bizarre we find his desires—should be counted as being for this person truly pleasant or painful, and as being for that reason good or bad for him. There may still be cases where it is plausible to claim that it would be bad for someone if he enjoys certain kinds of pleasure. This might be claimed, for instance, about sadistic pleasure. But there may be few such cases.

If instead we appeal to the Success Theory, we are not concerned only with the experienced quality of our conscious life. We are concerned with such things as whether we are achieving what we are trying to achieve, whether we are being deceived, and the like. When considering this theory, we can more often plausibly claim that, even if someone knew the facts, his preferences might go astray, and fail to correspond to what would be good or bad for him.

Which of these different theories should we accept? I shall not attempt an answer here. But I shall end by mentioning another theory, which might be claimed to combine what is most plausible in these conflicting theories. It is a striking fact that those who have addressed this question have disagreed so fundamentally. Many philosophers have been convinced Hedonists; many others have been as much convinced that Hedonism is a gross mistake.

Some Hedonists have reached their view as follows. They consider an opposing view, such as that which claims that what is good for someone is to have knowledge, to engage in rational activity, and to be aware of true beauty. These Hedonists ask, 'Would these states of mind be good, if they brought no enjoyment, and if the person in these states of mind had not the slightest desire that they continue?' Since they answer No, they conclude that the value of these states of mind must lie in their being liked, and in their arousing a desire that they continue.

This reasoning assumes that the value of a whole is just the sum of the value of its parts. If we remove the part to which the Hedonist appeals, what is left seems to have no value, hence Hedonism is the truth.

Suppose instead that we claim that the value of a whole may not be a mere sum of the value of its parts. We might then claim that what is best for people is a composite. It is not just their being in the conscious states that they want to be in. Nor is it just their having knowledge, engaging in rational activity, being aware of true beauty, and the like. What is good for someone is neither just what Hedonists claim, nor just what is claimed by Objective List Theorists. We might believe that if we had *either* of these, *without the other*, what we had would have little or no value. We might claim, for example, that what is good or bad for someone is to have knowledge, to be engaged in rational activity, to experience mutual love, and to be aware of beauty, while strongly wanting just these things. On this view, each side in this disagreement saw only half of the truth. Each put forward as sufficient something that was only necessary. Pleasure with many other kinds of object has no value. And, if they are entirely devoid of pleasure, there is no value in knowledge, rational activity, love, or the awareness of beauty. What is of value, or is good for someone, is to have both; to be engaged in these activities, and to be strongly wanting to be so engaged.

50

The Diversity of Goods

CHARLES TAYLOR

Charles Taylor (b. 1931) is Professor of Philosophy and Political Science at McGill University. His books include Hegel, Sources of the Self, *and* The Ethics of Authenticity. *This selection is from Amartya Sen and Bernard Williams, eds.,* Utilitarianism and Beyond.

Taylor defends a strong form of value-pluralism. His position is not merely that a variety of irreducibly different things are good. He holds, as well, that we distinguish between what is admirable and what is contemptible in a variety of different idioms, and that the different vocabularies impose conflicting and incommensurable demands. As examples, he cites the demands of fidelity to one's deepest convictions, of Christian charity, and of freedom from domination by natural and social forces.

There are, of course, strategies for reconciling these demands. A utilitarian might rate each in accordance with its contribution to happiness or desire-satisfaction. But Taylor argues that this merely elevates one ideal—the utilitarian model of rational calculation—above the rest. He also argues that it distorts various elements of our moral experience—for example, our reactions of admiration and contempt and our sense that "to recognize something as a higher goal is to recognize it as one that men ought to follow." For a utilitarian discussion that is sensitive to some of these considerations, see John Stuart Mill's comparison of Socrates and the fool in reading 23.

1

What did utilitarianism have going for it? A lot of things undoubtedly: its seeming compatibility with scientific thought; its this-worldly humanist focus, its concern with suffering. But one of the powerful background factors behind much of this appeal was *epistemological.* A utilitarian ethic seemed to be able to fit the canons of rational validation as these were understood in the intellectual culture nourished by the epistemological revolution of the seventeenth century and the scientific outlook which partly sprang from it.

In the utilitarian perspective, one validated an ethical position by hard evidence. You count the consequences for human happiness of one or another course, and you go with the one with the highest favourable total. What counts as human happiness was thought to be something conceptually unproblematic, a scientifically establishable domain of facts like others. One could abandon all the metaphysical or theological factors—commands of God, natural rights, virtues—which made ethical questions scientifically undecidable. Bluntly, we could calculate.

Ultimately, I should like to argue that this is but another example of the baleful effect of the classical epistemological model, common to Cartesians and empiricists, which has had such a distorting effect on the theoretical self-understanding of moderns. This is something which is above all visible in the sciences of man, but I think it has wreaked as great havoc in ethical theory.

The distortive effect comes in that we tend to start formulating our meta-theory of a given domain with an already formed model of valid reasoning, all the more dogmatically held because we are oblivious to the alternatives. This model then makes us quite incapable of seeing how reason does and can really function in the domain, to the degree that it does not fit the model. We cut and chop the reality of, in this case, ethical thought to fit the Procrustean bed of our model of validation. Then, since meta-theory and theory cannot be isolated from one another, the distortive conception begins to shape our ethical thought itself.

A parallel process, I should like to argue, has been visible in the sciences of man, with similar stultifying effects on the practice of students of human behaviour. The best, most insightful, practice of history, sociology, psychology is either devalued or misunderstood, and as a consequence we find masses of researchers engaging in what very often turns out to be futile exercises, of no scientific value whatever, sustained only by the institutional inertia of a professionalised discipline. The history of behaviourism stands as a warning of the virtual immortality that can be attained by such institutionalised futility.

In the case of ethics, two patterns of thought have especially benefited from the influence of the underlying model of validation. One is utilitarianism, which as I have just mentioned seemed to offer calculation over verifiable empirical quantities in the place of metaphysical distinctions. The other is various species of formalism. Kant is the originator of one of the most influential variants, without himself having fallen victim, I believe, to the narrowing consequences that usually follow the adoption of a formalism.

Formalisms, like utilitarianism, have the apparent value that they would allow us to ignore the problematic distinctions between different qualities of action or modes of life, which play such a large part in our actual moral decisions, feelings of admiration, remorse, etc., but which are so hard to justify when others controvert them. They offer the hope of deciding ethical questions without having to determine which of a number of rival languages of moral virtue and vice, of the admirable and the contemptible, of unconditional versus conditional obligation, are valid. You could finesse all this, if you could determine the cases where a maxim of action would be unrealisable if everyone adopted it, or where its universal realisation was something you could not possibly desire; or if you could determine what actions you could approve no matter whose standpoint you adopted of those persons affected; or if you could circumscribe the principles that would be adopted by free rational agents in certain paradigm circumstances.

Of course, all these formulae for ethical decision repose on some substantive moral insights; otherwise they would not seem even plausible candidates as models of *ethical* reasoning. Behind these Kant-derived formulae stands one of the most fundamental insights of modern Western civilisation, the universal attribution of moral personality: in fundamental ethical matters, everyone ought to count, and all ought to count in the same way. Within this outlook, one absolute requirement of ethical thinking is that we respect other human agents as subjects of practical reasoning on the same footing as ourselves.

In a sense, this principle is historically parochial. This is not the way the average Greek in ancient times, for instance, looked on his Thracian slave. But, in a sense, it also corresponds to something very deep in human moral reasoning. All moral reasoning is carried on within a community; and it is essential to the very existence of this community that each accord the other interlocutors this status as moral agents. The Greek who may not have accorded it to his Thracian slave most certainly did to his compatriots. That was part and parcel of there being recognised issues of justice between them. What modern civilisation has done, partly under the influence of Stoic natural law and Christianity, has been to lift all the parochial restrictions that surrounded this recognition of moral personality in earlier civilisations.

The modern insight, therefore, flows very naturally from one of the basic preconditions of moral thinking itself, along with the view—overwhelmingly plausible, to us moderns—that there is no defensible distinction to be made in this regard between different classes of human beings. This has become so widespread that even discrimination and domination is in fact justified on universalist grounds. (Even South Africa has an official ideology of *apartheid*, which can allow theoretically for the peoples concerned to be not unequal, but just different.)

So we seem on very safe ground in adopting a decision procedure which can be shown to flow from this principle. Indeed, this seems to be a moral principle of a quite different order from the various contested languages of moral praise, condemnation, aspiration or aversion, which distinguish rival conceptions of virtue and paradigm modes of life. We might even talk ourselves into believing that it is not a moral principle in any substantive contestable sense at all, but some kind of limiting principle of moral reasoning. Thus we might say with Richard Hare, for example, that in applying this kind of decision procedure we are following not moral intuitions, but rather our linguistic intuitions concerning the use of the word 'moral'.

Classical utilitarianism itself incorporated this universal principle in the procedural demand that in calculating the best course, the happiness of each agent count for one, and of no agent for more than one. Here again one of the fundamental issues of modern thought is decided by what looks like a formal principle, and utilitarianism itself got a great deal of its *prima facie* plausibility from the strength of the same principle. If everyone counts as a moral agent, then what they desire and aim at ought to count, and the right course of action should be what satisfies all, or the largest number possible. At least this chain of reasoning can appear plausible.

But clear reasoning ought to demand that we counteract this tendency to slip over our deepest moral convictions unexamined. They look like formal principles only because they are so foundational to the moral thinking of our civilisation. We should strive to formulate the underlying moral insights just as clearly and expressly as we do all others.

When we do so, of course, we shall find that they stand in need of justification like the others. This points us to one of the motives for construing them as formal principles. For those who despair of reason as the arbiter of moral disputes (and the epistemological tradition has tended to induce this despair in many), making the fundamental insights into a formal principle has seemed a way of avoiding a moral scepticism which was both implausible and distasteful.

But, I want to argue, the price of this formalism, as also of the utilitarian reduction, has been a severe distortion of our understanding of our moral thinking. One of the big illusions which grows from either of these reductions is the belief that there is a single consistent domain of the 'moral', that there is one set of considerations, or mode of calculations, which determines what we ought 'morally' to do. The unity of the moral is a question which is conceptually decided from the first on the grounds that moral reasoning just is equivalent to calculating consequences for human happiness, or determining the universal applicability of maxims, or something of the sort.

But once we shake ourselves clear from the formalist illusion, of the utilitarian reduction—and this means resisting the blandishments of their underlying model of rational validation—we can see that the boundaries of the moral are an open question; indeed, the very appropriateness of a single term here can be an issue.

We could easily decide—a view which I would defend—that the universal attribution of moral personality is valid, and lays obligations on us which we cannot ignore; but that there are also other moral ideals and goals—e.g., of less than universal solidarity, or of personal excellence—which cannot be easily coordinated with universalism, and can even enter into conflict with it. To decide *a priori* what the bounds of the moral are is just to obfuscate the question whether and to what degree this is so, and to make it incapable of being coherently stated.

2

I should like to concentrate here on a particular aspect of moral language and moral thinking that gets obscured by the epistemologically-motivated: reduction and homogenisation of the 'moral' we find in both utilitarianism and formalism. These are the qualitative distinctions we make between different actions, or feelings, or modes of life, as being in some way morally higher or lower, noble or base, admirable or contemptible. It is these languages of qualitative contrast that get marginalised, or even expunged together, by the utilitarian or formalist reductions. I want to argue, in opposition to this, that they are central to our moral thinking and ineradicable from it.

Some examples might help here of such qualitative distinctions which are commonly subscribed to. For some people, personal integrity is a central goal: what matters is that one's life express what one truly senses as important, admirable, noble, desirable. The temptations to be avoided here are those of conformity to established standards which are not really one's own, or of dishonesty with oneself concerning one's own convictions or affinities. The chief threat to integrity is a lack of courage in face of social demands, or in face of what one has been brought up to see as the unthinkable. This is a recognisable type of moral outlook.

We can see a very different type if we look at a Christian model of *agapê*, such as one sees, e.g., with Mother Theresa. The aim here is to associate oneself with, to become in a sense a channel of, God's love for men, which is seen as having the power to heal the divisions among men and take them beyond what they usually recognise as the limits to their love for one another. The obstacles to this are seen as various forms of refusal of God's *agapê*, either through a sense of self-sufficiency, or despair. This outlook understands human moral transformations in terms of images of healing, such as one sees in the New Testament narratives.

A very different, yet historically related, modern view centres around the goal of liberation. This sees the dignity of human beings as consisting in their directing their own lives, in their deciding for themselves the conditions of their own existence, as against falling prey to the domination of others, or to impersonal natural or social mechanisms which they fail to understand, and therefore cannot control or transform. The inner obstacles to this are ignorance, or lack of courage, or falsely self-depreciatory images of the self; but these are connected with external obstacles in many variants of modern liberation theory. This is particularly so of the last: self-depreciating images are seen as inculcated by others who benefit from the structures of domination in which subject groups are encased. Fanon has made this kind of analysis very familiar for the colonial context, and his categories have been transposed to a host of others, especially to that of women's liberation.

Let us look briefly at one other such language, that of rationality, as this is understood, for instance, by utilitarians. We have here the model of a human being who is clairvoyant about his goals, and capable of objectifying and understanding himself and the world which surrounds him. He can get a clear grasp of the mechanisms at work in self and world, and can thus direct his action clear-sightedly and deliberately. To do this he must resist the temptations offered by the various comforting illusions that make the self or the world so much more attractive than they really are in the cold light of science. He must fight off the self-indulgence which consists of giving oneself a picture of the world which is satisfying to one's *amour propre*, or one's sense of drama, or one's craving for meaning, or any of these metaphysical temptations. The rational man has the courage of austerity; he is marked by his ability to adopt an objective stance to things.

I introduce these four examples so as to give some intuitive basis to an otherwise abstract discussion. But I did not have to look far. These moral outlooks are very familiar to us from our own moral reasoning and sensibility, or those of people we know (and sometimes of people we love to hate). I am sure that some of the details of my formulation will jar with just about any reader. But that is not surprising. Formulating these views is a very difficult job. Like all self-interpretive activity it is open to potentially endless dispute. This is, indeed, part of the reason why these outlooks have fallen under the epistemological cloud and therefore have tended to be excluded from the formalist and utilitarian meta-ethical pictures. But one or some of these, or others like them, underlie much of our deciding what to do, our moral admirations, condemnations, contempts, and so on.

Another thing that is evident straight off is how different they are from each other. I mean by that not only that they are based on very different pictures of man, human possibility and the human condition; but that they frequently lead to incompatible prescriptions in our lives—incompatible with each other, and also with the utilitarian calculation which unquestionably plays some part in the moral reasoning of most moderns. (The modern dispute about utilitarianism is not about whether it occupies some of the space of moral reason, but whether it fills the whole space.) It could be doubted whether giving comfort to the dying is the highest util-producing activity possible in contemporary Calcutta. But, from another point of view, the dying are in an extremity that makes calculation irrelevant.

But, nevertheless, many people find themselves drawn by more than one of these views, and are faced with the job of somehow making them compatible in their lives. This is where the question can arise whether all the demands that we might consider moral and which we recognise as valid can be coherently combined. This question naturally raises another one, whether it is really appropriate to talk of a single type of demand called 'moral'. This is the more problematic when we reflect that we all recognise other qualitative distinctions which we would not class right off as moral, or perhaps even on reflection would refuse the title to; for instance, being 'cool', or being macho, or others of this sort. So that the question of drawing a line around the moral becomes a difficult one. And it may even come to appear as an uninteresting verbal one in the last analysis. The really important question may turn out to be how we combine in our lives two or three or four different goals, or virtues, or standards, which we feel we cannot repudiate but which seem to demand incompatible things of us. Which of these we dignify with the term 'moral', or whether we so designate all of them, may end up appearing a mere question of labelling—unless, that is, it confuses us into thinking that there is in principle only one set of goals or standards which can be accorded ultimate significance. In certain contexts, it might help clarity to drop the word, at least provisionally, until we get over the baleful effects of reductive thinking on our meta-ethical views.

3

Before going on to examine further the implications of this for social theory, it will be useful to look more closely at these languages of qualitative contrast. What I am gesturing at with the term 'qualitative contrast' is the sense that one way of acting or living is higher than others, or in other cases that a certain way of living is debased. It is essential to the kind of moral view just exemplified that this kind of contrast be made. Some ways of living and acting have a special status, they stand out above others; while, in certain cases, others are seen as despicable.

This contrast is essential. We should be distorting these views if we tried to construe the difference between higher and lower as a mere difference of degree in the attainment of some common good, as utilitarian theory would have us do. Integrity, charity, liberation, and the like stand out as worthy of pursuit in a special way, incommensurably with other goals we might have, such as the pursuit of wealth, or comfort, or the approval of those who surround us. Indeed, for those who hold to such views of the good, we ought to be ready to sacrifice some of these lesser goods for the higher.

Moreover, the agent's being sensible of this distinction is an essential condition of his realising the good concerned. For our recognising the higher value of integrity, or charity, or rationality, etc., is an essential part of our being rational, charitable, having integrity and so on. True, we recognise such a thing as unconscious virtue, which we ascribe to people who are good but quite without a sense of their superiority over others. This lack of self-congratulation we consider itself to be a virtue, as the deprecatory expression 'holier than thou' implies. But the absence of self-conscious superiority does not mean an absence of sensitivity to the higher goal. The saintly person is not 'holier than thou', but he is necessarily moved by the demands of charity in a special way, moved to recognise that there is something special here; in this particular case, he has a sense of awe before the power of God, or of wonder at the greatness of man as seen by God. And a similar point could be made for the other examples: an essential part of achieving liberation is sensing the greatness of liberated humanity—and consequently being sensible of the degradation of the dominated victim; an essential part of integrity is the recognition that it represents a demand on us of a special type, and so on.

Another way of making this point is to say that motivation enters into the definition of the higher activity or way of being in all these cases. The aspiration to achieve one of these goods is also an aspiration to be motivated in a certain way, or to have certain motivations win out in oneself. This is why we can speak of these aspirations as involving 'second-order' motivations (as I have tried to do elsewhere, following Harry Frankfurt).

We can articulate the contrast or incommensurability involved here in a number of ways. One way of saying it is via the notion of obligation. Ordinary goals, e.g., for wealth or comfort, are goals that a person may have or not. If he does, then there are a number of instrumental things that he ought to do—

hypothetically, in Kant's sense—to attain them. But if he lacks these goals, no criticism attaches to him for neglecting to pursue them. By contrast, it is in the nature of what I have called a higher goal that it is one we *should* have. Those who lack them are not just free of some additional instrumental obligations which weigh with the rest of us; they are open to censure. For those who subscribe to integrity, the person who cares not a whit for it is morally insensitive, or lacks courage, or is morally coarse. A higher goal is one from which one cannot detach oneself just by expressing a sincere lack of interest, because to recognise something as a higher goal is to recognise it as one that men ought to follow. This is, of course, the distinction that Kant drew between hypothetical and categorical imperatives.

Or rather, I should say that it is a closely related distinction. For Kant the boundary between the categorical and the hypothetical was meant to mark the line between the moral and the non-moral. But there are languages of qualitative contrast which we are quite ready to recognise as non-moral, even bearing in mind the fuzzy boundaries of the domain which this word picks out. We often apply such languages in what we call the aesthetic domain. If I see something especially magnificent in the music of Mozart as against some of his humdrum contemporaries, then I will judge you as insensitive in some way if you rate them on a par. The word 'insensitive' here is a word of depreciation. This is a difference one *should* be sensible of, in my view.

Of course, I would not speak of this as a *moral* condemnation, but condemnation it would be nevertheless. I do not react to this difference as I do to differences of taste which correspond to no such incommensurability, e.g., whether you like the symphonies of Bruckner or not.

The criterion for incommensurability I am offering here is therefore not the same as Kant's for the moral. But, as I have already indicated, I do not think that a line can be drawn neatly and unproblematically around the moral. Of course, if someone professes to see no distinction between his concern for the flowers in his garden and that for the lives of refugees faced with starvation, so that he proposes to act in both cases just to the degree that he feels interested at the time, we are rightly alarmed, and take this more seriously than the failure to appreciate Mozart over Boieldieu. We feel more justified in intervening here, and remonstrating with him, even forcing him to act, or subjecting him to some social or other penalty for non-acting. We feel, in other words, that the obligation here is 'categorical' in the stronger sense that licenses our intervention even against his will.

But the boundary here is necessarily fuzzier and very much open to dispute. Whereas the weaker sense of 'categorical' that could apply to the distinction I am drawing above turns on the question whether a declared lack of interest in a certain good simply neutralises it for you, or whether on the contrary, it redounds to your condemnation, shows you up as being blind, or coarse, or insensitive, or cowardly, or brutalised, too self-absorbed, or in some other way subject to censure. This, I would like to argue, is a relatively firm boundary— although the languages in which we draw it, each of us according to his own outlook, are very much in dispute between us—but it does not mark the moral from the non-moral. The languages of qualitative contrast embrace more than the moral.

A second way in which we can articulate this contrast is through the notions of admiration and contempt. People who exhibit higher goods to a signal degree are objects of our admiration; and those who fail are sometimes objects of our contempt. These emotions are bound up with our sense that there are higher and lower goals and activities. I would like to claim that if we did not mark these contrasts, if we did not have a sense of the incommensurably higher, then these emotions would have no place in our lives.

In the end, we can find ourselves experiencing very mitigated admiration for feats which we barely consider worthy of special consideration. I have a sort of admiration, mixed with tolerant amusement, for the person who has just downed 22 pancakes to win the eating contest. But that is because I see some kind of victory over self in the name of something which resembles a self-ideal. He wanted to be first, and he was willing to go to great lengths for it; and that goal at least stands out from that of being an average person, living just like everybody else. It is only because I see the feat in these terms, which are rather a caricature than an example of a higher aspiration, that the feeling of admiration can get even a mitigated grip on this case.

But we also find ourselves admiring people where there is no victory over self, where there is no recognisable achievement in the ordinary sense at all. We can admire people who are very beautiful, or have a striking grace or personal style, even though we may recognise that it is none of their doing. But we do so only because the aura of something higher, some magic quality contrasting with the ordinary and the humdrum, surrounds such people. The reasons why this should be so go very deep into the human psyche and the human form of life, and we find them hard to understand, but a special aura of this kind contributes often to what we call the 'charisma' of public figures (a word which conveys just this sense of a gift from on high, something we have not done for ourselves). Those who consider this kind of aura irrational, who resist the sense of something higher here, are precisely those who refuse their admiration to the 'charismatic', or to 'beautiful people'. Or at least they are those who claim to do so; for sometimes one senses that they are fighting a losing battle with their own feelings on this score.

In this way, admiration and contempt are bound up with our sense of the qualitative contrasts in our lives, of there being modes of life, activities, feeling, qualities, which are incommensurably higher. Where these are moral qualities, we can speak of moral admiration. These emotions provide one of the ways that we articulate this sense of the higher in our lives.

A third way we do so is in the experience we can call very loosely 'awe'. I mentioned above that a sensibility to the higher good is part of its realisation. The sense that a good occupies a special place, that it is higher, is the sense that it somehow commands our respect. This is why there is a dimension of human emotion, which we can all recognise, and which Kant again tried to articulate with his notion of the *Achtung* which we feel before the moral law. Once again, I propose to extend a Kantian analysis beyond the case of the unambiguously moral. Just as our admiration for the virtuosi of some higher goal extends to other contexts than the moral, so our sense of the incommensurable value of the goal does. For this sense, as a term of art translating Kant's *Achtung,* I propose 'awe'.

4

It is this dimension of qualitative contrast in our moral sensibility and thinking that gets short shrift in the utilitarian and formalist reductions. One of the main points of utilitarianism was to do away with this and reduce all judgements of ethical preference to quantitative form in a single dimension. In a different way, formalisms manage to reduce these contrasts to irrelevance; ethical reasoning can finesse them through a procedure of determining what is right which takes no account of them, or allows them in merely as subjective preferences, and therefore is not called upon to judge their substantive merits.

Now my argument was that a big part of the motivation for both reductions was epistemological; that they seemed to allow for a mode of ethical reasoning which fitted widely held canons of validation. We can now see better why this was so.

It is partly because these languages of contrast are so hard to validate once they come into dispute. If someone does not see that integrity is a goal one should seek, or that liberation is alone consistent with the dignity of man, how do you go about demonstrating this? But this is not the whole story. That argument is difficult in this area does not mean that it is impossible, that there is no such thing as a rationally induced conviction. That so many who have opted for utilitarianism or formalism can jump to this latter conclusion as far as higher goals are concerned is due to two underlying considerations which are rarely spelled out.

The first is that the ethical views couched in languages of contrast seem to differ in contestability from those which underlie utilitarianism and formalism. No-one seems very ready to challenge the view that, other things being equal, it is better that men's desires be fulfilled than that they be frustrated, that they be happy rather than miserable. Counter-utilitarians challenge rather whether the entire range of ethical issues can be put in these terms, whether there are not other goals which can conflict with happiness, whose claims have to be adjudicated together with utility. Again, as we saw, formalistic theories get their plausibility from the fact that they are grounded on certain moral intuitions which are almost unchallenged in modern society, based as they are in certain preconditions of moral discourse itself combined with a thesis about the racial homogeneity of humanity which it is pretty hard to challenge in a scientific, de-parochialised and historically sensitive contemporary culture.

The premises of these forms of moral reasoning can therefore easily appear to be of a quite different provenance from those that deal with qualitative contrast. Against these latter, we can allow ourselves to slip into ethical skepticism while exempting the former, either on the grounds that they are somehow self-evident, or even that they are not based on ethical insight at all but on something firmer, like the logic of our language.

But, in fact, these claims to firmer foundation are illusory. What is really going on is that some forms of ethical reasoning are being privileged over others because in our civilisation they come less into dispute or look easier to defend. This has all the rationality of the drunk in the well-known story (which the reader may forgive me for repeating) who was looking for his latch key late one night under a street lamp. A passer-by, trying to be helpful, asked him where he had dropped it. 'Over there' answered the drunk, pointing to a dark corner. 'Then why are you looking for it here?' 'Because there's so much more light here', replied the drunk.

In a similar way, we have been manoeuvred into a restrictive definition of ethics, which takes account of some of the goods we seek, e.g., utility, and universal respect for moral personality, while excluding others, viz., the virtues and goals like those mentioned above, largely on the grounds that the former are subject to less embarrassing dispute.

This may seem a little too dismissive of the traditions of reductive meta-ethics, because in fact there is a second range of considerations which have motivated the differential treatment of languages of contrast. That is that they seem to have no place in a naturalistic account of man.

The goal of a naturalist account of man comes in the wake of the scientific revolution of the seventeenth century. It is the aim of explaining human beings like other objects in nature. But a part of the practice of the successful natural science of modern times consists in its eschewing what we might call subject-related properties. By this I mean properties which things bear only insofar as they are objects of experience of subjects. The classical example of these in the seventeenth-century discussion were the so-called secondary properties, like colour or felt temperature. The aim was to account for what happens invoking only properties that the things concerned possessed absolutely, as one might put it (following Bernard Williams' use in his discussion of a related issue in Williams 1978), properties, that is, which they would possess even if (even when) they are not experienced.

How can one follow this practice in a science of animate beings, i.e., of beings who exhibit motivated action? Presumably, one can understand moti-vated action in terms of a tendency of the beings concerned to realise certain consummations in certain conditions. As long as these consummations are characterised absolutely, the demands of a naturalistic science of animate sub-jects seem to be met. Hence we get a demand which is widely recognised as a requirement of materialism in modern times: that we explain human behaviour in terms of goals whose consummations can be characterised in physical terms. This is what, e.g., for many Marxists establishes the claim that their theory is a materialist one: that it identifies as predominant the aim of getting the means to life (which presumably could ultimately be defined in physical terms).

But without being taken as far as materialism, the requirement of absolute-ness can serve to discredit languages of qualitative contrast. For these designate different possible human activities and modes of life as higher and lower.

And these are plainly subject-related notions. In the context of a naturalist explanation, one goal may be identified as more strongly desired than others, e.g., if the subject concerned gave it higher priority. But there is no place for the notion of a higher goal, which in the very logic of the contrast must be distinguishable from the strongest motive—else the term would have no function in moral discourse at all.

For those who cleave to naturalism, the languages of contrast must be suspect. They correspond to nothing in reality, which we may interpret as what we need to invoke in our bottom line explanatory language of human behaviour. They appear therefore to designate purely 'subjective' factors. They express the way we feel, not the way things are. But then this gives a rational basis to ethical scepticism, to the view that there is no rational way of arbitrating between rival outlooks expressed in such languages of contrast. This seems to give a strong intellectual basis to downgrading ethical reasoning, at least that cast in contrastive languages. For those who are impressed by naturalist considerations, but still want to salvage some valid form of ethical reasoning, utilitarianism or formalism seem attractive.

But this ground for scepticism is faulty. It leaves undefended the premiss that our accounts of man should be naturalistic in just this sense. Purging subject-related properties makes a lot of sense in an account of inanimate things. It cannot be taken as *a priori* self-evident that it will be similarly helpful in an account of human beings. We would have to establish *a posteriori* that such an absolute account of human life was possible and illuminating before we could draw conclusions about what is real, or know even how to set up the distinction objective/subjective.

In fact, though there is no place to examine the record here, it does not seem that absolute accounts offer a very plausible avenue. Put in other terms, it may well be that much of human behaviour will be understandable and explicable only in a language which characterises motivation in a fashion which marks qualitative contrasts and which is therefore not morally neutral. In this it will be like what we recognise today as the best example of clairvoyant self-understanding by those who have most conquered their illusions. If a science which describes consummations in exclusively physical terms cannot fill the bill, and if we therefore have to take account of the significances of things for agents, how can we know *a priori* that the best account available of such significances will not require some use of languages of qualitative contrast? It seems to me rather likely that it will.

In the absence of some demonstration of the validity of naturalism of this kind, the utilitarian and formalist reductions are clearly arbitrary. For they have little foundation in our ethical sensibility and practice. Even utilitarians and formalists make use of languages of contrast in their lives, decisions, admirations and contempts. One can see that in my fourth example above. 'Rational' as used by most utilitarians is a term in a qualitative contrast; it is the basis of moral admiration and contempt; it is a goal worthy of respect. The fact that it finds no place in their own meta-theory says a lot about the value of this theory.

5

Once we get over the epistemologically-induced reductions of the ethical, the problems of moral reasoning appear in a quite different light. I just have space here to mention some of the consequences for social theory.

An obviously relevant point is that we come to recognise that the ethical is not a homogeneous domain, with a single kind of good, based on a single kind of consideration. We have already noted at least three kinds of consideration which are morally relevant. The first is captured by the notion of utility, that what produces happiness is preferable to its opposite. The second is what I call the universal attribution of moral personality. These can combine to produce modern utilitarianism, as a theory that lays on us the obligation of universal benevolence in the form of the maximisation of general happiness. But the second principle is also the source of moral imperatives that conflict with utilitarianism; and this in notorious ways, e.g., demanding that we put equal distribution before the goal of maximising utility. Then, thirdly, there are the variety of goals that we express in languages of qualitative contrast, which are of course very different from each other.

The goods we recognise as moral, which means at least as laying the most important demands on us, over-riding all lesser ones, are therefore diverse. But the habit of treating the moral as a single domain is not just gratuitous or based on a mere mistake. The domain of ultimately important goods has a sort of prescriptive unity. Each of us has to answer all these demands in the course of a single life, and this means that we have to find some way of assessing their relative validity, or putting them in an order of priority. A single coherent order of goods is rather like an idea of reason in the Kantian sense, something we always try to define without ever managing to achieve it definitively.

The plurality of goods ought to be evident in modern society, if we could set aside the blinkers that our reductive meta-ethics imposes on us. Certainly we reason often about social policies in terms of utility. And we also take into account considerations of just distribution, as also of the rights of individuals, which are grounded on the principle of universal moral personality. But there are also considerations of the contrastive kind which play an important role. For instance, modern Western societies are all citizen republics, or strive to be. Their conception of the good is partly shaped by the tradition of civic humanism. The citizen republic is to be valued not just as a guarantee of general utility, or as a bulwark of rights. It may even endanger these in certain circumstances. We value it also because we generally hold that the form of life in which men govern themselves, and decide their own fate through common deliberation, is higher than one in which they live as subjects of even an enlightened despotism.

But just as the demands of utility and rights may diverge, so those of the citizen republic may conflict with both. For instance, the citizen republic requires a certain sense of community, and what is needed to foster this may go against the demands of maximum utility. Or it may threaten to enter into conflict with some of the rights of minorities. And there is a standing divergence between the demands of international equality and those of democratic self-rule in advanced Western societies. Democratic electorates in these societies will probably never agree to the amount of redistribution consistent with redressing the past wrongs of imperialism, or meeting in full the present requirements of universal human solidarity. Only despotic régimes, like Cuba and the DDR, bleed themselves for the Third World—not necessarily for the best of motives, of course.

It ought to be clear from this that no single-consideration procedure, be it that of utilitarianism, or a theory of justice based on an ideal contract, can do justice to the diversity of goods we have to weigh together in normative political thinking. Such one-factor functions appeal to our epistemological squeamishness which makes us dislike contrastive languages. And they may even have a positive appeal of the same kind insofar as they seem to offer the prospect of exact calculation of policy, through counting utils, or rational choice theory. But this kind of exactness is bogus. In fact, they only have a semblance of validity through leaving out all that they cannot calculate.

The other strong support for single-factor theory comes from the radical side. Radical theories, such as for instance Marxism, offer an answer to the demand for a unified theory—which we saw is a demand we cannot totally repudiate, at least as a goal—by revolutionary doctrines which propose sweeping away the plurality of goods now recognised in the name of one central goal which will subsume what is valuable in all of them. Thus the classless society will allegedly make unnecessary the entrenching of individual rights, or the safeguarding of 'bourgeois' civic spirit. It will provide an unconstrained community, in which the good of each will be the goal of all, and maximum utility a by-product of free collaboration, and so on.

But Marxism at least does not make the error of holding that all the goods we now seek can be reduced to some common coinage. At least it proposes to bring about unity through radical change. In the absence of such change, commensurability cannot be achieved. Indeed, it is of the essence of languages of contrast that they show our goals to be incommensurable.

If this is so, then there is no way of saving single-consideration theory however we try to reformulate it. Some might hope for instance to salvage at least the consequentialism out of utilitarianism: we would give up the narrow view that all that is worth valuing is states of happiness, but we would still try to evaluate different courses of action purely in terms of their consequences, hoping to state everything worth considering in our consequence-descriptions.

But unless the term 'consequentialism' is to be taken so widely as to lose all meaning, it has to contrast with other forms of deliberation, for instance one in which it matters whether I act in a certain way and not just what consequences I bring about. To put it differently, a non-consequentialist deliberation is one which values actions in ways which cannot be understood as a function of the consequences they have. Let us call this valuing actions intrinsically.

The attempt to reconstruct ethical and political thinking in consequentialist terms would in fact be another *a priori* fiat determining the domain of the good on irrelevant grounds. Not as narrow as utilitarianism perhaps, it would still legislate certain goods out of existence. For some languages of contrast involve intrinsic evaluation: the language of integrity, for instance. I have integrity to the degree to which my actions and statements are true expressions of what is really of importance to me. It is their intrinsic character as revelations or expressions that count, not their consequences. And the same objection would hold against a consequentialist social choice function. We may value our society for the way it makes integrity possible in its public life and social relations, or criticise a society for making it impossible. It may also be the case, of course, that we value the integrity for its effects on stability, or republican institutions, or something of the kind. But this cannot be all. It will certainly matter to us intrinsically as well as consequentially.

A consequentialist theory, even one which had gone beyond utilitarianism, would still be a Procrustes bed. It would once again make it impossible for us to get all the facets of our moral and political thinking in focus. And it might induce us to think that we could ignore certain demands because they fail to fit into our favoured mode of calculation. A meta-ethics of this kind stultifies thought.

Our political thinking needs to free itself both from the dead hand of the epistemological tradition, and the utopian monism of radical thought, in order to take account of the real diversity of goods that we recognise.

VIII

APPLICATIONS

Moral theory and real-life problems intersect in several ways. By bringing our theories to bear on actual problems, we draw out the theories' full implications. By pitting competing principles against one another, we learn their strengths and weaknesses. By attending to the complexities of the actual world, we notice new theoretical issues that we might otherwise overlook. And, conversely, by drawing on our theoretical findings, we gain new insight into how we ought to act.

Thus, consider first the problem of famine. Millions around the world are malnourished or starving, and millions more will surely die if population levels keep increasing. Those of us who live comfortably can influence these events. We can contribute to famine relief, work toward a lowering of the birthrate, or support egalitarian policies that would enable the very poor to buy more food. We can also do nothing, and simply let events take their course. Where do our responsibilities lie? What proportion of our time, energy, and wealth, if any, are we obligated to devote to preventing starvation? And upon what principles do our obligations rest?

Peter Singer (reading 51) argues that our obligations extend quite far. He appeals to the principle that when we can prevent something very bad from happening without sacrificing anything of comparable moral importance, we morally ought to do so. Because this principle says nothing about obligations to promote positive happiness, it differs from the principle of utility. However, like utilitarianism, it makes a person's obligations depend on the consequences of the acts open to him. As Singer interprets it, his principle assigns no weight to a needy person's proximity to, or prior acquaintance with, the agent. Thus, it implies that our obligations extend not only to persons we know, but also to distant strangers. To follow the principle, Singer writes, "we would have to give away enough to insure that the consumer society, dependent as it is on people spending on trivia rather than giving to famine relief, would slow down and perhaps disappear altogether."

But John Arthur (reading 52) denies that our shared morality demands this much. He argues that although "our code expects us to help people in need," it also imposes limits on what we are required to do. In particular, our code asserts both that persons have rights to property that they have legitimately acquired and that they deserve what they have gotten through their hard work. In Arthur's view, these elements usually outweigh the needs of distant persons whom we do not know. Thus, he concludes that "we are not usually obligated to give to strangers."

Of course, even if our shared moral code does not require large-scale donations, that code itself may not be defensible. But in Arthur's view, much of it is. He argues that the ideal moral code is the one that would best promote the general welfare, and that the welfare-maximizing code would recognize property rights of a familiar sort. Because Arthur appeals to the general welfare, his approach, like Singer's, is consequentialist. However, because he believes that "the welfare-maximizing moral code would not require us to maximize welfare in each individual case," Arthur's position is rule-utilitarian rather than act-utilitarian.

The problem of famine relief raises difficult questions about rights. In the next two readings, similar questions arise in another context. In reading 53, Judith Thomson takes up the controversial issue of abortion. Although the most obvious question here is whether an embryo or fetus should be considered a person with a right to life, Thomson does not address that question. Instead, she argues that even if we grant that fetuses are persons, it does not follow that abortion is impermissible. Although all persons have a right to life, Thomson argues that this is not a right to use whatever is necessary to sustain one's life. In particular, a person has no right to use what he needs to survive if another has a prior right to control that thing. Because Thomson believes that women do have a prior right to control the use of their bodies, she concludes that a fetus has no right to remain in a woman's body until it is born. Hence, expelling a fetus, and thus causing its death, does not violate its right to life.

But Joel Feinberg (reading 54) suggests that Thomson has overlooked a morally relevant complication—namely, that a woman may herself be responsible for the existence of the dependent fetus. He suggests that "whether or not a woman has a duty to continue her pregnancy depends, at least in part, on how responsible she is for being pregnant in the first place, that is, on the extent to which her pregnancy is the consequence of her own voluntary actions." Armed with this principle, Feinberg considers a spectrum of cases ranging from pregnancy resulting from rape through pregnancy caused by contraceptive failure to pregnancy that was deliberately chosen. He concludes that abortion is clearly permissible in some instances, clearly impermissible in others, and of uncertain status in yet others. However, like Thomson, Feinberg ends by pointing out that he has assumed, for purposes of discussion, that the fetus is, morally speaking, a person. If it is not, then abortion will be permissible in almost all cases.

In the readings examined so far, the conflict between consequentialism and deontology has lurked in the backgorund. In the last two readings it occupies center stage. In reading 55, Thomas Nagel argues that the moral limits on what may be done in wars—even just wars—cannot be understood in utilitarian terms. The prohibitions against attacking noncombatants and using weapons such as poison gas are not just indirect ways of maximizing happiness or minimizing suffering. Rather, these prohibitions reflect the fact that even hostile activity places us in a certain relationship to our victims and that we therefore ought never to treat those persons in ways that we could not justify to them. However, Nagel acknowledges that we may need to violate such prohibitions when the stakes are high enough. Thus, he concludes that the world may confront "a previously innocent person with a choice between morally abominable courses of action, and leave him no way to escape with his honor."

This theme is developed further by Michael Walzer in reading 56. Although Walzer's topic is politics rather than war, he agrees that persons sometimes *should* do what is wrong in order to bring good results. For example, a superior candidate for public office may have to compromise his principles if he is to be elected or put his program into effect. As Walzer notices, this need to get one's hands dirty raises a whole new set of questions about the agent's subsequent attitude. Should the successful politician simply be content to accept his moral defilement? Should he be perpetually wracked with guilt about it? Or should he pay some form of determinate penalty? If so, what is the penalty, and who should exact it?

51

Famine, Affluence,
and Morality

PETER SINGER

*Peter Singer (b. 1946) teaches philosophy at Monash University in
Australia. He has written many books and essays on social and political
problems. His book,* Animal Liberation, *was influential in bringing many
people to reflect on the way we treat animals.*

In this selection, which first appeared in Philosophy and Public Affairs
*(Spring 1972), Singer discusses the moral status of providing food to
persons who are starving. Many people believe that while it is praiseworthy
and charitable to help the destitute, the affluent have no moral obligation
to do so. However, Singer challenges this way of distinguishing charity
from obligation. His argument rests on the principle that "if it is in our
power to prevent something bad from happening, we ought, morally, to do
it." If we accept this principle, Singer argues, then we ought to forgo many
of the luxuries we currently enjoy so that we may prevent others from
starving. In Singer's view, the fact that the starving live in far-off lands and
that others could help them as easily as we could are not good reasons for
withholding aid.*

*Quite obviously, the success of Singer's argument depends on the
acceptability of his central premise. Although most utilitarians would
accept it, many deontologists would not. On various accounts, the
obligation not to cause harm is more stringent or far-reaching, or leaves the
agent less discretion in its application, than the obligation to take positive
steps to prevent harm. Whether this distinction has a rational basis, or
whether it is merely an excuse for nonaction, are questions left for further
consideration.*

As I write this, in November 1971, people are dying in East Bengal
from lack of food, shelter, and medical care. The suffering and death that are
occurring there now are not inevitable, not unavoidable in any fatalistic sense
of the term. Constant poverty, a cyclone, and a civil war have turned at least
nine million people into destitute refugees; nevertheless, it is not beyond the
capacity of the richer nations to give enough assistance to reduce any further
suffering to very small proportions. The decisions and actions of human beings
can prevent this kind of suffering. Unfortunately, human beings have not made

the necessary decisions. At the individual level, people have, with very few exceptions, not responded to the situation in any significant way. Generally speaking, people have not given large sums to relief funds; they have not written to their parliamentary representatives demanding increased government assistance; they have not demonstrated in the streets, held symbolic fasts, or done anything else directed toward providing the refugees with the means to satisfy their essential needs. At the government level, no government has given the sort of massive aid that would enable the refugees to survive for more than a few days. Britain, for instance, has given rather more than most countries. It has, to date, given £14,750,000. For comparative purposes, Britain's share of the nonrecoverable development costs of the Anglo-French Concorde project is already in excess of £275,000,000, and on present estimates will reach £440,000,000. The implication is that the British government values a supersonic transport more than thirty times as highly as it values the lives of the nine million refugees. Australia is another country which, on a per capita basis, is well up in the "aid to Bengal" table. Australia's aid, however, amounts to less than one-twelfth of the cost of Sydney's new opera house. The total amount given, from all sources, now stands at about £65,000,000. The estimated cost of keeping the refugees alive for one year is £464,000,000. Most of the refugees have now been in the camps for more than six months. The World Bank has said that India needs a minimum of £300,000,000 in assistance from other countries before the end of the year. It seems obvious that assistance on this scale will not be forthcoming. India will be forced to choose between letting the refugees starve or diverting funds from her own development program, which will mean that more of her own people will starve in the future.[1]

These are the essential facts about the present situation in Bengal. So far as it concerns us here, there is nothing unique about this situation except its magnitude. The Bengal emergency is just the latest and most acute of a series of major emergencies in various parts of the world, arising both from natural and from man-made causes. There are also many parts of the world in which people die from malnutrition and lack of food independent of any special emergency. I take Bengal as my example only because it is the present concern, and because the size of the problem has ensured that it has been given adequate publicity. Neither individuals nor governments can claim to be unaware of what is happening there.

What are the moral implications of a situation like this? In what follows, I shall argue that the way people in relatively affluent countries react to a situation like that in Bengal cannot be justified; indeed, the whole way we look at moral issues—our moral conceptual scheme—needs to be altered, and with it, the way of life that has come to be taken for granted in our society.

In arguing for this conclusion I will not, of course, claim to be morally neutral. I shall, however, try to argue for the moral position that I take, so

---

1 There was also a third possibility: that India would go to war to enable the refugees to return to their land. Since I wrote this paper, India has taken this way out. The situation is no longer that described above, but this does not affect my argument, as the next paragraph indicates.

that anyone who accepts certain assumptions, to be made explicit, will, I hope, accept my conclusion.

I begin with the assumption that suffering and death from lack of food, shelter, and medical care are bad. I think most people will agree about this, although one may reach the same view by different routes. I shall not argue for this view. People can hold all sorts of eccentric positions, and perhaps from some of them it would not follow that death by starvation is in itself bad. It is difficult, perhaps impossible, to refute such positions, and so for brevity I will henceforth take this assumption as accepted. Those who disagree need read no further.

My next point is this: if it is in our power to prevent something bad from happening, without thereby sacrificing anything of comparable moral importance, we ought, morally, to do it. By "without sacrificing anything of comparable moral importance" I mean without causing anything else comparably bad to happen, or doing something that is wrong in itself, or failing to promote some moral good, comparable in significance to the bad thing that we can prevent. This principle seems almost as uncontroversial as the last one. It requires us only to prevent what is bad, and not to promote what is good, and it requires this of us only when we can do it without sacrificing anything that is, from the moral point of view, comparably important. I could even, as far as the application of my argument to the Bengal emergency is concerned, qualify the point so as to make it: if it is in our power to prevent something very bad from happening, without thereby sacrificing anything morally significant, we ought, morally, to do it. An application of this principle would be as follows: if I am walking past a shallow pond and see a child drowning in it, I ought to wade in and pull the child out. This will mean getting my clothes muddy, but this is insignificant, while the death of the child would presumably be a very bad thing.

The uncontroversial appearance of the principle just stated is deceptive. If it were acted upon, even in its qualified form, our lives, our society, and our world would be fundamentally changed. For the principle takes, firstly, no account of proximity or distance. It makes no moral difference whether the person I can help is a neighbor's child ten yards from me or a Bengali whose name I shall never know, ten thousand miles away. Secondly, the principle makes no distinction between cases in which I am the only person who could possibly do anything and cases in which I am just one among millions in the same position.

I do not think I need to say much in defense of the refusal to take proximity and distance into account. The fact that a person is physically near to us, so that we have personal contact with him, may make it more likely that we *shall* assist him, but this does not show that we *ought* to help him rather than another who happens to be further away. If we accept any principle of impartiality, universalizability, equality, or whatever, we cannot discriminate against someone merely because he is far away from us (or we are far away from him). Admittedly, it is possible that we are in a better position to judge what needs to be done to help a person near to us than one far away, and perhaps also to provide the assistance we judge to be necessary. If this were the case, it would be a reason for helping those near to us first. This may once have been a justification for being more concerned with the poor in one's own town than with famine victims in India. Unfortunately for those who like to keep their moral responsibilities limited, instant communication and swift transportation have changed the situation. From the moral point of view, the development of the world into a "global village" has made an important, though still unrecognized, difference to our moral situation. Expert observers and supervisors, sent out by famine relief organizations or permanently stationed in famine-prone areas, can direct our aid to a refugee in Bengal almost as effectively as we could get it to someone in our own block. There would seem, therefore, to be no possible justification for discriminating on geographical grounds.

There may be a greater need to defend the second implication of my principle—that the fact that there are millions of other people in the same position, in respect to the Bengali refugees, as I am, does not make the situation significantly different from a situation in which I am the only person who can prevent something very bad from occurring. Again, of course, I admit that there is a psychological difference between the cases; one feels less guilty about doing nothing if one can point to others, similarly placed, who have also done nothing. Yet this can make no real difference to our moral obligations.[2] Should I consider that I am less obliged to pull the drowning child out of the pond if on looking around I see other people, no further away than I am, who have also noticed the child but are doing nothing? One has only to ask this question to see the absurdity of the view that numbers lessen obligation. It is a view that is an ideal excuse for inactivity; unfortunately most of the major evils—poverty, overpopulation, pollution—are problems in which everyone is almost equally involved.

The view that numbers do make a difference can be made plausible if stated in this way: if everyone in circumstances like mine gave £5 to the Bengal Relief Fund, there would be enough to provide food, shelter, and medical care for the refugees; there is no reason why I should give more than anyone else in the same circumstances as I am; therefore I have no obligation to give more than £5. Each premise in this argument is true, and the argument looks sound. It may convince us, unless we notice that it is based on a hypothetical premise, although the conclusion is not stated hypothetically. The argument would be sound if the conclusion were: if everyone in circumstances like mine were to give £5, I would have no obligation to give more than £5. If the conclusion were so stated, however, it would be obvious that the argument has no bearing on a situation in which it is not the case that everyone else gives £5. This, of

---

2 In view of the special sense philosophers often give to the term, I should say that I use "obligation" simply as the abstract noun derived from "ought," so that "I have an obligation to" means no more, and no less, than "I ought to." This usage is in accordance with the definition of "ought" given by the *Shorter Oxford English Dictionary*: "the general verb to express duty or obligation." I do not think any issue of substance hangs on the way the term is used; sentences in which I use "obligation" could all be rewritten, although somewhat clumsily, as sentences in which a clause containing "ought" replaces the term "obligation."

course, is the actual situation. It is more or less certain that not everyone in circumstances like mine will give £5. So there will not be enough to provide the needed food, shelter, and medical care. Therefore by giving more than £5 I will prevent more suffering than I would if I gave just £5.

It might be thought that this argument has an absurd consequence. Since the situation appears to be that very few people are likely to give substantial amounts, it follows that I and everyone else in similar circumstances ought to give as much as possible, that is, at least up to the point at which by giving more one would begin to cause serious suffering for oneself and one's dependents—perhaps even beyond this point to the point of marginal utility, at which by giving more one would cause oneself and one's dependents as much suffering as one would prevent in Bengal. If everyone does this, however, there will be more than can be used for the benefit of the refugees, and some of the sacrifice will have been unnecessary. Thus, if everyone does what he ought to do, the result will not be as good as it would be if everyone did a little less than he ought to do, or if only some do all that they ought to do.

The paradox here arises only if we assume that the actions in question—sending money to the relief funds—are performed more or less simultaneously, and are also unexpected. For if it is to be expected that everyone is going to contribute something, then clearly each is not obliged to give as much as he would have been obliged to had others not been giving too. And if everyone is not acting more or less simultaneously, then those giving later will know how much more is needed, and will have no obligation to give more than is necessary to reach this amount. To say this is not to deny the principle that people in the same circumstances have the same obligations, but to point out that the fact that others have given, or may be expected to give, is a relevant circumstance: those giving after it has become known that many others are giving and those giving before are not in the same circumstances. So the seemingly absurd consequence of the principle I have put forward can occur only if people are in error about the actual circumstances—that is, if they think they are giving when others are not, but in fact they are giving when others are. The result of everyone doing what he really ought to do cannot be worse than the result of everyone doing less than he ought to do, although the result of everyone doing what he reasonably believes he ought to do could be.

If my argument so far has been sound, neither our distance from a preventable evil nor the number of other people who, in respect to that evil, are in the same situation as we are, lessens our obligation to mitigate or prevent that evil. I shall therefore take as established the principle I asserted earlier. As I have already said, I need to assert it only in its qualified form: if it is in our power to prevent something very bad from happening, without thereby sacrificing anything else morally significant, we ought, morally, to do it.

The outcome of this argument is that our traditional moral categories are upset. The traditional distinction between duty and charity cannot be drawn, or at least, not in the place we normally draw it. Giving money to the Bengal Relief Fund is regarded as an act of charity in our society. The bodies which collect money are known as "charities." These organizations see themselves in this way—if you send them a check, you will be thanked for your "generosity." Because giving money is regarded as an act of charity, it is not thought that there is anything wrong with not giving. The charitable man may be praised, but the man who is not charitable is not condemned. People do not feel in any way ashamed or guilty about spending money on new clothes or a new car instead of giving it to famine relief. (Indeed, the alternative does not occur to them.) This way of looking at the matter cannot be justified. When we buy new clothes not to keep ourselves warm but to look "well-dressed" we are not providing for any important need. We would not be sacrificing anything significant if we were to continue to wear our old clothes, and give the money to famine relief. By doing so, we would be preventing another person from starving. It follows from what I have said earlier that we ought to give money away, rather than spend it on clothes which we do not need to keep us warm. To do so is not charitable, or generous. Nor is it the kind of act which philosophers and theologians have called "supererogatory"—an act which it would be good to do, but not wrong not to do. On the contrary, we ought to give the money away, and it is wrong not to do so.

I am not maintaining that there are no acts which are charitable, or that there are no acts which it would be good to do but not wrong not to do. It may be possible to redraw the distinction between duty and charity in some other place. All I am arguing here is that the present way of drawing the distinction, which makes it an act of charity for a man living at the level of affluence which most people in the "developed nations" enjoy to give money to save someone else from starvation, cannot be supported. It is beyond the scope of my argument to consider whether the distinction should be redrawn or abolished altogether. There would be many other possible ways of drawing the distinction—for instance, one might decide that it is good to make other people as happy as possible but not wrong not to do so.

Despite the limited nature of the revision in our moral conceptual scheme which I am proposing, the revision would, given the extent of both affluence and famine in the world today, have radical implications. These implications may lead to further objections, distinct from those I have already considered. I shall discuss two of these.

One objection to the position I have taken might be simply that it is too drastic a revision of our moral scheme. People do not ordinarily judge in the way I have suggested they should. Most people reserve their moral condemnation for those who violate some moral norm, such as the norm against taking another person's property. They do not condemn those who indulge in luxury instead of giving to famine relief. But given that I did not set out to present a morally neutral description of the way people make moral judgments, the way people do in fact judge has nothing to do with the validity of my conclusion. My conclusion follows from the principle which I advanced earlier, and unless that principle is rejected, or the arguments shown to be unsound, I think the conclusion must stand, however strange it appears.

It might, nevertheless, be interesting to consider why our society, and most other societies, do judge differently from the way I have suggested they should.

In a well-known article, J. O. Urmson suggests that the imperatives of duty, which tell us what we must do, as distinct from what it would be good to do but not wrong not to do, function so as to prohibit behavior that is intolerable if men are to live together in society.[3] This may explain the origin and continued existence of the present division between acts of duty and acts of charity. Moral attitudes are shaped by the needs of society, and no doubt society needs people who will observe the rules that make social existence tolerable. From the point of view of a particular society, it is essential to prevent violations of norms against killing, stealing, and so on. It is quite inessential, however, to help people outside one's own society.

If this is an explanation of our common distinction between duty and supererogation, however, it is not a justification of it. The moral point of view requires us to look beyond the interests of our own society. Previously, as I have already mentioned, this may hardly have been feasible, but it is quite feasible now. From the moral point of view, the prevention of the starvation of millions of people outside our society must be considered at least as pressing as the upholding of property norms within our society.

It has been argued by some writers, among them Sidgwick and Urmson, that we need to have a basic moral code which is not too far beyond the capacities of the ordinary man, for otherwise there will be a general breakdown of compliance with the moral code. Crudely stated, this argument suggests that if we tell people that they ought to refrain from murder and give everything they do not really need to famine relief, they will do neither, whereas if we tell them that they ought to refrain from murder and that it is good to give to famine relief but not wrong not to do so, they will at least refrain from murder. The issue here is: Where should we draw the line between conduct that is required and conduct that is good although not required, so as to get the best possible result? This would seem to be an empirical question, although a very difficult one. One objection to the Sidgwick-Urmson line of argument is that it takes insufficient account of the effect that moral standards can have on the decisions we make. Given a society in which a wealthy man who gives five percent of his income to famine-relief is regarded as most generous, it is not surprising that a proposal that we all ought to give away half our incomes will be thought to be absurdly unrealistic. In a society which held that no man should have more than enough while others have less than they need, such a proposal might seem narrowminded. What it is possible for a man to do and what he is likely to do are both, I think, very greatly influenced by what people around him are doing and expecting him to do. In any case, the possibility that by spreading the idea that we ought to be doing very much more than we are to relieve famine we shall bring about a general breakdown of moral behavior seems remote. If the stakes are an end to widespread starvation, it is worth the risk. Finally, it should be emphasized that these considerations are

3 J. O. Urmson, "Saints and Heroes," in *Essays in Moral Philosophy*, ed. Abraham I. Melden (Seattle and London, 1958), p. 214. For a related but significantly different view see also Henry Sidgwick, *The Methods of Ethics*, 7th edn. (London, 1907), pp. 220–221, 492–493.

relevant only to the issue of what we should require from others, and not to what we ourselves ought to do.

The second objection to my attack on the present distinction between duty and charity is one which has from time to time been made against utilitarianism. It follows from some forms of utilitarian theory that we all ought, morally, to be working full time to increase the balance of happiness over misery. The position I have taken here would not lead to this conclusion in all circumstances, for if there were no bad occurrences that we could prevent without sacrificing something of comparable moral importance, my argument would have no application. Given the present conditions in many parts of the world, however, it does follow from my argument that we ought, morally, to be working full time to relieve great suffering of the sort that occurs as a result of famine or other disasters. Of course, mitigating circumstances can be adduced—for instance, that if we wear ourselves out through overwork, we shall be less effective than we would otherwise have been. Nevertheless, when all considerations of this sort have been taken into account, the conclusion remains: we ought to be preventing as much suffering as we can without sacrificing something else of comparable moral importance. This conclusion is one which we may be reluctant to face. I cannot see, though, why it should be regarded as a criticism of the position for which I have argued, rather than a criticism of our ordinary standards of behavior. Since most people are self-interested to some degree, very few of us are likely to do everything that we ought to do. It would, however, hardly be honest to take this as evidence that it is not the case that we ought to do it.

It may still be thought that my conclusions are so wildly out of line with what everyone else thinks and has always thought that there must be something wrong with the argument somewhere. In order to show that my conclusions, while certainly contrary to contemporary Western moral standards, would not have seemed so extraordinary at other times and in other places, I would like to quote a passage from a writer not normally thought of as a way-out radical, Thomas Aquinas.

> Now, according to the natural order instituted by divine providence, material goods are provided for the satisfaction of human needs. Therefore the division and appropriation of property, which proceeds from human law, must not hinder the satisfaction of man's necessity from such goods. Equally, whatever a man has in superabundance is owed, of natural right, to the poor for their sustenance. So Ambrosius says, and it is also to be found in the *Decretum Gratiani*: "The bread which you withhold belongs to the hungry; the clothing you shut away, to the naked; and the money you bury in the earth is the redemption and freedom of the penniless."[4]

I now want to consider a number of points, more practical than philosophical, which are relevant to the application of the moral conclusion we have

---

4 *Summa Theologica*, II–II, Question 66, Article 7, in *Aquinas, Selected Political Writings*, ed. A. P. d'Entreves, trans. J. G. Dawson (Oxford, 1948), p. 171.

reached. These points challenge not the idea that we ought to be doing all we can to prevent starvation, but the idea that giving away a great deal of money is the best means to this end.

It is sometimes said that overseas aid should be a government responsibility, and that therefore one ought not to give to privately run charities. Giving privately, it is said, allows the government and the noncontributing members of society to escape their responsibilities.

This argument seems to assume that the more people there are who give to privately organized famine relief funds, the less likely it is that the government will take over full responsibility for such aid. This assumption is unsupported, and does not strike me as at all plausible. The opposite view—that if no one gives voluntarily, a government will assume that its citizens are uninterested in famine relief and would not wish to be forced into giving aid—seems more plausible. In any case, unless there were a definite probability that by refusing to give one would be helping to bring about massive government assistance, people who do refuse to make voluntary contributions are refusing to prevent a certain amount of suffering without being able to point to any tangible beneficial consequence of their refusal. So the onus of showing how their refusal will bring about government action is on those who refuse to give.

I do not, of course, want to dispute the contention that governments of affluent nations should be giving many times the amount of genuine, no-strings-attached aid that they are giving now. I agree, too, that giving privately is not enough, and that we ought to be campaigning actively for entirely new stan-dards for both public and private contributions to famine relief. Indeed, I would sympathize with someone who thought that campaigning was more important than giving oneself, although I doubt whether preaching what one does not practice would be very effective. Unfortunately, for many people the idea that "it's the government's responsibility" is a reason for not giving which does not appear to entail any political action either.

Another, more serious reason for not giving to famine relief funds is that until there is effective population control, relieving famine merely postpones starvation. If we save the Bengal refugees now, others, perhaps the children of these refugees, will face starvation in a few years' time. In support of this, one may cite the now well-known facts about the population explosion and the relatively limited scope for expanded production.

This point, like the previous one, is an argument against relieving suffering that is happening now, because of a belief about what might happen in the future; it is unlike the previous point in that very good evidence can be adduced in support of this belief about the future. I will not go into the evidence here. I accept that the earth cannot support indefinitely a population rising at the present rate. This certainly poses a problem for anyone who thinks it important to prevent famine. Again, however, one could accept the argument without drawing the conclusion that it absolves one from any obligation to do anything to prevent famine. The conclusion that should be drawn is that the best means of preventing famine, in the long run, is population control. It would then follow from the position reached earlier that one ought to be doing all one can to promote population control (unless one held that all forms of population control were wrong in themselves, or would have significantly bad consequences). Since there are organizations working specifically for population control, one would then support them rather than more orthodox methods of preventing famine.

A third point raised by the conclusion reached earlier relates to the question of just how much we all ought to be giving away. One possibility, which has already been mentioned, is that we ought to give until we reach the level of marginal utility—that is, the level at which, by giving more, I would cause as much suffering to myself or my dependents as I would relieve by my gift. This would mean, of course, that one would reduce oneself to very near the material circumstances of a Bengali refugee. It will be recalled that earlier I put forward both a strong and a moderate version of the principle of preventing bad occurrences. The strong version, which required us to prevent bad things from happening unless in doing so we would be sacrificing something of comparable moral significance, does seem to require reducing ourselves to the level of marginal utility. I should also say that the strong version seems to me to be the correct one. I proposed the more moderate version—that we should prevent bad occurrences unless, to do so, we had to sacrifice something morally significant—only in order to show that even on this surely undeniable principle a great change in our way of life is required. On the more moderate principle, it may not follow that we ought to reduce ourselves to the level of marginal utility, for one might hold that to reduce oneself and one's family to this level is to cause something significantly bad to happen. Whether this is so I shall not discuss, since, as I have said, I can see no good reason for holding the moderate version of the principle rather than the strong version. Even if we accepted the principle only in its moderate form, however, it should be clear that we would have to give away enough to ensure that the consumer society, dependent as it is on people spending on trivia rather than giving to famine relief, would slow down and perhaps disappear entirely. There are several reasons why this would be desirable in itself. The value and necessity of economic growth are now being questioned not only by conservationists, but by economists as well.[5] There is no doubt, too, that the consumer society has had a distorting effect on the goals and purposes of its members. Yet looking at the matter purely from the point of view of overseas aid, there must be a limit to the extent to which we should deliberately slow down our economy; for it might be the case that if we gave away, say, forty percent of our Gross National Product, we would slow down the economy so much that in absolute terms we would be giving less than if we gave twenty-five percent of the much larger GNP that we would have if we limited our contribution to this smaller percentage.

I mention this only as an indication of the sort of a factor that one would have to take into account in working out an ideal. Since Western societies

---

5 See, for instance, John Kenneth Galbraith, *The New Industrial State* (Boston, 1967); and E. J. Mishan, *The Costs of Economic Growth* (London, 1967).

generally consider one percent of the GNP an acceptable level for overseas aid, the matter is entirely academic. Nor does it affect the question of how much an individual should give in a society in which very few are giving substantial amounts.

It is sometimes said, though less often now than it used to be, that philosophers have no special role to play in public affairs, since most public issues depend primarily on an assessment of facts. On questions of fact, it is said, philosophers as such have no special expertise, and so it has been possible to engage in philosophy without committing oneself to any position on major public issues. No doubt there are some issues of social policy and foreign policy about which it can truly be said that a really expert assessment of the facts is required before taking sides or acting, but the issue of famine is surely not one of these. The facts about the existence of suffering are beyond dispute. Nor, I think, is it disputed that we can do something about it, either through orthodox methods of famine relief or through population control or both. This is therefore an issue on which philosophers are competent to take a position. The issue is one which faces everyone who has more money than he needs to support himself and his dependents, or who is in a position to take some sort of political action. These categories must include practically every teacher and student of philosophy in the universities of the Western world. If philosophy is to deal with matters that are relevant to both teachers and students, this is an issue that philosophers should discuss.

Discussion, though, is not enough. What is the point of relating philosophy to public (and personal) affairs if we do not take our conclusions seriously? In this instance, taking our conclusion seriously means acting upon it. The philosopher will not find it any easier than anyone else to alter his attitudes and way of life to the extent that, if I am right, is involved in doing everything that we ought to be doing. At the very least, though, one can make a start. The philosopher who does so will have to sacrifice some of the benefits of the consumer society, but he can find compensation in the satisfaction of a way of life in which theory and practice, if not yet in harmony, are at least coming together.

52

Equality, Entitlements, and the Distribution of Income

JOHN ARTHUR

John Arthur (b. 1946) is Professor of Philosophy at the State University of New York at Binghamton. He is the author of Words That Bind: Judicial Review and the Grounds of Modern Constitutional Theory. *This essay first appeared in Vincent Barry, ed.,* Applying Ethics.

Arthur contests Peter Singer's claim (reading 51) that we are obligated to contribute heavily to famine relief. He argues that Singer's position rests on a principle—roughly, do whatever you can to prevent serious harm without sacrificing anything of comparable moral importance—which is not a part of our shared moral code. Because our code asserts that people may keep what they own and deserve, it does not require nearly as much sacrifice as Singer's principle. Moreover, according to Arthur, this is a good thing. If our code did require as much sacrifice as Singer's principle, then many people wouldn't follow it. Such a code would lead many to feel guilty and would foster conflict between those who did and did not conform to it. Also, it might actually elicit less sacrifice than a less demanding code. Because he rejects Singer's principle on the grounds that it would not be part of a welfare-maximizing moral code, Arthur in effect advances a version of rule-utilitarianism. For further discussion of the view that act-utilitarian (and other act-consequentialist) views are too demanding, see Bernard Williams, reading 39. For further discussion of the rule-utilitarian response, see Richard Brandt, reading 46.

INTRODUCTION

My guess is that everyone who reads these words is wealthy by comparison with the poorest millions of people on our planet. Not only do we have plenty of money for food, clothing, housing, and other necessities, but a fair amount is left over for far less important purchases like phonograph records, fancy clothes, trips, intoxicants, movies, and so on. And what's more, we don't usually give thought to whether or not we ought to spend our money on such luxuries rather than to give it to those who need it more; we just assume it's ours to do with as we please.

Peter Singer, "Famine, Affluence, and Morality," and Richard Watson, "Reason and Morality in a World of Limited Food" argue that our assumption is wrong, that we should not buy luxuries when others are in severe need. But are they correct? In the first two sections of this paper my aim is to get into focus just what their arguments are, and to evaluate them. Both Singer and Watson, it seems to me, ignore an important feature of our moral code, namely that it allows people who deserve or have rights to their earnings to keep them.

But the fact that our code encourages a form of behavior is not a complete defense, for it is possible that our current moral attitudes are mistaken. Sections 3 and 4 consider this possibility from two angles: universalizability and the notion of an ideal moral code. Neither of these approaches, I argue, requires that desert and rights be sacrificed in the name of redistribution.

1. Equality and the Duty to Aid

What does our moral code have to say about helping people in need? Watson emphasizes what he calls the "principle of equity." Since "all human life is of equal value," and difference in treatment should be "based on freely chosen actions and not accidents of birth or environment," he thinks that we have "equal rights to the necessities of life." To distribute food unequally assumes that some lives are worth more than others, an assumption which, he says, we do not accept. Watson believes, in fact, that we put such importance on the "equity principle" that it should not be violated even if unequal distribution is the only way for anybody to survive. (Leaving aside for the moment whether or not he is correct about our code, it seems to me that if it really did require us to commit mass suicide rather than allow inequality in wealth, then we would want to abandon it for a more suitable set of rules. But more on that later.)

Is Watson correct in assuming that all life is of equal value? Did Adolph Hitler and Martin Luther King, for example, lead two such lives? Clearly one did far more good and less harm than the other. Nor are moral virtues like courage, kindness, and trustworthiness equally distributed among people. So there are at least two senses in which people are not morally equal.

Yet the phrase "All men are equal" has an almost platitudinous ring, and many of us would not hesitate to say that equality is a cornerstone of our morality. But what does it mean? It seems to me that we might have in mind one of two things. First is an idea that Thomas Jefferson expressed in the *Declaration of Independence*. "All men are created equal" meant, for him, that no man is the moral inferior of another, that, in other words, there are certain rights which all men share equally, including life and liberty. We are entitled to pursue our own lives with a minimum of interference from others, and no person is the natural slave of another. But, as Jefferson also knew, equality in that sense does not require equal distribution of the necessities of life, only that we not interfere with one another, allowing instead every person the liberty to pursue his own affairs, so long as he does not violate the rights of his fellows.

Others, however, have something different in mind when they speak of human equality. I want to develop this second idea by recounting briefly the details of Singer's argument in "Famine, Affluence, and Morality." He first argues that two general moral principles are widely accepted, and then that those principles imply an obligation to eliminate starvation.

The first principle is simply that "suffering and death from lack of food, shelter and medical care are bad." Some may be inclined to think that the mere existence of such an evil in itself places an obligation on others, but that is, of course, the problem which Singer addresses. I take it that he is not begging the question in this obvious way and will argue from the existence of evil to the obligation of others to eliminate it. But how, exactly, does he establish this? The second principle, he thinks, shows the connection, but it is here that controversy arises.

This principle, which I will call the greater moral evil rule, is as follows:

> If it is in our power to prevent something bad from happening, without thereby sacrificing anything of comparable moral importance, we ought, morally, to do it.[1]

In other words, people are entitled to keep their earnings only if there is no way for them to prevent a greater evil by giving them away. Providing others with food, clothing, and housing would generally be of more importance than buying luxuries, so the greater moral evil rule now requires substantial redistribution of wealth.

Certainly there are few, if any, of us who live by that rule, although that hardly shows we are *justified* in our way of life; we often fail to live up to our own standards. Why does Singer think our shared morality requires that we follow the greater moral evil rule? What arguments does he give for it?

He begins with an analogy. Suppose you came across a child drowning in a shallow pond. Certainly we feel it would be wrong not to help. Even if saving the child meant we must dirty our clothes, we would emphasize that those clothes are not of comparable significance to the child's life. The greater moral evil rule thus seems a natural way of capturing why we think it would be wrong not to help.

But the argument for the greater moral evil rule is not limited to Singer's claim that it explains our feelings about the drowning child or that it appears "uncontroversial." Moral equality also enters the picture. Besides the Jeffersonian idea that we share certain rights equally, most of us are also attracted to another type of equality, namely that like amounts of suffering (or happiness) are of equal significance, no matter who is experiencing them. I cannot reasonably say that, while my pain is no more severe than yours, I am somehow special and it's more important that mine be alleviated. Objectivity requires

---

1 Singer also offers a "weak" version of this principle which, it seems to me, is *too* weak. It requires giving aid only if the gift is of *no* moral significance to the giver. But since even minor embarrassment or small amounts of happiness are not completely without moral importance, this weak principle implies little or no obligation to aid, even to the drowning child.

us to admit the opposite, that no one has a unique status which warrants such special pleading. So equality demands equal consideration of interests as well as respect for certain rights.

But if we fail to give to famine relief and instead purchase a new car when the old one will do, or buy fancy clothes for a friend when his or her old ones are perfectly good, are we not assuming that the relatively minor enjoyment we or our friends may get is as important as another person's life? And that is a form of prejudice; we are acting as if people were not equal in the sense that their interests deserve equal consideration. We are giving special consideration to ourselves or to our group, rather like a racist does. Equal consideration of interests thus leads naturally to the greater moral evil rule.

2. Rights and Desert

Equality, in the sense of giving equal consideration to equally serious needs, is part of our moral code. And so we are led, quite rightly I think, to the conclusion that we should prevent harm to others if in doing so we do not sacrifice anything of comparable moral importance. But there is also another side to the coin, one which Singer and Watson ignore. This can be expressed rather awkwardly by the notion of entitlements. These fall into two broad categories, rights and desert. A few examples will show what I mean.

All of us could help others by giving away or allowing others to use our bodies. While your life may be shortened by the loss of a kidney or less enjoyable if lived with only one eye, those costs are probably not comparable to the loss experienced by a person who will die without any kidney or who is totally blind. We can even imagine persons who will actually be harmed in some way by your not granting sexual favors to them. Perhaps the absence of a sexual partner would cause psychological harm or even rape. Now suppose that you can prevent this evil without sacrificing anything of comparable importance. Obviously such relations may not be pleasant, but according to the greater moral evil rule, that is not enough; to be justified in refusing, you must show that the unpleasantness you would experience is of equal importance to the harm you are preventing. Otherwise, the rule says you must consent.

If anything is clear, however, it is that our code does not *require* such heroism; you are entitled to keep your second eye and kidney and not bestow sexual favors on anyone who may be harmed without them. The reason for this is often expressed in terms of rights; it's your body, you have a right to it, and that weighs against whatever duty you have to help. To sacrifice a kidney for a stranger is to do more than is required, it's heroic.

Moral rights are normally divided into two categories. Negative rights are rights of noninterference. The right to life, for example, is a right not to be killed. Property rights, the right to privacy, and the right to exercise religious freedom are also negative, requiring only that people leave others alone and not interfere.

Positive rights, however, are rights of recipience. By not putting their children up for adoption, parents give them various positive rights, including the rights to be fed, clothed, and housed. If I agree to share in a business venture, my promise creates a right of recipience, so that when I back out of the deal, I've violated your right.

Negative rights also differ from positive in that the former are natural; the ones you have depend on what you are. If lower animals lack rights to life or liberty it is because there is a relevant difference between them and us. But the positive rights you may have are not natural; they arise because others have promised, agreed, or contracted to give you something.

Normally, then, a duty to help a stranger in need is not the result of a right he has. Such a right would be positive, and since no contract or promise was made, no such right exists. An exception to this would be a lifeguard who contracts to watch out for someone's children. The parent whose child drowns would in this case be doubly wronged. First, the lifeguard should not have cruelly or thoughtlessly ignored the child's interests, and second, he ought not to have violated the rights of the parents that he help. Here, unlike Singer's case, we can say there are rights at stake. Other bystanders also act wrongly by cruelly ignoring the child, but unlike the lifeguard they do not violate anybody's rights. Moral rights are one factor to be weighed, but we also have other obligations; I am not claiming that rights are all we need to consider. That view, like the greater moral evil rule, trades simplicity for accuracy. In fact, our code expects us to help people in need as well as to respect negative and positive rights. But we are also entitled to invoke our own rights as justification for not giving to distant strangers or when the cost to us is substantial, as when we give up an eye or a kidney.

Rights come in a variety of shapes and sizes, and people often disagree about both their shape and size. Can a woman kill an unborn child because of her right to control her body? Does mere inheritance transfer rights to property? Do dolphins have a right to live? While some rights are widely accepted, others are controversial.

One more comment about rights, then we'll look at desert. Watson's position, which I criticized for other reasons earlier, is also mistaken because he ignores important rights. He claims that we must pay no attention to "accidents of birth and environment" and base our treatment of people on "what they freely choose." But think about how you will (or did) select a spouse or lover. Are you not entitled to consider such "accidents of birth or environment" as attractiveness, personality, and intelligence? It is, after all, your future, and it is certainly a part of our shared moral code that you have a right to use those (or whatever) criteria you wish in selecting a mate. It is at best an exaggeration to say we must always "ignore accidents of birth and environment" in our treatment of people.

Desert is a second form of entitlement. Suppose, for example, an industrious farmer manages through hard work to produce a surplus of food for the winter while a lazy neighbor spends his summer fishing. Must our industrious farmer ignore his hard work and give the surplus away because his neighbor or his family will suffer? What again seems clear is that we have more than one factor to weigh. Not only should we compare the consequences of his keeping it with his giving it away; we also should weigh the fact that one farmer deserves the food, he earned it through his hard work. Perhaps his deserving the product of his labor is outweighed by the greater need of his lazy neighbor, or perhaps it isn't, but being outweighed is in any case not the same as weighing nothing!

Desert can be negative, too. The fact that the Nazi war criminal did what he did means he deserves punishment, that we have a reason to send him to jail. Other considerations, for example the fact that nobody will be deterred by his suffering, or that he is old and harmless, may weigh against punishment and so we may let him go; but again that does not mean he doesn't still deserve to be punished.

Our moral code gives weight to both the greater moral evil principle and entitlements. The former emphasizes equality, claiming that from an objective point of view all comparable suffering, whoever its victim, is equally significant. It encourages us to take an impartial look at all the various effects of our actions; it is thus forward-looking. When we consider matters of entitlement, however, our attention is directed to the past. Whether we have rights to money, property, eyes, or whatever, depends on how we came to possess them. If they were acquired by theft rather than from birth or through gift exchange, then the right is suspect. Desert, like rights, is also backward-looking, emphasizing past effort or past transgressions which now warrant reward or punishment.

Our commonly shared morality thus requires that we ignore neither consequences nor entitlements, neither the future results of our action nor relevant events in the past. It encourages people to help others in need, especially when it's a friend or someone we are close to geographically, and when the cost is not significant. But it also gives weight to rights and desert, so that we are not usually obligated to give to strangers.

One path is still open as a defense of the greater moral evil rule, and it deserves comment. I have assumed throughout that Singer wants to emphasize the great disparity in the amount of enjoyment someone may get from, say, a new car, as compared with the misery that could be prevented by using the money to save another's life. The fact that the two are not comparable means that the money should not be spent on the car. It is possible to interpret the rule differently, however. By admitting that having rights and deserving things are also of moral significance, Singer could accept what I have said so that the greater moral evil rule would survive intact.

The problem with this response, however, is that the greater moral evil rule has now become an almost empty platitude, urging nothing more than that we should prevent something bad unless we have adequate moral reason not to do so. Since rights and desert often provide such reasons, the rule would say nothing useful about our obligation to help others, and it certainly would not require us to "reduce ourselves to the level of marginal utility" so that the "consumer society" would "slow down and perhaps disappear" as Singer claims. I will therefore assume he would not accept such an interpretation of his view, that entitlements are not among the sacrifices which could balance off the suffering caused by failing to help people in need.

But unless we are moral relativists, the mere fact that entitlements are an important part of our moral code does not in itself justify such a role. Singer and Watson can perhaps best be seen as moral reformers, advocating the rejection of rules which provide for distribution according to rights and desert. Certainly the fact that in the past our moral code condemned suicide and racial mixing while condoning slavery should not convince us that a more enlightened moral code, one which we would want to support, would take such positions. Rules which define acceptable behavior are continually changing, and we must allow for the replacement of inferior ones.

Why should we not view entitlements as examples of inferior rules we are better off without? What could justify our practice of evaluating actions by looking backward to rights and desert instead of just to their consequences? One answer is that more fundamental values than rights and desert are at stake, namely fairness, justice, and respect. Failure to reward those who earn good grades or promotions is wrong because it's *unfair;* ignoring past guilt shows a lack of regard for *justice;* and failure to respect rights to life, privacy, or religious choice suggests a lack of *respect for other persons.*

Some people may be persuaded by those remarks, feeling that entitlements are now on an acceptably firm foundation. But an advocate of equality may well want to question why fairness, justice, and respect for persons should matter. But since it is no more obvious that preventing suffering matters than that fairness, respect, and justice do, we again seem to have reached an impasse.

3. Universalizability

It is sometimes thought that we can choose between competing moral rules by noting which ones are compatible with some more fundamental rule. One such fundamental standard is attributed to Kant, though it is also rooted in traditional Christian thought. "Do unto others as you would have them do unto you" and the Kantian categorical imperative, "Act only on maxims that you can will would become universal laws," express an idea some think is basic to *all* moral rules. The suggestion is that if you think what you're doing is right, then you have got to be willing to universalize your judgment, that is, to acknowledge that anyone in similar circumstances would be correct if he were to follow the same rule.

Such familiar reasoning can be taken in two very different ways. The first requires only that a person not make himself an exception, that he live up to his own standard. This type of universalizability, however, cannot help choose between the two rules. An advocate of rights and desert would surely agree that whether he were the deserving or undeserving one, whether he had the specific right or did not have it, entitlements still should not be ignored. Nothing about the position of those supporting rights and desert suggests that they must make exceptions for themselves; such rules are in that sense universalizable. But the advocate of the greater moral evil rule can also be counted on to claim that he too should not be made an exception, and that *ignoring* entitlements in favor of the greater moral evil rule is the proper course whether or not he would benefit from the policy. Both views, then, could be universalized in the first sense.

But if we understand universalizability in another sense, neither of the rules passes the test. If being "willing to universalize the judgment" means that a supporter of a particular moral rule would be equally happy with the result were the roles reversed, then there is doubt whether either is universalizable. The rights advocate cannot promise always to like the outcome; he probably would *prefer*, were the tables turned and his life depended on somebody not keeping his rightfully owned income, that entitlements be ignored in that instance. But his opponent cannot pass the test either, since he would likely prefer that rights and desert *not* be ignored were he in a position to benefit from them. But in any case it is not at all clear why we should expect people who make moral judgments to be neutral as to which position they occupy. Must a judge who thinks justice requires that a murderer go to jail agree that he would prefer jail if he were the murderer? It seems that all he must do to universalize his judgment is agree that it would be *right* that he go to jail if the tables were turned, that, in other words, he is not exempt from the rules. But that is a test, as I said, which supporters of entitlements can pass.

So the test of universalizability does not provide grounds for rejecting entitle-ment rules, and we are once again at an impasse. A second possibility is to view the egalitarian as a moral reformer. Then, perhaps, the criticism of entitlements can be defended as part of a more reasonable and effective moral system. In the final section I look in detail at the idea that rights and desert would not be part of a such ideal moral code, one which we would support if we were fully rational.

4. Entitlements and the Ideal Moral Code

The idea I want now to consider is that part of our code should be dropped, so that people could no longer invoke rights and desert as justification for not making large sacrifices for strangers. In place of entitlements would be a rule regarding that any time we can prevent something bad without sacrificing anything of comparable moral significance we ought to do it. Our current code, however, allows people to say that while they would do more good with their earnings, still they have rights to the earnings, the earnings are deserved, and so need not be given away. The crucial question is whether we want to have such entitlement rules in our code, or whether we should reject them in favor of the greater moral evil rule.

Universalizability, I argued, gives no clear answer to this. Each position also finds a certain amount of support within our code, either from the idea of equal consideration of interests or from our concerns about fairness, justice, and respect for other persons. The problem to be resolved, then, is whether there are other reasons to drop entitlement rules in favor of the greater moral evil rule.

I believe that our best procedure is not to think about this or that specific rules, drawing analogies, refining it, and giving counterexamples, but to focus instead on the nature of morality as a whole. What is a moral code? What do we want it to do? What type of code do we want to support? These questions will give us a fresh perspective from which to consider the merits of rules which allow people to appeal to rights and desert and to weigh the issue of whether our present code should be reformed.

We can begin with the obvious: A moral code is a system of rules designed to guide people's conduct. As such, it has characteristics in common with other systems of rules. Virtually every organization has rules which govern the conduct of members; clubs, baseball leagues, corporations, bureaucracies, professional associations, even *The* Organization all have rules. Another obvious point is this: What the rules are depends on why the organization exists. Rules function to enable people to accomplish goals which lead them to organize in the first place. Some rules, for example, "Don't snitch on fellow mafioso," "Pay dues to the fraternity," and "Don't give away trade secrets to competing companies," serve in obvious ways. Other times the real purposes of rules are controversial, as when doctors do not allow advertising by fellow members of the AMA.

Frequently rules reach beyond members of a specific organization, obligating everyone who is capable of following them to do so. These include costs of civil and criminal law, etiquette, custom, and morality. But before discussing the specific purposes of moral rules, it will be helpful to look briefly at some of the similarities and differences between these more universal codes.

First, the sanctions imposed on rule violators vary among different types of codes. While in our legal code, transgressions are punished by fines, jail, or repayment of damages, informal sanctions of praise, blame, or guilt encourage conformity to the rules of morality and etiquette. Another difference is that while violation of a moral rule is always a serious affair, this need not be so for legal rules of etiquette and custom. Many of us think it unimportant whether a fork is on the left side of a plate or whether an outmoded and widely ignored Sunday closing law is violated, but violation of a moral rule is not ignored. Indeed, that a moral rule has lost its importance is often shown by its demotion to status of mere custom.

A third difference is that legal rules, unlike rules of morality, custom, and etiquette, provide for a specific person or procedure that is empowered to alter the rules. If Congress acts to change the tax laws, then as of the date stated in the statute the rules are changed. Similarly for the governing rules of social clubs, government bureaucracies, and the AMA. Rules of custom, morals, and etiquette also change, of course, but they do so in a less precise and much more gradual fashion, with no person or group specifically empowered to make changes.

This fact, that moral rules are *in a sense* beyond the power of individuals to change, does not show that rules of morality, any more than those of etiquette, are objective in the same sense that scientific laws are. All that needs to happen for etiquette or morality to change is for people to change certain practices, namely the character traits they praise and blame, or the actions they approve and disapprove. Scientific laws, however, are discovered, not invented by society, and so are beyond human control. The law that the boiling point of water increases as its pressure increases cannot be changed by humans, either individually or collectively. Such laws are a part of the fabric of nature.

But the fact that moral rules, like legal ones, are not objective in the same sense as scientific ones does not mean that there is no objective standard of right or wrong, that one code is as good as another, or even that the "right thing to do" is just what the moral code currently followed in our society teaches is right. Like the rules of a fraternity or corporation, legal and moral rules can serve their purposes either well or poorly, and whether they do is a matter of objective fact. Further, if a moral code doesn't serve its purpose, we have good reason to think of a way to change it, just as its serving us well provides a good reason to obey. In important respects morality is not at all subjective.

Take, for example, a rule which prohibits homosexual behavior. Suppose it serves no useful purpose, but only increases the burdens of guilt, shame, and social rejection borne by 10% of our population. If this is so, we have good reason to ignore the rule. On the other hand, if rules against killing and lying help us to accomplish what we want from a moral code, we have good reason to support those rules. Morality is created, and as with other systems of rules which we devise, a particular rule may or may not further the shared human goals and interests which motivated its creation. There is thus a connection between what we ought to do and how well a code serves its purposes. If a rule serves well the general purposes of a moral code, then we have reason to support it, and if we have reason to support it, we also have reason to obey it. But if, on the other hand, a rule is useless, or if it frustrates the purposes of morality, we have reason neither to support nor to follow it. All of this suggests the following conception of a right action: Any action is right which is approved by an ideal moral code, one which it is rational for us to support. Which code we would want to support would depend, of course, on which one is able to accomplish the purposes of morality.

If we are to judge actions in this way, by reference to what an ideal moral code would require, we must first have a clear notion of just what purposes morality is meant to service. And here again the comparison between legal and moral rules is instructive. Both systems discourage certain types of behavior—killing, robbing, and beating—while encouraging others—repaying debts, keeping important agreements, and providing for one's children. The purpose which both have in discouraging various behaviors is obvious. Such negative rules help keep people from causing harm. Think, for example, of how we are first taught it is wrong to hit a baby brother or sister. Parents explain the rule by emphasizing that it hurts the infant when we hit him. Promoting the welfare of ourselves, our friends and family, and to a lesser degree all who have the capacity to be harmed is the primary purpose of negative moral rules. It's how we learn them as children and why we support them as adults.

The same can be said of positive rules, rules which encourage various types of behavior. Our own welfare, as well as that of friends, family, and others, depends on general acceptance of rules which encourage keeping promises, fulfilling contracts, and meeting the needs of our children. Just try to imagine a society in which promises or agreements mean nothing, or where family members took no concern for one another. A life without positive or negative rights would be as Thomas Hobbes long ago observed: nasty, brutish, and short.

Moral rules thus serve two purposes. They promote our own welfare by discouraging acts of violence and promoting social conventions like promising and paying debts, and second, they perform the same service for our family, friends, and others. We have reason to support a moral code because we care about our own welfare, and because we care about the well-being of others. For most of us the ideal moral code, the one we would support because it best fulfills these purposes, is the code which is most effective in promoting general welfare.

But can everyone be counted on to share these concerns? Think, for example, of an egoist, who only desires that *he* be happy. Such a person, if he existed, would obviously like a code which maximizes his own welfare. How can we hope to get agreement about which code it is rational to support, if different people expect different things from moral rules?[2]

Before considering these questions, I want to mention two preliminary points. First, the problem with egoism is that it tends to make morality relative. If we are going to decide moral disputes by considering what would be required by the code which it is rational for people to support, then we must reach agreement about what that code is. Otherwise the right action for an altruist, the one which is required by the code which it's rational for him to support, may be the wrong act for the egoist. Yet how can the very same act done in identical circumstances be wrong for one person yet right for another? Maybe morality is relative in that way, but if so the prospects for peaceful resolution of important disputes is lessened, a result not to be hoped for.

My second point is that while we certainly do not want to assume people are perfect altruists, we also do not want to give people less credit than they deserve. There is some evidence, for example, that concern for others in our species is part of our biological heritage. Some geneticists think that many animals, particularly higher ones, take an innate interest in the welfare of other members of their species.[3] Other researchers argue that feelings of benevolence originate naturally, through classical conditioning; we develop negative associations with our own pain behavior (since we are then in pain) and this attitude becomes generalized to the pain behavior of others.[4] If either of these is true, egoism might be far more unusual than is commonly supposed, perhaps rare enough that it can be safely ignored.

---

2 This difficulty leads many to think the choice of a code should be made behind a "veil of ignorance" about one's particular station in life, talents, class, and religious or other moral values. The major proponent of this view is John Rawls, *A Theory of Justice* (Cambridge: Harvard University Press, 1971).

3 Stephen Jay Gould, "So Cleverly Kind an Animal" in *Ever Since Darwin* (New York: W. W. Norton Co., 1977).

4 Richard B. Brandt, *A Theory of the Good and the Right* (New York: Oxford University Press, 1979).

There is also a line of reasoning which suggests that disagreement about which moral code to support need not be as deep as is often thought. What sort of code in fact *would* a rational egoist support? He would first think of proposing one which allows him to do anything whatsoever that he desires, while requiring that others ignore their own happiness and do what is in his interests. But here enters a family of considerations which will bring us back to the merits of entitlements versus the greater moral evil rule. Our egoist is contemplating what code to *support*, which means going before the public and trying to win general acceptance of his proposed rules. Caring for nobody else, he might secretly prefer the code I mentioned, yet it would hardly make sense for him to work for its public adoption since others are unlikely to put his welfare above the happiness of themselves and their families. So it looks as if the code an egoist would actually support might not be all that different from the ideal (welfare maximizing) code; he would be wasting his time to advocate rules that serve only his own interests because they have no chance of public acceptance.

The lesson to be learned here is a general one: The moral code it is rational for us to support must be practical; it must actually work. This means, among other things, that it must be able to gain the support of almost everyone.

But the code must be practical in other respects as well. I have emphasized that it is wrong to ignore the possibilities of altruism, but it is also important that a code not assume people are more unselfish than they are. Rules that would work only for angels are not the ones it is rational to support for humans. Second, an ideal code cannot assume we are more objective than we are; we often tend to rationalize when our own interests are at stake, and a rational person will also keep that in mind when choosing a moral code. Finally, it is not rational to support a code which assumes we have perfect knowledge. We are often mistaken about the consequences of what we do, and a workable code must take that into account as well.

I want now to bring these various considerations together in order to decide whether or not to reject entitlements in favor of the greater moral evil rule. I will assume that the egoist is not a serious obstacle to acceptance of a welfare maximizing code, either because egoists are, like angels, merely imaginary, or because a practical egoist would only support a code which can be expected to gain wide support. We still have to ask whether entitlements would be included in a welfare maximizing code. The initial temptation is to substitute the greater moral evil rule for entitlements, requiring people to prevent something bad whenever the cost to them is less significant than the benefit to another. Surely, we might think, total welfare would be increased by a code requiring people to give up their savings if a greater evil can be prevented.

I think, however, that this is wrong, and that an ideal code would provide for rights and would encourage rewarding according to desert. My reasons for thinking this stem from the importance of insuring that a moral code really does, in fact, work. Each of the three practical considerations mentioned above now enters the picture. First, it will be quite difficult to get people to accept a code which requires that they give away their savings, extra organs, or anything else merely because they can avoid a greater evil for a stranger. Many people simply wouldn't do it: they aren't that altruistic. If the code attempts to require it anyway, two results would likely follow. First, because many would not live up to the rules, there would be a tendency to create feelings of guilt in those who keep their savings in spite of having been taught it is wrong, as well as conflict between those who meet their obligations and those who do not. And, second, a more realistic code, one which doesn't expect more than can be accomplished, may actually result in more giving. It's a bit like trying to influence how children spend their money. Often they will buy less candy if rules allow them to do so occasionally but they are praised for spending on other things than if its purchase is prohibited. We cannot assume that making a charitable act a requirement will always encourage such behavior. Impractical rules not only create guilt and social conflict, they often tend to encourage the opposite of the desired result. By giving people the right to use their savings for themselves, yet praising those who do not exercise the right but help others instead, we have struck a good balance; the rules are at once practical yet reasonably effective.

Similar practical considerations would also influence our decision to support rules that allow people to keep what they deserve. For most people, working is not their favorite activity. If we are to prosper, however, goods and services must be produced. Incentives are therefore an important motivation, and one such incentive for work is income. Our code encourages work by allowing people to keep a large part of what they earn, indeed that's much the point of entitlements. "I worked hard for it, so I can keep it" is an oft-heard expression. If we eliminate this rule from our code and ask people to follow the greater moral evil rule instead, the result would likely be less work done and so less total production. Given a choice between not working and continuing to work knowing the efforts should go to benefit others, many would choose not to work.

Moral rules should be practical in a third sense, too. They cannot assume people are either more unbiased or more knowledgeable than they are. This fact has many implications for the sorts of rules we would want to include in a welfare maximizing code. For example, we may be tempted to avoid slavish conformity to counterproductive rules by allowing people to break promises whenever they think doing so would increase total welfare. But again we must not ignore human nature, in this case our tendency to give special weight to our own welfare and our inability to be always objective in tracing the effects of our actions. While we would not want to teach that promises must never be broken no matter what the consequences, we also would not want to encourage breaking promises any time a person can convince himself the results of doing so would be better than if he kept his word.

Similar considerations apply to the greater moral evil rule. Imagine a situation where someone feels he can prevent an evil befalling himself by taking what he needs from a large store. The idea that he's preventing something bad from happening (to himself) without sacrificing anything of comparable moral significance (the store won't miss the goods) would justify robbery. Although sometimes a particular act of theft really is welfare maximizing, it does not follow that we should support a *rule* which allows theft whenever the robber is preventing a greater evil. Such a rule, to work, would require more objectivity and more knowledge of long-term consequences than we have. Here again, including rights in our moral code serves a useful role, discouraging the tendency to rationalize our behavior by underestimating the harm we may cause to others or exaggerating the benefits that may accrue to ourselves.

The first sections of this paper attempted to show that our moral code is a bit schizophrenic. It seems to pull us in opposite directions, sometimes toward helping people who are in need, other times toward the view that rights and desert justify keeping things we have even if greater evil could be avoided were we to give away our extra eye or our savings account. This apparent inconsistency led us to a further question: Is the emphasis on entitlements really defensible, or should we try to resolve the tension in our own code by adopting the greater moral evil rule and ignoring entitlements? In this section I considered the idea that we might choose between entitlements and the greater moral evil rule by paying attention to the general nature of a moral code; and in particular to the sort of code we might want to support. I argued that all of us, including egoists, have reason to support a code which promotes the welfare of everyone who lives under it. That idea, of an ideal moral code which it is rational for everyone to support, provides a criterion for deciding which rules are sound and which ones we should support.

My conclusion is a conservative one: Concern that our moral code encourages production and not fail because it unrealistically assumes people are more altruistic or objective than they are means that our rules giving people rights to their possessions and encouraging distribution according to desert should be part of an ideal moral code. And since this is so, it is not always wrong to invoke rights or claim that money is deserved as justification for not giving aid, even when something worse could be prevented by offering help. The welfare maximizing moral code would not require us to maximize welfare in each individual case.

I have not yet discussed just how much weight should be given to entitlements, only that they are important and should not be ignored as Singer and Watson suggest. Certainly an ideal moral code would not allow people to overlook those in desperate need by making entitlements absolute, any more than it would ignore entitlements. But where would it draw the line?

It's hard to know, of course, but the following seems to me to be a sensible stab at an answer. Concerns about discouraging production and the general adherence to the code argue strongly against expecting too much; yet on the other hand, to allow extreme wealth in the face of grinding poverty would seem to put too much weight on entitlements. It seems to me, then, that a reasonable code would require people to help when there is no substantial cost to themselves, that is, when what they are sacrificing would not mean *significant* reduction in their own or their families' level of happiness. Since most people's savings accounts and nearly everybody's second kidney are not insignificant, entitlements would in those cases outweigh another's need. But if what is at stake is trivial, as dirtying one's clothes would normally be, then an ideal moral code would not allow rights to override the greater evil that can be prevented. Despite our code's unclear and sometimes schizophrenic posture, it seems to me that these judgments are not that different from our current moral attitudes. We tend to blame people who waste money on trivia when they could help others in need, yet not to expect people to make large sacrifices to distant strangers. An ideal moral code thus might not be a great deal different from our own.

53

A Defense
of Abortion[1]

JUDITH JARVIS THOMSON

Judith Jarvis Thomson is Professor of Philosophy at MIT. Her books include Acts and Other Events *and* The Realm of Rights, *and she has written many articles on topics in ethics and social philosophy. This widely reprinted essay first appeared in* Philosophy and Public Affairs *(Fall 1971).*

In the essay, Thomson discusses the morality of abortion. Although much debate has centered on the question of whether fetuses are persons, Thomson simply assumes, for purposes of argument, that they are. Even so, she contends, it does not follow that aborting a fetus is wrong. Although all persons have a right to life, this does not mean that they have a right to be provided with everything necessary to sustain life. To drive this home, Thomson imagines a person who awakes to find that a sick violinist has been attached to his kidneys while he slept. Even though the violinist will die if detached, Thomson maintains that he has no right not to be detached. Since each person has a prior right to the use of his or her own body, nobody else can have a right to the use of that body.

Does this mean that abortion is always justified? Interestingly, Thomson does not say this. For one thing, she seems to acknowledge that a woman's degree of care in trying to avoid pregnancy may be relevant. For another, she suggests that it would be "indecent" to have a late abortion to avoid postponing a trip abroad. Thus, even if having an abortion would violate no one's rights, there may be other good reasons not to have one.

Most opposition to abortion relies on the premise that the fetus is a human being, a person, from the moment of conception. The premise is argued for, but, as I think, not well. Take, for example, the most common argument. We are asked to notice that the development of a human being from conception through birth into childhood is continuous; then it is said that to draw a line, to choose a point in this development and say "before this point the thing is not a person, after this point it is a person" is to make an arbitrary choice, a choice for which in the nature of things no good reason can be given. It is

[1] I am very much indebted to James Thomson for discussion, criticism, and many helpful suggestions.

concluded that the fetus is, or anyway that we had better say it is, a person from the moment of conception. But this conclusion does not follow. Similar things might be said about the development of an acorn into an oak tree, and it does not follow that acorns are oak trees, or that we had better say they are. Arguments of this form are sometimes called "slippery slope arguments"— the phrase is perhaps self-explanatory—and it is dismaying that opponents of abortion rely on them so heavily and uncritically.

I am inclined to agree, however, that the prospects for "drawing a line" in the development of the fetus look dim. I am inclined to think also that we shall probably have to agree that the fetus has already become a human person well before birth. Indeed, it comes as a surprise when one first learns how early in its life it begins to acquire human characteristics. By the tenth week, for example, it already has a face, arms and legs, fingers and toes; it has internal organs, and brain activity is detectable.[2] On the other hand, I think that the premise is false, that the fetus is not a person from the moment of conception. A newly fertilized ovum, a newly implanted clump of cells, is no more a person than an acorn is an oak tree. But I shall not discuss any of this. For it seems to me to be of great interest to ask what happens if, for the sake of argument, we allow the premise. How, precisely, are we supposed to get from there to the conclusion that abortion is morally impermissible? Opponents of abortion commonly spend most of their time establishing that the fetus is a person, and hardly any time explaining the step from there to the impermissibility of abortion. Perhaps they think the step too simple and obvious to require much comment. Or perhaps instead they are simply being economical in argument. Many of those who defend abortion rely on the premise that the fetus is not a person, but only a bit of tissue that will become a person at birth; and why pay out more arguments than you have to? Whatever the explanation, I suggest that the step they take is neither easy nor obvious, that it calls for closer examination than it is commonly given, and that when we do give it this closer examination we shall feel inclined to reject it.

I propose then, that we grant that the fetus is a person from the moment of conception. How does the argument go from here? Something like this, I take it. Every person has a right to life. So the fetus has a right to life. No doubt the mother has a right to decide what shall happen in and to her body, everyone would grant that. But surely a person's right to life is stronger and more stringent than the mother's right to decide what happens in and to her body, and so outweighs it. So the fetus may not be killed; an abortion may not be performed.

It sounds plausible. But now let me ask you to imagine this. You wake up in the morning and find yourself back to back in bed with an unconscious violinist. A famous unconscious violinist. He has been found to have a fatal

---

2 Daniel Callahan, *Abortion: Law, Choice and Morality* (New York, 1970), p. 373. This book gives a fascinating survey of the available information on abortion. The Jewish tradition is surveyed in David M. Feldman, *Birth Control in Jewish Law* (New York, 1968), Part 5; the Catholic tradition in John T. Noonan, Jr., "An Almost Absolute Value in History," in *The Morality of Abortion*, ed. John T. Noonan, Jr. (Cambridge, MA, 1970).

kidney ailment, and the Society of Music Lovers has canvassed all the available medical records and found that you alone have the right blood type to help. They have therefore kidnapped you, and last night the violinist's circulatory system was plugged into yours, so that your kidneys can be used to extract poisons from his blood as well as your own. The director of the hospital now tells you, "Look, we're sorry the Society of Music Lovers did this to you—we would never have permitted it if we had known. But still, they did it, and the violinist now is plugged into you. To unplug you would be to kill him. But never mind, it's only for nine months. By then he will have recovered from his ailment, and can safely be unplugged from you." Is it morally incumbent on you to accede to this situation? No doubt it would be very nice of you if you did, a great kindness. But do you *have* to accede to it? What if it were not nine months, but nine years? Or longer still? What if the director of the hospital says, "Tough luck, I agree, but you've now got to stay in bed, with the violinist plugged into you, for the rest of your life. Because remember this. All persons have a right to life, and violinists are persons. Granted you have a right to decide what happens in and to your body, but a person's right to life outweighs your right to decide what happens in and to your body. So you cannot ever be unplugged from him." I imagine you would regard this as outrageous, which suggests that something really is wrong with that plausible-sounding argument I mentioned a moment ago.

In this case, of course, you were kidnapped; you didn't volunteer for the operation that plugged the violinist into your kidneys. Can those who oppose abortion on the ground I mentioned make an exception for a pregnancy due to rape? Certainly. They can say that persons have a right to life only if they didn't come into existence because of rape; or they can say that all persons have a right to life, but that some have less of a right to life than others, in particular, that those who came into existence because of rape have less. But these statements have a rather unpleasant sound. Surely the question of whether you have a right to life at all, or how much of it you have, shouldn't turn on the question of whether or not you are the product of a rape. And in fact the people who oppose abortion on the ground I mentioned do not make this distinction, and hence do not make an exception in case of rape.

Nor do they make an exception for a case in which the mother has to spend the nine months of her pregnancy in bed. They would agree that would be a great pity, and hard on the mother; but all the same, all persons have a right to life, the fetus is a person, and so on. I suspect, in fact, that they would not make an exception for a case in which, miraculously enough, the pregnancy went on for nine years, or even the rest of the mother's life.

Some won't even make an exception for a case in which continuation of the pregnancy is likely to shorten the mother's life; they regard abortion as impermissible even to save the mother's life. Such cases are nowadays very rare, and many opponents of abortion do not accept this extreme view. All the same, it is a good place to begin: a number of points of interest come out in respect to it.

1. Let us call the view that abortion is impermissible even to save the mother's life "the extreme view." I want to suggest first that it does not issue

from the argument I mentioned earlier without the addition of some fairly powerful premises. Suppose a woman has become pregnant, and now learns that she has a cardiac condition such that she will die if she carries the baby to term. What may be done for her? The fetus, being a person, has a right to life, but as the mother is a person too, so has she a right to life. Presumably they have an equal right to life. How is it supposed to come out that an abortion may not be performed? If mother and child have an equal right to life, shouldn't we perhaps flip a coin? Or should we add to the mother's right to life her right to decide what happens in and to her body, which everybody seems to be ready to grant—the sum of her rights now outweighing the fetus' right to life?

The most familiar argument here is the following. We are told that performing the abortion would be directly killing[3] the child, whereas doing nothing would not be killing the mother, but only letting her die. Moreover, in killing the child, one would be killing an innocent person, for the child has committed no crime, and is not aiming at his mother's death. And then there are a variety of ways in which this might be continued. (1) But as directly killing an innocent person is always and absolutely impermissible, an abortion may not be performed. Or, (2) as directly killing an innocent person is murder, and murder is always and absolutely impermissible, an abortion may not be performed.[4] Or, (3) as one's duty to refrain from directly killing an innocent person is more stringent than one's duty to keep a person from dying, an abortion may not be performed. Or, (4) if one's only options are directly killing an innocent person or letting a person die, one must prefer letting the person die, and thus an abortion may not be performed.[5]

Some people seem to have thought that these are not further premises which must be added if the conclusion is to be reached, but that they follow from the very fact that an innocent person has a right to life.[6] But this seems to me to be a mistake, and perhaps the simplest way to show this is to bring out that

3 The term "direct" in the arguments I refer to is a technical one. Roughly, what is meant by "direct killing" is either killing as an end in itself, or killing as a means to some end, for example, the end of saving someone else's life. See note 6, below, for an example of its use.

4 Cf. *Encyclical Letter of Pope Pius XI on Christian Marriage,* St. Paul Editions (Boston, n.d.), p. 32: "however much we may pity the mother whose health and even life is gravely imperiled in the performance of the duty allotted to her by nature, nevertheless what could ever be a sufficient reason for excusing in any way the direct murder of the innocent? This is precisely what we are dealing with here." Noonan (*The Morality of Abortion,* p. 43) reads this as follows: "What cause can ever avail to excuse in any way the direct killing of the innocent? For it is a question of that."

5 The thesis in (4) is in an interesting way weaker than those in (1), (2), and (3): they rule out abortion even in cases in which both mother *and* child will die if the abortion is not performed. By contrast, one who held the view expressed in (4) could consistently say that one needn't prefer letting two persons die to killing one.

6 Cf. the following passage from Pius XII, *Address to the Italian Catholic Society of Midwives:* "The baby in the maternal breast has the right to life immediately from God.—Hence there is no man, no human authority, no science, no medical, eugenic, social, economic or moral 'indication' which can establish or grant a valid juridical ground for a direct deliberate disposition of an innocent human life, that is a disposition which looks to its destruction either as an end or as a means to another end perhaps in itself not illicit.—The baby, still not born, is a man in the same degree and for the same reason as the mother" (quoted in Noonan, *The Morality of Abortion,* p. 45).

while we must certainly grant that innocent persons have a right to life, the theses in (1) through (4) are all false. Take (2), for example. If directly killing an innocent person is murder, and thus is impermissible, then the mother's directly killing the innocent person inside her is murder, and thus is impermissible. But it cannot seriously be thought to be murder if the mother performs an abortion on herself to save her life. It cannot seriously be said that she *must* refrain, that she *must* sit passively by and wait for her death. Let us look again at the case of you and the violinist. There you are, in bed with the violinist, and the director of the hospital says to you, "It's all most distressing, and I deeply sympathize, but you see this is putting an additional strain on your kidneys, and you'll be dead within the month. But you *have* to stay where you are all the same. Because unplugging you would be directly killing an innocent violinist, and that's murder, and that's impermissible." If anything in the world is true, it is that you do not commit murder, you do not do what is impermissible, if you reach around to your back and unplug yourself from that violinist to save your life.

The main focus of attention in writings on abortion has been on what a third party may or may not do in answer to a request from a woman for an abortion. This is in a way understandable. Things being as they are, there isn't much a woman can safely do to abort herself. So the question asked is what a third party may do, and what the mother may do, if it is mentioned at all, is deduced, almost as an afterthought, from what it is concluded that third parties may do. But it seems to me that to treat the matter in this way is to refuse to grant to the mother that very status of person which is so firmly insisted on for the fetus. For we cannot simply read off what a person may do from what the third party may do. Suppose you find yourself trapped in a tiny house with a growing child. I mean a very tiny house, and a rapidly growing child—you are already up against the wall of the house and in a few minutes you'll be crushed to death. The child on the other hand won't be crushed to death; if nothing is done to stop him from growing he'll be hurt, but in the end he'll simply burst open the house and walk out a free man. Now I could well understand it if a bystander were to say, "There's nothing we can do for you. We cannot choose between your life and his, we cannot be the ones to decide who is to live, we cannot intervene." But it cannot be concluded that you too can do nothing, that you cannot attack it to save your life. However innocent the child may be, you do not have to wait passively while it crushes you to death. Perhaps a pregnant woman is vaguely felt to have the status of house, to which we don't allow the right of self-defense. But if the woman houses the child, it should be remembered that she is a person who houses it.

I should perhaps stop to say explicitly that I am not claiming that people have a right to do anything whatever to save their lives. I think, rather, that there are drastic limits to the right of self-defense. If someone threatens you with death unless you torture someone else to death, I think you have not the right, even to save your life, to do so. But the case under consideration here is very different. In our case there are only two people involved, one whose life is threatened, and one who threatens it. Both are innocent: the one who is threatened is not threatened because of any fault, the one who threatens does not threaten because of any fault. For this reason we may feel that we bystanders cannot intervene. But the person threatened can.

In sum, a woman surely can defend her life against the threat to it posed by the unborn child, even if doing so involves its death. And this shows not merely that the theses in (1) through (4) are false; it shows also that the extreme view of abortion is false, and so we need not canvass any other possible ways of arriving at it from the argument I mentioned at the outset.

2. The extreme view could of course be weakened to say that while abortion is permissible to save the mother's life, it may not be performed by a third party, but only by the mother herself. But this cannot be right either. For what we have to keep in mind is that the mother and the unborn child are not like two tenants in a small house which has, by an unfortunate mistake, been rented to both: the mother *owns* the house. The fact that she does adds to the offensiveness of deducing that the mother can do nothing from the supposition that third parties can do nothing. But it does more than this: it casts a bright light on the supposition that third parties can do nothing. Certainly it lets us see that a third party who says "I cannot choose between you" is fooling himself if he thinks this is impartiality. If Jones has found and fastened on a certain coat, which he needs to keep him from freezing, but which Smith also needs to keep him from freezing, then it is not impartiality that says "I cannot choose between you" when Smith owns the coat. Women have said again and again "This body is *my* body!" and they have reason to feel angry, reason to feel that it has been like shouting into the wind. Smith, after all, is hardly likely to bless us if we say to him, "Of course it's your coat, anybody would grant that it is. But no one may choose between you and Jones who is to have it."

We should really ask what it is that says "no one may choose" in the face of the fact that the body that houses the child is the mother's body. It may be simply a failure to appreciate this fact. But it may be something more interesting, namely the sense that one has a right to refuse to lay hands on people, even where it would be just and fair to do so, even where justice seems to require that somebody do so. Thus justice might call for somebody to get Smith's coat back from Jones, and yet you have a right to refuse to be the one to lay hands on Jones, a right to refuse to do physical violence to him. This, I think, must be granted. But when what should be said is not "no one may choose," but only "*I* cannot choose," and indeed not even this, but "*I* will not *act*," leaving it open that somebody else can or should, and in particular that anyone in a position of authority, with the job of securing people's rights, both can and should. So this is no difficulty. I have not been arguing that any given third party must accede to the mother's request that he perform an abortion to save her life, but only that he may.

I suppose that in some views of human life the mother's body is only on loan to her, the loan not being one which gives her any prior claim to it. One who held this view might well think it impartiality to say "I cannot choose." But I shall simply ignore this possibility. My own view is that if a human being has any just, prior claim to anything at all, he has a just, prior claim to his own body. And perhaps this needn't be argued for here anyway, since, as I mentioned, the arguments against abortion we are looking at do grant that the woman has a right to decide what happens in and to her body.

But although they do grant it, I have tried to show that they do not take seriously what is done in granting it. I suggest the same thing will reappear even more clearly when we turn away from cases in which the mother's life is at stake, and attend, as I propose we now do, to the vastly more common cases in which a woman wants an abortion for some less weighty reason than preserving her own life.

3. Where the mother's life is not at stake, the argument I mentioned at the outset seems to have a much stronger pull. "Everyone has a right to life, so the unborn person has a right to life." And isn't the child's right to life weightier than anything other than the mother's own right to life, which she might put forward as ground for an abortion?

This argument treats the right to life as if it were unproblematic. It is not, and this seems to me to be precisely the source of the mistake.

For we should now, at long last, ask what it comes to, to have a right to life. In some views having a right to life includes having a right to be given at least the bare minimum one needs for continued life. But suppose that what in fact *is* the bare minimum a man needs for continued life is something he has no right at all to be given? If I am sick unto death, and the only thing that will save my life is the touch of Henry Fonda's cool hand on my fevered brow, then all the same, I have no right to be given the touch of Henry Fonda's cool hand on my fevered brow. It would be frightfully nice of him to fly in from the West Coast to provide it. It would be less nice, no doubt well meant, if my friends flew out to the West Coast and carried Henry Fonda back with them. But I have no right at all against anybody that he should do this for me. Or again, to return to the story I told earlier, the fact that for continued life that violinist needs the continued use of your kidneys does not establish that he has a right to be given the continued use of your kidneys. He certainly has no right against you that *you* should give him continued use of your kidneys. For nobody has any right to use your kidneys unless you give him such a right; and nobody has the right against you that you shall give him this right—if you do allow him to go on using your kidneys, this is a kindness on your part, and not something he can claim from you as his due. Nor has he any right against anybody else that *they* should give him continued use of your kidneys. Certainly he has no right against the Society of Music Lovers that they should plug him into you in the first place. And if you now start to unplug yourself, having learned that you will otherwise have to spend nine years in bed with him, there is nobody in the world who must try to prevent you, in order to see to it that he is given something he has a right to be given.

Some people are rather stricter about the right to life. In their view, it does not include the right to be given anything, but amounts to, and only to, the right not to be killed by anybody. But here a related difficulty arises. If everybody is to refrain from killing that violinist, then everybody must refrain from doing a great many different sorts of things. Everybody must refrain from slitting his throat, everybody must refrain from shooting him—and everybody must refrain from unplugging you from him. But does he have a right against everybody that they shall refrain from unplugging you from him? To refrain from doing this is to allow him to continue to use your kidneys. It could be argued that he has a right against us that *we* should allow him to continue to use your kidneys. That is, while he had no right against us that we should give him the use of your kidneys, it might be argued that he anyway has a right against us that we shall not now intervene and deprive him of the use of your kidneys. I shall come back to third-party interventions later. But certainly the violinist has no right against you that *you* shall allow him to continue to use your kidneys. As I said, if you do allow him to use them, it is a kindness on your part, and not something you owe him.

The difficulty I point to here is not peculiar to the right to life. It reappears in connection with all the other natural rights; and it is something which an adequate account of rights must deal with. For present purposes it is enough just to draw attention to it. But I would stress that I am not arguing that people do not have a right to life—quite to the contrary, it seems to me that the primary control we must place on the acceptability of an account of rights is that it should turn out in that account to be a truth that all persons have a right to life. I am arguing only that having a right to life does not guarantee having either a right to be given the use of or a right to be allowed continued use of another person's body—even if one needs it for life itself. So the right to life will not serve the opponents of abortion in the very simple and clear way in which they seem to have thought it would.

4. There is another way to bring out the difficulty. In the most ordinary sort of case, to deprive someone of what he has a right to is to treat him unjustly. Suppose a boy and his small brother are jointly given a box of chocolates for Christmas. If the older boy takes the box and refuses to give his brother any of the chocolates, he is unjust to him, for the brother has been given a right to half of them. But suppose that, having learned that otherwise it means nine years in bed with that violinist, you unplug yourself from him. You surely are not being unjust to him, for you gave him no right to use your kidneys, and no one else can have given him any such right. But we have to notice that in unplugging yourself, you are killing him; and violinists, like everybody else, have a right to life, and thus in the view we were considering just now, the right not to be killed. So here you do what he supposedly has a right you shall not do, but you do not act unjustly to him in doing it.

The emendation which may be made at this point is this: the right to life consists not in the right not to be killed, but rather in the right not to be killed unjustly. This runs a risk of circularity, but never mind: it would enable us to square the fact that the violinist has a right to life with the fact that you do not act unjustly toward him in unplugging yourself, thereby killing him. For if you do not kill him unjustly, you do not violate his right to life, and so it is no wonder you do him no injustice.

But if this emendation is accepted, the gap in the argument against abortions stares us plainly in the face: it is by no means enough to show that the fetus is a person, and to remind us that all persons have a right to life—we need to be shown also that killing the fetus violates its right to life, i.e., that abortion is unjust killing. And is it?

I suppose we may take it as a datum that in a case of pregnancy due to rape the mother has not given the unborn person a right to the use of her body for food and shelter. Indeed, in what pregnancy could it be supposed that the mother has given the unborn person such a right? It is not as if there were unborn persons drifting about the world, to whom a woman who wants a child says "I invite you in."

But it might be argued that there are other ways one can have acquired a right to the use of another person's body than by having been invited to use it by that person. Suppose a woman voluntarily indulges in intercourse, knowing of the chance it will issue in pregnancy, and then she does become pregnant; is she not in part responsible for the presence, in fact the very existence, of the unborn person inside her? No doubt she did not invite it in. But doesn't her partial responsibility for its being there itself give it a right to the use of her body?[7] If so, then her aborting it would be more like the boy's taking away the chocolates, and less like your unplugging yourself from the violinist—doing so would be depriving it of what it does have a right to, and thus would be doing it an injustice.

And then, too, it might be asked whether or not she can kill it even to save her own life: If she voluntarily called it into existence, how can she now kill it, even in self-defense?

The first thing to be said about this is that it is something new. Opponents of abortion have been so concerned to make out the independence of the fetus, in order to establish that it has a right to life, just as its mother does, that they have tended to overlook the possible support they might gain from making out that the fetus is *dependent* on the mother, in order to establish that she has a special kind of responsibility for it, a responsibility that gives it rights against her which are not possessed by any independent person—such as an ailing violinist who is a stranger to her.

On the other hand, this argument would give the unborn person a right to its mother's body only if her pregnancy resulted from a voluntary act, undertaken in full knowledge of the chance a pregnancy might result from it. It would leave out entirely the unborn person whose existence is due to rape. Pending the availability of some further argument, then, we would be left with the conclusion that unborn persons whose existence is due to rape have no right to the use of their mothers' bodies, and thus that aborting them is not depriving them of anything they have a right to and hence is not unjust killing.

And we should also notice that it is not at all plain that this argument really does go even as far as it purports to. For there are cases and cases, and the details make a difference. If the room is stuffy, and I therefore open a window to air it, and a burglar climbs in, it would be absurd to say, "Ah, now he can stay, she's given him a right to the use of her house—for she is partially

---

[7] The need for a discussion of this argument was brought home to me by members of the Society for Ethical and Legal Philosophy, to whom this paper was originally presented.

responsible for his presence there, having voluntarily done what enabled him to get in, in full knowledge that there are such things as burglars, and that burglars burgle." It would be still more absurd to say this if I had had bars installed outside my windows, precisely to prevent burglars from getting in, and a burglar got in only because of a defect in the bars. It remains equally absurd if we imagine it is not a burglar who climbs in, but an innocent person who blunders or falls in. Again, suppose it were like this: people-seeds drift about in the air like pollen, and if you open your windows, one may drift in and take root in your carpets or upholstery. You don't want children, so you fix up your windows with fine mesh screens, the very best you can buy. As can happen, however, and on very, very rare occasions does happen, one of the screens is defective; and a seed drifts in and takes root. Does the person-plant who now develops have a right to the use of your house? Surely not—despite the fact that you voluntarily opened your windows, you knowingly kept carpets and upholstered furniture, and you knew that screens were sometimes defective. Someone may argue that you are responsible for its rooting, that it does have a right to your house, because after all you *could* have lived out your life with bare floors and furniture, or with sealed windows and doors. But this won't do—for by the same token anyone can avoid a pregnancy due to rape by having a hysterectomy, or anyway by never leaving home without a (reliable!) army.

It seems to me that the argument we are looking at can establish at most that there are *some* cases in which the unborn person has a right to the use of its mother's body, and therefore *some* cases in which abortion is unjust killing. There is room for much discussion and argument as to precisely which, if any. But I think we should sidestep this issue and leave it open, for at any rate the argument certainly does not establish that all abortion is unjust killing.

5. There is room for yet another argument here, however. We surely must all grant that there may be cases in which it would be morally indecent to detach a person from your body at the cost of his life. Suppose you learn that what the violinist needs is not nine years of your life, but only one hour: all you need do to save his life is to spend one hour in that bed with him. Suppose also that letting him use your kidneys for that one hour would not affect your health in the slightest. Admittedly you were kidnapped. Admittedly you did not give anyone permission to plug him into you. Nevertheless it seems to me plain you *ought* to allow him to use your kidneys for that hour—it would be indecent to refuse.

Again, suppose pregnancy lasted only an hour, and constituted no threat to life or health. And suppose that a woman becomes pregnant as a result of rape. Admittedly she did not voluntarily do anything to bring about the exis-tence of a child. Admittedly she did nothing at all which would give the unborn person a right to the use of her body. All the same it might well be said, as in the newly emended violinist story, that she *ought* to allow it to remain for that hour—that it would be indecent in her to refuse.

Now some people are inclined to use the term "right" in such a way that it follows from the fact that you ought to allow a person to use your body for the hour he needs, that he has a right to use your body for the hour he needs, even though he has not been given that right by any person or act. They may say that it follows also that if you refuse, you act unjustly toward him. This use of the term is perhaps so common that it cannot be called wrong; nevertheless it seems to me to be an unfortunate loosening of what we would do better to keep a tight rein on. Suppose that box of chocolates I mentioned earlier had not been given to both boys jointly, but was given only to the older boy. There he sits, stolidly eating his way through the box, his small brother watching enviously. Here we are likely to say "You ought not to be so mean. You ought to give your brother some of those chocolates." My own view is that it just does not follow from the truth of this that the brother has any right to any of the chocolates. If the boy refuses to give his brother any, he is greedy, stingy, callous—but not unjust. I suppose that the people I have in mind will say it does follow that the brother has a right to some of the chocolates, and thus that the boy does act unjustly if he refuses to give his brother any. But the effect of saying this is to obscure what we should keep distinct, namely the difference between the boy's refusal in this case and the boy's refusal in the earlier case, in which the box was given to both boys jointly, and in which the small brother thus had what was from any point of view clear title to half.

A further objection to so using the term "right" from that the fact that A ought to do a thing for B, it follows that B has a right against A that A do it for him, is that it is going to make the question of whether or not a man has a right to a thing turn on how easy it is to provide him with it; and this seems not merely unfortunate, but morally unacceptable. Take the case of Henry Fonda again. I said earlier that I had no right to the touch of his cool hand on my fevered brow, even though I needed it to save my life. I said it would be frightfully nice of him to fly from the West Coast to provide me with it, but that I had no right against him that he should do so. But suppose he isn't on the West Coast. Suppose he has only to walk across the room, place a hand briefly on my brow—and lo, my life is saved. Then surely he ought to do it, it would be indecent to refuse. Is it to be said "Ah, well, it follows that in this case she has a right to the touch of his hand on her brow, and so it would be an injustice in him to refuse"? So that I have a right to it when it is easy for him to provide it, though no right when it's hard? It's rather a shocking idea that anyone's rights should fade away and disappear as it gets harder and harder to accord them to him.

So my own view is that even though you ought to let the violinist use your kidneys for the one hour he needs, we should not conclude that he has a right to do so—we should say that if you refuse, you are, like the boy who owns all the chocolates and will give none away, self-centered and callous, indecent in fact, but not unjust. And similarly, that even supposing a case in which a woman pregnant due to rape ought to allow the unborn person to use her body for the hour he needs, we should not conclude that he has a right to do so; we should conclude that she is self-centered, callous, indecent, but not unjust, if she refuses. The complaints are no less grave; they are just different. However, there is no need to insist on this point. If anyone does wish to deduce "he has a right" from "you ought," then all the same he must surely grant that there are cases in which it is not morally required of you that you allow that violinist to use your kidneys, and in which he does not have a right to use them, and in which you do not do him an injustice if you refuse. And so also for mother and unborn child. Except in such cases as the unborn person has a right to demand it—and we were leaving open the possibility that there may be such cases—nobody is morally *required* to make large sacrifices, of health, of all other interests and concerns, of all other duties and commitments, for nine years, or even for nine months, in order to keep another person alive.

6. We have in fact to distinguish between two kinds of Samaritan: the Good Samaritan and what we might call the Minimally Decent Samaritan. The story of the Good Samaritan, you will remember, goes like this:

> A certain man went down from Jerusalem to Jericho, and fell among thieves, which stripped him of his raiment, and wounded him, and departed, leaving him half dead.
>
> And by chance there came down a certain priest that way; and when he saw him, he passed by on the other side.
>
> And likewise a Levite, when he was at the place, came and looked on him, and passed by on the other side.
>
> But a certain Samaritan, as he journeyed, came where he was; and when he saw him he had compassion on him.
>
> And went to him, and bound up his wounds, pouring in oil and wine, and set him on his own beast, and brought him to an inn, and took care of him.
>
> And on the morrow, when he departed, he took out two pence, and gave them to the host, and said unto him, "Take care of him; and whatsoever thou spendest more, when I come again, I will repay thee."
>
> (Luke 10:30–35)

The Good Samaritan went out of his way, at some cost to himself, to help one in need of it. We are not told what the options were, that is, whether or not the priest and the Levite could have helped by doing less than the Good Samaritan did, but assuming they could have, then the fact they did nothing at all shows they were not even Minimally Decent Samaritans, not because they were not Samaritans, but because they were not even minimally decent.

These things are a matter of degree, of course, but there is a difference, and it comes out perhaps most clearly in the story of Kitty Genovese, who, as you will remember, was murdered while thirty-eight people watched or listened, and did nothing at all to help her. A Good Samaritan would have rushed out to give direct assistance against the murderer. Or perhaps we had better allow that it would have been a Splendid Samaritan who did this, on the ground that it would have involved a risk of death for himself. But the thirty-eight not only did not do this, they did not even trouble to pick up a phone to call the police. Minimally Decent Samaritanism would call for doing at least that, and their not having done it was monstrous.

After telling the story of the Good Samaritan, Jesus said "Go, and do thou likewise." Perhaps he meant that we are morally required to act as the Good

Samaritan did. Perhaps he was urging people to do more than is morally required of them. At all events it seems plain that it was not morally required of any of the thirty-eight that he rush out to give direct assistance at the risk of his own life, and that it is not morally required of anyone that he give long stretches of his life—nine years or nine months—to sustaining the life of a person who has no special right (we were leaving open the possibility of this) to demand it.

Indeed, with one rather striking class of exceptions, no one in any country in the world is *legally* required to do anywhere near as much as this for anyone else. The class of exceptions is obvious. My main concern here is not the state of the law in respect to abortion, but it is worth drawing attention to the fact that in no state in this country is any man compelled by law to be even a Minimally Decent Samaritan to any person; there is no law under which charges could be brought against the thirty-eight who stood by while Kitty Genovese died. By contrast, in most states in this country women are compelled by law to be not merely Minimally Decent Samaritans, but Good Samaritans to unborn persons inside them. This doesn't by itself settle anything one way or the other, because it may well be argued that there should be laws in this country—as there are in many European countries—compelling at least Minimally Decent Samaritanism.[8] But it does show that there is a gross injustice in the existing state of the law. And it shows also that the groups currently working against liberalization of abortion laws, in fact working toward having it declared unconstitutional for a state to permit abortion, had better start working for the adoption of Good Samaritan laws generally, or earn the charge that they are acting in bad faith.

I should think, myself, that Minimally Decent Samaritan laws would be one thing, Good Samaritan laws quite another, and in fact highly improper. But we are not here concerned with the law. What we should ask is not whether anybody should be compelled by law to be a Good Samaritan, but whether we must accede to a situation in which somebody is being compelled—by nature, perhaps—to be a Good Samaritan. We have, in other words, to look now at third-party interventions. I have been arguing that no person is morally required to make large sacrifices to sustain the life of another who has no right to demand them, and this even where the sacrifices do not include life itself; we are not morally required to be Good Samaritans or anyway Very Good Samaritans to one another. But what if a man cannot extricate himself from such a situation? What if he appeals to us to extricate him? It seems to me plain that there are cases in which we can, cases in which a Good Samaritan would extricate him. There you are, you were kidnapped, and nine years in bed with that violinist lie ahead of you. You have your own life to lead. You are sorry, but you simply cannot see giving up so much of your life to the sustaining of his. You cannot extricate yourself, and ask us to do so. I should have thought that—in light of his having no right to the use of your body—

---

8 For a discussion of the difficulties involved, and a survey of the European experience with such laws, see *The Good Samaritan and the Law,* ed. James M. Ratcliffe (New York, 1966).

it was obvious that we do not have to accede to your being forced to give up so much. We can do what you ask. There is no injustice to the violinist in our doing so.

7. Following the lead of the opponents of abortion, I have throughout been speaking of the fetus merely as a person, and what I have been asking is whether or not the argument we began with, which proceeds only from the fetus' being a person, really does establish its conclusion. I have argued that it does not.

But of course there are arguments and arguments, and it may be said that I have simply fastened on the wrong one. It may be said that what is important is not merely the fact that the fetus is a person, but that it is a person for whom the woman has a special kind of responsibility issuing from the fact that she is its mother. And it might be argued that all my analogies are therefore irrelevant—for you do not have that special kind of responsibility for that violinist, Henry Fonda does not have that special kind of responsibility for me. And our attention might be drawn to the fact that men and women both *are* compelled by law to provide support for their children.

I have in effect dealt (briefly) with this argument in section 4 above; but a (still briefer) recapitulation now may be in order. Surely we do not have any such "special responsibility" for a person unless we have assumed it, explicitly or implicitly. If a set of parents do not try to prevent pregnancy, do not obtain an abortion, and then at the time of birth of the child do not put it out for adoption, but rather take it home with them, then they have assumed responsibility for it, they have given it rights, and they cannot *now* withdraw support from it at the cost of its life because they now find it difficult to go on providing for it. But if they have taken all reasonable precautions against having a child, they do not simply by virtue of their biological relationship to the child who comes into existence have a special responsibility for it. They may wish to assume responsibility for it, or they may not wish to. And I am suggesting that if assuming responsibility for it would require large sacrifices, then they may refuse. A Good Samaritan would not refuse—or anyway, a Splendid Samaritan, if the sacrifices that had to be made were enormous. But then so would a Good Samaritan assume responsibility for that violinist; so would Henry Fonda, if he is a Good Samaritan, fly in from the West Coast and assume responsibility for me.

8. My argument will be found unsatisfactory on two counts by many of those who want to regard abortion as morally permissible. First, while I do argue that abortion is not impermissible, I do not argue that it is always permissible. There may well be cases in which carrying the child to term requires only Minimally Decent Samaritanism of the mother, and this is a standard we must not fall below. I am inclined to think it a merit of my account precisely that it does *not* give a general yes or a general no. It allows for and supports our sense that, for example, a sick and desperately frightened fourteen-year-old schoolgirl, pregnant due to rape, may *of course* choose abortion, and that any law which rules this out is an insane law. And it also allows for and supports our sense that in other cases resort to abortion is even positively indecent. It would be indecent in the woman to request an abortion, and

indecent in a doctor to perform it, if she is in her seventh month, and wants the abortion just to avoid the nuisance of postponing a trip abroad. The very fact that the arguments I have been drawing attention to treat all cases of abortion, or even all cases of abortion in which the mother's life is not at stake, as morally on a par ought to have made them suspect at the outset.

Secondly, while I am arguing for the permissibility of abortion in some cases, I am not arguing for the right to secure the death of the unborn child. It is easy to confuse these two things in that up to a certain point in the life of the fetus it is not able to survive outside the mother's body; hence removing it from her body guarantees its death. But they are importantly different. I have argued that you are not morally required to spend nine months in bed, sustaining the life of that violinist; but to say this is by no means to say that if, when you unplug yourself, there is a miracle and he survives, you then have a right to turn round and slit his throat. You may detach yourself even if this costs him his life; you have no right to be guaranteed his death, by some other means, if unplugging yourself does not kill him. There are some people who will feel dissatisfied by this feature of my argument. A woman may be utterly devastated by the thought of a child, a bit of herself, put out for adoption and never seen or heard of again. She may therefore want not merely that the child be detached from her, but more, that it die. Some opponents of abortion are inclined to regard this as beneath contempt—thereby showing insensitivity to what is surely a powerful source of despair. All the same, I agree that the desire for the child's death is not one which anybody may gratify, should it turn out to be possible to detach the child alive.

At this place, however, it should be remembered that we have only been pretending throughout that the fetus is a human being from the moment of conception. A very early abortion is surely not the killing of a person, and so is not dealt with by anything I have said here.

54

Abortion and the Conflict of Claims

JOEL FEINBERG

For biographical information about Joel Feinberg, see reading 1. This selection first appeared in Tom Regan, ed., Matters of Life and Death.

In the selection, Feinberg assumes, for purposes of argument, that the fetus is a person with a right (or "claim") to life. His question is whether its claim is outweighed by that of a woman who wants an abortion. His answer is that women have no right that always outweighs the fetus's right to life.

To support his answer, Feinberg examines a number of rights that women are said to possess. These include property rights over their own bodies, rights to self-defense, and rights to bodily autonomy. In each case, Feinberg argues that the right is more complicated than many have realized. For example, when we exercise a right of self-defense, it matters whether the person who poses the threat is innocent or morally culpable. When we exercise our right to bodily autonomy, it matters whether we are responsible for the plight of the person whose claims require that our autonomy be restricted. These complexities lead Feinberg to conclude that if the fetus is a person, the permissibility of aborting it depends on various contextual factors. As an exercise, you may wish to compare this view with Judith Thomson's conclusion in reading 53.

The problem of the status of the fetus is the first and perhaps the most difficult of the questions that must be settled before we can come to a considered view about the moral justifiability of abortion, but its solution does not necessarily resolve all moral perplexities about abortion. Even if we were to grant that the fetus is a moral person and thus has a valid claim to life, it would not follow that abortion is always wrong. For there are other moral persons, in addition to the fetus, whose interests are involved. The woman in whose uterus the fetus abides, in particular, has needs and interests that may well conflict with bringing the fetus to term. Do any of these needs and interests of the woman provide grounds for her having a genuine claim to an abortion and, if they do, which of the two conflicting claims—the woman's claim to an abortion or the fetus's claim to life—ought to be respected if they happen to conflict? This is the second major moral question that needs to be examined with all the care we can muster. To do this, one very important assumption must be made—namely, that the fetus is a moral person and so has a valid claim to life. As we have seen in the previous section, this assumption might very well be unfounded and is unfounded in fact if we accept what appears to be the most reasonable criterion for moral personhood—namely, the actual-possession criterion. For purposes of the present section, however, we shall assume that the fetus is a moral person; this will enable us to investigate whose claim, the fetus's or the woman's, ought to be honored if both have genuine but conflicting claims.

FORMULATION OF THE "RIGHT TO AN ABORTION"

The right to an abortion that is often claimed on behalf of all women is a *discretionary right* to be exercised or not, on a given occasion, as the woman sees fit. For that reason it is sometimes called a "right to choose." If a pregnant woman has such a right, then it is up to her, and her alone, whether to bear the child or to have it aborted. She is at liberty to bear it if she chooses and at liberty to have it aborted if she chooses. She has no duty to bear it, but neither can she have a duty, imposed from without, to abort it. In respect to the fetus, her choice is sovereign. Correlated with this liberty is a duty of others not to interfere with its exercise and not to withhold the necessary means for its exercise. These duties are owed to her if she has a discretionary right to abortion, and she can claim their discharge as her due.

As a discretionary right, a right to an abortion would resemble the "right to liberty," or the right to move about or travel as one wishes. One is under no obligation to leave or stay home or to go to one destination rather than another, so that it is one's own choice that determines one's movements. But the right to move about at will, like other discretionary rights, is subject to limits. One person's liberty of movement, for example, comes to an end at the boundary of another person's property. The discretionary right to an abortion may be limited in similar ways, so that the statement of a specific right of a particular woman in a definite set of concrete circumstances may need to be qualified by various exceptive clauses—for example, ". . . may choose to have an abortion *except* when the fetus is viable." Which exceptive clauses, if any, must be appended to the formulation of the right to an abortion depends on what the basis of this discretionary right is thought to be. For example, if a woman is thought to have a right to an abortion because she has a right to property *and* because the fetus is said to be her property, then the only exceptions there could be to exercising the right to an abortion would be those that restrict the disposing of one's property. What we must realize, then, is that the alleged right to an abortion cannot be understood in a vacuum; it is a right that can only be understood by reference to the other, more fundamental rights from which it has often been claimed to be derived. Three of these rights and their possible association with the right to an abortion deserve our closest scrutiny. These are (1) the previously mentioned property rights, (2) the right to self-defense, and (3) the right to bodily autonomy. We shall consider each in its turn.

POSSIBLE GROUNDS FOR THE WOMAN'S RIGHT

Property Rights over One's Body

Within very wide limits any person has a right to control the uses of his or her own body. With only rare exceptions, surgeons are required to secure the consent of the patient before operating because the body to be cut open, after all, is the patient's own, and he or she has the chief interest in it, and should therefore have the chief "say" over what is done to it. If we think of a fetus as literally a "part" of a woman's body in the same sense as, say, an organ, or as a mere growth attached to a part of the body on the model of a tumor or a wart, then it would seem to follow that the woman may choose to have it removed if she wishes just as she may refuse to have it removed if she prefers. It is highly implausible, however, to think of a human fetus, even if it does fall short of moral personhood, as no more than a temporary organ or a parasitic growth. A fetus is not a constituent organ of the mother, like her vermiform appendix, but rather an independent entity temporarily growing inside the mother.

It would be still less plausible to derive a maternal right to an abortion from a characterization of the fetus as the *property* of its mother and thus in the same category as the mother's wristwatch, clothing, or jewelry. One may abandon or destroy one's personal property if one wishes; one's entitlement to do those things is one of the "property rights" that define ownership. But one would think that the father would have equal or near-equal rights of disposal if the fetus were "property." It is not in his body, to be sure, but he contributed as much genetically to its existence as did the mother and might therefore make just as strong (or just as weak) a claim to ownership over it. But neither claim would make very good conceptual sense. If fetuses were property, we would find nothing odd in the notion that they can be bought and sold, rented out, leased, used as collateral on loans, and so on. But no one has ever seriously entertained such suggestions. Finally, we must remember the methodological assumption that we shall make throughout this section, at least for the sake of the argument, that the fetus is a full moral person, with a right to life like yours and mine. On this assumption it would probably be contradictory to think of the fetus as *anyone's* property, especially if property rights include what we might call "the right of disposal"—to abandon or destroy as one chooses.

It is more plausible at first sight to claim that the pregnant woman owns not the fetus but the body in which she shelters the fetus. On this analogy, she owns her body (and particularly her womb) in roughly the way an innkeeper owns a hotel or a homeowner her house and garden. These analogies, however, are also defective. To begin with, it is somewhat paradoxical to think of the relation between a person and her body as similar to that of ownership. Is it possible to sell or rent or lease one's body without selling, renting, or leasing oneself? If one's body were one's property the answer would be affirmative, but in fact one's relationship to one's own body is much more intimate than the ownership model suggests. More important for our present purposes, the legal analogies to the right of innkeepers and householders will not bear scrutiny. One cannot conceive of what it would be like for a fetus to enter into a contract with a woman for the use of her womb for nine months or to fall in arrears in its payments and thus forfeit its right of occupancy. Surely that cannot be the most apt analogy on which to base the woman's abortion rights! Besides, whatever this, that, or the other legal statute may say about the matter, one is not *morally* entitled, in virtue of one's property rights, to expel a weak and helpless person from one's shelter when that is tantamount to consigning the person to a certain death, and surely one is not entitled to shoot and kill a trespasser who will not, or cannot, leave one's property. In no department of human life does the vindication of property rights justify homicide. The maternal right to an abortion, therefore, cannot be founded on the more basic right to property.

Self-Defense and Proportionality

Except for the most extreme pacifists, moralists agree that killing can be justified if done in self-defense. If, for example, one man (A) is attacked with a lethal weapon by another (B), we think that A has a right to defend himself against B's attack. Sometimes, in fact, we think that A would be justified in killing B if this were the only way for A to defend himself. Now, some of those who urge the maternal right to an abortion believe that this right is associated with the more basic right to self-defense. There are many difficulties standing in the way to rational acceptance of this view. In particular, the innocence and the nonaggressive nature of the fetus need our special attention. We shall turn to these matters shortly. First, though, it is important to realize what reasons would not count as morally good reasons for an abortion if the right to an abortion were supposed to be founded on the more basic right of self-defense.

All parties to the abortion dispute must agree that many women can be harmed if they are required to bring an unwanted fetus to term. Unwanted sexual intercourse imposed on a woman by a rapist can inflict on its victim severe psychological trauma of a sort deemed so serious by the law that a woman is entitled under some rules to use deadly force if necessary to prevent it. Similarly, an unwanted pregnancy in some circumstances can inflict severe psychological injury on a woman who is forced to carry her child to birth. There are various familiar examples of such harm. To borrow an example from Judith Thomson, a philosophy professor at the Massachusetts Institute of Technology: A terrified fourteen-year-old high schoolgirl whose pregnancy has been caused by rape has already suffered one severe trauma. If she is now required, over her protests, to carry the child to full term despite her fear, anguish, deep depression, and fancied public mortification, the harmful ramifications may be multiplied a hundredfold. The forty-year-old housewife who has exhausted herself raising a large family in unfavorable economic circumstances while dependent upon an unreliable and unsympathetic husband may find herself, to her horror, pregnant again and rightly feel that if she is forced to give birth to another child, she will forfeit her last opportunity to escape the intolerably squalid conditions of her life. A man must be morally blind not to acknowledge the severe harms that enforced continuance of unwanted pregnancies can inflict on women. An unwanted child need not literally cost the woman her life, but it can effectively ruin her life from her point of view, and it is a useful moral exercise for men to put themselves imaginatively in the woman's place to share that point of view.

At this stage in the argument the antiabortionist has a ready rejoinder. A woman need not keep her child, assume the responsibilities of raising it to adulthood, and forfeit her opportunities for self-fulfillment, he might reply, simply because she forgoes an abortion. She can always put the child up for adoption and be assured in the process that it will find loving foster parents who will give it a good upbringing. All she really has to suffer, the rejoinder concludes, is nine months of minor physical inconvenience. This is an argument that comes easily to the lips of men, but it betrays the grossest sort of masculine insensitivity. In the first place, it is not always true that a woman can have her baby adopted. If she is married, that transaction may require the consent of her husband, and the consent might not be forthcoming. But waiving that point, the possibility of adoption does not give much comfort to the unhappily pregnant woman, for it imposes on her a cruel dilemma and an anguish that far surpasses "minor inconvenience." In effect, she has two choices, both of which are intolerable to her. She can carry the child to term and keep it, thus incurring the very consequences that make her unwilling to remain pregnant, *or* she can nourish the fetus to full size, go into labor, give birth to her baby, and then have it rudely wrenched away, never to be seen by her again. Let moralistic males imagine what an emotional jolt that must be!

Still, on the scale of harms, mere traumas and frustrations are not exactly equal to death. Few women would choose their own deaths in preference to the harms that may come from producing children. According to a common interpretation of the self-defense rule, however, the harm to be averted by a violent act in self-defense need not be identical in severity to that which is inflicted upon one's assailant but only somehow "proportional" to it. Both our prevailing morality and our legal traditions permit the use of lethal force to prevent harms that are less serious than death, so it is plausible to assume that the rule of "proportionality" can be satisfied by something less than equality of harms. But how much less? The late Jane English, a philosopher from the University of North Carolina, offers an answer that, though vague, is in accordance with the moral sentiments of most people when they think of situations other than that involving abortion:

> How severe an injury may you inflict in self-defense? In part this depends upon the severity of the injury to be avoided: you may not shoot someone merely to avoid having your clothes torn. This might lead one to the mistaken conclusion

that the defense may only equal the threatened injury in severity; that to avoid death you may kill, but to avoid a black eye you may only inflict a black eye or the equivalent. Rather our laws and customs seem to say that you may create an injury *somewhat but not enormously greater* than the injury to be avoided. To fend off an attack whose outcome would be as serious as rape, a severe beating, or the loss of a finger, you may shoot; to avoid having your clothes torn, you may blacken an eye.[1] [Emphasis added.]

Applying English's answer to the abortion case, and assuming that both the fetus and the woman have legitimate claims, we derive the conclusion that killing the "fetal person" would not be justified when it is done merely to prevent relatively trivial harms to the mother's interests. Not *all* cases of abortion, therefore, can morally be justified, even if there is a maternal right to abortion derived from the more basic right to self-defense.

Self-Defense: The Problem of the Innocent Aggressor

Suppose, however, that the harms that will probably be caused to the mother if the fetus is brought to term are not trivial but serious. Here we have a case where the mother's right to have her important interests respected clashes with the assumed right to life of the fetus. In these circumstances, don't the mother's claims outweigh the fetus's? Doesn't self-defense in these circumstances justify abortion?

There is a serious, previously undiscussed difficulty that calls out for attention. Consider a case where someone aggressively attacks another. The reason we think that, to use English's expression, we may in self-defense create a "somewhat but not enormously greater injury" than would have been caused by the aggressor is because we think of the aggressor as the party who is morally at fault. If he had not launched the aggression in the first place, there should have been no occasion for the use of force. Since the whole episode was the aggressor's fault, his interests should not count for as much as those of the innocent victim. It is a shame that anybody has to be seriously hurt, but if it comes down to an inescapable choice between the innocent party suffering a serious harm or the culpable party suffering a still more serious harm, then the latter is the lesser of the two evils. Aggressors of course, for all their guilt, remain human beings, and consequently they do not forfeit all their human rights in launching an attack. We still may not kill them to prevent them from stealing $10. But their culpability does cost them their right to equal consideration; we may kill them to prevent them from causing serious harm.

But now suppose that the party who threatens us, even though he is the aggressor who initiates the whole episode, is not morally at fault. Suppose the person cannot act otherwise in the circumstances and thus cannot justly be held morally responsible. For example, he was temporarily (or permanently) insane, or it was a case of mistaken identity (he mistook you for a former

---

[1] Jane English, "Abortion and the Concept of a Person," *Canadian Journal of Philosophy* 5 (1975), p. 242.

Gestapo agent to whom you bear a striking resemblance), or someone had drugged the person's breakfast cereal and his behavior was influenced by the drug. George Fletcher, a Columbia law professor, provides a vivid illustration of the problem in what he calls "the case of the psychotic aggressor":

> Imagine that your companion in an elevator goes berserk and attacks you with a knife. There is no escape: the only way to avoid serious bodily harm or even death is to kill him. The assailant acts purposively in the sense that his means further his aggressive end . . . [but] he does act in a frenzy or a fit . . . [and] it is clear that his conduct is non-responsible. If he were brought to trial for his attack, he would have a valid defense of insanity.[2]

The general problem, as lawyers would put it, is "whether self-defense applies against an excused but unjustified aggression."[3] To *justify* an act is to show that it was the right thing to do in the circumstances; to *excuse* an act is to show that although it was unjustified, the actor didn't mean it or couldn't help it, that it was not, properly speaking, his doing at all. In the "excused but unjustified aggression" we have a more plausible model for the application of self-defense to the problem of abortion, for the *fetus is surely innocent* (not because of insanity but because of immaturity, and because *it* did not choose to threaten its mother—it did not "ask to be born").

Upon reflection, most of us would agree, I think, that one would be justified in killing even an innocent aggressor if that seemed necessary to save one's own life or to prevent one from suffering serious bodily injury. Surely we would not judge harshly the slightly built lady who shoots the armed stranger who goes berserk in the elevator. If we were in her shoes, we too would protect ourselves at all costs to the assailant, just as we would against wild animals, runaway trucks, or impersonal forces of nature. But while the berserk assailant, as well as those persons mentioned in the last paragraph, all are innocent— are not *morally* responsible for what they do—they are *all* assailants, and in this respect they differ in a quite fundamental respect from the fetus. For the fetus is not only innocent but also not an aggressor. *It* didn't start the trouble in any fashion. Thus, it would seem that while we are justified in killing an innocent assailant if this is the only way to prevent him from killing us, it does not follow that we are similarly justified in killing a fetal person, since, unlike the innocent aggressor, the fetus is not an aggressor at all.

Judith Thomson has challenged this argument. She presents the following farfetched but coherent hypothetical example:

> Aggressor is driving his tank at you. But he has taken care to arrange that a baby is strapped to the front of the tank so that if you use your anti-tank gun, you will not only kill Aggressor, you will kill the baby. Now Aggressor, admittedly, is in the process of trying to kill you; but that baby isn't. Yet you can presumably

---

2 George Fletcher, "Proportionality and the Psychotic Aggressor: A Vignette in the Comparative Criminal Law Theory," *Israel Law Review* 8 (1973), p. 376.

3 Fletcher, loc. cit.

go ahead and use the gun, even though this involves killing the baby as well as Aggressor.[4]

The baby in this example is not only "innocent" but also the "innocent shield of a threat."[5] Still it is hard to quarrel with Thomson's judgment that you *may* (not that you *should*) take the baby's life if necessary to save your own, that it is morally permissible, even if it is not morally obligatory, to do so. After all, you are (by hypothesis) perfectly innocent too. This example makes a better analogy to the abortion situation than any we have considered thus far, but there are still significant dissimilarities. Unless the fetus is the product of rape, it cannot conceivably be the shield of some third-party aggressor. There is simply no interpersonal "aggression" involved at all in the normal pregnancy. There may nevertheless be a genuine *threat* to the well-being of the mother, and if that threat is to her very life, then perhaps she does have a right to kill it, if necessary, in self-defense. At any rate, if the threatened victim in Thomson's tank example is justified in killing the innocent shield, then the pregnant woman threatened with similar harm is similarly entitled. But all that this would establish is that abortion is justified only if it is probably required to save the mother's life. So not only could we not use the self-defense argument to justify abortion for trivial reasons, as was argued earlier; it appears that the only reason that authorizes its use is the one that cites the fact that the mother will probably die if the fetus is not aborted.

Bodily Autonomy: The Example of the Plugged-in Violinist

The trouble with the use of self-defense as a model for abortion rights is that none of the examples of self-defense makes an *exact* analogy to the abortion situation. The examples that come closest to providing models for justified abortion are the "innocent aggressor cases" and these would apply, as we have seen, only to abortions that are necessary to prevent death to the mother. Even these examples do not fit the abortion case exactly, since the fetus is in no way itself an aggressor, culpable or innocent, but is at most a "nonaggressive, nonculpable threat," in some respects like an innocent shield.[6] And the more we change the examples to bring them closer to the situation of the fetus, the

---

4 Judith Jarvis Thomson, "Self-Defense and Rights," The Lindley Lecture, 1976 (Lawrence, KS: University of Kansas Philosophy Department, 1977).

5 The term comes from Robert Nozick, *Anarchy, State, and Utopia* (New York: Basic Books, 1974), p. 35.

6 Even when self-defense is acceptable as a defense to homicide in the case of forced killings of nonaggressive innocents, that may be because it is understood in those cases to be an excuse or a mitigation rather than a justification. If a criminal terrorist from a fortified position throws a bomb at my feet and I can escape its explosion only by quickly throwing it in the direction of a baby buggy whose infant occupant is enjoying a nap, perhaps I can be *excused* for saving my life by taking the baby's, perhaps the duress under which I acted mitigates my guilt, perhaps the law ought not to be too severe with me. But it is not convincing to argue that I was entirely justified in what I did because I was acting in self-defense. But the problem is a difficult one, and the case may be borderline.

less clear is their resemblance to the central models of self-defense. Once we are allowed to protect ourselves (and especially to protect interests less weighty than self-preservation) at the expense of nonaggressive innocents, it becomes difficult to distinguish the latter from innocent bystanders whom we kill as means to our own good, and that, in turn, begins to look like unvarnished murder. The killing of an innocent person simply because his continued existence in the circumstances would make the killer's life miserable is a homicide that cannot be justified. It is not self-defense to kill your boss because he makes your work life intolerable and you are unable to find another job, or to kill your spouse because he or she nags you to the point of extreme misery, and will not agree to a divorce,[7] or (closer to the point) to kill your shipwrecked fellow passenger in the lifeboat because there are provisions sufficient for only one to survive and he claims half of them, or to kill your innocent rival for a position or a prize because you can win only if he is out of the running. In all these cases the victim is either innocent or relatively innocent and in no way a direct aggressor.

Partly because of deficiencies in the hypothetical examples of self-defense, Thomson invented a different sort of example intended at once to be a much closer analogy to the abortion situation and also such that the killing can be seen to be morally justified for reasons less compelling than defense of the killer's very life:

> You wake up in the morning and find yourself back to back in bed with an unconscious violinist. A famous unconscious violinist. He has been found to have a fatal kidney ailment, and the Society of Music Lovers has canvassed all the available medical records and found that you alone have the right blood type to help. They have therefore kidnapped you, and last night the violinist's circulatory system was plugged into yours, so that your kidneys can be used to extract poisons from his blood as well as your own. The director of the hospital now tells you, "Look, we're sorry the Society of Music Lovers did this to you—we would never have permitted it if we had known. But still they did it, and the violinist now is plugged into you. To unplug you would be to kill him. But never mind, it's only for nine months. By then he will have recovered from his ailment, and can safely be unplugged from you." Is it morally incumbent on you to accede to this situation? No doubt it would be very nice of you if you did, a great kindness. But do you have to accede to it? . . . What if the director . . . says . . . "Granted you have a right to decide what happens in and to your body, but a person's right to life outweighs your right to decide what happens in and to your body. So you cannot . . . be unplugged from him." I imagine you would regard this as outrageous. . . .[8]

Suppose that you defy the director on your own, and exercise your control over your own body by unplugging the unconscious violinist, thereby causing

7 See Ludwig Lewisohn's remarkable novel, *The Case of Mr. Crump* (New York: Farrar, Straus, 1947).

8 Judith Jarvis Thomson, "A Defense of Abortion," *Philosophy and Public Affairs* 1 (1971), pp. 48–49.

his death. This would be to kill in defense of an interest far less important than self-preservation or the prevention of serious injury to oneself. And it would be to kill an innocent nonaggressor, indeed a victim who remains unconscious throughout the entire period during which he is a threat. We have, therefore, an example which—if it works—offers far more encouragement to the proabortion position than the model of self-defense does. We must now pose two questions: (1) Would you in fact be morally justified in unplugging the violinist? and (2) How close an analogy does this bizarre example make to the abortion situation?

There is no way to argue conclusively that unplugging the violinist would be morally justified. Thomson can only make the picture as vividly persuasive as possible and then appeal to her reader's intuitions. It is not an easy case, and neither an affirmative nor a negative judgment will seem self-evident to everyone. Still the verdict for justification seems as strong as in some of the other examples of killing innocent threats, and some additional considerations can be brought to bear in its support. There is, after all, a clear "intuition" in support of a basic right "to decide what happens in and to one's own body," even though the limits of that right are lost in a fog of controversy. So unless there is some stronger competing claim, anyone has a right to refuse to consent to surgery or to enforced attachment to a machine. Or indeed to an unconscious violinist. But what of the competing claim in this example, the violinist's right to life? That is another basic right that is vague around the edges.

In its noncontroversial core, the right to life is a right not to be killed directly (except under very special circumstances) and to be rescued from impending death whenever this can be done without unreasonable sacrifice. But as Warren has pointed out, one person's right to life does not impose a correlative duty on another person to do "whatever is necessary to keep him alive."[9] And though we all have general duties to come to the assistance of strangers in peril, we cannot be forced to make enormous sacrifices or to run unreasonably high risks to keep people alive when we stand in no special relationship to them, like "father" or "lifeguard." The wife of the violinist perhaps would have a duty to stay plugged to him (if that would help) for nine months; but the random stranger has no such duty at all. So there is good reason to grant Thomson her claim that a stranger would have a right to unplug the violinist from herself.

But how close an analogy after all is this to the normal case of pregnancy? Several differences come immediately to mind. In the normal case of pregnancy, the woman is not confined to her bed for nine months but can continue to work and function efficiently in the world until the final trimester at least. This difference, however, is of doubtful significance, since Thomson's argument is not based on a right to the protection of one's interest in efficient mobility but

[9] Mary Anne Warren, "On the Moral and Legal Status of Abortion," *The Monist* 57 (1973), pp. 43–61. Reprinted in J. Feinberg and H. Gross (eds.), *Liberty: Selected Readings*, pp. 133–143. The quotation is from the latter source, p. 135.

rather on a right to *decide* on the uses of one's own body, which is quite another thing. Another difference is that the mother and her fetus are not exactly "random strangers" in the same sense that the woman and the violinist are. Again the relationship between the mother and fetus seems to be in a class by itself. If the person who needs to use the woman's body for nine months in order to survive is her mother, father, sister, brother, son, daughter, or close friend, then the relationship would seem close enough to establish a special obligation in the woman to permit that use. If the needy person is a total stranger, then that obligation is missing. The fetus no doubt stands somewhere between these two extremes, but it is at least as close to the "special relationship" end of the spectrum as to the "total stranger" end.

The most important difference, however, between the violinist case and the normal pregnancy is that in the former the woman had absolutely nothing to do with creating the situation from which she wishes to escape. She bears no responsibility whatever for being in a state of "plugged-in-ness" with the violinist. As many commentators have pointed out, this makes Thomson's analogy fit at most one very special class of pregnancies, namely those imposed upon a woman entirely against her will, as in rape. In the "normal case" of pregnancy, the voluntary action of the woman herself (knowingly consenting to sexual intercourse) has something to do with her becoming pregnant. So once again, we find that a proabortion argument fails to establish an *unrestricted* moral right to abortion. Just as self-defense justifies abortion at most in the case where it is necessary to save the mother's life, the Thomson defense justifies abortion only when the woman shares no responsibility for her pregnancy, as, for example, when it has been caused by rape (force or fraud).

Voluntariness and Responsibility

If we continue the line of reasoning suggested by our criticism of the violinist example, we will soon reach a general principle, namely, that whether or not a woman has a duty to continue her pregnancy depends, at least in part, on how responsible she is for being pregnant in the first place, that is, on the extent to which her pregnancy is the consequence of her own voluntary actions. This formula, in turn, seems to be an application of a still more general moral principle, one that imposes duties on one party to rescue or support another, even a stranger and even when that requires great personal sacrifice or risk, to the degree that the first party, through his own voluntary actions or omissions, was responsible for the second party's dependence on him. A late-arriving bystander at the seaside has no duty to risk life or limb to save a drowning swimmer. If, however, the swimmer is in danger only because the bystander erroneously informed him that there was no danger, then the bystander has a duty to make some effort at rescue (though not a suicidal one), dangerous as it may be. If the swimmer is in the water only because the "bystander" has pushed him out of a boat, however, then the bystander has a duty to attempt rescue at any cost to personal safety,[10] since the bystander's own voluntary action was the whole cause of the swimmer's plight.

Since the voluntariness of an action or omission is a matter of degree, so is the responsibility that stems from it, as is the stringency of the duty that derives from that responsibility. The duty to continue a pregnancy, then, will be stronger (other things being equal) in the case where the pregnancy was entered into in a fully voluntary way than it will be in the case that fits the violinist model, where the pregnancy is totally involuntary. But in between these two extremes is a whole range of cases where moral judgments are more difficult to make. We can sketch the whole spectrum as follows:

1. Pregnancy caused by rape (totally involuntary).
2. Pregnancy caused by contraceptive failure, where the fault is entirely that of the manufacturer or pharmaceutical company.
3. Pregnancy caused by contraceptive failure within the advertised 1 percent margin of error (no one's fault).
4. Pregnancy caused by the negligence of the woman (or the man, or both). They are careless in the use of the contraceptive or else fail to use it at all, being unaware of a large risk that they *ought* to have been aware of.
5. Pregnancy caused by the recklessness of the woman (or the man, or both). They think of the risk but get swept along by passion and consciously disregard it.
6. Pregnancy caused by intercourse between partners who are genuinely indifferent at the time whether or not pregnancy results.
7. Pregnancy caused by the deliberate decision of the parties to produce it (completely, voluntary).

There would be a somewhat hollow ring to the claim in case 7 that one has no obligation to continue one's bodily support for a moral person whose dependence on that support one has deliberately caused. That would be like denying that one has a duty to save the drowning swimmer that one has just pushed out of the boat. The case for cessation of bodily support is hardly any stronger in 6 and 5 than in 7. Perhaps it is misleading to say of the negligence case (4) that the pregnancy is only partially involuntary, or involuntary "to a degree," since the parents did not *intentionally* produce or run the risk of producing a fetus. But there is no need to haggle over that terminological question. Whether wholly or partially involuntary, the actions of the parents in the circumstances were faulty and the pregnancy resulted from the fault (negligence), so they are to a substantial degree responsible (to blame) for it. It was within their power to be more careful or knowledgeable, and yet they were careless or avoidably ignorant. So they cannot plead, in the manner of the lady plugged to the violinist, that they had no control over their condition whatever. In failing to exercise due care, they were doing something else and doing *it* "to a degree voluntarily." In these cases—4, 5, 6, and 7—the woman

---

[10] The examples are Sissela Bok's. See her article "Ethical Problems of Abortion," *Hastings Center Studies* 2 (1974), p. 35.

and her partner are therefore responsible for the pregnancy, and on the analogy with the case of the drowning swimmer who was pushed from the boat, they have a duty not to kill the fetus or permit it to die.

Cases 2 and 3 are more perplexing. In case 2, where the fault was entirely that of the manufacturer, the woman is no more responsible for being pregnant than in case 1 where she is the unwilling victim of a rape. In neither case did she choose to become pregnant. In neither case was she reckless or negligent in respect to the possibility of becoming pregnant. So if she has no duty to continue to provide bodily support for the dependent fetus in the rape case, then equally she has no duty in the other case. To be sure, there is always *some* risk of pregnancy whenever there is intercourse, no matter how careful the partners are. There may be only 1 chance in 10,000 that a contraceptive pill has an undetectable flaw, but there is no chance whatever of pregnancy without intercourse. The woman in case 2, then, would seem to have *some* responsibility, even if vanishingly small, for her pregnancy. She could have been even more careful by abstaining from sex altogether. But notice that much the same sort of thing could be said of the rape victim. By staying home in a locked building patrolled round the clock by armed guards, she could have reduced the chances of bodily assault from, say, 1 in 50,000 to effectively nil. By staying off the dangerous streets, she would have been much more careful than she was in respect to the risk of rape. But surely that does not entitle us to say that she was "partially responsible" for the rape that made her pregnant. When a person takes all the precautions that she can *reasonably* be expected to take against a certain outcome, then that outcome cannot fairly be described as her responsibility. So in case 2, where the negligence of the manufacturer of the contraceptive is the cause of the pregnancy, the woman cannot be held responsible for her condition, and that ground for ascribing to her a duty not to abort is not present.

Case 3 brings us very close to the borderline. The couple in this example do not choose to have a baby and, indeed, they take strong precautions against pregnancy. Still they know that there is a 1 percent danger and they deliberately choose to run that risk anyway. As a result, a woman becomes pregnant against her will. Does she then have a right to abandon to a certain death a newly formed moral person who is even less responsible for his dependence on her than she is? When one looks at the problem in this way from the perspective of the fetus to whom we have suppositively ascribed full moral rights, it becomes doubtful that the pregnant woman's very minimal responsibility for her plight can permit her to abandon a being who has no responsibility for it whatever. She ran a very small risk, but the fetus ran no risk at all. Nevertheless, this is a borderline case for the following reason. If we extend to this case the rule we applied to case 2, then we might be entitled to say that the woman is no more responsible than the fetus for the pregnancy. To reach that conclusion we have to judge the 1 percent chance of pregnancy to be a *reasonable* risk for a woman to run in the circumstances. That appraisal itself is a disguised moral judgment of pivotal importance, and yet it is very difficult to know how to go about establishing it. Nevertheless, *if* it is correct, then the woman is, for all practical purposes, relieved of her responsibility for the pregnancy just as she is in cases 1 and 2, and in that event the fetus's "right to life" does not entail a duty on her part to make extreme sacrifices.

SUMMARY AND CONCLUSION

Assuming that the fetus is a moral person, under what conditions, if any, is abortion justifiable homicide? If the woman's right to an abortion is derived from her right to own property in her body (which is not very plausible), then abortion is never justifiable homicide. Property rights simply can't support that much moral weight. If the right is derived from self-defense, then it justifies abortion at most when necessary to save the woman from death. That is because the fetus, while sometimes a threat to the interests of the woman, is an innocent and (in a sense) nonaggressive threat. The doctrine of proportionality, which permits a person to use a degree of force in self-defense that is likely to cause the assailant harm greater (within reasonable limits) than the harm the assailant would otherwise cause the victim, has application only to the case where the assailant is culpable. One can kill an "innocent threat" in order to save one's life but not to save one's pocketbook. The right of bodily autonomy (to decide what is to be done in and to one's own body) is a much solider base for the right to abortion than either the right to property or the right to self-defense, since it permits one to kill innocent persons by depriving them of one's "life-support system," even when they are threats to interests substantially less important than self-preservation. But this justification is probably available at most to victims of rape, or contraceptive failure caused by the negligence of other parties, to the risk of which the woman has not consented. That narrow restriction on the use of this defense stems from the requirement, internal to it, that the woman be in no way responsible for her pregnancy.

It does not follow automatically that because the victim of a homicide was "innocent," the killing cannot have been justified. But abortion can plausibly be construed as justifiable homicide only on the basis of inexact analogies, and then only (1) to save the mother from the most extreme harm or else (2) to save the mother from a lesser harm when the pregnancy was the result of the wrongful acts of others for which the woman had no responsibility. Another possibility that was only suggested here is (3) when it can be claimed for a defective or diseased fetus that it has a right *not* to be born. These narrow restrictions on the right of the woman to an abortion will not satisfy many people in the proabortion camp. But if the assumption of the moral personhood of the fetus is false, as was argued in the first part of this essay, then the woman's right to bodily autonomy will normally prevail, and abortions at all but the later stages, at least, and for the most common reasons, at least, are morally permissible.

55

War and Massacre[1]

THOMAS NAGEL

For biographical information on Thomas Nagel, see reading 20. This essay first appeared in Philosophy and Public Affairs *(Winter 1972).*

Nagel's topic here is the rules of war, which have been widely taken to forbid such acts as the use of poison gas, the bombing of population centers, and attacks on medical personnel. If killing soldiers in other ways is permitted, what justifies these prohibitions? For utilitarians, the answer can lie only in the proscribed actions' consequences. But Nagel argues that the answer goes deeper. Even in the conduct of hostilities, he argues, some acts are absolutely forbidden.

What distinguishes acceptable from unacceptable hostile behavior? According to Nagel, even objects of hostility must be treated as persons. This means, first, that violence must be directed only against those who actually pose a threat. Attacks on noncombatants are unjustified even if tactically effective. And, second, even attacks on combatants must be directed at the threat they pose. Weapons that cause more pain or damage than necessary—napalm, dum-dum bullets, poison—are not sufficiently relevant to be permissible.

Two further aspects of Nagel's position warrant mention. First, he observes that we sometimes cannot avoid causing death to one or another innocent person. To square this with the prohibitions he is discussing, Nagel suggests that "what absolutism forbids is doing *certain things to people, rather than bringing about certain results." Second, Nagel notes that the costs of observing the prohibitions are sometimes unacceptably high. According to some theories, such as that of W. D. Ross (reading 29), the duty to avoid unacceptable costs may override the prohibitions. But Nagel sees another possibility. In these cases, he suggests, there may simply be* no right answer. *We may be guilty whatever* we *do.*

From the apathetic reaction to atrocities committed in Vietnam by the United States and its allies, one may conclude that moral restrictions in the conduct of war command almost as little sympathy among the general public as they do among those charged with the formation of U.S. military policy.

1 This paper grew out of discussions at the Society for Ethical and Legal Philosophy, and I am indebted to my fellow members for their help.

Even when restrictions on the conduct of warfare are defended, it is usually on legal grounds alone: their moral basis is often poorly understood. I wish to argue that certain restrictions are neither arbitrary nor merely conventional, and that their validity does not depend simply on their usefulness. There is, in other words, a moral basis for the rules of war, even though the conventions now officially in force are far from giving it perfect expression.

I

No elaborate moral theory is required to account for what is wrong in cases like the Mylai massacre, since it did not serve, and was not intended to serve, any strategic purpose. Moreover, if the participation of the United States in the Indo-Chinese war is entirely wrong to begin with, then that engagement is incapable of providing a justification for *any* measures taken in its pursuit—not only for the measures which are atrocities in every war, however just its aims.

But this war has revealed attitudes of a more general kind, that influenced the conduct of earlier wars as well. After it has ended, we shall still be faced with the problem of how warfare may be conducted, and the attitudes that have resulted in the specific conduct of this war will not have disappeared. Moreover, similar problems can arise in wars or rebellions fought for very different reasons, and against very different opponents. It is not easy to keep a firm grip on the idea of what is not permissible in warfare, because while some military actions are obvious atrocities, other cases are more difficult to assess, and the general principles underlying these judgments remain obscure. Such obscurity can lead to the abandonment of sound intuitions in favor of criteria whose rationale may be more obvious. If such a tendency is to be resisted, it will require a better understanding of the restrictions than we now have.

I propose to discuss the most general moral problem raised by the conduct of warfare: the problem of means and ends. In one view, there are limits on what may be done even in the service of an end worth pursuing—and even when adherence to the restriction may be very costly. A person who acknowledges the force of such restrictions can find himself in acute moral dilemmas. He may believe, for example, that by torturing a prisoner he can obtain information necessary to prevent a disaster, or that by obliterating one village with bombs he can halt a campaign of terrorism. If he believes that the gains from a certain measure will clearly outweigh its costs, yet still suspects that he ought not to adopt it, then he is in a dilemma produced by the conflict between two disparate categories of moral reason: categories that may be called *utilitarian* and *absolutist*.

Utilitarianism gives primacy to a concern with what will *happen*. Absolutism gives primacy to a concern with what one is *doing*. The conflict between them arises because the alternatives we face are rarely just choices between *total outcomes*: they are also choices between alternative pathways or measures to be taken. When one of the choices is to do terrible things to another person, the problem is altered fundamentally; it is no longer merely a question of which outcome would be worse.

Few of us are completely immune to either of these types of moral intuition, though in some people, either naturally or for doctrinal reasons, one type will be dominant and the other suppressed or weak. But it is perfectly possible to feel the force of both types of reason very strongly; in that case the moral dilemma in certain situations of crisis will be acute, and it may appear that every possible course of action or inaction is unacceptable for one reason or another.

II

Although it is this dilemma that I propose to explore, most of the discussion will be devoted to its absolutist component. The utilitarian component is straightforward by comparison, and has a natural appeal to anyone who is not a complete skeptic about ethics. Utilitarianism says that one should try, either individually or through institutions, to maximize good and minimize evil (the definition of these categories need not enter into the schematic formulation of the view), and that if faced with the possibility of preventing a great evil by producing a lesser, one should choose the lesser evil. There are certainly problems about the formulation of utilitarianism, and much has been written about it, but its intent is morally transparent. Nevertheless, despite the addition of various refinements, it continues to leave large portions of ethics unaccounted for. I do not suggest that some form of absolutism can account for them all, only that an examination of absolutism will lead us to see the complexity, and perhaps the incoherence, of our moral ideas.

Utilitarianism certainly justifies *some* restrictions on the conduct of warfare. There are strong utilitarian reasons for adhering to any limitation which seems natural to most people—particularly if the limitation is widely accepted already. An exceptional measure which seems to be justified by its results in a particular conflict may create a precedent with disastrous long-term effects.[2] It may even be argued that war involves violence on such a scale that it is never justified on utilitarian grounds—the consequences of refusing to go to war will never be as bad as the war itself would be, even if atrocities were not committed. Or in a more sophisticated vein it might be claimed that a uniform policy of never resorting to military force would do less harm in the long run, if followed consistently, than a policy of deciding each case on utilitarian grounds (even though on occasion particular applications of the pacifist policy might have worse results than a specific utilitarian decision). But I shall not consider these

---

2 Straightforward considerations of national interest often tend in the same direction: the inadvisability of using nuclear weapons seems to be overdetermined in this way.

arguments, for my concern is with reasons of a different kind, which may remain when reasons of utility and interest fail.[3]

In the final analysis, I believe that the dilemma cannot always be resolved. While not every conflict between absolutism and utilitarianism creates an insoluble dilemma, and while it is certainly right to adhere to absolutist restrictions unless the utilitarian considerations favoring violation are overpoweringly weighty and extremely certain—nevertheless, when that special condition is met, it may become impossible to adhere to an absolutist position. What I shall offer, therefore, is a somewhat qualified defense of absolutism. I believe it underlies a valid and fundamental type of moral judgment—which cannot be reduced to or overridden by other principles. And while there may be other principles just as fundamental, it is particularly important not to lose confidence in our absolutist intuitions, for they are often the only barrier before the abyss of utilitarian apologetics for large-scale murder.

III

One absolutist position that creates no problems of interpretation is pacifism: the view that one may not kill another person under any circumstances, no matter what good would be achieved or evil averted thereby. The type of absolutist position that I am going to discuss is different. Pacifism draws the conflict with utilitarian considerations very starkly. But there are other views according to which violence may be undertaken, even on a large scale, in a clearly just cause, so long as certain absolute restrictions on the character and direction of that violence are observed. The line is drawn somewhat closer to the bone, but it exists.

The philosopher who has done most to advance contemporary philosophical discussion of such a view, and to explain it to those unfamiliar with its extensive treatment in Roman Catholic moral theology, is G. E. M. Anscombe. In 1958 Miss Anscombe published a pamphlet entitled *Mr. Truman's Degree*,[4] on the occasion of the award by Oxford University of an honorary doctorate to Harry Truman. The pamphlet explained why she had opposed the decision to award

---

3 These reasons, moreover, have special importance in that they are available even to one who denies the appropriateness of utilitarian considerations in international matters. He may acknowledge limitations on what may be done to the soldiers and civilians of other countries in pursuit of his nation's military objectives, while denying that one country should in general consider the interests of nationals of other countries in determining its policies.

4 (Privately printed.) See also her essay "War and Murder," in *Nuclear Weapons and Christian Conscience*, ed. Walter Stein (London, 1963). The present paper is much indebted to these two essays throughout. These and related subjects are extensively treated by Paul Ramsey in *The Just War* (New York, 1968). Among recent writings that bear on the moral problem are Jonathan Bennett, "Whatever the Consequences," *Analysis* 26, no. 3 (1966): 83–102; and Philippa Foot, "The Problem of Abortion and the Doctrine of the Double Effect," *The Oxford Review* 5 (1967): 5–15. Miss Anscombe's replies are "A Note on Mr. Bennett," *Analysis* 26, no. 3 (1966): 208, and "Who Is Wronged?" *The Oxford Review* 5 (1967): 16–17.

that degree, recounted the story of her unsuccessful opposition, and offered some reflections on the history of Truman's decision to drop atom bombs on Hiroshima and Nagasaki, and on the difference between murder and allowable killing in warfare. She pointed out that the policy of deliberately killing numbers of civilians either as a means or as an end in itself did not originate with Truman, and was common practice among all parties during World War II for some time before Hiroshima. The Allied area bombings of German cities by conventional explosives included raids which killed more civilians than did the atomic attacks; the same is true of certain fire-bomb raids on Japan.

The policy of attacking the civilian population in order to induce an enemy to surrender, or to damage his morale, seems to have been widely accepted in the civilized world, and seems to be accepted still, at least if the stakes are high enough. It gives evidence of a moral conviction that the deliberate killing of noncombatants—women, children, old people—is permissible if enough can be gained by it. This follows from the more general position that any means can in principle be justified if it leads to a sufficiently worthy end. Such an attitude is evident not only in the more spectacular current weapons systems but also in the day-to-day conduct of the nonglobal war in Indochina: the indiscriminate destructiveness of antipersonnel weapons, napalm, and aerial bombardment; cruelty to prisoners; massive relocation of civilians; destruction of crops; and so forth. An absolutist position opposes to this the view that certain acts cannot be justified no matter what the consequences. Among those acts is murder—the deliberate killing of the harmless: civilians, prisoners of war, and medical personnel.

In the present war such measures are sometimes said to be regrettable, but they are generally defended by reference to military necessity and the importance of the long-term consequences of success or failure in the war. I shall pass over the inadequacy of this consequentialist defense in its own terms. (That is the dominant form of moral criticism of the war, for it is part of what people mean when they ask, "Is it worth it?") I am concerned rather to account for the inappropriateness of offering any defense of that kind for such actions.

Many people feel, without being able to say much more about it, that something has gone seriously wrong when certain measures are admitted into consideration in the first place. The fundamental mistake is made there, rather than at the point where the overall benefit of some monstrous measure is judged to outweigh its disadvantages, and it is adopted. An account of absolutism might help us to understand this. If it is not allowable to *do* certain things, such as killing unarmed prisoners or civilians, then no argument about what will happen if one doesn't do them can show that doing them would be all right.

Absolutism does not, of course, require one to ignore the consequences of one's acts. It operates as a limitation on utilitarian reasoning, not as a substitute for it. An absolutist can be expected to try to maximize good and minimize evil, so long as this does not require him to transgress an absolute prohibition like that against murder. But when such a conflict occurs, the prohibition takes complete precedence over any consideration of consequences. Some of the results of this view are clear enough. It requires us to forgo certain potentially useful military measures, such as the slaughter of hostages and prisoners or indiscriminate attempts to reduce the enemy civilian population by starvation, epidemic infectious diseases like anthrax and bubonic plague, or mass incineration. It means that we cannot deliberate on whether such measures are justified by the fact that they will avert still greater evils, for as intentional measures they cannot be justified in terms of any consequences whatever.

Someone unfamiliar with the events of this century might imagine that utilitarian arguments, or arguments of national interest, would suffice to deter measures of this sort. But it has become evident that such considerations are insufficient to prevent the adoption and employment of enormous antipopulation weapons once their use is considered a serious moral possibility. The same is true of the piecemeal wiping out of rural civilian populations in airborne antiguerrilla warfare. Once the door is opened to calculations of utility and national interest, the usual speculations about the future of freedom, peace, and economic prosperity can be brought to bear to ease the consciences of those responsible for a certain number of charred babies.

For this reason alone it is important to decide what is wrong with the frame of mind which allows such arguments to begin. But it is also important to understand absolutism in the cases where it genuinely conflicts with utility. Despite its appeal, it is a paradoxical position, for it can require that one refrain from choosing the lesser of two evils when that is the only choice one has. And it is additionally paradoxical because, unlike pacifism, it permits one to do horrible things to people in some circumstances but not in others.

IV

Before going on to say what, if anything, lies behind the position, there remain a few relatively technical matters which are best discussed at this point.

First, it is important to specify as clearly as possible the kind of thing to which absolutist prohibitions can apply. We must take seriously the proviso that they concern what we deliberately do to people. There could not, for example, without incoherence, be an absolute prohibition against *bringing about* the death of an innocent person. For one may find oneself in a situation in which, no matter what one does, some innocent people will die as a result. I do not mean just that there are cases in which someone will die no matter what one does, because one is not in a position to affect the outcome one way or the other. That, it is to be hoped, is one's relation to the deaths of most innocent people. I have in mind, rather, a case in which someone is bound to die, but who it is will depend on what one does. Sometimes these situations have natural causes, as when too few resources (medicine, lifeboats) are available to rescue everyone threatened with a certain catastrophe. Sometimes the situations are man-made, as when the only way to control a campaign of terrorism is to employ terrorist tactics against the community from which it has arisen. Whatever one does in cases such as these, some innocent people will die as a result.

If the absolutist prohibition forbade doing what would result in the deaths of innocent people, it would have the consequence that in such cases nothing one could do would be morally permissible.

This problem is avoided, however, because what absolutism forbids is *doing* certain things to people, rather than bringing about certain *results*. Not everything that happens to others as a result of what one does is something that one has *done* to them. Catholic moral theology seeks to make this distinction precise in a doctrine known as the law of double effect, which asserts that there is a morally relevant distinction between bringing about the death of an innocent person deliberately, either as an end in itself or as a means, and bringing it about as a side effect of something else one does deliberately. In the latter case, even if the outcome is foreseen, it is not murder, and does not fall under the absolute prohibition, though of course it may still be wrong for other reasons (reasons of utility, for example). Briefly, the principle states that one is sometimes permitted knowingly to bring about as a side effect of one's actions something which it would be absolutely impermissible to bring about deliberately as an end or as a means. In application to war or revolution, the law of double effect permits a certain amount of civilian carnage as a side effect of bombing munitions plants or attacking enemy soldiers. And even this is permissible only if the cost is not too great to be justified by one's objectives.

However, despite its importance and its usefulness in accounting for certain plausible moral judgments, I do not believe that the law of double effect is a generally applicable test for the consequences of an absolutist position. Its own application is not always clear, so that it introduces uncertainty where there need not be uncertainty.

In Indochina, for example, there is a great deal of aerial bombardment, strafing, spraying of napalm, and employment of pellet- or needle-spraying antipersonnel weapons against rural villages in which guerrillas are suspected to be hiding, or from which small-arms fire has been received. The majority of those killed and wounded in these aerial attacks are reported to be women and children, even when some combatants are caught as well. However, the government regards these civilian casualties as a regrettable side effect of what is a legitimate attack against an armed enemy.

It might be thought easy to dismiss this as sophistry: if one bombs, burns, or strafes a village containing a hundred people, twenty of whom one believes to be guerrillas, so that by killing most of them one will be statistically likely to kill most of the guerrillas, then isn't one's attack on the group of one hundred a *means* of destroying the guerrillas, pure and simple? If one makes no attempt to discriminate between guerrillas and civilians, as is impossible in an aerial attack on a small village, then one cannot regard as a mere side effect the deaths of those in the group that one would not have bothered to kill if more selective means had been available.

The difficulty is that this argument depends on one particular description of the act, and the reply might be that the means used against the guerrillas is not: killing everybody in the village—but rather: obliteration bombing of the *area* in which the twenty guerrillas are known to be located. If there are civilians in the area as well, they will be killed as a side effect of such action.[5]

Because of casuistical problems like this, I prefer to stay with the original, unanalyzed distinction between what one does to people and what merely happens to them as a result of what one does. The law of double effect provides an approximation to that distinction in many cases, and perhaps it can be sharpened to the point where it does better than that. Certainly the original distinction itself needs clarification, particularly since some of the things we do to people involve things happening to them as a result of other things we do. In a case like the one discussed, however, it is clear that by bombing the village one slaughters and maims the civilians in it. Whereas by giving the only available medicine to one of two sufferers from a disease, one does not kill the other, even if he dies as a result.

The second technical point to take up concerns a possible misinterpretation of this feature of the position. The absolutist focus on actions rather than outcomes does not merely introduce a new, outstanding item into the catalogue of evils. That is, it does not say that the worst thing in the world is the deliberate murder of an innocent person. For if that were all, then one could presumably justify one such murder on the ground that it would prevent several others, or ten thousand on the ground that they would prevent a hundred thousand more. That is a familiar argument. But if this is allowable, then there is no absolute prohibition against murder after all. Absolutism requires that we *avoid* murder at all costs, not that we *prevent* it at all costs.[6]

Finally, let me remark on a frequent criticism of absolutism that depends on a misunderstanding. It is sometimes suggested that such prohibitions depend on a kind of moral self-interest, a primary obligation to preserve one's own moral purity, to keep one's hands clean no matter what happens to the rest of the world. If this were the position, it might be exposed to the charge of self-indulgence. After all, what gives one man a right to put the purity of his soul or the cleanness of his hands above the lives or welfare of large numbers of other people? It might be argued that a public servant like Truman has no right to put himself first in that way; therefore if he is convinced that the alternatives would be worse, he must give the order to drop the bombs, and take the burden of those deaths on himself, as he must do other distasteful things for the general good.

But there are two confusions behind the view that moral self-interest under-lies moral absolutism. First, it is a confusion to suggest that the need to preserve one's moral purity might be the *source* of an obligation. For if by committing murder one sacrifices one's moral purity or integrity, that can only be because

---

5 This counterargument was suggested by Rogers Albritton.

6 Someone might of course acknowledge the *moral relevance* of the distinction between deliberate and nondeliberate killing, without being an absolutist. That is, he might believe simply that it was *worse* to bring about a death deliberately than as a secondary effect. But that would be merely a special assignment of value, and not an absolute prohibition.

there is *already* something wrong with murder. The general reason against committing murder cannot therefore be merely that it makes one an immoral person. Secondly, the notion that one might sacrifice one's moral integrity justifiably, in the service of a sufficiently worthy end, is an incoherent notion. For if one were justified in making such a sacrifice (or even morally required to make it), then one would not be sacrificing one's moral integrity by adopting that course: one would be preserving it.

Moral absolutism is not unique among moral theories in requiring each person to do what will preserve his own moral purity in all circumstances. This is equally true of utilitarianism, or of any other theory which distinguishes between right and wrong. Any theory which defines the right course of action in various circumstances and asserts that one should adopt that course, ipso facto asserts that one should do what will preserve one's moral purity, simply because the right course of action *is* what will preserve one's moral purity in those circumstances. Of course utilitarianism does not assert that this is *why* one should adopt that course, but we have seen that the same is true of absolutism.

V

It is easier to dispose of false explanations of absolutism than to produce a true one. A positive account of the matter must begin with the observation that war, conflict, and aggression are relations between persons. The view that it can be wrong to consider merely the overall effect of one's actions on the general welfare comes into prominence when those actions involve relations with others. A man's acts usually affect more people than he deals with directly, and those effects must naturally be considered in his decisions. But if there are special principles governing the manner in which he should *treat* people, that will require special attention to the particular persons toward whom the act is directed, rather than just to its total effect.

Absolutist restrictions in warfare appear to be of two types: restrictions on the class of persons at whom aggression or violence may be directed and restrictions on the manner of attack, given that the object falls within that class. These can be combined, however, under the principle that hostile treatment of any person must be justified in terms of something *about that person* which makes the treatment appropriate. Hostility is a personal relation, and it must be suited to its target. One consequence of this condition will be that certain persons may not be subjected to hostile treatment in war at all, since nothing about them justifies such treatment. Others will be proper objects of hostility only in certain circumstances, or when they are engaged in certain pursuits. And the appropriate manner and extent of hostile treatment will depend on what is justified by the particular case.

A coherent view of this type will hold that extremely hostile behavior toward another is compatible with treating him as a person—even perhaps as an end in himself. This is possible only if one has not automatically stopped treating him as a person as soon as one starts to fight with him. If hostile, aggressive, or combative treatment of others always violated the condition that they be treated as human beings, it would be difficult to make further distinctions on that score *within* the class of hostile actions. That point of view, on the level of international relations, leads to the position that if complete pacifism is not accepted, no holds need be barred at all, and we may slaughter and massacre to our hearts' content, if it seems advisable. Such a position is often expressed in discussions of war crimes.

But the fact is that ordinary people do not believe this about conflicts, physical or otherwise, between individuals, and there is no more reason why it should be true of conflicts between nations. There seems to be a perfectly natural conception of the distinction between fighting clean and fighting dirty. To fight dirty is to direct one's hostility or aggression not at its proper object, but at a peripheral target which may be more vulnerable, and through which the proper object can be attacked indirectly. This applies in a fist fight, an election campaign, a duel, or a philosophical argument. If the concept is general enough to apply to all these matters, it should apply to war—both to the conduct of individual soldiers and to the conduct of nations.

Suppose that you are a candidate for public office, convinced that the election of your opponent would be a disaster, that he is an unscrupulous demagogue who will serve a narrow range of interests and seriously infringe the rights of those who disagree with him; and suppose you are convinced that you cannot defeat him by conventional means. Now imagine that various unconventional means present themselves as possibilities: you possess information about his sex life which would scandalize the electorate if made public; or you learn that his wife is an alcoholic or that in his youth he was associated for a brief period with a proscribed political party, and you believe that this information could be used to blackmail him into withdrawing his candidacy; or you can have a team of your supporters flatten the tires of a crucial subset of his supporters on election day; or you are in a position to stuff the ballot boxes; or, more simply, you can have him assassinated. What is wrong with these methods, given that they will achieve an overwhelmingly desirable result?

There are, of course, many things wrong with them: some are against the law; some infringe the procedures of an electoral process to which you are presumably committed by taking part in it; very importantly, some may back-fire, and it is in the interest of all political candidates to adhere to an unspoken agreement not to allow certain personal matters to intrude into a campaign. But that is not all. We have in addition the feeling that these measures, these methods of attack are *irrelevant* to the issue between you and your opponent, that in taking them up you would not be directing yourself to that which makes him an object of your opposition. You would be directing your attack not at the true target of your hostility, but at peripheral targets that happen to be vulnerable.

The same is true of a fight or argument outside the framework of any system of regulations or law. In an altercation with a taxi driver over an excessive fare, it is inappropriate to taunt him about his accent, flatten one of his tires, or smear chewing gum on his windshield; and it remains inappropriate even if he casts aspersions on your race, politics, or religion, or dumps the contents of your suitcase into the street.[7]

The importance of such restrictions may vary with the seriousness of the case; and what is unjustifiable in one case may be justified in a more extreme one. But they all derive from a single principle: that hostility or aggression should be directed at its true object. This means both that it should be directed at the person or persons who provoke it and that it should aim more specifically at what is provocative about them. The second condition will determine what form the hostility may appropriately take.

It is evident that some idea of the relation in which one should stand to other people underlies this principle, but the idea is difficult to state. I believe it is roughly this: whatever one does to another person intentionally must be aimed at him as a subject, with the intention that he receive it as a subject. It should manifest an attitude to *him* rather than just to the situation, and he should be able to recognize it and identify himself as its object. The procedures by which such an attitude is manifested need not be addressed to the person directly. Surgery, for example, is not a form of personal confrontation but part of a medical treatment that can be offered to a patient face to face and received by him as a response to his needs and the natural outcome of an attitude toward *him*.

Hostile treatment, unlike surgery, is already addressed *to* a person, and does not take its interpersonal meaning from a wider context. But hostile acts can serve as the expression or implementation of only a limited range of attitudes to the person who is attacked. Those attitudes in turn have as objects certain real or presumed characteristics or activities of the person which are thought to justify them. When this background is absent, hostile or aggressive behavior can no longer be intended for the reception of the victim as a subject. Instead it takes on the character of a purely bureaucratic operation. This occurs when one attacks someone who is not the true object of one's hostility—the true object may be someone else, who can be attacked through the victim; or one may not be manifesting a hostile attitude toward anyone, but merely using the easiest available path to some desired goal. One finds oneself not facing or addressing the victim at all, but operating on him—without the larger context of personal interaction that surrounds a surgical operation.

If absolutism is to defend its claim to priority over considerations of utility, it must hold that the maintenance of a direct interpersonal response to the people one deals with is a requirement which no advantages can justify one in abandoning. The requirement is absolute only if it rules out any calculation of what would justify its violation. I have said earlier that there may be circumstances so extreme that they render an absolutist position untenable. One may

---

7 Why, on the other hand, does it seem appropriate, rather than irrelevant, to punch someone in the mouth if he insults you? The answer is that in our culture it is an insult to punch someone in the mouth, and not just an injury. This reveals, by the way, a perfectly unobjectionable sense in which convention may play a part in determining exactly what falls under an absolutist restriction and what does not. I am indebted to Robert Fogelin for this point.

find then that one has no choice but to do something terrible. Nevertheless, even in such cases absolutism retains its force in that one cannot claim *justification* for the violation. It does not become *all right*.

As a tentative effort to explain this, let me try to connect absolutist limitations with the possibility of justifying *to the victim* what is being done to him. If one abandons a person in the course of rescuing several others from a fire or a sinking ship, one *could* say to him, "You understand, I have to leave you to save the others." Similarly, if one subjects an unwilling child to a painful surgical procedure, one can say to him, "If you could understand, you would realize that I am doing this to help you." One could *even* say, as one bayonets an enemy soldier, "It's either you or me." But one cannot really say while torturing a prisoner, "You understand, I have to pull out your fingernails because it is absolutely essential that we have the names of your confederates"; nor can one say to the victims of Hiroshima, "You understand, we have to incinerate you to provide the Japanese government with an incentive to surrender."

This does not take us very far, of course, since a utilitarian would presumably be willing to offer justifications of the latter sort to his victims, in cases where he thought they were sufficient. They are really justifications to the world at large, which the victim, as a reasonable man, would be expected to appreciate. However, there seems to me something wrong with this view, for it ignores the possibility that to treat someone else horribly puts you in a special relation to him, which may have to be defended in terms of other features of your relation to him. The suggestion needs much more development; but it may help us to understand how there may be requirements which are absolute in the sense that there can be no justification for violating them. If the justification for what one did to another person had to be such that it could be offered to him specifically, rather than just to the world at large, that would be a significant source of restraint.

If the account is to be deepened, I would hope for some results along the following lines. Absolutism is associated with a view of oneself as a small being interacting with others in a large world. The justifications it requires are primarily interpersonal. Utilitarianism is associated with a view of oneself as a benevolent bureaucrat distributing such benefits as one can control to countless other beings, with whom one may have various relations or none. The justifications it requires are primarily administrative. The argument between the two moral attitudes may depend on the relative priority of these two conceptions.[8]

VI

Some of the restrictions on methods of warfare which have been adhered to from time to time are to be explained by the mutual interests of the involved parties: restrictions on weaponry, treatment of prisoners, etc. But that is not

---

[8] Finally, I should mention a different possibility, suggested by Robert Nozick: that there is a strong general presumption against benefiting from the calamity of another, whether or not it has been deliberately inflicted for that or any other reason. This broader principle may well lend its force to the absolutist position.

all there is to it. The conditions of directness and relevance which I have argued apply to relations of conflict and aggression apply to war as well. I have said that there are two types of absolutist restrictions on the conduct of war: those that limit the legitimate targets of hostility and those that limit its character, even when the target is acceptable. I shall say something about each of these. As will become clear, the principle I have sketched does not yield an unambiguous answer in every case.

First let us see how it implies that attacks on some people are allowed, but not attacks on others. It may seem paradoxical to assert that to fire a machine gun at someone who is throwing hand grenades at your emplacement is to treat him as a human being. Yet the relation with him is direct and straightforward.[9] The attack is aimed specifically against the threat presented by a dangerous adversary, and not against a peripheral target through which he happens to be vulnerable but which has nothing to do with that threat. For example, you might stop him by machine-gunning his wife and children, who are standing nearby, thus distracting him from his aim of blowing you up and enabling you to capture him. But if his wife and children are not threatening your life, that would be to treat them as means with a vengeance.

This, however, is just Hiroshima on a smaller scale. One objection to weapons of mass annihilation—nuclear, thermonuclear, biological, or chemical—is that their indiscriminateness disqualifies them as direct instruments for the expression of hostile relations. In attacking the civilian population, one treats neither the military enemy nor the civilians with that minimal respect which is owed to them as human beings. This is clearly true of the direct attack on people who present no threat at all. But it is also true of the character of the attack on those who *are* threatening you, viz., the government and military forces of the enemy. Your aggression is directed against an area of vulnerability quite distinct from any threat presented by them which you may be justified in meeting. You are taking aim at them through the mundane life and survival of their countrymen, instead of aiming at the destruction of their military capacity. And of course it does not require hydrogen bombs to commit such crimes.

This way of looking at the matter also helps us to understand the importance of the distinction between combatants and noncombatants, and the irrelevance of much of the criticism offered against its intelligibility and moral significance. According to an absolutist position, deliberate killing of the innocent is murder, and in warfare the role of the innocent is filled by noncombatants. This has been thought to raise two sorts of problems: first, the widely imagined difficulty of making a division, in modern warfare, between combatants and noncombatants; second, problems deriving from the connotation of the word "innocence."

Let me take up the latter question first.[10] In the absolutist position, the operative notion of innocence is not moral innocence and it is not opposed to

---

9 It has been remarked that according to my view, shooting at someone establishes an I-thou relationship.

10 What I say on this subject derives from Anscombe.

moral guilt. If it were, then we would be justified in killing a wicked but noncombatant hairdresser in an enemy city who supported the evil policies of his government, and unjustified in killing a morally pure conscript who was driving a tank toward us with the profoundest regrets and nothing but love in his heart. But moral innocence has very little to do with it, for in the definition of murder "innocent" means "currently harmless," and it is opposed not to "guilty" but to "doing harm." It should be noted that such an analysis has the consequence that in war we may often be justified in killing people who do not deserve to die, and unjustified in killing people who do deserve to die, if anyone does.

So we must distinguish between combatants from noncombatants on the basis of their immediate threat or harmfulness. I do not claim that the line is a sharp one, but it is not so difficult as is often supposed to place individuals on one side of it or the other. Children are not combatants even though they may join the armed forces if they are allowed to grow up. Women are not combatants just because they bear children or offer comfort to the soldiers. More problematic are the supporting personnel, whether in or out of uniform, from drivers of munitions trucks and army cooks to civilian munitions workers and farmers. I believe they can be plausibly classified by applying the condition that the prosecution of conflict must direct itself to the cause of danger, and not to what is peripheral. The threat presented by an army and its members does not consist merely in the fact that they are men, but in the fact that they are armed and are using their arms in the pursuit of certain objectives. Contributions to their arms and logistics are contributions to this threat; contributions to their mere existence as men are not. It is therefore wrong to direct an attack against those who merely serve the combatants' needs as human beings, such as farmers and food suppliers, even though survival as a human being is a necessary condition of efficient functioning as a soldier.

This brings us to the second group of restrictions: those that limit what may be done even to combatants. These limits are harder to explain clearly. Some of them may be arbitrary or conventional, and some may have to be derived from other sources; but I believe that the conditions of directness and relevance in hostile relations accounts for them to a considerable extent.

Consider first a case which involves both a protected class of noncombatants and a restriction on the measures that may be used against combatants. One provision of the rules of war which is universally recognized, though it seems to be turning into a dead letter in Vietnam, is the special status of medical personnel and the wounded in warfare. It might be more efficient to shoot medical officers on sight and to let the enemy wounded die rather than be patched up to fight another day. But someone with medical insignia is supposed to be left alone and permitted to tend and retrieve the wounded. I believe this is because medical attention is a species of attention to completely general human needs, not specifically the needs of a combat soldier, and our conflict with the soldier is not with his existence as a human being.

By extending the application of this idea, one can justify prohibitions against certain particularly cruel weapons: starvation, poisoning, infectious diseases (supposing they could be inflicted on combatants only), weapons designed to maim or disfigure or torture the opponent rather than merely to stop him. It is not, I think, mere casuistry to claim that such weapons attack the men, not the soldiers. The effect of dum-dum bullets, for example, is much more extended than necessary to cope with the combat situation in which they are used. They abandon any attempt to discriminate in their effects between the combatant and the human being. For this reason the use of flamethrowers and napalm is an atrocity in all circumstances that I can imagine, whoever the target may be. Burns are both extremely painful and extremely disfiguring—far more than any other category of wound. That this well-known fact plays no (inhibiting) part in the determination of U.S. weapons policy suggests that moral sensitivity among public officials has not increased markedly since the Spanish Inquisition.[11]

Finally, the same condition of appropriateness to the true object of hostility should limit the scope of attacks on an enemy country: its economy, agriculture, transportation system, and so forth. Even if the parties to a military conflict are considered to be not armies or governments but entire nations (which is usually a grave error), that does not justify one nation in warring against every aspect or element of another nation. That is not justified in a conflict between individuals, and nations are even more complex than individuals, so the same reasons apply. Like a human being, a nation is engaged in countless other pursuits while waging war, and it is not in those respects that it is an enemy.

The burden of the argument has been that absolutism about murder has a foundation in principles governing all one's relations to other persons, whether aggressive or amiable, and that these principles, and that absolutism, apply to warfare as well, with the result that certain measures are impermissible no matter what the consequences.[12] I do not mean to romanticize war. It is sufficiently utopian to suggest that when nations conflict they might rise to the

11 Beyond this I feel uncertain. Ordinary bullets, after all, can cause death, and nothing is more permanent than that. I am not at all sure why we are justified in trying to kill those who are trying to kill us (rather than merely in trying to stop them with force which may also result in their deaths). It is often argued that incapacitating gases are a relatively humane weapon (when not used, as in Vietnam, merely to make people easier to shoot). Perhaps the legitimacy of restrictions against them must depend on the dangers of escalation, and the great utility of maintaining *any* conventional category of restriction so long as nations are willing to adhere to it.

Let me make clear that I do not regard my argument as a defense of the moral immutability of the Hague and Geneva Conventions. Rather, I believe that they rest partly on a moral foundation, and that modifications of them should also be assessed on moral grounds.

But even this connection with the actual laws of war is not essential to my claims about what is permissible and what is not. Since completing this paper I have read an essay by Richard Wasserstrom entitled "The Laws of War" (forthcoming in *The Monist*), which argues that the existing laws and conventions do not even attempt to embody a decent moral position: that their provisions have been determined by other interests, that they are in fact immoral in substance, and that it is a grave mistake to refer to them as standards in forming moral judgments about warfare. This possibility deserves serious consideration, and I am not sure what to say about it, but it does not affect my view of the moral issues.

12 It is possible to draw a more radical conclusion, which I shall not pursue here. Perhaps the technology and organization of modern war are such as to make it impossible to wage as an acceptable form of interpersonal or even international hostility. Perhaps it is too impersonal and large-scale for that. If so, then absolutism would in practice imply pacifism, given the present state of things. On the other hand, I am skeptical about the unstated assumption that a technology dictates its own use.

level of limited barbarity that typically characterizes violent conflict between individuals, rather than wallowing in the moral pit where they appear to have settled, surrounded by enormous arsenals.

VII

Having described the elements of the absolutist position, we must now return to the conflict between it and utilitarianism. Even if certain types of dirty tactics become acceptable when the stakes are high enough, the most serious of the prohibited acts, like murder and torture, are not just supposed to require unusually strong justification. They are supposed *never* to be done, because no quantity of resulting benefit is thought capable of *justifying* such treatment of a person.

The fact remains that when an absolutist knows or believes that the utilitarian cost of refusing to adopt a prohibited course will be very high, he may hold to his refusal to adopt it, but he will find it difficult to feel that a moral dilemma has been satisfactorily resolved. The same may be true of someone who rejects an absolutist requirement and adopts instead the course yielding the most acceptable consequences. In either case, it is possible to feel that one has acted for reasons insufficient to justify violation of the opposing principle. In situations of deadly conflict, particularly where a weaker party is threatened with annihilation or enslavement by a stronger one, the argument for resorting to atrocities can be powerful, and the dilemma acute.

There may exist principles, not yet codified, which would enable us to resolve such dilemmas. But then again there may not. We must face the pessimistic alternative that these two forms of moral intuition are not capable of being brought together into a single, coherent moral system, and that the world can present us with situations in which there is no honorable or moral course for a man to take, no course free of guilt and responsibility for evil.

The idea of a moral blind alley is a perfectly intelligible one. It is possible to get into such a situation by one's own fault, and people do it all the time. If, for example, one makes two incompatible promises or commitments— becomes engaged to two people, for example—then there is no course one can take which is not wrong, for one must break one's promise to at least one of them. Making a clean breast of the whole thing will not be enough to remove one's reprehensibility. The existence of such cases is not morally disturbing, however, because we feel that the situation was not unavoidable: one had to do something wrong in the first place to get into it. But what if the world itself, or someone else's actions, could face a previously innocent person with a choice between morally abominable courses of action, and leave him no way to escape with his honor? Our intuitions rebel at the idea, for we feel that the constructibility of such a case must show a contradiction in our moral views. But it is not in itself a contradiction to say that someone can do X or not do X, and that for him to take either course would be wrong. It merely contradicts the supposition that *ought* implies *can*—since presumably one ought to refrain from what is wrong, and in such a case it is impossible to do so.[13] Given the limitations on human action, it is naïve to suppose that there is a solution to every moral problem with which the world can face us. We have always known that the world is a bad place. It appears that it may be an evil place as well.

13 This was first pointed out to me by Christopher Boorse.

56

Political Action: The Problem of Dirty Hands[1]

MICHAEL WALZER

Michael Walzer (b. 1935) is a Senior Fellow at the Institute for Advanced Study in Princeton, New Jersey. Previously he taught government at Harvard University. His books include Obligations, Just and Unjust Wars, Radical Principles, *and* Spheres of Justice.

In this reading from Philosophy and Public Affairs *(Winter 1973), Walzer takes up a variant of the problem raised by Thomas Nagel in reading 55. Nagel observes that in war, soldiers sometimes must choose between violating moral prohibitions and failing to prevent great disasters. Similarly, Walzer notes that politicians often must choose between using morally unsavory tactics (say, for example, making deals with corrupt bosses) and failing to implement worthwhile policies. Because implementing worthwhile policies is the aim of the best people who enter politics, such people must, as Machiavelli puts it, "learn not to be good." But how can this be?*

One answer is given by utilitarianism. According to many utilitarians, moral prohibitions have no absolute force. Rather, they are guidelines as to what generally maximizes utility. If the prohibitions seem absolute, it is because utility is served by our tendency to feel guilty when we violate them. (For pertinent discussion, see reading 23, by Mill, and reading 24, by Hare.)

But Walzer rejects all such suggestions. According to him, the decent politician may not simply dismiss the prohibitions he violates. Instead, he must acknowledge these even while he transgresses against them. This requires not only that he feel guilt, but also that he pay some more public penalty. Yet this raises a further problem. Since successful politicians receive power and honor rather than punishment, how is the penalty to be exacted?

---

[1] An earlier version of this paper was read at the annual meeting of the Conference for the Study of Political Thought in New York, April 1971. I am indebted to Charles Taylor, who served as commentator at that time and encouraged me to think that its arguments might be right.

In an earlier issue of *Philosophy & Public Affairs* there appeared a symposium on the rules of war which was actually (or at least more importantly) a symposium on another topic.[2] The actual topic was whether or not a man can ever face, or ever has to face, a moral dilemma, a situation where he must choose between two courses of action both of which it would be wrong for him to undertake. Thomas Nagel worriedly suggested that this could happen and that it did happen whenever someone was forced to choose between upholding an important moral principle and avoiding some looming disaster.[3] R. B. Brandt argued that it could not possibly happen, for there were guidelines we might follow and calculations we might go through which would necessarily yield the conclusion that one or the other course of action was the right one to undertake in the circumstances (or that it did not matter which we undertook). R. M. Hare explained how it was that someone might wrongly suppose that he was faced with a moral dilemma: sometimes, he suggested, the precepts and principles of an ordinary man, the products of his moral education, come into conflict with injunctions developed at a higher level of moral discourse. But this conflict is, or ought to be, resolved at the higher level; there is no real dilemma.

I am not sure that Hare's explanation is at all comforting, but the question is important even if no such explanation is possible, perhaps especially so if this is the case. The argument relates not only to the coherence and harmony of the moral universe, but also to the relative ease or difficulty—or impossibility—of living a moral life. It is not, therefore, merely a philosopher's question. If such a dilemma can arise, whether frequently or very rarely, any of us might one day face it. Indeed, many men have faced it, or think they have, especially men involved in political activity or war. The dilemma, exactly as Nagel describes it, is frequently discussed in the literature of political action—in novels and plays dealing with politics and in the work of theorists too.

In modern times the dilemma appears most often as the problem of "dirty hands," and it is typically stated by the Communist leader Hoerderer in Sartre's play of that name: "I have dirty hands right up to the elbows. I've plunged them in filth and blood. Do you think you can govern innocently?"[4] My own answer is no, I don't think I could govern innocently; nor do most of us believe that those who govern us are innocent—as I shall argue below—even the best of them. But this does not mean that it isn't possible to do the right thing while governing. It means that a particular act of government (in a political

2 *Philosophy & Public Affairs* 1, no. 2 (Winter 1971/72): Thomas Nagel, "War and Massacre," pp. 123–144 [reprinted in this volume, reading 55]; R. B. Brandt, "Utilitarianism and the Rules of War," pp. 145–165; and R. M. Hare, "Rules of War and Moral Reasoning," pp. 166–181.

3 For Nagel's description of a possible "moral blind alley," see "War and Massacre," pp. 142–144. Bernard Williams has made a similar suggestion, though without quite acknowledging it as his own: "many people can recognize the thought that a certain course of action is, indeed, the best thing to do on the whole in the circumstances, but that doing it involves doing something wrong" (*Morality: An Introduction to Ethics* [New York, 1972], p. 93).

4 Jean-Paul Sartre, *Dirty Hands*, in *No Exit and Three Other Plays*, trans. Lionel Abel (New York, n.d.), p. 224.

party or in the state) may be exactly the right thing to do in utilitarian terms and yet leave the man who does it guilty of a moral wrong. The innocent man, afterwards, is no longer innocent. If on the other hand he remains innocent, chooses, that is, the "absolutist" side of Nagel's dilemma, he not only fails to do the right thing (in utilitarian terms), he may also fail to measure up to the duties of his office (which imposes on him a considerable responsibility for consequences and outcomes). Most often, of course, political leaders accept the utilitarian calculation; they try to measure up. One might offer a number of sardonic comments on this fact, the most obvious being that by the calculations they usually make they demonstrate the great virtues of the "absolutist" position. Nevertheless, we would not want to be governed by men who consistently adopted that position.

The notion of dirty hands derives from an effort to refuse "absolutism" without denying the reality of the moral dilemma. Though this may appear to utilitarian philosophers to pile confusion upon confusion, I propose to take it very seriously. For the literature I shall examine is the work of serious and often wise men, and it reflects, though it may also have helped to shape, popular thinking about politics. It is important to pay attention to that too. I shall do so without assuming, as Hare suggests one might, that everyday moral and political discourse constitutes a distinct level of argument, where content is largely a matter of pedagogic expediency.[5] If popular views are resistant (as they are) to utilitarianism, there may be something to learn from that and not merely something to explain about it.

I

Let me begin, then, with a piece of conventional wisdom to the effect that politicians are a good deal worse, morally worse, than the rest of us (it is the wisdom of the rest of us). Without either endorsing it or pretending to disbelieve it, I am going to expound this convention. For it suggests that the dilemma of dirty hands is a central feature of political life, that it arises not merely as an occasional crisis in the career of this or that unlucky politician but systematically and frequently.

Why is the politician singled out? Isn't he like the other entrepreneurs in an open society, who hustle, lie, intrigue, wear masks, smile and are villains? He is not, no doubt, for many reasons, three of which I need to consider. First of all, the politician claims to play a different part than other entrepreneurs. He doesn't merely cater to our interests; he acts on our behalf, even in our name. He has purposes in mind, causes and projects that require the support and redound to the benefit, not of each of us individually, but of all of us together. He hustles lies, and intrigues *for us*—or so he claims. Perhaps he is

---

[5] Hare, "Rules of War and Moral Reasoning," pp. 173–178, esp. p. 174: "the simple principles of the deontologist . . . have their place at the level of character-formation (moral education and self-education)."

right, or at least sincere, but we suspect that he acts for himself also. Indeed, he cannot serve us without serving himself, for success brings him power and glory, the greatest rewards that men can win from their fellows. The competition for these two is fierce; the risks are often great, but the temptations are greater. We imagine ourselves succumbing. Why should our representatives act differently? Even if they would like to act differently, they probably can not: for other men are all too ready to hustle and lie for power and glory, and it is the others who set the terms of the competition. Hustling and lying are necessary because power and glory are so desirable—that is, so widely desired. And so the men who act for us and in our name are necessarily hustlers and liars.

Politicians are also thought to be worse than the rest of us because they rule over us, and the pleasures of ruling are much greater than the pleasures of being ruled. The successful politician becomes the visible architect of our restraint. He taxes us, licenses us, forbids and permits us, directs us to this or that distant goal—all for our greater good. Moreover, he takes chances for our greater good that put us, or some of us, in danger. Sometimes he puts himself in danger too, but politics, after all, is his adventure. It is not always ours. There are undoubtedly times when it is good or necessary to direct the affairs of other people and to put them in danger. But we are a little frightened of the man who seeks, ordinarily and every day, the power to do so. And the fear is reasonable enough. The politician has, or pretends to have, a kind of confidence in his own judgment that the rest of us know to be presumptuous in any man.

The presumption is especially great because the victorious politician uses violence and the threat of violence—not only against foreign nations in our defense but also against us, and again ostensibly for our greater good. This is a point emphasized and perhaps overemphasized by Max Weber in his essay "Politics as a Vocation."[6] It has not, so far as I can tell, played an overt or obvious part in the development of the convention I am examining. The stock figure is the lying, not the murderous, politician—though the murderer lurks in the background, appearing most often in the form of the revolutionary or terrorist, very rarely as an ordinary magistrate or official. Nevertheless, the sheer weight of official violence in human history does suggest the kind of power to which politicians aspire, the kind of power they want to wield, and it may point to the roots of our half-conscious dislike and unease. The men who act for us and in our name are often killers, or seem to become killers too quickly and too easily.

Knowing all this or most of it, good and decent people still enter political life, aiming at some specific reform or seeking a general reformation. They are then required to learn the lesson Machiavelli first set out to teach: "how not to be good."[7] Some of them are incapable of learning; many more profess to

---

6 In *From Max Weber: Essays in Sociology*, trans. and ed. Hans H. Gerth and C. Wright Mills (New York, 1946), pp. 77–128.

7. See *The Prince*, chap. XV; cf. *The Discourses*, bk. I, chaps. IX and XVIII. I quote from the Modern Library edition of the two works (New York, 1950), p. 57.

be incapable. But they will not succeed unless they learn, for they have joined the terrible competition for power and glory; they have chosen to work and struggle as Machiavelli says, among "so many who are not good." They can do no good themselves unless they win the struggle, which they are unlikely to do unless they are willing and able to use the necessary means. So we are suspicious even of the best of winners. It is not a sign of our perversity if we think them only more clever than the rest. They have not won, after all, because they were good, or not only because of that, but also because they were not good. No one succeeds in politics without getting his hands dirty. This is conventional wisdom again, and again I don't mean to insist that it is true without qualification. I repeat it only to disclose the moral dilemma inherent in the convention. For sometimes it is right to try to succeed, and then it must also be right to get one's hands dirty. But one's hands get dirty from doing what it is wrong to do. And how can it be wrong to do what is right? Or, how can we get our hands dirty by doing what we ought to do?

II

It will be best to turn quickly to some examples. I have chosen two, one relating to the struggle for power and one to its exercise. I should stress that in both these cases the men who face the dilemma of dirty hands have in an important sense chosen to do so; the cases tell us nothing about what it would be like, so to speak, to fall into the dilemma; nor shall I say anything about that here. Politicians often argue than they have no right to keep their hands clean, and that may well be true of them, but it is not so clearly true of the rest of us. Probably we do have a right to avoid, if we possibly can, those positions in which we might be forced to do terrible things. This might be regarded as the moral equivalent of our legal right not to incriminate ourselves. Good men will be in no hurry to surrender it, though there are reasons for doing so sometimes, and among these are or might be the reasons good men have for entering politics. But let us imagine a politician who does not agree to that: he wants to do good only by doing good, or at least he is certain that he can stop short of the most corrupting and brutal uses of political power. Very quickly that certainty is tested. What do we think of him then?

He wants to win the election, someone says, but he doesn't want to get his hands dirty. This is meant as a disparagement, even though it also means that the man being criticized is the sort of man who will not lie, cheat, bargain behind the backs of his supporters, shout absurdities at public meetings, or manipulate other men and women. Assuming that this particular election ought to be won, it is clear, I think, that the disparagement is justified. If the candidate didn't want to get his hands dirty, he should have stayed at home; if he can't stand the heat, he should get out of the kitchen, and so on. His decision to run was a commitment (to all of us who think the election important) to try to win, that is, to do within rational limits whatever is necessary to win. But the candidate is a moral man. He has principles and a history of adherence to those principles. That is why we are supporting him. Perhaps when he refuses to dirty his hands, he is simply insisting on being the sort of man he is. And isn't that the sort of man we want?

Let us look more closely at this case. In order to win the election the candidate must make a deal with a dishonest ward boss, involving the granting of contracts for school construction over the next four years. Should he make the deal? Well, at least he shouldn't be surprised by the offer, most of us would probably say (a conventional piece of sarcasm). And he should accept it or not, depending on exactly what is at stake in the election. But that is not the candidate's view. He is extremely reluctant even to consider the deal, puts off his aides when they remind him of it, refuses to calculate its possible effects upon the campaign. Now, if he is acting this way because the very thought of bargaining with that particular ward boss makes him feel unclean, his reluctance isn't very interesting. His feelings by themselves are not important. But he may also have reasons for his reluctance. He may know, for example, that some of his supporters support him precisely because they believe he is a good man, and this means to them a man who won't make such deals. Or he may doubt his own motives for considering the deal, wondering whether it is the political campaign or his own candidacy that makes the bargain at all tempting. Or he may believe that if he makes deals of this sort now he may not be able later on to achieve those ends that make the campaign worthwhile, and he may not feel entitled to take such risks with a future that is not only his own future. Or he may simply think that the deal is dishonest and therefore wrong, corrupting not only himself but all those human relations in which he is involved.

Because he has scruples of this sort, we know him to be a good man. But we view the campaign in a certain light, estimate its importance in a certain way, and hope that he will overcome his scruples and make the deal. It is important to stress that we don't want just *anyone* to make the deal; we want *him* to make it, precisely because he has scruples about it. We know he is doing right when he makes the deal because he knows he is doing wrong. I don't mean merely that he will feel badly or even very badly after he makes the deal. If he is the good man I am imagining him to be, he will feel guilty, that is, he will believe himself to be guilty. That is what it means to have dirty hands.

All this may become clearer if we look at a more dramatic example, for we are, perhaps, a little blasé about political deals and disinclined to worry much about the man who makes one. So consider a politician who has seized upon a national crisis—a prolonged colonial war—to reach for power. He and his friends win office pledged to decolonization and peace; they are honestly committed to both, though not without some sense of the advantages of the commitment. In any case, they have no responsibility for the war; they have steadfastly opposed it. Immediately, the politician goes off to the colonial capital to open negotiations with the rebels. But the capital is in the grip of a terrorist campaign, and the first decision the new leader faces is this: he is asked to authorize the torture of a captured rebel leader who knows or probably knows the location of a number of bombs hidden in apartment buildings around the city, set to go off within the next twenty-four hours. He orders the man tortured, convinced that he must do so for the sake of the people who might otherwise die in the explosions—even though he believes that torture is wrong, indeed abominable, not just sometimes, but always.[8] He had expressed this belief often and angrily during his own campaign; the rest of us took it as a sign of his goodness. How should we regard him now? (How should he regard himself?)

Once again, it does not seem enough to say that he should feel very badly. But why not? Why shouldn't he have feelings like those of St. Augustine's melancholy soldier, who understood both that his war was just and that killing, even in a just war, is a terrible thing to do?[9] The difference is that Augustine did not believe that it was wrong to kill in a just war; it was just sad, or the sort of thing a good man would be saddened by. But he might have thought it wrong to torture in a just war, and later Catholic theorists have certainly thought it wrong. Moreover, the politician I am imagining thinks it wrong, as do many of us who supported him. Surely we have a right to expect more than melancholy from him now. When he ordered the prisoner tortured, he committed a moral crime and he accepted a moral burden. Now he is a guilty man. His willingness to acknowledge and bear (and perhaps to repent and do penance for) his guilt is evidence, and it is the only evidence he can offer us, both that he is not too good for politics and that he is good enough. Here is the moral politician: it is by his dirty hands that we know him. If he were a moral man and nothing else, his hands would not be dirty; if he were a politician and nothing else, he would pretend that they were clean.

III

Machiavelli's argument about the need to learn how not to be good clearly implies that there acts known to be bad quite apart from the immediate circumstances in which they are performed or not performed. He points to a distinct set of political methods and stratagems which good men must study (by reading his books), not only because their use does not come naturally, but also because they are explicitly condemned by the moral teachings good men accept—and whose acceptance serves in turn to mark men as good. These methods may be

---

8. I leave aside the question of whether the prisoner is himself responsible for the terrorist campaign. Perhaps he opposed it in meetings of the rebel organization. In any case, whether he deserves to be punished or not, he does not deserve to be tortured.

9. Other writers argued that Christians must never kill, even in a just war; and there was also an intermediate position which suggests the origins of the idea of dirty hands. Thus Basil the Great (Bishop of Caesarea in the fourth century A.D.): "Killing in war was differentiated by our fathers from murder . . . nevertheless, perhaps it would be well that those whose hands are unclean abstain from communion for three years." Here dirty hands are a kind of impurity or unworthiness, which is not the same as guilt, though closely related to it. For a general survey of these and other Christian views, see Roland H. Bainton, *Christian Attitudes Toward War and Peace* (New York, 1960), esp. chaps. 5–7.

condemned because they are thought contrary to divine law or to the order of nature or to our moral sense, or because in prescribing the law to ourselves we have individually or collectively prohibited them. Machiavelli does not commit himself on such issues, and I shall not do so either if I can avoid it. The effects of these different views are, at least in one crucial sense, the same. They take out of our hands the constant business of attaching moral labels to such Machiavellian methods as deceit and betrayal. Such methods are simply bad. They are the sort of thing that good men avoid, at least until they have learned how not to be good.

Now, if there is no such class of actions, there is no dilemma of dirty hands, and the Machiavellian teaching loses what Machiavelli surely intended it to have, its disturbing and paradoxical character. He can then be understood to be saying that political actors must sometimes overcome their moral inhibitions, but not that they must sometimes commit crimes. I take it that utilitarian philosophers also want to make the first of these statements and to deny the second. From their point of view, the candidate who makes a corrupt deal and the official who authorizes the torture of a prisoner must be described as good men (given the cases as I have specified them), who ought, perhaps, to be honored for making the right decision when it was a hard decision to make. There are three ways of developing this argument. First, it might be said that every political choice ought to be made solely in terms of its particular and immediate circumstances—in terms, that is, of the reasonable alternatives, available knowledge, likely consequences, and so on. Then the good man will face difficult choices (when his knowledge of options and outcomes is radically uncertain), but it cannot happen that he will face a moral dilemma. Indeed, if he always makes decisions in this way, and has been taught from childhood to do so, he will never have to overcome his inhibitions, whatever he does, for how could he have acquired inhibitions? Assuming further that he weighs the alternatives and calculates the consequences seriously and in good faith, he cannot commit a crime, though he can certainly make a mistake, even a very serious mistake. Even when he lies and tortures, his hands will be clean, for he has done what he should do as best he can, standing alone in a moment of time, forced to choose.

This is in some ways an attractive description of moral decision-making, but it is also a very improbable one. For while any one of us may stand alone, and so on, when we make this or that decision, we are not isolated or solitary in our moral lives. Moral life is a social phenomenon, and it is constituted at least in part by rules, the knowing of which (and perhaps the making of which) we share with our fellows. The experience of coming up against these rules, challenging their prohibitions, and explaining ourselves to other men and women is so common and so obviously important that no account of moral decision-making can possibly fail to come to grips with it. Hence the second utilitarian argument: such rules do indeed exist, but they are not really prohibitions of wrongful actions (though they do, perhaps for pedagogic reasons, have that form). They are moral guidelines, summaries of previous calculations.

They ease our choices in ordinary cases, for we can simply follow their injunctions and do what has been found useful in the past; in exceptional cases they serve as signals warning us against doing too quickly or without the most careful calculations what has not been found useful in the past. But they do no more than that; they have no other purpose, and so it cannot be the case that it is or even might be a crime to override them.[10] Nor is it necessary to feel guilty when one does so. Once again, if it is right to break the rule in some hard case, after conscientiously worrying about it, the man who acts (especially if he knows that many of his fellows would simply worry rather than act) may properly feel pride in his achievement.

But this view, it seems to me, captures the reality of our moral life no better than the last. It may well be right to say that moral rules ought to have the character of guidelines, but it seems that in fact they do not. Or at least, we defend ourselves when we break the rules as if they had some status entirely independent of their previous utility (and we rarely feel proud of ourselves). The defenses we normally offer are not simply justifications; they are also excuses. Now, as Austin says, these two can *seem* to come very close together—indeed, I shall suggest that they can appear side by side in the same sentence—but they are conceptually distinct, differentiated in this crucial respect: an excuse is typically an admission of fault; a justification is typically a denial of fault and an assertion of innocence.[11] Consider a well-known defense from Shakespeare's *Hamlet* that has often reappeared in political literature: "I must be cruel only to be kind."[12] The words are spoken on an occasion when Hamlet is actually being cruel to his mother. I will leave aside the possibility that she deserves to hear (to be forced to listen to) every harsh word he utters, for Hamlet himself makes no such claim—and if she did indeed deserve that, his words might not be cruel or he might not be cruel for speaking them. "I must be cruel" contains the excuse, since it both admits a fault and suggests that Hamlet has no choice but to commit it. He is doing what he has to do; he can't help himself (given the ghost's command, the rotten state of Denmark, and so on). The rest of the sentence is a justification, for it suggests that Hamlet intends and expects kindness to be the outcome of his actions—we must assume that he means greater kindness, kindness to the right persons, or some such. It is not, however, so complete a justification that Hamlet is able to say that he is not *really* being cruel. "Cruel" and "kind" have exactly the same status;

---

10 Brandt's rules do not appear to be of the sort that can be overridden—except perhaps by a soldier who decides that he just *won't* kill any more civilians, no matter what cause is served—since all they require is careful calculation. But I take it that rules of a different sort, which have the form of ordinary injunctions and prohibitions, can and often do figure in what is called "rule-utilitarianism."

11 J. L. Austin, "A Plea for Excuses," in *Philosophical Papers*, ed. J. O. Urmson and G. J. Warnock (Oxford, 1961), pp. 123–152.

12 *Hamlet* 3.4.178

they both follow the verb "to be," and so they perfectly reveal the moral dilemma.[13]

When rules are overridden, we do not talk or act as if they had been set aside, canceled, or annulled. They still stand and have this much effect at least: that we know we have done something wrong even if what we have done was also the best thing to do on the whole in the circumstances.[14] Or at least we feel that way, and this feeling is itself a crucial feature of our moral life. Hence the third utilitarian argument, which recognizes the usefulness of guilt and seeks to explain it. There are, it appears, good reasons for "overvaluing" as well as for overriding the rules. For the consequences might be very bad indeed if the rules were overridden every time the moral calculation seemed to go against them. It is probably best if most men do not calculate too nicely, but simply follow the rules; they are less likely to make mistakes that way, all in all. And so a good man (or at least an ordinary good man) will respect the rules rather more than he would if he thought them merely guidelines, and he will feel guilty when he overrides them. Indeed, if he did not feel guilty, "he would not be such a good man."[15] It is by his feelings that we know him. Because of those feelings he will never be in a hurry to override the rules, but will wait until there is no choice, acting only to avoid consequences that are both imminent and almost certainly disastrous.

The obvious difficulty with this argument is that the feeling whose usefulness is being explained is most unlikely to be felt by someone who is convinced only of its usefulness. He breaks a utilitarian rule (guideline), let us say, for good utilitarian reasons: but can he then feel guilty, also for good utilitarian reasons, when he has no reason for believing that he *is* guilty? Imagine a moral philosopher expounding the third argument to a man who actually does feel guilty or to the sort of man who is likely to feel guilty. Either the man won't accept the utilitarian explanation as an account of his feeling about the rules (probably the best outcome from a utilitarian point of view) or he will accept it and then cease to feel that (useful) feeling. But I do not want to exclude the possibility of a kind of superstitious anxiety, the possibility, that is, that some men will continue to feel guilty even after they have been taught, and have agreed, that they cannot possibly *be* guilty. It is best to say only that the more fully they accept the utilitarian account, the less likely they are to feel that (useful) feeling. The utilitarian account is not at all useful, then, if political

13 Compare the following lines from Bertold Brecht's poem "To Posterity": "Alas, we/Who wished to lay the foundations of kindness/Could not ourselves be kind . . . " (*Selected Poems*, trans. H. R. Hays [New York, 1969], p. 177). This is more of an excuse, less of a justification (the poem is an *apologia*).

14 Robert Nozick discusses some of the possible effects of overriding a rule in his "Moral Complications and Moral Structures," *Natural Law Forum* 13 (1968): 34–35 and notes. Nozick suggests that what may remain after one has broken a rule (for good reasons) is a "duty to make reparations." He does not call this "guilt," though the two notions are closely connected.

15 Hare, "Rules of War and Moral Reasoning," p. 179.

actors accept it, and that may help us to understand why it plays, as Hare has pointed out, so small a part in our moral education.[16]

IV

One further comment on the third argument: it is worth stressing that to feel guilty is to suffer, and that the men whose guilt feelings are here called useful are themselves innocent according to the utilitarian account. So we seem to have come upon another case where the suffering of the innocent is permitted and even encouraged by utilitarian calculation.[17] But surely an innocent man who has done something painful or hard (but justified) should be helped to avoid or escape the sense of guilt; he might reasonably expect the assistance of his fellow men, even of moral philosophers, at such a time. On the other hand, if we intuitively think it true of some other man that he *should* feel guilty, then we ought to be able to specify the nature of his guilt (and if he is a good man, win his agreement). I think I can construct a case which, with only small variation, highlights what is different in these two situations.

Consider the common practice of distributing rifles loaded with blanks to some of the members of a firing squad. The individual men are not told whether their own weapons are lethal, and so though all of them look like executioners to the victim in front of them, none of them know whether they are really executioners or not. The purpose of this stratagem is to relieve each man of the sense that he is a killer. It can hardly relieve him of whatever moral responsibility he incurs by serving on a firing squad, and that is not its purpose, for the execution is not thought to be (and let us grant this to be the case) an

16 There is another possible utilitarian position, suggested in Maurice Merleau-Ponty's *Humanism and Terror*, trans. John O'Neill (Boston, 1970). According to this view the agony and the guilt feelings experienced by the man who makes a "dirty hands" decision derive from his radical uncertainty about the actual outcome. Perhaps the awful thing he is doing will be done in vain; the results he hopes for won't occur; the only outcome will be the pain he has caused or the deceit he has fostered. Then (and only then) he will indeed have committed a crime. On the other hand, if the expected good does come, then (and only then) he can abandon his guilt feelings; he can say, and the rest of us must agree, that he is justified. This is a kind of delayed utilitarianism, where justification is a matter of actual and not at all of predicted outcomes. It is not implausible to imagine a political actor anxiously awaiting the "verdict of history." But suppose the verdict is in his favor (assuming that there is a *final* verdict or a statute of limitations on possible verdicts): he will surely feel relieved—more so, no doubt, than the rest of us. I can see no reason, however, why he should think himself justified, if he is a good man and knows that what he did was wrong. Perhaps the victims of his crime, seeing the happy result, will absolve him, but history has no powers of absolution. Indeed, history is more likely to play tricks on our moral judgment. Predicted outcomes are at least thought to follow from our own acts (this is the prediction), but actual outcomes almost certainly have a multitude of causes, the combination of which may well be fortuitous. Merleau-Ponty stresses the risks of political decision-making so heavily that he turns politics into a gamble with time and circumstance. But the anxiety of the gambler is of no great moral interest. Nor is it much of a barrier, as Merleau-Ponty's book makes all too clear, to the commission of the most terrible crimes.

17 Cf. the cases suggested by David Ross, *The Right and the Good* (Oxford, 1930), pp. 56–57, and E. F. Carritt, *Ethical and Political Thinking* (Oxford, 1947), p. 65.

immoral or wrongful act. But the inhibition against killing another human being is so strong that even if the men believe that what they are doing is right, they will still feel guilty. Uncertainty as to their actual role apparently reduces the intensity of these feelings. If this is so, the stratagem is perfectly justifiable, and one can only rejoice in every case where it succeeds—for every success subtracts one from the number of innocent men who suffer.

But we would feel differently, I think, if we imagine a man who believes (and let us assume here that we believe also) either that capital punishment is wrong or that this particular victim is innocent, but who nevertheless agrees to participate in the firing squad for some overriding political or moral reason— I won't try to suggest what that reason might be. If he is comforted by the trick with the rifles, then we can be reasonably certain that his opposition to capital punishment or his belief in the victim's innocence is not morally serious. And if it is serious, he will not merely feel guilty, he will know that he is guilty (and we will know it too), though he may also believe (and we may agree) that he has good reasons for incurring the guilt. Our guilt feelings can be tricked away when they are isolated from our moral beliefs, as in the first case, but not when they are allied with them, as in the second. The beliefs themselves and the rules which are believed in can only be *overridden*, a painful process which forces a man to weigh the wrong he is willing to do in order to do right, and which leaves pain behind, and should do so, even after the decision has been made.

V

That is the dilemma of dirty hands as it has been experienced by political actors and written about in the literature of political action. I don't want to argue that it is only a political dilemma. No doubt we can get our hands dirty in private life also, and sometimes, no doubt, we should. But the issue is posed most dramatically in politics for the three reasons that make political life the kind of life it is, because we claim to act for others but also serve ourselves, rule over others, and use violence against them. It is easy to get one's hands dirty in politics and it is often right to do so. But it is not easy to teach a good man how not to be good, nor is it easy to explain such a man to himself once he has committed whatever crimes are required of him. At least, it is not easy once we have agreed to use the word "crimes" and to live with (because we have no choice) the dilemma of dirty hands. Still, the agreement is common enough, and on its basis there have developed three broad traditions of explanation, three ways of thinking about dirty hands, which derive in some very general fashion from neoclassical, Protestant, and Catholic perspectives on politics and morality. I want to try to say something very briefly about each of them, or rather about a representative example of each of them, for each seems to me partly right. But I don't think I can put together the compound view that might be wholly right.

The first tradition is best represented by Machiavelli, the first man, so far as I know, to state the paradox that I am examining. The good man who aims to found or reform a republic must, Machiavelli tells us, do terrible things to reach his goal. Like Romulus, he must murder his brother; like Numa, he must lie to the people. Sometimes, however, "when the act accuses, the result excuses."[18] This sentence from *The Discourses* is often taken to mean that the politician's deceit and cruelty are justified by the good results he brings about. But if they were justified, it wouldn't be necessary to learn what Machiavelli claims to teach: how not to be good. It would only be necessary to learn how to be good in a new, more difficult, perhaps roundabout way. That is not Machiavelli's argument. His political judgments are indeed consequentialist in character, but not his moral judgments. We know whether cruelty is used well or badly by its effects over time. But that it is bad to use cruelty we know in some other way. The deceitful and cruel politician is excused (if he succeeds) only in the sense that the rest of us come to agree that the results were "worth it" or, more likely, that we simply forget his crimes when we praise his success.

It is important to stress Machiavelli's own commitment to the existence of moral standards. His paradox depends upon that commitment as it depends upon the general stability of the standards—which he upholds in his consistent use of words like good and bad.[19] If he wants the standards to be disregarded by good men more often than they are, he has nothing with which to replace them and no other way of recognizing the good men except by their allegiance to those same standards. It is exceedingly rare, he writes, that a good man is willing to employ bad means to become prince.[20] Machiavelli's purpose is to persuade such a person to make the attempt, and he holds out the supreme political rewards, power and glory, to the man who does so and succeeds. The good man is not rewarded (or excused), however, merely for his willingness to get his hands dirty. He must do bad things well. There is no reward for doing bad things badly, though they are done with the best of intentions. And so political action necessarily involves taking a risk. But it should be clear that what is risked is not personal goodness—*that is thrown away*—but power and glory. If the politician succeeds, he is a hero; eternal praise is the supreme reward for not being good.

What the penalties are for not being good, Machiavelli doesn't say, and it is probably for this reason above all that his moral sensitivity has so often been questioned. He is suspect not because he tells political actors they must get their hands dirty, but because he does not specify the state of mind appropriate to a man with dirty hands. A Machiavellian hero has no inwardness. What he thinks of himself we don't know. I would guess, along with most other readers of Machiavelli, that he basks in his glory. But then it is difficult to account for the strength of his original reluctance to learn how not to be

---

18 *The Discourses*, bk. I, chap. IX (p. 139).

19 For a very different view of Machiavelli, see Isaiah Berlin, "The Question of Machiavelli," *The New York Review of Books*, 4 November 1971.

20 *The Discourses*, bk. I, chap. XVIII (p. 171).

good. In any case, he is the sort of man who is unlikely to keep a diary and so we cannot find out what he thinks. Yet we do want to know; above all, we want a record of his anguish. That is a sign of our own conscientiousness and of the impact on us of the second tradition of thought that I want to examine, in which personal anguish sometimes seems the only acceptable excuse for political crimes.

The second tradition is best represented, I think, by Max Weber, who outlines its essential features with great power at the very end of his essay "Politics as a Vocation." For Weber, the good man with dirty hands is a hero still, but he is tragic hero. In part, his tragedy is that though politics is his vocation, he has not been called by God and so cannot be justified by Him. Weber's hero is alone in a world that seems to belong to Satan, and his vocation is entirely his own choice. He still wants what Christian magistrates have always wanted, both to do good in the world and to save his soul, but now these two ends have come into sharp contradiction. They are contradictory because of the necessity for violence in a world where God has not instituted the sword. The politician takes the sword himself, and only by doing so does he measure up to his vocation. With full consciousness of what he is doing, he does bad in order to do good, and surrenders his soul. He "lets himself in," Weber says, "for the diabolic forces lurking in all violence." Perhaps Machiavelli also meant to suggest that his hero surrenders salvation in exchange for glory, but he does not explicitly say so. Weber is absolutely clear: "the genius or demon of politics lives in an inner tension with the god of love . . . [which] can at any time lead to an irreconcilable conflict."[21] His politician views this conflict when it comes with a tough realism, never pretends that it might be solved by compromise, chooses politics once again, and turns decisively away from love. Weber writes about this choice with a passionate high-mindedness that makes a concern for one's soul seem no more elevated than a concern for one's flesh. Yet the reader never doubts that his mature, superbly trained, relentless, objective, responsible, and disciplined political leader is also a suffering servant. His choices are hard and painful, and he pays the price not only while making them but forever after. A man doesn't lose his soul one day and find it the next.

The difficulties with this view will be clear to anyone who has ever met a suffering servant. Here is a man who lies, intrigues, sends other men to their death—and suffers. He does what he must do with a heavy heart. None of us can know, he tells us, how much it costs him to do his duty. Indeed, we cannot, for he himself fixes the price he pays. And that is the trouble with this view of political crime. We suspect the suffering servant of either masochism or hypocrisy or both, and while we are often wrong, we are not always wrong. Weber attempts to resolve the problem of dirty hands entirely within the

---

21 "Politics as a Vocation," pp. 125–126. But sometimes a political leader does choose the "absolutist" side of the conflict, and Weber writes (p. 127) that it is "immensely moving when a *mature* man . . . aware of a responsibility for the consequences of his conduct . . . reaches a point where he says: 'Here I stand; I can do no other.' " Unfortunately, he does not suggest just where that point is or even where it might be.

confines of the individual conscience, but I am inclined to think that this is neither possible nor desirable. The self-awareness of the tragic hero is obviously of great value. We want the politician to have an inner life at least something like that which Weber describes. But sometimes the hero's suffering needs to be socially expressed (for like punishment, it confirms and reinforces our sense that certain acts are wrong). And equally important, it sometimes needs to be socially limited. We don't want to be ruled by men who have lost their souls. A politician with dirty hands needs a soul, and it is best for us all if he has some hope of personal salvation, however that is conceived. It is not the case that when he does bad in order to do good he surrenders himself forever to the demon of politics. He commits a determinate crime, and he must pay a determinate penalty. When he has done so, his hands will be clean again, or as clean as human hands can ever be. So the Catholic Church has always taught, and this teaching is central to the third tradition that I want to examine.

Once again I will take a latter-day and a lapsed representative of the tradition and consider Albert Camus' *The Just Assassins*. The heroes of this play are terrorists at work in nineteenth-century Russia. The dirt on their hands is human blood. And yet Camus' admiration for them, he tells us, is complete. We consent to being criminals, one of them says, but there is nothing with which anyone can reproach us. Here is the dilemma of dirty hands in a new form. The heroes are innocent criminals, just assassins, because, having killed, they are prepared to die—*and will die*. Only their execution, by the same despotic authorities they are attacking, will complete the action in which they are engaged: dying, they need make no excuses. That is the end of their guilt and pain. The execution is not so much punishment as self-punishment and expiation. On the scaffold they wash their hands clean and, unlike the suffering servant, they die happy.

Now the argument of the play when presented in so radically simplified a form may seem a little bizarre, and perhaps it is marred by the moral extremism of Camus' politics. "Political action has limits," he says in a preface to the volume containing *The Just Assassins*, "and there is no good and just action but what recognizes those limits and if it must go beyond them, at least accepts death."[22] I am less interested here in the violence of that "at least"—what else does he have in mind?—than in the sensible doctrine that it exaggerates. That doctrine might best be described by an analogy: just assassination, I want to suggest, is like civil disobedience. In both men violate a set of rules, go beyond a moral or legal limit, in order to do what they believe they should do. At the same time, they acknowledge their responsibility for the violation by accepting punishment or doing penance. But there is also a difference between the two, which has to do with the difference between law and morality. In most cases of civil disobedience the laws of the state are broken for moral reasons, and the state provides the punishment. In most cases of dirty hands moral rules are broken for reasons of state, and no one provides the punishment. There is rarely a Czarist executioner waiting in the wings for politicians with dirty

---

[22] *Caligula and Three Other Plays* (New York, 1958), p. x. (The preface is translated by Justin O'Brian, the plays by Stuart Gilbert.)

hands, even the most deserving among them. Moral rules are not usually enforced against the sort of actor I am considering, largely because he acts in an official capacity. If they were enforced, dirty hands would be no problem. We would simply honor the man who did bad in order to do good, and at the same time we would punish him. We would honor him for the good he has done, and we would punish him for the bad he has done. We would punish him, that is, for the same reasons we punish anyone else; it is not my purpose here to defend any particular view of punishment. In any case, there seems no way to establish or enforce the punishment. Short of the priest and the confessional, there are no authorities to whom we might entrust the task.

I am nevertheless inclined to think Camus' view the most attractive of the three, if only because it requires us at least to imagine a punishment or a penance that fits the crime and so to examine closely the nature of the crime. The others do not require that. Once he has launched his career, the crimes of Machiavelli's prince seem subject only to prudential control. And the crimes of Weber's tragic hero are limited only by *his* capacity for suffering and not, as they should be, by *our* capacity for suffering. In neither case is there any explicit reference back to the moral code, once it has, at great personal cost to be sure, been set aside. The question posed by Sartre's Hoerderer (whom I suspect of being a suffering servant) is rhetorical, and the answer is obvious (I have already given it), but the characteristic sweep of both is disturbing. Since it is concerned only with those crimes that ought to be committed, the dilemma of dirty hands seems to exclude questions of degree. Wanton or excessive cruelty is not at issue, any more than is cruelty directed at bad ends. But political action is so uncertain that politicians necessarily take moral as well as political risks, committing crimes that they only think ought to be committed. They override the rules without ever being certain that they have found the best way to the results they hope to achieve, and we don't want them to do that too quickly or too often. So it is important that the moral stakes be very high—which is to say, that the rules be rightly valued. That, I suppose, is the reason for Camus' extremism. Without the executioner, however, there is no one to set the stakes or maintain the values except ourselves, and probably no way to do either except through philosophic reiteration and political activity.

"We shall not abolish lying by refusing to tell lies," says Hoerderer, "but by using every means at hand to abolish social classes."[23] I suspect we shall not abolish lying at all, but we might see to it that fewer lies were told if we contrived to deny power and glory to the greatest liars—except, of course, in the case of those lucky few whose extraordinary achievements make us forget the lies they told. If Hoerderer succeeds in abolishing social classes, perhaps he will join the lucky few. Meanwhile, he lies, manipulates, and kills, and we must make sure he pays the price. We won't be able to do that, however, without getting our own hands dirty, and then we must find some way of paying the price ourselves.

23 *Dirty Hands*, p. 223.

Copyrights and Acknowledgments

The authors are indebted to the following for permission to reprint from copyrighted material:

PART I

JOEL FEINBERG, Psychological Egoism
From *Reason and Responsibility,* Fourth Edition by Joel Feinberg. Copyright © 1978 Wadsworth Publishing Company. Reprinted by permission.

PLATO, The Ring of Gyges
From Plato's *Republic,* translated by G. M. A. Grube. Copyright © 1974, Hackett Publishing Company, Inc. Reprinted by permission.

THOMAS HOBBES, Morality and Self-Interest
From *Leviathan.*

DAVID GAUTHIER, Morality and Advantage
From "Morality and Advantage" by David Gauthier which appeared in *The Philosophical Review,* Volume 76, Number 4 (October 1967).

ALAN GEWIRTH, The Is-Ought Problem Resolved
From "The Is-Ought Problem Resolved" by Alan Gewirth which appeared in *Proceedings and Addresses of the American Philosophical Association,* Volume 47 (1973–74). Reprinted by permission of the author.

PHILIPPA FOOT, Morality as a System of Hypothetical Imperatives
From "Morality as a System of Hypothetical Imperatives" by Philippa Foot which appeared in *The Philosophical Review,* Volume 81, No. 3 (1972). Reprinted by permission of the author.

JEAN-PAUL SARTRE, Existentialism Is a Humanism
From *Existentialism and Human Emotions* by Jean-Paul Sartre. Copyright © 1957, Philosophical Library, New York, NY. Reprinted by permission.

PART II

DAVID HUME, Morality and Natural Sentiment
From *A Treatise of Human Nature.*

PART IV

PART VII

PART VIII